Willmington's
COMPLETE GUIDE TO
BIBLE KNOWLEDGE

Introduction to Theology

Introduction to Theology

Willmington's
Complete
GUIDE
to
BIBLE
KNOWLEDGE

HAROLD L. WILLMINGTON

Tyndale House Publishers, Inc.
WHEATON, ILLINOIS

This book, the sixth in the series *Willmington's Complete Guide to Bible Knowledge,* is dedicated to Dr. Wendell Hawley, senior vice-president, Editorial, Tyndale House Publishers.

Scripture quotations, unless otherwise noted, are from the King James Version of the Bible. Scripture quotations marked NIV are from the *Holy Bible,* New International Version®. Copyright © 1973, 1978, 1984 by International Bible Society. Used by permission of Zondervan Publishing House. All rights reserved. The *"NIV"* and *"New International Version"* trademarks are registered in the United States Patent and Trademark Office by International Bible Society. Use of either trademark requires the permission of International Bible Society. Scripture quotations marked TLB are from *The Living Bible,* copyright © 1971 owned by assignment by KNT Charitable Trust. All rights reserved. Scripture quotations marked NASB are from the *New American Standard Bible,* copyright © 1960, 1962, 1963, 1968, 1971, 1972, 1973, 1975, 1977 by The Lockman Foundation. Used by permission. Scripture quotations marked ASV are from the *Holy Bible,* American Standard Version, copyright © 1901 by Thomas Nelson and Sons, and © 1929 by International Council of Religious Education. Used by permission.

Library of Congress Cataloging-in-Publication Data

Willmington, H. L.
  Willmington's complete guide to Bible knowledge.

  Vol. 6 has bibliographical references.
  Contents: v. 1. Old Testament people — [2] New Testament people — [etc.] — [6] Introduction to theology.
  1. Bible—Biography—Dictionaries. 2. Bible—Dictionaries. 3. Bible—Theology—Dictionaries. I. Title.
  BS417.W49 1990   220.3   90-70187
  ISBN 0-8423-8166-x (v. 6)

Printed in the United States of America

99 98 97 96 95 94 93
7   6   5   4   3   2   1

CONTENTS

THE DOCTRINE OF THE HOLY SPIRIT 195

INTRODUCTION
The Theological Method

Perhaps no other single word has been so successfully twisted by the devil today as has the biblical word *doctrine*. In the minds of millions, doctrine involves the following concepts:

1. Doctrine is that silly and useless practice of arguing (in the spirit and tradition of medieval monks) such things as: "How many angels can dance on the head of a pin?" "Could God create a stone so heavy that he couldn't lift it?" "Could he plant an immovable post in the ground and then throw an unstoppable rock at it?"
2. Doctrine divides, whereas love unites.
3. One cannot mix doctrine with soul-winning.
4. Doctrine is dull and impractical.
5. Doctrine is over the heads of most people.
6. Why learn a lot of doctrine when we don't live up to the light we already have?
7. The key goal is to let the Bible master us, and not spend our energies mastering the Bible.

In answering these charges, one could say that they are as far removed from the truth as the Babe in Bethlehem is from Rudolph the Red-Nosed Reindeer. Each argument needs but a brief refutation.

1. True biblical doctrine has nothing whatsoever to do with dancing angels, massive rocks, sturdy posts, and speeding stones. The word *doctrine,* as found in the Bible, refers to the systematic (and often simple) gathering and presentation of the facts concerning any great body of truth.
2. True doctrine does indeed divide. It divides light from darkness, right from wrong, and life from death. But it also unites, for God's love cannot be known or appropriated by sinful men without the involvement of doctrine.
3. These two not only *can* be mixed, they *must* be mixed if God's commands are to be followed. It is thrilling to note that the greatest soul winner of all time and the greatest theologian who ever lived were one and the same—the Apostle Paul. The same man who went door to door, pleading with tears for men to accept Christ (Acts 20:20-21, 26) also wrote some 50 percent of books of the New Testament, including that most profound of all doctrinal books, the Epistle to the Romans.
4. To the contrary, doctrine will put both a fire and a song in the hearts of those who read and heed its tremendous truths. "And they said one to another, Did not our heart burn within us, while he talked with us by the way, and while he opened to us the scriptures?" (Luke 24:32). "Speaking to yourselves in psalms and hymns and spiritual songs, singing and making melody in your heart to the Lord" (Eph. 5:19). "Blessed is he that readeth, and they that hear the words of this prophecy, and keep those things which are written therein: for the time is at hand" (Rev. 1:3). "Behold, I come quickly: blessed is he that keepeth the sayings of the prophecy of this book" (Rev. 22:7).

5. This is simply not true, as refuted by Christ himself. "At that time Jesus answered and said, I thank thee, O Father, Lord of heaven and earth, because thou has hid these things from the wise and prudent, and hast revealed them unto babes. . . . Come unto me, all ye that labour and are heavy laden, and I will give you rest. Take my yoke upon you,and learn of me; for I am meek and lowly in heart; and ye shall find rest unto your souls. For my yoke is easy, and my burden is light" (Matt. 11:25, 28-30).

6. To follow this twisted logic would mean never to go beyond the first commandment (Exod. 20:3), which says we are to have no gods or interests placed before the true God. But who has not on occasion been guilty of this? Should we therefore conclude that the sixth and seventh commandments ("Thou shalt not kill; thou shalt not commit adultery," Exod. 20:13-14) should not be kept simply because we do not always obey the first commandment?

7. This statement is pious nonsense, for one cannot possibly be even remotely influenced, let alone mastered, by that which he or she knows nothing about. It is true that the goal of Bible study is to become Spirit controlled. But the *fruit* of the Spirit can never come apart from the *root* of personal study.

Having listed and answered those objections to studying doctrine, let us now give some important advantages for doing it.

1. Doctrine will help save us from theological food poisoning. "Till I come, give attendance to reading, to exhortation, to doctrine. Neglect not the gift that is in thee, which was given thee by prophecy, with the laying on of the hands of the presbytery. Meditate upon these things; give thyself wholly to them; that thy profiting may appear to all. Take heed unto thyself, and unto the doctrine; continue in them: for in doing this thou shalt both save thyself, and them that hear thee" (1 Tim. 4:13-16). "Now the Spirit speaketh expressly, that in the latter times some shall depart from the faith, giving heed to seducing spirits, and doctrines of devils" (1 Tim. 4:1).

   "I charge thee therefore before God, and the Lord Jesus Christ, who shall judge the quick and the dead at his appearing and his kingdom; Preach the word; be instant in season, out of season; reprove, rebuke, exhort with all longsuffering and doctrine. For the time will come when they will not endure sound doctrine; but after their own lusts shall they heap to themselves teachers, having itching ears; And they shall turn away their ears from the truth, and shall be turned unto fables" (2 Tim. 4:1-4).

2. Doctrine will help settle us. "That we henceforth be no more children, tossed to and fro, and carried about with every wind of doctrine, by the sleight of men, and cunning craftiness, whereby they lie in wait to deceive" (Eph. 4:14).

3. Doctrine will acquaint us with the details of God's eternal plan.
   a. Concerning the history of Israel—"Moreover, brethren, I would not that ye should be ignorant, how that all our fathers were under the cloud, and all passed through the sea" (1 Cor. 10:1).
   b. Concerning the restoration of Israel—"For I would not, brethren, that ye should be ignorant of this mystery, lest ye should be wise in your own conceits; that blindness in part is happened to Israel, until the fulness of the Gentiles be come in" (Rom. 11:25).
   c. Concerning spiritual gifts—"Now concerning spiritual gifts, brethren, I would not have you ignorant" (1 Cor. 12:1).

    d. Concerning the Rapture—"But I would not have you to be ignorant, brethren, concerning them which are asleep, that ye sorrow not, even as others which have no hope" (1 Thess. 4:13).

    e. Concerning the destruction of this earth—"But, beloved, be not ignorant of this one thing, that one day is with the Lord as a thousand years, and a thousand years as one day. But the day of the Lord will come as a thief in the night; in the which the heavens shall pass away with a great noise, and the elements shall melt with fervent heat, the earth also and the works that are therein shall be burned up" (2 Pet. 3:8, 10).

4. Doctrine helps us edify ourselves. "Study to show thyself approved unto God, a workman that needeth not to be ashamed, rightly dividing the word of truth" (2 Tim. 2:15).

5. Doctrine helps us equip ourselves. "But evil men and seducers shall wax worse and worse, deceiving, and being deceived. But continue thou in the things which thou hast learned and hast been assured of, knowing of whom thou hast learned them; and that from a child thou hast known the holy scriptures, which are able to make thee wise unto salvation through faith which is in Christ Jesus. All scripture is given by inspiration of God, and is profitable for doctrine, for reproof, for correction, for instruction in righteousness: That the man of God may be perfect, thoroughly furnished unto all good works" (2 Tim. 3:13-17).

    "Finally, my brethren, be strong in the Lord, and in the power of his might. Put on the whole armour of God, that ye may be able to stand against the wiles of the devil. For we wrestle not against flesh and blood, but against principalities, against powers, against the rulers of the darkness of this world, against spiritual wickedness in high places. Wherefore take unto you the whole armour of God, that ye may be able to withstand in the evil day, and having done all, to stand. Stand therefore, having your loins girt about with truth, and having on the breastplate of righteousness; And your feet shod with the preparation of the gospel of peace; Above all, taking the shield of faith, wherewith ye shall be able to quench all the fiery darts of the wicked. And take the helmet of salvation, and the sword of the Spirit, which is the word of God" (Eph. 6:10-17).

THE DOCTRINE OF THE TRINITY

INTRODUCTION

Some 1,500 years B.C. an arrogant pagan in Egypt demanded from an 80-year-old Jew: "Who is the Lord, that I should obey his voice . . . ?" (Exod. 5:2).

Nearly 1,000 years later a similar question was raised by another pagan in Babylon, this time addressed to three young Jewish men: "Who is that God, that shall deliver you out of my hands?" (Dan. 3:15).

As both Pharaoh (the Egyptian pagan) and Nebuchadnezzar (the Babylonian pagan) would soon learn, the God they had reviled was able to punish his enemies (through the ten plagues), and protect his elect (in the fiery furnace).

This chapter provides a simple but systematic study of that God, the Creator, Sustainer, Redeemer, and Judge of all things and all men.

I. Non-Christian Views of God
  A. The atheistic view—This denies the existence of any God or gods.
  B. The agnostic view—This holds that the existence and nature of God are unknown and unknowable.
  C. The polytheistic view—This holds that there are many gods.
  D. The dualistic view—This assumes that there are two distinct, eternal, irreducible realities (one good and the other evil) that oppose each other.
  E. The pantheistic view—This believes that all things are merely aspects, modifications, or parts of the one eternal self-existing being or principle; that God is everything and everything is God.
  F. The deistic view

> This holds the existence of God but rejects his having any relation to the world or self-revelation. As pantheism accepts the immanence of God to the exclusion of his transcendence, so deism accepts the transcendence of God to the exclusion of his immanence. For deism, God is an absentee landlord who, having made the universe like a vast machine, allows it to operate on its own by inherent natural law without his personal supervision. It claims that all truths are discoverable by reason and that the Bible is merely a book on the principles of natural religion, which are discernible by the light of nature. (Floyd Barackman, *Practical Christian Theology*, p. 24)

II. The Existence of God—The greatest and most profound idea the human mind can ever conceivably entertain concerns the possibility of the existence of a personal God. The sheer importance of man's response to this idea cannot be exaggerated, for it will not only govern his life down here but will also determine his ultimate destiny. Unless one satisfactorily answers the *who* question, he cannot possibly solve the *how, why, when,* and *where* problems of his own existence.

A. Some philosophical arguments for the existence of God—Throughout the centuries certain extrabiblical arguments have been advanced to confirm the existence of a supreme being. While there is a valid place for them, it must be kept in mind the only acceptable approach to God is by faith and faith alone. "But without faith it is impossible to please him; for he that cometh to God must believe that he is, and that he is a rewarder of them that diligently seek him" (Heb. 11:6).

Thus, in a real sense, the following arguments apply more to the believer than the unbeliever, serving to confirm that which has already been accepted by faith.

1. The universal belief argument—The universal belief argument says that all mankind has some idea of a supreme Being. This argument has often been challenged, but never refuted. While the concepts of God found among many cultures and civilizations differ greatly on the number, name and nature of this supreme being, nevertheless, the idea remains.

A classic example of this is the amazing story of Helen Keller (1880–1968). From the age of two, Miss Keller was blind, deaf, and without the sense of smell. After two months of agonizing and fruitless attempts on the part of her teacher to communicate with this young girl, a miracle occurred. One day Helen suddenly understood the concept and meaning of running water. From this humble foundation Miss Keller built a lofty tower of thought, including the ability to use her voice in speaking. She became an educated and articulate human being. Sometime after she had progressed to the point that she could engage in conversation, she was told of God and his love in sending Christ to die on the cross. She is said to have responded with joy, "I always knew he was there, but I didn't know his name!"

2. The cosmological argument—This argument says that every effect must have an adequate cause. Robert Culver writes:

> One of the great names in British science, mathematics, and philosophy is Sir Isaac Newton (1642–1727). Sir Isaac had a miniature model of the solar system made. A large golden ball representing the sun was at its center and around it revolved smaller spheres, representing planets—Mercury, Venus, Earth, Mars, Jupiter, and the others. They were each kept in an orbit relatively the same as in the real solar system. By means of rods, cogwheels, and belts they all moved around the center golden ball in exact precision. A friend called on the noted man one day while he was studying the model. The friend was not a believer in the biblical doctrine of divine creation. According to reports, their conversation went as follows:
> Friend: "My, Newton, what an exquisite thing! Who made it for you?"
> Newton: "Nobody."
> Friend: "Nobody?"
> Newton: "That's right! I said, 'Nobody!' All of these balls and cogs and belts and gears just happened to come together, and wonder of wonders, by chance they began revolving in their set orbits with perfect timing!"
> Of course, the visitor understood the unexpressed argument: "In the beginning, God created the heaven and the earth." (*The Living God*, pp. 29–30)

3. The teleological argument—This argument says every design must have a designer. The entire universe is characterized by order and useful arrangement.

This is readily seen by the constant speed of light, laws of gravity, the arrangement of the planets around the sun, the complexity of the tiny atom, and the amazing makeup of the human body. All this design literally cries out for a divine designer.

4. The ontological argument—This argument says:

> Man has an idea of a Most Perfect Being. This idea includes the idea of existence, since a being, otherwise perfect, who did not exist would not be as perfect as a perfect being who did exist. Therefore, since the idea of existence is contained in the idea of the Most Perfect Being, the Most Perfect Being must exist. (Charles Ryrie, *Basic Theology*, p. 32)

5. The anthropological argument—This argument says that the conscience and moral nature of man demands a self-conscious and moral Maker. This built-in barometer supplies no information, and the information on which it passes judgment may be incorrect. But nevertheless, conscience tells us we *ought* to do what is right regarding the information we have. Robert Culver writes as follows:

> This sense of duty may be weak (1 Corinthians 8:12), good (1 Peter 3:16), defiled (1 Corinthians 8:7), seared (1 Timothy 4:2), strong or pure (1 Corinthians 8:7, 9). But it is never absent. The only accurate explanation is that the great Moral Being, who created us all, planted the moral sense in us. No other explanation is adequate. (*The Living God*, p. 31)

The following letter, reportedly received by the Internal Revenue Service, underlines this argument in an amusing way:

> Dear Sir,
>   Some years ago I cheated on my income tax return by failing to report a large sum of money I had made that year. As a result, my conscience has bothered me terribly. Please find my enclosed check as part payment on my debt. . . .
>   P.S. If my conscience continues to plague me, I'll send you more money at a later date!

B. Scriptural arguments for the existence of God—None! The Bible simply assumes the existence of God. "The fool hath said in his heart, 'There is no God.' They are corrupt, they have done abominable works, there is none that doeth good" (Psa. 14:1). "But without faith it is impossible to please him; for he that cometh to God must believe that he is, and that he is a rewarder of them that diligently seek him" (Heb. 11:6).

Clark Pinnock aptly summarizes all this when he writes:

> For the Scripture then, the existence of God is both a historical truth (God acted into history), and an existential truth (God reveals himself to every soul). His existence is both objectively and subjectively evident. It is necessary *logically* because our assumption of order, design, and rationality rests upon it. It is necessary *morally* because there is no explanation for the shape of morality apart from it. It is necessary *personally* because the exhaustion of all material possibilities still cannot give satisfaction to the heart. The deepest proof for God's existence apart from history is just life itself. God has

created man in His image, and man cannot elude the implications of this fact. Everywhere his identity pursues him. (*Set Forth Your Case*, p. 77)

III. The Names of God—One of the most well-known passages in Shakespeare's *Romeo and Juliet* can be found in the second scene of the second act. As the story opens, Juliet is lamenting the fact that her parents (the Capulets) intensely dislike the parents of her lover, Romeo (the Montagues).

In an attempt to play down the situation, she sighs: "What's Montague? It is nor hand, nor foot, nor arm, nor face, nor any other part belonging to a man. O, be some other name! What's in a name? That which we call a rose by any other name would smell as sweet."

Thus, to Juliet a person's name meant little or nothing. This is, however, decidedly not the case as one approaches the Bible. In fact, to the contrary, one may learn a great deal about a person simply by examining the names ascribed to him or her. This is especially true concerning the names for God.

A. Elohim—Used 2,570 times, it refers to God's power and might. "In the beginning God created the heaven and the earth" (Gen. 1:1). "The heavens declare the glory of God; and the firmament sheweth his handiwork" (Psa. 19:1).

B. El—There are four compounds of the name El.

1. Elyon, "the strongest strong one"—There are two significant places where this name was used in the Old Testament. One came from the lips of Jerusalem's first sovereign, and the other from history's first sinner.

   a. Jerusalem's first sovereign, Melchizedek—"And Melchizedek king of Salem brought forth bread and wine: and he was the priest of the most high God. And he blessed him, and said, Blessed be Abram of the most high God, possessor of heaven and earth: And blessed be the most high God, which hath delivered thine enemies into thy hand. And he gave him tithes of all" (Gen. 14:18-20).

   b. History's first sinner, Satan—"For thou has said in thine heart, I will ascend into heaven, I will exalt my throne above the stars of God: I will sit also upon the mount of the congregation, in the sides of the north: I will ascend above the heights of the clouds; I will be like the most High" (Isa. 14:13-14).

2. Roi, "the strong one who sees"—In Genesis 16 an angered and barren Sarai had cast into the wilderness her pregnant and arrogant handmaiden, Hagar. When all hope for survival had fled, this pagan Egyptian girl was visited and ministered to by El Roi himself—the strong God who sees. "And she called the name of the Lord that spake unto her, Thou God seest me: for she said, Have I also here looked after him that seeth me?" (Gen. 16:13).

3. El Shaddai, "the breasted one"—Used 48 times in the Old Testament, the Hebrew word *shad* is used often to designate the bosom of a nursing mother. "And when Abram was ninety years old and nine, the Lord appeared to Abram, and said unto him, I am the Almighty God; walk before me, and be thou perfect" (Gen. 17:1).

   This revelation of God came to Abraham at a much needed time in his life. His sin in marrying Hagar (Gen. 16) had doubtless prevented that full and unhindered fellowship which had previously flowed between him and God. In addition, his wife, Sarah, was now an old woman, nearly 90, humanly unable to give birth to Abraham's long-anticipated heir.

"He that dwelleth in the secret place of the most High shall abide under the shadow of the Almighty" (Psa. 91:1).

4. Olam, "the everlasting God"—Isaiah 40 is usually regarded as being one of the greatest Old Testament chapters. The prophet begins by predicting both the first and second advent of Christ. He then contrasts the awesome power of the true God with the miserable impotence of all idols. But carnal Israel had trouble accepting all this, wondering just how these wonderful events could transpire. To answer these doubts, Isaiah declares: "Hast thou not known? Hast thou not heard, that the everlasting God, the Lord, the Creator of the ends of the earth, fainteth not, neither is weary? There is no searching of his understanding. He giveth power to the faint; and to them that have no might he increaseth strength. Even the youths shall faint and be weary, and the young men shall utterly fall: But they that wait upon the Lord shall renew their strength, they shall mount up with wings as eagles; they shall run, and not be weary; and they shall walk, and not faint" (Isa. 40:28-31).

C. Adonai—The name means "Master, Lord." The Hebrew Old Testament name *Adonai* and its Greek New Testament counterpart *Kurios* describe the relationship between master and slave. God owns all his children. Thus, *Adonai* carries with it a twofold implication:

1. The master has a right to expect obedience—Robert Lightner writes:

> In Old Testament times the slave was the absolute possession of his master, having no rights of his own. His chief business was to carry out the wishes of his master. The slave had a relationship and responsibility different from that of the hired servant. The hired servant could quit if he did not like the orders of his master. But not so with the slave. He could do nothing but obey (cf. Gen. 24:1-12). (*The God of the Bible*, p. 116)

2. The slave may expect provision—Again, to quote Lightner:

> The slave had no worry of his own. It was the master's business to provide food, shelter, and the necessities of life. Since the slave is the possession of the master, his needs become the master's. Obedience is the only condition for this provision. This truth is marvelously displayed in Paul, who was himself a bond slave, when he assured the Philippians that God would supply all their needs (Phil. 4:19). Only the obedient slave can expect this from his master. (Ibid., p. 117)

> "A son honoreth his father, and a servant his master: if then I be a father, where is mine honor? and if I be a master, where is my fear? saith the Lord of hosts unto you, O priests, that despise my name. And ye say, Wherein have we despised thy name?" (Mal. 1:6).

D. Jehovah—This is the most common name for God, occurring 6,823 times. It means the "self-existent one, the God of the covenant." "And Moses said unto God, Behold, when I come unto the children of Israel, and shall say unto them, The God of your fathers hath sent me unto you; and they shall say to me, What is his name? What shall I say unto them? And God said unto Moses, I AM THAT I AM: and he said, Thus shalt thou say unto the children of Israel, I AM hath sent me unto you" (Exod. 3:13-14).

"And God spake unto Moses, and said unto him, I am the LORD: And I appeared unto Abraham, unto Isaac, and unto Jacob, by the name of God Almighty, but by my name JEHOVAH was I not known to them. And I have also established my covenant with them, to give them the land of Canaan, the land of their pilgrimage, wherein they were strangers" (Exod. 6:2-4).

The name Jehovah here in Exodus 6:3 is the Hebrew tetragrammaton (a four-lettered expression) YHWH. Because of the sacredness of it, the Jewish reader would not even pronounce it, substituting the word *Adonai* in its place when read aloud.

There are nine compound names of Jehovah:

1. Jireh, "The Lord (Jehovah) will provide"—This is the name given by Abraham to the place where God provided a ram to be offered in sacrifice instead of Isaac. "And Abraham lifted up his eyes, and looked, and behold, behind him a ram caught in a thicket by his horns; and Abraham went and took the ram, and offered him up for a burnt offering in the stead of his son. And Abraham called the name of that place Jehovah-jireh: as it is said to this day, In the mount of the Lord it shall be seen" (Gen. 22:13-14).

2. Nissi, "The Lord (Jehovah) is my banner"—"And Moses built an altar, and called the name of it Jehovah-nissi" (Exod. 17:15). This passage is significant, for it marks the first battle and subsequent victory of Israel on its march after leaving Egypt. The great lawgiver, Moses, mounted a hill and, with outstretched arms, prayed for the Israelite armies, headed up by Joshua, in their pitched battle against the fierce Amalekites.

3. Shalom, "The Lord (Jehovah) is peace"—"Then Gideon built an altar there unto the Lord and called it Jehovah-shalom: unto this day it is yet in Ophrah of the Abiezrites" (Judg. 6:24).

   As one studies the thrilling account of Gideon, he reads how Jehovah-shalom did indeed bring peace to Israel over the Midianites through this warrior and his 300 trumpet-blowing soldiers. Our Lord Jesus would, of course, become both the Bringer and Giver of peace. Note: "The sceptre shall not depart from Judah, nor a lawgiver from between his feet, until Shiloh come; and unto him shall the gathering of the people be" (Gen. 49:10). The word *Shiloh* here (meaning peace) is no doubt in reference to the Messiah.

   "For unto us a child is born, unto us a son is given: and the government shall be upon his shoulder: and his name shall be called Wonderful, Counsellor, the mighty God, the everlasting Father, The Prince of Peace" (Isa. 9:6). "Glory to God in the highest and on earth peace, good will toward men" (Luke 2:14). "For he is our peace, who hath made both one, and hath broken down the middle wall of partition between us" (Eph. 2:14).

4. Sabaoth, "The Lord (Jehovah) of hosts"—*Sabaoth* is derived from the Hebrew word *tsaba,* meaning "hosts." The "Lord of hosts" is a reference to the captain of heaven's armies. These armies are said to be composed of angels.

   "The chariots of God are twenty thousand, even thousands of angels: the Lord is among them, as in Sinai, in the holy place" (Psa. 68:17). "Who maketh his angels spirits; his ministers a flaming fire" (Psa. 104:4). "Praise ye him, all his angels: praise ye him, all his hosts." (Psa. 148:2).

   The great prophet Isaiah described his vision in which he was allowed to see Jehovah-Sabaoth—the Lord of hosts: "In the year that king Uzziah died I saw also the Lord sitting upon a throne, high and lifted up, and his train filled the temple. Above it stood the seraphim: each one had six wings; with twain he covered his face, and with twain he covered his feet, and with twain he did fly.

And one cried unto another, and said, Holy, holy, holy, is the LORD of hosts; the whole earth is full of his glory" (Isa. 6:1-3).

In Revelation 5 we read that John saw angels, "ten thousand times ten thousand and thousands and thousands"—an uncountable number. Jehovah Sabaoth is the Lord of hosts.

In the New Testament Christ himself is pictured as the leader of these angels. (See Matthew 26:53.) When Jesus was arrested, our Lord himself (the Lord Sabaoth) made an interesting comment when Simon Peter pulled out his sword and did violence to one of the servants of the high priest by cutting off his ear: "Then said Jesus unto him, Put up again thy sword into his place: for all they that take the sword shall perish with the sword. Thinkest thou that I cannot now pray to my Father, and he shall presently give me more than twelve legions of angels?" (Matt. 26:52-53).

5. Maccaddeschem, "The Lord (Jehovah) thy sanctifier" ("the God who desires to set his people apart")—"Speak thou also unto the children of Israel, saying, Verily my sabbaths ye shall keep: for it is a sign between me and you throughout your generations; that ye may know that I am the LORD that doth sanctify you" (Exod. 31:13).

This great name for God, first mentioned in Exodus, appears many times in the following book, Leviticus. To be sanctified is to be set apart, and that is what God desired to do for his people—to set them apart for special service.

In the New Testament we read how the Great Sanctifier set himself apart that he might set apart the sanctified. "And for their sakes I sanctify myself, that they also might be sanctified through the truth" (John 17:19). "For this is the will of God, even your sanctification, that ye should abstain from fornication" (1 Thess. 4:3). "And the very God of peace sanctify you wholly; and I pray God your whole spirit and soul and body be preserved blameless unto the coming of our Lord Jesus Christ" (1 Thess. 5:23).

6. Rohi (Raah), "The Lord (Jehovah) my shepherd"—Of all the compound names of Jehovah, this is at once the most easily understood title because it literally means that good, and great, and chief Shepherd God—"the Lord, my shepherd."

"I am the good shepherd: the good shepherd giveth his life for the sheep" (John 10:11). "Now the God of peace, that brought again from the dead our Lord Jesus, that great shepherd of the sheep" (Heb. 13:20). "Feed the flock of God. . . . And when the chief shepherd shall appear, ye shall receive a crown of glory that fadeth not away" (1 Pet. 5:4).

How wonderful to think upon Christ as one's good, and great, and chief shepherd. But even more glorious to know him as David did when he wrote, "The Lord is *my* shepherd; I shall not want" (Psa. 23:1).

7. Tsidkenu, "The Lord (Jehovah) of righteousness"—According to the prophet Jeremiah, the official name for the Messiah during the future Millennium will be Jehovah-Tsidkenu. "In his days Judah shall be saved, and Israel shall dwell safely: and this is his name whereby he shall be called, THE LORD OUR RIGHTEOUSNESS" (Jer. 23:6).

8. Shammah, "The Lord (Jehovah) who is present"—"It was round about eighteen thousand measures: and the name of the city from that day shall be, The Lord is there" (Ezek. 48:35). In this passage Ezekiel describes for us the dimensions of the millennial temple and then gives us the new name for the earthly city of

Jerusalem during earth's Golden Age: Jehovah-Shammah. Of course, the obvious meaning is that God himself will be in that city. The psalmist had this idea when he wrote Psalm 46: "God is our refuge and strength, a very present help in trouble. Therefore will not we fear, though the earth be removed, and though the mountains be carried into the midst of the sea" (Psa. 46:1-2).

He is a very present help in time of trouble. He is an ever-present help in time of need. He is Jehovah-Shammah at weddings. He is an ever present strength in times of sorrow. He is our joy in times of rejoicing. Jehovah-Shammah—the Lord who is present.

The greatest thing about heaven is probably connected to the worst thing about hell. The worst thing about hell is not the terrible pain and the eternality, but rather that hell will be a place where Jesus Christ will be conspicuously absent throughout all eternity. On the other hand, the greatest thing about heaven is not the pearly gates, the ivory palaces, the jasper walls, or the streets of gold, but rather, heaven will be a place where Jesus Christ will be conspicuously present throughout all eternity. Jehovah-Shammah—the Lord who is present.

"And when she had so said, she went her way, and called Mary her sister secretly, saying, 'The Master is come, and calleth for thee'" (John 11:28).

9. Rapha, "The Lord (Jehovah) our healer"—By this new name God introduced to Israel the terms of his heavenly "medicare" health plan while they were on their way to Canaan. If only they had accepted this gracious policy. The Israelites were challenged to obey God, and God would instruct them in every area of life, including health and nutrition, in order to keep them from disease and illness. "If thou wilt diligently hearken to the voice of the Lord thy God, and wilt do that which is right in his sight, and wilt give ear to his commandments, and keep all his statutes, I will put none of these diseases upon thee, which I have brought upon the Egyptians: for I am the LORD that healeth thee" (Exod. 15:26).

God desires to heal many things:

a. He desires to heal nations—"If my people, which are called by my name, shall humble themselves, and pray, and seek my face, and turn from their wicked ways; then will I hear from heaven, and will forgive their sin, and will heal their land" (2 Chron. 7:14). "In the midst of the street of it, and on either side of the river, was there the tree of life, which bare twelve manner of fruits, and yielded her fruit every month: and the leaves of the tree were for the healing of the nations" (Rev. 22:2).

b. He desires to heal backsliders—In Jeremiah 3:22 we are told, "Return, ye backsliding children, and I will heal your backslidings."

c. He desires to heal broken hearts—David says in Psalm 147:3, "He healeth the broken in heart and bindeth up their wounds."

d. He desires to heal sinful souls—Note the words of David in Psalm 41:4: "I said, Lord, be merciful unto me: heal my soul; for I have sinned against thee."

e. Sometimes, but not all times, Jehovah Rapha heals human bodies—It is not always God's will to heal broken bodies belonging to believers. In 2 Corinthians 1:7, we are told of Paul's infirmity in the flesh. Paul asked God to heal him. God said, "My grace is sufficient." Many believe this infirmity of Paul's was an actual physical infirmity because of what Paul said in

Galatians 4:13-15: "Ye know how through infirmity of the flesh I preached the gospel unto you . . . my temptation which was in my flesh ye despised not, nor rejected, but received me as an angel of God . . . if it had been possible, ye would have plucked out your own eyes, and have given them to me." Based on this passage, many believe that Paul's infirmity was poor eyesight; Galatians 6:11 seems to strengthen their position: "Ye see how large a letter I have written unto you with mine own hand."

Truly, God—Jehovah Rapha—is our healer. Note two other related passages of Scripture: "See now that I, even I, am he, and there is no god with me: I kill, and I make alive; I wound, and I heal: neither is there any that can deliver out of my hand" (Deut. 32:39). "For, behold, the day cometh that shall burn as an oven; and all the proud, yea, and all that do wickedly, shall be stubble: and the day that cometh shall burn them up, saith the Lord of hosts, that it shall leave them neither root nor branch. But unto you that fear my name shall the Sun of righteousness arise with healing in his wings; and ye shall go forth, and grow up as calves of the stall" (Mal. 4:1-2).

IV. The Attributes of God—Reduced to its simplest definition, an attribute of God is whatever God has in any way revealed as being true of himself. Some theologians prefer the word *perfection* to that of attribute. A. W. Tozer has written:

> In the awful abyss of the Divine being may be attributes of which we know nothing and which can have no meaning for us, just as the attributes of mercy and grace can have no personal meaning for seraphim or cherubim. These holy beings may know of these qualities of God but be unable to feel them sympathetically for the reason that they have not sinned and so do not call forth God's mercy and grace. So there may be, and I believe there surely are, other aspects of God's essential being which He has not revealed even to His ransomed and Spirit-illuminated children. (*The Knowledge of the Holy,* p. 52)

Thus, it must be concluded that there are hidden facts of God's nature wholly unknown (and perhaps unknowable) by any created being, even angels. They are known only by Jehovah God himself. Let us now consider some 30 attributes, or perfections, of God.

A. God is Spirit—Jesus made this clear when he told the Samaritan woman: "God is a Spirit: and they that worship him must worship him in Spirit and in truth" (John 4:24).

Emery Bancroft has written: "God as Spirit is incorporeal, invisible, without material substance, without physical parts or passions and therefore free from all temporal limitations" (*Elemental Theory,* p. 23).

Some have been disturbed as they compare these statements with certain Old Testament expressions that speak of God's arms (Deut. 33:27), his eyes (Psa. 33:18), his ears (2 Kings 19:16), and his mouth (Isa. 58:14). However, these terms are simply anthropomorphic expressions, terms used to explain some function or characteristic of God by using words descriptive of human elements. Robert Lightner writes: "Such expressions do not mean that God possesses these physical parts. He is Spirit (John 4:24). Rather, they mean since God is Spirit and eternal, He is capable of doing precisely the functions which are performed by these physical properties in man" (*The God of the Bible,* p. 67).

B. God is a Person—One of the greatest books ever written on the person of God is entitled *The Pursuit of God*, by the late A. W. Tozer. In this book Dr. Tozer wrote the following:

> In this hour of all but universal darkness, one cheering gleam appears. Within the fold of conservative Christianity, there are to be found increasing numbers of persons whose religious lives are marked by a growing hunger after God Himself. They are eager for spiritual realities, and will not be put off with words, nor will they be content with correct "interpretations" of truth. They are athirst for God, and they will not be satisfied until they have drunk deep at the fountain of living water.
>
> The modern scientist has lost God amid the wonders of His world. We Christians are in real danger of losing God amid the wonders of His Word. We have almost forgotten that God is a person; and, as such, can be cultivated as any person can. It is inherent in personality to be able to know other personalities, but full knowledge of one personality by another cannot be achieved in one encounter. It is only after long and loving mental communication that the full possibilities both can be explored. (*The Pursuit of God*, pp. 7, 13)

Dr. Robert Lightner has written the following about the personality of God:

> Personality involves existence with the power of self-consciousness and self-determination. To be self-conscious means to be able to be aware of one's own self among others. It is more than mere consciousness. Even animals possess something which makes them aware of things around them. The brute, however, is not able to objectify himself. Man, in contrast to the brute, possesses both consciousness and self-consciousness. Self-determination has to do with the ability to look to the future and prepare an intelligent course of action. It also involves the power of choice. The brute also has determination, but he does not have self-determination—the power to act from his own free will and to thus determine his acts. It is usually admitted that there are three elements of personality—intellect, emotion and will. (*The God of the Bible*, p. 65)

Thus, as a person, God exhibits all those elements involved in personality. Let us now look at some of the things God does which prove that he is indeed not some mystical principle, but an actual person.

1. He creates—"In the beginning God created the heaven and the earth" (Gen. 1:1).
2. He destroys—"And the Lord said, Because the cry of Sodom and Gomorrah is great, and because their sin is very grievous. . . . Then the Lord rained upon Sodom and upon Gomorrah brimstone and fire from the Lord out of heaven. And he overthrew those cities, and all the plain, and all the inhabitants of the cities, and that which grew upon the ground" (Gen. 18:20; 19:24-25).
3. He provides—"These wait all upon thee; that thou mayest give them their meat in due season. That thou givest them they gather; thou openest thine hands, they are filled with good. Thou hidest thy face, they are troubled: thou takest away their breath, they die, and return to their dust. Thou sendest forth thy spirit, they are created: and thou renewest the face of the earth" (Psa. 104:27-30). "Consider the ravens: for they neither sow nor reap; which neither have storehouse nor barn, and God feedeth them: how much more are ye better than the fowls?" (Luke 12:24).
4. He promotes—"For promotion cometh neither from the east, nor from the west,

nor from the south. But God is the judge: he putteth down one, and setteth up another" (Psa. 75:6-7).

5. He cares—"Humble yourselves therefore under the mighty hand of God, that he may exalt you in due time: Casting all you care upon him; for he careth for you" (1 Pet. 5:6-7). "Cast not away therefore your confidence, which hath great recompense of reward" (Heb. 10:35).

No principle can care. Only a person can care for another person or another object. Poet Thomas Baird wrote these thrilling words concerning these verses in 1 Peter and Hebrews:

> *It is His will that I should cast my cares on him each day,*
> *He also bids me not to cast my confidence away;*
> *But oh! how foolishly I act when taken unaware,*
> *I cast away my confidence and carry all my care.*

6. He hears—"He that planteth the ear, shall he not hear? He that formed the eye, shall he not see? He that chastiseth the heathen, shall not he correct? He that teacheth man knowledge, shall not he know?" (Psa. 94:9-10).

The fact that God hears is mentioned nearly 70 times in the Psalms alone. In almost all cases this fact is connected to hearing our prayers. For example, in Psalm 6:8 God says that he hears in time of sorrow. Then in Psalm 34:6 we are told God hears in time of trouble. Perhaps the greatest passage is found in Psalm 55:17, where we are told that God hears us anytime we pray. David says: "Evening and morning, and at noon, will I pray, and cry aloud: and he shall hear my voice."

7. He hates—There are certain things that God hates, and only a person can be involved in this manner. "These six things doth the Lord hate: yea, seven are an abomination unto him. A proud look, a lying tongue, and hands that shed innocent blood, A heart that deviseth wicked imaginations, feet that be swift in running to mischief, A false witness that speaketh lies and he that soweth discord among brethren" (Prov. 6:16-19).

8. He grieves—"And it repented the Lord that he had made man on the earth, and it grieved him at his heart" (Gen. 6:6). As humans are grieved, God grieves. In the New Testament we are told concerning the ministry of the Holy Spirit, "Grieve not the Holy Spirit of God, whereby ye are sealed unto the day of redemption" (Eph. 4:30).

9. He loves—"For God so loved the world that he gave his only begotten Son, that whosoever believeth in him should not perish, but have everlasting life" (John 3:16).

Perhaps the greatest song ever written is a song that we sometimes limit the singing of to little children. It is the song that, as small children, we learned in Sunday school:

> *Jesus loves me, this I know;*
> *For the Bible tells me so.*
> *Little ones to him belong,*
> *They are weak, but he is strong.*

C. God is one—God is not only a Spirit, he is not only a Person, but he is one. Probably the greatest and most descriptive summary statement in the entire Bible about God is found in Deuteronomy 6. It could be called the theme of the entire Old

Testament, and indeed, of the whole Bible: "Hear, O Israel: The LORD our God is one LORD: and thou shalt love the LORD thy God with all thine heart, and with all thy soul, and with all thy might" (Deut. 6:4-5).

There are so many passages in both the Old and the New Testaments that speak of the unity of God. Listed here are but a few: "That all people of the earth may know that the LORD is God, and that there is none else" (1 Kings 8:60). "I am the LORD, and there is none else, there is no God beside me: I girded thee, though thou hast not known me: that they may know from the rising of the sun and from the west, that there is none beside me. I am the LORD, and there is none else" (Isa. 45:5-6). "There is one body, and one Spirit, even as ye are called in one hope of your calling; one Lord, one faith, one baptism, one God and Father of all, who is above all, and through all, and in you all" (Eph. 4:4-6). "For there is one God, and one mediator between God and man, the man Christ Jesus" (1 Tim. 2:5).

D. God is a Trinity—B. B. Warfield has suggested the following definition concerning the Trinity: "There is only one God, but in the unity of the Godhead, there are three eternal and co-equal Persons, the same in substance, but distinct in subsistence" (James Orr, ed., *International Standard Bible Encyclopedia*, vol. 5, p. 3,012).

Robert Culver writes:

Two expressions have been traditionally employed to designate certain inner relations between the Father and the Son, and the Father and the Son with the Spirit. These two expressions are the eternal generation of the Son by the Father and the eternal spiration (or procession) of the Spirit from the Father and the Son. They began to be employed about the time of Nicea (A.D. 325). They expressed in Scriptural language the idea that the Son and the Spirit were eternally with the Godhead. John 1:14 refers to our Lord as the "only begotten of the Father." John 14:16, 26 and 15:26 speak of the Spirit as "proceeding from the Father and the Son." (*The Living God*, p. 96)

1. False views concerning the Trinity—There are serious errors about the doctrine of the Trinity.
   a. The error of tri-theism—This says that the Trinity consists of three separate (but cooperating) Gods.
   b. The error of modalism—According to this view there is but one God who simply reveals himself through three different modes, or roles. For example, a particular man could be considered a "husband" to his wife, a "father" to his children, and an "employee" to his boss.
   Both tri-theism and modalism are totally unscriptural.
2. Proposed illustrations demonstrating the Trinity—Throughout church history various illustrations have been offered to demonstrate the Trinity. Eight such examples are as follows. The first four are totally unscriptural, while the final four possess some limited possibilities.
   a. A three-leaf clover—Each leaf enjoys the same stem, but this is a poor illustration of the Trinity because these leaves can be separated one from the other, and you cannot separate the Trinity.
   b. The three states of water (liquid, vapor, and solid)—In its natural form, water is liquid. When boiled it turns into vapor, and when frozen, it becomes solid. This, too, is a poor illustration of the Trinity.
   c. The threefold nature of man (body, soul, spirit)—Man possesses body, soul, and spirit, but they can be separated. At death the body is buried; the soul

(the spirit) goes to be with the Lord. You cannot separate the Trinity. Therefore this, too, is a poor illustration.
   d. The three parts of an egg (shell, white, yolk)—These three parts can be separated, thus making a bad illustration.
   e. The nature of light, consisting of three kinds of rays:
      (1) chemical rays—Rays that are invisible, and can neither be felt nor seen
      (2) light rays—Rays that are seen, but cannot be felt
      (3) heat rays—Rays that are felt, but never seen
         Some have said this is a good illustration of the Trinity, because chemical rays are invisible and could illustrate a type of the Father (can neither be felt nor seen). Light rays can be seen but cannot be felt, thus illustrating a type of the Son. Heat rays illustrate a type of the Holy Spirit because they are felt but never seen. This is a possible illustration of the Trinity.
   f. The dimensional example—A book has height, width, and length. This is my favorite example of the Trinity because these three factors cannot be separated, yet they are not the same.
   g. A triangle—This is a fairly good example of the Trinity because it has three sides, and yet, it is a triangle.
   h. Fire—A fire must have three things to exist. They are not the same, but if any ingredient is absent the fire ceases to be. These are: fuel, heat, and oxygen.
      (1) Remove the fuel and the fire goes out.
      (2) Lower the heat and the fire goes out.
      (3) Take away the oxygen and the fire goes out.
3. Old Testament passages regarding the Trinity
   a. The usage of the Hebrew word *Elohim*—The very first verse in the Bible contains God's great name Elohim (Gen. 1:1): "In the beginning God created the heaven and the earth."
      (1) Elohim is a plural name—However, when used in reference to the one true God, it is constantly joined with verbs and adjectives in the singular. "Hear, O Israel: The LORD our God is one LORD" (Deut. 6:4). "See not that I, even I, am he" (Deut. 32:39).
      (2) In many Old Testament passages Elohim is plurally used—"And God said, Let us make man in our image, after our likeness" (Gen. 1:26). "And the LORD God said, Behold, the man is become as one of us, to know good and evil" (Gen. 3:22). "Go to, let us go down, and there confound their language" (Gen. 11:7).
      (3) Certain variants of Elohim are plural—Often one must go back to the original Hebrew translation to see that certain variants of Elohim are plural, although the more current writing would indicate that they are singular. "Remember now thy Creator in the days of thy youth" (Eccles. 12:1). In the original, this is literally "thy Creators." "For thy Maker is thine husband" (Isa. 54:5). Here, *Maker* should be translated "Makers."
   b. The triune conversations in Isaiah—"Also I heard the voice of the Lord saying, Whom shall I send, and who will go for us? Then said I, Here am I; send me" (Isa. 6:8). This passage is a reference to the Trinity.
      "Come ye near unto me, hear ye this; I have not spoken in secret, from the beginning; from the time that it was, there am I; and now the Lord God, and his Spirit, hath sent me" (Isa. 48:16). In this passage the "Son" is speaking about the "Father" who sent him, and the "Holy Spirit."

"In all their affliction he was afflicted, and the angel of his presence saved them; in his love and in his pity he redeemed them; and he bare them, and carried them all the days of old. But they rebelled, and vexed his holy Spirit; therefore he was turned to be their enemy" (Isa. 63:9-10). In this passage there is a reference to the "Father," the "Son," and the "Holy Spirit."

   c. The conversation between the Father and the Son in the Psalms—"The kings of the earth set themselves, and the rulers take counsel together, against the LORD, and against his anointed, saying, Let us break their bands asunder, and cast away their cords from us. . . . I will declare the decree: the LORD hath said unto me, Thou art my Son; this day have I begotten thee" (Psa. 2:2-3, 7). "The LORD said unto my Lord, Sit thou at my right hand, until I make thine enemies thy footstool." (Psa. 110:1)

4. New Testament passages regarding the Trinity.

   a. The baptism of Christ—"And Jesus, when he was baptized, went up straightway out of the water; and lo, the heavens were opened unto him, and he saw the Spirit of God descending like a dove, and lighting upon him: And lo, a voice from heaven saying, This is my beloved Son, in whom I am well pleased" (Matt. 3:16-17).

   b. The temptation of Christ—"Then was Jesus led up of the Spirit into the wilderness to be tempted of the devil" (Matt. 4:1).

   c. The teachings of Jesus—"And I will pray the Father, and he shall give you another Comforter, that he may abide with you forever" (John 14:16). The Greek word here translated "another" is *allos*, meaning another of the same kind. *Heteros* is the Greek word for another of a different kind. It is never used in referring to the Trinity.

     "But the Comforter, which is the Holy Ghost, whom the Father will send in my name, he shall teach you all things, and bring all things to your remembrance, whatsoever I have said unto you" (John 14:26).

   d. The baptismal formula—"Go ye therefore and teach all nations, baptizing them in the name of the Father, and of the Son, and of the Holy Ghost: teaching them to observe all things whatsoever I have commanded you; and lo, I am with you alway, even unto the end of the world. Amen" (Matt. 28:19-20).

   e. The apostolic benediction—"The grace of the Lord Jesus Christ, and the love of God, and the communion of the Holy Ghost, be with you all. Amen" (2 Cor. 13:14).

5. A scriptural summary of the Trinity

   a. The Father is God—"No man can come to me, except the Father which hath sent me draw him: and I will raise him up at the last day" (John 6:44). "Grace to you and peace from God our Father, and the Lord Jesus Christ" (Rom. 1:7). "Elect according to the foreknowledge of God the Father, through sanctification of the Spirit, unto obedience and sprinkling of the blood of Jesus Christ: Grace unto you, and peace, be multiplied" (1 Pet. 1:2).

   b. The Son is God—"For unto us a child is born, unto us a son is given: and the government shall be upon his shoulder: and his name shall be called Wonderful, Counselor, The mighty God, The everlasting Father, The Prince of Peace" (Isa. 9:6). "In the beginning was the Word [Christ], and the Word was with God, and the Word was God" (John 1:1). "And Thomas answered and said unto him [the Son], My Lord and my God" (John 20:28). "Looking for that blessed hope, and the glorious appearing of the great God and our Savior, Jesus Christ" (Titus 2:13). "But unto the Son he saith, Thy throne, O God, is for ever and ever" (Heb. 1:8).

c. The Spirit is God—"But Peter said, Ananias, why hath Satan filled thine heart to lie to the Holy Ghost, and to keep back part of the price of the land? While it remained, was it not thine own? and after it was sold, was it not in thine own power? why hast thou conceived this thing in thine heart? thou has not lied unto men, but unto God" (Acts 5:3-4). "How much more shall the blood of Christ, who through the eternal Spirit offered himself without spot to God, purge your conscience from dead works to serve the living God?" (Heb. 9:14).

Actually, Reginald Hernber, the great songwriter, put the doctrine of the Trinity in poetic form when he wrote the beautiful hymn:

> *Holy, Holy, Holy, Lord God Almighty,*
> *Early in the morning, our song shall rise to Thee;*
> *Holy, Holy, Holy, merciful and mighty,*
> *God in three Persons, blessed Trinity.*

E. God is self-existent—This is simply to say (with staggering implications) that God exists because he exists. He is not dependent upon anything or anyone for his thoughts (Rom.11:33-34), his will (Rom. 9:19; Eph. 1:5), his power (Psa. 115:3), or his counsel (Psa. 33:10-11). "And Moses said unto God, Behold, when I come unto the children of Israel, and shall say unto them, The God of your fathers hath sent me unto you; and they shall say to me, What is his name? what shall I say unto them? And God said unto Moses, I AM THAT I AM; and he said, Thus shalt thou say unto the children of Israel, I AM hath sent me unto you" (Exod. 3:13-14).

In a nutshell, *we* exist because our *parents* existed (past tense), but *God* exists because *he* exists (eternal tense).

F. God is self-sufficient—"For every beast of the forest is mine, and the cattle upon a thousand hills. I know all the fowls of the mountains: and the wild beasts of the field are mine. If I were hungry, I would not tell thee: for the world is mine, and the fulness thereof" (Psa. 50:10-12).

This attribute is closely connected to the attribute of self-existence, but carries it a step further. This means God has never had in eternity past, nor can ever have in the ages to come, a single need for which his own divine nature has not already provided.

G. God is eternal—Simply defined, this means God is absolutely free from the tyranny of time. In him there is no past or future, but one always and never-ending present. He is neither conditioned nor confined by time. "The eternal God is thy refuge, and underneath are the everlasting arms: and he shall thrust out the enemy from before thee; and shall say, Destroy them" (Deut. 33:27). "My days are like a shadow that declineth; and I am withered like grass. But thou, O Lord, shalt endure forever; and thy remembrance unto all generations" (Psa. 102:11-12).

During one of his dialogues with the wicked Pharisees, the Son of God made reference to his attribute of eternality. Note his declaration: "Your father Abraham rejoiced to see my day: and he saw it, and was glad. Then said the Jews unto him, Thou art not yet fifty years old, and hast thou seen Abraham?" (John 8:56-57). In response, it should be noted that Jesus did not say, "Before Abraham was, I *was*," but, "Before Abraham was, I *am*" (John 8:58).

"Before the mountains were brought forth, or ever thou hadst formed the earth and the world, even from everlasting to everlasting, thou art God" (Psa. 90:2).

We see things only as they occur, if we see them at all. Man may be pictured as peeking through a small knothole in a huge fence, watching the parade of life go by. He can only see that tiny section of the parade that passes immediately before his eyes. This section he calls the present. That part of the parade already gone by is the past, while the final part of the parade he calls the future. But the eternal God stands on top of the fence and sees easily the entire panorama. He views the beginning (the past to us), the middle (our present), and looks upon the coming parade (the future to us).

H. God is infinite—God has no limitations. He is bound only by his own nature and will.

"And Solomon stood before the altar of the LORD in the presence of all the congregation of Israel, and spread forth his hands toward heaven: And he said, LORD God of Israel, there is no God like thee, in heaven above, or on earth beneath, who keepest covenant and mercy with thy servants that walk before thee with all their heart. But will God indeed dwell on the earth? Behold, the heaven and heaven of heavens cannot contain thee; how much less this house that I have builded?" (1 Kings 8:22-23, 27). "Can any hide himself in secret places that I shall not see him? said the LORD. Do not I fill heaven and earth? said the LORD" (Jer. 23:24).

These verses totally refute the "God-in-a-box" charge, namely, that the Old Testament God was confined to the Ark of the Covenant in the holy of holies.

I. God is perfect—"As for God, his way is perfect: the word of the LORD is tried: he is a buckler to all those that trust in him" (Psa. 18:30). "Be ye therefore perfect, even as your Father which is in heaven is perfect" (Matt. 5:48). "Every good gift and every perfect gift is from above, and cometh down from the Father of lights, with whom is no variableness, neither shadow of turning" (James 1:17).

The word *perfect* means "complete," without the slightest flaw. This states, therefore, that anything God *is, has,* or *does* is perfect.

1. His various characteristics (attributes) are perfect—His love is a perfect love, his grace is perfect, his holiness is perfect, etc.

2. His law is perfect—"The law of the LORD is perfect, converting the soul: the testimony of the LORD is sure, making wise the simple" (Psa. 19:7).

3. His actions toward believers are perfect—"The LORD will perfect that which concerneth me: thy mercy, O LORD, endureth forever: forsake not the works of thine own hands" (Psa. 138:8).

Thus, all of God's dealings with his people are perfect, that is to say, complete, without the slightest flaw or mistake.

J. God is omnipresent—The great theologian A. H. Strong defines this attribute as follows: "God, in the totality of His essence, without diffusion or expansion, multiplication or division, penetrates and fills the universe in all its parts" (*Systematic Theology,* p. 279).

The omnipresence of God thus means he is present everywhere with his whole being at the same time. The great danger to avoid in rightly understanding this attribute is the grievous error of pantheism, which says that God is everywhere, and everything is God. This is totally false. God is everywhere, but everything is not God.

Paul Enns writes: "The doctrine of omnipresence is a comfort to the believer who recognizes that no calamity can befall him that God is not present with him; it is also a warning to the disobedient person that he cannot escape the presence of God" (*Moody Handbook of Theology,* p. 194).

Two aspects should be kept in mind as one studies the omnipresence of God.

1. God's immanence—This speaks of God being in the world, acting within and through his creation. "For where two or three are gathered together in my name, there am I in the midst of them" (Matt. 18:20).
2. God's transcendence—This affirms that God is above and beyond his creation. "Whither shall I go from thy spirit? Or whither shall I flee from thy presence? If I ascend up into heaven, thou art there: if I make my bed in hell, behold, thou art there. If I take the wings of the morning, and dwell in the uttermost parts of the sea; even there shall thy hand lead me, and thy right hand shall hold me. If I say, Surely the darkness shall cover me; even the night shall be light about me. Yea, the darkness hideth not from thee; but the night shineth as the day; the darkness and the light are both alike to thee" (Psa. 139:7-12).

   Charles Ryrie observes:

   > Omnipresent does not mean that the immediacy of His presence does not vary. It does. His presence on His throne (Rev. 4:2), in Solomon's temple (2 Chron. 7:2), or in the believer (Gal. 2:20) certainly differs in its immediacy from His presence in the lake of fire (Rev. 14:10). Though in the lake of fire people will be separated from the face-presence of God (2 Thess. 1:9, "prosopon"), they will never be separated from Him who is omnipresent (Rev. 14:10, "enopion"). There is obviously no presence of fellowship (for His face will be turned away from the wicked in the lake of fire) as exists when He indwells believers. (*Basic Theology,* p. 41)

K. God is omnipotent (all powerful)—"Is there anything too hard for the LORD? At the time appointed I will return unto thee, according to the time of life, and Sarah shall have a son" (Gen. 18:14). "And I heard as it were the voice of a great multitude, and as the voice of many waters, and as the voice of mighty thunderings, saying, Alleluia: for the Lord God omnipotent reigneth" (Rev. 19:6).

This means God can do anything if it can be done and if it does not contradict his own nature. To illustrate these two things: God *cannot* create a rock so heavy that he couldn't lift it, because the very nature of this act would be impossible to perform. God *cannot* lie, or steal, for these things would contradict his own nature. Here are some areas in which God's omnipotence is clearly seen:

1. Over nature
   a. He separates light from darkness (Gen. 1:4).
   b. He separates the waters by the firmament (space) (Gen. 1:7).
   c. He separates the seas from the dry land (Gen. 1:10).
   d. He measures oceans in his hands (Isa. 40:12).
   e. He weighs mountains in his scale (Isa. 40:12).
   f. He regards nations as a drop in the bucket (Isa. 40:15).
   g. He looks upon the islands as small particles of dirt (Isa. 40:15).
2. Over men—"The king spake and said, Is not this great Babylon, that I have built for the house of the kingdom by the might of my power, and for the honor of my majesty? While the word was in the king's mouth, there fell a voice from heaven saying, O king Nebuchadnezzar, to thee it is spoken; The kingdom is departed from thee. And they shall drive thee from men, and thy dwelling shall be with the beasts of the field: they shall make thee to eat grass as oxen, and

seven times shall pass over thee, until thou know that the most High ruleth in the kingdom of men, and giveth it to whomsoever he will" (Dan. 4:30-32).

3. Over angels—"Bless the Lord, ye his angels, that excel in strength, that do his commandments, hearkening unto the voice of his word" (Psa. 103:20).

4. Over Satan—The first two chapters of Job deal with Satan's accusations against the patriarch before God. The devil then subjects Job to various fierce and fiery trials, but not before being granted the needed specific permission from the omnipotent God himself. (See Job 1:12; 2:6.)

5. Over death—"I am he that liveth, and was dead; and, behold, I am alive for evermore, Amen; and have the keys of hell and of death" (Rev. 1:18). "Forasmuch then as the children are partakers of flesh and blood, he also himself likewise took part of the same; that through death he might destroy him that had the power of death, that is, the devil; and deliver them who through fear of death were all their lifetime subject to bondage" (Heb. 2:14-15).

L. God is omniscient (all knowing)—God possesses (without prior discovery of facts) complete and universal knowledge of all things past, present, and future. This includes not only the actual, but also the possible. This total and immediate knowledge is based on his eternality (he has always and will always exist), and his omnipresence (he has been, is, and will always be everywhere at the same time).

In essence, God knows everything completely, perfectly, independently, simultaneously, and innately. Thus:

- The quantity of his knowledge—complete.
- The quality of his knowledge—perfect.
- The source of his knowledge—independent.
- The time involved concerning his knowledge—simultaneous.
- The method of his knowledge—innate.

"Great is our Lord, and of great power: his understanding is infinite" (Psa. 147:5). "Who hath directed the Spirit of the LORD, or being his counselor hath taught him? With whom took he counsel, and who instructed him, and taught him in the path of judgment, and taught him knowledge, and showed to him the way of understanding? (Isa. 40:13-14). "Neither is there any creature that is not manifest in his sight: but all things are naked and opened unto the eyes of him with whom we have to do" (Heb. 4:13). "O LORD, how manifold are thy works! In wisdom hast thou made them all: the earth is full of thy riches" (Psa. 104:24).

1. He sees all things—"The eyes of the LORD are in every place, beholding the evil and the good" (Prov. 15:3).

2. He knows all things—"He telleth the number of the stars; he calleth them by their names" (Psa. 147:4). "Are not two sparrows sold for a farthing? and one of them shall not fall on the ground without your Father. But the very hairs of your head are all numbered" (Matt. 10:29-30).

3. He knows mankind.

   a. Our thoughts—"Thou understandest my thought afar off" (Psa. 139:2b). "Shall not God search this out? For he knoweth the secrets of the heart" (Psa. 44:21).

   b. Our words—"For there is not a word in my tongue, but lo, O LORD, thou knowest it altogether" (Psa. 139:4). "Then they that feared the LORD spake often one to another: and the LORD hearkened, and heard it, and a book of remembrance was written before him for them that feared the LORD, and that thought upon his name" (Mal. 3:16).

   c. Our deeds—"Thou knowest my downsitting and mine uprising" (Psa.
      139:2a). "I know thy works, and charity, and service, and faith, and thy
      patience" (Rev. 2:19). (See also Psa. 139:3; Rev. 2:2, 9, 13; 3:1, 8, 15.)
   d. Our sorrows—"And the LORD said, I have surely seen the affliction of my
      people which are in Egypt, and have heard their cry by reason of their
      taskmasters; for I know their sorrows" (Exod. 3:7).
   e. Our needs—"(For after all these things do the Gentiles seek;) for your
      heavenly Father knoweth that ye have need of all these things" (Matt. 6:32).
   f. Our devotion—"And the LORD said, Shall I hide from Abraham that thing
      which I do; seeing that Abraham shall surely become a great and mighty nation,
      and all the nations of the earth shall be blessed in him? For I know him, that he
      will command his children and his household after him, and they shall keep the
      way of the LORD, to do justice and judgment; that the LORD may bring upon
      Abraham that which he hath spoken of him" (Gen. 18:17-19).
         "And the angel of the LORD called unto him out of heaven, and said,
      Abraham, Abraham; and he said, Here am I. And he said, Lay not thine
      hand upon the lad, neither do thou anything unto him: for now I know that
      thou fearest God, seeing thou hast not withheld thy son, thine only son from
      me" (Gen. 22:11-12).
         "For the eyes of the LORD run to and fro throughout the whole earth, to
      shew himself strong in the behalf of them whose heart is perfect toward him.
      Herein thou hast done foolishly: Therefore from henceforth thou shalt have
      wars" (2 Chron. 16:9).
         To illustrate this, imagine yourself in the vicinity of the Garden of
      Gethsemane on a warm April night some 2,000 years ago. As you watch, a
      man walks up to Jesus and begins kissing him. You would probably
      conclude, "How this man must love the Master!" Shortly after this you are
      shocked to hear another man bitterly cursing Christ. Now your conclusion
      would be, "How this man must hate the Master!" But both times you would
      be wrong. Judas, the man who kissed Christ, really hated him, and Peter, the
      one who cursed him, really loved him.
   g. Our frailties—"For he knoweth our frame; he remembereth that we are
      dust" (Psa. 103:14).
   h. Our foolishness—"O God, thou knowest my foolishness; and my sins are
      not hid from thee" (Psa. 69:5).
4. He knows his own—"I am the good shepherd, and know my sheep, and am
   known of mine" (John 10:14). "Nevertheless the foundation of God standeth
   sure, having this seal, The Lord knoweth them that are his. And, Let every one
   that nameth the name of Christ depart from iniquity" (2 Tim. 2:19).
5. He knows the past, present and future—"Known unto God are all his works
   from the beginning of the world" (Acts 15:18).
6. He knows what might or could have been—"And thou, Capernaum, which art
   exalted unto heaven, shalt be brought down to hell: for if the mighty works,
   which have been done in thee, had been done in Sodom, it would have
   remained until this day" (Matt. 11:23).
      A. W. Tozer has written:

   God perfectly knows Himself and, being the source and author of all things,
   it follows that He knows all that can be known. And this He knows instantly

and with a fulness of perfection that includes every possible item of knowledge concerning everything that exists or could have existed anywhere in the universe at any time in the past or that may exist in the centuries or ages yet unborn. God knows instantly and effortlessly all matter and all matters, all mind and every mind, all spirit and all spirits, all beings and every being, all creaturehood and all creatures, every plurality and all pluralities, and every law, all relations, all causes, all thoughts, all mysteries, all enigmas, all feeling all desires, every unuttered secret, all thrones and dominions, all personalities, all things visible and invisible in heaven and in earth, motion, space, time, life, death, good, evil, heaven, and hell. (*The Knowledge of The Holy*, p. 62)

M. God is wise—We have already noted that God's omniscience is based upon his eternality and omnipresence. We may now suggest his wisdom is grounded upon his omniscience. Robert Lightner writes:

> Though very closely related, knowledge and wisdom are not the same. Nor do they always accompany each other. No doubt we have all known those who have acquired a great deal of facts but who lacked the ability to use them wisely. Both knowledge and wisdom are imperfect in man but perfect and perfectly related to each other in God. Only He knows how to use His infinite knowledge to the best possible end. Through His wisdom God applies His knowledge to the fulfillment of His own purposes in ways which will bring the most glory to Him. (*The God of the Bible*, p. 99)

A single definition of knowledge and wisdom would read: Knowledge is the accumulation of facts. Wisdom is the ability to rightfully apply those facts.

Following are but a few of the passages that declare the wisdom of God. "To him that by wisdom made the heavens: for his mercy endureth forever" (Psa. 136:5). "The LORD by wisdom hath founded the earth; by understanding hath he established the heavens" (Prov. 3:19). "But we speak the wisdom of God in a mystery, even the hidden wisdom, which God ordained before the world unto our glory" (1 Cor. 2:7). "Now unto the King eternal, immortal, invisible, the only wise God, be honour and glory forever and ever. Amen" (1 Tim. 1:17). "To the only wise God our Savior, be glory and majesty, dominion and power, both now and ever. Amen" (Jude 25).

N. God is immutable—In a sentence, this says that God never differs from himself. He may on occasion alter his dealings with men in a dispensational sense, but his divine character remains constant. This is a vital attribute of God, without which he could not be God. For example, a person may only change in two directions. He may go from better to worse, or from worse to better. But it is unthinkable that God could travel down either of these roads. To go from worse to better implies *past* imperfection. To go from better to worse implies *present* imperfection. However, how can we understand those occasions when we read of God repenting? In fact, this is recorded no less than 15 times in the Old Testament. Note but a few examples:

"And it repented the LORD that he had made man on the earth, and it grieved him at his heart" (Gen. 6:6). "And the LORD repented of the evil which he thought to do unto his people" (Exod. 32:14). "And Samuel came no more to see Saul until the day of his death: nevertheless Samuel mourned for Saul: and the LORD repented that he had made Saul king over Israel" (1 Sam. 15:35). "And God saw their works, that they turned from their evil way; and God repented of the evil, that he had said that he would do unto them; and he did it not" (Jon. 3:10).

Here it is vital to observe God's immutable plan in dealing with man as stated in the Bible. In a nutshell:

1. God will always bless when men do good.
2. God will always judge when men do evil.
3. God will always forgive when men repent.

Thus, in the above cases it was *man* who changed, not God.

"And, Thou, Lord, in the beginning has laid the foundation of the earth; and the heavens are the works of thine hands: They shall perish, but thou remainest: and they all shall wax old as doth a garment; And as a vesture shalt thou fold them up, and they shall be changed: but thou art the same, and thy years shall not fail" (Heb. 1:10-12). "Every good gift and every perfect gift is from above, and cometh down from the Father of lights, with whom is no variableness, neither shadow of turning" (1:17). "Which also said, Ye men of Galilee, why stand ye gazing up into heaven? this same Jesus, which is taken up from you into heaven, shall so come in like manner as ye have seen him go into heaven" (Acts 1:11). "Jesus Christ the same yesterday and today and forever" (Heb. 13:8).

O. God is sovereign—This means that God is the absolute and sole ruler in the universe. To be truly sovereign demands that one have the total freedom, power, knowledge, wisdom, and determination to carry out a predetermined course of action. God possesses all these in infinite measure, and he is thus sovereign.

> The word means principal, chief, supreme. It speaks first of position (God is the chief Being in the universe), then of power (God is supreme in power in the universe). How He exercises that power is revealed in the Scriptures. A sovereign could be a dictator (God is not), or a sovereign could abdicate the use of his powers (God has not). Ultimately God is in complete control of all things, though He may choose to let certain events happen according to natural laws which He has ordained. (Charles Ryrie, *Basic Theology*, p. 43)

Two ancient problems usually surface during any discussion of the sovereignty of God.

1. If God is sovereign, how do we explain the presence of sin and evil? A. W. Tozer writes:

> The Zend-Avesta, sacred book of Zoroastrianism, loftiest of the great non-biblical religions, got around this difficulty neatly enough by postulating a theological dualism. There were two gods, Ormazd and Ahriman, and these between them created the world. The good Ormazd made all good things and the evil Ahriman made the rest. It was quite simple. Ormazd had no sovereignty to worry about, and apparently did not mind sharing his prerogatives with another. (*The Knowledge of the Holy*, p. 117)

This explanation is, of course, totally unscriptural. The only positive statement in our present ignorance is that the sovereign God has indeed allowed (but not arranged) for sin to enter this universe, that through it all he might receive the most glory (Rev. 4:11), and that the elect (Rom. 8:28) might receive the most good.

2. If God is sovereign, how do we reconcile the responsibility and freedom of man? Again, to quote from A. W. Tozer:

Here is my view: God sovereignly decreed that man should be free to exercise moral choice, and man from the beginning has fulfilled that decree by making his choice between good and evil. When he chooses to do evil, he does not thereby countervail the sovereign will of God, but fulfills it, inasmuch as the eternal decree decided not which choice man should make, but that he should be free to make it. (Ibid., p. 118)

"Whatsoever the LORD pleased, that did he in heaven, and in earth, in the seas, and all deep places" (Psa. 135:6). "Remember the former things of old: for I am God, and there is none else; I am God, and there is none like me, declaring the end from the beginning, and from ancient times the things that are not yet done, saying, My counsel shall stand, and I will do all my pleasure: Calling a ravenous bird from the east, the man that executeth my counsel from a far country: yea, I have spoken it, I will also bring it to pass; I have purposed it, I will also do it" (Isa. 46:9-11).

Charles Ryrie aptly summarizes:

The sovereignty of God seems to contradict the freedom or actual responsibility of man. But even though it may seem to do so, the perfection of sovereignty is clearly taught in the Scriptures so must not be denied because of our inability to reconcile it with freedom or responsibility. Also, if God is sovereign, how can the creation be so filled with evil?

Man was created with genuine freedom, but the exercise of that freedom in rebellion against God introduced sin into the human race. Though God was the Designer of the plan, He was in no way involved in the commission of evil either on the part of Satan originally, or of Adam subsequently. Even though God hates sin, for reasons not revealed to us, sin is present by His permission. Sin must be within God's eternal plan (or God would not be sovereign) in some way in which He is not the author of it (or God could not be holy). (*Basic Theology*, p. 43)

P. God is incomprehensible—By this it is stated that no one except God himself can even remotely understand and comprehend God. "Yet man is born unto trouble, as the sparks fly upward. I would seek unto God, and unto God would I commit my cause: Which doeth great things and unsearchable; marvelous things without number" (Job 5:7-9). "Canst thou by searching find out God? Canst thou find out the Almighty unto perfection? It is as high as heaven; what canst thou do? deeper than hell; what canst thou know? The measure thereof is longer than the earth, and broader than the sea" (Job 11:7-9).

"Thy mercy, O LORD, is in the heavens; and thy faithfulness reacheth unto the clouds. Thy righteousness is like the great mountains; thy judgments are a great deep: O LORD, thou preservest man and beast" (Psa. 36:5-6). "O the depth of the riches both of the wisdom and knowledge of God! how unsearchable are his judgments, and his ways past finding out! (Rom. 11:33).

To illustrate this attribute, consider the following: Let us suppose in heaven we are able to double our learning each year concerning the person and attributes of God. This is not at all an unreasonable assumption, for the Christian will possess a sinless and glorified body, along with a holy and tireless desire to know more about Jesus. So here is a believer who begins eternity with *x* amount of knowledge about God. At the beginning of the second year he has doubled this, the third year he learns four times as much, the fourth year, eight times as much, etc. By the end of his eleventh year he will have increased his knowledge concerning God a thousandfold. At the conclusion of year number 21 the figure jumps to one million. At the end of the thirty-first year the number leaps to one billion. Following the forty-first year it reaches one trillion. As he finishes his first century in eternity his knowledge of God (doubling each year) would reach 10^{30} (one followed by 30 zeroes) times his original amount of knowledge. This figure is thousands of times more than the combined total of all the grains of sand on all the seashores of the earth. But this number simply marks his first 100 years. How much knowledge-doubling will he have experienced at the end of his first one million years? This staggering figure cannot even be comprehended by the mortal mind, but whatever it is, and however many zeroes it represents, it will double itself the very next year.

The point of all the above is simply this: Throughout the untold and unnumbered trillions and trillions of years in timeless eternity, each child of God can double his or her learning about the Creator each year and yet never even remotely exhaust the awesome height, depth, or length to be known of the person of God.

Q. God is inscrutable—"How unsearchable are his judgments, and his ways past finding out" (Rom. 11:33).

This attribute refers to the inexplicable and mysterious ways of God. It raises the most painful question of all: Why does a loving and wise God allow certain terrible tragedies to occur? As an example, here is a young, spirit-filled pastor. He has spent a number of years diligently preparing for the ministry. His wife has sacrificed to help put him through school. But now all this is paying off. His church is experiencing an amazing growth. Souls are saved weekly. New converts are baptized each Sunday. Additional Sunday school buses are purchased, and a new building is planned. A skeptical community slowly finds itself being profoundly influenced by this vibrant and exciting pastor and his people. Suddenly, without any warning, the minister is killed in a freak accident. Shortly after the funeral the still confused and stunned congregation extends a call to another man. But the new minister shows little compassion and less leadership ability. Soon the flock is scattered and the once thrilling testimony of a growing and glowing work is all but stilled.

How many times since Abel's martyrdom at the dawn of human history have similar tragedies taken place? One need only change the names, places, and rearrange some of the details. But the searing and searching question remains: Why does God permit such terrible things? A clue (and only a clue) to this question is seen in the tenth chapter of Revelation: "But in the days of the voice of the seventh angel, when he shall begin to sound, the mystery of God should be finished, as he hath declared to his servants the prophets" (Rev. 10:7). But until the sound of that blessed trumpet, the perplexed child of God can arrive at no better conclusion than once offered by Abraham: "Shall not the Judge of all the earth do right" (Gen. 18:25).

This sublime statement is amplified on at least three other biblical occasions:

1. By Moses—"He is the Rock, his work is perfect: for all his ways are judgment: a God of truth and without iniquity, just and right is he" (Deut. 32:4).
2. By Job—"Naked came I out of my mother's womb, and naked shall I return thither. The Lord gave, and the Lord hath taken away; blessed be the name of the Lord" (Job 1:21). "Though he slay me, yet will I trust in him" (Job 13:15).
3. By a Galilean crowd in Jesus' day—"He hath done all things well" (Mark 7:37).

R. God is holy—Without a doubt, the most prominent attribute of God as presented by both Old and New Testament Scriptures is his holiness. This one single perfection would perhaps come closer to describing the eternal Creator than any other characteristic he possesses. It has been suggested that his holiness is the union of all other attributes, as pure white light is the union of all the colored rays of the spectrum. Note but a few biblical references: "Speak unto all the congregation of the children of Israel, and say unto them, Ye shall be holy: for I the LORD your God am holy" (Lev. 19:2). "Exalt the LORD our God, and worship at his holy hill; for the LORD our God is holy" (Psa. 99:9). "But as he which hath called you is holy, so be ye holy in all manner of conversation" (1 Pet. 1:15).

A. W. Tozer writes:

"Holy" is the way God is. To be holy He does not conform to a standard. He *is* that standard. He is absolutely holy with an infinite, incomprehensible fullness of purity that is incapable of being other than it is. Because He is holy, all His attributes are holy; that is, whatever we think of as belonging to God must be thought of as holy.

God is holy and He made holiness the moral condition necessary to the health of His universe. Sin's temporary presence in the world only accents this. Whatever is holy is healthy: evil is a moral sickness that must end ultimately in death. The formation of the language itself suggests this, the English word "holy" deriving from the Anglo-Saxon "halig, hal," meaning "well, whole."

Since God's first concern for His universe is its moral health, that is, its holiness, whatever is contrary to this is necessarily under His eternal displeasure. To preserve His creation God must destroy whatever would destroy it. When He arises to put down iniquity and save the world from inseparable moral collapse, He is said to be angry. Every wrathful judgment in the history of the world has been a holy act of preservation. The holiness of God, the wrath of God, and the health of the creation are inseparably united. God's wrath is His utter intolerance of whatever degrades and destroys. He hates iniquity as a mother hates the polio that would take the life of her child. (*The Knowledge of the Holy*, p. 113)

In a sense there are both negative and positive aspects to God's holiness:
• Negative—The absence of any unclean or evil element
• Positive—The abundance of every clean and pure element

In the Bible God underlines his holiness by direct commands, objects, personal visions, and individual judgments.

1. Direct commandments
   a. The moral law (Ten Commandments) (Exod. 19:10-25; 20:1-17)
   b. The spiritual law (feasts and offerings) (Exod. 35–40; Lev. 1–7; 23)
   c. The ceremonial law (diet, sanitation, etc.) (Lev. 11:15)
2. Objects—The main object was the tabernacle itself.
3. Personal visions
   a. Moses' vision—"And he said, I beseech thee, shew me thy glory. And he said, I will make all my goodness pass before thee, and I will proclaim the name of the LORD before thee; and will be gracious to whom I will be gracious, and will shew mercy on whom I will shew mercy. And he said, Thou canst not see my face: for there shall no man see me, and live. And the

LORD said, Behold, there is a place by me, and thou shalt stand upon a rock: And it shall come to pass, while my glory passeth by, that I will put thee in a clift of the rock, and will cover thee with my hand while I pass by: And I will take away mine hand, and thou shalt see my back parts: but my face shall not be seen" (Exod. 33:18-23).

b. Isaiah's vision—"In the year that King Uzziah died I saw also the Lord sitting upon a throne, high and lifted up, and his train filled the temple. Above it stood the seraphims: each one had six wings; with twain he covered his face, and with twain he covered his feet, and with twain he did fly. And one cried unto another, and said, Holy, holy, holy, is the LORD of hosts: the whole earth is full of his glory. And the posts of the door moved at the voice of him that cried, and the house was filled with smoke. Then said I, Woe is me! for I am undone; because I am a man of unclean lips, and I dwell in the midst of a people of unclean lips: for mine eyes have seen the King, the LORD of hosts" (Isa. 6:1-5).

c. Daniel's vision—"I beheld till the thrones were cast down, and the Ancient of days did sit, whose garment was white as snow, and the hair of his head like the pure wool; his throne was like the fiery flame, and his wheels as burning fire. A fiery stream issued and came forth from before him: thousand thousands ministered unto him, and ten thousand times ten thousand stood before him: the judgment was set, and the books were opened. I beheld then because of the voice of the great words which the horn spake: I beheld even till the beast was slain, and his body destroyed, and given to the burning flame. As concerning the rest of the beasts, they had their dominion taken away: yet their lives were prolonged for a season and time. I saw in the night visions, and, behold, one like the Son of man came with the clouds of heaven, and came to the Ancient of days, and they brought him near before him. And there was given him dominion, and glory, and a kingdom, that all people, nations, and languages, should serve him: his dominion is an everlasting dominion, which shall not pass away, and his kingdom that which shall not be destroyed" (Dan. 7:9-14).

d. John's vision—"And the four beasts had each of them six wings about him; and they were full of eyes within: and they rest not day and night, saying, Holy, holy, holy, Lord God Almighty, which was, and is, and is to come. And when those beasts give glory and honor and thanks to him that sat on the throne, who liveth forever and ever, the four and twenty elders fall down before him that sat on the throne, and worship him that liveth forever and ever, and cast their crowns before the throne, saying, Thou art worthy, O Lord, to receive glory and honor and power: for thou has created all things, and for thy pleasure they are and were created" (Rev. 4:8-11).

Note the threefold usage of the word *holy* here. In the Scriptures we never read the expression, "grace, grace, grace, Lord God Almighty", or "love, love, love, Lord God Almighty." But on two specific occasions we do read, "Holy, holy, holy, Lord God Almighty" (Isa. 6:3; Rev. 4:8). It is as if this attribute of God is so important that one "holy" will not suffice.

4. Individual judgments
   a. Upon Nadab and Abihu, for offering strange fire (Lev. 10:1-3)
   b. Upon Korah, for rebellion (Num. 16:4-12, 31-33)
   c. Upon Uzziah, for intruding into the office of the priest (2 Chron. 26:16-21)

      d. Upon Herod, for blasphemy (Acts 12:20-23)

      e. Upon Christ, for the sins of the world (Isa. 53:1-10; Psa. 22:1; Heb. 2:7; 1 Pet. 2:21-25; 3:18)—Without a doubt, the greatest historical example of God's holiness was Calvary.

S. God is righteous and just—Righteousness can be defined as moral equity. Justice is the illustration of this moral equity. In righteousness, God reveals his love for holiness. In justice, God reveals his hatred for sin. The Scriptures present this twin attribute in a threefold light.

  1. The intrinsic righteousness and justice of God—"And Pharaoh sent, and called for Moses and Aaron, and said unto them, I have sinned this time: the LORD is righteous, and I and my people are wicked" (Exod. 9:27). "O LORD God of Israel, thou art righteous: for we remain yet escaped, as it is this day: behold, we are before thee in our trespasses: for we cannot stand before thee because of this" (Ezra 9:15).

  2. The legislative righteousness and justice of God—"O let the nations be glad and sing for joy: for thou shalt judge the people righteously, and govern the nations upon earth. Selah" (Psa. 67:4). "Oh let the wickedness of the wicked come to an end; but establish the just: for the righteous God trieth the hearts and reins" (Psa. 7:9). "Say among the heathen that the LORD reigneth: the world also shall be established that it shall not be moved: he shall judge the people righteously" (Psa. 96:10). "Righteous art thou, O LORD, and upright are thy judgments" (Psa. 119:137).

      a. Rewarding the good—"Henceforth there is laid up for me a crown of righteousness, which the Lord, the righteous judge, shall give me at that day, and not to me only, but unto all them that love his appearing" (2 Tim. 4:8).

      It should be pointed out, however, that while God's righteousness guarantees rewards, it does not bestow them. A. H. Strong writes as follows:

> Neither justice or righteousness bestows reward. This follows from the fact that obedience is due to God, instead of being optional or a gratuity. No creature can claim anything for his obedience. If God rewards, He rewards by virtue of His goodness and faithfulness, but not by virtue of His justice or His righteousness. (*Systematic Theology*, p. 293)

      b. Punishing the evil—"Alexander, the coppersmith, did me much evil: the Lord reward him according to his works" (2 Tim. 4:14). "And I heard the angel of the waters say, Thou art righteous, O Lord, which art, and wast, and shalt be, because thou hast judged thus. For they have shed the blood of saints and prophets, and thou hast given them blood to drink; for they are worthy. And I heard another out of the altar say, Even so, Lord God Almighty, true and righteous are thy judgments" (Rev. 16:5-7).

  3. The imputed righteousness of God—"And what saith the scripture? Abraham believed God, and it was counted unto him for righteousness" (Rom. 4:3). (See also Rom. 4:6-8; Phil. 3:7-9; 1 Pet. 2:24.)

T. God is true—"Paul, a servant of God, and an apostle of Jesus Christ, according to the faith of God's elect, and the acknowledging of the truth which is after godliness; in hope of eternal life, which God, that cannot lie, promised before the world began" (Titus 1:1-2). "And this is life eternal, that they might know thee, the only true God, and Jesus Christ, whom thou hast sent" (John 17:3). (See also 1 Thess. 1:9; Rom. 3:4.)

A. H. Strong makes the following statement: "By truth we mean that attribute of the Divine nature in virtue of which God's being and God's knowledge eternally conform to each other" (*Systematic Theology*, p. 260).

Truth is therefore anything factual about God. The child of God may well say, "I speak (or serve) the truth," but only the Son of God can say, "I *am* the truth" (John 14:6). Again to quote from A. H. Strong:

> Since Christ is the truth of God, we are successful in our search for truth only as we recognize Him. Whether all roads lead to Rome depends upon which way your face is turned. Follow a point of land out into the sea, and you find only ocean. With the back turned upon Jesus Christ all following after truth leads only into mist and darkness. (Ibid., p. 262)

God is the ultimate and only source and standard of truth. This is why the Bible describes the "God that cannot lie" (Titus 1:2), and concludes that it is utterly "impossible for God to lie" (Heb. 6:18).

This may be taken a step further and stated that he not only *cannot* lie, but he *need not* lie. A lie is almost always resorted to by human beings to get out of a tight spot, to impress someone, to gain an advantage, etc. But Almighty God never finds himself in any of these situations. In Psalms he speaks to us concerning this: "For every beast of the forest is mine, and the cattle upon a thousand hills. I know all the fowls of the mountains: and the wild beasts of the field are mine. If I were hungry, I would not tell thee: for the world is mine, and the fullness thereof" (Psa. 50:10-12).

To summarize this attribute:

1. God is true because his character and reputation are identical.
2. In light of this, he is both the source and standard of all truth, which is derived from him and defined by him. Thus, as *all* truth resides in him, then *any* truth must be revealed by him. This includes every fact concerning time, space, the universe, angels, man, animals, and the very atoms themselves.
3. How does this attribute relate to man? Consider the following illustration, which may be referred to as "Nile River knowledge."

    One's first flight over Egypt is a remarkable experience. To describe the sight from the air, imagine a sheet of light brown construction paper. Take a blue felt-tip pen and make a line down the center of the sheet from top to bottom. Now take a green felt-tip pen and make two lines, one on each side of the blue line. This is how Egypt looks from a plane; the blue line is the Nile, and the green line on either side is the fertile and productive strip of land created by the life-giving waters. The brown sheet itself represents the desert.

    All knowledge possessed by human beings can be pictured as the untold grains of sand represented by that brown sheet. It is there, but totally useless and unproductive in and by itself. But allow the waters of the Word of God to occupy the central place, then suddenly any and all facts become fertile, useful, and productive wisdom.

U. God is faithful—God's faithfulness refers to his self-loyalty and to his loyalty to his entire creation. He will not (indeed, he cannot) change his character nor fail to perform all he has promised.

"Know therefore that the LORD thy God, he is God, the faithful God, which keepeth covenant and mercy with them that love him and keep his commandments to a thousand generations" (Deut. 7:9). "Thy mercy, O LORD, is in the heavens; and thy faithfulness reacheth unto the clouds" (Psa. 36:5). "I will sing of the mercies of the LORD forever: with my mouth will I make known thy faithfulness to all generations. For I have said, Mercy shall be built up forever: thy faithfulness shalt thou establish in the very heavens" (Psa. 89:1-2). "It is of the LORD's mercies that we are not consumed, because his compassions fail not. They are new every morning: great is thy faithfulness" (Lam. 3:22-23).

God's faithfulness is seen in many areas.

1. In nature—"Thy faithfulness is unto all generations: thou hast established the earth, and it abideth" (Psa. 119:90). "While the earth remaineth, seedtime and harvest, and cold and heat, and summer and winter, and day and night shall not cease" (Gen. 8:22). "And he is before all things, and by him all things consist" (Col. 1:17).

2. In keeping his promises to his friends
   a. Adam—He promised Adam that someday a Savior would come from the seed of a woman. (Compare Gen. 3:15 with Gal. 4:4.)
   b. Abraham—He promised Abraham he would father a son in his old age. (Compare Gen. 15:4; 18:14 with Gen. 21:1-2.)
   c. Moses—He promised Moses that Israel would not leave Egypt empty-handed. (Compare Exod. 3:2 with Exod. 12:35-36.)
   d. Joshua—He promised Joshua glorious victory. (Compare Josh. 1:1-5 with Josh. 23:14.)
   e. David—He promised David a king would come from his line who would rule eternally. (Compare 2 Sam. 7:12-13 with Luke 1:31-33.)

3. In keeping his warnings against his enemies
   a. Ahab—He warned wicked King Ahab that because he had murdered godly Naboth, the very location "where dogs licked the blood of Naboth shall dogs lick thy blood." (Compare 1 Kings 21:17-19 with 1 Kings 22:34-38.)
   b. Jezebel—He warned wicked Jezebel that the wild dogs of Jezreel would someday eat her dead body beside the city wall. (Compare 1 Kings 21:23 with 2 Kings 9:30-37.)

4. In times of temptation—"There hath no temptation taken you but such as is common to man; but God is faithful, who will not suffer you to be tempted above that ye are able; but will with the temptation also make a way to escape, that ye may be able to bear it" (2 Cor. 10:13).

5. In chastening his children—"I know, O LORD, that thy judgments are right, and that thou in faithfulness hast afflicted me" (Psa. 119:75). "For whom the Lord loveth he chasteneth, and scourgeth every son whom he receiveth" (Heb. 12:6).

6. In forgiving our sins—"If we confess our sins, he is faithful and just to forgive us our sins, and to cleanse us from all unrighteousness" (1 John 1:9).

7. In answering our prayers—"Hear my prayer, O LORD, give ear to my supplications; in thy faithfulness answer me, and in thy righteousness" (Psa. 143:1).

8. In keeping the saved saved—"Who shall also confirm you unto the end, that ye may be blameless in the day of our Lord Jesus Christ. God is faithful, by whom ye were called unto the fellowship of his son Jesus Christ our Lord" (1 Cor. 1:8-9). "And the very God of peace sanctify you wholly; and I pray God your whole spirit and soul and body be preserved blameless unto the coming of our Lord Jesus Christ. Faithful is he that calleth you, who also will do it" (1 Thess.

5:23-24). "But the Lord is faithful, who shall stablish you and keep you from evil" (2 Thess. 3:3).

9. In defending his people—God defended the city of Jerusalem against its enemies on at least three occasions.

   a. In the days of King Asa (2 Chron. 14:9-15)

   b. In the days of King Jehoshaphat (2 Chron. 20:1-25)

   c. In the days of King Hezekiah (2 Kings 19:32-35)

   "For the LORD will not forsake his people for his great name's sake: because it hath pleased the LORD to make you his people" (1 Sam. 12:22). "If we believe not, yet he abideth faithful: he cannot deny himself" (2 Tim. 2:13).

V. God is light—He is both the source and strength of all illumination. This refers not only to those golden beams of energy radiating from the sun and stars, but also to moral, mental, and spiritual rays of information and inspiration. "For with thee is the fountain of life: in thy light shall we see light" (Psa. 36:9). "Who coverest thyself with light as with a garment: who stretchest out the heavens like a curtain" (Psa. 104:2).

"But ye are a chosen generation, a royal priesthood, an holy nation, a peculiar people; that ye should shew forth the praises of him who hath called you out of darkness into his marvelous light" (1 Pet. 2:9). "But if we walk in the light, as he is in the light, we have fellowship one with another, and the blood of Jesus Christ his Son cleanseth us from all sin" (1 John 1:7). "For God, who commanded the light to shine out of darkness, hath shined in our hearts, to give the light of the knowledge of the glory of God in the face of Jesus Christ" (2 Cor. 4:6). "Who only hath immortality, dwelling in the light which no man can approach unto; whom no man hath seen, nor can see; to whom be honour and power everlasting. Amen" (1 Tim. 6:16). "Every good gift and every perfect gift is from above, and cometh down from the Father of lights, with whom is no variableness, neither shadow of turning" (1:17). "This then is the message which we have heard of him, and declare unto you, that God is light, and in him is no darkness at all" (1 John 1:5).

This attribute of God is referred to some 100 times in the Bible.

1. The first occasion has to do with the earth and creation—"And God said, Let there be light: and there was light" (Gen. 1:3).

2. The final occasion has to do with the heavenly city and redemption—"And there shall be no night there; and they need no candle, neither light of the sun; for the Lord God giveth them light: and they shall reign for ever and ever" (Rev. 22:5).

3. This attribute as related to the saints—"The LORD is my light and my salvation; whom shall I fear? the LORD is the strength of my life; of whom shall I be afraid?" (Psa. 27:1). (See also Psa. 43:3; 89:15; 112:4; 119:105; 139:11-12.)

4. This attribute as related to the Savior—"Then spake Jesus again unto them, saying, I am the light of the world: he that followeth me shall not walk in darkness, but shall have the light of life" (John 8:12). (See also Isa. 9:2; 42:6; 49:6; Matt. 4:16; 17:2; Luke 2:32; John 1:4-5, 7-9; 3:19-21; 9:5; 12:35-36, 46.)

W. God is good—A. H. Strong defines goodness as follows: "Goodness is the eternal principle of God's nature which leads Him to communicate of His own life and blessedness to those who are like Him in moral character" (*Systematic Theology*, p. 289).

A. W. Tozer writes in similar fashion as follows:

The goodness of God is that which disposes Him to be kind, cordial, benevolent, and full of good will toward men. He is tenderhearted and of quick sympathy, and His unfailing attitude toward all moral beings is open, frank, and friendly. By His nature He is inclined to bestow blessedness, and He takes holy pleasure in the happiness of His people. (*The Knowledge of the Holy.* p. 88)

"Oh that men would praise the LORD for his goodness and for his wonderful works to the children of men! (Psa. 107:8). "Surely goodness and mercy shall follow me all the days of my life; and I will dwell in the house of the LORD for ever" (Psa. 23:6). "Or despisest thou the riches of his goodness and forbearance and long-suffering; not knowing that the goodness of God leadeth thee to repentance?" (Rom. 2:4).

X. God is patient and long-suffering—This attribute has to do with God's restraint concerning his righteous wrath and judgment in the face of rebellion and sin. "And the Lord passed by before him, and proclaimed, The LORD, The LORD God, merciful and gracious, longsuffering, and abundant in goodness and truth" (Exod. 34:6). "But thou, O Lord, art a God full of compassion and gracious, longsuffering and plenteous in mercy and truth" (Psa. 86:15). "The LORD is merciful and gracious, slow to anger, and plenteous in mercy" (Psa. 103:8).

"Or despisest thou the riches of his goodness and forbearance and longsuffering; not knowing that the goodness of God leadeth thee to repentance?" (Rom. 2:4). "The Lord is not slack concerning his promise, as some men count slackness; but is longsuffering to us-ward, not willing that any should perish, but that all should come to repentance" (2 Pet. 3:9).

Y. God is merciful—Mercy is that eternal principle of God's nature that leads him to seek the temporal good and eternal salvation of those who have opposed themselves to his will, even at the cost of infinite self-sacrifice. God's mercy is optional, in that he is in no way obligated to save sinners. However, he chooses to do so.

The Old Testament speaks four times as much about the mercy of God as does the New Testament. It is mentioned twenty-six times in Psalm 136 alone. Mercy then, among other things, is not getting what we deserve, namely, hell.

1. The example of David—Psalm 51 is the confessional psalm prayed by David after his shameful sin with Bathsheba, which included both adultery and murder. He begins by pleading for mercy and ends by acknowledging that no animal sacrifice could cleanse his sin. He then bypasses the Levitical offerings and throws himself completely upon the mercy of God (see Psalm 51). "Have mercy upon me, O God, according to thy lovingkindness: according unto the multitude of thy tender mercies blot out my transgressions. . . . For thou desirest not sacrifice; else would I give it: thou delightest not in burnt offering. The sacrifices of God are a broken spirit: a broken and a contrite heart, O God, thou wilt not despise" (Psa. 51:1, 16-17).

2. The example of Israel—"The LORD is merciful and gracious, slow to anger, and plenteous in mercy. He will not always chide; neither will he keep his anger forever. He hath not dealt with us after our sins; nor rewarded us according to our iniquities. For as the heaven is high above the earth, so great is his mercy toward them that fear him. As far as the east is from the west, so far hath he removed our transgressions from us. Like as a father pitieth his children, so the Lord pitieth them that fear him. For he knoweth our frame; he remembereth that we are dust. As for man, his days are as grass; as a flower of the field, so he

flourisheth. For the wind passeth over it, and it is gone; and the place thereof shall know it no more. But the mercy of the LORD is from everlasting to everlasting upon them that fear him, and his righteousness unto children's children" (Psa. 103:8-17).

"For finding fault with them, he saith, Behold, the days come, saith the Lord, when I will make a new covenant with the house of Israel and with the house of Judah. . . . For I will be merciful to their unrighteousness, and their sins and their iniquities will I remember no more" (Heb. 8:8, 12).

3. The example of Jonah—"And he prayed unto the LORD, and said, I pray thee, O LORD, was not this my saying, when I was yet in my country? Therefore I fled before unto Tarshish: for I knew that thou art a gracious God, and merciful, slow to anger, and of great kindness, and repentest thee of the evil." (Jon. 4:2).

4. The example of Paul—"Who was before a blasphemer, and a persecutor, and injurious; but I obtained mercy, because I did it ignorantly in unbelief. . . . Howbeit for this cause I obtained mercy, that in me first Jesus Christ might shew forth all longsuffering, for a pattern to them which should hereafter believe on him to life everlasting" (1 Tim. 1:13, 16).

Z. God is gracious—The very simplest definition of this beautiful attribute is unmerited favor. It is helpful at this point to contrast mercy with grace. God's *mercy* allows him to withhold *merited* punishment. God's *grace* allows him to freely bestow *unmerited* favor. *Mercy* is not getting what we deserve, namely, hell. *Grace* is getting what we do not deserve, namely, heaven.

Consider the following illustration: A young man has been sentenced to life imprisonment for leading a violent rebellion against his king. One day the king himself visits the prisoner. To the amazement of the young rebel, his ruler sets him free. After releasing him, the king then offers to provide a permanent place in the royal palace for the ex-convict. Finally, the ruler states his intention to adopt the former rebel as his own son. At this point, the prisoner has experienced both mercy and grace. When released, he experienced mercy, that is, he did *not* receive that which he deserved, namely, the life of a prisoner. When adopted, he experienced grace, that is he *did* receive that which he did not deserve, namely, the life of a prince.

"He hath made his wonderful works to be remembered: the LORD is gracious and full of compassion" (Psa. 111:4). "Gracious is the LORD, and righteous; yea, our God is merciful" (Psa. 116:5). "If so be ye have tasted that the Lord is gracious" (1 Pet. 2:3). "But the God of all grace, who hath called us into his eternal glory by Christ Jesus, after that ye have suffered a while, make you perfect, stablish, strengthen, settle you" (1 Pet. 5:10).

1. God's grace is seen through all dispensations in history—God's grace is first mentioned on the eve of the first universal world destruction: "But Noah found grace in the eyes of the Lord" (Gen. 6:8). The last reference to grace occurs in Scripture's final verse: "The grace of our Lord Jesus Christ be with you all. Amen" (Rev. 22:21).

2. God's grace is always a free gift—"Being justified freely by his grace through the redemption that is in Christ Jesus" (Rom. 3:24). "For by grace are ye saved through faith; and that not of yourselves; it is the gift of God: not of works, lest any man should boast" (Eph. 2:8-9).

3. God's grace always precedes his peace—"To all that be in Rome, beloved of God, called to be saints: Grace to you and peace from God our Father, and the Lord Jesus Christ" (Rom. 1:7).

The phrase "Grace to you and peace," a common salutation in that day, is found many times in the New Testament, but always in this order—never "peace and grace." It is spiritually true that one cannot experience God's peace until he has first appropriated his grace.

4. God's grace was incarnate in Christ—"For the law was given by Moses, but grace and truth came by Jesus Christ" (John 1:17). "And the Word was made flesh, and dwelt among us (and we beheld his glory, the glory as of the only begotten of the Father), full of grace and truth" (John 1:14). "For the grace of God that bringeth salvation hath appeared to all men" (Titus 2:11).

5. God's grace is greater than man's sin—"Moreover the law entered, that the offence might abound. But where sin abounded, grace did much more abound" (Rom. 5:20).

6. God's grace was displayed at Calvary—"But we see Jesus, who was made a little lower than the angels for the suffering of death, crowned with glory and honour; that he by the grace of God should taste death for every man" (Heb. 2:9).

7. God's grace makes a man what he is—"My grace is sufficient for thee: for my strength is made perfect in weakness. Most gladly therefore will I rather glory in my infirmities, that the power of Christ may rest upon me" (2 Cor. 12:9). "But by the grace of God I am what I am: and his grace which was bestowed upon me was not in vain; but I laboured more abundantly than they all: yet not I, but the grace of God which was with me" (1 Cor. 15:10). "Let us therefore come boldly unto the throne of grace, that we may obtain mercy, and find grace to help in time of need" (Heb. 4:16).

8. God's grace was perhaps the attribute that prompted him to create the world in the first place. (See Ephesians 2.)

AA. God is love—This is at once the most universally known and universally misunderstood attribute of all. Millions have simply equated love with God, thus weakening or totally denying his other perfections. A man and woman may have an affair hidden from their spouses and justify their adulterous relationship by their great "love" for each other. But God's love cannot be separated or isolated from his holiness and hatred for sin. Having said all this, however, it must be admitted that of all his attributes, God's love is probably more quickly seized upon by seeking sinners than any other perfection. The smallest child can sing with great understanding, "Jesus loves me, this I know, for the Bible tells me so!"

1. Definitions of love
   a. Love is unselfish concern about another's welfare.
   b. Love is that act of one person seeking the highest good for another person.
      Of all the 30 attributes presented during this study, three of them (mercy, grace, love) will probably be the most difficult to explain to angels, who have never experienced them. It would be like attempting to explain the breathtaking majesty of the Grand Canyon during a magnificent sunset and the glorious sound coming from a nearby symphony orchestra to a friend who was born blind and deaf.

2. Important truths concerning God's love
   a. It is impartial—"Or despisest thou the riches of his goodness and forbearance and longsuffering; not knowing that the goodness of God leadeth thee to repentance?" (Rom. 2:4). (See also Deut. 10:17; Acts 10:34-35.)
   b. It is universal (John 3:16).

    c. It is everlasting—"The LORD hath appeared of old unto me, saying, Yea, I have loved thee with an everlasting love: therefore with lovingkindness have I drawn thee" (Jer. 31:3).

    d. It is independent—The Greek word used in describing God's love for man is *agape*. This kind of love is absolutely unique, for it is not dependent upon the beauty of the object being loved. Naturally, human love does not function this way. We love others because they love us or because we see some beauty or value in them. But note how and when God loved us: "But God commendeth his love toward us, in that, while we were yet sinners, Christ died for us" (Rom. 5:8).

    e. It is proven love—God demonstrated his love for us at Calvary. "In this was manifested the love of God toward us, because that God sent his only begotten Son into the world, that we might live through him" (1 John 4:9).

3. Objects of God's love

    a. God loves Israel—"The LORD did not set his love upon you, nor choose you, because ye were more in number than any people; for ye were the fewest of all people. But because the LORD loved you, and because he would keep the oath which he had sworn unto your father, hath the LORD brought you out with a mighty hand, and redeemed you out of the house of bondmen, from the hand of Pharaoh, king of Egypt" (Deut. 7:7-8). "Can a woman forget her suckling child, that she should not have compassion on the son of her womb? yea, they may forget, yet will I not forget thee" (Isa. 49:15). "The LORD hath appeared of old unto me saying, Yea, I have loved thee with an everlasting love: therefore with lovingkindness have I drawn thee" (Jer. 31:3). "When Israel was a child, then I loved him, and called my son out of Egypt" (Hosea 11:1). "I have loved you, saith the Lord. Yet ye say, Wherein hast thou loved us? Was not Esau Jacob's brother? saith the LORD: yet I loved Jacob" (Mal. 1:2).

    b. God loves the world—"For God so loved the world, that he gave his only begotten Son, that whosoever believeth in him should not perish, but have everlasting life" (John 3:16). "For this is good and acceptable in the sight of God our Savior; who will have all men to be saved, and to come to the knowledge of the truth" (1 Tim. 2:3-4). "The Lord is not slack concerning his promise, as some men count slackness; but is longsuffering to us-ward, not willing that any should perish, but that all should come to repentance" (2 Pet. 3:9).

    c. God loves the church—"Husbands, love your wives, even as Christ also loved the church, and gave himself for it; that he might sanctify and cleanse it with the washing of water by the word, that he might present it to himself a glorious church, not having spot, or wrinkle, or any such thing; but that it should be holy and without blemish. So ought men to love their wives as their own bodies. He that loveth his wife loveth himself. For no man ever yet hated his own flesh; but nourisheth and cherisheth it, even as the Lord the church; for we are members of his body, of his flesh, and of his bones. For this cause shall a man leave his father and mother, and shall be joined unto his wife, and they two shall be one flesh. This is a great mystery: but I speak concerning Christ and the church" (Eph. 5:25-32).

    d. God loves the sinner—"But God commendeth his love toward us, in that, while we were yet sinners, Christ died for us" (Rom. 5:8).

   e. God loves the spiritual Christian—"I am crucified with Christ: nevertheless,
      I live; yet not I, but Christ liveth in me: and the life which I now live in the
      flesh I live by the faith of the Son of God, who loved me, and gave himself
      for me" (Gal. 2:20).
   f. God loves the carnal Christian (Luke 15:12-24).
   g. God loves his Son—"The Father loveth the Son, and hath given all things
      into his hand" (John 3:35). "Therefore doth my Father love me, because I lay
      down my life, that I might take it again" (John 10:17). "As the Father hath
      loved me, so have I loved you; continue ye in my love" (John 15:9). "I in
      them, and thou in me, that they may be made perfect in one; and that the
      world may know that thou hast sent me, and hast loved them, as thou hast
      loved me. Father, I will that they also, whom thou hast given me, be with me
      where I am; that they may behold my glory, which thou hast given me; for
      thou lovedst me before the foundation of the world" (John 17:23-24).
         "And lo a voice from heaven saying, This is my beloved Son, in whom I
      am well pleased" (Matt. 3:17). "While he yet spake, behold, a bright cloud
      overshadowed them: and behold a voice out of the cloud, which said, This is
      my beloved Son, in whom I am well pleased; hear ye him" (Matt. 17:5).
   h. God loves the cheerful giver—"Every man according as he purposeth in his
      heart, so let him give; not grudgingly, or of necessity: for God loveth a
      cheerful giver" (2 Cor. 9:7).
   Consider one final illustration: When God was about to create man, says a
Jewish legend, he took into his counsel the angels that stood about his throne.
"Create him not," said the angel of Justice, "for if thou dost he will commit all kinds
of wickedness against his fellow men; he will be hard and cruel and dishonest and
unrighteous." "Create him not," said the angel of Truth, "for he will be false and
deceitful to his brother-man, and even to thee. "Create him not," said the angel of
Holiness, "he will follow that which is impure in thy sight, and dishonor thee to thy
face. Then stepped forward the angel of Love (God's best beloved) and said: "Create
him, our heavenly Father, for when he sins and turns from the path of right and
truth and holiness, I will take him tenderly by the hand, and speak loving words to
him, and then lead him back to thee."
BB. God is glorious—This attribute is referred to perhaps more than any other, being
   mentioned over 150 times. Some of these instances are: "Who is like unto thee, O
   LORD, among the gods? who is like thee, glorious in holiness, fearful praises, doing
   wonders? (Exod. 15:11). "Glory and honour are in his presence; strength and gladness are in his place" (1 Chron. 16:27). "O LORD our Lord, how excellent is thy
   name in all the earth! who hast set thy glory above the heavens" (Psa. 8:1). "And
   blessed be his glorious name forever: and let the whole earth be filled with his
   glory; Amen, and Amen" (Psa. 72:19).
      The basic Old Testament word for glory is *kabed*, meaning, "to be weighted down
   with riches, beauty, honor, and fame." The basic New Testament word for glory is
   doxazo, meaning, "brilliance, brightness, radiance, shining." Thus, God is glorious in
   that he is weighted down with brilliant and dazzling riches, beauty, honor, and fame.
      This glory, furthermore, is seen in all his possessions. These include:
   1. His name (Neh. 9:5; Psa. 72:9)
   2. His voice (Isa. 30:30)
   3. His arm (Isa. 63:12)
   4. His hand (Exod. 15:6)

    5. His feet (Isa. 60:13)

    6. His kingdom (Psa. 145:12)

    7. His city (Psa. 87:3; Rev. 21:11, 23)

    8. His temple (Isa. 60:7)

    9. His throne (Matt. 19:28; 25:31)

    10. His power (Col. 1:12)

    11. His work (Psa. 111:3)

    12. His gospel (1 Tim. 1:11)

    13. His Son (John 17:5, 24; Acts 3:13; 1 Cor. 2:8)

    14. His church (Eph. 5:27)

CC. God is unique—This attribute is inescapable in light of the first 28 attributes. Certainly he is absolutely, eternally, and infinitely unique from anything and anyone in his creation. The following passages bring this out:

    "Unto thee it was shewed, that thou mightest know that the LORD he is God; there is none else beside him. . . . Know therefore this day, and consider it in thine heart, that the LORD he is God in heaven above, and upon the earth beneath: there is none else" (Deut. 4:35, 39). "Fear ye not, neither be afraid: have not I told thee from that time, and have declared it? ye are even my witnesses. Is there a God beside me? yea, there is no God; I know not any" (Isa. 44:8). "I am the LORD, and there is none else, there is no God beside me: I girded thee, though thou hast not known me: That they may know from the rising of the sun, and from the west, that there is none beside me. I am the LORD, and there is none else. I form the light, and create darkness: I make peace, and create evil: I the LORD do all these things" (Isa. 45:5-7). "To whom will ye liken me, and make me equal, and compare me, that we may be like? . . . Remember the former things of old: for I am God, and there is none else; I am God, and there is none like me" (Isa. 46:5, 9).

DD. God is a God of wrath—"For the wrath of God is revealed from heaven against all ungodliness and unrighteousness of men, who hold the truth in unrighteousness" (Rom. 1:18).

    1. Definition of God's wrath—It may be defined as God's immediate and continuous response to man's wickedness. It is the settled opposition of his holiness to evil. "God judgeth the righteous, and God is angry with the wicked every day" (Psa. 7:11).

    2. Objects of God's wrath

       a. Upon the nations

         (1) Israel—"Yea, I will gather you, and blow upon you in the fire of my wrath, and ye shall be melted in the midst thereof. As silver is melted in the midst of the furnace, so shall ye be melted in the midst thereof; and ye shall know that I the LORD have poured out my fury upon you" (Ezek. 22:21-22).

            (a) For idolatry (Exod. 32:10; Deut. 11:17; 2 Chron. 34:25; Psa. 106:40)

            (b) For slanderous complaining (Num. 11:33; Psa. 78:31)

            (c) For disobedience (Deut. 29:23, 28)

            (d) For mocking his prophets (2 Chron. 36:16; Zech. 7:12)

            (e) For intermarriage with pagan women (Ezra 10:14)

            (f) For unbelief (Psa. 95:11; Heb. 3:11; 4:3)

         (2) Babylon (Jer. 50:13; Rev. 16:19)

         (3) Gog and Magog (Ezek. 38:18-19)

         (4) All pagan nations (Psa. 9:17; Rev. 11:18)

b. Upon individuals
   (1) Those who mistreat widows and orphans (Exod. 22:24)
   (2) Job's three friends (Job 42:7)
   (3) Saul (Hos. 13:11)
   (4) Achan (Josh. 22:20)
   (5) Moses (Exod. 4:14)
   (6) Hezekiah (2 Chron. 32:25)
   (7) Balaam (Num. 22:22)
   (8) The sexually impure (Eph. 5:6; Col. 3:6)
   (9) Worshippers of Antichrist (Rev. 14:10)
   (10) Truth rejecters (Rom. 1:18)
   (11) Christ rejecters (Psa. 2:5; John 3:36; 1 Thess. 2:16)
3. Special demonstrations of God's wrath
  a. The universal flood (Gen. 6–8)
  b. Calvary (1 Pet. 3:18; 2 Cor. 5:21)
  c. The coming great tribulation (Psa. 110:5-6; Isa. 13:9, 11; Zeph. 1:14-15, 18; Jer. 10:10; 1 Thess. 1:10; Rev. 15:1, 7; 16:1)—"And said to the mountains and rocks, Fall on us, and hide us from the face of him that sitteth on the throne, and from the wrath of the Lamb: for the great day of his wrath is come; and who shall be able to stand?" (Rev. 6:16-17).
  d. Armageddon (Rev. 14:19; 19:15)
  e. Great White Throne Judgment (Rev. 11:18)
  f. Eternal hell (Rev. 14:10)
4. Only protection from God's wrath—"Much more then, being now justified by his blood, we shall be saved from wrath through him" (Rom. 5:9). "And to wait for his Son from heaven, whom he raised from the dead, even Jesus, which delivered us from the wrath to come" (1 Thess. 1:10).

THE DOCTRINE OF THE BIBLE

PART ONE: A TWOFOLD DESCRIPTION OF THE BIBLE
(Written by Unknown Authors)

I. This Book contains the mind of God, the state of man, the way of salvation, the doom of sinners and the happiness of believers. Its doctrines are holy, its precepts are binding, its histories are true, and its decisions are immutable. Read it to be wise, believe it to be safe, and practice it to be holy. It contains light to direct you, food to support you, and comfort to cheer you. It is the traveler's map, the pilgrim's staff, the pilot's compass, the soldier's sword and the Christian's character. Here paradise is restored, heaven opened, and the gates of hell disclosed. Christ is its grand object, our good is its design, and the glory of God its end. It should fill the memory, rule the heart, and guide the feet. Read it slowly, frequently, and prayerfully. It is given you in life and will be opened in the judgment and will be remembered forever. It involves the highest responsibility, will reward the greatest labour, and will condemn all who trifle with its sacred contents.

II. The Bible is a beautiful palace built of 66 blocks of solid marble—the 66 books. In the first chapter of *Genesis* we enter the vestibule, filled with the mighty acts of creation.

The vestibule gives access to the law courts—the *five books of Moses*—passing through which we come to the picture gallery of the *historical* books. Here we find hung upon the walls scenes of battlefields, representations of heroic deeds, and portraits of eminent men belonging to the early days of the world's history.

Beyond the picture gallery we find the philosopher's chamber—the book of *Job*—passing through which we enter the music room—the book of *Psalms*—where we listen to the grandest strains that ever fell on human ears.

Then we come to the business office—the book of *Proverbs*—where right in the center of the room, stands facing us the motto, "Righteousness exalteth a nation, but sin is a reproach to any people."

From the business office we pass into the chapel—*Ecclesiastes*, or the *Song of Solomon* with the rose of Sharon and the lily of the valley, and all manner of fine perfume and fruit and flowers and singing birds.

Finally we reach the observatory—the *Prophets*, with their telescopes fixed on near and distant stars, and all directed toward "the Bright and Morning Star," that was soon to arise.

Crossing the court we come to the audience chamber of the King—the *Gospels*—where we find four vivid lifelike portraits of the King himself. Next we enter the workroom of the Holy Spirit—the *Acts of the Apostles*—and beyond that the correspondence room—the *Epistles*—where we see Paul and Peter and James and John and Jude busy at their desks.

Before leaving we stand a moment in the outside gallery—the *Revelation*—where we look upon some striking pictures of the judgments to come, and the glories to be revealed, concluding with an awe-inspiring picture of the throne room of the King.

PART TWO: GENERAL STATISTICS ON THE BIBLE
I. Facts about the Old and New Testaments
  A. The Old Testament
      1. 39 books
      2. 929 chapters
      3. 23,214 verses
      4. 593,493 words
      5. Longest book—Psalms
      6. Shortest book—Obadiah
      7. 17 historical books
      8. 5 poetical books
      9. 17 prophetical books
  B. The New Testament
      1. 27 books
      2. 260 chapters
      3. 7,959 verses
      4. 181,253 words
      5. Longest book—Acts
      6. Shortest book—3 John
      7. 4 Gospels
      8. 1 historical book
      9. 22 epistles
  C. The ten longest books in the Bible
      1. Psalms—150 chapters, 2,461 verses, 43,743 words
      2. Jeremiah—52 chapters, 1,364 verses, 42,659 words
      3. Ezekiel—48 chapters, 1,273 verses, 39,407 words
      4. Genesis—50 chapters, 1,533 verses, 38,267 words
      5. Isaiah—66 chapters, 1,292 verses, 37,044 words
      6. Numbers—36 chapters, 1,288 verses, 32,902 words
      7. Exodus—40 chapters, 1,213 verses, 32,602 words
      8. Deuteronomy—34 chapters, 959 verses, 28,461 words
      9. 2 Chronicles—36 chapters, 822 verses, 26,074 words
      10. Luke—24 chapters, 1,151 verses, 25,944 words
  D. The ten shortest books in the Bible
      1. 3 John—1 chapter, 14 verses, 299 words
      2. 2 John—1 chapter, 13 verses, 303 words
      3. Philemon—1 chapter, 25 verses, 445 words
      4. Jude—1 chapter, 25 verses, 613 words
      5. Obadiah—1 chapter, 21 verses, 670 words
      6. Titus—3 chapters, 46 verses, 921 words
      7. 2 Thessalonians—3 chapters, 47 verses, 1,042 words
      8. Haggai—2 chapters, 38 verses, 1,131 words
      9. Nahum—3 chapters, 47 verses, 1,285 words
      10. Jonah—4 chapters, 48 verses, 1,321 words
  E. The ten Old Testament books most referred to in the New Testament

1. Isaiah—referred to 419 times in 23 New Testament books
2. Psalms—referred to 414 times in 23 books
3. Genesis—referred to 260 times in 21 books
4. Exodus—referred to 250 times in 19 books
5. Deuteronomy—referred to 208 times in 21 books
6. Ezekiel—referred to 141 times in 15 books
7. Daniel—referred to 133 times in 17 books
8. Jeremiah—referred to 125 times in 17 books
9. Leviticus—referred to 107 times in 15 books
10. Numbers—referred to 73 times in 4 books

F. The ten New Testament books containing material from the greatest number of Old Testament books
   1. Revelation—material from 32 Old Testament books
   2. Luke—material from 31 Old Testament books
   3. John—material from 26 Old Testament books
   4. Acts—material from 25 Old Testament books
   5. Mark—material from 24 Old Testament books
   6. Romans—material from 23 Old Testament books
   7. Hebrews—material from 21 Old Testament books
   8. 1 Corinthians—material from 18 Old Testament books
   9. James—material from 17 Old Testament books
   10. 1 Peter—material from 15 Old Testament books

G. The ten Old Testament verses most frequently cited in the New Testament
   1. Psalm 110:1—quoted 18 times (Matt. 22:44; 26:64; Mark 12:36; 14:62; 16:19; Luke 20:42-43; 22:69; Acts 2:34-35; Rom. 8:34; 1 Cor. 15:25; Eph. 1:20; Col. 3:1; Heb. 1:3, 13; 8:1; 10:12-13; 12:2)
   2. Ezekiel 1:26-28—quoted 12 times (Rev. 4:2-3, 9-10; 5:1, 7, 13; 6:16; 7:10, 15; 19:14; 21:5)
   3. Daniel 12:1—quoted 11 times (Matt. 24:21; Mark 13:19; Phil. 4:3; Jude 9; Rev. 3:5; 7:14; 12:7; 13:8; 16:18; 17:8; 20:12)
   4. Isaiah 6:1—quoted 11 times (Rev. 4:2, 9-10; 5:1, 7, 13; 6:16; 7:10, 15; 19:4; 21:5)
   5. 2 Chronicles 18:18; Psalm 47:8; and 1 Kings 22:19—each quoted 11 times (Rev. 4:2, 9-10; 5:1, 7, 13; 6:16; 7:10, 15; 19:4; 21:5)
   6. Psalm 2:7—quoted ten times (Matt. 3:17; 17:5; Mark 1:11; 9:7; Luke 3:22; 9:35; John 1:49; Acts 13:33; Heb. 1:5; 5:5)
   7. Isaiah 53:7—quoted ten times (Matt. 26:63; 27:12, 14; Mark 14:60-61; 15:4-5; 1 Cor. 5:7; 1 Pet. 2:23; Rev. 5:6, 12; 13:8)
   8. Amos 3:13—quoted ten times (Rev. 1:8; 4:8, 13; 11:17; 15:3; 16:7, 14; 19:6, 15; 21:22)
   9. Amos 4:13—quoted ten times (2 Cor. 6:18; Rev. 1:8; 4:8; 11:17; 15:3; 16:7, 14; 19:6, 15; 21:22)
   10. Leviticus 19:18—quoted ten times (Matt. 5:43; 19:19; 22:39; Mark 12:31, 33; Luke 10:27; Rom. 12:19; 13:9; Gal. 5:14; James 2:8)

H. Old Testament events and quotes found in the New Testament—The New Testament writers refer to at least 161 Old Testament events and quote from over 246 Old Testament passages. Some of these events and passages are as follows:
   1. Old Testament events referred to in the New Testament—Of the 161 events, 22 of the more important ones are listed here:
      a. Creation (Gen. 1:1; Heb. 11:3)

b. Man made in God's image (Gen. 1:26; 1 Cor. 11:7)
c. God resting (Gen. 2:2-3; Heb. 4:4)
d. The institution of marriage (Gen. 2:24; Matt. 19:4-6)
e. The fall (Gen. 3:6-8; Rom. 5:12-19)
f. The murder of Abel (Gen. 4:8; 1 John 3:12)
g. Enoch's translation (Gen. 5:21-24; Heb. 11:5)
h. The ark of Noah (Gen. 6:14-16; 7:1-12; Luke 17:26-27; 2 Pet. 3:6)
i. The call of Abraham (Gen. 12:1; Heb. 11:8)
j. The meeting of Abraham and Melchizedek (Gen. 14:18-20; Heb. 7:1-4)
k. The destruction of Sodom (Gen. 19; Matt. 11:24; Luke 17:32)
l. Isaac's birth (Gen. 19:26; Gal. 4:23)
m. The offering up of Isaac (Gen. 22:10; Heb. 11:17-19)
n. The burning bush (Exod. 3:2; Luke 20:37; Acts 7:30)
o. The Exodus (Exod. 12-14; Acts 7:36; Heb. 11:29; 1 Cor. 10:1)
p. The giving of manna (Exod. 16:15; John 6:31)
q. The giving of the law (Exod. 20; Gal. 3:19)
r. The serpent of brass (Num. 21:8-9; John 3:14)
s. Elijah and the drought (1 Kings 17; Luke 4:25; James 5:17)
t. The healing of Naaman (2 Kings 5:14; Luke 4:27)
u. Daniel in the lions' den (Dan. 6:22; Heb. 11:33)
v. Jonah in the belly of the fish (Jon. 1:17; Matt. 12:40; 16:4)
2. Old Testament passages referred to in the New Testament
  a. "Be ye holy, for I am holy" (Lev. 11:44; 1 Pet. 1:16).
  b. "I will never leave thee nor forsake thee" (Josh. 1:5; Heb. 13:5).
  c. "Be ye angry and sin not" (Psa. 4:4; Eph. 4:26).
  d. "There is none righteous, no not one" (Psa. 14:1; Rom. 3:10).
  e. "Whom the Lord loveth he chasteneth" (Prov. 3:12; Heb. 12:6).
  f. "God shall wipe away all tears from their eyes" (Isa. 25:8; Rev. 21:4).
  g. "Death is swallowed up in victory" (Hos. 13:14; 1 Cor. 15:54).
  h. "I will pour out my Spirit upon all flesh" (Joel 2:28; Acts 2:17).
  i. "Whomsoever shall call on the name of the Lord shall be saved" (Joel 2:32; Rom. 10:13).
  j. "The earth is the LORD's and the fulness thereof" (Psa. 24:1; 1 Cor. 10:26).
  k. "My son, despise not the chastening of the Lord" (Prov. 3:11; Heb. 12:5).
  l. "Blessed is he that cometh in the name of the Lord" (Psa. 118:26; Matt. 21:9).
  m. "Charity covereth a multitude of sins" (Prov. 10:12; 1 Pet. 4:8).
  n. "How beautiful are the feet of them that preach the gospel" (Isa. 52:7; Rom. 10:15).
II. The Authors of the Bible
  1. Moses wrote Genesis, Exodus, Leviticus, Numbers, Deuteronomy, and Psalm 90.
  2. Joshua wrote the book named after him.
  3. Job may have written his own story.
  4. Samuel may have written Judges, Ruth, and 1 Samuel.
  5. David wrote most of the Psalms (2 Sam. 23:2).
  6. Sons of Korah wrote Psalms 42, 44–49, 84–85, 87.
  7. Asaph wrote Psalms 50, 73–83.
  8. Heman wrote Psalm 88.
  9. Ethan wrote Psalm 89.

10. Hezekiah wrote Psalms 120–123. 128–130, 132, 134–136 (Isa. 38:20).
11. Solomon wrote Psalms 72, 127, Proverbs 1–29, Ecclesiastes, Song of Solomon.
12. Agur wrote Proverbs 30.
13. Lemuel wrote Proverbs 31.
14. Jeremiah wrote Jeremiah, probably Lamentations, and possibly 1 and 2 Kings.
15. Ezra wrote Ezra and possibly 1 and 2 Chronicles and 2 Samuel.
16. Mordecai may have written Esther.
17. Luke wrote Acts as well as the Gospel of Luke.
18. John wrote the Gospel of John, 1 John, 2 John, 3 John, and Revelation.
19. Paul wrote Romans, 1 Corinthians, 2 Corinthians, Galatians, Ephesians, Philippians, Colossians, 1 Thessalonians, 2 Thessalonians, 1 Timothy, 2 Timothy, Titus, and Philemon.
20. Apollos may have written Hebrews.
21. The books of Old Testament prophecy were written by the prophets whose names they bear. The New Testament Epistles and Gospels, with the exceptions noted above, were also named after their authors.

III. Important B.C. and A.D. Biblical Dates
  A. B.C. dates
    1. 2165 B.C.—Birth of Abram (Gen. 11:26)
    2. 2090—Abram enters Canaan (Gen. 12)
    3. 2066—Destruction of Sodom (Gen. 19)
    4. 2065—Birth of Isaac (Gen. 21)
    5. 2045?—Sacrifice of Isaac on Mount Moriah (Gen. 22)
    6. 2025—Marriage of Isaac and Rebekah (Gen. 24)
    7. 2005—Birth of Esau and Jacob (Gen. 25)
    8. 1990—Death of Abraham (Gen. 25)
    9. c. 1990?—Life of Job (Job)
    10. 1928—Jacob deceives his father, Isaac, and flees to Haran (Gen. 27)
    11. 1920—Marriage of Jacob to Leah and Rachel (Gen. 29:28)
    12. 1897—Joseph is sold into Egypt (Gen. 37)
    13. 1884—Joseph is exalted by Pharaoh (Gen. 41)
    14. 1875—Jacob and his family enter Egypt (Gen. 46)
    15. 1858—Death of Jacob (Gen. 49)
    16. 1804—Death of Joseph; Israel enjoys prosperity for 75 years (Gen. 50; Exod. 1:1-7)
    17. 1730—Egyptian oppression begins (Exod. 1:8–12:42)
    18. 1525—Birth of Moses (Exod. 2:1-4)
    19. 1485—Moses flees Egypt (Exod. 2:11-15)
    20. 1445—Moses returns to Egypt (Exod. 4:20)
    21. 1445—The Exodus (Exod. 12–15)
    22. June 15, 1445—Arrival at Mount Sinai (Exod. 19:1)
    23. 1444–1405—Wandering in wilderness (Num. 15:1—Deut. 34)
    24. October 7, 1405—Death of Moses (Deut. 34:1-7)
    25. April 10, 1404—The crossing of the Jordan (Josh. 1:5)
    26. 1404–1397—The conquering of Canaan (Josh. 6–12)
    27. 1390—Death of Joshua (Josh. 23–24)
    28. 1374–1334—Judgeship of Othniel (Judg. 3:7-11)
    29. 1316–1236—Judgeship of Ehud (Judg. 3:12-14)
    30. 1216–1176—Judgeship of Deborah and Barak (Judg. 4–5)

31. 1169–1129—Judgeship of Gideon (Judg. 6–8)
32. c. 1150?—Life of Ruth (Ruth)
33. c. 1087—Judgeship of Jephthah (Judg. 11–12)
34. c. 1069—Judgeship of Samson (Judg. 13–16)
35. c. 1107—Judgeship of Eli (1 Sam. 1–4)
36. 1105—Birth of Samuel (1 Sam. 1:19-20)
37. 1043—Saul anointed first king of Israel by Samuel (1 Sam. 10)
38. 1025—The anointing of David (1 Sam. 16)
39. 1011—Death of Saul (1 Sam. 31)
40. 1011—Reign of David over one tribe begins (2 Sam. 2:4)
41. 1005—Jerusalem becomes the capital (2 Sam. 2:4)
42. 1004—Reign of David over all Israel begins (2 Sam. 5:3)
43. 971—Death of David (1 Kings 2:10)
44. 971—Reign of Solomon begins (1 Kings 1:39)
45. 959—Completion of the temple (1 Kings 6:38)
46. 931—Kingdom splits into two kingdoms, Israel and Judah, after Solomon's death (1 Kings 12)
47. 874—The reign of Ahab begins in Israel (1 Kings 16–22)
48. 860–852—The ministry of Elijah (1 Kings 17–19, 21; 2 Kings 1–2)
49. 852–795—The ministry of Elisha (2 Kings 2–9, 13)
50. 850—Book of Obadiah
51. 848—Book of Joel
52. 785—Book of Jonah
53. 760—Book of Amos
54. 758—Book of Hosea
55. 739—Book of Isaiah
56. 735—Book of Micah
57. 721—The capture of the Northern Kingdom by the Assyrians (2 Kings 17)
58. 716—Reign of Hezekiah begins (2 Kings 18–21)
59. 701—Jerusalem saved from the Assyrians by the angel of the Lord (2 Kings 19)
60. 697—Reign of Manasseh begins (2 Kings 21)
61. 650—Book of Nahum
62. 641—Reign of Josiah begins (2 Kings 22–23)
63. 640—Book of Zephaniah
64. 636–605—The ministry of Daniel (Dan.)
65. 627—Book of Jeremiah
66. 612—Fall of Nineveh
67. 608—Book of Habakkuk
68. 605—The first siege of Jerusalem; Daniel taken (2 Kings 24)
69. 597—The second siege of Jerusalem; Ezekiel taken (2 Kings 24)
70. 593–560—The ministry of Ezekiel (Ezek.)
71. 587—Third siege of Jerusalem (2 Kings 24)
72. 587—Fall of Jerusalem to the Babylonians (2 Kings 25)
73. 586—The Book of Lamentations
74. October 29, 539—The fall of Babylon to Persia (Dan. 5)
75. 538—The edict of Cyrus for the Jews' return to Judea (Ezra 1)
76. 536—First return to Judea under Zerubbabel (Ezra 1–6)
77. June 535—Work on the temple begun (Ezra 3)
78. 520—Ministry of Haggai (Ezra 5:1; Hag.)

79. 520—Ministry of Zechariah (Ezra 5:1; Zech.)
80. February 18, 516—Work on temple completed (Ezra 6:15)
81. 478—Esther becomes queen of Persia (Esther 2)
82. March 455—Second return to Judea under Ezra (Ezra 7:10)
83. September 444—The walls of Jerusalem are completed (Neh. 6:15)
84. 437—Ministry of Malachi
85. 425—Completion of the Old Testament
86. 331–323—Career of Alexander the Great
87. 260—Translation of the Old Testament into Greek (The Septuagint)
88. 175–169—Reign of Antiochus Epiphanes, who defiled the temple
89. 166—Revolt of the Maccabees, Jewish freedom fighters
90. 164—Roman general Pompey conquers Jerusalem
91. 40—Herod the Great appointed king
92. 20—Herod begins enlarging the second temple
93. 5—Birth of John the Baptist (Luke 1:57-60)
94. 5—Birth of Jesus Christ (Luke 2:1-20)
95. 4—Visit of the wise men (Matt. 2:1-12)
96. 4—Flight into Egypt (Matt. 2:13-15)
97. 4—Slaughter of the innocent Bethlehem babies (Matt. 2:16)
98. 4—Death of Herod (Matt. 2:19)
99. 4—Journey from Egypt to Nazareth (Matt. 2:20-23)

B. A.D. dates
1. A.D. 8—Temple discussion when Christ was 12 (Luke 2:41-52)
2. 26—Baptism of Christ (Matt. 3:16-17)
3. 28—Choosing of the Twelve (Matt. 10:1-4)
4. Spring 29—Death of John the Baptist (Matt. 14:1-12)
5. Fall 29—Feast of Tabernacles message (John 7:14-39)
6. Winter 29—Lazarus raised (John 11:1-46)
7. April, 30—Death and resurrection of Christ (Matt. 27–28)
8. May, 30—Ascension of Christ (Acts 1)
9. June, 30—Pentecost (Acts 2)
10. 31—Death of Ananias and Sapphira (Acts 5:1-11)
11. 32—Seven deacons selected (Acts 6:1-7)
12. 34—Martyrdom of Stephen (Acts 6:8–7:60)
13. 35—Conversion of Paul (Acts 9:1-7)
14. 37—Paul's first visit in Jerusalem as a believer (Acts 9:26-29; Gal. 1:18)
15. 40—Conversion of Cornelius (Acts 10)
16. 42—Antioch ministry of Paul and Barnabas (Acts 11:19-30)
17. 44—Martyrdom of the Apostle James (Acts 12:1-2)
18. 45—Letter of James
19. 47—Beginning of Paul's first missionary journey (Acts 13:1-3)
20. 49—Completion of first missionary journey (Acts 14:26)
21. 49—Letter to the Galatians
22. 49—Jerusalem Council (Acts 15)
23. 50—Beginning of Paul's second missionary journey (Acts 15:40-41)
24. 51—First Letter to the Thessalonians
25. 52—Second Letter to the Thessalonians
26. 52—Completion of second missionary journey (Acts 18:22)
27. 53—Beginning of Paul's third missionary journey (Acts 18:23)

28. 55—First Letter to the Corinthians
29. 56—Second Letter to the Corinthians
30. 57—Letter to the Romans
31. 57—Completion of third missionary journey (Acts 21:15)
32. 57—Arrest of Paul in Jerusalem (Acts 21:27)
33. 57—Beginning of Paul's imprisonment in Caesarea (Acts 23:33)
34. 59—Paul's voyage to Rome (Acts 27:1–28:15)
35. 60—Paul's arrival in Rome (Acts 28:16)
36. 60—Beginning of Paul's first Roman imprisonment (Acts 28:16)
37. 60—Letter to the Ephesians
38. 60—Letter to the Colossians
39. 61—Letter to Philemon
40. 61—Letter to the Philippians
41. 61—Gospel of Luke
42. 61—Book of Acts
43. 61—Letter to the Hebrews
44. 62—Paul released from first Roman imprisonment (Philem. 22)
45. 62—Martyrdom of James, the Lord's brother
46. 62—First Letter to Timothy
47. 64—Letter to Titus
48. 64—First Letter of Peter
49. 65—Second Letter of Peter
50. 65—Martyrdom of Peter
51. 65—Gospel of Matthew
52. 65—Gospel of Mark
53. 66—Final Roman imprisonment of Paul (2 Tim. 1:8)
54. 66—Jewish revolt against Rome
55. 67—Second Letter to Timothy
56. 67—Martyrdom of Paul
57. 70—Destruction of Jerusalem by the Romans
58. 85—Letter of Jude
59. 90—Gospel of John
60. 92—First, Second, and Third Letters of John
61. 95—Book of Revelation, signifying completion of New Testament (Rev. 22:21)

PART THREE: THE FORMATION OF THE BIBLE

Everybody knows the Bible has been and continues to be the world's best seller, but not everybody knows just how this amazing Book came down to us today. It *could* have happened this way: At some early ecumenical "scripture session," a group of prophets and priests got together in Jerusalem to write a religious best-seller. A committee was soon formed which assigned the books, appointed the authors, and arranged for all other details. Upon completion, the publicity chairman commissioned the Palestinian Press to print up the first one million copies. We said it *could* have happened that way. But of course it didn't! God used three wonderful methods as he carefully carved out that most blessed of all books, the Bible! These three "tools of the Trinity" are referred to as *revelation, inspiration,* and *illumination.* Let us use an earthly story to illustrate this.

Over 70 years ago a famous German scientist named Albert Einstein developed a very important mathematical concept of the nature of the universe. Let us suppose that during this time he suddenly summons you into his home for a secret conference. He invites you to be seated and immediately explains why you have been asked to come. He begins: "I have just completed one of the most comprehensive scientific theories since the days of Sir Isaac Newton. I want you to write this all down on paper and send it to the news media of the world. Here is my astonishing theory—energy equals the mass times the speed of light squared ($E=mc^2$)!"

He then goes on to explain how mass and energy are equivalent, and that the property called mass is simply concentrated energy. You are awed as he continues with his amazing grasp of the universe. Finally he stops and says: "Now I want you to write this all down in your own words, but in order to make sure you get everything right, I want to help you in choosing those words."

So the next few hours are spent in this manner. Dr. Einstein gently but firmly guides you in the selection of the verbs and nouns from your own vocabulary. At long last you have it all down, the exact and complete revelation of truth from Albert Einstein described perfectly in your own handwriting and from your personal reservoir of words.

Before you leave, the aged scientist speaks once again: "One final thing that will encourage you: I plan to call every important newspaper and television editor, telling them the message they will receive from you is true and they should believe it and publish it!"

Here we have an example (however weak) of God's three tools and how they function. *Revelation* occurred when Dr. Einstein called you in and imparted to you his great truth. *Inspiration* took place when he guided you as you wrote it down. *Illumination* happened when he encouraged the news editor to accept his report as given by you.

How then did we receive our Bible? Well, around 1400 B.C. God began to quietly call some 40 men and women into his presence. Oh, he didn't call them in all at once, mind you. In fact, it took him nearly 15 centuries to complete the job. He spoke the burden of his great heart in simple but sublime language to those chosen 40. With a holy hush they heard him tell of creation and corruption, of condemnation, of justification, sanctification, and glorification! Weighty words, indeed. When he had finished, the first tool in carving out the Bible was set aside. *Revelation* had occurred.

Now we see this almighty Author as he quickly but carefully guides each chosen human vessel in his assigned writing task. Each of the 40 is dealt with individually. Job, a rich farmer, will write differently than will Amos, a poor farmer. The words of the educated Paul will be more complicated on occasion than those of the uneducated John or Peter. But all will carry with them the divine approval of heaven itself.

Finally, the last scribe lays down his (or her) pen. The angels watch as their Creator lays aside the second tool in the making of his manuscript. *Inspiration* has taken place.

Soon many thousands of men and women join the ranks of those original 40 and begin their assigned task of taking God's glory story to the uttermost parts of the earth. As they do, untold multitudes are stopped in their tracks, convinced in their hearts, and saved from their sins! By what secret power did all this take place? The answer is simple: the Author of the Bible is using the third and final tool. *Illumination* continues to take place.

And so the Scriptures are shaped. To summarize thus far, think of the three tools as follows:

Revelation: From God to man (man hears that which God wants written)
Inspiration: From man to paper (man writes that which God wants written)
Illumination: From paper to heart (man receives that which God has written)
Now that we have observed the purpose of these three tools, let us turn our thoughts

to the nature of each weapon. We have examined the fruit of the tools, but what of the root? How did God make the weapon itself? We first consider:

I. Revelation—We know God spoke to man, but how did he speak? Hebrews 1:1 informs us he spoke to the fathers and prophets in many ways. A careful examination of the Bible reveals at least 11 different modes of communication. These are:

A. He often spoke to men through angels. Consider:
   1. Angels reassured Abraham of the birth of Isaac and informed him of God's decision to destroy Sodom (Gen. 18).
   2. Angels warned Lot to flee Sodom before that awful destruction took place (Gen. 19).
   3. The angel Gabriel explained the nature of the tribulation to Daniel (Dan. 9:21-27).
   4. Gabriel informed Zacharias he would have a son who would become the forerunner of Christ (Luke 1:11-20).
   5. Gabriel informed Mary that God had chosen her as his vessel for Christ's birth (Luke 1:26-37).
   6. Angels announced the birth of Christ to the shepherds (Luke 2:8-14).
   7. An angel announced the resurrection of Christ to some women (Matt. 28:5-7).
   8. An angel directed Philip to the seeking eunuch (Acts 8:26).
   9. An angel directed Peter out of a Roman prison (Acts 12:7-10).

B. He spoke to men through a loud voice.
   1. He spoke directly to Adam (Gen. 3:9-19).
   2. He spoke directly to Noah (Gen. 6:13-21).
   3. He spoke directly to Abraham (Gen. 12:1-3).
   4. He spoke directly to Moses (Exod. 20:1-17).
   5. He spoke directly to Joshua (Josh. 1:1-9).
   6. He spoke directly to Samuel (1 Sam. 3:1-14).
   7. He spoke directly to Nathan, about David (2 Sam. 7:4-16).
   8. He spoke directly to Elijah (1 Kings 17:2-4).
   9. He spoke directly to Jeremiah (Jer. 1:4-5).

C. He spoke to men through a still, small voice (1 Kings 19:11-12; Psa. 32:8).

D. He spoke to men through nature (Psa. 19:1-3; Rom. 1:18-20; Acts 14:15-17).

E. He spoke to one man through the mouth of an ass (Num. 22:28)—This simply has to be one of the funniest moments in the Bible!

F. He spoke to men through dreams—On a number of occasions God chose this method.
   1. Jacob received the confirmation of the Abrahamic Covenant in a dream (Gen. 28:12).
   2. Solomon received both wisdom and a warning in a dream (1 Kings 3:5; 9:2).
   3. Joseph in the New Testament received three messages in three dreams.
      a. Assuring him of Mary's purity (Matt. 1:20)
      b. Commanding him to flee to Egypt (Matt. 2:13)
      c. Ordering him to return to Palestine (Matt. 2:19-22)
   4. The wise men were warned of Herod's evil intentions in a dream (Matt. 2:12).

G. He spoke to men through visions—*Unger's Bible Dictionary* defines a vision as: "A supernatural presentation of certain scenery or circumstances to the mind of a person while awake." It may be noted that many great truths in the Scriptures were related to men through this unique method.

1. Jacob was instructed in a vision to go to Egypt (Gen. 46:2).
2. David was warned of judgment in a vision (1 Chron. 21:16).
3. Isaiah saw God's holiness in a vision (Isa. 6:1-8).
4. Daniel saw the great Gentile powers in a vision (Dan. 7–8).
5. Daniel saw the glories of Christ in a vision (Dan. 10:5-9).
6. Daniel saw the rise and fall of Alexander the Great in a vision (Dan. 8).
7. Ezekiel saw the regathering of Israel in a vision (Ezek. 37).
8. Ananias was ordered to minister to Saul in a vision (Acts 9:10).
9. Cornelius was instructed to send for Peter in a vision (Acts 10:3-6).
10. Peter was ordered to minister to Cornelius in a vision (Acts 10:10-16).
11. Paul was ordered to Macedonia in a vision (Acts 16:9).
12. Paul was comforted at Corinth in a vision (Acts 19:9).
13. Paul was comforted at Jerusalem in a vision (Acts 23:11).
14. Paul viewed the glories of the third heaven in a vision (2 Cor. 12:1-4).
15. The Apostle John received the book of Revelation in a vision.

H. He spoke to men through the Urim and Thummin (Exod. 28:30; Num. 27:21).
I. He spoke to men through the casting of lots.
1. To select a scapegoat (Lev. 16:8)
2. To divide the land of Canaan among the 12 tribes (Num. 26:55; Josh. 18:10)
3. To determine who would live in Jerusalem (Neh. 11:1)
4. To replace Judas (Acts 1:26)

J. He spoke to men through the Old Testament Christophanies—A Christophany is a pre-Bethlehem appearance of Christ. Some theologians have seen a number of these appearances in the Old Testament, believing that the term "the Angel of the Lord" is actually another name of Christ. If this is true, the following examples of Christophany communication could be submitted.
1. The Angel of the Lord wrestled with Jacob (Gen. 32:24-30).
2. The Angel of the Lord redeemed Jacob from all evil (Gen. 48:16).
3. The Angel of the Lord spoke to Moses from the burning bush (Exod. 3:2).
4. The Angel of the Lord protected Israel at the Red Sea (Exod. 14:19).
5. The Angel of the Lord prepared Israel for the Promised Land (Exod. 23:20-23; Psa. 34:7; Isa. 63:9; 1 Cor. 10:1-4).
6. The Angel of the Lord commissioned Gideon (Judg. 6:11).
7. The Angel of the Lord ministered to Elijah (1 Kings 19:7).
8. The Angel of the Lord reassured Joshua (Josh. 5:13-15).
9. The Angel of the Lord saved Jerusalem (Isa. 37:36).
10. The Angel of the Lord preserved three godly Hebrew men (Dan. 3:25).

K. He spoke to men through the New Testament incarnation of Christ—Charles Ryrie observes: "Undebatably the incarnation of Jesus Christ was a major avenue of special revelation. He exegeted the Father (John 1:14), revealing the nature of God (14:9), the power of God (3:2), the wisdom of God (7:46), the glory of God (1:14), the life of God (1 John 1:1-3), and the love of God (Rom. 5:8). Our Lord did all this by both his acts (John 2:11) and his words (Matt. 16:17)" (*Basic Theology*, p. 64).

How then did God communicate his revelation to the 40 human authors? To be truthful, we simply do not know. He could have used any one or a combination of these 11 modes of communication as have been described above.

L. Basic review and overview—Paul Enns suggests all divine revelation can be

placed under one of two categories, that of General Revelation and that of
Special Revelation.
1. General revelation (threefold)
   a. In nature
      (1) Psalm 19:1-6
         (a) Reveals that God exists
         (b) Reveals God's glory
      (2) Romans 1:18-21
         (a) Reveals that God is omnipotent
         (b) Reveals that God will judge
   b. In providence
      (1) Matthew 5:45—Reveals that God is benevolent to all people
      (2) Acts 14:15-17—Reveals that God provides food for all people
      (3) Daniel 2:21—Reveals that God raises up and removes rulers
   c. In conscience—Romans 2:14-15 reveals that God has placed his law within
      the hearts of all people.
2. Special revelation (twofold)
   a. In Christ
      (1) John 1:18—Reveals what the Father is like
      (2) John 5:36-37—Reveals the Father's compassion
      (3) John 6:63; 14:10—Reveals that the Father gives life to those who believe
      in the Son
   b. In Scripture
      (1) 2 Timothy 3:16-17—Reveals all the doctrine, rebuke, correction, and
      guidance that the Christian needs for good living
      (2) 2 Peter 1:21—Reveals all that God has chosen to disclose through
      human authors directed by the Holy Spirit (*Moody Handbook of
      Theology*, p. 157).
II. Inspiration
   A. The definition of inspiration—"Inspiration may be defined as the Holy Spirit's
      superintending over the writers so that while writing according to their own styles
      and personalities, the result was God's Word written—authoritative, trustworthy,
      and free from error in the original autographs" (Ibid. p. 160).

      While many theological viewpoints would be willing to say the Bible is
      inspired, one finds little uniformity as to what is meant by inspiration. Some
      focus it on the writers; others, on the writings; still others, on the readers. Some
      relate it to the general message of the Bible; others, to the thoughts; still others,
      to the words. Some include inerrancy; many don't.
         These differences call for precision in stating the biblical doctrine. Formerly
      all that was necessary to affirm one's belief in full inspiration was the statement
      "I believe in the inspiration of the Bible." But when some did not extend
      inspiration to the words of the text it became necessary to say, "I believe in the
      verbal inspiration of the Bible." To counter the teaching that not all parts of the
      Bible were inspired, one had to say, "I believe in the verbal, plenary inspiration
      of the Bible." Then because some did not want to ascribe total accuracy to the
      Bible, it was necessary to say, "I believe in the verbal, plenary, infallible, inerrant
      inspiration of the Bible." But then "infallible" and "inerrant" began to be
      limited to matters of faith only rather than also embracing all that the Bible

records (including historical facts, genealogies, accounts of creation, etc.), so it became necessary to add the concept of "unlimited inerrancy." Each addition to the basic statement arose because of an erroneous teaching. (Charles Ryrie, *Basic Theology*, p. 67)

The term *inspiration* is found but once in the New Testament. This occurs in 2 Timothy 3:16. Here Paul says, "All scripture is given by inspiration of God." The Greek word is *theopneustos*, and literally means "God-breathed."

B. Scripture texts on inerrancy and inspiration

1. Concerning inerrancy—Psalms 12:6; 18:30; 19:7, 9; 119:89, 151, 160, 172; Proverbs 30:5-6; Matthew 4:4; Luke 24:25; John 10:35; 17:17; Acts 24:14

2. Concerning inspiration—Exodus 4:12-16; 17:14; 20:1; 31:18; 34:27; Numbers 22:38; 23:5; 24:12-13, 15-16; 32:2; Deut. 18:18; Isa. 8:1; 30:8-9; Jer. 1:9; 5:14; 25:13; 30:1-2; Ezekiel 24:1; Habakkuk 2:2; Matthew 4:4; John 15:26; 16:12-15; Acts 4:25; 1 Corinthians 2:13; 14:37; 2 Corinthians 13:2-3; 1 Thessalonians 2:13; 2 Timothy 3:16-17; Hebrews 3:7-8; 2 Peter 1:20-21; 3:16.

   Note but a few of these verses that strongly proclaim the inerrancy and inspiration of the Scriptures: "And the LORD said unto Moses, Write thou these words: for after the tenor of these words I have made a covenant with thee and with Israel" (Exod. 34:27). "Now these be the last words of David. David the son of Jesse said, and the man who was raised up on high, the anointed of the God of Jacob, and the sweet psalmist of Israel, said, The Spirit of the LORD spake by me, and his word was in my tongue" (2 Sam. 23:1-2). "Then the LORD put forth his hand, and touched my mouth. And the LORD said unto me, Behold, I have put my words in thy mouth" (Jer. 1:9). "For ever, O LORD, thy word is settled in heaven" (Psa. 119:89). "Every word of God is pure: he is a shield unto them that put their trust in him. Add thou not unto his words, lest he reprove thee, and thou be found a liar" (Prov. 30:5-6).

   "But he answered and said, It is written, Man shall not live by bread alone, but by every word that proceedeth out of the mouth of God" (Matt. 4:4). "Then he said unto them, O fools, and slow of heart to believe all that the prophets have spoken" (Luke 24:25). "If he called them gods, unto whom the word of God came, and the scripture cannot be broken" (John 10:35). "Which things also we speak, not in the words which man's wisdom teacheth, but which the Holy Ghost teacheth; comparing spiritual things with spiritual" (1 Cor. 2:13). "All scripture is given by inspiration of God, and is profitable for doctrine, for reproof, for correction, for instruction in righteousness: That the man of God may be perfect, thoroughly furnished unto all good works" (2 Tim. 3:16-17). "Knowing this first, that no prophecy of the scripture is of any private interpretation For the prophecy came not in old time by the will of man: but holy men of God spake as they were moved by the Holy Ghost" (2 Pet. 1:20-21).

C. The early church and inspiration—The early church fathers, having lived during the time of, or in the few centuries following, the New Testament era, would doubtless have been greatly influenced by those beliefs held by the original apostles (Peter, Paul, John, etc.). These men would include:

1. Ignatius of Antioch (A.D. 35–107)

2. Polycarp (69–155)

3. Justin Martyr (100–165)

4. Tertullian (160–220)
5. Eusebius of Caesarea (263–340)
6. Athanasius (295–373)
7. Augustine (354–430)

Question: What did these men believe concerning the doctrine of inspiration? Dr. Robert Lightner writes: "The inspiration and therefore infallibility of the Bible was believed by the majority of Christians from the earliest days of the church. This belief dominated until the rise of materialistic rationalism and mysticism in the 18th and 19th centuries. . . . There is abundant evidence in the writings of the earliest church fathers and historians of their commitment to the infallibility of Scripture" (Evangelical Theology, *pp. 5–6).*

*Charles Ryrie cites a quote from Augustine as a representative statement: "The most disastrous consequences must follow upon our believing that anything false is found in the sacred books. . . . If you once admit into such a high sanctuary of authority one false statement, there will not be left a single sentence of those books, which . . . may not be explained away" (*Basic Theology, *p. 81).*

During the third, fourth, and fifth centuries the church held no less than 184 councils, not to deal with civil rights, ecology problems, or political ills, but to deal with any and all heresy that would dare tamper with the pure Word of God. In summary, the early church fathers would surely have agreed with that conclusion drawn by Charles Wesley centuries later concerning the inspiration of the Bible:

The Bible must be the invention either of good men or angels, bad men or devils, or of God.

> *1. It could not be the invention of good men or angels; for they neither would or could make a book, and tell lies all the time they were writing it, saying "Thus saith the Lord," when it was their own invention.*
>
> *2. It could not be the invention of bad men or devils; for they would not make a book which commands all duty, forbids all sin, and condemns their souls to hell to all eternity.*
>
> *3. Therefore, I draw this conclusion, that the Bible must be given by divine inspiration."*

(A General Introduction to the Bible, *p. 199*)

D. The false views concerning inspiration
  1. The natural theory—This says the Bible writers were inspired in the same sense William Shakespeare was inspired. In other words, that spark of divine inspiration that supposedly is in all men simply burned a little brighter in the hearts of the Bible writers. This theory is totally rejected by the Apostle Peter (2 Pet. 1:20). "Knowing this first, that no prophecy of the scripture is of any private interpretation."
  2. The content (or concept) theory—This theory says that only the main thought of a paragraph or chapter is inspired. This theory is immediately refuted by many biblical passages. "For verily I say unto you, Till heaven and earth pass, one jot or one tittle shall in no wise pass from the law, till all be fulfilled" (Matt. 5:18). "Now these be the last words of David. David the son of Jesse said, and the man who was raised up on high, the anointed of the God of Jacob, and the sweet psalmist of Israel, said, The Spirit of the LORD spake by me, and his word was in my tongue" (2 Sam. 23:1-2).

3. The partial theory—This says that only certain parts of the Bible are inspired. This of course is the position of the liberal theologian who would cheerfully accept those portions of the Bible which deal with love and brotherhood, but quickly reject the passages dealing with sin, righteousness, and future judgment. But let it be said that heaven and hell are like up and down—you can't have one without the other. Paul refutes the partial theory in 2 Timothy 3:16.

In his textbook, *Dispensational Theology*, Dr. Charles F. Baker writes:

A certain bishop is purported to have said that he believed the Bible to have been inspired in spots. When asked for his authority for such a statement, he quoted Hebrews 1:1, stating that this meant that God spoke at various times in varying degrees. Thus, some spots were fully inspired, others were only partially inspired, and still others were not inspired at all. The bishop was embarrassed when a layman asked: "How do you know that Hebrews 1:1, the one scripture upon which you base your argument, is one of those fully inspired spots?" (*A Dispensational Theology*, p. 38)

4. The spiritual-rule-only theory—This says the Bible may be regarded as our infallible rule of faith and practice in all matters of religious, ethical, and spiritual value, but not in other matters such as some of the historical and scientific statements found in the Word of God. This is pious nonsense. Consider the following: Here is a pastor greatly beloved by his congregation. How would this man of God feel if only his "moral" and "spiritual" statements made in the pulpit were accepted by his members? How would he react when the members would smile and take lightly any scientific or historical statements he might make? The fallacy of the spiritual-rule-only theory is that any book or man whose scientific or historical statements are open to question can certainly neither be trusted in matters of moral and spiritual pronouncements. This theory is soundly refuted by Jesus himself in John 3:12. "If I have told you earthly things, and ye believe not, how shall ye believe, if I tell you of heavenly things?"

5. The mechanical theory—This says that God coldly and woodenly dictated the Bible to his writers as an office manager would dictate an impersonal letter to his secretary. It should be noted here that the Bible is the story of divine love, and God is anything but mechanical or cold concerning this subject. The Holy Spirit therefore never transgressed the limits of the writer's vocabulary. Thus, the educated Paul uses many of the "eighty-five-cent" words, while the less educated John employs more of the "twenty-five-cent" words. But both writings are equally inspired by God. (See 2 Tim. 3:16.)

Dr. Charles Hodge has well written:

The Church has never held what has been stigmatized as the mechanical theory of inspiration. The sacred writers were not machines. Their self-consciousness was not suspended; nor were their intellectual powers super-seded. Holy men spoke as they were moved by the Holy Ghost. It was men not machines; not unconscious instruments, but living, thinking, willing minds, whom the Spirit used as his organs. . . . The sacred writers impressed their peculiarities on their several productions as plainly as though they were the subjects of no extraordinary influence." (*Systematic Theology*, vol. I, p. 157)

E. The scriptural view concerning inspiration—As previously noted, this is referred to as the plenary-verbal view. It says, in essence, that all (plenary) the very words (verbal) of the Bible are inspired by God. The Bible strongly claims its writings are from God. In fact, no less than 3,800 times the Scriptures say, "Thus saith the Lord," or, "God said." Summarizing these occurrences we learn that:

1. No Old Testament Scripture was thought up by the prophet himself (2 Pet. 1:20).
2. All Old Testament Scriptures were given by the Holy Spirit as he moved upon men (2 Pet. 1:21).
3. This Spirit-breathed inspiration was given in many ways (Heb. 1:1).
4. Once it was given, this inspired writing:
   a. Could not be broken or shaken down (John 10:35)
   b. Is exact in all details, down to the smallest stroke and letter (Matt. 5:18)
   c. Would abide forever (Matt. 5:18; 1 Pet. 1:25)
5. The Old Testament writers did not always understand the nature of everything they wrote about (1 Pet. 1:10-12; Luke 10:23-24).
   a. They did not completely understand the details of Christ's suffering.
   b. They did understand the mysteries would be clear to a generation other than theirs.
6. The four gospels were given by inspiration of God (Heb. 1:1; 2 Pet. 3:2).
7. Paul believed his writings were inspired by God (1 Cor. 2:4; 15:3; 1 Thess. 2:13; 4:15).
8. The scriptures claim to be inspired as a whole, in parts, in words, and in the very letters.
   a. Inspiration of the whole—"Think not that I am come to destroy the law, or the prophets: I am not come to destroy, but to fulfil" (Matt. 5:17). "All scripture is given by inspiration of God, and is profitable for doctrine, for reproof, for correction, for instruction in righteousness" (2 Tim. 3:16).
   b. Inspiration of the parts—"And Jesus, when he had found a young ass, sat thereon; as it is written, Fear not, daughter of Sion: behold, thy King cometh, sitting on an ass's colt. These things understood not his disciples at the first: but when Jesus was glorified, then remembered they that these things were written of him, and that they had done these things unto him" (John 12:14-16).
   c. Inspiration of the words—"But he answered and said, It is written, Man shall not live by bread alone, but by every word that proceedeth out of the mouth of God" (Matt. 4:4).
   d. Inspiration of the very letters—"For verily I say unto you, Till heaven and earth pass, one jot or one tittle shall in no wise pass from the law, till all be fulfilled" (Matt. 5:18).
9. Paul used the Holy Spirit's words to explain the Holy Spirit's facts (1 Cor. 2:13).
10. Paul's writings were received through a special revelation from Christ (Gal. 1:11-12).
11. Paul's writings were to be read by all (Col. 4:6; 1 Thess. 5:27).
    Note: Some have felt Paul claimed no inspiration when he wrote certain passages in 1 Corinthians 7. Consider the following:
    a. "But I speak this by permission, and not of commandment" (v.6).

b. "But to the rest speak I, not the Lord" (v. 12).

c. "Now concerning virgins I have no commandment of the Lord; yet I give my judgment" (v. 25).

d. "But she is happier if she so abide, after my judgment: and I think also that I have the Spirit of God" (v. 40).

Let us now briefly examine each of these passages:

e. The word *permission* is literally "a joint opinion," and may refer to the inspired "considered opinion" of both Paul and Sosthenes. At any rate, Paul was simply saying this opinion was not a command but rather a divine suggestion. For a comparable passage, see Romans 12:1.

f. Verse 12 can be explained by comparing it with verse 10. There, Paul quotes a command uttered by the Lord Jesus himself while he was upon the earth (see Matt. 19:6). But here is a group situation (one partner saved, one unsaved) to which Jesus issued no command while on earth, but now does so in heaven through Paul's inspired pen.

g. The same answer given for verse 12 also applies here in verse 25.

h. The word *think* here could also be translated "persuaded." (See Matt. 22:42; 1 Cor. 8:2, where the same Greek word is used.)

12. Peter believed his writings were inspired by God (2 Pet. 3:2).

13. Peter believed Paul's writings were inspired by God (2 Pet. 3:15-16).

14. John believed his writings were inspired by God (Rev. 22:18-19)—John warned:

a. That if anyone added to his words, God would add horrible plagues to him

b. That if anyone subtracted from his words, God would remove his name from the Holy City

F. The implications of inspiration—As one considers the subject of inspiration, he is led to the following nine conclusions:

1. Plenary-verbal inspiration does not teach that all parts of the Bible are equally important, but only that they are equally inspired—For example, Judges 3:16 is obviously not as important as John 3:16, but both these verses were inspired by God: "But Ehud made him a dagger which had two edges, of a cubit length; and he did gird it under his raiment upon his right thigh" (Judg. 3:16). "For God so loved the world, that he gave his only begotten Son, that whosoever believeth in him should not perish, but have everlasting life" (John 3:16).

2. Plenary-verbal inspiration does not guarantee the inspiration of any modern or ancient translation of the Bible, but deals only with the original Hebrew and Greek languages.

3. Plenary-verbal inspiration does not allow for any false teaching, but it does on occasion record the lie of someone—For example, Satan distorts the truth and lies to Eve (Gen. 3:4). Therefore we have an accurate record of the devil's words. As one reads the Bible, he must carefully distinguish between what God records and what he sanctions. Thus, while lying, murder, adultery, and polygamy are to be found in the Word of God, they are never approved by the God of the Word.

4. Plenary-verbal inspiration does not permit any historical, scientific, or prophetical error whatsoever—While it is admitted that the Bible is not a textbook on science, it is nevertheless held that every scientific statement in the Scriptures is absolutely true.

5. Plenary-verbal inspiration does not prohibit personal research—The New Testament writer Luke begins his Gospel account with the following words:

"Inasmuch as many have undertaken to compile an account of the things accomplished among us, just as those who from the beginning were eyewitnesses and servants of the Word have handed them down to us, it seemed fitting for me as well, having investigated everything carefully from the beginning, to write it out" (Luke 1:1-3, NASB).

6. Plenary-verbal inspiration does not deny the use of extrabiblical sources—Here several examples come to mind.
   a. On at least two occasions, Paul quotes from heathen authors (Acts 17:28; Titus 1:12).
   b. Jude quotes from an ancient Hebrew book, one not included in the Bible (Jude 14-15).
7. Plenary-verbal inspiration does not overwhelm the personality of the human author—The Bible writers experienced no coma-like trances as do some mediums during a séance, but on the contrary, always retained their physical, mental, and emotional powers. Various passages testify to this. (See Isa. 6:1-11; Dan. 12.)
8. Plenary-verbal inspiration does not exclude the usage of pictorial and symbolic language—This is to say the Holy Spirit does not demand we accept every word in the Bible in a wooden and legalistic way. For example, a case could not be made that God has feathers like a bird by referring to Psalm. 91:4. Here the thought is simply that the persecuted believer can flee to his heavenly Father for protection and warmth.
9. Plenary-verbal inspiration does not mean uniformity in all details given in describing the same event—Here an Old Testament and a New Testament example come to mind.
   a. Old Testament example: The wicked reign of King Manasseh is vividly described for us in two separate chapters. These are 2 Kings 21:1-18 and 2 Chronicles 33:1-20. In 2 Kings we read only of his sinful ways, but in 2 Chronicles we are told of his eventual prayers for forgiveness and subsequent salvation. The reason for this may be that God allowed the author of 2 Kings to describe the reign of Manasseh from an earthly standpoint (even though he inspired the pen of the author), while he guided the pen of the author of 2 Chronicles to record Manasseh's reign from a heavenly viewpoint. God alone of course knows true repentance when he sees it coming from the human heart.
   b. New Testament example: There are four different accounts concerning the superscription on the cross at Calvary.
      (1) Matthew says—"THIS IS JESUS THE KING OF THE JEWS" (Matt. 27:37).
      (2) Mark says—"THE KING OF THE JEWS" (Mark 15:26).
      (3) Luke says—"THIS IS THE KING OF THE JEWS" (Luke 23:38).
      (4) John says—"JESUS OF NAZARETH THE KING OF THE JEWS" (John 19:19).
      The entire title probably read, "This is Jesus of Nazareth, the King of the Jews."
10. Plenary-verbal inspiration assures us God included all the necessary things he wanted us to know, and excluded everything else (2 Tim. 3:15-17).
G. The importance of inspiration—Of the three tools involved in the making of our Bible, inspiration is the most important. This is true because:

1. One may have inspiration without revelation—We have already seen how Luke carefully checked out certain facts concerning the life of Christ and was then led to write them on paper (Luke 1:1-4; 1 John 1:1-4).
2. One may have inspiration without illumination—Peter tells us (1 Pet. 1:11) the Old Testament prophets did not always understand everything they wrote about. But without inspiration, the Bible falls.

H. The completion of inspiration—Is inspiration still going on today? Has God inspired the writing (or will he someday) of a sixty-seventh book of the Bible? For nearly 20 centuries now, evangelical Christians everywhere have held to the belief that when John the apostle wrote Revelation 22:21 and wiped his pen, inspiration stopped. Furthermore, it is generally believed his warning not to add to nor to subtract from his book included not only the book of Revelation, but the entire Bible. (See Rev. 22:18-19.) It is of utmost importance that this is clearly understood, else the following tragic conclusions take place. If inspiration is still going on today, then one is forced to admit that:
   1. God could have inspired the weird and wicked writings of a Joseph Smith, or a Mary Baker Eddy, or a Charles Russell, or a Herbert W. Armstrong.
   2. Perhaps we still do not possess all the details concerning the plan of salvation, details vital to escape hell and enter heaven.
   3. God has allowed millions of devoted and faithful Christians to believe a horrible lie for some 2,000 years.

I. The betrayal of inspiration—Here the word *betrayal* is used rather than the phrase "the attack against," thus indicating the source of the action. Stated another way, one can be *attacked* by his enemies, but only *betrayed* by his friends.
   Richard Belcher of Concordia Theological Seminary writes:

> It is commonly assumed in scholarly circles, even among many evangelicals, that the doctrine of verbal inspiration of Scripture is dead. However, the corpse awaits burial, because many of the laity and untrained pastors still hold tenaciously to it and refuse to admit what the scholars claim. The doctors of theology have examined the body, read the pulse, assessed the life signs, and concluded (not always sadly) that verbal inspiration choked on the claim of inerrancy and the too rigid concept of mechanical dictation. The laity must now be re-educated so that it will know and agree with what the scholars already know to be a certainty. Care must be taken to work slowly and inconspicuously at that task lest the uneducated and uninformed be sent into shock over the truth of their beloved's passing. The news, however, must be filtered to them through the schools and publishing houses and from more enlightened pulpits. In time the majority will agree with the decree of the scholars that the concept of verbal inspiration is dead and has given way to a more excellent concept.
>
> For several years now the process of reeducation has been descending upon us. Many persons have been convinced by the scholars; others feel it really makes no difference; another large group is puzzled by it all. A few understand the problem and its implications. (*The Inerrancy Debate*, pp. 9–10)

Charles Ryrie adds the following words: "Attacks on the inerrancy of the Bible are not new and seem to be somewhat cyclical. However, the contemporary debate seems to be an intramural one; that is, it is among evangelicals, rather than between liberals and conservatives. Perhaps this makes it even more significant, for the debate has drawn lines among evangelicals that needed to be drawn. It has also served to sharpen distinctions that surround the concept of inerrancy" (*Basic Theology*, p.77).

In a lead article in the Spring 1974 issue of *Review & Expositor*, well-known evangelical author Bernard Ramm concluded in essence that the Scripture is indeed the Word of God, but not in any infallible or inerrant sense regarding its wording. He went on to say that while Scripture is the canonical Word of God, the canon is not necessarily fixed but is still open. This means God could and may add additional books to the original 66. Richard Belcher responds to Ramm's article as follows:

> Ramm's position is a supreme example of the evangelical double-talk that is going on concerning the nature of Scripture. High sounding statements, using traditional evangelical language, are made about Scripture. But then the meaning of that language is undermined by further statements and observations. Scripture is the Word of God—but not fully. Scripture is the revelation of God—but not infallible and inerrant. Scripture is the canonical Word of God—but the canon is potentially still open. Scripture is the authoritative Word of God—but it only reflects the mind of God in some measure or to some degree. Scripture is the doctrinal Word of God—but only potentially. Such use of evangelical language enables modern evangelicals who do not hold to inerrancy still to answer "yes" to probing questions concerning the nature of Scripture. (*The Inerrancy Debate*, p. 54)

Norman Geisler summarizes:

> In summary, for a neo-evangelical the Bible is a religious book, a book of salvation. Its purpose is to save and it is infallible in accomplishing that purpose. But it is not inerrant in all its statements. Only the saving "core" is true, not the cultural "husk" in which it is presented. Inspiration is dynamic and "organic." It does not guarantee the inerrancy of all historical and scientific statements in Scripture but only the infallibility of the saving purpose of Scripture.
>
> Neo-evangelicals vary on the issue of the precise *means* of inspiration. Some hold that God inspired the *idea*, and the writers put it into their own erring *words*. Others affirm that God inspired only the *core* redemptive truths, not the *cultural* mode in which it was expressed. Some stress that the *purposes* (intentions) of the Bible are inspired of God, but not all its *propositions* (affirmations). But all neo-evangelicals allow for actual errors (i.e., mistakes) in the biblical record. That is in strong contrast to the historic orthodox and contemporary evangelical view of the Bible as an infallible and inerrant record. (*A General Introduction to the Bible*, pp. 180, 189)

J. The Chicago statement on inerrancy and inspiration—It was my privilege to represent Liberty University of Lynchburg, Virginia, at the first International Council on Biblical Inerrancy Conference, which took place in Chicago on October 26–28, 1978. The Articles of Affirmation and Denial presented at the conference are as follows. This Chicago statement was signed by nearly 300 scholars, representing almost every major evangelical organization in the United States and several foreign countries.

Article I

We affirm that the Holy Scriptures are to be received as the authoritative Word of God.

We deny that the Scriptures receive their authority from the Church, tradition, or any other human source.

Article II

We affirm that the Scriptures are the supreme written norm by which God binds the conscience, and that the authority of the Church is subordinate to that of Scripture.

We deny that Church creeds, councils, or declarations have authority greater than or equal to the authority of the Bible.

Article III

We affirm that the written Word in its entirety is revelation given by God.

We deny that the Bible is merely a witness to revelation, or only becomes revelation in encounter, or depends on the responses of men for its validity.

Article IV

We affirm that God who made mankind in his image has used language as a means of revelation.

We deny that human language is so limited by our creatureliness that it is rendered inadequate as a vehicle for divine revelation. We further deny that the corruption of human culture and language through sin has thwarted God's work of inspiration.

Article V

We affirm that God's revelation in the Holy Scriptures was progressive.

We deny that later revelation, which may fulfill earlier revelation, ever corrects or contradicts it. We further deny that any normative revelation has been given since the completion of the New Testament writings.

Article VI

We affirm that the whole of Scripture and all its parts, down to the very words of the original, were given by divine inspiration.

We deny that the inspiration of Scripture can rightly be affirmed of the whole without the parts, or of some parts but not the whole.

Article VII

We affirm that inspiration was the work in which God by his Spirit, through human writers, gave us his Word. The origin of Scripture is divine. The mode of divine inspiration remains largely a mystery to us.

We deny that inspiration can be reduced to human insight, or to heightened states of consciousness of any kind.

Article VIII

We affirm that God in his Word of inspiration utilized the distinctive personalities and literary styles of the writers whom he had chosen and prepared.

We deny that God, in causing these writers to use the very words that he chose, overrode their personalities.

Article IX

We affirm that inspiration, though not conferring omniscience, guaranteed true and trustworthy utterance on all matters of which the Biblical authors were moved to speak and write.

We deny that the finitude or fallenness of these writers, by necessity or otherwise, introduced distortion or falsehood into God's Word.

Article X

We affirm that inspiration, strictly speaking, applies only to the autographic text of Scripture, which in the providence of God can be ascertained from available manuscripts with great accuracy. We further affirm that copies and translations of Scripture are the Word of God to the extent that they faithfully represent the original.

We deny that any essential element of the Christian faith is affected by the absence of the autographs. We further deny that this absence renders the assertions of Biblical inerrancy invalid or irrelevant.

Article XI

We affirm that Scripture, having been given by divine inspiration, is infallible, so that, far from misleading us, it is true and reliable in all the matters it addresses.

We deny that it is possible for the Bible to be at the same time infallible and errant in its assertions. Infallibility and inerrancy may be distinguished, but not separated.

Article XII

We affirm that Scripture in its entirety is inerrant, being free from all falsehood, fraud, or deceit.

We deny that Biblical infallibility and inerrancy are limited to spiritual, religious, or redemptive themes, exclusive of assertions in the fields of history and science. We further deny that scientific hypotheses about earth history may properly be used to overturn the teaching of Scripture on creation and the flood.

Article XIII

We affirm the propriety of using inerrancy as a theological term with reference to the complete truthfulness of Scripture.

We deny that it is proper to evaluate Scripture according to standards of truth and error that are alien to its usage or purpose. We further deny that inerrancy is negated by Biblical phenomena such as a lack of modern technical precision, irregularities of grammar or spelling, observational descriptions of nature, the reporting of falsehoods, the use of hyperbole and round numbers, the topical arrangement of material, variant selections of material in parallel accounts, or the use of free citations.

Article XIV

We affirm the unity and internal consistency of Scripture.

We deny that alleged errors and discrepancies that have not yet been resolved vitiate the truth claims of the Bible.

Article XV

We affirm that the doctrine of inerrancy is grounded in the teaching of the Bible about inspiration.

We deny that Jesus' teaching about Scripture may be dismissed by appeals to accommodation or to any natural limitation of his humanity.

Article XVI

We affirm that the doctrine of inerrancy has been integral to the Church's faith throughout its history.

We deny that the inerrancy is a doctrine invented by Scholastic Protestantism, or is a reactionary position postulated in response to negative higher criticism.

Article XVII

We affirm that the Holy Spirit bears witness to the Scriptures, assuring believers of the truthfulness of God's written Word.

We deny that this witness of the Holy Spirit operates in isolation from or against Scripture.

Article XVIII

We affirm that the text of Scripture is to be interpreted by grammatico-historical exegesis, taking account of its literary forms and devices, and that Scripture is to interpret Scripture.

We deny the legitimacy of any treatment of the text or quest for sources lying behind it that leads to relativizing, dehistoricizing, or discounting its teaching, or rejecting its claims to authorship.

Article XIX

We affirm that a confession of the full authority, infallibility, and inerrancy of Scripture is vital to a sound understanding of the whole of the Christian faith.

We further affirm that such confession should lead to increasing conformity to the image of Christ.

We deny that such confession is necessary for salvation. However, we further deny that inerrancy can be rejected without grave consequences, both to the individual and to the Church.

III. Illumination—We have already stated that without inspiration, no Scripture would have ever been written. We may now claim that without illumination, no sinner would have ever been saved! Illumination, then, is that method used by the Holy Spirit to shed divine light upon all seeking men as they look into the Word of God. Illumination is from the written word to the human heart. Consider:

  A. The reasons for illumination—Why is this third step necessary? Why cannot sinful man simply read and heed the biblical message without divine aid?

    1. It is necessary because of natural blindness—Paul writes of this: "But the natural man receiveth not the things of the Spirit of God: for they are foolishness unto him: neither can he know them, because they are spiritually discerned" (1 Cor. 2:14).

      Our Lord also commented on this during his earthly ministry. "And Simon Peter answered and said, Thou art the Christ, the Son of the living God. And Jesus answered and said unto him, Blessed art thou, Simon Bar-jona: for flesh and blood hath not revealed it unto thee, but my Father which is in heaven" (Matt. 16:16-17).

    2. It is necessary because of satanic blindness—Again we note the sober words of

Paul: "But if our gospel be hid, it is hid to them that are lost: in whom the god of this world hath blinded the minds of them which believe not" (2 Cor. 4:3-4).

3. It is necessary because of carnal blindness (Heb. 5:12-14; 1 Cor. 3; 2 Pet. 1).

4. It is necessary (in the case of Israel) because of divine judicial blindness. (See Matt. 23:37-39; John 9:39; Acts 28:25-27; Rom. 11:25.)

B. Results of illumination

1. Sinners are saved—"The LORD openeth the eyes of the blind: the LORD raiseth them that are bowed down: the LORD loveth the righteous" (Psa. 146:8). "The entrance of thy words giveth light; it giveth understanding unto the simple" (Psa. 119:130).

2. Christians are strengthened—"As newborn babes, desire the sincere milk of the word, that ye may grow thereby" (1 Pet. 2:2). "But God hath revealed them unto us by his Spirit: for the Spirit searcheth all things, yea,the deep things of God" (1 Cor. 2:10). "For God, who commanded the light to shine out of darkness, hath shined in our hearts, to give the light of the knowledge of the glory of God in the face of Jesus Christ" (2 Cor. 4:6). "Thy word is a lamp unto my feet, and a light unto my path" (Psa. 119:105).

C. Implications of illumination

1. The Holy Spirit looks for a certain amount of sincerity before he illuminates any human heart—We are quick to point out sincerity is not enough to save anyone. However, it should be also noted that it is equally impossible for an insincere person to be saved. This first implication is brought out in several passages. "But without faith it is impossible to please him: for he that cometh to God must believe that he is, and that he is a rewarder of them that diligently seek him" (Heb. 11:6). "God is a Spirit: and they that worship him must worship him in spirit and in truth" (John 4:24).

Furthermore, it should be stated here that no Christian should ever look upon illumination as automatic. That is to say, God has never promised to reveal precious and profound biblical truths to any believer who will not search the Scriptures for himself. Note the following admonitions: "But he answered and said, It is written, Man shall not live by bread alone, but by every word that proceedeth out of the mouth of God" (Matt. 4:4). "But these are written, that ye might believe that Jesus is the Christ, the Son of God; and that believing ye might have life through his name" (John 20:31). "These were more noble than those in Thessalonica, in that they received the word with all readiness of mind, and searched the scriptures daily, whether those things were so" (Acts 17:11). "Study to shew thyself approved unto God, a workman that needeth not to be ashamed, rightly dividing the word of truth" (2 Tim. 2:15). "As newborn babes, desire the sincere milk of the word, that ye may grow thereby" (1 Pet. 2:2).

2. The Holy Spirit often seeks out the aid of a believer in performing his task of illuminating the hearts of others—This is seen:

a. In the ministry of Philip to the Ethiopian eunuch—"And Philip ran thither to him, and heard him read the prophet Esaias, and said, Understandest thou what thou readest? And he said, How can I, except some man should guide me? . . . Then Philip opened his mouth, and began at the same scripture, and preached unto him Jesus" (Acts 8:30-31, 35).

b. In the ministry of Paul, to the Jews at Thessalonica—"And Paul, as his manner was, went in unto them, and three sabbath days reasoned with them out of the scriptures" (Acts 17:2).

   c. In the ministry of Aquila and Priscilla to Apollos—"And he began to speak
      boldly in the synagogue: whom when Aquila and Priscilla had heard, they
      took him unto them, and expounded unto him the way of God more
      perfectly" (Acts 18:26).
   d. In the ministry of Apollos to the Jews at Corinth—"For he mightily
      convinced the Jews, and that publicly, shewing by the scriptures that Jesus
      was Christ" (Acts 18:28).

PART FOUR: CHRIST AND THE BIBLE
I. The Unfolding of Christ in the Scriptures
   A. Descriptions of Christ in the 39 Old Testament books
      1. Seed of the woman; Shiloh (Gen. 3:15; 49:10)
      2. Passover Lamb (Exod. 12:3)
      3. Anointed High Priest (Lev. 8:7-9)
      4. Star of Jacob; brazen serpent (Num. 21:8; 24:17)
      5. Prophet like Moses; the great rock (Deut. 18:15; 32:4)
      6. Captain of the Lord's hosts (Josh. 5:14)
      7. Messenger of the Lord (Judg. 2:1)
      8. Kinsman-Redeemer (Ruth 2:1)
      9. Great judge (1 Sam. 2:10)
      10. Seed of David (2 Sam. 7:13)
      11. Lord God of Israel (1 Kings 8:15, 26)
      12. God of the cherubim (2 Kings 19:15)
      13. God of our salvation (1 Chron. 16:35)
      14. God of our fathers (2 Chron. 20:6)
      15. Lord of heaven and earth (Ezra 1:2)
      16. Covenant-keeping God (Neh. 1:5)
      17. The God of providence (Esther)
      18. Risen and returning Redeemer (Job 19:25)
      19. The anointed Son; the Holy One; the Good Shepherd; the King of glory (Psa.
          2:7, 12; 16:10; 23:1; 24:7-10)
      20. The wisdom of God (Prov. 8)
      21. The one above the sun (Eccles.)
      22. Chief among ten thousand; altogether lovely (Song of Sol. 5:10, 16)
      23. Virgin-born Immanuel; wonderful counselor, the mighty God, the everlasting
          Father, the Prince of Peace; the man of sorrows (Isa. 7:14; 9:6; 52:13; 53:3)
      24. The Lord our righteousness (Jer. 23:6; 33:16)
      25. The faithful and compassionate (Lam. 3:22-23, 31-33)
      26. The Lord is there (Ezek.)
      27. Stone; Son of God; Son of Man (Dan. 2:34; 3:25; 7:13)
      28. King of the resurrection (Hos. 13:9, 14)
      29. God of the battle and giver of the Spirit (Joel 2:11, 28-32; 3:2, 9-17)
      30. God of hosts and the plumbline (Amos 4:13; 7:7)
      31. Destroyer of the proud (Obad. 8, 15)
      32. The risen prophet; God of second chance; the long-suffering one (Jon. 2:10; 3:1;
          4:9-11)
      33. God of Jacob; the Bethlehem-born; the pardoning God (Mic. 4:1-5; 5:2; 7:18-19)
      34. The avenging God; the bringer of good tidings (Nah. 1:2, 15)
      35. The everlasting, pure, glorious, and anointed one (Hab. 1:12-13; 2:14; 3:13)

36. The King of Israel (Zeph. 3:15)
37. Desire of all nations (Hag. 2:7)
38. Branch; builder of temple; King of triumphal entry; pierced one; King of the earth (Zech. 3:8; 6:12-13; 9:9; 12:10; 14:9)
39. The sun of righteousness (Mal. 4:2)

B. Descriptions of Christ in the 27 New Testament books
1. King of the Jews (Matt. 2:2; 27:37)
2. Servant (Mark 9:35; 10:43-44)
3. Perfect man (Luke 2:40, 52; 9:22, 56, 58; 22:48)
4. Eternal God (John 1:1-5; 20:28, 31)
5. Ascended Lord (Acts 1:9)
6. The Lord our righteousness (Rom. 10:4)
7. Our resurrection (1 Cor. 15)
8. God of all comfort (2 Cor. 1:3)
9. Redeemer from the law (Gal. 4:4-5)
10. Head of the church; giver of gifts (Eph. 1:22; 2:20; 3:23–4:8)
11. Supplier of every need; obedient servant (Phil. 1:19; 4:19; 2:5-8)
12. Fullness of the Godhead (Col. 1:19; 2:9)
13. The coming Christ (1 Thess. 4:13-18; 5:2)
14. The consuming Christ (2 Thess. 2:8)
15. Savior of sinners (1 Tim. 2:15; 3:16; 1:15)
16. Righteous and rewarding Judge; author of Scripture (2 Tim. 4:8; 3:16-17)
17. Our great God and Savior (Titus 1:3; 2:10, 13; 3:4)
18. Payer of our debt (Philem.)
19. Appointed heir of all things; one greater than the prophets or angels (Heb. 1:2, 4; 3:3)
20. Ever-present God; Great Physician; the coming one (James 4:6-8; 5:15; 5:7-8)
21. Unblemished lamb; great example; chief shepherd; Lord of glory (1 Pet. 1:19; 2:21-24; 5:4; 3:22)
22. The beloved Son (2 Pet. 1:17)
23. Word of life; advocate; propitiation; Son of God (1 John 1:1; 2:1; 3:8; 4:15; 5:5)
24. Son of the Father (2 John 3)
25. The truth (3 John 4, 8)
26. Preserver and only wise God (Jude 1-25)
27. The Alpha and Omega; the Lion of Judah; King of kings (Rev. 1:8; 5:5; 19:16)

II. The Unity Between Christ and the Scriptures—A marvelous and manifold unity is seen as one compares the Savior with the Scriptures.
A. Both are known as the Word of God.
1. One is the written Word—"And he gave unto Moses, when he had made an end of communing with him upon mount Sinai, two tables of testimony, tables of stone, written with the finger of God" (Exod. 31:18).
2. One is the Living Word—"And the Word was made flesh, and dwelt among us, (and we beheld his glory, the glory as of the only begotten of the Father,) full of grace and truth" (John 1:14).
B. Both are eternal.
1. The Scriptures—"Being born again, not of corruptible seed, but of incorruptible, by the word of God, which liveth and abideth for ever" (1 Pet. 1:23).

2. The Savior—"Jesus Christ the same yesterday, and to day, and for ever" (Heb. 13:8).

C. Both came from heaven.
    1. The Scriptures—"For ever, O LORD, thy word is settled in heaven" (Psa. 119:89).
    2. The Savior—"And no man hath ascended up to heaven, but he that came down from heaven, even the Son of man which is in heaven" (John 3:13).

D. Both came to bless a lost world.
    1. The Scriptures—"But he said, Yea rather, blessed are they that hear the word of God, and keep it" (Luke 11:28).
    2. The Savior—"Unto you first God, having raised up his Son Jesus, sent him to bless you, in turning away every one of you from his iniquities" (Acts 3:26).

E. Both partook of the human and divine.
    1. The Scriptures—"And without controversy great is the mystery of godliness: God was manifest in the flesh, justified in the Spirit, seen of angels, preached unto the Gentiles, believed on in the world, received up into glory" (1 Tim. 3:16).
    2. The Savior—"For the prophecy came not in old time by the will of man: but holy men of God spake as they were moved by the Holy Ghost" (2 Pet. 1:21).

F. Both enjoyed angelic support.
    1. The Scriptures—"Who have received the law by the disposition of angels, and have not kept it" (Acts 7:53). "The Law . . . was ordained by angels" (Gal. 3:19). "The Word spoken by angels" (Heb. 2:2).
    2. The Savior—"Then the devil leaveth him, and, behold, angels came and ministered unto him" (Matt. 4:11). "And there appeared an angel unto him from heaven, strengthening him" (Luke 22:43).

G. Both are faultless.
    1. The Scriptures—"Every word of God is pure: he is a shield unto them that put their trust in him" (Prov. 30:5).
    2. The Savior—"And ye know that he was manifested to take away our sins; and in him is no sin" (1 John 3:5).

H. Both are sources of life.
    1. The Scriptures—"For the word of God is quick, and powerful [living and active]" (Heb. 4:12a).
    2. The Savior—"Jesus saith unto him, I am the way, the truth, and the life: no man cometh unto the Father, but by me" (John 14:6).

I. Both are sources of light.
    1. The Scriptures—"The entrance of thy words giveth light; it giveth understanding unto the simple" (Psa. 119:130).
    2. The Savior—"That was the true Light, which lighteth every man that cometh into the world" (John 1:9).

J. Both are absolute truth.
    1. The Scriptures—"Sanctify them through thy truth: thy word is truth" (John 17:17).
    2. The Savior—"Jesus saith unto him, I am the way, the truth, and the life: no man cometh unto the Father, but by me" (John 14:6).

K. Both provide food for the soul.
    1. The Scriptures—"And he humbled thee, and suffered thee to hunger, and fed thee with manna, which thou knewest not, neither did thy fathers know; that he might make thee know that man doth not live by bread only, but by every word that proceedeth out of the mouth of the LORD doth man live" (Deut. 8:3).

2. The Savior—"And Jesus said unto them, I am the bread of life: he that cometh to me shall never hunger; and he that believeth on me shall never thirst" (John 6:35).

L. Both provide cleansing.
1. The Scriptures—"Now ye are clean through the word which I have spoken unto you" (John 15:3).
2. The Savior—"If we confess our sins, he is faithful and just to forgive us our sins, and to cleanse us from all unrighteousness" (1 John 1:9).

M. Both produce fruit.
1. The Scriptures—"But he that received seed into the good ground is he that heareth the word, and understandeth it; which also beareth fruit, and bringeth forth, some an hundredfold, some sixty, some thirty" (Matt. 13:23).
2. The Savior—"I am the vine, ye are the branches: He that abideth in me, and I in him, the same bringeth forth much fruit: for without me ye can do nothing" (John 15:5).

N. Both give peace.
1. The Scriptures—"Great peace have they which love thy law: and nothing shall offend them" (Psa. 119:165).
2. The Savior—"Peace I leave with you, my peace I give unto you: not as the world giveth, give I unto you. Let not your heart be troubled, neither let it be afraid" (John 14:27).

O. Both are likened to a sword.
1. The Scriptures—"And take the helmet of salvation, and the sword of the Spirit, which is the word of God" (Eph. 6:17).
2. The Savior—"And out of his mouth goeth a sharp sword, that with it he should smite the nations: and he shall rule them with a rod of iron: and he treadeth the winepress of the fierceness and wrath of Almighty God" (Rev. 19:15).

P. Both are called wonderful.
1. The Scriptures—"Open thou mine eyes, that I may behold wondrous things out of thy law" (Psa. 119:18).
2. The Savior—"For unto us a child is born, unto us a son is given: and the government shall be upon his shoulder: and his name shall be called Wonderful, Counsellor, The mighty God, The everlasting Father, The Prince of Peace" (Isa. 9:6).

Q. Both are called the power of God.
1. The Scriptures—"For I am not ashamed of the gospel of Christ: for it is the power of God unto salvation to every one that believeth; to the Jew first, and also to the Greek" (Rom. 1:16).
2. The Savior—"But unto them which are called, both Jews and Greeks, Christ the power of God, and the wisdom of God" (1 Cor. 1:24).

R. Both successfully complete their original assignment.
1. The Scriptures—"For as the rain cometh down, and the snow from heaven, and returneth not thither, but watereth the earth, and maketh it bring forth and bud, that it may give seed to the sower, and bread to the eater: so shall my word be that goeth forth out of my mouth: it shall not return unto me void, but it shall accomplish that which I please, and it shall prosper in the thing whereto I sent it" (Isa. 55:10-11).
2. The Savior—"I have glorified thee on the earth: I have finished the work which thou gavest me to do. . . . When Jesus therefore had received the vinegar, he

said, It is finished: and he bowed his head, and gave up the ghost" (John 17:4; 19:30).
S. Both must be received for salvation.
    1. The Scriptures—"Wherefore lay apart all filthiness and superfluity of naughtiness, and receive with meekness the engrafted word, which is able to save your souls" (James 1:21).
    2. The Savior—"But as many as received him, to them gave he power to become the sons of God, even to them that believe on his name" (John 1:12).
T. Both were rejected by sinful men.
    1. The Scriptures—"And he said unto them, Full well ye reject the commandment of God, that ye may keep your own tradition" (Mark 7:9).
    2. The Savior—"He is despised and rejected of men; a man of sorrows, and acquainted with grief: and we hid as it were our faces from him; he was despised, and we esteemed him not" (Isa. 53:3).
U. Both were subjected to attacks by sinful men.
    1. The Scriptures—"Then the word of the LORD came to Jeremiah, after that the king had burned the roll, and the words which Baruch wrote at the mouth of Jeremiah, saying, Take thee again another roll, and write in it all the former words that were in the first roll, which Jehoiakim the king of Judah hath burned" (Jer. 36:27-28).
    2. The Savior—"Then the Jews took up stones again to stone him" (John 10:31).
V. Both will eventually judge all sinful men.
    1. The Scriptures—"For as many as have sinned without law shall also perish without law: and as many as have sinned in the law shall be judged by the law. . . . Now we know that what things soever the law saith, it saith to them who are under the law: that every mouth may be stopped, and all the world may become guilty before God" (Rom. 2:12; 3:19).
    2. The Savior—"For the Father judgeth no man, but hath committed all judgment unto the Son" (John 5:22).
III. The Usage by Christ of the Scriptures
  A. The Old Testament events and individuals he mentioned
    1. The creation of Adam and Eve (Gen. 1:27; 2:24; Mark 10:6-8)
    2. The murder of Abel (Gen. 4:10; Luke 11:51)
    3. The corruption of Noah's day and the flood (Gen. 6–7; Luke 17:26-27)
    4. The corruption of Lot's day and the fire (Gen. 19; Luke 17:28-29)
    5. The worldliness of Lot's wife (Gen. 19:26; Luke 17:32)
    6. The faith of Abraham, Isaac, and Jacob (Matt. 22:32)
    7. Moses and the burning bush (Exod. 3; Mark 12:26)
    8. Moses and the heavenly manna (Exod. 16:15; John 6:31)
    9. Moses and the brazen serpent (Num. 21:18; John 3:14)
    10. David and some shewbread (1 Sam. 21:6; Matt. 12:3-4)
    11. Solomon and the Queen of Sheba (1 Kings 10:1; Matt. 12:42)
    12. Elijah, a widow, and the famine (1 Kings 17:1, 9; Luke 4:25-26)
    13. Naaman and his leprosy (2 Kings 5; Luke 4:27)
    14. The murder of Zechariah (2 Chron. 24:20-21; Luke 11:51)
    15. Daniel and the abomination of desolation (Dan. 9:27; 11:31; 12:11; Matt. 24:15)
    16. Jonah and the fish (Jon. 1:17; Matt. 12:40; 16:4)
    17. Jonah and the repentance of the Ninevites (Jon. 3:4-10; Luke 11:30; Matt. 12:41)
  B. The Old Testament passages he quoted from

1. During his temptations
    a. The first temptation—In Matthew 4:4 he quotes Deuteronomy 8:3.
    b. The second temptation—In Matthew 4:7 he quotes Deuteronomy 6:16.
    c. The third temptation—In Matthew 4:10 he quotes Deuteronomy 6:13.
2. During his Sermon on the Mount
    a. In Matthew 5:21 he quotes Exodus 20:13, the sixth commandment.
    b. In Matthew 5:27 he quotes Exodus 20:14, the seventh commandment— Also
    compare Matthew 5:31 with Deuteronomy 24:1. Note: He later quotes some
    of the same commandments during his talk with a rich young ruler. See
    Mark 10:19.
3. During his hometown sermon—In Luke 4:18-19 he quotes Isaiah 61:1-2.
4. During various confrontations with Jewish rulers
    a. As he defended his associating with sinners—In Matthew 9:13 he quotes
    Hosea 6:6.
    b. As he expounds on marriage—In Mark 10:7-8 he quotes Genesis 2:24.
    c. As he is asked concerning the greatest of the commandments—in Mark
    12:29-30 he quotes Deuteronomy 6:4-5.
    d. As he rebukes their vain traditions—In Matthew 15:7-9 he quotes Isaiah
    29:13.
    e. As the Pharisees question his authority—In John 8:17 he quotes
    Deuteronomy 17:6.
5. During his tribute to John the Baptist—In Luke 7:27 he quotes Malachi 3:1.
6. During his triumphal entry day—In Matthew 21:16 he quotes Psalm 8:2.
7. During his cleansing of the temple—In Luke 19:46 he quotes Isaiah 56:7.
8. During a parable about Israel—In Matthew 21:42, 44 he quotes Psalm 118:22-23;
    Isaiah 8:14-15.
9. During a question session in the temple—In Mark 12:36 he quotes Psalm 110:1.
10. During his last Passover night—Predicting the world would hate the disciples
    as they hated him—in John 15:25 he quotes Psalms 35:19; 69:4.
11. On the cross
    a. His fourth utterance—In Matthew 27:46 he quotes Psalm 22:1.
    b. His seventh utterance—In Luke 23:46 he quotes Psalm 31:5.
In summary, our Lord said the Law would be fulfilled (Matt. 5:18) and the Scriptures
could not be broken (John 10:35).

It has been estimated that over one-tenth of Jesus' recorded New Testament words
were taken from the Old Testament. In the four Gospels, 180 of the 1,800 verses that
report his discourses are either Old Testament quotes or Old Testament allusions.

PART FIVE: ISRAEL AND THE BIBLE
"The people of Israel. Theirs is the adoption as sons; theirs the divine glory, the cove-
nants, the receiving of the law, the temple worship and the promises. Theirs are the patri-
archs, and from them is traced the human ancestry of Christ, who is God over all, forever
praised! Amen" (Rom. 9:4-5, NIV).
 I. Moses and the Scriptures—In the book of Deuteronomy Israel's great lawgiver writes
  the following concerning the holy Scriptures:
  A. It was not to be added to or taken from (4:2).
  B. To obey God's Word meant to live (4:1; 6:25; 11:13-15, 22-25; 28:1-14).
  C. To disobey God's Word was to die (11:16-17, 28; 28:15-68).
  D. It would be the source of Israel's wisdom and understanding (4:6).

E. It would be the envy of pagan nations (4:6-8).

F. The Word was to be diligently taught to one's sons, grandsons, etc. (4:9-10; 6:2, 7-9).

G. Future kings were to be guided by it (17:18-20).

H. The blessings and curses of the Law were to be read from the two mountains of Gerizim and Ebal after Israel entered the promised land (27:12-13).

II. Joshua

A. God told him he would prosper if the Law was read and obeyed (Josh. 1:7-9).

B. Joshua commanded the Law to be read from Mounts Gerizim and Ebal as Moses had instructed (8:34).

C. During his final message to Israel's leaders, Joshua reminded them of God's faithfulness in keeping his word (23:14).

III. Samuel

A. He taught the Scriptures throughout Israel (1 Sam. 3:19-21; 4:1; 7:15-17).

B. He reviewed it to Saul, hoping (unsuccessfully) to keep Israel's first king in the center of God's will (1 Sam. 9:27; 15:1).

IV. David

A. David testified concerning the inspiration and inerrancy of the Scriptures (2 Sam. 23:2).

B. He wrote Psalm 119, by far the Bible's most lengthy chapter, a chapter given completely in describing the titles, functions, and importance of the Scriptures.

V. Solomon—Israel's most fabulous king writes the following concerning the Scriptures:

A. They will direct one's feet (Prov. 3:6-7).

B. They bring great peace (Prov. 3:24-26).

C. They bring God's favor (Prov. 8:35).

D. They produce happiness and result in great honor (Prov. 3:13; 4:8).

E. They are better than silver, gold, or rubies (Prov. 3:14-15; 8:19).

F. They are of utmost importance (Prov. 4:7).

G. They become "the whole duty of man" (Eccl. 12:13).

VI. Isaiah

A. He wrote concerning the *eternality* of the Scriptures (40:6-8).

B. He wrote concerning the *effectiveness* of the Scriptures (55:10-11).

VII. Jehoshaphat—This godly Judean king sent teachers throughout all Israel to instruct the people concerning the Scriptures (2 Chron. 17:9).

VIII. Josiah—During his reign a copy of the Law of Moses was found in the temple. Upon reading it the king led his people in a revival (2 Chron. 34:14).

IX. Ezekiel—This prophet was commanded to literally eat a portion of the Word (Ezek. 3:1-3). Later, John the apostle was given the same instructions (Rev. 10:9).

X. Daniel

A. Daniel's reading of Jeremiah helped prepare him for the prophecy of the 70 weeks (Dan. 9:1-2, 24).

B. Following this, an angel personally instructed Daniel from "the Scriptures of truth" (Dan. 10:21).

XI. Ezra—His faithful and fearless proclamation of the Scriptures produced a twofold reaction:

A. The first occasion led to a great repentance among God's people (Ezra 10).

B. The second occasion led to a great rejoicing among God's people (Neh. 8).

XII. Jesus—Our Lord said Israel had failed God "not knowing the Scriptures, nor the power of God" (Matt. 22:29).

XIII. Stephen—He totally condemned the Jewish leaders for their unforgivable sin of rejecting the Spirit of God, the Word of God, and the Son of God (Acts 7:51-53).
XIV. Paul
　　A. He said Israel had understood the letter of the Law (its morality) but would not
　　　　obey it (Rom. 2:17-23).
　　B. He said Israel had not understood the spirit of the Law (its Messiah) and would
　　　　not receive him (Acts 13:27; 2 Cor. 3:14-15).

PART SIX: SATAN AND THE BIBLE
　I. Satan Twists the Word of God (Gen. 3:1).
　II. He denies it (Gen. 3:4-5).
　III. He takes it out of context (Matt. 4:6).
　IV. He attempts to destroy it (Jer. 36:27-29).
　V. He attempts to muzzle it.
　　A. As experienced by Micaiah (2 Chron. 18:12-13)
　　B. As experienced by Amos (Amos 7:10-13)
　　C. As experienced by Peter and John (Acts 4:13-18; 5:28)
　VI. He tries to add to it (Acts 15:1).
　VII. He steals it from human hearts (Matt. 13:4, 19).
VIII. He ridicules it.
　　A. As seen at Pentecost (Acts 2:4, 12-13)
　　B. As seen at Athens (Acts 17:18-21, 32)
　　C. As seen at Caesarea (Acts 26:24)
　IX. He attempts to identify with it (Acts 16:16-18).
　X. He will cause men to totally turn from it in the last days (1 Tim. 4:1; 2 Tim. 3:1-5; 4:1-4).

PART SEVEN: FALSE POSITIONS ON THE BIBLE
　I. The Position of Agnosticism—Dr. Bertrand Russell makes the following statement:

> An agnostic regards the Bible exactly as enlightened clerics regard it. He does not
> think it is divinely inspired; he thinks its early history legendary, and no more
> exactly true than that in Homer; he thinks its moral teaching sometimes good, but
> sometimes very bad. For example: Samuel ordered Saul, in a war, to kill not only
> every man, woman, and child of the enemy, but also all the sheep and cattle. Saul,
> however, let the sheep and cattle live, and for this we are told to condemn him. I
> have never been able to admire Elisha for cursing the children who laughed at him,
> or to believe (what the Bible asserts) that a benevolent Deity would send two
> she-bears to kill the children. (*A Guide to the Religions of America*, Leo Rosten, ed.,
> p. 152)

　II. The Position of Liberalism—Probably the most famous liberal of the twentieth century
was the late Harry Emerson Fosdick. He has written the following words which typify
the liberal attitude:

> When one moves back to the Scriptures with a mind accustomed to work in
> modern ways he finds himself in a strange world. . . . Knowing modern astronomy
> he turns to the Bible to find the sun and moon standing still or the shadow
> retreating on a sundial. Knowing modern biology he hears that when Elisha had
> been so long dead that only his bones were left, another dead body, thrown into the
> cave where he was buried, touched his skeleton and sprang to life again, or that

after our Lord's resurrection many of the saints long deceased arose and appeared in Jerusalem. Knowing modern physics he turns to the Bible to read that light was created three days before the sun and that an axe-head floated when Elisha threw a stick into the water. Knowing modern medicine he finds in the scripture many familiar ailments, epilepsy, deafness, dumbness, blindness, insanity, ascribed to the visitation of demons. . . . We live in a new world. We have not kept the forms of thought and categories of explanation in astronomy, geology, biology, which the Bible contains. We have definitely and irrevocably gotten new ones. (Ibid., p. 160)

But at the end of his life Fosdick may have seen the error of this false liberal approach to the Word of God. Note his evaluation:

Today, however, looking back over forty years of ministry, I see an outstanding difference between then and now with regard to what is standard and who must do the adjusting. What man in his senses can now call our modern civilization standard? It is not Christ's message that needs to be accommodated to this mad scene; it is this mad scene into which our civilization has collapsed that needs to be judged and saved by Christ's message. This is the most significant change distinguishing the beginning of my ministry from now. Then we were trying to accommodate Christ to our scientific civilization; now we face the desperate need of accommodating our scientific civilization to Christ. (Quoted in Norman Geisler and William Nix, *A General Introduction to the Bible*, p. 168)

III. The Position of the Cults—In general it may be said the major cults and sects of Christianity give lip service to the Bible; they nevertheless look upon the writings of their various founders as equal if not superior to the Scriptures.
   A. Christian Scientist—Founded by Mary Baker Eddy (1821–1910). George Channing, an international Christian Science lecturer and practitioner, writes the following: "Each person, of any religion, can find what is satisfying to him as the spiritual meaning in the Bible. But Christian Scientists feel that Mrs. Mary Baker Eddy's book, *Science and Health with Key to the Scriptures*, offers the complete spiritual meaning of the Bible. They believe that this full meaning would not have been available to them without Mrs. Eddy's discovery" (*The Reason for Our Hope*, p. 67).
   B. Jehovah's Witnesses—Founded by Charles Taze Russell (1851–1916). Mr. Russell calmly announces in the opening pages of his *Studies in the Scriptures* that it would be far better to leave the Bible unread but read his comments on it than to omit his writings and read the Bible.
   C. Mormonism—Founded by Joseph Smith 1805–1844). This cult teaches that the *Book of Mormon*, first printed in 1830, must be regarded on an equal basis with the Bible.
IV. The Position of Romanism—Rome believes that the church is the divinely appointed custodian of the Bible and has the final word on what is meant in any specific passage. It accepts the apocryphal books as a part of the inspired Scriptures. Rome's position on the Bible could be diagrammed as a triangle, with the pope at the top, and the Bible and church tradition at the bottom.
 V. The Position of Mysticism—Those holding this view lean heavily upon that divine "inner light" to reveal and guide them into all truth. Thus the personal experiences, feelings, etc. of an individual are looked upon as vital to discovering divine truth as the Word of God itself.
VI. The Position of Neoorthodoxy (popularized by Karl Barth in his *Epistle to the Romans*,

first published in 1918)—This position holds that the Bible may well indeed contain the Word of God, but that, until it becomes such, it is as dead and uninspired as any other ancient or modern historical book might be. Thus the Bible is not to be viewed as objective, but subjective in nature. It is only the Word of God as it becomes the Word of God to me. Neoorthodoxy would thus view the first 11 chapters of Genesis as "religious myths." This term is defined as a "conveyer of theological truth in a historical garb, but which theological truth is not dependent upon the historicity of the garb itself for its validity."

Norm Geisler concludes:

> To sum it up, the neo-orthodox view is that the Bible is a fallible human book. Nevertheless, it is the instrument of God's revelation to us, for it is a record of God's personal revelation in Christ. Revelation, however, is personal; the Bible is not a verbally inspired revelation from God. It is merely an errant human means through which one can encounter the personal revelation who is Christ. In itself it is not the Word of God: at best, the Bible only becomes the Word of God to the individual when he encounters Christ through it. (*A General Introduction to the Bible*, p. 175)

VII. Higher Criticism—"The Documentary Hypothesis developed in the 19th century in association with the work of Hupfeld, K. H. Graf, and Julius Wellhausen, resulted in the analysis of the Pentateuch into four or more documents usually labeled J (Jahwistic), E (Elohistic), D (Deuteronomic), and P (Priestly)" (*Beacon Dictionary of Theology* Beacon Hill Press. Kansas City, Mo. 1983, p. 144).

In essence, the Documentary Hypothesis, without the slightest evidence, boldly concludes Moses did not write the Pentateuch (in spite of repeated scriptural statements saying he did—see Deut. 31:24; Josh. 8:31; John 1:17), but that it represents a forgery, produced by at least four separate sources.

Jewish historian and novelist Herman Wouk, a man well versed in the religion and culture of his people has written concerning the Documentary Hypothesis:

> I have read Wellhausen's *Prolegomena,* and I have checked all his textual references in the Old Testament in Hebrew. It may well be that I am the last man on earth who will ever accomplish this feat. The book is a museum piece now, and even young Bible scholars are not required to plow through it. But I thought I owed it to the readers of this discussion to perform the task. I will try to describe the book, which was for a while a sort of inside-out Bible for non-believers.

Wellhausen starts by announcing his grand theme: the forging priests, the non-existent tabernacle, and the phony doctrine of central worship. Then he plunges into his main task: getting the Bible to retell its story according to Wellhausen, in its own words.

His method is simple, but the working out in detail is grandiose. Whatever passages of Scripture support his thesis, or at least do not oppose it, are authentic. Wherever the text contradicts him, the verses are spurious. His attack on each verse that does not support him is violent. He shows bad grammar, or internal inconsistency, or corrupt vocabulary, or jerkiness of continuity, every time. There is no passage he cannot explain away or annihilate. If he has to change the plain meaning of Hebrew words he does that too. He calls this "conjectural emendation."

The puzzle today is how such a work ever captured, even for a few decades, a serious scholastic field. But the history of science shows that any vigorously asserted hypothesis can have a good run, in the absence of solid facts. The main thing, probably, was that in 1875 evolution was in the air. The battles over Darwin were still being fought, but it was obvious who was going to win. A theory that imposed evolution on Old Testament religion radiated chic and excitement, even though it stood the Bible on its head. Wellhausen's job of documentation, shrill and twisted though it was, lacking any scientific precision, nevertheless was overpowering in its sheer mass of minute scholarly detail. His construction lasted, with increasing shakiness, until the 1930s. It still lingers to some extent in popular culture, which does not turn on a dime. Serious Bible scholarship has dropped it. (*This Is My God*, pp. 275–276)

PART EIGHT: STATEMENTS FROM GREAT PERSONALITIES
          CONCERNING THE BIBLE
I. United States Presidents
   A. George Washington (First)—"It is impossible to rightly govern the world without the Bible."
   B. John Adams (Second)—"The Bible is the best book in the world. It contains more . . . than all the libraries I have seen."
   C. Thomas Jefferson (Third)—"The Bible makes the best people in the world."
   D. John Quincy Adams (Sixth)—"It is an invaluable and inexhaustible mine of knowledge and virtue."
   E. Andrew Jackson (Seventh)—"That book, sir, is the rock on which our Republic rests."
   F. Zachary Taylor (Twelfth)—"It was for the love of the truths of this great book that our fathers abandoned their native shore for the wilderness."
   G. Abraham Lincoln (Sixteenth)—"But for this Book we could not know right from wrong. I believe the Bible is the best gift God has ever given to man."
   H. Ulysses S. Grant (Eighteenth)—"The Bible is the Anchor of our liberties."
   I. Rutherford B. Hayes (Nineteenth)—"The best religion the world has ever known is the religion of the Bible. It builds up all that is good."
   J. Benjamin Harrison (Twenty-third)—"It is out of the Word of God that a system has come to make life sweet."
   K. William McKinley (Twenty-fifth)—"The more profoundly we study this wonderful Book . . . the better citizens we will become."
   L. Theodore Roosevelt (Twenty-sixth)—"No educated man can afford to be ignorant of the Bible."
   M. Woodrow Wilson (Twenty-eighth)—"The Bible is the one supreme source of revelation of the meaning of life."
   N. Herbert Hoover (Thirty-first)—"The whole of the inspirations of our civilization springs from the teachings of Christ . . . to read the Bible . . . is a necessity of American life."
   O. Franklin D. Roosevelt (Thirty-second)—"It is a fountain of strength. I feel that a comprehensive study of the Bible is a liberal education for anyone.
   P. Dwight D. Eisenhower (Thirty-fourth)—"In the highest sense the Bible is to us the unique repository of eternal spiritual truths."
II. World Leaders
   A. William Gladstone—"I have known 95 great men of the world in my time, and of these, 87 were followers of the Bible."
   B. Winston Churchill—"We rest with assurance upon the impregnable rock of Holy Scripture."

C. Chiang Kai-Shek—"The Bible is the voice of the Holy Spirit."

D. Haile Selassie—"The Bible is not only a great book of historical reference, but it also is a guide for daily life, and for this reason I respect it and I love it."

E. Syngman Rhee—"Fellow prisoners held the Bible and turned the pages for me because my fingers were so crushed that I could not use them. I read the Bible, and I have read it the rest of my life."

III. Military Men

A. Douglas MacArthur—"Believe me, sir, never a night goes by, be I ever so tired, but I read the Word of God before I go to bed."

B. William K. Harrison—"The Bible is the Word of God, given by His inspiration for our use and benefit."

C. Robert E. Lee—"The Bible is a book in comparison with which all others in my eyes are of minor importance, and in which in all my perplexities and distresses has never failed to give me light and strength."

D. Stonewall Jackson—"God's promises change not . . . let us endeavor to adorn the doctrine of Christ in all things."

E. Oliver Cromwell (upon hearing Phil. 4:11-13 read as he lay dying)—"He that was Paul's Christ is my Christ too."

IV. Scientists

A. Sir Isaac Newton—"We account the Scriptures of God to be the most sublime philosophy. I find more sure marks of authenticity in the Bible than in any profane history whatsoever."

B. Sir Francis Bacon—"The volume of Scriptures . . . reveal the will of God."

C. Sir John Herschel—"All human discoveries seem to be made only for the purpose of confirming more and more strongly the truths come from on high and contained in the sacred writings."

D. Michael Faraday—"Why will people go astray when they have this blessed Book to guide them?"

E. James Dwight Dana—"Young men, as you go forth, remember that I, an old man, who has known only science all his life, say unto you that there is no truer facts than the facts found within the Holy Scriptures."

V. Historians

A. Arnold J. Toynbee—"It pierces through the Intellect and plays directly upon the heart."

B. H. G. Wells—"The Bible has been the Book that held together the fabric of Western civilization. . . . The civilization we possess could not come into existence and could not have been sustained without it."

C. Thomas Carlyle—"A Noble book! All men's book! . . . grand in its sincerity, in its simplicity, and in its epic melody."

VI. Physicians

A. Mark Hopkins—"Thus we have every conceivable species of historical proof, both external and internal. Thus do the very stones cry out."

B. Charles W. Mayo—"In sickness or in health, one can find comfort and constructive advice in the Bible."

VII. Lawyers

A. Daniel Webster—"I believe the Scriptures of the Old and New Testament to be the will and the Word of God."

B. Benjamin Franklin—"Young men, my advice to you is that you cultivate an acquaintance with, and a firm belief in, the Holy Scriptures."

C. Patrick Henry—"This is a Book worth more than all the others that were ever printed."

VIII. Educators

A. Timothy Dwight—"The Bible is a window in this prison world through which we may look into eternity."

B. William Lyon Phelps—"Everyone who has a thorough knowledge of the Bible may truly be called educated. . . . I believe knowledge of the Bible without a college course is more valuable than a college course without the Bible."

C. Henry Van Dyke—"No other book in the world has had such a strange vitality, such an outgoing power of influence and inspiration. . . . No man is poor or desolate who has this treasure for his own."

IX. Philosophers and Writers

A. Charles Dana—"Of all the books, the most indispensable and the most useful, the one whose knowledge is the most effective, is the Bible."

B. Horace Greeley—"It is impossible to mentally or socially enslave a Bible-reading people."

C. Immanuel Kant—"The existence of the Bible as a book for the people is the greatest benefit which the human race has ever experienced."

D. John Locke—"It has God for its Author, salvation for its end, and truth, without any mixture of error, for its matter: it is all pure, sincere, nothing too much, nothing wanting."

E. Count Leo Tolstoy—"Without the Bible the education of a child in the present state of society is impossible."

F. John Ruskin—"All I have taught in art, everything I have written, whatever greatness there has been in any thought of mine, whatever I have done in my life, has simply been due to the fact that, when I was a child, my mother daily read with me a part of the Bible, and daily made me learn a part of it by heart."

G. John Milton—"There are no songs like the songs of the Scriptures, no orations like the orations of the prophets."

H. William Cowper—"A Glory gilds the sacred page, Majestic like the sun: It gives a light to every age—It gives, but borrows none."

I. John Dryden—"It speaks no less than God in every line; Commanding words whose force is still the same."

J. Sir Walter Scott—"Within this awful volume lies the Mystery of mysteries."

K. Charles Dickens—"It is the best Book that ever was or ever will be in the world."

X. Various Fields

A. J. Edgar Hoover—"The Bible is the unfailing guide which points the way for men to the perfect life."

B. Bernard Baruch—"I have always placed the Bible as number one among the four books I think everyone should read and study. Therein one will find all the problems that beset mankind."

C. Helen Keller—"In the Bible I find a confidence mightier than the utmost evil."

D. Lowell Thomas—"The Bible is of vital importance in teaching freedom."

E. King George V—"The English Bible is . . . the most valuable thing that this world affords."

XI. From the Church Fathers

A. Augustine—"Let us give in and yield our assent to the authority of Holy Scripture, which knows not how either to be deceived or to deceive."

B. John Chrysostom—"It is a great thing, this reading of the Scriptures! For it is not possible, I say, not possible ever to exhaust the mines of the Scriptures. It is a well which has no bottom."

C. Athanasius—"They were spoken and written by God through men who spoke of God. . . . Let no man add to these, neither let him take aught from these."

D. Origen—"For my part, I believe that not one jot or tittle of the divine instruction is in vain. We are never to say that there is anything impertinent or superfluous in the Scriptures of the Holy Spirit."

E. Jerome—"Give ear for a moment that I may tell you how you are to walk in the Holy Scriptures. All that we read in the Divine Book, while glistening and shining without, is yet far sweeter within."

F. Luther—"It cannot be otherwise, for the Scriptures are Divine; in them God speaks, and they are His Word. To hear or to read the Scriptures is nothing else than to hear God."

G. Calvin—"The Scriptures is the school of the Holy Spirit, in which, as nothing necessary and useful to be known is omitted, so nothing is taught which is not beneficial to know."

H. Charles Wesley—"The Bible must be the invention either of good men or angels, bad men or devils, or of God.

"1. It could not be the invention of good men or angels; for they neither would or could make a book, and tell lies all the time they were writing it, saying, "Thus saith the Lord," when it was their own invention.

"2. It could not be the invention of bad men or devils; for they would not make a book which commands all duty, forbids all sin, and condemns their souls to hell to all eternity.

"3. Therefore, I draw this conclusion, that the Bible must be given by divine inspiration."

In concluding this section it may be necessary to stop here and consider some anticipated objections about all these "pious commercials" for the Bible. Some have felt the statements made by political persons, such as U.S. presidents, were made solely for election purposes, for, it is claimed, no atheist could ever be voted into the White House. But to say this is to deny the integrity of almost every American president. It should be also pointed out that many of these statements were made at a time when either the man was not a candidate for reelection or had already moved out of the White House.

Furthermore, while history shows many famous "Bible haters" who later became "Bible lovers," it never records the opposite. To take this a step further, it can be shown that no evil and murderous dictator or tyrant in history was ever a friend of the Bible and that no good and wise leader was ever an enemy of God's Word. Thus to deny the authority of the Bible is to set oneself against practically every great leader in Western civilization. While it is true that this in itself constitutes no absolute proof of the Scriptures, it does, nevertheless, lend itself to Abraham Lincoln's famous proverb: "You can fool some of the people all of the time, and all of the people some of the time, but you can't fool all of the people all of the time!"

PART NINE: SYMBOLS FOR THE BIBLE

I. A Mirror—"For if a person just listens and doesn't obey, he is like a man looking at his face in a mirror; As soon as he walks away, he can't see himself anymore or remember what he looks like. But if he keeps looking steadily into God's law for free men he will not only remember it, but do what it says, and God will greatly bless that man in everything he does" (James 1:23-25, TLB). It is called a mirror because it reflects the mind of God and the true condition of man.

II. A Seed—"Being born again, not of corruptible seed, but of incorruptible, by the word of God, which liveth and abideth forever" (1 Pet. 1:23). "Of his own will begat he us with the word of truth, that we should be a kind of firstfruits of his creatures" (1:18). "But he that received seed into the good ground is he that heareth the word, and understandeth it; which also beareth fruit, and bringeth forth, some an hundredfold, some sixty, some thirty" (Matt. 13:23). It is called a seed because, once properly planted, it brings forth life, growth, and fruit.

III. Water—"Husbands, love your wives, even as Christ also loved the church, and gave himself for it; that he might sanctify and cleanse it with the washing of water by the word, that he might present it to himself a glorious church, not having spot, or wrinkle, or any such thing; but that it should be holy and without blemish" (Eph. 5:25-27). It is called water because of its cleansing, quenching, and refreshing qualities. (See Psa. 42:1; 119:9; Prov. 25:25; Isa. 55:10; Heb. 10:22; Rev. 22:17.)

IV. A Lamp—"Thy word is a lamp unto my feet, and a light unto my path" (Psa. 119:105). "For the commandment is a lamp; and the law is light; and reproofs of instruction are the way of life" (Prov. 6:23). "We have also a more sure word of prophecy; whereunto ye do well that ye take heed, as unto a light that shineth in a dark place, until the day dawn, and the day star arise in your hearts" (2 Pet. 1:19). It is called a lamp because it shows us where we are now, it guides us in the next step, and it keeps us from falling.

V. A Sword—"For the word of God is quick, and powerful, and sharper than any two-edged sword, piercing even to the dividing asunder of soul and spirit, and of the joints and marrow, and is a discerner of the thoughts and intents of the heart" (Heb. 4:12). "And take the helmet of salvation, and the sword of the Spirit, which is the word of God" (Eph. 6:17). It is called a sword because of its piercing ability, operating with equal effectiveness upon sinners, saints and Satan! Of the various armour pieces mentioned in Ephesians 6:11-17, all to be worn by the believer, the only offensive piece is the "sword of the Spirit, which is the Word of God."

VI. Precious Metals
   A. Gold (Psa. 19:10; 119:127)—"Therefore I love thy commandments above gold; yea above fine gold" (Psa. 119:127).
   B. Silver (Psa. 12:6)—"The words of the LORD are pure words: as silver tried in a furnace of earth, purified seven times" (Psa. 12:6). It is referred to as precious metals because of its desirability, its preciousness, its beauty, and its value.

VII. Nourishing Food
   A. Milk—"As newborn babes, desire the sincere milk of the word, that ye may grow thereby" (1 Pet. 2:2).
   B. Meat—"For when for the time ye ought to be teachers, ye have need that one teach you again which be the first principles of the oracles of God; and are become such as have need of milk, and not of strong meat. For every one that useth milk is unskillful in the word of righteousness: for he is a babe. But strong meat belongeth to them that are of full age, even those who by reason of use have their senses exercised to discern both good and evil" (Heb. 5:12-14).
   C. Bread—"I am the living bread which came down from heaven: if any man eat of this bread, he shall live for ever: and the bread that I will give is my flesh, which I will give for the life of the world" (John 6:51).
   D. Honey—"More to be desired are they than gold, yea, than much fine gold: sweeter

also than honey and the honeycomb" (Psa. 19:10). It is referred to as nourishing food because of the strength it imparts. The Bible is the original "soul food."

VIII. A Hammer—"Is not my word like as a fire? saith the LORD; and like a hammer that breaketh the rock in pieces?" (Jer. 23:29). It is referred to as a hammer because of its ability to both tear down and to build up. (See Acts 9:4; Jude 20.)

IX. A Fire—"Then I said, I will not make mention of him, nor speak any more in his name. But his word was in mine heart as a burning fire shut up in my bones, and I was weary with forbearing, and I could not stay" (Jer. 20:9). "And they said one to another, Did not our heart burn within us, while he talked with us by the way, and while he opened to us the scriptures?" (Luke 24:32). It is called a fire because of its judging, purifying, and consuming abilities.

PART TEN: THE SUPREME AUTHORITY OF THE BIBLE

I. Over Human Reason—God gave us our minds and desires that we should use them! This is seen in two classic passages, one directed to the unsaved, the other to the saved. "Come now, and let us reason together, saith the LORD: though your sins be as scarlet, they shall be as white as snow; though they be red like crimson, they shall be as wool" (Isa. 1:18). "I beseech you therefore, brethren, by the mercies of God, that ye present your bodies a living sacrifice, holy, acceptable unto God, which is your reasonable service. And be not conformed to this world: but be ye transformed by the renewing of your mind, that ye may prove what is that good, and acceptable, and perfect, will of God" (Rom. 12:1-2).

However, there are times when God desires us to submit our human reasoning to him. Note the following admonition: "Trust in the LORD with all thine heart; and lean not unto thine own understanding. In all thy ways acknowledge him, and he shall direct thy paths. Be not wise in thine own eyes: fear the LORD, and depart from evil" (Prov. 3:5-7).

Often our reasoning is as the thinking of Naaman, who when asked to take a sevenfold bath in Jordan's muddy waters, angrily replied: "But Naaman was wroth, and went away, and said, Behold, I thought, He will surely come out to me, and stand, and call on the name of the LORD his God, and strike his hand over the place, and recover the leper" (2 Kings 5:11).

But Elisha did not do so! Often God's ways are different from our ways. "For my thoughts are not your thoughts, neither are your ways my ways, saith the LORD. For as the heavens are higher than the earth, so are my ways higher than your ways, and my thoughts than your thoughts" (Isa. 55:8-9).

II. Over the Church—The New Testament abounds with passages which declare Christ is the Head of the church. (See Eph. 1:22; 2:19-20; 4:15-16; 5:23-30; Col. 1:18; 2:9.) The Savior, it must be remembered, gave birth to the church, and not the other way around. (See Matt. 16:18.) Thus the Christian must look to the Bible and not to any earthly church for final instruction. Sometimes even those local churches mentioned in the Bible itself were grievously wrong. Note the following description of New Testament churches, some of which were started by Paul himself.

A. The church at Ephesus—"Nevertheless I have somewhat against thee, because thou hast left thy first love. Remember therefore from whence thou art fallen, and repent, and do the first works; or else I will come unto thee quickly, and will remove thy candlestick out of his place, except thou repent" (Rev. 2:4-5).

B. The church at Pergamos—"But I have a few things against thee, because thou hast there them that hold the doctrine of Balaam, who taught Balac to cast a stumblingblock before the children of Israel, to eat things sacrificed unto idols, and to commit fornication. So hast thou also them that hold the doctrine of the Nicolaitans, which thing I hate. Repent; or else I will come unto thee quickly, and will fight against them with the sword of my mouth" (Rev. 2:14-16).

C. The church at Thyatira—"Notwithstanding I have a few things against thee, because thou sufferest that woman Jezebel, which calleth herself a prophetess, to teach and to seduce my servants to commit fornication, and to eat things sacrificed unto idols" (Rev. 2:20).

D. The church at Sardis—"And unto the angel of the church in Sardis write; These things saith he that hath the seven Spirits of God, and the seven stars; I know thy works, that thou hast a name that thou livest, and art dead. Be watchful, and strengthen the things which remain, that are ready to die: for I have not found thy works perfect before God. Remember therefore how thou hast received and heard, and hold fast, and repent. If therefore thou shalt not watch, I will come on thee as a thief, and thou shalt not know what hour I will come upon thee" (Rev. 3:1-3).

E. The church at Laodicea—"I know thy works, that thou art neither cold nor hot: I would thou wert cold or hot. So then because thou art lukewarm, and neither cold nor hot, I will spue thee out of my mouth. Because thou sayest, I am rich, and increased with goods, and have need of nothing; and knowest not that thou art wretched, and miserable, and poor, and blind, and naked: I counsel thee to buy of me gold tried in the fire, that thou mayest be rich; and white raiment, that thou mayest be clothed, and that the shame of thy nakedness do not appear; and anoint thine eyes with eyesalve, that thou mayest see. As many as I love, I rebuke and chasten: be zealous therefore, and repent" (Rev. 3:15-19).

III. Over Tradition—In this atomic and space age in which we live today where change occurs at rocket speed, it will doubtless cause many to appreciate even more some of our beautiful traditions of the past. And rightly so. But traditions, like changes, can be wrong. If a thing was in error when it began, it is still in error regardless of the centuries that separate it from us today. Often in the past, hurtful "traditions of the fathers" have crept into the church of the Living God. Our Savior himself was grieved over some harmful Jewish traditions. Note his words:

"And honour not his father or his mother, he shall be free. Thus have ye made the commandment of God of none effect by your tradition" (Matt. 15:6). Later Paul would warn also of this. "Beware lest any man spoil you through philosophy and vain deceit, after the tradition of men, after the rudiments of the world, and not after Christ" (Col. 2:8).

IV. Over Religious Leaders—"Remember them which have the rule over you, who have spoken unto you the word of God: whose faith follow, considering the end of their conversation. . . . Obey them that have the rule over you, and submit yourselves: for they watch for your souls, as they that must give account, that they may do it with joy, and not with grief: for that is unprofitable for you" (Heb. 13:7, 17). As important as these verses are, they do *not* teach spiritual leaders are to become our source of authority. While godly pastors are indeed called to serve as role models (1 Cor. 11:1; 1 Tim. 4:12; 1 Pet. 5:3), the Bible alone must be our ultimate guide and standard.

V. Over Feelings and Experiences—At times Christians fall unto error because they "felt led" to do or say certain things. However we must learn that at times our feelings can be treacherous and totally untrustworthy. The psalmist often spoke of this: "I had fainted, unless I had believed to see the goodness of the LORD in the land of the living" (Psa. 27:13). "Why art thou cast down, O my soul? and why art thou disquieted in me? hope thou in God: for I shall yet praise him for the help of his countenance" (Psa. 42:5).

"I cried unto God with my voice, even unto God with my voice; and he gave ear unto me. In the day of my trouble I sought the Lord: my sore ran in the night, and ceased not: my soul refused to be comforted. I remembered God, and was troubled: I complained, and my spirit was overwhelmed. Selah. Thou holdest mine eyes waking: I am so troubled that I cannot speak. I have considered the days of old, the years of ancient times. I call to remembrance my song in the night: I commune with mine own heart: and my spirit made diligent search. Will the Lord cast off for ever? and will he be favourable no more? Is his mercy clean gone for ever? doth his promise fail for evermore? Hath God forgotten to be gracious? hath he in anger shut up his tender mercies? Selah. And I said, This is my infirmity: but I will remember the years of the right hand of the most High" (Psa. 77:1-10). "I said in my haste, All men are liars" (Psa. 116:11).

This is not only the case with our feelings, but also our experiences. One of Job's three "friends," Eliphaz, based all his advice to the suffering Job on experience (Job 4:12-16). He is later severely rebuked by God himself for doing this. (See Job 42:7.)

Thus as valuable as personal experiences may be, it is no substitute for the revealed Word of God.

PART ELEVEN: THE COLLECTIONS OF THE 66 BOOKS OF THE BIBLE

I. The Writing Materials of the Bible—The Spirit of God moved upon the authors of the Bible to record their precious messages upon whatever object was in current use at the time of the writing. Thus once again we see the marvelous condescension of God. These writing materials would include:
  A. Clay (Jer. 17:13; Ezek. 4:1)
  B. Stone (Exod. 24:12; 31:18; 32:15-16; 34:1, 28; Deut. 5:22; 27:2-3; Josh. 8:31-32)
  C. Papyrus (made by pressing and gluing two layers of split papyrus reeds together in order to form a sheet) (2 John 12; Rev. 5:1)
  D. Vellum (calfskin), parchment (lambskin), leather (cowhide) (2 Tim. 4:13)
  E. Metal (Exod. 28:36; Job 19:24; Matt. 22:19-20)

II. The Language of the Bible
  A. The Old Testament was written in Hebrew, with the following exceptions appearing in Aramaic—These are: Ezra 4:8–6:18; 7:12-26; Daniel 2:4–7:28; Jeremiah 10:11. Why did God choose Hebrew? In their book, *A General Introduction to the Bible,* authors Geisler and Nix note the following:

> It is a pictorial language, speaking with vivid, bold metaphors which challenge and dramatize the story. The Hebrew language possesses a facility to present "pictures" of the events narrated. "The Hebrew thought in pictures, and consequently his nouns are concrete and vivid. There is no such thing as neuter gender, for the Semite everything is alive. Compound words are lacking. . . . There is no wealth of adjectives. . . ." The language shows "vast powers of association and, therefore, of imagination." Some of this is lost in the English translation, but even so, "much of the vivid, concrete, and forthright character of our English Old Testament is really a carrying over into English of something of the genius of the Hebrew tongue." As a pictorial language, Hebrew presents a vivid picture of the acts of God among a people who became examples or

illustrations for future generations (cf. 1 Cor. 10:11). The Old Testament was intended to be presented graphically in a "picture-language."

Further, Hebrew is a personal language. It addresses itself to the heart and emotions rather than merely to the mind or reason. Sometimes even nations are given personalities (cf. Mal. 1:2-3). Always the appeal is to the person in concrete realities of life and not to the abstract or theoretical. Hebrew is a language through which the message is felt rather than thought. As such, the language was highly qualified to convey to the individual believer as well as to the worshiping community the personal relation of the living God in the events of the Jewish nation. It was much more qualified to record the realization of revelation in the life of a nation than to propositionalize that revelation for the propagation among all nations. (pp. 219–220)

B. The entire New Testament was written in Greek. Again, to quote from Geisler and Nix:

Greek was an intellectual language. It was more a language of the mind than of the heart, a fact to which the great Greek philosophers gave abundant evidence. Greek was more suited to codifying a communication or reflecting on a revelation of God in order to put it into simple communicable form. It was a language that could more easily render the credible into the intelligible than could Hebrew. It was for this reason that New Testament Greek was a most useful medium for expressing the propositional truth of the New Testament, as Hebrew was for expressing the biographical truth of the Old Testament. Since Greek possessed a technical precision not found in Hebrew, the theological truths which were more generally expressed in the Hebrew of the Old Testament were more precisely formulated in the Greek of the New Testament.

Furthermore, Greek was a nearly universal language. The truth of God in the Old Testament, which was initially revealed to one nation (Israel), was appropriately recorded in the language of the nation (Hebrew). But the fuller revelation given by God in the New Testament was not restricted in that way. In the words of Luke's gospel, the message of Christ was to "be preached in his name to all nations" (Luke 24:47). The language most appropriate for the propagation of this message was naturally the one that was most widely spoken throughout the world. Such was the common (Koine) Greek, a thoroughly international language of the first century Mediterranean world.

It may be concluded, then, that God chose the very languages to communicate His truth which had, in His providence, been prepared to express most effectively the kind of truth He desired at that particular time, in the unfolding of His overall plan. Hebrew, with its pictorial and personal vividness, expressed well the biographical truth of the Old Testament. Greek, with its intellectual and universal potentialities, served well for the doctrinal and evangelistic demands of the New Testament. (Ibid., p. 221)

III. The Reason for the Writing of the Bible—Perhaps the one supreme difference between man and all other creatures (apart from his immortal soul, of course) is his God-given ability to express his thoughts on paper. It has been observed that while it was no doubt desirable to speak *to* the prophets "in diverse manners" in time past, the best way to communicate with *all* men of *all* ages is through the written record. The advantages of the written method are many, of course:

A. Precision—One's thoughts must be somewhat precise to be written.
B. Propagation—The most accurate way to communicate a message is usually through writing.
C. Preservation—Men die, and memories fail, but the written record remains. It may be said the New Testament especially was written for the following reasons:
  1. Because of the demands of the early church (1 Thess. 5:27; 1 Tim. 4:13; 2 Tim. 3:16-17)
  2. Because of false doctrines (to counteract it)
  3. Because of missionary endeavors (to propagate it)
  4. Because of persecution and politics
IV. The Possible Order of the Writing of the Bible
A. Old Testament books
  1. Job—2000 B.C. (?)
  2. Genesis through Deuteronomy—1405 B.C.
  3. Joshua—1390 B.C.
  4. Judges—1025 B.C.
  5. Ruth—1025 B.C.
  6. Psalms—1000–930 B.C. (for the most part)
  7. Proverbs—930 B.C.
  8. Ecclesiastes—930 B.C.
  9. Song of Solomon—930 B.C.
  10. 1 and 2 Samuel—920 B.C. (?)
  11. Obadiah—850 B.C.
  12. Joel—848 B.C.
  13. Jonah—785 B.C.
  14. Amos—760 B.C.
  15. Hosea—758 B.C.
  16. Isaiah—739 B.C.
  17. Micah—735 B.C.
  18. Nahum—650 B.C.
  19. Zephaniah—640 B.C.
  20. Jeremiah—627 B.C.
  21. Habakkuk—608 B.C.
  22. 1 and 2 Kings—590 B.C.
  23. 1 and 2 Chronicles—590 B.C.
  24. Lamentations—586 B.C.
  25. Ezekiel—560 B.C.
  26. Daniel—538 B.C.
  27. Haggai—520 B.C.
  28. Zechariah—520 B.C.
  29. Esther—470 B.C.
  30. Ezra—455 B.C.
  31. Nehemiah—445 B.C.
  32. Malachi—435 B.C.

Special Note:
The 39 books in our English Old Testament appear somewhat differently in a present-day Hebrew

Bible. They cover the identical material except they number 24 and are arranged in a threefold division.

 I. *The Law—5 books*
  A. *Genesis*
  B. *Exodus*
  C. *Leviticus*
  D. *Numbers*
  E. *Deuteronomy*
 II. *The Prophets—8 books*
  A. *Former Prophets—4*
   1. *Joshua*
   2. *Judges*
   3. *1 & 2 Samuel*
   4. *1 & 2 Kings*
  B. *Latter Prophets—4*
   1. *Isaiah*
   2. *Jeremiah*
   3. *Ezekiel*
   4. *The 12—Hosea, Joel, Amos, Obadiah, Jonah, Micah, Nahum, Habakkuk, Zephaniah, Haggai, Zechariah, Malachi*
 III. *The Writings—11 books*
  A. *The poetical books—3*
   1. *Psalms*
   2. *Proverbs*
   3. *Job*
  B. *The Scrolls, or Rolls—5*
   1. *Song of Solomon*
   2. *Ruth*
   3. *Lamentations*
   4. *Esther*
   5. *Ecclesiastes*
  C. *The historical books—3*
   1. *Daniel*
   2. *Ezra—Nehemiah*
   3. *1 & 2 Chronicles*

 B. New Testament books
  1. James—A.D. 45
  2. Galatians—A.D. 49
  3. 1 Thessalonians—A.D. 51
  4. 2 Thessalonians—A.D. 52
  5. 1 Corinthians—A.D. 55
  6. 2 Corinthians—A.D. 56
  7. Romans—A.D. 57
  8. Ephesians—A.D. 60
  9. Colossians—A.D. 60
  10. Philemon—A.D. 61
  11. Philippians—A.D. 61

12. Luke—A.D. 61
13. Acts—A.D. 61
14. Hebrews—A.D. 61
15. 1 Timothy—A.D. 62
16. Titus—A.D. 64
17. 1 Peter—A.D. 64
18. 2 Peter—A.D. 65
19. Matthew—A.D. 65
20. Mark—A.D. 65
21. 2 Timothy—A.D. 67
22. Jude—A.D. 85
23. John—A.D. 90
24. 1, 2, 3 John—A.D. 92
25. Revelation—A.D. 95

PART TWELVE: THE CANON OF THE BIBLE
 I. Definition of the Word *Canon*—Charles Ryrie suggests:
    1. Its derivation—"The word comes from the Greek word *kanon,* which refers to a measuring instrument. It therefore came to mean a rule of action (Gal. 6:16; Phil. 3:16)."
    2. History of the use of the word—"In the early church the word *canon* was used to refer to the creeds. In the middle of the fourth century it came to be used of the Bible (i.e., of the list of accepted books that were acknowledged to make up the Bible)."
    3. Its meaning—"Actually the word *canon* has a twofold meaning. It refers to the list of books that met certain tests or rules and thus were considered authoritative and canonical. But it also means that the collection of canonical books becomes our rule of life" (p. 105).
 II. Location of the Canonical Books
  A. Old Testament
    1. Before the Babylonian captivity—Prior to this period (606 B.C.) the Old Testament books were apparently laid beside the Ark of the Covenant in the temple. This is indicated in the following passages:
      "And Moses came and told the people all the words of the LORD, and all the judgments: and all the people answered with one voice, and said, All the words which the LORD hath said will we do. And Moses wrote all the words of the LORD, and rose up early in the morning, and builded an altar under the hill, and twelve pillars, according to the twelve tribes of Israel. . . . And he took the book of the covenant, and read in the audience of the people: and they said, All that the LORD hath said will we do, and be obedient" (Exod. 24:3-4, 7).
      "And it came to pass, when Moses had made an end of writing the words of this law in a book, until they were finished, that Moses commanded the Levites, which bare the ark of the covenant of the LORD, saying, Take this book of the law, and put it in the side of the ark of the covenant of the LORD your God, that it may be there for a witness against thee" (Deut. 31:24-26).
      "And Hilkiah the high priest said unto Shaphan the scribe, I have found the book of the law in the house of the LORD. And Hilkiah gave the book to Shaphan, and he read it. And Shaphan the scribe came to the king, and brought the king word again, and said, Thy servants have gathered the money that was

found in the house, and have delivered it into the hand of them that do the work, that have the oversight of the house of the LORD. And Shaphan the scribe shewed the king, saying, Hilkiah the priest hath delivered me a book. And Shaphan read it before the king" (2 Kings 22:8-10).

"So Joshua made a covenant with the people that day, and set them a statute and an ordinance in Shechem. And Joshua wrote these words in the book of the law of God, and took a great stone, and set it up there under an oak, that was by the sanctuary of the LORD" (Josh. 24:25-26).

"Then Samuel told the people the manner of the kingdom, and wrote it in a book, and laid it up before the LORD. And Samuel sent all the people away, every man to his house" (1 Sam. 10:25).

2. During the Babylonian captivity—The books were probably carried to Babylon and later collected by Daniel. In 9:2 of his book, the prophet Daniel writes: "In the first year of his reign I Daniel understood by books the number of the years, whereof the word of the Lord came to Jeremiah the prophet that he would accomplish seventy years in the desolations of Jerusalem" (Dan. 9:2). Here Daniel specifically states he was reading Jeremiah and "the books," a reference no doubt to the other Old Testament books written up to that time.

3. After the Babylonian captivity—These books may have been taken back to Jerusalem by Ezra the prophet and kept in the newly completed temple. (See Ezra 3:10-11; 6:15-18; Neh. 8:1-8.)

B. New Testament—"And when this epistle is read among you, cause that it be read also in the church of the Laodiceans; and that ye likewise read the epistle from Laodicea" (Col. 4:16). "I charge you by the Lord that this epistle be read unto all the holy brethren" (1 Thess. 5:27).

It seems certain the New Testament books were *not* kept in the temple area as the Old Testament books were. This was the case for at least two reasons:

1. Some of the New Testament books were written after the destruction of the temple in A.D. 70.

2. No New Testament book would have been accepted by the Jewish rabbis as an inspired addition to the Old Testament canon—However, from the above verses it appears various churches may have cared for and circulated among the Christian community the New Testament books.

III. Tests Given to the Canonical Books—The books were subjected to various tests. These included:

A. Authorship—Who wrote the book or the epistle?

B. Local church acceptance—Had it been read by the various churches? What was their opinion?

C. Church fathers' recognition—Had the pupils of the disciples quoted from the book? As an example, a man named Polycarp was a disciple of John the apostle. Therefore one test of a book might be, What did Polycarp think of it?

D. Book subject matter (content)—What did the book teach? Did it contradict other recognized books?

E. Personal edification—Did the book have the ability to inspire, convict, and edify local congregations and individual believers?

In closing this section it should be stated it was a combination of these five steps, and not just one alone, which helped determine whether a book was inspired or not. Contrary to what may have seemed vital, canonicity was *not* determined at all by either the age or the language of a given book. For example, there were many ancient books mentioned in the Old Testament (see Num. 21:14; Josh. 10:3) that were not in the Old Testament canon. Also, some of the apocryphal books (such as Tobit) were written in Hebrew but were not included in the Old Testament, while some books (like portions of Daniel) written in Aramaic were included in the canon.

IV. Disputed Books of the Canon—Some canonical books were at first doubted but later fully accepted. During the first few years of early church history there were some 11 biblical books that were temporarily objected to for various reasons. These were:

A. Old Testament books
1. The Song of Solomon because it seemed to some to be a mere poem on human love.
2. Ecclesiastes because some felt it taught atheism. (See 9:5.)
3. Esther because it did not mention the word *God* in the entire book.
4. Ezekiel because it seemed to contradict the Mosaic Law.
5. Proverbs because it seemed to contradict itself. (See 26:4-5.)

B. New Testament books
1. Hebrews because of the uncertainty about the book's authorship.
2. James because it seemed to contradict the teachings of Paul. (Compare James 2:20 with Eph. 2:8-9.)
3. 2 and 3 John because they seemed to be simply two personal letters.
4. Jude because the author refers to an uncanonical Old Testament book, the book of Enoch.
5. Revelation because of the uncertainty about the book's authorship and because of its many mysterious symbols.

V. The Recognition of the Canon
A. The Old Testament—By the year 300 B.C. (at the latest) all Old Testament books had been written, collected, revered, and recognized as official, canonical books. Many believe Ezra the prophet led the first recognition council.
B. The New Testament—During the Third Council of Carthage, held in A.D. 397, the 27 New Testament books were declared to be canonical. However, it absolutely *must* be understood that the Bible is *not* an authorized collection of books, but rather a collection of authorized books. In other words, the 27 New Testament books were not inspired because the Carthage Council proclaimed them to be, but rather the Council proclaimed them to be such because they were already inspired.

Norm Geisler has suggested the following:
1. "The church is the *discoverer* of and not the *determiner* of the canon."
2. "It is the *child* and not the *mother* of the canon."
3. "It is the *minister* and not the *magistrate* of the canon."
4. "It is the *recognizer* and not the *regulator* of the canon."
5. "It is the *witness* and not the *judge* of the canon."
6. "It is the *servant* and not the *master* of the canon" (*A General Introduction to the Bible*, p. 221).

VI. The Accuracy of the Canon
A. The bad news—As every Christian knows, none of the actual 66 books has been preserved. Our Bible today is thus a translation of a copy (or copies) of a copy, etc., of the original writings. Often it is asked why God did not preserve the original books. Only the Holy Spirit knows the ultimate and complete answer to this. However, at least three possible reasons have been suggested.
1. To prevent the text from being tampered with—To illustrate this, let us suppose there existed only one single account of the American Civil War, and that one

record was totally controlled by a man or perhaps a small group of men. No other copies from this original account were in existence. If this were true, it can be readily seen how easy it would be for the actual story of the War Between the States to be altered in any manner desired by the custodians of the one single record. Thus, through a stroke of the pen (or eraser), lost battles could be turned into victories, villains could suddenly appear as heroes, etc.

However, imagine the original record did not exist but there was in circulation literally thousands of copies of copies taken from the first Civil War story account. Now it can be seen no man or small group of individuals could corrupt the true record. This is exactly the Bible situation today, for there are literally thousands of manuscript copies covering both the Old Testament and New Testament books in circulation worldwide.

2. To guard against a misguided worship—The very nature of man demands he worship something, be it power, money, sex, a pagan idol, or the true God. Had God preserved any or all of the 66 original manuscripts, they undoubtedly would have become the objects of superstition and worship. There are at least two biblical examples where even well-intentioned individuals were guilty of worshipping the wrong thing.
   a. Israel's sin in worshipping Moses' serpent of brass (2 Kings 18:4)
   b. John the apostle's sin in (attempting) to worship an angel—This occurred not once but twice. (See Rev. 19:10; 22:8-9.)
3. To stimulate intense Bible study—Only eternity itself will reveal the multiplied millions of hours invested by devout scholars examining the manuscript copies to determine the exact contents of the original scriptural text.
B. The good news—Even though the original books are lost, there is overwhelming evidence our translated Bibles today represent amazingly accurate copies of the first manuscripts themselves. Consider the following:
   1. The number of existing both Old Testament and New Testament Hebrew and Greek manuscript fragments runs literally into the thousands. There are some 5,300 New Testament Greek manuscripts alone.
   2. The favorable comparison of all these manuscripts—Note the testimony of the scholars regarding the text of the New Testament.
      a. Westcott and Hort estimated it is 98.33% pure.
      b. Ezra Abbott raises it to 99.75% pure.
      c. A. T. Robertson gives the number at 99.9% pure.
   3. The discovery of the Dead Sea Scrolls

   Prior to the discovery of the scrolls at Qumran the oldest extant manuscripts were dated from approximately A.D. 900. Some manuscripts of the Dead Sea Scrolls, which included copies of Isaiah, Habakkuk, and others, were dated back to 125 B.C., providing manuscripts 1,000 years older than previously available. The major conclusion was that there was no significant difference between the Isaiah scroll at Qumran and the Masoretic Hebrew text dated one thousand years later. This confirmed the reliability of our present Hebrew text. (Paul Enns, *Moody Handbook of Theology,* p. 173)

   4. The biblical quotations from the early church fathers—During the second and third centuries important church fathers such as Justin Martyr, Irenaeus, Clement of Alexandria, Origen, Tertullian, Hippolytus, and Eusebius quoted from the New Testament in their writings for a total of over 36,000 occasions.

With the possible exception of 11 verses, every single New Testament passage is to be found in these 36,000 quotations. Thus, had Satan succeeded in destroying every copy of the Greek manuscripts, the entire New Testament could have been almost totally reconstructed from the writings of the church fathers.

Edward Goodrick offers the following concerning the amazing accuracy of the Old Testament canon.

> Do we have hard evidence that copies of the Old Testament autographs were called "Scripture" (*graphe*) in the New Testament? A search of the 50 appearances of *graphe* in the New Testament reveals that Jesus read from the Scripture (*graphe*) in the synagogue at Nazareth (Luke 4:21) and Paul from the Scripture (*graphe*) in the synagogue at Thessalonica (Acts 17:2). The Ethiopian eunuch riding in his chariot on his way home from Jerusalem was reading a portion of Scripture (*graphe*, Acts 8:32-33). These were not autographs; they were copies. And copies contain scribal errors. Yet the Bible calls them *graphe*, and every *graphe* is inspired (2 Timothy 3:16). Yes, copies of the autographs are inspired. (*Is My Bible the Inspired Word of God?* p. 62)

VII. The Completion of the Canon—Is the 66-book biblical canon closed? This question may be answered by both a yes and no response.

A. Hypothetically and theoretically . . . *yes*—Although all known evidence would seem to be a trillion to one against it, it remains nevertheless theoretically possible that God may, through some totally unexpected circumstances and for some hitherto inconceivable reason, suddenly decide to add a sixty-seventh book to the canon prior to Christ's return.

B. Practically and realistically . . . *no*—This is concluded by a threefold line of evidence.

1. Scriptural evidence—Dr. Robert Lightner writes:

> The first reason is stated in two passages of Scripture. Jude 3 refers to *the faith which was once for all delivered to the saints,* a body of truth more authoritative than one's personal belief. When Jude wrote his epistle, the only books not yet written were those of John. John then warned against adding to or taking from *the prophecy of this book* (Rev. 22:18-19). This warning applies to the book of Revelation, the last book of the Bible and the culmination of God's recorded revelation. Therefore John's warning seems to apply to all Scripture and relates to the matter of canonicity.
>
> As for the Old Testament canon, Christ accepted the same books received by the Jews of his day. He referred to the first and last books of the Jewish canon in one breath (Matt. 23:35; Luke 11:51), indicating his acceptance of its entirety. So this canon was clearly closed by Jesus' time. (*Evangelical Theology,* pp. 21–22)

2. Historical evidence—Norm Geisler observes:

> The immediate successors of the apostles did not claim new revelation, nor did they claim special confirmatory gifts. In fact, they looked on the apostolic revelations as full and final. When new cults have arisen since the time of the apostles, their leaders have claimed to be apostles in order that their books could gain recognition. Historically, the canon is closed with the 27 books written in the apostolic period. They alone are and have been the

books of the canon through all the intervening centuries. No other non-apostolic books have been accepted since the earliest centuries, and no new books written by the apostles have come to light. In His providence, God has guided the church in the preservation of all the canonical books. (*A General Introduction to the Bible*, pp. 217–218)

3. Providential evidence

What if a truly prophetic or apostolic book were found today: would it belong in the canon? Of course, the question is only hypothetical, and so the answer is only hypothetical, too. But it is an interesting question, and it does focus an important issue not yet stressed: *the providence of God.* It seems highly unlikely that God would have inspired a book He did not preserve. Why should He give a revelation for the church but not provide for the preservation of it? It is understandable that God might give special guidance to certain individuals, which He did not deem necessary to do for the broader body of believers. But to provide instruction in the Christian faith by way of a revelation He did not preserve for others is another matter altogether. (Ibid., p. 217)

In regard to an almost-certainly closed canon, consider another (but similar) question: "Is it possible for a believer to live a sinless life following his or her salvation?" This question also involves a yes and no answer.

  I. Hypothetically and theoretically . . . yes—There is no doubt whatsoever that God provides the needed supernatural power for every Christian to defeat all his enemies, to conquer every temptation, to be victorious over every sin, to experience total and continuous spiritual success. The following verses give testimony to this available and adequate power over sin: Romans 6:1-14; 1 Corinthians 10:13; 15:57; Philippians 4:13.

  II. Practically and realistically . . . no—To boast of sinless perfection is to claim that which Paul, John, and James could not and would not claim for themselves.

   A. Paul's testimony (Phil. 3:12; 1 Tim. 1:15)

   B. John's testimony (1 John 1:8)

   C. James's testimony (James 3:2)

PART THIRTEEN: IMPORTANT HISTORICAL TRANSLATIONS OF THE BIBLE
Perhaps the most thrilling story in mankind's history is the true account of the earnest (and sometimes agonizing) efforts to translate God's precious Word in the language of a particular day. Literally billions of intensive man-hours have been spent doing this. We shall now briefly examine some of the better-known fruits of all this sweat and study.

  I. Publications up to the Time of Jesus

   A. The Dead Sea Scrolls—During 1947, in a series of caves near the Dead Sea, a discovery was made that would soon excite the entire religious world. These were the Dead Sea Scrolls. Dr. William F. Albright states this find was "the most important discovery ever made concerning the Old Testament manuscripts." These scrolls were probably hidden there sometime during the second century B.C. by a Jewish group called the Essenes. They included fragments of every Old Testament book in the Hebrew Bible with the exception of the book of Esther.

   Especially exciting was a complete scroll on the book of Isaiah. The reason this discovery was so important was that until this event the earliest copy we had of Isaiah's writings were made during the twelfth century A.D. Now scholars could move back over 1,000 years closer to the time when the prophet actually wrote (around 700 B.C.). When a comparison was made between the Dead Sea copy and the twelfth-century-A.D. copy, they were found to be almost identical, there once again reassuring us that our copy of God's Word today is indeed accurate and reliable.

B. The Greek Septuagint—The Septuagint is a translation of the Old Testament Hebrew into the Greek language. This was done around 280 B.C. at the request of some Jewish leaders. The reason was because many Jews had moved into Egypt and other places outside of Palestine, and as a result, were unable to read or speak Hebrew. So a translation was prepared in the common Greek language of the day. It was called the "Septuagint" (the Greek word for 70) because, according to tradition, it was supposedly translated by 70 Jewish scholars in 70 days. The Septuagint was the Bible in Jesus' day.

II. Publications up to the Seventh Century A.D.

A. The Papyri—This consisted of hundreds of sheets found in central Egypt in 1895. Some were stuffed in mummy cases and embalmed crocodile bodies. Among the various sheets was a three-by-two-inch fragment containing John 18:31-38. Carbon-14 dating has shown this to have been written around A.D. 125. Thus this fragment is the oldest known Bible manuscript.

B. The Latin Vulgate—During the fourth century A.D. it was felt a new translation of the Bible was needed in Latin, which was then the common language in the Western world. Thus, in A.D. 382 the great scholar Jerome was appointed by Damascus, the Bishop of Rome, to begin doing this. For the next 25 years Jerome worked on this translation, going right to the Hebrew and Greek. The term *vulgate* comes from the Latin word that means "common." Thus, until the King James Version in 1611, the Latin Vulgate became the recognized Bible for nearly 1,200 years. In 1228 the Vulgate was divided into chapters by Stephen Langton, archbishop of Canterbury. It was divided into verses by Robert Stephens in 1551, and these verses were numbered by Montanus around A.D. 1571. The Vulgate was also the first Bible to be printed by John Gutenburg in 1455. One of these printed copies now resides in the U.S. Library of Congress and is valued at $350,000.

C. Codex Sinaiticus—This was an ancient manuscript of the Greek Septuagint, written approximately A.D. 330. It was discovered by the German Bible scholar Tischendorf in the monastery of St. Catherine on Mount Sinai in 1844. He noticed in a wastebasket, waiting to be burned, vellum pages with Greek writings on them. The Codex Sinaiticus contained 199 leaves of the Old Testament and the entire New Testament. On December 24, 1933, this codex that came so close to being burned was sold to the British government by the Russians for $510,000, making it the most expensive book purchase of all time.

D. Codex Vaticanus—Also written around A.D. 330, it has been in the Vatican Library in Rome since 1481. Roman Catholic popes had constantly refused to allow competent Bible scholars to study it until the nineteenth century. It is thought that both this codex and the Mount Sinai copy are 2 of the original 50 copies ordered by Emperor Constantine shortly after he assumed power over the Roman Empire in A.D. 312. It is however, incomplete, omitting the Pastoral Epistles, Philemon, Revelation, and the last few chapters of Hebrews.

E. Codex Alexandrinus—This is dated around A.D. 450 and was written in Egypt. In

1708 it was given to the Patriarch of Alexandria (where it got its name). In 1757 it was transferred to the British museum.

F. The Coptic Version—During the second century a new kind of language came into being which was sort of a cross between Greek and Egyptian. It became known as Coptic. Several translations of God's Word were made around A.D. 350 from the Greek into Coptic.

G. The Ethiopic Version—Ethiopia is the land south of Egypt in Africa. The Ethiopian eunuch of Acts 8:26-39 probably introduced Christianity there. This translation was a good verbal rendering of the Greek. It was fluent, readable, and helpful, and dates at around A.D. 350.

H. The Gothic Version—The land of the Goths was located north of the Danube River and west of the Black Sea. The Goths were an extremely warlike people. During one of their raids in Asia Minor they captured a young man named Ulfilos. Ulfilos was a Christian and a scholar who later translated the Scriptures into Gothic—with the exception of 1 and 2 Samuel and 1 and 2 Kings. The reason for this was due to the many wars recorded in these four Old Testament books. Ulfilos did not want to encourage the Goths along this line. The Gothic Version, dated about A.D. 350, thus became the first translation of the Bible into a barbarian language. One of Ulfilos's versions still exists. It is called the Codex Argentus and was written in gold and silver letters upon purple vellum. It now resides in the University Library at Upsala, Sweden.

I. The Armenian Version—Armenia is north of Mesopotamia. About A.D. 406 a great missionary and writer named Mesrob began translating into Armenian after reducing their language to a writing alphabet. The Armenian Version has been called "the most beautiful and accurate of all ancient versions—the Queen of Versions."

III. Publications in English from the Seventh Century to the Present—Historians have classified the English language into three main periods: Old English (from A.D. 450 to 1100), Middle English (from A.D. 1100 to 1500), Modern English (from A.D. 1500 to date)

Keeping this in mind we shall now consider some major attempts to publish the Bible in English.

A. Old English Period (A.D. 450 to 1100)—There were at least 10 known translators of the Bible during this period. The list would include a servant, two bishops, two monks, a king, two priests, an archbishop, and a hermit. Of these 10, we will examine the following 3:

1. Caedmon (died in 680)—This stable worker at a monastery in North England did not translate the Bible on paper but rather memorized great portions of it and sang it with his harp in short lines of beautiful Celtic-Saxon verse wherever he traveled. He sang the story of Genesis, Exodus, a part of Daniel, the doctrines of the resurrection, ascension, and the second coming of Christ, and of heaven and hell.

2. Bede (674–735)—This godly monk, scholar, historian, and theologian is often called today by the title of "the Father of English History." In his textbook, *General Biblical Introduction*, author H. S. Miller writes the following about Bede:

> His important work is the translation of the Gospel of John, which he finished just as he was breathing his last. All the day before Ascension Day, 735, the good old monk . . . had been dictating his translations, for he said, 'I do not want my boys to read a lie, or to work to no purpose after I am gone."
> The next day he was very weak, and suffered much. His scribe said,

"Dear master, there is yet one chapter to do, but it seems very hard for you to speak." Bede replied, "Nay, it is easy, take up thy pen and write quickly." In blinding tears the scribe wrote on. "And now father, there is just one sentence more." Bede dictated it and said, "write quickly." The scribe said, "It is finished, master." "Ay, it is finished!" echoed the dying saint, and with the Gloria chant upon his lips he passed to the great Master whom he had loved and served so long. (p. 320)

3. Alfred (King of England, 871–901)—Here Miller writes:

Alfred loved . . . the Bible. He was King, lawgiver, teacher, writer, translator. His wish was "that all the freeborn youth of his kingdom should employ themselves on nothing till they could first read well the English scriptures." He translated the ten commandments and other Old Testament laws, placing them at the head of his laws for England. He also translated the Psalms and the Gospels." (Ibid., p. 321)

B. Middle English Period (A.D. 1100 to 1500)—Here we will examine but one name—that of John Wycliffe.

John Wycliffe (1320–1384) has often been called "The Morning Star of Reformation." He was a great Oxford University teacher, preacher, reformer, and translator. Wycliffe was the first man to completely translate the entire Bible into the English language. By placing God's Word in common language he thus did for England what Martin Luther would later do for Germany. His was the only English Bible for 145 years. As a sample of his English, note the following translation of the Lord's prayer:

"Our Fadir that art in hevenes, halewid be thi name; Thi kingdom comme to, Be thi wille done in heven so in erthe; Gyve to us this dai oure breed over other substance, and forgive to us oure dettis as we forgyven to oure detouris; and leede us not into tempacioun, but delyvere us fro yvel."

C. Modern English Period (A.D. 1500 to date)

1. Tyndale's Version (1525)—If Wycliffe was known as the "Morning Star of Reformation," then Tyndale could rightly be called "The Milky Way of the Modern Bible." No other single man in history perhaps did as much in translating the Word of God for the people of God as did William Tyndale. Tyndale worked in constant danger, for under Catholic King Charles V it was a crime punishable by horrible torture, burning at the stake, or actual burial alive for anyone to read, purchase, or possess any New Testament book. But prior to Tyndale's martyrdom it is estimated that some 50,000 copies of the New Testament were circulated by this fearless and faithful servant of God. Early in 1526, Tyndale's New Testaments began pouring into England concealed in cases of merchandise, barrels, bales of cloth, sacks of flour and corn, and every other secret way that could be found. For every one the devil burned, God would allow Tyndale to publish three more to take its place.

It is thought that Tyndale's New Testament was based on the printed Greek New Testament text of the great scholar Erasmus (first printed on March 1, 1516), and that his Old Testament text was taken in part from the 1488 Hebrew publication. He also consulted the Latin Vulgate and Martin Luther's translation.

2. The Coverdale Version (A.D. 1535)—Miles Coverdale was born in 1488. He was

converted to Christ and developed a strong love for the Scripture. He was a friend of Tyndale and later finished Tyndale's Old Testament translation and revised his New Testament. It was a secondary translation; that is, it was based on previous translations of the Bible into Latin, German, and English. The reason for this is that Coverdale was not familiar with the Greek or Hebrew. The first edition came off the press on October 4, 1535. This was indeed a milestone for God's Word, as it marked the first whole Bible printed in English.

3. Matthew's Version (1537)—This version was prepared by John Rogers, who used the pseudonym Thomas Matthew. The reason for this was that Rogers, a known friend of Tyndale, felt his work would be more acceptable to various authorities if this relationship was not known. Rogers would later be burned to death during the reign of Bloody Mary in 1555. Matthew's Version was the first revision of the Tyndale Bible. It was approved by King Henry VIII, who had hated Tyndale and his work. A divine irony is seen here.

4. The Great Bible (1539)—The notes and prefaces of Tyndale's and Coverdale's translations aroused so much argument that Henry VIII authorized a new version that would include no controversial footnote material. It was called the Great Bible because of its size. Due to its extreme value it was usually chained to a "reading post" within a church. In 1538 the king issued an injunction to all churches to purchase a copy of the Great Bible. This was to be paid for by the parson and parishioners. The importance of the Great Bible is that it became the first official English Bible "appointed to be read in all the churches." The King James Bible is basically a revision of the Great Bible.

5. The Geneva Bible (1557)—During the vicious Protestant persecution under Bloody Mary, many Reformers fled to Geneva, Switzerland, and enjoyed the protection of Geneva's great leader John Calvin. It was here that Calvin's brother-in-law, William Whittingham, translated the Scriptures into the Geneva Bible. The text of the Geneva Bible was based on that of the Great Bible. This Bible became important for the following reasons:
   a. It was the first version to divide the text into verses.
   b. It was the first to omit the Apocrypha.
   c. It was kissed by Queen Elizabeth (daughter of Henry VIII) at her coronation, a policy which is still followed by English kings and queens.
   d. It was the most-beloved Bible of the common people up to that time and went through more than 160 editions.
   e. It was the Bible of Shakespeare and John Bunyan.
   f. It was the Bible the pilgrims brought with them on the Mayflower in 1620 to America.

6. The Bishop's Bible (1568)—This version was translated because of the following reasons:
   a. The Church of England did not like the notes in the Geneva Bible.
   b. The Geneva Bible was undermining the authority of the Great Bible and that of the bishops.
It was translated by Matthew Parker, archbishop of Canterbury, who was aided by nine other bishops; thus its name, the Bishop's Bible. The Bishop's Bible was the second "authorized version" of the church, but it was never accepted by the common people. In fact, Queen Elizabeth simply ignored it. The Bishop's Bible has gone down in history as the most unsatisfactory and useless of all the old translations.

7. The Rheims-Douai Bible (1582)—This version was an attempt by the pope to win England back to the Roman fold, but he utterly failed. It was headed by William Allen and Gregory Martin, two Protestant turncoats from Oxford University. The name comes from the two places where the Old Testament and New Testament were produced. The Douai Version was therefore the first Catholic English Bible and was taken almost literally from the Latin Vulgate. The footnotes in this version strongly attacked all Protestant "heresies," and defended all Roman Catholic doctrine and practices.

8. The King James Version (1611)—One of the first tasks King James I faced upon mounting his throne at the beginning of the seventeenth century was the reconciliation of various religious parties within his kingdom. The King James Version began with a request by Puritan spokesman Dr. Reynolds of Oxford concerning the feasibility of a new Bible translation. James agreed almost at once. He had disliked the popular Geneva Bible because of its footnotes. He also realized that neither the Geneva, nor the Great, nor the Bishop's Bible could be held up by him as a rallying point for Christians.

The following quote is from H. S. Miller:

> On July 22, 1604, the King announced that he had appointed 54 men as translators. The only indispensable qualification was that they should have proven efficiency as Biblical scholars. . . . A list of 47 revisers has been preserved; the other seven may have died or resigned before the work had really begun.
>
> The revisers were organized into six groups, two meeting at Westminster, two at Cambridge, two at Oxford. One group at Westminster had Genesis to 2 Kings, the other had Romans to Jude: one group at Cambridge had 1 Chronicles to Ecclesiastes, the other had the Apocrypha; one group at Oxford had Isaiah to Malachi, the other had Matthew to Acts and Revelation. These men were the great Hebrew and Greek scholars of this day.
>
> Each reviser first made his own translation, then passed it on to be reviewed by each member of his group; then when each group had completed a book, a copy of it was sent to each of the other five groups for their independent criticism. Thus each book went through the hands of the entire body of revisers. Then the entire version, thus amended, came before a select committee of six, two from each of the three companies, and they ironed out ultimate differences of opinion, put the finishing touches . . . and prepared it for the printer.
>
> The revisers were governed by 15 rules, the gist of a few of them being: (1) The Bishop's Bible shall be followed and as little altered as the truth of the original will permit; (2) The old ecclesiastical words shall be retained; (3) The chapter divisions shall not be changed, unless very necessary; (4) No marginal notes at all, except explanation of Hebrew and Greek words which cannot be briefly and fitly expressed in the text; (5) Whenever the Tyndale, Matthew, Coverdale, the Great Bible, or the Geneva agrees better with the text than the Bishop's Bible, they are to be used. (*General Biblical Introduction,* pp. 363–364)

The King James Version also doubtless made usage of the four available printed Hebrew Old Testament Bibles at that time, the Erasmos's fifth edition of the Greek New Testament.

The King James Version is remarkable for many reasons. It was, first of all, undoubtedly the most beautiful, beloved, and popular translation of all time. It was also probably the only translation in which no parties involved had an axe to grind. In other words, it was a national undertaking in which no one had any interest at heart, save that of producing the best possible version of the Scriptures.

It must be said however, that the King James Version was not immediately accepted by the general public. The Roman Catholics claimed it favored Protestantism. The Arminians said it leaned toward Calvinism. The Puritans disliked certain words, such as "bishop," "ordain," and "Easter." But after some 40 years it overtook the popular Geneva Bible and had retained its tremendous lead for almost three and a half centuries.

9. The English (1881–1885) and American (1901) Revision—By the latter part of the nineteenth century, the Church of England felt a new revision of the King James Version was needed for the following reasons:
   a. The change in the meaning of some of the English words
   b. The discovery of new manuscripts since 1611
   c. The improved science of biblical criticism
Thus, on May 3, 1870, the initial formalities began. The Canterbury Convocation adopted five resolutions.
   a. "We do not contemplate any new translation of the Bible, or any alteration of the language, except when in the judgment of the most competent scholars such change is necessary."
   b. It offered a uniformity of renderings—that is, it translated the same Hebrew and Greek word by the same English word. The King James Version did not do this, but used a great variety of English words to translate a single Greek word. (For example, the Greek word *meno,* which means "to remain," is translated by ten different words in the King James Version. The Greek word *dunamis,* meaning "power," is translated by 13 different English words.)
   c. It translated the Greek tenses more accurately, especially the aorist and imperfect tenses.
   d. It translated the Greek definite article more accurately.
   e. It translated the Greek preposition more accurately.
The English revised New Testament was published in England on May 17, 1881, and sale in the United States began on May 20. The excitement in this country about receiving a new version of the Bible was at an unbelievable high. For example, the people of Chicago wanted the New Testament about the same time New York would have it, and they could not wait until a fast train could bring it. So two Chicago dailies (the *Tribune* and the *Times*) had the first six books (Matthew to Romans, about 118,000 words) telegraphed from New York to Chicago (978 miles), by far the largest message ever sent over the wire. These papers then published all this on May 22, 1881.

But to the great disappointment of its friends, the English Version of 1881–1885 whose popularity had risen so high so fast almost immediately cooled off. People soon realized how much they would miss the familiar and loved words, phrases, grace, ease, poetry, and rhythm of the King James Version.

In 1901 the American Standard Version was published. This version offered several changes and improvements over its English cousin:

   a. The substitution of "demon" for "devil," where the Greek read *daimon*.
   b. The uniform rendering of "Holy Spirit" for "Holy Ghost."
   c. The use of "who" instead of "which" in reference to persons. The King
      James Version phrase "Our Father, which art in heaven" became "Our
      Father, who art in heaven."
         Although the American Standard Version enjoyed better permanent
      reception than the English one, it still has not seriously cut into the lead of
      the King James Version.
10. The Revised Standard Version (1952)—This work has been one of the most
    controversial versions of the Bible ever published. The Revised Standard
    Version was authorized by the National Council of Churches of Christ in the
    U.S.A. and is the "official" version of this group. Hebrew scholar Dr. Merrill F.
    Unger summarizes the Revised Standard Version in the following way:
    "Although this version has many excellencies, it is weak and obscure in its
    translation of certain key Old Testament messianic passages" (*Unger's Bible
    Handbook*, p. 893).
11. *The Amplified Bible* (1954)—This is a literal translation with multiple expressions
    using associated words to convey the original thought. The New Testament
    uses the Greek text of Westcott and Hort plus 27 translations and revisions. The
    Old testament is similarly extensive. The version is intended to supplement
    other translations authentically, concisely, and in convenient form.
12. *Good News for Modern Man* (1966)—This translation of the New Testament by
    Dr. Robert G. Bratcher (plus a distinguished review committee) is a paraphrase
    that gained enormous popularity in a short period of time. It was intended to
    communicate the Scriptures to the masses of English-speaking people around
    the world and has been much used as an instrument of evangelism for persons
    outside the church. It has since become available as a complete Bible called the
    Good News Bible.
13. *The Jerusalem Bible* (1966)—This is a translation from the Hebrew Masoretic,
    Greek Septuagint, Dead Sea Scrolls, and accepted Greek and Aramaic New
    Testament texts—all compared with the French Version. It was produced by 28
    principal collaborators in translation and literary revision under Alexander
    Jones, general editor.
14. The *New American Bible* (1970)—This is a Catholic translation that is a highlight
    of Bible publishing in the present century. All basic texts were consulted, and
    the work was 26 years in the making. Over 50 recognized biblical scholars, the
    majority of them college professors, labored to produce this outstanding
    version. Scholars were Catholic, Protestant, and Jewish. The purpose was to
    produce a more accurate translation from the older manuscripts, and this was
    made possible by the pope in 1943. Prior to this version, Catholics had been
    required to use the Latin Vulgate as the basis for translation.
15. *The Living Bible* (1971)—An extremely popular paraphrase, this is the work of a
    single translator, Kenneth N. Taylor. The initial source was the American
    Standard Version of 1901, but Dr. Taylor and the Greek and Hebrew specialists
    he consulted for accuracy also used the most respected texts available.
16. The *New American Standard Bible* (1971)—This Bible was translated by an
    editorial board of 54 Greek and Hebrew scholars and required nearly 11 years
    to complete.
17. New International Version (1978)—Revised in 1984, this version was translated

by over one hundred scholars using the most reliable original-language texts. This version has overtaken the King James Version in annual sales.

18. New King James Version (1982)—This version is a faithful revision of the King James Bible. The major changes that have been made were to modernize antiquated verb and pronoun forms, to update punctuation, vocabulary, and grammar, and to capitalize deity pronouns.

19. New Century Version (*International Children's Bible* or *The Everyday Bible* (1988)—Striving for simplicity and clarity in phrases, the translators worked from the original languages to produce a version that would be easy to understand for both adults and children.

PART FOURTEEN: THE APOCRYPHA AND THE BIBLE

After the Old Testament canon had been recognized by the Jews as being officially closed, and prior to the New Testament period, there arose a section of literature called the Apocrypha. This word literally means "that which is hidden" and consists of 14 books.

I. The Contents of the Apocrypha

A. 1 Esdras—This book covers much of the material found in Ezra, Nehemiah, and 2 Chronicles but it also includes a fanciful story concerning three Jewish servants in Persia. They were all asked a question by King Darius concerning what the greatest thing in the world was. One said wine, another replied women, while the third claimed truth was. He won, and when offered a reward, suggested the King allow the Jews to rebuild the temple in Jerusalem.

B. 2 Esdras—This contains certain visions given to Ezra dealing with God's government of the world and the restoration of certain lost Scriptures.

C. Tobit—Tobit is the story of a pious Jew (Tobit) who is accidentally blinded (by sparrow dung) and is later healed by an angel named Raphael, who applies a concoction of fish heart, liver, and gall to his eye.

D. Judith—This is the story of a beautiful and devout Jewish princess who saves Jerusalem from being destroyed by Nebuchadnezzar's invading armies. This she does by beguiling the enemy general through her beauty, then returning to Jerusalem with his head in her handbag!

E. The remainder of Esther—There are additional inserts to this book to show the hand of God in the narrative by putting the word *God* in the text. The word *God* does not appear in the Old Testament book of Esther.

F. The Wisdom of Solomon—This book has been called "The Gem of the Apocrypha," and is one of the loftier books of the Apocrypha.

G. Ecclesiasticus—Also called "the Wisdom of Jews, the Son of Sirach," it resembles the book of Proverbs and gives rules for personal conduct in all details of civil, religious, and domestic life.

H. 1 Maccabees—This historical account of the Maccabean period relates events of the Jews' heroic struggle for liberty (175–135 B.C.)

I. 2 Maccabees—This work covers in part the same period as 1 Maccabees but is somewhat inferior content-wise.

J. Baruch—Supposedly written by Jeremiah's secretary, Baruch, it contains prayers and confessions of the Jews in exile, with promises of restoration.

K. The Song of the Three Children—Inserted in the book of Daniel, right after the fiery furnace episode (Dan. 3:23), It contains an eloquent prayer of Azariah, one of the three Hebrew men thrown in the fire.

L. The story of Susanna—This story relates how the godly wife of a wealthy Jew in Babylon, falsely accused of adultery, was cleared by the wisdom of Daniel.

M. Bel and the Dragon—This is also added to the book of Daniel. The book contains two stories:
  1. The first concerns how Daniel proves to the king his great god Bel is a dead idol and that the Bel priests are religious crooks.
  2. *Unger's Bible Handbook* describes this event in the following words:

> The other legend concerns a dragon worshiped in Babylon. Daniel, sum-moned to do it homage, feeds it a mixture of pitch, hair, and fat, which causes it to explode. The enraged populace compels the King to throw Dan-iel in the den of lions where he is fed on the sixth day by the prophet Habak-kuk, who is angelically transported to Babylon by the hair of his head while carrying food and drink to the reapers in Judea. On the seventh day the King rescues Daniel and throws his would-be destroyers to the hungry lions. (p. 459)

N. The Prayer of Manasseh—This is the supposed confessional prayer of wicked King Manasseh of Judah after he was carried away prisoner to Babylon by the Assyrians.

II. Reasons for Rejecting the Apocrypha—"Why don't you Protestants have all the books of the Bible in your King James Version?" Often Christians and Bible lovers are con-fronted with this question by those who have accepted the Apocrypha into their trans-lations of the Bible. Why indeed do we *not* include these 14 books? There are many sound scriptural reasons for not doing this.

A. The Apocrypha was never included in the Old Testament canon by such recog-nized authorities as the Pharisees, Ezra the prophet, etc.

B. It was never quoted by either Jews or any other New Testament writers.

C. The great Jewish historian Josephus excluded it.

D. The well-known Jewish philosopher Philo did not recognize it.

E. The early church fathers excluded it.

F. The Bible translator Jerome did not accept them as inspired, although he was forced by the pope to include them into the Latin Vulgate Bible.

G. None of the 14 books claim divine inspirations; in fact, some actually disclaim it.

H. Some books contain historical and geographical errors.

I. Some books teach false doctrine, such as praying for the dead.

J. No apocryphal book can be found in any catalogue list of canonical books com-posed during the first four centuries A.D. In fact, it was not until 1596 at the Council of Trent that the Roman Catholic church officially recognized these books, basically in an attempt to strengthen its position, which had been grievously weakened by the great reformer Martin Luther.

PART FIFTEEN: FACTS INDICATING THE DIVINE ORIGIN OF THE BIBLE

Often the unbeliever hurls the following accusation at the believer: "Oh, you Christians—you're all alike! You're so dogmatic! You think you alone are right and everybody else is dead wrong! How can you possibly be so sure what you believe is true?" This question, even though often asked in a scoffing manner, is nevertheless a fair one. How *does* the child of God know his faith is the only correct one?

Let us suppose you are invited to an important social function in your hometown. Attending this gathering are people from all over the world. As the introductions are being made, it slowly dawns on you that the only professing Christian there is yourself.

You are subsequently introduced to a Buddhist, a Confucianist, a Shintoist, a Muslim, and other individuals, all belonging to various non-Christian religions. After a pleasant dinner, the conversation gradually turns to matters of religion. Your hostess, realizing this subject to be of general interest, suddenly announces: "I have a wonderful idea! Since everyone here seems to have a great interest in religion, may I suggest we share with one another by doing the following: Each person will be allowed to speak uninterrupted for ten minutes on the subject, Why I feel my faith is the right one."

The group quickly agrees with this unique and provocative idea. Then, with no warning, she suddenly turns to you and exclaims, "You go first!" All talk immediately ceases. Every eye is fixed on you. Every ear is tuned to pick up your first words. What, pray tell, would you say? How would you start? Let us quickly list a few arguments you could not use.

- You *couldn't* say, "I know I'm right because I *feel* I'm right! Christ lives in my heart!"— This of course is a wonderful truth experienced by all believers, but it would not convince the Buddhist who would doubtless feel Buddha lived in his heart.
- You *couldn't* say, "I know I'm right because Christianity has more followers in this world than any other religion"—This is simply not true today. Actually, the sad truth is that evangelical, Bible-believing Christianity is a distinct minority in the world today. The Muslim would doubtless quickly point this out to you.
- You *couldn't* say, "I know I'm right because Christianity is the oldest of all religions"— Ultimately, of course, this is true. But the Confucianist might contend that Confucius presented his teachings centuries before the Bethlehem scene. Of course, he would not understand the eternal existence of our Lord Jesus Christ.

These then are arguments you could not use. What then *could* you say? In reality you would have at your disposal only one single argument. But that argument, that weapon, used in the right way, would be more than enough to overwhelmingly convince any honest and sincere listener at a social gathering. That wonderful weapon, that unanswerable argument is one's own personal copy of the Bible. What could you say? Well, you could hold up your Bible and confidently proclaim: "Look at this! I know I'm right because the author of my faith has given me a Book that is completely unlike any of the books of your faiths."

You could then continue (until your time runs out) by pointing out the unity, the indestructibility, and the universal influence of the Bible. You could discuss its historical, scientific, and prophetical accuracy. Finally, you might relate exciting examples of perhaps the greatest single proof of the supernaturalness of the Bible, and that is its marvelous, life-transforming power.

Of course it must be pointed out that neither the Word of God nor the God of the Word can be scientifically analyzed in a laboratory test tube. The Divine Creator still desires and demands faith on the part of his creation. (See Heb. 11:1-6.) But he has presented us with a heavenly textbook to aid us in this needed faith. In fact, the Gospel of John was specifically written "that ye might believe that Jesus is the Christ, the Son of God; and that believing ye might have life through his name" (John 20:31).

During this phase of the study we will but briefly touch upon each of these "supernatural signs of the Scriptures," all of which indicate our Bible did in fact come from the very hand of God. As the Christian acquaints himself with these amazing arguments, he is then qualified to: "Sanctify the Lord God in your hearts: and be ready always to give an answer to every man that asketh you a reason of the hope that is in you with meekness and fear" (1 Pet. 3:15).

I. First Supernatural Element: Its Amazing Unity—That the Bible is a unity is a fact no honest reader can deny. In the preface of most Bibles, the 39 Old Testament and 27

New Testament books are listed in two parallel columns down the page. But a more accurate way would be to place the entire 66-book collection in a clock-like circle, with Genesis occupying the first minute past 12:00, Exodus the second, Leviticus the third, and so on. Finally, the book of Revelation would be placed on the number 12, right next to Genesis. It is simply thrilling how these two books, Genesis the first and Revelation the last, perfectly dovetail together in a unity only God could create. For example:

In Genesis we read: "In the beginning God created the heaven and the earth" (1:1). In Revelation we read: "I saw a new heaven and a new earth" (21:1).

In Genesis we see described the first Adam with his wife, Eve, in the Garden of Eden, reigning over the earth (1:27-28). In Revelation we see described the last Adam with his wife, the church, in the City of God, reigning over all the universe (21:9).

In Genesis we are told: "And the gathering of the waters called he Seas" (1:10). In Revelation we are told: "And there was no more sea" (21:1).

In Genesis God created the sun and moon, the day and the night (1:5, 16). In Revelation "there shall be no night there" (22:5). "And the City had no need of the sun, neither of the moon, to shine in it: for the glory of God did lighten it, and the Lamb is the light thereof" (21:23).

In Genesis the Tree of Life is denied to sinful man (3:22). In Revelation the Tree of Life "yielded her fruit every month: and the leaves of the tree were for the healing of the nations" (22:2).

In Genesis man hears God say: "Cursed is the ground for thy sake" (3:17). In Revelation man will hear God say: "And there shall be no more curse" (22:3).

In Genesis Satan appears to torment man (3:1). In Revelation Satan disappears, himself to be tormented forever (20:10).

In Genesis the old earth was punished through a flood (7:12). In Revelation the new earth shall be purified through a fire (2 Peter 3:6-12; Rev. 21:1)

In Genesis man's early home was beside a river (2:10). In Revelation man's eternal home will be beside a river: "And he shewed me a pure river of water of life, clear as crystal, proceeding out of the throne of God and of the Lamb" (22:1).

In Genesis the patriarch Abraham weeps for Sarah (23:2). In Revelation the children of Abraham will have God himself wipe away all tears from their eyes (21:4)

In Genesis God destroys an earthly city, wicked Sodom, from the sands (chapter 19). In Revelation God presents a heavenly city, new Jerusalem, from the skies (21:1).

Genesis ends with a believer in Egypt, lying in a coffin (50:1-3). Revelation ends with all believers in eternity, reigning forever (21:4).

A. This unity is achieved in spite of the long period of time involved in its writing.
    1. More than 15 centuries elapsed between the writing of Genesis and Revelation.
    2. Nearly 400 years elapsed between the writing of Malachi and Matthew.
B. This unity is achieved in spite of the many authors (some 40) and their various occupations (approximately 17)—"The Lord gave the word: great was the company of those who published it" (Psa. 68:11).
    1. Moses was an Egyptian prince.
    2. Joshua was a soldier.
    3. Samuel was a priest.
    4. David was a king.
    5. Job was a rich farmer.
    6. Amos was a poor farmer.

7. Ezra was a scribe.
8. Isaiah was a prophet.
9. Daniel was a prime minister.
10. Nehemiah was a cupbearer.
11. Matthew was a tax collector.
12. Mark was an evangelist.
13. Luke was a physician.
14. John was a wealthy fisherman.
15. Peter was a poor fisherman.
16. Jude and James were probably carpenters.
17. Paul was a tentmaker.
C. This unity is achieved in spite of the different geographical places where the Bible was written.
1. In the desert (Exod. 17)
2. On Mount Sinai (Exod. 20)
3. In Palestine (most)
4. In Egypt (Jeremiah?)
5. On the Isle of Patmos (Revelation)
6. In Babylon (Daniel)
7. In Persia (Esther)
8. In Corinth (1 and 2 Thessalonians)
9. In Ephesus (Galatians?)
10. In Caesarea (Luke?)
11. From Rome (2 Timothy)
D. This unity is achieved in spite of the many different styles of its writing.
1. As history
2. As prophecy
3. As biography
4. As autobiography
5. As poetry
6. As law
7. In letter form
8. In symbolic form
9. In proverb form
10. In doctrinal form

Let us imagine a religious novel of 66 chapters that was begun by a single writer around the sixth century A.D. After the author had completed but five chapters he suddenly dies. But during the next 1,000 years, up to the sixteenth century, around 30 amateur "free-lance" writers felt constrained to contribute to this unfinished religious novel. Few of these authors shared anything in common. Some of them were black, others white, still others yellow, and a few brown. They spoke different languages, lived at different times, in different countries, had totally different backgrounds and occupations, and wrote in different styles.

Let us furthermore imagine that at the completion of the thirty-ninth chapter the writing for some reason suddenly stops. Not one word is therefore added from the sixteenth until the twentieth century. After this long delay it begins once again by eight new authors who add the final 27 chapters.

With all this in mind, what would be the chances of this religious novel becoming a moral, scientific, prophetic, and historical unity? The answer is obvious—not one in a million. And yet this is the story of the Bible.

II. Second Supernatural Element: Its Indestructibility—The story is told of a visitor who toured a blacksmith shop. Viewing heaps of discarded hammers but only one huge anvil, he asked: "How often do you replace your anvil?" With a smile the owner replied, "Never! It is the anvil that wears out the hammers, you know!"

So it is with the Word of God. The hammers of persecution, ridicule, higher criticism, liberalism, and atheism have for centuries pounded out their vicious blows upon the divine anvil, but all to no avail. There they lay, in rusting piles, while the mighty anvil of the Scriptures stands unbroken, unshaken, and unchipped.

A. Its indestructibility in spite of political persecutions (from the Roman emperors)—In A.D. 303, Emperor Diocletian thought he had destroyed every hated Bible. After many tireless years of ruthless slaughter and destruction, he erected a column of victory over the embers of a burned Bible. The title on the column read: "Extinct is the Name of Christian." Twenty years later, the new Emperor Constantine offered a reward for any remaining Bibles. Within 24 hours no less than 50 copies were brought out of hiding and presented to the king.

B. Its indestructibility in spite of religious persecutions

1. As seen through the persecutions by Roman Catholic popes—Almost without exception, the early popes opposed the reading and translating of the Bible. In 1199, Pope Innocent III ordered the burning of all Bibles.

2. As seen through the persecutions leveled against John Wycliffe and William Tyndale—Of all the heroes in church history no two other names are so closely associated with the Word of God than the names of Wycliffe and Tyndale. The very mention of these two men was no doubt sufficient to turn the devil livid with rage. It is therefore no surprise to read of the vicious attacks leveled against them.

   a. John Wycliffe (c. 1330–1384)—Wycliffe lived at a time (the early part of the fourteenth century) when the burning question was: Who shall rule England, the king or the pope? Wycliffe believed the best way to break the grievous yoke of Romanism would be to place the Bible into the hands of the common people. This he did by translating (for the first time in history) the complete Bible into English. He then organized and sent forth a group of preachers (called the Lollards) to teach the Word of God all across England.

   On December 28, 1384, while conducting a service in the Lutterworth Church, he was suddenly stricken with paralysis and died three days later. After his death, those who hated his Bible translation activities said the following things about Wycliffe:

   > John Wycliffe, the organ of the devil, the enemy of the Church, the confusion of the common people, the idol of heretics, the looking glass of hypocrites, the encourager of schism, the sower of hatred, the storehouse of lies, the sink of flattery, was suddenly struck by the judgment of God . . . that mouth which was to speak huge things against God and against His Saints or holy church, was miserably drawn aside . . . showing plainly that the curse which God had thundered forth against Cain who also inflicted upon him. [From the mouth of a Monk]

   > That pestilent wretch John Wycliffe, the son of the old serpent, the

forerunner of Antichrist, who had completed his iniquity by inventing a new translation of the Scriptures. (*General Biblical Introduction*, p. 329)

One would almost conclude the Savior had this in mind when he spoke the following words: "These things have I spoken unto you, that ye should not be offended. They shall put you out of the synagogues: yea, the time cometh, that whosoever killeth you will think that he doeth God service. And these things will they do unto you, because they have not known the Father, nor me" (John 16:1-3).

One final quotation from Miller's book seems appropriate here:

In 1415, the Council of Constance which consigned John Hus and Jerome of Prague to a cruel death, demanded that the bones of the notorious heretic Wycliffe . . . be taken out of the consecrated ground and scattered at a distance from the sepulchre. Thirteen years later (1428), 44 years after his death, Pope Clement VIII ordered no further delay; the grave was torn up, the coffin and skeleton borne down to the bank of the River Swift, a fire was kindled, the bones were burned, and the ashes thrown into the river. In the words of Thomas Fuller, so often quoted: "The Swift conveyed them into the Avon, the Avon into the Severn, the Severn into the narrow seas; they into the main ocean; and thus the ashes of Wycliffe are the emblem of his doctrine, which is now dispersed all the world over." (Ibid., p. 330)

b. William Tyndale (1484–1536)—Tyndale was one of the greatest translators of God's Word who ever lived. He was born in England, and so skilled in seven languages (Hebrew, Greek, Latin, Italian, Spanish, English, and Dutch) that whichever he might be speaking one would believe that language was his native tongue. Our own King James Version is practically a fifth revision of Tyndale's, and it retains many of the words and much of the character, form, and style of his version. In 1525, he printed the first copy ever produced of the New Testament in English. His overall goal in life was perhaps best expressed through a statement he made in 1521: "I defy the Pope and all his laws; if God spares my life, ere many years I will cause a boy that driveth the plough shall know . . . the Scripture" (Ibid., p. 334).

In 1529, an amusing and thrilling event happened in England and Europe concerning the Word of God. Tyndale had been driven from England and had fled to Germany, but had continued producing New Testaments and slipping them back into England. One day the Bishop of London (Bishop Tunstall) remarked to a British merchant, a man named Packington and a secret friend of Tyndale, of his desire to buy up all copies of the New Testament.

Said Packington, "My Lord, if it be your pleasure, I can buy them, for I know where they are sold, if it be in your Lord's pleasure to pay for them. I will then assure you to have every book of them that is imprinted."

Said the Bishop, "Gentle master Packington, do your diligence and get them; and with all my heart I will pay for them whatsoever they cost you, for the books are erroneous . . . and I intend to destroy them all, and burn them at St. Paul's Cross."

Packington then came to Tyndale and said, "William, I know that thou art a poor man, and hast a heap of New Testaments and books by thee, by the which thou hast endangered thy friends and beggared thyself; and I have now gotten thee a merchant, which with ready money shall dispatch thee of all that thou hast, if you think it so profitable to thyself."

"Who is the merchant," asked Tyndale.

"The Bishop of London," answered Packington.

"Oh, that is because he will burn them."

"Yes, marry, but what of that? The Bishop will burn them anyhow, and it is best that you should have the money for enabling you to imprint others instead."

"I shall do this," said Tyndale, "for these two benefits shall come thereof: First, I shall get money to bring myself out of debt, and the whole world will cry out against the burning of God's Word; and Second, the overplus of the money that shall remain to me shall make me more studious to correct the said New Testament, and so newly to imprint the same once again, and I trust the second will be much better than ever was the first." So the bargain was made. The bishop had the books, Packington had the thanks, and Tyndale had the money. Later, a man named Constantine was being tried as a heretic, and the judge promised him favor if he would tell how Tyndale received so much help in printing so many Testaments.

He replied, "My Lord, I will tell you truly: It is the Bishop of London that hath helped, for he hath bestowed among us a great deal of money upon the New Testaments to burn them, and that hath been, and yet is, our chief help and comfort." (Ibid., p. 339)

Again, to quote from Miller's textbook:

On Friday, October 6, 1536, Tyndale was executed. By the Emperor's laws, only Anabaptists were burned alive, so he escaped that fate. He was led out and permitted to engage in a few moments of prayer. With fervent zeal and a loud voice he cried, "Lord, open the King of England's eyes!" Then his feet were bound to the stake, the iron chain was fastened around his neck, with a hemp rope loosely tied in a noose, and fagots and straw were heaped around him. At a given signal the rope was tightened, and Tyndale was strangled to death. Then the torch was applied, and the body was quickly consumed. (Ibid., p. 340)

C. Its indestructibility in spite of philosophical persecution—Here several cases come to mind:

1. Voltaire—He once said, "Another century and there will be not a Bible on the earth." The century is gone, and the circulation of the Bible is one of the marvels of the age. After he died, his old printing press and the very house where he lived was purchased by the Geneva Bible Society and made a depot for Bibles.

   On December 24, 1933, the British Government bought the valuable Codex Sinaiticus from the Russians for half a million dollars. On that same day a first edition of Voltaire's work sold for 11 cents in Paris book shops.

2. Thomas Paine—He once said, "I have gone through the Bible as a man would go through a forest with an axe to fell trees. I have cut down tree after tree; here they lie. They will never grow again." Tom Paine thought he had demolished the Bible, but since he crawled into a drunkard's grave in 1809, the Bible has leaped forward as never before.

3. Joseph Stalin—This bloody butcher took over all of Russia at the death of Lenin in the late twenties. From this point on until his death in the fifties, Stalin instituted a "ban the Bible" purge from the USSR such as had never been witnessed before. This miserable man literally attempted to wipe the Word of God and the God of the Word from the Russian minds. Did he succeed? A recent poll taken in Russia shows that today more people than ever believe in God and his Word.

III. Third Supernatural Element: Its Historical Accuracy—Less than a century ago, the agnostic took great glee in sneeringly referring to the "hundreds of historical mistakes" in the Bible. But then came the science of archaeology, and with each shovel full of dirt the sneers have become less visible, until today they scarcely can be seen. When one thinks of historical scholarship and the Bible, three brilliant scholars of giant intellect and achievement come to mind. These three are:

A. Sir William Ramsay—For many years Ramsay was professor of humanity at the University of Aberdeen, Scotland. He was, in his time, the world's most eminent authority on the geography and history of ancient Asia Minor (Turkey today). In his zeal to study every available early document concerning that period and area, he undertook an intensive research of the New Testament book of Acts and also the Gospel of Luke. This study, however, was approached with much skepticism. At that time he penned the following description of the book of Acts: "A highly imaginative and carefully colored account of primitive Christianity."

But after many years of intensive study, this scholar, who began an unbeliever, became a staunch defender of the Word of God. The absolute historical accuracy of Luke's writings, even in the most minute details, captured first his brain and then his heart. Ramsay authored many books, but one of his better known is entitled *The Bearing of Recent Discovery on the Trustworthiness of the New Testament*. Ramsay's overall opinion of the Bible is perhaps best seen in the following quote: "I take the view that Luke's history is unsurpassed in regard to its trustworthiness . . . you may press the words of Luke in a degree beyond any other historian's and they stand the keenest scrutiny and the hardest treatment."

B. William F. Albright—One of the greatest and most respected oriental scholars who ever lived was William F. Albright. The list of his earned doctorate degrees reminds one of the "New Deal" alphabetical organizations. These degrees included the Ph.D., Litt.D., D.H.L., Th.D., and LL.D. Dr. Albright writes the following concerning the Bible and his historical findings: "The reader may rest assured: nothing has been found to disturb a reasonable faith, and nothing has been discovered which can disprove a single theological doctrine. . . . We no longer trouble ourselves with attempts to 'harmonize' religion and science, or to 'prove' the Bible. The Bible can stand for itself" (Robert Young, *Young's Analytical Concordance to the Bible*, p. 51).

C. Robert Dick Wilson—Probably the most qualified Old Testament linguist of all time was Robert Dick Wilson. His skill along this line staggers the imagination. Dr. Wilson was born in 1856 and took his undergraduate work at Princeton

University, graduating in 1876. He then completed both the M.A. and the Ph.D. After this, two years were spent at the University of Berlin in further postgraduate studies. Wilson taught Old Testament courses at Western Theological Seminary in Pittsburgh and returned to Princeton, where he received international fame as a Hebrew scholar without peer. He was perfectly at home in over 40 ancient Semitic languages. Dr. Wilson writes the following about himself:

> If a man is called an expert, the first thing to be done is to establish the fact that he is such. One expert may be worth more than a million other witnesses that are not experts. Before a man has the right to speak about the history and the language . . .of the Old Testament, the Christian Church has the right to demand that a man should establish his ability to do so. For 45 years continuously, since I left college, I have devoted myself to the one great study of the Old Testament, in all its languages, in all its archaeology, in all its translations, and as far as possible in everything bearing upon its text and history. I tell you this so that you may see why I can and do speak as an expert. I may add that the result of my 45 years of study of the Bible has led me all the time to a firmer faith that in the Old Testament we have a true historical account of the history of the Israelite people; and I have a right to commend this to some of those bright men and women who think that they can laugh at the old-time Christian and believer in the Word of God. . . . I have claimed to be an expert. Have I the right to do so? Well, when I was in the Seminary I used to read my New Testament in nine different languages. I learned my Hebrew by heart, so that I could recite it without the intermission of a syllable . . . as soon as I graduated from the Seminary, I became a teacher of Hebrew for a year and then I went to Germany. When I got to Heidelberg, I made a decision. I decided—and did it with prayer—to consecrate my life to the study of the Old Testament. I was 25 then; and I judged from the life of my ancestors that I should live to be 70; so that I should have 45 years to work. I divided the period into three parts. The first 15 years I would devote to the study of the languages necessary. For the second 15 I was going to devote myself to the study of the text of the Old Testament; and I reserved the last 15 years for the work of writing the results of my previous studies and investigations, so as to give them to the world. And the Lord has enabled me to carry out that plan almost to a year. (*Which Bible?* pp. 40–41)

Thus did Robert Dick Wilson write. One of the stirring moments in the experience of his students occurred when, after a dissertation on the complete trustworthiness of Scripture, the renowned scholar said with tears: "Young men, there are many mysteries in this life I do not pretend to understand, many things hard to explain. But I can tell you this morning with the fullest assurance that—

> "*Jesus loves me, this I know*
> *For the Bible tells me so.*" (Ibid., p. 42)

Of course, it must be admitted that no human intellect, however brilliant or accomplished, is infallible. But this fact should be kept in mind—no three other men among the many, who have criticized and ridiculed the Bible, were probably even half as qualified to speak with the authority as possessed by Ramsey, Albright, and Wilson.

D. Authenticated by Archaeology—The fact is, many biblical events and places are strongly supported by archaeological findings. These would include:
1. Creation (Gen. 1:1)
2. Original monotheism (Gen. 1:1)
3. The Garden of Eden (Gen. 2:8-17)
4. The fall of man (Gen. 3)
5. Earliest civilization (Gen. 4:1-26)
6. Pre-flood longevity (Gen. 5:1-32)
7. The universal flood (Gen. 6–8)
8. Mount Ararat as the site of Noah's ark (Gen. 8:4)
9. The table of nations (Gen. 10)
10. The tower of Babel (Gen. 11:1-9)
11. Ur of the Chaldeans (Gen. 11:31)
12. Haran (Gen. 12:5)
13. The battle route of Chedorlaomer (Gen. 14:1-12)
14. The Hittite empire (Gen. 15:20)
15. Nahor (Gen. 24:10)
16. The employment of camels in patriarchal times (Gen. 24:11)
17. The cities of Sodom and Gomorrah (Gen. 19)
18. The commonness in inscriptions of biblical names such as Adam, Eve, Lamech, Jabal, Noah, Hagar, Keturah, and Bilhah (Gen. 2:19; 3:20; 4:19-20; 5:29; 16:1; 25:1; 29:29)
19. The abundance of food in Gerar in time of famine (Gen. 26:1)
20. Joseph and Potiphar's wife (Gen. 39)
21. The bricks without straw (Exod. 5:7-19)
22. The death of the firstborn in Egypt (Exod. 12)
23. The destruction of Pharaoh and his armies in the Red Sea (Exod. 14)
24. The parting of the Jordan River (Josh. 3)
25. The destruction of Jericho (Josh. 6)
26. The altar used by Joshua when Israel crossed into the promised land (Josh. 8:30-35)
27. The wealth of Gibeon (Josh. 10:2)
28. The springs of Kirjath-sepher (Josh. 15:13-19)
29. Shiloh, where the tabernacle resided after Israel crossed into the promised land (Josh. 18:1)
30. The use of the hornet in conquering Palestine (Josh. 24:12)
31. The burial of Joshua (Josh. 24:30)
32. Cities in the book of Judges (Judg. 1:21-29)
33. The Philistine's use of iron weapons (Judg. 1:19)
34. The Deborah and Barak battle (Judg. 4)
35. Gideon's hidden grain pit (Judg. 6:11)
36. The destruction of Gibeah (Judg. 20)
37. The taking of the Ark (1 Sam. 4)
38. Saul's house in Gibeah (1 Sam. 10:26)
39. Jonathan's victory over the Philistines (1 Sam. 14)
40. The music of David (1 Sam. 16:18, 23; 1 Chron. 15:16)
41. The pool of Gibeon (2 Sam. 2:13)
42. The capture of Jerusalem (2 Sam. 5:6-10)
43. The wealth of Solomon (1 Kings 4:26; 9:26; 10:22)

44. Solomon's fortresses, built to defend his cities in the Negev (1 Kings 9:15)
45. The invasion of Judah by Pharaoh Shisak of Egypt (1 Kings 14:25-28; 2 Chron. 12:2-9)
46. The reign of northern King Omri (1 Kings 16:22-28)
47. The rebuilding of Jericho (Josh. 6:26; 1 Kings 16:34)
48. The victory of Elijah on Mount Carmel (1 Kings 18)
49. Ahab's house of ivory (1 Kings 22:39)
50. The pool of Samaria (1 Kings 22:37-38)
51. The war between Israel and Moab (2 Kings 3)
52. The building where the Judean king Joash was murdered (2 Kings 12:20-21)
53. The punishment of King Jehu (2 Kings 10:29-33)
54. The official seal of the servant of Jeroboam II (2 Kings 14:23-29)
55. Repentance of Nineveh (Jon. 3)
56. The tribute money King Menahem of Israel paid to Assyrian King Pul (2 Kings 15:19)
57. The accomplishments and judgment of King Uzziah (2 Chron. 26)
58. The capture of Israel by Assyrian King Shalmaneser (2 Kings 17)
59. Ahaz's money tribute to King Tiglath-pileser (2 Kings 16:5-9)
60. The seal and tomb of Shebna, Hezekiah's scribe (Isa. 22:15-16)
61. A seal bearing the name "Gemariah, the son of Shaphan," who served as official scribe to the Judean king Jehoiakim (Jer. 36:9-12)
62. The destruction of Lachish by Sennacherib (2 Chron. 32:9)
63. Sennacherib's failure to capture Jerusalem (2 Kings 18–19; 2 Chron. 32; Isa. 36–37)
64. The murder of Sennacherib by his own sons (Isa. 37:37-38)
65. The imprisonment of King Manasseh by the Assyrians (2 Chron. 33:11)
66. The discovery of the book of the law in the temple during Josiah's reign (2 Chron. 34:8-32)
67. Hezekiah's water tunnel (2 Kings 20:20; 2 Chron. 32:30)
68. Hezekiah's wall repairs (2 Chron. 32:5)
69. The destruction of Lachish by Nebuchadnezzar (Jer. 34:7)
70. The captivity of Jehoiachin and the appointment of Zedekiah (2 Kings 24:10-19; 25:27-30)
71. The futile hope of Zedekiah in looking to Egypt to aid against Babylon (Jer. 37:1, 5-11)
72. The treachery of Ishmael against Gedaliah and his officials (Jer. 41:1-15)
73. The great stones buried by Jeremiah in Tahpanhes, Egypt (Jer. 43:8-13)
74. The great statue and fiery furnace of Nebuchadnezzar (Dan. 3)
75. The pride of Nebuchadnezzar and the greatness of Babylon (Dan. 4)
76. The insanity of Nebuchadnezzar (Dan. 4)
77. The capture of Babylon and execution of Belshazzar (Dan. 5)
78. Daniel and the lions' den (Dan. 6)
79. Ahasuerus, the Persian king (Esther)
80. The edict of King Cyrus (Ezra 1:1-4)
81. The wall constructed by Nehemiah (Neh. 1–6)
82. The enemies of Nehemiah (Neh. 2; 4; 6)
83. The synagogue in Capernaum where Jesus preached (Mark 1:21-25; Luke 7:1-10)
84. Simon Peter's home in Capernaum (Mark 1:21, 29)
IV. Fourth Supernatural Element: Its Scientific Accuracy—It has previously been dis-

cussed in this study that although the Bible is primarily a spiritual message from God and not a specific scientific textbook, all scientific statements found in the Scriptures must nevertheless be taken literally and at face value. The devoted believer will find little time for the claim that while we may look to God for the who and why of creation, we must depend upon the scientist for the how and when of this creation. Actually the Bible contains far more specific scientific statements than one might realize. Some of these precepts would include:

A. The fact that the earth is spherical—Some seven centuries B.C. the Hebrew prophet Isaiah wrote: "It is he that sitteth upon the circle of the earth" (Isa. 40:22).

While it is true that a few Greek philosophers did postulate this as early as 540 B.C., the common man held the earth to be flat until the introduction of the compass and the fifteenth-century voyages of Columbus and Magellan.

B. The fact that the earth is suspended in space—The book of Job is thought to be one of the oldest in the Bible, written perhaps earlier than 1500 B.C. At this time one of the most advanced "scientific" theories concerning the earth was that our planet was flat and rested securely upon the back of a gigantic turtle who was slowly plodding through a cosmic sea of some sort. But note the refreshing (and accurate) words of Job: "He stretcheth out the north over the empty place, and hangeth the earth upon nothing" (Job 26:7). All this was not known by the scientists of the world until the writings of Sir Isaac Newton in 1687.

C. The fact that the stars are innumerable—Nearly 20 centuries B.C., God spoke to Abraham one night and said: "Look now toward heaven, and tell the stars if thou be able to number them: and he said unto him. So shall thy seed be" (Gen. 15:5).

Abraham must have at first wondered about this. God was promising him to be the founder of a nation whose descendants would be as uncountable as the stars. But Abraham could count the stars. There they were—a little under 1,200 visible to the naked eye. Was his future nation to be limited to this number? Although we are not told so, he must have reasoned that perhaps there were "a few more" up there that he couldn't see. And he would not be disappointed, for today scientists tell us there are probably as many stars in the heavens as there are grains of sand on all the sea shores of the world. In fact, in a previous conversation with Abraham, God used this very comparison. "And I will make thy seed as the dust of the earth: so that if a man can number the dust of the earth, then shall thy seed also be numbered" (Gen. 13:16).

Thus does the Bible describe the heavens. (See also Jer. 33:22; Heb. 11:12.) But what about the scientific opinion of that day? As late as A.D. 150, the famous astronomer Ptolemy dogmatically declared the number of the stars to be exactly 1,056.

D. The fact that there are mountains and canyons in the sea—As recently as a century or so ago, the ocean's volume and size was viewed as a watery bowl, which sloped from the coastline gently downward until the middle, where it was deepest. It then was thought to proceed upward to the other side. Of course we now know this to be totally untrue. Some of the highest mountains and deepest canyons are located on the floor of the Pacific Ocean. In fact, the deepest hole yet found is the Marianas Trench, just off the Philippines; it is over seven miles deep.

But long before ocean science discovered this, the Bible graphically described it. During one of his songs of deliverance, David spoke of the canyons of the sea (2 Sam. 22:16), and a backslidden prophet described the submerged mountains during the world's first submarine trip. (See Jon. 2:6.)

E. The fact that there are springs and fountains in the sea—Shortly after World War II, research ships discovered many underwater volcanoes. The number is estimated today to be at least 10,000. Further research by Dr. William W. Rubey of the U.S. Geological Survey has shown the present rate of water increase from underwater volcanic outlets to be 430 million tons each year. The earth's heat drives the entrapped water from underground molten rock and forces it out through one of these natural openings. This interesting fact is vividly described in at least three Old Testament passages. (See Gen. 7:11; 8:2; Prov. 8:28.)

F. The fact that there are watery paths (ocean currents) in the sea—In his booklet, *Has God Spoken?* author A. O. Schnabel writes the following: "David said in Psalms 8:8 that God had subjected all things to men, including: 'Whatsoever passeth through the path of the sea'" (p. 38). The Hebrew word *paths* carries the literal meaning of "customary roads."

Matthew Fountaine Maury is called the "Pathfinder of the Seas." This American is the father of today's oceanography and responsible for the establishment of Annapolis Academy. A statue of Maury stands in Richmond, Virginia—charts of the sea in one hand, and Bible in the other. Until Maury's efforts there were no charts or sailing lanes. One day during a temporary illness, his eldest son was reading to him from the Bible and came to Psalm 8:8. Maury stopped him and said, "Read that again." After hearing it again, he exclaimed, "It is enough—if the Word of God says there are paths in the sea, they must be there, and I am going to find them." Within a few years he had charted the sea lanes and currents. His *Physical Geography of the Sea* was the first textbook of modern oceanography.

G. The fact of the invisible atom structure of matter—The modern era of atomic physics did not begin until 1895 with the discovery of X-rays. Prior to this, men reasoned that all matter was built from visible things. But scientists now understand that all matter is held together by attraction and energy—things that are not apparent. With all this in mind, consider the following Scripture passages:

"Who being the brightness of his glory, and the express image of his person, and upholding all things by the word of his power, when he had by himself purged our sins, sat down on the right hand of the Majesty on high" (Heb. 1:3) "Now faith is the substance of things hoped for, the evidence of things not seen" (Heb. 11:1). "And he is before all things, and by him all things consist" (Col. 1:17). "For the invisible things of him from the creation of the world are clearly seen, being understood by the things that are made, even his eternal power and Godhead; so that they are without excuse" (Rom. 1:20).

H. The fact that all living things are reproduced after their own kind—"And God created great whales, and every living creature that moveth, which the waters brought forth abundantly, after their kind, and every winged fowl after his kind: and God saw that it was good" (Gen. 1:21). "And of every living thing of all flesh, two of every sort shalt thou bring into the ark, to keep them alive with thee; they shall be male and female" (Gen. 6:19).

For hundreds of years scientists followed the spontaneous generation theory of Aristotle (350 B.C.). They believed eggs of all lower animals (insects, etc.) were formed out of rotting substance. Frogs and other small sea life had their origin in slime pools. In fact, it was not until 1862 that Louis Pasteur proved once for all that there was no such thing as spontaneous generation. Then, in 1865, a monk named Gregor Mendel demonstrated even more forcibly the rigid laws of heredity. But one could learn all this in the first few chapters of the Bible.

I. The facts involved in health and sanitation—The great law giver in the Bible was Moses, of course, who established hundreds of rules to govern health and sanitation. Moses grew up in the court of Pharaoh, spending the first 40 years of his life there. About this time a famous ancient medical book called *The Papyrus Ebers* was being written in Egypt. Because of Egypt's role in the world at that time, this work soon achieved fame as the official standard for its day. Actually it was filled with quack cures, old wives' tales, and practically every false superstition of its day. In his book *None of These Diseases,* author S. McMillen writes:

> Several hundred remedies for diseases are advised in the Papyrus Ebers. The drugs include "lizard's blood, swine's teeth, putrid meat, stinking fat, moisture from pig's ears, milk goose grease, asses' hoofs, animal fats from various sources, excreta from animals, including human beings, donkey's, antelopes, dogs, cats, and even flies." (p. 11)

The point of all the above is simply this—Moses was well acquainted with all the medical knowledge of his day. Yet in all his writings and proven remedies concerning health and sanitation, he never once even indirectly refers to the false "cures" found in the Papyrus Ebers.

J. The facts involved concerning the human bloodstream—The Bible is, among other matters, an expert on human blood. In Leviticus 17:11, God lays down one of his key statements concerning this subject. Here he declares: "For the life of the flesh is in the blood."

One searches in vain to read in this ancient Book any reference whatsoever to that false medical practice known as bloodletting that plagued mankind from the fourth century B.C. until the nineteenth century A.D. Only eternity will reveal how many sick individuals were actually killed through this "cure." No other nonbiblical writer understood the nature of the blood. In fact, many scientists (for example, Herophilos, a physician in the medical museum at Alexandria, Egypt) believed blood to be a carrier of *disease* instead of life. The death of our own George Washington is thought to have been due in part to excessive bloodletting.

K. The facts involved in the two laws of thermodynamics—Apart from gravity itself, two of the most solid and immutable laws in all physics are the first and second laws of thermodynamics. Albert Einstein himself testified that in all the known universe there is no time nor place where the two do not apply.

The first law of thermodynamics—that of energy conservation. This law states that although energy can change forms, it cannot be either created or destroyed, and therefore the sum total remains constant. Thus no energy is now being created or destroyed anywhere in the known universe.

The second law of thermodynamics—that of energy deterioration. This law states that when energy is being transformed from one state to another, some of it is turned into heat energy that cannot be converted back into useful forms. In other words this universe may be looked upon as a wound up clock that is slowly running down.

These two absolute laws were not fully realized nor established by scientists until around A.D. 1850. Yet there are literally dozens of specific references to these laws in the Word of God.

1. Passages describing the first law (Gen. 2:1-3; Psa. 33:6-9; 102:25; Heb. 4:3, 10)
2. Passages describing the second law (Psa. 102:26; Rom. 8:18-23; Heb. 1:10-12)

It may be furthermore stated that God brought the first law into being after the original creation (see Gen. 1:31) and instituted the second law after man's fall (Gen. 3:17). Finally, it may be said that both laws will be rescinded after the Great White Throne Judgment. "For, behold, I create new heavens and a new earth: and the former shall not be remembered, nor come into mind" (Isa. 65:17). "For as the new heavens and the new earth, which I will make, shall remain before me, saith the LORD, so shall your seed and your name remain" (Isa. 66:22) "Nevertheless we, according to his promise, look for new heavens and a new earth, wherein dwelleth righteousness" (2 Pet. 3:13). (See also Rev. 21:1-5.)

Here then are at least 12 scientific principles accurately described in the Bible, some of them centuries before man discovered them. Not only does the Word of God include that which is scientifically correct, but it also totally avoids the scientific nonsense that is found in all other ancient religious writings.

The Egyptians believed the world was hatched from a great cosmic egg. The egg had wings and flew. This resulted in mitosis. They also believed the sun was a reflection of earth's light, and that man sprang from little white worms they found in the slime and ooze after the overflow of the Nile.

In the sacred Vedas of India we read: "The moon is 50,000 leagues higher than the sun, and shines by its own light; night is caused by the sun's setting behind a huge mountain, several thousand feet high, located in the center of the earth; that this world, flat and triangular is composed of seven states - one of honey, another of sugar, a third of butter, and still another of wine, and the whole mass is borne on the heads of countless elephants which in shaking produce earthquakes."

In the Library of the Louvre in Paris there are three and a half miles of obsolete science books. In 1861 the French Academy of Science published a brochure of 51 "scientific facts" that supposedly contradicted the Bible. These were used by the atheists of that day in ridiculing Christians. Today all 51 of those "facts" are *un*acceptable to modern scientists.

Surely the devout Christian can utter a hearty amen with Dr. James Dwight Dana of Yale University, probably the most eminent geologist in American history, who once addressed a graduating class in these words: "Young men! As you go out into the world to face scientific problems, remember that I, an old man who has known only science all his life long, say to you, that there is nothing t ruer in all the universe than the scientific statements contained in the Word of God!"

V. Fifth Supernatural Element: Its Prophetical Accuracy—One of the acid tests of any religion is its ability to predict the future. In this area (as in all other areas) the Bible reigns supreme. One searches in vain through the pages of other sacred writings to find even a single line of accurate prophecy. Some seven centuries B.C. the Hebrew prophet Isaiah wrote: "Let them . . . shew us what shall happen . . . or declare us things for to come. Shew the things that are to come hereafter, that we may know that ye are gods" (Isa. 41:22-23).

For a detailed listing of both fulfilled and unfulfilled biblical predictions, see the chapter entitled Doctrine of Prophecy in this book.

VI. Sixth Supernatural Element: Its Universal Influence

  A. Upon civilization

    1. Western civilization is founded directly upon the Bible and its teachings—
Its very manner of life had its origin in Acts 16:9, when Paul, obedient to his heavenly vision, directed his second missionary journey toward Europe instead of Asia and the East.

2. The world's calendar and most of its holidays stem from the Bible.
3. It was the Bible that elevated the blood-drinking savages of the British Isles to decency.
4. The Bible has influenced, if not directed, the advancement of all fine arts.
   a. Literature—Ruskin quotes over 5,000 scriptural references in his writings. Milton's greatest works are rooted in the Word of God, as are Shakespeare's and others such as Coleridge, Scott, Pope, Bryant, Longfellow, Kipling, Carlyle, Macaulay, Hawthorne, Irving, Thoreau, and others.
   b. Art—Over 52 world-famous paintings depicting well-known scenes in the Old Testament, along with over 65 in the New Testament are preserved today. These paintings can be found in every important museum on earth. They have been done by the greatest and most talented artists of all time. These would include Leonardo da Vinci, Rembrandt, Raphael, Michelangelo, and others.
   c. Music—The Bible has produced more inspiring music than all other combined books in the world.
      (1) Bach—History has concluded that Johann Sebastian Bach "anticipated every important [musical] idea that has been born since his day. He is the inspiration of the pianist, the organist, and the composer." Bach was a zealous Lutheran who devoted most of his genius to church-centered music.
      (2) Mendelssohn—*St. Paul, Elijah*
      (3) Brahms—*Requiem*
      (4) Beethoven—*Mount of Olives, Samson and Delilah*
      (5) Handel—*Messiah* (he quotes from 15 books of the Bible)
      (6) Haydn—*The Creation*
5. The Bible has produced the law of the Western world—Early attempts of governing forms such as the English common law, the Bill of Rights, the Magna Carta, and our own Constitution are all rooted in God's gift to Moses on Mount Sinai, the Ten Commandments.

B. Upon America
   1. The Bible led to the discovery of our country. According to a written statement from his own pen, Columbus testified it was certain texts in Isaiah that prompted his fateful trip in 1492. He later wrote, "In the Name of the most Holy Trinity who inspired me with the idea and afterwards made it perfectly clear to me that I could go to the Indies from Spain by traversing the ocean westwardly."
   2. It was Bible lovers desiring to read this blessed Book in personal freedom who populated our shores—There were the Puritans in England, the Huguenots in France, the Dunkers in Germany, and the Anabaptists from all over Europe who came here. The Pilgrims came to Plymouth in 1620 because of the Bible.
   3. The charter of every colony includes Bible language.
      a. Salem, Massachussetts—"We covenant with the Lord . . . to walk together in all His ways . . . as He has revealed . . . in His blessed word of truth."
      b. Rhode Island—"We submit . . . to the Lord Jesus Christ, the King of Kings and the Lord of Lords."
      c. Delaware—"For the further propagation of the Holy Gospel."
      d. Maryland—"A pious zeal for extending the Christian religion."

e. Massachusetts—"To the knowledge and obedience of the only true God and the Saviour of mankind."

f. Connecticut—"To preserve the liberty and purity of the Gospel of our Lord Jesus Christ."

As one considers the almost desperate (and often vicious) attacks on God from all American educational and political systems, he is forced to this painful conclusion: The actual establishment of the original 13 colonies would have been strictly prohibited under existing laws today. Thus one atheist owes the very rights she enjoys today in the state of Maryland to those "narrow-minded Puritan bigots" whose love for God and freedom she so passionately hates. It is indeed a strange world.

4. Less than one percent of the total adult population in 1776 were not members of a Protestant church.

5. The American Revolution was produced by the Bible—The Liberty Bell itself bears a scriptural injunction: "proclaim liberty throughout all the land unto the inhabitants thereof" (Lev. 25:10). Even today our most important capitol buildings and monuments display scriptural truths. These include: the Capitol building, the Supreme Court building, the White House, the Library of Congress, the Washington Monument, the Thomas Jefferson Memorial, the Lincoln Memorial, the Tomb of the Unknown Soldier, the Union Station and others. Every single charter of the 50 United States includes the word *God* and other biblical phrases.

6. Our presidents are still sworn into their high office by placing their right hand on an ancient book, *the Bible*.

7. American education has its roots in the Bible—The New England Primer was a Bible primer. In 1642 Massachusetts law required schools to operate. The stated reason was: "It being one chief project of that old deluder Satan to keep men from the knowledge of the Scriptures." Of the ten first colleges in America, nine were founded by churches, and the tenth by evangelist George Whitefield. Ninety-five percent of the colleges and universities in America today were founded by Christian bodies. In 1780 Robert Raikes in England initiated the Sunday school movement, which led to the establishment of the American public school system.

8. Abraham Lincoln's Gettysburg Address was inspired by John Wycliffe's introduction to the New Testament when he wrote, "The Bible is for the government of the people, by the people, and for the people."

9. Julia Ward Howe's great Civil War song "The Battle Hymn of the Republic" was taken from the pages of the Bible. Other patriotic songs are likewise grounded in biblical terms, such as "The Star-Spangled Banner" by Frances Scott Key; "America the Beautiful" by Katherine Lee Bates, and others.

10. American altruism (humanitarianism) has been originated by those people who have loved the message of the Bible—This would include:

a. Reforms in penal systems

b. Reforms in child labor injustices

c. Reforms in mental institutions

d. Creation of mercy organizations such as the Salvation Army, YMCA, YWCA, crippled children's associations, homes for the aged, orphanages, rescue missions, etc. Since our beginning as a nation, we have donated a total of over $50 billion to practically every nation in the world for

the purposes of good will, and in many cases to stave off mass star-
vation.

e. The modern nursing system is taken from Luke 10:30-37, the parable of the
Good Samaritan.

VII. Seventh Supernatural Element: Its Care and Copy

A. No book in history has been copied as many times with as much care as has been
the Word of God. The Talmud lists the following rules for copying the Old Testament:

1. The parchment had to be made from the skin of a clean animal, prepared by a
Jew only, and had to be fastened by strings from clean animals.

2. Each column must have no less than 48 or more than 60 lines.

3. The ink must be of no other color than black, and had to be prepared according
to a special recipe.

4. No word nor letter could be written from memory; the scribe must have an
authentic copy before him, and he had to read and pronounce aloud each word
before writing it.

5. He had to reverently wipe his pen each time before writing the Word of God,
and had to wash his whole body before writing the sacred name of Jehovah.

6. One mistake on a sheet condemned the sheet; if three mistakes were found on
any page, the entire manuscript was condemned.

7. Every word and every letter was counted, and if a letter were omitted, an extra
letter inserted, or if one letter touched another, the manuscript was condemned
and destroyed at once.

The old rabbi gave the solemn warning to each young scribe: "Take heed how thou
dost do thy work, for thy work is the work of heaven; lest thou drop or add a letter
of a manuscript and so become a destroyer of the world!"

The scribe was also told that while he was writing if even a king would enter the
room and speak with him, the scribe was to ignore him until he finished the page he
was working on, lest he make a mistake. In fact, some texts were actually
annotated—that is, each letter was individually counted. Thus in copying the Old
Testament they would note the letter *aleph* (first letter in the Hebrew alphabet)
occurred 42,377 times, and so on.

According to Westcott and Hort, the points in which we cannot be sure of the
original words are microscopic in proportion to the bulk of the whole, some one in
one thousand. Thus only one letter out of 1,580 in the Old Testament is open to
question, and none of these uncertainties would change in the slightest any
doctrinal teaching.

B. Today there are almost 5,000 ancient Greek manuscripts of the New Testament.
This perhaps does not seem like many, until one considers that:

1. Fifteen hundred years after Herodotus wrote his history there was only one
copy in the entire world.

2. Twelve hundred years after Plato wrote his classic there was only one
manuscript.

3. Today there exist but a few manuscripts of Sophocles, Euripedes, Virgil, and
Cicero.

VIII. Eighth Supernatural Element: Its Amazing Circulation—When David Hume said,
"I see the twilight of Christianity and the Bible," he was much confused, for he could
not tell the sunrise from the sunset. Consider the following facts about this amazing
Book:

A. The Bible is now (1991) in 1,946 languages. Eighteen new languages were added alone in 1990.
B. Bible societies are currently working with translators on 406 language projects in which one part of the Bible is being translated for the first time.
C. More than 80 percent of the world's population now has access to at least some portions of the Bible in a language they can speak or understand. A summary of worldwide translations is as follows:

Africa	556
Asia	483
Australia/New Zealand/Pacific Islands	311
Europe	187
North America	69
Mexico/Central & South America	337
Constructed languages	3
Total	1,946

D. Only one-half of one percent of all books published survive seven years—Eighty percent of all books are forgotten in one year. For example, let us imagine that during this year 200 new books are published in America. Statistics show that by next year only 40 of these 200 will remain. At the end of the seventh year, of the original 200, only one lonely book will survive.
E. During the Civil War, the ABS produced 7,000 Bibles a day for both sides—When Grant's armies marched through Tennessee, horse-drawn Bible vans followed. In 1864, the Memphis Bible Society sent a shipment of cotton to New York in return for 50,000 Scripture portions.

What other ancient religious book can even remotely be compared to all this? Where could one go today to purchase a copy of Zen Vedas, or the Egyptian Book of the Dead? In fact, dozens of religions that once flourished have simply disappeared from the face of the earth without leaving the slightest trace. Other ancient religions may be viewed behind glass cases in the rare book section of dusty museums. But the smallest child can walk into almost any dime store in America and pick up a copy of the Word of God.

IX. Ninth Supernatural Element: Its Absolute Honesty—Perhaps no other single statement so completely summarizes the Bible as does the following: "The Bible is not a Book that man *could* write if he *would*, or would write if he could." Let us analyze this one section at a time.

"Man could not write the Bible if he would." Even if a man had all the necessary spirituality, he could not know the facts involved in the historical, scientific, and prophetical statements we have previously already seen in the Bible. Thus, without God's direction the Bible is not a book that man could write if he would.

"Man would not write the Bible if he could." Suppose God would give sinful man all the necessary facts and abilities to write the Bible. What then? Man still *would* not write it correctly if he *could*. Note the following reasons:

A. Because of the bad things God writes about some of his friends—Here five men immediately come to mind. Most of these individuals are mentioned in the Faith Hall of Fame (Hebrews 11).
   1. Noah—Indeed a man of God. He walked with God; he was a just man (Gen. 6:9), and he obeyed God (Heb. 11:7). Yet after the flood this great hero of the faith gets dead drunk and exposes his nakedness and shame to his entire family (Gen. 9:20-24). Surely a mere human author would not have written all this.

2. Moses—The meekest man in all the earth during his time (Num. 12:3), and a leader who single-handedly led an entire nation of enslaved Hebrews out of captivity in Egypt. But en route to Palestine we read of his anger and direct disobedience to the clearly revealed word of God. (See Num. 20:7-12.) Surely man would have eliminated this part of Moses' record.

3. David—Without exception the grandest human king whoever sat upon a throne. God himself would testify that here was a man after his own heart (see 1 Sam. 13:14; 16:7, 12-13). David's fearlessness (1 Sam. 17:34-36, 49), love for God (Psa. 18; 103; etc.), and kindness (1 Sam. 24:6-7) were universally known. But in 2 Samuel 11 this same king is accurately accused of lust, adultery, lying, and cold-blooded murder. Who but God would write in such a manner?

4. Elijah—Few other Old Testament prophets are as colorful and exciting as Elijah the Tishbite. In 1 Kings 18 he champions the cause of God against 450 priests of Satan, but in the very next chapter he is pictured as running for his very life from a mere woman.

5. Peter—self-appointed spokesman for Christ who so confidently assured the Savior that "though all men shall be offended because of thee, yet will I never be offended" (Matt. 26:33). But in the hour of Jesus' great need we read of Peter: "Then began he to curse and to swear, saying, I know not the man" (Matt. 26:74).

B. Because of the good things God writes about some of his enemies—On TV the bad guys wear black hats and never do anything good, while the good guys wear white hats and rarely do anything wrong. But not in the Bible. As we have already seen, on many occasions God records bad things about the white hats, and he often mentions good things about the black hats. This can be seen in the accounts of Esau (Gen. 33), Artaxerxes (Neh. 2), Darius (Dan. 6), Gamaliel (Acts 5:34-39), Julius (Acts 27:1-3), etc.

The point of all the above is simply this—the Bible is *not* an edited book. God literally "tells it like it is." Human authors, however sincere, simply do not consistently write this way.

C. Because of certain doctrines repugnant to the natural mind—Many examples could be listed here, but the following three will demonstrate this:

1. The doctrine of eternal hell (See Rev. 14:10-11.)
2. The doctrine of man's total helplessness (See Eph. 2:8-9; Rom. 7:18.)
3. The doctrine of final judgment upon saved and unsaved (See 1 Cor. 3:9-15; Rev. 20:11-15.)

X. Tenth Supernatural Element: Its Life-Transforming Power—According to an ancient proverb, "The proof of the pudding is in the eating." So it is. Undoubtedly the greatest proof of all that the Bible is indeed God's Word is its amazing ability to change corrupt humanity.

It is said that a socialist once stood on a soapbox in New York and, pointing to an old ragged bum, proudly announced, "Socialism will put a new suit of clothes on that old man there." As he stepped down, a Christian mounted the box and proclaimed, "The Bible will put a new man in that old suit of clothes there."

An atheist once sneeringly asked a new convert the question, "Do you believe Jesus actually turned water into wine?" The convert answered: "Yes, I believe he did! But let me tell you something. For years I was a hopeless drunkard. All my money went for booze. But then God's Word gripped my soul, and I'm here to say that Jesus performed an even greater miracle, for he turned wine into milk for my children!"

A. Examples from among the multiplied millions that could be offered to demonstrate the power of this Book of God.

1. As illustrated by Henry Stanley:

> Why is it that, when Henry Stanley journeyed into the tangled forest of Africa to find David Livingstone, he started out with 180 pounds of books, but as hunger and illness forced the sacrifice of unessentials, he discarded volume after volume until all he had was an edition of Shakespeare, a copy of Carlyle, two treatises on navigation, and the Bible; and concerning these five books he said on his return to the United States, "Poor Shakespeare was afterwards burned up; Carlyle and the navigation books were abandoned by the way, and I had only the Bible left!" During this time, Stanley read his Bible through three times. He is quoted as follows: "During my first attack of African fever, I took up the Bible to while away the tedious hours. I read Job, and then the Psalms. Its powerful verses had a different meaning in the silence of the wilds. I came to feel a strange glow. . . . Alone in my tent I flung myself on my knees and poured out my soul utterly in secret prayer to Him." (Vernon Grounds, *The Reason for Our Hope*, p. 47)

2. As illustrated by Captain Bligh:

> Probably there is no more sensational example of the life-transforming power of the Bible than the unbelievable story of Mutiny on the Bounty. In 1887 the Bounty, under Captain Bligh, set sail for the island of Tahiti in the South Seas. After a voyage of ten months, the ship arrived at her destination, and further six months were spent collecting palm saplings. The sailors meanwhile had become so attached to the native girls that upon receiving the order to embark, mutinied, set the captain and a few men adrift in an open boat, and returned to the island. Captain Bligh, however, survived his ordeal and eventually arrived home in England. A punitive expedition was sent out, which captured 14 of the mutineers. But nine of them had transferred to another island, where they formed a new colony. Here, in the language of the Encyclopedia Britannica, they degenerated so fast and became so fierce as to make the life of the colony a hell on earth. The chief reason for this was the distillation of whiskey from a native plant. Quarrels, orgies, and murders were a common feature of their life. Finally all the men except one were killed or had died off. Alexander Smith was left alone with a crowd of native women and half-breed children. Then a strange thing happened. In a battered chest, he found a Bible. He read it, believed it, and began to live it. Determining to make amends for his past evil life, he gathered the women and children around him and taught them too. Time rolled on. The children grew up and became Christians. The community prospered exceedingly. Nearly 20 years later an American ship visited the island and brought back to Europe and England word of its peaceful state. The British government took no further action. There was no need. The island was a Christian community. There was no disease, no insanity, no crime, and no illiteracy, and no strong drink. Life and property were safe, and the

moral standards of the people were as high as anywhere in the world. It was a veritable Utopia on a small scale. What had brought about this astounding transformation? Just the reading of a book, and that book was the Bible. (Ibid., p. 89)

3. As illustrated by Billy Graham:

   Among the many thousands of conversions in the London Crusade were those of a medical doctor and the man who sat next to him in the arena. Before the service began, the two strangers engaged in conversation, criticizing the campaign and expressing the utmost skepticism. As Graham preached, throwing out one truth of Scripture after another, the doctor was gripped by an unseen power. When the invitation was given, he said to the man next to him. "I don't know about you, but I'm going forward to receive Christ." The other hesitated a moment, then reached into his pocket and replied, "I'm going too, and here's your wallet. I'm a pickpocket." (G. M. Day, *The Wonder of the Word*, p. 28)

4. As illustrated by Captain Mitsuo Fuchida:

   When Captain Mitsuo Fuchida, the Japanese squadron commander who led the air raid on Pearl Harbor in 1941, and Jacob DeShazer, one of the famed Doolittle flyers who participated in the bombing of Tokyo in 1942, sat on a platform together in a Christian evangelistic meetings in Japan they created a great sensation. And so they should! Bitter national enemies who had delighted in sending fiery death and destruction to each other, were united in a tremendous cooperative effort for Christian evangelism. (Ibid., p. 30)

5. As illustrated by Augustine—"Shortly after his new birth experience, Augustine met a prostitute on the street. Pretending not to see her, he attempted to pass by without recognition, but she called, 'Augustine, it is I.' He turned to her then and answered, 'Yes, but it is not I!'" (Ibid., p. 34).

6. As illustrated by Sir Walter Scott—There is not a more familiar story in the annals of literature than the story that describes the death of the immortal Scot poet and novelist, Sir Walter Scott. As he lay dying he turned to his son-in-law, Lockhart, and said to him, "Son, bring me the Book." There was a vast library in Walter Scott's home and bewildered, the son-in-law said, "Sir, what book?" "Which book?" The dying bard replied, "My son, there is just one Book. Bring me the Book." It is then that Lockhart went to the library and brought to Sir Walter Scott the Bible.

   "There's just one book," cried the dying sage,
   "Read me the old, old story."
   And the winged words that can never age
   Wafted him home to glory.
   There's just one Book.
   There's just one book for the tender years,
   One book of love's own guiding,
   —The little feet through the joys and fears,
   The unknown days are hiding
   There's just one Book!
   There's just one book for the bridal hour,

> *One book of love's own coining,*
> *Its truths alone lend beauty and power,*
> *To vows that lives are joining.*
> *There's just one Book!*
>
> *There's just one book for life's gladness,*
> *One book for the toilsome days.*
> *One book that can cure life's madness,*
> *One book that can voice life's praise.*
> *There's just one Book!*
> *There's just one book for the dying,*
> *One book for the starting tears,*
> *And one for the soul that is going home,*
> *For the measureless years.*
> *There's just one Book!* (W. A. Criswell, The Bible for Today's World, *p. 25*)

7. As illustrated by the Apostle Paul—According to his own testimony, Paul was the "chief of sinners" (1 Tim. 1:13). To show this was no empty claim, Paul sadly relates his pre-Christian sinful activities:
   a. He took care of the coats of Stephen's murderers as they stoned him (Acts 7:58).
   b. He arrested Christians and threw them into prison (Acts 8:3; 22:4).
   c. He beat Christians (Acts 22:19).
   d. He compelled them to use abusive language (Acts 26:11).
   e. He persecuted them unto death (Acts 22:4).
   f. He attempted to destroy the Christian faith (Gal. 1:23).
   g. He wasted the church of God and made havoc of it (Gal. 1:13; Acts 8:3). This word *havoc* occurs but once here in the Greek New Testament and refers to a wild boar which charges into a vineyard and viciously uproots it. But then this ravaging wolf heard the voice of the Shepherd and became one of God's best sheepdogs.

B. Examples of those who have refused the power of this Book of God—Most Americans are aware of the perverted poison of the notorious atheist Madalyn Murray O'Hair. This person, like most atheists, finds a fiendish glee in ridiculing Christians and the Christian faith. "That pie-in-the-sky is a great big lie!" they sneer. But what do they offer in place of Christ and the Bible? The following statements come from the mouths of various atheists:
   1. Byron—"Count o'er the joys thine hours have seen,/Count o'er thy days from anguish free,/And know, whatever thou hast been,/Tis something better not to be."
   2. Ingersoll—"For, whether in mid-sea or among the breakers of the farther shore, a wreck must mark at last the end of each and all. And every life, no matter if its every hour is rich with love and every moment jeweled with a joy, will, at its close, become a tragedy, as sad, and deep, and dark as can be woven of the warp and woof of mystery and death. Life is a narrow vale between the cold and barren peaks of two eternities. We strive in vain to look beyond the heights. We cry aloud, and the only answer is the echo of our wailing cry. From the voiceless lips of the unreplying dead there comes no word."
   3. Strauss—"In the enormous machine of the universe, amid wheel and hiss of its jagged iron wheels, amid the deafening clash of its stamps and hammers, in the

midst of this whole terrific commotion, man finds himself placed with no security for a moment, that a wheel might not seize and render him, or a hammer crash him to pieces."

4. Anatole France—"'In all the world the unhappiest creature is man.' He takes my hands in his and his are trembling and feverish. He looks me in the eyes. His are full of tears. His face is haggard. He sighs: 'There is not in all the universe a creature more unhappy than I. People think me happy. I have never been happy for one day, not for a single hour.'"

5. Bertrand Russell—"The life of Man is a long march through the night, surrounded by invisible foes, tortured by weariness and pain, towards a goal that few can hope to reach, and where none may tarry long."

6. Mark Twain—"A myriad of men are born; they scramble for little mean advantages over each other; age creeps upon them and infirmities follow; shame and humiliations bring down their prides and vanities. Those they love are taken from them and the joy of life is turned into aching grief. The burden of pain, care, misery, grows heavier year by year. At length ambition is dead, pride is dead, vanity is dead; longing for release is in their place. It comes at last—the only unpoisoned gift earth ever had for them—and they vanish from a world where they were of no consequence, where they left no sign that they have existed—a world that will lament them for a day and forget them forever."

7. Schopenhauer—"Life is necessarily and hopelessly wretched. To live is to desire, to desire is to want, to want is to suffer, and hence to live is to suffer. No man is happy except when drunk or deluded; his happiness is only like that of a beggar who dreams that he is a king. Nothing is worth the trouble which it costs us. Wretchedness always outweighs felicity. The history of man is a long, confused, and painful dream."

8. Charles Darwin—"I have everything to make me happy and contented, but life has become very wearisome to me."

9. Teller—"As the sun loses weight at the rate of more than four million tons a second, its gravitational hold is rapidly decreasing, and we are each year headed, in an ever-increasing spiral course, toward the great, yawning abyss beyond. While there is no immediate danger of our being swept into oblivion, the time will arrive when all earthly things will be doomed to perish, when the earth will be too cold to sustain life, and the finest of human thoughts will have been lost forever. Then our earth, like all things else, will have joined the billions of lifeless globes" (James Bales, *Atheism's Faith and Fruits*, pp. 72, 76, 80).

Thus is life without the God of the Bible.

As we conclude this section, the words of the familiar song come to mind:

> *The B-I-B-L-E! Yes, that's the book for me!*
> *I stand alone on the Word of God—*
> *The B-I-B-L-E!*

PART SIXTEEN: THE PURPOSE OF THE BIBLE
   I. The Bible and the Sovereign God
      A. It was written to give us the twofold account of God's labor.
         1. As defined—Everything that God has done, is doing, or shall do can be placed under one of two categories, his work in creation and his work in redemption.

2. As described—There are two special days, four special chapters, and nine special feasts that remind us of God's great labor in creation and redemption.
   a. Two special days
     (1) Saturday, reminding us of his work in creation—"Remember the sabbath day, to keep it holy. Six days shalt thou labour, and do all thy work: But the seventh day is the sabbath of the LORD thy God: in it thou shalt not do any work, thou, nor thy son, nor thy daughter, thy manservant, nor thy maidservant, nor thy cattle, nor thy stranger that is within thy gates: For in six days the LORD made heaven and earth, the sea, and all that in them is, and rested the seventh day: wherefore the LORD blessed the sabbath day, and hallowed it" (Exod. 20:8-11).
     (2) Sunday, reminding us of his work in redemption—"In the end of the sabbath, as it began to dawn toward the first day of the week, came Mary Magdalene and the other Mary to see the sepulchre. And, behold, there was a great earthquake: for the angel of the Lord descended from heaven, and came and rolled back the stone from the door, and sat upon it. His countenance was like lightning, and his raiment white as snow: And for fear of him the keepers did shake, and became as dead men. And the angel answered and said unto the women, Fear not ye: for I know that ye seek Jesus, which was crucified. He is not here: for he is risen, as he said. Come, see the place where the Lord lay" (Matt. 28:1-6).
   b. Four special chapters
     (1) Genesis 1—The account of man being made in the image of God. This speaks of Creation. "And God said, Let us make man in our image, after our likeness: and let them have dominion over the fish of the sea, and over the fowl of the air, and over the cattle, and over all the earth, and over every creeping thing that creepeth upon the earth" (Gen. 1:26).
     (2) Luke 2—The account of God being made in the image of man. This speaks of redemption. "And she brought forth her firstborn son, and wrapped him in swaddling clothes, and laid him in a manger; because there was no room for them in the inn" (Luke 2:7).
     (3) Revelation 4—The account of heaven thanking God for his first great work. "Thou art worthy, O Lord, to receive glory and honour and power: for thou hast created all things, and for thy pleasure they are and were created" (Rev. 4:11).
     (4) Revelation 5—The account of heaven thanking God for his final great work. "And they sung a new song, saying, Thou art worthy to take the book, and to open the seals thereof: for thou wast slain, and hast redeemed us to God by thy blood out of every kindred, and tongue, and people, and nation" (Rev. 5:9).
   c. Nine special feasts—His creative work, as seen by:
     (1) The weekly Sabbath (Exod. 20:8-11; Lev. 23:1-3)
     (2) The seven-year Sabbath feast (Exod. 23:10-11; Lev. 25:2-7)
     (3) The fiftieth year Sabbath feast (Lev. 25:8-16)
   His redemptive work, as seen by:
     (4) The Passover feast (Lev. 23:4-8)—This speaks of Calvary (1 Cor. 5:7).
     (5) The Feast of Firstfruits (Lev. 23:9-14)—This speaks of the Resurrection (1 Cor. 15:23).

(6) The Feast of Pentecost (Lev. 23:15-25)—This speaks of the coming of the Holy Spirit (Acts 2:1).

(7) The Feast of Trumpets (Lev. 23:23-25)—This speaks of the Rapture and Second Coming (1 Thess. 4:13-18; Rev. 11:15).

(8) The Day of Atonement feast (Lev. 23:26-32)—This speaks of the Tribulation (Rev. 6-19).

(9) The Feast of Tabernacles (Lev. 23:33-44)—This speaks of the Millennium (Rev. 20:1-6).

B. It was written to give us the fivefold account of God's Lamb.

1. The Old Testament records the preparation for the life of Jesus.

a. That we might be aware of his coming—"And beginning at Moses and all the prophets, he expounded unto them in all the scriptures the things concerning himself" (Luke 24:27). "Search the scriptures; for in them ye think ye have eternal life: and they are they which testify of me" (John 5:39).

b. That we might be assured by his coming—"For whatsoever things were written aforetime were written for our learning, that we through patience and comfort of the scriptures might have hope" (Rom. 15:4). "Now all these things happened unto them for ensamples: and they are written for our admonition, upon whom the ends of the world are come" (1 Cor. 10:11).

2. The Gospels record the manifestation of the life of Jesus.

a. The fact of his birth (Luke 2:1-20)

b. The fact of his death (Matt. 27; Mark 15; Luke 23; John 19)

c. The fact of his resurrection (Matt. 28; Mark 16; Luke 24; John 20)

d. The fact of his ascension (Mark 16:19; Luke 24:51)

3. The book of Acts records the propagation of the life of Jesus.

a. The origin of the church (Acts 2:1-13)

b. The obedience of the (early) church

(1) Its message—"And daily in the temple, and in every house, they ceased not to teach and preach Jesus Christ" (Acts 5:42).

(2) Its ministers—Serving in Jerusalem, Judea, and Samaria were Peter, James the half-brother of Christ, John, Philip and Stephen (Acts 1-12).

(3) Its missionaries—Serving throughout the known world were Paul, Barnabas, Timothy, Luke, Titus, and Silas (Acts 13-28).

4. The Epistles record the interpretation of the life of Jesus.

a. The reason for his birth—"This is a faithful saying, and worthy of all acceptation, that Christ Jesus came into the world to save sinners; of whom I am chief" (1 Tim. 1:15). "For it is not possible that the blood of bulls and of goats should take away sins. Wherefore when he cometh into the world, he saith, Sacrifice and offering thou wouldest not, but a body hast thou prepared me: In burnt offerings and sacrifices for sin thou hast had no pleasure. Then said I, Lo, I come (in the volume of the book it is written of me,) to do thy will, O God" (Heb. 10:4-7).

b. The reason for his death—"Who was delivered for our offenses" (Rom. 4:25a). "But God commendeth his love toward us, in that, while we were yet sinners, Christ died for us. Much more then, being now justified by his blood, we shall be saved from wrath through him" (Rom. 5:8-9). "Forasmuch then as the children are partakers of flesh and blood, he also himself likewise took part of the same; that through death he might destroy him that had the power of death, that is, the devil; and deliver them who through fear of death were all their lifetime subject to bondage" (Heb. 2:14-15).

c. The reason for his resurrection—"and was raised again for our justification" (Rom. 4:25b). "But now is Christ risen from the dead, and become the firstfruits of them that slept" (1 Cor. 15:20).

d. The reason for his ascension—"Who is he that condemneth? It is Christ that died, yea rather, that is risen again, who is even at the right hand of God, who also maketh intercession for us" (Rom. 8:34). "Seeing then that we have a great high priest, that is passed into the heavens, Jesus the Son of God, let us hold fast our profession. For we have not an high priest which cannot be touched with the feeling of our infirmities; but was in all points tempted like as we are, yet without sin. Let us therefore come boldly unto the throne of grace, that we may obtain mercy, and find grace to help in time of need" (Heb. 4:14-16). "For Christ is not entered into the holy places made with hands, which are the figures of the true; but into heaven itself, now to appear in the presence of God for us" (Heb. 9:24).

5. The book of Revelation records the coronation of the eternal Jesus—"And the seventh angel sounded; and there were great voices in heaven, saying, The kingdoms of this world are become the kingdoms of our Lord, and of his Christ; and he shall reign for ever and ever" (Rev. 11:15). "And I saw heaven opened, and behold a white horse; and he that sat upon him was called Faithful and True, and in righteousness he doth judge and make war. . . . And he hath on his vesture and on his thigh a name written, KING OF KINGS, AND LORD OF LORDS" (Rev. 19:11, 16).

a. Revelation 1–3: The witnesses of the Lamb—"The mystery of the seven stars which thou sawest in my right hand, and the seven golden candlesticks. The seven stars are the angels of the seven churches: and the seven candlesticks which thou sawest are the seven churches" (Rev. 1:20).

b. Revelation 4–5: The worship of the Lamb—"And the four beasts had each of them six wings about him; and they were full of eyes within: and they rest not day and night, saying, Holy, holy, holy, Lord God Almighty, which was, and is, and is to come" (Rev. 4:8).

"And I beheld, and I heard the voice of many angels round about the throne and the beasts and the elders: and the number of them was ten thousand times ten thousand, and thousands of thousands; saying with a loud voice, Worthy is the Lamb that was slain to receive power, and riches, and wisdom, and strength, and honour, and glory, and blessing. And every creature which is in heaven, and on the earth, and under the earth, and such as are in the sea, and all that are in them, heard I saying, Blessing, and honour, and glory, and power, be unto him that sitteth upon the throne, and unto the Lamb for ever and ever. And the four beasts said, Amen. And the four and twenty elders fell down and worshipped him that liveth for ever and ever" (Rev. 5:11-14).

c. Revelation 6–19: The wrath of the Lamb—"And the stars of heaven fell unto the earth, even as a fig tree casteth her untimely figs, when she is shaken of a mighty wind. And the heaven departed as a scroll when it is rolled together; and every mountain and island were moved out of their places. And the kings of the earth, and the great men, and the rich men, and the chief captains, and the mighty men, and every bondman, and every free man, hid themselves in the dens and in the rocks of the mountains; and said to the mountains and rocks, Fall on us, and hide us from the face of him that sitteth on the throne, and from the wrath of the Lamb: for the great day of his wrath is come; and who shall be able to stand?" (Rev. 6:13-17).

    d. Revelation 20: The wonder of the Lamb's reign—"And I saw thrones, and they sat upon them, and judgment was given unto them: and I saw the souls of them that were beheaded for the witness of Jesus, and for the word of God, and which had not worshipped the beast, neither his image, neither had received his mark upon their foreheads, or in their hands; and they lived and reigned with Christ a thousand years" (Rev. 20:4).

    e. Revelation 21–22: The wife of the Lamb—"And there came unto me one of the seven angels which had the seven vials full of the seven last plagues, and talked with me, saying, Come hither, I will shew thee the bride, the Lamb's wife. And he carried me away in the spirit to a great and high mountain, and shewed me that great city, the holy Jerusalem, descending out of heaven from God, having the glory of God: and her light was like unto a stone most precious, even like a jasper stone, clear as crystal" (Rev. 21:9-11).

II. The Bible and the Saints of God

  A. What the Bible does for the believer

    1. It upholds (Psa. 119:116).
    2. It orders steps (Psa. 119:133).
    3. It produces joy (Psa. 119:162).
    4. It strengthens (Psa. 119:28; 1 John 2:14).
    5. It gives hope (Psa. 119:74, 81).
    6. It gives light (Psa. 119:105, 130).
    7. It gives understanding (Psa. 119:169).
    8. It shows God's will (Isa. 55:11).
    9. It builds up (Acts 20:32).
   10. It produces fruit (John 15:7).
   11. It convicts of sin (Heb. 4:12).
   12. It converts the soul (James 1:18; 1 Pet. 1:23).
   13. It cleanses the conscience (John 15:3).
   14. It consecrates life (John 17:17).
   15. It corrects the wrong (2 Tim. 3:16).
   16. It confirms the right (John 8:31).
   17. It comforts the heart (Psa. 119:50, 54).

  B. What the Bible demands from the believer—Because of the above, the Christian is exhorted to:

    1. Read it (Col. 3:16; Deut. 31:11; Rev. 1:3; Isa. 34:16; Luke 4:16; Eph. 3:4; 1 Thess. 5:27; 2 Tim. 4:13; Col. 4:1).
    2. Heed it (Psa. 119:9; 1 Tim. 4:16).
    3. Seed it (Matt. 28:19-20).
    4. Desire it (1 Pet. 2:2).
    5. Preach it (2 Tim. 4:2).
    6. Rightly divide it (2 Tim. 2:15).
    7. Live by it (Matt. 4:4).
    8. Use it (Eph. 6:17).
    9. Suffer for it, and if need be, die for it (Rev. 1:9; 6:9; 20:4).

The child of God is to *know* it in his head, *stow* it in his heart, *show* it in his life, and *sow* it in the world. See also the following Scriptures: Deuteronomy 4:1-10; 12:32; Joshua 1:8; Psalm 33:6; Proverbs 30:5-6; Mark 4:24; Luke 8:12; John 12:48-50; Romans 8:7; 1 Corinthians 2:14; Hebrews 1:1-3; 2:1-4; Revelation 1:1-3; 20:12; 22:18-19.

Thus the authority of God's Word is as a *stethoscope,* for it probes within, as a *microscope,* for it looks upon, and as a *telescope,* for it sees beyond.

Perhaps the grandest and most conclusive description of the Bible was penned by the Apostle Paul in a letter to a young pastor. Here he wrote: "And that from a child thou hast known the holy scriptures, which are able to make thee wise unto salvation through faith which is in Christ Jesus. All scripture is given by inspiration of God, and is profitable for doctrine, for reproof, for correction, for instruction in righteousness: That the man of God may be perfect, thoroughly furnished unto all good works" (2 Tim. 3:15-17).

In this remarkable passage Paul claims the Bible is profitable:

1. For doctrine—That is, it may be used as the perfect textbook to present the systematic teachings of the great truths relating to God himself.
2. For reproof—That is, the Bible is to be used to convict us of the wrong in our lives.
3. For correction—That is, it will then show us the right way.
4. For instruction in righteousness—That is, God's Word provides all the necessary details that will allow a Christian to become fully equipped for every good work.

THE DOCTRINE OF THE FATHER

INTRODUCTION
Imagine yourself among a group of Christians who have been given a biblical test with but three essay questions on it. Here are the questions:

Number one: Put down everything you know about the person and work of Jesus Christ, the Second Person in the Trinity. (Probably most of the group could fill several pages of material about the Savior in a reasonable amount of time. So far, so good!)

Number two: Put down everything you know about the person and work of the Holy Spirit, the Third Person in the Trinity. (Now the pens do not move as rapidly or as confidently as before. There are long pauses between sentences. At the end of the given time period the average believer has probably written at least half a page or more.)

Number three: Put down everything you know about the person and work of the God the Father, the First Person in the Trinity. (Oh, how silent the room now becomes! Finally, one statement is written: "He is the Father of Jesus Christ." But what can be added to this? It is my opinion that precious few in that group of Christians would be able to write even half a dozen lines about the Father.)

This all but universal ignorance about the Father is inexcusable because of the number of *references* and the various *relationships* ascribed to him!

I. The References Involved
  A. He is referred to as Father on 271 occasions in the Scriptures.
    1. 13 times in the Old Testament
    2. 258 times in the New Testament
      a. 178 times in the Gospels
      b. 80 times from Acts through Revelation
  B. He is mentioned by the title *Father* in six Old Testament books (2 Samuel, 1 Chronicles, Psalms, Isaiah, Jeremiah, Malachi) and in every New Testament book, with the single exception of 3 John.
    1. The Old Testament first and final references
      a. First: 2 Samuel 7:14
      b. Final: Malachi 1:6
    2. The New Testament first and final references
      a. First: Matthew 5:16
      b. Final: Revelation 14:1
  C. Jesus refers to him as "Father" on all but 2 of the 178 occasions in the Gospels. The two exceptions are John 13:1, 3. He mentions him:
    1. 17 times during the Sermon on the Mount (Matt. 5–7)
    2. 22 times in the Upper Room (John 13–14)
    3. 22 times during his final discourse (John 15–16)

4. 6 times during his great high priestly prayer (John 17)

D. Our Lord began and concluded his ministry by referring to the Father.

    1. The beginning, in the temple of Herod—"And he said unto them, How is it that ye sought me? wist ye not that I must be about my Father's business?" (Luke 2:49).

    2. The concluding, on the Mount of Olives—"And, behold, I send the promise of my Father upon you: but tarry ye in the city of Jerusalem, until ye be endued with power from on high" (Luke 24:49).

E. Jesus began and concluded his Calvary experience by praying to the Father.

    1. His first statement—"Then said Jesus, Father, forgive them; for they know not what they do. And they parted his raiment, and cast lots" (Luke 23:34).

    2. His final statement—"And when Jesus had cried with a loud voice, he said, Father, into thy hands I commend my spirit: and having said thus, he gave up the ghost" (Luke 23:46).

F. Jesus revealed basic facts concerning the nature of the Father.

    1. He is Spirit (John 4:24).

    2. He is invisible (John 1:18; 6:46).

       Question: Will we see the Father in heaven? There are two passages that seem to suggest we will (see Dan. 7:9-10; Rev. 4:2-3).

    3. He is perfect (Matt. 5:48).

    4. He is omnipotent (Matt. 19:26).

    5. He is omniscient (Matt. 10:29-30).

    6. He is holy (John 17:11).

    7. He is righteous (John 17:25).

    8. He is loving (John 3:16; 17:23).

    9. He is good (Matt. 6:26, 28-30).

II. The Relationships Involved

A. The Father and Creation—"For with thee is the fountain of life: in thy light shall we see light" (Psa. 36:9). "For as the Father hath life in himself; so hath he given to the Son to have life in himself" (John 5:26). "God that made the world and all things therein, seeing that he is Lord of heaven and earth, dwelleth not in temples made with hands; neither is worshipped with men's hands, as though he needed any thing, seeing he giveth to all life, and breath, and all things" (Acts 17:24-25). "This I say therefore, and testify in the Lord, that ye henceforth walk not as other Gentiles walk, in the vanity of their mind, having the understanding darkened, being alienated from the life of God through the ignorance that is in them, because of the blindness of their heart" (Eph. 4:17-18). "The heavens declare the glory of God; and the firmament sheweth his handiwork" (Psa. 19:1). "Praise ye him, all his angels: praise ye him, all his hosts. Praise ye him, sun and moon: praise him, all ye stars of light. Praise him, ye heavens of heavens, and ye waters that be above the heavens. Let them praise the name of the LORD: for he commanded, and they were created" (Psa. 148:2-5).

    1. He tends and cares for vegetation—"He causeth the grass to grow for the cattle, and herb for the service of man: that he may bring forth food out of the earth . . . the trees of the LORD are full of sap; the cedars of Lebanon, which he hath planted" (Psa. 104:14, 16). "And why take ye thought for raiment? Consider the lilies of the field, how they grow; they toil not, neither do they spin: and yet I say unto you, That even Solomon in all his glory was not arrayed like one of these. Wherefore, if God so clothe the grass of the field, which to day is, and to

morrow is cast into the oven, shall he not much more clothe you, O ye of little faith?" (Matt. 6:28-30).
2. He tends and cares for brute nature—"He causeth the grass to grow for the cattle, and herb for the service of man: that he may bring forth food out of the earth. . . . The trees of the LORD are full of sap; the cedars of Lebanon, which he hath planted; where the birds make their nests: as for the stork, the fir trees are her house. The high hills are a refuge for the wild goats; and the rocks for the conies. . . . Thou makest darkness, and it is night: wherein all the beasts of the forest do creep forth. The young lions roar after their prey, and seek their meat from God. . . . These wait all upon thee; that thou mayest give them their meat in due season" (Psa. 104:14, 16-18, 20-21, 27). "Behold the fowls of the air: for they sow not, neither do they reap, nor gather into barns; yet your heavenly Father feedeth them. Are ye not much better than they?" (Matt. 6:26). "Are not two sparrows sold for a farthing? and one of them shall not fall on the ground without your Father" (Matt. 10:29).
3. He tends and cares for the weather—"Whatsoever the LORD pleased, that did he in heaven, and in earth, in the seas, and all deep places. He causeth the vapours to ascend from the ends of the earth; he maketh lightnings for the rain; he bringeth the wind out of his treasuries" (Psa. 135:6-7). "Who covereth the heaven with clouds, who prepareth rain for the earth, who maketh grass to grow upon the mountains. . . . He giveth snow like wool: he scattereth the hoarfrost like ashes. He casteth forth his ice like morsels: who can stand before his cold? He sendeth out his word, and melteth them: he causeth his wind to blow, and the waters flow" (Psa. 147:8, 16-18). "Fire, and hail; snow, and vapour; stormy wind fulfilling his word" (Psa. 148:8).
4. He tends and cares for the seasons—"While the earth remaineth, seedtime and harvest, and cold and heat, and summer and winter, and day and night shall not cease" (Gen. 8:22). "Nevertheless he left not himself without witness, in that he did good, and gave us rain from heaven, and fruitful seasons, filling our hearts with food and gladness" (Acts 14:17).

B. The Father and Angels
1. They worship and minister to him—"I beheld till the thrones were cast down, and the Ancient of days did sit, whose garment was white as snow, and the hair of his head like the pure wool: his throne was like the fiery flame, and his wheels as burning fire. A fiery stream issued and came forth from before him: thousand thousands ministered unto him, and ten thousand times ten thousand stood before him: the judgment was set, and the books were opened" (Dan. 7:9-10). "And immediately I was in the spirit: and, behold, a throne was set in heaven, and one sat on the throne. And he that sat was to look upon like a jasper and a sardine stone: and there was a rainbow roundabout the throne, in sight like unto an emerald. . . . The four and twenty elders fall down before him that sat on the throne, and worship him that liveth for ever and ever, and cast their crowns before the throne, saying, Thou art worthy, O Lord, to receive glory and honour and power: for thou hast created all things, and for thy pleasure they are and were created" (Rev. 4:2-3, 10-11).
2. He commanded them to worship the babe at Bethlehem—"And again, when he bringeth in the first begotten into the world, he saith, And let all the angels of God worship him" (Heb. 1:6).
3. He controls their activities—"The chariots of God are twenty thousand, even

thousands of angels: the Lord is among them, as in Sinai, in the holy place" (Psa. 68:17). "Thinkest thou that I cannot now pray to my Father, and he shall presently give me more than twelve legions of angels?" (Matt. 26:53).

4. He sent them to aid believers—"Are they not all ministering spirits, sent forth to minister for them who shall be heirs of salvation?" (Heb. 1:14).

C. The Father and Israel

1. He is viewed as the source and strength of Israel's very existence—"Wherefore David blessed the LORD before all the congregation: and David said, Blessed be thou, LORD God of Israel our father, for ever and ever. Thine, O LORD, is the greatness, and the power, and the glory, and the victory, and the majesty: for all that is in the heaven and in the earth is thine; thine is the kingdom, O LORD, and thou art exalted as head above all. Both riches and honour come of thee, and thou reignest over all; and in thine hand is power and might; and in thine hand it is to make great, and to give strength unto all" (1 Chron. 29:10-12).

2. He is the potter, and Israel is the clay—"But now, O LORD, thou art our father; we are the clay, and thou our potter; and we all are the work of thy hand" (Isa. 64:8).

3. He is Israel's eternal Redeemer—"Doubtless thou art our father, though Abraham be ignorant of us, and Israel acknowledge us not: thou, O LORD, art our father, our redeemer; thy name is from everlasting" (Isa. 63:16).

4. He dearly loves Israel—"Like as a father pitieth his children, so the LORD pitieth them that fear him" (Psa. 103:13).

5. He protects her widows and orphans—"A father of the fatherless, and a judge of the widows, is God in his holy habitation" (Psa. 68:5).

6. He had a special relationship with Israel's most beloved king, David (2 Sam. 7:4-17; 1 Chron. 17:3-15; Psa. 89:20-37)—"I have found David my servant; with my holy oil have I anointed him. . . . But my faithfulness and my mercy shall be with him: and in my name shall his horn be exalted. . . . He shall cry unto me, Thou art my father, my God, and the rock of my salvation. . . . His seed shall endure for ever, and his throne as the sun before me" (Psa. 89:20, 24, 26, 36).

7. He received, however, no respect or honor from Israel (Mal. 1:6; 2:10).

8. In fact, he described himself as the faithful husband married to an unfaithful wife—"Surely as a wife treacherously departeth from her husband, so have ye dealt treacherously with me, O house of Israel, saith the LORD" (Jer. 3:20).

9. He anticipates the day when Israel will acknowledge him as Father (Jer. 3:19).

10. He then will forgive and restore his erring children—"They shall come with weeping, and with supplications will I lead them: I will cause them to walk by the rivers of waters in a straight way, wherein they shall not stumble: for I am a father to Israel, and Ephraim is my firstborn" (Jer. 31:9).

D. The Father and Our Lord Jesus Christ

1. The Father sent his Son—"Then said Jesus to them again, Peace be unto you: as my Father hath sent me, even so send I you" (John 20:21). "As the living Father hath sent me, and I live by the Father" (John 6:57a). "The Father that sent me beareth witness of me" (John 8:18b). "But when the fulness of the time was come, God sent forth his Son, made of a woman" (Gal. 4:4). "And we have seen and do testify that the Father sent the Son to be the Savior of the world" (1 John 4:14). "For God so loved the world, that he gave his only begotten Son, that whosoever believeth in him should not perish, but have everlasting life" (John 3:16). "And yet if I judge, my judgment is true: for I am not alone, but I and the

Father that sent me" (John 8:16). "For I have not spoken of myself; but the Father which sent me, he gave me a commandment, what I should say, and what I should speak" (John 12:49).

2. The Father commanded the angels to worship his Son—"And again, when he bringeth in the first begotten into the world, he saith, And let all the angels of God worship him" (Heb. 1:6). (See also Luke 2:8-15.)

3. He sealed his Son—"Labour not for the meat which perisheth, but for that meat which endureth unto everlasting life, which the Son of man shall give unto you: for him hath God the Father sealed" (John 6:27).

4. He honored (and honors) his Son—"Jesus answered, If I honour myself, my honour is nothing: it is my Father that honoureth me; of whom ye say, that he is your God" (John 8:54).

5. He bore witness to his Son—"The Father that sent me beareth witness of me" (John 8:18b).

6. He loved (and loves) his Son—"Therefore doth my Father love me, because I lay down my life, that I might take it again" (John 10:17).

7. He glorified his Son—"Now is my soul troubled; and what shall I say? Father, save me from this hour: but for this cause came I unto this hour. Father, glorify thy name. Then came there a voice from heaven, saying, I have both glorified it, and will glorify it again" (John 12:27-28). "These words spake Jesus, and lifted up his eyes to heaven, and said, Father, the hour is come; glorify thy Son, that thy Son also may glorify thee. . . . And now, O Father, glorify thou me with thine own self with the glory which I had with thee before the world was" (John 17:1, 5).

8. He taught his Son—"Then said Jesus unto them, When ye have lifted up the Son of man, then shall ye know that I am he, and that I do nothing of myself; but as my Father hath taught me, I speak these things" (John 8:28).

9. He anointed his Son—"And he came to Nazareth, where he had been brought up: and, as his custom was, he went into the synagogue on the sabbath day, and stood up for to read. And there was delivered unto him the book of the prophet Esaias. And when he had opened the book, he found the place where it was written, The Spirit of the Lord is upon me, because he hath anointed me to preach the gospel to the poor; he hath sent me to heal the brokenhearted, to preach deliverance to the captives, and recovering of sight to the blind, to set at liberty them that are bruised, to preach the acceptable year of the Lord. And he closed the book, and he gave it again to the minister, and sat down. And the eyes of all them that were in the synagogue were fastened on him. And he began to say unto them, This day is this scripture fulfilled in your ears" (Luke 4:16-21). "For he whom God hath sent speaketh the words of God: for God giveth not the Spirit by measure unto him" (John 3:34).

10. He delighted in his Son—"Behold my servant, whom I uphold; mine elect, in whom my soul delighteth; I have put my spirit upon him: he shall bring forth judgment to the Gentiles" (Isa. 42:1). "And lo a voice from heaven, saying, This is my beloved Son, in whom I am well pleased" (Matt. 3:17). "While he yet spake, behold, a bright cloud overshadowed them: and behold a voice out of the cloud, which said, This is my beloved Son, in whom I am well pleased; hear ye him" (Matt. 17:5). "For he received from God the Father honour and glory, when there came such a voice to him from the excellent glory, This is my beloved Son, in whom I am well pleased" (2 Pet. 1:17).

11. He listened to his Son—"Then they took away the stone from the place where the dead was laid. And Jesus lifted up his eyes, and said, Father, I thank thee that thou hast heard me. And I knew that thou hearest me always: but because of the people which stand by I said it, that they may believe that thou hast sent me" (John 11:41-42). "Then said Jesus unto him, Put up again thy sword into his place: for all they that take the sword shall perish with the sword. Thinkest thou that I cannot now pray to my Father, and he shall presently give me more than twelve legions of angels?" (Matt. 26:52-53). (See also John 12:27-28.)

12. He offered his Son—"Then said Jesus unto Peter, Put up thy sword into the sheath: the cup which my Father hath given me, shall I not drink it?" (John 18:11). "He that spared not his own Son, but delivered him up for us all, how shall he not with him also freely give us all things?" (Rom. 8:32). "In this was manifested the love of God toward us, because that God sent his only begotten Son into the world, that we might live through him. Herein is love, not that we loved God, but that he loved us, and sent his Son to be the propitiation for our sins" (1 John 4:9-10).

13. He was totally satisfied by his Son—"And he that sent me is with me: the Father hath not left me alone; for I do always those things that please him" (John 8:29).

14. He raised his Son—"Paul, an apostle, (not of men, neither by man, but by Jesus Christ, and God the Father, who raised him from the dead)" (Gal. 1:1). "Which he wrought in Christ, when he raised him from the dead, and set him at his own right hand in the heavenly places" (Eph. 1:20).

15. He exalts his Son—"Wherefore God also hath highly exalted him, and given him a name which is above every name: that at the name of Jesus every knee should bow, of things in heaven, and things in earth, and things under the earth; and that every tongue should confess that Jesus Christ is Lord, to the glory of God the Father" (Phil. 2:9-11). "Far above all principality, and power, and might, and dominion, and every name that is named, not only in this world, but also in that which is to come" (Eph. 1:21).

16. He makes his Son head of the church—"And hath put all things under his feet, and gave him to be the head over all things to the church" (Eph. 1:22).

17. He commits judgment unto his Son—"The Father loveth the Son, and hath given all things into his hand" (John 3:35). "For the Father judgeth no man, but hath committed all judgment unto the Son: and hath given him authority to execute judgment also, because he is the Son of man" (John 5:22, 27).

18. He will some day send his Son back to earth again with great glory—"For the Son of man shall come in the glory of his Father with his angels; and then he shall reward every man according to his works" (Matt. 16:27).

Lewis Chafer aptly summarizes the relationship between the Father and the Son:

> The relationship of the second person to the first person has from all eternity been that of a Son, and, like all else, related to the Godhead, is not only eternal but is unchangeable. He did not become a Son of the Father, as some say that He did, by His incarnation, or by His resurrection, nor is He a Son by mere title, nor is He temporarily assuming such a relationship that He may execute His part in the covenant of Redemption.
>
> He was the only begotten of the Father from all eternity, having no other relation to time and creation than that He is the Creator of them. It is evident

that the Father and Son relationship sets forth only the features of emanation and manifestation and does not include the usual conception of derivation, inferiority, or distinction as to the time of beginning.

It is probable that the terms Father and Son, as applied to the first and second persons in the Godhead, are somewhat anthropomorphic in character. That sublime and eternal relationship which existed between these two persons is best expressed to human understanding in the terms of Father and Son, but wholly without implication that the two Persons, on the divine side, are not equal in every particular. (*Systematic Theology*, vol. 1, pp. 313–315)

E. The Father and the Christian—"Behold, what manner of love the Father hath bestowed upon us, that we should be called the sons of God: therefore the world knoweth us not, because it knew him not" (1 John 3:1).

  1. He foreknew the believer—"For whom he did foreknow, he also did predestinate to be conformed to the image of his Son, that he might be the firstborn among many brethren" (Rom. 8:29). "Elect according to the foreknowledge of God the Father, through sanctification of the Spirit, unto obedience and sprinkling of the blood of Jesus Christ: Grace unto you, and peace, be multiplied" (1 Pet. 1:2).

  2. He predestinated the believer—"Having predestinated us unto the adoption of children by Jesus Christ to himself, according to the good pleasure of his will, in whom also we have obtained an inheritance, being predestinated according to the purpose of him who worketh all things after the counsel of his own will" (Eph. 1:5, 11). (See also Rom. 8:29.)

  3. He elected the believer—"And shall not God avenge his own elect, which cry day and night unto him, though he bear long with them?" (Luke 18:7). "Who shall lay any thing to the charge of God's elect? It is God that justifieth" (Rom. 8:33). "According as he hath chosen us in him before the foundation of the world, that we should be holy and without blame before him in love" (Eph. 1:4). "Put on therefore, as the elect of God, holy and beloved, bowels of mercies, kindness, humbleness of mind, meekness, longsuffering" (Col. 3:12). "Knowing, brethren beloved, your election of God" (1 Thess. 1:4). "But we are bound to give thanks alway to God for you, brethren beloved of the Lord, because God hath from the beginning chosen you to salvation through sanctification of the Spirit and belief of the truth" (2 Thess. 2:13). "Paul, a servant of God, and an apostle of Jesus Christ, according to the faith of God's elect, and the acknowledging of the truth which is after godliness" (Titus 1:1). "Peter, an apostle of Jesus Christ, to the strangers scattered throughout Pontus, Galatia, Cappadocia, Asia, and Bithynia, elect according to the foreknowledge of God the Father, through sanctification of the Spirit, unto obedience and sprinkling of the blood of Jesus Christ: Grace unto you, and peace, be multiplied" (1 Pet. 1:1-2). "But ye are a chosen generation, a royal priesthood, an holy nation, a peculiar people; that ye should shew forth the praises of him who hath called you out of darkness into his marvellous light" (1 Pet. 2:9).

  4. He gave all the elected believers to Christ—"All that the Father giveth me shall come to me; and him that cometh to me I will in no wise cast out" (John 6:37). "No man can come to me, except the Father which hath sent me draw him: and I will raise him up at the last day" (John 6:44). "My Father, which gave them me, is greater than all; and no man is able to pluck them out of my Father's

hand" (John 10:29). "Jesus knowing that the Father had given all things into his hands, and that he was come from God, and went to God" (John 13:3).

5. He called the believer—"And we know that all things work together for good to them that love God, to them who are the called according to his purpose" (Rom. 8:28). "Moreover whom he did predestinate, them he also called" (Rom. 8:30a). "God is faithful, by whom ye were called unto the fellowship of his Son Jesus Christ our Lord" (1 Cor. 1:9). "Whereunto he called you by our gospel, to the obtaining of the glory of our Lord Jesus Christ" (2 Thess. 2:14).

6. He conforms the believer to the image of Christ—"For whom he did foreknow, he also did predestinate to be conformed to the image of his Son, that he might be the firstborn among many brethren" (Rom. 8:29). "But we all, with open face beholding as in a glass the glory of the Lord, are changed into the same image from glory to glory, even as by the Spirit of the Lord" (2 Cor. 3:18).

7. He redeemed the believer—"Blessed be the God and Father of our Lord Jesus Christ, who hath blessed us with all spiritual blessings in heavenly places in Christ: according as he hath chosen us in him before the foundation of the world, that we should be holy and without blame before him in love: having predestinated us unto the adoption of children by Jesus Christ to himself, according to the good pleasure of his will, to the praise of the glory of his grace, wherein he hath made us accepted in the beloved. In whom we have redemption through his blood, the forgiveness of sins, according to the riches of his grace; wherein he hath abounded toward us in all wisdom and prudence; having made known unto us the mystery of his will, according to his good pleasure which he hath purposed in himself: That in the dispensation of the fulness of times he might gather together in one all things in Christ, both which are in heaven, and which are on earth; even in him" (Eph. 1:3-10).

8. He justified the believer—"Who shall lay any thing to the charge of God's elect? It is God that justifieth" (Rom. 8:33).

9. He indwells the believer—"Jesus answered and said unto him, If a man love me, he will keep my words: and my Father will love him, and we will come unto him, and make our abode with him" (John 14:23).

10. He sealed the believer with the Holy Spirit—"In whom ye also trusted, after that ye heard the word of truth, the gospel of your salvation: in whom also after that ye believed, ye were sealed with that holy Spirit of promise" (Eph. 1:13). "And grieve not the holy Spirit of God, whereby ye are sealed unto the day of redemption" (Eph. 4:30).

It was, of course, the Father who sent the Holy Spirit at the request of Christ to the believer in the first place. "And I will pray the Father, and he shall give you another Comforter, that he may abide with you for ever. . . . But the Comforter, which is the Holy Ghost, whom the Father will send in my name, he shall teach you all things, and bring all things to your remembrance, whatsoever I have said unto you" (John 14:16, 26). "But when the Comforter is come, whom I will send unto you from the Father, even the Spirit of truth, which proceedeth from the Father, he shall testify of me" (John 15:26).

11. He keeps the believer—"My Father, which gave them me, is greater than all; and no man is able to pluck them out of my Father's hand" (John 10:29). "And now I am no more in the world, but these are in the world, and I come to thee. Holy Father, keep through thine own name those whom thou hast given me, that they may be one, as we are" (John 17:11).

12. He honors the believer—"If any man serve me, let him follow me; and where I am, there shall also my servant be: if any man serve me, him will my Father honour" (John 12:26).
13. He blesses the believer—"Blessed be the God and Father of our Lord Jesus Christ, who hath blessed us with all spiritual blessings in heavenly places in Christ" (Eph. 1:3).
14. He loves the believer—"Now our Lord Jesus Christ himself, and God, even our Father, which hath loved us, and hath given us everlasting consolation and good hope through grace" (2 Thess. 2:16). "He that hath my commandments, and keepeth them, he it is that loveth me: and he that loveth me shall be loved of my Father, and I will love him, and will manifest myself to him" (John 14:21). "I in them, and thou in me, that they may be made perfect in one; and that the world may know that thou hast sent me, and hast loved them, as thou hast loved me" (John 17:23). (See also John 14:23.)
15. He comforts the believer—"Blessed be God, even the Father of our Lord Jesus Christ, the Father of mercies, and the God of all comfort; who comforteth us in all our tribulation, that we may be able to comfort them which are in any trouble, by the comfort wherewith we ourselves are comforted of God. For as the sufferings of Christ abound in us, so our consolation also aboundeth by Christ. And whether we be afflicted, it is for your consolation and salvation, which is effectual in the enduring of the same sufferings which we also suffer: or whether we be comforted, it is for your consolation and salvation. And our hope of you is stedfast, knowing, that as ye are partakers of the sufferings, so shall ye be also of the consolation" (2 Cor. 1:3-7). "And God shall wipe away all tears from their eyes; and there shall be no more death, neither sorrow, nor crying, neither shall there be any more pain: for the former things are passed away" (Rev. 21:4). (See also 2 Thess. 2:16.)
16. He sanctifies the believer—"Jude, the servant of Jesus Christ, and brother of James, to them that are sanctified by God the Father, and preserved in Jesus Christ, and called" (Jude 1). "Sanctify them through thy truth: thy word is truth" (John 17:17).
17. He bestows peace upon the believer—"Peace I leave with you, my peace I give unto you: not as the world giveth, give I unto you. Let not your heart be troubled, neither let it be afraid" (John 14:27). (See also 1 Cor. 1:3; Gal. 1:3; Eph. 1:2; Phil. 1:2; Col. 1:2; 1 Thess. 1:1; 2 Thess. 1:2; Titus 1:4.)
18. He is glorified when the believer bears fruit—"Herein is my Father glorified, that ye bear much fruit; so shall ye be my disciples" (John 15:8).
19. He reveals truth to the believer—"At that time Jesus answered and said, I thank thee, O Father, Lord of heaven and earth, because thou hast hid these things from the wise and prudent, and hast revealed them unto babes" (Matt. 11:25). "And Jesus answered and said unto him, Blessed art thou, Simon Bar-jona: for flesh and blood hath not revealed it unto thee, but my Father which is in heaven" (Matt. 16:17). "That the God of our Lord Jesus Christ, the Father of glory, may give unto you the spirit of wisdom and revelation in the knowledge of him" (Eph. 1:17). (See also Luke 10:21.)
20. He supplies the needs of the believer—"(For after all these things do the Gentiles seek:) for your heavenly Father knoweth that ye have need of all these things. But seek ye first the kingdom of God, and his righteousness; and all

these things shall be added unto you" (Matt. 6:32-33). "But my God shall supply all your need according to his riches in glory by Christ Jesus" (Phil. 4:19).

21. He seeks the worship of the believer—"But the hour cometh, and now is, when the true worshippers shall worship the Father in spirit and in truth: for the Father seeketh such to worship him" (John 4:23).

22. He chastens the believer—"And ye have forgotten the exhortation which speaketh unto you as unto children, My son, despise not thou the chastening of the Lord, nor faint when thou art rebuked of him: for whom the Lord loveth he chasteneth, and scourgeth every son whom he receiveth. If ye endure chastening, God dealeth with you as with sons; for what son is he whom the father chasteneth not? But if ye be without chastisement, whereof all are partakers, then are ye bastards, and not sons. Furthermore we have had fathers of our flesh which corrected us, and we gave them reverence: shall we not much rather be in subjection unto the Father of spirits, and live? For they verily for a few days chastened us after their own pleasure; but he for our profit, that we might be partakers of his holiness. Now no chastening for the present seemeth to be joyous, but grievous: nevertheless afterward it yieldeth the peaceable fruit of righteousness unto them which are exercised thereby" (Heb. 12:5-11).

23. He restores the believer—"He restoreth my soul: he leadeth me in the paths of righteousness for his name's sake" (Psa. 23:3). "Restore unto me the joy of thy salvation; and uphold me with thy free spirit" (Psa. 51:12). "And the son said unto him, Father, I have sinned against heaven, and in thy sight, and am no more worthy to be called thy son. But the father said to his servants, Bring forth the best robe, and put it on him; and put a ring on his hand, and shoes on his feet: and bring hither the fatted calf, and kill it; and let us eat, and be merry: for this my son was dead, and is alive again; he was lost, and is found. And they began to be merry" (Luke 15:21-24).

24. He will someday gather all believers in Christ—"That in the dispensation of the fulness of times he might gather together in one all things in Christ, both which are in heaven, and which are on earth; even in him" (Eph. 1:10).

25. He will someday reward all believers—"Take heed that ye do not your alms before men, to be seen of them: otherwise ye have no reward of your Father which is in heaven" (Matt. 6:1). "But without faith it is impossible to please him: for he that cometh to God must believe that he is, and that he is a rewarder of them that diligently seek him" (Heb. 11:6). "Henceforth there is laid up for me a crown of righteousness, which the Lord, the righteous judge, shall give me at that day: and not to me only, but unto all them also that love his appearing" (2 Tim. 4:8).

26. He will someday glorify all believers—"Moreover whom he did predestinate, them he also called: and whom he called, them he also justified: and whom he justified, them he also glorified" (Rom. 8:30).

27. He has prepared a kingdom for believers—"Then shall the righteous shine forth as the sun in the kingdom of their Father. Who hath ears to hear, let him hear" (Matt. 13:43). "Then shall the King say unto them on his right hand, Come, ye blessed of my Father, inherit the kingdom prepared for you from the foundation of the world" (Matt. 25:34). "But I say unto you, I will not drink henceforth of this fruit of the vine, until that day when I drink it new with you in my Father's kingdom" (Matt. 26:29). "Fear not, little flock; for it is your Father's good pleasure to give you the kingdom" (Luke 12:32).

THE DOCTRINE OF CHRIST

INTRODUCTION

The Old Testament opens with man made in the likeness of God. The New Testament opens with God made in the likeness of man.

In the Old Testament the sovereign Creator created his creatures. In the New Testament, the sinful creatures crucified their sovereign Creator.

These statements, in essence, summarize the person and work of Jesus Christ, who is both the Lamb of God and the Lion of Judah.

It has been estimated that some 40 billion individuals have lived upon this earth since Adam. What a contrast can be seen in this vast multitude of humanity. It includes black men, white men, brown men, and yellow men. These men have explored and settled in every corner of this earth. They speak dozens of languages, practice multitudes of religions, and have formulated numerous cultures.

But every single human being in this 40 billion number shares one vital thing in common. His purpose of life down here and his eternal destiny afterwards depend completely upon his personal relationship with the subject of this study—the Lord Jesus Christ. It is therefore absolutely impossible to overemphasize the importance of his life. The key question of the universe continues to be, "What think ye of Christ?" (Matthew 22:42).

Jesus said, "Search the scriptures; for in them ye think ye have eternal life: and they are they which testify of me" (John 5:39). Note the following:

To the artist he is the one altogether lovely (Song of Sol. 5:16).

To the architect he is the chief Cornerstone (1 Pet. 2:6).

To the astronomer he is the Sun of righteousness (Mal. 4:2).

To the baker he is the Bread of Life (John 6:35).

To the banker he is the hidden treasure (Matt. 13:44).

To the builder he is the sure foundation (Isa. 28:16).

To the carpenter he is the door (John 10:7).

To the doctor he is the Great Physician (Jer. 8:22).

To the educator he is the new and living way (Heb. 10:20).

To the farmer he is the sower and the Lord of the harvest (Luke 10:2).

I. The Preexistence of Jesus Christ as God—It is possible (as some have done) to hold to his preexistence without believing in his deity. For instance, the Jehovah's Witnesses cult brazenly declares that Christ preexisted as Michael the archangel prior to Bethlehem. But the Bible dogmatically declares both his preexistence *and* his deity.

  A. The fact of his divine preexistence

      1. As taught by Isaiah—"For unto us a child is born, unto us a son is given: and the government shall be upon his shoulder: and his name shall be called

Wonderful, Counsellor, The mighty God, The everlasting Father, The Prince of Peace" (Isa. 9:6).

    a. His eternal preexistence is seen through the title "the everlasting Father," a phrase that can also be translated "the Father of Eternity"—The Hebrew word for father is *ab*, which can also be rendered "source," and "inventor." In other words Jesus is the father and source of eternity itself.

    b. His divine preexistence is seen by the twin titles "wonderful," and "mighty God."

        (1) Wonderful—The Hebrew word for *wonderful* is *pehleh*. The same phrase occurs in Isaiah 28:29: "This also cometh forth from the LORD of hosts, which is wonderful in counsel, and excellent in working."

        (2) The mighty God—Here the Hebrew is *el gibbor* and can be found in many Old Testament passages, all of which refer to God himself! (See Deut. 10:17; Judg. 5:23; Psa. 24:8; 45:3; Isa. 10:21; 42:13; Jer. 32:18.)

2. As taught by Micah—"But you, Bethlehem Ephrathah, though you are small among the clans of Judah, out of you will come for me one who will be ruler over Israel, whose origins are from of old, from ancient times" (Mic. 5:2, NIV).

3. As taught by John the Baptist—"John bare witness of him, and cried, saying, This was he of whom I spake, He that cometh after me is preferred before me: for he was before me" (John 1:15).

    What does this verse mean? According to Luke 1:36, John's birth to Elisabeth occurred some six months prior to Jesus' birth. Even though, humanly speaking, John the Baptist was born before Jesus was born, John declares in these verses that Jesus existed before him and that he recognizes Jesus as our Messiah . . . "the Lamb of God, which taketh away the sin of the world" (John 1:29).

4. As taught by the Apostle John—"In the beginning was the Word, and the Word was with God, and the Word was God" (John 1:1). "(For the life was manifested, and we have seen it, and bear witness, and shew unto you that eternal life, which was with the Father, and was manifested unto us;)" (1 John 1:2).

    In these verses the Apostle John connects Jesus' preexistence to his deity.

5. As taught by the Apostle Paul—"For by him were all things created, that are in heaven, and that are in earth, visible and invisible, whether they be thrones, or dominions, or principalities, or powers: all things were created by him, and for him: and he is before all things, and by him all things consist" (Col. 1:16-17). (See also 2 Cor. 8:9; Phil. 2:6-8.)

6. As taught by the Apostle Peter—"Who verily was foreordained before the foundation of the world, but was manifest in these last times for you" (1 Pet. 1:20).

7. As taught by Christ himself—"For I came down from heaven, not to do mine own will, but the will of him that sent me" (John 6:38). "I am the living bread which came down from heaven: if any man eat of this bread, he shall live for ever: and the bread that I will give is my flesh, which I will give for the life of the world. . . . When Jesus knew in himself that his disciples murmured at it, he said unto them, Doth this offend you? What and if ye shall see the Son of man ascend up where he was before?" (John 6:51, 61-62). "Jesus said unto them, Verily, verily, I say unto you, Before Abraham was, I am" (John 8:58).

    "And now, O Father, glorify thou me with thine own self with the glory which I had with thee before the world was" (John 17:5). Here Christ requests that the Father share his glory with the Son. But note the Father's previous statement about his glory in Isaiah: "I am the LORD: that is my name: and my glory will I not give to another" (Isa. 42:8).

Óne is forced to conclude that either Christ was God indeed and had a rightful claim to this glory, or he was an arrogant imposter demanding something the Father would never give him. Of course Jesus' divine preexistence is inescapable. Jesus Christ is God. (See also Rev. 1:8, 11; 22:13.)

8. As taught by the book of Hebrews—"But unto the Son he saith, Thy throne, O God, is for ever and ever: a sceptre of righteousness is the sceptre of thy kingdom" (Heb. 1:8). "Jesus Christ the same yesterday, and to day, and for ever" (Heb. 13:8). (See also Heb. 1:10-12.)

B. The activities of the divine preexistent Christ—What was our Savior doing prior to his Bethlehem appearance? The Scriptures make it plain he was busy indeed.

1. He was creating the universe—"All things were made by him; and without him was not any thing made that was made" (John 1:3). "For by him were all things created, that are in heaven, and that are in earth, visible and invisible, whether they be thrones, or dominions, or principalities, or powers: all things were created by him, and for him" (Col. 1:16). "Hath in these last days spoken unto us by his Son, whom he hath appointed heir of all things, by whom also he made the worlds; and, Thou, Lord, in the beginning hast laid the foundation of the earth; and the heavens are the works of thine hands" (Heb. 1:2, 10).

Moses, in Genesis 1:1, tells us, "In the beginning God created the heaven and the earth." In other words, Moses, who wrote the book of Genesis, tells us that the universe was created by God. However, in the above verses John tells us that the world and the universe were made by Christ. Of course there is no contradiction. Jesus *was* God, and he created all things. This creation included everything, from electrons to galaxies, and from angels to Adam.

2. He was controlling this created universe—"Who being the brightness of his glory, and the express image of his person, and upholding all things by the word of his power, when he had by himself purged our sins, sat down on the right hand of the Majesty on high" (Heb. 1:3). "And he is before all things, and by him all things consist" (Col. 1:17).

From the time he created the earth and placed it some 93 million miles from the sun right on up to this very day he is controlling that distance. If the earth would suddenly venture too close to the sun—get a few million miles closer to it—we would all "boil away." If the earth would stray a few more million miles from the sun in its orbit around the sun, we would freeze to death. However, we have the assurance he is controlling the universe.

3. He was communing with the Father—"Father, I will that they also, whom thou hast given me, be with me where I am; that they may behold my glory, which thou hast given me: for thou lovedst me before the foundation of the world" (John 17:24).

II. The Old Testament Ministry of Jesus Christ—The Old Testament records a number of theophanies. A theophany is a pre-Bethlehem appearance of Christ. Most Bible theologians hold that the recurring angel of the Lord episodes in the Old Testament are to be identified with Christ himself. This theological position is strongly suggested by two key passages.

The first is found in Genesis 48, where the dying patriarch Jacob is blessing his two grandchildren. The old founder of Israel prays: "The angel which redeemed me from all evil, bless the lads" (Gen. 48:16a). As no regular angel can redeem men, it is assumed the angel here is actually Jesus Christ.

The second passage is found in Judges 13, where a barren couple has just learned from the angel of the Lord about the future birth of Samson. In gratitude, Manoah (the father) requests the name of the angel, that he might call the babe after him. Note the answer, however: "And the angel of the LORD said unto him, Why askest thou thus after my name, seeing it is secret?" (Judg. 13:18).

This word *secret* is from the same Hebrew root word found in Isaiah 9:6, where it is translated "Wonderful." "For unto us a child is born, unto us a son is given: and the government shall be upon his shoulder: and his name shall be called Wonderful, Counsellor, The mighty God, The everlasting Father, The Prince of Peace" (Isa. 9:6). Since we know the "Wonderful" in this verse is a reference to Christ, it is highly probable the "secret" in Judges 13:18 is also referring to Christ.

Let us now examine some other Old Testament theophanies.

A. He appeared to Hagar, Abraham's Egyptian wife, on two occasions.
   1. First occasion, prior to the birth of her son Ishmael (Gen. 16:7-14)—The first biblical reference to the angel of the Lord occurs here as he tenderly ministers to a pagan and pregnant Egyptian girl.
   2. Second occasion, following the birth of Ishmael (Gen. 21:16-20)
B. He appeared to Abraham.
   1. Concerning the birth of Isaac (Gen.18:10)
   2. Concerning the destruction of Sodom (Gen.18:17)
   3. Concerning the sacrifice of Isaac (Gen. 22:11)
C. He appeared to Jacob.
   1. At Bethel (Gen. 28:12-15)
   2. By the brook Jabbok (Gen. 32:24-30)
D. He appeared to Moses—These three occasions were all connected with Mount Sinai.
   1. The first occasion was *near* the mountain—"And when the LORD saw that he turned aside to see, God called unto him out of the midst of the bush, and said, Moses, Moses. And he said, Here am I. And he said, Draw not nigh hither: put off thy shoes from off thy feet, for the place whereon thou standest is holy ground" (Exod. 3:4-5).
   2. The second occasion was *on* the mountain—"Behold, I send an Angel before thee, to keep thee in the way, and to bring thee into the place which I have prepared" (Exod. 23:20).
   3. The last occasion was *in* the mountain—"And it shall come to pass, while my glory passeth by, that I will put thee in a clift of the rock, and will cover thee with my hand while I pass by" (Exod. 33:22).
E. He appeared to Joshua (Josh. 5:13-15)—He appeared to Joshua on the eve of the battle against Jericho and introduced himself as "captain of the host of the LORD."
F. He appeared to Gideon (Judg. 6:11-24)—The angel of the Lord found a very discouraged Gideon threshing wheat beside a wine press to hide it from the opposing Midianites.
G. He appeared to Samson's parents (Judg. 13).
H. He appeared to Isaiah (Isa. 6:1-13)—A study of the book of Isaiah reveals that Isaiah was allowed to see more of the glory of the preincarnate Christ than any other Old Testament prophet.

I. He appeared to three young Hebrews in the fiery furnace—How exciting are the astonished words of the pagan king Nebuchadnezzar as he witnessed this appearance. "Then Nebuchadnezzar the king was astonied, and rose up in haste, and spake, and said unto his counsellors, Did not we cast three men bound into the midst of the fire? They answered and said unto the king, True, O king. He answered and said, Lo, I see four men loose, walking in the midst of the fire, and they have no hurt; and the form of the fourth is like the Son of God" (Dan. 3:24-25).

J. He appeared to Daniel.

　1. The first of these appearances was in a lions' den—"Then said Daniel unto the king, O king, live for ever. My God hath sent his angel, and hath shut the lions' mouths, that they have not hurt me" (Dan. 6:21-22).

　2. The second occurred during the beginning of King Belshazzar's reign—"I saw in the night visions, and, behold, one like the Son of man came with the clouds of heaven, and came to the Ancient of days, and they brought him near before him. And there was given him dominion, and glory, and a kingdom, that all people, nations, and languages, should serve him: his dominion is an everlasting dominion, which shall not pass away, and his kingdom that which shall not be destroyed" (Dan. 7:13-14).

　3. The third occurred by the Tigris River—"Then I lifted up mine eyes, and looked, and behold a certain man clothed in linen, whose loins were girded with fine gold of Uphaz: His body also was like the beryl, and his face as the appearance of lightning, and his eyes as lamps of fire, and his arms and his feet like in colour to polished brass, and the voice of his words like the voice of a multitude" (Dan. 10:5-6).

K. He appeared to Zechariah (Zech. 1:8-13; 2:8-11; 3:10; 6:12-15)—In his book Zechariah describes Christ as protecting Jerusalem (1:8-13), measuring Jerusalem (2:8-11), cleansing Jerusalem (3:10), and building Jerusalem (6:12-15).

As you can see, from the above study of the Old Testament ministry of Christ, he was busily at work, even before his Bethlehem appearance. John MacArthur summarizes:

> The ministry of the Angel of the Lord in the Old Testament parallels the ministry of Jesus Christ in the New Testament:
>
> 1. He revealed God's Word (Exod. 3:2-6; John 1:18).
>
> 2. He called leaders like Moses, Gideon, and Samson into God's service just as Christ called his disciples (Exod. 3:6-10); Judg. 6:14-16; 13:1-5, 24-25; Matt. 10:1-4).
>
> 3. He delivered his people through Moses, Gideon, and Samson just as Christ delivered his people through his work on the cross (Exod. 14:19-20; Judg. 6:14-16; Gal. 5:1).
>
> 4. He protected his people. Psalm 34:7 says, "The angel of the Lord encampeth around about those who fear him, and delivereth them." Christ protects us as well.
>
> 5. He interceded for Israel (Zech. 1:12). Similarly Christ is our intercessor (Heb. 7:25).
>
> 6. He defended believers against the attacks of Satan (Zech. 3:1-6), which is precisely what Christ does (1 John 2:1-2).
>
> 7. He confirmed the covenant with Abraham (Gen. 22:15-18), and Christ sealed the New Covenant with his blood (Matt. 26:28).
>
> 8. He comforted Hagar (Gen. 16:7-11), which is reminiscent of how Jesus comforts us (Matt. 11:28-30). (*God, Satan, and Angels,* p. 147)

III. The Virgin Birth Incarnation of Jesus Christ—"And the Word was made flesh, and dwelt among us, (and we beheld his glory, the glory as of the only begotten of the Father,) full of grace and truth" (John 1:14). "Hereby know ye the Spirit of God: Every spirit that confesseth that Jesus Christ is come in the flesh is of God" (1 John 4:2). "For what the law could not do, in that it was weak through the flesh, God sending his own Son in the likeness of sinful flesh, and for sin, condemned sin in the flesh" (Rom. 8:3). "And without controversy great is the mystery of godliness: God was manifest in the flesh, justified in the Spirit, seen of angels, preached unto the Gentiles, believed on in the world, received up into glory" (1 Tim. 3:16).

  A. False views concerning the Incarnation

    1. The Ebionites—The Ebionites denied the reality of Jesus' divine nature. Their error is refuted by the Apostle John in the first verse of his Gospel account: "In the beginning was the Word, and the Word was with God, and the Word was God" (John 1:1).

    2. The Gnostics—The Gnostics denied the reality of Jesus' human nature. Their error is refuted by the Apostle John in the first verse of his first epistle: "That which was from the beginning, which we have heard, which we have seen with our eyes, which we have looked upon, and our hands have handled, of the Word of life" (1 John 1:1).

    3. The Arians—The Arians affirmed Jesus' preexistence but denied his deity. This is the position of the present-day Jehovah's Witnesses.

    4. The Nestorians—The Nestorians believed two persons actually indwelt the body of Christ, the human person and the divine person.

    5. The Eutychians—The Eutychians went to the opposite extreme and said both natures (the human and the divine) mingled to make up a third and totally different nature from the original two natures.

  B. The true view of the Incarnation

    1. The definition involved

> The word *incarnation* means "in flesh" and denotes the act whereby the eternal Son of God took to Himself an additional nature, humanity, through the virgin birth. The result is that Christ remains forever unblemished deity, which He has had from eternity past; but He also possesses true, sinless humanity in one Person forever (cf. John 1:14; Phil. 2:7-8; 1 Tim. 3:6).

> The virgin birth was the *means* whereby the incarnation took place and guaranteed the sinlessness of the Son of God. For this reason the virgin birth was essential. Isaiah 7:14 predicted the virgin birth and Matthew 1:23 provides the commentary, indicating its fulfillment in the birth of Christ. Matthew 1:23 identifies Mary as a "virgin" (Gk. *parthenos*, clearly denoting a virgin). (Paul Enns, *Moody Handbook of Theology*, p. 222)

> Note: This Greek word *parthenos* is used 14 times in the New Testament, and on every occasion it refers to a virgin. (See Matt. 1:23; 25:1, 7, 11; Luke 1:27—twice; Acts 21:9; 1 Cor. 7:25, 28, 34, 36-37; 2 Cor. 11:2; Rev. 14:4.)

> In the one person, Jesus Christ, there are two natures—a human nature and a divine nature, each in its completeness and integrity, and these two natures are organically and indissolubly united, yet so that no third nature is formed thereby. (A. H. Strong, *Systematic Theology*, p. 673)

Charles Ryrie suggests:

More concisely one may describe the person of Christ incarnate as being full Deity and perfect humanity united without mixture, change, division, or separation in one Person forever. The key components of the description include "full Deity" (no diminution of any attribute of Deity), "perfect humanity" ("perfect" rather than "full" in order to emphasize his sinlessness), "one Person" (not two), and "forever" (for He continues to have a body, though resurrected, Acts 1:11; Rev. 5:6). (*Basic Theology*, p. 247)

2. The illustration involved—The great evangelist D. L. Moody often related the story of a young biologist who came across an especially large and active ant hill during his walk in a forest. Delighted with his find, the biologist sat down on a nearby rock, and taking out pen and notebook, began writing down what he saw. Soon, however, the entire ant hill was in an upheaval as the tiny creatures became aware of his presence. Frustrated, the biologist walked away wishing he could in some manner communicate with them, assuring the little creatures of his interest and that no harm would be forthcoming.

He concluded, however, the only way this could happen would be to take upon himself the body of an ant and thus become part of their existence, sharing his story in a way they could comprehend.

This is exactly what occurred at the Incarnation. The infinite, holy, eternal, and sinless Son of God agreed to take upon himself a finite and fleshly body that he, the lofty Creator, might personally communicate with us, his lowly creatures.

3. The nature involved—The term "hypostatic union" is often employed in explaining the nature of the Incarnation. Consider the following three quotations describing the hypostatic union:
   a. From Paul Enns

   The hypostatic union may be defined as "the second person, the preincarnate Christ came and took to Himself a human nature and remains forever undiminished Deity and true humanity united in one person forever." When Christ came, a Person came, not just a nature; He took on an additional nature, a human nature—He did not simply dwell in a human person. The result of the union of the two natures is the theanthropic Person (the God-Man). (*Moody Handbook of Theology*, p. 227)

   b. From Robert Lightner

   To deny either the undiminished deity or the perfect humanity of Christ is to put oneself outside the pale of orthodoxy. Equally as essential to orthodox theology is the belief that these two are inseparable and will remain eternally united in the person of Christ. The hypostatic union is the theological description of this and refers to the two hypostases, or natures, forming the one person of Christ.

   Apart from this union Christ could not have been mediator between God and man. If he had only been man, his death could not have atoned for man's sin. If he had been only God, he could not have died, since God cannot die. If he had not been man, he would not have had a genuine link with humanity and would not have had perfect sympathy with man. (*Biblical Theology*, p.81.)

c. From Charles Ryrie

This simply means that the attributes of both natures belong to the one Person without mixing the natures or dividing the Person. Practically speaking, it is the basis for Christ being seen to be weak, yet omnipotent; ignorant, yet omniscient; limited, yet infinite.

I have said that attributes cannot be transferred from one nature to the other. To do so would change the mix of the complex of attributes and thus the nature. If infinity can be transferred to humanity, then Deity loses infinity and is no longer full Deity. However, attributes of both natures must be expressed through the one Person. Thus the Person can seem to "transfer" back and forth from the expression of one or the other natures, though the attributes themselves must remain as part of whichever nature they properly belong to. Thus theologians have developed a system to classify the actions of the person of Christ with respect to origination of the action.

Some examples include (a) actions predicated on the whole Person, like redemption (both natures being involved); (b) actions predicated on the divine nature (though the whole Person is the subject), like preexistence (true only of the divine nature); and (c) actions predicated on the human nature, like being thirsty.

Whatever help such a classification may give, it seems more important to remember that the Person does whatever He does, revealing whatever attribute of whichever nature He reveals. The Person thirsted; the Person knew all things; the Person does not know the day or the hour; and (probably the hardest one) the Person died. Of course, Deity does not die or thirst, but the Person, Jesus Christ, the God-Man, did both. (*Basic Theology*, p. 247.)

4. The miracle involved—The miracle of the virgin birth was not the actual birth, but rather the conception of Christ's earthly body. Furthermore, the conception was not only supernatural, but unique also, for God had already performed supernatural births for Sarah, Hannah, Elisabeth, and others. Finally it should be noted that we are not to speak of the virgin birth as the Immaculate Conception. This is the false religious dogma that Mary was conceived and born without original sin.

5. The duration (or perpetuity) involved—When the Son of God joined himself to a body at Bethlehem it was an eternal arrangement. He will continue to manifest himself in this body (in its resurrected state, of course) throughout the ages.

6. The prophecies involved:
   a. Old Testament prophecies
      (1) The fact of his birth—"And I will put enmity between thee and the woman, and between thy seed and her seed; it shall bruise thy head, and thou shalt bruise his heel" (Gen. 3:15). Genesis 3:15 is known to Bible students as the protoevangel verse. This literally means, "first Gospel" verse, that is, the first mention of Christ's birth. This is important to note, for neither Adam or Eve (to whom these words were first spoken) had experienced physical birth. Both were directly created, one from the dust

of the ground (Gen. 2:7), and the other from a human side (Gen. 2:21-22). But the Messiah would be born.

(2) The method of his birth

    (a) He was to be born of a woman—This too must have been a shocker, for originally the woman had come from the man, but not so with the future Messiah. He would proceed from the seed of the woman (Gen. 3:15).

    (b) He was to be born of a virgin woman—"Therefore the Lord himself shall give you a sign; Behold, a virgin shall conceive, and bear a son, and shall call his name Immanuel" (Isa. 7:14). This woman would conceive and bear the Christ child without the aid of a man.

(3) The nature of his birth—"For unto us a child is born, unto us a son is given: and the government shall be upon his shoulder: and his name shall be called Wonderful, Counsellor, The mighty God, The everlasting Father, The Prince of Peace" (Isa. 9:6). In a nutshell, he would become the God-man.

    (a) The phrase "a child is born" refers to his humanity.

    (b) The phrase "a son is given" refers to his deity.

(4) The nationality of his birth

    (a) First, he would come from the nation Israel (Gen. 12:3)—This prophecy was especially remarkable, for Israel did not officially become a nation until the days of Moses, many centuries later (Exod. 19–20). Even then it would remain a small and insignificant country in the Middle East. In matters of military strength, cultural accomplishments, inventions, etc., Israel would contribute nothing. Her mission, however, was to be far more important, for the Savior of all men would come from her borders.

    (b) Second, he would come from Judah, one of Israel's 12 tribes (Gen. 49:10)—The oldest tribe was Reuben, and perhaps the most influential tribe was Ephraim, but the Messiah would come from the tribe of Judah.

    (c) Third, he would come from the house of David, of the tribe of Judah in Israel (2 Sam. 7:12-13)—David was the eighth son of a poor Bethlehem sheep herder, but this family would produce the Savior of the world.

(5) The time of his birth—According to Daniel 9:24-27, his death would occur some 483 years after the beginning of the project to rebuild the Jerusalem walls. He was born, of course, some 33 years prior to his death.

(6) The place of his birth—It was to be in the little town of Bethlehem. "But thou, Bethlehem Ephratah, though thou be little among the thousands of Judah, yet out of thee shall he come forth unto me that is to be ruler in Israel; whose goings forth have been from of old, from everlasting" (Mic. 5:2). God could have chosen Rome, or Babylon, or even the Jewish religious center of Jerusalem, but instead he picked Bethlehem, the house of Bread.

(7) The sign accompanying his birth—A special supernatural light in the form of a star would brighten the heavens and point to his birth place (Num. 24:17).

(8) The unusual interest at his birth

(a) Wise men would come to Bethlehem to worship him (Isa. 60:3, 6, 9; Psa. 72:10).

(b) Wicked men would come to Bethlehem to kill him (Jer. 31:15).

b. New Testament prophecies—Heavenly announcements were given to at least eight individuals or groups concerning the Incarnation in the New Testament.

(1) To Zacharias—"And he shall go before him in the spirit and power of Elias, to turn the hearts of the fathers to the children, and the disobedient to the wisdom of the just; to make ready a people prepared for the Lord. . . . And thou, child, shalt be called the prophet of the Highest: for thou shalt go before the face of the Lord to prepare his ways" (Luke 1:17, 76). This prophecy was given to Zacharias concerning his son, John the Baptist.

(2) To Mary—"And, behold, thou shalt conceive in thy womb, and bring forth a son, and shalt call his name JESUS. . . . And the angel answered and said unto her, The Holy Ghost shall come upon thee, and the power of the Highest shall overshadow thee: therefore also that holy thing which shall be born of thee shall be called the Son of God" (Luke 1:31, 35). In these verses the angel Gabriel appears to Mary and tells her that she has found favor among women and God is going to allow her the privilege of bearing the Messiah into the world.

(3) To Elisabeth—"And she spake out with a loud voice, and said, Blessed art thou among women, and blessed is the fruit of thy womb. And whence is this to me, that the mother of my Lord should come to me?" (Luke 1:42-43).

(4) To Joseph—The angel Gabriel appeared to Joseph, the distraught would-be husband of Mary, to reassure him. "But while he thought on these things, behold, the angel of the Lord appeared unto him in a dream, saying, Joseph, thou son of David, fear not to take unto thee Mary thy wife: for that which is conceived in her is of the Holy Ghost. And she shall bring forth a son, and thou shalt call his name JESUS: for he shall save his people from their sins" (Matt. 1:20-21).

(5) To the shepherds—"And the angel said unto them, Fear not: for, behold, I bring you good tidings of great joy, which shall be to all people. For unto you is born this day in the city of David a Saviour, which is Christ the Lord. And this shall be a sign unto you; Ye shall find the babe wrapped in swaddling clothes, lying in a manger" (Luke 2:10-12).

(6) To the Wise Men—"Now when Jesus was born in Bethlehem of Judaea in the days of Herod the king, behold, there came wise men from the east to Jerusalem, saying, Where is he that is born King of the Jews? for we have seen his star in the east, and are come to worship him" (Matt. 2:1-2). "When they saw the star, they rejoiced with exceeding great joy. And when they were come into the house, they saw the young child with Mary his mother, and fell down, and worshipped him: and when they had opened their treasures, they presented unto him gifts; gold, and frankincense, and myrrh. And being warned of God in a dream that they should not return to Herod, they departed into their own country another way" (Matt. 2:10-12).

(7) To Simeon—"And it was revealed unto him by the Holy Ghost, that he should not see death, before he had seen the Lord's Christ" (Luke 2:26).

(8) To Anna—"And she coming in that instant gave thanks likewise unto the Lord, and spake of him to all them that looked for redemption in Jerusalem" (Luke 2:38).

7. The reasons involved—Why the Virgin Birth incarnation? God never does anything without a good reason, and in this case, there were some 12 excellent reasons for the Incarnation.

   a. To reveal the invisible God—"No man hath seen God at any time; the only begotten Son, which is in the bosom of the Father, he hath declared him" (John 1:18). "Jesus saith unto him, Have I been so long time with you, and yet hast thou not known me, Philip? he that hath seen me hath seen the Father; and how sayest thou then, Shew us the Father?" (John 14:9).

      God loved the world, and how could he get his message across? He sent Jesus into the world to become man and tell God's story in man's language to reveal the invisible God.

   b. To fulfill prophecy—"And I will put enmity between thee and the woman, and between thy seed and her seed; it shall bruise thy head, and thou shalt bruise his heel" (Gen. 3:15). This was the first promise of Bethlehem—the seed of woman shall bruise the head of the serpent.

   c. To guarantee the Davidic Covenant—In 2 Samuel 7 David was discouraged because he wanted to build the temple, and the Lord would not allow him to do so. Because he was a man of war, the Lord would instead allow his son, Solomon, to build the temple. However, God promised David something far more precious, and it was what theologians refer to today as the Davidic Covenant. This covenant assured David that someday an heir from his own seed would rule over Israel on his throne forever.

      "And, behold, thou shalt conceive in thy womb, and bring forth a son, and shalt call his name JESUS. He shall be great, and shall be called the Son of the Highest: and the Lord God shall give unto him the throne of his father David: And he shall reign over the house of Jacob for ever; and of his kingdom there shall be no end" (Luke 1:31-33). In this Scripture from Luke 1, the angel Gabriel reminded Mary of the fact that the Incarnation was the fulfillment of the Davidic Covenant.

   d. To make a sacrifice for our sins—Jesus left the ivory palaces of heaven to come down to this world and enter the womb of Mary, to make sacrifice for our sins. "But we see Jesus, who was made a little lower than the angels for the suffering of death, crowned with glory and honour; that he by the grace of God should taste death for every man" (Heb. 2:9).

      "For it is not possible that the blood of bulls and of goats should take away sins. Wherefore when he cometh into the world, he saith, Sacrifice and offering thou wouldest not, but a body hast thou prepared me. . . . By the which will we are sanctified through the offering of the body of Jesus Christ once for all. . . . But this man, after he had offered one sacrifice for sins for ever, sat down on the right hand of God" (Heb. 10:4-5, 10, 12).

      "And ye know that he was manifested to take away our sins; and in him is no sin" (1 John 3:5). "For even the Son of man came not to be ministered unto, but to minister, and to give his life a ransom for many" (Mark 10:45).

   e. To reconcile man to God—"To wit, that God was in Christ, reconciling the world unto himself, not imputing their trespasses unto them; and hath committed unto us the word of reconciliation" (2 Cor. 5:19). "For there is one

God, and one mediator between God and men, the man Christ Jesus; Who gave himself a ransom for all, to be testified in due time" (1 Tim. 2:5-6).

f. To provide an example for believers—We are told in the Scriptures that Christ suffered, and that he left an example for us, that we should follow his steps. The world often misunderstands the Incarnation. The world thinks Christ is the example for *un*believers. That's not what 1 Peter 2:21 says. It says that Christ has come to be an example for **believers**. He is not an example for unbelievers. He is the Savior. He came to *save* unbelievers and make them believers. Once we are saved we study the life of Christ because he is our example. But there could be no example apart from the Incarnation.

"For even hereunto were ye called: because Christ also suffered for us, leaving us an example, that ye should follow his steps" (1 Pet. 2:21). "He that saith he abideth in him ought himself also so to walk, even as he walked" (1 John 2:6).

g. To provide the believer with a high priest—In order to provide believers with a high priest, it was necessary that Christ should be made like unto his brethren. He passed sinlessly through all human experiences, that he might be a merciful and faithful High Priest in things pertaining to God, to make atonement for our sins. He was obliged to become completely like his brethren—apart from sin, of course.

"Wherefore in all things it behoved him to be made like unto his brethren, that he might be a merciful and faithful high priest in things pertaining to God, to make reconciliation for the sins of the people" (Heb. 2:17). "Wherefore, holy brethren, partakers of the heavenly calling, consider the Apostle and High Priest of our profession, Christ Jesus" (Heb. 3:1). "For we have not an high priest which cannot be touched with the feeling of our infirmities; but was in all points tempted like as we are, yet without sin" (Heb. 4:15).

h. To destroy the devil and his works—"Forasmuch then as the children are partakers of flesh and blood, he also himself likewise took part of the same; that through death he might destroy him that had the power of death, that is, the devil" (Heb. 2:14). "He that committeth sin is of the devil; for the devil sinneth from the beginning. For this purpose the Son of God was manifested, that he might destroy the works of the devil" (1 John 3:8).

i. To escape the historical curse
  (1) Upon Adam's seed—"Wherefore, as by one man sin entered into the world, and death by sin; and so death passed upon all men, for that all have sinned" (Rom. 5:12).
  (2) Upon King Jehoiakim and his son, Jehoiachin—Both King Jehoiakim and his son, Jehoiachin, were wicked rulers (Jer. 22:30; Jer. 36:27-31). They were both judged by God and warned that their physical seed would never prosper upon the throne of David. Jesus escaped that judgment by being born of a virgin.

j. To preach, heal, and liberate—"The Spirit of the Lord is upon me, because he hath anointed me to preach the gospel to the poor; he hath sent me to heal the brokenhearted, to preach deliverance to the captives, and recovering of sight to the blind, to set at liberty them that are bruised, to preach the acceptable year of the Lord" (Luke 4:18-19).

k. To give life—abundant life—"He that believeth on the Son hath everlasting life: and he that believeth not the Son shall not see life; but the wrath of God abideth on him" (John 3:36). "The thief cometh not, but for to steal, and to kill, and to destroy: I am come that they might have life, and that they might have it more abundantly" (John 10:10).

l. To glorify the Father—"Therefore, when he was gone out, Jesus said, Now is the Son of man glorified, and God is glorified in him" (John 13:31). "And whatsoever ye shall ask in my name, that will I do, that the Father may be glorified in the Son" (John 14:13). "I have glorified thee on the earth: I have finished the work which thou gavest me to do" (John 17:4).

IV. The Biblical Names and Titles of Jesus Christ—It may be true that a rose by another name would smell as sweet. But not so concerning Bible names, which often give keen insight into the lives of those who bear the titles. This is especially true concerning Christ. A wealth of information concerning his person and work can be obtained from studying some of the names and titles ascribed to him. Note some of these:

Adam (1 Cor. 15:45)
Advocate (1 John 2:1)
Almighty (Rev. 1:8)
Alpha (Rev. 1:8; 21:6)
Amen (Rev. 3:14)
Angel of the Lord (Gen. 16:9-14; Judg. 6:11-24)
Anointed (Psa. 2:2)
Apostle (Heb. 3:1)
Author (Heb. 12:2)
Babe (Luke 2:16)
Beginning of Creation (Rev. 3:14)
Begotten of the Father (John 1:14)
Beloved (Eph. 1:6)
Beloved son (Mark 1:11)
Bishop (1 Pet. 2:25)
Blessed (1 Tim. 6:15)
Branch (Zech. 3:8)
Bread of Life (John 6:35)
Bridegroom (Matt. 9:15; John 3:29)
Bright and Morning Star (Rev. 22:16)
Captain (Josh. 5:14)
Carpenter (Mark 6:3)
Child (Isa. 9:6)
Christ (Matt. 1:16; 2:4)
Commander (Isa. 55:4)
Consolation of Israel (Luke 2:25)
Corner Stone (Eph. 2:20)
Counselor (Isa. 9:6)
Dayspring from on High (Luke 1:78)
Day Star (2 Pet. 1:19)
Deliverer (Rom. 11:26)
Desire of all Nations (Hag. 2:7)
Door of the Sheep (John 10:7)
Emmanuel (Matt. 1:23)
Eternal Life (1 John 5:20)

Everlasting Father (Isa. 9:6)
Express Image of God (Heb. 1:3)
Faithful Witness (Rev. 1:5; 3:14)
Faithful and True (Rev. 19:11)
First Fruits (1 Cor. 15:23)
Forerunner (Heb. 6:20)
Foundation (Isa. 28:16)
Fountain (Zech. 13:1)
Friend of Sinners (Matt. 11:19)
Gift of God (2 Cor. 9:15)
Glory of the Lord (Isa. 60:1)
God (John 1:1; Rom. 9:5; 1 Tim. 3:16)
Good Master (Mark 10:17)
Governor (Matt. 2:6)
Guide (Psa. 48:14)
Head of the Church (Col. 1:18)
Heir of all things (Heb. 1:2)
High Priest (Heb. 2:17; 3:1)
Holy Child (Acts 4:30)
Holy One of God (Mark 1:24)
Holy One of Israel (Isa. 41:14)
Horn of Salvation (Psa. 18:2)
I Am—He calls himself this name seven times in John's Gospel:
    I am the Bread of Life (John 6:35)
    I am the Light of the World (John 9:5)
    I am the Good Shepherd (John 10:11)
    I am the Door (John 10:9)
    I am the Resurrection (John 11:25)
    I am the True Vine (John 15:1)
    I am the Way (John 14:6)
Jehovah (Isa. 26:4)
Jesus (Matt. 1:21)
Judge (Mic. 5:1; Acts 10:42)
King
    King of Israel (Matt. 27:42; John 1:49)
    King of Kings (Rev. 17:14; 19:16)
Lamb of God (John 1:29, 36)
Lawgiver (Isa. 33:22)
Lily of the Valley (Song of Sol. 2:1)
Lion of the Tribe of Judah (Rev. 5:5)
Living Bread (John 6:51)
Lord of Lords (Rev. 19:16)
Man (Acts 17:31; 1 Tim. 2:5)
Master (Matt. 8:19)
Mediator (1 Tim. 2:5)
Messiah (Dan. 9:25; John 1:41)
Mighty God (Isa. 9:6)
Minister (Heb. 8:2)
Nazarene (Matt. 2:23)

Only Begotten Son (John 1:18)
Passover (1 Cor. 5:7)
Physician (Matt. 9:12)
Potentate (1 Tim. 6:15)
Power of God (1 Cor. 1:24)
Priest (Heb. 4:14)
Prince (Acts 3:15; 5:31)
Prince of Peace (Isa. 9:6)
Prophet (Acts 3:22)
Propitiation (1 John 2:2; 4:10)
Purifier (Mal. 3:3)
Rabbi—On three well-known occasions he was called by this name:
    By Nicodemus (John 3:2)
    By Judas (Matt. 26:25)
    By Mary Magdalene (John 20:16)
Ransom (1 Tim. 2:6)
Redeemer (Isa. 59:20; 60:16)
Refiner (Mal. 3:3)
Refuge (Isa. 25:4)
Righteousness (Jer. 23:6; 33:16)
Rock (Deut. 32:15)
Rod (Isa. 11:1)
Root of David (Rev. 22:16)
Rose of Sharon (Song of Sol. 2:1)
Sacrifice (Eph. 5:2)
Savior—He was called Savior by:
    His mother (Luke 1:47)
    The angels (Luke 2:11)
    The men of Samaria (John 4:42)
Second Man (1 Cor. 15:47)
Seed of Abraham (Gal. 3:16, 19)
Seed of David (2 Tim. 2:8)
Seed of the Woman (Gen. 3:15)
Servant (Isa. 42:1; 49:5-7)
Shepherd
    The Chief Shepherd (1 Pet. 5:4)
    The Good Shepherd (John 10:11, 14)
    The Great Shepherd (Heb. 13:20)
    My Shepherd (Psa. 23:1)
Shiloh (Gen. 49:10)
Son of David—He was called by this name by the following:
    Two blind men in Capernaum (Matt. 9:27)
    The Syro-Phoenician woman (Matt. 15:22)
    Two blind men in Jericho (one named Bartimaeus—Matt. 20:30; Mark 10:46-47)
    The Palm Sunday crowd (Matt. 21:9)
Son of God—Christ referred to himself by this name on only two occasions: (John 9:35; 10:36), but many others in the Gospels also called him by this name. He was called the Son of God by:
    Satan (Matt. 4:3, 6)

Gabriel (Luke 1:35)
A demon (Matt. 8:29; Luke 4:41)
A disciple (Matt. 14:33)
Peter (Matt. 16:16)
Martha (John 11:27)
Nathanael (John 1:49)
A centurion (Matt. 27:54)

Son of Man—This was his favorite name for himself. According to his own testimony, the Son of Man:

Came not to be ministered unto (Matt. 20:28)
Came to save that which was lost (Matt. 18:11)
Can forgive sins (Matt. 9:6)
Had nowhere to lay his head (Matt. 8:20)
Is Lord of the Sabbath (Luke 6:5)
Would be betrayed (Matt. 17:22)
Would suffer (Matt. 17:12)
Would be lifted up (John 3:14)
Would be three days in the heart of the earth (Matt. 12:40)
Would be raised from the dead (Matt. 17:9)
Will come again in the glory of his Father (Matt. 16:27; 24:30)
Will send forth his angels (Matt. 13:41)
Shall sit upon the throne of his glory (Matt. 19:28)

Son of Mary (Mark 6:3)
Son of the Highest (Luke 1:32)
Stone (Matt. 21:42; Mark 12:10; Acts 4:11; Rom. 9:32-33; Eph. 2:20; 1 Pet. 2:6-7)
Sun of Righteousness (Mal. 4:2)
Teacher (Master) (Matt. 26:18; John 3:2; 11:28)
Wonderful (Isa. 9:6)
Word—the Apostle John's favorite name for Christ (John 1:1; 1 John 5:7; Rev. 19:13)

V. The Humanity of Jesus Christ—Jesus was as much man as if he had never been God.
  A. He had a human parentage—"And, behold, thou shalt conceive in thy womb, and bring forth a son, and shalt call his name JESUS" (Luke 1:31). "But when the fulness of the time was come, God sent forth his Son, made of a woman, made under the law" (Gal. 4:4).
  B. He had a human body, soul, and spirit.
    1. Body—"For in that she hath poured this ointment on my body, she did it for my burial" (Matt. 26:12).
    2. Soul—"Then saith he unto them, My soul is exceeding sorrowful, even unto death: tarry ye here, and watch with me" (Matt. 26:38). "Now is my soul troubled; and what shall I say? Father, save me from this hour: but for this cause came I unto this hour" (John 12:27).
    3. Spirit—"And immediately when Jesus perceived in his spirit that they so reasoned within themselves, he said unto them, Why reason ye these things in your hearts?" (Mark 2:8). "And when Jesus had cried with a loud voice, he said, Father, into thy hands I commend my spirit: and having said thus, he gave up the ghost" (Luke 23:46).
  C. He looked like a man.
    1. To the Samaritan woman—The Samaritan woman assumed at first that Jesus was just another man. "Then saith the woman of Samaria unto him, How is it

that thou, being a Jew, askest drink of me, which am a woman of Samaria? for the Jews have no dealings with the Samaritans" (John 4:9).

2. To the Jews—"Then said the Jews unto him, Thou art not yet fifty years old, and hast thou seen Abraham?" (John 8:57).

3. To Mary Magdalene—"Jesus saith unto her, Woman, why weepest thou? whom seekest thou? She, supposing him to be the gardener, saith unto him, Sir, if thou have borne him hence, tell me where thou hast laid him, and I will take him away" (John 20:15).

D. He possessed flesh and blood—"Forasmuch then as the children are partakers of flesh and blood, he also himself likewise took part of the same; that through death he might destroy him that had the power of death, that is, the devil" (Heb. 2:14)).

E. He grew—"And the child grew, and waxed strong in spirit, filled with wisdom: and the grace of God was upon him" (Luke 2:52).

F. He asked questions—"And it came to pass, that after three days they found him in the temple, sitting in the midst of the doctors, both hearing them, and asking them questions" (Luke 2:46).

G. He increased in wisdom—"And Jesus increased in wisdom and stature, and in favour with God and man" (Luke 2:52).

H. He was limited in knowledge—Here it should be pointed out that this limitation was self-imposed. According to Philippians 2:5-8 (a passage we will examine in great detail in a later part of the study), Christ voluntarily abstained from using (yet always retained) certain divine attributes while here on earth, that he might totally depend upon the power and wisdom of the Holy Spirit. This fact helps explain the following passages:

"And Jesus, immediately knowing in himself that virtue had gone out of him, turned him about in the press, and said, Who touched my clothes?" (Mark 5:30). "And said, Where have ye laid him? They said unto him, Lord, come and see" (John 11:34). "And seeing a fig tree afar off having leaves, he came, if haply he might find any thing thereon: and when he came to it, he found nothing but leaves; for the time of figs was not yet" (Mark 11:13). "But of that day and that hour knoweth no man, no, not the angels which are in heaven, neither the Son, but the Father" (Mark 13:32).

I. He prayed—"And in the morning, rising up a great while before day, he went out, and departed into a solitary place, and there prayed" (1:35). "And it came to pass, that, as he was praying in a certain place, when he ceased, one of his disciples said unto him, Lord, teach us to pray, as John also taught his disciples" (Luke 11:1).

J. He was tempted—"Then was Jesus led up of the Spirit into the wilderness to be tempted of the devil" (Matt. 4:1). "For in that he himself hath suffered being tempted" (Heb. 2:18). "For we have not an high priest which cannot be touched with the feeling of our infirmities; but was in all points tempted like as we are, yet without sin" (Heb. 4:15).

K. He learned obedience—"Though he were a Son, yet learned he obedience by the things which he suffered" (Heb. 5:8).

L. He hungered—"And when he had fasted forty days and forty nights, he was afterward an hungered" (Matt. 4:2). "Now in the morning as he returned into the city, he hungered" (Matt. 21:18).

M. He thirsted—"There cometh a woman of Samaria to draw water: Jesus saith unto her, Give me to drink" (John 4:7). "After this, Jesus knowing that all things were now accomplished, that the scripture might be fulfilled, saith, I thirst" (John 19:28).

N. He was weary—"Now Jacob's well was there. Jesus therefore, being wearied with his journey, sat thus on the well: and it was about the sixth hour" (John 4:6).

O. He slept—"And, behold, there arose a great tempest in the sea, insomuch that the ship was covered with the waves: but he was asleep" (Matt. 8:24).

P. He loved—"Then Jesus beholding him loved him, and said unto him, One thing thou lackest: go thy way, sell whatsoever thou hast, and give to the poor, and thou shalt have treasure in heaven: and come, take up the cross, and follow me" (Mark 10:21).

Q. He had compassion—"But when he saw the multitudes, he was moved with compassion on them, because they fainted, and were scattered abroad, as sheep having no shepherd" (Matt. 9:36).

R. He was angered and grieved—"And when he had looked round about on them with anger, being grieved for the hardness of their hearts, he saith unto the man, Stretch forth thine hand. And he stretched it out: and his hand was restored whole as the other" (Mark 3:5).

S. He wept—"Jesus wept" (John 11:35). "And when he was come near, he beheld the city (Jerusalem), and wept over it" (Luke 19:41).

T. He experienced joy—"In that hour Jesus rejoiced in spirit, and said, I thank thee, O Father, Lord of heaven and earth, that thou hast hid these things from the wise and prudent, and hast revealed them unto babes: even so, Father; for so it seemed good in thy sight" (Luke 10:21). "Looking unto Jesus the author and finisher of our faith; who for the joy that was set before him endured the cross, despising the shame, and is set down at the right hand of the throne of God" (Heb. 12:2).

U. He was troubled—"When Jesus therefore saw her weeping, and the Jews also weeping which came with her, he groaned in the spirit, and was troubled" (John 11:33). "Now is my soul troubled; and what shall I say? Father, save me from this hour: but for this cause came I unto this hour" (John 12:27). "When Jesus had thus said, he was troubled in spirit, and testified, and said, Verily, verily, I say unto you, that one of you shall betray me" (John 13:21). "And he taketh with him Peter and James and John, and began to be sore amazed, and to be very heavy; And saith unto them, My soul is exceeding sorrowful unto death: tarry ye here, and watch" (Mark 14:33-34).

V. He sweat drops as of blood—"And being in an agony he prayed more earnestly: and his sweat was as it were great drops of blood falling down to the ground" (Luke 22:44).

W. He suffered—"Forasmuch then as Christ hath suffered for us in the flesh, arm yourselves likewise with the same mind: for he that hath suffered in the flesh hath ceased from sin" (1 Pet. 4:1).

X. He bled—"But one of the soldiers with a spear pierced his side, and forthwith came there out blood and water" (John 19:34).

Y. He died—"Jesus, when he had cried again with a loud voice, yielded up the ghost" (Matt. 27:50). "For I delivered unto you first of all that which I also received, how that Christ died for our sins according to the scriptures;" (1 Cor. 15:3).

Z. He was buried—"And when Joseph had taken the body, he wrapped it in a clean linen cloth, And laid it in his own new tomb, which he had hewn out in the rock: and he rolled a great stone to the door of the sepulchre, and departed" (Matt. 27:59-60).

VI. The Deity of Jesus Christ—Jesus Christ was as much God as had he never been man.

We shall examine this tremendous theological truth by considering the preeminence, the prophecies, and the proof involved.

A. The preeminence involved—The person of Jesus Christ is given the highest preeminence and priority in the Scriptures.

1. His identity as God himself is declared—"In the beginning was the Word, and the Word was with God, and the Word was God" (John 1:1). "Looking for that blessed hope, and the glorious appearing of the great God and our Saviour Jesus Christ" (Titus 2:13). "And we know that the Son of God is come, and hath given us an understanding, that we may know him that is true, and we are in him that is true, even in his Son Jesus Christ. This is the true God, and eternal life" (1 John 5:20). "To the only wise God our Saviour, be glory and majesty, dominion and power, both now and ever. Amen" (Jude 25). (See also John 20:28; Acts 8:37; Gal. 2:20.)

2. His equality with God himself is described—"That all men should honour the Son, even as they honour the Father. He that honoureth not the Son honoureth not the Father which hath sent him" (John 5:23). "I and my Father are one" (John 10:30). "For in Christ all the fullness of the Deity lives in bodily form, and you have been given fullness in Christ, who is the head over every power and authority" (Col. 2:9, NIV).

   Note: John Davis writes concerning Colossians 2:9, "The Greek has two words for 'live' or 'have your home.' The weaker one suggests that your abode is temporary; you may move on. He does not use this word, *paroikein*, but the much stronger word, *katoikein*, which means to 'make your permanent abode.' The fullness of deity has its permanent location in Jesus" (*Handbook of Basic Bible Texts*, p. 72). (See also John 14:8-10; Phil. 25-6.)

B. The prophecies involved—Various Old Testament passages speak of the deity of the coming Messiah.

1. As described by David—"Thy throne, O God, is for ever and ever: the sceptre of thy kingdom is a right sceptre. Thou lovest righteousness, and hatest wickedness: therefore God, thy God, hath anointed thee with the oil of gladness above thy fellows" (Psa. 45:6-7). "The LORD said unto my Lord, Sit thou at my right hand, until I make thine enemies thy footstool" (Psa. 110:1).

2. As described by Solomon—"The LORD possessed me in the beginning of his way, before his works of old. I was set up from everlasting, from the beginning, or ever the earth was. . . . Then I was by him, as one brought up with him: and I was daily his delight, rejoicing always before him" (Prov. 8:22, 23, 30).

3. As described by Isaiah (Isa. 9:6)

4. As described by Daniel—"I saw in the night visions, and, behold, one like the Son of man came with the clouds of heaven, and came to the Ancient of days, and they brought him near before him. And there was given him dominion, and glory, and a kingdom, that all people, nations, and languages, should serve him: his dominion is an everlasting dominion, which shall not pass away, and his kingdom that which shall not be destroyed" (Dan. 7:13-14).

5. As described by Micah—"But you, Bethlehem Ephrathah, though you are small among the clans of Judah, out of you will come for me one who will be ruler over Israel, whose origins are from of old, from ancient times" (Micah 5:2, NIV).

6. As described by Zechariah—"Rejoice greatly, O daughter of Zion; shout, O daughter of Jerusalem: behold, thy King cometh unto thee: he is just, and having salvation; lowly, and riding upon an ass, and upon a colt the foal of an

ass" (Zech. 9:9). "And the LORD shall be king over all the earth: in that day shall there be one LORD, and his name one" (Zech. 14:9). Note: In 9:9 Zechariah describes the Messiah as Israel's king and here in 14:9 as the Lord God himself.

C. The proof involved—While upon this earth, both the words and works of Jesus Christ strongly cried out that he was indeed the incarnate God.

   1. He is omnipresent—"And no man hath ascended up to heaven, but he that came down from heaven, even the Son of man which is in heaven" (John 3:13). "For where two or three are gathered together in my name, there am I in the midst of them" (Matt. 18:20). "Teaching them to observe all things whatsoever I have commanded you: and, lo, I am with you alway, even unto the end of the world. Amen" (Matt. 28:20).

   2. He is omnipotent—"And Jesus came and spake unto them, saying, All power is given unto me in heaven and in earth" (Matt. 28:18). "Who being the brightness of his glory, and the express image of his person, and upholding all things by the word of his power, when he had by himself purged our sins, sat down on the right hand of the Majesty on high" (Heb. 1:3).

     a. Over disease—"And Jesus went about all Galilee, teaching in their synagogues, and preaching the gospel of the kingdom, and healing all manner of sickness and all manner of disease among the people" (Matt. 4:23).

     b. Over Satan—"Then saith Jesus unto him, Get thee hence, Satan: for it is written, Thou shalt worship the Lord thy God, and him only shalt thou serve" (Matt. 4:10). "Now is the judgment of this world: now shall the prince of this world be cast out" (John 12:31). "Forasmuch then as the children are partakers of flesh and blood, he also himself likewise took part of the same; that through death he might destroy him that had the power of death, that is, the devil" (Heb. 2:14).

     c. Over demons—"When the even was come, they brought unto him many that were possessed with devils: and he cast out the spirits with his word, and healed all that were sick" (Matt. 8:16).

     d. Over men—"As thou hast given him power over all flesh, that he should give eternal life to as many as thou hast given him" (John 17:2).

     e. Over nature—"And he saith unto them, Why are ye fearful, O ye of little faith? Then he arose, and rebuked the winds and the sea; and there was a great calm. But the men marvelled, saying, What manner of man is this, that even the winds and the sea obey him!" (Matt. 8:26-27).

     f. Over sin—"And ye know that he was manifested to take away our sins; and in him is no sin" (1 John 3:5).

     g. Over traditions—"Why do thy disciples transgress the tradition of the elders? for they wash not their hands when they eat bread. But he answered and said unto them, Why do ye also transgress the commandment of God by your tradition?" (Matt. 15:2-3). (See also Matt. 9:10-17.)

     h. Over the Sabbath—"For the Son of man is Lord even of the sabbath day" (Matt. 12:8).

     i. Over the temple—"But I say unto you, That in this place is one greater than the temple" (Matt. 12:6).

     j. Over death itself

       (1) Physical death—"Marvel not at this: for the hour is coming, in the which all that are in the graves shall hear his voice, and shall come forth; they

that have done good, unto the resurrection of life; and they that have done evil, unto the resurrection of damnation" (John 5:28-29).

Note: While on earth Jesus raised three from the dead. This included a young man at Nain (Luke 7:14-15), the daughter of Jairus (Luke 8:54-56), and Lazarus (John 11:43).

(2) Spiritual death—"Verily, verily, I say unto you, He that heareth my word, and believeth on him that sent me, hath everlasting life, and shall not come into condemnation; but is passed from death unto life" (John 5:24). "And deliver them who through fear of death were all their lifetime subject to bondage" (Heb. 2:15).

3. He is omniscient—"Now are we sure that thou knowest all things, and needest not that any man should ask thee: by this we believe that thou camest forth from God" (John 16:30).

   a. He knew the fickleness of the crowds—"Now when he was in Jerusalem at the passover, in the feast day, many believed in his name, when they saw the miracles which he did. But Jesus did not commit himself unto them, because he knew all men, and needed not that any should testify of man: for he knew what was in man" (John 2:23-25).

   b. He knew the wickedness of the scribes and Pharisees—"And, behold, certain of the scribes said within themselves, This man blasphemeth. And Jesus knowing their thoughts said, Wherefore think ye evil in your hearts?" (Matt. 9:3-4). "And Jesus knew their thoughts, and said unto them, Every kingdom divided against itself is brought to desolation; and every city or house divided against itself shall not stand" (Matt. 12:25).

   c. He knew the problem of his disciples—"Then there arose a reasoning among them, which of them should be greatest. And Jesus, perceiving the thought of their heart, took a child, and set him by him" (Luke 9:46-47).

   d. He knew the whereabouts of Nathanael—"Nathanael saith unto him, Whence knowest thou me? Jesus answered and said unto him, Before that Philip called thee, when thou wast under the fig tree, I saw thee" (John 1:48).

   e. He knew the history of the Samaritan woman—"Come, see a man, which told me all things that ever I did: is not this the Christ?" (John 4:29).

   f. He knew the true nature of Judas—"Jesus answered them, Have not I chosen you twelve, and one of you is a devil?" (John 6:70). "For he knew who should betray him; therefore said he, Ye are not all clean" (John 13:11).

4. He receives worship—"Then saith Jesus unto him, Get thee hence, Satan: for it is written, Thou shalt worship the Lord thy God, and him only shalt thou serve" (Matt. 4:10). Having said these words, he then accepted the worship of men, thus proving he looked upon himself as God. He received this worship:

   a. From the angels—"And again, when he bringeth in the first begotten into the world, he saith, And let all the angels of God worship him" (Heb. 1:6).

   b. From the Wise Men—"And when they were come into the house, they saw the young child with Mary his mother, and fell down, and worshipped him: and when they had opened their treasures, they presented unto him gifts; gold, and frankincense, and myrrh" (Matt. 2:11).

   c. From a leper—"And, behold, there came a leper and worshipped him, saying, Lord, if thou wilt, thou canst make me clean" (Matt. 8:2).

   d. From a Jewish ruler—"While he spake these things unto them, behold, there came a certain ruler, and worshipped him, saying, My daughter is even now dead: but come and lay thy hand upon her, and she shall live" (Matt. 9:18).

e. From a heartbroken mother—"Then came she and worshipped him, saying, Lord, help me" (Matt. 15:25).

f. From the mother of James and John—"Then came to him the mother of Zebedee's children with her sons, worshipping him, and desiring a certain thing of him" (Matt. 20:20).

g. From the maniac of Gadara—"But when he saw Jesus afar off, he ran and worshipped him" (Mark 5:6).

h. From the man born blind—"And he said, Lord, I believe. And he worshipped him" (John 9:38).

i. From Thomas—"And Thomas answered and said unto him, My Lord and my God" (John 20:28).

j. From the women at the empty tomb—"And as they went to tell his disciples, behold, Jesus met them, saying, All hail. And they came and held him by the feet, and worshipped him" (Matt. 28:9).

k. From his disciples—"Then they that were in the ship came and worshipped him, saying, Of a truth thou art the Son of God" (Matt. 14:33). "Then the eleven disciples went away into Galilee, into a mountain where Jesus had appointed them. "And when they saw him, they worshipped him: but some doubted" (Matt. 28:16-17).

5. He forgives sin—"When Jesus saw their faith, he said unto the sick of the palsy, Son, thy sins be forgiven thee" (Mark 2:5). Our Lord warned that to reject him meant to die in one's sins: "I said therefore unto you, that ye shall die in your sins: for if ye believe not that I am he, ye shall die in your sins" (John 8:24).

6. He possesses all authority—"For he taught them as one having authority, and not as the scribes" (Matt. 7:29). (See also Phil. 2:9-11.)

7. He is the source of life itself—"And the Word was made flesh, and dwelt among us, (and we beheld his glory, the glory as of the only begotten of the Father,) full of grace and truth" (John 1:4). "For as the Father hath life in himself; so hath he given to the Son to have life in himself" (John 5:26).

8. He is Creator of all things—"All things were made by him; and without him was not any thing made that was made" (John 1:3). "For by him were all things created, that are in heaven, and that are in earth, visible and invisible, whether they be thrones, or dominions, or principalities, or powers: all things were created by him, and for him" (Col. 1:16). "Hath in these last days spoken unto us by his Son, whom he hath appointed heir of all things, by whom also he made the worlds" (Heb. 1:2).

9. He is preserver of all things—"And he is before all things, and by him all things consist" (Col. 1:17). "Who being the brightness of his glory, and the express image of his person, and upholding all things by the word of his power, when he had by himself purged our sins, sat down on the right hand of the Majesty on high" (Heb. 1:3).

10. He alone can meet all our needs—"In the last day, that great day of the feast, Jesus stood and cried, saying, If any man thirst, let him come unto me, and drink" (John 7:37). "Jesus saith unto him, I am the way, the truth, and the life: no man cometh unto the Father, but by me" (John 14:6). "Come unto me, all ye that labour and are heavy laden, and I will give you rest. Take my yoke upon

you, and learn of me; for I am meek and lowly in heart: and ye shall find rest unto your souls" (Matt. 11:28-29).

11. He receives our prayers—"And they stoned Stephen, calling upon God, and saying, Lord Jesus, receive my spirit" (Acts 7:59).

12. He is the final judge—"When the Son of man shall come in his glory, and all the holy angels with him, then shall he sit upon the throne of his glory: and before him shall be gathered all nations: and he shall separate them one from another, as a shepherd divideth his sheep from the goats" (Matt. 25:31-32). "For the Father judgeth no man, but hath committed all judgment unto the Son. . . . And hath given him authority to execute judgment also, because he is the Son of man" (John 5:22, 27). "Because he hath appointed a day, in the which he will judge the world in righteousness by that man whom he hath ordained; whereof he hath given assurance unto all men, in that he hath raised him from the dead" (Acts 17:31).

13. He is both the Lord of Glory and King of kings (see 2:1; Rev. 19:16)—Dr. John Walvoord in his book, *Jesus Christ, Our Lord*, quotes the following from Charles Hodge:

> All divine names and titles are applied to Him. He is called God, the mighty God, the great God, God over all; Jehovah; Lord; the Lord of lords and King of kings. All divine attributes are ascribed to Him. He is declared to be omnipresent, omniscient, almighty, and immutable, the same yesterday, today, and forever. He is set forth as the creator and upholder and ruler of the universe. All things were created by Him and for Him; and by Him all things consist. He is the object of worship to all intelligent creatures, even the highest; all the angels (i.e., all creatures between man and God) are commanded to prostrate themselves before Him. He is the object of all the religious sentiments; of reverence, love, faith, and devotion. To Him men and angels are responsible for their character and conduct. He required that man should honour Him as they honoured the Father; that they should exercise the same faith in Him that they do in God. He declares that He and the Father are one; that those who had seen Him had seen the Father also. He calls all men unto Him; promises to forgive their sins; to send them the Holy Spirit; to give them rest and peace; to raise them up at the last day; and to give them eternal life. God is not more, and cannot promise more, or do more than Christ is said to be, to promise, and to do. He has, therefore, been the Christian's God from the beginning, in all ages and in all places. (p. 31)

VII. The Impeccability of Jesus—The doctrine of impeccability (from the Latin, meaning "not able to sin") deals with the absolute moral purity found within both the character and conduct of Jesus Christ while he was upon this earth.

A. The problem of impeccability—There exists no disagreement whatsoever among Bible believers as to whether Christ *did* sin, but rather whether he *could have* sinned. Paul Enns observes:

> Those who hold to the peccability of Christ do so on the basis of Hebrews 4:15: He "has been tempted in all things as we are, yet without sin." If the temptation was genuine then Christ had to be able to sin, otherwise the temptation was not a genuine temptation. Charles Hodge, a Reformed theologian, is perhaps the best representative of this view. He states:

"If He was a true man He must have been capable of sinning. That He did not sin under the greatest provocation; that when He was reviled He blessed; when He suffered He threatened not; that He was dumb, as a sheep before its shearers, is held up to us as an example. Temptation implies the possibility of sin. If from the constitution of his person it was impossible for Christ to sin, then his temptation was unreal and without effect, and He cannot sympathize with his people." (*Moody Handbook of Theology*, p. 236)

As opposed to Hodge, the great champion for Christ's impeccability William Shedd writes:

It is objected to the doctrine of Christ's impeccability that it is inconsistent with his temptability. A person who cannot sin, it is said, cannot be tempted to sin. This is not correct, any more than it would be correct to say that because an army cannot be conquered, it cannot be attacked. (*Dogmatic Theology*, vol. II, p. 336)

In refuting the doctrine of peccability, Paul Enns concludes:

The weaknesses of this view are that it does not sufficiently consider Christ in his Person as God as well as man. Additionally, the word *temptation* (Gk. *peirazo*) is also used of God the Father (Acts 15:10; 1 Cor. 10:9; Heb. 3:9) and the Holy Spirit (Acts 5:9). It is unlikely that anyone would say the Father or the Holy Spirit could have sinned. The conclusion is that temptation does not demand the ability to sin. The people genuinely tempted God the Father and the Holy Spirit, but there was no likelihood of those Persons of the Trinity sinning.

The evidence for the impeccability of Christ is set forth by Shedd and others in the following way.

(1) The immutability of Christ (Heb. 13:8). Christ is unchangeable and therefore could not sin. If Christ could have sinned while on earth, then he could sin now because of his immutability. If he could have sinned on earth, what assurance is there that he will not sin now?

(2) The omnipotence of Christ (Matt. 28:18). Christ was omnipotent and therefore could not sin. Weakness is implied where sin is possible, yet there was no weakness of any kind in Christ. How could he be omnipotent and still be able to sin?

(3) The omniscience of Christ (John 2:25). Christ was omniscient and therefore could not sin. Sin depends on ignorance in order that the sinner may be deceived, but Christ could not be deceived because he knows all things, including the hypothetical (Matt. 11:21). If Christ could have sinned then he really did not know what would happen if he would sin.

(4) The deity of Christ. Christ is not only man but also God. If he were only a man then he could have sinned, but God cannot sin and in a union of the two natures, the human nature submits to the divine nature (otherwise the finite is stronger than the infinite). United in the one Person of Christ are the two natures, humanity and deity; because Christ is also deity he could not sin.

(5) The nature of temptation (James 1:14-15). The temptation that came to Christ was *from without*. However, for sin to take place, there must be an *inner* response to the outward temptation. Since Jesus did not possess a sin nature,

there was nothing within him to respond to the temptation. People sin because there is an inner response to the outer temptation.

(6) The will of Christ. In moral decisions, Christ could have only one will: to do the will of his Father; in moral decisions the human will was subservient to the divine will. If Christ could have sinned then his human will would have been stronger than the divine will.

(7) The authority of Christ (John 10:18). In his deity, Christ had complete authority over his humanity. For example, no one could take the life of Christ except He would lay it down willingly (John 10:18). If Christ had authority over life and death, He certainly had authority over sin; if He could withhold death at will, He could also withhold sin at will. (*Moody Handbook of Theology*, pp. 236–237)

The question is asked, however, that, if Christ could not have sinned, then what was the purpose of the temptations in the wilderness? Here it should be observed that these trials were not to see *if* Christ would sin, but to *prove* he would not. It is possible for a tiny Chihuahua dog to attack a huge lion, but it is impossible for the little creature to conquer the big cat. A row boat may declare war on a mighty nuclear equipped battleship, but it could never sink it.

B. The proofs for impeccability
1. The testimony of Gabriel—"And the angel answered and said unto her, The Holy Ghost shall come upon thee, and the power of the Highest shall overshadow thee: therefore also that holy thing which shall be born of thee shall be called the Son of God" (Luke 1:35).
2. His own testimony—"Which of you convinceth me of sin? And if I say the truth, why do ye not believe me? (John 8:45). "Hereafter I will not talk much with you: for the prince of this world cometh, and hath nothing in me" (John 14:30). "If ye keep my commandments, ye shall abide in my love; even as I have kept my Father's commandments, and abide in his love" (John 15:10).
3. The testimony from his enemies
   a. Judas—"Saying, I have sinned in that I have betrayed the innocent blood. And they said, What is that to us? see thou to that" (Matt. 27:4).
   b. Herod Antipas (Luke 23:15)
   c. Pilate—On at least four separate occasions Pilate speaks concerning the innocence of Jesus. "Pilate saith unto him, What is truth? And when he had said this, he went out again unto the Jews, and saith unto them, I find in him no fault at all" (John 18:38). "When Pilate saw that he could prevail nothing, but that rather a tumult was made, he took water, and washed his hands before the multitude, saying, I am innocent of the blood of this just person: see ye to it" (Matt. 27:24). (See also John 19:4, 6.)
   d. Pilate's wife—"When he was set down on the judgment seat, his wife sent unto him, saying, Have thou nothing to do with that just man: for I have suffered many things this day in a dream because of him" (Matt. 27:19).
   e. The repentant dying thief—"And one of the malefactors which were hanged railed on him, saying, If thou be Christ, save thyself and us. But the other answering rebuked him, saying, Dost not thou fear God, seeing thou art in the same condemnation? And we indeed justly; for we receive the due reward of our deeds: but this man hath done nothing amiss" (Luke 23:39-41).

        f. The Roman centurion—"Now when the centurion saw what was done, he
           glorified God, saying, Certainly this was a righteous man" (Luke 23:47).
    4. The testimony of Paul—"For he hath made him to be sin for us, who knew no
       sin; that we might be made the righteousness of God in him" (2 Cor. 5:21).
    5. The testimony of Peter—"But ye denied the Holy One and the Just, and desired
       a murderer to be granted unto you" (Acts 3:14). "But with the precious blood of
       Christ, as of a lamb without blemish and without spot" (1 Pet. 1:19). "Who did
       no sin, neither was guile found in his mouth" (1 Pet. 2:22).
    6. The testimony of John—"And ye know that he was manifested to take away
       our sins; and in him is no sin" (1 John 3:5).
    7. The testimony of Hebrews—"For we have not an high priest which cannot be
       touched with the feeling of our infirmities; but was in all points tempted like as
       we are, yet without sin" (Heb. 4:15). "For such an high priest became us, who is
       holy, harmless, undefiled, separate from sinners, and made higher than the
       heavens; who needeth not daily, as those high priests, to offer up sacrifice, first
       for his own sins, and then for the people's: for this he did once, when he offered
       up himself" (Heb. 7:26-27).
VIII. The Character of Jesus Christ—What kind of man was our Lord? What were some of
    his characteristics? Consider:
    A. His zeal—"And his disciples remembered that it was written, The zeal of thine
       house hath eaten me up" (John 2:17).
      1. His zeal forced him to remain behind in Jerusalem as a boy—"And he said unto
        them, How is it that ye sought me? wist ye not that I must be about my Father's
        business?" (Luke 2:49).
      2. His zeal led him to become the first circuit preacher—"And when it was day, he
        departed and went into a desert place: and the people sought him, and came
        unto him, and stayed him, that he should not depart from them. And he said
        unto them, I must preach the kingdom of God to other cities also: for therefore
        am I sent. And he preached in the synagogues of Galilee" (Luke 2:42-44). "And
        it came to pass afterward, that he went throughout every city and village,
        preaching and shewing the glad tidings of the kingdom of God: and the twelve
        were with him," (Luke 8:1).
      3. His zeal caused his friends to think him mad—"And when his friends heard of
        it, they went out to lay hold on him: for they said, He is beside himself" (Mark
        3:21). The words "He is beside himself" may be paraphrased, "He has gone
        crazy over religion."
      4. His zeal prompted him to risk his life in purifying the temple—"And his
        disciples remembered that it was written, The zeal of thine house hath eaten
        me up" (John 2:17).
      5. His zeal gave him no rest until he accomplished his mission—"I am come to
        send fire on the earth; and what will I, if it be already kindled? But I have a
        baptism to be baptized with; and how am I straitened till it be accomplished!"
        (Luke 12:49-50).
    B. His compassion—"Who can have compassion on the ignorant, and on them that
       are out of the way; for that he himself also is compassed with infirmity" (Heb. 5:2).
      1. Upon the shepherdless multitudes—"But when he saw the multitudes, he was
        moved with compassion on them, because they fainted, and were scattered
        abroad, as sheep having no shepherd" (Matt. 9:36).
      2. Upon the sick multitudes—"And Jesus went forth, and saw a great multitude,

and was moved with compassion toward them, and he healed their sick" (Matt. 14:14).

3. Upon the hungry multitudes—"Then Jesus called his disciples unto him, and said, I have compassion on the multitude, because they continue with me now three days, and have nothing to eat: and I will not send them away fasting, lest they faint in the way" (Matt. 15:32).

4. Upon a widow—"And when the Lord saw her, he had compassion on her, and said unto her, Weep not" (Luke 7:13).

5. Upon a leper—"And Jesus, moved with compassion, put forth his hand, and touched him, and saith unto him, I will; be thou clean" (Mark 1:41).

6. Upon a father—"And ofttimes it hath cast him into the fire, and into the waters, to destroy him: but if thou canst do any thing, have compassion on us, and help us. Jesus said unto him, If thou canst believe, all things are possible to him that believeth" (Mark 9:22-23).

7. Upon a demoniac—"Howbeit Jesus suffered him not, but saith unto him, Go home to thy friends, and tell them how great things the Lord hath done for thee, and hath had compassion on thee" (Mark 5:19).

It did not take a sinner long to know that, while Jesus hated *sin*, he loved the *sinner*. Our Lord was very compassionate. People instantly knew this about him. That's the great secret in winning people to Christ or in ministering to the saints—the manifestation of a real, genuine love for those being ministered to.

C. His meekness and gentleness—"Now I Paul myself beseech you by the meekness and gentleness of Christ, who in presence am base among you, but being absent am bold toward you" (2 Cor. 10:1). "For even hereunto were ye called: because Christ also suffered for us, leaving us an example, that ye should follow his steps" (1 Pet. 2:21-23).

1. In dealing with our infirmities—"Behold my servant, whom I have chosen; my beloved, in whom my soul is well pleased: I will put my spirit upon him, and he shall shew judgment to the Gentiles. He shall not strive, nor cry; neither shall any man hear his voice in the streets. A bruised reed shall he not break, and smoking flax shall he not quench, till he send forth judgment unto victory. And in his name shall the Gentiles trust" (Matt. 12:18-21). "Like as a father pitieth his children, so the LORD pitieth them that fear him. For he knoweth our frame; he remembereth that we are dust" (Psa. 103:13-14).

2. In washing the feet of the disciples—"He riseth from supper, and laid aside his garments; and took a towel, and girded himself. After that he poureth water into a basin, and began to wash the disciples' feet, and to wipe them with the towel wherewith he was girded" (John 13:4-5).

3. In his own words—"Come unto me, all ye that labour and are heavy laden, and I will give you rest. Take my yoke upon you, and learn of me; for I am meek and lowly in heart: and ye shall find rest unto your souls. For my yoke is easy, and my burden is light" (Matt. 11:28-30).

4. In his sufferings and death—"He was oppressed, and he was afflicted, yet he opened not his mouth: he is brought as a lamb to the slaughter, and as a sheep before her shearers is dumb, so he openeth not his mouth" (Isa. 53:7).

D. His courage

1. As seen in his hometown proclamation (Luke 4:16-30)—During this, his first recorded sermon in Nazareth, he boldly pointed out Israel's historical unbelief which prompted God even back in Old Testament times to bypass, on occasion,

the chosen people and bless believing Gentiles instead. A murderous attempt
was made on his life at the end of the message.

2. As seen in his two cleansings of the temple (John 2:13-17; Matt. 21:12-16)—The
first of these took place at the beginning of his ministry and the second during
the final week. Both took great personal courage.

3. As seen in his fearless ministry to a madman (Mark 5:1-9)—No coward would
have dared confront (as did our Lord) this raging lunatic who doubtless
possessed superhuman and satanic strength.

4. As seen in risking his life to raise Lazarus (John 11:7, 8, 16, 53)—He was fully
aware (as were his frightened disciples) that a trip to Bethany at this time
would simply invite the enraged Jews to attempt to stone him again (see John
11:8). But he went anyway.

5. As seen in denouncing the wicked Pharisees (Matt. 23)—Never in written
history was a group of religious hypocrites so soundly and severely rebuked as
were the wicked Pharisees by the Savior here in Matthew 23. Furthermore, he
condemned this powerful and perverted group to their face.

6. As seen in his approach to Calvary—"And they were in the way going up to
Jerusalem; and Jesus went before them: and they were amazed; and as they
followed, they were afraid. And he took again the twelve, and began to tell
them what things should happen unto him, saying, Behold, we go up to
Jerusalem; and the Son of man shall be delivered unto the chief priests, and
unto the scribes; and they shall condemn him to death, and shall deliver him to
the Gentiles: and they shall mock him, and shall scourge him, and shall spit
upon him, and shall kill him: and the third day he shall rise again" (Mark
10:32-34). "And it came to pass, when the time was come that he should be
received up, he stedfastly set his face to go to Jerusalem" (Luke 9:51). (See also
Matt. 26:46.)

E. His obedience—"For I came down from heaven, not to do mine own will, but the
will of him that sent me" (John 6:38).

1. The demonstrations
   a. In the temple—"And he said unto them, How is it that ye sought me? wist
   ye not that I must be about my Father's business?" (Luke 2:49).
   b. In the garden—"And he was withdrawn from them about a stone's cast, and
   kneeled down, and prayed, saying, Father, if thou be willing, remove this
   cup from me: nevertheless not my will, but thine, be done" (Luke 22:41-42).

2. The declarations
   a. By Paul—"For as by one man's disobedience many were made sinners, so
   by the obedience of one shall many be made righteous" (Rom. 5:19). "And
   being found in fashion as a man, he humbled himself, and became obedient
   unto death, even the death of the cross" (Phil. 2:8).
   b. By Hebrews—"Though he were a Son, yet learned he obedience by the
   things which he suffered; and being made perfect, he became the author of
   eternal salvation unto all them that obey him" (Heb. 5:8-9).

F. His love—"Greater love hath no man than this, that a man lay down his life for his
friends" (John 15:13). As a member of the Trinity, Christ naturally loves that which
his Father loves. However, while he was on earth, he especially loved:

1. His Father—"But that the world may know that I love the Father; and as the
Father gave me commandment, even so I do. Arise, let us go hence" (John

14:31). "If ye keep my commandments, ye shall abide in my love; even as I have kept my Father's commandments, and abide in his love" (John 15:10).

2. His disciples (John 13:34, 17:2, 9, 12; 19:25-27)—"A new commandment I give unto you, That ye love one another; as I have loved you, that ye also love one another" (John 13:34).

3. Little children—"And they brought young children to him, that he should touch them: and his disciples rebuked those that brought them. But when Jesus saw it, he was much displeased, and said unto them, Suffer the little children to come unto me, and forbid them not: for of such is the kingdom of God. Verily I say unto you, Whosoever shall not receive the kingdom of God as a little child, he shall not enter therein. And he took them up in his arms, put his hands upon them, and blessed them" (Mark 10:13-16).

4. Certain close friends (John 11:1-3; 13:23)—"Now there was leaning on Jesus' bosom one of his disciples, whom Jesus loved" (John 13:23).

5. The city of Jerusalem—"O Jerusalem, Jerusalem, thou that killest the prophets, and stonest them which are sent unto thee, how often would I have gathered thy children together, even as a hen gathereth her chickens under her wings, and ye would not!" (Matt. 23:37). "And when he was come near, he beheld the city, and wept over it" (Luke 19:41).

IX. The Kenosis (Divine Emptying) of Jesus Christ—Perhaps the most profound theological passage in the entire Bible is found in Philippians 2:5-11.

"Let this mind be in you, which was also in Christ Jesus: who, being in the form of God, thought it not robbery to be equal with God: but made himself of no reputation, and took upon him the form of a servant, and was made in the likeness of men: and being found in fashion as a man, he humbled himself, and became obedient unto death, even the death of the cross. Wherefore God also hath highly exalted him, and given him a name which is above every name: that at the name of Jesus every knee should bow, of things in heaven, and things in earth, and things under the earth; and that every tongue should confess that Jesus Christ is Lord, to the glory of God the Father" (Phil. 2:5-11).

This great doctrinal truth in essence summarizes both what the Savior *gave up* and what he *gained* as a result of his earthly ministry.

A. What he gave up

1. He left heaven's glory—"And now, O Father, glorify thou me with thine own self with the glory which I had with thee before the world was" (John 17:5). "For ye know the grace of our Lord Jesus Christ, that, though he was rich, yet for your sakes he became poor, that ye through his poverty might be rich" (2 Cor. 8:9).

2. He made himself of no reputation—The Greek word found in Philippians 2:7 is *kenoo* and means "to empty." Just what did Christ empty himself of?

  a. Negative—He did *not* lay aside, in any sense of the word, his deity. He was, is, and ever shall be the total Son of God. (See John 1:1, 2 Cor. 4:4; Col. 1:15; 2:9; Heb. 1:3.)

  In the late eighties a well-known TV evangelist wrote a book entitled *Jesus Was Not Poor*, the purpose being to "prove" from the Scriptures that the Savior was actually a very wealthy man, and that he now desires that all his people also be rich. Some of the incredible "proofs" in this bizarre book include:

The fact that Jesus owned a large home, based on John 1:39. In reality, this verse does not even hint of this.

The fact that Jesus wore "designer clothes," as seen by the seamless garment at the cross referred to in John 19:23-24. No comment is necessary here.

The fact that he could afford to hire a chief financial officer, Judas by name, as recorded in John 12:6. Again, no comment needed.

When asked however, to explain 2 Cor. 8:9, where Paul says that Christ "though he was rich, yet for your sakes became poor, that ye through his poverty might be rich," the evangelist confidently replied: "The poverty spoken of here did not refer to Christ's money, but rather his deity! In other words, Jesus gave up his deity at Bethlehem!" If this statement be true, then both Isaiah (7:14) and Matthew (1:23) were wrong for each had predicted the virgin's babe would be known as Immanuel, which means, "God with us."

b. Positive—He did, for awhile, hide his heavenly fame in an earthly frame. Even though he retained every single attribute of deity while on earth, he did, nevertheless, surrender the independent exercise of those divine characteristics.

There is a common false view of the *kenosis* that teaches that Jesus emptied himself of his *relative* attributes (omniscience, omnipotence, omnipresence) while retaining his *immanent* attributes (his holiness, love, and truth). But this is in error. He did, it is true, abstain for awhile from using some of these relative attributes, but he never gave them up.

(1) He abstained from his omnipresence for a period—"Then said Jesus unto them plainly, Lazarus is dead. And I am glad for your sakes that I was not there, to the intent ye may believe; nevertheless let us go unto him" (John 11:14-15).

(2) He abstained from his omniscience for a period—"But of that day and that hour knoweth no man, no, not the angels which are in heaven, neither the Son, but the Father" (Mark 13:32). "And Jesus said, Who touched me? When all denied, Peter and they that were with him said, Master, the multitude throng thee and press thee, and sayest thou, Who touched me? And Jesus said, Somebody hath touched me: for I perceive that virtue is gone out of me" (Luke 8:45-46).

(3) He abstained from his omnipotence for a period—"Then answered Jesus and said unto them, Verily, verily, I say unto you, The Son can do nothing of himself, but what he seeth the Father do: for what things soever he doeth, these also doeth the Son likewise" (John 5:19).

Two phrases found in Philippians 2:6 need to be examined at this point.

The form of God: This does not mean that Christ had a physical shape prior to the Incarnation. It refers to that inner, essential, and abiding nature of a person or thing. As an example, we might say, "The tennis player was in rare form today."

Robbery to be equal with God: That is, he did not hold or consider the outer manifestation of his deity in Heaven as a treasure to be grasped and retained at all costs. Christ in his incarnation did not concern himself with retaining all this.

3. He was made in the likeness of men—"And the Word was made flesh, and dwelt among us, (and we beheld his glory, the glory as of the only begotten of the Father,) full of grace and truth" (John 1:14). "But when the fulness of the

time was come, God sent forth his Son, made of a woman, made under the Law" (Gal. 4:4).

This simple but absolutely staggering fact cannot be even remotely grasped by human minds. The infinite, holy Creator suddenly becomes in the likeness of his finite and sinful creatures (yet without sin). Who can comprehend such unbelievable condescension? It is as if a mighty and magnificent earthly king would determine to lay aside for awhile his fantastic storehouse of wealth and, leaving behind an adoring and amazed court, take upon himself the body of a lowly ant. The "Son of Man" was, by the way, our Lord's favorite name for himself while on earth. He took upon himself the form of a servant. He did not come as a mighty human Caesar or some world-renowned human philosopher. Even this would have been a condescension of colossal proportions. He came, rather, as a lowly servant.

4. He humbled himself—That is, he submitted to authority. "For even hereunto were ye called: because Christ also suffered for us, leaving us an example, that ye should follow his steps: who did no sin, neither was guile found in his mouth: who, when he was reviled, reviled not again; when he suffered, he threatened not; but committed himself to him that judgeth righteously: who his own self bare our sins in his own body on the tree, that we, being dead to sins, should live unto righteousness: by whose stripes ye were healed" (1 Pet. 2:21-24).

He agreed to talk our language, to wear our clothes, to eat our food, to breathe our air, and to endure our vile and vicious treatment. Contrast his statement in the garden with Lucifer's statement.

Jesus: "And he went a little further, and fell on his face, and prayed, saying, O my Father, if it be possible, let this cup pass from me: nevertheless not as I will, but as thou wilt" (Matt. 26:39). "He went away again the second time, and prayed, saying, O my Father, if this cup may not pass away from me, except I drink it, thy will be done" (Matt. 26:42).

Lucifer: "For thou hast said in thine heart, I will ascend into heaven, I will exalt my throne above the stars of God: I will sit also upon the mount of the congregation, in the sides of the north: I will ascend above the heights of the clouds; I will be like the most High" (Isa. 14:13-14).

5. He became obedient unto death—"No man taketh it from me, but I lay it down of myself. I have power to lay it down, and I have power to take it again. This commandment have I received of my Father" (John 10:18). (See Matt. 26:39; John 10:18; Heb. 5:8; 12:2.)

6. He died on a cross—Jesus did not just die, but he suffered the worst kind of death both physically and judicially. (See Psa. 22; Isa. 53.) "Christ hath redeemed us from the curse of the law, being made a curse for us: for it is written, Cursed is every one that hangeth on a tree" (Gal. 3:13).

B. What he received

1. He has been highly exalted by the Father himself—"Behold, my servant shall deal prudently, he shall be exalted and extolled, and be very high" (Isa. 52:13). "These words spake Jesus, and lifted up his eyes to heaven, and said, Father, the hour is come; glorify thy Son, that thy Son also may glorify thee" (John 17:1). "Therefore being by the right hand of God exalted, and having received of the Father the promise of the Holy Ghost, he hath shed forth this, which ye now see and hear" (Acts 2:33). "But we see Jesus, who was made a little lower than the

angels for the suffering of death, crowned with glory and honour; that he by the grace of God should taste death for every man" (Heb. 2:9).

2. He has been given a name (a position and place of authority) above all other names—"Which he wrought in Christ, when he raised him from the dead, and set him at his own right hand in the heavenly places, far above all principality, and power, and might, and dominion, and every name that is named, not only in this world, but also in that which is to come" (Eph. 1:20-21). "Being made so much better than the angels, as he hath by inheritance obtained a more excellent name than they (Heb. 1:4).

3. He will be universally acknowledged as Lord of all.
   a. The how of this acknowledgment—By the bowing of the knee and the confession of the tongue.
   b. The who of this acknowledgment—"And every creature which is in heaven, and on the earth, and under the earth, and such as are in the sea, and all that are in them, heard I saying, Blessing, and honour, and glory, and power, be unto him that sitteth upon the throne, and unto the Lamb for ever and ever" (Rev. 5:13).
      This includes:
      (1) Those in heaven (the world of saints and angels)
      (2) Those on earth (the world of sinners)
      (3) Those under the earth (the world of demons)

Thus, to confess him in this life as Lord means salvation. But to wait until the next life to confess him as Lord means damnation. The bottom line here is all will eventually confess him as Lord. Concerning this there is no choice. The only choices are *where* and *when* and *how* we confess him.

X. The Offices of Jesus Christ—It is extremely important to know not only the names that Jesus has, but the offices that were connected to him while he was on this earth. Although he has other offices, there were three great offices in the Old Testament that were created by God to meet the spiritual and material needs of God's chosen people.
   A. Those offices as overviewed by the Old Testament men of God.
      1. The prophet, an individual who represented God before man—A prophet thus exercised:
         a. Hindsight—He knew the secrets of the past. Moses wrote of man's creation, his fall, the universal flood, and other early events that transpired centuries before he himself was born in Egypt.
         b. Insight—He knew the problems and needs of the present. Prophets like Isaiah, Amos, Joel, Jeremiah, and others thundered out God's wrath against the sin and decay of their times.
         c. Foresight—He knew the secrets of the future. Daniel wrote of the coming tribulation, and Ezekiel described the glorious Millennium.
      2. The priest, an individual who represented man before God—Qualifications of the priesthood were:
         a. He must be taken from among men, a man with compassion for other men—"For every high priest taken from among men is ordained for men in things pertaining to God, that he may offer both gifts and sacrifices for sins: who can have compassion on the ignorant, and on them that are out of the way; for that he himself also is compassed with infirmity" (Heb. 5:1-2).
         b. He must be chosen by God—"And he spake unto Korah and unto all his company, saying, Even tomorrow the LORD will shew who are his, and who

is holy; and will cause him to come near unto him: even him whom he hath chosen will he cause to come near unto him" (Num. 16:5). "And no man taketh this honour unto himself, but he that is called of God, as was Aaron" (Heb. 5:4).

    c. He must be consecrated to God—"They shall be holy unto their God, and not profane the name of their God: for the offerings of the LORD made by fire, and the bread of their God, they do offer: therefore they shall be holy" (Lev. 21:6).

  3. The king, an individual who ruled for God

    a. He was to come from the tribe of Judah—"The sceptre shall not depart from Judah, nor a lawgiver from between his feet, until Shiloh come" (Gen. 49:10).

    b. He was to come from the seed of David (2 Sam. 7:8-17; Psa. 89:3-4)—"I have made a covenant with my chosen, I have sworn unto David my servant, thy seed will I establish for ever, and build up thy throne to all generations. Selah" (Psa. 89:3-4).

B. Those offices as occupied by the New Testament Son of God

  1. The prophet

    a. The requirements involved—Our Lord fulfilled this office as was predicted concerning him by Moses. "I will raise them up a Prophet from among their brethren, like unto thee, and will put my words in his mouth; and he shall speak unto them all that I shall command him" (Deut. 18:18). Some 14 centuries later the Pharisees demanded to know from John the Baptist if he was this prophet (see John 1:21-23).

      As a prophet, our Lord demonstrated:

    (1) Hindsight—He knew the failures of the Samaritan woman (John 4:16-18).

    (2) Insight—He knew the fears of the disciples (John 14:1-3).

    (3) Foresight—He knew the fate of the temple (Matt. 24:1-2).

    b. The recognition involved—Christ was looked upon as a prophet by many during his earthly ministry.

    (1) By the Samaritan woman—"The woman saith unto him, Sir, I perceive that thou art a prophet" (John 4:19).

    (2) By the people of Galilee—"And there came a fear on all: and they glorified God, saying, That a great prophet is risen up among us; and, That God hath visited his people" (Luke 7:16).

    (3) By the crowd in Jerusalem—"And the multitude said, This is Jesus the prophet of Nazareth of Galilee" (Matt. 21:11). "Many of the people therefore, when they heard this saying, said, Of a truth this is the Prophet" (John 7:40).

    (4) By his enemies—"And when they had blindfolded him, they struck him on the face, and asked him, saying, Prophesy, who is it that smote thee?" (Luke 22:64).

    (5) By the two disciples on the Emmaus Road—"And he said unto them, What things? And they said unto him, Concerning Jesus of Nazareth, which was a prophet mighty in deed and word before God and all the people" (Luke 24:19).

  2. The priest

    a. He met the requirements for the priest's office.

    (1) He was taken from among men—"For verily he took not on him the nature of angels; but he took on him the seed of Abraham" (Heb. 2:16).

"For we have not an high priest which cannot be touched with the feeling of our infirmities; but was in all points tempted like as we are, yet without sin" (Heb. 4:15).

(2) He was chosen by God—"And Jesus, when he was baptized, went up straightway out of the water: and, lo, the heavens were opened unto him, and he saw the Spirit of God descending like a dove, and lighting upon him: and lo a voice from heaven, saying, This is my beloved Son, in whom I am well pleased" (Matt. 3:16-17). (See also Matt. 17:5.)

"And no man taketh this honour unto himself, but he that is called of God, as was Aaron. So also Christ glorified not himself to be made an high priest; but he that said unto him, Thou art my Son, to day have I begotten thee. As he saith also in another place, Thou art a priest for ever after the order of Melchisedec" (Heb. 5:4-6).

(3) He was consecrated to God—"And the angel answered and said unto her, The Holy Ghost shall come upon thee, and the power of the Highest shall overshadow thee: therefore also that holy thing which shall be born of thee shall be called the Son of God" (Luke 1:35). "For such an high priest became us, who is holy, harmless, undefiled, separate from sinners, and made higher than the heavens" (Heb. 7:26).

b. He performed the responsibilities of the priest's office.

(1) He offered himself upon Calvary—"But we see Jesus, who was made a little lower than the angels for the suffering of death, crowned with glory and honour; that he by the grace of God should taste death for every man" (Heb. 2:9).

(2) He prayed (and prays) for his people (John 17; Rom. 8:34; Heb. 7:25)—"I pray not that thou shouldest take them out of the world, but that thou shouldest keep them from the evil. They are not of the world, even as I am not of the world. Sanctify them through thy truth: thy word is truth" (John 17:15-17). "Who is he that condemneth? It is Christ that died, yea rather, that is risen again, who is even at the right hand of God, who also maketh intercession for us" (Rom. 8:34). "Wherefore he is able also to save them to the uttermost that come unto God by him, seeing he ever liveth to make intercession for them" (Heb. 7:25).

(3) He blesses his people (Eph. 1:3; 2:11-22)—"Blessed be the God and Father of our Lord Jesus Christ, who hath blessed us with all spiritual blessings in heavenly places in Christ" (Eph. 1:3).

3. The king—He will fulfill the office of the king.

a. He comes from the tribe of Judah.

b. He comes from the seed of David—"And one of the elders saith unto me, Weep not: behold, the Lion of the tribe of Judah, the Root of David, hath prevailed to open the book, and to loose the seven seals thereof" (Rev. 5:5).

Jesus *was* a prophet. He *is* a priest. He *shall be* the King of kings and Lord of lords when he comes. You see, this is the reason God, in the Old Testament, pronounced judgment upon men like Saul and Uzziah, who were both kings and who both usurped the office of the priest. (Read about these two men for a clearer understanding.) There is only one man in whom God is going to entrust these offices of prophet, priest, and king. This man Jesus Christ our Lord, the mediator between God and man.

Thus, to summarize his three offices: His role as a *prophet* began at the River

Jordan and ended at Calvary. His role as a *priest* began at Calvary (where he offered up himself), and continues today in heaven (where he prays for his people), and will end at the Second Coming. His role as a *king* will begin at the Battle of Armageddon and continue through the Millennium.

XI. The Death of Jesus Christ—Henry Thiessen writes:

> The death of Christ has a prominent place in the New Testament. The last three days of our Lord's earthly life occupy about one-fifth of the narratives in the four Gospels. If all the three and a half years of his public ministry had been written out as fully as the last three days, we would have a Life of Christ of some 8,400 pages! . . . Torrey claims that the death of Christ is mentioned directly in the New Testament more than 175 times. Since there are 7,959 verses in the New Testament, this would mean that one out of every 53 verses refers to this theme.
>
> The death of Christ is the essential thing in Christianity. Other religions base their claim to recognition on the teaching of their founders; Christianity is distinguished from all of them by the importance it assigns to the death of its Founder. Take away the death of Christ as interpreted by the Scriptures, and you reduce Christianity to the level of the ethic religions. Though we would still have a higher system of ethics, were we to take away the cross of Christ, we would have no more salvation than these other religions. Napoleon said, when banished to St. Helena, that Alexander, Caesar, Charlemagne, and he had founded mighty kingdoms on force, but that Jesus Christ had founded his on love. This is true, if we mean love expressed in his substitutionary death.
>
> *It is of Supreme Interest in Heaven.* The death of Christ is the subject of supreme interest in heaven. We may expect those who have gone to heaven to have a fuller and truer conception of life's values than those who are still limited in their vision by their existence in the body. We are told that when Moses and Elijah appeared on the Mount of Transfiguration, they conversed with Christ about the decease which he was about to accomplish at Jerusalem (Luke 9:30-31). We also find that the four living creatures and the twenty-four elders sang the song of redemption through the death of Christ (Revelation 5:8-10). Even the multitude of angels around the throne, though not in need of redemption themselves, joined in the song of the Lamb that was slain (Revelation 5:11-12). Since those who have the veil of human limitations completely removed from their eyes—those who have entered into the fuller fruits of redemption through the blood of Christ—extol Christ's death above everything else, we mortals ought to study into the true meaning of that death. (*Systematic Theology*, pp. 313–314)

A. The awesomeness of it—As considered from a national perspective—Israel killing its own Messiah. As considered from an international perspective—sinful creatures killing their own sinless Creator. This incredible, mind-boggling event was pondered by both men and angels.

   1. As pondered by the Old Testament prophets—"Of which salvation the prophets have enquired and searched diligently, who prophesied of the grace that should come unto you: searching what, or what manner of time the Spirit of Christ which was in them did signify, when it testified beforehand the sufferings of Christ, and the glory that should follow" (1 Pet. 1:10-11). "And these all, having obtained a good report through faith, received not the promise" (Heb. 11:39).

     In essence, these verses teach the Old Testament writers did *not* always fully understand all the prophecies concerning the Messiah the Holy Spirit directed them to write about. For example:

    a. Moses may have pondered his prophecy—"And I will put enmity between thee and the woman, and between thy seed and her seed; it shall bruise thy head, and thou shalt bruise his heel" (Gen. 3:15).

    b. David may have pondered his prophecies—"My God, my God, why hast thou forsaken me? why art thou so far from helping me, and from the words of my roaring? . . . For dogs have compassed me: the assembly of the wicked have inclosed me: they pierced my hands and my feet. . . . They part my garments among them, and cast lots upon my vesture" (Psa. 22:1, 16, 18). "They gave me also gall for my meat; and in my thirst they gave me vinegar to drink" (Psa. 69:21).

    c. Isaiah may have pondered his prophecies—"I gave my back to the smiters, and my cheeks to them that plucked off the hair: I hid not my face from shame and spitting" (Isa. 50:6). "As many were astonied at thee; his visage was so marred more than any man, and his form more than the sons of men" (Isa. 52:14).

       "Surely he hath borne our griefs, and carried our sorrows: yet we did esteem him stricken, smitten of God, and afflicted. But he was wounded for our transgressions, he was bruised for our iniquities: the chastisement of our peace was upon him; and with his stripes we are healed. All we like sheep have gone astray; we have turned every one to his own way; and the LORD hath laid on him the iniquity of us all. He was oppressed, and he was afflicted, yet he opened not his mouth: he is brought as a lamb to the slaughter, and as a sheep before her shearers is dumb, so he openeth not his mouth" (Isa. 53:4-7).

    d. Daniel may have pondered his prophecy—"And after threescore and two weeks shall Messiah be cut off, but not for himself" (Dan. 9:26a).

    e. Zechariah may have pondered his prophecy—"So they weighed for my price thirty pieces of silver" (Zech. 11:12). "And I will pour upon the house of David, and upon the inhabitants of Jerusalem, the spirit of grace and of supplications: and they shall look upon me whom they have pierced, and they shall mourn for him, as one mourneth for his only son, and shall be in bitterness for him, as one that is in bitterness for his firstborn" (Zech. 12:10).

2. As pondered by the heavenly angels—"Unto whom it was revealed, that not unto themselves, but unto us they did minister the things, which are now reported unto you by them that have preached the gospel unto you with the Holy Ghost sent down from heaven; which things the angels desire to look into" (1 Pet. 1:12). "To the intent that now unto the principalities and powers in heavenly places might be known by the church the manifold wisdom of God" (Eph. 3:10).

    We are told that angels desire to look into the things of salvation (1 Pet. 1:12). Surely some of these accompanying things that transpired during the earthly life of our Lord must have filled them with joy and pride. They marveled at his birth. They were inspired by his sermons and thrilled by his miracles. But how did those holy, heavenly creatures react when they watched their beloved celestial Creator being systematically slaughtered by brutal mortal sinners? We cannot tell, but surely astonishment and outrage must have flooded their beings.

3. As predicted by the Savior himself—Our Lord spoke concerning his suffering and death on at least nine separate occasions.
   a. After cleansing the temple—"Jesus answered and said unto them, Destroy this temple, and in three days I will raise it up" (John 2:19).
   b. During his conversation with Nicodemus—"And as Moses lifted up the serpent in the wilderness, even so must the Son of man be lifted up" (John 3:14).
   c. After promising to build his church—"From that time forth began Jesus to shew unto his disciples, how that he must go unto Jerusalem, and suffer many things of the elders and chief priests and scribes, and be killed, and be raised again the third day" (Matt. 16:21).
   d. After the Transfiguration event—"And while they abode in Galilee, Jesus said unto them, The Son of man shall be betrayed into the hands of men: and they shall kill him, and the third day he shall be raised again. And they were exceeding sorry" (Matt. 17:22-23).
   e. During his final trip to Jerusalem—"And Jesus going up to Jerusalem took the twelve disciples apart in the way, and said unto them, Behold, we go up to Jerusalem; and the Son of man shall be betrayed unto the chief priests and unto the scribes, and they shall condemn him to death, and shall deliver him to the Gentiles to mock, and to scourge, and to crucify him: and the third day he shall rise again" (Matt. 20:17-19).
   f. During his parable of the wicked vineyard workers—"Then said the lord of the vineyard, What shall I do? I will send my beloved son: it may be they will reverence him when they see him. But when the husbandmen saw him, they reasoned among themselves, saying, This is the heir: come, let us kill him, that the inheritance may be ours. So they cast him out of the vineyard, and killed him. What therefore shall the lord of the vineyard do unto them?" (Luke 20:13-15).
   g. Following his Triumphal Entry—"Verily, verily, I say unto you, Except a corn of wheat fall into the ground and die, it abideth alone: but if it die, it bringeth forth much fruit. . . . And I, if I be lifted up from the earth, will draw all men unto me. This he said, signifying what death he should die" (John 12:24, 32-33).
   h. In the Upper Room—"And as they were eating, Jesus took bread, and blessed it, and brake it, and gave it to the disciples, and said, Take, eat; this is my body. And he took the cup, and gave thanks, and gave it to them, saying, Drink ye all of it; for this is my blood of the new testament, which is shed for many for the remission of sins" (Matt. 26:26-28).
   i. En route to Gethsemane—"Then saith Jesus unto them, All ye shall be offended because of me this night: for it is written, I will smite the shepherd, and the sheep of the flock shall be scattered abroad" (Matt. 26:31).
B. The source of it—This is to say, who killed Christ? How did his death come about? What caused it?
   1. The secondary sources involved
      a. Judas (Matt. 26:14-16, 47-50)
      b. Annas and Caiaphas (John 18:12-13, 24; Matt. 26:57, 65)
      c. Pilate (Matt. 27:26)
      d. The Jewish leaders (Matt. 26:3-4; 27:1)
      e. The Roman soldiers (Matt. 27:27-31)

f. All sinners (Heb. 2:9)

2. The primary source: The Father himself—"All we like sheep have gone astray; we have turned every one to his own way; and the LORD hath laid on him the iniquity of us all. . . . Yet it pleased the LORD to bruise him; he hath put him to grief: when thou shalt make his soul an offering for sin, he shall see his seed, he shall prolong his days, and the pleasure of the LORD shall prosper in his hand" (Isa. 53:6, 10). "For he hath made him to be sin for us, who knew no sin; that we might be made the righteousness of God in him" (2 Cor. 5:21).

C. The scope of it—For whom did Christ die? In general it may be said he died for the world, the elect, and for each man.

1. His death for the world—"For God so loved the world, that he gave his only begotten Son, that whosoever believeth in him should not perish, but have everlasting life" (John 3:16). "The next day John seeth Jesus coming unto him, and saith, Behold the Lamb of God, which taketh away the sin of the world" (John 1:29). "And he is the propitiation for our sins: and not for ours only, but also for the sins of the whole world" (1 John 2:2). "For the grace of God that bringeth salvation hath appeared to all men" (Titus 2:11). "The Lord is not slack concerning his promise, as some men count slackness; but is longsuffering to us-ward, not willing that any should perish, but that all should come to repentance" (2 Pet. 3:9). "Who gave himself a ransom for all, to be testified in due time" (1 Tim. 2:6).

2. His death for the elect—"According as he hath chosen us in him before the foundation of the world, that we should be holy and without blame before him in love" (Eph. 1:4). "Husbands, love your wives, even as Christ also loved the church, and gave himself for it" (Eph. 5:25). "And all that dwell upon the earth shall worship him, whose names are not written in the book of life of the Lamb slain from the foundation of the world" (Rev. 13:8).

3. His death for each man—"But we see Jesus, who was made a little lower than the angels for the suffering of death, crowned with glory and honour; that he by the grace of God should taste death for every man" (Heb. 2:9).

D. Old Testament examples of it—During that first Easter Sunday afternoon the resurrected Christ appeared unrecognized to two disciples on their way to Emmaus. After listening to their despair over the recent crucifixion of Israel's Messiah, our Lord admonished them as follows:

"Then he said unto them, O fools, and slow of heart to believe all that the prophets have spoken: ought not Christ to have suffered these things, and to enter into his glory? And beginning at Moses and all the prophets, he expounded unto them in all the scriptures the things concerning himself" (Luke 24:25-27).

The following Old Testament events that speak of Jesus' death were no doubt referred to by our Lord to those disciples during that afternoon conversation.

1. The coats of skins (Gen. 3:21)—"Unto Adam also and to his wife did the LORD God make coats of skins, and clothed them." God probably killed a lamb and from that lamb provided coats of skins for Adam and Eve, representing the righteousness of Christ and the costliness of salvation.

2. The ark of Noah (1 Pet. 3:18-22)—This is not a reference to the Ark of the Covenant, but to the ark of safety. Just as the ark delivered Noah and his family from the judgment of the flood, likewise salvation through Jesus Christ delivers believers from the judgment of God.

3. The offering up of Isaac (Gen. 22:1-14)—"By faith Abraham, when he was tried,

offered up Isaac: and he that had received the promises offered up his only begotten son. . . accounting that God was able to raise him up, even from the dead; from whence also he received him in a figure" (Heb. 11:17, 19).

4. The Passover lamb (Exod. 12)—In Exodus 12 a lamb was taken and killed, then its blood was sprinkled upon the door post. That blood then saved the life of that household's eldest child when God himself passed over all the homes in Egypt on that fateful night during the tenth plague. The New Testament says that Christ has become our Passover. (See 1 Cor. 5:7.)

5. The passage through the Red Sea (1 Cor. 10:1-2)—This was perhaps the greatest miracle in the Old Testament. Paul, in 1 Corinthians 10, likens this event in Israel's history to the death of Christ. God spared the nation of Israel from annihilation by the Egyptian army in making a way of escape across the Red Sea. God spares individuals from spiritual death because of sin by making a way of escape through the sacrificial death of his Son.

6. The branch cast into the waters of Marah (Exod. 15:23-26)—While the Israelites were out in the desert, the waters were bitter. Moses cried unto the Lord, and the Lord showed him a tree. When he had cast the tree into the waters, the waters were made sweet (v. 25). This is symbolic of the death of Christ—the work of Jesus on the cross. Through this work on the cross the bitter waters of experience in the life of the believer can be made sweet.

7. The smitten rock (1 Cor. 10:4)—In Exodus 17:6 Moses had only to strike the rock once and it gave them water. Paul, in 1 Corinthians 10:4, refers to the "rock" as representing Jesus Christ, the real source of their sustenance. The typology is this: Christ has only been smitten one time. We need not offer a sacrifice now—we need not kill a lamb, as in the Old Testament. All we need do is speak to him and ask him to save us. So the smitten rock in the Old Testament was certainly a type of the death of Christ.

8. The brazen serpent (John 3:14; Num. 21)—In John 3:14 Jesus illustrates, from Numbers 21, the redemptive plan of God. The Son of Man must be lifted up (as Moses lifted up the serpent in the wilderness) so that man, bitten by sin, might have eternal life. Then John 3:16 tells us, "For God so loved the world, that he gave his only begotten Son, that whosoever believeth in him should not perish, but have everlasting life."

9. The Levitical offerings (Leviticus 1–5)—If you read these five chapters in Leviticus, you will notice there are five offerings. The meal offering is not a type of Christ's death, but rather a type of his sinless life. However, the other four—the burnt offering, the trespass offering, the peace offering, and the sin offering—speak of his death.

10. The ordinance of the red heifer (Numbers 19)—Laws had already been given whereby a living person coming in contact with a corpse would be considered unclean (that is, disqualified from religious life and service) for a period of seven days. But a crisis had probably now arisen. Due to the recent plague (16:49), no less than 14,700 corpses had come upon the scene. This event alone had, doubtless, contributed to the defilement of tens of thousands of people. What could be done about this? The rite of the red heifer was God's answer to this problem. The cleansing of a defiled Israelite was fourfold: (1) Eleazar was to slaughter an unblemished red heifer outside the camp (vv. 2-3). (2) Its blood was to be sprinkled toward the tabernacle seven times. (v. 4). (3) The red heifer was to be burned along with cedar, wood, hyssop, and some scarlet cloth

material (vv. 5-6). (4) Finally, water was to be added to the ashes of the heifer and sprinkled upon the defiled Israelite (vv. 17-19). This whole rite was to cleanse or purify them from being defiled by coming in contact with a corpse. This cleansing purified the Jew and kept him from being cut off from Israel, just as the cleansing of Christ keeps us from being cut off from God.

11. The sacrifice on the Day of Atonement (Leviticus 16)—While Exodus 12 refers to a sacrifice for each family (the Passover lamb), Leviticus 16 refers to one sacrifice for the Jewish nation. This Day of Atonement is celebrated as Yom Kippur and is the single most important day in the entire Jewish calendar. On this day the high priest would actually take two goats and lay his hands upon one, and that goat would make its way out into the wilderness. That goat would be the scape goat, symbolically carrying away the sins of Israel. However, the other goat was killed, and its blood was sprinkled upon the mercy seat in the holy of holies. This Day of Atonement was a time annually to make an atonement for the children of Israel for all their sins. This is portrayed in Hebrews 9:7. Hebrews 9:12 contrasts this with the work of Christ when it says, "Neither by the blood of goats and calves, but by his own blood he entered in once into the holy place, having obtained *eternal* redemption for us" (emphasis mine).

12. The two memorials (Joshua 3–4)—When God rolled the waters of the Jordan River back and allowed the Israelites to pass through to dry ground, Joshua built a memorial of two piles of stones. One pile was in the Jordan River itself, and the other was on the western bank. The pile of stones in the Jordan River was symbolic of Christ because God allowed the waters of sin to come rushing in upon Christ, as God allowed these waters of the Jordan to come in with all their fury upon those 12 memorial stones.

E. Theories concerning it

1. The false positions

a. The recapitulation theory, advocated by Irenaeus (130–202)—This theory says Christ recapitulated in himself all the stages of human life that related to sin. In this way he reversed the course of Adam, who by his sin started humanity. Here it should be said Jesus Christ did not *reverse* Adam's course, but rather by his death *redeemed* all those of Adam's race who would believe from the road leading to destruction. (See Rom. 5:12-21.)

b. The payment-to-Satan theory, advocated by Origen (185–254)—This says man had sold his immortal soul to Satan through sin and that Christ's death was the devil's "pound of flesh" ransom note. This is wholly untrue, for Christ's death assured the final and eternal damnation of the devil. The only thing God owes Satan is a place in Gehenna hell forever.

c. The satisfaction theory, advocated by Anselm (1033–1109)—This teaches that Jesus died to appease God's offended honor. It acted somewhat like a pistol duel at dawn, where an insulted man takes revenge for prior insult and injury. While this theory is closer to the truth than the former ones, it still smacks of error. There was absolutely no revenge involved in the death of Christ.

d. The moral influence theory, advocated by (Abelard (1079–1142)—Here we are told God allowed Christ to die to show that he can enter into man's sufferings. By this act God thus may stimulate man's sympathy for Christ. This too is false, for (among other reasons) the very ones who put him to death continue to hate him and his followers the most. Furthermore, God's eternal plan is not to "share man's sufferings with him," but rather to save him, that man might someday share the riches of Christ.

    e. The example theory, advocated by Socinus (1539–1604)—Christ's death simply showed how one man can give his life for others. But what would this single act accomplish? Soldiers, law officers, mothers, and other individuals had done this very thing thousands of times prior to and following Christ's death. What could Calvary add to all this?

2. The substitutional (and orthodox) theory—This alone is the correct view. Dr. John Walvoord writes:

> Christ in his death fully satisfied the demands of a righteous God for judgment upon sinners and, as their infinite sacrifice, provided a ground not only for the believer's forgiveness, but for his justification and sanctification. (*Jesus Christ, Our Lord*, p. 162)

Moody Press in Chicago has printed an excellent tract written by Major D. W. Whittle entitled *Willie Lear, the Substitute* that aptly illustrates this point.

Willie Lear lived near Palmyra, Missouri. In 1862 he was a young man of about 18 years of age. Like most of those who lived in his neighborhood, he sympathized with the south in the Civil War, which was at that time in progress. The Union forces occupied Palmyra and had control of the district. Outrages were committed on both sides, and many indefensible deeds are recorded in the local histories of those sad times. Union soldiers were shot down from behind hedges, and Union men were driven away from their homes, and sometimes foully treated. To avenge these things, and to check them, the Federal commander arrested and imprisoned a large number of citizens. They were all charged with being "guerrillas," and, after trial by court-martial, were all sentenced to be shot. Willie Lear was among the number.

After this condemnation, the general decided to select 10 of the number of those condemned for immediate execution, and reserve the remainder under hope of pardon if outrages in the neighborhood ceased, or for future punishment if not. These 10 men were drawn by lot. Willie Lear was not of this number.

A neighbor of Lear's, who was among the number to be shot, was terribly distressed at the thought of his situation. He was the father of a large family, a poor man, and the thought of the helpless condition in which he would leave his loved ones was very distressing to him.

Lear saw this, and it deeply moved him. He stepped forward to the commanding officer and offered to *take his neighbor's place*. The officer had no objection. The order had been issued that 10 men of the number should be shot, and if that number was made up, the law would be satisfied. The neighbor with the deepest of gratitude accepted Lear as his substitute: and so, by the acquiescence of the three parties concerned, the representative of the law, the condemned by the law, and the satisfier of the law by substitution, the matter was settled.

Willie Lear took the place of his friend in the line with the nine men drawn up before a detachment prepared with loaded rifles, and at the command, "Fire!" he, with the others, fell, riddled with bullets, his blood soaking the earth.

As the man for whom he died looked upon that blood, and beheld that mangled body, what would be his thought? Would he not say, with streaming eyes: "He died for me. I owe my life to him. O that I could do anything to show my gratitude to one who has done so much for me!

If he were asked, "How is it that you are delivered from the sentence that was hanging over you? would he be apt to ignore the work of his substitute by magnifying the importance of some fancied work of his own in the acceptance of the substitute? Would he say, "Oh, I was saved by my faith, and by my determination to live a better life. It is all by faith and development of character?" Would he have been so ungrateful as to leave out all mention of the death of that noble young man in his stead as the alone cause of his escape? If he would, he was not worth dying for, and it was a curse to his family and the community that he was spared. But no. He never returned such answers. He could not treat the act of his friend with such indifference.

Men for whom Christ died on the cross talk that way; but this man never did. He never tired of telling how Willie Lear had saved him, and gladly acknowledged his obligation to him.

"Who his own self bare our sins in his own body on the tree, that we, being dead to sins, should live unto righteousness: by whose stripes ye were healed" (1 Pet. 2:24).

F. The need for it—Henry Thiessen writes:

At first God and man stood face to face with each other. In sinning, Adam turned his back upon God. Then God turned His back upon Adam. Christ's death has satisfied the demands of God and now God has again turned His face toward man. It remains for man to turn round about and face God. Since God has been reconciled by the death of His Son, man is now entreated to be reconciled to God. (*Systematic Theology*, pp. 327–328)

The need, therefore, for Christ's death was twofold:
1. It was necessary because of God's holiness—"For I am the LORD your God: ye shall therefore sanctify yourselves, and ye shall be holy; for I am holy: neither shall ye defile yourselves with any manner of creeping thing that creepeth upon the earth" (Lev. 11:44). "The way of the wicked is an abomination unto the LORD: but he loveth him that followeth after righteousness" (Prov. 15:9).
2. It was necessary because of man's sinfulness—"What then? are we better than they? No, in no wise: for we have before proved both Jews and Gentiles, that they are all under sin; as it is written, There is none righteous, no, not one: there is none that understandeth, there is none that seeketh after God. They are all gone out of the way, they are together become unprofitable; there is none that doeth good, no, not one. Their throat is an open sepulchre; with their tongues they have used deceit; the poison of asps is under their lips: whose mouth is full of cursing and bitterness: their feet are swift to shed blood: destruction and misery are in their ways: and the way of peace have they not known: there is no fear of God before their eyes" (Rom. 3:9-18).

G. The results from it
1. In relation to sinners: Redemption—"In whom we have redemption through his blood, the forgiveness of sins, according to the riches of his grace" (Eph. 1:7). "Christ hath redeemed us from the curse of the law, being made a curse for us: for it is written, Cursed is every one that hangeth on a tree" (Gal. 3:13). "And they sung a new song, saying, Thou art worthy to take the book, and to open

the seals thereof: for thou wast slain, and hast redeemed us to God by thy blood out of every kindred, and tongue, and people, and nation" (Rev. 5:9).

2. In relation to saints: Sanctification—"Who gave himself for our sins, that he might deliver us from this present evil world, according to the will of God and our Father" (Gal. 1:4). "By the which will we are sanctified through the offering of the body of Jesus Christ once for all" (Heb. 10:10). "Having therefore, brethren, boldness to enter into the holiest by the blood of Jesus, by a new and living way, which he hath consecrated for us, through the veil, that is to say, his flesh" (Heb. 10:19-20).

3. In relation to Satan: Destruction—"Forasmuch then as the children are partakers of flesh and blood, he also himself likewise took part of the same; that through death he might destroy him that had the power of death, that is, the devil" (Heb. 2:14). "And having spoiled principalities and powers, he made a shew of them openly, triumphing over them in it" (Col. 2:15). "He that committeth sin is of the devil; for the devil sinneth from the beginning. For this purpose the Son of God was manifested, that he might destroy the works of the devil" (1 John 3:8).

4. In relation to the Savior: Expectation—"But this man, after he had offered one sacrifice for sins for ever, sat down on the right hand of God; from henceforth expecting till his enemies be made his footstool" (Heb. 10:12-13).

XII. The Heart of the Earth Descent of Jesus Christ—"For as Jonas was three days and three nights in the whale's belly; so shall the Son of man be three days and three nights in the heart of the earth" (Matt. 12:40). "For Christ also hath once suffered for sins, the just for the unjust, that he might bring us to God, being put to death in the flesh, but quickened by the Spirit: by which also he went and preached unto the spirits in prison; which sometime were disobedient, when once the longsuffering of God waited in the days of Noah, while the ark was a preparing, wherein few, that is, eight souls were saved by water" (1 Pet. 3:18-20). "Now that he ascended, what is it but that he also descended first into the lower parts of the earth?" (Eph. 4:9).

On the strength of these verses, the following events are suggested. Between his death and resurrection, our Lord descended into the lower parts of this earth to perform a twofold ministry:

A. To depopulate the "saved" compartment of hades (Luke 16:19-31)—"I knew a man in Christ above fourteen years ago, (whether in the body, I cannot tell; or whether out of the body, I cannot tell: God knoweth;) such an one caught up to the third heaven" (2 Cor. 12:2).

B. To preach judgment upon the fallen angels who had attempted to corrupt human flesh and thus prevent the promised incarnation of Christ (Gen. 3:15; 6:1-4)—The theme of Christ's message therefore was, "It didn't work!" "For if God spared not the angels that sinned, but cast them down to hell, and delivered them into chains of darkness, to be reserved unto judgment" (2 Pet. 2:4). "And the angels which kept not their first estate, but left their own habitation, he hath reserved in everlasting chains under darkness unto the judgment of the great day" (Jude 6).

XIII. The Resurrection of Jesus Christ

A. The Resurrection, denied—There is surely no other single doctrine in all the Bible so hated by Satan as the resurrection of Christ. He has attempted (always unsuccessfully) to ridicule it, downplay it, deny it, or simply explain it away.

Here are but a few theories he has inspired his children (ungodly men) to promote concerning this precious doctrine:

1. The fraud theory—This says that either Jesus or his disciples (or both) simply invented the entire thing. It would have us believe that Christ was simply a clever crook who read the prophecies regarding the Messiah in the Old Testament and set about arranging for them to be fulfilled by himself. However, it would have been somewhat difficult for an imposter to arrange the place where he was to be born (it had to be Bethlehem) or for some Roman soldiers to cooperate by not breaking his bones on the cross. The only fraud here is on the part of those who offer this silly and sinful explanation.

2. The swoon theory—We are informed here that Christ merely fainted on the cross and was later revived by the cool, dark air of the tomb. But how did he get out of that tomb? What bright light did he use to blind and terrify the Roman soldiers who stood guard outside?

3. The vision theory—This would advocate that the early disciples were guilty of using some kind of primitive LSD. If this be true, then the practice was certainly widespread, for on one occasion alone over 500 claimed to have seen him. There is not one speck of biblical or secular evidence to support such an empty theory.

4. The spirit theory—This holds that only his spirit arose. But Jesus is said to have eaten in his resurrected body. The very nail prints were still there. This view, like the above, cannot for one second stand the logic of reason.

5. The heart theory—Here we are to believe that he was only resurrected in the hearts of his friends. The trouble here, however, is that none of those friends actually believed he would literally rise from the dead until they saw him with their own eyes and heard his words with their ears.

B. The Resurrection, declared

1. David predicted it—"For thou wilt not leave my soul in hell; neither wilt thou suffer thine Holy One to see corruption" (Psa. 16:10). We know David here was not referring to himself but to the coming Messiah, for Israel's great Old Testament king did indeed die and see corruption.

   Both Peter and Paul used this fact in proving to Israel that Jesus Christ was indeed their Messiah.

   a. Peter's testimony—"Because thou wilt not leave my soul in hell, neither wilt thou suffer thine Holy One to see corruption" (Acts 2:27).

   b. Paul's testimony—"Wherefore he saith also in another psalm, Thou shalt not suffer thine Holy One to see corruption. For David, after he had served his own generation by the will of God, fell on sleep, and was laid unto his fathers, and saw corruption: But he, whom God raised again, saw no corruption" (Acts 13:35-37).

2. Isaiah predicted it—"Yet it pleased the LORD to bruise him; he hath put him to grief: when thou shalt make his soul an offering for sin, he shall see his seed, he shall prolong his days, and the pleasure of the LORD shall prosper in his hand. He shall see of the travail of his soul, and shall be satisfied: by his knowledge shall my righteous servant justify many; for he shall bear their iniquities. Therefore will I divide him a portion with the great, and he shall divide the spoil with the strong; because he hath poured out his soul unto death: and he was numbered with the transgressors; and he bare the sin of many, and made intercession for the transgressors" (Isa. 53:10-12).

3. Zechariah predicted it—"And I will pour upon the house of David, and upon the inhabitants of Jerusalem, the spirit of grace and of supplications: and they

shall look upon me whom they have pierced, and they shall mourn for him, as one mourneth for his only son, and shall be in bitterness for him, as one that is in bitterness for his firstborn" (Zech. 12:10).

4. Jesus himself predicted it many times.

   a. After the first temple cleansing—"Jesus answered and said unto them, Destroy this temple, and in three days I will raise it up" (John 2:19).

   b. Upon being asked by the Pharisees to show them a sign

      (1) First occasion—"But he answered and said unto them, An evil and adulterous generation seeketh after a sign; and there shall no sign be given to it, but the sign of the prophet Jonas: for as Jonas was three days and three nights in the whale's belly; so shall the Son of man be three days and three nights in the heart of the earth" (Matt. 12:39-40).

      (2) Second occasion (Matt. 16:4)

   c. After promising to build his church—"From that time forth began Jesus to shew unto his disciples, how that he must go unto Jerusalem, and suffer many things of the elders and chief priests and scribes, and be killed, and be raised again the third day" (Matt. 16:21).

   d. After the Transfiguration event—"And they shall kill him, and the third day he shall be raised again. And they were exceeding sorry" (Matt. 17:23).

   e. During his final trip to Jerusalem—"Behold, we go up to Jerusalem; and the Son of man shall be betrayed unto the chief priests and unto the scribes, and they shall condemn him to death, And shall deliver him to the Gentiles to mock, and to scourge, and to crucify him: and the third day he shall rise again" (Matt. 20:18-19).

   f. During his sermon on the Good Shepherd—"Therefore doth my Father love me, because I lay down my life, that I might take it again. No man taketh it from me, but I lay it down of myself. I have power to lay it down, and I have power to take it again. This commandment have I received of my Father" (John 10:17-18).

   g. Following the Triumphal Entry—"Verily, verily, I say unto you, Except a corn of wheat fall into the ground and die, it abideth alone: but if it die, it bringeth forth much fruit" (John 12:24).

   h. In the Upper Room—"For this is my blood of the new testament, which is shed for many for the remission of sins. But I say unto you, I will not drink henceforth of this fruit of the vine, until that day when I drink it new with you in my Father's kingdom" (Matt. 26:28-29).

   i. En route to Gethsemane—"But after I am risen again, I will go before you into Galilee" (Matt. 26:33).

C. The Resurrection, doubted—It is ironic and sad that the predicted resurrection of Christ was only remembered by his enemies, the Pharisees, and not by his friends.

"Now the next day, that followed the day of the preparation, the chief priests and Pharisees came together unto Pilate, saying, Sir, we remember that that deceiver said, while he was yet alive, After three days I will rise again. Command therefore that the sepulchre be made sure until the third day, lest his disciples come by night, and steal him away, and say unto the people, He is risen from the dead: so the last error shall be worse than the first" (Matt. 27:62-64).

So much for his enemies. But what about his friends?

  1. The women did not remember—"And when the sabbath was past, Mary Magdalene, and Mary the mother of James, and Salome, had bought sweet

spices, that they might come and anoint him. And very early in the morning the first day of the week, they came unto the sepulchre at the rising of the sun. And they said among themselves, Who shall roll us away the stone from the door of the sepulchre?" (Mark 16:1-3).

2. Mary Magdalene did not remember—"And they say unto her, Woman, why weepest thou? She saith unto them, Because they have taken away my Lord, and I know not where they have laid him. And when she had thus said, she turned herself back, and saw Jesus standing, and knew not that it was Jesus. Jesus saith unto her, Woman, why weepest thou? whom seekest thou? She, supposing him to be the gardener, saith unto him, Sir, if thou have borne him hence, tell me where thou hast laid him, and I will take him away" (John 20:13-15).

3. Peter and John did not remember—"For as yet they knew not the scripture, that he must rise again from the dead" (John 20:9). "Then arose Peter, and ran unto the sepulchre; and stooping down, he beheld the linen clothes laid by themselves, and departed, wondering in himself at that which was come to pass" (Luke 24:12).

4. The apostles did not remember—"And returned from the sepulchre, and told all these things unto the eleven, and to all the rest. It was Mary Magdalene, and Joanna, and Mary the mother of James, and other women that were with them, which told these things unto the apostles. And their words seemed to them as idle tales, and they believed them not" (Luke 24:9-11).

5. The two disciples on the Emmaus Road did not remember (Luke 24:13-31)—"Then he said unto them, O fools, and slow of heart to believe all that the prophets have spoken: ought not Christ to have suffered these things, and to enter into his glory?" (Luke 24:25-26).

6. Thomas did not remember (John 20:24-29)—"But Thomas, one of the twelve, called Didymus, was not with them when Jesus came. The other disciples therefore said unto him, We have seen the Lord. But he said unto them, Except I shall see in his hands the print of the nails, and put my finger into the print of the nails, and thrust my hand into his side, I will not believe" (John 20:24-25).

D. The Resurrection, described—By far the most lengthy and detailed overview of Christ's glorious resurrection from a theological perspective in the entire Bible is found in 1 Corinthians 15. Here Paul describes the following:

1. The prominence of the resurrection of Christ (15:1-4)
   a. It is the focal point in reference to salvation (15:1-2).
   b. It is the focal point in reference to the Scriptures (15:3-4).

2. The proof of the resurrection of Christ (15:5-11)—In these verses Paul lists a twofold proof:
   a. The resurrection appearances of Christ (15:5-8)
   b. The conversion experience of Paul himself (15:9-11)

3. The priority of the resurrection of Christ (15:12-19)—"Now if Christ be preached that he rose from the dead, how say some among you that there is no resurrection of the dead? But if there be no resurrection of the dead, then is Christ not risen: And if Christ be not risen, then is our preaching vain, and your faith is also vain. Then they also which are fallen asleep in Christ are perished. If in this life only we have hope in Christ, we are of all men most miserable" (15:12-14, 18-19).

The resurrection of Christ is the Constitution, Bill of Rights, and Declaration of Independence of the Christian faith. The sign of Christianity is really not the cross, but an empty tomb. If one denies the Resurrection, he is forced to six horrible conclusions:

    a. All gospel preaching has been, is now, and always will be, utterly and completely useless.

    b. All past, present, and future faith is futile.

    c. All preachers become notorious liars.

    d. All living Christians are still in their sins.

    e. All departed Christians are in hell.

    f. All reason and purpose for life itself is destroyed.

4. The program of the resurrection of Christ (15:20-28)—"For as in Adam all die, even so in Christ shall all be made alive. But every man in his own order" (15:22, 23). The Greek word for "order" here is *tagma*, a military term referring to troops in order of rank, as in a victorious homecoming parade. This resurrection parade consists of three sections:

    a. First part, the resurrection of Christ—"Christ the first fruits" (15:23b). The resurrection of Christ is represented here as being the first of its kind, thus indicating that previous miracles, such as the raising of Lazarus, were more on the order of restoring a dead, mortal body to a living, mortal body. True resurrection carries with it *glorification.*

    b. Second part, the Rapture resurrection—"Afterward they that are Christ's at his coming" (15:23c).

    c. Final part, the resurrection of Old Testament and tribulational believers at the beginning of the Millennium—"Then cometh the end, when he shall have delivered up the kingdom to God, even the Father; when he shall have put down all rule and all authority and power" (15:24).

5. The prompting of the resurrection of Christ (15:29-34)—The resurrection factor should motivate me to pick up the fallen banner of departed believers. This is what Paul is saying in verse 29: "Else what shall they do which are baptized for the dead, if the dead rise not at all? why are they then baptized for the dead?"

6. The pattern of the resurrection of Christ (15:35-38)—The apostle illustrates the Resurrection by a grain of wheat."When you sow, you do not plant the body that will be, but just a seed, perhaps of wheat or of something else" (15:37, NIV).

7. The perfection of the resurrection of Christ (15:39-50)—Paul here contrasts the new body to the old body. "It is sown a natural body; it is raised a spiritual body. There is a natural body, and there is a spiritual body" (15:44).

    What kind of body did Jesus have after his resurrection? This is of great importance to the believer, for we someday will have a similar body. "Who, by the power that enables him to bring everything under his control, will transform our lowly bodies so that they will be like his glorious body" (Phil. 3:21, NIV). "Beloved, now are we the sons of God, and it doth not yet appear what we shall be: but we know that, when he shall appear, we shall be like him; for we shall see him as he is" (1 John 3:2).

    a. His new body had flesh and bone—"Behold my hands and my feet, that it is I myself: handle me, and see; for a spirit hath not flesh and bones, as ye see me have. And when he had thus spoken, he shewed them his hands and his feet" (Luke 24:39-40).

b. He ate food in this new body—"And while they yet believed not for joy, and wondered, he said unto them, Have ye here any meat? And they gave him a piece of a broiled fish, and of an honeycomb. And he took it, and did eat before them" (Luke 24:41-43). "Jesus saith unto them, Come and dine. And none of the disciples durst ask him, Who art thou? knowing that it was the Lord. Jesus then cometh, and taketh bread, and giveth them, and fish likewise" (John 21:12-13).

c. His new body still bore the marks of his crucifixion—"The other disciples therefore said unto him, We have seen the Lord. But he said unto them, Except I shall see in his hands the print of the nails, and put my finger into the print of the nails, and thrust my hand into his side, I will not believe. And after eight days again his disciples were within, and Thomas with them: then came Jesus, the doors being shut, and stood in the midst, and said, Peace be unto you. Then saith he to Thomas, Reach hither thy finger, and behold my hands; and reach hither thy hand, and thrust it into my side: and be not faithless, but believing" (John 20:25-27). "And when he had thus spoken, he shewed them his hands and his feet" (Luke 24:40). "And I beheld, and, lo, in the midst of the throne and of the four beasts, and in the midst of the elders, stood a Lamb as it had been slain, having seven horns and seven eyes, which are the seven Spirits of God sent forth into all the earth" (Rev. 5:6).

d. His new body was not subjected to material laws—"Then the same day at evening, being the first day of the week, when the doors were shut where the disciples were assembled for fear of the Jews, came Jesus and stood in the midst, and saith unto them, Peace be unto you" (John 20:19). "And their eyes were opened, and they knew him; and he vanished out of their sight. . . . and as they thus spake, Jesus himself stood in the midst of them, and saith unto them, Peace be unto you" (Luke 24:31, 36).

Thus: The new body is as superior to the old body as: Man is to beast, heaven is to the earth, and the sun is to the moon.

8. The promise of the resurrection of Christ (15:51-53)
   a. At the Rapture the bodies of living believers will be changed without dying.
   b. At the Rapture the bodies of departed believers will be raised without corruption.

9. The purpose of the Resurrection (15:54-57)—Simply stated, his resurrection assures victory over man's final enemy, physical death. "So when this corruptible shall have put on incorruption, and this mortal shall have put on immortality, then shall be brought to pass the saying that is written, Death is swallowed up in victory. O death, where is thy sting? O grave, where is thy victory?" (15:54-55).

10. The practical value of the resurrection of Christ (15:57)—"But thanks be to God, which giveth us the victory through our Lord Jesus Christ."

E. The Resurrection, documented—The Scriptures offer a number of facts that serve to strongly document the reality of Christ's resurrection.

1. The empty tomb—If Christ did not rise again, what happened to his body?
   a. His friends did not remove it, for they were as surprised concerning the empty tomb as the rest (John 20:1-9).
   b. His enemies did not remove it, for they were bribed to tell a lie concerning the empty tomb—"And when they were assembled with the elders, and had

taken counsel, they gave large money unto the soldiers, saying, Say ye, His disciples came by night, and stole him away while we slept. And if this come to the governor's ears, we will persuade him, and secure you. So they took the money, and did as they were taught: and this saying is commonly reported among the Jews until this day" (Matt. 28:12-15).

2. The tremendous and sudden change in the lives of the disciples—Two examples will suffice here:
   a. That of Simon Peter
      (1) Just prior to the Resurrection Peter is seen bitterly denying his Savior (Matt. 26:69-74).
      (2) Just after the Resurrection he is seen boldly declaring his Savior (Acts 2:14-40).
   b. That of John the apostle
      (1) Just prior to the Resurrection John displayed total contempt toward the Samaritans—"And when his disciples James and John saw this, they said, Lord, wilt thou that we command fire to come down from heaven, and consume them, even as Elias did?" (Luke 9:54).
      (2) Just after the Resurrection he displays total compassion toward the Samaritans—"Now when the apostles which were at Jerusalem heard that Samaria had received the word of God, they sent unto them Peter and John: And they, when they had testified and preached the word of the Lord, returned to Jerusalem, and preached the gospel in many villages of the Samaritans" (Acts 8:14, 25).

3. The silence from both the Romans and Pharisees—Not once did either of these enemy groups ever attempt to deny Christ's resurrection. They hated it and tried to suppress it, but could not refute it.

4. The change from Saturday to Sunday as the main day of worship—Imagine the following: While visiting a foreign country you are suddenly seized by some terrorists and held hostage in solitary confinement for 90 days. During this time you are permitted absolutely no contact with the outside world. After three months (for no apparent reason) you are released and allowed to return home. Upon arrival however, you learn some incredible news. During your absence all Christian churches everywhere no longer gather for worship on Sunday, but instead assemble on Monday of each week. Your immediate question of course would be what in the world could have happened during those 90 days causing Christians to abandon their 2,000-year-old custom of worshipping on Sunday.

   Yet this is exactly what happened in Palestine shortly after the resurrection of Christ. As ingrained as the Sabbath was in the hearts and history of the apostles, it would have taken some fantastic event to change their thinking here.

5. The existence of the church—In less than 50 years after Christ's death, the Christian church had become a mighty power, causing the Roman government to view with growing concern its influence upon men and women. Legends and religions do not develop this quickly.

6. The various appearances of Christ following his resurrection—During the 40 days between his resurrection and ascension, our Lord made ten specific appearances before individuals or groups of individuals.
   a. The first day (Easter Sunday)
      (1) To Mary Magdalene (Mark 16:9-11; John 20:11-18)
      (2) To some women (Matt. 28:9-15)

(3) To Simon Peter (Luke 24:34; 1 Cor. 15:5)
(4) To two disciples en route to Emmaus (Mark 16:12-13; Luke 24:13-35)
(5) To ten apostles in the upper room (Mark 16:14; Luke 24:36-48; John 20:19-23)
b. The final 39 days
(1) To Thomas and the 10 apostles in the Upper Room (John 20:24-31)
(2) To seven apostles by the Galilean Sea (John 21)
(3) To the apostles and 500 disciples (Matt. 28:16-20; Mark 16:15-18; 1 Cor. 15:6)
(4) To James, the half brother of Christ (1 Cor. 15:7)
(5) To the 11 apostles on the Mount of Olives (Luke 24:49-50; Acts 1:3-8)
John Walvoord writes: "Taken as a whole, the appearances are of such various character and to so many people under so many different circumstances that proof of the resurrection of Christ is as solid as any historical fact that could be cited in the first century" (*Jesus Christ, Our Lord*, pp. 193–195).
F. The Resurrection, discerned—What are the results of the Resurrection?
1. In relation to the believer, there are immediate blessings we have because of the Resurrection.
a. A guarantee of our justification—How dare the devil tell a person he is not saved if that person has accepted Jesus Christ, because what he is saying is that the Resurrection did not have the power to get a person saved and to keep him saved, and that is a terrible lie.
b. A guarantee of present-day power and strength (Eph. 1:18–2:10)
c. A guarantee of fruitful labor—This is a guarantee that the things we do down here for Jesus will not be forgotten in heaven. "Therefore, my beloved brethren, be ye stedfast, unmoveable, always abounding in the work of the Lord, forasmuch as ye know that your labour is not in vain in the Lord" (1 Cor. 15:58).
d. A guarantee of our own resurrection—"Knowing that he which raised up the Lord Jesus shall raise up us also by Jesus, and shall present us with you" (2 Cor. 4:14).
There are also future blessings.
e. Exchanging corruption for incorruption—"So also is the resurrection of the dead. It is sown in corruption; it is raised in incorruption" (1 Cor. 15:42).
f. Exchanging dishonor for glory—"It is sown in dishonour; it is raised in glory: it is sown in weakness; it is raised in power" (1 Cor. 15:43).
g. Exchanging weakness for power (1 Cor. 15:43)
h. Exchanging a material body for a spiritual body—"It is sown a natural body; it is raised a spiritual body. There is a natural body, and there is a spiritual body" (1 Cor. 15:44).
2. In relation to the Savior
a. It is the mark of his deity—"And declared to be the Son of God with power, according to the spirit of holiness, by the resurrection from the dead" (Rom. 1:4). "Him God raised up the third day, and shewed him openly" (Acts 10:40).
b. It is the springboard of his exaltation—"The God of our fathers raised up Jesus, whom ye slew and hanged on a tree. Him hath God exalted with his right hand to be a Prince and a Saviour, for to give repentance to Israel, and

forgiveness of sins" (Acts 5:30-31). "Wherefore God also hath highly exalted him, and given him a name which is above every name: that at the name of Jesus every knee should bow, of things in heaven, and things in earth, and things under the earth; And that every tongue should confess that Jesus Christ is Lord, to the glory of God the Father" (Phil. 2:9-11).

    c. It marks the beginning of his headship over the church—"And what is the exceeding greatness of his power to us-ward who believe, according to the working of his mighty power, which he wrought in Christ, when he raised him from the dead, and set him at his own right hand in the heavenly places, far above all principality, and power, and might, and dominion, and every name that is named, not only in this world, but also in that which is to come: and hath put all things under his feet, and gave him to be the head over all things to the church, which is his body, the fulness of him that filleth all in all" (Eph. 1:19-23).

  3. In relation to the sinner, it warns him of a coming judgment day—"Because he hath appointed a day, in the which he will judge the world in righteousness by that man whom he hath ordained; whereof he hath given assurance unto all men, in that he hath raised him from the dead" (Acts 17:31).

  4. In relation to the devil, it seals his doom forever—"Forasmuch then as the children are partakers of flesh and blood, he also himself likewise took part of the same; that through death he might destroy him that had the power of death, that is, the devil" (Heb. 2:14). "And the devil that deceived them was cast into the lake of fire and brimstone, where the beast and the false prophet are, and shall be tormented day and night for ever and ever" (Rev. 20:10).

  5. In relation to the Sabbath, it transfers the worship day from Saturday to Sunday—"And upon the first day of the week, when the disciples came together to break bread, Paul preached unto them, ready to depart on the morrow; and continued his speech until midnight" (Acts 20:7). "Upon the first day of the week let every one of you lay by him in store, as God hath prospered him, that there be no gatherings when I come" (1 Cor. 16:2).

  G. The Resurrection, depicted—Both Christ's death and resurrection are pictured by the ordinance of baptism. "Therefore we are buried with him by baptism into death: that like as Christ was raised up from the dead by the glory of the Father, even so we also should walk in newness of life. For if we have been planted together in the likeness of his death, we shall be also in the likeness of his resurrection" (Rom. 6:4-5).

XIV. The Ascension of Jesus Christ

  A. The prophecies involved

    1. As predicted by David, the King of Israel—"Thou hast ascended on high, thou hast led captivity captive: thou hast received gifts for men; yea, for the rebellious also, that the LORD God might dwell among them" (Psa. 68:18).

    2. As predicted by Jesus, the King of kings—"What and if ye shall see the Son of man ascend up where he was before?" (John 6:62). "I came forth from the Father, and am come into the world: again, I leave the world, and go to the Father" (John 16:28). "Jesus saith unto her, Touch me not; for I am not yet ascended to my Father: but go to my brethren, and say unto them, I ascend unto my Father, and your Father; and to my God, and your God" (John 20:17).

  B. The parting involved—"So then after the Lord had spoken unto them, he was received up into heaven, and sat on the right hand of God" (Mark 16:19). "And it came to pass, while he blessed them, he was parted from them, and carried up into heaven" (Luke 24:51). "And when he had spoken these things, while they beheld, he was taken up; and a cloud received him out of their sight" (Acts 1:9).

C. The promise involved—"And while they looked stedfastly toward heaven as he went up, behold, two men stood by them in white apparel; which also said, Ye men of Galilee, why stand ye gazing up into heaven? this same Jesus, which is taken up from you into heaven, shall so come in like manner as ye have seen him go into heaven" (Acts 1:10-11).

D. The place involved—"Then returned they unto Jerusalem from the mount called Olivet, which is from Jerusalem a sabbath day's journey" (Acts 1:12).

XV. The Present Ministry of Jesus Christ

A. The place involved: The right hand of God—The place here is in reality a position of highest honor. In essence, the Lord Jesus Christ now occupies the most prominent, privileged, and powerful position in all the universe.

1. This place is verified by many New Testament authors—"So then after the Lord had spoken unto them, he was received up into heaven, and sat on the right hand of God" (Mark 16:19). "Now of the things which we have spoken this is the sum: We have such an high priest, who is set on the right hand of the throne of the Majesty in the heavens" (Heb. 8:1). "But this man, after he had offered one sacrifice for sins for ever, sat down on the right hand of God" (Heb. 10:12). "Who is gone into heaven, and is on the right hand of God; angels and authorities and powers being made subject unto him" (1 Pet. 3:22). (See also: Luke 22:69; Acts 2:33; 5:31; Rom. 8:34; Eph. 1:20; Col. 3:1; Heb. 1:3, 13.)

2. This place is viewed by one New Testament martyr—"But he, being full of the Holy Ghost, looked up stedfastly into heaven, and saw the glory of God, and Jesus standing on the right hand of God, and said, Behold, I see the heavens opened, and the Son of man standing on the right hand of God" (Acts 7:55-56).

B. The performance involved—Just what kind of ministry does our Lord perform for us at the Father's right hand? In essence, he is there:

1. To be our forerunner—"Which hope we have as an anchor of the soul, both sure and stedfast, and which entereth into that within the veil; whither the forerunner is for us entered, even Jesus, made an high priest for ever after the order of Melchisedec" (Heb. 6:19-20).

2. To prepare a place for us—"In my Father's house are many mansions: if it were not so, I would have told you. I go to prepare a place for you" (John 14:2).

3. To give spiritual gifts to his followers—"(He that descended is the same also that ascended up far above all heavens, that he might fill all things.) And he gave some, apostles; and some, prophets; and some, evangelists; and some, pastors and teachers; for the perfecting of the saints, for the work of the ministry, for the edifying of the body of Christ: till we all come in the unity of the faith, and of the knowledge of the Son of God, unto a perfect man, unto the measure of the stature of the fulness of Christ: that we henceforth be no more children, tossed to and fro, and carried about with every wind of doctrine, by the sleight of men, and cunning craftiness, whereby they lie in wait to deceive" (Eph. 4:10-14).

4. To offer encouragement to his followers—"Seeing then that we have a great high priest, that is passed into the heavens, Jesus the Son of God, let us hold fast our profession. For we have not an high priest which cannot be touched with the feeling of our infirmities; but was in all points tempted like as we are, yet

without sin. Let us therefore come boldly unto the throne of grace, that we may obtain mercy, and find grace to help in time of need" (Heb. 4:14-16).

"Wherefore seeing we also are compassed about with so great a cloud of witnesses, let us lay aside every weight, and the sin which doth so easily beset us, and let us run with patience the race that is set before us, looking unto Jesus the author and finisher of our faith; who for the joy that was set before him endured the cross, despising the shame, and is set down at the right hand of the throne of God. For consider him that endured such contradiction of sinners against himself, lest ye be wearied and faint in your minds" (Heb. 12:1-3).

5. To make high priestly prayers for us—"Who is he that condemneth? It is Christ that died, yea rather, that is risen again, who is even at the right hand of God, who also maketh intercession for us" (Rom. 8:34). "For Christ is not entered into the holy places made with hands, which are the figures of the true; but into heaven itself, now to appear in the presence of God for us:" (Heb. 9:25).

Here he functions in a twofold manner:

a. Acting as our intercessor (due to the weakness and frailties of the believer)—While on earth, our Lord once told Peter: "Simon, Simon, behold, Satan hath desired to have you, that he may sift you as wheat: but I have prayed for thee, that thy faith fail not" (Luke 22:31-32).

According to many New Testament passages, the Savior continues to perform this blessed ministry for his people from heaven. "Wherefore he is able also to save them to the uttermost that come unto God by him, seeing he ever liveth to make intercession for them" (Heb. 7:25).

b. Acting as our advocate (due to the sins of the believer)—"If we confess our sins, he is faithful and just to forgive us our sins, and to cleanse us from all unrighteousness" (1 John 1:9). "My little children, these things write I unto you, that ye sin not. And if any man sin, we have an advocate with the Father, Jesus Christ the righteous" (1 John 2:1). "And I heard a loud voice saying in heaven, Now is come salvation, and strength, and the kingdom of our God, and the power of his Christ: for the accuser of our brethren is cast down, which accused them before our God day and night" (Rev. 12:10).

6. To send the promise of the Father (John 16; Acts 1:4; 2:33)—"And, being assembled together with them, commanded them that they should not depart from Jerusalem, but wait for the promise of the Father, which, saith he, ye have heard of me" (Acts 1:4).

Much ink has been used attempting to explain the five words "the promise of the Father." Various passages of Scripture make it clear that the promise of the Father (Joel 2:28; Acts 2:16) and also the promise of the Son (John 14:16-26; 15:26; 16:7) were references to the arrival of the Holy Spirit of God. "Therefore being by the right hand of God exalted, and having received of the Father the promise of the Holy Ghost, he hath shed forth this, which ye now see and hear" (Acts 2:33). The exaltation of Christ allows him to sit at the right hand of the Father and thus send the Holy Spirit of God on his believers.

7. To care for his churches (Rev. 1:10-3:22)—In this amazing passage the Apostle John, on the Isle of Patmos, sees the resurrected and glorified Christ standing among seven golden lampstands, dressed in the garb of a high priest. He is told that the lampstands symbolize local churches on earth.

8. To work through his people—"Verily, verily, I say unto you, He that believeth

on me, the works that I do shall he do also; and greater works than these shall he do; because I go unto my Father" (John 14:12).

9. To wait until his enemies become his footstool—"But this man, after he had offered one sacrifice for sins for ever, sat down on the right hand of God; from henceforth expecting till his enemies be made his footstool" (Heb. 10:12-13).

XVI. The Future Twofold Return of Jesus Christ

A. At the Rapture, where he comes *for* his people (thus introducing the great tribulation)

1. As predicted by the Savior himself—"Let not your heart be troubled: ye believe in God, believe also in me. In my Father's house are many mansions: if it were not so, I would have told you. I go to prepare a place for you. And if I go and prepare a place for you, I will come again, and receive you unto myself; that where I am, there ye may be also" (John 14:1-3).

2. As predicted by the Apostle Paul—"Behold, I shew you a mystery; We shall not all sleep, but we shall all be changed, in a moment, in the twinkling of an eye, at the last trump: for the trumpet shall sound, and the dead shall be raised incorruptible, and we shall be changed. For this corruptible must put on incorruption, and this mortal must put on immortality" (1 Cor. 15:51-53).

"For the Lord himself shall descend from heaven with a shout, with the voice of the archangel, and with the trump of God: and the dead in Christ shall rise first: then we which are alive and remain shall be caught up together with them in the clouds, to meet the Lord in the air: and so shall we ever be with the Lord" (1 Thess. 4:16-17).

B. At the Second Coming, where he comes *with* his people (thus concluding the great tribulation)

1. As foretold:

a. By Enoch—"And Enoch also, the seventh from Adam, prophesied of these, saying, Behold, the Lord cometh with ten thousands of his saints" (Jude 14).

b. By David—"Lift up your heads, O ye gates; even lift them up, ye everlasting doors; and the King of glory shall come in. Who is this King of glory? The LORD of hosts, he is the King of glory. Selah" (Psa. 24:9-10).

c. By Isaiah—"He will swallow up death in victory; and the Lord GOD will wipe away tears from off all faces; and the rebuke of his people shall he take away from off all the earth: for the LORD hath spoken it. And it shall be said in that day, Lo, this is our God; we have waited for him, and he will save us: this is the LORD; we have waited for him, we will be glad and rejoice in his salvation" (Isa. 25:8-9).

"And the glory of the LORD shall be revealed, and all flesh shall see it together: for the mouth of the LORD hath spoken it. . . . Behold, the Lord GOD will come with strong hand, and his arm shall rule for him: behold, his reward is with him, and his work before him" (Isa. 40:5, 10).

d. By Christ himself—"For the Son of man shall come in the glory of his Father with his angels; and then he shall reward every man according to his works" (Matt. 16:27). "And then shall appear the sign of the Son of man in heaven: and then shall all the tribes of the earth mourn, and they shall see the Son of man coming in the clouds of heaven with power and great glory" (Matt. 24:30). "Jesus saith unto him, Thou hast said: nevertheless I say unto you, Hereafter shall ye see the Son of man sitting on the right hand of power, and coming in the clouds of heaven" (Matt. 26:64).

e. By Paul—"And to you who are troubled rest with us, when the Lord Jesus shall be revealed from heaven with his mighty angels" (2 Thess. 1:7). "And then shall that Wicked be revealed, whom the Lord shall consume with the spirit of his mouth, and shall destroy with the brightness of his coming" (2 Thess. 2:8).

2. As fulfilled

   a. The wedding involved—"Let us be glad and rejoice, and give honour to him: for the marriage of the Lamb is come, and his wife hath made herself ready. And to her was granted that she should be arrayed in fine linen, clean and white: for the fine linen is the righteousness of saints. And he saith unto me, Write, Blessed are they which are called unto the marriage supper of the Lamb. And he saith unto me, These are the true sayings of God" (Rev. 19:7-9).

   b. The warfare involved

      (1) The warrior—"And I saw heaven opened, and behold a white horse; and he that sat upon him was called Faithful and True, and in righteousness he doth judge and make war. His eyes were as a flame of fire, and on his head were many crowns; and he had a name written, that no man knew, but he himself. And he was clothed with a vesture dipped in blood: and his name is called The Word of God. . . . And he hath on his vesture and on his thigh a name written, KING OF KINGS, AND LORD OF LORDS" (Rev. 19:11-13, 16).

      (2) The war—"And I saw the beast, and the kings of the earth, and their armies, gathered together to make war against him that sat on the horse, and against his army. And the beast was taken, and with him the false prophet that wrought miracles before him, with which he deceived them that had received the mark of the beast, and them that worshipped his image. These both were cast alive into a lake of fire burning with brimstone. And the remnant were slain with the sword of him that sat upon the horse, which sword proceeded out of his mouth: and all the fowls were filled with their flesh" (Rev. 19:19-21).

XVII. The Millennial Reign of Jesus Christ

   A. As foretold

      1. By David and the Psalm writers (47:7-8; 93:1; 96:10; 97:1; 98:8-9; 99:1; 103:19; 145:13; 146:10)
      2. By Isaiah (9:6-7; 24:23; 32:1; 52:7)
      3. By Micah (4:7; 5:2)
      4. By Joel (3:20-21)
      5. By Daniel (2:44; 4:3, 17, 32; 7:14, 18, 22, 27)
      6. By Jeremiah (23:5-6)
      7. By Gabriel (Luke 1:32-33)
      8. By Christ himself (Matt. 8:11; 13:43; 25:34; 26:29)
      9. By James, the half brother of Christ (Acts 15:15-17)
      10. By Peter (Acts 3:19-21)
      11. By Paul (Rom. 8:16-23; 15:11-12)

   B. As fulfilled—"And I saw thrones, and they sat upon them, and judgment was given unto them: and I saw the souls of them that were beheaded for the witness of Jesus, and for the word of God, and which had not worshipped the beast, neither his image, neither had received his mark upon their foreheads, or in their hands;

and they lived and reigned with Christ a thousand years. Blessed and holy is he that hath part in the first resurrection: on such the second death hath no power, but they shall be priests of God and of Christ, and shall reign with him a thousand years" (Rev. 20:4, 6).

XVIII. The Old Testament Witnesses of Jesus Christ—The Bible is a Christ-centered book. Jesus himself said the Old Testament spoke of him. "Search the scriptures; for in them ye think ye have eternal life: and they are they which testify of me" (John 5:39).

The following is a brief panorama of his story in history, as demonstrated by some Old Testament men and women. Events in their lives remind us of some aspect in the Savior's New Testament ministry.

A. Adam—His headship over a new creation (Gen. 1:28; Rom. 5:17-19; 1 Cor. 15:22, 45, 47; Heb. 2:7-9)

B. Moses—His prophetical ministry (Deut. 18:15-18; Heb. 3:5-6)

C. Melchizedek—His priestly ministry (Gen. 14:18-20; Psa. 110:4; Heb. 5–8)

D. David—His kingly ministry (2 Sam. 7:1-17; Mark 11:10; Rev. 5:5; 22:16)

E. Jeremiah—His sorrows (Jer. 3:20; 5:1-5; 8:20-22; 9:1; 10:19; 11:19)

F. Joseph—His sufferings (the most perfect type of Christ in the Old Testament)
   1. Hated without a cause (Gen. 37:4, 8; John 15:25)
   2. Ridiculed (Gen. 37:19; Luke 22:63)
   3. Plotted against (Gen. 37:20; John 11:53)
   4. Stripped of his robe (Gen. 37:23; John 19:23-24)
   5. Sold for silver (Gen. 37:28; Matt. 26:14-16)
   6. Lied about (Gen. 39:14; Matt. 26:61)
   7. Placed in captivity with two guilty men (Gen. 40:1-3; Luke 23:32-33)
   8. Unrecognized by his own (Gen. 42:8; John 1:11)

G. Isaac—His death (Gen. 22:2, 8, 10; Matt. 26:36, 42-43)

H. Jonah—His resurrection (Jonah 1:17; Matt. 12:40; 16:4; Luke 11:29)

I. Joshua—His victorious life (Joshua 1:3, 5-6, 8-9; John 10:17-18; 19:30)

J. Noah—His saving life (Gen. 6:13-14, 17-18; 1 Pet. 3:18-22)

K. Abraham—His father (Gen. 22:7-8; Matt. 26:36, 42-43)

L. Daniel—His acceptance by the Father (Dan. 9:23; 10:11, 19; Matt. 3:17; 17:5)

M. Elijah—His forerunner (Isa. 40:3-4; Matt. 17:11-12)

N. Elisha—His miracles (2 Kings 2:9; John 3:2): Elisha performed 14 miracles, nearly double those of any other Old Testament man, except Moses.

O. Ezekiel—His parables (Ezek. 17:2; 20:49; Matt. 13:3): There are 69 parables in the Old Testament; 23 are to be found in Ezekiel's book alone.

P. Ruth—His church (Ruth 2–4; 2 Cor. 11:2)

Q. Boaz—His love for the church (Ruth 2–4; Eph. 5:25-27)

R. Ezra—His zeal for the Scriptures (Neh. 8; Matt. 21:42; 22:29; Mark 12:10, 12:24; Luke 4:21; 24:27; John 10:35)

S. Nehemiah—His zeal for the Holy City (Neh. 1–2; Matt. 23:37-39; Luke 19:41)

T. Absalom: His opposition
   1. From Judas—Absalom was a betrayer and member of David's inner circle, as was Judas of Jesus' inner circle (2 Sam. 15; Matt. 26:14).
   2. From the coming Antichrist—Absalom plotted against the Davidic throne, as will the Antichrist (2 Sam. 15; Rev. 13)

U. Solomon—His wisdom (1 Kings 3:11-13; Luke 4:22; John 7:46)

V. Lot—His backslidden followers (Gen. 19; 2 Pet. 2:7)

THE DOCTRINE OF THE HOLY SPIRIT

INTRODUCTION

During one of his missionary trips, the Apostle Paul questioned a group of Ephesian "church members" (actually, they were disciples of John the Baptist) about the doctrine of the Holy Spirit. Their answer must have shocked him somewhat, for they replied, "We have not so much as heard whether there be any Holy Ghost" (Acts 19:2).

If Paul was shocked, surely the Father and Son were saddened as they viewed yet another example of the almost universal ignorance concerning the ministry of the blessed third Person in the Trinity. This statement by these Ephesian disciples, perhaps as no other in the Bible, illustrates the sorry and shameful treatment often given him. His very existence has been ignored and his ministry misunderstood.

If the Bible teaches anything, it teaches that there is a Trinity, and that the Trinity consists of three persons—the Father, who is a person; the Son, who is a person; and the Holy Spirit, who is a person. The Holy Spirit of God is a person, as much as the Father and the Son are persons.

The Holy Spirit is mentioned over 100 times in the Old Testament. In the New Testament alone there are some 261 passages that refer to the Holy Spirit. He is mentioned 56 times in the Gospels, 57 times in the book of Acts, 112 times in the Pauline Epistles, and 36 times in the remaining books of the New Testament.

These passages make it clear that the Holy Spirit is that blessed Third Person of the Godhead who lives in the heart of every Christian.

Even prior to considering the details of this study it can be said the one overriding and all-important mission prompting the various appearances and activities of the Holy Spirit was to introduce and clarify God's two great *Words* and God's two great *works*.

A. God's two great Words
  1. The written Word—"Knowing this first, that no prophecy of the scripture is of any private interpretation. For the prophecy came not in old time by the will of man: but holy men of God spake as they were moved by the Holy Ghost" (2 Pet. 1:20-21).
    "But as it is written, Eye hath not seen, nor ear heard, neither have entered into the heart of man, the things which God hath prepared for them that love him. But God hath revealed them unto us by his Spirit: for the Spirit searcheth all things, yea, the deep things of God. . . . But the natural man receiveth not the things of the Spirit of God: for they are foolishness unto him: neither can he know them, because they are spiritually discerned" (1 Cor. 2:9-10, 14).
  2. The Living Word—"But when the Comforter is come, whom I will send unto you from the Father, even the Spirit of truth, which proceedeth from the Father,

he shall testify of me. . . . He shall glorify me: for he shall receive of mine, and shall shew it unto you" (John 15:26; 16:14).

B. God's two great works

1. Creation—"And the earth was without form, and void; and darkness was upon the face of the deep. And the Spirit of God moved upon the face of the waters" (Gen. 1:2).

2. Redemption—"And the Spirit and the bride say, Come. And let him that heareth say, Come. And let him that is athirst come. And whosoever will, let him take the water of life freely" (Rev. 22:17).

I. The Personality of the Holy Spirit—The Holy Spirit of God is a Person, as much as the Father and Son are Persons, and, therefore, experiences all the sinless elements involved within a divine personality. Personality consists of possessing intellect, emotions, and will. The Holy Spirit has all three.

Both John and Paul often use masculine pronouns for the Holy Spirit, contrary to the normal Greek usage. The Greek word *pneuma*, translated "spirit" is neuter in gender. Note: "The Spirit of truth . . . *he* shall testify of me. . . . *He* shall not speak of himself" (John 15:26; 16:13). "That Holy Spirit of promise . . . *who* is the earnest of our inheritance" (Eph. 1:13-14).

A. He has a mind—"And he that searcheth the hearts knoweth what is the mind of the Spirit, because he maketh intercession for the saints according to the will of God" (Rom. 8:27). The first *he* in this verse is a reference to the Son of God, as seen in verse 34 of Romans 8, while the second *he* refers to the Holy Spirit himself. What a fantastic truth is seen here, for the believer enjoys the intercessory ministry of both the Son and Holy Spirit. "Who is he that condemneth? It is Christ that died, yea rather, that is risen again, who is even at the right hand of God, who also maketh intercession for us" (Rom. 8:34).

B. He searches out the human mind—"But God hath revealed them unto us by his Spirit: for the Spirit searcheth all things, yea, the deep things of God" (1 Cor. 2:10). In the verse just prior to this, Paul paraphrases from Isaiah 64:4 and writes: "But as it is written, Eye hath not seen, nor ear heard, neither have entered into the heart of man, the things which God hath prepared for them that love him" (1 Cor. 2:9).

C. He has a will—"But all these worketh that one and the selfsame Spirit, dividing to every man severally as he will" (1 Cor. 12:11). This is a reference to the various spiritual gifts that the Holy Spirit imparts to believers as he determines.

D. He forbids—"Now when they had gone throughout Phrygia and the region of Galatia, and were forbidden of the Holy Ghost to preach the word in Asia, after they were come to Mysia, they assayed to go into Bithynia: but the Spirit suffered them not" (Acts 16:6-7). Here, Paul, Silas, and Timothy were prohibited from going to two possible mission fields by the Spirit.

E. He permits—"And after he had seen the vision, immediately we endeavoured to go into Macedonia, assuredly gathering that the Lord had called us for to preach the gospel unto them" (Acts 16:10). This explains the reason for the previous prohibition.

F. He speaks—Note to whom he speaks.

1. To Philip in a desert—"Then the Spirit said unto Philip, Go near, and join thyself to this chariot" (Acts 8:29).

2. To Peter on a housetop—"While Peter thought on the vision, the Spirit said unto him, Behold, three men seek thee" (Acts 10:19).

3. To some elders in Antioch—"As they ministered to the Lord, and fasted, the

Holy Ghost said, Separate me Barnabas and Saul for the work whereunto I have called them" (Acts 13:2).

4. To seven churches in Asia Minor (see Rev. 2–3). On no less than seven occasions (one to each church) do we read the words: "He that hath an ear, let him hear what the Spirit saith unto the churches" (Rev. 2:7a; see also Rev. 2:11, 17, 29; 3:6, 13, 22.)

Note: What language did he use? Apparently he spoke Hebrew in the Old Testament, for young Samuel first mistook his voice for Eli's voice (see 1 Sam. 3:1-10). In the New Testament, inasmuch as his words are recorded in Greek, it can be assumed he spoke in Greek.

G. He loves—"Now I beseech you, brethren, for the Lord Jesus Christ's sake, and for the love of the Spirit, that ye strive together with me in your prayers to God for me" (Rom. 15:30). "As many as I love, I rebuke and chasten: be zealous therefore, and repent. He that hath an ear, let him hear what the Spirit saith unto the churches" (Rev. 3:19, 22).

It is glorious to know that each believer is loved by the Father (John 14:21; 16:27), Son (Gal. 2:20), and Holy Spirit.

H. He grieves—"And grieve not the holy Spirit of God, whereby ye are sealed unto the day of redemption" (Eph. 4:30). The command here is, literally, "Stop grieving the Holy Spirit of God." They were already doing this. (For further details concerning the nature of this grievance, see Rev. 2:4.) This grieving attribute of the Holy Spirit is really an extension of his love, for while one may be angered by his enemies, he can only be grieved by those he loves. "Nevertheless I have somewhat against thee, because thou hast left thy first love" (Rev. 2:4).

I. He prays—"Likewise the Spirit also helpeth our infirmities: for we know not what we should pray for as we ought: but the Spirit itself maketh intercession for us with groanings which cannot be uttered" (Rom. 8:26). In the difficult moments of our lives, how comforting it is to know we are being prayed for, perhaps by family members or some godly pastor, but how much more blessed to realize that the Holy Spirit of God offers up fervent and effective prayer for us.

II. The Deity of the Holy Spirit—In a sentence, the Holy Spirit is not only a person, but a divine person. The Scriptures declare this by a threefold argument.

A. He possesses the attributes of God.

1. He possesses divine life—"For the law of the Spirit of life in Christ Jesus hath made me free from the law of sin and death" (Rom. 8:2).

2. He possesses divine holiness (Matt. 12:32; Rom. 1:4).

3. He possesses divine righteousness (Rom. 8:4).

4. He possesses divine truth (John 14:17).

5. He possesses divine grace (Heb. 10:29).

6. He possesses divine love (Rom. 5:5; 15:30; Gal. 5:22)—"And hope maketh not ashamed; because the love of God is shed abroad in our hearts by the Holy Ghost which is given unto us" (Rom. 5:5).

7. He is eternal (Heb. 9:14).

8. He is sovereign (1 Cor. 12:11).

9. He is omnipresent—"Whither shall I go from thy spirit? Or whither shall I flee from thy presence? If I ascend up into heaven, thou art there: if I make my bed in hell, behold, thou art there. If I take the wings of the morning, and dwell in the uttermost parts of the sea; even there shall thy hand lead me, and thy right hand shall hold me. If I say, Surely the darkness shall cover me; even the night

shall be light about me. Yea, the darkness hideth not from thee; but the night shineth as the day: the darkness and the light are both alike to thee" (Psa. 139:7-12).

10. He is omnipotent (Job 33:4; Gen. 1:1; Psa. 104:30; Mic. 3:8; Zech. 4:6).

   a. In shaping us—"The Spirit of God hath made me, and the breath of the Almighty hath given me life" (Job 33:4).

   b. In strengthening us—"But truly I am full of power by the spirit of the LORD, and of judgment, and of might, to declare unto Jacob his transgression, and to Israel his sin" (Mic. 3:8). "Then he answered and spake unto me, saying, This is the word of the LORD unto Zerubbabel, saying, Not by might, nor by power, but by my spirit, saith the LORD of hosts" (Zech. 4:6).

11. He is omniscient (Isa. 40:13-14; John 16:13; 1 Cor. 2:10-12)—"O LORD, thou hast searched me, and known me. Thou knowest my downsitting and mine uprising, thou understandest my thought afar off. Thou compassest my path and my lying down, and art acquainted with all my ways. For there is not a word in my tongue, but, lo, O LORD, thou knowest it altogether. Thou hast beset me behind and before, and laid thine hand upon me. Such knowledge is too wonderful for me; it is high, I cannot attain unto it" (Psa. 139:1-6).

B. He is called God (Acts 5:3-4).

C. He is made equal with the Father and the Son—While the Holy Spirit does indeed occupy a place of submission in the Trinity, he is nevertheless not one whit behind the Father or Son in all their divine attributes. His perfect equality with the Father and Son is demonstrated through the following New Testament examples.

   1. In the baptismal experience of Christ—"And Jesus, when he was baptized, went up straightway out of the water: and, lo, the heavens were opened unto him, and he saw the Spirit of God descending like a dove, and lighting upon him: and lo a voice from heaven, saying, This is my beloved Son, in whom I am well pleased" (Matt. 3:16-17).

   2. As declared by Jesus in the Upper Room—"And I will pray the Father, and he shall give you another Comforter, that he may abide with you for ever" (John 14:16).

   3. As declared by Jesus on the Mount of Olives—"Go ye therefore, and teach all nations, baptizing them in the name of the Father, and of the Son, and of the Holy Ghost: Teaching them to observe all things whatsoever I have commanded you: and, lo, I am with you alway, even unto the end of the world. Amen" (Matt. 28:19-20).

   4. As declared by Paul—"The grace of the Lord Jesus Christ, and the love of God, and the communion of the Holy Ghost, be with you all. Amen" (2 Cor. 13:14).

   5. As declared by Peter—"Elect according to the foreknowledge of God the Father, through sanctification of the Spirit, unto obedience and sprinkling of the blood of Jesus Christ: Grace unto you, and peace, be multiplied" (1 Pet. 1:2).

III. The Names and Titles of the Holy Spirit—Often in the Scriptures, one may learn much about someone simply by studying the names and titles given to that person. So it is with the Holy Spirit. The 13 titles ascribed to him provide much insight into his true nature. He is called:

A. The Spirit of God (1 Cor. 3:16)

B. The Spirit of Christ (Rom. 8:9)—Theologically considered, he is the Spirit *from* Christ.

C. The eternal Spirit (Heb. 9:14)—Thus, to overemphasize the temporary things down here grieves him, for they are passing, and he is the eternal Spirit.

D. The Spirit of truth (John 16:13)—Any deceit, deception, distortion, or dishonesty grieves him, for he is the Spirit of truth.

E. The Spirit of grace (Heb. 10:29)—The curse of legalism grieves him, for he is the Spirit of grace.

F. The Spirit of glory (1 Pet. 4:14)—Earthly greed, materialism, corrupt doctrine such as prosperity theology grieve him, for he is the Spirit of glory.

G. The Spirit of life—Any deadness or lukewarmness on our part grieves him, for he is the Spirit of life. Dr. Lewis Sperry Chafer writes:

> A dead leaf that may have clung to the twig through the external raging storms of winter, will silently fall to the ground when the new flow of sap from within has begun in the spring. The leaf falls because there is a new manifestation of life pressing from within outward. A dead leaf cannot remain where a new bud is springing, nor can worldliness remain where the blessings of the Spirit are flowing. We are not called upon to preach against dead leaves. We have a message of the imperishable spring. It is the outflowing of the limitless life of God. (*He That Is Spiritual,* p. 69)

H. The Spirit of wisdom and revelation (Eph. 1:17)—Thus, to neglect a careful and prayerful reading of one's Bible grieves the Holy Spirit, for he is the Spirit of wisdom and revelation. Note the warnings of Hosea and Jesus concerning this: "My people are destroyed for lack of knowledge: because thou hast rejected knowledge, I will also reject thee, that thou shalt be no priest to me: seeing thou hast forgotten the law of thy God, I will also forget thy children" (Hos. 4:6). "Jesus answered and said unto them, Ye do err, not knowing the scriptures, nor the power of God" (Matt. 22:29).

I. The Comforter—"But the Comforter, which is the Holy Ghost, whom the Father will send in my name, he shall teach you all things, and bring all things to your remembrance, whatsoever I have said unto you" (John 14:26).

> C. I. Scofield observes the following concerning the word *comforter* in this passage.

> It is the Greek *parakletos,* meaning, "one called alongside to help," thus, a counselor. It is translated "advocate" in 1 John 2:1. Christ is the Christian's Paraclete with the Father when the Christian sins; the Holy Spirit is the Christian's indwelling Paraclete to help his ignorance and infirmity, and to make intercession (Rom. 8:26-27). (*New Scofield Reference Bible,* p. 1147)

J. The Spirit of promise (Acts 1:4-5)

K. The Spirit of adoption (Rom. 8:15)

L. The Spirit of holiness (Rom. 1:4)—Any uncleanness, defilement, impurity grieves him, for he is the Spirit of holiness. It can be said one's understanding of the hideousness of sin is directly related to his understanding of the holiness of God. The great prophet Isaiah realized this when he "saw also the LORD sitting upon a throne, high and lifted up" (Isa. 6:1) and heard the angels cry, "Holy, holy, holy, is the LORD of hosts; the whole earth is full of his glory" (Isa. 6:3). Note the prophet's immediate reaction to all this: "Then said I, Woe is me! for I am undone; because I am a man of unclean lips, and I dwell in the midst of a people of unclean lips: for mine eyes have seen the King, the LORD of hosts" (Isa. 6:5).

M. The Spirit of faith (2 Cor. 4:13). Any unbelief, doubt, fear, or worry on the part of a believer grieves the Holy Spirit, for he is the Spirit of faith.

IV. The Emblems of the Holy Spirit—Like his 13 names and titles, his eight designated emblems shed light upon both his nature and his mission.

A. The dove—The dove indicates purity, peace, and modesty. "And John bare record, saying, I saw the Spirit descending from heaven like a dove, and it abode upon him" (John 1:32).

B. Water—Water indicates life and cleansing. "For I will pour water upon him that is thirsty, and floods upon the dry ground: I will pour my spirit upon thy seed, and my blessing upon thine offspring" (Isa. 44:3).

"In the last day, that great day of the feast, Jesus stood and cried, saying, If any man thirst, let him come unto me, and drink. He that believeth on me, as the scripture hath said, out of his belly shall flow rivers of living water. (But this spake he of the Spirit, which they that believe on him should receive: for the Holy Ghost was not yet given; because that Jesus was not yet glorified)" (John 7:37-39).

C. Oil—Oil indicates light, healing, and anointing for service. "The Spirit of the Lord is upon me, because he hath anointed me to preach the gospel to the poor; he hath sent me to heal the brokenhearted, to preach deliverance to the captives, and recovering of sight to the blind, to set at liberty them that are bruised" (Luke 4:18). "How God anointed Jesus of Nazareth with the Holy Ghost and with power: who went about doing good, and healing all that were oppressed of the devil; for God was with him" (Acts 10:38). "Thou hast loved righteousness, and hated iniquity; therefore God, even thy God, hath anointed thee with the oil of gladness above thy fellows" (Heb. 1:9). "But ye have an unction from the Holy One, and ye know all things" (1 John 2:20).

In the Old Testament there were three kinds of individuals anointed for special service. These were the office of the prophet, of the priest, and of the king. In a very real sense, the Holy Spirit desires to anoint us as we serve in these roles:

1. That of a prophet, as we represent God to man
2. That of a priest, as we represent man to God
3. That of a king, as we prepare to rule with God

D. A seal—A seal indicates ownership, finished transaction, identification, security, genuineness, value, and authority. "In whom ye also trusted, after that ye heard the word of truth, the gospel of your salvation: in whom also after that ye believed, ye were sealed with that holy Spirit of promise" (Eph. 1:13). "And grieve not the holy Spirit of God, whereby ye are sealed unto the day of redemption" (Eph. 4:30). "Who hath also sealed us, and given the earnest of the Spirit in our hearts" (2 Cor. 1:22).

There are three important occasions in the Bible when a seal is used.

1. As used by the Persian king Darius to secure Daniel in the lions' den (Dan. 6:16-17)
2. As used by the Persian king Ahasuerus (upon the advice of wicked Haman) to plot the wholesale murder of the Jews (Esther 3:8-12)
3. As used by Pilate to seal the tomb of Jesus (Matt. 27:66)

E. Wind—Wind indicates unseen power. "The wind bloweth where it listeth, and thou hearest the sound thereof, but canst not tell whence it cometh, and whither it goeth: so is every one that is born of the Spirit" (John 3:8). "And when the day of Pentecost was fully come,they were all with one accord in one place. And suddenly there came a sound from heaven as of a rushing mighty wind, and it filled all the house where they were sitting" (Acts 2:1-2).

F. Fire—Fire indicates presence, approval, protection, purifying, gift, and judgment.

   1. The presence of the Lord—"And the angel of the LORD appeared unto him in a flame of fire out of the midst of a bush: and he looked, and, behold, the bush burned with fire, and the bush was not consumed" (Exod. 3:2).

   2. The approval of the Lord—"And there came a fire out from before the LORD, and consumed upon the altar the burnt offering and the fat: which when all the people saw, they shouted, and fell on their faces" (Lev. 9:24).

   3. The protection of the Lord—"And the LORD went before them by day in a pillar of a cloud, to lead them the way; and by night in a pillar of fire, to give them light; to go by day and night" (Exod. 13:21).

   4. The purifying from the Lord (Isa. 6:1-8).

   5. The gift of the Lord—"And there appeared unto them cloven tongues like as of fire, and it sat upon each of them" (Acts 2:3).

   6. The judgment of the Lord—"For our God is a consuming fire" (Heb. 12:29).

G. An earnest—An earnest indicates firstfruits, down payment, a pledge, an assurance of the eventual complete payment. "Who hath also sealed us, and given the earnest of the Spirit in our hearts" (2 Cor. 1:22). "Now he that hath wrought us for the selfsame thing is God, who also hath given unto us the earnest of the Spirit" (2 Cor. 5:5). "Which is the earnest of our inheritance until the redemption of the purchased possession, unto the praise of his glory" (Eph. 1:14).

    The earnest mentioned here may be the blood of Christ, or perhaps the presence of the Holy Spirit himself. The believer's eternal security is assured by the earnest of the Holy Spirit as seen by the following: A man securing an object by earnest money can eventually react in one of four ways:

   1. He can decide he doesn't want or need it.

   2. He can conclude he can't afford it.

   3. He can forget about it.

   4. He can keep his word and secure it.

H. Clothing—"And, behold, I send the promise of my Father upon you: but tarry ye in the city of Jerusalem, until ye be endued with power from on high" (Luke 24:49). The word *endued* here is a transliteration of the Greek word *enduo*, referring to clothes one would wear. It is used in describing:

   1. The clothes worn by John the Baptist (Mark 1:6)

   2. The purple robe put on Jesus by the Roman soldiers (Mark 15:17)

   3. The high priestly garment the Savior now wears in heaven (Rev. 1:13)

   4. The pure white linen the saints will wear (Rev. 19:14)

In light of this, it can be concluded that the "clothes" mentioned here in Luke 24:49 are a reference to the coming of the Holy Spirit at Pentecost. (See Acts 2:1-3.)

V. The Various Ministries of the Holy Spirit—Many erroneously believe the Holy Spirit first came to earth at Pentecost in Acts 2. This is not true. The Word of God assigns no less than 11 mighty ministries of the Spirit, and many were performed in Old Testament times. Let us consider these separately.

A. His ministry concerning the universe—According to David, the Father created all things. "The heavens declare the glory of God; and the firmament sheweth his handiwork" (Psa. 19:1).

    However, John declares the Son did it. "All things were made by him; and without him was not any thing made that was made. In him was life; and the life was the light of men" (John 1:3-4).

Finally, in other passages, the Holy Spirit is said to have performed the initial act of Creation. What are we to believe? The answer is, of course, that all three persons in the Trinity had a part. As an illustration let us consider an important executive who determines to build a spacious and expensive home. He, thus, employs an architect to design the necessary plans for this home. The architect thereupon secures a competent contractor to follow his blueprints. In this illustration the executive is the Father, the architect is the Son, and the contractor is the Holy Spirit. The following verses, then, refer to the work of this divine Contractor.

1. In creating the stars—"By the word of the LORD were the heavens made; and all the host of them by the breath of his mouth" (Psa. 33:6).
2. In creating the earth—"And the earth was without form, and void; and darkness was upon the face of the deep. And the Spirit of God moved upon the face of the waters" (Gen. 1:2).

   Note: The Hebrew word *rachaph,* here translated "moved," occurs only one other time in the Old Testament, where Moses describes God's gentle dealings with Israel: "As an eagle stirreth up her nest, fluttereth over her young, spreadeth abroad her wings, taketh them, beareth them on her wings" (Deut. 32:11).

   Here the Hebrew is translated "flutter." All this suggests the gentle motion of an eagle as she quietly hovers over her nest, imparting her body heat upon the eggs until they are hatched. The Holy Spirit thus acted in similar fashion in regards to the earth.
3. In creating the trees, birds, animals, and fish
   a. The trees (Psa. 104:16)
   b. The birds (Psa. 104:11, 17, 20)
   c. The animals (Psa. 104:12, 18, 21-22, 25)
   d. The fish (Psa. 104:25)

   "Thou sendest forth thy spirit, they are created: and thou renewest the face of the earth" (Psa. 104:30).
4. In creating man—"The Spirit of God hath made me, and the breath of the Almighty hath given me life" (Job 33:4).

B. His ministry concerning the Scriptures—In a word, the Holy Spirit is the author of the Word of God. Furthermore, he has chosen three basic methods in the preparation and reception of his divine manuscript, the Bible. These "steps of the Spirit" are:

   • Revelation—That process whereby the Holy Spirit spoke to the 40 human writers of the Bible the message he wanted them to transmit. This process flowed from God to man.
   • Inspiration—That process whereby the Holy Spirit guided the very pen of these 40 writers so that the spoken message would be accurately written. This process flowed from man to paper.
   • Illumination—That process whereby the Holy Spirit takes the written Word when it is preached and read and enlightens those human ears who will hear it. This process flows from paper to heart.

   The following passages bear all this out.
1. The Holy Spirit is the Author of the Old Testament.

a. According to David—"The spirit of the Lord spake by me, and his word was in my tongue" (2 Sam. 23:2).

b. According to Isaiah—"As for me, this is my covenant with them, saith the Lord; My spirit that is upon thee, and my words which I have put in thy mouth, shall not depart out of thy mouth, nor out of the mouth of thy seed, nor out of the mouth of thy seed's seed, saith the Lord, from henceforth and for ever" (Isa. 59:21).

c. According to Jeremiah—"Then the Lord put forth his hand, and touched my mouth. And the Lord said unto me, Behold, I have put my words in thy mouth" (Jer. 1:9).

d. According to Jesus—"For verily I say unto you, Till heaven and earth pass, one jot or one tittle shall in no wise pass from the law, till all be fulfilled" (Matt. 5:18). "Unto whom the word of God came, and the scripture cannot be broken" (John 10:35).

e. According to Peter—"For the prophecy came not in old time by the will of man: but holy men of God spake as they were moved by the Holy Ghost" (2 Pet. 1:21).

f. According to Paul—"And that from a child thou hast known the holy scriptures, which are able to make thee wise unto salvation through faith which is in Christ Jesus. All scripture is given by inspiration of God, and is profitable for doctrine, for reproof, for correction, for instruction in righteousness: That the man of God may be perfect, throughly furnished unto all good works" (2 Tim. 3:15-17).

2. The Holy Spirit is the Author of the New Testament.

a. According to Jesus—"These things have I spoken unto you, being yet present with you. But the Comforter, which is the Holy Ghost, whom the Father will send in my name, he shall teach you all things, and bring all things to your remembrance, whatsoever I have said unto you" (John 14:25-26).

b. According to Paul—"If any man think himself to be a prophet, or spiritual, let him acknowledge that the things that I write unto you are the commandments of the Lord" (1 Cor. 14:37).

c. According to John—"I was in the Spirit on the Lord's day, and heard behind me a great voice, as of a trumpet, saying, I am Alpha and Omega, the first and the last: and, What thou seest, write in a book, and send it unto the seven churches which are in Asia; unto Ephesus, and unto Smyrna, and unto Pergamos, and unto Thyatira, and unto Sardis, and unto Philadelphia, and unto Laodicea" (Rev. 1:10-11).

C. His ministry concerning the nation of Israel

1. He came upon Israel's leaders—No less than 16 Old Testament individuals are said to have experienced the anointing of the Holy Spirit.

a. Upon Joseph—"And Pharaoh said unto his servants, Can we find such a one as this is, a man in whom the Spirit of God is?" (Gen. 41:38).

b. Upon Moses—"And I will come down and talk with thee there: and I will take of the spirit which is upon thee, and will put it upon them; and they shall bear the burden of the people with thee, that thou bear it not thyself alone" (Num. 11:17).

c. Upon Joshua—"And the Lord said unto Moses, Take thee Joshua the son of

Nun, a man in whom is the spirit, and lay thine hand upon him" (Num. 27:18).

d. Upon Othniel—"And the Spirit of the LORD came upon him, and he judged Israel, and went out to war: and the LORD delivered Chushan-rishathaim king of Mesopotamia into his hand; and his hand prevailed against Chushan-rishathaim" (Judg. 3:10).

e. Upon Gideon—"But the Spirit of the LORD came upon Gideon, and he blew a trumpet; and Abi-ezer was gathered after him" (Judg. 6:34).

f. Upon Jephthah—"Then the Spirit of the LORD came upon Jephthah, and he passed over Gilead, and Manasseh, and passed over Mizpeh of Gilead, and from Mizpeh of Gilead he passed over unto the children of Ammon" (Judg. 11:29).

g. Upon Samson—At least three times we read of the Holy Spirit coming upon this Hebrew strong man. "And when he came unto Lehi, the Philistines shouted against him: and the Spirit of the LORD came mightily upon him, and the cords that were upon his arms became as flax that was burnt with fire, and his bands loosed from off his hands. And he found a new jawbone of an ass, and put forth his hand, and took it, and slew a thousand men therewith" (Judg. 15:14-15). (See also 14:6, 19.)

h. Upon Saul
   (1) After he was anointed king by Samuel—"And when they came thither to the hill, behold, a company of prophets met him; and the Spirit of God came upon him, and he prophesied among them" (1 Sam. 10:10).
   (2) Just before his victory at Jabesh-gilead—"And the Spirit of God came upon Saul when he heard those tidings, and his anger was kindled greatly" (1 Sam. 11:6).

i. Upon David—Unlike Saul's case, we are never told that the Holy Spirit departed from David. However, on one occasion David was afraid he might indeed withdraw himself. "Cast me not away from thy presence; and take not thy holy spirit from me" (Psa. 51:11). "Then Samuel took the horn of oil, and anointed him in the midst of his brethren: and the Spirit of the LORD came upon David from that day forward" (1 Sam. 16:13).

j. Upon Elijah
   (1) As testified to by Obadiah (1 Kings 18:12)
   (2) As testified to by some prophets at Jericho (2 Kings 2:16)

k. Upon Elisha (2 Kings 2:15)

l. Upon Ezekiel—"And the spirit entered into me when he spake unto me, and set me upon my feet, that I heard him that spake unto me" (Ezek. 2:2).

m. Upon Daniel
   (1) As testified to by King Nebuchadnezzar (Dan. 4:9)
   (2) As testified by a frightened queen (Dan. 5:1)
   (3) As testified by King Darius (Dan. 6:3)

n. Upon Micah—"But truly I am full of power by the spirit of the LORD, and of judgment, and of might, to declare unto Jacob his transgression, and to Israel his sin" (Mic. 3:8).

o. Upon Azariah the prophet—"And the Spirit of God came upon Azariah the son of Oded" (2 Chron. 15:1).

p. Upon Zechariah the high priest—"And the Spirit of God came upon Zechariah the son of Jehoiada the priest, which stood above the people, and said unto them, Thus saith God, Why transgress ye the commandments of the LORD, that ye cannot prosper? because ye have forsaken the LORD, he hath also forsaken you" (2 Chron. 24:20).

2. He came upon Israel's elders—"And the LORD came down in a cloud, and spake unto him, and took of the spirit that was upon him, and gave it unto the seventy elders: and it came to pass, that, when the spirit rested upon them, they prophesied, and did not cease" (Num. 11:25).

3. He came upon Israel's tabernacle—"Then a cloud covered the tent of the congregation, and the glory of the LORD filled the tabernacle" (Exod. 40:34).

4. He came upon Israel's temple—"And it came to pass, when the priests were come out of the holy place, that the cloud filled the house of the LORD" (1 Kings 8:10).

5. He led Israel through the desert—"Thou gavest also thy good spirit to instruct them, and withheldest not thy manna from their mouth, and gavest them water for their thirst" (Neh. 9:20).

   In spite of his goodness to them, Israel grieved the blessed Holy Spirit. "But they rebelled, and vexed his holy Spirit: therefore he was turned to be their enemy, and he fought against them" (Isa. 63:10).

6. He will come upon Israel during the tribulation. (See Joel 2:28-32; Rev. 7:24.)

7. He will come upon Israel during the Millennium—"Neither will I hide my face any more from them: for I have poured out my spirit upon the house of Israel, saith the Lord GOD" (Ezek. 39:29). (See also Ezek. 37:13-14; Zech. 12:10.)

D. His ministry concerning the devil—The Holy Spirit now acts as a divine dam, holding back and limiting the full power of Satan and of sin.

1. As stated by Isaiah—"So shall they fear the name of the LORD from the west, and his glory from the rising of the sun. When the enemy shall come in like a flood, the Spirit of the LORD shall lift up a standard against him" (Isa. 59:19).

2. As stated by Paul—In his second letter to the church at Thessalonica Paul describes the coming Antichrist. The apostle writes, "And now you know what is holding him back, so that he may be revealed at the proper time. For the secret power of lawlessness is already at work; but the one who now holds it back will continue to do so till he is taken out of the way. And then the lawless one will be revealed, whom the Lord Jesus will overthrow with the breath of his mouth and destroy by the splendour of his coming" (2 Thess. 2:6-8, NIV).

   The one described in these verses holding back the onslaught of evil is thought by many to be the Holy Spirit. Here, Paul states that at the beginning of the tribulation the restraining power of the Holy Spirit will be somewhat removed, thus allowing Satan and his hateful Antichrist to briefly reign over the earth for a seven-year period.

E. His ministry concerning the Savior—From his bodily conception to his final ascension, the Lord Jesus Christ was led by the Holy Spirit.

1. The Savior was begotten by the Holy Spirit.

   a. As explained by the angel to Mary—"And the angel answered and said unto her, The Holy Ghost shall come upon thee, and the power of the Highest shall overshadow thee: therefore also that holy thing which shall be born of thee shall be called the Son of God" (Luke 1:35).

   b. As explained by the angel to Joseph—"Now the birth of Jesus Christ was on this wise: When as his mother Mary was espoused to Joseph, before they came together, she was found with child of the Holy Ghost. Then Joseph her husband, being a just man, and not willing to make her a publick example, was minded to put her away privily. But while he thought on these things, behold, the angel of the Lord appeared unto him in a dream, saying, Joseph, thou son of David, fear not to take unto thee Mary thy wife: for that which is conceived in her is of the Holy Ghost" (Matt. 1:18-20).

Thus, the real Father of Christ's body was the Holy Spirit, and the real miracle was not in the Savior's birth, but in his supernatural conception.

2. The Savior was anointed by the Holy Spirit—"And Jesus, when he was baptized, went up straightway out of the water: and, lo, the heavens were opened unto him, and he saw the Spirit of God descending like a dove, and lighting upon him" (Matt. 3:16). "The Spirit of the Lord is upon me, because he hath anointed me to preach the gospel to the poor; he hath sent me to heal the brokenhearted, to preach deliverance to the captives, and recovering of sight to the blind, to set at liberty them that are bruised" (Luke 4:18).

"How God anointed Jesus of Nazareth with the Holy Ghost and with power: who went about doing good, and healing all that were oppressed of the devil; for God was with him" (Acts 10:38). "Thou hast loved righteousness, and hated iniquity; therefore God, even thy God, hath anointed thee with the oil of gladness above thy fellows" (Heb. 1:9).

3. The Savior was sealed by the Holy Spirit—"Labour not for the meat which perisheth, but for that meat which endureth unto everlasting life, which the Son of man shall give unto you: for him hath God the Father sealed" (John 6:27). The seal here demonstrated the Son's identification with both the Father and the Holy Spirit. It also spoke of his genuineness, value, and authority.

4. The Savior was led by the Holy Spirit—"Then was Jesus led up of the Spirit into the wilderness to be tempted of the devil" (Matt. 4:1).

5. The Savior was empowered by the Holy Spirit—"But if I cast out devils by the Spirit of God, then the kingdom of God is come unto you" (Matt. 12:28).

According to Philippians 2:5-8, Christ abstained from using, in an independent way, his divine attributes (his omnipresence, omniscience, etc.) while on earth, but chose, rather, to depend completely upon the Holy Spirit for strength and guidance. "Let this mind be in you, which was also in Christ Jesus: who, being in the form of God, thought it not robbery to be equal with God: but made himself of no reputation, and took upon him the form of a servant, and was made in the likeness of men: and being found in fashion as a man, he humbled himself, and became obedient unto death, even the death of the cross" (Phil. 2:5-8).

6. The Savior was filled by the Holy Spirit—"For he whom God hath sent speaketh the words of God: for God giveth not the Spirit by measure unto him" (John 3:34). "And Jesus being full of the Holy Ghost returned from Jordan, and was led by the Spirit into the wilderness," (Luke 4:1). The words *filled* and *full* refer, simply, to "control." Thus, the Savior was totally controlled by the Holy Spirit while on this earth.

7. The Savior sorrowed in the Holy Spirit—"When Jesus therefore saw her weeping, and the Jews also weeping which came with her, he groaned in the spirit, and was troubled" (John 11:33).

8. The Savior rejoiced in the Holy Spirit—"In that hour Jesus rejoiced in spirit, and said, I thank thee, O Father, Lord of heaven and earth, that thou hast hid these

things from the wise and prudent, and hast revealed them unto babes: even so, Father; for so it seemed good in thy sight" (Luke 10:21).

9. The Savior offered himself at Calvary through the Holy Spirit—"How much more shall the blood of Christ, who through the eternal Spirit offered himself without spot to God, purge your conscience from dead works to serve the living God?" (Heb. 9:14).

10. The Savior was resurrected by the Holy Spirit—"And declared to be the Son of God with power, according to the spirit of holiness, by the resurrection from the dead" (Rom. 1:4). "For Christ also hath once suffered for sins, the just for the unjust, that he might bring us to God, being put to death in the flesh, but quickened by the Spirit" (1 Pet. 3:18).

11. The Savior commanded his disciples through the Holy Spirit—"Until the day in which he was taken up, after that he through the Holy Ghost had given commandments unto the apostles whom he had chosen" (Acts 1:2).

12. The Savior will return and raise the dead in Christ through the Holy Spirit—"But if the Spirit of him that raised up Jesus from the dead dwell in you, he that raised up Christ from the dead shall also quicken your mortal bodies by his Spirit that dwelleth in you" (Rom. 8:11).

The point of this particular section of our study should be painfully obvious. If the sinless Son of God found it necessary to depend totally upon the Holy Spirit to form every word and guide every step, how much more is this absolutely vital for us?

F. His ministry concerning the sinner—During his midnight discourse, just prior to entering Gethsemane, our Lord spoke the following words to his sorrowing disciples about the Holy Spirit: "Nevertheless I tell you the truth; It is expedient for you that I go away: for if I go not away, the Comforter will not come unto you; but if I depart, I will send him unto you. And when he is come, he will reprove the world of sin, and of righteousness, and of judgment: of sin, because they believe not on me; of righteousness, because I go to my Father,and ye see me no more; of judgment, because the prince of this world is judged" (John 16:7-11).

The key word in this passage is the word *reprove*. In the Greek it is *elegcho*, which is elsewhere translated as follows: To convince: "Which of you convinceth me of sin? And if I say the truth, why do ye not believe me?" (John 8:46). To convict: "And they which heard it, being convicted by their own conscience, went out one by one, beginning at the eldest, even unto the last: and Jesus was left alone, and the woman standing in the midst" (John 8:9). To tell someone his fault: "Moreover if thy brother shall trespass against thee, go and tell him his fault between thee and him alone: if he shall hear thee, thou hast gained thy brother" (Matt. 18:15).

Thus, the holy Hound of Heaven, as he has been called, will track down the sinner, and, upon "catching" him, will (1) convince him; (2) convict him; and (3) tell him his faults.

1. He convicts man.

a. Of sin—Here the sin is not sex, smoking, or swearing, but rejecting Christ's sacrifice on Calvary. This is, of course, the one ultimate sin which will damn a man's soul to hell forever. "He that believeth on him is not condemned: but he that believeth not is condemned already, because he hath not believed in the name of the only begotten Son of God" (John 3:18).

It is important to fully understand this fact. Often the seeking sinner is left confused and uncertain. How many sins must he be expected to repent of to be saved? What about those sins he may have forgotten? Not only is this concept confusing to the particularly immoral unsaved man, but it is equally so to the moral unsaved man. After all, he does not drink, gamble, smoke, or even fudge on his income tax report. Thus, he concludes he has no need of salvation. But, in fact, he too, like the drunkard, is guilty of rejecting Christ's sacrifice on the cross and, therefore, is in desperate need of repentance and salvation.

    b. Of Christ's righteousness—Later, the Holy Spirit directed the Apostle Paul to write an entire epistle on this one word *righteousness.* In this epistle (the book of Romans) Paul stresses three things:

        (1) God *is* righteousness.

        (2) God *demands* righteousness.

        (3) God *provides* righteousness.

    c. Of future judgment—In this area, the Holy Spirit would point out to the sinner that:

        (1) All unsaved people belong to Satan—"Ye are of your father the devil, and the lusts of your father ye will do. He was a murderer from the beginning, and abode not in the truth, because there is no truth in him. When he speaketh a lie, he speaketh of his own: for he is a liar, and the father of it" (John 8:44).

        (2) Satan's doom is already in the making—"And the God of peace shall bruise Satan under your feet shortly. The grace of our Lord Jesus Christ be with you. Amen" (Rom. 16:20).

        (3) All unsaved people will share his doom—"Then shall he say also unto them on the left hand, Depart from me, ye cursed, into everlasting fire, prepared for the devil and his angels" (Matt. 25:41).

2. Seven classic examples of the Holy Spirit's convicting ministry found in the book of Acts

    a. The crowd at Pentecost (upon hearing the sermon preached by Peter)—"Now when they heard this, they were pricked in their heart, and said unto Peter and to the rest of the apostles, Men and brethren, what shall we do?" (Acts 2:37).

    b. The Ethiopian eunuch (Acts 8:29-38)

    c. Saul of Tarsus (Acts 9:1-6)

    d. A centurion named Cornelius and the Gentiles at Caesarea—"While Peter yet spake these words, the Holy Ghost fell on all them which heard the word" (Acts 10:44).

    e. The Philippian jailor (Acts 16:25-34)—"Then he called for a light, and sprang in, and came trembling, and fell down before Paul and Silas, and brought them out, and said, Sirs, what must I do to be saved?" (Acts 16:29-30).

    f. A governor named Felix—"And after certain days, when Felix came with his wife Drusilla, which was a Jewess, he sent for Paul, and heard him concerning the faith in Christ. And as he reasoned of righteousness, temperance, and judgment to come, Felix trembled, and answered, Go thy way for this time; when I have a convenient season, I will call for thee" (Acts 24:24-25).

    g. A king named Agrippa (Acts 26:23-28)—"Then Agrippa said unto Paul, Almost thou persuadest me to be a Christian" (Acts 26:28).

In conclusion, it may be stated that the chief ministry performed by the Holy Spirit to the sinner is that of old fashioned, pulse-pounding, blood-racing conviction.

G. His ministry concerning the church—Of the three basic institutions in the Bible (marriage, human government, and the church), none is more important to the Holy Spirit than the church. It was to aid the growth of the church that he formally came at Pentecost.

1. The Holy Spirit and the universal church—In a sentence, he both founded and formed it. "Now therefore ye are no more strangers and foreigners, but fellow citizens with the saints, and of the household of God; and are built upon the foundation of the apostles and prophets, Jesus Christ himself being the chief corner stone; in whom all the building fitly framed together groweth unto an holy temple in the Lord: in whom ye also are builded together for an habitation of God through the Spirit" (Eph. 2:19-22).

2. The Holy Spirit and the local church

   a. He desires to inspire its worship and service—"For we are the circumcision, which worship God in the spirit, and rejoice in Christ Jesus, and have no confidence in the flesh" (Phil. 3:3). If allowed by the pastor and the people, the Spirit of God can guarantee both the presence and power of God at each church meeting.

   b. He desires to direct its missionary work—"Then the Spirit said unto Philip, Go near, and join thyself to this chariot" (Acts 8:29). "As they ministered to the Lord, and fasted, the Holy Ghost said, Separate me Barnabas and Saul for the work whereunto I have called them. . . . So they, being sent forth by the Holy Ghost, departed unto Seleucia; and from thence they sailed to Cyprus" (Acts 13:2, 4).

   "Now when they had gone throughout Phrygia and the region of Galatia, and were forbidden of the Holy Ghost to preach the word in Asia, after they were come to Mysia, they assayed to go into Bithynia: but the Spirit suffered them not. . . . And after he had seen the vision, immediately we endeavoured to go into Macedonia, assuredly gathering that the Lord had called us for to preach the gospel unto them" (Acts 16:6-7, 10).

   c. He desires to aid in its singing services—"And be not drunk with wine, wherein is excess; but be filled with the Spirit; speaking to yourselves in psalms and hymns and spiritual songs, singing and making melody in your heart to the Lord" (Eph. 5:18-19). Many times a visiting speaker in a church has discovered to his delight that the music director has unknowingly chosen those songs and special music which correspond perfectly to the message. Obviously, both speaker and song leader were sensitive to the ministry of the Spirit.

   d. He desires to appoint its preachers—"Take heed therefore unto yourselves, and to all the flock, over the which the Holy Ghost hath made you overseers, to feed the church of God, which he hath purchased with his own blood" (Acts 20:28).

   It must be understood, the Holy Spirit alone appoints the true undershepherds of Christ. "And no man taketh this honour unto himself, but he that is called of God, as was Aaron" (Heb. 5:4). "And he gave some, apostles; and some, prophets; and some, evangelists; and some, pastors and teachers" (Eph. 4:11). (See also Acts 26:16; Rom. 15:16; 1 Tim. 1:12.)

   All too often, however (especially in these final days), the tragic words of

God to the prophet Jeremiah apply: "I have not sent these prophets, yet they ran: I have not spoken to them, yet they prophesied" (Jer. 23:21). "For they prophesy falsely unto you in my name: I have not sent them, saith the LORD" (Jer. 29:9).

e. He desires to anoint its preachers—"And my speech and my preaching was not with enticing words of man's wisdom, but in demonstration of the Spirit and of power" (1 Cor. 2:4). Here we see the divine order of service. He first appoints and then anoints his servants. The appointing is a once-for-all event, but the anointing must be sought daily.

f. He desires to warn its members—"Now the Spirit speaketh expressly, that in the latter times some shall depart from the faith, giving heed to seducing spirits, and doctrines of devils" (1 Tim. 4:1).

g. He desires to determine its decisions—"For it seemed good to the Holy Ghost, and to us, to lay upon you no greater burden than these necessary things" (Acts 15:28).

This all-important decision made at the Jerusalem Council concerning circumcision is a beautiful example of the teamwork between a local church and the Holy Spirit. Those assemblies governed by congregational vote often pride themselves on their democratic policies. But the real goal can only be achieved through a democratic-theocratic combined team effort.

h. He desires to condemn or bless its efforts as needed—"He that hath an ear, let him hear what the Spirit saith unto the churches." This admonition is found no less than seven times in the opening chapters of Revelation. (See 2:7, 11, 17, 29; 3:6, 13, 22.)

Churches are often overly concerned about improving their image in the eyes of the younger generation, society, the business world, academic circles, etc. But the real concern should be directed toward that one who, alone, is properly qualified to improve and correct—namely, the Holy Spirit.

i. He desires to head up its visitation and evangelistic programs—"And the Spirit and the bride say, Come. And let him that heareth say, Come. And let him that is athirst come. And whosoever will, let him take the water of life freely" (Rev. 22:17).

In this, the Scripture's final invitation, we see the Holy Spirit speaking through the church urging the unsaved to come to Christ.

H. His ministry concerning the day of Pentecost—Of all the important days in history, the day of Pentecost must surely be ranked near the top. At this time, the Holy Spirit performed one of his greatest and most far-reaching works.

"And when the day of Pentecost was fully come, they were all with one accord in one place. And suddenly there came a sound from heaven as of a rushing mighty wind, and it filled all the house where they were sitting. And there appeared unto them cloven tongues like as of fire, and it sat upon each of them. And they were all filled with the Holy Ghost, and began to speak with other tongues, as the Spirit gave them utterance" (Acts 2:1-4).

1. The background of Pentecost—Just minutes before his dramatic ascension, our resurrected Lord commanded his disciples: "And, being assembled together with them, commanded them that they should not depart from Jerusalem, but wait for the promise of the Father, which, saith he, ye have heard of me" (Acts 1:4).

Much ink has been used attempting to explain these five words, "the promise of the Father." What was this promise of the Father? Various passages of Scripture make it clear that this promise of the Father, and also of the Son, was a reference to the arrival of the Holy Spirit. "And it shall come to pass afterward, that I will pour out my spirit upon all flesh; and your sons and your daughters shall prophesy, your old men shall dream dreams, your young men shall see visions" (Joel 2:28). "But this is that which was spoken by the prophet Joel; And it shall come to pass in the last days, saith God, I will pour out of my Spirit upon all flesh: and your sons and your daughters shall prophesy, and your young men shall see visions, and your old men shall dream dreams" (Acts 2:16-17).

The Holy Spirit had, of course, already performed an Old Testament ministry, but now his work was to introduce three completely new elements.

a. His new ministry was to be universal—Previously the Holy Spirit had confined his work among humanity to the nation Israel. There is no record before the book of Acts that he fell upon the Greeks, or Romans, or Babylonians, etc. But here in Acts he came to bless all repenting sinners everywhere.

b. His new ministry was to be permanent—Although the Holy Spirit did come upon certain Old Testament men, he often departed from them also.

(1) As illustrated by Samson—This Hebrew strongman enjoyed the presence of the Holy Spirit on various occasions. (See Judg. 14:6, 19; 15:15.) But then, because of sin and immorality, God's Spirit left Samson. One of the most tragic verses in the Bible records this event, when Samson awakes to hear Delilah say: "The Philistines be upon thee, Samson. And he awoke out of his sleep, and said, I will go out as at other times before, and shake myself. And he wist not that the LORD was departed from him" (Judg. 16:20).

(2) As illustrated by Saul—As with Samson, the Holy Spirit came upon Saul, but later left him, as demonstrated by the following: "And when they came thither to the hill, behold, a company of prophets met him; and the Spirit of God came upon him, and he prophesied among them" (1 Sam. 10:10). "But the Spirit of the LORD departed from Saul, and an evil spirit from the LORD troubled him" (1 Sam. 16:14).

(3) As illustrated by David—The Spirit of God came upon David when he was anointed by Samuel: "Then Samuel took the horn of oil, and anointed him in the midst of his brethren: and the Spirit of the LORD came upon David from that day forward. So Samuel rose up, and went to Ramah" (1 Sam. 16:13).

So far as it can be determined, the Holy Spirit remained with him until death. But David realized the Holy Spirit could depart, and on at least one occasion, he pleaded with the Lord about this matter. "Cast me not away from thy presence; and take not thy holy spirit from me" (Psa. 51:11).

No Christian today need ever pray this prayer. However, millions of believers could probably, with profit, pray the next phrase of David's psalm of confession: "Restore unto me the joy of thy salvation; and uphold me with thy free spirit" (Psa. 51:12). David offered this prayer after his great sin with Bathsheba.

The point of all the above is that in the Old Testament the Holy Spirit, on occasion, in a temporary sense, came upon, filled, and indwelled certain believers, but never in a permanent way. However, as promised by Christ himself in the Upper Room just prior to Calvary, this would soon change. Note his words: "And I will pray the Father, and he shall give you another Comforter, that he may abide with you for ever" (John 14:16). (See also John 14:26; 15:26; 16:7.)

For Old Testament examples where believers were temporarily indwelt, see Genesis 41:38; Numbers 27:18; Daniel 4:8; 5:11-14; 6:3. For Old Testament examples where believers were temporarily filled, see Exodus 31:3; 35:31.

   c. His new ministry was to be perfecting—That is to say, his new ministry would now be to make all repenting sinners grow in grace and be like Jesus. This was not the case in the Old Testament. There is no indication that the moral and spiritual nature of either Saul or Samson was advanced by the presence of the Holy Spirit. They apparently derived only his power, not his purity.

In essence, it can be said that the all-important mission of the Holy Spirit regarding the believer is to make him or her as much like Jesus in the shortest amount of time. Note Paul's words concerning this: "Now the Lord is that Spirit: and where the Spirit of the Lord is, there is liberty. But we all, with open face beholding as in a glass the glory of the Lord, are changed into the same image from glory to glory, even as by the Spirit of the Lord" (2 Cor. 3:17-18).

2. The chronology of Pentecost—Pentecost (from a Greek word that simply means "50") is the third of six great Israelite feasts mentioned in Leviticus 23. These feasts actually summarize the entire future work of the Trinity in the New Testament. Consider:

   a. The Passover and the Feast of Unleavened Bread—A reference to Calvary (see Lev. 23:4-8; 1 Cor. 5:6-8)

   b. The Sheaf of Firstfruits—A reference to the Resurrection (see Lev. 23:9-14; 1 Cor. 15:23)

   c. The Feast of Seven Weeks—A reference to Pentecost (see Lev. 23:15-21; Acts 2:1)

   d. The Feast of Trumpets—A reference to the Rapture (see Lev. 23:23-25; 1 Thess. 4:13-18)

   e. The Day of Atonement—A reference to the great tribulation (see Lev. 23:26-32; Matt. 24:21)

   f. The Feast of Tabernacles—A reference to the Millennium (see Lev. 23:33-43; Rev. 21:3)

3. The comparisons of Pentecost

   a. New Testament Pentecost may be compared with Old Testament Pentecost.

     (1) Old Testament Pentecost occurred 50 days after Israel left Egypt.

Note: The Passover lamb was slain on April 14, 1491 B.C., and Israel left Egypt the next night. "And the LORD spake unto Moses and Aaron in the land of Egypt, saying, This month shall be unto you the beginning of months: it shall be the first month of the year to you" (Exod. 12:1-2). "And ye shall keep it up until the fourteenth day of the same month: and the whole assembly of the congregation of Israel shall kill it in the evening" (Exod. 12:6). "For I will pass through the land of Egypt this night, and will smite all the firstborn in the land of Egypt, both man and beast; and against all the gods of Egypt I will execute judgment: I am the LORD" (Exod. 12:12). "And he called for Moses and Aaron by night, and said, Rise up, and get you forth from among my people, both ye and the children of Israel; and go, serve the LORD, as ye have said" (Exod. 12:31).

Exactly 50 days later, they arrived at Mount Sinai during the first week of June. "In the third month, when the children of Israel were gone forth out of the land of Egypt, the same day came they into the wilderness of Sinai" (Exod. 19:1).

(2) New Testament Pentecost occurred 50 days after Christ rose from the dead.

Note: Our Lord was, of course, crucified during the Passover week in April. "And it was the preparation of the passover, and about the sixth hour: and he saith unto the Jews, Behold your King!" (John 19:14).

He then spent 40 days with his disciples after the Resurrection. "To whom also he shewed himself alive after his passion by many infallible proofs, being seen of them forty days, and speaking of the things pertaining to the kingdom of God" (Acts 1:3).

Then, some 10 days later, New Testament Pentecost occurred. "For John truly baptized with water; but ye shall be baptized with the Holy Ghost not many days hence" (Acts 1:5). "And when the day of Pentecost was fully come, they were all with one accord in one place" (Acts 2:1).

(3) Old Testament Pentecost celebrated a birthday—that of the nation Israel—"Now therefore, if ye will obey my voice indeed, and keep my covenant, then ye shall be a peculiar treasure unto me above all people: for all the earth is mine" (Exod. 19:5).

The Scriptures tell us that angels were involved in the giving of the law at Mount Sinai. "Who have received the law by the disposition of angels, and have not kept it" (Acts 7:53). "Wherefore then serveth the law? It was added because of transgressions, till the seed should come to whom the promise was made; and it was ordained by angels in the hand of a mediator" (Gal. 3:19).

(4) New Testament Pentecost celebrated a birthday—that of the church—"Then they that gladly received his word were baptized: and the same day there were added unto them about three thousand souls. And they continued stedfastly in the apostles' doctrine and fellowship, and in breaking of bread, and in prayers. And fear came upon every soul: and many wonders and signs were done by the apostles. And all that believed were together, and had all things common; and sold their possessions and goods, and parted them to all men, as every man had need. And they, continuing daily with one accord in the temple, and breaking bread from house to house, did eat their meat with gladness and singleness of heart, praising God, and having favour with all the people. And the Lord added to the church daily such as should be saved" (Acts 2:41-47).

(5) Old Testament Pentecost witnessed the slaying of some 3,000 souls—"And the children of Levi did according to the word of Moses: and there fell of the people that day about three thousand men" (Exod.

32:28). Israel's worship of the golden calf while encamped at the base of Mount Sinai was a tragic episode in its history.

(6) New Testament Pentecost witnessed the saving of some 3,000 souls—"Then they that gladly received his word were baptized: and the same day there were added unto them about three thousand souls" (Acts 2:41).

What an amazing contrast is seen here between these two Pentecosts. In fact, the difference is so important that Paul takes an entire chapter in one of his epistles to discuss it. Note these two verses in this chapter: "Not that we are sufficient of ourselves to think any thing as of ourselves; but our sufficiency is of God; who also hath made us able ministers of the new testament; not of the letter, but of the spirit: for the letter killeth, but the spirit giveth life" (2 Cor. 3:5-6).

(7) Old Testament Pentecost was introduced in a mighty way—"And it came to pass on the third day in the morning, that there were thunders and lightnings, and a thick cloud upon the mount, and the voice of the trumpet exceeding loud; so that all the people that was in the camp trembled" (Exod. 19:16). "And mount Sinai was altogether on a smoke, because the LORD descended upon it in fire: and the smoke thereof ascended as the smoke of a furnace, and the whole mount quaked greatly" (Exod. 19:18).

(8) New Testament Pentecost was introduced in a mighty way—"And suddenly there came a sound from heaven as of a rushing mighty wind, and it filled all the house where they were sitting. And there appeared unto them cloven tongues like as of fire, and it sat upon each of them" (Acts 2:2-3).

b. New Testament Pentecost may be compared to Bethlehem.

(1) At Bethlehem, God the Father was preparing a body for his Son to work through—"Wherefore when he cometh into the world, he saith, Sacrifice and offering thou wouldest not, but a body hast thou prepared me" (Heb. 10:5).

(2) At Pentecost, God the Father was preparing a body for his Spirit to work through—"What? know ye not that your body is the temple of the Holy Ghost which is in you, which ye have of God, and ye are not your own?" (1 Cor. 6:19). "And what agreement hath the temple of God with idols? for ye are the temple of the living God; as God hath said, I will dwell in them, and walk in them; and I will be their God, and they shall be my people" (2 Cor. 6:16).

Because of this, Pentecost can never be repeated in the same sense that Bethlehem can never again happen. It is, therefore, as unscriptural to have a "tarrying meeting" to pray down another Pentecost as it would be to have a meeting and plead for the shepherds and Wise Men to reappear. The events occurring in Luke 2 and Acts 2 are forever in the past.

c. New Testament Pentecost may be compared to Old Testament Babel.

(1) At Babel, we see sinful men working for their own glory—"And they said, Go to, let us build us a city and a tower, whose top may reach unto heaven; and let us make us a name, lest we be scattered abroad upon the face of the whole earth" (Gen. 11:4).

(2) At Pentecost, we see saved men waiting for God's glory—"These all continued with one accord in prayer and supplication, with the women, and Mary the mother of Jesus, and with his brethren" (Acts 1:14).

(3) At Babel, God confounded man's language—"Therefore is the name of it called Babel; because the LORD did there confound the language of all the earth: and from thence did the LORD scatter them abroad upon the face of all the earth" (Gen. 11:9).

(4) At Pentecost, God clarified man's language—"And how hear we every man in our own tongue, wherein we were born?" (Acts 2:8).

(5) At Babel, God scattered men throughout the world—"Therefore is the name of it called Babel; because the LORD did there confound the language of all the earth: and from thence did the LORD scatter them abroad upon the face of all the earth" (Gen. 11:9).

(6) At Pentecost, God gathered men within the church—"That in the dispensation of the fulness of times he might gather together in one all things in Christ, both which are in heaven, and which are on earth; even in him" (Eph. 1:10).

I. His ministry concerning the believer—Thus far, we have discussed the ministry of the Holy Spirit in regard to the universe, the Scriptures, Israel, Satan, Christ, sinners, the church, and Pentecost. But what ministry does he perform for that special group of New Testament people called Christians? The instant an unsaved person prays, "God be merciful to me, a sinner," the Holy Spirit immediately effects a fivefold work in him.

1. The Holy Spirit regenerates the believer—He literally re-creates him and gives him the nature of God. The Holy Spirit thus functions as a divine "midwife" to the repenting sinner as he ushers him into the kingdom of God. This is accomplished by the instrument of "water," which is symbolic language for the Word of God. The following passages bear this out:

"Not by works of righteousness which we have done, but according to his mercy he saved us, by the washing of regeneration, and renewing of the Holy Ghost" (Titus 3:5). "Jesus answered and said unto him, Verily, verily, I say unto thee, Except a man be born again, he cannot see the kingdom of God. Nicodemus saith unto him, How can a man be born when he is old? can he enter the second time into his mother's womb, and be born? Jesus answered, Verily, verily, I say unto thee, Except a man be born of water and of the Spirit, he cannot enter into the kingdom of God. That which is born of the flesh is flesh; and that which is born of the Spirit is spirit. Marvel not that I said unto thee, Ye must be born again" (John 3:3-7).

"Being born again, not of corruptible seed, but of incorruptible, by the word of God, which liveth and abideth for ever" (1 Pet. 1:23). "Of his own will begat he us with the word of truth, that we should be a kind of firstfruits of his creatures" (James 1:18).

This regenerating ministry was of course, not a new one, as inferred by Jesus, who rebuked Nicodemus for not being aware of it. "Nicodemus answered and said unto him, How can these things be? Jesus answered and said unto him, Art thou a master of Israel, and knowest not these things?" (John 3:9-10).

In fact, his ministry of regeneration will continue throughout both the great tribulation and glorious Millennium. (See Jer. 32:39; Ezek. 11:19; 36:25-27.)

2. The Holy Spirit baptizes the believer—"Know ye not, that so many of us as were baptized into Jesus Christ were baptized into his death? Therefore we are buried with him by baptism into death: that like as Christ was raised up from the dead by the glory of the Father, even so we also should walk in newness of life" (Rom. 6:3-4). "For by one Spirit are we all baptized into one body, whether we be Jews or Gentiles, whether we be bond or free; and have been all made to drink into one Spirit" (1 Cor. 12:13).

"For as many of you as have been baptized into Christ have put on Christ" (Gal. 3:27). "There is one body, and one Spirit, even as ye are called in one hope of your calling; one Lord, one faith, one baptism" (Eph. 4:4-5). "Buried with him in baptism, wherein also ye are risen with him through the faith of the operation of God, who hath raised him from the dead" (Col. 2:12).

The question is often asked: Does a person have to be baptized to be saved? The answer is an emphatic yes—*but not by water baptism.* The purpose of the Holy Spirit's placing the believer into the body of Christ is twofold:

a. He does it to answer Christ's prayer for Christian unity—"That they all may be one; as thou, Father, art in me, and I in thee, that they also may be one in us: that the world may believe that thou hast sent me" (John 17:21).

b. He does it to prepare a bride for Christ, composed of all believers saved from Pentecost until the Rapture—"So we, being many, are one body in Christ, and every one members one of another" (Rom. 12:5). "For we being many are one bread, and one body: for we are all partakers of that one bread" (1 Cor. 10:17). "For by one Spirit are we all baptized into one body, whether we be Jews or Gentiles, whether we be bond or free; and have been all made to drink into one Spirit" (1 Cor. 12:13). "Now ye are the body of Christ, and members in particular" (1 Cor. 12:27). (See also Eph. 1:22-23; 4:4, 12; 5:30; Col. 3:15; 2 Cor. 11:2; Rev. 19:6-9.)

Note the prophetical, historical, and doctrinal aspects of this baptism.

(1) The prophetical aspect (Matt. 3:11; Mark 1:8; Luke 3:16; John 1:33; Acts 1:5)

(2) The historical aspect (Acts 2:1-4; 11:15-17)

(3) The doctrinal aspect (1 Cor. 12:12-13; Rom. 6:1-4)

3. The Holy Spirit indwells the believer—In other words, he not only joins us to the Savior (through the baptism), but he joins himself to us. Jesus, prior to his crucifixion, predicted both of these ministries. He said: "At that day ye shall know that I am in my Father, and ye in me, and I in you" (John 14:20). "Know ye not that ye are the temple of God, and that the Spirit of God dwelleth in you?" (1 Cor. 3:16). "What? know ye not that your body is the temple of the Holy Ghost which is in you, which ye have of God, and ye are not your own?" (1 Cor. 6:19). (See also John 7:37-39; 14:16; Rom. 8:9; 1 Cor. 2:12; 1 John 3:24.)

The purpose of this indwelling ministry is to control the newly created nature. "Therefore if any man be in Christ, he is a new creature: old things are passed away; behold, all things are become new" (2 Cor. 5:17). "This I say then, Walk in the Spirit, and ye shall not fulfil the lust of the flesh. For the flesh lusteth against the Spirit, and the Spirit against the flesh: and these are contrary the one to the other: so that ye cannot do the things that ye would. But if ye be led of the Spirit, ye are not under the law" (Gal. 5:16-18). "That he would grant you, according to the riches of his glory, to be strengthened with might by his Spirit in the inner man" (Eph. 3:16).

4. The Holy Spirit seals the believer—"Who hath also sealed us, and given the earnest of the Spirit in our hearts" (2 Cor. 1:22). "In whom ye also trusted, after that ye heard the word of truth, the gospel of your salvation: in whom also after that ye believed, ye were sealed with that holy Spirit of promise," (Eph. 1:13). "And grieve not the holy Spirit of God, whereby ye are sealed unto the day of redemption" (Eph. 4:30).

The presence of the Holy Spirit himself seems to be the seal here, who is given by the Father to assure the believer of his eternal salvation. This seal is also referred to as an earnest. "Who hath also sealed us, and given the earnest of the Spirit in our hearts" (2 Cor. 1:22). "Now he that hath wrought us for the selfsame thing is God, who also hath given unto us the earnest of the Spirit" (2 Cor. 5:5). "Which is the earnest of our inheritance until the redemption of the purchased possession, unto the praise of his glory" (Eph. 1:14).

Charles Ryrie observes:

> Registered mail furnishes a good example of the security concept in sealing. When registering a piece of mail, it not only has to be sealed carefully but then the post office stamps it a number of times across the edges of the seal to be able to detect any tampering with that seal. Only two people can legitimately break the seal, the recipient or the sender (if it is delivered back to him). In the case of believers, God is the Sender and God is the recipient, and God is the One who does the sealing. So only God can break the seal and He has promised not to do so until the day of redemption. (*Basic Theology,* p. 360)

5. The Holy Spirit fills the believer—"And they were all filled with the Holy Ghost, and began to speak with other tongues, as the Spirit gave them utterance" (Acts 2:4).

A great deal of controversy and misunderstanding throughout church history has come into existence concerning this ministry of the Holy Spirit. For example, what is the difference between the indwelling and the filling of the Holy Spirit? To aid in understanding this vital distinction, consider the following illustration.

A guest is invited into a home. But upon entering that home he is immediately confined to a small room somewhere near the front door. For awhile, he may even be forgotten by his host. Finally, however, the owner of the house is convicted concerning his shabby treatment of the houseguest. He thereupon gives his guest free access to every room in the house.

In this illustration the Holy Spirit is, of course, the invited guest. The host is the believing sinner, and the house stands for his life. The difference, then, between the indwelling and the filling is the difference between being confined in a small room somewhere and being given free access to all the rooms. The filling, therefore, does not mean the believer gets more of the Holy Spirit, but rather, the Holy Spirit gets more of the believer.

In the light of these five ministries we may observe that:

a. All five of these ministries happen instantaneously to the believer—They all occur by faith and are not in the least dependent upon one's personal emotional feelings at the time.

b. The first four ministries can never be lost and therefore, need not be and should not be asked for again—Nowhere in the Bible are we commanded to ask God to baptize us by his Spirit, or to seal us with his Spirit, or to regenerate and indwell us. If a man has accepted Christ, he has for all eternity been regenerated, indwelled, baptized and sealed by the Holy Spirit.

c. The fifth ministry, however, can be lost, and therefore should be asked for as many times as needed—The following passages bring this out:

"And be not drunk with wine, wherein is excess; but be filled with the Spirit" (Eph. 5:18). "This I say then, Walk in the Spirit, and ye shall not fulfil the lust of the flesh" (Gal. 5:16).

Believers in the book of Acts experienced the filling of the Holy Spirit often in their lives.

(1) The apostles (Acts 2:4; 4:31-32; 13:52)

(2) Peter (Acts 4:8; 6:3)

(3) Stephen (Acts 7:55)

(4) Paul (Acts 9:17; 13:9)

(5) Barnabas (Acts 11:24)

d. The first four ministries give us peace *with* God—"Therefore being justified by faith, we have peace with God through our Lord Jesus Christ" (Rom. 5:1).

e. The fifth ministry assures us the *peace* of God—"And the peace of God, which passeth all understanding, shall keep your hearts and minds through Christ Jesus" (Phil. 4:7).

Thus, all Christians, regardless of how backslidden they might be, enjoy peace *with* God, but only Spirit-controlled believers can know that blessed peace *of* God.

f. The fifth ministry is lost whenever disobedience is found in the life of the believer—This disobedience may manifest itself in either (or both) of the following ways:

(1) The sin of quenching the Holy Spirit—"Quench not the Spirit" (1 Thess. 5:19). This sin involves not doing that which the Holy Spirit would have us do. It is negative in nature. The same word is used elsewhere in reference to the putting out of a fire. Note: "A bruised reed shall he not break, and smoking flax shall he not quench, till he send forth judgment unto victory" (Matt. 12:20). "Above all, taking the shield of faith, wherewith ye shall be able to quench all the fiery darts of the wicked" (Eph. 6:16).

(2) The sin of grieving the Holy Spirit—"And grieve not the holy Spirit of God, whereby ye are sealed unto the day of redemption" (Eph. 4:30). This sin involves doing that which the Holy Spirit would not have us do. It is positive in nature.

To illustrate: A believer boards a plane in Chicago for Los Angeles and finds himself seated next to an unsaved man. In flight the Holy Spirit attempts to witness to the unsaved man through the testimony of the Christian, but he remains silent and fails to witness. At this point, the believer has quenched the Holy Spirit. He has not done that which the Spirit of God wanted him to do.

As the flight continues, however, the two men introduce themselves and begin talking, but not about spiritual things. In fact, to the shame of the Christian, several off-color stories are passed between the two men. Now the saved man has gone the second step and grieved the Holy Spirit—he has done that which the Holy Spirit did not want him to do.

These two sins, if left unchecked for a long period of time, can eventually lead to that "sin unto death" as described in the following passages: "To deliver such an one unto Satan for the destruction of the flesh, that the spirit may be saved in the day of the Lord Jesus" (1 Cor. 5:5). The sin unto death, in this case, was immorality on the part of a totally carnal believer in Corinth. "For this cause many are weak and sickly among you, and many sleep" (1 Cor. 11:30).

In the case of Ananias and Sapphira, gross dishonesty and blatant hypocrisy led to the sin unto death. (See Acts 5:1-11.) That Ananias was indeed a believer is proven by the question Peter asked him: "But Peter said, Ananias, why hath Satan filled thine heart to lie to the Holy Ghost, and to keep back part of the price of the land?" (Acts 5:3).

"If any man see his brother sin a sin which is not unto death, he shall ask, and he shall give him life for them that sin not unto death. There is a sin unto death: I do not say that he shall pray for it" (1 John 5:16). The sin unto death does not mean one loses salvation, but it does imply the possibility that God will remove him from the scene down here earlier than originally planned. This seemed to have been in the thoughts of Paul when he wrote: "I therefore so run, not as uncertainly; so fight I, not as one that beateth the air. But I keep under my body, and bring it into subjection: lest that by any means, when I have preached to others, I myself should be a castaway" (1 Cor. 9:26-27).

g. The fifth ministry may (and should be) instantly regained—This can be accomplished:
   (1) By knowing God's method of forgiveness and cleansing—the blood of Christ—"But if we walk in the light, as he is in the light, we have fellowship one with another, and the blood of Jesus Christ his Son cleanseth us from all sin" (1 John 1:7).
   (2) By knowing God's means of forgiveness and cleansing—the confession of the Christian—"If we confess our sins, he is faithful and just to forgive us our sins, and to cleanse us from all unrighteousness" (1 John 1:9). This confession is absolutely vital, for while Christ's blood will cleanse us from all sins, it will not cleanse us from a single excuse.

   God does not demand golden vessels, nor does he require silver ones, but he must have clean ones. Thus, the union with the Spirit is so strong that nothing can break it, but the communion with the Spirit is so fragile that the smallest sin can shatter it.

   Consider another illustration: A family leaves California to visit friends in New York. The first half of their trip is rather uneventful, but while they are in the Chicago area, their automobile breaks down. After some difficulty, the services of a mechanic are secured and the car is repaired. What action does the family take now? Does the driver head back to California and take another run for New York? All would agree that this, of course, would be sheer stupidity. What does this family do? They simply continue on from the spot where they first broke down.

   This little travel story has a direct application to the Spirit-filled life. When God saves a man, he puts him on the road to heaven. For a while the trip may go smoothly for the new convert. But there will come a time when he will break down somewhere along the line. Perhaps the spiritual motor trouble will be caused by some angry words, or a wicked deed, or some careless act. The Spirit has been quenched and grieved and all forward progress ceases immediately. There the man sits.

What should he do? He should immediately secure the services of that divine mechanic, the Holy Spirit. If he confesses his sins and depends upon Christ's blood, his broken testimony will once again be restored. Then what should the believer do? The answer is obvious. However, there is a false concept among Christians today that once a child of God sins (particularly if it is a serious sin) he automatically loses all previous progress and must start all over. This simply is not the case. The secret of the Spirit-filled life is the knowledge that broken fellowship can be instantly restored by confession and by Christ's blood.

h. The fifth ministry assures the believer of the following blessings:

(1) The Holy Spirit will pray for him—"Likewise the Spirit also helpeth our infirmities: for we know not what we should pray for as we ought: but the Spirit itself maketh intercession for us with groanings which cannot be uttered" (Rom. 8:26).

In the original text, the word *infirmities* is in the singular. Thus, the one infirmity in mind here is our inability to pray as we ought to pray. It is for this reason that the Spirit comes to our aid. However, it should be kept in mind that the Bible says he "helpeth" us, which simply means he desires the Christian to do his part also. Therefore, to be effectively prayed for, we ourselves must pray. (See also Eph. 6:18; Jude 20.)

(2) The Holy Spirit will guide him—"Howbeit when he, the Spirit of truth, is come, he will guide you into all truth: for he shall not speak of himself; but whatsoever he shall hear, that shall he speak: and he will shew you things to come" (John 16:13). "For as many as are led by the Spirit of God, they are the sons of God" (Rom. 8:14).

(3) The Holy Spirit will teach him—"But the anointing which ye have received of him abideth in you, and ye need not that any man teach you: but as the same anointing teacheth you of all things, and is truth, and is no lie, and even as it hath taught you, ye shall abide in him" (1 John 2:27). "But the Comforter, which is the Holy Ghost, whom the Father will send in my name, he shall teach you all things, and bring all things to your remembrance, whatsoever I have said unto you" (John 14:26).

(4) The Holy Spirit will empower him for witnessing—"But ye shall receive power, after that the Holy Ghost is come upon you: and ye shall be witnesses unto me both in Jerusalem, and in all Judaea, and in Samaria, and unto the uttermost part of the earth" (Acts 1:8).

(5) The Holy Spirit will impart the love of Christ to him and through him—"And hope maketh not ashamed; because the love of God is shed abroad in our hearts by the Holy Ghost which is given unto us" (Rom. 5:5).

(6) The Holy Spirit will conform him to the image of Christ—"But we all, with open face beholding as in a glass the glory of the Lord, are changed into the same image from glory to glory, even as by the Spirit of the Lord" (2 Cor. 3:18).

The ultimate goal and stated intention of the Father is to conform the believer throughout eternity into the image of Christ. This is made clear in such passages as Philippians 3:21 and 1 John 3:2. But God the Spirit desires to start this glorious work in each child of God at the moment of salvation. (See Phil. 3:10.)

"Who shall change our vile body, that it may be fashioned like unto his glorious body, according to the working whereby he is able even to subdue all things unto himself" (Phil. 3:21). "Beloved, now are we the sons of God, and it doth not yet appear what we shall be: but we know that, when he shall appear, we shall be like him; for we shall see him as he is" (1 John 3:2). "That I may know him, and the power of his resurrection, and the fellowship of his sufferings, being made conformable unto his death" (Phil. 3:10).

(7) The Holy Spirit will strengthen his new nature—"That he would grant you, according to the riches of his glory, to be strengthened with might by his Spirit in the inner man" (Eph. 3:16). This he does through Bible study and prayer. "As newborn babes, desire the sincere milk of the word, that ye may grow thereby" (1 Pet. 2:2). "But ye, beloved, building up yourselves on your most holy faith, praying in the Holy Ghost" (Jude 20).

(8) The Holy Spirit will reveal biblical truth to him—"But God hath revealed them unto us by his Spirit: for the Spirit searcheth all things, yea, the deep things of God" (1 Cor. 2:10).

(9) The Holy Spirit will assure him concerning salvation and service—"The Spirit itself beareth witness with our spirit, that we are the children of God" (Rom. 8:16). "And he that keepeth his commandments dwelleth in him, and he in him. And hereby we know that he abideth in us, by the Spirit which he hath given us" (1 John 3:24).

(10) The Holy Spirit will give him liberty—"For the law of the Spirit of life in Christ Jesus hath made me free from the law of sin and death" (Rom. 8:2). "Now the Lord is that Spirit: and where the Spirit of the Lord is, there is liberty" (2 Cor. 3:17).

(11) The Holy Spirit will fill his mouth with appropriate things—"But when they shall lead you, and deliver you up, take no thought before hand what ye shall speak, neither do ye premeditate: but whatsoever shall be given you in that hour, that speak ye: for it is not ye that speak, but the Holy Ghost" (Mark 13:11). Several instances come to mind in the book of Acts where this blessed prophecy was fulfilled. (See Acts 4:8-22; 5:29-33; 7:55.)

Finally, in regards to the ministry of the Holy Spirit in filling the believer, consider the following.

In Acts 2:13 and Ephesians 5:18 a comparison is made between being filled with the Spirit and being filled with wine. "Others mocking said, These men are full of new wine" (Acts 2:13). "And be not drunk with wine, wherein is excess; but be filled with the Spirit" (Eph. 5:18).

In all fairness, a comparison can be made between these two:
- Both control the user and give him a new boldness, one in the good sense and the other in the bad sense of the word.
- Both produce a desire for more.

J. His ministry concerning spiritual gifts—"There is one body, and one Spirit, even as ye are called in one hope of your calling; one Lord, one faith, one baptism, one God and Father of all, who is above all, and through all, and in you all. But unto every one of us is given grace according to the measure of the gift of Christ. Wherefore he saith, When he ascended up on high, he led captivity captive, and gave gifts unto men" (Eph. 4:4-8).

In the Bible, the entire Trinity is often described in the act of giving. God loves to give. It was the Father who gave his dearly beloved Son. "For God so loved the world, that he gave his only begotten Son, that whosoever believeth in him should not perish, but have everlasting life" (John 3:16).

It was the Son who freely gave his precious blood. "And he took bread, and gave thanks, and brake it, and gave unto them, saying, This is my body which is given for you: this do in remembrance of me" (Luke 22:19).

Finally, after his arrival at Pentecost, the Holy Spirit began his ministry of gift-giving to the church, and will continue it until the Rapture. "Now there are diversities of gifts, but the same Spirit. . . . But the manifestation of the Spirit is given to every man to profit withal" (1 Cor. 12:4, 7).

1. The definition of a spiritual gift—A spiritual gift is a supernatural ability given by Christ through the Holy Spirit to the believer at the moment of his salvation. At this point two distinctives should be made.

   a. The distinction between the *gift* of the Spirit and the *gifts* of the Spirit—The gift occurred at Pentecost when the Holy Spirit came in answer to the promise of Christ. The gifts occur today.

   b. The distinction between gifts and talents—A talent is a human and natural ability given at birth. It may be in the area of music, speech, organization, etc. But no natural talent, however great it might be, can be used by its owner to glorify God until it is sanctioned by the Holy Spirit. When this occurs, the talent then may become a gift.

     To illustrate this, let's consider an individual who is a brilliant and talented musician. His ability is acclaimed by millions. But the performer is not a Christian and, thus, his talent can never be used by the Holy Spirit for the glory of God. But, let us assume the man hears the gospel and accepts Christ as Savior. Now, the Holy Spirit may determine to transform the man's natural talent into a supernatural gift. As there is no specific gift of music as such, the musician's new efforts for Christ would probably fall under that of exhortation, which is a listed gift.

     A fivefold comparison, can be seen between natural talents and spiritual gifts:

    (1) Natural talents
      (a) Source—From God through parents
      (b) Possessed—From birth
      (c) Purpose—To benefit mankind on the natural level
      (d) Process—Must be recognized, developed, exercised
      (e) Function—Ought to be dedicated by believers to God for his use and glory
    (2) Spiritual gifts
      (a) Source—From God, independent of parents
      (b) Possessed—Probably from conversion
      (c) Purpose—To benefit mankind on the spiritual level.
      (d) Process—Must be recognized, developed, exercised
      (e) Function—Ought to be used to God's glory

2. The extent of the spiritual gifts

a. Each believer possesses at least one spiritual gift—"As every man hath received the gift, even so minister the same one to another, as good stewards of the manifold grace of God" (1 Pet. 4:10). "But unto every one of us is given grace according to the measure of the gift of Christ" (Eph. 4:7).

"For I would that all men were even as I myself. But every man hath his proper gift of God, one after this manner, and another after that" (1 Cor. 7:7). "But the manifestation of the Spirit is given to every man to profit withal" (1 Cor. 12:7). "But all these worketh that one and the selfsame Spirit, dividing to every man severally as he will" (1 Cor. 12:11).

b. No believer possesses all the gifts—"Are all apostles? are all prophets? are all teachers? are all workers of miracles? Have all the gifts of healing? do all speak with tongues? do all interpret?" (1 Cor. 12:29-30).

Thus, in light of this:

(1) To claim that one possesses *all* the gifts is to defy the decision of the Spirit.

(2) To claim that one possesses *none* of the gifts is to deny the decision of the Spirit.

3. The purpose of the spiritual gifts
   a. To glorify the Father—"Thou art worthy, O Lord, to receive glory and honour and power: for thou hast created all things, and for thy pleasure they are and were created" (Rev. 4:11).
   b. To edify the church—"For the perfecting of the saints, for the work of the ministry, for the edifying of the body of Christ: till we all come in the unity of the faith, and of the knowledge of the Son of God, unto a perfect man, unto the measure of the stature of the fulness of Christ" (Eph. 4:12-13).
4. The abuse of the spiritual gifts
   a. Not using those gifts imparted to us—"Wherefore I put thee in remembrance that thou stir up the gift of God, which is in thee by the putting on of my hands" (2 Tim. 1:6). "Neglect not the gift that is in thee, which was given thee by prophecy, with the laying on of the hands of the presbytery" (1 Tim. 4:14).
   b. Attempting to use those gifts not imparted to us—See 1 Corinthians 12–13.
   c. Not using the gifts in love—"Though I speak with the tongues of men and of angels, and have not charity, I am become as sounding brass, or a tinkling cymbal" (1 Cor. 13:1). How often are those blessed gifts abused? Only eternity will reveal the number of men in the ministry who should never have been there. On the other hand (and just as tragic), there has doubtless been a great company of men who were called into God's service, but never answered it. But perhaps the greatest abuse of all is the use of gifts without love.

      If one rightly comprehends the material given thus far on gifts, he can understand why God sometimes seems to use a carnal Christian in a great way in spite of glaring (or often secret) sins in his life. However, in such cases God is only blessing the gift and not the man personally. At the judgment seat of Christ (see 1 Cor. 3) there will doubtless be many surprises as perhaps a number of world-famous Christian leaders receive so little actual personal reward from Christ because of their sins and carnality.
5. The number of the spiritual gifts—In three main passages, the Apostle Paul lists 18 separate spiritual gifts for us. These are Romans 12; 1 Corinthians 12; and Ephesians 4.

6. The nature of the spiritual gifts—It would seem that these 18 gifts can be placed into two basic categories, the permanent stewardship gifts and the temporary sign gifts.
   a. The sign gifts (the passing gifts)
      (1) Apostleship
      (2) Prophecy
      (3) Miracles
      (4) Healing
      (5) Tongues
      (6) Interpretation of tongues
      (7) Knowledge
   b. The stewardship gifts (the permanent gifts)
      (1) Wisdom
      (2) Discernment of spirits
      (3) Giving
      (4) Exhortation
      (5) Ministering
      (6) Mercy showing
      (7) Ruling, administration
      (8) Faith
      (9) Teaching
      (10) Evangelism
      (11) Pastor/teacher

At this point it is relevant to ask by what right do we designate the sign gifts as temporary in duration. In fact, at first glance this would seem to contradict Hebrews 13:8, "Jesus Christ, the same yesterday, and today, and forever."

In other words, if Jesus once instructed the Holy Spirit to impart all the gifts to believers (he did, see Eph. 4:7-8), and he never changes (he doesn't), then how can it be said some of the gifts are not for today?

In answering, it should be pointed out one must distinguish between the person of God, and the program of God. This is to say that while his person never changes (Heb. 1:10-12; James 1:17), on occasion his program does. For example, God's program once called for believers to enter an ark, and centuries later, to sacrifice lambs in the Jerusalem temple. But today God's program does not include these things. The little poem is wrong which says: "Every promise in the Bible is mine/Every chapter, every verse, every line." This is simply not the case. While all the Bible was indeed written for us (1 Cor. 10:11), not all the Bible was written specifically to us. Two examples can be cited here:
   • No 90-year old barren woman today could rightfully expect to bear a son based on God's promise to Sarah in Genesis 17:19, 21.
   • No terminally stricken man today could rightfully expect an additional 15 years to be added to his life based on God's promise to Hezekiah in 2 Kings 20:5-6.

Assuming, however, all the above is true, it still does not explain why some of the gifts are not for today.

The answer is found in the miraculous nature of the gift itself. Imagine yourself to be a spokesman sent from God some 20 centuries ago, before most of the New Testament was written. You have a message from the Lord. But how can your listeners be sure you are not one more false prophet among the many of the day? One dramatic indication of your genuineness would be the ability to perform miraculous signs. Note the following verses that bring this out.

a. As seen in the ministry of Jesus—"The same came to Jesus by night, and said unto him, Rabbi, we know that thou art a teacher come from God: for no man can do these miracles that thou doest, except God be with him" (John 3:2).

"And when he had called unto him his twelve disciples, he gave them power against unclean spirits, to cast them out, and to heal all manner of sickness and all manner of disease. . . . And as ye go, preach, saying, The kingdom of heaven is at hand. Heal the sick, cleanse the lepers, raise the dead, cast out devils: freely ye have received, freely give" (Matt. 10:1, 7-8).

"Now when John had heard in the prison the works of Christ, he sent two of his disciples, and said unto him, Art thou he that should come, or do we look for another? Jesus answered and said unto them, Go and shew John again those things which ye do hear and see: the blind receive their sight, and the lame walk, the lepers are cleansed, and the deaf hear, the dead are raised up, and the poor have the gospel preached to them" (Matt. 11:2-5).

"And many other signs truly did Jesus in the presence of his disciples, which are not written in this book: but these are written, that ye might believe that Jesus is the Christ, the Son of God; and that believing ye might have life through his name" (John 20:30-31).

b. As seen in the ministry of Paul—"For I will not dare to speak of any of those things which Christ hath not wrought by me, to make the Gentiles obedient, by word and deed" (Rom. 15:18). "Truly the signs of an apostle were wrought among you in all patience, in signs, and wonders, and mighty deeds" (2 Cor. 12:12).

c. As seen in the ministry of the apostles—"God also bearing them witness, both with signs and wonders, and with divers miracles, and gifts of the Holy Ghost, according to his own will?" (Heb. 2:4).

The sign gifts were given primarily to validate the authority of the Savior and his apostles prior to the writing of the New Testament. Afterward, this miraculous proof was no longer needed, for the Scriptures themselves reveal the true from the false.

The amazing power of the Scriptures and the Scriptures alone, apart from any signs and wonders to totally accomplish God's will, is vividly brought out by Paul in his final epistle before suffering martyrdom: "And that from a child thou hast known the holy scriptures, which are able to make thee wise unto salvation through faith which is in Christ Jesus. All scripture is given by inspiration of God, and is profitable for doctrine, for reproof, for correction, for instruction in righteousness" (2 Tim. 3:15-16).

With this somewhat lengthy introduction, we now consider the seven sign gifts.

1. The gift of apostleship (Eph. 4:11; 1 Cor. 12:28)—A reference to certain men called by Christ himself and endued with special power to function as the official "charter members" of the newly organized church.

Here a distinction should be made between an apostle (literally, "one sent forth"), and a disciple (meaning, "a learner"). Thus, while all the apostles were (hopefully) disciples, not all the disciples were apostles. Note the following account: "From that time many of his disciples went back, and walked no more with him. Then said Jesus unto the twelve, Will ye also go away?" (John 6:66-67).

    a. Apostolic requirements—One must have seen the resurrected Christ. "Beginning from the baptism of John, unto that same day that he was taken up from us, must one be ordained to be a witness with us of his resurrection" (Acts 1:22). "Am I not an apostle? am I not free? have I not seen Jesus Christ our Lord? are not ye my work in the Lord?" (1 Cor. 9:1).

    b. Apostolic number—The original 12. "And when it was day, he called unto him his disciples: and of them he chose twelve, whom also he named apostles" (Luke 6:13).

        The total number of the early apostles was not, however, limited to these 12.

      (1) Matthias was an apostle (Acts 1:26).

      (2) Paul was an apostle (Rom. 1:1; 11:13; 1 Cor. 9:1; 2 Cor. 11:15; 12:12)—"For I speak to you Gentiles, inasmuch as I am the apostle of the Gentiles, I magnify mine office" (Rom. 11:13).

      (3) Barnabas was an apostle (Acts 14:14).

      (4) James, the half brother of Christ, was an apostle (1 Cor. 15:7; Gal. 1:19).

2. The gift of prophecy (Rom. 12:6; 1 Cor. 12:10; 14:1, 3-6; Eph. 4:11)—This was, in essence, a twofold gift: to correctly foretell the future, and to correctly forthtell the present—Paul exhibited this twofold gift when writing 1 Corinthians.

    a. He foretold the future in 1 Corinthians 15—This is foresight. "Behold, I shew you a mystery; We shall not all sleep, but we shall all be changed, in a moment, in the twinkling of an eye, at the last trump: for the trumpet shall sound, and the dead shall be raised incorruptible, and we shall be changed. For this corruptible must put on incorruption, and this mortal must put on immortality. So when this corruptible shall have put on incorruption, and this mortal shall have put on immortality, then shall be brought to pass the saying that is written, Death is swallowed up in victory. O death, where is thy sting? O grave, where is thy victory?" (1 Cor. 15:51-55).

    b. He forthtold the present in 1 Corinthians 3—This is insight. "And I, brethren, could not speak unto you as unto spiritual, but as unto carnal, even as unto babes in Christ. I have fed you with milk, and not with meat: for hitherto ye were not able to bear it, neither yet now are ye able. For ye are yet carnal: for whereas there is among you envying, and strife, and divisions, are ye not carnal, and walk as men?" (1 Cor. 3:1-3).

3. The gift of miracles (1 Cor. 12:28)—The gift of miracles is the supernatural ability to perform those events outside and beyond the realm of nature; the ability to set aside for a time the regular laws of nature.

    a. The purpose of miracles—The purpose was to prove the God-sent authority of the one doing the miracle. It thus served to validate both the messenger and the message. As we have previously noted, this was the ultimate purpose and reason for all the sign gifts. (See John 3:2; 20:30-31; Rom. 15:18; 2 Cor. 12:12; Heb. 2:4.)

    b. The threefold division of Bible miracles—In the Word of God there are three periods which witnessed a great outpouring of miracles.

      (1) During the time of Moses and Joshua (approximately 25 miracles)

      (2) During the time of Elijah and Elisha (approximately 21; Elijah performed 7, and Elisha, 14)

(3) During the time of Christ and his apostles (approximately 50)
The Bible student will readily agree that during these three periods there
was a real need for the miracles to awaken Israel from her indifference and
immorality.

4. The gift of healing (1 Cor. 12:9, 28, 30)—The gift of healing is a supernatural
ability to cure human ills, whether of physical, mental, or demonic origin.
   a. The purpose of the gift of healing—As in the case of miracles, this gift was
   apparently given to attest to the authority and power of the one doing the
   healing.
   b. The limitation of the gift of healing
      (1) Christ did not heal all those he encountered. (See Luke 4:25-27.)
      (2) Paul was limited in his healing abilities.
         (a) As seen in his own affliction (2 Cor. 12:7-10)
         (b) As seen in the case of Epaphroditus (Phil. 2:26-27)
         (c) As seen in the case of Timothy—"Drink no longer water, but use a
         little wine for thy stomach's sake and thine often infirmities" (1 Tim.
         5:23).
         (d) As seen in the case of Trophimus—"Erastus abode at Corinth: but
         Trophimus have I left at Miletum sick" (2 Tim. 4:20).

At this point, the following question may arise: If the gifts of miracles and
healing were temporary, does this mean that God does not heal today? It does
not. It simply means that the gift of healing, through an individual, is no longer
in existence. It is through prayers of faith that miraculous healings can come.
Furthermore, healing can only come if it is God's will. Contrary to what faith
healers teach, it is not always God's will to heal.

5. The gift of tongues (1 Cor. 12:10)—There is perhaps no other subject in all the
Bible that has generated more heat, confusion, and division than that of
speaking in tongues.
   a. Passages referring to tongues
      (1) Prophetical—The promise in Mark: "And these signs shall follow them
      that believe; In my name shall they cast out devils; they shall speak with
      new tongues" (Mark 16:17).
      (2) Historical—The three accounts in Acts
         (a) Occurring in Jerusalem (at Pentecost)—"And when the day of
         Pentecost was fully come, they were all with one accord in one place.
         And suddenly there came a sound from heaven as of a rushing
         mighty wind, and it filled all the house where they were sitting. And
         there appeared unto them cloven tongues like as of fire, and it sat
         upon each of them. And they were all filled with the Holy Ghost, and
         began to speak with other tongues, as the Spirit gave them utterance"
         (Acts 2:1-4).
         (b) Occurring in Caesarea—"While Peter yet spake these words, the Holy
         Ghost fell on all them which heard the word. And they of the
         circumcision which believed were astonished, as many as came with
         Peter, because that on the Gentiles also was poured out the gift of the
         Holy Ghost. For they heard them speak with tongues, and magnify
         God. Then answered Peter, Can any man forbid water, that these
         should not be baptized, which have received the Holy Ghost as well
         as we?" (Acts 10:44-47).

(c) Occurring in Ephesus—Here Paul meets 12 apostles of John the Baptist. When he brought them up to date about the crucifixion, resurrection, and ascension of Christ, and the events of Pentecost, they experienced a twofold baptism, both physical and spiritual. "When they heard this, they were baptized in the name of the Lord Jesus. And when Paul had laid his hands upon them, the Holy Ghost came on them; and they spake with tongues, and prophesied" (Acts 19:5-6).

(3) Doctrinal—The overview in 1 Corinthians: "I would that ye all spake with tongues, but rather that ye prophesied: for greater is he that prophesieth than he that speaketh with tongues, except he interpret, that the church may receive edifying. If any man speak in an unknown tongue, let it be by two, or at the most by three, and that by course; and let one interpret" (1 Cor. 14:5, 27).

b. Views on the biblical record of tongues—There are at least three views concerning their nature.

(1) That all accounts of tongues-speaking refer to the same event, that is, the supernatural ability to suddenly speak previously unlearned human languages.

Arguments:

(a) Because the word _glossa_ is found 50 times in the Greek New Testament. Of these, 16 times it refers to the physical organ (see James 3:5); once it refers to flames of fires (Acts 2:3); 33 times it refers to human language.

(b) Because of the description of the events at Pentecost (Acts 2:6-11). Also, Peter says that the tongues-speaking he witnessed at Caesarea was identical to that at Pentecost (Acts 11:15).

(2) That all accounts of tongues-speaking refer to the same event, that is, the supernatural ability to speak in a nonhuman ecstatic language. This has often been called "the language of angels."

Arguments:

(a) The tongues-speaking disciples at Pentecost are accused of drunkenness (Acts 2:13), a charge that would not be made if the language was of an earthly nature.

(b) Because of Paul's words in 1 Corinthians 14:2, "For he that speaketh in an unknown tongue speaketh not unto men, but unto God: for no man understandeth him."

(c) Paul had the gift of tongues (1 Cor. 14:18), yet he could not understand the human speech of Lycaonia in Acts 14:11.

(d) Because of the phrase "other tongues" in Acts 2:4. This is a translation of the Greek word _heteros_, which means "another of a different kind." (See also Gal. 1:6-7.)

(3) That some of the accounts (as in Acts 2) refer to unlearned human language, while other accounts (as in 1 Cor. 14) refer to an angelic language—Concerning this last view, Dr. John Walvoord writes:

The use of identical terms in reference to speaking with tongues in Acts and in 1 Corinthians leaves no foundation for a distinction. In all passages, the same vocabulary is used: _laleo_ and _glossa_, in various grammatical constructions. On the basis of the Greek and statement of the text no distinction is found. (*The Holy Spirit*, p. 183)

c. The purpose of tongues
  (1) Negative
    (a) It was not for church edification—"He that speaketh in an unknown tongue edifieth himself; but he that prophesieth edifieth the church. . . . Yet in the church I had rather speak five words with my understanding, that by my voice I might teach others also, than ten thousand words in an unknown tongue" (1 Cor. 14:4, 19).
    (b) It probably was not for personal edification—Here an objection may be raised, for does not Paul say, "He that speaketh in an unknown tongue edifieth himself?" He does indeed. (See 1 Cor. 14:4.) However, a problem is seen here. *If* tongues are for personal edification, and *if* the church house was filled with those having this gift (as the context actually indicates, see 14:23), then why is it that apart from the church at Laodicea (Rev. 3:14-18), this group was probably the most carnal, confused, and even corrupt Christian congregation in the entire New Testament? The answer may center in the fact that no gift was to be used for personal edification in a selfish way. In other words, Paul may be actually rebuking them for their unscriptural usage of this gift.
    (c) It was not to demonstrate either salvation or Spirit baptism—These false concepts are totally refuted in 1 Corinthians 12:13; Romans 6:3-4; Colossians 2:9-12; Ephesians 4:5; Galatians 3:27-28. "For by one Spirit are we all baptized into one body, whether we be Jews or Gentiles, whether we be bond or free; and have been all made to drink into one Spirit" (1 Cor. 12:13).
  (2) Positive
    (a) To reassure—This is to say the sign gift of tongues (like all other sign gifts) served to validate both the messenger and the spoken message.
    (b) To rebuke—"In the law it is written, With men of other tongues and other lips will I speak unto this people; and yet for all that will they not hear me, saith the Lord. Wherefore tongues are for a sign, not to them that believe, but to them that believe not: but prophesying serveth not for them that believe not, but for them which believe" (1 Cor. 14:21-22).
       Question: How can tongues possibly be a sign "to them that believe not?" Who are these "that believe not"? The answer concerning both the how and the who is found in the phrase, "In the law it is written" (14:21). Here Paul quotes from Isaiah 28:11-12. At this point, some historical background is vital.
       In 721 B.C. the northern 10 tribes of Israel were carried off into captivity by the Assyrians. In chapter 28 of his book Isaiah warns the remaining southern two tribes (Judah and Benjamin) the same judgment awaited them unless they repented. He is, however, ridiculed by a group of drunken priests and prophets who denounce his message.
       "But they also have erred through wine, and through strong drink are out of the way; the priest and the prophet have erred through

strong drink, they are swallowed up of wine, they are out of the way through strong drink; they err in vision, they stumble in judgment. . . . Wherefore hear the word of the LORD, ye scornful men, that rule this people which is in Jerusalem. Because ye have said, We have made a covenant with death, and with hell are we at agreement; when the overflowing scourge shall pass through, it shall not come unto us: for we have made lies our refuge, and under falsehood have we hid ourselves. . . . And your covenant with death shall be disannulled, and your agreement with hell shall not stand; when the overflowing scourge shall pass through, then ye shall be trodden down by it" (Isa. 28:7, 14-15, 18).

In essence, God says to Judah through Isaiah: "All right, since I cannot reach you in the Hebrew language, I will nevertheless command your attention when, through the mouth of enemy soldiers I speak to you in the Assyrian and Babylonian language!" (author's paraphrase). Thus, to be addressed by God in a non-Hebrew language was a symbol of judgment to the Hebrew mind. Both Moses and Jeremiah, along with Isaiah, wrote in similar fashion: "The LORD shall bring a nation against thee from far, from the end of the earth, as swift as the eagle flieth; a nation whose tongue thou shalt not understand" (Deut. 28:49). "Lo, I will bring a nation upon you from far, O house of Israel, saith the LORD: it is a mighty nation, it is an ancient nation, a nation whose language thou knowest not, neither understandest what they say" (Jer. 5:15).

Tongues then, served as a sign to unbelieving Israel. Peter later clearly reaffirmed all this on the day of Pentecost: "And they were all filled with the Holy Ghost, and began to speak with other tongues, as the Spirit gave them utterance. . . . Ye men of Israel, hear these words; Jesus of Nazareth, a man approved of God among you by miracles and wonders and signs, which God did by him in the midst of you, as ye yourselves also know: him, being delivered by the determinate counsel and foreknowledge of God, ye have taken, and by wicked hands have crucified and slain. . . . And with many other words did he testify and exhort, saying, Save yourselves from this untoward generation" (Acts 2:4, 22-23, 40).

(c) To reveal—When Paul sat down and wrote 1 Corinthians 14, there was in existence at that time (A.D. 53) only four of the 27 New Testament books (James, Galatians, 1 and 2 Thessalonians). There was no written record available concerning such important issues as:

  i) The doctrine of the church (later discussed in Ephesians and Colossians)
  ii) The doctrine of justification, sanctification, and glorification (later written about in Romans)
  iii) The doctrine of apostasy (Jude)
  iv) Christian forgiveness (Philemon)
  v) The priesthood of Christ (Hebrews)
  vi) The life of Christ (4 Gospels)
  vii) Practical Christian service (1 and 2 Peter)
  viii) Christian love (as found in 1, 2, and 3 John)

ix) Advice to pastors and deacons (as discussed in 1 and 2 Timothy, and Titus)

In view of all this, no believer could quote or claim the blessed truth in 2 Timothy 3:16-17—simply because it had not yet been written. "All scripture is given by inspiration of God, and is profitable for doctrine, for reproof, for correction, for instruction in righteousness: That the man of God may be perfect." Thus, one of the reasons for tongues was to reveal needed spiritual truths prior to the completion of the New Testament.

d. General facts about tongues
  (1) Speaking in a known tongue helps all—"But he that prophesieth speaketh unto men to edification, and exhortation, and comfort" (1 Cor. 14:3).
  (2) Speaking in tongues helps no Christian in the church—"He that speaketh in an unknown tongue edifieth himself; but he that prophesieth edifieth the church" (1 Cor. 14:4).
  (3) The tongue, like a musical instrument, is useless unless heard and distinctly understood—"And even things without life giving sound, whether pipe or harp, except they give a distinction in the sounds, how shall it be known what is piped or harped?" (1 Cor. 14:7).
  (4) The distinction can sometimes mean the difference between life and death—"For if the trumpet give an uncertain sound, who shall prepare himself to the battle?" (1 Cor. 14:8).
  (5) Although Paul is said to have spoken in tongues (see 1 Cor. 14:18), there is no stress on this whatsoever during any of his testimonies (as before Felix and Agrippa) or missionary trips—While he did not forbid the speaking in tongues, neither did he especially encourage it, for he realized that not all Christians even during those days had the gift. "Have all the gifts of healing? do all speak with tongues? do all interpret?" (1 Cor. 12:30). "Wherefore, brethren, covet to prophesy, and forbid not to speak with tongues" (1 Cor. 14:39).
  (6) Therefore, the teaching today that all Christians must speak in tongues for salvation or sanctification is totally unscriptural.
  (7) Paul taught that in the church, preaching (both foretelling and forthtelling) was to be preferred 2,000 times over tongues. "Yet in the church I had rather speak five words with my understanding, that by my voice I might teach others also, than ten thousand words in an unknown tongue" (1 Cor. 14:19).

e. Regulations concerning tongues
  (1) Unanimous tongues-speaking was forbidden—"If therefore the whole church be come together into one place, and all speak with tongues, and there come in those that are unlearned, or unbelievers, will they not say that ye are mad?" (1 Cor. 14:23).
  (2) Preaching, not tongues, is God's method for saving the lost—"But if all prophesy, and there come in one that believeth not, or one unlearned, he is convinced of all, he is judged of all: and thus are the secrets of his heart made manifest; and so falling down on his face he will worship God, and report that God is in you of a truth" (1 Cor. 14:24-25).
  (3) Tongues-speaking was to be limited in number, with each to speak in

turn—"If any man speak in an unknown tongue, let it be by two, or at the most by three, and that by course; and let one interpret" (1 Cor. 14:27).

(4) Women were absolutely forbidden to speak in tongues—"Let your women keep silence in the churches: for it is not permitted unto them to speak; but they are commanded to be under obedience, as also saith the law" (1 Cor. 14:34). Note: In 1 Corinthians 11 Paul had previously allowed a woman to both pray and offer prophecies in a local church (1 Cor. 11:5), but here in chapter 14 he forbids her to speak in tongues.

(5) All things in God's house are to be done decently and in order—"Let all things be done decently and in order" (1 Cor. 14:40). In light of the above, all honest observers would have to admit that approximately 90 percent of the modern tongue movement would immediately fall, if the rules in 1 Corinthians 14 were obeyed.

f. Conclusions about tongues—Are they for today? While one cannot dogmatically prove the gift of tongues was temporary, there are, nevertheless, strong indications that this gift of tongues has indeed ceased. Consider the following:

(1) Tongues are never mentioned by Paul again after 1 Corinthians 14.

(2) Peter, James, John, and Jude, the remaining New Testament writers, never once refer to tongues.

(3) Tongues are not mentioned as a fruit of the Spirit—"But the fruit of the Spirit is love, joy, peace, longsuffering, gentleness, goodness, faith, meekness, temperance: against such there is no law" (Gal. 5:22-23).

(4) Paul indicates that tongues would cease—"Charity never faileth: but whether there be prophecies, they shall fail; whether there be tongues, they shall cease; whether there be knowledge, it shall vanish away" (1 Cor. 13:8).

(5) Tongues are not mentioned as a qualification for a pastor or a deacon in 2 Timothy 3 and Titus 1.

(6) In Revelation 2–3 Christ speaks to his seven churches in Asia Minor but never refers to tongues.

(7) In the three centuries that followed the Apostolic period, there are only two references in the writings of the church fathers concerning tongues.

Question: Is there a "smoking gun" verse proving that tongues have indeed ceased? Many would answer in the affirmative, pointing to 1 Corinthians 13:8. "Charity never faileth: but whether there be prophecies, they shall fail; whether there be tongues, they shall cease; whether there be knowledge, it shall vanish away."

However, the pro-tongues movement would quickly point out that inasmuch as prophecies have not "failed," nor has knowledge "vanished away," then it must be concluded that tongues have not ceased. Here it must be said, however, that the King James rendering of the Greek verbs is misleading to say the least. Note the more accurate New American Standard Bible: "Love never fails; but if there are gifts of prophecy, they will be done away; if there are tongues, they will cease; if there is knowledge, it will be done away."

In other words, the original Greek verb *katargeo* (used in describing both prophecies and knowledge) never says these two gifts will "fail," but rather be phased out. Furthermore, the Greek word *pauo* (translated the same way in both the KJV and the NASB) used in describing tongues does indeed mean to cease, to stop, or to refrain. Finally, observe the three spiritual gifts mentioned in 1 Corinthians 13:8. They are prophecy, tongues, and knowledge. This study has already dealt with the first two, but what was the gift of knowledge? In reality this gift may refer to that supernatural ability to both receive and transmit on paper a book or section of the New Testament. This gift will be examined in more detail in a later section. Thus, in light of all this, a strong case can be made that tongues, along with at least two other sign gifts, have indeed been phased out.

6. The gift of the interpretation of tongues (1 Cor. 14:13, 27-32)—The gift of interpretation of tongues is the supernatural ability to clarify and interpret those messages uttered in an unknown language. "But God hath revealed them unto us by his Spirit: for the Spirit searcheth all things, yea, the deep things of God" (1 Cor. 2:10).

Instructions concerning the employment of this gift:
   a. This gift can be used in one of two ways:
      (1) To interpret one's own tongues speaking (1 Cor. 14:13)
      (2) To interpret another's tongues speaking (1 Cor. 14:27)
   b. Two interpretations should not be given at the same time in a meeting (1 Cor. 14:29-32)
   c. Unless one who has the gift of interpretation is present, another should not attempt to use the gift of tongues (1 Cor. 14:28).

7. The gift of knowledge (1 Cor. 12:8)—This is perhaps one of the least understood of all the gifts. Some believe it involves the supernatural ability to *accumulate* facts, as opposed to the gift of wisdom, which seems to be the supernatural ability to rightfully *apply* those facts.

But there is a problem with this view, for 1 Corinthians 13:8 states the gift of knowledge will be phased out.

Those claiming to possess this gift today, however, view it as the supernatural ability to correctly diagnose a disease by special revelation and then to heal the diseased person. Here it should be simply noted that the gift of knowledge is referred to five times (1 Cor. 12:8; 13:2, 8; 1 Cor. 14:6; 2 Cor. 8:7) but is never in any way associated with healing.

What then is the gift of knowledge? It may have involved the following twofold aspect:
   a. The supernatural ability to receive an oral revelation concerning the person of God, another human being, etc.
   b. The supernatural ability to receive a written revelation to be added as part of the New Testament.

Having considered the 7 temporary sign gifts, we now examine the 11 permanent stewardship gifts.

1. The gift of wisdom (1 Cor. 12:8)—There are four kinds of wisdom mentioned in the Bible.
   a. Natural wisdom—The Pharisee lawyer Gamaliel displayed this kind of wisdom when he cautioned the Jewish Sanhedrin who were determined to kill the apostles by the following advice: "And now I say unto you, Refrain from these men, and let them alone: for if this counsel or this work be of

men, it will come to nought: but if it be of God, ye cannot overthrow it; lest haply ye be found even to fight against God" (Acts 5:38-39).

b. Worldly wisdom—This is, in reality, that anti-God philosophical wisdom condemned by the Bible in 1 Corinthians 1:17-31. Note Paul's description at this point: "For Christ sent me not to baptize, but to preach the gospel: not with wisdom of words, lest the cross of Christ should be made of none effect. For the preaching of the cross is to them that perish foolishness; but unto us which are saved it is the power of God. For it is written, I will destroy the wisdom of the wise, and will bring to nothing the understanding of the prudent. Where is the wise? where is the scribe? where is the disputer of this world? hath not God made foolish the wisdom of this world? For after that in the wisdom of God the world by wisdom knew not God, it pleased God by the foolishness of preaching to save them that believe. . . . Because the foolishness of God is wiser than men; and the weakness of God is stronger than men" (1 Cor. 1:17-21, 25).

c. Sanctifying wisdom—This is the wisdom God desires to impart to all his people. "If any of you lack wisdom, let him ask of God, that giveth to all men liberally, and upbraideth not; and it shall be given him" (1:15).

d. Stewardship wisdom—This is the supernatural ability to correctly and concisely apply spiritual principles to contemporary problems. This is the gift of wisdom.

2. The gift of discernment of spirits (1 Cor. 12:10)—"Beloved, believe not every spirit, but try the spirits whether they are of God: because many false prophets are gone out into the world" (1 John 4:1).

This seems to involve the supernatural ability to distinguish between the actions of demons, humans, and the Holy Spirit in the life of another person.

a. Both Peter and Paul had this gift.

(1) Peter's usage (in condemning Simon the sorcerer)—"Repent therefore of this thy wickedness, and pray God, if perhaps the thought of thine heart may be forgiven thee. For I perceive that thou art in the gall of bitterness, and in the bond of iniquity" (Acts 8:22-23).

(2) Paul's usage (in condemning a false prophet named Bar-jesus)—"Then Saul, (who also is called Paul,) filled with the Holy Ghost, set his eyes on him, and said, O full of all subtilty and all mischief, thou child of the devil, thou enemy of all righteousness, wilt thou not cease to pervert the right ways of the Lord?" (Acts 13:9-10).

b. A personal survey taken among several hundred pastors concerning this gift revealed the following:

(1) Over 90 percent felt they did *not* possess the gift of discernment.

(2) Over 90 percent felt their wives *did* possess the gift of discernment.

3. The gift of giving (Rom. 12:8)—This gift may be defined as the supernatural ability to sacrificially invest large amounts of one's time and (or) money into the life of another. This priceless gift is probably the least coveted but the most needed in the body of Christ today. Few, if any, of those Christian leaders loudly promoting those exotic gifts (signs and wonders, healings, prophecy, tongues, etc.) would show the slightest interest in this humble, selfless, and nonsensational gift. Individuals in various New Testament churches gave example of the gift of giving.

a. The Jerusalem church (Acts 4:32-37)

b. The Galatian church (Gal. 4:15)

c. The Philippian church (Phil. 4:10-18)

d. The churches at Macedonia (2 Cor. 8:1-5)

Note: A pre-Pentecost example of this gift is seen in the account of the widow's mite: "And he looked up, and saw the rich men casting their gifts into the treasury. And he saw also a certain poor widow casting in thither two mites. And he said, Of a truth I say unto you, that this poor widow hath cast in more than they all: for all these have of their abundance cast in unto the offerings of God: but she of her penury hath cast in all the living that she had" (Luke 21:1-4).

It has been correctly observed: (a) "What I earned, I spent"; (b) "What I saved, I lost"; and (c) "What I gave, I have!"

4. The gift of exhortation (Rom. 12:8)—The gift of exhortation is that supernatural ability to help someone by motivating him in a positive way to fruitful action. Rick Yohn writes:

> The word exhortation is derived from two Greek words, *para* (alongside) and *kaleo* (to call). You may be familiar with the term "paraclete." Jesus calls the Holy Spirit a paraclete (comforter: one who is called to aid or support another). (*Discover Your Spiritual Gift and Use It*, p. 83.)

With this in mind, it can be said (in a certain sense) that the one possessing the gift of exhortation functions as a human Holy Spirit.

This spiritual gift was used in the New Testament in a threefold manner, namely, to challenge, to encourage, and to rebuke. The same Greek word is in mind here concerning all three terms. Thus:

a. The exhorter challenges.

(1) He challenges concerning the flesh of the believer—"I beseech you therefore, brethren, by the mercies of God, that ye present your bodies a living sacrifice, holy, acceptable unto God, which is your reasonable service" (Rom. 12:1).

(2) He challenges concerning the finances of the believer—"So I thought it necessary to urge the brothers to visit you in advance and finish the arrangements for the generous gift you had promised. Then it will be ready as a generous gift, not as one grudgingly given" (2 Cor. 9:5, NIV).

(3) He challenges concerning the faith of the believer—"Beloved, when I gave all diligence to write unto you of the common salvation, it was needful for me to write unto you, and exhort you that ye should earnestly contend for the faith which was once delivered unto the saints" (Jude 3).

b. The exhorter encourages—"Sufficient to such a man is this punishment, which was inflicted of many" (2 Cor. 2:6).

The one referred to here was an immoral and (for awhile) unrepentant church member once excommunicated from the assembly at Corinth by Paul's command (see 1 Cor. 5). Sometime after this, however, the man had apparently repented, but was not being restored back into fellowship by the fickle church. Note Paul's admonition at this point: "So that contrariwise ye ought rather to forgive him, and comfort him, lest perhaps such a one should be swallowed up with overmuch sorrow. Wherefore I beseech you that ye would confirm your love toward him" (2 Cor. 2:7-8). Here the word *beseech* is from the Greek *parakaleo*.

c. The exhorter rebukes.
   (1) Paul gently rebukes two pouting women in the church at Philippi. "I beseech Euodias, and beseech Syntyche, that they be of the same mind in the Lord" (Phil. 4:2).
   (2) Paul sternly rebukes Peter at Antioch because of his legalism—"But when Peter was come to Antioch, I withstood him to the face, because he was to be blamed" (Gal. 2:11).
   One final quote from Rick Yohn:

> To summarize the uses of this gift, consider the case of a man living immorally with a woman. The exhorter *rebukes* the man for his conduct. Not only do the Scriptures condemn his action, but his own conscience condemns him. The man has felt guilty, even though he has probably told himself that love makes it all right. The exhorter then *challenges* the man to change his way of life. "Flee immorality" (1 Corinthians 6:18). "Break off your relationship with this woman." "You are sinning against your own body" (1 Corinthians 6:18). "God wants you to be pure" (1 Thessalonians 4:3-8). "The thief sins alone, but the adulterer causes another to sin."
>
> If the individual repents of his sin and seeks God's forgiveness, the need to rebuke has ended. There is no need to challenge him to turn to Christ. The exhorter now accepts and encourages him. (Ibid., p. 86)

5. The gift of ministering (Rom. 12:7; 1 Cor. 12:28)—The gift of ministering is the supernatural ability to render practical help in both physical and spiritual matters.

   This gift is called the gift of helps in 1 Corinthians 12:28. How sorely needed is the gift of helps in local churches today. There seems to be an abundance of eloquent pastors and colorful evangelists, but where are the helpers? This is sometimes known as the Benjamin gift, which name means "son of my right hand" (see Gen. 35:18).

   Perhaps the most outstanding Old Testament illustration concerning this gift is seen through the ministry offered to Moses by his brother, Aaron, and his brother-in-law, Hur. Note the account:

   "Then came Amalek, and fought with Israel in Rephidim. And Moses said unto Joshua, Choose us out men, and go out, fight with Amalek: to morrow I will stand on the top of the hill with the rod of God in mine hand. So Joshua did as Moses had said to him, and fought with Amalek: and Moses, Aaron, and Hur went up to the top of the hill. And it came to pass, when Moses held up his hand, that Israel prevailed: and when he let down his hand, Amalek prevailed. But Moses' hands were heavy; and they took a stone, and put it under him, and he sat thereon; and Aaron and Hur stayed up his hands, the one on the one side, and the other on the other side; and his hands were steady until the going down of the sun" (Exod. 17:8-12).

   A number of New Testament people possessed this gift.
   a. Dorcas (Acts 9:36-39)
   b. Phoebe (Rom. 16:1-2)
   c. Onesiphorus (2 Tim. 1:16-18)
6. The gift of mercy showing (Rom. 12:8)—The gift of the showing of mercy is the

supernatural ability to minister to those sick and afflicted. This gift, perhaps as no other gift, stands out like a flashing diamond when contrasted to the unspeakable cruelty displayed in these final days. The ultimate scriptural role model concerning this gift is the Good Samaritan (see Luke 10:30-37).

7. The gift of ruling, or administration (Rom. 12:8; 1 Cor. 12:28)—The gift of ruling, or administration, is the supernatural ability to organize, administer, and promote the various affairs in a local church. It has also been defined as the ability to direct others towards a common objective. A local church will not grow beyond a certain point unless it employs the ministry of those individuals empowered with this gift.

    The New Testament pastor Titus had this gift, as testified by the Apostle Paul. "To Titus, mine own son after the common faith: Grace, mercy, and peace, from God the Father and the Lord Jesus Christ our Savior. For this cause left I thee in Crete, that thou shouldest set in order the things that are wanting, and ordain elders in every city, as I had appointed thee" (Titus 1:4-5).

8. The gift of faith (1 Cor. 12:9)—The Bible describes three kinds of faith:
    a. Saving faith—This faith is given to all repenting sinners. "And they said, Believe on the Lord Jesus Christ, and thou shalt be saved, and thy house" (Acts 16:31). "But to him that worketh not, but believeth on him that justifieth the ungodly, his faith is counted for righteousness" (Rom. 4:5). "Therefore being justified by faith, we have peace with God through our Lord Jesus Christ" (Rom. 5:1). "So then faith cometh by hearing, and hearing by the word of God" (Rom. 10:17).
    b. Sanctifying faith—Sanctifying faith is available to all believers. "I am crucified with Christ: nevertheless I live; yet not I, but Christ liveth in me: and the life which I now live in the flesh I live by the faith of the Son of God, who loved me, and gave himself for me" (Gal. 2:20). "But that no man is justified by the law in the sight of God, it is evident: for, The just shall live by faith" (Gal. 3:11). "But the fruit of the Spirit is love, joy, peace, longsuffering, gentleness, goodness, faith" (Gal. 5:22). "Above all, taking the shield of faith, wherewith ye shall be able to quench all the fiery darts of the wicked" (Eph. 6:16).
    c. Stewardship faith—Stewardship faith is given to some believers. This is the gift of faith, and is a supernatural ability to believe and expect great things from God.

        C. Peter Wagner has defined this gift as follows: "The gift of faith is the special ability that God gives to some members of the body of Christ to discern with extraordinary confidence the will and purposes of God for the future of His work" (*Your Spiritual Gifts Can Help Your Church Grow*, p. 158).

9. The gift of teaching (Rom. 12:7; Eph. 4:11; 1 Cor. 12:28)—The gift of teaching is the supernatural ability to communicate and clarify the details of the Word of God causing spiritual growth in the body of Christ.

    At least three steps are involved in successfully accomplishing this spiritual growth:
    a. Information (that is, correctly relating the scriptural text)—In other words, what does this passage say?
    b. Interpretation (that is, correctly explaining the scriptural text)—In other words, what does this passage mean?

    c. Application (that is, correctly directing the scriptural text)—In other words, how does this passage apply to my life?

      While no one can present a better gospel than that in the Bible, there are those who can teach that gospel better. This is the gift of teaching.

      A number of New Testament individuals possessed this gift. These would include:

    a. Paul (Acts 20:27)

    b. Apollos (Acts 18:24-25)

    c. Aquila and Priscilla (Acts 18:26)

10. The gift of evangelism (Eph. 4:11)—This gift seems to be twofold:

    a. The personal aspect—Here the gift of evangelism is the supernatural ability to point sinners to Christ and to burden Christians about soul winning. All believers are to witness for Christ whether they have this special gift or not. Timothy, for example, was not an evangelist, but he was a soul winner. "But watch thou in all things, endure afflictions, do the work of an evangelist, make full proof of thy ministry" (2 Tim. 4:5).

      There are others, however, who were given this gift.

    (1) Philip possessed it (Acts 8:5-12; 21:8).

    (2) Peter possessed it (Acts 2:37-42).

    (3) Paul possessed it (Acts 19:18-20).

    b. The pioneering aspect—This involves the supernatural ability to found and establish new churches in previously unchurched areas. The Apostle Paul had both the personal and pioneering aspect of this gift.

    (1) The personal aspect (Acts 13:12; 14:9-10; 16:18, 31; 17:4; 20:31; 24:24-25; 26:27-28)

    (2) The pioneering aspect (Acts 14:21-23; 15:41; Rom. 15:20)

11. The gift of the pastor/teacher (Eph. 4:11)—The gift of pastor/teacher is the supernatural ability to preach and teach the Word of God and to feed and lead the flock of God.

    C. Peter Wagner writes:

> The pastor of a group of Christians is the person responsible under Jesus, who is the Master Shepherd; for teaching, feeding, healing the wounds, developing unity, helping people find their gifts, and doing whatever else is necessary to see that they continue in the faith and grow in their spiritual lives. (Ibid., p. 143)

At this point some would distinguish between the *office* of the pastor and the *gift* of the pastor. Charles Ryrie comments:

> The gift is the ability and can be exercised whether one holds an office in a local church or not. In this regard much confusion exists over the gift of pastor. The gift is the ability to shepherd people. This can be done by the person who occupies what we call, in our modern ecclesiology, the office of the pastorate. Or it can be done, say, by a dean of men or a dean of women in a school. Or it can be done by the wife and mother in a home. (*Basic Theology*, pp. 367–368)

The words of two successful New Testament pastors aptly describe this shepherding gift.

    a. The testimony of Paul—"Take heed therefore unto yourselves, and to all the flock, over the which the Holy Ghost hath made you overseers, to feed the church of God, which he hath purchased with his own blood" (Acts 20:28).

   b. The testimony of Peter—"The elders which are among you I exhort, who am also an elder, and a witness of the sufferings of Christ, and also a partaker of the glory that shall be revealed: feed the flock of God which is among you, taking the oversight thereof, not by constraint, but willingly; not for filthy lucre, but of a ready mind; neither as being lords over God's heritage, but being ensamples to the flock. And when the chief Shepherd shall appear, ye shall receive a crown of glory that fadeth not away" (1 Pet. 5:1-4).

K. His ministry concerning the fruit of the Spirit—We now come to the eleventh and final recorded ministry performed by the Holy Spirit of God. In a very real sense it best demonstrates his ultimate goal here on earth, namely, to bear fruit for Christ through believers.

   "But now being made free from sin, and become servants to God, ye have your fruit unto holiness, and the end everlasting life" (Rom. 6:22). "Wherefore, my brethren, ye also are become dead to the law by the body of Christ; that ye should be married to another, even to him who is raised from the dead, that we should bring forth fruit unto God" (Rom. 7:4). "That ye might walk worthy of the Lord unto all pleasing, being fruitful in every good work, and increasing in the knowledge of God" (Col. 1:10).

   1. The commands to bear fruit
      a. God desires his new creation to do the same as he ordered his old creation to do—"And God blessed them, and God said unto them, Be fruitful, and multiply, and replenish the earth, and subdue it: and have dominion over the fish of the sea, and over the fowl of the air, and over every living thing that moveth upon the earth" (Gen. 1:28).
      b. God desires the believer to fulfill the prophecy concerning Joseph—"Joseph is a fruitful bough, even a fruitful bough by a well; whose branches run over the wall" (Gen. 49:22).
      c. God desires his children to experience the blessings of Psalm 1—"And he shall be like a tree planted by the rivers of water, that bringeth forth his fruit in his season; his leaf also shall not wither; and whatsoever he doeth shall prosper" (Psa. 1:3).
      d. God desires his children of light to function today as his tree of life will function in eternity—"And he shewed me a pure river of water of life, clear as crystal, proceeding out of the throne of God and of the Lamb. In the midst of the street of it, and on either side of the river, was there the tree of life, which bare twelve manner of fruits, and yielded her fruit every month: and the leaves of the tree were for the healing of the nations" (Rev. 22:1-2).

   2. The prerequisites for bearing fruit
      a. One must die to this world—"Verily, verily, I say unto you, Except a corn of wheat fall into the ground and die, it abideth alone: but if it die, it bringeth forth much fruit" (John 12:24).
      b. One must abide in the Savior—"I am the true vine, and my Father is the husbandman. Every branch in me that beareth not fruit he taketh away: and every branch that beareth fruit,he purgeth it, that it may bring forth more fruit. Now ye are clean through the word which I have spoken unto you. Abide in me, and I in you. As the branch cannot bear fruit of itself, except it abide in the vine; no more can ye, except ye abide in me. I am the vine, ye

are the branches. He that abideth in me, and I in him, the same bringeth forth much fruit: for without me ye can do nothing" (John 15:1-5). "Ye have not chosen me, but I have chosen you, and ordained you, that ye should go and bring forth fruit, and that your fruit should remain: that whatsoever ye shall ask of the Father in my name, he may give it you" (John 15:16).

(1) In the Old Testament the nation Israel was God's chosen vine vessel—"Thou hast brought a vine out of Egypt: thou hast cast out the heathen, and planted it" (Psa. 80:8).

(2) But Israel refused to bear fruit—"Israel is an empty vine, he bringeth forth fruit unto himself: according to the multitude of his fruit he hath increased the altars; according to the goodness of his land they have made goodly images" (Hos. 10:1).

(3) Thus, that nation was eventually set aside by Jesus—"Therefore say I unto you, The kingdom of God shall be taken from you, and given to a nation bringing forth the fruits thereof" (Matt. 21:43).

(4) In the Gospels, Christ was God's chosen vine vessel while he was on this earth—"I am the true vine, and my Father is the husbandman" (John 15:1). (See also Isa. 11:1; 53:2.)

(5) In the present dispensation since Pentecost the believer is to be God's vine-branch vessel—To be this one must submit to pruning. "Now no chastening for the present seemeth to be joyous, but grievous: nevertheless afterward it yieldeth the peaceable fruit of righteousness unto them which are exercised thereby" (Heb. 12:11).

(6) This pruning and purifying process is absolutely vital to fruit-bearing according to Jesus—It will result in:
   (a) Fruit—"Every branch in me that beareth not fruit he taketh away: and every branch that beareth fruit, he purgeth it" (John 15:2).
   (b) More fruit—"That it may bring forth more fruit" (John 15:2).
   (c) Much fruit—"I am the vine, ye are the branches. He that abideth in me, and I in him, the same bringeth forth much fruit: for without me ye can do nothing. . . . Herein is my Father glorified, that ye bear much fruit; so shall ye be my disciples" (John 15:5, 8).
   (d) And permanent fruit—"Ye have not chosen me, but I have chosen you, and ordained you, that ye should go and bring forth fruit, and that your fruit should remain: that whatsoever ye shall ask of the Father in my name, he may give it you" (John 15:16).

(7) Jesus told his disciples they were to be branches—The only useful function of a branch is to bear fruit. A branch does not produce fruit, it simply bears it.

3. The two kinds of fruit
   a. Outer fruit: soul winning (John 4:35-36; Rom. 1:13)—"The fruit of the righteous is a tree of life; and he that winneth souls is wise" (Prov. 11:30).
   b. Inner fruit: Christlikeness (Gal. 5:22-23; Eph. 5:9)—"But the fruit of the Spirit is love, joy, peace, longsuffering, gentleness, goodness, faith, meekness, temperance: against such there is no law" (Gal. 5:22-23).

   It should be noted that the word *fruit* in both of these passages is in the singular. Paul does not say "the fruits of the Spirit are," but rather "the fruit of the Spirit is." The reason is this: all the fruit of the Spirit, unlike all the gifts of the Spirit, are to be possessed by every believer.

Consider the following illustration: Upon salvation the believer is ushered into an orchard and a vineyard.

(1) The official name of the orchard is the Gifts of the Spirit orchard. Upon entering, the believer notes that there are 18 "apples" (gifts) hanging from each tree. The Holy Spirit then selects several "apples" and gives them to the believer.

(2) The official name of the vineyard is the Fruit of the Spirit vineyard. Upon entering, the believer notes that there are 11 "grapes" hanging from each cluster on the vines. The Holy Spirit then selects an entire cluster and gives it to the believer. In other words, the Christian receives some of the apples, but all of the grapes.

4. The elevenfold fruit of the Spirit

a. Love—"And above all these things put on charity, which is the bond of perfectness" (Col. 3:14).

In the Greek vocabulary there are four main words for love:

(1) *Stergein*—*Stergein* is a natural, gravitational love; an instinctive concern for one's offspring. It is found in animals and humans alike, and used but two times in the Greek New Testament. "Without understanding, covenant breakers, without natural affection, implacable, unmerciful" (Rom. 1:31). "This know also, that in the last days perilous times shall come. For men shall be lovers of their own selves, covetous, boasters, proud, blasphemers, disobedient to parents, unthankful, unholy, without natural affection, trucebreakers, false accusers, incontinent, fierce, despisers of those that are good" (2 Tim. 3:1-3).

(2) *Eros*—*Eros* is a sexual, passionate (and often lustful and perverted) love. In mythology Eros was the son of Aphrodite, the Greek goddess of love. This word for love is not found in the Greek New Testament.

(3) *Phileo*—*Phileo* is a beautiful and friendly love. This is the love that David had for Jonathan. "And it came to pass, when he had made an end of speaking unto Saul, that the soul of Jonathan was knit with the soul of David, and Jonathan loved him as his own soul" (1 Sam. 18:1).

In the New Testament this love is often referred to, as seen by the following:

(a) Jesus' love for John (John 20:2)

(b) Jesus' love for Lazarus (John 11:3)

(c) The Father's love for Jesus (John 5:20)

(d) Christians' love for Paul (Titus 3:15)

(e) The love that all Christians should have for each other (Rom. 12:10; Heb. 13:1)

(f) The love a pastor should have for his people (Titus 1:8)

(g) The love husbands should have for their wives (Eph. 5:25)

(4) *Agapao*—*Agapao* is a divine love, found only in God. This love is not dependent upon the beauty of the object being loved. It is found 320 times in the Greek New Testament, but rarely in classical writings. Homer used it two times, and Euripedes used it three times.

"But God commendeth his love toward us, in that, while we were yet sinners, Christ died for us" (Rom. 5:8).

This love is never found in the heart of any man prior to the ascension of Christ. In fact, Jesus asks Peter on three occasions if he really loved him. "So when they had dined, Jesus saith to Simon Peter, Simon, son of Jonas, lovest thou me more than these? He saith unto him, Yea, Lord; thou knowest that I love thee. He saith unto him, Feed my lambs. He saith to him again the second time, Simon, son of Jonas, lovest thou me? He saith unto him,Yea, Lord; thou knowest that I love thee. He saith unto him, Feed my sheep. He saith unto him the third time, Simon, son of Jonas, lovest thou me? Peter was grieved because he said unto him the third time, Lovest thou me? And he said unto him, Lord, thou knowest all things; thou knowest that I love thee. Jesus saith unto him, Feed my sheep. Verily, verily, I say unto thee, When thou wast young, thou girdedst thyself, and walkedst whither thou wouldest: but when thou shalt be old, thou shalt stretch forth thy hands, and another shall gird thee, and carry thee whither thou wouldest not. This spake he, signifying by what death he should glorify God. And when he had spoken this, he saith unto him, Follow me" (John 21:15-19).

The first two times Jesus uses the fourth kind of love and asks the following question: "Peter, do you *agapao* me?" On both occasions Peter answers by choosing the third word. He says, "Lord, you know I *phileo* you." Finally, our Lord uses the third word also. The reason for all this (as Peter would later find out) is explained by Paul in his epistle to the church at Rome. "And hope maketh not ashamed; because the love of God is shed abroad in our hearts by the Holy Ghost which is given unto us" (Rom. 5:5).

Thus, the reason why Peter answered the way he did was because the Holy Spirit had not yet come at Pentecost and it was therefore impossible for him to love Christ with this divine *agapao* love. In John 11 we have a similar case where we are told that Lazarus loved Jesus with a *phileo* love, but that Jesus loved Lazarus with an *agapao* love. "Therefore his sisters sent unto him, saying, Lord, behold, he whom thou lovest is sick. . . . Now Jesus loved Martha, and her sister, and Lazarus" (John 11:3, 5).

There are two beloved New Testament passages where this *agapao* love is in view. "For God so loved the world, that he gave his only begotten Son, that whosoever believeth in him should not perish, but have everlasting life" (John 3:16). "Husbands, love your wives, even as Christ also loved the church, and gave himself for it" (Eph. 5:25).
  b. Joy (Gal. 5:22; Rom. 14:17; 1 Thess. 1:6)—This is the same kind of joy that:
    (1) The angels brought to the shepherds—"And the angel said unto them, Fear not: for, behold, I bring you good tidings of great joy, which shall be to all people" (Luke 2:10).
    (2) The wise men experienced when they found Christ—"When they saw the star, they rejoiced with exceeding great joy" (Matt. 2:10).
    (3) The angels have when a soul is saved—"Likewise, I say unto you, there is joy in the presence of the angels of God over one sinner that repenteth" (Luke 15:10).
    (4) Faithful and rewarded servants will someday have—"His lord said unto him, Well done, thou good and faithful servant: thou hast been faithful over a few things, I will make thee ruler over many things: enter thou into the joy of thy lord" (Matt. 25:21).
    (5) The women had at the news of the Resurrection—"And they departed

quickly from the sepulchre with fear and great joy; and did run to bring his disciples word" (Matt. 28:8).

(6) The Savior had in redeeming us—"Looking unto Jesus the author and finisher of our faith; who for the joy that was set before him endured the cross, despising the shame, and is set down at the right hand of the throne of God" (Heb. 12:2).

(7) The disciples had at the ascension of Christ—"And they worshipped him, and returned to Jerusalem with great joy" (Luke 24:52).

(8) This joy may be experienced even in terrible trials—"My brethren, count it all joy when ye fall into divers temptations" (1:2). "Wherein ye greatly rejoice, though now for a season, if need be, ye are in heaviness through manifold temptations" (1 Pet. 1:6).

c. Peace—There are two kinds of peace.

(1) The peace *with* God—"Therefore being justified by faith, we have peace with God through our Lord Jesus Christ" (Rom. 5:1). This peace is positional peace and includes all believers at the moment of their salvation.

(2) The peace *of* God—"And the peace of God, which passeth all understanding, shall keep your hearts and minds through Christ Jesus" (Phil. 4:7). This peace is experienced, and includes only those believers who are filled with God's Spirit. It can be defined as reassurance in tribulation.

"Great peace have they which love thy law: and nothing shall offend them" (Psa. 119:165). "I will both lay me down in peace, and sleep: for thou, LORD, only makest me dwell in safety" (Psa. 4:8). "Peace I leave with you, my peace I give unto you: not as the world giveth, give I unto you. Let not your heart be troubled, neither let it be afraid" (John 14:27).

d. Long-suffering—Long-suffering is the ability to gracefully bear an unbearable situation and to patiently endure the unendurable. "By pureness, by knowledge, by longsuffering, by kindness, by the Holy Ghost, by love unfeigned" (2 Cor. 6:6).

e. Gentleness—Gentleness is a quiet and respectful kindness. "And the servant of the Lord must not strive; but be gentle unto all men, apt to teach, patient" (2 Tim. 2:24). "To speak evil of no man, to be no brawlers, but gentle, shewing all meekness unto all men" (Titus 3:2).

f. Faith—This is sanctifying faith and seems to include, among other things, the ability to trust God for those things one cannot see. "For therein is the righteousness of God revealed from faith to faith: as it is written, The just shall live by faith" (Rom. 1:17). "Above all, taking the shield of faith, wherewith ye shall be able to quench all the fiery darts of the wicked" (Eph. 6:16). "But without faith it is impossible to please him: for he that cometh to God must believe that he is, and that he is a rewarder of them that diligently seek him" (Heb. 11:6).

This sanctifying faith also includes the ability to trust him and accept those things one cannot understand.

(1) As demonstrated by Job—"Then Job arose, and rent his mantle, and shaved his head, and fell down upon the ground, and worshipped, and said, Naked came I out of my mother's womb, and naked shall I return

thither: the LORD gave, and the LORD hath taken away; blessed be the name of the LORD" (Job 1:20-21).

    (2) As demonstrated by Abraham—"Who against hope believed in hope, that he might become the father of many nations, according to that which was spoken, So shall thy seed be" (Rom. 4:18). "By faith Abraham, when he was tried, offered up Isaac: and he that had received the promises offered up his only begotten son . . . accounting that God was able to raise him up, even from the dead; from whence also he received him in a figure" (Heb. 11:17, 19).

g. Righteousness—Righteousness may be defined as right acts; going the appointed mile. "For the fruit of the Spirit is in all goodness and righteousness and truth" (Eph. 5:9). "Now no chastening for the present seemeth to be joyous, but grievous: nevertheless afterward it yieldeth the peaceable fruit of righteousness unto them which are exercised thereby" (Heb. 12:11).

h. Goodness—Goodness may be defined as wholesome acts; going the extra mile. "And whosoever shall compel thee to go a mile, go with him twain" (Matt. 5:41). (See also Eph. 5:9.)

i. Meekness—Meekness may be defined as subdued strength.

    (1) Paul used this trait in dealing with the Corinthian church—"What will ye? shall I come unto you with a rod, or in love, and in the spirit of meekness?" (1 Cor. 4:21).

    (2) This is the trait to be used by spiritual people in restoring a backslider—"Brethren, if a man be overtaken in a fault, ye which are spiritual, restore such an one in the spirit of meekness; considering thyself, lest thou also be tempted" (Gal. 6:1).

    (3) It is the trait to be used in keeping unity within a church—"With all lowliness and meekness, with longsuffering, forbearing one another in love; endeavouring to keep the unity of the Spirit in the bond of peace" (Eph. 4:2-3).

    (4) It is the trait to be used in dealing with all men—"And the servant of the Lord must not strive; but be gentle unto all men, apt to teach, patient, in meekness instructing those that oppose themselves; if God peradventure will give them repentance to the acknowledging of the truth" (2 Tim. 2:24-25).

j. Temperance—Temperance may be defined as self-control. The great New Testament example of this is the Apostle Paul. Observe his testimony:

"For though I be free from all men, yet have I made myself servant unto all, that I might gain the more. And unto the Jews I became as a Jew, that I might gain the Jews; to them that are under the law, as under the law, that I might gain them that are under the law; to them that are without law, as without law, (being not without law to God, but under the law to Christ,) that I might gain them that are without law. To the weak became I as weak, that I might gain the weak: I am made all things to all men, that I might by all means save some. And this I do for the gospel's sake, that I might be partaker thereof with you. Know ye not that they which run in a race run all, but one receiveth the prize? So run, that ye may obtain. And every man that striveth for the mastery is temperate in all things. Now they do it to obtain a corruptible crown; but we an incorruptible. I therefore so run, not as uncertainly; so fight I, not as one that beateth the air: but I keep under my body, and bring it into subjection: lest that by any means, when I have preached to others, I myself should be a castaway" (1 Cor. 9:19-27).

k. Truth—Truth may be defined as living an open life, without guile and hypocrisy. "Therefore seeing we have this ministry, as we have received mercy, we faint not; but have renounced the hidden things of dishonesty, not walking in craftiness, nor handling the word of God deceitfully; but by manifestation of the truth commending ourselves to every man's conscience in the sight of God" (2 Cor. 4:1-2).

THE DOCTRINE OF MAN

INTRODUCTION

Some 10 centuries before Christ, a young shepherd lad near Jerusalem gazed into the starry sky and exclaimed, "When I consider thy heavens, the work of thy fingers, the moon and the stars, which thou hast ordained; what is man, that thou art mindful of him? and the son of man, that thou visitest him?" (Psa. 8:3-4).

What indeed is man? Who is he? Where did he come from? Why is he here? Where is he going? These questions are among the $64 billion ones in nature. Furthermore, the way in which a man answers these questions will determine his conduct of life. As the Bible declares: "For as he thinketh in his heart, so is he" (Prov. 23:7a).

Worldly materialism can be defined as that bloodless philosophy that knows the *price* of everything, but the *value* of nothing. What is the true worth of a human? Is there any reliable standard to determine the value of a man?

The following article appeared in the April 1977 issue of *Reader's Digest*.

Six-Million-Dollar Original

Tired of hearing that the human body is worth only about three dollars? And of the humbling and humiliating realization that a chicken or a salmon sells for more than you are worth? There's news to heal our bruised egos.

Yale University biophysicist Harold J. Morowitz says that the human body is actually worth $6 million. And that price covers only the raw materials—hormones, proteins, enzymes, etc. The intricate work of fashioning the material into human cells might cost six thousand trillion dollars. And assembling these cells into a functioning human being would drain all the world's treasures. "Each human being is priceless" is the professor's understatement. (p. 144)

The scientist has thus placed a surprisingly high figure upon each human. After all, $6 million is nothing to sneeze at. However, this huge price tag is less than nothing when compared to the worth God places upon each and everyone of his creatures. Here is the divine estimate: "For God so loved the world, that he gave his only begotten Son, that whosoever believeth in him should not perish, but have everlasting life" (John 3:16). "But we see Jesus, who was made a little lower than the angels for the suffering of death, crowned with glory and honour; that he by the grace of God should taste death for every man" (Heb. 2:9).

What then are we worth to God? The simple but staggering truth is he gladly sacrificed his only and beloved Son to redeem us back to himself out of sin's slave market. This study briefly reviews the past, present, and future state of God's multitrillion-dollar investment—man himself.

I. The Origin of Man—There are (at least) four main theories concerning the origin of man.

   A. Atheistic evolution—This theory holds that man is the accidental and random product of a blind and nonpersonal series of chemical and biological events. Simply defined, evolution is that process by which all living organisms have developed from the simple to the more complex forms. This theory would have us believe that our world and all it contains came into being through evolving mud in time past. We are assured that if we but allow a little mud enough time it will, of and by itself, produce the music of a Beethoven, the paintings of a Raphael, the writings of a Shakespeare, and the teachings of a Christ.

   Question: How long would it take one million monkeys typing away day and night on one million typewriters for just one monkey to accidentally type out the first 10 words in the Bible? ("In the beginning God created the heaven and the earth.")

   Answer: Consider a rock that reached from the earth to the nearest star (some 26 trillion miles away). Once every million years a tiny bird flies to this massive rock and removes the smallest grain of sand from it. When four rocks this size have been completely carried away, then one of those monkeys will have accidentally typed out Genesis 1:1.

   But this accomplishment would be absolutely nothing as compared to the probabilities that a living cell would by random processes be formed. Consider the following: Dr. Harold Morowitz of Yale estimated the theoretical limits for the smallest free-living thing that could duplicate itself. It would require 239 individual protein molecules. What are the chances that the first protein molecule would form all its amino acids into left-handed chains? (For some unknown reason, all life consists only of these left-handed protein molecule chains). Well, the minimal number of amino acids in a protein is 410. This then would be like flipping a coin 410 times and coming up with heads every time. The answer is one chance in 10^{123} (the figure 1 followed by 123 zeros). But then even *if* this occurred in one protein, it would have to be repeated in at least 238 other proteins also. The chances are now one in 10^{29345} (one followed by 29,345 zeros). This would be about 20 8½-by-11 pages of typed zeros.

   How big is this number? Consider the following: There are 10^{18} seconds in 15 billion years.

   The universe contains 10^{130} electrons.

   Conclusion: It has been demonstrated time and again from a mathematical perspective the utter impossibility for life to have come about accidentally. But all this is curtly brushed aside by those closed-minded "scholars" who according to Peter, are "willingly . . . ignorant" of the facts involved. Having thus dismissed the mathematical barrier, they compound their error attempting to demonstrate the evolution of the human race through various supposed subhuman-creature discoveries that are claimed to link ancient man to modern man. Here are but a few:

      1. Neanderthal man—Found in Neander Valley, near Dusseldorf, Germany, in 1856 by Johann C. Fuhlrott. The find consisted of a skull and several bones. He was first portrayed as a semierect brutish subhuman. It is now believed these "creatures" were real people who suffered severely from rickets, caused by a deficiency of vitamin D. This condition results in the softening of bones and consequent malformation.

It is now known that Neanderthal man was fully erect and in most details was indistinguishable from modern man, his cranial capacity even exceeding that of modern man. It is said that if he were dressed in a business suit, and were to walk down one of our city streets, he would be given no more attention than any other individual. Today he is classified *Homo Sapiens*— full human. (Duane T. Gish, *Evolution? The Fossils Say No*, p. 103)

2. Java man (*Pithecanthropus erectus*, "erect ape man")—Found in Trinil, Java, in 1891, by Eugene Dubois, a Dutch physician. The "find" consisted of a single skull cap. One year later a thigh bone, along with two molar teeth, was discovered 50 feet from where the skullcap had been. Dubois estimated they all belonged together, and dated back half a million years. He did not reveal, however, until 31 years later, that he had also found two obviously human skulls at the same time and in the same level. Most evolutionists of the day were convinced of the validity of this 500,000-year-old creature. But prior to his death, Dubois sadly concluded his Java man was actually the remains of a large gibbon.

3. Piltdown man (*Eanthropus dawsoni*, "Dawn man")—Found in Piltdown, England, in 1912, by Charles Dawson. The find was a skull part and a few teeth. Soon the consensus of the world's greatest authorities was that here indeed was a genuine link in the evolution of man. It was dated to be from 500,000 to 750,000 years old. The praises of the Piltdown man were sung by Dr. Arthur Smith Woodward, eminent paleontologist at the British Museum, and Dr. Henry Fairfield Osborn, paleontologist of the American Museum of Natural History. However, in 1950 the Piltdown bones were carefully examined by fluoride tests and discovered to be a colossal hoax. The "skull" had been stained with iron salts and the teeth filed down to give it the appearance of age. Thus, the world-famous Piltdown man was simply the doctored remains of a recent age.

4. Peking man—Found near Peking, China, in 1912 (and 1937) by Davidson Bolack. The find consisted of the fragments of 30 skulls and 147 teeth. This find disappeared in 1941 when it was moved from Peking by a U.S. Marine detachment to escape the oncoming Japanese invasion. It is now believed by some that this find was simply the remains of some large monkeys or baboons killed and eaten by workers in an ancient lime-burning quarry.

5. Nebraska man ("Western ape man")—Found in western Nebraska in 1922 by Harold Cook. The find was exactly one tooth. It was immediately declared by Dr. H. F. Osborn of the American Museum to be the vaunted missing link. He placed it at the very bottom of the tree of man's ancestry. Dr. William K. Gregory, curator of the American Museum of Natural History and professor of paleontology at Columbia University, called it "the million dollar tooth." Sir Grafton Elliott Smith of the *London Illustrated News* assigned an imaginative artist to draw the ape man that once carried the tooth around in his mouth some six thousand centuries ago. During the famous Scopes evolutionary trial in Dayton, Tennessee, William Jennings Bryan (Bible defender) was confronted and ridiculed for his ignorance concerning this tooth and other "facts" of evolution by H. H. Newman of the University of Chicago. In 1927, to the supreme embarrassment of many, the tooth was discovered to be that of an extinct pig.

6. East Africa ape (*Zinjanthropus*)—Found in 1959 in Olduvia, Tanzania, by Louis S. B. Leakey. Find consisted of a skull cap and a few bone fragments. This "discovery" was sensationalized through the *National Geographic Magazine*, which society had sponsored Leakey. His find was dated from two to four million years in age, thus making East Africa man by far the oldest "link" known at the time. However, prior to his death, Leakey indicated he felt his vaunted discovery was but a variety of *australopithecus* (Southern ape) found in 1924.

B. The pre-Adamic, gap theory—Did something horrible take place between the first and second verse in the Bible? Many believe something terrible indeed occurred, and that something was the fall of Satan. The following arguments have been offered to support this.

1. The phrase in Genesis 1:2, "without form and void" (Hebrew: *tohu wa-bohu*), appears elsewhere in Isaiah 34:11; 45:18; and Jeremiah 4:23 and speaks of judgment. However, in other passages it simply means space (see Job 26:7; Deut. 32:10; Job 6:18; 12:24; Psa. 107:40).

2. The verb translated "was" in Gen. 1:2 (Hebrew: *hayetha*) should be translated "became." Scriptural evidence, however, would deny this. The Hebrew verb *hayetha* is found 264 times in the Pentateuch, and of these, in 258 instances the word is correctly translated "was." See, for example, Jonah 3:3.

3. There is a difference between the verbs *bara* ("created," Genesis 1:1) and *asah* ("made," Genesis 1:7). But, to the contrary, these verbs are used synonymously. Note:

   a. "And God *created [bara]* the great sea monsters" (1:21).
   b. "And God *made [asah]* the beast of the earth" (1:25).
   c. "Let us *make [asah]* man in our image" (1:26).
   d. "So God *created [bara]* man in his own image" (1:27).

4. Genesis 1:2 says "darkness was upon the face of the deep," and darkness is a symbol of evil. This is not always the case, as seen in Psalm 104:20: "Thou makest darkness, and it is night, wherein all the beasts of the forest do creep forth."

Although traces of this theory can be traced back in Christian writings as early as the fourth century A.D., it was not until the ministries of Dr. Thomas Chalmers, Scottish scholar, and George H. Pember (1876) that the theory really caught on. In 1917 C. I. Scofield included it in his notes and its popularity was assured. These last two dates are significant, for by 1880 Darwin's theory of evolution, as propounded in his book *The Origin of Species* was universally accepted by the scientific world. This theory taught that the world was many millions of years old, as indicated by the vast fossil record and the claims of uniformitarian geology. The Christian theologian was then confronted with a serious problem. How could all this be reconciled with Genesis 1? An answer was found—uncounted millions of years could be conveniently tucked into that bottomless hole that was thought to exist between Genesis 1:1 and 1:2. Thus the gap theory may be viewed in part as an attempt by the Christian theologian to appease the non-Christian evolutionist.

In summary, the gap theory faces a real problem in the New Testament, for Paul states in Romans 5:12 and 8:20-22 that man's sin brought about death, even of animals. But the gap theory would have Adam walking on top of a gigantic fossilized animal graveyard. One may thus conclude that Genesis 1:1 is a summary statement for the first two chapters. In this verse God tells us *what* he originally did. In the remaining verses he then informs us *how* he did it.

The pre-Adamic, Gap theory is also known as the "Twin Adam theory."

This theory attributes early human fossils to pre-Adamites in the first creation in Gen. 1:1, who were destroyed before the rest of the creation events in Gen. 1. The two Adams theory states that the first Adam of Gen. 1 was the old stone age Adam, which has since been extinct, and the second Adam of Gen. 2 was the new stone age Adam, who is the ancestor of mankind today. This theory suggests the rest of the Bible is concerned with the fall and salvation of the new stone age Adam and his descendants. (Walter Elwell, ed., *Evangelical Dictionary of Theology*, p. 389)

C. Theistic evolution—This view, as the name implies, says there is a God and that he used the method of evolution to bring about the universe and the world.

In essence it attempts to harmonize Moses and Darwin, suggesting we look to the first for the *who* and *why* of all things, and to the second concerning the *how* and *when* of all things. It has been observed, however, that a theistic evolutionist is a man attempting to ride two horses that are going in opposite directions. There are two basic variations of theistic evolution:

  1. The original, classical view
     a. The philosophy involved—This says, in effect, God selected, originated, employed, and created the processes of naturalistic evolution to bring into being the world of plants, animals, and man. Actually, according to this view the only direct intervention by God was in arranging the pre-life chemical circumstances that would, in and by themselves, produce the first living organism.
     b. The problems involved
        (1) Genesis states that life began on dry ground, while evolution says it began on the surface of some ancient sea (Gen. 1:11-12).
        (2) Genesis declares that birds existed before insects, while evolution reverses this order (Gen. 1:20, 24).
        (3) Genesis states that birds and fishes were created at the same time, but evolution says fishes evolved hundreds of millions of years before birds developed (Gen. 1:21).
        (4) Genesis stresses (10 times) that the entities created were to reproduce "after their kinds," while evolution postulates the slow ascent of all organisms from a common ancestor.
        (5) Genesis says that Adam was made from the dust of the ground into the image of God, while evolution claims Adam descended from a sub-ape creature—"And the LORD God formed man of the dust of the ground, and breathed into his nostrils the breath of life; and man became a living soul."
        (6) Genesis records woman's coming from man's side, while evolution teaches both man and woman developed simultaneously—"And the LORD God caused a deep sleep to fall upon Adam, and he slept: and he took one of his ribs, and closed up the flesh instead thereof; and the rib, which the LORD God had taken from man, made he a woman, and brought her unto the man" (Gen. 2:21-22).

(7) Genesis tells us that man was originally a vegetarian, while evolution teaches he was probably a head-hunting cannibal (Gen. 1:29).

2. The recent, revised view

a. The philosophy involved—This position is known both as progressive creationism and threshold evolution. Charles Ryrie explains:

> But many who fall into the general category of theistic evolutionists perceive God as being involved not only at the beginning of the process but at various points along the way. God stepped in to create at the major states of life throughout geologic history (e.g., the vertebrates, the birds, the mammals, and man). But He also permitted and used naturalistic evolution processes throughout the long periods of geologic time. This view is known as progressive creationism or threshold evolution and often is linked with the day-age view of Genesis 1. (*Basic Theology*, p. 172)

Pattle P. T. Pun, an advocate of this view writes:

> Progressive creationists are willing to reinterpret the Scriptures if this is necessitated by the findings of modern science. Therefore in light of the overwhelming evidence supporting the antiquity of the earth, they accept the traditional day-age theory of the creation account in Genesis. This view revolves around the usage of "day" as depiction of a period of time rather than a twenty-four hour solar day. (Walter Elwell, ed., *Evangelical Dictionary of Theology*, p. 389)

b. The problems involved—Henry Morris observes:

> Among evangelicals, a popular semantic variant of theistic evolution is a system called progressive creationism. There are many Christian intellectuals who feel it inexpedient to adopt a full-blown evolutionary position, and so they allow for a number of acts of special creation interspersed at various points throughout the long evolutionary process. That is, they suggest that perhaps God supernaturally created the first protozoan, then later possibly the different phyla, and eventually the first man and woman. Depending on the particular writer, there may have been few or many acts of special creation inserted by God at strategic states in evolutionary history, but the overall process was still evolution. In progressive creationism, the same system of evolutionary geological ages and the same mechanisms of evolution (whatever they may be) are accepted as those used by the theistic evolutionist, or even by the atheistic evolutionist. The only differences are these occasional interjections of creation. This system allows its proponents to say that they believe in "special creation" instead of evolution, without experiencing the intellectual opprobrium attached to belief in "six-day creationism" or "flood geology."
>
> Such a semantic game, however, is rightly repudiated by most scientists, who consider it unworthy of the scientific world view, as a mere "god-of-the-gaps" device. That is, wherever there currently seems to be a significant gap in the fossil record or in the mechanism of evolutionary progress, then this might have been a point, they would say, where God stepped in to create something. As the gaps are filled in, however, by further paleontological collections or genetic manipulations, then God's role

becomes progressively smaller and evolution's role progressively greater. Thus progressive creation eventually yields to progressive evolution. In the final analysis, it is almost impossible, either scientifically or Biblically, to distinguish between progressive creation and theistic evolution.

In fact, if one were forced to choose between only these two alternatives, theistic evolution would surely be the better choice. Not only would it be more acceptable to the scientific establishment, but it would also be less dishonoring to God. That is, the theistic evolutionist at least gives God credit for being able to design and energize the entire evolutionary process right from the beginning. The progressive creationist, however, visualizes a bumbling sort of god, one who has to come down at intervals to redirect the evolutionary process whenever it veers off target, or to reenergize the process whenever it plays out. Furthermore, the same objections we have already lodged against theistic evolution can also be lodged against progressive creation. Nothing whatever is gained—except semantic dissimulation—by advocating progressive creation instead of theistic evolution. (*The Biblical Basis For Modern Science*, p. 114)

D. Special creation—This is the view that man is a direct product from the hand of God and that the statements in Genesis 1 and 2 are to be taken at face value in a literal and normal way. In addition to this, a number of Bible students see in these first two chapters a clear case for believing in a special 24-hour, 6-day creation week. This, it is believed, can be seen:

    1. As indicated by the Hebrew language—If the days were really long periods of time, the Hebrew word *olam* (meaning a long, indefinite time) would doubtless have been used, rather than the Hebrew word *yom* (which means day).

    "The use of a numerical adjective with the word *day* in Genesis 1 limits it to a normal day . . . in historical narratives the numerical adjective always limits the word to a 24-hour period (cf. Numbers 7 for a remarkable parallel)" (Dr. John C. Whitcomb, Jr., *Creation According to God's Word*, p. 4).

    Departmental professors of Oriental language in nine leading universities were once asked the following question by a research scholar: "Do you consider that the Hebrew word *yom* (day) as used in Genesis 1 accompanied by a numeral should properly be translated as (a) a day, as commonly understood, (b) an age, or (c) either a day or an age without preference?"

    The nine universities polled were: Oxford, Cambridge, London, Harvard, Yale, Columbia, Toronto, McGill, and Manitoba. Of these, seven universities responded that it should be translated as a day as commonly understood.

    2. As indicated by the genealogies found in Genesis 5; 11—If evolution is correct and man is really a million years old, then we would be forced to allow a 50,000 year gap between each name in these two chapters. Furthermore, if life itself is nearly one billion years old, then each day in Genesis 1 would have to stand for approximately 125 million years.

    3. As indicated by Moses at Mount Sinai—"Remember the sabbath day, to keep it holy. Six days shalt thou labour, and do all thy work . . . for in six days the LORD made heaven and earth, the sea, and all that in them is, and rested the seventh day: wherefore the LORD blessed the sabbath day, and hallowed it" (Exod. 20:8-9, 11). (See also Exod. 31:16-17.)

4. As indicated by David—"By the word of the LORD were the heavens made; and all the host of them by the breath of his mouth. He gathereth the waters of the sea together as an heap: he layeth up the depth in storehouses. . . . For he spake, and it was done; he commanded, and it stood fast" (Psa. 33:6-7, 9).

5. As indicated by Luke—In his genealogy, Luke traces Jesus' biological line back from Mary to the first man. His last three names were Enos, Seth, and Adam. Luke writes: "Enos, who was the son of Seth, who was the son of Adam, who was the son of God" (Luke 3:38). (See also Gen. 4:25; 5:6.) In other words, Luke leads us to believe Adam came directly from God, as Seth came directly from Adam (and Eve), thus indicating special creation.

6. As indicated by Jesus—The Savior evidently accepted in a literal way the early chapters of Genesis. "And he answered and said unto them, Have ye not read, that he which made them at the beginning made them male and female" (Matt. 19:4). "If I have told you earthly things, and ye believe not, how shall ye believe, if I tell you of heavenly things?" (John 3:12). "For had ye believed Moses, ye would have believed me: for he wrote of me. But if ye believe not his writings, how shall ye believe my words?" (John 5:46-47).

7. As indicated by Paul—"For the man is not of the woman; but the woman of the man. Neither was the man created for the woman; but the woman for the man. . . . For as the woman is of the man, even so is the man also by the woman; but all things of God" (1 Cor. 11:8-9, 12). "For Adam was first formed, then Eve. And Adam was not deceived, but the woman being deceived was in the transgression" (1 Tim. 2:13-14).

   In addition to these verses, there are two all-important theological passages where Paul contrasts the first Adam with the last Adam (Christ).

   a. In Rom. 5:12-21—The contrast is between condemnation (as introduced by the first Adam) with that of justification (as brought about by the last Adam).

   b. In 1 Cor. 15:22, 45-47—The contrast is between the mortal, fleshly body of the first Adam (given to all his seed) with the immortal, spiritual body of the last Adam (to be given to all his seed).

      In light of all this, it can be seen these references and analogies concerning the two Adams are both historically wrong and theologically worthless if special creation is denied.

8. As indicated by Benjamin Warfield—Benjamin Warfield was one of the greatest orthodox theologians of modern time. Although Warfield admitted the possibility of man existing for over 100,000 years, he personally believed man's creation date to be no earlier than 5,000 to 10,000 B.C. (*Biblical and Theological Studies*, p. 248).

9. As indicated by Edward Young—Edward Young was an outstanding Hebrew scholar. In one of his journals, he stated: "The six days are to be understood in a chronological sense, that is, one day following another in succession. This fact is emphasized in that the days are designated one, two, three, etc." (Edward Young, *Westminster Theological Journal*, May 1963, p. 169).

10. As indicated by the *Interpreter's Bible*,

    there can be no question but that by "day" the author means just what we mean—the time required for one revolution of the earth on its axis. Had he meant an aeon he would have certainly, in view of his fondness for numbers, have stated the number of millenniums each period embraces. (Vol. I, p. 417)

Even though the *Interpreter's Bible* (a very liberal work) would doubtless consider the first 11 chapters of Genesis as pure myth, it nevertheless holds that the Genesis writer believed in a literal six-day creation account.

One of the most respected scholars of the twentieth century is Dr. Mortimer J. Adler, coeditor of the monumental 54-volume set *Great Books of the Western World*. In one of his many books, *Great Ideas from the Great Books*, Adler answers a question asked him concerning the difference between men and animals.

Dear Dr. Adler,

Is there any basic difference between man and animals, or is man an animal like all the others? Some people say that man is the only creature that can think and learn. But I don't regard this as a real distinction, since biologists and psychologists have demonstrated that animals can construct things and solve problems. I have known some very intelligent dogs and some very thoughtless human beings. What is the essential difference between man and the animals?

A.M.P.

Dear A.M.P.,

Until comparatively recent times, few philosophers doubted that man was essentially different from all other animals. In the great tradition of Western thought, from Plato right down to the 19th century, it was almost universally held that man and man alone is a rational animal. This philosophical view of man's distinctive nature accords with the Biblical view that man and man alone is created in the image of God—a person, not a thing.

Since the time of Darwin, the opposite view has come to prevail, not only among scientists but among the educated classes generally. The Darwinian theory of man's origin, as you know, is that man and that anthropoid apes have descended from a common ancestral form; and along with this view of man's evolutionary origin goes the view that man and the higher mammals differ only in degree. Thus, for example, instead of regarding man alone as rational, the evolutionists find the same kind of intelligence in man and other animals. Man simply has more of it.

You say in your letter that you think the traditional arguments for man's distinctive nature are weak, because animals as well as men can reason, because animals as well as men can make things, etc. Let me answer your question by defending the traditional point of view about man as a very special creature.

The strongest evidence that men have certain powers which no other animals possess in any degree whatsoever consists in the things which men can do but which other animals cannot do at all. One such indication is man's power of making things.

I know that bees make hives, birds make nests, and beavers make dams. But such productions are entirely instinctive on their part. A given species of bird makes its nests in the same way generation after generation. This shows that the nest is a product of instinct not of art, which involves reason and free will. In making houses, bridges, or any other of their artifacts, men invent and select. They are truly artists, as animals are not.

In addition, only men build machines which are themselves productive. Other animals may use rough tools, but no other animal makes a die press which stamps out an indefinite number of a product when the raw materials are fed into it. This is another indication of man's special power as a maker of things.

You say that other animals can reason. In my opinion it is more correct to say that other animals can solve problems when they are confronted by the biological urgency of finding a way of getting what they need. All so-called "thinking" by animals is on this level. But no animal ever sits down to think, the way a philosopher or a mathematician does when he has no biologically urgent need to do so.

The fact that human thinking is discursive and involves language is another indication that it is quite different from animal problem-solving. Animals, of course, do make sounds and communicate their emotions or impulses to one another. But no animal communicates thought; no animal ever utters a sentence which asserts something to be true or false. Only a rational animal can do that.

I could go on and give you many other items of evidence that man has certain powers which no other animal possesses in the least degree. But I shall content myself with one more fact.

Man is the only animal with an historical development. Other animals may change in their biological constitution over the course of hundreds of thousands of generations; but such changes result entirely from changes in the germ plasm, which is the only thing that is transmitted from one generation to another. Men transmit ideas and institutions, a whole tradition of culture, from one generation to another, and it is this which accounts for the history of the human race.

In my opinion the empirical evidence is overwhelmingly in favor of the view that men are essentially different in kind from the brutes. Like the brutes, they, too, are animals. But unlike them, men are rational. This, of course, if true, would require us to reject Darwin's theory of man's evolutionary origin. But theories after all must be made to fit the facts, not facts theories. (pp. 173-175)

II. The Nature of Man—In dealing with man's nature, we will ask, and attempt to answer, six basic questions.

   A. How is man made in the image and likeness of God? "And God said, Let us make man in our image, after our likeness: and let them have dominion over the fish of the sea, and over the fowl of the air, and over the cattle, and over all the earth, and over every creeping thing that creepeth upon the earth. So God created man in his own image, in the image of God created he him; male and female created he them" (Gen. 1:26-27).

     How are we to understand these words? Throughout the history of the Christian church various theories have been propounded.

     1. That this likeness means God possesses a physical body similar to man—It is amazing (indeed, shocking) to discover the number of people holding this

totally unscriptural and bizarre theory. The Mormon cult of course has taught this since its inception. Josh McDowell writes:

> The Mormon doctrine of God is contradictory to what the Bible teaches. The Mormons believe in many gods and teach that God himself was once a man. Moreover, Mormon males have the possibility of attaining godhood. Joseph Smith made this clear in *The King Follet Discourse:*
>
> "I am going to inquire after God: for I want you all to know him and be familiar with him. . . . I will go back to the beginning before the world was, to show you what kind of a being God is.
>
> "God was once as we are now, and is an exalted man, and sits enthroned in yonder heavens. . . . I say, if you were to see him today, you would see him like a man in a form like yourselves in all the person, image, and very form of a man.
>
> "I am going to tell you how God came to be God. We have imagined and supposed that God was God from all eternity. I will refute that idea and take away the veil so that you may see.
>
> "It is the first principle of the gospel to know for certainty the character of God and to know that we may converse with him as one man with another, and that he was once a man like us; yea, that God himself, the father of us all, dwelt on an earth, the same as Jesus Christ did.
>
> "Here then, is eternal life—to know the only wise and true God; and you have got to learn how to be Gods yourselves, and to be kings and priests to God, the same as all Gods have done before you" (Joseph Smith, Jr., *King Follet Discourses*, pp. 8–10). (*Handbook of Today's Religions*, p. 69)

The Worldwide Church of God, initiated by Herbert W. Armstrong also advocates this same heresy. "The final destiny of man is to become God. You are setting out on a training to become creator—to become God! We shall then be God!" (Ibid., p. 117).

The New Age movement, of course, also holds this view. In essence it says the next great step in the evolutionary process of mankind will not be physical, but spiritual, that is, the realization that we are actually all divine, growing into little gods.

All this perhaps could be expected from the cults. However, it is truly shocking to hear this apostasy coming from those who profess to be in the evangelical camp. "Just as dogs have puppies and cats have kittens, so God has little gods. . . . Until we comprehend that we are little gods and we begin to act like little gods, we cannot manifest the kingdom of God!" (Earl Paulk, *Satan Unmasked*, p. 96).

"You don't *have* a God in you. You *are* one" (Kenneth Copeland, *The Force of Love*, tape message).

"I believe that in this divine Godhead there are three separate and distinct persons—each having His own personal spirit *body*, personal soul, and personal spirit" (Jimmy Swaggart, *Questions and Answers*, p. 199).

2. That this likeness is a reference to the triunity of man—In other words, as God is triune in nature (Father, Son, and Holy Spirit), he created man a triune creature consisting of spirit, soul, and body.

3. That this likeness is associated with man's self-consciousness and sense of morality—This theory states that man is created in the image of God in that his

Creator gave him self-consciousness and a sense of morality as God himself possesses.

4. That this likeness is tied in with the Incarnation—This theory states that when God spoke these words he was thinking of the future incarnation of Christ, the God-man, and his present-day work in making the Christian like himself. We note the following verses:

"For our conversation is in heaven; from whence also we look for the Saviour, the Lord Jesus Christ: who shall change our vile body, that it may be fashioned like unto his glorious body, according to the working whereby he is able even to subdue all things unto himself" (Phil. 3:20-21). "For whom he did foreknow, he also did predestinate to be conformed to the image of his Son, that he might be the firstborn among many brethren" (Rom. 8:29). "Beloved, now are we the sons of God, and it doth not yet appear what we shall be: but we know that, when he shall appear, we shall be like him; for we shall see him as he is" (1 John 3:2). At any rate, there seems to be an image of God in all men which cannot be lost, and an image which can be lost.

   a. The image that cannot be lost—"For a man indeed ought not to cover his head, forasmuch as he is the image and glory of God: but the woman is the glory of the man" (1 Cor. 11:7). "But the tongue can no man tame; it is an unruly evil, full of deadly poison. Therewith bless we God, even the Father; and therewith curse we men, which are made after the similitude of God" (James 3:8-9).

   In the following verse God institutes capital punishment and justifies it on the grounds that a murderer should die for taking the life of another creature made in the image of God. "Whoso sheddeth man's blood, by man shall his blood be shed: for in the image of God made he man" (Gen. 9:6).

   The Bible therefore indicates that all unsaved men still display certain traces of the original image of God's creation. It has been suggested that fallen man resembles a beautiful European cathedral after it has been gutted by a Nazi bomb.

   b. The image that can be lost—"Lie not one to another, seeing that ye have put off the old man with his deeds; and have put on the new man, which is renewed in knowledge after the image of him that created him" (Col. 3:9-10). "And that ye put on the new man, which after God is created in righteousness and true holiness" (Eph. 4:24).

   Thus it would seem evident from these verses that there is a part of God's image that was lost after Adam sinned and must now be restored by the Holy Spirit at the moment of salvation. This lost image would thus seem to be the inability to know God and the desire to love and serve him.

B. What is the nature of man's body? Paul Enns writes:

Views concerning the purpose of the body. (1) The body is the prison house of the soul. This was the view of the Greek philosophers who placed a great dichotomy between the body and soul. The soul was nonmaterial and good; the body was material and evil. In this view, therefore, the body was depreciated. However, it is unbiblical to place this kind of dichotomy between the material and nonmaterial. The Bible does not refer to the body as intrinsically evil. In fact, the Song of Solomon in its entirety focuses on the value of the human body and the bliss of married love and sexual expression. Divine revelation makes it clear that "man is. . . a unity—one being—and the material and immaterial can be separated only by physical death."

(2) The body is the only part of man that is important. This view is called *hedonism* and represents the opposite of the preceding view. Hedonists suggest a person should seek to please the body by doing what he enjoys doing. This philosophy is a denial of the soul. The testimony of Jesus Christ invalidates this view inasmuch as Christ spoke of the enormous value of the soul as distinct from the body (Matt. 10:28; 16:26). Other Scriptures also affirm the existence of the soul (2 Cor. 5:8; Eccles. 12:7).

(3) The body is the partner of the soul. The body is the means of glorifying God since it is the temple of God (1 Cor. 6:19). The body is not to be the master so that the believer caters to it in self-indulgence, nor is it to be an enemy that needs to be punished. The body is to be submitted to God (Rom. 12:1) in order that Christ may be glorified in that body (Phil. 1:20). Ultimately, the believer will be rewarded for deeds done in the body (2 Cor. 5:10). (*Moody Handbook of Theology*, p. 304)

C. Is man a dichotomous or trichotomous being? Is man a dichotomous (two-part) being, or is he a trichotomous (three-part) being? That is, does he consist of body and soul, or does he possess body, soul, and spirit?
   1. The theory that man is a dichotomous being—This view offers the following two arguments to support dichotomy.
      a. Material and nonmaterial—Man is a dichotomous being not just because of the plan of God, but because of the very nature of the universe, which only recognizes material and nonmaterial. In other words, man's body belongs to the material and his soul to the nonmaterial. What else is left? Therefore, as man's spirit is decidedly nonmaterial, it must be placed into the camp of the nonmaterial and thus becomes identical with that of the soul.
      b. Terms *soul* and *spirit* used interchangeable in the Bible—Often in the Bible the terms *soul* and *spirit* are used interchangeably. The Virgin Mary seems to do this very thing during her hymn of praise to God. "And Mary said, My soul doth magnify the Lord, and my spirit hath rejoiced in God my Saviour" (Luke 1:46-47).

         Advocates of this view would also compare the following verses claiming the interchangeable usage of soul and spirit in both cases. "Having therefore these promises, dearly beloved, let us cleanse ourselves from all filthiness of the flesh and spirit, perfecting holiness in the fear of God" (2 Cor. 7:1). "Dearly beloved, I beseech you as strangers and pilgrims, abstain from fleshly lusts, which war against the soul" (1 Pet. 2:11). "Let him know, that he which converteth the sinner from the error of his way shall save a soul from death, and shall hide a multitude of sins" (James 5:20). "To deliver such an one unto Satan for the destruction of the flesh, that the spirit may be saved in the day of the Lord Jesus" (1 Cor. 5:5).
   2. The theory that man is a trichotomous being—Basic evidences for trichotomy would include:
      a. Both terms used interchangeably does not mean no distinction whatsoever— The fact that some passages use both terms interchangeably does not mean there is no distinction whatsoever. For example, the phrases "Kingdom of God" and "Kingdom of Heaven" are on occasion used interchangeably, yet

most Bible students would recognize a general and decided difference between them.

    b. The New Testament carefully distinguishes between body and soul—In at least two essential passages the New Testament carefully distinguishes between body and soul. "And the very God of peace sanctify you wholly; and I pray God your whole spirit and soul and body be preserved blameless unto the coming of our Lord Jesus Christ" (1 Thess. 5:23). "For the word of God is quick, and powerful, and sharper than any two-edged sword, piercing even to the dividing asunder of soul and spirit, and of the joints and marrow, and is a discerner of the thoughts and intents of the heart" (Heb. 4:12).

    c. The Hebrew word *nephesh* translated "soul," "beast," and "creature"—The Hebrew word *nephesh* is translated by the word "soul" 428 times in the Old Testament. But on two occasions it is rendered "beast," and in nine other passages we find the word "creature" being used.

        "And he that killeth a beast shall make it good; beast for beast" (Lev. 24:18). "And the LORD God formed man of the dust of the ground, and breathed into his nostrils the breath of life; and man became a living soul" (Gen. 2:7). "And out of the ground the LORD God formed every beast of the field, and every fowl of the air; and brought them unto Adam to see what he would call them: and whatsoever Adam called every living creature, that was the name thereof" (Gen. 2:19).

        The point of the above is simply this: The Bible on occasion pictures animals as possessing souls. Therefore, as man is different than animals, he must have something higher, and that higher thing is the spirit. Nowhere in the Scriptures do we read of an animal possessing a spirit.

    d. The three levels of consciousness in all men—Trichotomy is the best theory to explain the three levels of consciousness in all men, that of self-consciousness (through the soul), world-consciousness (through the body) and God-consciousness (through the spirit).

These, then, are the arguments for dichotomy and trichotomy. What are we to believe? Hebrew scholar Dr. Merrill F. Unger has written the following concerning this question:

> The two terms are often used interchangeably . . . however, *soul* and *spirit* as synonymous terms are not always employed interchangeably. The soul is said to be lost, for example, but not the spirit. When no technical distinctions are set forth, the Bible is dichotomous, but otherwise it is trichotomous. Theologians have pored over these distinctions ceaselessly. (*Unger's Bible Dictionary*, p. 1043)

D. Where and how does man receive his soul? There are three distinct theories concerning this subject.

    1. Preexistence—This says that in a previous existence men were angelic spirits, and as a punishment and discipline for sin they were sent down here to indwell human bodies. Henry Thiessen writes:

> Some have felt the disciples of Christ were influenced by this view when they said of the man born blind, "Who sinned, this man or his parents, that he should be born blind?" (John 9:2). This is not certain, but we know that Plato, Philo, and Origen held this view. Plato taught it to explain man's

possession of ideas which he had not derived from sense; Philo, to account for the soul's imprisonment in the body; and Origen, to justify the disparity of conditions in which men enter the world. (*Lectures in Systematic Theology,* p. 164)

Needless to say, there is absolutely no scriptural evidence whatsoever to support the preexistence theory.

2. Creationism—According to this theory each human soul is an immediate and special creation by God and enters the developing body at an early stage, probably at conception. The following verses are offered to support creationism:

"Then shall the dust return to the earth as it was: and the spirit shall return unto God who gave it" (Eccles. 12:7). "The burden of the word of the LORD for Israel, saith the LORD, which stretcheth forth the heavens, and layeth the foundation of the earth, and formeth the spirit of man within him" (Zech. 12:1). "Furthermore we have had fathers of our flesh which corrected us, and we gave them reverence: shall we not much rather be in subjection unto the Father of spirits, and live?" (Heb. 12:9).

However, there are several problems with creationism:

a. It cannot account for the fact that children resemble their parents in intellectual and spiritual as well as in physical respects.

b. It cannot explain the universality of sin—If God creates each soul in heaven separately and sends it down into the developing body, then why are all men sinners? It is wrong, furthermore, to say the soul is thereupon corrupted by the body, for nowhere do the Scriptures teach that the source of sin in man stems from his body of flesh and blood and bones. Quite the contrary, for sin is said to come from man's stubborn and rebellious will, and his will is an aspect of his soul. In other words, does God create a sinful soul in the first place? If he does, he then becomes the author of sin. But if, instead, he creates a pure and innocent soul, then why and how and when does man become a sinner? Would not one of the more than 40 billion individuals who have lived, or are living on this earth, have decided to keep his pure soul unspotted and sinless?

3. Traducianism—Both body and soul are passed on through natural generations. This is called the traducian theory and is the view of most theologians (with notable exceptions, such as Charles Hodge). Passages that would tend to support this view are as follows:

"Behold, I was shapen in iniquity, and in sin did my mother conceive me" (Psa. 51:5). "Who can bring a clean thing out of an unclean? not one" (Job 14:4). "The wicked are estranged from the womb: they go astray as soon as they be born, speaking lies" (Psa. 58:3). "That which is born of the flesh is flesh; and that which is born of the Spirit is spirit" (John 3:6). "Among whom also we all had our conversation in times past in the lusts of our flesh, fulfilling the desires of the flesh and of the mind; and were by nature the children of wrath, even as others" (Eph. 2:3).

However, as in the case of the theory of creationism, a serious charge is likewise levelled at the traducian view. The problem is this: If the child receives his soul from his parents, then how did Jesus escape the sin-tainted nature of Mary and remain the pure and perfect Savior that he was? But it would seem this argument overlooks one basic but absolutely vital fact—the personality of the Lord Jesus Christ did not come into existence at Bethlehem through either the creation or traducian method. The indisputable scriptural fact is that as God he always existed. Thus, while he could pray, "A body hast thou prepared me" (Heb. 10:5), he also would pray later, "And now, O Father, glorify thou me with thine own self with the glory which I had with thee before the world was" (John 17:5).

E. What is the soul? The nature of man's soul is, like that of the doctrine of the Trinity, a mystery that simply cannot be grasped by mortal mind. Only a fool would attempt a dogmatic answer to this question. The following statements are therefore but suggestions and not absolute answers. In the opinion of this writer it would seem the Bible indicates not so much that I *have* a soul, but rather I *am* a soul. I have a body and I have a spirit, but the soul is me. If this be true (and again, who can be dogmatic here?), then the following proposed illustration would not seem to be inappropriate.

Let us consider Adam in the Garden of Eden. Prior to his fall, the first man could be likened to a driver guiding his beautiful new automobile down a smooth and scenic super highway. As he drives along, his car is filled with lovely Christian music and inspiring scriptural messages coming from His Father's Broadcasting House nearby and is being picked up by his stereo unit. In this illustration, the driver (Adam) would be the soul of man, the car would be his body, and the radio his spirit. For a while everything goes well. Then the driver deliberately twists the car off the highway and smashes it into a tree.

Almost instantly three tragic events take place:

1. The three events initiated by the driver
   a. The automobile—The automobile is badly damaged with a cracked block. While it will still run for awhile, it is evident that soon the entire mechanical system will break down completely.
   b. The radio—The radio is hopelessly wrecked. No sound whatsoever can now come through its system.
   c. The driver—The driver, although still alive, is under the condemnation of the righteous Judge for his foolish and wicked act. His punishment is twofold:
      (1) To continue driving—The first punishment is to continue on down life's highway in a dying car with no soothing and comforting messages from the radio.
      (2) To be eventually forced from the car—The second punishment is to be forced from the car after it stops completely and to be then confined to a lake of fire forever.
2. The three actions generated by the Holy Spirit—This, then, is the situation all unsaved men find themselves in today. But in keeping with this illustration, when the sinner turns to Christ for salvation, the Holy Spirit of God immediately effects three things:
   a. His action concerning the car (body)—Although he does not fix up the old wrecked car, he does nevertheless promise eventually to transform the entire automobile. "Behold, I shew you a mystery; We shall not all sleep, but we shall all be changed, in a moment, in the twinkling of an eye, at the last trump: for the trumpet shall sound, and the dead shall be raised incorruptible, and we shall be changed. For this corruptible must put on incorruption, and this mortal must put on immortality. So when this

corruptible shall have put on incorruption, and this mortal shall have put on immortality, then shall be brought to pass the saying that is written, Death is swallowed up in victory" (1 Cor. 15:51-54).

b. His action concerning the radio (spirit)—The Holy Spirit immediately repairs the smashed radio, and soon the car is once again filled with the blessed sounds of God. "Now we have received, not the spirit of the world, but the spirit which is of God; that we might know the things that are freely given to us of God. Which things also we speak, not in the words which man's wisdom teacheth, but which the Holy Ghost teacheth; comparing spiritual things with spiritual. But the natural man receiveth not the things of the Spirit of God: for they are foolishness unto him: neither can he know them, because they are spiritually discerned" (1 Cor. 2:12-14).

c. His action concerning the driver (soul)—The driver is assured that whereas he once was subjected to God's wrath, he now can enjoy his peace. "Therefore being justified by faith, we have peace with God through our Lord Jesus Christ" (Rom. 5:1). "There is therefore now no condemnation to them which are in Christ Jesus, who walk not after the flesh, but after the Spirit" (Rom. 8:1).

He needs no longer fear hell, as heaven is now his future home. "Let not your heart be troubled: ye believe in God, believe also in me. In my Father's house are many mansions: if it were not so, I would have told you. I go to prepare a place for you. And if I go and prepare a place for you, I will come again, and receive you unto myself; that where I am, there ye may be also" (John 14:1-3).

F. What are the basic characteristics of the soul? As one consults various theological works on the makeup of man, he soon discovers the discussion usually centers around four basic words. These are: *Intellect, sensibility, conscience,* and *will.* Here again let it be emphasized that no absolute and all-inclusive definition can be forthcoming but the following statements are offered as guidelines.

1. Intellect—Intellect is that aspect of the soul which tells man whether a given issue is right or wrong.

2. Sensibility—Sensibility is that aspect which tells man what he would like to do about the issue.

3. Conscience—Conscience is that aspect which tells man what he should do about the issue. The Bible lists several kinds of conscience:

a. An evil conscience—"Let us draw near with a true heart in full assurance of faith, having our hearts sprinkled from an evil conscience, and our bodies washed with pure water" (Heb. 10:22).

b. A defiled conscience—"Unto the pure all things are pure: but unto them that are defiled and unbelieving is nothing pure; but even their mind and conscience is defiled" (Titus 1:15).

c. A weak conscience—"Howbeit there is not in every man that knowledge: for some with conscience of the idol unto this hour eat it as a thing offered unto an idol; and their conscience being weak is defiled. . . . But when ye sin so against the brethren, and wound their weak conscience, ye sin against Christ" (1 Cor. 8:7, 12).

d. A good conscience—"And Paul, earnestly beholding the council, said, Men and brethren, I have lived in all good conscience before God until this day" (Acts 23:1; see also 1 Tim. 1:5, 19; Heb. 13:18; 1 Pet. 3:16, 21).

       e. A pure conscience—"Holding the mystery of the faith in a pure conscience" (1 Tim. 3:9).

       f. A seared conscience—"Speaking lies in hypocrisy; having their conscience seared with a hot iron" (1 Tim. 4:2).

    4. Will—Will is the aspect that tells man what he shall do about the issue.

III. The Purpose for the Creation of Man—Why did God create man? Before giving the various reasons why he did, it should be strongly stated that God did not make man because he was lonely. Long before he created angels or man, the Father was having blessed fellowship with his beloved Son.

    "And now, O Father, glorify thou me with thine own self with the glory which I had with thee before the world was. . . . Father, I will that they also, whom thou hast given me, be with me where I am; that they may behold my glory, which thou hast given me: for thou lovedst me before the foundation of the world" (John 17:5, 24). "The LORD possessed me in the beginning of his way, before his works of old. I was set up from everlasting, from the beginning, or ever the earth was. When there were no depths, I was brought forth; when there were no fountains abounding with water. Before the mountains were settled, before the hills was I brought forth: while as yet he had not made the earth, nor the fields, nor the highest part of the dust of the world. When he prepared the heavens, I was there: when he set a compass upon the face of the depth: when he established the clouds above: when he strengthened the fountains of the deep: when he gave to the sea his decree, that the waters should not pass his commandment: when he appointed the foundations of the earth: then I was by him, as one brought up with him: and I was daily his delight, rejoicing always before him" (Prov. 8:22-30).

    But why, then, did he create man?

A. Historically speaking, man was created to demonstrate and display the glory of God—"O LORD our Lord, how excellent is thy name in all the earth! who hast set thy glory above the heavens. . . . When I consider thy heavens, the work of thy fingers, the moon and the stars, which thou hast ordained; what is man, that thou art mindful of him? and the son of man, that thou visitest him? For thou hast made him a little lower than the angels, and hast crowned him with glory and honour" (Psa. 8:1, 3-5). "Thou art worthy, O Lord, to receive glory and honour and power: for thou hast created all things, and for thy pleasure they are and were created" (Rev. 4:11).

B. Prophetically speaking, man was created to demonstrate and display the grace of God—"But God, who is rich in mercy, for his great love wherewith he loved us, even when we were dead in sins, hath quickened us together with Christ, (by grace ye are saved;) and hath raised us up together, and made us sit together in heavenly places in Christ Jesus: that in the ages to come he might shew the exceeding riches of his grace in his kindness toward us through Christ Jesus" (Eph. 2:4-7).

IV. The Original Responsibilities and Restrictions of Man

A. His responsibilities

    1. Man was to assume the headship over all nature—"And God said, Let us make man in our image, after our likeness: and let them have dominion over the fish of the sea, and over the fowl of the air, and over the cattle, and over all the earth, and over every creeping thing that creepeth upon the earth" (Gen. 1:26). "Thou madest him to have dominion over the works of thy hands; thou hast put all things under his feet: all sheep and oxen, yea, and the beasts of the field;

the fowl of the air, and the fish of the sea, and whatsoever passeth through the paths of the seas" (Psa. 8:6-8).

The New Testament makes it clear that man was made to eventually assume headship over the entire universe. "For unto the angels hath he not put in subjection the world to come, whereof we speak. But one in a certain place testified, saying, What is man, that thou art mindful of him? or the son of man, that thou visitest him? Thou madest him a little lower than the angels; thou crownedst him with glory and honour, and didst set him over the works of thy hands: thou hast put all things in subjection under his feet. For in that he put all in subjection under him, he left nothing that is not put under him. But now we see not yet all things put under him" (Heb. 2:5-8).

2. Man was to make his headquarters in Eden and especially to care for this beautiful garden paradise—"And the LORD God took the man, and put him into the garden of Eden to dress it and to keep it" (Gen. 2:15).
3. Man was to provide names for every living creatures—"And out of the ground the LORD God formed every beast of the field, and every fowl of the air; and brought them unto Adam to see what he would call them: and whatsoever Adam called every living creature, that was the name thereof. And Adam gave names to all cattle, and to the fowl of the air, and to every beast of the field; but for Adam there was not found an help meet for him" (Gen. 2:19-20).
4. Man was to love and protect his wife.
   a. Eve is removed from the side of Adam (Gen. 2:18, 21).
   b. Eve is returned to the side of Adam (Gen. 2:22-24)—"Therefore shall a man leave his father and his mother, and shall cleave unto his wife: and they shall be one flesh" (Gen. 2:24).
5. Man was to reproduce himself and populate the earth with his kind—"And God blessed them, and God said unto them, Be fruitful, and multiply, and replenish the earth, and subdue it: and have dominion over the fish of the sea, and over the fowl of the air, and over every living thing that moveth upon the earth" (Gen. 1:28).
6. Man was to enjoy all the fruits of the various trees (except one)—"And the LORD God commanded the man, saying, Of every tree of the garden thou mayest freely eat" (Gen. 2:16).

B. His restrictions—Man was forbidden to partake of the fruit of the tree of the knowledge of good and evil—"But of the tree of the knowledge of good and evil, thou shalt not eat of it: for in the day that thou eatest thereof thou shalt surely die" (Gen. 2:17).

V. The Tragic Sin and Fall of Man
   A. The temptation preceding the Fall
      1. The tempter—"Now the serpent was more subtle than any beast of the field which the Lord God had made" (Gen. 3:1).
      2. The tactics—"Lest Satan should get an advantage of us: for we are not ignorant of his devices" (2 Cor. 2:11).
         a. Satan begins by *doubting* the Word of God—"And he said unto the woman, yea, hath God said, Ye shall not eat of every tree of the garden?" (Gen. 3:1b).
            Note the woman's response: "And the woman said unto the serpent, We may eat of the fruit of the trees of the garden: but of the fruit of the tree which is in the midst of the garden, God hath said, Ye shall not eat of it, neither shall ye touch it, lest ye die" (Gen. 3:2-3).

b. Satan ends by *denying* the Word of God—"And the serpent said unto the woman, Ye shall not surely die: for God doth know that in the day ye eat thereof, then your eyes shall be opened, and ye shall be as gods, knowing good and evil" (Gen. 3:4-5).

    In these verses Eve commits two fatal mistakes. She adds to God's word (God did not say, "Neither shall ye touch it"), and then she takes from God's Word (she omitted the original command, "Thou shalt surely die").

B. The transgression causing the Fall—"And when the woman saw that the tree was good for food, and that it was pleasant to the eyes, and a tree to be desired to make one wise, she took of the fruit thereof, and did eat, and gave also unto her husband with her; and he did eat" (Gen. 3:6).

C. The trials following the Fall

  1. The pain involved

    a. Shame—"And the eyes of them both were opened, and they knew that they were naked; and they sewed fig leaves together, and made themselves aprons" (Gen. 3:7).

    b. Fear—"And they heard the voice of the LORD God walking in the garden in the cool of the day: and Adam and his wife hid themselves from the presence of the LORD God amongst the trees of the garden" (Gen. 3:8).

    c. Excuses—"And the man said, The woman whom thou gavest to be with me, she gave me of the tree, and I did eat. And the LORD God said unto the woman, What is this that thou hast done? And the woman said, The serpent beguiled me, and I did eat" (Gen. 3:12-13).

  2. The parties involved—At this point the righteous Judge sets up his court in Eden and indicts the following:

    a. The serpent

    b. Satan

    c. Adam and Eve

    d. Mother nature

  3. The punishment involved

    a. Upon the serpent—"And the LORD God said unto the serpent, Because thou hast done this, thou art cursed above all cattle, and above every beast of the field; upon thy belly shalt thou go, and dust shalt thou eat all the days of thy life" (Gen. 3:14).

      Isaiah indicates that this judgment will continue to be binding upon the serpent even during the Millennium: "The wolf and the lamb shall feed together, and the lion shall eat straw like the bullock: and dust shall be the serpent's meat. They shall not hurt nor destroy in all my holy mountain, saith the LORD" (Isa. 65:25).

    b. Upon Satan—In essence, Satan would suffer a crushing and fatal head wound (Gen. 3:15).

    c. Upon Adam and Eve

      (1) Corporately

        (a) Physical death—This involves the separation of the soul from the body. "And all the days that Adam lived were nine hundred and thirty years: and he died" (Gen. 5:5). "The days of our years are threescore years and ten; and if by reason of strength they be fourscore years, yet is their strength labour and sorrow; for it is soon cut off, and we fly away" (Psa. 90:10).

(b) Spiritual death—This involves the separation of the sinner from the Savior. "Then shall he say also unto them on the left hand, Depart from me, ye cursed, into everlasting fire, prepared for the devil and his angels" (Matt. 25:41). "But the fearful, and unbelieving, and the abominable, and murderers, and whoremongers, and sorcerers, and idolaters, and all liars, shall have their part in the lake which burneth with fire and brimstone: which is the second death" (Rev. 21:8).

(2) Individually

(a) Adam, weary labor—"And unto Adam he said, Because thou hast hearkened unto the voice of thy wife, and hast eaten of the tree, of which I commanded thee, saying, Thou shalt not eat of it: cursed is the ground for thy sake; in sorrow shalt thou eat of it all the days of thy life; thorns also and thistles shall it bring forth to thee; and thou shalt eat the herb of the field; in the sweat of thy face shalt thou eat bread, till thou return unto the ground; for out of it wast thou taken: for dust thou art, and unto dust shalt thou return" (Gen. 3:17-19).

(b) Eve—"Unto the woman he said, I will greatly multiply thy sorrow and thy conception; in sorrow thou shalt bring forth children; and thy desire shall be to thy husband, and he shall rule over thee" (Gen. 3:16). Paul Enns observes:

> The woman would experience pain in childbirth. The pain (Heb. *yizabon*) in childbirth is similarly used of Adam's toil (Gen. 3:17). Both would suffer in their respective roles. The desire of the woman would be toward her husband. This is a difficult phrase and may mean (a) sexual desire (Song of Sol. 7:10), (b) desire for security under her husband's authority, or (c) desire to rule over her husband (cf. Gen. 4:7). A final aspect of the judgment upon the woman was that the husband would rule over her. (*Moody Handbook of Theology*, p. 309)

d. Upon nature itself—"Cursed is the ground for thy sake. . . . Thorns also and thistles shall it bring forth" (Gen. 3:17-18). "The creation waits in eager expectation for the sons of God to be revealed. For the creation was subjected to frustration, not by its own choice, but by the will of the one who subjected it, in hope that the creation itself will be liberated from its bondage to decay and brought into the glorious freedom of the children of God. We know that the whole creation has been groaning as in the pains of childbirth right up to the present time" (Rom. 8:19-22, NIV).

4. The promise involved—"And I will put enmity between thee and the woman, and between thy seed and her seed; it shall bruise thy head, and thou shalt bruise his heel" (Gen. 3:15). At first glance this verse would merely seem to predict the natural hatred of man for snakes. But for centuries devout Bible students have seen a far more precious and profound truth underlying these words. For in this verse they claim to see no less than a thrilling prediction of the cross and the resurrection, of the Savior's great victory over Satan. Theologically, then, verse 15 may be translated as follows: "And there will be an intense hatred between Satan and Christ. Eventually Christ shall crush the head of Satan, while suffering a heel wound in the process."

"But he was wounded for our transgressions, he was bruised for our iniquities: the chastisement of our peace was upon him; and with his stripes we are healed" (Isa. 53:5). "And the God of peace shall bruise Satan under your feet shortly. The grace of our Lord Jesus Christ be with you. Amen" (Rom. 16:20).

D. The theories explaining the Fall—Were the effects of Adam's fall merely confined to himself, or do they continue somehow to make themselves known in the lives of twentieth-century men?

1. The liberal position—This position holds that, as the entire story is simply a silly Hebrew legend, there can, of course, be absolutely no effect whatsoever.

2. The Pelagian position—Pelagius was a fifth-century British monk who taught that Adam's sin affected only himself, for God imputes to men only those sins which they personally and consciously perform. Pelagius said the only effect of Adam's sin on posterity was that of a bad example. The doctrine of Pelagianism was condemned by the council of Carthage in A.D. 418.

3. The Arminian position—Arminius (1560–1609) was a professor who lived and taught in Holland. This theory teaches that, while Adam's sin definitely weakened the will of his posterity to remain sinless, it did not, nevertheless, destroy the possibility.

4. The Augustinian position—Augustine was one of the greatest of the early church fathers. He taught that because of the unity of the human race in Adam, man's sin therefore is imputed to his posterity. Thus, corrupted nature begets corrupted nature. This final view is the only position which is amply supported by the Scriptures.

"Wherefore, as by one man sin entered into the world, and death by sin; and so death passed upon all men, for that all have sinned. . . . Therefore as by the offence of one judgment came upon all men to condemnation; even so by the righteousness of one the free gift came upon all men unto justification of life. For as by one man's disobedience many were made sinners, so by the obedience of one shall many be made righteous" (Rom. 5:12, 18-19). "For as in Adam all die, even so in Christ shall all be made alive" (1 Cor. 15:22).

At this point it should be said that in the New Testament the Apostle Paul often distinguishes between "sin" and "sins." According to Paul:

Sin is the root of man's problems and a reference to his corrupted nature which he received from Adam. *Sins* are the fruit of man's problems and a reference to those actions resulting from his corrupted nature.

It is vital to understand this distinction, for God will not deal with man favorably concerning his sins until he allows him to treat his sin nature. Man sins (commits individual transgressions) because he is a sinner and therefore does not become a sinner because he sins. Thus modernism is content to treat the boils on the skin of mankind (his sins), but the real disease is in the bloodstream (his sin nature). Paul summarizes all this in a single verse, which should be literally translated: "For all have sinned [past tense in Adam], and are [present time, in daily experience] falling short of God's glory" (Rom. 3:23).

From all this man therefore concludes that Adam's individual transgression resulted in a sin nature for him, but with mankind it is the other way around—his sin nature results in individual transgressions.

VI. The Present-Day Condition of Man

A. The fallacies

1. Man is dirt and therefore cannot be saved—This is the view of the materialist and the communist. According to this position, the only real difference between

a mushroom, a man, and a mountain is simply in the accidental arrangement of the atoms.

2. Man is divine, and therefore need not be saved—This is the view of liberalism. For example, according to this view, as Christian witnesses, our primary ministry to the poor, lost, helpless drunkard is to simply inform him that he is made in God's image and carries the divine spark of divinity within him. He therefore need only to fan that small flame and begin living that victorious life God wants him to live.

B. The facts—In his first epistle to the church at Corinth, Paul places all living men into three spiritual categories:

1. The natural man—"But the natural man receiveth not the things of the Spirit of God: for they are foolishness unto him: neither can he know them, because they are spiritually discerned" (1 Cor. 2:14).

The Bible describes all unsaved men (the natural man) as being spiritually depraved. As some confusion has centered itself around the scriptual doctrine of human depravity, let us examine the facts.

a. Negative aspects of depravity

(1) Depravity does not mean that all unsaved men are as depraved as they can possibly become—Most American men, for example, do not run around murdering little children or robbing banks. But some do. Also, few housewives suddenly abandon their families and become professional harlots.

(2) Depravity does not hold that a sinner has no sense of God, nor of good and evil—Often, to the shame of the Christian, unsaved men and women demonstrate a higher morality than shown by their professing neighbors and family members.

(3) Depravity does not teach that an unsaved man cannot admire the noble, or even perform noble and heroic acts—Many battle accounts record the bravery of unsaved soldiers who pay the supreme sacrifice to save the lives of their endangered buddies. On other occasions unsaved firemen and policemen have laid down their lives to protect individuals they may not have even known.

b. Positive aspects of depravity

(1) Depravity means that all sinners are capable of all wicked things—This means that a freedom-loving Winston Churchill still possessed within his nature all the potential cruelty of an Adolf Hitler.

(2) Depravity teaches that no sinner has the power to please God.—In essence then, the doctrine of depravity says that man, without God, is not as bad as he can be, but rather as bad off as he can be.

The following Scriptures aptly describe the natural man: "But I know you, that ye have not the love of God in you" (John 5:42). "As it is written, There is none righteous, no, not one: there is none that understandeth, there is none that seeketh after God. They are all gone out of the way, they are together become unprofitable; there is none that doeth good, no, not one" (Rom. 3:10-12). "For I know that in me (that is, in my flesh,) dwelleth no good thing: for to will is present with me; but how to perform that which is good I find not" (Rom. 7:18). "Because the carnal mind is enmity against God: for it is not subject to the law of God, neither indeed can be. So then they that are in the flesh cannot please

God" (Rom. 8:7-8). "That at that time ye were without Christ, being aliens from the commonwealth of Israel, and strangers from the covenants of promise, having no hope, and without God in the world" (Eph. 2:12).

2. The carnal man—"And I, brethren, could not speak unto you as unto spiritual, but as unto carnal, even as unto babes in Christ. I have fed you with milk, and not with meat: for hitherto ye were not able to bear it, neither yet now are ye able. For ye are yet carnal: for whereas there is among you envying, and strife, and divisions, are ye not carnal, and walk as men?" (1 Cor. 3:1-3).

Here Paul sadly describes a Christian who is indwelt by the Holy Spirit, but who still allows himself to be controlled by the passions of the flesh. Paul calls him a baby, for he has never learned to grow.

3. The Spirit-controlled man—"But he that is spiritual judgeth all things, yet he himself is judged of no man" (1 Cor. 2:15).

Thus, to summarize this section concerning the present-day condition of man, we may state that all men in the sight of God are (1) corpses—the natural man, (2) crybabies—the carnal man, or (3) conquerors—the Spirit-controlled man.

VII. The Destiny of Man—In the throes of despair, the suffering patriarch Job once cried out: "Man that is born of a woman is of few days, and full of trouble. He cometh forth like a flower, and is cut down: he fleeth also as a shadow, and continueth not" (Job 14:1-2).

Later during the same dialogue Job would sigh and ask: "If a man die, shall he live again? all the days of my appointed time will I wait, till my change come" (Job 14:14).

Finally, in the nineteenth chapter of his book, Job reaffirms his own personal faith in God and the destiny of man. Job exclaims: "For I know that my redeemer liveth, and that he shall stand at the latter day upon the earth: and though after my skin worms destroy this body, yet in my flesh shall I see God" (Job 19:25-26).

It has been said that the three most asked, anxious, and for the most part, unanswered, questions of mankind are as follows: Where did I come from? Why am I here? Where am I going?

Thus far in this study, questions one and two have been answered. This section will answer the third question.

A. False views concerning the destiny of man

1. Nirvana—This is an oriental Hindu philosophy (which at certain periods in history has wormed its way into Christian thought) that teaches that at death a man ceases all personal existence and is absorbed by some great life-giving principle in the universe. According to this thought, a man, while he lives, can be pictured as a small wave ripple, skimming the top of a mighty ocean. But when the wind stops (the moment of death), the wave is then received back into the ocean from whence it came, and forever loses its previous identity. Among the many biblical verses refuting Nirvana is Matthew 17:3: "And, behold, there appeared unto them Moses and Elijah talking with him" (Matt. 17:3).

Here we see Moses (who had died 1,400 years earlier) and Elijah (who had departed over seven centuries back) both reappearing on the Mount of Transfiguration to Peter, James, and John. This, of course, proves that absence from this earth does not mean the termination of personality or personhood. (See also 1 Cor. 15:12-20, 42-49.)

2. Reincarnation—This is the belief in the transmigration or rebirth of the soul which has been fundamental to most religions and philosophies of India. As one sows in the present life, so one shall reap in the next, good deeds resulting in a good state of rebirth, bad deeds in a bad state of rebirth. Thus a man's state of life is seen not as something fortuitous or meaningless, but as the working out, for good or ill, of the effects of a previous existence and the predetermining of a future state. This theory is totally without scriptural support.

   A recent *Newsweek* poll, taken on December 21, 1988, showed that 24 percent of Americans believe in reincarnation.

3. Materialism—This is the atheistic belief that man, like a weasel in the woods, upon death, forever ceases to be and quietly rots into nothingness. This philosophy has been aptly described on an ancient tombstone that read: "I was not, I became not, I am not, I care not."

   To the contrary, the Scriptures teach both the saved and lost will eventually be raised and give an account of themselves to God himself.

   a. The unsaved—"And I saw a great white throne, and him that sat on it, from whose face the earth and the heaven fled away; and there was found no place for them. And I saw the dead, small and great, stand before God; and the books were opened: and another book was opened, which is the book of life: and the dead were judged out of those things which were written in the books, according to their works" (Rev. 20:11-12).

   b. The saved—"For we must all appear before the judgment seat of Christ; that every one may receive the things done in his body, according to that he hath done, whether it be good or bad" (2 Cor. 5:10).

4. Universalism

   The general decline in belief in an everlasting hell has not only contributed to the increasing use of the word "hell" to describe conditions on earth (as in "the hell of Stalingrad" and "the hell of Dachau") but has also been accompanied within the churches by the assumption that most, if not all, humanity will get to heaven. Universalism is the word normally used by theologians to describe the doctrine that ultimately and finally all humanity without exception will enter into the everlasting life. Another way of expressing it is to say that it is the doctrine that since no soul can have been created for final condemnation no soul can in the end be lost. Not all those who would call themselves (or be called by others) universalists necessarily suppose that there will be no hell (for there may be a "temporary" hell for some) or that the total number in heaven will be equivalent to the total number of human beings and angels originally created (for some angels and humans may be annihilated). What universalism does require is that finally from everlasting to everlasting there be no person left in hell or not included in the kingdom of heaven. (Peter Toon, *Heaven and Hell*, p. 183)

   John Braun expands Peter Toon's definition when he writes:

   At rock bottom, the doctrine of universalism is a speculative philosophical system. Universalists do not begin with either the biblical material on the subject of eternal punishment or with the historic church's interpretation of that data. Instead, they start with two philosophical assumptions born in their own imaginations.

The first is that God's love is so perfectly good and perfectly sovereign that there is no way it could suffer the defeat of allowing one of His creatures to end up being eternally punished. That would mean, they contend, that there is something more powerful than the love of God. The second assumption has to do with the free will of man. Stripped of all the fancy philosophical language, it boils down to the argument that if man stands at a crossroads with only two opinions, one leading to heaven and the other leading to eternal torment, he doesn't really have free will at all. He is forced to choose one or the other. How, they contend, under such pressure could free will truly be exercised? According to D. P. Walker, a contemporary writer whose book, *The Decline of Hell,* favors universalism, these two assumptions stretch all the way back to Origen:

"The whole of Origen's eschatology is based on two principles: first, the justice and goodness of an omnipotent Creator; secondly, the absolute free will of every rational being (man, animated star, angel, demon)." (*Whatever Happened to Hell?* p. 42)

Origen actually taught that even Satan himself would eventually be reconciled to God. In addition to his grievous error concerning universalism, Origen was also the father of Arianism, which denied the deity of Jesus Christ. His teaching on both issues was soundly condemned at the Council of Constantinople in A.D. 543.

   a. The argument for universalism reviewed—The following Scripture passages are offered to support universalism: "And I, if I be lifted up from the earth, will draw all men unto me" (John 12:32). "And he shall send Jesus Christ, which before was preached unto you: whom the heaven must receive until the times of restitution of all things, which God hath spoken by the mouth of all his holy prophets since the world began" (Acts 3:20-21).

"Therefore as by the offence of one judgment came upon all men to condemnation; even so by the righteousness of one the free gift came upon all men unto justification of life" (Rom. 5:18). "For as in Adam all die, even so in Christ shall all be made alive" (1 Cor.15:22). "That in the dispensation of the fulness of times he might gather together in one all things in Christ, both which are in heaven, and which are on earth; even in him" (Eph. 1:10). "That at the name of Jesus every knee should bow, of things in heaven, and things in earth, and things under the earth; and that every tongue should confess that Jesus Christ is Lord, to the glory of God the Father" (Phil. 2:10-11).

   b. The argument for universalism refuted

     (1) First, Origen's hope for Satan's final salvation will definitely not be realized—In fact, to the contrary, he, along with the Antichrist and false prophet will suffer the judgment of eternal hell. "And the devil that deceived them was cast into the lake of fire and brimstone, where the beast and the false prophet are, and shall be tormented day and night for ever and ever" (Rev. 20:10).

     (2) Second, we must realize that the Bible frequently uses the word *all* in a restricted sense, as pertaining to all in a certain category rather than all without exception—Examples are numerous.

       Matthew tells us that "all Judea" went out to hear John the Baptist (3:5-6). Luke records that a decree went out that "a census be taken of all the inhabited earth" (2:1). And the disciples of John the Baptist complained that "all men" were following Christ. In the passages written by Paul, it is clear that all who are in Adam die, whereas all who are in Christ shall be made alive. The *all* has limitations built into it by the context. (Erwin Lutzer, *Coming to Grips with Hell*, p. 14)

(3) Third, the passage in Philippians does not teach all will *accept* Christ as Savior, but rather that all will eventually *acknowledge* him as Sovereign—"And every creature which is in heaven, and on the earth, and under the earth, and such as are in the sea, and all that are in them, heard I saying, Blessing, and honour, and glory, and power, be unto him that sitteth upon the throne, and unto the Lamb for ever and ever" (Rev. 5:13).

This "creature confession" of their creator includes the world of demons also. "And there was in their synagogue a man with an unclean spirit; and he cried out, saying, Let us alone; what have we to do with thee, thou Jesus of Nazareth? art thou come to destroy us? I know thee who thou art, the Holy One of God" (Mark 1:23-24).

5. Restorationism—This is the belief that in a future life all men will be given a second chance to make that choice for God they did not make during this life.

  a. Reasons for this position—Restorationists use the following scriptures to "prove" their view: "For this is good and acceptable in the sight of God our Saviour; who will have all men to be saved, and to come unto the knowledge of the truth" (1 Tim. 2:3-4). "For therefore we both labour and suffer reproach, because we trust in the living God, who is the Saviour of all men, specially of those that believe" (1 Tim. 4:10). "For Christ also hath once suffered for sins, the just for the unjust, that he might bring us to God, being put to death in the flesh, but quickened by the Spirit: by which also he went and preached unto the spirits in prison" (1 Pet. 3:18-19).

    However, a quick glance at the context of the above verses show that all the "restored" here are those who have accepted Christ as Savior. The passage in 1 Peter has been the subject of some controversy, but whatever else, it does not teach restorationism. The verb "preached" in verse 19 in the original Greek does not refer to gospel preaching.

  b. Rejection of this position—Restorationism is refuted by the following verses: "He, that being often reproved hardeneth his neck, shall suddenly be destroyed, and that without remedy" (Prov. 29:1). "Many will say to me in that day, Lord, Lord, have we not prophesied in thy name? and in thy name have we cast out devils? and in thy name done many wonderful works? And then will I profess unto them, I never knew you: depart from me, ye that work iniquity" (Matt. 7:22-23). "And whosoever speaketh a word against the Son of man, it shall be forgiven him: but whosoever speaketh against the Holy Ghost, it shall not be forgiven him, neither in this world, neither in the world to come" (Matt. 12:32).

    "And beside all this, between us and you there is a great gulf fixed: so that they which would pass from hence to you cannot; neither can they pass to us, that would come from thence" (Luke 16:26). "He that is unjust, let him be unjust still: and he which is filthy, let him be filthy still: he that is righteous, let him be righteous still: and he that is holy, let him be holy still. . . . For I testify unto every man that heareth the words of the prophecy of this book, If any man shall add unto these things, God shall add unto him the plagues that are written in this book: and if any man shall take away from the words of the book of this prophecy, God shall take away his part out of the book of life, and out of the holy city, and from the things which are written in this book" (Rev. 22:11, 18-19).

If these verses teach anything, they strongly and sternly declare that at the moment of death there exists absolutely no chance for the salvation of an unsaved person. We may be tempted to argue with God concerning the why of the matter, but not the what of the matter.

6. Conditionalism—Erwin Lutzer writes:

> Whereas universalism sought to take the "forever" out of hell, we now come to a theory that attempts to take the hell out of forever. Conditional immortality is more attractive to evangelicals than universalism. This teaching contends that all will not be saved, but neither will any be in conscious torment forever. God resurrects the wicked to judge them, then they are thrown into the fire and consumed. The righteous are granted eternal life while the unbelievers are granted eternal death. Hell is annihilation. (Ibid., p. 15)

This false doctrine will be dealt with in more detail under the discussion of annihilation. In a sense, conditionalism is even a greater heresy than that of universalism or restorationism, for it teaches that all human beings were originally created without immortal souls, which is clearly refuted by the Scriptures. "And many of them that sleep in the dust of the earth shall awake, some to everlasting life, and some to shame and everlasting contempt" (Dan. 12:2). Note here the souls of both saved and lost are said to be everlasting.

7. Annihilationism—This theory, espoused by the Jehovah's Witnesses, along with various other groups, teaches that all the ungodly will someday literally be "uncreated," or annihilated, by God. Harold Bryson observes:

> Annihilationism takes several forms for its expression. One is that at death every unsaved person ceases to exist. Another form claims that annihilation does not come immediately. According to this variation, the unsaved remain in hell in a conscious state until the day of judgment. After judgment they cease to exist. This form of annihilationism allows time of the suffering of the full penalty of sins. (Harold Bryson, *Yes, Virginia, There Is a Hell*, p. 39)

Peter Toon quotes from a modern-day defender of annihilationism:

Already we have referred to this position, espoused this century by leading Anglican writers. Most recently Brian Hebblethwaite has written:

"If creatures can rebel against the divine ground of their being to such an extent as to render themselves absolutely unredeemable then there seems no point in God's keeping them in being for ever in such an unending state of deprivation. It is much more plausible to suppose that the language of damnation and everlasting loss is symbolic language, designed to bring out the awesome possibility that a man may by his actions and his attitudes forfeit his eternal destiny and render himself incapable of being drawn into the love and life of God. But if such a terrible possibility is fulfilled, it must mean that the lost one brings about his own annihilation and disappears from being rather than that he is raised for ever and held in a state of everlasting damnation. The sheer pointlessness of such a state being allowed to continue for ever shows clearly that conditional immortality is more religiously and morally plausible than everlasting punishment."

But he really does not want to believe in annihilation, for he continues:

"One would like to be able to hope that even the possibility of eternal loss in the sense of annihilation is never in fact realized. To suppose that there comes a time when the God of love, who went to the lengths of the Cross of Christ to win men's love in return, has to write off a created person as absolutely unredeemable is a hard supposition for a Christian to make."

In fact he wants to believe in a second chance after death in a process which is like a purgatory for all (baptized and unbaptized alike). He says:

"Once we free ourselves from the old idea that opportunities to repent and respond to God's love are restricted to a single life-span on earth, we may be the readier to hope that God's patient, self-sacrificial love will in the end prevail over even the most recalcitrant sinner. In other words, the notion of conditional immortality makes greater sense in conjunction with the old idea of the finality of death." (*Heaven and Hell*, pp. 186–187)

Tragically, in recent times, two scholars from the evangelical camp have come down on the side of annihilation. These men are Clark Pinnock and Edward Fudge.

Erwin Lutzer writes concerning Pinnock:

Clark Pinnock of McMaster University in Toronto, Canada, asks how one can imagine for a moment that the God who gave His Son to die on the cross would "install a torture chamber somewhere in the new creation in order to subject those who reject him in everlasting pain? He observes that it is difficult enough to defend Christianity in light of the problem of evil and suffering without having to explain hell too.

Pinnock believes that the fire of God consumes the lost. Thus God does not raise the wicked to torture them but rather to declare judgment on them and condemn them to extinction, which is the second death. Everlasting punishment, according to Pinnock, means God sentences the lost to final, definitive death. (*Coming to Grips with Hell*, p. 16)

An angry John Braun writes concerning Fudge:

A 1976 *Christianity Today* article, "Putting Hell in Its Place," provides a typical example of a careless, unchecked "soft line" on hell. Here author Edward Fudge dangerously hedges on the biblical teaching of the degree and extent of eternal punishment.

Admitting there is such a place and that the wicked go there, Fudge sets out with an obvious backhanded slap at great preachers such as Charles Haddon Spurgeon and Isaac Watts. The obvious implication, apparent even from the title of the article, is that these preachers—not hell's critics—removed hell from its proper place.

Then, dismissing these two giants of the past with the all-soothing evangelical shibboleth, "But enough of that; let us look to the Scriptures" (as if Spurgeon and Watts didn't preach the Scriptures!), he makes an incredibly shallow attempt to demonstrate why we should speak of the torments of hell as "aionic" or "new age" instead of "eternal" or "everlasting."

"In our common versions, this word [*aionos*, the Greek word for eternal] is usually translated 'everlasting' or 'eternal.' A better translation would probably be the transliteration 'aionic' or 'new age.' *Aionos* designates a quality of the Age to Come."

Suddenly, the word *aionos* no longer really can mean "everlasting" or "eternal." It's now a quality—whatever on earth, in heaven, or in hell that might be.

In the article, Fudge begins his conclusion with a discussion of this portion of Matthew 25:46, "Then these will go away into eternal punishment but the righteous to eternal life." Fudge comments:

"Here is 'punishment'—punishment that expresses both wrath and justice. There stands 'life.' Both terms are rich in meaning for inhabitants of the Present Age. But both are here qualified by the same word 'aionic.' Both punishment and life are of a quality belonging to the Age to Come and may be described finally only by 'aionic.'"

Come on now! This arbitrary tampering with words has gone far enough. "Aionic" life *is* everlasting life, not some quality of unknown duration, and "aionic" punishment may be described finally only by "everlasting." . . . Where the New Testament Scriptures are dealt with, the word refers to an endless period of time, *not* a quality. Tell me now, who would be excited about having "aionic" life and who would be scared of "aionic" punishment?

Who on earth knows what "aionic" means? Talk about taking the stinger out of hell! Furthermore, there is no way Fudge's shoddy attempt at a linguistic treatment of a handful of Bible verses holds up—as if no Bible expert but him in the last two thousand years caught the "error" of using the term "eternal" instead of "new age" or "aionic!"

The article's insipid conclusion is shocking, not only that Fudge would write it, but that *Christianity Today* would print it. Wrote Fudge:

"Hell is *one* New Testament picture portraying the fate of the unsaved. But, as we have seen, it is not the only one: *it is not even the primary one. Nor is it the definitive one* [italics mine]."

What a far cry this lukewarm stance is from that of the founders of the evangelical movement. (*Whatever Happened to Hell?* pp. 96–97)

Those believing in annihilationism attempt to undergird their claims by quoting certain Scripture verses in the Psalms: "For evildoers shall be cut off: but those that wait upon the LORD, they shall inherit the earth" (Psa. 37:9). "The LORD preserveth all them that love him: but all the wicked will he destroy" (Psa. 145:20).

However, it should be observed that the same Hebrew word *karath* translated "cut off" in Psalm 37:9 is also used in reference to the crucifixion of the Messiah as prophesied in Daniel 9:26. Christ was certainly not annihilated at Calvary. In Psalm 145:20 the identical Hebrew word here rendered "destroy" is found describing the punishment of both Egypt (Exod. 10:7) and Israel (Hosea 13:9), neither of which nation has yet to suffer annihilation.

Concerning the New Testament, annihilationists attempt to show that whenever the words *eternal* or *everlasting* are linked to words of action, it refers to the result of the action, not to the action itself. For example, the phrase "eternal judgment" does not mean that the judgment itself will go on eternally, though there will be consequences that will. "Eternal redemption" does not mean that the act of Christ goes on forever, though the consequences do.

Erwin Lutzer, however, quickly refutes this claim:

> Unfortunately, that interpretation will not survive careful analysis. Robert A. Morey in his book *Death and the Afterlife* points out that the word *destroyed* as used in the Bible does not mean "to annihilate." The Greek word *apollumi* is used in passages such as Matthew 9:17; Luke 15:4; and John 6:12, 17. In none of those instances does it mean "to pass out of existence." Morey writes, "There isn't a single instance in the New Testament where *apollumi* means annihilation in the strict sense of the word." Thayer's *Greek-English Lexicon* defines it as "to be delivered up to eternal misery." (*Coming to Grips with Hell*, p. 18)

8. Soul sleep—This says both the departed saved and unsaved sleep in their graves, awaiting the final resurrection.

   a. This position reviewed—The following verses are offered to support soul sleep. "These things said he: and after that he saith unto them, Our friend Lazarus sleepeth; but I go, that I may awake him out of sleep. . . . Then said Jesus unto them plainly, Lazarus is dead" (John 11:11, 14). "And they stoned Stephen, calling upon God, and saying, Lord Jesus, receive my spirit. And he kneeled down, and cried with a loud voice, Lord, lay not this sin to their charge. And when he had said this, he fell asleep" (Acts 7:59-60). "But now is Christ risen from the dead, and become the firstfruits of them that slept" (1 Cor. 15:20). "For if we believe that Jesus died and rose again, even so them also which sleep in Jesus will God bring with him" (1 Thess. 4:14).

   b. This position refuted—Here it should be noted that while soul sleep is not nearly as heretical as the previous seven positions we have thus mentioned, it is, nevertheless, a false view. The context of the above verses describe the body as sleeping, not the soul. Note the wording relating to an event that occurred after the death of Christ: "And the graves were opened; and many bodies of the saints which slept arose" (Matt. 27:52).

   Key verses refuting soul sleep and reaffirming soul consciousness after death are as follows: "And, behold, there appeared unto them Moses and Elijah talking with him" (Matt. 17:3). "I am the God of Abraham, and the God of Isaac, and the God of Jacob. God is not the God of the dead, but of the living" (Matt. 22:32). "We are confident, I say, and would prefer to be away from the body and at home with the Lord." (2 Cor. 5:8, NIV). "For I am in a strait betwixt two, having a desire to depart, and to be with Christ; which is far better:" (Phil. 1:23).

   "And when he had opened the fifth seal, I saw under the altar the souls of them that were slain for the word of God, and for the testimony which they held: and they cried with a loud voice, saying, How long, O Lord, holy and true, dost thou not judge and avenge our blood on them that dwell on the earth? And white robes were given unto every one of them; and it was said unto them, that they should rest yet for a little season, until their fellow servants also and their brethren, that should be killed as they were, should be fulfilled" (Rev. 6:9-11).

9. Purgatory—This is the belief of Roman Catholics that all those who die at peace with the church but are not perfect must undergo penal and purifying sufferings. However, this is only for those who die in venial (lesser) sin, for all dying in mortal sin are forever condemned to hell. Roman doctrine teaches that a person's stay in purgatory may be shortened by the gifts or services rendered by living people in behalf of the beloved dead one through the Roman Catholic church.

   a. This position reviewed—The doctrine of purgatory is based upon two main sources, neither of which is scriptural.

      (1) A church council decree—In 1563 the Roman Catholic Council of Trent approved the Decree Concerning Purgatory. It reads:

> Whereas the Catholic Church, instructed by the Holy Spirit, has, from the Sacred Writings and the ancient tradition of the Fathers, taught, in sacred Councils, and very recently in this ecumenical Synod, that there is a Purgatory and that the souls there detained are helped by the suffrages of the faithful, but principally by the acceptable sacrifice of the altar—the holy Synod enjoins on bishops that they diligently endeavor that the sound doctrine concerning Purgatory, transmitted by the holy Fathers and sacred Councils, be believed, maintained, taught, and everywhere proclaimed by the faithful of Christ.

      (2) A reference from 2 Maccabees, a noncanonical book—Following his victory over an enemy in battle, Jewish hero Judas received an offering of some 12,000 pieces of silver and sent it to Jerusalem "for sacrifice to be offered for the sins of the dead (soldiers who had fallen in battle)," concluding, "It is therefore a holy and wholesome thought to pray for the dead, that they may be loosed from sins" (2 Macc. 12:43, 46).

   b. This position refuted

      (1) The Scriptures teach a repenting sinner is saved by faith in the grace of God alone, apart from any good works, including suffering in purgatory. (See Eph. 2:8-9; Titus 3:5.)

      (2) The Scriptures teach Christ's work on the cross was sufficient to save all sinners. (See Heb. 9:11-14, 24-28; 10:12, 16-17.)

10. Limbo—This is another aspect of Roman Catholic theology that teaches that all unbaptized children and the mentally incompetent, upon death, proceed to a permanent place of "natural happiness," but not heaven. Jesus himself refuted this view on at least two occasions:

"At the same time came the disciples unto Jesus, saying, Who is the greatest in the kingdom of heaven? And Jesus called a little child unto him, and set him in the midst of them, and said, Verily I say unto you, Except ye be converted, and become as little children, ye shall not enter into the kingdom of heaven" (Matt. 18:1-3). "But Jesus said, Suffer little children, and forbid them not, to come unto me: for of such is the kingdom of heaven" (Matt. 19:14).

B. Scriptural considerations concerning the destiny of man

   1. Before the cross—Where was the abode of the dead prior to Calvary? It is held by a number of Bible students that before Jesus died, the souls of all men descended into an abode located somewhere in the earth known as hades in the

New Testament and Sheol in the Old Testament. Originally, there were two sections of hades, one for the saved and one for the lost. The saved section is sometimes called paradise, and is at other times referred to as "Abraham's bosom." "And Jesus said unto him, Verily I say unto thee, To day shalt thou be with me in paradise" (Luke 23:43). "And it came to pass, that the beggar died, and was carried by the angels into Abraham's bosom: the rich man also died, and was buried" (Luke 16:22).

There is no name given for the unsaved section apart from the general designation of hades. In Luke 16:19-31 the Savior relates the account of a poor believer who died and went to the saved part of hades and of a rich unbeliever who died and went to the unsaved section.

A number of extremely interesting conclusions may be derived from this historical account as related by Christ.

a. The activities of angels in carrying believers to their reward
b. The possibilities of an intermediate, preresurrection body for the lost as well as the saved
c. The irony of an occupant in hell desiring to become a soul winner
d. The nature of the rich man's request to send Lazarus to testify to his five lost brothers, reasoning that "if one went unto them from the dead, they will repent"

This pathetic request was of course denied, simply because it would not have worked. The fact of the matter is that Christ did actually raise a man with the same name as Lazarus a few months later. What were the results of this? Did it cause the unbelieving Jews to come to the Savior? Hardly. In fact, just the opposite occurred, for the wicked Pharisees not only decided to kill Jesus for his action (John 11:53), but actually planned (if necessary) to murder the resurrected Lazarus also (John 12:10-11). "Then from that day forth they took counsel together for to put him to death" (John 11:53). "But the chief priests consulted that they might put Lazarus also to death; because that by reason of him many of the Jews went away, and believed on Jesus" (John 12:10-11).

However, many believe that all this changed after Christ had made full payment for the believer's sins on Calvary. The *Scofield Bible* suggests that during the time of his death and resurrection our Lord descended into hades, depopulated paradise, and led a spiritual triumphal entry into the heavenlies with all the saved up to that time. The following is offered as proof of this: "Wherefore he saith, When he ascended up on high, he led captivity captive, and gave gifts unto men. (Now that he ascended, what is it but that he also descended first into the lower parts of the earth? He that descended is the same also that ascended up far above all heavens, that he might fill all things)" (Eph. 4:8-10).

In his book *Revelation* the late Dr. Donald Barnhouse writes: "When He ascended on High He emptied Hell of Paradise and took it straight to the presence of God. Captivity was taken captive. . . . From that moment onward there was to be no separation whatsoever for those who believe in Christ. The gates of Hell would never more prevail against any believer" (*Revelation*, p. 380).

"And I say also unto thee, That thou art Peter, and upon this rock I will build my church; and the gates of hell shall not prevail against it" (Matt. 16:18).

2. After the cross—The state of the unsaved dead remained (and remains) unchanged after the cross. They remain in hades awaiting the final Great White Throne Judgment.

"And I saw a great white throne, and him that sat on it, from whose face the earth and the heaven fled away; and there was found no place for them. And I saw the dead, small and great, stand before God; and the books were opened: and another book was opened, which is the book of life: and the dead were judged out of those things which were written in the books, according to their works. And the sea gave up the dead which were in it; and death and hell delivered up the dead which were in them: and they were judged every man according to their works. And death and hell were cast into the lake of fire. This is the second death. And whosoever was not found written in the book of life was cast into the lake of fire" (Rev. 20:11-15).

This means the lost rich man is still in hades, there having since been joined by Judas, Herod, Nero, Hitler, etc., and will remain there until after the Millennium and the resurrection of the unjust. "But the rest of the dead lived not again until the thousand years were finished" (Rev. 20:5).

But a glorious change has occurred concerning the state of those who fall asleep in Jesus. Note the following Scriptures: "But he, being full of the Holy Ghost, looked up stedfastly into heaven, and saw the glory of God, and Jesus standing on the right hand of God. . . . And they stoned Stephen, calling upon God, and saying, Lord Jesus, receive my spirit. And he kneeled down, and cried with a loud voice, Lord, lay not this sin to their charge. And when he had said this, he fell asleep" (Acts 7:55, 59-60).

"For to me to live is Christ, and to die is gain. . . . For I am in a strait betwixt two, having a desire to depart, and to be with Christ; which is far better" (Phil. 1:21, 23). "We are confident, I say, and willing rather to be absent from the body, and to be present with the Lord" (2 Cor. 5:8).

Thus, according to these verses, both Stephen and Paul, along with all other departed believers, are now in the heavenlies with Christ. In the Scriptures Paul refers to this place as "the third heaven." (See 2 Cor. 12:1-4.)

VIII. The Final Place for Unsaved Man: Hell—"But I will forewarn you whom ye shall fear: Fear him, which after he hath killed hath power to cast into hell; yea, I say unto you, Fear him." (Luke 12:5). "And if thine eye offend thee, pluck it out: it is better for thee to enter into the kingdom of God with one eye, than having two eyes to be cast into hell fire: where their worm dieth not, and the fire is not quenched" (Mark 9:47-48).

A. The denial of hell—Of all the many doctrines in the Bible, undoubtedly the very first that the unbeliever will deny and the weak believer will question is the doctrine of hell. Satan has successfully accomplished this coveted goal through the following three methods:

1. Rationalism—"There is no God, and therefore there can be no hell." This rationalism often disguises itself in the garb of "science." Harold Bryson writes:

Other people deny the existence of hell on the basis of modern thinking. Some assume that many scientific discoveries of the 20th century render belief in a future life impossible. Using scientific study of the dissolution of the chemical elements of the body, they deny any possibility of a bodily resurrection. Also, the theory of organic evolution tries to demonstrate man's common origin with lower life forms. Evolution destroys the basis for believing that man has a higher destiny than any other creature. Some naively insist that the penetration of space leaves no place for the biblical teachings on heaven and hell. It has been assumed that if man finds no evidence of heaven in space then there is likewise no hell located in the opposite direction. (*Yes, Virginia, There Is a Hell*, p. 12)

Charles Darwin rejected the doctrine of hell: "Disbelief crept over me at a very slow rate, but was at last complete. I can hardly see how anyone ought to wish Christianity to be true; for, if so, the plain language of the text seems to show that the men who do not believe—and this would include my father, brother, and almost all my best friends—will be everlastingly punished. And this is a damnable doctrine" (Ibid., p. 164).

The English agnostic clergyman John A. T. Robinson, bishop of Woolwich, writes: "There are still a few who would like to bring back hell, as some want to bring back . . . hanging. They are usually the same types who wish to purge Britain of . . . sex and violence" (*But That I Can't Believe*, p. 69).

A *Newsweek* article on the after life says: "Today, hell is theology's H-word, a subject too trite for serious scholarship. When well-known church historian Martin Marty prepared a Harvard lecture on the disappearance of hell, he consulted the indices of several scholarly journals, including one dating back to 1889, and failed to find a single entry" (*Newsweek*, 27 March 1989, 54).

Marty thus concluded: "Hell disappeared. And no one noticed!"

2. Ridicule—"There may be a God, but it is silly to speculate about multitudes of disembodied spirits frying in some literal lake of fire somewhere."

One of America's most famous atheists was Robert G. Ingersoll, who ridiculed the idea of hell whenever and wherever he could. When asked to coin a slogan to help promote a cigar that bore his name, he quipped, "Smoke in this world, and not in the one to come!" Ingersoll loved the writings of the great poet Robert Burns. He often stated that one page of Burns had more literary merit than an entire book by Moses. Upon Ingersoll's death, some wag suggested that an appropriate epitaph for his tombstone would be to simply print the name of his favorite author: "Robert Burns!"

On the subject of hell, Ingersoll said: "The idea of hell was born of revenge and brutality on the one side, and cowardice on the other. . . . I have no respect for any man who preaches it. . . . I dislike this doctrine, I hate it, I despise it, I defy this doctrine!"

The famous news editor Horace Greeley is said to have refused to make a contribution to a religious group who solicited funds to be used in "keeping people out of hell." His reason was that, in his opinion, there were not nearly enough people going to hell at that present time.

3. Religion—"There is a God, but he is a God of love and therefore would not and could not send anyone to hell." This, of course, is the position of liberalism. Recent theologians such as Karl Barth, Emil Brunner, Paul Tillich, and others either denied or downplayed the doctrine of hell. The cults have at least one common ground, and that is, there is no hell.

   a. The Christian Science church defines hell as error of mortal mind.

   b. The Jehovah's Witnesses teach that the wicked will simply be annihilated.

c. The Mormons believe in hell, but not as an endless existence—They teach that life after death involves three levels: celestial, terrestrial, and telestial. The celestial level includes Mormons in an intermediate state, who will eventually become gods. The terrestrial level includes Christians and other persons who rejected the Mormon message. The telestial level is reserved for those currently in hell who await a final resurrection. Mormons teach that these will ultimately be saved and not suffer punishment forever.

d. The Seventh-Day Adventists claim that God will someday blot out all sin and sinners and establish a clean universe again.

The late Bishop James Pike wrote:

> A Heaven of infinite bliss and a Hell of infinite torment is an impossible contradiction. The kind of people who would qualify for Heaven would not be in bliss knowing that there were a lot of people in suffering with no chance whatever for change—the have-nots, the underprivileged. Those suitable for Heaven would want to go to Hell to be alongside them in their needs. Jesus, as shown by the reports of his ministry on earth, would be there alongside them too. God in his Heaven would find himself lonely and might well join everybody there—or change the whole scheme. (William C. Oursler, *Protestant Power and the Coming Revolution*, p. 173)

Regardless of the doubts and denials of men, the Bible dogmatically declares the existence and reality of hell. Here the devout believer would agree with the Apostle Paul: "Yea, let God be true, but every man a liar" (Rom. 3:4a).

B. The church's belief in hell—John Hunt has observed:

> If there be any doctrine ever taught in the name of Christianity which can claim to be really catholic, it is the doctrine of never-ending punishment. This has been believed by the majority of Christians in all ages, in all Churches, and, with very insignificant exceptions, in all sects. Fathers, Schoolmen, and Reformers, zealous Roman Catholics and ardent Protestants, have agreed that this is an undeniable portion of the Catholic faith. (*Contemporary Review*, April 1878)

John Braun's helpful book *Whatever Happened to Hell?* documents for us the almost universal belief in the doctrine of eternal Hell as testified by the most important and influential church fathers. Note their statements:

1. Ignatius of Antioch, a pupil of John the apostle (A.D. 35–107)—When describing the kind of man who corrupts families, Ignatius warns: "Such a man becomes filthy and will go to the unquenchable fire" (p. 105).

2. Polycarp, another disciple of John the apostle (69–155)—When threatened by the Roman proconsul to burn him with fire if he refused to renounce Christ, Polycarp replied: "You threaten fire which burns for an hour and is soon quenched; for you are ignorant of the fire of the coming judgment and eternal punishment received for the wicked" (p. 106).

3. Justin Martyr (100–165)—"We say that the souls of the wicked, being united to the same bodies, shall be consigned over to eternal torment" (p. 106).

4. Irenaeus (130–202)—"Thus also the punishment of those who do not believe the Word of God is not merely temporal, but is . . . eternal. . . these shall be damned forever" (p. 107).

5. Tertullian (160–220)—"The profane and all who are not true worshippers of God . . . shall be consigned to the punishment of everlasting fire" (p. 107).

6. Cyprian, Bishop of Carthage (200–258)—"An ever burning Gehenna will burn up the condemned, and a punishment devouring with living flames; nor will there be any time whence they may have either rest or end to their torments. The pain of punishment will be without the fruit of penitence; weeping will be useless, and prayers ineffectual. Too late they will believe in eternal punishment who do not believe in eternal life" (p. 108).

7. Athanasius, Bishop of Alexandria (296–372)—"Therefore the divine word does not allow them (sinners) to have peace . . . for there is no hope . . . the last fire, prepared for the devil and his angels, awaits those who disregarded divine light" (p. 108).

8. John Chrysostom (347–407)—"Neither will any severity of torment destroy the soul, nor will the body be able, in that time, to be consumed by burning" (p. 110).

It will be noted that all the above lived during the first few centuries of church history. At least two of them (Ignatius and Polycarp) were personally instructed by a leading apostle of Christ, who himself authored five New Testament epistles (John).

All this is extremely important and should not be overlooked. Apparently the early church fathers were totally unaware that the scriptural words *forever, eternal,* and *everlasting* do not really mean what they imply, as advocated by recent "enlightened" evangelicals. The fact remains—the original Christians believed in an eternal hell. Note Martin Luther's testimony: "Moreover, this article [eternal punishment] has been unanimously believed and held from the beginning of the Christian church to the present hour, as may be shown from the books and writings of the fathers, both in Greek and Latin languages; which testimony of the entire holy Christian Church ought to be sufficient for us" (p. 104).

C. The vocabulary of hell—Four key words must be considered if one desires to understand the concept of hell. These are: *Sheol, hades, Tartarus,* and *Gehenna.*

1. Sheol—*Sheol* is a Hebrew word, found 65 times in the Hebrew Old Testament. It is translated "hell" 31 times, "grave" 31 times, and "pit" 3 times.

Two locations and meanings may be in view by these 65 references, with the scriptural context determining the particular location.

a. The dwelling place of the dead human body (the grave)—There are (at least) four Old Testament instances where Sheol means simply the grave.

(1) Jacob's sorrow over the (assumed) death of his beloved son Joseph— "And all his sons and all his daughters rose up to comfort him; but he refused to be comforted; and he said, For I will go down into the grave unto my son mourning. Thus his father wept for him" (Gen. 37:35).

(2) Job's desire to end his suffering by way of death—"O that thou wouldest hide me in the grave, that thou wouldest keep me secret, until thy wrath be past, that thou wouldest appoint me a set time, and remember me!" (Job 14:13).

(3) David's prophecy concerning the resurrection of Christ from the grave— "For thou wilt not leave my soul in hell; neither wilt thou suffer thine Holy One to see corruption" (Psa. 16:10).

(4) The psalmist's fear of death—"For my soul is full of troubles: and my life

draweth nigh unto the grave. I am counted with them that go down into the pit: I am as a man that hath no strength" (Psa. 88:3-4).

b. The dwelling place of the departed human spirit (consisting of two separate compartments)

(1) Saved human spirits

(a) The place where Samuel came from to meet Saul (1 Sam. 28:14)

(b) The place where David expected to meet his dead infant son (2 Sam. 12:21-23)

(2) Lost human spirits

(a) Those Israelites who rebel against God—"For a fire is kindled in mine anger, and shall burn unto the lowest hell, and shall consume the earth with her increase, and set on fire the foundations of the mountains" (Deut. 32:22).

(b) Those Gentiles who rebel against God—"The wicked shall be turned into hell, and all the nations that forget God" (Psa. 9:17).

2. Hades—In essence, *hades* may be looked upon as the counterpart Greek New Testament word for the Hebrew Old Testament word *Sheol*. The word *hades* is translated by the word "hell" ten times in the New Testament, and on one occasion is rendered "grave" (1 Cor. 15:55).

a. Three of the hell references have the grave in mind (Matt. 16:18; Acts 2:27, 31).

b. Seven of the hell references have punishment in mind (Matt. 11:23; Luke 10:15; 16:23; Rev. 1:18; 6:8; 20:13-14).

3. Tartarus—This word is used but once in the New Testament, and is translated by the word "hell." "For if God spared not the angels that sinned, but cast them down to hell, and delivered them into chains of darkness, to be reserved unto judgment" (2 Pet. 2:4).

In light of this passage it is not unreasonable to suggest tartarus may be the underground prison house for a special group of fallen angels already in chains awaiting final judgment. Both Luke and Jude seem to indicate this. "And they besought him that he would not command them to go out into the deep" (Luke 8:31). "And the angels which kept not their first estate, but left their own habitation, he hath reserved in everlasting chains under darkness unto the judgment of the great day" (Jude 6). The sin causing the early imprisonment of these particular fallen angels may have been associated with the events in Genesis 6. (See also 1 Peter 3:18-20.)

4. Gehenna—We have already seen that, following the Tribulation, all the unsaved dead will be resurrected from Hades in the heart of the earth to appear before the Great White Throne judgment. (This is clearly stated in Revelation 20:11-15, see above.) They will then be cast into Gehenna hell forever. *Gehenna* is a New Testament word with an Old Testament background. It is found 12 times in the Greek New Testament, 11 of those instances coming from the mouth of the Savior himself (Matt. 5:22, 29-30; 10:28; 18:9; 25:15, 33; Mark 9:43, 45, 47; Luke 12:5; James 3:6). On each occasion it is translated by the word "hell." A brief etymology of the word *Gehenna* will be helpful here.

In the Old Testament, a wicked Israelite king named Ahaz forsook the worship of Jehovah and followed the devil-god Molech. In his insane and immoral attempt to please Molech, the king actually sacrificed his own children in the fires as burnt offerings to his abominable idol. (See 2 Chron. 28:1-4; 2 Kings 23:10.)

This all took place in a deep and narrow valley to the south of Jerusalem called the Valley of Hinnom. It was called by this name because of its owners, the sons of Hinnom.

This terrible practice was stopped under the reign of godly King Josiah, but the Valley of Hinnom continued to be used as the dumping ground for the garbage and filth of the city of Jerusalem.

Jeremiah the prophet also writes about both the Valley of Hinnom and Tophet: "And they have built the high places of Tophet, which is in the valley of the son of Hinnom, to burn their sons and their daughters in the fire; which I commanded them not, neither came it into my heart. Therefore, behold, the days come, saith the LORD, that it shall no more be called Tophet, nor the valley of the son of Hinnom, but the valley of slaughter: for they shall bury in Tophet, till there be no place. And the carcasses of this people shall be meat for the fowls of the heaven, and for the beasts of the earth; and none shall fray them away" (Jer. 7:31-33).

Walter Price writes:

Tophet was probably the point south of Jerusalem where three valleys met. The Tyropoeon Valley which runs through the old city and down by the Western Wall of the temple mount, intersects here with the Valley of Hinnom. The Valley of the son of Hinnom sweeps around the western side of the city and turns east below the Ophel to meet the Valley of Kidron. All three of these valleys converge at the spot where ancient Israel offered sacrifices to the Ammonite god Molech (2 Chron. 28:3; 33:6). Here also the field of Akeldama is located (Matt. 27:7-8; Acts 1:18-19). The Talmud places the mouth of Hell in this place. The Arabs also call this lower end of the Hinnom Valley where it meets Kidron, at Topheth, the Valley of Hell. In Jesus' day the city garbage dump was located there. The fighting between Jews and Romans ended here in A.D. 70. As many as 600,000 bodies of dead Jews, slain in the defense of Jerusalem against the Romans, were carried out through the Dung Gate to be buried in Tophet. (*The Coming Antichrist*, pp. 202–203)

As one therefore combines both Old Testament and New Testament meanings, he has described for him a place of filth and sorrow, of smoke and pain, of fire and death. This, then, is the word the Holy Spirit chose to employ in describing the final destiny for the unsaved. With all these things in mind, one is forced to the sobering conclusion that Gehenna hell is God's final dumping and burning place for all unsaved men and apostate angels.

D. The location of hell—The Bible definitely indicates that hades is somewhere down in the heart of the earth. "And the earth opened her mouth, and swallowed them up, and their houses, and all the men that appertained unto Korah, and all their goods. They, and all that appertained to them, went down alive into the pit, and the earth closed upon them: and they perished from among the congregation" (Num. 16:32-33).

It teaches, however, the following about Gehenna: "But the children of the kingdom shall be cast out into outer darkness: there shall be weeping and gnashing of teeth" (Matt. 8:12). "Then said the king to the servants, Bind him hand and foot, and take him away, and cast him into outer darkness; there shall be weeping and gnashing of teeth" (Matt. 22:13). "And cast ye the unprofitable servant into outer darkness: there shall be weeping and gnashing of teeth" (Matt. 25:30). "These are wells without water, clouds that are carried with a tempest; to whom the mist of darkness is reserved for ever" (2 Pet. 2:17). "Raging waves of the sea, foaming out their own shame; wandering stars, to whom is reserved the blackness of darkness for ever" (Jude 13).

From these five verses it becomes immediately clear that Gehenna hell is located away from this earth, a place of outer darkness, to be found, perhaps, in some remote spot near the edge of God's universe. If one thus distinguishes between hades hell and Gehenna hell, he will understand the words of John in describing the final resurrection of the wicked dead and their judgment. John writes: "And death and hell were cast into the lake of fire. This is the second death" (Rev. 20:14).

By this John meant that both death (which claimed the bodies of all dead unbelievers) and hell (that is, hades hell, which had held the spirits of all unsaved men) gave up their possessions, thus resulting in the joined bodies and spirits of all the unsaved being cast into Gehenna hell.

E. The nature and characteristics of hell—What will Gehenna really be like? Consider: Hell is:
  1. A place of unquenchable fire—"Whose fan is in his hand, and he will throughly purge his floor, and gather his wheat into the garner; but he will burn up the chaff with unquenchable fire" (Matt. 3:12). "The Son of man shall send forth his angels, and they shall gather out of his kingdom all things that offend, and them which do iniquity; and shall cast them into a furnace of fire: there shall be wailing and gnashing of teeth" (Matt. 13:41-42). "And if thy hand offend thee, cut it off: it is better for thee to enter into life maimed, than having two hands to go into hell, into the fire that never shall be quenched" (Mark 9:43).

     Opposing positions have been taken concerning whether the fire here is literal fire. It has been suggested that the fire is not real fire but something far worse. However, the Greek language would indicate otherwise. The same Greek word for fire (*pur*) used in Matthew 13:42 is also found in Matthew 17:15 and Luke 17:29. "And shall cast them into a furnace of fire: there shall be wailing and gnashing of teeth" (Matt. 13:42). "Lord, have mercy on my son: for he is lunatick, and sore vexed: for ofttimes he falleth into the fire, and oft into the water" (Matt. 17:15). "But the same day that Lot went out of Sodom it rained fire and brimstone from heaven, and destroyed them all" (Luke 17:29).
  2. A place of memory and remorse—In Luke 16:19-31 the unsaved rich man experienced memory and remorse over his lost condition in hades. Surely these experiences will not be lessened in Gehenna.
     a. Like David, those in hell will always be able to say—"For I acknowledge my transgressions: and my sin is ever before me" (Psa. 51:3).
     b. Unlike David, they will never be able to say—"Blessed is he whose transgression is forgiven, whose sin is covered" (Psa. 32:1).
        The poet John Greenleaf Whittier has written: "For of all sad words of tongue or pen, the saddest are these: 'It might have been.' "
  3. A place of thirst—Again in the Luke 16 account we read: "And he cried and said, Father Abraham, have mercy on me, and send Lazarus, that he may dip the tip of his finger in water, and cool my tongue; for I am tormented in this flame" (Luke 16:24).

It would seem difficult indeed to accept this account literally unless the fire in hell is literal. But what of Lazarus's finger and the rich man's tongue? Can this be interpreted literally?

It has been speculated, on the basis of this passage and also the one in 2 Corinthians 5, that temporary bodies of some sort are given to both unsaved and saved until the final resurrection of all.

4. A place of misery and pain—"The same shall drink of the wine of the wrath of God, which is poured out without mixture into the cup of his indignation; and he shall be tormented with fire and brimstone in the presence of the holy angels, and in the presence of the Lamb: and the smoke of their torment ascendeth up for ever and ever: and they have no rest day nor night, who worship the beast and his image, and whosoever receiveth the mark of his name" (Rev. 14:10-11).

5. A place of frustration and anger—"And shall cast them into a furnace of fire: there shall be wailing and gnashing of teeth" (Matt. 13:42). "And shall cut him asunder, and appoint him his portion with the hypocrites: there shall be weeping and gnashing of teeth" (Matt. 24:51).

6. A place of separation—Often the unsaved man jokes about hell in the following manner: "Well, if I do go to hell, I won't be lonely; all my friends will be there too." But quite the opposite is true. In at least four separate passages Gehenna hell is called "the second death."

"He that hath an ear, let him hear what the Spirit saith unto the churches; He that overcometh shall not be hurt of the second death" (Rev. 2:11). "Blessed and holy is he that hath part in the first resurrection: on such the second death hath no power, but they shall be priests of God and of Christ, and shall reign with him a thousand years. . . . And whosoever was not found written in the book of life was cast into the lake of fire" (Rev. 20:6, 15). "But the fearful, and unbelieving, and the abominable, and murderers, and whoremongers, and sorcerers, and idolaters, and all liars, shall have their part in the lake which burneth with fire and brimstone: which is the second death" (Rev. 21:8).

As we have already noted, "death" in the Bible refers to separation. Thus hell is literally the second death, for the sinner will be forever separated from God, and, inasmuch as Gehenna is a place of darkness, this separation will doubtless isolate him from the companionship of unsaved friends as well.

Thus, the worst thing about hell is closely connected to the best thing about heaven, and that is, the first is a place where Jesus Christ will be conspicuously absent while the second location is a place where he will be conspicuously present.

7. A place of undiluted divine wrath—Man has already experienced some of God's wrath on this earth, but not in its pure state. After the flood there has been the rainbow, for up to this point God has always heard and answered the prophet Habakkuk's prayer: "O LORD, I have heard thy speech, and was afraid: O LORD, revive thy work in the midst of the years, in the midst of the years make known; in wrath remember mercy" (Hab. 3:2).

But no more! All living unsaved men should carefully ponder over the following frightful words: "The same shall drink of the wine of the wrath of God, which is poured out without mixture into the cup of his indignation; and he shall be tormented with fire and brimstone in the presence of the holy angels, and in the presence of the Lamb" (Rev. 14:10).

8. A place originally prepared for Satan and his hosts—Perhaps the saddest fact about hell is that unsaved man goes there as an uninvited guest, so to speak. Note Jesus' words: "Then shall he say also unto them on the left hand, Depart from me, ye cursed, into everlasting fire, prepared for the devil and his angels" (Matt. 25:41).

How tragic, therefore, that the sinner will refuse heaven, the place prepared for all repenting men, only to eventually descend into hell, a place originally not created for him. "In my Father's house are many mansions: if it were not so, I would have told you. I go to prepare a place for you" (John 14:2).

Note: In Gethsemane on three occasions our Lord prayed, "Thy will be done." In a very real sense those four simple words determine heaven or hell for each human being. To explain:

a. If the sinner rejects Christ, then the Father says to him, "Thy will be done," resulting in hell.

b. If the sinner accepts Christ, then he himself says to the Father, "Thy will be done," resulting in heaven.

9. A place created for all eternity—The Greek word for "everlasting" is *aionios*, and it is found 71 times in the New Testament. Sixty-four of these instances are in reference to God, such as his eternal power, spirit, kingdom, covenant, etc. The remaining seven instances are directly related to the duration of hell. In other words, hell will continue as long as God's works continue, which is forever. Many passages bring this truth out.

"And many of them that sleep in the dust of the earth shall awake, some to everlasting life, and some to shame and everlasting contempt" (Dan. 12:2). "And these shall go away into everlasting punishment: but the righteous into life eternal" (Matt. 25:46). "Even as Sodom and Gomorrah, and the cities about them in like manner, giving themselves over to fornication, and going after strange flesh, are set forth for an example, suffering the vengeance of eternal fire" (Jude 7).

How long is eternity? Imagine the sun (which is well over a million times the size of our earth) being made of solid granite rock. Also imagine a little bird from our planet flying to this incredibly huge rock once each thousand years and removing from it a tiny grain of sand. When the last particle has been carried away, the first moment of eternity would have scarcely begun.

What Christian has not thrilled with the singing of the last stanza of John Newton's great hymn, "Amazing Grace." Note its words: "When we've been there ten thousand years, bright shining as the sun, we've no less days to sing God's praise than when we first begun."

But let me reverse this and apply it to those in hell: "When *they've* been there ten thousand years, fire hotter than the sun, *they've* no less days to curse and rave, than when *they* first begun!" Sobering thought indeed!

Without doubt the most difficult truth to accept, even for Christians, is the duration of hell. One might understand a 65-year old sinner going to Hell for 65 years, or 650, or 6,500, or even 65 million years. But why the endless ages? How can a just God rightfully punish forever those sins that were committed in a brief period of time on earth?

A full answer to this exists only in the mind of God. However, hell does vividly demonstrate the heinousness of sin and the holiness of God. Thus, sins against God's eternal holiness can only be punished by God's eternal justice.

F. The degrees of punishment in hell—The Scriptures clearly teach there is neither injustice or partiality with God. Note: "Who will render to every man according to his deeds. . . . For there is no respect of persons with God" (Rom. 2:6, 11).

It naturally follows therefore that the degrees of suffering in hell (as is also the case concerning the rewards in heaven) will vary greatly, being in direct relationship to the sinner's life here on earth. A number of Scriptures bear this out:

1. Christ's words concerning some unbelieving cities—"Then began he to upbraid the cities wherein most of his mighty works were done, because they repented not: Woe unto thee, Chorazin! woe unto thee, Bethsaida! for if the mighty works, which were done in you, had been done in Tyre and Sidon, they would have repented long ago in sackcloth and ashes. But I say unto you, It shall be more tolerable for Tyre and Sidon at the day of judgment, than for you. And thou, Capernaum, which art exalted unto heaven, shalt be brought down to hell: for if the mighty works, which have been done in thee, had been done in Sodom, it would have remained until this day. But I say unto you, That it shall be more tolerable for the land of Sodom in the day of judgment, than for thee" (Matt. 11:20-24).

2. Christ's words concerning the unfaithful servant—"And that servant, which knew his lord's will, and prepared not himself, neither did according to his will, shall be beaten with many stripes. But he that knew not, and did commit things worthy of stripes, shall be beaten with few stripes. For unto whomsoever much is given, of him shall be much required: and to whom men have committed much, of him they will ask the more" (Luke 12:47-48).

3. Christ's words concerning the dishonest scribes—"Then in the audience of all the people he said unto his disciples, Beware of the scribes, which desire to walk in long robes, and love greetings in the markets, and the highest seats in the synagogues, and the chief rooms at feasts; which devour widows' houses, and for a shew make long prayers: the same shall receive greater damnation" (Luke 20:45-47).

4. Christ's words concerning the Jewish leaders involved in his crucifixion—"Then saith Pilate unto him, Speakest thou not unto me? knowest thou not that I have power to crucify thee, and have power to release thee? Jesus answered, Thou couldest have no power at all against me, except it were given thee from above: therefore he that delivered me unto thee hath the greater sin" (John 19:10-11).

5. Paul's words concerning the unbeliever's relationship to the Law of God—"All who sin apart from the law will also perish apart from the law, and all who sin under the law will be judged by the law" (Rom. 2:12, NIV).

G. The occupants of hell—Who shall be someday confined to Gehenna forever?

1. Satan—"And the God of peace shall bruise Satan under your feet shortly. The grace of our Lord Jesus Christ be with you. Amen" (Rom. 16:20). "And the devil that deceived them was cast into the lake of fire and brimstone, where the beast and false prophet are, and shall be tormented day and night for ever and ever" (Rev. 20:10).

2. The Antichrist—"And then shall that Wicked be revealed, whom the Lord shall consume with the spirit of his mouth, and shall destroy with the brightness of his coming" (2 Thess. 2:8).

3. The false prophet—"And the beast was taken, and with him the false prophet that wrought miracles before him, with which he deceived them that had

received the mark of the beast, and them that worshipped his image. These
both were cast alive into a lake of fire burning with brimstone" (Rev. 19:20).
4. Fallen angels—"For if God spared not the angels that sinned, but cast them
down to hell, and delivered them into chains of darkness, to be reserved unto
judgment" (2 Pet. 2:4).

   According to Paul, the believer will take part in the passing of judgment
upon fallen angels. "Know ye not that we shall judge angels? how much more
things that pertain to this life?" (1 Cor. 6:3).
5. Judas Iscariot—The betrayer of Jesus Christ is singled out here in particular
because there are those (notably the late beloved Kenneth S. Wuest of the
Moody Bible Institute faculty) who believe Judas will be consigned to a special
place in Gehenna on the basis of Peter's words concerning him in the Upper
Room just prior to Pentecost: "That he may take part of this ministry and
apostleship, from which Judas by transgression fell, that he might go to his own
place" (Acts 1:25).
6. All unsaved people—In Rev. 21:8 John classifies all sinners into eight general
categories: "But the fearful, and unbelieving, and the abominable, and
murderers, and whoremongers, and sorcerers, and idolaters, and all liars, shall
have their part in the lake which burneth with fire and brimstone: which is the
second death" (Rev. 21:8).

   These categories are:
   a. The fearful—At first glance it might seem strange to find the fearful at the
top of this divine "rogues of Gehenna" listing, but many obviously will
wind up in hell because they fear the cost of claiming the Savior's name.

   "The fear of man bringeth a snare: but whoso putteth his trust in the
LORD shall be safe" (Prov. 29:25). "These words spake his parents, because
they feared the Jews: for the Jews had agreed already, that if any man did
confess that he was Christ, he should be put out of the synagogue" (John
9:22). "Nevertheless among the chief rulers also many believed on him; but
because of the Pharisees they did not confess him, lest they should be put
out of the synagogue: for they loved the praise of men more than the praise
of God" (John 12:42-43).
   b. The unbelieving—Literally, these are the disbelieving. No man ever goes to
hell because he can't believe, but rather because he won't believe. There is
no such thing as an honest agnostic. "He that believeth on the Son hath
everlasting life: and he that believeth not the Son shall not see life; but the
wrath of God abideth on him" (John 3:36).
   c. The abominable—Literally, this refers to those defiled with abominations.
"These six things doth the LORD hate: yea, seven are an abomination unto
him: a proud look, a lying tongue, and hands that shed innocent blood, an
heart that deviseth wicked imaginations, feet that be swift in running to
mischief, a false witness that speaketh lies, and he that soweth discord
among brethren" (Prov. 6:16-19).
   d. Murderers—This refers not only to a human-killer, but also to a human-
hater as well. "Whosoever hateth his brother is a murderer: and ye know
that no murderer hath eternal life abiding in him" (1 John 3:15).
   e. Whoremongers—This describes those guilty of sexual sins. "For this ye
know, that no whoremonger, nor unclean person, nor covetous man, who is
an idolater, hath any inheritance in the kingdom of Christ and of God" (Eph.

5:5). "Marriage is honourable in all, and the bed undefiled: but whore-mongers and adulterers God will judge" (Heb. 13:4).

For some reason not fully revealed in the Scriptures, God especially hates the sin of sexual immorality, perhaps considering it, with the exception of pride and self-will, the most offensive transgression of all.

This sin invoked the death penalty upon those guilty of it in the Old Testament (Lev. 20:10; Deut. 22:22-24). It was for this sin God wiped out the ancient city of Sodom (Gen. 13:13; 18:20-21; 19:24). Sexual perversion probably led to the destruction of the Canaanite society by Joshua at the command of God (Compare Deut. 20:17-18; Josh. 6:21 with 1 Kings 14:24).

Finally, in the New Testament Paul links this sin to the ultimate degradation of the human race. In fact, it is the *only* recorded sin prompting God to "give up" on those nations and cultures practicing it.

"Therefore God gave them over in the sinful desires of their hearts to sexual impurity for the degrading of their bodies with one another. They exchanged the truth of God for a lie, and worshiped and served created things rather than the Creator—who is forever praised. Amen. Because of this, God gave them over to shameful lusts. Even their women exchanged natural relations for unnatural ones. In the same way the men also abandoned natural relations with women and were inflamed with lust for one another. Men committed indecent acts with other men, and received in themselves the due penalty for their perversion. Furthermore, since they did not think it worthwhile to retain the knowledge of God, he gave them over to a depraved mind, to do what ought not to be done." (Rom. 1:24-28, NIV).

f. Sorcerers—The Greek word is *pharmakos*, which refers to an enchanter with drugs. In a general sense the word also covers those who commune with Satan through fortunetellers, mediums, and astrology.

"Neither repented they of their murders, nor of their sorceries, nor of their fornication, nor of their thefts" (Rev. 9:21). "And the light of a candle shall shine no more at all in thee; and the voice of the bridegroom and of the bride shall be heard no more at all in thee: for thy merchants were the great men of the earth; for by thy sorceries were all nations deceived" (Rev. 18:23).

g. Idolaters—Those who worship something or someone else in place of the true God are described as idolaters. "Professing themselves to be wise, they became fools, and changed the glory of the uncorruptible God into an image made like to corruptible man, and to birds, and fourfooted beasts, and creeping things" (Rom. 1:22-23).

h. Liars—"I know thy works, and thy labour, and thy patience, and how thou canst not bear them which are evil: and thou hast tried them which say they are apostles, and are not, and hast found them liars" (Rev. 2:2). "Ye are of your father the devil, and the lusts of your father ye will do. He was a murderer from the beginning, and abode not in the truth, because there is no truth in him. When he speaketh a lie, he speaketh of his own: for he is a liar, and the father of it" (John 8:44). "Who is a liar but he that denieth that Jesus is the Christ? He is antichrist, that denieth the Father and the Son" (1 John 2:22).

It is sobering to contemplate that all the above passages concern religious liars!

H. The possible present-day existence of Gehenna hell—We know, according to Jesus, that heaven is still being prepared. "Let not your heart be troubled: ye believe in God, believe also in me. In my Father's house are many mansions: if it were not so, I would have told you. I go to prepare a place for you. And if I go and prepare a place for you, I will come again, and receive you unto myself; that where I am, there ye may be also" (John 14:1-3).

But what about hell? There are several scriptural and scientific facts that would strongly indicate that Gehenna hell is right now in existence. Consider Jesus' words: "Then shall he say also unto them on the left hand, Depart from me, ye cursed, into everlasting fire, prepared for the devil and his angels" (Matt. 25:41).

Dr. J. Dwight Pentecost writes:

The word "prepared" literally is "having been prepared," suggesting that the lake of fire is already in existence and awaiting its occupants. It is the thesis of C. T. Schwarze, then of New York University, that such a place as a lake of fire is known to science today. He writes: "The word *lake* must connote a body of matter having liquid form. Therefore, if Scripture is truth, this eternal fire must be in liquid form.

". . . The very simple proof of the portions of Scripture we have been discussing lies in the existence of the singular phenomena of the skies known as midget or white dwarf stars! . . . A midget star is one which, because of some things which have happened to it (not quite clear at this time), should be roughly 5,000 or more times as big as it really is! Applying this idea for illustration to such a planet as the earth, you must conceive the earth as having shrunk to such an extent that its diameter would be about 400 miles . . . instead of being 8,000 miles in diameter as it really is.

"This enormous density . . . has a great deal to do with our subject. Most people know the sun, our nearest star, is rather hot. . . . There is general agreement that the temperature at or near the center of stars is between 25 million and 30 million degrees Fahrenheit! . . . At such temperatures, much can happen, like the bursting of atoms, which helps to explain the phenomenon of the white dwarf.

". . . A temperature of 30 million degrees Fahrenheit could explode atoms. . . . It would cause the atoms to lose their electrons, even though the attraction between nucleus and electrons is an octillion times the attraction of gravity. The separated parts could then be better packed in, particularly under such great pressure. . . . With the constant activity of X rays, atom walls could not be reformed; therefore enormous densities, such as are found in the midgets, can be attained. Now, please note, at such high temperatures all matter would be in the form of gas; . . . in a white dwarf the pressure is so great that gasses become compressed to the consistency of a liquid, although they may still respond to the characteristics of a gas.

". . . Before such a star would cool off and gradually become dark it would have to expand to normal proportions. That is, it would have to get to be more than 5,000 times its present size. Here is the difficulty. Such expansion would cause enormous heat which, in turn, would absolutely keep the star compressed, so that, insofar as astronomers and physicists know, the midget stars can never cool off! . . . The white dwarf, to all intents, can never burn out." (*Things to Come*, pp. 559–560)

Thus wrote Dr. Schwarze. Pentecost then concludes:

May I summarize to show that the Bible, God's Word, is scientifically accurate? We find, first, an eternal fire which cannot burn out. Being of a liquid consistency it is, secondly, a lake of fire. In the third place, it cannot be quenched, for any quenching material such as water, would immediately have its atoms stripped of electrons and be packed in with the rest. In the fourth place, since astronomers have been, and still are, studying this strange phenomenon, it is only too evident that the lake of fire has been prepared and is now ready. Although we cannot say that God will actually use these lakes of fire in fulfilling His Word, the answer to the skeptic is in the heavens where there are lakes of fire. (Ibid., p. 561)

Perhaps an even more likely (certainly more frightening) location for Gehenna hell is known by astronomers as a black hole. Stated as simply as possible, a black hole is the hypothetical result of a runaway or uncontrolled gravitational collapse of a supernova. Eventually a collapsing object, such as a star, will reach a limited size, called the Schwarzschild Radius, which depends upon the mass of the object. For the sun the Schwarzschild Radius would be about two miles. If the contracting object continues to contract to less than its Schwarzschild Radius, it becomes a black hole. The gravitational forces exerted by this object are so strong that no matter or radiation can escape from it. The light emanating from this object is trapped and effectively removed from the "observable universe."

Dr. Kip Thorne, of the California Institute of Technology, one of the world's authorities on collapsed stars writes:

We believe a black hole is an extremely smooth structure; it can never have ripples or mountains. Anything it traps can never escape. The black hole can neither split nor decrease in size; it can only grow. . . .

Ultimately, if the universe itself does not collapse and die first, the black holes will eat up all the matter in our galaxy. Already, as much as one ten-thousandth of the universe might be down black holes. We would like to sweep this fact under the rug, but occasionally we drag it out and look it in the face and shudder. (*National Geographic,* May 1974, 620)

According to Dr. Paul Ho, researcher at the Harvard-Smithsonian Center for Astrophysics, a black hole, one million times more massive than our sun, has been discovered in the center of the Milky Way, about 30,000 light years from earth in the constellation Sagittarius. This was reported by various U.S. newspapers in 1989.

IX. The Final Place for Saved Man: Heaven—Both heaven and hell are either ignored, ridiculed, or denied by the world today. In his book *The Biblical Doctrine of Heaven,* Dr. Wilbur Smith lists two significant quotes from a world-famous theologian and a scientist about heaven:

"It is unwise for Christians to claim any knowledge of either the furniture of heaven or the temperature of hell"—Dr. Reinhold Niebuhr (p. 12).

"As for the Christian theology, can you imagine anything more appallingly idiotic than the Christian idea of Heaven?"—Dr. Alfred Whitehead (p. 21).

William Inge, dean of St. Paul's Cathedral, once wrote:

The discovery that the earth, instead of being the centre of a finite universe, like a dish with a dish-cover above it, is a planet revolving round the sun, which itself is only one of millions of stars, tore into shreds the Christian map of the universe.

Until that time the ordinary man, whether educated or uneducated, had pictured the sum of things as a three-storied building, consisting of heaven, the abode of God, the angels, and beatified spirits; our earth; and the infernal regions, where the devil, his angels, and lost souls are imprisoned and tormented. . . . The Copernican astronomy, and all the knowledge about the heavens which has been built upon this foundation, leave no room for a geographical heaven. Space seems to be infinite, or as some prefer to say, boundless—a distinction not very intelligible except to the mathematicians; and among all the stars, planets, satellites, and nebulae which are sparsely scattered over its vast empty distances we can hardly imagine that one has been chosen as the abode of the Creator and the site of the heavenly Jerusalem" (*The Church in the World*, p. 156)

A common approach of the liberal clergyman is that he does indeed believe in a literal heaven and hell, but limits them both to this earth. In other words, life's good experiences are "heaven," and its bad moments "hell." Without him probably being at all aware of it, his Bible-denying philosophy does contain a very potent truth. The facts are that this world is indeed the only hell the believer will ever experience, and the only heaven the unbeliever will ever know.

Sometimes a "pious" objection is raised concerning the very study of heaven. The protest goes: "But don't you think we can become so heavenly minded that we're no earthly good?" This may be, but for every one like this, there are probably ten believers who are so earthly minded that they are no heavenly good. "If ye then be risen with Christ, seek those things which are above, where Christ sitteth on the right hand of God. Set your affection on things above, not on things on the earth. For ye are dead, and your life is hid with Christ in God" (Col. 3:1-3).

A poll taken by sociologist Andrew Greeley refutes the oft-repeated claims of Freud, Marx, and Nietzsche who argued that hope in a heaven inhibits individuals from enjoying or caring about earthly life. To the contrary, the poll revealed those who believe in an after life lead happier and more productive lives than those who do not.

In reality, we are told a surprising number of things in the Word of God about our future home. Contrary to popular opinion, heaven is discussed far more than hell in the Scriptures.

A. The categories of heaven—In the Bible we read of four heavens. Briefly, these are:

1. The first heaven—This heaven is the home of the birds and clouds, the atmospheric heaven. "The leaves thereof were fair, and the fruit thereof much, and in it was meat for all: the beasts of the field had shadow under it, and the fowls of the heaven dwelt in the boughs thereof, and all flesh was fed of it" (Dan. 4:12). "Behold the fowls of the air: for they sow not, neither do they reap, nor gather into barns; yet your heavenly Father feedeth them. Are ye not much better than they?" (Matt. 6:26).

2. The second heaven—The second heaven is the home of the sun, moon, and stars. "That in blessing I will bless thee, and in multiplying I will multiply thy seed as the stars of the heaven, and as the sand which is upon the sea shore; and thy seed shall possess the gate of his enemies" (Gen. 22:17). "The heavens declare the glory of God; and the firmament sheweth his handiwork" (Psa. 19:1).

   In the 1960s (beginning with the Russian orbit in 1961 and climaxing with the U.S. moon landing in 1969) man for the first time in history succeeded in developing a spacecraft that would transport him out of the first heaven into the second heaven. But as wide and wonderful as it is, the second heaven (like the first) cannot be confused with the heaven of salvation.

3. The third heaven—The third heaven is the home of God. "I knew a man in Christ above fourteen years ago, (whether in the body, I cannot tell; or whether out of the body, I cannot tell: God knoweth;) such an one caught up to the third heaven" (2 Cor. 12:2). "But will God indeed dwell on the earth? behold, the heaven and heaven of heavens cannot contain thee; how much less this house that I have builded? . . . And hearken thou to the supplication of thy servant, and of thy people Israel, when they shall pray toward this place: and hear thou in heaven thy dwelling place: and when thou hearest, forgive" (1 Kings 8:27, 30).

This and this alone is the true third heaven. It has already been noted how man's brain power recently transported him from the first to the second heaven. But no space vehicle can ever be devised which will take him from the second to the third heaven. This journey can only be effected by blood, and not by brain. In fact, Jesus once told Nicodemus a man could not even see this heaven, let alone enter it, apart from the new birth. "Jesus answered and said unto him, Verily, verily, I say unto thee, Except a man be born again, he cannot see the kingdom of God" (John 3:3).

In Matthew 6:9 our Lord taught his disciples to pray: "After this manner therefore pray ye: Our Father which art in heaven, hallowed be thy name" (Matt. 6:9).

4. The fourth heaven—"For, behold, I create new heavens and a new earth: and the former shall not be remembered, nor come into mind" (Isa. 65:17). "Nevertheless we, according to his promise, look for new heavens and a new earth, wherein dwelleth righteousness" (2 Pet. 3:13). "And I saw a new heaven and a new earth: for the first heaven and the first earth were passed away; and there was no more sea" (Rev. 21:1).

B. The capital of heaven—For all intents and purposes, the believer, in contemplating his or her final heavenly home, should think of it in terms of a literal, physical, incredibly large and costly, dazzling bright, and blessed *city* located among the stars.

1. This city is anticipated in the Old Testament.
   a. By Abraham—"For he looked for a city which hath foundations, whose builder and maker is God" (Heb. 11:10).
   b. By David—"There is a river, the streams whereof shall make glad the city of God, the holy place of the tabernacles of the most High" (Psa. 46:4). "Glorious things are spoken of thee, O city of God. Selah" (Psa. 87:3).
   c. By all the men and women of faith—"These all died in faith, not having received the promises, but having seen them afar off, and were persuaded of them, and embraced them, and confessed that they were strangers and pilgrims on the earth. . . . But now they desire a better country, that is, an heavenly: wherefore God is not ashamed to be called their God: for he hath prepared for them a city" (Heb. 11:13, 16).

2. This city is promised in the Gospels—"Let not your heart be troubled: ye believe in God, believe also in me. In my Father's house are many mansions: if it were not so, I would have told you. I go to prepare a place for you. And if I go and prepare a place for you, I will come again, and receive you unto myself; that where I am, there ye may be also" (John 14:1-3).

3. This city is referred to in the Epistles—"Jerusalem which is above. . . " (Gal. 4:26). "But ye are come unto mount Sion, and unto the city of the living God, the heavenly Jerusalem, and to an innumerable company of angels" (Heb. 12:22). "For here have we no continuing city, but we seek one to come" (Heb. 13:14).

4. This city is described in the book of Revelation—"And I John saw the holy city, new Jerusalem, coming down from God out of heaven, prepared as a bride adorned for her husband" (Rev. 21:2).

C. The characteristics of heaven (facts about the new Jerusalem)

1. The size—"And he measured the city with the reed, twelve thousand furlongs. The length and the breadth and the height of it are equal" (Rev. 21:16b). According to our present-day measurements this city would be roughly 1,400 miles long, high, and wide. If placed in America, it would reach from New York City to Denver, Colorado, and from Canada to Florida.

How big is a city this size? Our earth has approximately 120 million square miles of water surface and 60 million square miles of land surface. If one multiplies 1,400 by 1,400 by 1,400 (the dimensions of the new Jerusalem), he arrives at the total cubic miles of the city, a staggering figure of 2.744 billion. This is some 14 times the combined surface of the entire earth, including both land and water area.

It has been estimated that approximately 40 billion people have lived on our planet since the creation of Adam. Of this number, over 5 billion are living today. Density studies of city populations assure us that every single one of these 40 billion could easily be accomodated upon just the first "foundational floor" of this marvelous 1,400-layer metropolis.

Taking a different approach, heaven will consist of 396,000 stories (at 20 feet per story) each having an area as big as half the size of the United States.

2. The shape—"And the city lieth foursquare, and the length is as large as the breadth. . . . The length and the breadth and the height of it are equal" (Rev. 21:16).

This description allows for two possibilities, namely that the new Jerusalem is either in the shape of a tetragon (a perfect cube) or of a vast pyramid.

a. Arguments for a cubical city—John's statement in Rev. 21:3 seems to indicate it. "Behold, the tabernacle of God is with men."

Gary Cohen writes in "Some Questions Concerning the New Jerusalem":

It is interesting to note that the Holy of Holies inside the Tabernacle is cubical-shaped (20 x 20 x 20 cubits).

The suggestion that the entire city is a huge Holy of Holies, cubical in shape as was the sacred inner sanctuary of the Temple (1 Kings 6:20), perfectly fits the truth that this city will be the very place in which God makes His dwelling. (*Grace Journal*, vol. 6, 24)

b. Arguments for a triangular city—H. A. Ironside writes:

I rather think of that holy city as the mountain of God, a vast pyramid resting on a foursquare base, 12 thousand furlongs each way, and rising to a height as great as its length and breadth, and the throne of God and of the Lamb, the very apex of it, from which flows the river of the water of life, winding about the mountain, in the midst of the one street of gold on either side of that river. But in either case, whether we think of a cube or a pyramid, the thought is the same: it is a city of absolute perfection. (*Revelation,* p. 357)

Dr. J. Vernon McGee, however, takes a different approach from the two above views:

> The shape of this city is difficult to describe. . . . Some have envisioned it as a cube, others as a pyramid. In view of the fact that it is hanging in space as a planet or star, it seems that it would be a globe. . . . The city is inside the globe. . . . The light would shine through the 12 foundations, giving a fantastic and startling coloring to the new universe. . . . From the outside, the city looks like a diamond. The gold is transparent and the diamond is the setting for the gold on the inside. . . . We live on the outside of the planet called earth, but the Bride will dwell within the planet called the New Jerusalem. The glory of light streaming through this crystal clear prism, will break up into a polychromed rainbow of breathtaking beauty. The sphere will have the circumference of 8,164 miles. The diameter of the moon is about 2,160 miles and that of the New Jerusalem sphere is about 2,600 miles: thus the New Jerusalem will be about the size of the moon. And it will be a sphere, as are the other heavenly bodies.
>
> While the Bible definitely pictures the New Jerusalem as floating in space, it should not be thought of as a satellite city to the earth, but rather the opposite, that is, the earth as a satellite planet encircling the New Jerusalem. (*Reveling through Revelation,* pp. 86–87, 105)

3. The names—At least seven names and titles are given for this celestial city.
  a. New Jerusalem (Rev. 3:12; 21:2)
  b. The Holy City (Rev. 21:2; 22:19)
  c. The heavenly Jerusalem (Heb. 11:16; 12:22)
  d. Mount Zion (Heb. 12:22)
  e. The Bride, the Lamb's wife (Rev. 21:9)
  f. Paradise—"He that hath an ear, let him hear what the Spirit saith unto the churches; To him that overcometh will I give to eat of the tree of life, which is in the midst of the paradise of God" (Rev. 2:7).

    Judson Cornwall observes:

> Both the Old and the New Testaments speak of paradise. In the King James version of the Old Testament the Hebrew word for paradise is translated as, "an orchard" (Song of Solomon 4:13; Eccles. 2:5), and "a forest" (Neh. 2:8), probably because it is actually a Persian word that was coined to describe the magnificent parks and gardens that were designed for the Persian kings. Later this word was picked up by the Latin scholars who produced the Septuagint version of the Old Testament scriptures (a translation from Hebrew into Greek) who used this word as a name for the garden of Eden. Whereas our English Bible calls the first habitation of God's special creation "Eden," the Greek translation calls Adam's home "paradise." (Judson Cornwall, *Heaven,* p. 32)

  g. The Father's house (John 14:2)

4. The foundations (Rev. 21:14, 19-20)—The city rests upon 12 layers of foundation stones, with each layer being inlaid with a different precious gem. These are:
   a. First foundation—The first foundation is inlaid with jasper, a crystal clear diamond, as bright as a transparent icicle in the sunshine.
   b. Second foundation—The second foundation is inlaid with sapphire, a blue opaque stone with gold specks.
   c. Third foundation—The third foundation is inlaid with chalcedony, a sky-blue stone with stripes of other colors running through it.
   d. Fourth foundation—The fourth foundation is inlaid with emerald, a bright green stone.
   e. Fifth foundation—The fifth foundation is inlaid with sardonyx, a white stone with layers of red.
   f. Sixth foundation—The sixth foundation is inlaid with sardius, a fiery red stone.
   g. Seventh foundation—The seventh foundation is inlaid with chrysolyte, a transparent golden yellow stone.
   h. Eighth foundation—The eighth foundation is inlaid with beryl, a sea-green stone.
   i. Ninth foundation—The ninth foundation is inlaid with topaz, a transparent golden-green stone.
   j. Tenth foundation—The tenth foundation is inlaid with chrysoprasus, a blue-green stone.
   k. Eleventh foundation—The eleventh foundation is inlaid with jacinth, a violet stone.
   l. Twelfth foundation—The twelfth foundation is inlaid with amethyst, a flashing purple stone.

   These 12 foundations were not only inlaid with costly gems, but each foundational layer carried the name of one of the 12 apostles of the New Testament. "And the wall of the city had twelve foundations, and in them the names of the twelve apostles of the Lamb" (Rev. 21:14).

   It should be noted that these jewels roughly parallel the 12 stones in the breastplate of the high priest (Exod. 28:17-20).

5. The walls—The walls of the new Jerusalem are some 216 feet high and are made of jasper (Rev. 21:17-18). The wall is obviously not for protection, but for design and beauty only. In comparison to size, a 216-foot wall around a 1,400-mile-high city would be like a one-inch curb around the Empire State building.

6. The gates—There are 12 gates to this city, 3 gates on each side. On each gate is the name of one of the tribes of Israel. Each gate is composed of a beautiful solid white pearl (Rev. 21:12-13, 21).

   It has been observed that the "coat of arms" in the new Jerusalem is not the 12-jeweled foundation (Rev. 21:19-20), nor the jasper wall (Rev. 21:18), nor the streets of gold (Rev. 21:21), nor the ivory towers (indicated by Psa. 45:8), but rather the gates of pearl. In reality the believer will literally be surrounded by pearls. Whether one looks to the north, south, east, or west, the prominent object catching the eye will be the pearl! Why is this? Several suggestions have been offered.
   a. The pearl was the precious gem God selected to depict the church (Matt. 13:45, 46).

    b. The pearl comes from a body of water, which is often used to symbolize
       Gentile peoples—The church will consist mostly of Gentiles.
    c. The pearl is created (unlike a diamond or piece of gold) by a living
       organism—An oyster experiences a grain of sand in its side. To protect
       itself, the little creature coats the foreign object with layer upon layer of its
       own substance until finally a beautiful pearl is formed. Thus, the gates of
       heaven may be made of pearl to remind the redeemed that each person was
       once a tiny little grain of sinful sand in the sight and side of almighty God.
       To solve this problem he forgave our iniquities by coating us with layer
       upon layer of his own love. We thus become "the pearl of great price" by the
       marvelous grace of God.
7. The main street—The central boulevard of the new Jerusalem is composed of
   pure transparent gold. ". . . and the street of the city was pure gold, as it were
   transparent glass" (Rev. 21:21b). When one considers the price of gold, the total
   worth of this city becomes incomprehensible.
8. The throne—"The LORD hath prepared his throne in the heavens; and his
   kingdom ruleth over all" (Psa. 103:19).
      At least three biblical men were allowed to gaze upon the awesome sight of
   God's throne.
    a. Isaiah—"In the year that king Uzziah died I saw also the Lord sitting upon a
       throne, high and lifted up, and his train filled the temple. Above it stood the
       seraphims: each one had six wings; with twain he covered his face, and with
       twain he covered his feet, and with twain he did fly. And one cried unto
       another, and said, Holy, holy, holy, is the LORD of hosts: the whole earth is
       full of his glory" (Isa. 6:1-3).
    b. Daniel—"I beheld till the thrones were cast down, and the Ancient of days
       did sit, whose garment was white as snow, and the hair of his head like the
       pure wool: his throne was like the fiery flame, and his wheels as burning
       fire. A fiery stream issued and came forth from before him: thousand
       thousands ministered unto him, and ten thousand times ten thousand stood
       before him: the judgment was set, and the books were opened" (Dan. 7:9-10).
    c. John—"And immediately I was in the spirit: and, behold, a throne was set in
       heaven, and one sat on the throne. . . . And before the throne there was a sea
       of glass like unto crystal: and in the midst of the throne, and round about the
       throne, were four beasts full of eyes before and behind" (Rev. 4:2, 6).
    God's throne is referred to more than 40 times in the New Testament alone.
9. The river of life—"And he shewed me a pure river of water of life, clear as
   crystal, proceeding out of the throne of God and of the Lamb" (Rev. 22:1).
      The Holy Spirit doubtless meant to make at least some reference to this river
   when he inspired David to write: "And he shall be like a tree planted by the
   rivers of water, that bringeth forth his fruit in his season; his leaf also shall not
   wither; and whatsoever he doeth shall prosper" (Psa. 1:3). "There is a river, the
   streams whereof shall make glad the city of God, the holy place of the
   tabernacles of the most High" (Psa. 46:4).
10. The tree of life—"In the midst of the street of it, and on either side of the river,
    was there the tree of life, which bare twelve manner of fruits, and yielded her
    fruit every month: and the leaves of the tree were for the healing of the nations"
    (Rev. 22:2).
      When God created man and placed him in the Garden of Eden, he placed at

Adam's disposal (among many other things) the tree of life. But when man sinned, he was driven from Eden and from this tree (Gen. 2:9; 3:24). At this point in human history the tree of life disappears, but here in the new Jerusalem it will blossom and bloom as never before.

In his book *Reveling through Revelation* Dr. J. Vernon McGee writes the following words concerning this river and this tree.

> Up to this chapter, the New Jerusalem seems to be all mineral and no vegetable. Its appearance is as the dazzling display of a fabulous jewelry store, but there is no soft grass to sit upon, no green trees to enjoy, and no water to drink or food to eat. However, here introduced are the elements which add a rich softness to this city of elaborate beauty. (p. 91)

Paul Lee Tan writes:

> Because of the location of the tree of life "on either side of the river," theologians have understood the "tree" to be not a single tree, but a single kind of tree . . . a row of trees on either side of the river. Others, however, see one tree planted at the middle of the river, with branches extending to both banks. The tree is large enough to span the river, so that the river is in the midst of the street, and the tree is on both sides of the river. (*The New Jerusalem*, p. 28)

D. The citizens of heaven—Who will dwell in this magnificent metropolis beyond the Milky Way?
  1. The holy and elect angels
    a. By name—There are but two holy angels referred to by name in the scriptures.
      (1) Michael (Dan. 10:13, 21; 12:1; Jude 9; Rev. 12:7)
      (2) Gabriel (Dan. 8:16; 9:21; Luke 1:19, 26)
    b. By number—God, of course, knows their number, but they are presented to men as uncountable. There may be as many angels as there are stars in the heavens, for angels are often associated with the stars.
      "The chariots of God are twenty thousand, even thousands of angels: the Lord is among them, as in Sinai, in the holy place" (Psa. 68:17). "But ye are come unto mount Sion, and unto the city of the living God, the heavenly Jerusalem, and to an innumerable company of angels" (Heb. 12:22). "And I beheld, and I heard the voice of many angels round about the throne and the beasts and the elders: and the number of them was ten thousand times ten thousand, and thousands of thousands" (Rev. 5:11).
    c. By notation—Several ranks of angels are described in the Bible:
      (1) Seraphim (Isa. 6:1-7)
      (2) Cherubim (Gen. 3:24; Exod. 25:18-20; Ezek. 1:4-28; 10:1-22)
      (3) Living creatures (Rev. 4:6-9; 5:8; 6:1-7)
      (4) Ruling angels (Eph. 1:12; 3:10; Col. 1:16; 2:10; 1 Pet. 3:22)
      (5) Guardian angels (Matt. 18:10; Heb. 1:14)
      (6) Angels associated with horses and chariots (2 Kings 2:11; 6:17; Psa. 68:17; Zech. 1:8-11; Rev. 19:14)
      (7) Archangels (1 Thess. 4:16; Jude 9)
  2. The church—"And after these things I heard a great voice of much people in heaven, saying, Alleluia; Salvation, and glory, and honour, and power, unto the

Lord our God. . . . Let us be glad and rejoice, and give honour to him: for the marriage of the Lamb is come, and his wife hath made herself ready. And to her was granted that she should be arrayed in fine linen, clean and white: for the fine linen is the righteousness of saints" (Rev. 19:1, 7-8).

"And there came unto me one of the seven angels which had the seven vials full of the seven last plagues, and talked with me, saying, Come hither, I will shew thee the bride, the Lamb's wife" (Rev. 21:9). "And the Spirit and the bride say, Come. And let him that heareth say, Come. And let him that is athirst come. And whosoever will, let him take the water of life freely" (Rev. 22:17).

3. Saved Israel—Although the new Jerusalem is basically a wedding present from the Bridegroom (Christ) to the bride (the church), Israel nevertheless is also invited to dwell within these jasper walls. The following passages bear this out:

"But now they desire a better country, that is, an heavenly: wherefore God is not ashamed to be called their God: for he hath prepared for them a city" (Heb. 11:16). "And while they went to buy, the bridegroom came; and they that were ready went in with him to the marriage: and the door was shut. . . . His lord said unto him, Well done, good and faithful servant; thou hast been faithful over a few things, I will make thee ruler over many things: enter thou into the joy of thy lord" (Matt. 25:10, 23).

Our Lord quotes these words during his Olivet Discourse. In relating two parables he likens saved Israel to some prepared wedding guests (parable of the Ten Virgins), and later as two faithful servants (parable of the Talents). He thus pictures saved Israel as joining the bride and the Bridegroom.

4. All the redeemed who ever lived—"And they sung a new song, saying, Thou art worthy to take the book, and to open the seals thereof: for thou wast slain, and hast redeemed us to God by thy blood out of every kindred, and tongue, and people, and nation" (Rev. 5:9). "After this I beheld, and, lo, a great multitude, which no man could number, of all nations, and kindreds, and people, and tongues, stood before the throne, and before the Lamb, clothed with white robes, and palms in their hands" (Rev. 7:9).

5. The Father—We have previously noted those occasions when Isaiah (Isa. 6:1-3), Daniel (Dan. 7:9-10), and John (Rev. 4:2, 6) saw heaven's throne and someone seated upon it. The context of all three passages strongly indicate this figure was the Father himself.

6. The Son—"And I beheld, and, lo, in the midst of the throne and of the four beasts, and in the midst of the elders, stood a Lamb as it had been slain, having seven horns and seven eyes, which are the seven Spirits of God sent forth into all the earth" (Rev. 5:6).

Here we learn that not only is the Lamb of God an occupant of heaven, but the very source and strength and center of heaven, without which there could be no heaven. Thus we see:

The *light* of heaven is the face of Jesus.

The *joy* of heaven is the presence of Jesus.

The *song* of heaven is the name of Jesus.

The *theme* of heaven is the work of Jesus.

The *fullness* of heaven is the person of Jesus.

   a. In the book of Revelation John refers to Jesus as a Lamb no less than 27 times—From these verses we see that heaven's Hero will be:

      (1) A slain Lamb (5:6)

(2) A redeeming Lamb (5:9)

(3) A worthy Lamb (5:12)

(4) A comforting Lamb (7:17)

(5) A life-giving Lamb (13:8)

(6) An overcoming Lamb (12:11; 17:14)

(7) An eternal Lamb (5:13)

(8) An angry Lamb (6:18)

(9) A loving Lamb (19:7)

(10) A glorious Lamb (21:23)

b. In addition to the title of Lamb, the following names should be added for this "Jewel of the new Jerusalem," Jesus Christ:

(1) The Faithful Witness (1:5a)

(2) The First Begotten of the Dead (1:5b)

(3) The Prince of the Kings of the Earth (1:5c)

(4) The Alpha and Omega (1:8)

(5) The Beginning and the End (1:8b)

(6) The Son of man (1:13)

(7) The Son of God (2:18)

(8) The Lion of the tribe of Judah (5:5a)

(9) The Root of David (5:5b)

(10) The King of Saints (15:3)

(11) The Lord of Lords (17:14a)

(12) The King of Kings (17:14b)

(13) The Word of God (19:13)

(14) The Bright and Morning Star (22:16)

(15) Jesus (22:16)

7. The Holy Spirit—Although the Spirit of God is not as prominent as the Father or Son, he is unquestionably an occupant of the new Jerusalem, as attested by the following passages: "And I heard a voice from heaven saying unto me, Write, Blessed are the dead which die in the Lord from henceforth: Yea, saith the Spirit, that they may rest from their labours; and their works do follow them" (Rev. 14:13). "And the Spirit and the bride say, Come. And let him that heareth say, Come. And let him that is athirst come. And whosoever will, let him take the water of life freely" (Rev. 22:17).

E. The counterpart of heaven (the relationship of the heavenly Jerusalem with the earthly Jerusalem)—There will be two fabulous cities of God in the future. One is located on the earth. It will be known as Jehovah Tsidkenu, meaning "the LORD our righteousness," (Jer. 23:6; 33:16), and as Jehovah Shammah, meaning "the LORD is there" (Ezek. 48:35).

The circumference of the earthly Jerusalem during the Millennium will be "eighteen thousand measures" (Ezek. 48:35), or about six miles. The heavenly city is suspended in space, and, as we have previously noted, is many times larger. To summarize, it would seem all resurrected and raptured believers will reside in the heavenly city, but will reign upon the earthly city. There is disagreement concerning whether the earthly Jerusalem will be phased out after the Millennium or continue alongside the heavenly city forever.

F. The challenges in heaven—A popular but totally perverted concept of heaven would describe that future life in the skies in terms of some disembodied spirits piously perched on fleecy clouds and strumming their golden harps. This may be heaven according to Walt Disney, but not according to the New Testament. The Scriptures would indicate:

1. Heaven will be a place of singing—"Serve the LORD with gladness: come before his presence with singing" (Psa. 100:2). "Sing, O heavens; and be joyful, O earth; and break forth into singing, O mountains: for the LORD hath comforted his people, and will have mercy upon his afflicted" (Isa. 49:13).

   "And they sung a new song, saying, Thou art worthy to take the book, and to open the seals thereof: for thou wast slain, and hast redeemed us to God by thy blood out of every kindred, and tongue, and people, and nation" (Rev. 5:9). "And they sung as it were a new song before the throne, and before the four beasts, and the elders: and no man could learn that song but the hundred and forty and four thousand, which were redeemed from the earth" (Rev. 14:3). "And they sing the song of Moses the servant of God, and the song of the Lamb, saying, Great and marvelous are thy works, Lord God Almighty; just and true are thy ways, thou King of saints. Who shall not fear thee, O Lord, and glorify thy name? for thou only art holy: for all nations shall come and worship before thee; for thy judgments are made manifest" (Rev. 15:3-4).

2. Heaven will be a place of fellowship—One of the most beloved gospel songs is entitled "Leaning on the Everlasting Arms." The first stanza begins: "What a fellowship, what a joy divine. . . ." Sometimes, however, as one observes the petty squabbling that goes on in local churches, this verse might be rephrased to read: "What? A Fellowship? What? A joy divine?" But in heaven real and eternal fellowship will prevail.

   Not only will believers enjoy blessed fellowship with other believers but, even more important, we shall know and be known by the Savior in a far more intimate way than ever possible here on earth. Note the things this Good and Great and Chief Shepherd will do for his sheep in heaven as listed by John:

   (a) He will feed us that hidden heavenly manna; he will give us a new name (Rev. 2:17).
   (b) He will lead us beside the living waters and dry all our tears (Rev. 7:17).
   (c) He will allow us to sit with him on his throne (Rev. 3:21).
   (d) He will array us in fine linen (Rev. 19:8).
   (e) He will reward us (Rev. 22:12).

3. Heaven will be a place of serving—"Therefore are they before the throne of God, and serve him day and night in his temple: and he that sitteth on the throne shall dwell among them" (Rev. 7:15). "And there shall be no more curse: but the throne of God and of the Lamb shall be in it; and his servants shall serve him:" (Rev. 22:3). While we cannot be dogmatic on the exact nature of this service, we do know from the following passage that a portion of our labor for the Lamb will be that of exercising authority and judgment over angels.

   Erwin Lutzer suggests:

   That word *servant* is found frequently in the book of Revelation for it pictures a continuation of the relationship we even now have with Christ. However, the word *serve* used here is used primarily in the New Testament for service that is carried on within the Temple or church (Matt. 4:10; Luke 2:37; Acts 24:14). Thus we shall serve Him in that special, intimate relationship available only to those who are included within the inner circle of the redeemed. David Gregg gives his conception of what that kind of work will be like:

"It is work as free from care and toil and fatigue as is the wing-stroke of the jubilant lark when it soars into the sunlight of a fresh, clear day and, spontaneously and for self-relief, pours out its thrilling carol. Work up there is a matter of self-relief, as well as a matter of obedience to the ruling will of God. It is work according to one's tastes and delight and ability. If tastes vary there, if abilities vary there, then occupations will vary there." (*Coming to Grips with Heaven*, p. 31)

4. Heaven will be a place of learning—"For we know in part, and we prophesy in part. But when that which is perfect is come, then that which is in part shall be done away" (1 Cor. 13:9-10).

"Wherefore I also, after I heard of your faith in the Lord Jesus, and love unto all the saints, cease not to give thanks for you, making mention of you in my prayers; that the God of our Lord Jesus Christ, the Father of glory, may give unto you the spirit of wisdom and revelation in the knowledge of him: the eyes of your understanding being enlightened; that ye may know what is the hope of his calling, and what the riches of the glory of his inheritance in the saints, and what is the exceeding greatness of his power to us-ward who believe, according to the working of his mighty power, which he wrought in Christ, when he raised him from the dead, and set him at his own right hand in the heavenly places, far above all principality, and power, and might, and dominion, and every name that is named, not only in this world, but also in that which is to come" (Eph. 1:15-21).

It is evident, as one ponders the theology of Paul's prayer here in Ephesians, that all these glorious spiritual truths cannot possibly be learned in their fullest sense by the believer down here. These precious principles must surely find their consummation in eternity. This is also true concerning his later prayer in the same epistle: "For this cause I bow my knees unto the Father of our Lord Jesus Christ, . . . that Christ may dwell in your hearts by faith; that ye, being rooted and grounded in love, may be able to comprehend with all saints what is the breadth, and length, and depth, and height; and to know the love of Christ, which passeth knowledge, that ye might be filled with all the fulness of God" (Eph. 3:14, 17-19).

What will we learn about in Heaven?

a. We will learn concerning the *person* of God—Let us suppose in heaven we are able to double our learning each year concerning the person and attributes of God. This is not at all an unreasonable assumption, for the Christian will possess a sinless and glorified body, along with a holy and tireless desire to know more about Jesus! So here is a believer who begins eternity with x amount of knowledge about God. At the beginning of his second year he has double this, the third year four times as much, the fourth year he knows eight times as much, etc. By the end of his eleventh year he will increase his knowledge concerning God a thousandfold. At the conclusion of his twenty-first year the figure jumps to one million. At the end of the thirty-first year the number leaps to one billion. Following the forty-first year it reaches one trillion. As he finishes his first century in eternity his knowledge of God (doubling each year) would reach 10^{30} (one followed by 30 zeros) times what it originally was.

This figure is thousands of times more than the combined total of all the grains of sand on all the seashores of the earth. But this number marks his first 100 years. How much knowledge doubling will he have experienced at the end of his first one million years? This staggering figure cannot even be comprehended by the mortal mind, but whatever it is, and however many zeros it represents, it will double itself the very next year. The point of all the above is simply this. Throughout the untold and unnumbered trillions and trillions of years in timeless eternity, each child of God can double his or her learning about the Creator each year and yet never even remotely exhaust the awesome height, depth, or length of the Person of God. Our testimony will continuously be: "O the depth of the riches both of the wisdom and knowledge of God! how unsearchable are his judgments, and his ways past finding out!" (Rom. 11:33).

b. We will learn concerning the *precepts* of God, the Bible itself—Dedicated and brilliant godly scholars have throughout history given their lives in the study of but a handful of verses, testifying they only dipped their feet in the mighty ocean of the truths involved. Surely one could spend billions of years pondering each of the 31,173 scriptural verses without fully probing their awesome depths.

c. We will learn concerning the *plan* of God—One of the most painful questions asked here on earth by Christians is why a loving and wise God allows certain terrible tragedies to occur. As an example, here is a young, spirit-filled pastor. He has spent a number of years diligently preparing for the ministry. His wife has sacrificed to help put him through school. Now all this is paying off. His church is experiencing amazing growth. Souls are saved weekly. New converts are baptized each Sunday. Additional Sunday school busses are purchased and a new building is planned. A skeptical community slowly finds itself being profoundly influenced by this vibrant and exciting pastor and his people. Suddenly, without any warning, the minister is killed in a freak accident. Shortly after the funeral the still-confused and stunned congregation extends a call to another man. But the new minister shows little compassion and less leadership ability. Soon the flock is scattered and the once-thrilling testimony of a growing and glowing work is all but stilled.

How many times since Abel's martyrdom at the dawn of human history have similar tragedies like this taken place? But the searing and searching question remains: Why does God permit such terrible things? We may rest assured that in heaven God will take each of us aside and explain fully the reason for all our suffering and trials. We then will say the words once stated by a Galilean crowd in Jesus' day: "He hath done all things well" (Mark 7:37).

d. We will learn concerning the *power* of God—"In the beginning God created the heaven and the earth" (Gen. 1:1).

Just how vast is our universe? It is so huge that it takes a beam of light (which travels some 700 million miles per hour) over 10 billion years to cross the known universe. Within this universe are untold trillions of stars, planets, and other heavenly bodies. God made them all to instruct man concerning his power and glory: "The heavens declare the glory of God; and the firmament sheweth his handiwork" (Psa. 19:1). "He telleth the number of the stars; he calleth them all by their names" (Psa. 147:4). "Lift up your eyes on high, and behold who hath created these things, that bringeth out their host by number: he calleth them all by names by the greatness of his might, for that he is strong in power; not one faileth" (Isa. 40:26). We shall someday therefore visit each star and explore every corner of our Father's universe.

5. Heaven will be a place of testifying—"Let the redeemed of the Lord say so" (Psa. 107:2).

"Jesus . . . saith . . . Go . . . tell them how great things the Lord hath done for thee, and hath had compassion on thee" (Mark 5:19).

G. The clarifications concerning heaven—Here are some suggested answers to at least five of the most frequently asked questions concerning heaven.

1. What kind of bodies will we have in Heaven? In essence, our bodies will be like the glorified body of Jesus. "Who shall change our vile body, that it may be fashioned like unto his glorious body, according to the working whereby he is able even to subdue all things unto himself" (Phil. 3:21). "Beloved, now are we the sons of God, and it doth not yet appear what we shall be: but we know that, when he shall appear, we shall be like him; for we shall see him as he is" (1 John 3:2).

Note the features of Christ's resurrected body:

a. It consisted of flesh and bone—"Behold my hands and my feet, that it is I myself: handle me, and see; for a spirit hath not flesh and bones, as ye see me have. And when he had thus spoken, he shewed them his hands and his feet" (Luke 24:39-40).

b. He ate in this body, partaking of fish, honeycomb, and bread (Luke 24:41-43; John 21:12-15).

c. His body was not subjected to the regular laws of time and gravity (John 20:19; Luke 24:31, 36).

In 1 Corinthians 15 Paul answers questions concerning this transformation. In verse 44 he writes, "There is a natural body and there is a spiritual body." What is the difference?

Consider a book with a sheet of plain white paper stuck inside it. In this illustration the book is man's body and the paper sheet is his spirit. Down here the book "bosses" the spirit. It has the final say. This is the natural body, governed by the physical laws of gravity and time. But now take the white sheet out of the book and wrap it around the book like a cover. Now the sheet (spirit) is on top. It has the final say. This is the spiritual body, unaffected by the physical laws of gravity or time, but enjoys the blessings of eternity.

2. Will our bodies be recognizable? In other words, will we know each other? In this the Scriptures answer with an emphatic yes. During his transfiguration, our Lord spoke freely with Moses and Elijah centuries after both these Old Testament heroes departed from this earth. "And, behold, there appeared unto them Moses and Elias talking with him" (Matt. 17:3).

Yet they are still recognized as Moses and Elijah. In addition to this, the Apostle John, during his vision of the Revelation, sees and recognizes the differences between elders, angels, and various redeemed peoples from all the nations of the earth. Perhaps the apex of this beautiful truth is found in Paul's love chapter: "For now we see through a glass, darkly; but then face to face: now I know in part; but then shall I know even as also I am known" (1 Cor. 13:12).

3. What age will we be in heaven? Thomas Aquinas believed (based on Ephesians 4:13) that the human body would have the development appropriate to the age of 30, which was that of the risen Christ in his full, human maturity. Thus those who were younger and those who were older would be resurrected and transformed to look like what they were when they were 30 or what they would have looked like had they reached the age of 30.

Of course this is but sheer speculation. We simply do not know, but it is not at all unreasonable to conclude whatever the age, every believer will enjoy the maximum physically, spiritually, socially, and intellectually.

4. What about loved ones not in heaven? Erwin Lutzer offers the following:

> The question is often asked how we can be happy in Heaven if one or more of our relatives is in Hell. Can a child, for example, enjoy the glories of eternity knowing that a father or a mother will always be absent from the celebration? Or can a godly mother serve and worship with joy knowing that her precious son will be in torment forever? That question has so vexed the minds of theologians that some have actually asserted that in Heaven God will blank out a part of our memory. The child will not know that his parents are lost in Hell; the mother will not remember that she had a son.
>
> However, it is unlikely that we will know less in Heaven than we do on earth. It is not characteristic of God to resolve a problem by expanding the sphere of human ignorance. That is especially true in Heaven, where we will have better mental faculties than on earth. In Heaven we shall be comforted, not because we know less than we did on earth but because we know more.
>
> It is more likely that God will wipe away all tears by explaining His ultimate purposes. We will look at Heaven and Hell from His viewpoint and say that He did all things well. If God can be content knowing that unbelievers are in Hell, so will we.
>
> I expect that all who are in Heaven will live with the knowledge that justice was fully served and that God's plan was right. And with such an explanation and perspective, our emotions will mirror those of our heavenly Father. Jonathan Edwards said that Heaven will have no pity for Hell, not because the saints are unloving but because they are perfectly loving. They will see everything in conformity with God's love, justice, and glory. Thus with both head and heart we will worship the Lord without regret, sorrow, or misgivings about our Father's plan. (*Coming to Grips with Heaven*, pp. 38–39)

Obviously not all would agree with Lutzer's conclusions. We simply do not know how God will solve this problem.

5. What will our relationships be with our loved ones in heaven? In other words, will a special rapport still exist between husband and wife, father and son, mother and daughter? Again, we are not specifically told. We do know glorified believers in heaven will not marry and raise children (Matt. 22:30). However, it would seem (at least to this author) that certain individuals in heaven will continue to be perhaps closer to me than others. Here I would refer to Sue (my wife), Matthew (my son), etc.

6. What about those who die as babies? The vast majority of Bible students hold all infants and very young children go to heaven upon dying. Both David and Jesus definitely indicated this.

   a. David's testimony—"And he said, While the child was yet alive, I fasted and wept: for I said, Who can tell whether GOD will be gracious to me, that the child may live? But now he is dead, wherefore should I fast? can I bring him back again? I shall go to him, but he shall not return to me" (2 Sam. 12:22-23).

   b. Jesus' testimony—"And Jesus called a little child unto him, and set him in the midst of them, and said, Verily I say unto you, Except ye be converted, and become as little children, ye shall not enter into the kingdom of heaven" (Matt. 18:2-3). "But Jesus said, Suffer little children, and forbid them not, to come unto me: for of such is the kingdom of heaven" (Matt. 19:14).

H. The contrasts and comparisons concerning heaven

  1. Those elements absent in heaven:

    a. No more sea (Rev. 21:1)

    b. No more tears, pain, or death (1 Cor. 15:54-57; Rev. 21:4)

    c. No more insecurity or night (Rev. 21:25)

    d. No more sin (Rev. 21:27)

    e. No more sickness nor curse (Rev. 22:2)

    f. No more satanic opposition (Rev. 20:10)

    g. No more thirst, hunger, or excessive heat (Rev. 7:16)

    h. No more condemnation (John 5:24)

    i. No more corruption (1 Cor. 15:54; 1 Pet. 1:4)

  2. Those elements present in heaven:

    a. Glory (John 17:24; Rom. 8:18; Rev. 21:23)—"And the city had no need of the sun, neither of the moon, to shine in it: for the glory of God did lighten it, and the Lamb is the light thereof" (Rev. 21:23).

    b. Beauty—"Out of Zion, the perfection of beauty, God hath shined" (Psa. 50:2).

      Try to imagine the excitement of walking on the lower level of heaven and looking straight up through 1,400 levels of pure gold streets all sparkling as crystal, strong and glorious—incalculable tons of gold, all worth some $300 an ounce by American monetary standards. Then look around you, and behold majestic mansions and magnificent houses as far as the eye can see, all made of this same highly purified gold. It is, indeed, a crystal city with nothing to hinder the flow of light and color. Everything is constructed of durable materials; nothing that could decay, rot, mold, or rust is used here, for this city will endure eternally.

    c. Divine light (Isa. 60:1-3, 19-20; Rev. 21:23-24)—"And the city had no need of the sun, neither of the moon, to shine in it: for the glory of God did lighten it, and the Lamb is the light thereof" (Rev. 21:23).

    d. Unity—"That in the dispensation of the fulness of times he might gather together in one all things in Christ, both which are in heaven, and which are on earth; even in him" (Eph. 1:10).

    e. Joy—"Thou wilt shew me the path of life: in thy presence is fulness of joy; at thy right hand there are pleasures for evermore" (Psa. 16:11).

    f. Righteousness—"Nevertheless we, according to his promise, look for new heavens and a new earth, wherein dwelleth righteousness" (2 Pet. 3:13).

THE DOCTRINE OF SATAN

I. The Existence of Satan—There is scarcely a culture, tribe, or society to be found in this world that does not have some concept or fear of an invisible evil power. This has been attested by Christian missionaries and secular anthropologists alike. Witch doctors, shrunken heads, voodoo dolls, and totem poles all give dramatic evidence of this universal fear. One may well ask where this fear came from and of whom are they afraid. The study of the doctrine of Satan may not thrill the soul of man, but it will answer these questions.

A. His existence is doubted by the world.
   1. As shown by the typical "Walt Disney cartoon concept"—Most of the world today pictures the devil as a medieval and mythical two-horned, fork-tailed impish creature, dressed in red flannel underwear, busily pitching coal into the furnace of hell. Satan is ignored or downplayed by the world.
   2. As shown by the denial from liberal pulpits—Satan is ignored or downplayed in liberal churches today. These Christ-denying liberals have, of course, long since thrown out such concepts as the "old devil" and the "new birth." They now leave out the *d* in devil and add an *o* to God. It's a shame, but most words like *hell, damned,* and *devil* are found in the vocabularies of factory workers, politicians, school children, college students, and even professional people. They are not heard from behind pulpits of liberal churches—where they should be heard. These liberal churches are the places from which people need to hear these words. In the fifties, a national secular magazine took a poll of some 5,000 American clergymen and discovered that a full 73 percent ridiculed the concept of a personal devil of any sort.
   3. As shown by the silence from conservative pulpits—Satan is even ignored or downplayed among many Bible-believers. Many Bible-believing pastors and lay people are, it would seem, extremely reluctant to "give the devil his due." Some time ago, this author wrote an article entitled, "If I Were the Devil." In this article the following points were stressed:

   > The first thing I would do would be to deny my own existence. The Bible informs us that God desires, perhaps above all else, to be fully believed in. "But without faith it is impossible to please him: for he that cometh to God must believe that he is, and that he is a rewarder of them that diligently seek him" (Heb. 11:6). But this is not so with Satan! This disciple of doubt seems to thrive best when he is either underestimated, ignored or denied.
   >
   > Suppose there is a Bible-believing church which is going through a spiritual crisis. For some months no soul has walked its aisles. The attendance

and offerings are down and the members are becoming restless. All Bible pastors have had these experiences. Finally, in desperation, a special committee is appointed by the congregation to discover the source of this coldness and lifelessness. After considerable prayer and probing, the committee submits its report. What are its findings? I believe it may be safely assumed that the average committee would lay the blame on one or more of the following: (1) the pastor; (2) certain officials; (3) a cold congregation; or (4) a difficult neighborhood.

But what fact-finding group would return the following indictment? "We believe the main source of our heartaches for the past few months is satanic! We believe the reason no souls have been saved recently is due to an all-out attack on our church by the devil! We close this report with a strong recommendation that the congregation call a special meeting, rebuke Satan, plead the blood of Christ and claim the victory!"

If I were the devil I would deny my existence in the world and downplay it in the local church, thus freeing me to go about my business unheeded, unhindered, and unchecked. (*The Baptist Bulletin,* Dec. 1971, p. 13)

The following poem by an unknown author vividly describes this devil-denying attitude:

The Devil

Men don't believe in a devil now, as their fathers used to do.
They've opened the door to the broadest creed to let his majesty thru.
There isn't a print of his cloven feet or a fiery dart from his bow
To be found on earth or anywhere, for the world has voted it so.
But who is mixing the fatal draught that kills both heart and brain,
And loads the earth each passing year with ten hundred thousand slain?
Who blights the bloom of the land today with the fiery breath of hell?
If the devil isn't or never was - won't somebody please rise and tell?
Who dogs the steps of the toiling saint and digs the pits for his feet?
Who sows the tares in the field of time when God is sowing pure wheat.
But the devil is voted just not to be - and of course the thing is true—
But who is doing the kind of work the devil is supposed to do?
Won't somebody step to the front right now—and immediately begin to show—
How the frauds and the crimes of the day spring up—for surely we want to know!
The devil was fairly voted out—and of course the devil's gone—
But simply folk would like to know, who carries his business on?

This overall scriptural ignorance concerning the person of Satan has, in all probability, greatly contributed to one of the most frightening developments in the final decades of the twentieth century, namely, the worship of Satan.
Josh McDowell observes:

In a chapter on Satanism today, William Petersen in *Those Curious New Cults* comments on the fact that since the mid-1960s Satanism is making a comeback. He points to the catalyst for the strong upswing as being the box office smash of *Rosemary's Baby.* Of the film he states:

"Anton Szandor La Vey, self-styled high priest of San Francisco's First Church of Satan and author of *The Satanic Bible,* played the role of the devil.

Later, he called the film the 'best paid commercial for Satanism since the Inquisition.' No doubt it was" (p. 75).

Many people are becoming involved in Satanism from all walks of life. They vary in age, occupation and educational background. (*Handbook of Today's Religions,* p. 237)

The Satanic Bible has reportedly sold over 250,000 copies and is now in its third printing. Concerning the doctrine of Satanism, La Vey writes: "It is a blatantly selfish, brutal religion. It is based on the belief that man is inherently a selfish, violent creature, that life is a Darwinian struggle for survival of the fittest, that the earth will be ruled by those who fight to win" (Ibid., p. 238).

B. His existence is declared by the Bible.

1. The devil is mentioned in seven Old Testament books—Genesis, 1 Chronicles, Job (12 times), Psalms, Isaiah, Ezekiel, and Zechariah.

2. He is to be found in 19 New Testament books and is referred to by every New Testament writer.

3. He is referred to by our Lord Jesus Christ some 15 times—Note but a few of these.

   a. In Matthew 4, Jesus was not arguing with some type of principle in the desert, but with a vile person by the name of Satan—"Then saith Jesus unto him, Get thee hence, Satan: for it is written, Thou shalt worship the Lord thy God, and him only shalt thou serve" (Matt. 4:10).

   b. In Matthew 16, Jesus realized that Satan was prompting or influencing Simon Peter to rebuke him—"But he turned, and said unto Peter, Get thee behind me, Satan: thou art an offence unto me: for thou savourest not the things that be of God, but those that be of men" (Matt. 16:23).

   c. In Luke 22, Jesus speaks again to Simon Peter—"And the Lord said, Simon, Simon, behold, Satan hath desired to have you, that he may sift you as wheat" (Luke 22:31).

   d. In Luke 10, Jesus speaks of seeing Satan fall—"And he said unto them, I beheld Satan as lightning fall from heaven" (Luke 10:18).

   e. In Matthew 25, Jesus speaks of the final abode of Satan and his followers (the unsaved)—"Then shall he say also unto them on the left hand, Depart from me, ye cursed, into everlasting fire, prepared for the devil and his angels" (Matt. 25:41).

   f. In John 8, Jesus accuses a group of ungodly Pharisees of being from their father, the devil—"Ye are of your father the devil, and the lusts of your father ye will do. He was a murderer from the beginning, and abode not in the truth, because there is no truth in him. When he speaketh a lie, he speaketh of his own: for he is a liar, and the father of it" (John 8:44).

   g. In John 6, Jesus reveals that one of his disciples, one of the Twelve, was at that point (early in his ministry) being influenced by Satan—Later on, that person (Judas) would become possessed by Satan. "Jesus answered them, Have not I chosen you twelve, and one of you is a devil?" (John 6:70).

   Thus, we cannot believe in the Bible and deny the existence of Satan.

II. The Origin of Satan—Often a twofold question is asked concerning Satan: "Why did God create the devil, and why doesn't God destroy him?" A simple answer to these questions would be: "He didn't, and he will!"

There are two important passages in the Word of God concerning the origin and fall of the devil.

A. His origin and fall as related by the prophet Ezekiel—In his book, Ezekiel predicts coming judgment upon the wicked city of Tyre in chapters 26, 27 and the first part of chapter 28. This has already been fulfilled, for the city was sacked by Nebuchadnezzar in 573 B.C. and later destroyed by Alexander in 332 B.C. But in verses 12-19 of Ezekiel 28, the prophet goes beyond the earthly scene of pronouncing judgment on the king (or prince) of Tyre at that time (whose name was Ithabaal II). Ezekiel describes for us the creation and judgment of a vile and vicious, nonhuman creature whose name we find out later to be Lucifer.

God often uses a backdoor approach—that is, he often addresses Satan through another source. For example, in Genesis 3 God pronounced doom upon the devil by addressing the serpent. Another example is in Matthew 16:23, when Jesus rebuked Satan by talking to Simon Peter. In Ezekiel 28 God used the king (or prince) of Tyre in order to really make a wider prophecy—actually, to get at the devil.

"Son of man, take up a lamentation upon the king of Tyrus, and say unto him, Thus saith the Lord GOD; Thou sealest up the sum, full of wisdom, and perfect in beauty. Thou hast been in Eden the garden of God; every precious stone was thy covering, the sardius, topaz, and the diamond, the beryl, the onyx, and the jasper, the sapphire, the emerald, and the carbuncle, and gold: the workmanship of thy tabrets and of thy pipes was prepared in thee in the day that thou wast created. Thou art the anointed cherub that covereth; and I have set thee so: thou wast upon the holy mountain of God; thou hast walked up and down in the midst of the stones of fire. Thou wast perfect in thy ways from the day that thou wast created, till iniquity was found in thee. By the multitude of thy merchandise they have filled the midst of thee with violence, and thou hast sinned: therefore I will cast thee as profane out of the mountain of God: and I will destroy thee, O covering cherub, from the midst of the stones of fire. Thine heart was lifted up because of thy beauty, thou hast corrupted thy wisdom by reason of thy brightness: I will cast thee to the ground, I will lay thee before kings, that they may behold thee" (Ezek. 28:12-17).

We now note in some detail the key phrases in this passage.

1. "Thou sealest up the sum"—This is literally, "You set the seal on perfection."
2. "Full of wisdom, and perfect in beauty"—This was thus the most brilliant and beautiful creature ever to exist. Lucifer became the pattern of perfection and beauty.
3. "Thou hast been in Eden, the garden of God"—The word *Eden* means "delight." What garden did Ezekiel refer to here? There are at least three suggestions:
   a. A reference to the earthly, Adamic garden, man's original home (see Gen. 2:8, 10, 15; 3:23-24; 4:16)
   b. A reference to a heavenly, angelic garden—If it exists, this garden would thus serve as a pattern for the earthly one, as did the heavenly tabernacle (see Exod. 25:9, 40; Heb. 8:1-2, 5; 9:23; Rev. 15:5).
   c. A reference to both gardens
4. "Every precious stone was thy covering"—Lucifer was decked with dazzling stones, somewhat resembling the display of costly gems in an expensive and exclusive jewelry store. This marks the second of three listings of these stones in the Bible. These are:
   a. In the high priest's breastplate, relating to the grace of God (Exod. 39:10-13)
   b. In the new Jerusalem, relating to the glory of God (Rev. 21:14, 19-21)

c. Surrounding the person of Lucifer, relating to the guardian of God (this is indicated in Ezek. 28:14)

5. "The workmanship of thy timbrels and of thy flutes"—Dr. J. Dwight Pentecost writes:

> Musical instruments were originally designed to be means of praising and worshiping God. It was not necessary for Lucifer to learn to play a musical instrument in order to praise God. If you please, he had a built-in pipe organ, or, he was an organ! That's what the prophet meant when he said, "The workmanship of thy tabrets and of thy pipes. . . ." Lucifer, because of his beauty, did what a musical instrument would do in the hands of a skilled musician—bring forth a psalm of praise to the glory of God. Lucifer didn't have to look for someone to play the organ so that he could sing the doxology—he was a doxology. (*Your Adversary, the Devil*, p. 16)

6. "Thou art the anointed cherub that covereth"—The word *cherub* is derived from the Hebrew root word *charab*, meaning "to cut," "to engrave," a meaning that carries with it the engraving on a coin, the idea of representation. F. C. Jennings writes: "The cherub, we gather from the word itself, was to be the representative of God . . . as the image cut on a coin represents fully the sovereign, or governor, that issues it. Compare Matt. 22:20-21" (*Satan, His Person, Work, Place, and Destiny*, p. 40).

Note the following concerning this cherub:

a. He was anointed—In the Old Testament there were three anointed offices—that of prophet, priest, and king. Here is a suggestion that Lucifer may have originally been created to function (under Christ) as heaven's prophet, priest, and king. But he failed. This may be the reason God separated these offices. It also may be that after the fall of Lucifer, God determined never again to entrust this power to only one person, whether it be a human being or an angel. We note this separation of the offices of "priest" and "king" in two specific Old Testament passages.

(1) In 1 Samuel 13 King Saul usurped the priest's office by offering a sacrifice—He was reproved by Samuel and punished by God (13:9-14).

(2) King Uzziah was a good and wise king, but like Lucifer, he allowed his heart to become power-hungry—In 2 Chronicles 26 King Uzziah usurped the priest's office. He was reproved by Azariah and 80 other priests, and he was punished by God.

> "But when he was strong, his heart was lifted up to his destruction: for he transgressed against the LORD his God, and went into the temple of the LORD to burn incense upon the altar of incense. And Azariah the priest went in after him, and with him fourscore priests of the LORD, that were valiant men: and they withstood Uzziah the king, and said unto him, It appertaineth not unto thee, Uzziah, to burn incense unto the LORD, but to the priests the sons of Aaron, that are consecrated to burn incense: go out of the sanctuary; for thou hast trespassed; neither shall it be for thine honour from the LORD God. Then Uzziah was wroth, and had a censer in his hand to burn incense: and while he was wroth with the priests, the leprosy even rose up in his forehead before the priests in the house of the LORD, from beside the incense altar. And Azariah the chief priest, and all the priests, looked upon him, and, behold, he was

leprous in his forehead, and they thrust him out from thence; yea, himself hasted also to go out, because the LORD had smitten him. And Uzziah the king was a leper unto the day of his death, and dwelt in a several house, being a leper; for he was cut off from the house of the LORD: and Jotham his son was over the king's house, judging the people of the land" (2 Chron. 26:16-21).

b. He was a guardian cherub—A cherub was a special kind of angelic being whose purpose was to protect God's holiness (see Gen. 3; Exod. 25; 1 Kings 6; Ezek. 1; Rev. 4). Both archaeological and biblical evidences suggest they bore the likeness of a lion, a calf, a man, and an eagle.

Apparently Lucifer was created (among other purposes) to demonstrate the earthly work of Christ, as pictured by the four Gospel writers:
(1) Matthew presents Christ as the lionlike king.
(2) Mark presents Christ as the calflike servant.
(3) Luke presents Christ as the perfect man.
(4) John presents Christ as the eaglelike God.
The book of Revelation seems to indicate that in heaven also this power was to be distributed among these four special cherubim—one with the appearance of a lion, one with the appearance of a calf, one with the appearance of an eagle, and the other with the appearance of a man. (See Rev. 4:6-8.)

7. "I have set thee so"—Stated another way, "I have appointed you to serve in this lofty position." Thus, angels, like men, owe both their creation and commission to God and God alone. (See John 15:16; Heb. 5:4.)

8. "Thou wast upon the holy mountain of God; thou hast walked up and down in the midst of the stones of fire"—Note two phrases here.
   a. "The holy mountain of God"—Both Isaiah and John speak of this mountain.
      (1) Isaiah connects it to the enemy of God—"For thou hast said in thine heart, I will ascend into heaven, I will exalt my throne above the stars of God: I will sit also upon the mount of the congregation, in the sides of the north" (Isa. 14:13).
      (2) John connects it to the Son of God and the glory of God—"And I looked, and, lo, a Lamb stood on the mount Sion, and with him an hundred forty and four thousand, having his Father's name written in their foreheads" (Rev. 14:1). "And he carried me away in the spirit to a great and high mountain, and shewed me that great city, the holy Jerusalem, descending out of heaven from God" (Rev. 21:10).
   b. "The stones of fire"—Compare what Ezekiel says here with what Moses said when he was allowed to see the glory of God: "Moses and Aaron, Nadab and Abihu, and the seventy elders of Israel went up and saw the God of Israel. Under his feet was something like a pavement made of sapphire, clear as the sky itself. . . . And the glory of the LORD settled on Mount Sinai. For six days the cloud covered the mountain, and on the seventh day the LORD called to Moses from within the cloud. To the Israelites the glory of the LORD looked like a consuming fire on top of the mountain" (Exod. 24:9-10, 16-17, NIV).

"The appearance of the living creatures was like burning coals of fire or like torches. Fire moved back and forth among the creatures; it was bright, and lightning flashed out of it" (Ezek. 1:13, NIV).

9. "Till iniquity was found in thee"—What was the nature of this iniquity? In a nutshell, pride and self-will.
   a. Pride—"Thine heart was lifted up because of thy beauty" (Ezek. 28:17a).
   b. Self-will—"For thou has said in thine heart, I will" (Isa. 14:13.). Thus, the very *worst* sin was the very *first* sin. "Pride goeth before destruction, and an haughty spirit before a fall" (Prov. 16:18). "Not a novice, lest being lifted up with pride he fall into the condemnation of the devil" (1 Tim. 3:6).

10. "By the multitude of thy merchandise . . . by the iniquity of thy traffick"—The word *merchandise* (also, *traffick*) is from the Hebrew root word meaning "to go about, for either the purpose of trade or slanderous gossip." Here the latter is in view.

11. "I will cast thee as profane out of the mountain of God"—The word *profane* is from the Hebrew *chalal,*, meaning, "to pollute, prostitute, stain, defile."

B. His origin and fall as related by the prophet Isaiah—"How art thou fallen from heaven, O Lucifer, son of the morning! how art thou cut down to the ground, which didst weaken the nations! For thou hast said in thine heart, I will ascend into heaven, I will exalt my throne above the stars of God: I will sit also upon the mount of the congregation, in the sides of the north: I will ascend above the heights of the clouds; I will be like the most High. Yet thou shalt be brought down to hell, to the sides of the pit" (Isa. 14:12-15).

The name Lucifer means "light bearer, day star, shining one." Note his five fatal "I wills."

1. I will ascend into heaven—Obviously Satan had the third heaven in mind here, the very abode of God. Paul speaks of this third heaven in 2 Corinthians 12:2: "Such a one caught up to the third heaven."

2. I will exalt my throne above the stars of God—Probably "the stars of God" is a reference to angels. Satan desired the worship of angels. (See Job 38:7; Ezek. 28:9; Dan. 8:10.)

3. I will sit upon the mount of the congregation, in the sides of the north—Lucifer now seeks to enter God's "executive office" somewhere in the north and sit at his very desk. He would attempt to control not only the angels, but also the size and number of the starry galaxies. Note two phrases here:
   a. "The mount of the congregation"—This is an expression related to the millennial kingdom of God (see Isa. 2:1-4).
   b. "The sides of the north"—This has to do with the location of Christ's reign during the Millennium. "Great is the LORD, and greatly to be praised in the city of our God, in the mountain of his holiness. Beautiful for situation, the joy of the whole earth, is mount Zion, on the sides of the north, the city of the great King" (Psa. 48:1-2). "For promotion cometh neither from the east, nor from the west, nor from the south. But God is the judge: he putteth down one, and setteth up another" (Psa. 75:6-7).

   It should be observed that the direction north is left out here, indicating promotion does indeed proceed from here. In Babylonian mythology the gods assembled in the north.

4. I will ascend above the heights of the clouds—This may well refer to that special shekinah glory cloud of God, where God's glory dwells, that is found so frequently in the Bible. Satan would take that glory also upon himself. A clear reference to this "glory cloud" is found in Number 9:15-23, where God used this "cloud" to direct the children of Israel.

"And on the day that the tabernacle was reared up the cloud covered the tabernacle, namely, the tent of the testimony: and at even there was upon the tabernacle as it were the appearance of fire, until the morning. So it was alway: the cloud covered it by day, and the appearance of fire by night. And when the cloud was taken up from the tabernacle, then after that the children of Israel journeyed: and in the place where the cloud abode, there the children of Israel pitched their tents" (Num. 9:15-17).

5. I will be like the most High—It is revealing to note the name for God that Satan uses here. He wanted to be like El Elyon, the most High. This name literally means "the strongest strong one." The devil could have picked other names for God. He could have used El Shaddai, which means "the breasted one, the one who feeds his children," but he didn't. He might have selected Jehovah-Rohi, which means, "the shepherd God," but he avoided this title also. The reason is obvious. Satan coveted God's strength, but was not the least bit interested in his feeding and leading attributes.

We should note the contrast of the five foolish "I wills" of Lucifer in the garden of God with the prayer of our Lord Jesus in the Garden of Gethsemane, where he prayed. "O my Father, if it be possible, let this cup pass from me: nevertheless not as I will, but as thou wilt" (Matt. 26:39).

Therein we see one great example of the differences between Satan and our Lord Jesus, God's dear Son. Jesus came to do the will of the Father, while Satan viciously fought for his own will.

III. The Personality of Satan

A. He is a real person—In view of the fact that Satan is a fallen angel from the celestial world, it is not, some believe, unreasonable to suggest that he, too, possesses a body. Not a flesh-and-blood terrestrial body, of course, but perhaps a body of some substance nevertheless. He is a person and has a personality. Paul distinguishes between heavenly bodies and earthly bodies in 1 Corinthians 15: "All flesh is not the same flesh: but there is one kind of flesh of men, another flesh of beasts, another of fishes, and another of birds. There are also celestial bodies, and bodies terrestrial: but the glory of the celestial is one, and the glory of the terrestrial is another" (1 Cor. 15:39-40).

B. He possesses intelligence—Even though sin has corrupted his original perfect wisdom, Satan is still the most knowledgeable creature in the universe. In addition to the innate knowledge given at his creation, he has acquired much experiential knowledge in his war against God and man throughout the centuries after his fall. He was fully aware, for example, of the strength of Job (Job 1:6-12; 2:1-7) and the weakness of Peter (Luke 22:31).

C. He possesses memory—Again, to quote from the author's article entitled "If I Were the Devil":

The second thing I would do if I were the devil would be to read the Bible carefully. We are often reminded of how Jesus answered Satan's temptations in the wilderness with Scripture (Matthew 4). But note that Satan also used Scripture! During the second temptation the devil quoted Psalm 91:11-12 to Christ.

"For it is written, he shall give his angels charge concerning thee; and in their hands they shall bear thee up, lest at any time thou dash thy foot against a stone" (Matt. 4:6).

To be sure he took it completely out of context and twisted it, but Shakespeare was right: "The devil doth quote Scripture." Another example of this "Scripture-reading serpent" is found in Revelation 12:

"Therefore rejoice, ye heavens, and ye that dwell in them. Woe to the inhabiters of the earth and of the sea! for the devil is come down unto you, having great wrath, because he knoweth that he hath but a short time" (Rev. 12:12).

Satan will be thrown out of Heaven during the middle of the tribulation and will come down to earth, "having great wrath, because he knoweth that he hath but a short time." How does he know this? The apparent answer is that he has carefully read the ninth chapter of Daniel! If I were the devil I'd read the Bible. I could then so twist and turn the Scriptures in such a way as to mislead saints and sinners alike. (*The Baptist Bulletin,* Dec. 1971, p. 13)

D. He possesses a will—Paul instructed Timothy in dealing with backslidden Christians. He said to be gentle, but firm, "that they may recover themselves out of the snare of the devil, who are taken captive by him at his will" (2 Tim. 2:26).
E. He possesses emotions.
  1. Desire—He has certain goals; he has things that he wants to see accomplished. "And the Lord said, Simon, Simon, behold, Satan hath desired to have you, that he may sift you as wheat" (Luke 22:31).
  2. Pride—In describing the qualifications of a deacon, Paul lists the following restriction: "Not a novice, lest being lifted up with pride he fall into the condemnation of the devil" (1 Tim. 3:6).
  3. Wrath—"Therefore rejoice, ye heavens, and ye that dwell in them. Woe to the inhabiters of the earth and of the sea! for the devil is come down unto you, having great wrath, because he knoweth that he hath but a short time" (Rev. 12:12).
F. He possesses great organizational ability—The Bible speaks of Satan's synagogues, doctrines, and deep things. "Now the Spirit speaketh expressly, that in the latter times some shall depart from the faith, giving heed to seducing spirits, and doctrines of devils" (1 Tim.4:1). "I know thy works, and tribulation, and poverty, (but thou art rich) and I know the blasphemy of them which say they are Jews, and are not, but are the synagogue of Satan" (Rev. 2:9). "But unto you I say, and unto the rest in Thyatira, as many as have not this doctrine, and which have not known the depths of Satan, as they speak; I will put upon you none other burden" (Rev. 2:24).
  1. It was the devil who organized and led the first rebellion against God—His organizational ability was proven when he convinced one-third of heaven's angels to march with him. "And his tail drew the third part of the stars of heaven, and did cast them to the earth: and the dragon stood before the woman which was ready to be delivered, for to devour her child as soon as it was born" (Rev. 12:4).
    Note: The word *drew* in this passage is from the Greek word *suro,* which means "to drag, or carry something." It is also found in Acts 14:19 when Paul's unconscious body was dragged out of the city of Lystra by his enemies. Thus, Lucifer was able to drag down from their lofty position one-third of heaven's angels.
  2. It will be the devil who will organize and lead the last rebellion against God—

"And when the thousand years are expired, Satan shall be loosed out of his prison, and shall go out to deceive the nations which are in the four quarters of the earth, Gog and Magog, to gather them together to battle: the number of whom is as the sand of the sea. And they went up on the breadth of the earth, and compassed the camp of the saints about, and the beloved city: and fire came down from God out of heaven, and devoured them" (Rev. 20:7-9).

Satan's organizational ability will be proven prophetically after the Millennium, when he is loosed from the bottomless pit and once again gathers his army, the number of whom is as the sand of the sea. There will apparently be millions of children born to parents saved during the tribulation, and these children will be raised during the Millennium. For one thousand years these children will have to give lip service to King Jesus and King David, but many of them will never be born again. We believe it will be from these unsaved children of the Millennium that Satan will gather together and organize his final rebellion. According to the Bible, he will be highly successful, as he was with his first rebellion. I will again call your attention to Revelation 20:7-8: "Satan shall . . . deceive the nations . . . of the earth . . . gather them together to battle: the number of whom is as the sand of the sea."

3. It was the devil who systematically subjected the Old Testament patriarch Job to fiery trials in an attempt to break him—See Job 1–2.

We need to understand Satan's tremendous organizational ability, because we are dealing with the enemy of our soul—Satan.

IV. The Names of Satan—There are no less than 27 names and titles of this perverted ex-prince of paradise, which study by itself gives much insight into his evil character. These names and titles, given in alphabetical order, are:

A. Abaddon, Apollyon, "destroyer"—"And they had a king over them, which is the angel of the bottomless pit, whose name in the Hebrew tongue is Abaddon, but in the Greek tongue hath his name Apollyon" (Rev. 9:11). The frightful extent of his destructive power is seen during the sixth trumpet judgment, at which time his hellish army of demons 200 million strong will kill one-third of all humanity. (See Rev. 9:18.)

B. Accuser of the brethren—"And I heard a loud voice saying in heaven, Now is come salvation, and strength, and the kingdom of our God, and the power of his Christ: for the accuser of our brethren is cast down, which accused them before our God day and night" (Rev. 12:10).
   1. He accused Job before God (Job 1:6-12; 2:1-7).
   2. He accused Joshua the high priest before God (Zech. 3:1).

C. Adversary, "to bind, cause distress, oppose"—"O God, how long shall the adversary reproach? shall the enemy blaspheme thy name for ever?" (Psa. 74:10). "Be sober, be vigilant; because your adversary the devil, as a roaring lion, walketh about, seeking whom he may devour" (1 Pet. 5:8). (See also 1 Tim. 5:14-15.)

D. Angel of light—"And no marvel; for Satan himself is transformed into an angel of light" (2 Cor. 11:14).

E. Anointed cherub—"Thou art the anointed cherub that covereth; and I have set thee so: thou wast upon the holy mountain of God; thou hast walked up and down in the midst of the stones of fire" (Ezek. 28:14).

F. Beelzebub, "prince of demons"—"But when the Pharisees heard it, they said, This fellow doth not cast out devils, but by Beelzebub the prince of the devils" (Matt. 12:24).

G. Belial, "worthless, reckless, lawless"—"And what concord hath Christ with Belial? or what part hath he that believeth with an infidel?" (2 Cor. 6:15).

H. Deceiver, "to lead astray"
   1. The first deception involved Adam and Eve in the Garden of Eden (Gen. 3:1-7).
   2. The final deception will involve millions at the close of the Millennium (Rev. 20:7-8).

   It is sobering indeed to observe that both deceptions took place in a perfect environment.

I. Devil, "slanderer"—"Ye are of your father the devil, and the lusts of your father ye will do. He was a murderer from the beginning, and abode not in the truth, because there is no truth in him. When he speaketh a lie, he speaketh of his own: for he is a liar, and the father of it. . . . Then answered the Jews, and said unto him, Say we not well that thou art a Samaritan, and hast a devil?" (John 8:44, 48).

   This is his second most referred to title, used 35 times.

J. Dragon—"And there appeared another wonder in heaven; and behold a great red dragon" (Rev. 12:3). The title dragon is used 12 times, and each instance appears in the book of Revelation.
   1. He is a *great* red dragon because of his power.
   2. He is a great *red* dragon because of the horrible blood-letting he has caused throughout the centuries.
   3. He is a great red *dragon* because of his frightful appearance in the spiritual realm.

K. Enemy, "one's foe who causes distress"—"The enemy that sowed them is the devil; the harvest is the end of the world; and the reapers are the angels" (Matt. 13:39). "So shall they fear the name of the LORD from the west, and his glory from the rising of the sun. When the enemy shall come in like a flood, the Spirit of the LORD shall lift up a standard against him" (Isa. 59:19).

L. God of this world—"In whom the god of this world hath blinded the minds of them which believe not, lest the light of the glorious gospel of Christ, who is the image of God, should shine unto them" (2 Cor. 4:4). "Thy word is a lamp unto my feet, and a light unto my path" (Psa. 119:105). How sad to observe that the true God brightens the path of his people, while in stark contrast the false god blinds the minds of his followers.

M. King of death—"Forasmuch then as the children are partakers of flesh and blood, he also himself likewise took part of the same; that through death he might destroy him that had the power of death, that is, the devil" (Heb. 2:14). "But of the tree of the knowledge of good and evil, thou shalt not eat of it: for in the day that thou eatest thereof thou shalt surely die" (Gen. 2:17). "Wherefore, as by one man sin entered into the world, and death by sin; and so death passed upon all men, for that all have sinned" (Rom. 5:12).

   He is called the King of death because by successfully tempting Adam, the devil helped to bring about both physical and spiritual death upon all mankind.
   1. Physical death—"The days of our years are threescore years and ten; and if by reason of strength they be fourscore years, yet is their strength labour and sorrow; for it is soon cut off, and we fly away" (Psa. 90:10).
   2. Spiritual death—"But the fearful, and unbelieving, and the abominable, and murderers, and whoremongers, and sorcerers, and idolaters, and all liars, shall have their part in the lake which burneth with fire and brimstone: which is the second death" (Rev. 21:8).

N. Leviathan, "one who dwells in the sea of humanity"—"In that day the LORD with his sore and great and strong sword shall punish leviathan the piercing serpent, even leviathan that crooked serpent; and he shall slay the dragon that is in the sea" (Isa. 27:1).

O. Liar—"Ye are of your father the devil, and the lusts of your father ye will do. He was a murderer from the beginning, and abode not in the truth, because there is no truth in him. When he speaketh a lie, he speaketh of his own: for he is a liar, and the father of it" (John 8:44).

Satan was the source of both the first and final lie in the Bible concerning the very nature of God.

1. First lie—"And the serpent said unto the woman, Ye shall not surely die: for God doth know that in the day ye eat thereof, then your eyes shall be opened, and ye shall be as gods, knowing good and evil" (Gen. 3:4-5).

2. Final lie—"Let no man deceive you by any means: for that day shall not come, except there come a falling away first, and that man of sin be revealed, the son of perdition; who opposeth and exalteth himself above all that is called God, or that is worshipped; so that he as God sitteth in the temple of God, shewing himself that he is God. . . . Even him, whose coming is after the working of Satan with all power and signs and lying wonders. . . . And for this cause God shall send them strong delusion, that they should believe a lie" (2 Thess. 2:3-4, 9, 11).

P. Lucifer, "light bearer, daystar, shining one"—"How art thou fallen from heaven, O Lucifer, son of the morning! how art thou cut down to the ground, which didst weaken the nations!" (Isa. 14:12).

Q. Murderer—"For this is the message that ye heard from the beginning, that we should love one another. Not as Cain, who was of that wicked one, and slew his brother. And wherefore slew he him? Because his own works were evil, and his brother's righteous" (1 John 3:11-12).

R. Prince of the power of the air—"Wherein in time past ye walked according to the course of this world, according to the prince of the power of the air, the spirit that now worketh in the children of disobedience" (Eph. 2:2).

S. Prince of this world—"After these things Jesus shewed himself again to the disciples at the sea of Tiberias; and on this wise shewed he himself" (John 12:31). "Hereafter I will not talk much with you: for the prince of this world cometh, and hath nothing in me" (John 14:30).

T. Roaring lion—"Be sober, be vigilant; because your adversary the devil, as a roaring lion, walketh about, seeking whom he may devour" (1 Pet. 5:8). As an angel of light, Satan is a wolf in sheep's clothing. As a roaring lion, he wears his own clothing.

U. Ruler of darkness—"Put on the whole armour of God, that ye may be able to stand against the wiles of the devil. For we wrestle not against flesh and blood, but against principalities, against powers, against the rulers of the darkness of this world, against spiritual wickedness in high places" (Eph. 6:11-12).

V. Satan, "hateful accuser, adversary, opposer"—This is his most referred to title, used 52 times.

W. Serpent—"But I fear, lest by any means, as the serpent beguiled Eve through his subtilty, so your minds should be corrupted from the simplicity that is in Christ" (2 Cor. 11:3). "That old serpent, called the Devil, and Satan" (Rev. 12:9). "And he laid hold on the dragon, that old serpent, which is the Devil, and Satan, and bound him a thousand years" (Rev. 20:2). "Now the serpent was more subtil than any beast of the field which the LORD God had made. And he said unto the woman, Yea, hath God said, Ye shall not eat of every tree of the garden?" (Gen. 3:1).

F. C. Jennings writes:

> The word for "serpent" in Hebrew is *nachash,* which may come from the root, to hiss; or, as Dr. Taylor Lewis writes, "is far more likely to have had its sense from the secondary meaning of that root—to shine, whence brass, the shining metal." This gives, as the first thought in the word for serpent, "splendor," "glistening," "bright," "shining," either from its glossy appearance, or, more likely, from the bright glistening of the eye. The first impressions of mankind in regards to the serpent were of the splendid and terrible kind—beauty and awe. (*Satan, His Person, Work, Place, and Destiny,* p. 15)

X. Son of the morning—"How art thou fallen from heaven, O Lucifer, son of the morning! how art thou cut down to the ground, which didst weaken the nations!" (Isa. 14:12).

How tragic to realize this mighty and magnificent angel who was originally created to serve as Son of the morning will someday be eternally condemned to outer darkness, the lake of fire. "And the angels which kept not their first estate, but left their own habitation, he hath reserved in everlasting chains under darkness unto the judgment of the great day" (Jude 6). "And the devil that deceived them was cast into the lake of fire and brimstone, where the beast and the false prophet are, and shall be tormented day and night for ever and ever" (Rev. 20:10).

Y. Tempter, "one who entices another to evil"—"Then was Jesus led up of the Spirit into the wilderness to be tempted of the devil" (Matt. 4:1). "For in that he himself hath suffered being tempted, he is able to succour them that are tempted" (Heb. 2:18).

Z. Thief—"The thief cometh not, but for to steal, and to kill, and to destroy: I am come that they might have life, and that they might have it more abundantly" (John 10:10).

AA. Wicked one, "bad, malignant"—"When any one heareth the word of the kingdom, and understandeth it not, then cometh the wicked one, and catcheth away that which was sown in his heart. This is he which received seed by the way side" (Matt. 13:19). "Above all, taking the shield of faith, wherewith ye shall be able to quench all the fiery darts of the wicked" (Eph. 6:16).

V. The Activities of Satan—Whatever else Satan is, he can never be accused of being lazy. He has been working, apparently ever since his fall, 24 hours a day, seven days a week, 52 weeks out of every year. He never sleeps (apparently he doesn't need sleep). He is continuously at work attempting to keep sinners from being saved and saints from growing in grace. Let's examine some of his activities.

A. His imitation of God—The great ambition and determination of Satan is to be like God. The boast of Lucifer was "I will be like the Most High." In Satan's great scheme he imitates and counterfeits the things God is doing, and so fine is his imitation that vast multitudes of people who are actually following Satan's error think they are serving God. Satan is not an initiator, but an imitator.

Satan is far more effective in matters of imitation than in matters of opposition. We often think of Satan as the great opposer of the plan of God—and certainly he is—but sometimes the best opposition against something is a clever imitation.

1. In regard to the Trinity
   a. The true Trinity—"The grace of the Lord Jesus Christ, and the love of God, and the communion of the Holy Ghost, be with you all. Amen" (2 Cor. 13:14).
   b. The false trinity—In this arrangement Satan assumes the role of the Father, the Antichrist that of the Son, and the false prophet that of the Holy Spirit. (See Rev. 13:2, 11-12; 2 Thess. 2:8-9.)
2. In regard to ministers
   a. True ministers—"Ye have not chosen me, but I have chosen you, and ordained you, that ye should go and bring forth fruit, and that your fruit should remain: that whatsoever ye shall ask of the Father in my name, he may give it you" (John 15:16).
   b. False ministers—"For such are false apostles, deceitful workers, transforming themselves into the apostles of Christ" (2 Cor. 11:13).
3. In regard to teachers
   a. True teachers (Acts 13:1; Eph. 4:11; 1 Tim. 2:7)
   b. False teachers—"But there were false prophets also among the people, even as there shall be false teachers among you, who privily shall bring in damnable heresies, even denying the Lord that bought them, and bring upon themselves swift destruction" (2 Pet. 2:1).
4. In regard to spiritual children
   a. The true seed—"Behold, what manner of love the Father hath bestowed upon us, that we should be called the sons of God: therefore the world knoweth us not, because it knew him not. . . . In this the children of God are manifest, and the children of the devil: whosoever doeth not righteousness is not of God, neither he that loveth not his brother" (1 John 3:1, 10).
   b. The false seed—"The field is the world; the good seed are the children of the kingdom; but the tares are the children of the wicked one" (Matt. 13:38). "Ye are of your father the devil, and the lusts of your father ye will do. He was a murderer from the beginning, and abode not in the truth, because there is no truth in him. When he speaketh a lie, he speaketh of his own: for he is a liar, and the father of it" (John 8:44).
5. In regard to worshippers
   a. The true ones—"But the hour cometh, and now is, when the true worshippers shall worship the Father in spirit and in truth: for the Father seeketh such to worship him" (John 4:23). "Who shall not fear thee, O Lord, and glorify thy name? for thou only art holy: for all nations shall come and worship before thee; for thy judgments are made manifest" (Rev. 15:4).
   b. The false ones—"And they worshipped the dragon which gave power unto the beast: and they worshipped the beast, saying, Who is like unto the beast? who is able to make war with him? . . . And all that dwell upon the earth shall worship him, whose names are not written in the book of life of the Lamb slain from the foundation of the world" (Rev. 13:4, 8).
6. In regard to angels
   a. The elect ones—"But ye are come unto mount Sion, and unto the city of the living God, the heavenly Jerusalem, and to an innumerable company of angels" (Heb. 12:22).
   b. The evil ones—"Then shall he say also unto them on the left hand, Depart from me, ye cursed, into everlasting fire, prepared for the devil and his angels" (Matt. 25:41).

7. In regard to miracles
   a. Divine miracles—"And Jesus went about all Galilee, teaching in their synagogues, and preaching the gospel of the kingdom, and healing all manner of sickness and all manner of disease among the people" (Matt. 4:23). "The same came to Jesus by night, and said unto him, Rabbi, we know that thou art a teacher come from God: for no man can do these miracles that thou doest, except God be with him" (John 3:2).
   b. Devilish miracles—"Even him, whose coming is after the working of Satan with all power and signs and lying wonders" (2 Thess. 2:9). "Not every one that saith unto me, Lord, Lord, shall enter into the kingdom of heaven; but he that doeth the will of my Father which is in heaven. Many will say to me in that day, Lord, Lord, have we not prophesied in thy name? and in thy name have cast out devils? and in thy name done many wonderful works? And then will I profess unto them, I never knew you: depart from me, ye that work iniquity" (Matt. 7:21-23).
8. In regard to marks of identification
   a. Divine mark—"And grieve not the holy Spirit of God, whereby ye are sealed unto the day of redemption" (Eph. 4:30). "Saying, Hurt not the earth, neither the sea, nor the trees, till we have sealed the servants of our God in their foreheads" (Rev. 7:3).
   b. Devilish mark—"And he causeth all, both small and great, rich and poor, free and bond, to receive a mark in their right hand, or in their foreheads" (Rev. 13:16).
9. In regard to ruling headquarters
   a. God's capital—"And he built altars in the house of the LORD, of which the LORD said, In Jerusalem will I put my name" (2 Kings 21:4).
   b. Satan's capital
      (1) Original, Babylon (Gen. 11:1-9)
      (2) Old Testament times, possibly Babylon and Tyre (Isa. 14:4-17; Ezek. 28:1-19)
      (3) New Testament times, Pergamos—"And to the angel of the church in Pergamos write; These things saith he which hath the sharp sword with two edges; I know thy works, and where thou dwellest, even where Satan's seat is: and thou holdest fast my name, and hast not denied my faith, even in those days wherein Antipas was my faithful martyr, who was slain among you, where Satan dwelleth" (Rev. 2:12-13).
      (4) Final, Babylon (Zech. 5:5-11; Rev. 17:5; 18:2)—"And upon her forehead was a name written, MYSTERY, BABYLON THE GREAT, THE MOTHER OF HARLOTS AND ABOMINATIONS OF THE EARTH" (Rev. 17:5). "And the voice of harpers, and musicians, and of pipers, and trumpeters, shall be heard no more at all in thee; and no craftsman, of whatsoever craft he be, shall be found any more in thee; and the sound of a millstone shall be heard no more at all in thee" (Rev. 18:2).
10. In regard to kingdoms
    a. God's kingdom—"Thy kingdom come. Thy will be done in earth, as it is in heaven" (Matt. 6:10). "And the seventh angel sounded; and there were great voices in heaven, saying, The kingdoms of this world are become the kingdoms of our Lord, and of his Christ; and he shall reign for ever and ever" (Rev. 11:15).

b. Satan's kingdom—"And the devil, taking him up into an high mountain, shewed unto him all the kingdoms of the world in a moment of time. And the devil said unto him, All this power will I give thee, and the glory of them: for that is delivered unto me; and to whomsoever I will I give it" (Luke 4:5-6). "And the fifth angel poured out his vial upon the seat of the beast; and his kingdom was full of darkness; and they gnawed their tongues for pain" (Rev. 16:10).

11. In regard to mysteries
    a. The mystery of godliness: The fullness of God in the person of Christ—"And without controversy great is the mystery of godliness: God was manifest in the flesh, justified in the Spirit, seen of angels, preached unto the Gentiles, believed on in the world, received up into glory" (1 Tim. 3:16).
    b. The mystery of iniquity: The fullness of Satan in the person of Antichrist—"Don't let anyone deceive you in any way, for that day will not come until the rebellion occurs and the man of lawlessness is revealed, the man doomed to destruction. . . . For the secret power of lawlessness is already at work; but the one who now holds it back will continue to do so till he is taken out of the way" (2 Thess. 2:3, 7, NIV).

12. In regard to doctrine
    a. The theology of God—"All scripture is given by inspiration of God, and is profitable for doctrine, for reproof, for correction, for instruction in righteousness" (2 Tim. 3:16). "But as it is written, Eye hath not seen, nor ear heard, neither have entered into the heart of man, the things which God hath prepared for them that love him. But God hath revealed them unto us by his Spirit: for the Spirit searcheth all things, yea, the deep things of God" (1 Cor. 2:9-10).
    b. The theology of Satan—"Now the Spirit speaketh expressly, that in the latter times some shall depart from the faith, giving heed to seducing spirits, and doctrines of devils" (1 Tim. 4:1). "For the time will come when they will not endure sound doctrine; but after their own lusts shall they heap to themselves teachers, having itching ears" (2 Tim. 4:3). "But unto you I say, and unto the rest in Thyatira, as many as have not this doctrine, and which have not known the depths of Satan, as they speak; I will put upon you none other burden" (Rev. 2:24).

B. His activities against God
    1. Concerning the Scriptures—Simon Peter ends his second epistle as follows: "And account that the longsuffering of our Lord is salvation; even as our beloved brother Paul also according to the wisdom given unto him hath written unto you; as also in all his epistles, speaking in them of these things; in which are some things hard to be understood, which they that are unlearned and unstable wrest, as they do also the other scriptures, unto their own destruction" (2 Pet. 3:15-16).
        a. Satan adds to the Scriptures—"For I testify unto every man that heareth the words of the prophecy of this book, If any man shall add unto these things, God shall add unto him the plagues that are written in this book" (Rev. 22:18).

        This is, in essence, what the cults do. The *Book of Mormon* and the writings of a Mary Baker Eddy or a Charles Taze Russell represent foolish and futile attempts to add to the Word of God.

b. Satan deletes from the Scriptures—"And if any man shall take away from the words of the book of this prophecy, God shall take away his part out of the book of life, and out of the holy city, and from the things which are written in this book" (Rev. 22:19).

This is, in essence, what the liberals do. They brazenly strike out certain biblical truths such as the literal Virgin Birth of Christ, his bodily resurrection, the doctrine of hell, etc.

c. Satan denies the inerrancy of the Scriptures—During the 1950s a disturbing sound was heard coming from certain sections of the evangelical world that said, in effect, that while the Bible was indeed inspired, it was not necessarily inerrant. This said one could accept at face value all the spiritual and moral statements in the Word of God, but must carefully examine for possible human error the scientific, historical, and geographical statements.

d. Satan misinterprets the Scriptures—By doing this, he has led people to believe:

(1) That one must be baptized to be saved, based on Acts 2:38

(2) That one is saved by faith plus works, based on James 2:14, 24

(3) That one can sin away his day of grace, based on Matthew 12:31-32

(4) That God desires to keep all Christians in perfect health, based on Matthew 8:17 and 3 John 2

(5) That a believer may achieve sinless perfection here on earth, based on 1 John 3:9

(6) That speaking in tongues is the sign of the baptism of the Holy Spirit, based on Acts 2 and 1 Corinthians 14

(7) That an unmarried believer is more spiritual than a married believer, based on 1 Corinthians 7:32-34

This is not to say, of course, that all those holding one or more of the views are unsaved and demon-possessed. Not in the least, for many of God's choice Christians have at one time or another in their lives fallen victim to one of these misinterpretations. The point is simply this: All misinterpretations come from either human error or satanic influence, and probably more often than not the latter is involved.

e. Satan overemphasizes certain parts of the Scriptures.

(1) By stressing the sovereignty of God to the exclusion of the responsibility of man

(2) By stressing the responsibility of man to the exclusion of the sovereignty of God

f. Satan takes the Scriptures out of their proper context—This he did when tempting Jesus by quoting Psalm 91:11-12 out of its intended context. (See Matt. 4:6.)

g. Satan instigates false doctrine—"Now the Spirit speaketh expressly, that in the latter times some shall depart from the faith, giving heed to seducing spirits, and doctrines of devils" (1 Tim. 4:1). "For the time will come when they will not endure sound doctrine; but after their own lusts shall they heap to themselves teachers, having itching ears; and they shall turn away their ears from the truth, and shall be turned unto fables" (2 Tim. 4:3-4).

2. Concerning the Savior—There are at least six recorded occasions when Satan specifically attacked the Savior.

a. In Bethlehem, where he attempted to kill him—"And when they were departed, behold, the angel of the Lord appeareth to Joseph in a dream, saying, Arise, and take the young child and his mother, and flee into Egypt, and be thou there until I bring thee word: for Herod will seek the young child to destroy him" (Matt. 2:13).

b. In the wilderness, where he tempted him
   (1) In matters of independence (Matt. 4:3-4)
   (2) In matters of indulgence (Matt. 4:5-7)
   (3) In matters of idolatry (Matt. 4:8-10)
   Outline as suggested by Charles Ryrie (*Basic Theology*, p. 147).

c. At Caesarea Philippi, where he attempted to sidetrack him from Calvary (first occasion)—"From that time forth began Jesus to shew unto his disciples, how that he must go unto Jerusalem, and suffer many things of the elders and chief priests and scribes, and be killed, and be raised again the third day. Then Peter took him, and began to rebuke him, saying, Be it far from thee, Lord: this shall not be unto thee. But he turned, and said unto Peter, Get thee behind me, Satan: thou art an offence unto me: for thou savourest not the things that be of God, but those that be of men" (Matt. 16:21-23).

d. At the Feast of Passover, where he attempted to sidetrack him from Calvary (second occasion)—"Now is my soul troubled; and what shall I say? Father, save me from this hour: but for this cause came I unto this hour. . . . Now is the judgment of this world: now shall the prince of this world be cast out. And I, if I be lifted up from the earth, will draw all men unto me" (John 12:27, 31-32).

e. In the Upper Room, where he arranged to betray him—"When Jesus had thus said, he was troubled in spirit, and testified, and said, Verily, verily, I say unto you, that one of you shall betray me. . . . He then lying on Jesus' breast saith unto him, Lord, who is it? Jesus answered, He it is, to whom I shall give a sop, when I have dipped it. And when he had dipped the sop, he gave it to Judas Iscariot, the son of Simon. And after the sop Satan entered into him. Then said Jesus unto him, That thou doest, do quickly" (John 13:21, 25-27).

f. In Gethsemane, where he attempted to break him emotionally and physically. "And they came to a place which was named Gethsemane: and he saith to his disciples, Sit ye here, while I shall pray. And he taketh with him Peter and James and John, and began to be sore amazed, and to be very heavy; and saith unto them, My soul is exceeding sorrowful unto death: tarry ye here, and watch. And he went forward a little, and fell on the ground, and prayed that, if it were possible, the hour might pass from him. And he said, Abba, Father, all things are possible unto thee; take away this cup from me: nevertheless not what I will, but what thou wilt" (Mark 14:32-36). "And being in an agony he prayed more earnestly: and his sweat was as it were great drops of blood falling down to the ground" (Luke 22:44).

3. Concerning the saint
   a. He sows tares among God's wheat—"Another parable put he forth unto them, saying, The kingdom of heaven is likened unto a man which sowed good seed in his field: but while men slept, his enemy came and sowed tares

among the wheat, and went his way. But when the blade was sprung up, and brought forth fruit, then appeared the tares also. So the servants of the householder came and said unto him, Sir, didst not thou sow good seed in thy field? from whence then hath it tares? He said unto them, An enemy hath done this. The servants said unto him, Wilt thou then that we go and gather them up? But he said, Nay; lest while ye gather up the tares, ye root up also the wheat with them. Let both grow together until the harvest: and in the time of harvest I will say to the reapers, Gather ye together first the tares, and bind them in bundles to burn them: but gather the wheat into my barn" (Matt. 13:24-30).

One of the most dangerous characteristics of a tare is that, at least for awhile in the early stages, it is identical in appearance to a grain of wheat. So where would we go to find the tares? This may come as a shock, but probably we would not go to the liberal churches or the taverns. Instead we would look for tares in Bible-believing, evangelical, conservative, fundamental churches. Often Satan does plant his tares among the wheat of God's fundamental churches. They speak the same language, sing the same songs, and are familiar with the same theology. Yet they have never been born again—not because they do not know the plan of salvation, but because they are of Satan. So who are the real tares? Some day the question will be asked, "Will the real tares please stand up." And, of course, the Lord Jesus then, during the *harvest,* will weed them out from the wheat (the believers).

b. He hinders the work of God's servants—"Wherefore we would have come unto you, even I Paul, once and again; but Satan hindered us" (1 Thess. 2:18). He cannot do this, of course, except by the direct permission of God, who sometimes allows hindrances to teach the believer spiritual lessons.

c. He resists the prayers of God's servants—"Then said he unto me, Fear not, Daniel: for from the first day that thou didst set thine heart to understand, and to chasten thyself before thy God, thy words were heard, and I am come for thy words. But the prince of the kingdom of Persia withstood me one and twenty days: but, lo, Michael, one of the chief princes, came to help me; and I remained there with the kings of Persia" (Dan. 10:12-13).

Again, as in the former point, it should be noted that Satan cannot do this without God's approval. Understand this—God always answers all faithful prayers that he hears from believers. But sometimes there is a delay. It's a delay that God allows and that God permits, but it is a delay caused by satanic interference. So Satan does resist the prayers of God's servants.

d. He accuses Christians before God—"And I heard a loud voice saying in heaven, Now is come salvation, and strength, and the kingdom of our God, and the power of his Christ: for the accuser of our brethren is cast down, which accused them before our God day and night" (Rev. 12:10).

(1) He accused Job (Job 1:7-12; 2:3-6).

(2) He accused Joshua the high priest (Zech. 3:1).

These verses inform us of one of Satan's greatest ministries—that of bad-mouthing Christians. Job 1–2 and Zechariah 3 refer to Satan being at the right hand of the Father. So he has access to the very right hand of God. Even as you go about your daily activities of life, Satan, who never sleeps, is continuously at work at the right hand of the Father, making intercession *against* the believer and attempting to slander the child of God. Tragically, sometimes he doesn't even have to exaggerate. This is one of the reasons Christ had to ascend back to heaven—that he might function in the believer's defense. The following passages speak of this ministry.

"And the Lord said, Simon, Simon, behold, Satan hath desired to have you, that he may sift you as wheat: but I have prayed for thee, that thy faith fail not: and when thou art converted, strengthen thy brethren" (Luke 22:31-32). "Wherefore he is able also to save them to the uttermost that come unto God by him, seeing he ever liveth to make intercession for them" (Heb. 7:25). "Who shall lay any thing to the charge of God's elect? It is God that justifieth. Who is he that condemneth? It is Christ that died, yea rather, that is risen again, who is even at the right hand of God, who also maketh intercession for us" (Rom. 8:33-34).

e. He lays snares for believers—"Moreover he must have a good report of them which are without; lest he fall into reproach and the snare of the devil" (1 Tim. 3:7). "And that they may recover themselves out of the snare of the devil, who are taken captive by him at his will" (2 Tim. 2:26).

There is a little poem that reads: "When the danger least thou fearest, then the devil's snare is nearest."

In the verses above, Paul admonishes Timothy to warn other members of the church "that they may recover themselves out of the snare of the devil, who are taken captive by him at his will." Often the child of God becomes careless and feels he is past the point of being ensnared by a certain sin. Quite often a person will be aware he has problems in certain areas of his life and be on guard, but feels he doesn't have to worry about other areas of his life. Satan loves to go around and come in the back door. He hits quite often in the strong areas. The Bible is filled with instances where men failed God in their strong points and not in their weak points. Let's look at a few of these instances.

(1) Moses—If one analyzes the life of Moses and picks his strongest characteristic, it would be his meekness. The Bible says that the man Moses was a meek man—he was the meekest man on earth (Num. 12:3). He wasn't a *weak* man, but he was a *meek* man. This means he had sustained strength—he didn't lose his cool. He controlled his emotions. Yet, he was guilty of anger, which is the antithesis of meekness. This sin of anger kept him out of the promised land. Moses failed God on his strong point.

(2) Elijah—Elijah, the prophet, had boldness—this was his great source of strength. This fearless prophet stood up singlehandedly against 450 priests of Baal (1 Kings 18:17-46), and yet in 1 Kings 19 he ran for his life from a woman. He failed God in his strong point.

(3) David—David's two outstanding characteristics were his purity (here is the man who wrote the Twenty-Third Psalm) and his kindness. David refused on a number of occasions to kill his enemies. He refused to kill Saul. He refused to kill a man named Shimi. He refused to kill a man named Nabal. All of these were ungodly men who deserved to be killed. But David in his kindness could not kill them, and he said in matters pertaining to Saul, "God forbid that I should touch God's anointed." Yet

David failed God in matters of adultery and murder—the opposite of purity and kindness.

These men were, most likely, more concerned with their weak points than their strong points. Satan, thus, hit them on strong points in their lives by laying snares. Each of us should keep our guard up because Satan is determined to lay snares for anyone who stands for God in this world.

f. He tempts believers—"Put on the whole armour of God, that ye may be able to stand against the wiles of the devil" (Eph. 6:11).

   (1) God tests with the idea of making better, as seen in Genesis 22:1—"And it came to pass after these things, that God did tempt Abraham, and said unto him, Abraham: and he said, Behold, here I am."

   (2) Satan tempts by enticing people to do evil—It is no sin to be tempted. In fact, it is a tragedy if you claim to be a child of God and you are not tempted. It simply means you are so worthless in Satan's sight that he doesn't even give the command for one of his cohorts to tempt you. Many people feel that because they are tempted to do certain things they are not as close to God as they should be. However, this is not the case. In fact, to the contrary, the Bible says we are to rejoice in the hour and in the midst of temptation, because God is going to allow us to suffer for Christ, and he will purify us through the fire of temptation. Tempt, Satan does. However, the limitation of Satan's power to tempt the child of God is found in 1 Cor. 10:13: "There hath no temptation taken you but such as is common to man: but God is faithful, who will not suffer you to be tempted above that ye are able; but will with the temptation also make a way to escape, that ye may be able to bear it."

g. He afflicts believers—"So went Satan forth from the presence of the LORD, and smote Job with sore boils from the sole of his foot unto his crown" (Job 2:7). "And lest I should be exalted above measure through the abundance of the revelations, there was given to me a thorn in the flesh, the messenger of Satan to buffet me, lest I should be exalted above measure" (2 Cor. 12:7). "How God anointed Jesus of Nazareth with the Holy Ghost and with power: who went about doing good, and healing all that were oppressed of the devil; for God was with him" (Acts 10:38).

   The sobering fact to keep in mind here is that Satan's victims in these passages are believers. While Satan cannot *possess* a Christian, he can certainly *oppress* a child of God—mentally, emotionally, and physically. He afflicted Job with boils. He afflicted the Apostle Paul. Sometimes God allows the believer to be afflicted to *purify* him (as in the case of Job). There are times when God allows a believer to be afflicted to *punish* him for some sin. Paul writes about this in 1 Cor. 5:3-5: "For I verily, as absent in body, but present in spirit, have judged already, as though I were present, concerning him that hath so done this deed, in the name of our Lord Jesus Christ, when ye are gathered together, and my spirit, with the power of our Lord Jesus Christ, to deliver such an one unto Satan for the destruction of the flesh, that the spirit may be saved in the day of the Lord Jesus" (1 Cor. 5:3-5).

h. He influences believers to disobey God.

   (1) As seen by David—"And Satan stood up against Israel, and provoked David to number Israel" (1 Chron. 21:1).

   (2) As seen by Peter

(a) He influenced Peter to rebuke Jesus (Matt. 16:22-23).

(b) He influenced Peter to deny Jesus (John 13:38; 18:15-18, 25-27).

(3) As seen by Ananias and Sapphira (Acts 5:1-11)—"But Peter said, Ananias, why hath Satan filled thine heart to lie to the Holy Ghost, and to keep back part of the price of the land?" (Acts 5:3).

4. Concerning the sinner

a. He blinds the unsaved to the truth—"In whom the god of this world hath blinded the minds of them which believe not, lest the light of the glorious gospel of Christ, who is the image of God, should shine unto them" (2 Cor. 4:4).

b. He steals the Word of God from their hearts—"And he spake many things unto them in parables, saying, Behold, a sower went forth to sow; and when he sowed, some seeds fell by the way side, and the fowls came and devoured them up. . . . Hear ye therefore the parable of the sower. When any one heareth the word of the kingdom, and understandeth it not, then cometh the wicked one, and catcheth away that which was sown in his heart. This is he which received seed by the way side" (Matt. 13:3-4, 18-19).

c. He deceives the unsaved—The words *deceive, deceitful,* and *deceit* are found some 50 times in the New Testament. It is sobering to contemplate that the vast majority of these references have to do with satanic religious deception in the last days.

(1) The messengers of deception

(a) The men of sin—"For there shall arise false Christs, and false prophets, and shall shew great signs and wonders; insomuch that, if it were possible, they shall deceive the very elect" (Matt. 24:24).

"For such are false apostles, deceitful workers, transforming themselves into the apostles of Christ. And no marvel; for Satan himself is transformed into an angel of light. Therefore it is no great thing if his ministers also be transformed as the ministers of righteousness; whose end shall be according to their works" (2 Cor. 11:13-15). "But evil men and seducers shall wax worse and worse, deceiving, and being deceived" (2 Tim. 3:13).

(b) The man of sin—"Even him, whose coming is after the working of Satan with all power and signs and lying wonders, and with all deceivableness of unrighteousness in them that perish; because they received not the love of the truth, that they might be saved" (2 Thess. 2:9-10).

(2) The message of deception—"And Jesus answered and said unto them, Take heed that no man deceive you. For many shall come in my name, saying, I am Christ; and shall deceive many" (Matt. 24:4-5). "For many deceivers are entered into the world, who confess not that Jesus Christ is come in the flesh. This is a deceiver and an antichrist" (2 John 7).

(3) The means of deception—"And deceiveth them that dwell on the earth by the means of those miracles which he had power to do in the sight of the beast; saying to them that dwell on the earth, that they should make an image to the beast, which had the wound by a sword, and did live. And he had power to give life unto the image of the beast, that the image of the beast should both speak, and cause that as many as would not worship the image of the beast should be killed" (Rev. 13:14-15).

5. Concerning the systems—In the beginning God created four special institutions, or systems, for the overall well being of mankind. Because of their origin and purpose Satan has viciously and persistently attacked all four institutions.

  a. The institution of marriage

    (1) The birth—And the LORD God caused a deep sleep to fall upon Adam, and he slept: and he took one of his ribs, and closed up the flesh instead thereof; and the rib, which the LORD God had taken from man, made he a woman, and brought her unto the man. And Adam said, This is now bone of my bones, and flesh of my flesh: she shall be called Woman, because she was taken out of Man. Therefore shall a man leave his father and his mother, and shall cleave unto his wife: and they shall be one flesh" (Gen. 2:21-24).

    (2) The battle—"Let the husband render unto the wife due benevolence: and likewise also the wife unto the husband. The wife hath not power of her own body, but the husband: and likewise also the husband hath not power of his own body, but the wife. Defraud ye not one the other, except it be with consent for a time, that ye may give yourselves to fasting and prayer; and come together again, that Satan tempt you not for your incontinency" (1 Cor. 7:3-5).

      Very few marriage counselors ever take satanic activity into consideration when advising couples having marital problems. Sometimes the real fault lies not with the husband or wife, but squarely with Satan. The devil despises the very institution of marriage because it was originated and given by God himself.

  b. The institution of human government

    (1) The birth—It probably had its beginnings with the Cainite civilization (Gen. 4:16-22). Whatever the spiritual condition of this civilization might have been, the fact remains the powers that be are ordained of God. (See Dan. 4:25; Rom. 13:1-7; 1 Tim. 2:1-3; Titus 3:1; 1 Pet. 2:13-14, 17.)

    (2) The battle—"But chiefly them that walk after the flesh in the lust of uncleanness, and despise government. Presumptuous are they, selfwilled, they are not afraid to speak evil of dignities" (2 Pet. 2:10).

  c. The institution of the nation Israel

    (1) The birth—"Now the LORD had said unto Abram, Get thee out of thy country, and from thy kindred, and from thy father's house, unto a land that I will shew thee: and I will make of thee a great nation, and I will bless thee, and make thy name great; and thou shalt be a blessing" (Gen. 12:1-2).

    (2) The battle—"And when the dragon saw that he was cast unto the earth, he persecuted the woman which brought forth the man child. . . . And the dragon was wroth with the woman, and went to make war with the remnant of her seed, which keep the commandments of God, and have the testimony of Jesus Christ" (Rev. 12:13, 17).

      (a) Pharaoh—The Egyptian tried to drown them (Exod. 14).

      (b) Sennacherib—The Assyrian tried to starve them (2 Kings 19).

      (c) Nebuchadnezzar—The Babylonian tried to burn them (Dan. 3).

      (d) Haman—The Persian tried to hang them (Esther 3).

  d. The institution of the church

(1) The birth—"I will build my church; and the gates of hell shall not prevail against it" (Matt. 16:18). "And when the day of Pentecost was fully come, they were all with one accord in one place. And suddenly there came a sound from heaven as of a rushing mighty wind, and it filled all the house where they were sitting" (Acts 2:1-2).

(2) The battle—"For we wrestle not against flesh and blood, but against principalities, against powers, against the rulers of the darkness of this world, against spiritual wickedness in high places" (Eph. 6:12).

VI. The Various Geographical and Spiritual Locations of Satan—The devil is like a check forger in that he moves around constantly. Satan has been to, is in, or will occupy the following six locations.

A. Past location—In the heavenlies as God's choir leader (Ezek. 28:12-19; Isa. 14:12-14)

B. Present location—In the heavenlies as God's chief enemy (Job 1:6; 2:1; Zech. 3:1)

C. Future locations

  1. On earth during the great tribulation—"And the great dragon was cast out, that old serpent, called the Devil, and Satan, which deceiveth the whole world: he was cast out into the earth, and his angels were cast out with him. And I heard a loud voice saying in heaven, Now is come salvation, and strength, and the kingdom of our God, and the power of his Christ: for the accuser of our brethren is cast down, which accused them before our God day and night. . . . Therefore rejoice, ye heavens, and ye that dwell in them. Woe to the inhabiters of the earth and of the sea! for the devil is come down unto you, having great wrath, because he knoweth that he hath but a short time" (Rev. 12:9-10, 12).

  2. In the bottomless pit during the Millennium—"And I saw an angel come down from heaven, having the key of the bottomless pit and a great chain in his hand. And he laid hold on the dragon, that old serpent, which is the Devil, and Satan, and bound him a thousand years, and cast him into the bottomless pit, and shut him up, and set a seal upon him, that he should deceive the nations no more, till the thousand years should be fulfilled: and after that he must be loosed a little season" (Rev. 20:1-3).

  3. On earth following the Millennium—"And when the thousand years are expired, Satan shall be loosed out of his prison, and shall go out to deceive the nations which are in the four quarters of the earth, Gog and Magog, to gather them together to battle: the number of whom is as the sand of the sea" (Rev. 20:7-8).

  4. In the lake of fire forever—"And the devil that deceived them was cast into the lake of fire and brimstone, where the beast and the false prophet are, and shall be tormented day and night for ever and ever" (Rev. 20:10).

VII. The Limitations of Satan—As one compiles and analyzes the many Bible passages on Satan, it is evident that he is the most powerful creature in all God's universe. This depraved and deadly dragon possesses more strength and savvy than any archangel or saint. But in spite of all this, he is still a creature and not the Creator. Because of this blessed truth, his power and knowledge is limited. We shall now consider the restrictions of this red dragon.

A. He is not omnipresent—The devil cannot be in China, Chicago, and Cuba at the same instant. However, this is not to say that believers in those areas cannot be tempted at the same instant, for Satan has literally millions of fallen angels to do his bidding, thus extending his ministry universally. But only God is omnipresent.

Satan cannot say, as Jesus once said to his followers, "Lo, I am with you always, even to the end of the age." Satan is not omnipresent.

B. He is not omnipotent—While he is still the strongest creature in the universe, his power compared to God's is like an ant pitted against a mighty elephant. There are a number of things Satan cannot do. For example, he cannot so frustrate the Word of God that it will not bring its eventual fruit. According to the book of Isaiah, the Word of God shall not return void, but it shall accomplish the purpose for which God sent it (Isaiah 55:11). Satan cannot drag the saved soul of a believer to hell; he cannot cause a saved person to become lost. Satan is not omnipotent.

C. He is not omniscient—The devil has, admittedly, acquired an immense amount of knowledge by simply being around during the last 6,000+ years, but he is totally ignorant of many things known by the most humble and uneducated believer. He knows nothing of God's love, his mercy, his grace, and his forgiveness. The devil does not know the future, nor all the secrets of the past. The question is often asked if Satan doesn't know his doom is sealed and the lake of fire will be his eternal imprisonment. He is indeed aware of these prophecies, but it must be kept in mind that according to Ezekiel 28:17 sin has corrupted the wisdom of Satan to the point where he still thinks he can defeat God. Sometimes the most clever criminal is a psychopathic killer.

VIII. The Christian's Victory over Satan—The word *nako* is found 28 times in the Greek New Testament and is almost always translated as "overcome." There are three important verses where this word is used: "These things I have spoken unto you, that in me ye might have peace. In the world ye shall have tribulation: but be of good cheer; I have overcome the world" (John 16:33). "Ye are of God, little children, and have overcome them: because greater is he that is in you, than he that is in the world" (1 John 4:4). "He that overcometh shall inherit all things; and I will be his God, and he shall be my son" (Rev. 21:7).

If language means anything at all, these verses promise the child of God total victory over his enemy, the devil. But how does the Christian experience this promised victory? He does it by keeping the same fundamental facts in mind that any would-be victor would, whether in the secular or spiritual battlefield.

These four fundamental facts are: (a) he must know his own weakness; (b) he must know his own strength; (c) he must know the weakness of his enemy; and (d) he must know the strength of his enemy. To either overestimate or underestimate in any of these four areas could prove to be a fatal error.

In one of his parables, our Lord warns of this very thing. "For which of you, intending to build a tower, sitteth not down first, and counteth the cost, whether he have sufficient to finish it? Lest haply, after he hath laid the foundation, and is not able to finish it, all that behold it begin to mock him, saying, This man began to build, and was not able to finish. Or what king, going to make war against another king, sitteth not down first, and consulteth whether he be able with ten thousand to meet him that cometh against him with twenty thousand? Or else, while the other is yet a great way off, he sendeth an ambassage, and desireth conditions of peace" (Luke 14:28-32).

Let us now examine these four facts the victor must be aware of:

A. The weakness of the Christian—"I am the vine, ye are the branches: He that abideth in me, and I in him, the same bringeth forth much fruit: for without me ye can do nothing. If a man abide not in me, he is cast forth as a branch, and is withered; and men gather them, and cast them into the fire, and they are burned" (John 15:5-6).

When I was first saved, I felt the Christian life was a 50/50 proposition. That is to say, I would carry my 50 percent of the load, and God would assume the remaining half. But to my dismay, I kept dropping my end of the load. I then suggested to God that we alter the proportions whereby he would carry 60 percent and I would be responsible for the remaining 40 percent. But alas, this also proved too heavy. So, I reasoned, a 70/30 agreement would surely work. But again, failure. Finally, after many years in the work of the Lord, I sometimes think I have things down to a 98/2 arrangement. I still am tempted to feel that by *now* I must surely be able to carry on at least 2 percent of the Master's work by myself. There simply *has* to be something I can perform in the flesh for God. But Jesus said, "Without me ye can do nothing" (John 15:5).

In Romans 7:18 Paul refers to this very thing. "For I know that in me (that is, in my flesh,) dwelleth no good thing: for to will is present with me; but how to perform that which is good I find not" (Rom. 7:18).

So the first basic fact of which we as Christians must be aware in order to assure victory over Satan is our own weakness.

B. The strength of the Christian—This is the second vital principle to be observed in guaranteeing spiritual success. What, though, is our chief strength? The answer is found in the following passages.

"I am crucified with Christ: nevertheless I live; yet not I, but Christ liveth in me: and the life which I now live in the flesh I live by the faith of the Son of God, who loved me, and gave himself for me" (Gal. 2:20).

The power of the universe is owned by the Lord Jesus Christ. This power is described in Philippians 4:13: "I can do all things through Christ which strengtheneth me."

Keep in mind that the will of God will never lead you where the grace of God and the strength of God cannot sustain you.

C. The weakness of Satan—Third, we must fully understand the weakness of our enemy. According to the Scriptures, the devil is powerless in the following areas:

1. He cannot tempt a believer except by God's permission—"There hath no temptation taken you but such as is common to man: but God is faithful, who will not suffer you to be tempted above that ye are able; but will with the temptation also make a way to escape, that ye may be able to bear it" (1 Cor. 10:13).

   God knows exactly how much his child can bear. He will not allow Satan to go beyond this breaking point. Remember, when you are being tempted, Satan has had to first get the permission from God to tempt you. God only allows the temptation in the first place to strengthen and purify his children. "Wherein ye greatly rejoice, though now for a season, if need be, ye are in heaviness through manifold temptations: that the trial of your faith, being much more precious than of gold that perisheth, though it be tried with fire, might be found unto praise and honour and glory at the appearing of Jesus Christ" (1 Pet. 1:6-7).

2. He cannot stand to be resisted—"Submit yourselves therefore to God. Resist the devil, and he will flee from you" (James 4:7). But how does one go about resisting the devil? James answers this—by submitting first to God. "Neither give place to the devil" (Eph. 4:27). Satan enjoys a lively debate (like the one he

carried on with Eve in Genesis 3), but he cannot tolerate being resisted. The Christian can successfully resist the devil if he does the following:

a. The Christian must know how the devil attacks—"Lest Satan should get an advantage of us: for we are not ignorant of his devices" (2 Cor. 2:11).

But what are his devices? In section D of this study we will briefly consider the 16 deadly devices of Satan.

b. The Christian must stand guard waiting for Satan to attack—"Be sober, be vigilant; because your adversary the devil, as a roaring lion, walketh about, seeking whom he may devour" (1 Pet. 5:8).

Do you remember what you were doing on December 7, 1941? Perhaps this is just a date in history to you. This was the day the Japanese bombed Pearl Harbor. There had been all sorts of indirect evidence that Pearl Harbor would be subjected to an attack, even as much as six months earlier. Yet, on this particular Sunday morning in December 1941, 3,200 of our boys went out into eternity, and several of our ships were sunk. Why? Because even though there had been some indirect information concerning an attack, we were not standing guard when the Japanese did attack. So, as Peter warns us in the passage above, we must stand guard waiting for Satan to attack.

c. The Christian must have on the proper protection when Satan attacks— "Finally, my brethren, be strong in the Lord, and in the power of his might. Put on the whole armour of God, that ye may be able to stand against the wiles of the devil. For we wrestle not against flesh and blood, but against principalities, against powers, against the rulers of the darkness of this world, against spiritual wickedness in high places. Wherefore take unto you the whole armour of God, that ye may be able to withstand in the evil day, and having done all, to stand. Stand therefore, having your loins girt about with truth, and having on the breastplate of righteousness; and your feet shod with the preparation of the gospel of peace; above all, taking the shield of faith, wherewith ye shall be able to quench all the fiery darts of the wicked" (Eph. 6:10-17).

In this passage it seems very probable that the Holy Spirit led Paul to use the analogy of the pieces of armor worn by the Roman soldier of the day to illustrate the Christian's proper protection against Satan.

Warren Wiersbe aptly describes and applies each piece of this armor:

(1) The girdle of truth (v. 14a)

> Satan is a liar (John 8:44), but the believer whose life is controlled by truth will defeat him. The girdle holds the other parts of the armor together, and truth is the integrating force in the life of the victorious Christian. A man of integrity, with a clear conscience, can face the enemy without fear. The girdle also held the sword. Unless we practice the truth, we cannot use the Word of truth. Once a lie gets into the life of a believer, everything begins to fall apart. For over a year, King David lied about his sin with Bathsheba, and nothing went right. Psalms 32 and 51 tell of the price he paid.

(2) The breastplate of righteousness (v. 14b)

> This piece of armor, made of metal plates or chains, covered the body from the neck to the waist, both front and back. It symbolizes the

believer's righteousness in Christ (2 Cor. 5:21) as well as his righteous
life in Christ (Eph. 4:24). Satan is the accuser, but he cannot accuse the
believer who is living a godly life in the power of the Spirit. The life
we live either fortifies us against Satan's attacks or makes it easier for
him to defeat us (2 Cor. 6:1-10). When Satan accuses the Christian, it is
the righteousness of Christ that assures the believer of his salvation.
But our positional righteousness in Christ, without practical righteousness in the daily life, only gives Satan opportunity to attack us.

(3) The shoes of the gospel (v. 15)

The Roman soldier wore sandals with hobnails in the soles to give
him better footing for the battle. If we are going to "stand" and "withstand," then we need the shoes of the Gospel. Because we have the
peace with God (Rom. 5:1) that comes from the Gospel, we need not
fear the attack of Satan or men. We must be at peace with God and
with each other if we are to defeat the devil (Jas. 4:1-7). But the shoes
have another meaning. We must be prepared each day to share the
Gospel of peace with a lost world. The most victorious Christian is a
witnessing Christian. If we wear the shoes of the Gospel, then we
have the "beautiful feet" mentioned in Isaiah 52:7 and Romans 10:15.
Satan has declared war, but you and I are ambassadors of peace
(2 Cor. 5:18-21); and, as such, we take the Gospel of peace wherever
we go.

(4) The shield of faith (v. 16)

The shield was large, usually about four feet by two feet, made of
wood, and covered with tough leather. As the soldier held it before
him, it protected him from spears, arrows, and "fiery darts." The
edges of these shields were so constructed that an entire line of soldiers could interlock shields and march into the enemy like a solid
wall. This suggests that we Christians are not in the battle alone. The
"faith" mentioned here is not saving faith, but rather living faith, a
trust in the promises and power of God. Faith is a defensive weapon
which protects us from Satan's fiery darts.

In Paul's day, arrows, dipped in some inflammable substance and
ignited, were shot at the enemy. Satan shoots "fiery darts" at our
hearts and minds: lies, blasphemous thoughts, hateful thoughts about
others, doubts, and burning desires for sin. If we do not by faith
quench these darts, they will light a fire within and we will disobey
God. We never know when Satan will shoot a dart at us, so we must
always walk by faith and use the shield of faith.

(5) The helmet of salvation (v. 17)

Satan wants to attack the mind, the way he defeated Eve (Gen. 3;
2 Cor. 11:1-3). The helmet refers to the mind controlled by God. It is
too bad that many Christians have the idea that the intellect is not
important, when in reality it plays a vital role in Christian growth, service, and victory. When God controls the mind, Satan cannot lead the
believer astray. The Christian who studies his Bible and learns the

meaning of Bible doctrines is not going to be led astray too easily. We need to be "taught by Him, as the truth is in Jesus" (Eph. 4:21). We are to "grow in grace, and in the knowledge of our Lord and Savior Jesus Christ" (2 Peter. 3:18). Whenever Paul ministered, he taught the new converts the truths of the Word of God, and this helmet protected them from Satan's lies.

(6) The sword of the Spirit (v. 17b)

This sword is the offensive weapon God provides us. The Roman soldier wore on his girdle a short sword which was used for close-in fighting. Hebrews 4:12 compares the Word of God to a sword, because it is sharp and is able to pierce the inner man just as a material sword pierces the body. You and I were "cut to the heart" (Acts 2:37; 5:33) when the Word convicted us of our sins. Peter tried to use a sword to defend Jesus in the garden (Luke 22:47-51); but he learned at Pentecost that the "sword of the Spirit" does a much better job. Moses also tried to conquer with a physical sword (Exod. 2:11-15), only to discover that God's word alone was more than enough to defeat Egypt.

A material sword pierces the body, but the word of God pierces the heart. The more you use a physical sword, the duller it becomes; but using God's Word only makes it sharper in our lives. A physical sword requires the hand of a soldier, but the sword of the Spirit has its own power, for it is "living and powerful" (Heb. 4:12). The Spirit wrote the Word, and the Spirit wields the Word as we take it by faith and use it. A physical sword wounds to hurt and kill, while the sword of the Spirit wounds to heal and give life. But when we use the sword against Satan, we are out to deal him a blow that will cripple him and keep him from hindering God's work.

In one sense, the "whole armor of God" is a picture of Jesus Christ. Christ is the Truth (John 14:6), and He is our righteousness (2 Cor. 5:21) and our peace (Eph. 2:14). His faithfulness makes possible our faith (Gal. 2:20); He is our salvation (Luke 2:30); and He is the Word of God (John 1:1, 14). This means that when we trusted Christ, we received the armor. Paul told the Romans what to do with the armor (Rom. 13:11-14); wake up (Rom. 13:11), cast off sin, and "put on the armor of light" (Rom. 13:12). We do this by putting "on the Lord Jesus Christ" (Rom. 13:14). By faith, put on the armor and trust God for the victory. Once and for all, we have put on the armor at the moment of salvation. But there must be a daily appropriation. When King David put off his armor and returned to his palace, he was in greater danger than when he was on the battlefield (2 Sam. 11). We are never out of reach of Satan's devices, so we must never be without the whole armor of God." (*Be Rich [Ephesians]*, pp. 58–59)

One final thought concerning the action of the believer in regards to this equipment: As pilgrims we walk, as witnesses we talk, as contenders we run, but as fighters we stand.

3. He cannot stand the blood of Christ nor the Christian's testimony—"And they

overcame him by the blood of the Lamb, and by the word of their testimony; and they loved not their lives unto the death (Rev. 12:11).

The blood of Jesus Christ not only cleanses us from sin, but it defeats Satan in the process. If you need to check out a person theologically, ask that person what he thinks of the blood of Christ. Right away, his response to this will determine his spirituality or his lack of spirituality. If the person is unsaved or not in the right relationship with God, or if he is controlled by the devil, you will be able to determine it from his reaction to such a question. Satan cannot stand the blood of Christ nor the positive testimony of a Christian. We may rest assured that songs like "Power in the Blood" and "Nothing but the Blood" will never be put on the top ten of the Hades' Hit Parade.

D. The strength of Satan—The following list could well be called "The 16 Deadly *D*s of the Devil."

1. Disappointment: To be disappointed is to forget—"And we know that all things work together for good to them that love God, to them who are the called according to his purpose" (Rom. 8:28).

2. Discouragement: To be discouraged is to forget—"And David was greatly distressed; for the people spake of stoning him, because the soul of all the people was grieved, every man for his sons and for his daughters: but David encouraged himself in the LORD his God" (1 Sam. 30:6).

3. Despair: To despair is to forget—"We are troubled on every side, yet not distressed; we are perplexed, but not in despair" (2 Cor. 4:8).

4. Doubt: To doubt is to forget—"I will therefore that men pray every where, lifting up holy hands, without wrath and doubting" (1 Tim. 2:8).

5. Disbelief: To disbelieve is to forget—"Take heed, brethren, lest there be in any of you an evil heart of unbelief, in departing from the living God" (Heb. 3:12).

6. Distraction: To be distracted is to forget—"But when he saw the wind boisterous, he was afraid; and beginning to sink, he cried, saying, Lord, save me" (Matt. 14:30).

7. Doublemindedness: To be double-minded is to forget—"A double minded man is unstable in all his ways" (James 1:8).

8. Dishonesty: To be dishonest is to forget—"But have renounced the hidden things of dishonesty, not walking in craftiness, nor handling the word of God deceitfully; but by manifestation of the truth commending ourselves to every man's conscience in the sight of God" (2 Cor. 4:2).

9. Deceit: To be deceitful is to forget—"The heart is deceitful above all things, and desperately wicked: who can know it?" (Jer. 17:9).

10. Dullness: To suffer dullness is to forget—"Of whom we have many things to say, and hard to be uttered, seeing ye are dull of hearing" (Heb. 5:11).

11. Deadness: To suffer deadness is to forget—"How much more shall the blood of Christ, who through the eternal Spirit offered himself without spot to God, purge your conscience from dead works to serve the living God?" (Heb. 9:14). "And unto the angel of the church in Sardis write; These things saith he that hath the seven Spirits of God, and the seven stars; I know thy works, that thou hast a name that thou livest, and art dead" (Rev. 3:1).

12. Delay: To delay is to forget—"Boast not thyself of to morrow; for thou knowest not what a day may bring forth" (Prov. 27:1).

13. Defilement: To be defiled is to forget—"Know ye not that ye are the temple of God, and that the Spirit of God dwelleth in you? If any man defile the temple of

God, him shall God destroy; for the temple of God is holy, which temple ye are" (1 Cor. 3:16-17).

14. Defamation: to defame someone is to forget—"Whoso privily slandereth his neighbour, him will I cut off: him that hath an high look and a proud heart will not I suffer" (Psa. 101:5). "He that hideth hatred with lying lips, and he that uttereth a slander, is a fool" (Prov. 10:18).

15. Disobedience: To disobey is to forget—"And Samuel said, Hath the LORD as great delight in burnt offerings and sacrifices, as in obeying the voice of the LORD? Behold, to obey is better than sacrifice, and to hearken than the fat of rams" (1 Sam. 15:22).

     "For sin shall not have dominion over you: for ye are not under the law, but under grace. What then? shall we sin, because we are not under the law, but under grace? God forbid. Know ye not, that to whom ye yield yourselves servants to obey, his servants ye are to whom ye obey; whether of sin unto death, or of obedience unto righteousness? But God be thanked, that ye were the servants of sin, but ye have obeyed from the heart that form of doctrine which was delivered you. Being then made free from sin, ye became the servants of righteousness" (Rom. 6:14-18).

16. Discord: to sow discord is to forget—"Frowardness is in his heart, he deviseth mischief continually; he soweth discord." (Prov. 6:14). "These six things doth the LORD hate: yea, seven are an abomination unto him: A proud look, a lying tongue, and hands that shed innocent blood, an heart that deviseth wicked imaginations, feet that be swift in running to mischief, a false witness that speaketh lies, and he that soweth discord among brethren" (Prov. 6:16-19).

THE DOCTRINE OF ANGELS

INTRODUCTION

Throughout his long history, man has often wondered whether he is indeed the only intelligent being in his universe, and whether life as we know it is confined to the earth alone. One of the most recent scientific attempts is the search for extraterrestrial life. Coded messages are now being transmitted into the distant recesses of outer space by means of radio telescopes. The scientist then anxiously awaits the results of his bold probe. Will his signals be picked up by unearthly ears? If life is out there, will it prove friend or foe?

The following article entitled "Are We Alone?" appeared in the *1991 Information Please Almanac* (p. 353).

> Seventeen years ago, on November 16, 1974, the people of the planet Earth sent a purposeful message to interstellar space. Using a giant radio telescope in Puerto Rico, we beamed up a 3-minute message about ourselves to anyone listening in a cluster of stars in the constellation Hercules. We told them all about the solar system we live in, about the population of the world at the time, and about the atomic elements we're made of. We haven't heard back from anyone.
>
> Moving outward, our message has travelled 17 light years so far, nearly four times the distance to the nearest star, *Alpha Centauri,* but needs at least another 24,983 years to get to the 300,000 closely packed stars in the Hercules cluster. Then it will be another 25,000 before we should expect to hear anything back.
>
> Today, several programs around the world are tuned into the great beyond. Perhaps best known as SETI (for Search for Extra Terrestrial Intelligence), NASA is most heavily involved. Harvard runs the META (for Megachannel Extra Terrestrial Assay) receiver, which covers 64 times as many channels as its predecessor *Project Sentinel.* In 1992, a group of NASA scientists will begin a 10-year search for extraterrestrial intelligence using a radio spectrum analyzer that will tune into 10 million radio channels simultaneously. The radio telescopes used by the Naval Observatory are trained on 73 distant quasars, performing the essential mission-related work needed for precise navigation. They measure Earth rotation, and do astrometric research. In this program of observation, the same quasars are being monitored year after year.
>
> Finding a signal from the great beyond would be momentous, a turning point. Definitively finding that there existed intelligent life elsewhere in our Universe would perhaps be the greatest event in all of human history. Mankind's view of itself would change irrevocably, and forever.

In light of all this, it seems tragic that man does not turn to the Word of God in his search, for the Bible clearly answers this question, as it does all other questions that confront humanity.

Is there intelligent life in the universe? Are there other living and rational creatures "out there" besides man? There are, indeed. Are they friend or foe? They are both. Is their "civilization" older than ours is? It is. Will we ever learn to communicate with them? We not only *will*, but a number of human beings *already* have met and talked with them.

Who are these cosmic creatures? They are called *angels*.

Belief in angels is found in the history of all nations. The ancient Egyptians, Phoenicians, Greeks, and others all expressed their belief in angels. A. S. Joppie writes: "The Mohammedans believe in angels. They believe that two angels are assigned to each person. The angel on the right hand records all your good deeds. The angel on your left records all your evil deeds.

"The Hebrews taught there were four great angels: (1) Gabriel, who reveals the secrets of God to men. (2) Michael, who fights and avenges God's foes. (3) Raphael, who receives the departing spirits of the dead. (4) Uriel, who will summon everybody to judgment" (*All about Angels*, p. 43).

In the apocryphal book of Tobit is an account of an angel by the name of Raphael. The young man whom the angel accompanied was in danger of being devoured by a big fish. The angel saved him. Then he told the young man to use the heart and liver of the fish against demon influence, and the gall against eye diseases, etc.

According to Muslim legend, when Muhammad was transported to heaven he saw an angel there with "70,000 heads, each head had 70,000 faces, each face had 70,000 mouths, each mouth had 70,000 tongues, and each tongue spoke 70,000 languages." This would make more than 1.6 *septillion* languages, and nearly 343 trillion mouths!

The earliest archaeological evidence of angels to date appears on the stela of Ur-Nammus (2250 B.C.), and shows angels flying over the head of this king while he is in prayer.

But enough of tradition and history. What does the Bible say about angels?

I. The Existence of Angels
  A. The words involved
    1. Old Testament words
      a. *Malak*, translated "angel"—It is used 111 times. Note: The vast majority of these instances are in regards to the Angel of the Lord. Most Bible students feel this title as found in the Old Testament is always a Christophany, that is, a pre-Bethlehem appearance of Christ.
      b. *Ruach*, translated "spirit"—It is used 6 times.
      c. *Sair* and *shed*, translated "devils"—These are used 4 times.
    2. New Testament words
      a. *Aggellos*, translated "angel"—It is used 181 times.
      b. *Daimon*, translated "devil"—It is used 74 times.
  B. The witness involved—Many biblical individuals met and were ministered to by angels. Some of them were:
    1. Lot (Gen. 19:1)
    2. Jacob (Gen. 28:12; 31:1)
    3. Daniel (Dan. 8:16-19; 9:21-27; 10:10-15)
    4. Ezekiel (Ezek. 1:4-28; 10:1-22)
    5. Isaiah (Isa. 6:1-7)
    6. Zechariah (Zech. 1:10; 2:13) Old Testament prophet
    7. Zechariah (Luke 1:11-20) New Testament priest
    8. Mary (Luke 1:26)

9. The shepherds (Luke 2:9)
10. Joseph (Matt. 1:20; 2:13, 19)
11. Lazarus the beggar (Luke 16:22)
12. Mary Magdalene (John 20:12)
13. The women at the empty tomb (Matt. 28:5; Luke 24:23)
14. The apostles (Acts 5:19)
15. Philip (Acts 8:26)
16. Cornelius (Acts 10:3)
17. Peter (Acts 12:7)
18. Paul (Acts 27:23)
19. John the apostle—John experiences by far more encounters with angels than any other person in the entire Bible, witnessing these heavenly creatures on dozens of occasions.
    a. Personal encounters
        (1) He is commanded to eat the Word of God (Rev. 10:9-10).
        (2) He is commanded to measure the tribulational temple (Rev. 11:1).
        (3) He is invited to witness the judgment of the false church (Rev. 17:1).
        (4) He is invited to visit the heavenly Jerusalem (Rev. 21:9).
        (5) He is rebuked on two occasions for attempting to worship an angel.
            (a) First occasion (Rev. 19:10)
            (b) Second occasion (Rev. 22:8-9)
        (6) He is forbidden to seal up his book on prophecy (Rev. 22:10).
    b. Public encounters—John both sees and hears the angels doing and saying many things.
        (1) Proclaiming (Rev. 5:2; 10:1)
        (2) Worshipping (Rev. 4:8, 11; 5:11-12)
        (3) Judging
            (a) Via the trumpets (Rev. 8:2)
            (b) Via the bowls (Rev. 15:9)
        (4) Opening (Rev. 9:1)
        (5) Sealing (Rev. 7:3)
        (6) Offering incense (Rev. 8:3)
        (7) Warning (Rev. 14:9-10)
        (8) Reaping (Rev. 15:17)
        (9) Illustrating (Rev. 18:21)
        (10) Fighting (Rev. 12:7)
        (11) Preaching (Rev. 14:6-7)
        (12) Announcing doom (Rev. 14:8; 18:2)
        (13) Celebrating (Rev. 11:15)
        (14) Inviting (Rev. 19:17-18)
        (15) Binding (Rev. 20:1-3)
        (16) Torturing the unbelievers (Rev. 9:3-6)
        (17) Killing the unbelievers (Rev. 9:18)

II. The Origin of Angels
    A. The source of their origin—Angels, like everything else in this universe, were made by God the Father through Jesus Christ in the energy of the Holy Spirit. "In the beginning God created the heaven and the earth. And the earth was without form, and void; and darkness was upon the face of the deep. And the Spirit of God moved upon the face of the waters" (Gen. 1:1-2). "Thus the heavens and

the earth were finished, and all the host of them" (Gen. 2:1). "Thou, even thou, art LORD alone; thou hast made heaven, the heaven of heavens, with all their host, the earth, and all things that are therein, the seas, and all that is therein, and thou preservest them all; and the host of heaven worshippeth thee" (Neh. 9:6). "In the beginning was the Word, and the Word was with God, and the Word was God. The same was in the beginning with God. All things were made by him; and without him was not any thing made that was made" (John 1:1-3). "And to make all men see what is the fellowship of the mystery, which from the beginning of the world hath been hid in God, who created all things by Jesus Christ" (Eph. 3:9). "For by him were all things created, that are in heaven, and that are in earth, visible and invisible, whether they be thrones, or dominions, or principalities, or powers: all things were created by him, and for him" (Col. 1:16).

B. The method of their origin
1. Angels, like man, were created by a special act of God. They did not evolve into being. "Praise ye him, all his angels: praise ye him, all his hosts. Let them praise the name of the LORD: for he commanded, and they were created" (Psa. 148:2, 5).
2. Each angel is, therefore, a direct creation from God. This is perhaps why they are referred to as sons of God.
   a. As is indicated in the time of Noah (See Gen. 6:2, 4.)
   b. As indicated in the time of Job (See Job 1:6; 2:1.)—"Now there was a day when the sons of God came to present themselves before the LORD, and Satan came also among them" (Job 1:6).
3. The word "son" seems to indicate a direct creation of God, as Adam is also called the "son of God." (See Luke 3:38.)
4. Believers are also called this, as they are recreated in Christ, individually, as sons of God—"Behold, what manner of love the Father hath bestowed upon us, that we should be called the sons of God: therefore the world knoweth us not, because it knew him not" (1 John 3:1).
5. Their number, once completed at creation, was forever fixed. This is assumed because we never read of God creating more of them and Jesus said they do not reproduce themselves—"For in the resurrection they neither marry, nor are given in marriage, but are as the angels of God in heaven" (Matt. 22:30).
6. Furthermore, since we are told they cannot die (Luke 20:36) we conclude the original number of angels will never increase or decrease in size. For these reasons they must be considered a *company* of beings, and not a *race*—"Neither can they die any more: for they are equal unto the angels; and are the children of God, being the children of the resurrection" (Luke 20:36).

C. The time of their origin—"Then the LORD answered Job out of the whirlwind, and said, where wast thou when I laid the foundations of the earth? declare, if thou hast understanding. When the morning stars sang together, and all the sons of God shouted for joy?" (Job 38:1, 4, 7). In these verses God declares that the creation of angels took place prior to the creation of the earth.

D. The purpose of their origin: Angels were created to glorify Jesus Christ—"And again, when he bringeth in the first begotten into the world, he saith, And let all the angels of God worship him" (Heb. 1:6). "Thou art worthy, O Lord, to receive glory and honour and power: for thou hast created all things, and for thy pleasure they are and were created" (Rev. 4:11). (See also Col. 1:16.)

III. The Nature of Angels
   A. They are spirit beings—"Who maketh his angels spirits; his ministers a flaming
      fire" (Psa. 104:4)). "And of the angels he saith, Who maketh his angels spirits, and
      his ministers a flame of fire. Are they not all ministering spirits, sent forth to minis-
      ter for them who shall be heirs of salvation?" (Heb. 1:7, 14).

      Floyd Barackman writes, "Unlike our human nature with its body, soul and
      spirit, angels have a spirit kind of nature (Luke 24:37-39) that makes them spirits
      (Heb. 1:7, 14). However, we must not equate their spirit nature with God's
      uncreated essence that is spirit (John 4:24) or with our human spirit" (*Practical
      Christian Theology*, p. 171).
      1. While we are informed by Christ himself that spiritual beings do not possess
         flesh and bone (Luke 24:39), does this prove angels do not have any kind of
         body?
      2. Some have pointed to 1 Corinthians 15:40 as an indication that they *do* possess
         bodies—"There are also celestial bodies, and bodies terrestrial: but the glory of
         the celestial is one, and the glory of the terrestrial is another."
      3. At any rate, on two specific occasions angels are described as partaking of
         physical food, and on one occasion as applying physical force.
         a. They have been known to eat food.
            (1) Abraham served them under the oaks in Mamre (Gen. 18:1-8).
            (2) Lot served them in a home in Sodom (Gen. 19:1-3).
         b. They have been known to apply force—"And, behold, the angel of the Lord
            came upon him, and a light shined in the prison: and he smote Peter on the
            side, and raised him up, saying, Arise up quickly. And his chains fell off
            from his hands" (Acts 12:7).
   B. They are invisible beings. While on occasion they do manifest themselves, their
      normal practice is to remain invisible. Certainly one basic reason for this is to pre-
      vent both unsaved and saved men from worshipping them.
      1. Paul warned against angelic worship (Col. 2:18).
      2. John the apostle attempted to worship angels on two occasions.
         a. First occasion—"And I fell at his feet to worship him. And he said unto me,
            See thou do it not: I am thy fellow servant, and of thy brethren that have the
            testimony of Jesus: worship God: for the testimony of Jesus is the spirit of
            prophecy" (Rev. 19:10).
         b. Second occasion—"And I John saw these things, and heard them. And when
            I had heard and seen, I fell down to worship before the feet of the angel
            which shewed me these things. Then saith he unto me, See thou do it not:
            for I am thy fellow servant, and of thy brethren the prophets, and of them
            which keep the sayings of this book: worship God" (Rev. 22:8-9).
   C. They are innumerable.
      1. God, of course, knows their number, but they are presented to men as
         uncountable. There may be as many angels as there are stars in the heavens,
         for angels are associated with the stars. "Where wast thou when I laid the
         foundations of the earth? declare, if thou hast understanding. When the
         morning stars sang together, and all the sons of God shouted for joy?" (Job
         38:4, 7). (See also Psa. 148:1-3; Rev. 12:3, 4, 7-9.)
      2. If this be so, there would exist untold trillions of these heavenly beings, for
         modern astronomy tells us there are as many stars in the heavens as there are

grains of sand on all the seashores of the world! A hint of their huge number can be seen by the following:

    a. As indicated by Moses—"The LORD came from Sinai . . . with ten thousands of saints" (Deut. 33:2). The "saints" here are no doubt angels.

    b. As indicated by Daniel—"I beheld till the thrones were cast down, and the Ancient of days did sit, whose garment was white as snow, and the hair of his head like the pure wool: his throne was like the fiery flame, and his wheels as burning fire. A fiery stream issued and came forth from before him: thousand thousands ministered unto him, and ten thousand times ten thousand stood before him: the judgment was set, and the books were opened" (Dan. 7:9-10).

    c. As indicated by the Psalms—"The chariots of God are twenty thousand, even thousands of angels: the Lord is among them, as in Sinai, in the holy place" (Psa. 68:17).

    d. As indicated by the fallen angel possessing the maniac of Gadara—When Jesus demanded to know his name, the demon replied, "My name is Legion: for we are many" (Mark 5:9). A legion in the Roman army at that time consisted of 6,000 men. Apparently Satan controls so many fallen angels, he could afford to give over 6,000 of them to torment one poor, unimportant lunatic!

    e. As indicated by Jesus—"Thinkest thou that I cannot now pray to my Father, and he shall presently give me more than twelve legions of angels?" (Matt. 26:53).

    f. As indicated by the book of Hebrews—"But ye are come unto mount Sion, and unto the city of the living God, the heavenly Jerusalem, and to an innumerable company of angels" (Heb. 12:22).

    g. As indicated by John's heavenly vision—"And I beheld, and I heard the voice of many angels round about the throne and the beasts and the elders: and the number of them was ten thousand times ten thousand, and thousands of thousands" (Rev. 5:11).

D. They possess individual personalities. Angels possess separate and individual personalities, probably no two alike. They have the three necessary features required of personality:

  1. Intelligence

    a. Angels explained to Daniel the details concerning God's final plan for Israel (Dan. 9:21-22; 10:14).

    b. An angel revealed to John the mystery of religious Babylon, Satan's false church (Rev. 17:1, 7).

  2. Will

    a. Lucifer willfully left his first estate (Isa. 14:12-15).

    b. A number of angels willfully sided in with Lucifer during his revolt (Jude 6).

  3. Emotion

    a. They displayed joy at the birth of Christ (Luke 2:13).

    b. They desire to know the details of God's salvation (1 Pet. 1:12).

E. They are superior to man—"What is man, that thou art mindful of him? and the son of man, that thou visitest him? For thou hast made him a little lower than the angels, and hast crowned him with glory and honour" (Psa. 8:4-5). (See also Heb. 2:6-11.)

    However, someday, angels will be in subjection to believers—"Do ye not know that the saints shall judge the world? and if the world shall be judged by you, are ye unworthy to judge the smallest matters? Know ye not that we shall judge angels? how much more things that pertain to this life?" (1 Cor. 6:2-3).

1. They are stronger than man—"Bless the LORD, ye his angels, that excel in strength, that do his commandments, hearkening unto the voice of his word" (Psa. 103:20). "And to you who are troubled rest with us, when the Lord Jesus shall be revealed from heaven with his mighty angels" (2 Thess. 1:7). (See also 2 Pet. 2:11.)

2. They are smarter than man.
   a. They know the secrets of the past, having lived through it.
   b. They (probably) know the size and shape of the universe, being able to travel though it.
   c. They are swifter than man—"And I saw another angel fly in the midst of heaven" (Rev. 14:6).
      Their superiority in these areas seems to stem from two things:
      (1) They are unhindered by a fallen nature.
      (2) They are unbounded by the laws of gravity and time.

F. They are inferior to God.
   1. They are not omnipresent—"Then said he unto me, Fear not, Daniel: for from the first day that thou didst set thine heart to understand, and to chasten thyself before thy God, thy words were heard, and I am come for thy words" (Dan. 10:12). The angel, here, in Daniel 10 was in heaven at the time of Daniel's prayer and was sent by God to aid him. (See also Dan. 9:21.)
   2. They are not omnipotent—"But the prince of the kingdom of Persia withstood me one and twenty days: but, lo, Michael, one of the chief princes, came to help me; and I remained there with the kings of Persia" (Dan. 10:13). "Yet Michael the archangel, when contending with the devil he disputed about the body of Moses, durst not bring against him a railing accusation, but said, The Lord rebuke thee" (Jude 9). This same angel was experiencing satanic pressure, which hindered him for a full three weeks.
   3. They are not omniscient—"But of that day and hour knoweth no man, no, not the angels of heaven, but my Father only" (Matt. 24:36).

G. They, like man, may have been made in the image of God. How was man made in God's image? It has been suggested that this image consisted of two things:
   1. Personality: *Personality* gives the basic *capacity* to have fellowship with the person of God.
   2. Holiness: *Holiness* provides the basic *requirement* to enjoy that fellowship—"Follow peace with all men, and holiness, without which no man shall see the Lord" (Heb. 12:14).

If the above definition is correct, then angels can be said to have been made in the image of God, also.

IV. The Moral Classification of Angels
   A. It is believed that all angels were originally created without fault and, like Adam in the Garden, placed on a probation of some sort. They were theologically, during this time, *posse non pecarre* (able not to sin). But the probation period ended when heaven's chief angel, Lucifer by name, instigated a great revolt against Jehovah God Himself—"How art thou fallen from heaven, O Lucifer, son of the morning! how art thou cut down to the ground, which didst weaken the nations! For thou hast said in thine heart, I will ascend into heaven, I will exalt my throne above the stars of God: I will sit also upon the mount of the congregation, in the sides of the

north: I will ascend above the heights of the clouds; I will be like the most High. Yet thou shalt be brought down to hell, to the sides of the pit" (Isa. 14:12-15). (See also Ezek. 28:11-19.)

B. It is suggested by Revelation 12:3-4 that he was able to persuade one-third of heaven's angels to side with him in this terrible rebellion—"And there appeared another wonder in heaven; and behold a great red dragon, having seven heads and ten horns, and seven crowns upon his heads. And his tail drew the third part of the stars of heaven, and did cast them to the earth: and the dragon stood before the woman which was ready to be delivered, for to devour her child as soon as it was born" (Rev. 12:3-4).

Note: The word *drew* in this passage is from the Greek word *suro* , which means to drag or carry something. It is also found in Acts 14:19 when Paul's unconscious body was dragged out of the city of Lystra by his enemies. Thus Lucifer was able to drag down from their exalted position one-third of the angels.

C. The ones who did so, thus became *non posse non pecarre* (not able not to sin), while the remaining two-thirds were pronounced *non posse pecarre* (not able to sin).

D. From that point on, the *faithful* angels are referred to as holy and elect angels (Mark 8:38; 1 Tim. 5:21), while the *fallen* angels are known as the devil's angels (Matt. 25:41; Rev. 12:9).

   1. References to the holy and elect angels—"Whosoever therefore shall be ashamed of me and of my words in this adulterous and sinful generation; of him also shall the Son of man be ashamed, when he cometh in the glory of his Father with the holy angels" (Mark 8:38). "I charge thee before God, and the Lord Jesus Christ, and the elect angels, that thou observe these things without preferring one before another, doing nothing by partiality" (1 Tim. 5:21).

   2. References to the unholy and evil angels—"Then shall he say also unto them on the left hand, Depart from me, ye cursed, into everlasting fire, prepared for the devil and his angels" (Matt. 25:41). "And the great dragon was cast out, that old serpent, called the Devil, and Satan, which deceiveth the whole world: he was cast out into the earth, and his angels were cast out with him" (Rev. 12:9).

V. The Characteristics of Faithful Angels

A. Their rank

   1. The archangels

      a. Michael—His name means "Who is like God?" This should be contrasted to Satan's evil desire to "be like the most High": "I will ascend above the heights of the clouds; I will be like the most High" (Isa. 14:14).

      Michael is mentioned by name on four separate occasions in the Bible.

      (1) He helps a lesser-ranked angel get through to answer Daniel's prayer— "But the prince of the kingdom of Persia withstood me one and twenty days: but, lo, Michael, one of the chief princes, came to help me; and I remained there with the kings of Persia. But I will shew thee that which is noted in the scripture of truth: and there is none that holdeth with me in these things, but Michael your prince" (Dan. 10:13, 21).

      (2) He will stand up for Israel during the tribulation—"And at that time shall Michael stand up, the great prince which standeth for the children of thy people: and there shall be a time of trouble, such as never was since there was a nation even to that same time: and at that time thy people shall be delivered, every one that shall be found written in the book" (Dan. 12:1).

    (3) He disputes with Satan concerning the dead body of Moses—"Yet Michael the archangel, when contending with the devil he disputed about the body of Moses, durst not bring against him a railing accusation, but said, The Lord rebuke thee" (Jude 9).

    (4) He fights against Satan in the heavens—"And there was war in heaven: Michael and his angels fought against the dragon; and the dragon fought and his angels" (Rev. 12:7).

  b. Gabriel—His name means "The mighty one of God."

    (1) He explains the vision of the ram and goat battle to Daniel—"And I heard a man's voice between the banks of Ulai, which called, and said, Gabriel, make this man to understand the vision" (Dan. 8:16).

    (2) He explains the Seventy weeks to Daniel—"Yea, whiles I was speaking in prayer, even the man Gabriel, whom I had seen in the vision at the beginning, being caused to fly swiftly, touched me about the time of the evening oblation" (Dan. 9:21).

    (3) He predicts the birth of John the Baptist to Zacharias—"And the angel answering said unto him, I am Gabriel, that stand in the presence of God; and am sent to speak unto thee, and to shew thee these glad tidings" (Luke 1:19).

    (4) He predicts the birth of Jesus to Mary—"And in the sixth month the angel Gabriel was sent from God unto a city of Galilee, named Nazareth" (Luke 1:26).

    (5) He assures Joseph concerning the purity of Mary—"But while he thought on these things, behold, the angel of the Lord appeared unto him in a dream, saying, Joseph, thou son of David, fear not to take unto thee Mary thy wife: for that which is conceived in her is of the Holy Ghost" (Matt. 1:20).

    (6) He warns Joseph about the plot of Herod—"And when they were departed, behold, the angel of the Lord appeareth to Joseph in a dream, saying, Arise, and take the young child and his mother, and flee into Egypt, and be thou there until I bring thee word: for Herod will seek the young child to destroy him" (Matt. 2:13).

    (7) He tells Joseph about the death of Herod—"But when Herod was dead, behold, an angel of the Lord appeareth in a dream to Joseph in Egypt" (Matt. 2:19).

Note: Some Bible students have identified Gabriel with the various appearances of the Angel of the Lord in the remaining pages of the New Testament. If this is true, then Gabriel can be seen in the following 10 occasions.

    (8) He announces the birth of Christ to the shepherds—"And, lo, the angel of the Lord came upon them, and the glory of the Lord shone round about them: and they were sore afraid" (Luke 2:9).

    (9) He strengthens Christ in the Garden of Gethsemane—"And there appeared an angel unto him from heaven, strengthening him" (Luke 22:43).

    (10) He rolls the stone back at Christ's resurrection—"And, behold, there was a great earthquake: for the angel of the Lord descended from heaven, and came and rolled back the stone from the door, and sat upon it" (Matt. 28:2).

(11) He frees the apostles from prison—"But the angel of the Lord by night opened the prison doors, and brought them forth" (Acts 5:19).

(12) He sends Philip to the desert of Gaza to meet the eunuch—"And the angel of the Lord spake unto Philip, saying, Arise, and go toward the south unto the way that goeth down from Jerusalem unto Gaza, which is desert" (Acts 8:26).

(13) He instructs Cornelius to send for Peter—"He saw in a vision evidently about the ninth hour of the day an angel of God coming in to him, and saying unto him, Cornelius" (Acts 10:3).

(14) He frees Peter from prison—"And, behold, the angel of the Lord came upon him, and a light shined in the prison: and he smote Peter on the side, and raised him up, saying, Arise up quickly. And his chains fell off from his hands" (Acts 12:7).

(15) He executes wicked Herod for blasphemy—"And immediately the angel of the Lord smote him, because he gave not God the glory: and he was eaten of worms, and gave up the ghost" (Acts 12:23).

(16) He assures Paul on the deck of a sinking ship—"For there stood by me this night the angel of God, whose I am, and whom I serve" (Acts 27:23).

(17) He will sound the trumpet at the Rapture—"For the Lord himself shall descend from heaven with a shout, with the voice of the archangel, and with the trump of God: and the dead in Christ shall rise first" (1 Thess. 4:16).

2. The cherubim—"So he drove out the man; and he placed at the east of the garden of Eden Cherubims, and a flaming sword which turned every way, to keep the way of the tree of life" (Gen. 3:24). "And thou shalt make two cherubims of gold, of beaten work shalt thou make them, in the two ends of the mercy seat. And make one cherub on the one end, and the other cherub on the other end: even of the mercy seat shall ye make the cherubims on the two ends thereof. And the cherubims shall stretch forth their wings on high, covering the mercy seat with their wings, and their faces shall look one to another; toward the mercy seat shall the faces of the cherubims be" (Exod. 25:18-20). (See also Ezek. 1:4-28; 10:1-20.)

a. The description of the cherubim

(1) Each had four faces.

(a) The face in front is as a man.

(b) The face on the right is as a lion.

(c) The face on the left is as an ox.

(d) The face in back is as an eagle.

(2) Each has two pairs of wings.

(a) One pair spreads out from the middle of the back.

(b) The other pair is used to cover the body. These wings make a noise like waves crashing upon the seashore.

(3) They have the legs of men, but their feet are cloven like calves' feet, which shine like burnished brass.

(4) They have four human hands, with one located under each wing.

(5) They apparently travel in groups of four. The outstretched wings of each cherubim touches those of the remaining three companions, so that they form a square. When they move, they move as a group without turning their bodies.

   b. The duties of the cherubim:
      (1) They kept Adam from the Tree of Life after the Fall, lest he eat of it and live forever in his sin—"So he drove out the man; and he placed at the east of the garden of Eden Cherubims, and a flaming sword which turned every way, to keep the way of the tree of life" (Gen. 3:24).

   Note: There is an interesting analogy between the cherubim as guarding the entrance to paradise and the winged bulls and lions of Babylon and Assyria, colossal figures with human faces standing guard at the entrance of temples and palaces. Inasmuch as both these nations occupied the very spot where the original Garden of Eden may have been located, it is not unreasonable to suggest that these idols were perverted statue copies of the real cherubim.

      (2) Two golden cherubim were constructed at God's command and placed at either end on top of the Ark lid in the tabernacle Holy of Holies. (See also Exod. 25:18-20; Heb. 9:5.)
      (3) They appeared to Ezekiel—"Also out of the midst thereof came the likeness of four living creatures. And this was their appearance; they had the likeness of a man" (Ezek. 1:5). "Then I looked, and, behold, in the firmament that was above the head of the cherubims there appeared over them as it were a sapphire stone, as the appearance of the likeness of a throne" (Ezek. 10:1).
      (4) Prior to his fall, Satan (then known as Lucifer) was the chief cherub angel—"How art thou fallen from heaven, O Lucifer, son of the morning! how art thou cut down to the ground, which didst weaken the nations!" (Isa. 14:12) "Thou art the anointed cherub that covereth; and I have set thee so: thou wast upon the holy mountain of God; thou hast walked up and down in the midst of the stones of fire" (Ezek. 28:14).

3. The seraphim—"In the year that king Uzziah died I saw also the Lord sitting upon a throne, high and lifted up, and his train filled the temple. Above it stood the seraphim: each one had six wings; with twain he covered his face, and with twain he covered his feet, and with twain he did fly. And one cried unto another, and said, Holy, holy, holy, is the LORD of hosts: the whole earth is full of his glory. And the posts of the door moved at the voice of him that cried, and the house was filled with smoke. Then said I, Woe is me! for I am undone; because I am a man of unclean lips, and I dwell in the midst of a people of unclean lips: for mine eyes have seen the King, the LORD of hosts. Then flew one of the seraphim unto me, having a live coal in his hand, which he had taken with the tongs from off the altar: And he laid it upon my mouth, and said, Lo, this hath touched thy lips; and thine iniquity is taken away, and thy sin purged" (Isa. 6:1-7).

   The Hebrew word for *seraphim* means "burning ones" and probably speaks of the burning devotion to God on the part of these angelic beings. These beings are mentioned only once in the Bible.

4. The Four Living Creatures—"And before the throne there was a sea of glass like unto crystal: and in the midst of the throne, and round about the throne, were four beasts full of eyes before and behind. And the first beast was like a lion, and the second beast like a calf, and the third beast had a face as a man, and the fourth beast was like a flying eagle. And the four beasts had each of them six wings about him; and they were full of eyes within: and they rest not day and

night, saying, Holy, holy, holy, Lord God Almighty, which was, and is, and is to come. And when those beasts give glory and honour and thanks to him that sat on the throne, who liveth for ever and ever" (Rev. 4:6-9).

These special heavenly beings are in some ways similar to both the cherubim and the seraphim, but seem to be in a separate class by themselves. Their number appears to be limited to four. It has been suggested that they now hold those privileges and responsibilities once assigned to Lucifer, before he became the devil.

   a. John the apostle sees these four standing before the shining crystal sea in heaven surrounding God's throne.

   b. They are covered with eyes, both in front and behind.

   c. Each of the four has a different face.

      (1) One has the face of a lion.

      (2) One has the face of an ox.

      (3) One has the face of a man.

      (4) One has the face of an eagle.

   d. Each creature has six wings.

      Note: As it has been observed, there are similarities here between the cherubim and the living creatures. But differences may also be seen. The cherubim each have four faces, while the living creatures have but one. The cherubim possess four wings, whereas the living creatures have six.

   e. Without ceasing day or night, they proclaim God's praise, saying: "Holy, holy, holy, Lord God Almighty, which was, and is, and is to come" (Rev. 4:8).

   f. Each of the four living creatures will announce one of the first four great tribulational judgments of the seven-sealed book. (See Rev. 6:1, 3, 5, 7.)

   g. It has been suggested that the faces of both the cherubim and the living creatures are to remind the elect throughout all eternity of the earthly ministry performed by our blessed Lord. These faces correspond directly to the fourfold gospel presentation of Christ.

      (1) Matthew presents him as the lion of the tribe of Judah.

      (2) Mark presents him as the lowly ox.

      (3) Luke presents him as the perfect man.

      (4) John presents him as the mighty Godlike eagle.

5. Ruling angels—"Far above all principality, and power, and might, and dominion, and every name that is named, not only in this world, but also in that which is to come" (Eph. 1:21). "To the intent that now unto the principalities and powers in heavenly places might be known by the church the manifold wisdom of God" (Eph. 3:10). "For by him were all things created, that are in heaven, and that are in earth, visible and invisible, whether they be thrones, or dominions,or principalities, or powers: all things were created by him, and for him" (Col. 1:16). "And ye are complete in him, which is the head of all principality and power" (Col. 2:10). "Who is gone into heaven, and is on the right hand of God; angels and authorities and powers being made subject unto him" (1 Pet. 3:22).

In the above passages the following organizational features are mentioned.

   a. Principalities

   b. Powers

   c. Thrones

   d. Authorities

    e. Dominions

    f. Might

    While it is impossible to distinguish clearly among these six, it is nevertheless evident that they describe various levels of ruling positions assigned to angels, ranging perhaps (to use an earthly analogy) from generals to privates.

6. Guardian angels—"Take heed that ye despise not one of these little ones; for I say unto you, That in heaven their angels do always behold the face of my Father which is in heaven" (Matt. 18:10). "Are they not all ministering spirits, sent forth to minister for them who shall be heirs of salvation?" (Heb. 1:14).

    The Bible does not state whether each believer has a specific guardian angel, or whether various angels on occasion simply protect and aid the heirs of salvation. Both are logical possibilities.

7. Angels associated with horses and chariots—"And it came to pass, as they still went on, and talked, that, behold, there appeared a chariot of fire, and horses of fire, and parted them both asunder; and Elijah went up by a whirlwind into heaven" (2 Kings 2:11). "And Elisha prayed, and said, LORD, I pray thee, open his eyes, that he may see. And the LORD opened the eyes of the young man; and he saw: and, behold, the mountain was full of horses and chariots of fire round about Elisha" (2 Kings 6:17). "The chariots of God are twenty thousand, even thousands of angels: the Lord is among them, as in Sinai, in the holy place" (Psa. 68:17). (See also Zech. 1:8-11.) "And the armies which were in heaven followed him upon white horses, clothed in fine linen, white and clean" (Rev. 19:14).

    If these verses are to be taken in a literal sense, then one must conclude (whatever problems may be involved) that certain angels work closely with creatures of the animal kingdom in performing their ministry.

No discussion on the organization (and transportation) of angels would be perhaps complete without at least a brief consideration of the modern UFO phenomena. Is there a connection between angelic activity and flying saucer sightings? It cannot be denied that a similarity may exist between what Ezekiel viewed and the present-day reports of some UFOs as described by competent and reliable eyewitnesses.

The entire subject of UFOs has been aptly summarized in a book published by the Reader's Digest *entitled* Strange Stories, Amazing Facts *(pp. 585–589). The following items are some excerpts taken from this summary:*

Enigma of the UFO

Are they alien visitors, hallucinations, or natural phenomena?

To many people, unidentified flying objects are a harmless hoax. Yet they have been seen and photographed by astronauts, airline pilots, policemen, astronomers, housewives, meteorologists, and farmers.

The big mystery, which has remained unsolved since the popular term "flying saucers" was first coined in 1947, is: What are they, and where do they come from?

All kinds of explanations have been put forward to account for the worldwide sightings of discs, egg shapes, spheres, and other oddly formed aerial objects.

They have been explained away as unusual cloud formations, fireballs, meteorites, weather balloons, optical illusions, hallucinations, or simply fabrications engineered by publicity-seeking cranks.

But not every reported case can be dismissed in this way. The most logical attitude toward UFOs is that man is faced with a series of strange, at times inexplicable, phenomena.

The attitude of ufologists—students of UFOs—goes a step further. They usually claim that the earth is under surveillance by alien intelligences.

Tomorrow, perhaps, the truth will emerge. Meanwhile, mankind is left with a mass of evidence that ranges from impartial, level-headed accounts to the totally implausible.

The first saucers

The flying saucer story began on June 24, 1947, when a private pilot, Kenneth Arnold, who was taking part in a search for a missing transport aircraft, saw nine disc-shaped objects flying over Mount Rainier, Washington.

He described the objects as "flying like a saucer would if you skipped it across the water." Arnold's veracity and professional reputation were beyond question, and his account of the incident was accepted by the authorities. Newspapers picked up the story and labeled the objects "flying saucers."

Since then, there have been waves of reports of sightings. Even the House of Representatives' Committee on Science and Astronautics has held special hearings to take evidence from witnesses.

One of the most spectacular recent reports came from a Gemini 4 astronaut, James McDivitt, in June 1965. In orbit, about 90 miles above the earth, McDivitt saw a cylindrical object, apparently with arms sticking out of it, which he took to be another spacecraft with antennae. It appeared to be in free-drifting flight over the Pacific, somewhat higher than the Gemini capsule. McDivitt took one still photograph and some movie film.

He observed that the object was nearby and moving in a path toward his own spacecraft, but closing in fast. McDivitt and his fellow astronaut, Edward White, were hastily preparing to take evasive action when the UFO disappeared from view.

After splashdown the film was taken away, and McDivitt did not see it again for several days. When he did inspect the film, the object was "hazily" outlined against the sky. But he remained unalterably convinced it was a positive identification.

Originally, McDivitt thought he had seen some unmanned satellite. The official view was that he had spotted the unmanned photographic satellite Pegasus. But that was 1,200 miles away at the time.

However extraordinary their content, such reports have been given serious consideration. As highly trained observers, astronauts are unlikely to give way to speculation or imagination.

Capt. Ed Mitchell, the sixth man to walk on the moon, told a press conference in 1974: "I am completely convinced that some UFO sightings are real. The question isn't where the UFOs are from. The question is what are they?"

UFOs in orbit

A total of about 26 astronauts have reported seeing UFOs while in orbit. The first sighting was in 1962, and later reports include those made by men aboard Skylabs 1, 2, and 3. NASA (the National Aeronautics and Space Administration) takes the phenomenon seriously and checks into every sighting and analyzes all photographs.

During their stint of duty in Skylab 2, astronauts Jack Lousma, Owen Garriott, and Alan Bean watched and photographed a red UFO for ten minutes. They were then 270 miles above the earth. They said the object rotated every ten seconds and was 30 to 50 miles away in an orbit very close to their own.

In a prepared statement, put before the Committee on Science and Astronautics of the House of Representatives in 1968, Prof. James E. McDonald, a physicist from the University of Arizona, said: "My own present opinion, based on two years of careful study, is that UFOs are probably extraterrestrial devices engaged in something that might very tentatively be termed 'surveillance.'"

An "occupant sighting" was reported on April 24, 1964, in Socorro, New Mexico. State policeman Lonnie Zamora gave up chasing a speeding motorist to chase a UFO instead, when he saw one apparently coming in to land about a mile away.

Zamora reported that he found it outside the town, a bright, metallic oval, the size of an upturned car. Standing beside it, he said, were two humanoid figures, about the size of 10-year-old children. As he called headquarters to report, the figures retreated inside, and the object took off.

On July 1 the following year, a French lavender grower in the Provence village of Valensole saw what he thought were youths trying to steal his valuable plants. They were two diminutive figures, standing by an object "about the size of a Renault."

He got within five yards of them before one of the "boys" pointed an instrument at him and he claimed to have become paralyzed. The two figures then boarded their craft, and it sped away.

It was regarded as just another sighting—until an interviewer showed the lavender grower a photograph. The man became terrified, showing all the symptoms of sever shock. It was a picture of a model, constructed from the detailed description given by Zamora, 15 months earlier in New Mexico.

On October 11, 1973, two shipyard workers out fishing in Pascagoula, Mississippi, claimed to have been taken aboard an egg-shaped UFO and examined by three silvery-skinned creatures with no eyes. Charles Hickson, then 42, and Calvin Parker, 19, said the creatures kept them for about 20 minutes, "photographed" them, and then took them back to a riverside pier.

Parker said he fainted when he first saw the humanoid creatures. Each had a slit for a mouth and three pointed protrusions instead of a nose and ears. Their vehicle had descended from the sky to hover a few feet over the Pascagoula River.

After their ordeal the two men were interviewed by Dr. J. Allen Hynek, an astronomer who investigated UFOs for the U.S. Air Force. Later, the men were questioned under hypnosis by Dr. James Harder, of the University of California.

Traumatic experience

Dr. Hynek said: "They had undergone such a shocking thing that they couldn't put it exactly into words. Whatever happened to them definitely affected their rationality."

In Holsworthy, North Devon, England, two police constables on motor patrol got involved in a high-speed chase with an object resembling a shiny cross for about 50 minutes in the cold dawn of October 24, 1967. The two constables, Roger Willey and Clifford Wycott, later held a press conference. Willey said: "It looked like a star-spangled cross, radiating points of light from all angles. At times we drove at 90 miles an hour to keep up with it. It seemed to be watching us and would not let us catch up. It had terrific acceleration and knew we were chasing it."

The Ministry of Defense later said that the mysterious object was a giant jet tanker of the U.S. Air Force on a refueling mission. However, it was soon established that none of the tankers was airborne at the time.

UFOs appear to be attracted to western England. The town of Warminster is the UFO sightings' capital of the world. Since the mid-sixties there have been thousands of reports.

Thunderous explosion

The best substantiated incident was more a hearing than a sighting—by a whole company of Welsh Guards on Christmas morning 1964. Thirty of the men were awakened by "the sound of a thunderous explosion." The noise was repeated so many times that the men were alerted for duty. But outside there was nothing to be seen.

Later that morning a woman on her way to church was knocked down and pinned to the ground by some sort of sonic blast wave. The noise, described as a low drone with a beating rhythm, passed over several houses in the town, shaking foundations and lifting roof tiles.

Some months later there were reports that animals were suddenly and inexplicably collapsing "as if they hat been hit by some sort of ray."

Sightings and strange phenomena became so prevalent in and around Warminster that local people began to refer to anything unusual as the "Warminster Thing."

It has been said that the sights and sounds are caused by experiments with new weapons at the School of Infantry, near Warminster.

Twilight zone

The objects are generally seen in rural areas, but occasionally sightings are reported over cities. Most reports are in the two twilight periods, early morning and early evening, at a time when the glare of a city would make it difficult to observe a UFO in flight.

While most UFO sightings are reported by people on the ground, there are also many sightings by airline pilots and private-plane pilots. But it is more than likely that the number of such sightings greatly exceeds the number of actual reports. Pilots, particularly those with major airlines, are understandably reluctant to be thought of as cranks.

Most pilots relate to some strange object that often goes through aerial maneuvers that no man-made aircraft could execute—such as halting suddenly and hovering, after traveling at amazing speeds—then disappears.

But in one or two cases UFOs appear to have been linked with disasters. In 1953 the pilot of a DC-6, flying from Wake Island in the Pacific to Los Angeles, reported seeing some objects in the sky. Then communications ceased. The next morning searchers found fragments of the plane and 20 bodies.

Disappeared without a trace

In the same year two Air Force personnel in an F-89 jet chased a UFO over Lake Superior, on the U.S.-Canadian border. Tracked on radar, both the jet and the UFO appeared to merge on the radar screen. Then the jet disappeared, and the UFO passed out of range. Rescue aircraft and ships were sent out, but no trace of the jet or its occupants was found, despite the rigorous searches.

There are cases in which motorists claim their cars have been immobilized by UFOs. Other people say they were burned, put into trances, or knocked unconscious when approaching strange craft on the ground. There is even a police chief, Jeff Greenshaw, who claimed he chased a six-foot creature in a metallic suit in October 1973, at Falkville, Alabama. But, Greenshaw said, the humanoid outran the car.

But still no one has put forward a satisfactory explanation for all the strange happenings logged in UFO files, whether by amateurs or experts. Some believe that the earth is being watched by beings from another planet. If so, what is the purpose of these aliens?

Man, it seems, will simply have to wait until the extraterrestrials, if they exist, make themselves properly known to learn the answers to these and other questions. Either that, or find a more plausible explanation for the strange objects seen over and on the earth.

Having examined this information, is there a conclusion we can reach about the subject? Is a more plausible explanation for the objects that they are angels? If so, should we take the incidents of the missing plane and trances and burnings as angelic or demonic activity? Here we cannot be dogmatic.

B. Their appearance—A detailed description of the cherubim and seraphim has already been considered in our study. But what about the general appearance of angels? The Scriptures offer the following description.

"And entering into the sepulchre, they saw a young man sitting on the right side, clothed in a long white garment; and they were affrighted" (Mark 16:5). "His countenance was like lightning, and his raiment white as snow" (Matt. 28:3). "And it came to pass, as they were much perplexed thereabout, behold, two men stood by them in shining garments" (Luke 24:4). "And I saw another mighty angel come down from heaven, clothed with a cloud: and a rainbow was upon his head, and his face was as it were the sun, and his feet as pillars of fire" (Rev. 10:1). "And the seven angels came out of the temple, having the seven plagues, clothed in pure and white linen, and having their breasts girded with golden girdles" (Rev. 15:6). "And after these things I saw another angel come down from heaven, having great power; and the earth was lightened with his glory" (Rev. 18:1).

In view of their dazzling splendor and great glory, it is not difficult to understand why both unsaved (Col. 2:18) and saved men (Rev. 19:10; 22:8-9) have attempted to worship angels.

C. Their names and titles
  1. Ministers—This signifies their religious duties and spiritual service. "Bless the LORD, ye his angels, that excel in strength, that do his commandments, hearkening unto the voice of his word. Bless ye the LORD, all ye his hosts; ye ministers of his, that do his pleasure" (Psa. 103:20-21). "Who maketh his angels spirits; his ministers a flaming fire" (Psa. 104:4).
  2. Host—This name speaks of their military service.
      a. As testified by Jacob—"And Jacob went on his way, and the angels of God met him. And when Jacob saw them, he said, This is God's host: and he called the name of that place Mahanaim" (Gen. 32:1-2).
      b. As testified by Joshua—"And it came to pass, when Joshua was by Jericho, that he lifted up his eyes and looked, and, behold, there stood a man over against him with his sword drawn in his hand: and Joshua went unto him, and said unto him, Art thou for us, or for our adversaries? And he said, Nay; but as captain of the host of the LORD am I now come. And Joshua fell on his face to the earth, and did worship, and said unto him, What saith my lord unto his servant?" (Josh. 5:13-14).
      c. As testified by David—"Then said David to the Philistine, Thou comest to me with a sword, and with a spear, and with a shield: but I come to thee in the name of the LORD of hosts, the God of the armies of Israel, whom thou hast defied" (1 Sam. 17:45).
  3. Chariots—This may refer to their swiftness. "And he answered, Fear not: for they that be with us are more than they that be with them. And Elisha prayed, and said, LORD, I pray thee, open his eyes, that he may see. And the LORD opened the eyes of the young man; and he saw: and, behold, the mountain was full of horses and chariots of fire round about Elisha" (2 Kings 6:16-17). "The

chariots of God are twenty thousand, even thousands of angels: the Lord is among them, as in Sinai, in the holy place" (Psa.68:17). "And the angel answered and said unto me, These are the four spirits of the heavens, which go forth from standing before the Lord of all the earth" (Zech. 6:5).

4. Watchers—This speaks of their duties as supervisors and agents. "I saw in the visions of my head upon my bed, and, behold, a watcher and an holy one came down from heaven; this matter is by the decree of the watchers, and the demand by the word of the holy ones: to the intent that the living may know that the most High ruleth in the kingdom of men, and giveth it to whomsoever he will, and setteth up over it the basest of men" (Dan. 4:13, 17).

5. Sons of the mighty—This title may refer to their awesome strength and power. "Give unto the LORD, O ye mighty, give unto the LORD glory and strength" (Psa. 29:1). "For who in the heaven can be compared unto the LORD? who among the sons of the mighty can be likened unto the LORD?" (Psa. 89:6).

6. Sons of God—This title may indicate their relationship with God. "Now there was a day when the sons of God came to present themselves before the LORD, and Satan came also among them" (Job 1:6). "When the morning stars sang together, and all the sons of God shouted for joy?" (Job 38:7).

Dr. Lewis S. Chafer writes: "In Old Testament terminology, sometimes angels are called sons of God while men are called servants of God. In the New Testament this is reversed. Angels are servants and Christians are the sons of God. This particular order may be due to the fact that, in the Old Testament men are seen as related to this sphere over which angels are superior; while in the New Testament, saints are seen as related to their final exaltation into the likeness of Christ, compared to which the angels are inferior" (*Systematic Theology*, vol. II, p. 23).

7. Saints—Usually the term saints in the Bible refers to saved human beings. But on several occasions it is used in describing angels. "And he said, The LORD came from Sinai, and rose up from Seir unto them; he shined forth from mount Paran, and he came with ten thousands of saints: from his right hand went a fiery law for them" (Deut. 33:2). The "saints" Moses speaks of here accompanying God at the giving of the Law were angels, as attested to by three New Testament passages. (See Acts 7:53; Gal. 3:19; Heb. 2:2.) This title may refer to their total separation to the will of God. (See also Dan. 8:13; Zech. 14:5.)

8. Stars—"Where wast thou when I laid the foundations of the earth? declare, if thou hast understanding. When the morning stars sang together, and all the sons of God shouted for joy?" (Job 38:4, 7). (See also Rev. 12:3-4.) This may indicate both their number and their brightness.

D. Their work and ministry

1. Their activities in heaven

a. They worship the Person of God—"And he said, Hear thou therefore the word of the LORD: I saw the LORD sitting on his throne, and all the host of heaven standing by him on his right hand and on his left" (1 Kings 22:19). "Give unto the LORD, O ye mighty, give unto the LORD glory and strength. Give unto the LORD the glory due unto his name; worship the LORD in the beauty of holiness" (Psa. 29:1-2). "And one cried unto another, and said, Holy, holy, holy, is the LORD of hosts: the whole earth is full of his glory" (Isa. 6:3). "And the four beasts had each of them six wings about him; and they were full of eyes within: and they rest not day and night, saying, Holy,

holy, holy, Lord God Almighty, which was, and is, and is to come" (Rev. 4:8). "And the four and twenty elders and the four beasts fell down and worshipped God that sat on the throne, saying, Amen; Alleluia" (Rev. 19:4).

b. They observe the people of God—"Also I say unto you, Whosoever shall confess me before men, him shall the Son of man also confess before the angels of God: But he that denieth me before men shall be denied before the angels of God" (Luke 12:8-9).

   (1) In regards to our witnessing—"Likewise, I say unto you, there is joy in the presence of the angels of God over one sinner that repenteth" (Luke 15:10).

   (2) In regards to our testimony—"For I think that God hath set forth us the apostles last, as it were appointed to death: for we are made a spectacle unto the world, and to angels, and to men" (1 Cor. 4:9).

   (3) In regards to our submission—"For this cause ought the woman to have power on her head because of the angels" (1 Cor. 11:10).

   (4) In regards to our obedience—"I charge thee before God, and the Lord Jesus Christ, and the elect angels, that thou observe these things without preferring one before another, doing nothing by partiality" (1 Tim. 5:21).

   (5) In regards to our preaching—"Unto whom it was revealed, that not unto themselves, but unto us they did minister the things, which are now reported unto you by them that have preached the gospel unto you with the Holy Ghost sent down from heaven: which things the angels desire to look into" (1 Pet. 1:12).

c. They inquire into the prophetical plan of God—"Then I Daniel looked, and, behold, there stood other two, the one on this side of the bank of the river, and the other on that side of the bank of the river. And one said to the man clothed in linen, which was upon the waters of the river, How long shall it be to the end of these wonders?" (Dan. 12:5-6).

d. They rejoice in the works of God.

   (1) His work of creation—"When the morning stars sang together, and all the sons of God shouted for joy?" (Job 38:7). "Thou art worthy, O Lord, to receive glory and honour and power: for thou hast created all things, and for thy pleasure they are and were created" (Rev. 4:11).

   (2) His work of redemption—"And without controversy great is the mystery of godliness: God was manifest in the flesh, justified in the Spirit, seen of angels, preached unto the Gentiles, believed on in the world, received up into glory" (1 Tim. 3:16). "And I beheld, and I heard the voice of many angels round about the throne and the beasts and the elders: and the number of them was ten thousand times ten thousand, and thousands of thousands; saying with a loud voice, Worthy is the Lamb that was slain to receive power, and riches, and wisdom, and strength, and honour, and glory, and blessing" (Rev. 5:11-12).

e. They perform the will of God—"And he dreamed, and behold a ladder set up on the earth, and the top of it reached to heaven: and behold the angels of God ascending and descending on it" (Gen. 28:12). "Bless the LORD, ye his angels, that excel in strength, that do his commandments, hearkening unto the voice of his word" (Psa. 103:20). "A fiery stream issued and came forth from before him: thousand thousands ministered unto him, and ten thousand times ten thousand stood before him: the judgment was set, and the books were opened" (Dan. 7:10).

f. They witness the wrath of God—"The same shall drink of the wine of the wrath of God, which is poured out without mixture into the cup of his indignation; and he shall be tormented with fire and brimstone in the presence of the holy angels, and in the presence of the Lamb" (Rev. 14:10).

2. Their activities on earth

a. Concerning the saved—"Are they not all ministering spirits, sent forth to minister for them who shall be heirs of salvation?" (Heb. 1:14). "I Jesus have sent mine angel to testify unto you these things in the churches. I am the root and the offspring of David, and the bright and morning star" (Rev. 22:16).

(1) They inform, instruct, and interpret concerning both the will and Word of God. Note the following individuals who received that kind of ministry from angels:

(a) Daniel

i) Concerning the future ministry of the Antichrist (Dan. 7:16-25; 8:23-25)

ii) Concerning the purification of the Jewish temple (Dan. 8:13-14)

iii) Concerning the destruction of Persia by Greece (Dan. 8:15-22)

iv) Concerning the prophecy of the Seventy Weeks (Dan. 9:21-27)

(b) Zechariah, concerning the birth of John the Baptist (Luke 1:11-17)

(c) Mary, concerning the birth of Jesus (Luke 1:26-33)

(d) Joseph

i) Concerning the purity of Mary (Matt. 1:20)

ii) Concerning the evil intentions of Herod the Great (Matt. 2:13)

iii) Concerning the death of Herod (Matt. 2:19)

(e) The shepherds, concerning the birth of Jesus (Luke 2:9-12)

(f) The women at the empty tomb, concerning the resurrection of Christ (Luke 24:4-7)

(g) The apostles, concerning the return of Christ (Acts 1:10-11)

(h) Philip, concerning his mission in the desert of Gaza (Acts 8:26)

(i) Cornelius, concerning his need to hear Simon Peter (Acts 10:3-6)

(j) Paul, concerning the physical salvation of all 276 passengers on a sinking ship (Acts 27:23)

(k) John the apostle, concerning the mystery of religious Babylon (Rev. 17:1, 7)

(2) They protect—"The angel of the LORD encampeth round about them that fear him, and delivereth them" (Psa. 34:7). "For he shall give his angels charge over thee, to keep thee in all thy ways" (Psa. 91:11).

Dr. Billy Graham relates the following account:

The Reverend John G. Paton, a missionary in the New Hebrides Islands, tells a thrilling story involving the protective care of angels. Hostile natives surrounded his mission headquarters one night, intent on burning the Patons out and killing them. John Paton and his wife prayed all during that terror-filled night that God would deliver them. When daylight came they were amazed to see the attackers unaccountably leave. They thanked God for delivering them.

A year later, the chief of the tribe was converted to Jesus Christ, and Mr. Paton, remembering what had happened, asked the chief what had kept him and his men from burning down the house and killing them. The chief replied in surprise, "Who were all those men you had with you there?" The missionary answered, "There were no men there; just my wife and I." The chief argued that they had seen many men standing guard—hundreds of big men in shining garments with swords in their hands. They seemed to circle the mission station so that the natives were afraid to attack. Only then did Mr. Paton realize that God had sent His angels to protect them. The chief agreed that there was no other explanation. Could it be that God had sent a legion of angels to protect His servants, whose lives were being endangered? (*Angels: God's Special Agents*, p. 3)

(a) Angels protected Lot from the Sodomites—"But the men put forth their hand, and pulled Lot into the house to them, and shut to the door. And they smote the men that were at the door of the house with blindness, both small and great: so that they wearied themselves to find the door" (Gen. 19:10-11).

(b) Angels protected Elisha from the Syrians—"And when the servant of the man of God was risen early, and gone forth, behold, an host compassed the city both with horses and chariots. And his servant said unto him, Alas, my master! how shall we do? And he answered, Fear not: for they that be with us are more than they that be with them. And Elisha prayed, and said, LORD, I pray thee, open his eyes, that he may see. And the LORD opened the eyes of the young man; and he saw: and, behold, the mountain was full of horses and chariots of fire round about Elisha" (2 Kings 6:15-17).

(3) They comfort—"And as he lay and slept under a juniper tree, behold, then an angel touched him, and said unto him, Arise and eat" (1 Kings 19:5). "For there stood by me this night the angel of God, whose I am, and whom I serve, saying, Fear not, Paul; thou must be brought before Caesar: and, lo, God hath given thee all them that sail with thee" (Acts 27:23-24).

(4) They deliver—"But the angel of the Lord by night opened the prison doors, and brought them [the apostles] forth" (Acts 5:19). "And behold, the angel of the Lord came upon him, and a light shined in the prison: and he smote Peter on the side, and raised him up, saying, Arise up quickly. And his chains fell off from his hands" (Acts 12:7).

(5) They minister to the believer at the moment of death. "And it came to pass, that the beggar died, and was carried by the angels into Abraham's bosom" (Luke 16:22).

b. Concerning the unsaved

(1) They judged the Sodomites—"For we will destroy this place, because the cry of them is waxen great before the face of the LORD; and the LORD hath sent us to destroy it" (Gen. 19:13).

(2) They judged Herod—"And immediately the angel of the Lord smote him, because he gave not God the glory: and he was eaten of worms, and gave up the ghost" (Acts 12:23).

(3) They will judge the earth during the great tribulation—"And another

angel came out of the temple, crying with a loud voice to him that sat on the cloud, Thrust in thy sickle, and reap: for the time is come for thee to reap; for the harvest of the earth is ripe. And he that sat on the cloud thrust in his sickle on the earth; and the earth was reaped" (Rev. 14:15-16).

(4) They hold back the four winds of heaven—"And after these things I saw four angels standing on the four corners of the earth, holding the four winds of the earth, that the wind should not blow on the earth, nor on the sea, nor on any tree" (Rev. 7:1).

(5) They pronounce the seven trumpet judgments—"And I saw the seven angels which stood before God; and to them were given seven trumpets" (Rev. 8:2).

(6) They cast Satan and his angels out of heaven—"And there was war in heaven: Michael and his angels fought against the dragon; and the dragon fought and his angels, and prevailed not; neither was their place found any more in heaven" (Rev. 12:7-8).

(7) They announce the eternal hell awaiting all unbelievers—"The same shall drink of the wine of the wrath of God, which is poured out without mixture into the cup of his indignation; and he shall be tormented with fire and brimstone in the presence of the holy angels, and in the presence of the Lamb" (Rev. 14:10).

(8) They predict the fall of Babylon—"And there followed another angel, saying, Babylon is fallen, is fallen, that great city, because she made all nations drink of the wine of the wrath of her fornication" (Rev. 14:8).

(9) They announce the fall of Babylon—"And after these things I saw another angel come down from heaven, having great power; and the earth was lightened with his glory. And he cried mightily with a strong voice, saying, Babylon the great is fallen, is fallen, and is become the habitation of devils, and the hold of every foul spirit, and a cage of every unclean and hateful bird" (Rev. 18:1-2).

(10) They pour out the seven vial judgments—"And I saw another sign in heaven, great and marvellous, seven angels having the seven last plagues; for in them is filled up the wrath of God" (Rev. 15:1).

(11) They announce Armageddon—"I saw an angel standing in the sun; and he cried with a loud voice, saying to all the fowls that fly in the midst of heaven, Come and gather yourselves together unto the supper of the great God" (Rev. 19:17).

(12) They accompany Christ at his second coming.

"And to you who are troubled rest with us, when the Lord Jesus shall be revealed from heaven with his mighty angels, in flaming fire taking vengeance on them that know not God, and that obey not the gospel of our Lord Jesus Christ" (2 Thess. 1:7-8).

(13) They gather the unsaved for eternal hell—"The enemy that sowed them is the devil; the harvest is the end of the world; and the reapers are the angels. As therefore the tares are gathered and burned in the fire; so shall it be in the end of this world. The Son of man shall send forth his angels, and they shall gather out of his kingdom all things that offend, and them which do iniquity; and shall cast them into a furnace of fire: there shall be wailing and gnashing of teeth. Then shall the righteous shine forth as the

sun in the kingdom of their Father. Who hath ears to hear, let him hear" (Matt. 13:39-43).

(14) They bind Satan in the bottomless pit—"And I saw an angel come down from heaven, having the key of the bottomless pit and a great chain in his hand" (Rev. 20:1).

c. Concerning Israel

(1) Angels fought for Israel—"They fought from heaven; the stars in their courses fought against Sisera" (Judg. 5:20).

(2) They gave the law to Israel.

(a) According to Moses—"And he said, The LORD came from Sinai, and rose up from Seir unto them; he shined forth from mount Paran, and he came with ten thousands of saints: from his right hand went a fiery law for them" (Deut. 33:2).

(b) According to Stephen—"Who have received the law by the disposition of angels, and have not kept it" (Acts 7:53).

(c) According to Paul—"Wherefore then serveth the law? It was added because of transgressions, till the seed should come to whom the promise was made; and it was ordained by angels in the hand of a mediator" (Gal. 3:19).

(d) According to Hebrews—"For if the word spoken by angels was stedfast, and every transgression and disobedience received a just recompence of reward" (Heb. 2:2).

(3) They seal the 144,000 Israelites—"And after these things I saw four angels standing on the four corners of the earth, holding the four winds of the earth, that the wind should not blow on the earth, nor on the sea, nor on any tree. And I saw another angel ascending from the east, having the seal of the living God: and he cried with a loud voice to the four angels, to whom it was given to hurt the earth and the sea, saying, Hurt not the earth, neither the sea, nor the trees, till we have sealed the servants of our God in their foreheads" (Rev. 7:1-3).

(4) They will regather faithful Israel—"And he shall send his angels with a great sound of a trumpet, and they shall gather together his elect from the four winds, from one end of heaven to the other" (Matt. 24:31).

d. Concerning the Savior

(1) They worship him—"And again, when he bringeth in the first begotten into the world, he saith, And let all the angels of God worship him" (Heb. 1:6).

(2) They were made by him and for him—"And he is before all things, and by him all things consist" (Col. 1:17).

(3) They predicted his birth—"And, behold, thou shalt conceive in thy womb, and bring forth a son, and shalt call his name JESUS" (Luke 1:31). (See also Matt. 1:20-21.)

(4) They announced his birth—"And, lo, the angel of the Lord came upon them, and the glory of the Lord shone round about them: and they were sore afraid. And the angel said unto them, Fear not: for, behold, I bring you good tidings of great joy, which shall be to all people. For unto you is born this day in the city of David a Saviour, which is Christ the Lord. And this shall be a sign unto you; Ye shall find the babe wrapped in

swaddling clothes, lying in a manger. And suddenly there was with the angel a multitude of the heavenly host praising God" (Luke 2:9-13).

(5) They helped protect him—"And when they were departed, behold, the angel of the Lord appeareth to Joseph in a dream, saying, Arise, and take the young child and his mother, and flee into Egypt, and be thou there until I bring thee word: for Herod will seek the young child to destroy him" (Matt. 2:13).

(6) They ministered to him in the wilderness—"Then the devil leaveth him, and, behold, angels came and ministered unto him" (Matt. 4:11).

(7) They ministered to him in the garden—"And there appeared an angel unto him from heaven, strengthening him" (Luke 22:43).

(8) They rolled away the tombstone—"And, behold, there was a great earthquake: for the angel of the Lord descended from heaven, and came and rolled back the stone from the door, and sat upon it" (Matt. 28:2).

(9) They announced his resurrection—"He is not here: for he is risen, as he said. Come, see the place where the Lord lay" (Matt. 28:6).

(10) They predicted his second coming—"And while they looked stedfastly toward heaven as he went up, behold, two men stood by them in white apparel; which also said, Ye men of Galilee, why stand ye gazing up into heaven? this same Jesus, which is taken up from you into heaven, shall so come in like manner as ye have seen him go into heaven" (Acts 1:10-11).

(11) They will accompany him at his second coming—"And to you who are troubled rest with us, when the Lord Jesus shall be revealed from heaven with his mighty angels, in flaming fire taking vengeance on them that know not God, and that obey not the gospel of our Lord Jesus Christ" (2 Thess. 1:7-8).

(12) They are in total subjection to him—"Who is gone into heaven, and is on the right hand of God; angels and authorities and powers being made subject unto him" (1 Pet. 3:22).

Dr. Lewis S. Chafer quotes Dr. Cooke:

How constant their attendance on the Incarnate Saviour during his mysterious life amongst men! At his birth they are his heralds, and with songs exultant announce the glad tidings to mankind. In his temptation they minister to him; in his agonies they succour him; on his resurrection they are the first to proclaim his triumph; on his ascension they come to escort him to the mediatorial throne; in his glorified state they render him supreme homage as their Lord; and when he returns to judge the world they will form his retinue! What sublime thoughts would be suggested, what emotions of wonder and joy would be excited by the scenes they witnessed on earth and still witness in heaven, in reference to Christ, his twofold nature, and his great redeeming work.

God incarnate! This was new to them. They had seen the Son in his deity; but never till now enshrined in humanity. What amazing condescension! Obeying his own law as if he were a mere creature, and in the attitude of a servant! This was new. They had seen him as the governor of the universe; but never till now as a subject! Encountering Satan in conflict and prolonged temptation! This was new. They had seen him frown the arch-rebel from his presence and hurl him to perdition; but never till now submitting to be tempted by him whose subtlety and power had seduced myriads to eternal ruin. Suffering the scorn and reproach of sinful men! This was new. They had seen myriads of happy spirits worship, adore, and love him, but never till now had they seen him personally insulted, reproached, and maltreated by his creatures. Groaning in Gethsemane, and crucified between two thieves, and dying as a sacrificial victim! This was new. They had seen him supremely happy and glorious; but to see him agonize, to hear that dying wail, and to behold him a bloody corpse, and all this to save the world which had revolved from him! What mysterious love! To see him, after all this, enthroned and glorified in human nature. This was a new fact in the moral history of the universe. The whole scenes were full of interest, wonder, and mystery; a gradation of wonders rising in succession, until they culminated in the permanent presence of the God-man, resplendent with a glory that fills the heaven of heavens. Here were chapters of instruction for angelic minds to ponder; here were developments of hidden truths; here were discoveries of the Divine perfections, never known before, and still unfolding in brighter effulgence as ages roll on! (*Systematic Theology*, vol. II, p. 22)

Charles Ryrie aptly summarizes the activities of the faithful angels.

Angels appear to be unusually active when God institutes a new epoch in the sweep of history.
   —They joined in praise when the earth was created (Job 38:6-7).
   —They were involved in the giving of the Mosaic law (Gal. 3:19; Heb. 2:2).
   —They were active at the first advent of Christ (Matt. 1:20; 4:11).
   —They were active during the early years of the church (Acts 8:26; 10:3, 7; 12:11).
   —They will be involved in events surrounding the Second Advent of Christ (Matt. 25:31; 1 Thess. 4:1). (*Basic Theology*, p. 13)

E. Their destiny
   1. To spend eternity in the New Jerusalem along with the elect—"But ye are come unto mount Sion, and unto the city of the living God, the heavenly Jerusalem, and to an innumerable company of angels, to the general assembly and church of the firstborn, which are written in heaven, and to God the Judge of all, and to the spirits of just men made perfect" (Heb. 12:22-23).
   2. To learn throughout eternity of God's grace as exhibited by the elect—
   One of the reasons (perhaps the main reason) for the dispensation of the grace of God to all repenting sinners is stated by Paul in the book of Ephesians: "But God, who is rich in mercy, for his great love wherewith he loved us, Even when we were dead in sins, hath quickened us together with Christ, (by grace ye are saved;) And hath raised us up together, and made us sit together in heavenly places in Christ Jesus: That in the ages to come he might shew the exceeding riches of his grace in his kindness toward us through Christ Jesus" (Eph. 2:4-7). "To the intent that now unto the principalities and powers in heavenly places might be known by the church the manifold wisdom of God,

according to the eternal purpose which he purposed in Christ Jesus our Lord" (Eph. 3:10-11).

There is little doubt that much of this display of grace will be for the benefit of angels. Thus, if their number is, indeed, as large as it appears, then each redeemed sinner will have a vast congregation of *billions* of angels to preach and testify to.

VI. The Characteristics of Evil Angels

A. The names for fallen angels

1. Old Testament names

a. *Shedim,* "spoiler, destroyer"—"They [Israel] sacrificed unto devils, not to God; to gods whom they knew not, to new gods that came newly up, whom your fathers feared not" (Deut. 32:17).

The Hebrew word here translated "devils" is *shedim.* "Yea, they sacrificed their sons and their daughters unto devils" (Psa. 106:37). "But I say, that the things which the Gentiles sacrifice, they sacrifice to devils, and not to God: and I would not that ye should have fellowship with devils" (1 Cor. 10:20).

b. *Seirim, sair, satyr,* "hairy one"—"And they shall no more offer their sacrifices unto devils, after whom they have gone a whoring. This shall be a statute for ever unto them throughout their generations" (Lev. 17:7). "But wild beasts of the desert shall lie there; and their houses shall be full of doleful creatures; and owls shall dwell there, and satyrs shall dance there" (Isa. 13:21).

The word translated "he-goat" is *satyr* in the Hebrew, and is thought to be tied in to demon creatures of some sort.

Dr. Fred Dickason writes:

> "The Hebrews were to sacrifice at the altar of the Tabernacle and not to sacrifice in the desert to "he-goats." Jeroboam I appointed worship for the *Seirim* (2 Chron. 11:15), and Josiah "brake down the high places of the gates" which is to be read *Seirim* (2 Kings 23:8)." (*Angels, Elect and Evil,* p. 152.)

c. *Ruach,* "a spirit"

(1) Evil spirits

(a) Causing contention between wicked Abimelech and his followers (Judg. 9:23)

(b) Causing deep depression to fall upon King Saul (1 Sam. 16:14-15)

(c) Causing Saul to make attempts on David's life (1 Sam. 18:10; 19:9)

(2) Lying spirit (1 Kings 22:22-23)—This fallen angel plotted the death of King Ahab on the battle field.

(3) Perverse spirit (Isa. 19:14)—This fallen angel brought about the destruction of Egypt.

(4) Sexually impure spirits (Hosea 4:12; 5:4)—Israel turned from God after giving themselves over to these spirits.

(5) Unclean spirit (Zech. 13:2)—God will drive out from Israel this kind of spirit at the beginning of the millennium.

(6) Familiar spirits—This phrase (Heb., *ob*) is found 16 times in the Old Testament. In reality it refers not so much to the spirit itself, but rather to the medium (human vessel) who is the channel for its wickedness.

(a) God imposed the death penalty upon mediums (Lev. 20:6, 27).

(b) Saul sought advice from one (the witch of Endor; 1 Sam. 28) and was later killed by God for this act (1 Chron. 10:13).

(c) Wicked Judean king Manasseh relied upon them (2 Kings 21:6).

(d) Godly Judean king Josiah did away with them (2 Kings 23:24).

d. *Malek*, "angel"—"He cast upon them the fierceness of his anger, wrath, and indignation, and trouble, by sending evil angels among them" (Psa. 78:49).

2. New Testament name

a. *Pneuma*, "a spirit"—Fallen spirits possessing various characteristics are described in the New Testament.

(1) Unclean spirits—"And when he had called unto him his twelve disciples, he gave them power against unclean spirits, to cast them out, and to heal all manner of sickness and all manner of disease" (Matt. 10:1).

(2) Evil spirits—"And certain women, which had been healed of evil spirits and infirmities, Mary called Magdalene, out of whom went seven devils" (Luke 8:2).

(3) Foul spirits—"And he cried mightily with a strong voice, saying, Babylon the great is fallen, is fallen, and is become the habitation of devils, and the hold of every foul spirit, and a cage of every unclean and hateful bird" (Rev. 18:2).

(4) Wicked spirits—"Then goeth he, and taketh to him seven other spirits more wicked than himself; and they enter in, and dwell there: and the last state of that man is worse than the first" (Luke 11:26).

(5) Deaf and dumb spirits—"When Jesus saw that the people came running together, he rebuked the foul spirit, saying unto him, Thou dumb and deaf spirit, I charge thee, come out of him, and enter no more into him" (Mark 9:25).

(6) Seducing spirits—"Now the Spirit speaketh expressly, that in the latter times some shall depart from the faith, giving heed to seducing spirits, and doctrines of devils" (1 Tim. 4:1).

(7) Christ-denying spirits—"And every spirit that confesseth not that Jesus Christ is come in the flesh is not of God: and this is that spirit of antichrist, whereof ye have heard that it should come; and even now already is it in the world" (1 John 4:3).

(8) Miracle-working spirits—"For they are the spirits of devils, working miracles, which go forth unto the kings of the earth and of the whole world, to gather them to the battle of that great day of God Almighty" (Rev. 16:14).

(9) Disobedient spirits—"Wherein in time past ye walked according to the course of this world, according to the prince of the power of the air, the spirit that now worketh in the children of disobedience" (Eph. 2:2).

b. *Aggellos*, "angel"

(1) The devil's angels—"Then shall he say also unto them on the left hand, Depart from me, ye cursed, into everlasting fire, prepared for the devil and his angels" (Matt. 25:41).

(2) Angels which kept not their first estate—"And the angels which kept not their first estate, but left their own habitation, he hath reserved in everlasting chains under darkness unto the judgment of the great day" (Jude 6).

c. *Daimon*, "demon"—"And his fame went throughout all Syria: and they brought unto him all sick people that were taken with divers diseases and torments, and those which were possessed with devils, and those which were lunatick, and those that had the palsy; and he healed them" (Matt. 4:24). "Heal the sick, cleanse the lepers, raise the dead, cast out devils: freely ye have received, freely give" (Matt. 10:8).

The word *daimon* is found more than 75 times in the Greek New Testament. In each case it is translated (incorrectly) as "devil" in the King James Version. There are a number of theories concerning the origin of demons. Among these are the following:

(1) They are spirits of deceased wicked men—However, this cannot be, for the Bible declares the unsaved dead are in hades and not roaming the earth. "The wicked shall be turned into hell, and all the nations that forget God" (Psa. 9:17). "And in hell he lift up his eyes, being in torments, and seeth Abraham afar off, and Lazarus in his bosom" (Luke 16:23). "And the sea gave up the dead which were in it; and death and hell delivered up the dead which were in them: and they were judged every man according to their works" (Rev. 20:13).

(2) They are spirits of a pre-Adamic race—But there is no scriptural support whatsoever for this view. The Bible declares that Adam was the first man. "And so it is written, The first man Adam was made a living soul; the last Adam was made a quickening spirit" (1 Cor. 15:45).

(3) They are the spirits from the unnatural union between angels and women in Genesis 6—However, this view, like the previous two, is without the slightest biblical support.

(4) The most logical conclusion is that the word *demon* is simply another title or name for fallen angels—In fact, the terms *devils* and *spirits* are often used interchangeably. "When the even was come, they brought unto him many that were possessed with devils: and he cast out the spirits with his word, and healed all that were sick" (Matt. 8:16).

B. The location of fallen angels

   1. Unchained angels—There are unchained fallen angels who have a certain amount of freedom at the present time. "For we wrestle not against flesh and blood, but against principalities, against powers, against the rulers of the darkness of this world, against spiritual wickedness in high places" (Eph. 6:12). "And the great dragon was cast out, that old serpent, called the Devil, and Satan, which deceiveth the whole world: he was cast out into the earth, and his angels were cast out with him" (Rev. 12:9).

   2. Chained angels—There are chained fallen angels who have no freedom at the present time. "For if God spared not the angels that sinned, but cast them down to hell, and delivered them into chains of darkness, to be reserved unto judgment" (2 Pet. 2:4). "And the angels which kept not their first estate, but left their own habitation, he hath reserved in everlasting chains under darkness unto the judgment of the great day" (Jude 6). "And Jesus asked him, saying, What is thy name? And he said, Legion: because many devils were entered into him. And they besought him that he would not command them to go out into the deep" (Luke 8:30-31).

   There are two Greek words found in these verses, probably referring to the same place:

   a. *Tartarus*, translated "hell" in 2 Peter 2:4—Note: This is not the usual New

Testament word for *hell*, such as "hades," and "gehenna." In fact, *tartarus* is only found here in 2 Peter 2:4.

b. *Abussos*, translated "deep" in Luke 8:31—The word is also translated "bottomless pit" on seven occasions (see Rev. 9:1-2, 11; 11:7; 17:8; 20:1, 3). "And the fifth angel sounded, and I saw a star fall from heaven unto the earth: and to him was given the key of the bottomless pit. And he opened the bottomless pit; and there arose a smoke out of the pit, as the smoke of a great furnace; and the sun and the air were darkened by reason of the smoke of the pit" (Rev. 9:1-2).

From the various passages involved we learn three things concerning the bottomless pit.

(1) The name of the angelic leader of the bottomless pit—"And they had a king over them, which is the angel of the bottomless pit, whose name in the Hebrew tongue is Abaddon, but in the Greek tongue hath his name Apollyon" (Rev. 9:11). Note: The titles *Abaddon* and *Apollyon* both mean "destroyer."

(2) The Antichrist comes from the bottomless pit (see Rev. 11:3, 7; 17:8).

(3) Satan will be imprisoned there during the Millennium (see Rev. 20:1, 3).

C. The sin of the bound angels—It has already been observed that one-third of heaven's angels joined Lucifer in his rebellion against God. These, of course, are the fallen angels of the Bible. Someday they will be judged by God and thrown into Gehenna hell. But why have some of their number suffered imprisonment already? Many Bible students believe the answer to this question is found in Genesis 6: "And it came to pass, when men began to multiply on the face of the earth, and daughters were born unto them, that the sons of God saw the daughters of men that they were fair; and they took them wives of all which they chose. There were giants in the earth in those days; and also after that, when the sons of God came in unto the daughters of men, and they bare children to them, the same became mighty men which were of old, men of renown" (Gen. 6:1-2, 4).

Much controversy has surrounded these verses. Who were the "sons of God" who married the daughters of men? There are two basic approaches to this. The simple interpretation is that the sons of God were those individuals belonging to the line of Seth, while the daughters of men were the unsaved girls who belonged to the line of Cain. The second and more involved interpretation holds that the sons of God were wicked and fallen angelic beings of some kind who committed immoral and unnatural physical acts with women in general.

1. Basic arguments for the first view

   a. This is the most natural way to interpret the passage.

   b. The statement of Jesus in Matthew 22:30—"For in the resurrection they neither marry, nor are given in marriage, but are as the angels of God in heaven."

   c. The law of biogenesis—life begets similar life. This points to the repeated phrase "after its kind," found in Genesis 1 and 2, which seems to prohibit breeding between the species. In other words, a dog and a cat cannot mate and give birth to a "dat"! This biological law would also hold true concerning angels and humans.

   d. Paul's statement in 1 Corinthians 15:38-40—"These are also celestial bodies, and bodies terrestrial." This would indicate these two can never co-join.

e. Moses did not use the regular Hebrew word for angels, *malak*, which he later employs at least 28 times in the Pentateuch.

f. "Mighty men"—"Mighty men" (supposed offspring of angels and women) is the Hebrew word *gibbor*, (Gen. 6:4) which is used dozens of times in the Old Testament and always refers to human men (Judg. 6:12).

2. Basic arguments for the second view

a. The Hebrew phrase *bne-elohim*—This phrase, meaning "sons of God," always refers to angels in the Old Testament. "Now there was a day when the sons of God came to present themselves before the LORD, and Satan came also among them" (Job 1:6). "Again there was a day when the sons of God came to present themselves before the LORD, and Satan came also among them to present himself before the LORD" (Job 2:1). "When the morning stars sang together, and all the sons of God shouted for joy?" (Job 38:7). "He answered and said, Lo, I see four men loose, walking in the midst of the fire, and they have no hurt; and the form of the fourth is like the Son of God" (Dan. 3:25).

The Hebrew word *nephilim*—This word, translated "giants" in Genesis 6:4, actually should be rendered "fallen ones." The normal word for a huge man is *rapha*. Thus, men like Og and Goliath were described by the word *rapha*. (See Deut. 3:11; 1 Chron. 20:6.)

b. Ancient pagan legends—There is almost always a basis for commonly held ancient legends, however weird and distorted they might have become. In Genesis 6:4 we read concerning the "men of renown," which some believe is the historical basis for the legends of Hercules and other children of the gods of mythology. This later corresponds to such Babylonian figures as Gilgamesh, the supposed son of a goddess and a mortal. He was called "two-thirds god and one-third man."

c. The common opinion of Jewish scholars—Josephus, a great Jewish historian, brings this out in his writings. The Septuagint (the Greek translation of the Hebrew Old Testament and the Bible used by Jews) translates Genesis 6:2 as the "angels of God."

d. The interpretation of the early church—It was not until the fourth century that another view opposed to the angels of God theory was offered. The late Dr. James M. Gray, past president of Moody Bible Institute, writes, "There is reason to believe this view would not have changed . . . had it not been for certain erroneous opinions and practices of Christendom" (*Spiritism and the Fallen Angels*, p. 94).

Gray suggests two such reasons:

(1) Angel worship—The church sometime after the fourth century began worshipping angels, so the natural thing would be to deny any angel could do such vile things with humanity.

(2) Celibacy—If indeed these sons of God were human men, then the monks would have scriptural justification for indulging in sexual acts in spite of their official vows of celibacy.

e. The passage in 1 Peter 3—"For Christ also hath once suffered for sins, the just for the unjust, that he might bring us to God, being put to death in the flesh, but quickened by the Spirit: By which also he went and preached unto the spirits in prison; Which sometime were disobedient, when once the longsuffering of God waited in the days of Noah, while the ark was a preparing, wherein few, that is, eight souls were saved by water" (1 Pet. 3:18-20).

It is thought by some that these spirits here were those sons of God in Genesis 6. The reason for their iniquity was a satanic attempt to corrupt human flesh and thus prevent the promised Incarnation (Gen. 3:15) from taking place. But here Peter describes Christ as telling them their foul plan didn't work.

In conclusion it should be noted that a *third* view has been recently advocated which says the sons of God were indeed fallen angels who totally controlled and possessed all the evil men living before the flood. These demons may have even attempted to change (by genetic engineering, as we see today) the DNA code of future babies like some deadly virus.

D. The organization and rank of fallen angels—"For we wrestle not against flesh and blood, but against principalities, against powers, against the rulers of the darkness of this world, against spiritual wickedness in high places" (Eph. 6:12). This verse indicates that Satan's kingdom of evil angels is as organized as God's elect angelic group.

1. There are evil angels who rule over the nations of this world—"But the prince of the kingdom of Persia withstood me one and twenty days: but, lo, Michael, one of the chief princes, came to help me; and I remained there with the kings of Persia" (Dan. 10:13).

2. A wicked angel named Legion headed up a large group of fallen spirits that had possessed the maniac of Gadara—"And he asked him, What is thy name? And he answered, saying, My name is Legion: for we are many" (Mark 5:9).

3. The bottomless pit is under the control of an angel called Abaddon (in the Hebrew) and Apollyon (in the Greek)—"And they had a king over them, which is the angel of the bottomless pit, whose name in the Hebrew tongue is Abaddon, but in the Greek tongue hath his name Apollyon" (Rev. 9:11).

4. Four military angels will lead a hellish army 200 million strong during the latter part of the tribulation—"And the four angels were loosed, which were prepared for an hour, and a day, and a month, and a year, for to slay the third part of men" (Rev. 9:15).

5. Three angels organize events which lead to the battle of Armageddon—"And I saw three unclean spirits like frogs come out of the mouth of the dragon, and out of the mouth of the beast, and out of the mouth of the false prophet. For they are the spirits of devils, working miracles, which go forth unto the kings of the earth and of the whole world, to gather them to the battle of that great day of God Almighty" (Rev. 16:13-14).

E. The appearance of fallen angels—Fallen angels, like good angels, are invisible spirit beings. However, on occasion they do manifest themselves. There are three New Testament passages which offer some description of these corrupted creatures.

1. Revelation 9:7-10—The shapes of these creatures are absolutely hideous. They are like horses prepared for battle. Crowns of gold seem to be upon their heads. Their faces are like men's, their hair like women's, their teeth like lions'. They have on breastplates as iron. Their tails are like those of a scorpion. The sound of their wings is like that of many chariots rushing toward battle.

2. Revelation 9:13-21—These demons are mounted upon some type of hellish

horse. The horses' heads look much like lions' heads, with smoke, fire, and flaming sulfur billowing from their mouths. The riders wear fiery-red breast-plates.

3. Revelation 16:13—"And I saw three unclean spirits like frogs come out of the mouth of the dragon, and out of the mouth of the beast, and out of the mouth of the false prophet."

F. The personalities of fallen angels—Author John Phillips writes:

Modern man professes not to believe in demons, but they exist just the same. Moreover, they are clever with a diabolical cunning. Man's attitude toward the demon world may well be likened to man's attitude in the dark ages toward bacteria. If we could be transported back to London in the year 1666, we would find ourselves in a nightmare world. The great bubonic plague is at its height. The sights and sounds of the city are like the terrible climax of a horror movie. It is generally believed that fresh air is the culprit. The College of Physicians recommends the frequent firing of guns to blow away the deadly air. People seal themselves into their rooms and burn foul-smelling messes to ward off the fresh air. Chimneys are sealed, rooms are gray with smoke, and people choke in the suffocating stench. Outside, palls of black smoke hang over the city. People sit in the tightly sealed chambers, grimly determined to endure the smarting smoke, convinced they are thus immune to the plague. We tell them they are wrong, that the plague is not caused by fresh air but by germs, microscopic organisms spread by fleas- and they laugh us to scorn.

Modern man has adopted a similar attitude toward the demon world. We tell them that he (Satan) has countless host of invisible demons to aid him in his dark designs against mankind. We say that these unseen beings are intelligent, and that before long, they are to be joined by countless more of their kind worse even than themselves. People look at us with pitying scorn and suggest we peddle our theories to the publishers of science fiction. But it is true all the same. Once the pit is opened, the world of men will be invaded by a virus far more dreadful than the bubonic plague, a virus all the more deadly because it is able to think and because it directs its attack against the soul rather than the body." (*Exploring Revelation*, Moody Press, p. 137)

1. They have names—"And Jesus asked him, saying, What is thy name? And he said, Legion: because many devils were entered into him" (Luke 8:30). (See also Rev. 9:11.)

2. They speak—"Saying, Let us alone; what have we to do with thee, thou Jesus of Nazareth? art thou come to destroy us? I know thee who thou art; the Holy One of God. . .Thou art Christ the Son of God" (Luke 4:34, 41). "When he saw Jesus, he cried out, and fell down before him, and with a loud voice said, What have I to do with thee, Jesus, thou Son of God most high? I beseech thee, torment me not" (Luke 8:28). "And, behold, they cried out, saying, What have we to do with thee, Jesus, thou Son of God? art thou come hither to torment us before the time?" (Matt. 8:29).

"And all the devils besought him, saying, Send us into the swine, that we may enter into them" (Mark 5:12). "And the evil spirit answered and said, Jesus I know, and Paul I know; but who are ye?" (Acts 19:15). "And unclean spirits, when they saw him, fell down before him, and cried, saying, Thou art the Son of God" (Mark 3:11).

3. They possess intelligence.
   a. They know who Jesus is—"Saying, Let us alone; what have we to do with thee, thou Jesus of Nazareth? art thou come to destroy us? I know thee who thou art; the Holy One of God" (Luke 4:34).
   b. They know of future damnation—"And, behold, they cried out, saying, What have we to do with thee, Jesus, thou Son of God? art thou come hither to torment us before the time?" (Matt. 8:29).
   c. They know the saved from the unsaved—"And it came to pass, as we went to prayer, a certain damsel possessed with a spirit of divination met us, which brought her masters much gain by soothsaying: The same followed Paul and us, and cried, saying, These men are the servants of the most high God, which shew unto us the way of salvation" (Acts 16:16-17). "And it was commanded them that they should not hurt the grass of the earth, neither any green thing, neither any tree; but only those men which have not the seal of God in their foreheads" (Rev. 9:4).
   d. They are able to formulate a Satan-centered systematic theology—"Now the Spirit speaketh expressly, that in the latter times some shall depart from the faith, giving heed to seducing spirits, and doctrines of devils" (1 Tim. 4:1).
4. They experience emotion.
   a. Fear—"Thou believest that there is one God; thou doest well: the devils also believe, and tremble" (James 2:19). (See also Luke 8:28.)
   b. Desire—"And all the devils besought him, saying, Send us into the swine, that we may enter into them" (Mark 5:12).
   c. Cynicism—See Acts 16:15-18.
5. They possess great strength.
   a. As demonstrated in Egypt—"Then Pharaoh also called the wise men and the sorcerers: now the magicians of Egypt, they also did in like manner with their enchantments. For they cast down every man his rod, and they became serpents: but Aaron's rod swallowed up their rods" (Exod. 7:11-12).
   b. As demonstrated in Persia—"But the prince of the kingdom of Persia withstood me one and twenty days: but, lo, Michael, one of the chief princes, came to help me; and I remained there with the kings of Persia" (Dan. 10:13).
   c. As demonstrated in Gadara—"And when he was come out of the ship, immediately there met him out of the tombs a man with an unclean spirit, Who had his dwelling among the tombs; and no man could bind him, no, not with chains: Because that he had been often bound with fetters and chains, and the chains had been plucked asunder by him, and the fetters broken in pieces: neither could any man tame him" (Mark 5:2-4).
   d. As demonstrated in Ephesus—"And the man in whom the evil spirit was leaped on them, and overcame them, and prevailed against them, so that they fled out of that house naked and wounded" (Acts 19:16).
G. The activities of fallen angels
   1. They oppose God's program (see Dan. 10:10-14; Eph. 6:12).
   2. They execute Satan's program—"And I saw three unclean spirits like frogs come out of the mouth of the dragon, and out of the mouth of the beast, and out of the mouth of the false prophet. For they are the spirits of devils, working miracles, which go forth unto the kings of the earth and of the whole world, to gather them to the battle of that great day of God Almighty" (Rev. 16:13-14).
   3. They disseminate false doctrine—"Now the Spirit speaketh expressly, that in

the latter times some shall depart from the faith, giving heed to seducing spirits, and doctrines of devils" (1 Tim. 4:1). "But evil men and seducers shall wax worse and worse, deceiving, and being deceived. For the time will come when they will not endure sound doctrine; but after their own lusts shall they heap to themselves teachers, having itching ears; and they shall turn away their ears from the truth, and shall be turned unto fables" (2 Tim. 4:3-4). "But there were false prophets also among the people, even as there shall be false teachers among you, who privily shall bring in damnable heresies, even denying the Lord that bought them, and bring upon themselves swift destruction" (2 Pet. 2:1). "But evil men and seducers shall wax worse and worse, deceiving, and being deceived" (2 Tim. 3:13).

Without doubt, the most *unscriptural, unified*, and *universal* religious doctrinal heresy ever introduced upon this earth by demons is the New Age movement. Furthermore, if these are indeed the last days, it would become the *ultimate* anti-God blasphemy, eventually serving as the theological basis for Satan's false and filthy church! (See Rev. 17.)

Two gifted Christian scholars aptly summarize this deadly demonic doctrine for us.
  J. Kerby Anderson writes:

> *Rudyard Kipling once wrote that "East is East, and West is West, and never the twain shall meet." But that can no longer be said now that a pantheistic philosophy has spread to this country. The primary vehicle for this transmission of ideas has been through the New Age Movement.*
>
> *Evidence of Eastern philosophy's arrival can certainly be seen in many ways. Statements by movie stars, the growth of Eastern cults, and the popularity of films like the* Star Wars *trilogy testify to the growing influence of New Age ideas. In the movie* The Empire Strikes Back, *for example, Yoda espouses these pantheistic ideas to his Jedi disciple, Luke Skywalker: "You must feel the Force around you. Here, between you and me. Between the rock . . . everywhere. Yes, even the land."*
>
> *. . . The New Age Movement has taken on a variety of names including: the Human Potential Movement, the Third Force, the Aquarian Conspiracy, Cosmic Consciousness, and Cosmic Humanism. Although most refer to it as the New Age Movement, many in the movement do not like that label and many others would not even consider themselves part of the movement even though they may hold to many of the core beliefs of the New Age Movement.*
>
> *Accurately defining the New Age is a formidable task for several reasons. First, the New Age Movement is eclectic and diverse. It is not a cohesive movement but exceedingly diverse in its composition and ideology. The unifying factors are shared ideology rather than a shared organizational structure.*
>
> *Second, the New Age Movement is difficult to define because it emphasizes and encourages change. The New Age Movement is syncretistic and therefore evolutionary in its nature. Many proponents change their perspectives and so it is frequently difficult to pin down the major beliefs of the New Age Movement.*
>
> *The third major tenet of the New Age follows as a logical conclusion from the other two. If "all is one" and "all is god," then we should conclude that "we are gods." We are, according to New Agers, ignorant of our divinity. We are "gods in disguise." The goal therefore of the New Age Movement is to discover our own divinity.*

Fourth, we discover our own divinity by experiencing a change in consciousness. The human race suffers from a collective form of metaphysical amnesia. We have forgotten our true identity is divine and thus must undergo a change of consciousness to achieve our true human potential (hence the name, the Human Potential Movement).

A fifth tenet is reincarnation. Most New Agers believe in some form of reincarnation. In its classic form, the cycles of birth, death, and reincarnation are necessary to work off our bad karma and finally to reach perfection. The doctrine of karma says that one's present condition was determined by one's actions in a past life.

The Western version of reincarnation held by many New Agers places much less emphasis on bad karma and postulates an upward spiral toward perfection through reincarnation. This view has been espoused by such people as Shirley MacLaine, Sylvester Stallone, George Patton, and Henry Ford.

A final major tenet is moral relativism. New Agers think in terms of gray, rather than black or white. Denying the law of noncontradiction, New Agers will frequently believe that two conflicting statements can both be true. They will therefore teach that "all religions are true" and that "there are many paths to God." (From the pamphlet Confronting, *pp. 11–13)*

Dr. Geisler presents an overview of the New Age movement's apostate approach to six great scriptural subjects.

    I. Knowledge of truth—People must not be hindered by the strictures of logical thinking. The Bible is incomplete and inadequate. New Age revelation is superior to Scripture. Special revelation continues today through many New Age prophets.

   II. Nature of God—God is everything, and everything is God. God is energy, as everything—including humans—is energy. Some New Agers describe God as eternal, impersonal, infinite, and unchanging (pantheism). At other times God is described as a changing God, ever growing and increasing, so that God is actually finite though potentially infinite (panentheism). There exists an interdependent relationship between God and humankind. God needs man just as man needs God.

  III. Nature of Christ—The man Jesus is separate and distinct from the Christ Spirit. Jesus is not unique since all men are innately divine. Christ is part of the same force as Lucifer. The two are partners in bringing about mankind's salvation. Jesus did not die and therefore did not physically resurrect.

  IV. Sin and morality—Moral values are relative and are dependent upon the will of man, not the nature of God. There is really no such thing as sin (the breaking of moral law) and evil. One's present problems are rooted in "evil" deeds performed in past reincarnations. This is called "karma." The ultimate problem is that people have forgotten their divinity.

   V. Salvation—Salvation is self-earned, and is the realization of one's own divinity. Reincarnation is a vital part of the process of salvation.

  VI. Future events—Jesus of Nazareth is not the Christ who will reappear. The world will improve before the Christ appears. Christ will bring global peace and unity. He will teach the world, and communicate to mankind telepathically. He will set up a new world religion, a new economic system, and a new government. (Adapted from his book, The Infiltration of the New Age*)*

---

    4. They afflict human beings.
       a. Some cause insanity—"And when he was come to the other side into the country of the Gergesenes, there met him two possessed with devils, coming

out of the tombs, exceeding fierce, so that no man might pass by that way" (Matt. 8:28). "Lord, have mercy on my son: for he is lunatick, and sore vexed: for oft times he falleth into the fire, and oft into the water. And Jesus rebuked the devil; and he departed out of him: and the child was cured from that very hour" (Matt. 17:15, 18).

b. Some cause deafness and muteness of speech—"And when the devil was cast out, the dumb spake: and the multitudes marvelled, saying, It was never so seen in Israel" (Matt. 9:33). "When Jesus saw that the people came running together, he rebuked the foul spirit, saying unto him, Thou dumb and deaf spirit, I charge thee, come out of him, and enter no more into him" (Mark 9:25).

c. Some may cause immorality—This is suggested by the Old Testament prophet Hosea who warns concerning the "spirit of whoredoms" (Hos. 4:12; 5:4)

d. Some cause blindness—"Then was brought unto him one possessed with a devil, blind, and dumb: and he healed him, insomuch that the blind and dumb both spake and saw" (Matt. 12:22).

e. Some cause personal injuries—"And wheresoever he taketh him, he teareth him: and he foameth, and gnasheth with his teeth, and pineth away: and I spake to thy disciples that they should cast him out; and they could not" (Mark 9:18).

f. Some cause physical defects—"And, behold, there was a woman which had a spirit of infirmity eighteen years, and was bowed together, and could in no wise lift up herself" (Luke 13:11).

5. They can possess human beings.

a. In the Bible there are at least 14 major examples of individuals possessed by fallen angels.

(1) Saul—Israel's first king was often troubled by an evil spirit. "But the Spirit of the LORD departed from Saul, and an evil spirit from the LORD troubled him" (1 Sam. 16:14).

(a) Causing him to make attempts on David's life—"And Saul was very wroth, and the saying displeased him; and he said, They have ascribed unto David ten thousands, and to me they have ascribed but thousands: and what can he have more but the kingdom?" (1 Sam. 18:8).

i) By piercing him with a javelin (1 Sam. 18:10-11; 19:10)

ii) By trickery—"And Saul said, Thus shall ye say to David, The king desireth not any dowry, but an hundred foreskins of the Philistines, to be avenged of the king's enemies. But Saul thought to make David fall by the hand of the Philistines" (1 Sam. 18:25).

iii) By hunting him down like a wild animal (1 Sam. 24:1-2, 11; 26:1-2)

(b) Causing him to turn against his own son Jonathan for befriending David (1 Sam. 20:33)

(c) Causing him to murder Israel's High Priest and 85 other priests of God whom he believed had helped David (1 Sam. 22:17)

(d) Causing him to turn to the occult in the hour of death—"Then said Saul unto his servants, Seek me a woman that hath a familiar spirit, that I may go to her, and enquire of her. And his servants said to him,

Behold, there is a woman that hath a familiar spirit at Endor" (1 Sam. 28:7).

(e) Causing him to be forsaken by God—"And when Saul enquired of the LORD, the LORD answered him not, neither by dreams, nor by Urim, nor by prophets" (1 Sam. 28:6).

(f) Causing him to be killed by God—"So Saul died for his transgression which he committed against the LORD, even against the word of the LORD, which he kept not, and also for asking counsel of one that had a familiar spirit, to enquire of it; And enquired not of the LORD: therefore he slew him, and turned the kingdom unto David the son of Jesse" (1 Chron. 10:13-14).

(2) Those seven demon-possessed persons delivered by Jesus

(a) A boy, at the request of his father (Matt. 17:14-20; Mark 9:14-29; Luke 9:37-43)

(b) A girl, at the request of her mother (Matt. 15:21-28; Mark 7:24-30)

(c) A woman—"And, behold, there was a woman which had a spirit of infirmity eighteen years, and was bowed together, and could in no wise lift up herself. And when Jesus saw her, he called her to him, and said unto her, Woman, thou art loosed from this infirmity" (Luke 13:11-12).

(d) Four men

i) A man in Capernaum (Mark 1:21-28; Luke 4:31-37)

ii) A man in Gadara (Matt. 8:28-34; Mark 5:1-20; Luke 8:26-39)

iii) A man somewhere in Galilee—"As they went out, behold, they brought to him a dumb man possessed with a devil. And when the devil was cast out, the dumb spake: and the multitudes marvelled, saying, It was never so seen in Israel" (Matt. 9:32-33).

iv) A man with a threefold problem (Matt. 12:22; Luke 11:14)—He was blind, deaf and mute. "Then was brought unto him one possessed with a devil, blind, and dumb: and he healed him, insomuch that the blind and dumb both spake and saw" (Matt. 12:22).

Note especially the fearful results of demon-possession as seen by the two case studies involving the maniac of Gadara and the boy brought to Jesus by his father.

(3) The maniac

(a) He was exceedingly fierce, so that no man could control him.

(b) He had broken all the chains put upon him.

(c) He was living among the tombs.

(d) He was naked and controlled by 6,000 demons.

(e) He had been possessed for a long time.

(4) The boy

(a) He had been possessed since childhood.

(b) The demon would bruise him and rip at him.

(c) He would be thrown down into water and fire.

(d) He suffered severe convulsions.

(e) Often he was thrown violently to the ground and caused to roll around, foaming at the mouth.

(f) He was rendered unconscious and feared dead upon the removal of the demon by Jesus.

(5) Mary Magdalene—Mary had seven demons living in her prior to her conversion. "Now when Jesus was risen early the first day of the week, he appeared first to Mary Magdalene, out of whom he had cast seven devils" (Mark 16:9). "And certain women, which had been healed of evil spirits and infirmities, Mary called Magdalene, out of whom went seven devils" (Luke 8:2).

(6) Simon the sorcerer—A demon possessed Simon to twist the Gospel message into a perverted profit system. "And when Simon saw that through laying on of the apostles' hands the Holy Ghost was given, he offered them money, saying, Give me also this power, that on whomsoever I lay hands, he may receive the Holy Ghost. But Peter said unto him, Thy money perish with thee, because thou hast thought that the gift of God may be purchased with money. Thou hast neither part nor lot in this matter: for thy heart is not right in the sight of God. Repent therefore of this thy wickedness, and pray God, if perhaps the thought of thine heart may be forgiven thee. For I perceive that thou art in the gall of bitterness, and in the bond of iniquity. Then answered Simon, and said, Pray ye to the Lord for me, that none of these things which ye have spoken come upon me" (Acts 8:18-24).

(7) Elymas—This demon-possessed sorcerer attempted to frustrate Paul's efforts to win the governor of Cyprus to Christ. "But Elymas the sorcerer (for so is his name by interpretation) withstood them, seeking to turn away the deputy from the faith. Then Saul, (who also is called Paul,) filled with the Holy Ghost, set his eyes on him, and said, O full of all subtilty and all mischief, thou child of the devil, thou enemy of all righteousness, wilt thou not cease to pervert the right ways of the Lord? And now, behold, the hand of the Lord is upon thee, and thou shalt be blind, not seeing the sun for a season. And immediately there fell on him a mist and a darkness; and he went about seeking some to lead him by the hand" (Acts 13:8-11).

(8) A slave girl—In this amazing account a demon (through a possessed girl) tried to identify itself with the work of Paul, that the message of Christ might be confused in the minds of those in Philippi. "And it came to pass, as we went to prayer, a certain damsel possessed with a spirit of divination met us, which brought her masters much gain by soothsaying: The same followed Paul and us, and cried, saying, These men are the servants of the most high God, which shew unto us the way of salvation. And this did she many days. But Paul, being grieved, turned and said to the spirit, I command thee in the name of Jesus Christ to come out of her. And he came out the same hour" (Acts 16:16-18).

b. To this list could be added the many general references concerning demon-possessed people delivered by Jesus and his apostles.

(1) Those referred to by Matthew (4:24; 8:16; 10:1, 8)

(2) Those referred to by Mark (1:27, 32, 34, 39; 3:11, 15; 6:7, 13)

(3) Those referred to by Luke (4:36, 41; 6:18; 7:21; 8:2; 9:1; 10:17)

(4) Those referred to in the book of Acts (5:16; 8:7; 19:12-13)

6. They will inflict both destruction and death upon unsaved mankind during the great tribulation—The ninth chapter of Revelation, which contains both the fifth and sixth trumpet judgments, may be the most revealing section in all the

Bible concerning the subject of demonology. Prior to this, God has already made it known that there are two kinds of unfallen angels. These are the cherubim (Gen. 3:24; Exod. 25:18-22; Ezek. 10:1-20), and the seraphim (Isa. 6:1-8). Here he may be describing for us the two kinds of fallen angels.

The fifth trumpet judgment (Rev. 9:1-12)—This trumpet unleashes the first hellish invasion of demons upon the earth.

  a. Their location—"And he opened the bottomless pit; and there arose a smoke out of the pit, as the smoke of a great furnace; and the sun and the air were darkened by reason of the smoke of the pit" (Rev. 9:2).

  b. Their leader—"And they had a king over them, which is the angel of the bottomless pit, whose name in the Hebrew tongue is Abaddon, but in the Greek tongue hath his name Apollyon" (Rev. 9:11).

  c. Their torment—"And there came out of the smoke locusts upon the earth: and unto them was given power, as the scorpions of the earth have power" (Rev. 9:3). "And their torment was as the torment of a scorpion, when he striketh a man" (Rev. 9:5b). The sting of a scorpion, though not generally fatal, is perhaps the most intense pain that any animal can inflict upon the human body. The insect itself is the most malignant that lives, and its poison is like itself.

  d. Their victims—"And it was commanded them that they should not hurt the grass of the earth, neither any green thing, neither any tree; but only those men which have not the seal of God in their foreheads" (Rev. 9:4).

  e. Their duration—"And to them it was given that they should not kill them, but that they should be tormented five months" (Rev. 9:5a). "And in those days shall men seek death, and shall not find it; and shall desire to die, and death shall flee from them" (Rev. 9:6).

Charles Ryrie writes:

> Horrible as the torment will be, God will place certain limitations on the activity of these demons. They will be limited as to what they may strike and as to how far they may go and as to how long they may do what they will do. They will not attack the vegetation of the earth (as common locusts do); they may only attack certain men, that is, those who have not the seal of God in their foreheads (the 144,000, cf. 7:3). The wicked will persecute God's servants, the 144,000; but in turn they will be tormented by this plague which God allows. The demon-locusts will also be limited in that they may not kill men, just torment them. Further, the duration of this plague will be five months. The effect of this torment is to drive men to suicide, but they will not be able to die. Although men will prefer death to the agony of living, death will not be possible. Bodies will not sink and drown; poisons and pills will have no effect; and somehow even bullets and knives will not do their intended job. (*Revelation*, p. 62)

The reason men cannot die is probably because Satan has the key to the shaft and will not allow his followers to leave the earth scene where the battle of light and darkness is being fought.

  f. Their description—"And the shapes of the locusts were like unto horses prepared unto battle; and on their heads were as it were crowns like gold, and their faces were as the faces of men. And they had hair as the hair of women, and their teeth were as the teeth of lions. And they had breastplates, as it were breastplates of iron; and the sound of their wings was as the sound of chariots of many horses running to battle" (Rev. 9:7-9). "And they had tails like unto scorpions" (Rev. 9:10a).

The sixth trumpet judgment (Rev. 9:13-21)—This trumpet unleashes the second hellish invasion of demons upon the earth.

   a. Their four leaders and location—"Saying to the sixth angel which had the trumpet, Loose the four angels which are bound in the great river Euphrates" (Rev. 9:14).

      Note two phrases:

      (1) "The four angels"—These may function to Satan as the four living creatures do to God (see Rev. 4:6-8).

      (2) "The great river Euphrates"—This is where evil began on earth (Zech. 5:8-11; Gen. 1:10-14; 3:1-7), where false religion began (Gen. 4:3; 10:9-10; 11:4), and where it will come to its end (Rev. 17-18).

   b. Their mission—"And the four angels were loosed, which were prepared for an hour, and a day, and a month, and a year, for to slay the third part of men" (Rev. 9:15).

      One-third of humanity is killed through fire, smoke, and brimstone. One-fourth had already been slain by the fourth seal (6:8). This would be approximately one billion people. Now one-third is killed, meaning another billion die. This invasion is therefore the opposite of the fifth trumpet judgment, during which no man was able to die.

   c. Their number—"And the number of the army of the horsemen were two hundred thousand thousand: and I heard the number of them" (Rev. 9:16). By normal standards this mighty army would occupy a territory 1 mile wide and 87 miles long.

   d. Their description (Rev. 9:17, 19)—These demons, unlike those of the first invasion, seem to be mounted upon some type of hellish horse. The horses' heads look much like lions', with smoke, fire, and flaming sulfur billowing from their mouths. The riders wear fiery-red breastplates.

7. They are, on occasion, actually used by God to fulfill his divine purpose.

   a. A demon was used to punish wicked Abimelech (Judg. 9:23).

   b. A demon was used to plot the execution of king Ahab in battle (1 Kings 22:19-23).

   c. A demon brought out the true nature of unsaved king Saul (1 Sam. 16:14).

   d. Demons were used to punish rebellious Israel during the time of the Exodus wandering—"He cast upon them the fierceness of his anger, wrath, and indignation, and trouble, by sending evil angels among them" (Psa. 78:49).

   e. Demons will be used to bring ungodly nations to Armageddon for slaughter at the end of the tribulation (Rev. 16:13-16).

H. The destiny of unsaved angels

1. To be judged by Christ and his church—"Know ye not that we shall judge angels? how much more things that pertain to this life?" (1 Cor. 6:3).

2. To be cast into the lake of fire forever—"Then shall he say also unto them on the left hand, Depart from me, ye cursed, into everlasting fire, prepared for the devil and his angels" (Matt. 25:41). "For if God spared not the angels that sinned, but cast them down to hell, and delivered them into chains of darkness, to be reserved unto judgment" (2 Pet. 2:4). "And the angels which kept not their

first estate, but left their own habitation, he hath reserved in everlasting chains under darkness unto the judgment of the great day" (Jude 6).

Is there any chance whatsoever for the salvation of a fallen angel? Dr. Fred Dickason writes:

> Furthermore, we may deduce that evil angels are non-redeemable. Those that followed Satan in his sin, fell decisively and are permanently left in their evil state without recourse or even the possibility of redemption. They are irrevocably consigned to the lake of fire (Matt. 25:41).
>
> What evidence is there for such a position? First, there is no record of any angel ever being delivered from sin. True, this is an argument from silence, which is never too strong; but if Christ's redemption extended to angels, we could rightly expect some mention of it in God's revelation of the grace of His Son's work. We read of many other accomplishments of the death of Christ besides the redemption of man, but nothing of the salvation of angels. We read of His cross as their judgment (John 16:11; Col. 2:14, 15), but it is never presented as their blessing in any sense.
>
> Second, there is the definite statement that Christ did not take hold of angels to save them, but only of believing man (Heb. 2:16). He passed by angels to help man.
>
> Third, it is implied in Heb. 2:14-17 and is evident from the very nature of angels that Christ did not and could not take upon Himself the nature of angels. Hebrews tells us that Christ saves those who are His "brethren" (2:11). He had to be made like them, in fact one of them, to save them; so He took upon Himself "flesh and blood" (2:14). This means that He entered into the race of men by the virgin birth, retaining His deity in essence (though not always its expression) and adding to His person sinless but genuine humanity. As the God-man He is a genuine representative of the race because He is truly human, as well as divine. On the cross, Christ was the effective Mediator between God and men because He was the God-man, representing both God and man in the settlement of our debt of sin. For man He suffered the penalty as a genuine substitute, since He genuinely participated in our humanity.
>
> Christ could not lay hold on angels in like fashion to represent and to redeem them. Their very nature forbids it. Angels are not a race to which genuine additions may enter. They are individually separate creations of God, and they do not procreate (Matt. 22:28-30). Christ could not become their Kinsman-Redeemer by birth or creation and so represent angels as a class before God.
>
> But since Christ did become the last Adam, the Head of a new race of men reborn by faith in Christ, we have a song no angel can sing—of Jesus the God-man and His saving grace (John 1:12-13; Heb. 2:9-12).
>
> We must reject any teaching of universal restoration of all men, or even of Satan, to God. Only humans can be saved, and only those who trust Christ in this life will be saved. So taught Christ who died and rose again (Matt. 25:41; John 5:29; 8:24). The lake of fire is an eternal torment for wicked men and angels (Rev. 14:10-11; 19:20; 20:11-15). (*Angels, Elect and Evil*, pp. 40–42)

THE DOCTRINE OF SIN

INTRODUCTION

Man calls it an accident; God calls it an abomination.
Man calls it a blunder; God calls it a blight.
Man calls it a defect; God calls it a disease.
Man calls it a chance; God calls it a choice.
Man calls it an error; God calls it an enmity.
Man calls it a fascination; God calls it a fatality.
Man calls it an infirmity; God calls it an iniquity.
Man calls it a luxury; God calls it a leprosy.
Man calls it a liberty; God calls it lawlessness.
Man calls it a trifle; God calls it a tragedy.
Man calls it a mistake; God calls it a madness.
Man calls it a weakness; God calls it a willfulness.

What is this mysterious thing, so downplayed and on occasion actually denied by man, but utterly denounced by God? By actual count it is referred to over 700 times in the Word of God.

In a nutshell, one's concept of the holiness of God is directly connected to and governed by his understanding of the exceeding sinfulness of sin. The aim of this doctrinal study is to allow the student to clearly see both the purity of the one and the perversion of the other.

The word *sin* is found hundreds of times in the Bible in both Old and New Testaments. Its first mention is in Genesis 4:7, where it is said to have been lurking at the door of the world's first murderer, Cain. The second reference is found in Genesis 18:20, where it causes the fiery and fearsome destruction of Sodom. The final mention is in Revelation 18:5, where it brings down the full wrath of an angry God upon the political and economic systems of this entire world.

What is this deadly and damnable thing that is so hated by God and so harmful to man? The very word carries with it the hissing sound of a vicious viper.

Some 20 centuries ago the angel Gabriel appeared to a troubled carpenter named Joseph to reassure him of the purity of Mary. "But while he thought on these things, behold, the angel of the Lord appeared unto him in a dream, saying, Joseph, thou son of David, fear not to take unto thee Mary thy wife: for that which is conceived in her is of the Holy Ghost. And she shall bring forth a son, and thou shalt call his name JESUS: for he shall save his people from their sins" (Matt. 1:20-21).

Approximately 30 years after this angelic announcement, this babe, who had now grown into strong manhood, was publicly introduced by John the Baptist in the following manner: "Behold the Lamb of God, which taketh away the sin of the world" (John 1:29b).

From these verses we are told that the basic reason for the incarnation of God's Son was to deal with this terrible thing called sin.

I. The Definition and Meaning of Sin

The biblical concept of sin comes from a study of words used in both Testaments for sin. The terms are numerous, compared to the words for grace in the Bible. Only three words are needed to express grace (*chen* and *chesed* in the Old Testament and *charis* in the New). By contrast, there are at least eight basic words for sin in the Old Testament and a dozen in the New. Together they furnish the basic concepts involved in the doctrine.

Sin may properly be defined by using all these descriptive words for its various forms as recorded in the Old and New Testaments. Such a definition would be accurate though lengthy. Indeed, it might be a good idea to define it thus: sin is missing the mark, badness, rebellion, iniquity, going astray, wickedness, wandering, ungodliness, crime, lawlessness, transgression, ignorance, and a falling away. (Charles Ryrie, *Basic Theology*, pp. 209, 212)

The two most commonly used words for sin in the entire Bible are the words *chata* and *hamartia*.

A. The Old Testament word *chata*

In all of its forms this basic word for sin occurs about 522 times in the Old Testament. Its basic meaning is to miss the mark and is equivalent to the Greek word *hamartano*. But missing the mark also involves hitting some other mark; i.e., when one misses the right mark and thus sins, he also hits the wrong mark. The idea is not merely a passive one of missing, but also an active one of hitting. It is used of moral evil, idolatry, and ceremonial sins. Some important references include Exodus 20:20; Judges 20:16; Proverbs 8:36; and 19:2. (Ibid., p. 211)

B. The New Testament word *hamartia*

This is the most frequently used word for sin, occurring in its various forms about 227 times. When a writer wanted one inclusive word for sin, he used this one. The metaphor behind the word is missing the mark, but, as in the Old Testament, this is not only a negative idea but includes the positive idea of hitting some wrong mark. When it is used in the Gospels it almost always occurs in a context that speaks of forgiveness or salvation (Matt. 1:21; John 1:29). Other instructive references include Acts 2:38; Romans 5:12; 6:1; 1 Corinthians 15:3; 2 Corinthians 5:21; James 1:15; 1 Peter 2:22; 1 John 1:7; 2:2; Revelation 1:5. (Ibid., p. 211)

Various theological definitions would include:
"Sin is lack of conformity to the moral law of God, either in act, disposition, or state."—A. H. Strong
"Sin is a transgression of, or want of conformity to the divine law."—Charles Hodge
"Sin may be defined ultimately as anything in the creature which does not express, or which is contrary to, the holy character of the Creator."—James Oliver Buswell, Jr.

"Sin is a restless unwillingness on the part of the creature to abide in the sphere and limitation in which the Creator, guided by infinite wisdom, had placed him."—L. S. Chafer

II. The Origin of Sin
   A. The origin of sin into the universe—According to five key biblical passages of Scripture, a powerful angelic creature named Lucifer once (perhaps before the creation of the earth) led a wicked revolt against Jehovah God himself in an insane attempt to dethrone the rightful King, the Lord Jesus Christ. While this treachery proved unsuccessful, it did, nevertheless, introduce into the universe a new evil element hitherto unknown. This perverted principle was sin. Lucifer degenerated into the devil and became, therefore, the source and strength of sin.
      1. According to Isaiah—"How art thou fallen from heaven, O Lucifer, son of the morning! how art thou cut down to the ground, which didst weaken the nations! For thou hast said in thine heart, I will ascend into heaven, I will exalt my throne above the stars of God: I will sit also upon the mount of the congregation, in the sides of the north: I will ascend above the heights of the clouds; I will be like the most High" (Isa. 14:12-14).
      2. According to Ezekiel—"Son of man, take up a lament concerning the king of Tyre and say to him: 'This is what the Sovereign LORD says: You were the model of perfection, full of wisdom and perfect in beauty. You were in Eden, the garden of God; every precious stone adorned you: ruby, topaz and emerald, chrysolite, onyx and jasper, sapphire, turquoise and beryl. Your settings and mountings were made of gold; on the day you were created they were prepared. You were anointed as a guardian cherub, for so I ordained you. You were on the holy mount of God; you walked among the fiery stones. You were blameless in your ways from the day you were created till wickedness was found in you. Through your widespread trade you were filled with violence, and you sinned. So I drove you in disgrace from the mount of God, and I expelled you, O guardian cherub, from among the fiery stones. Your heart became proud on account of your beauty, and you corrupted your wisdom because of your splendor. So I threw you to the earth; I made a spectacle of you before kings. By your many sins and dishonest trade you have desecrated your sanctuaries. So I made a fire come out from you, and it consumed you, and I reduced you to ashes on the ground in the sight of all who were watching'" (Ezek. 28:12-18, NIV).
      3. According to Jesus—"And he said unto them, I beheld Satan as lightning fall from heaven" (Luke 10:18).
      4. According to 1 John—"He that committeth sin is of the devil; for the devil sinneth from the beginning. For this purpose the Son of God was manifested, that he might destroy the works of the devil" (1 John 3:8).
      5. According to Revelation—"And there appeared another wonder in heaven; and behold a great red dragon, having seven heads and ten horns, and seven crowns upon his heads. And his tail drew the third part of the stars of heaven, and did cast them to the earth: and the dragon stood before the woman which was ready to be delivered, for to devour her child as soon as it was born" (Rev. 12:3-4).
   B. The origin of sin into the world—While an angel introduced sin into the universe,

it was a man who invited it into the world. In the Old Testament Moses describes the act historically, and in the New Testament Paul describes it theologically.

1. The historical account
   a. The temptation of Adam and Eve—"And the LORD God commanded the man, saying, Of every tree of the garden thou mayest freely eat: but of the tree of the knowledge of good and evil, thou shalt not eat of it: for in the day that thou eatest thereof thou shalt surely die" (Gen. 2:16-17).
      (1) That they doubt God's Word—"Now the serpent was more subtil than any beast of the field which the LORD God had made. And he said unto the woman, Yea, hath God said, Ye shall not eat of every tree of the garden?" (Gen. 3:1).
      (2) That they deny God's Word—"And the serpent said unto the woman, Ye shall not surely die: For God doth know that in the day ye eat thereof, then your eyes shall be opened, and ye shall be as gods, knowing good and evil" (Gen. 3:4-5).
   b. The transgression by Adam and Eve—"And when the woman saw that the tree was good for food, and that it was pleasant to the eyes, and a tree to be desired to make one wise, she took of the fruit thereof, and did eat, and gave also unto her husband with her; and he did eat" (Gen. 3:6).
2. The theological account—"Wherefore, as by one man sin entered into the world, and death by sin; and so death passed upon all men, for that all have sinned" (Rom. 5:12). "For as in Adam all die, even so in Christ shall all be made alive" (1 Cor. 15:22).

III. The Nature of Sin
   A. Sin is not eternal—In the third century A.D. a Persian philosopher named Mani developed a school of thought called Manichaeism. In essence, this taught that there are two dual eternal and impersonal principles which exist side by side in this universe. One is the principle of good, and the other the principle of evil. This false philosophy would therefore spell God with two os and omit the letter *d* from devil.
   B. Sin is not merely the absence of good—Some teach that as darkness is merely the absence of light, sin is simply the nonpresence of goodness. This is unscriptural, for sin is as real and positive to the soul of man as cancer and leprosy are to his physical body.
   C. Sin is not simply the weakness or frailty of the human flesh—This false view would see sin as mere frailties of the flesh such as hunger, thirst, and weariness.
   D. Sin has no standard of its own—Sin must derive its measurements from that which is positive or good. One may assume good apart from evil (which indeed was true historically), but evil cannot exist apart from good. By its very nature sin (evil) must oppose and pervert something good. Every sin is, in reality, a perversion of some good principle.
   E. Sin and evil cannot really manifest themselves as such, but must (to some extent) be disguised as good—For example, Hitler's stated reason for the systematic slaughter of Jews and East Europeans was for the "protection and good" of his own people, Germany. A rebel feels free to rape and burn in order to "awaken the conscience" of a careless society unconcerned about the "plight" of his particular minority group. A hijacker threatens and terrifies an entire passenger plane to "correct" the wrongs a certain government may have done in holding some "innocent" political prisoners. Thus, even in a sin-cursed world, evil dare not expose itself in

the raw, as the vicious and vile wolf it really is, but is forced to assume in some form the garb of a sheep.

F. Sin must not only disguise itself *as* the good, but must also actually connect itself *to* the good—In itself it has no unifying power. Here sin may be likened to a virus, and the good to a healthy cell.

Much research is now going on concerning the nature and makeup of a virus. Some believe it is a bridge between the living and non-living. A virus contains DNA (deoxyribonucleic acid), that necessary genetic code of all living organisms, but it has no sugar or fat molecules, nor does it possess nucleotides or amino acids. It can play dead like a crystal for a long duration. Upon being revived, it fastens to the wall of a living cell like a mosquito, driving a tubular shaft in and injecting its own DNA genes. These genes take over the total function of the cell, gathering free-floating nucleotides, and produce copies of the original virus. The virus even secretes an enzyme which breaks down existing cell DNA and uses this for itself.

When several hundred virus DNAs have been assembled, the cell is milked dry. Then the original virus (outside the cell wall) secretes a final enzyme which dissolves the cell wall. An army of virus particles march forth, each seeking new cells to invade, leaving behind the empty broken husk of what had been, an hour before, a healthy, living cell. The operation is simple, ruthless, and effective.

Therefore (as we have already said), sin must disguise itself *as* and connect itself *to* the good. But not so with the good, which has no connection whatsoever with evil, and cannot disguise itself but must be manifested by its true nature.

G. Sin often must strive against itself—For example, a miser is at variance with a spendthrift. A proud stoic will view with contempt a glutton. A promiscuous heterosexual is sickened at the sexual perversions of a homosexual.

But this is not so with the good, where all its elements and attributes complement and do not contradict each other. Love, grace, truth, wisdom, righteousness, and justice are all the closest of friends. Thus, good has only one enemy, the evil; but any given evil has two enemies, the good and another conflicting evil. A classic example of this was seen during World War II, when the two most wicked men on earth hated each other with a passion seldom seen. These two bitter enemies were Adolf Hitler and Joseph Stalin.

H. Sin on some occasions is to be distinguished from evil—For example, sin is not always the exact same thing as evil. We often refer to cyclones, floods, fires, earthquakes, and such as evil, and well they may be. But these cannot be called sin. This fact should be understood, as many Christians have been troubled and confused over the words of God in Isaiah 45:7, where we read: "I form the light, and create darkness: I make peace, and create evil: I the LORD do all these things."

Here the Hebrew word *ra* is used, which can also be translated "calamity." Thus, while we read of God creating evil, the Scriptures assure us he does not create sin. "For he hath made him to be sin for us, who knew no sin; that we might be made the righteousness of God in him" (2 Cor. 5:21). "In hope of eternal life, which God, that cannot lie, promised before the world began" (Titus 1:2). "For we have not an high priest which cannot be touched with the feeling of our infirmities; but was in all points tempted like as we are, yet without sin" (Heb. 4:15). "Who did no sin, neither was guile found in his mouth" (1 Pet. 2:22). "And ye know that he was manifested to take away our sins; and in him is no sin" (1 John 3:5).

IV. The Universality of Sin—The indisputable fact that all men are sinners is attested to by the following five sources:

A. The testimony of history—It has been estimated that some 40 billion human beings have lived (or are living) upon this earth since Adam. It would not be unreasonable to suggest that perhaps one third of these 40 billion people lost their lives at the hand of another human being. Hundreds of millions of living flesh-and-blood creatures have been stabbed, stoned, strangled, shot, gassed, bombed, burned, buried alive, hung, and drowned by other living flesh-and-blood creatures.

B. The testimony of conscience—How often has man's built-in "sin gauge" smote him to despair and even to suicide over his sinful actions. This club of conscience strikes all men, regardless of their brains, brawn, bloodstream, or banking powers. Thus, while the voice of conscience can be defiled, it cannot be denied.

C. The testimony of religions—Louis Berkhof writes the following:

> The history of religions and of philosophy testify to it. The history of religions testifies to the universality of sin. The question of Job, "How shall a man be just with God?" is a question that was asked not merely in the realm of special revelation, but also outside of it in the Gentile world. (Job 9:2) The heathen religions testify to a universal consciousness of sin and of the need of reconciliation with a Supreme Being. There is a general feeling that the gods are offended and must be propititated in some way. There is a universal voice of conscience, testifying to the fact that man falls short of the ideal and stands condemned in the sight of some higher Power. Altars reeking with the blood of sacrifices, often the sacrifices of dear children, repeated confessions of wrongdoing, and prayers for deliverance from evil—all point to the consciousness of sin. Missionaries find this wherever they go. The history of philosophy is indicative of the same fact. Early Greek philosophers were already wrestling with the problem of moral evil, and since their day no philosopher of name was able to ignore it. They were all constrained to admit the universality of it, and that in spite of the fact they were not able to explain the phenomenon. There was, it is true, a superficial optimism in the 18th century, which dreamt of the inherent goodness of man, but in its stupidity flew in the face of the facts and was sharply rebuked by Kant. Many liberal theologians were induced to believe and to preach this inherent goodness of man as gospel truth, but today many of them qualify it as one of the most pernicious errors of the past. Surely the facts of life do not warrant such optimism. (*Systematic Theology*, pp. 239–240)

D. The testimony of the Scriptures
  1. General statements concerning the sinfulness of man—"For there is no man that sinneth not" (1 Kings 8:46a). "Who can say, I have made my heart clean, I am pure from my sin?" (Prov. 20:9). "The heart is deceitful above all things, and desperately wicked: who can know it?" (Jer. 17:9a). "For there is not a just man upon earth, that doeth good, and sinneth not" (Eccles. 7:20). "All we like sheep have gone astray" (Isa. 53:6a). "But we are all as an unclean thing, and all our righteousnesses are as filthy rags; and we all do fade as a leaf; and our iniquities, like the wind, have taken us away" (Isa. 64:6).

  "For all have sinned, and come short of the glory of God" (Rom. 3:23). "But the scripture hath concluded all under sin" (Gal. 3:22a). "For in many things we offend all" (James 3:2a). "If we say that we have no sin, we deceive ourselves, and the truth is not in us" (1 John 1:8). "If we say that we have not sinned, we make him a liar, and his word is not in us" (1 John 1:10).

2. Personal statements concerning the sinfulness of man—On at least eight separate occasions in the Bible an individual is forced to utter those three tragic but true words, "I have sinned."

   a. Pharaoh—"And Pharaoh sent, and called for Moses and Aaron, and said unto them, I have sinned this time: the LORD is righteous, and I and my people are wicked" (Exod. 9:27). "Then Pharaoh called for Moses and Aaron in haste; and he said, I have sinned against the LORD your God, and against you" (Exod. 10:16).

   b. Balaam—"And Balaam said unto the angel of the LORD, I have sinned; for I knew not that thou stoodest in the way against me: now therefore, if it displease thee, I will get me back again" (Num. 22:34).

   c. Achan—"And Achan answered Joshua, and said, Indeed I have sinned against the LORD God of Israel, and thus and thus have I done" (Josh. 7:20).

   d. Saul—"Then said Saul, I have sinned: return, my son David: for I will no more do thee harm, because my soul was precious in thine eyes this day: behold, I have played the fool, and have erred exceedingly" (1 Sam. 26:21).

   e. David—"And David said unto Nathan, I have sinned against the LORD. And Nathan said unto David, The LORD also hath put away thy sin; thou shalt not die" (2 Sam. 12:13). "And David's heart smote him after that he had numbered the people. And David said unto the LORD, I have sinned greatly in that I have done: and now, I beseech thee, O LORD, take away the iniquity of thy servant; for I have done very foolishly" (2 Sam. 24:10).

   f. Job—"I have sinned; what shall I do unto thee, O thou preserver of men? why hast thou set me as a mark against thee, so that I am a burden to myself?" (Job 7:20).

   g. The Prodigal Son—"And the son said unto him, Father, I have sinned against heaven, and in thy sight, and am no more worthy to be called thy son" (Luke 15:21).

   h. Judas—"Saying, I have sinned in that I have betrayed the innocent blood. And they said, What is that to us? see thou to that" (Matt. 27:4).

   A double tragedy is seen here, for out of these eight confessions, it would seem only three really were sincere and experienced the forgiveness of a gracious God. These three are David, Job, and the Prodigal Son.

E. The testimony of our children—The good must be taught to our children. The bad they know already. Sharing is not natural, but selfishness is.

V. The Exceeding Wickedness of Sin—There are two unfathomable areas that even the most spiritual believer can but penetrate slightly. One is the lofty heights of the Creator's holiness. The other is the fearful depths of the creature's sinfulness. Scripture offers three major proofs and illustrations of the exceeding wickedness of sin.

A. The angelic proof—Consider a kindly and highly experienced craftsman creating a magnificent figure out of nothing. Upon its creation this figure is given life, covered with dazzling precious gems, and equipped with a beautiful musical system. The craftsman then places his newly created being over all the universe, to rule (under him) and to enjoy. Millions of other created beings look to this creature for guidance. His only responsibility is to faithfully serve his wise and wonderful Creator. But one dark day, for absolutely no reason whatsoever, this privileged being who had received so much from the craftsman, viciously lashes out against his benevolent benefactor and leads a wicked rebellion to drive him from the very universe he originally created.

What base and perverted ingratitude all this would display. And yet, such was the case when Lucifer rebelled against his mighty Creator, Jehovah God. The depths and depravity of this sin, in light of its background, can never be comprehended by any creature, angelic or human. (See Isa. 14:12-15; Ezek. 28:11-19.)

B. The human proof—L. S. Chafer writes:

> One individual, the first of the human creation, committed one sin and that sin being apparently so innocuous men are prone to ridicule the thought that God would notice it at all; yet that one sin is, according to divine estimation, sufficiently evil to cause the degeneracy and depravity of the unfallen person who committed the sin, and to cause uncounted millions of his posterity to suffer in the flesh and die, and the vast majority of them to spend eternity in the realms of woe. (L. S. Chafer, *Systematic Theology*, vol. II, p. 252)

C. The divine proof
   1. As seen by the price paid by the Savior

   > The Son of God suffered to an infinite degree and died on the cross because of sin. There was no other way whereby redemption could be secured. However, had there never been but one sin committed in this world, the same depths of suffering and death by the Son of God would have been required as a righteous ground for divine forgiveness of that one sin and the justification of that sinner. (Ibid., p. 252)

   2. As seen by the price to be paid by the unrepentant sinner—"Then shall he say also unto them on the left hand, Depart from me, ye cursed, into everlasting fire, prepared for the devil and his angels" (Matt. 25:41).

   Undoubtedly the most difficult aspect of hell to comprehend is its eternal duration. Why could not the torment of even an Adolf Hitler be over after several billion years of suffering? A partial answer has to do with the awesome holiness of God. Any attempted attack against this holiness (as sin is) demands an eternal payment of some sort. Thus, when a sinner rejects the paid price effected by the crucified Savior, he must then spend all eternity paying for it himself.

VI. The Sources of Sin—We have previously discussed the origin of sin, but what are its present-day sources? What causes both unsaved and saved people to sin? Dr. Charles Ryrie observes that the poisonous waters of sin can proceed from one of three polluted fountains:
   A. The world—"Satan's world stands in opposition to God's people and promotes Satan's purposes. So the world system is a source of sin when anyone conforms to it (John 15:18-19)."
      1. Its description—"Satan stands as its head and controlling force. Its chief characteristic is counterfeiting, though Satan will use any tactic he can in order to defeat the believer. Often borderline issues are the most difficult to discern and decide."
      2. Our defense—"A number of things serve as the believer's defense against the counterfeit of the world—the armor (Eph. 6:13-18), knowledge of Satan's strategies (2 Cor. 2:11), sobriety, vigilance (1 Pet. 5:8). Perhaps faith should be placed at or near the top of the list. Our faith is the victory that

overcomes the world (1 John 5:4-5), the faith which identified us with Christ's work on the cross. Since every believer has such faith, he has an adequate defense against the world. Yet such faith needs to be constantly exercised to realize victory (1 Tim. 6:12)."

B. The flesh

    1. The concept—"The flesh is that principle of sin within all of us. Some equate the sin nature and flesh. The flesh produces works (Gal. 5:19), is characterized by lusts and passions (v. 24; 1 John 2:16), and it can enslave the believer (Rom. 7:25). In it is nothing good (v. 18), for the presence of the new life in Christ makes all that is associated with the flesh old and useless. This includes blatantly evil things as well as amoral things and sometimes things that might be good in themselves but which bring no pleasure to God because they are works of the flesh."

    2. The control—"The flesh can only be controlled by actualizing our co-crucifixion with Christ. We have crucified the flesh, that is, been separated from its domination by our association with Christ's dying *unto* (Gal. 5:24). We can experience victory not by eradication of the flesh but in walking in dependence on the Spirit to control it (v. 16)."

C. The devil—"Christ was acutely aware of the power, program, and procedures of Satan. Some have tried to suggest that the Lord really did not believe in the reality of Satan but was accommodating the ignorances of the people when He taught about Satan. However, He spoke of Satan on occasions when there was no need to unless He believed Satan actually existed (e.g., Luke 10:18). Our Lord acknowledged Satan as the ruler of this world (John 12:31), the head of his own kingdom (Matt. 12:26), the father of rebellious people (John 8:44), the father of lies (v. 44), the evil one who opposes the reception of the Gospel (Matt. 13:19), the enemy who sows tares among the good seed (v. 39), and thus the one who causes people to do these things which he promotes."

    1. His strategy is planned. "Satan devises methods, uses strategies, and employs all the craftiness of a superhuman creature to trap the believer (2 Cor. 2:11; Eph. 6:11)."

    2. His strategy is persistent. "He continually stalks the believer, waiting for the right moment to attack (1 Pet. 5:8)."

    3. His strategy is powerful. "The believer must wrestle in hand-to-hand combat against Satan, never underestimating his power (Eph. 6:12; 1 John 4:4; Jude 9)" (Charles Ryrie, *Basic Theology,* pp. 216, 231–232).

VII. The Kinds of Sin

A. A general listing—As might be expected, there are many types of sin recorded in the Word of God, all of which are tragically illustrated by various individuals. Here is a general alphabetical listing:

    1. Adultery (2 Sam. 11:4)

    2. Anger (Num. 20:7-11; Matt. 5:22)

    3. Anxiety (Phil. 4:6; 2 Kings 6:15)

    4. Apostasy (Jude)

    5. Arrogance (Exod. 5:2)

    6. Attempted genocide (Esther 3)

    7. Backbiting (Rom. 1:30; Psa. 15:3)

    8. Backsliding (Prov. 14:14; Jer. 3:14)

    9. Betrayal (Gen. 37:28; Luke 22:3-4)

    10. Bitterness (Job 10:1; Heb. 12:15)

11. Blasphemy (Luke 22:65; Rev. 13:1)
12. Bloodletting (2 Kings 11:1; 21:16)
13. Boasting (Prov. 25:14; James 3:5)
14. Brazenness (Num. 24:6; Dan. 5:1-4)
15. Bribery (1 Sam. 8:3; Amos 5:12)
16. Brutality (2 Kings 15:16)
17. Carelessness (Exod. 4:24-26)
18. Carnality (1 Cor. 3:1-4)
19. Child abuse (Matt. 18:6, 10)
20. Cursing God's anointed (2 Sam. 16:5)
21. Compromise (Judg. 2:2; 1 Kings 22:1-4)
22. Conspiracy (2 Sam. 15:12; Acts 23:12-13)
23. Covetousness (Josh. 7:1, 20-21; Luke 12:15)
24. Crucifying Christ (Acts 2:23)
25. Deceit (Gen. 12:12-13; 27:18-19)
26. Defrauding (Mark 10:19; 1 Cor. 6:8)
27. Delaying (Acts 24:24-25)
28. Denying Christ (Matt. 26:69-75)
29. Despising authority (2 Pet. 2:10-12)
30. Despising God's message (Jer. 36:22-25)
31. Despising God's messengers (Matt. 23:31-34)
32. Discouragement (1 Kings 19:4; 1 Sam. 27:1)
33. Dishonesty (2 Cor. 4:2)
34. Disloyalty (2 Sam. 15:31)
35. Disobedience (Gen. 2:17; 3:5; 1 Sam. 15:19, 22)
36. Divisiveness (Prov. 6:19; 1 Cor. 1:11-13)
37. Doublemindedness (James 1:5-8)
38. Doubt (Matt. 14:31; 1 Tim. 2:8)
39. Drunkenness (Gen. 9:20-21; Gal. 5:21)
40. Dullness (of hearing, Heb. 5:11-14; of seeing, 2 Pet. 1:9)
41. Enticement (Gen. 39:7, 10; Prov. 1:10)
42. Envy (1 Sam. 18:8-9; Gal. 5:21, 26)
43. Extortion (Matt. 23:25; 1 Cor. 5:10-11)
44. Faithlessness (Matt. 17:17; John 20:27)
45. False accusation (Gen. 39:13-15; 1 Kings 21:10-13)
46. False piety (Matt. 6:1-8, 16-18)
47. Fear (Prov. 29:25; Rom. 8:15; 1 John 4:18)
48. Foolish talking (Eph. 5:4; Titus 3:9)
49. Formalism (2 Tim. 3:5)
50. Fruitlessness (Hos. 10:1; John 15:2)
51. Gluttony (Prov. 23:21; Matt. 11:19)
52. Hatred (Gen. 27:41; 37:5; Titus 3:3)
53. Homosexuality (Gen. 19:5; Rom. 1:24-27)
54. Hypocrisy (Matt. 7:5; 23:28)
55. Idolatry (Exod. 32:6a; Judg. 2:12; 1 Kings 16:33)
56. Immorality (Exod. 32:6b; Judg. 16:1; Matt. 5:27-32)
57. Incest (Gen. 19:33-36)
58. Indulgence (1 Sam. 3:13)
59. Ingratitude (Rom. 1:21)

60. Intrusion into the priest's office (1 Sam. 13:9; 2 Chron. 26:16)
61. Irresponsible stewardship (Matt. 25:14-30; Luke 19:11-27)
62. Judging (Rom. 14:10-12; 1 Cor. 4:5; Matt. 7:1-5)
63. Lack of mercy (Matt. 18:23-35)
64. Lack of natural affection (Rom. 1:31; 2 Tim. 3:3)
65. Laziness (Titus 1:12; 2 Thess. 3:10)
66. Leaving first love (Rev. 2:4)
67. Legalism (Gal.)
68. Living in the flesh (Gal. 3:3)
69. Lust (1 John 2:15-17)
70. Lying (1 Sam. 21:2-3; Prov. 17:22; Eph. 4:25)
71. Malice (Rom. 1:29; 1 Cor. 5:8; Eph. 4:31)
72. Materialism (2 Tim. 3:1-2; Rev. 3:15-19)
73. Mocking (Gen. 21:9; 2 Kings 2:23; 2 Pet. 3:3-4)
74. Murder (Gen. 4:8)
75. Murmuring (Exod. 14:10-12; 16:7; 17:2-3)
76. Offering human sacrifices (2 Kings 17:17)
77. Partiality (James 1:2-4)
78. Polygamy (Deut. 17:17; 1 Kings 11:1-11)
79. Polluting God's house (Jer. 7:1-11; John 2:13-16)
80. Prayerlessness (1 Sam. 12:23; Luke 18:1-8)
81. Presumption (Josh. 7:3; 9:14-15)
82. Pride (Prov. 16:18; 2 Chron. 26:16)
83. Prophesying falsely (1 Kings 22:11-24; Rev. 2:20)
84. Prostitution (Gen. 38:15; 1 Cor. 6:15)
85. Rape (2 Sam. 13:14)
86. Rashness (Judg. 11:30-31; 1 Sam. 14:24)
87. Rebellion (Gen. 11:4; Num. 14:4-10; 16:1-3)
88. Revenge (2 Sam. 13:28-29)
89. Robbing God (Mal. 3:8-9; Hag. 1:3-11)
90. Sacrilege (Mark 11:15-18)
91. Scattering the sheep (Jer. 23:1; Ezek. 34:1-10; John 10:12-13)
92. Sedition (2 Sam. 15:1-6)
93. Selfishness (Luke 12:16-19)
94. Self-will (Isa. 14:12-14; 2 Pet. 2:10)
95. Self-worship (Rom. 1:25)
96. Slander (Prov. 10:18; 2 Sam. 19:27)
97. Strife (Gen. 13:7; Prov. 17:19; Phil. 2:3)
98. Stubbornness (1 Sam. 15:23; Acts 7:31)
99. Suicide (2 Sam. 17:23; Matt. 27:5)
100. Teaching false doctrine (Matt. 16:6; 1 Tim. 4:1-3; 2 Tim. 4:3)
101. Theft (Matt. 15:19; Rev. 9:21)
102. Treachery (Gen. 34:13-18, 25-29; 2 Sam. 3:27)
103. Unbelief (Matt. 13:58; Heb. 4:6, 11)
104. Unequal alliance (1 Cor. 5:9; 6:15; 2 Cor. 6:14-18)
105. Unthankfulness (Rom. 1:21; Psa. 103:2)
106. Willful ignorance (2 Pet. 3:5)
107. Wisdom rejecting (Prov. 1:20-29)
108. Witchcraft (1 Sam. 28:7-18; 2 Chron. 33:6; Gal. 5:20)

B. A group listing—Are some sins worse than other sins? While it is true that the Bible teaches in a general sense that to be guilty of one is to be guilty of all sins (James 2:10), it also indicates there are sins of greater degree and sins of lesser degree.

We note the following words of Jesus: "And that servant, which knew his lord's will, and prepared not himself, neither did according to his will, shall be beaten with many stripes. But he that knew not, and did commit things worthy of stripes, shall be beaten with few stripes. For unto whomsoever much is given, of him shall be much required: and to whom men have committed much, of him they will ask the more" (Luke 12:47-48).

Let us consider some of the various kinds of sins as indicated in the Word of God:

1. Sins of ignorance—"Then said Jesus, Father, forgive them; for they know not what they do" (Luke 23:34a). "Jesus answered [Pilate], . . . he that delivered me unto thee [the wicked Jews] hath the greater sin" (John 19:11). "For as many as have sinned without law shall also perish without law: and as many as have sinned in the law shall be judged by the law" (Rom. 2:12). "And I thank Christ Jesus our Lord, who hath enabled me, for that he counted me faithful, putting me into the ministry; who was before a blasphemer, and a persecutor, and injurious: but I obtained mercy, because I did it ignorantly in unbelief" (1 Tim. 1:12-13).

2. Sins of infirmity—"Who can understand his errors: cleanse thou me from secret faults" (Psa. 19:12). "He hath not dealt with us after our sins; nor rewarded us according to our iniquities. . . . For he knoweth our frame; he remembereth that we are dust" (Psa. 103:10, 14).

   "Likewise the Spirit also helpeth our infirmities: for we know not what we should pray for as we ought: but the Spirit itself maketh intercession for us with groanings which cannot be uttered" (Rom. 8:26). "For whatsoever is not of faith is sin" (Rom. 14:23b). "We then that are strong ought to bear the infirmities of the weak" (Rom. 15:1a). "Watch and pray, that ye enter not into temptation: the spirit indeed is willing, but the flesh is weak" (Matt. 26:41).

3. Sins of carelessness—"I said, I will take heed to my ways, that I sin not with my tongue" (Psa. 39:1a). "Take heed to yourselves, that your heart be not deceived" (Deut. 11:16a). "But take heed lest by any means this liberty of yours become a stumbling block to them that are weak" (1 Cor. 8:9). "Wherefore let him that thinketh he standeth take heed lest he fall" (1 Cor. 10:12). "Therefore we ought to give the more earnest heed to the things which we have heard, lest at any time we should let them slip" (Heb. 2:1).

4. Sins of presumption—"Keep back thy servant also from presumptuous sins" (Psa. 19:13a). "But chiefly them that walk after the flesh in the lust of uncleanness, and despise government. Presumptuous are they, selfwilled . . ." (2 Pet. 2:10). "Who knowing the judgment of God, that they which commit such things are worthy of death, not only do the same, but have pleasure in them that do them" (Rom. 1:32).

5. Sins related to physical and spiritual death
   a. Physical death: the sin unto death—"For this cause many are weak and sickly among you, and many sleep" (1 Cor. 11:30). "There is a sin unto death" (1 John 5:16b).

   As in the case of the unpardonable sin, the sin unto death has been the object of some controversy. The commonly accepted view is that the sin can only be committed by a child of God, and happens when the believer lives such a wretched life that the Father finally reaches down and takes him home to heaven earlier than he normally would have. In other words, just as there is a premature birth, there is a premature death. Evidence of this theory is thought by some to be seen in Acts 5:1-11; 1 Corinthians 5:1-5 (here, though, the Corinthian believer apparently repented—see 2 Cor. 2:6-11). Some who hold this theory use it as a theological basis for interpreting such difficult passages as Hebrews 6:4-10; 10:26-30.

b. Spiritual death: the unpardonable sin—"Wherefore I say unto you, All manner of sin and blasphemy shall be forgiven unto men: but the blasphemy against the Holy Ghost shall not be forgiven unto men. And whosoever speaketh a word against the Son of man, it shall be forgiven him: but whosoever speaketh against the Holy Ghost, it shall not be forgiven him, neither in this world, neither in the world to come" (Matt. 12:31-32).

Much ink has been spilled over these words. What is this unforgivable and unpardonable sin? Who can commit it? Can it be done today? Two main views have been offered to explain this sin.

(1) First view—The first view is that the sin can be committed by any unbeliever today and occurs when a sinner rejects the convicting voice of the Holy Spirit once too often. At this point, the Holy Spirit forever ceases to deal with the sinner and he is hopelessly condemned, with no chance of salvation, however he may later desire it. Genesis 6:3 is sometimes offered in support of this theory. "And the LORD said, My spirit shall not always strive with man, for that he also is flesh: yet his days shall be an hundred and twenty years."

However, an examination of the passage shows this meaning is taken completely out of its context. In reality there is no scriptural basis for the first theory.

(2) Second view—The second view is that the sin was dispensational in nature, that it was the sin of ascribing to Satan the earthly miracles performed by our Savior and therefore cannot be committed today. This theory is generally held by the majority of Bible students and the passage context would seem to support its accuracy.

"Then was brought unto him one possessed with a devil, blind, and dumb: and he healed him, insomuch that the blind and dumb both spake and saw. And all the people were amazed, and said, Is not this the son of David? But when the Pharisees heard it, they said, This fellow doth not cast out devils, but by Beelzebub the prince of the devils" (Matt. 12:22-24).

VIII. Symbols and Metaphors of Sin

A. Metaphors

1. Sin is *poisonous,* like a viper—"They have sharpened their tongues like a serpent; adders' poison is under their lips. Selah" (Psa. 140:3). "Ye serpents, ye generation of vipers, how can ye escape the damnation of hell?" (Matt. 23:33).

2. Sin is *stubborn,* like a mule—"For vain man would be wise, though man be born like a wild ass's colt" (Job 11:12).

3. Sin is *cruel,* like a bear—"And behold another beast, a second, like to a bear, and it raised up itself on one side, and it had three ribs in the mouth of it between the teeth of it: and they said thus unto it, Arise, devour much flesh (Dan. 7:5).

4. Sin is *destructive,* like a cankerworm—"And I will restore to you the years that

the locust hath eaten, the cankerworm, and the caterpillar, and the palmerworm, my great army which I sent among you" (Joel 2:25).

5. Sin is *unclean*, like a wild dog—"As a dog returneth to his vomit, so a fool returneth to his folly" (Prov. 26:11).

6. Sin is *cunning*, like a fox—"And he said unto them, Go ye, and tell that fox, Behold, I cast out devils, and I do cures today and tomorrow, and the third day I shall be perfected" (Luke 13:32).

7. Sin is *fierce*, like a wolf—"But he that is an hireling, and not the shepherd, whose own the sheep are not, seeth the wolf coming, and leaveth the sheep, and fleeth: and the wolf catcheth them, and scattereth the sheep" (John 10:12).

8. Sin *devours*, like a lion—"They gaped upon me with their mouths, as a ravening and a roaring lion" (Psa. 22:13). "The first was like a lion, and had eagle's wings: I beheld till the wings thereof were plucked, and it was lifted up from the earth, and made stand upon the feet as a man, and a man's heart was given to it" (Dan. 7:4).

9. Sin is *filthy*, like a swine—"But it is happened unto them according to the true proverb, The dog is turned to his own vomit again; and the sow that was washed to her wallowing in the mire" (2 Pet. 2:22). (Metaphors compiled by Emery Bancroft, in *Christian Theology*, p. 228.)

B. Symbols

1. A serpent—"Now the serpent was more subtle than any beast of the field". (Gen. 3:1a). "Ye serpents, ye generation of vipers, how can ye escape the damnation of hell?" (Matt. 23:33). "That old serpent, called the Devil and Satan" (Rev. 12:9).

2. Leprosy—"He is a leprous man, he is unclean: the priest shall pronounce him utterly unclean; his plague is in his head" (Lev. 13:44).

3. Leaven—"Then Jesus said unto them, Take heed and beware of the leaven of the Pharisees and of the Sadducees" (Matt. 16:6).

4. A woman—"And, behold, there was lifted up a talent of lead: and this is a woman that sitteth in the midst of the ephah. And he said, This is wickedness. And he cast it into the midst of the ephah; and he cast the weight of lead upon the mouth thereof" (Zech. 5:7-8).

"And the woman was arrayed in purple and scarlet colour, and decked with gold and precious stones and pearls, having a golden cup in her hand full of abominations and filthiness of her fornication: And upon her forehead was a name written, MYSTERY, BABYLON THE GREAT, THE MOTHER OF HARLOTS AND ABOMINATIONS OF THE EARTH" (Rev. 17:4-5).

IX. The Consequences of Sin

A. Upon Lucifer—As Lucifer was the first sinner, he naturally experienced the first terrible results of sin.

1. Immediate consequences

a. Lucifer lost his coveted position as heaven's anointed cherub—"Thou art the anointed cherub that covereth; and I have set thee so: thou wast upon the holy mountain of God; thou hast walked up and down in the midst of the stones of fire. Thou wast perfect in thy ways from the day that thou wast created, till iniquity was found in thee" (Ezek. 28:14-15).

b. He became earth's depraved dragon—"And there was war in heaven: Michael and his angels fought against the dragon; and the dragon fought and his angels, and prevailed not; neither was their place found any more in heaven" (Rev. 12:7-8).

2. Future consequences—The devil will someday be forever cast into the lake of fire, a place God himself prepared for the universe's first sinner. "Then shall he say also unto them on the left hand, Depart from me, ye cursed, into everlasting fire, prepared for the devil and his angels" (Matt. 25:41). "And the devil that deceived them was cast into the lake of fire and brimstone, where the beast and the false prophet are, and shall be tormented day and night for ever and ever" (Rev. 20:10).

B. Upon man—When Adam opened the door for sin, two vicious criminals also rushed in and immediately began tormenting the human race. The names of these two terrible gangsters are physical death and spiritual death. In the Bible the theological meaning for death is "separation."

1. Physical death—God created Adam with the possibilities of living forever (Gen. 2:9). But Adam sinned (Gen. 3:6-7). Therefore Adam had to later experience physical death, that is, the separation of his body from soul and spirit.

   "And all the days that Adam lived were nine hundred and thirty years: and he died" (Gen. 5:5). "The days of our years are threescore years and ten; and if by reason of strength they be fourscore years, yet is their strength labour and sorrow; for it is soon cut off, and we fly away" (Psa. 90:10).

2. Spiritual death—Because of sin, all unsaved people will someday be forever separated from God in the lake of fire. This is referred to as the second death. "And then will I profess unto them, I never knew you: depart from me, ye that work iniquity" (Matt. 7:23). "Then shall he say also unto them on the left hand, Depart from me, ye cursed, into everlasting fire, prepared for the devil and his angels" (Matt. 25:41).

   "He that hath an ear, let him hear what the Spirit saith unto the churches; He that overcometh shall not be hurt of the second death" (Rev. 2:11). "Blessed and holy is he that hath part in the first resurrection: on such the second death hath no power, but they shall be priests of God and of Christ, and shall reign with him a thousand years. And death and hell were cast into the lake of fire. This is the second death" (Rev. 20:6, 14). "But the fearful, and unbelieving, and the abominable, and murderers, and whoremongers, and sorcerers, and idolaters, and all liars, shall have their part in the lake which burneth with fire and brimstone: which is the second death" (Rev. 21:8).

   It should be furthermore stated that, although the second death as mentioned above is still future for the sinner, the Bible nevertheless teaches that all unsaved people right now are considered by God to be dead in trespasses and sins and separated even at this present time from his fellowship (Eph. 2:1-12). Both physical and spiritual death seem to be in the mind of God when he warned Adam about the consequences of sin. The Hebrew of Genesis 2:17 may be translated, "For in the day that thou eatest thereof, in dying thou shalt surely die."

   Cut flowers well illustrate living human beings doing good things but who nevertheless are spiritually dead. Is the blossom that has been cut from the plant alive or dead? At first it is beautiful, fragrant, and in combination with other cut flowers may grace the finest home, church, or occasion. It looks alive; it is useful; but it is in reality dead, for it has been severed from the life of the plant which produced it. At this point the illustration breaks down, for it is not possible to give the flower new and eternal life, something God can do for the one who believes in the Lord Jesus. (Charles Ryrie, *Basic Theology*, p. 219)

In summary it may be said then that sin:
a. Dulls man's ears—"For the heart of this people is waxed gross, and their ears are dull of hearing, and their eyes have they closed; lest they should see with their eyes, and hear with their ears, and understand with their heart, and should be converted, and I should heal them" (Acts 28:27).
b. Darkens his eyes of understanding—"Having the understanding darkened, being alienated from the life of God through the ignorance that is in them, because of the blindness of their heart" (Eph. 4:18).
c. Diverts his feet—"All we like sheep have gone astray; we have turned every one to his own way; and the LORD hath laid on him the iniquity of us all" (Isa. 53:6).
d. Defiles his tongue—"Their throat is an open sepulchre; with their tongues they have used deceit; the poison of asps is under their lips: whose mouth is full of cursing and bitterness" (Rom. 3:13-14).
e. Deceives his heart—"The heart is deceitful above all things, and desperately wicked: who can know it?" (Jer. 17:9).
f. Devours his intellect—"But the natural man receiveth not the things of the Spirit of God: for they are foolishness unto him: neither can he know them, because they are spiritually discerned" (1 Cor. 2:14).
g. Dooms his soul—"Behold, all souls are mine; as the soul of the father, so also the soul of the son is mine: the soul that sinneth, it shall die" (Ezek. 18:4).

C. Upon nature—After sin, man's paradise became a wilderness. The roses contained thorns and the docile tiger suddenly became a hungry meat-eater. This will continue to be the case until the curse is lifted during the Millennium. In the New Testament Paul writes about the consequences of sin upon nature:
"For the earnest expectation of the creature waiteth for the manifestation of the sons of God. For the creature was made subject to vanity, not willingly, but by reason of him who hath subjected the same in hope, because the creature itself also shall be delivered from the bondage of corruption into the glorious liberty of the children of God. For we know that the whole creation groaneth and travaileth in pain together until now" (Rom. 8:19-22).

D. Upon the holy angels—Man's sin apparently became an object lesson for angels as their Creator allowed them to enter into his blessed work of redeeming mankind. The following passages seem to bear this out: "For we are made a spectacle unto the world, and to angels, and to men" (1 Cor. 4:9b). "I charge thee before God, and the Lord Jesus Christ, and the elect angels" (1 Tim. 5:21a). "And it [the Law] was ordained by angels" (Gal. 3:19c). "Which things [matters concerning salvation] the angels desire to look into" (1 Pet. 1:12d). "Are they [angels] not all ministering spirits, sent forth to minister for them who shall be heirs of salvation?" (Heb. 1:14).

E. Upon God himself—What effect did man's sin have upon God? It meant that he could no longer rest as he had done when creation was completed. "And on the seventh day God ended his work which he had made; and he rested on the seventh day from all his work which he had made" (Gen. 2:2). It meant that he began his second and greatest work, that of redemption. To this very day, God continues to work in matters of redemption. "But Jesus answered them, My Father worketh hitherto, and I work" (John 5:17). "I must work the works of him that sent me" (John 9:4a). "He which hath begun a good work in you will perform it until the day of Jesus Christ" (Phil. 1:6b).

X. The Imputation of Sin—Were the effects of Adam's fall merely confined to himself, or do they continue somehow to make themselves known in the life of twentieth century man?

A. The liberal position—The entire story is simply a Hebrew legend.

B. The Pelagian position—Pelagius was a British monk who taught that Adam's sin affected only himself, for God imputes to men only those sins which they personally and consciously perform. Pelagius said the only effect of Adam's sin on posterity was that of a bad example. The doctrine of Pelagianism was condemned by the Council of Carthage in A.D. 418.

C. The Arminian position—Arminius (1560–1609) was a professor who lived and taught in Holland. His theory teaches that while Adam's sin definitely weakened the will of his posterity to remain sinless, it did not, however, destroy the possibility.

D. The Augustinian position—Paul Enns writes:

> This view is named after Augustine (A.D. 354–430) and has been more recently held by Calvin, Luther, Shedd, and Strong. This view teaches that the statement "all sinned" in Romans 5:12 suggests that all humanity was a participant in Adam's sin. Just as Levi (although not yet born) paid tithes to Melchizedek through Abraham in that Levi was "seminally present" in Abraham (Heb. 7:9-10), in a similar way, all humanity was "seminally present" in Adam when Adam sinned and therefore all humanity participated in the sin. Therefore, the sin of Adam and the resultant death is charged to all humanity because all humanity is guilty. God holds all humanity guilty because all humanity is guilty. (*Moody Handbook of Theology*, p. 312)

E. The federal position

> The federal view was originally propounded by Cocceius (1603–1669) and became a standard of belief in Reformed theology. It was taught by men like Charles Hodge; J. Oliver Buswell, Jr.; and Louis Berkhof. This view is called the federal view because Adam is seen as the federal head or representative of the entire human race. God entered into a covenant of works with Adam whereby He promised to bless Adam and thereby the entire human race with eternal life if Adam obeyed. Disobedience would bring suffering to the entire human race. As a result of Adam's sin, since he was the representative of the human race, his sin plunged the entire human race into suffering and death. Through the one sin of Adam, sin and death are imputed to all humanity because all humanity was represented in Adam. Charles Hodge defines the view: "In virtue of the union, federal and natural, between Adam and his posterity, his sin, although not their act, is so imputed to them that it is the judicial ground of the penalty threatened against him coming also upon them." (Ibid., p. 312)

> Note: Although these two final views are similar, they are not exactly the same.

1. The Augustinian view says that I actually sinned with Adam, even though unborn, being found in his "genetic pool," and thus had his sin imputed to me.

2. The federal view says that although I did not sin with Adam, yet inasmuch as he served to represent me, his sin was imputed to me.

Question: Which of the two views (Augustinian and federal) is supported by the Scriptures? In general, a case can be made for both positions. "Wherefore, as by one man sin entered into the world, and death by sin; and so death passed upon all men, for that all have sinned: therefore as by the offence of one judgment came upon all men to condemnation; even so by the righteousness of one the free gift came upon all men unto justification of life" (Rom. 5:12, 18).

At this point it will be helpful to read the summaries offered by two well-known theologians.

> *With respect to the origin of sin in the history of mankind, the Bible teaches that it began with the transgression of Adam in paradise, and therefore with a perfectly voluntary act on the part of man. The tempter came from the spirit world with the suggestion that man, by placing himself in opposition to God, might become like God. Adam yielded to the temptation and committed the first sin by eating of the forbidden fruit. But the matter did not stop there, for by that first sin Adam became the bond-servant of sin. That sin carried permanent pollution with it, and a pollution which, because of the solidarity of the human race, would affect not only Adam but all his descendants as well. As a result of the fall the father of the race could only pass on a depraved human nature to his off-spring. From that unholy source sin flows on as an impure stream to all the generations of men, polluting everyone and everything with which it comes in contact. It is exactly this state of things that made the question of Job so pertinent, "Who can bring a clean thing out of an unclean? not one" (Job 14:4). But even this is not all. Adam sinned not only as the father of the human race, but also as the representative head of all his descendants; and therefore the guilt of his sin is placed to their account, so that they are all liable to the punishment of death. It is primarily in that sense that Adam's sin is the sin of all. That is what Paul teaches us in Romans 5:12: "Through one man sin entered into the world, and death through sin; and so death passed unto all men, for that all sinned." The last words can only mean that they all sinned in Adam, and sinned in such a way as to make them all liable to the punishment of death. It is not sin considered merely as pollution, but sin as guilt that carries punishment with it. God adjudges all men to be guilty sinners in Adam, just as He adjudges all believers to be righteous in Jesus Christ. That is what Paul means, when he says: "So then as through one act of righteousness the free gift came unto all men to justification of life. For as through the one man's disobedience the many were made sinners, even so through the obedience of the one shall the many be made righteous" (Rom. 5:18-19). (Louis Berkhof,* Systematic Theology, *pp. 221–222)*

> *As a matter of fact the representative principle runs through the entire range of human life. Representative action is a sociological fact everywhere and is recognized in all orderly legal systems. For example, it may properly be said, I signed the Declaration of Independence as of the Fourth of July, 1776. I was not there, but my representatives acted as my representatives, and I am implicated in all the consequences of their action. Further, I declared war and entered World War II with the whole nation as of December 7, 1941. I was not present when the action was taken. I was only listening over the radio. I might have been an unborn child. Nevertheless, my representatives acted for me and as representing me, therefore it was my action, and I am implicated and involved in all the consequences of that action.*

> *Just so, I became a wicked, guilty sinner in the Garden of Eden. I turned my back*

upon fellowship with my holy God. I deliberately corrupted the character of godly holiness which God imparted to His creation. I willfully began to spread corruption through the creation over which God had intended me to rule. I was not there. No, but my representative was there, and he acted as such in my place and I was driven out from the garden and excluded from the tree of life." (J. Oliver Buswell, A Systematic Theology of the Christian Religion, *p. 295)*

XI. The Reasons for Sin—We have already observed the biblical teachings that God is nowhere pictured as the author of sin. But why did he allow it? Could he not have prevented it? The answer is, of course, that he could have, but chose not to. Why? Several suggestions have been offered along this line.

    A. First suggestion—God created both angels and men as intelligent creatures possessing moral natures that could determine and choose between right and wrong. Had God stopped Lucifer and Adam one second before their sin, he would, in effect, have violated their moral natures and reduced them to mere walking robots.

    B. Second suggestion—God allowed man to sin so that he might display his grace. Thus, prior to Adam, God was already exhibiting his omnipresence (in being everywhere at once), his omnipotence (in setting the galaxies into motion), and his omniscience (in creating angels). But there was one attribute, one characteristic perhaps closer to his heart than any other, and that was his grace. Where there is no sin there is no need of grace. As Paul would later write: "But where sin abounded, grace did much more abound" (Rom. 5:20b).

        Why then did God allow Adam to sin? No man knows. But it does not seem unreasonable to believe that part of the answer lies in the above suggestion, that is, for God to display his marvelous grace. Again, in the words of Paul: "Even when we were dead in sins [he] hath quickened us together with Christ, (by grace ye are saved;). . . . That in the ages to come he might shew the exceeding riches of his grace in his kindness toward us through Christ Jesus" (Eph. 2:5, 7).

XII. The Christian's Sin—One of the truly great and far-reaching blessings of salvation is God's dealings with the subject of our sin. The repenting sinner is immediately and eternally saved from the *penalty* of sin (in the past), provided with victory over the *power* of sin (in the present), and guaranteed final removal from the *presence* of sin (in the future). But what happens when the Christian fails to use the available power and falls into sin? How does God view sin in the life of his child? Is it indeed possible (as some have claimed) to remain sinless from the cross to the crown?

    A. The fact of sin—Let it be said up front that the one claiming sinless perfection ascribes to himself that which neither Paul, nor James, nor John claimed for themselves. Note the testimony of these three apostles:

        1. Paul—"Not as though I had already attained, either were already perfect: but I follow after, if that I may apprehend that for which also I am apprehended of Christ Jesus" (Phil. 3:12). "This is a faithful saying, and worthy of all acceptation, that Christ Jesus came into the world to save sinners; of whom I am chief" (1 Tim. 1:15).

        2. James—"For in many things we offend all. If any man offend not in word, the same is a perfect man, and able also to bridle the whole body" (James 3:2).

3. John—Charles Ryrie writes:

> Being a Christian does not free one from sinning. Of course there are some who teach eradication of the sin nature in this life, but the picture and doctrine of the New Testament seem to teach otherwise. In fact, John mentions three false claims which people in his day made in this regard in 1 John 1:8-10.
>
> "If we say that we have no sin, we deceive ourselves, and the truth is not in us. If we confess our sins, he is faithful and just to forgive us our sins, and to cleanse us from all unrighteousness. If we say that we have not sinned, we make him a liar, and his word is not in us" (1 John 1:8-10).
>
> Verse 8 speaks of denying the *presence* of the principle of sin.
>
> Verse 9 speaks of the denial of *particular* sins.
>
> Verse 10 speaks of the denial of *personally* sinning. (*A Survey of Bible Doctrine*, p. 112)

B. The effect of sin—The child of God immediately loses the following eight things upon sinning. The ninth may be lost.
   1. The loss of light—"If we say that we have fellowship with him, and walk in darkness, we lie, and do not the truth" (1 John 1:6).
   2. The loss of joy—"Restore unto me the joy of thy salvation; and uphold me with thy free spirit" (Psa. 51:12). "These things have I spoken unto you, that my joy might remain in you, and that your joy might be full" (John 15:11). "But the fruit of the Spirit is love, joy, peace, longsuffering, gentleness, goodness, faith" (Gal. 5:22). "And these things write we unto you, that your joy may be full" (1 John 1:4).
   3. The loss of peace—There are two kinds of peace enjoyed by the believer.
      a. The peace with God, enjoyed by *all* believers regardless of their spiritual condition (Rom. 5:1).
      b. The peace of God, enjoyed by *only* those believers living in the center of his will. This is the peace sin causes one to lose.
   4. The loss of love—"But whoso keepeth his word, in him verily is the love of God perfected: hereby know we that we are in him" (1 John 2:5). "Love not the world, neither the things that are in the world. If any man love the world, the love of the Father is not in him. For all that is in the world, the lust of the flesh, and the lust of the eyes, and the pride of life, is not of the Father, but is of the world. And the world passeth away, and the lust thereof: but he that doeth the will of God abideth for ever" (1 John 2:15-17). "No man hath seen God at any time. If we love one another, God dwelleth in us, and his love is perfected in us" (1 John 4:12).
   5. The loss of fellowship—"That which we have seen and heard declare we unto you, that ye also may have fellowship with us: and truly our fellowship is with the Father, and with his Son Jesus Christ. . . . If we say that we have fellowship with him, and walk in darkness, we lie, and do not the truth: But if we walk in the light, as he is in the light, we have fellowship one with another, and the blood of Jesus Christ his Son cleanseth us from all sin" (1 John 1:3, 6-7).
   6. The loss of confidence—"And hereby we know that we are of the truth, and shall assure our hearts before him. For if our heart condemn us, God is greater than our heart, and knoweth all things. Beloved, if our heart condemn us not, then have we confidence toward God. And whatsoever we ask, we receive of

him, because we keep his commandments, and do those things that are pleasing in his sight" (1 John 3:19-22).

7. The loss of testimony—"No one who is born of God will continue to sin, because God's seed remains in him; he cannot go on sinning, because he has been born of God. This is how we know who the children of God are and who the children of the devil are: Anyone who does not do what is right is not a child of God; neither is anyone who does not love his brother" (1 John 3:9-10, NIV).

8. The loss of rewards—"Therefore we ought to give the more earnest heed to the things which we have heard, lest at any time we should let them slip" (Heb. 2:1). "Cast not away therefore your confidence, which hath great recompence of reward" (Heb. 10:35). "Look to yourselves, that we lose not those things which we have wrought, but that we receive a full reward" (2 John 8).

9. The possible loss of health and even physical life—"For this cause many are weak and sickly among you, and many sleep" (1 Cor. 11:30).

C. The restoration following sin—How can a "sinning saint" be restored to full fellow-ship? In essence, he or she must know and apply both the means and the method of God's cleansing and forgiveness.

1. The means is the blood of Christ—"But if we walk in the light, as he is in the light, we have fellowship one with another, and the blood of Jesus Christ his Son cleanseth us from all sin" (1 John 1:7).

2. The method is the confession of the Christian—"If we confess our sins, he is faithful and just to forgive us our sins, and to cleanse us from all unrighteousness" (1 John 1:9).

D. The preventives against sin

1. The role played by the Word of God—"Thy word have I hid in mine heart, that I might not sin against thee" (Psa. 119:11). "If ye abide in me, and my words abide in you, ye shall ask what ye will, and it shall be done unto you" (John 15:7). "Sanctify them through thy truth: thy word is truth" (John 17:17). "All scripture is given by inspiration of God, and is profitable for doctrine, for reproof, for correction, for instruction in righteousness: That the man of God may be perfect, thoroughly furnished unto all good works" (2 Tim. 3:16-17).

   It has been often observed that the Bible will keep one from sin, or sin will keep one from the Bible.

2. The role played by the Son of God—"But I have prayed for thee, that thy faith fail not: and when thou art converted, strengthen thy brethren" (Luke 22:32). "I pray not that thou shouldest take them out of the world, but that thou shouldest keep them from the evil" (John 17:15). "Who is he that condemneth? It is Christ that died, yea rather, that is risen again, who is even at the right hand of God, who also maketh intercession for us" (Rom. 8:34). "And they truly were many priests, because they were not suffered to continue by reason of death: But this man, because he continueth ever, hath an unchangeable priesthood. Wherefore he is able also to save them to the uttermost that come unto God by him, seeing he ever liveth to make intercession for them" (Heb. 7:23-25).

3. The role played by the Spirit of God—"Then he answered and spake unto me, saying, This is the word of the LORD unto Zerubbabel, saying, Not by might, nor by power, but by my spirit, saith the LORD of hosts" (Zech. 4:6).

   a. As seen through his praying ministry—"Likewise the Spirit also helpeth our infirmities: for we know not what we should pray for as we ought: but the Spirit itself maketh intercession for us with groanings which cannot be uttered" (Rom. 8:26).

b. As seen through his teaching ministry—"Now we have received, not the spirit of the world, but the spirit which is of God; that we might know the things that are freely given to us of God" (1 Cor. 2:12).

XIII. The Ultimate and Final Victory over Sin—In three key passages New Testament writers Paul and John describe for us this thrilling victory.

"For he must reign, till he hath put all enemies under his feet. The last enemy that shall be destroyed is death. For he hath put all things under his feet. But when he saith all things are put under him, it is manifest that he is excepted, which did put all things under him. And when all things shall be subdued unto him, then shall the Son also himself be subject unto him that put all things under him, that God may be all in all" (1 Cor. 15:25-28).

"But ye are come unto mount Sion, and unto the city of the living God, the heavenly Jerusalem, and to an innumerable company of angels, to the general assembly and church of the firstborn, which are written in heaven, and to God the Judge of all, and to the spirits of just men made perfect, and to Jesus the mediator of the new covenant, and to the blood of sprinkling, that speaketh better things than that of Abel" (Heb. 12:22-24).

"And God shall wipe away all tears from their eyes; and there shall be no more death, neither sorrow, nor crying, neither shall there be any more pain: for the former things are passed away. And he that sat upon the throne said, Behold, I make all things new. And he said unto me, Write: for these words are true and faithful" (Rev. 21:4-5).

THE DOCTRINE OF SALVATION

INTRODUCTION

It has been observed that among the many thousands of English words, the three most *difficult* to repeat are "I was wrong," while the three most *delightful* to read are "Find check enclosed." Be that as it may, it can be safely concluded that the most *dynamic* single word in our language is the word *salvation*.

I. The Meaning of Salvation
 A. The meaning of the word *salvation*
  1. The Hebrew root word *yesha* (basis for the name of Joshua and Jesus) signifies freedom from what binds or restricts and thus effects deliverance.
  2. The Greek word is *soteria*, meaning "to cure, to provide recovery, to rescue, to effect one's welfare."
 B. The mention of the word *salvation*
  1. It is found 160 times in the Bible and is referred to by 32 books.
   a. The Old Testament includes 116 references as found in 16 books (Gen., Exod., Deut., 1 & 2 Sam., 1 & 2 Chron., Job, Psa., Isa., Jer., Lam., Jon., Mic., Hab., Zech.).
   b. The New Testament includes 44 references as found in 16 books (Luke, John, Acts, Rom., 2 Cor., Eph., Phil., 1 & 2 Thess., 2 Tim., Titus, Heb., 1 & 2 Pet., Jude, Rev.).
  2. Its first mention comes from a father in Egypt—"And Jacob called unto his sons, and said, Gather yourselves together, that I may tell you that which shall befall you in the last days. . . . I have waited for thy salvation, O LORD" (Gen. 49:1, 18).
  3. Its final mention comes from the faithful in heaven—"And after these things I heard a great voice of much people in heaven, saying, Alleluia; Salvation, and glory, and honour, and power, unto the Lord our God" (Rev. 19:1).
 C. The magnificence of the word *salvation*—Note the way it is employed in the following verses: "Salvation belongeth unto the LORD: thy blessing is upon thy people. Selah" (Psa. 3:8). "The LORD is my light and my salvation; whom shall I fear? the LORD is the strength of my life; of whom shall I be afraid?" (Psa. 27:1). "Restore unto me the joy of thy salvation; and uphold me with thy free spirit" (Psa. 51:12). "Truly my soul waiteth upon God: from him cometh my salvation. He only is my rock and my salvation; he is my defence; I shall not be greatly moved" (Psa. 62:1-2). "Blessed be the Lord, who daily loadeth us with benefits, even the God of our salvation. Selah" (Psa. 68:19). "Let all those that seek thee rejoice and be glad in thee: and let such as love thy salvation say continually, Let God be magnified" (Psa. 70:4).

"Behold, God is my salvation; I will trust, and not be afraid: for the LORD JEHOVAH is my strength and my song; he also is become my salvation" (Isa. 12:2). "Lift up your eyes to the heavens, and look upon the earth beneath: for the heavens shall vanish away like smoke, and the earth shall wax old like a garment, and they that dwell therein shall die in like manner: but my salvation shall be for ever, and my righteousness shall not be abolished" (Isa. 51:6). "How beautiful upon the mountains are the feet of him that bringeth good tidings, that publisheth peace; that bringeth good tidings of good, that publisheth salvation; that saith unto Zion, Thy God reigneth! . . . The LORD hath made bare his holy arm in the eyes of all the nations; and all the ends of the earth shall see the salvation of our God" (Isa. 52:7, 10). "I will greatly rejoice in the LORD, my soul shall be joyful in my God; for he hath clothed me with the garments of salvation, he hath covered me with the robe of righteousness, as a bridegroom decketh himself with ornaments, and as a bride adorneth herself with her jewels" (Isa. 61:10).

"But I will sacrifice unto thee with the voice of thanksgiving; I will pay that that I have vowed. Salvation is of the LORD" (Jon. 2:9). "For I am not ashamed of the gospel of Christ: for it is the power of God unto salvation to every one that believeth; to the Jew first, and also to the Greek" (Rom. 1:16). "For with the heart man believeth unto righteousness; and with the mouth confession is made unto salvation" (Rom. 10:10).

II. The Implications of Salvation—The very word itself carries with it a twofold implication.

A. That someone needs to be saved

1. The facts involved—People are lost.

a. Only a sick person needs a doctor, and man is desperately ill—"From the sole of the foot even unto the head there is no soundness in it; but wounds, and bruises, and putrefying sores: they have not been closed, neither bound up, neither mollified with ointment" (Isa. 1:6). "And he entered into a ship, and passed over, and came into his own city. And, behold, they brought to him a man sick of the palsy, lying on a bed: and Jesus seeing their faith said unto the sick of the palsy; Son, be of good cheer; thy sins be forgiven thee" (Matt. 9:1-2).

b. Only an accused person needs a lawyer, and man stands condemned before God—"Now we know that what things soever the law saith, it saith to them who are under the law: that every mouth may be stopped, and all the world may become guilty before God" (Rom. 3:19).

c. Only a drowning person needs a lifeguard, and man finds himself flooded by the waters of sin—"Save me, O God; for the waters are come in unto my soul. I sink in deep mire, where there is no standing: I am come into deep waters, where the floods overflow me" (Psa. 69:1-2).

d. Only a person unable to find his way needs a guide, and man is hopelessly lost—"For the Son of man is come to seek and to save that which was lost" (Luke 19:10). "That at that time ye were without Christ, being aliens from the commonwealth of Israel, and strangers from the covenants of promise, having no hope, and without God in the world" (Eph. 2:12).

A sinner may not be as *bad* as he can be (like an Adolf Hitler), but he is nevertheless as *bad off* as he can be. Man is both dead spiritually and dying physically (see Gen. 2:17). This can be likened to a condemned criminal on death row awaiting the electric chair and suffering from terminal cancer.

2. The focus involved—Why are people lost?
   a. Because of their rejection of biblical revelation—"The heavens declare the glory of God; and the firmament sheweth his handiwork" (Psa. 19:1). "Nevertheless he left not himself without witness, in that he did good, and gave us rain from heaven, and fruitful seasons, filling our hearts with food and gladness" (Acts 14:17). "Because that which may be known of God is manifest in them; for God hath shewed it unto them. For the invisible things of him from the creation of the world are clearly seen, being understood by the things that are made, even his eternal power and Godhead; so that they are without excuse" (Rom. 1:19-20).
   b. Because of disobeying their own conscience—"(Indeed, when Gentiles, who do not have the law, do by nature things required by the law, they are a law for themselves, even though they do not have the law, since they show that the requirements of the law are written on their hearts, their consciences also bearing witness, and their thoughts now accusing, now even defending them.) This will take place on the day when God will judge men's secrets through Jesus Christ, as my gospel declares" (Rom. 2:14-16, NIV).
   c. Because of their relationship to the world—"Wherein in time past ye walked according to the course of this world, according to the prince of the power of the air, the spirit that now worketh in the children of disobedience:" (Eph. 2:2). "Ye adulterers and adulteresses, know ye not that the friendship of the world is enmity with God? whosoever therefore will be a friend of the world is the enemy of God" (James 4:4). "Love not the world, neither the things that are in the world. If any man love the world, the love of the Father is not in him. For all that is in the world, the lust of the flesh, and the lust of the eyes, and the pride of life, is not of the Father, but is of the world" (1 John 2:15-16).
   d. Because of their relationship to Satan—"Ye are of your father the devil, and the lusts of your father ye will do. He was a murderer from the beginning, and abode not in the truth, because there is no truth in him. When he speaketh a lie, he speaketh of his own: for he is a liar, and the father of it" (John 8:44). "In whom the god of this world hath blinded the minds of them which believe not, lest the light of the glorious gospel of Christ, who is the image of God, should shine unto them" (2 Cor. 4:4). "In this the children of God are manifest, and the children of the devil: whosoever doeth not righteousness is not of God, neither he that loveth not his brother" (1 John 3:10).
   e. Because of their relationship to sin—"But of the tree of the knowledge of good and evil, thou shalt not eat of it: for in the day that thou eatest thereof thou shalt surely die" (Gen. 2:17). "For there is not a just man upon earth, that doeth good, and sinneth not" (Eccles. 7:20). "The heart is deceitful above all things, and desperately wicked: who can know it?" (Jer. 17:9).
   "And he said, That which cometh out of the man, that defileth the man. For from within, out of the heart of men, proceed evil thoughts, adulteries, fornications, murders, thefts, covetousness, wickedness, deceit, lasciviousness, an evil eye, blasphemy, pride, foolishness: All these evil things come from within, and defile the man" (Mark 7:20-23). "Wherefore, as by one man sin entered into the world, and death by sin; and so death passed upon all men, for that all have sinned" (Rom. 5:12).

f. Because of their relationship to God—"He that hath the Son hath life; and he that hath not the Son of God hath not life" (1 John 5:12). "These be they who separate themselves, sensual, having not the Spirit" (Jude 19).

B. That someone is able and willing to save—Such a Savior must fulfill both requirements

1. He must be able to save—It is possible for a person to have the desire but not the ability to save another individual. Many a physician has stood in utter frustration beside the bed of his dying patient, wanting so much to give aid, but totally helpless to do so.

2. He must be willing to save—It is possible for a person to have the ability but not the desire to save another individual. In 1978 a man in the United States in desperate need of a rare blood-type transfusion died. The tragedy of the story was that he suffered and died needlessly, for one of his own relatives possessed that rare type of blood and could have easily donated some, but stubbornly refused. Perhaps the greatest ability, after all, is *avail*ability.

III. The Source of Salvation—Jesus Christ is the source of salvation. He meets both requirements.

A. He is able to save—"Now unto him that is able to do exceeding abundantly above all that we ask or think, according to the power that worketh in us" (Eph. 3:20). "For the which cause I also suffer these things: nevertheless I am not ashamed: for I know whom I have believed, and am persuaded that he is able to keep that which I have committed unto him against that day" (2 Tim. 1:12).

"For in that he himself hath suffered being tempted, he is able to succour them that are tempted" (Heb. 2:18). "Wherefore he is able also to save them to the uttermost that come unto God by him, seeing he ever liveth to make intercession for them" (Heb. 7:25). "Now unto him that is able to keep you from falling, and to present you faultless before the presence of his glory with exceeding joy" (Jude 24).

B. He is willing to save—"And, behold, there came a leper and worshipped him, saying, Lord, if thou wilt, thou canst make me clean. And Jesus put forth his hand, and touched him, saying, I will; be thou clean. And immediately his leprosy was cleansed" (Matt. 8:2-3). "For this is good and acceptable in the sight of God our Saviour; who will have all men to be saved, and to come unto the knowledge of the truth" (1 Tim. 2:3-4). "The Lord is not slack concerning his promise, as some men count slackness; but is longsuffering to us-ward, not willing that any should perish, but that all should come to repentance" (2 Pet. 3:9).

As has been previously stated, the Lord Jesus Christ is the source, center, and sum total of salvation. This is clearly demonstrated in the following passages: "Rejoice greatly, O daughter of Zion; shout, O daughter of Jerusalem: behold, thy King cometh unto thee: he is just, and having salvation; lowly, and riding upon an ass, and upon a colt the foal of an ass" (Zech. 9:9).

"Blessed be the Lord God of Israel; for he hath visited and redeemed his people, and hath raised up an horn of salvation for us in the house of his servant David" (Luke 1:68-69). "Lord, now lettest thou thy servant depart in peace, according to thy word: For mine eyes have seen thy salvation" (Luke 2:29-30). "Every valley shall be filled, and every mountain and hill shall be brought low; and the crooked shall be made straight, and the rough ways shall be made smooth; and all flesh shall see the salvation of God" (Luke 3:5-6).

"Neither is there salvation in any other: for there is none other name under heaven given among men, whereby we must be saved" (Acts 4:12). "For I am not ashamed of the gospel of Christ: for it is the power of God unto salvation to every one that believeth; to the Jew first, and also to the Greek" (Rom. 1:16). "For the grace of God that bringeth salvation hath appeared to all men" (Titus 2:11). "And being made perfect, he became the author of eternal salvation unto all them that obey him" (Heb. 5:9).

IV. The False Hopes of Salvation—"There is a way which seemeth right unto a man, but the end thereof are the ways of death" (Prov. 14:12).

A. Education—On two separate occasions Paul warns Timothy about the folly of depending on education. "O Timothy, keep that which is committed to thy trust, avoiding profane and vain babblings, and oppositions of science falsely so called" (1 Tim. 6:20). "Ever learning, and never able to come to the knowledge of the truth" (2 Tim. 3:7).

B. Church membership—The scriptural reason for joining a local church is not for the obtaining of one's salvation, but rather for its outworking.

C. Good works—"For by grace are ye saved through faith; and that not of your-selves: it is the gift of God: Not of works, lest any man should boast" (Eph. 2:8-9).

D. Baptism—"For Christ sent me not to baptize, but to preach the gospel: not with wisdom of words, lest the cross of Christ should be made of none effect" (1 Cor. 1:17).

E. Proper environment—Being fortunate enough to have experienced a proper and comfortable environment may lead one to success, but never to salvation. In fact, to the contrary, the world's systems (on both sides of the tracks) are in the hands of the evil one (1 John 5:19). This is the case for the down-and-outers as well as the up-and-comers.

F. Keeping the law—"Knowing that a man is not justified by the works of the law, but by the faith of Jesus Christ, even we have believed in Jesus Christ, that we might be justified by the faith of Christ, and not by the works of the law: for by the works of the law shall no flesh be justified" (Gal. 2:16).

G. Confirmation—Religious confirmation is as far removed from redemption's trans-formation as a lump of coal from a glittering diamond.

H. Living by the Golden Rule—There is one very simple reason why an unsaved per-son cannot experience salvation living by the Golden Rule, and that reason is he cannot keep the Golden Rule. "But we are all as an unclean thing, and all our righteousnesses are as filthy rags; and we all do fade as a leaf; and our iniquities, like the wind, have taken us away" (Isa. 64:6).

I. Sincerity—While it is true that God cannot save an insincere man, sincerity in itself is not sufficient, for one can be sincerely wrong.

J. Lodge membership—A ring, however impressive, adds not the slightest iota to the owner's redemption.

K. Tithing—Paul commends the churches in Macedonia not simply for the financial help he received from them, but rather because they had first submitted their wills to the Lord and only then their wallets (see 2 Cor. 8:1-7).

L. Political organizations—During the coming great tribulation the combined secular, political, and economical organizations of this world will turn against the Father and attempt to dethrone his Son, only to be themselves utterly destroyed by the brightness of his coming. (See Psa. 2; Rev. 18.)

M. Religious organizations—The unified and false religious movement will likewise suffer destruction during the tribulation. (See Rev. 17.)

V. The Threefold Method of Salvation—While God has indeed dealt with his creatures under different dispensations (the pre-law stages, the age of the law, the post-law stage, etc.), he saves them all by the identical threefold method.

A. Salvation is always by the blood—"And almost all things are by the law purged with blood; and without shedding of blood is no remission" (Heb. 9:22). Furthermore, this blood must be innocent, shed, and applied.

1. Innocent—"How much more shall the blood of Christ, who through the eternal Spirit offered himself without spot to God, purge your conscience from dead works to serve the living God?" (Heb. 9:14).

2. Shed—"For this is my blood of the new testament, which is shed for many for the remission of sins" (Matt. 26:28).

3. Applied—"And from Jesus Christ, who is the faithful witness, and the first begotten of the dead, and the prince of the kings of the earth. Unto him that loved us, and washed us from our sins in his own blood" (Rev. 1:5).

B. Salvation is always through a person—"But I will sacrifice unto thee with the voice of thanksgiving; I will pay that that I have vowed. Salvation is of the LORD" (Jon. 2:9). "Neither is there salvation in any other: for there is none other name under heaven given among men, whereby we must be saved" (Acts 4:12). "For God hath not appointed us to wrath, but to obtain salvation by our Lord Jesus Christ" (1 Thess. 5:9). "And being made perfect, he became the author of eternal salvation unto all them that obey him" (Heb. 5:9).

C. Salvation is always by grace—"For by grace are ye saved through faith; and that not of yourselves: it is the gift of God: Not of works, lest any man should boast" (Eph. 2:8-9). "For the grace of God that bringeth salvation hath appeared to all men" (Titus 2:11).

1. This grace is appropriated by the sinner's faith—"Therefore being justified by faith, we have peace with God through our Lord Jesus Christ" (Rom. 5:1). "But without faith it is impossible to please him: for he that cometh to God must believe that he is, and that he is a rewarder of them that diligently seek him" (Heb. 11:6).

2. This grace is accompanied by the Savior's peace—"To all that be in Rome, beloved of God, called to be saints: Grace to you and peace from God our Father, and the Lord Jesus Christ" (Rom. 1:7). "Grace be unto you, and peace, from God our Father, and from the Lord Jesus Christ" (1 Cor. 1:3). (See also Gal. 1:3.)

VI. The Work of the Trinity in Salvation—The following poem quickly overviews the subject of salvation as it relates to heaven, earth, and hell.

The Father wrought it,
The Son bought it,
The Spirit taught it,
The devil fought it,
The rich man sought it,
The dying thief caught it,
Praise God, I've got it!

As shown by this little poem, the entire Trinity was totally involved in the work of salvation.

A. The work of the Father in salvation

1. He foreknew and predestinated us—"For whom he did foreknow, he also did predestinate" (Rom. 8:29a). "God hath not cast away his people which he

foreknew" (Rom. 11:2). "Having predestinated us unto the adoption of children by Jesus Christ to himself, according to the good pleasure of his will, in whom also we have obtained an inheritance, being predestinated according to the purpose of him who worketh all things after the counsel of his own will" (Eph. 1:5, 11).

2. He chose and elected us—"And he shall send his angels with a great sound of a trumpet, and they shall gather together his elect from the four winds, from one end of heaven to the other" (Matt. 24:31). "Who shall lay any thing to the charge of God's elect? It is God that justifieth" (Rom. 8:33). "According as he hath chosen us in him before the foundation of the world, that we should be holy and without blame before him in love" (Eph. 1:4). "God hath from the beginning chosen you to salvation" (2 Thess. 2:13). "Elect according to the foreknowledge of God the Father" (1 Pet. 1:2).

3. He called and conformed us—"And we know that all things work together for good to them that love God, to them who are the called according to his purpose" (Rom. 8:28). "To be conformed to the image of his son" (Rom. 8:29). "Moreover whom he did predestinate, them he also called" (Rom. 8:30).

4. He justified and glorified us—"And whom he called, them he also justified; and whom he justified, them he also glorified" (Rom. 8:30).

5. He sent his Son to us—"To wit, that God was in Christ, reconciling the world unto himself, not imputing their trespasses unto them; and hath committed unto us the word of reconciliation" (2 Cor. 5:19). "Thanks be unto God for his unspeakable gift" (2 Cor. 9:15).

B. The work of the Son in salvation—The following four action verbs depict the work of Jesus in our salvation.

1. Showing—"And he that seeth me seeth him that sent me" (John 12:45). "Philip saith unto him, Lord, shew us the Father, and it sufficeth us. Jesus saith unto him, Have I been so long time with you, and yet hast thou not known me, Philip? he that hath seen me hath seen the Father; and how sayest thou then, Shew us the Father?" (John 14:8-9)

2. Seeking—"For the Son of man is come to seek and to save that which was lost" (Luke 19:10).

3. Sacrificing—"I am the good shepherd: the good shepherd giveth his life for the sheep" (John 10:11).

4. Satisfying—"Whom God hath set forth to be a propitiation through faith in his blood, to declare his righteousness for the remission of sins that are past, through the forbearance of God; to declare, I say, at this time his righteousness: that he might be just, and the justifier of him which believeth in Jesus" (Rom. 3:25-26).

   Note: "Propitiation" here refers to satisfaction. This is simply to say Christ's death satisfied the holiness and righteousness of God.

C. The work of the Holy Spirit in salvation

1. He convicts, thus pointing us to Christ—"Nevertheless I tell you the truth; It is expedient for you that I go away: for if I go not away, the Comforter will not come unto you; but if I depart, I will send him unto you. And when he is come, he will reprove the world of sin, and of righteousness, and of judgment: of sin, because they believe not on me; of righteousness, because I go to my Father, and ye see me no more; of judgment, because the prince of this world is judged" (John 16:7-11).

2. He baptizes, thus placing us in Christ—"For by one Spirit are we all baptized into one body, whether we be Jews or Gentiles, whether we be bond or free; and have been all made to drink into one Spirit" (1 Cor. 12:13).

VII. The Costliness of Salvation

A. According to David and Moses, creation was effected by God's fingers and came about through his spoken word—"And God said, Let there be light: and there was light" (Gen. 1:3). "When I consider thy heavens, the work of thy fingers, the moon and the stars, which thou hast ordained; what is man, that thou art mindful of him? and the son of man, that thou visitest him?" (Psa. 8:3-4). "By the word of the LORD were the heavens made; and all the host of them by the breath of his mouth. . . . For he spake, and it was done; he commanded, and it stood fast" (Psa. 33:6, 9). (See also Gen. 1:6, 9, 11, 14, 20, 24, 26.)

B. According to Isaiah and Peter, salvation was effected by God's arms and came about through his shed blood—"Who hath believed our report? and to whom is the arm of the LORD revealed?" (Isa. 53:1). "Surely he hath borne our griefs, and carried our sorrows: yet we did esteem him stricken, smitten of God, and afflicted. But he was wounded for our transgressions, he was bruised for our iniquities: the chastisement of our peace was upon him; and with his stripes we are healed. All we like sheep have gone astray; we have turned every one to his own way; and the LORD hath laid on him the iniquity of us all" (Isa. 53:4-6). "Forasmuch as ye know that ye were not redeemed with corruptible things, as silver and gold, from your vain conversation received by tradition from your fathers; but with the precious blood of Christ, as of a lamb without blemish and without spot" (1 Pet. 1:18-19).

In the book of Revelation John records all of heaven praising Christ for his work in *creation* (4:11) and *salvation* (5:9). "Thou art worthy, O Lord, to receive glory and honour and power: for thou hast created all things, and for thy pleasure they are and were created" (Rev. 4:11). "And they sung a new song, saying, Thou art worthy to take the book, and to open the seals thereof: for thou wast slain, and hast redeemed us to God by thy blood out of every kindred, and tongue, and people, and nation" (Rev. 5:9).

VIII. The Old Testament Types of Salvation—These are depicted by *events* (the Passover, the serpent of brass, etc.), *institutions* (the Sabbath), *objects* (lamb, oil, tabernacle), *places* (Jerusalem, Egypt, Babylon, Canaan), or *individuals* (Adam, Isaac, Joseph, Jonah) that serve to foreshadow a particular New Testament aspect of salvation. The Greek word *tupos* (referring to a type) is found 18 times in the New Testament, translated by such words as *example, figure,* and *pattern.* Here are but a few *tupos* of salvation.

A. Adam and Eve, illustrating that salvation clothes us—"Unto Adam also and to his wife did the LORD God make coats of skins, and clothed them" (Gen. 3:21).

The first terrible result of sin upon Adam and Eve was the realization of their shame and nakedness before God. "And the eyes of them both were opened, and they knew that they were naked; and they sewed fig leaves together, and made themselves aprons" (Gen. 3:7). But the gracious Creator then forgave and clothed his two sinful citizens in Eden (see Gen. 3:21).

For a similar case describing how Joshua the high priest was clothed with divine righteousness during the rebuilding of the temple, see Zechariah 3:1-5.

B. Cain and Abel, illustrating that salvation guarantees us acceptance—The story of Cain and Abel also demonstrates (in Cain's example) the wrong way to be accepted. "And Abel, he also brought of the firstlings of his flock and of the fat thereof. And the LORD had respect unto Abel and to his offering" (Gen. 4:4). Abel made the first recorded "public profession of Christ" on earth when he offered the blood sacrifice, while Cain became the first religious rebel by offering a bloodless sacrifice. (See Eph. 1:7.)

C. The ark and the Passover, illustrating that salvation protects us from God's wrath

    1. The ark—"And the LORD said unto Noah, Come thou and all thy house into the ark; for thee have I seen righteous before me in this generation" (Gen. 7:1).

    2. The Passover—"For the LORD will pass through to smite the Egyptians; and when he seeth the blood upon the lintel, and on the two side posts, the LORD will pass over the door, and will not suffer the destroyer to come in unto your houses to smite you" (Exod. 12:23). The unprotected will be subjected to a future world judgment wrath (the message of the ark) and to a personal great white throne judgment (the lesson from the Passover).

       Consider also the following passages: "For the wrath of God is revealed from heaven against all ungodliness and unrighteousness of men, who hold the truth in unrighteousness" (Rom. 1:18). "For which things' sake the wrath of God cometh on the children of disobedience" (Col. 3:6). "And to wait for his Son from heaven, whom he raised from the dead, even Jesus, which delivered us from the wrath to come" (1 Thess. 1:10). "For the great day of his wrath is come; and who shall be able to stand?" (Rev. 6:17).

D. Abraham and Isaac, illustrating that salvation provides for us an acceptable substitute—"And he said, Lay not thine hand upon the lad, neither do thou any thing unto him: for now I know that thou fearest God, seeing thou hast not withheld thy son, thine only son from me. And Abraham lifted up his eyes, and looked, and behold behind him a ram caught in a thicket by his horns: and Abraham went and took the ram, and offered him up for a burnt offering in the stead of his son. And Abraham called the name of that place Jehovah-jireh: as it is said to this day, In the mount of the LORD it shall be seen" (Gen. 22:12-14).

       Some 20 centuries after Abraham offered up Isaac, another Father lifted up his only Son on that same spot, but this time there was no last minute reprieve. This was prophesied by Isaiah: "Surely he hath borne our griefs, and carried our sorrows: yet we did esteem him stricken, smitten of God, and afflicted. But he was wounded for our transgressions, he was bruised for our iniquities: the chastisement of our peace was upon him; and with his stripes we are healed. All we like sheep have gone astray; we have turned every one to his own way; and the LORD hath laid on him the iniquity of us all" (Isa. 53:4-6). (See 1 Pet. 3:18.)

E. The manna and the smitten rock, illustrating that salvation satisfies us—"And when the dew that lay was gone up, behold, upon the face of the wilderness there lay a small round thing, as small as the hoar frost on the ground" (Exod. 16:14). "Behold, I will stand before thee there upon the rock in Horeb; and thou shalt smite the rock, and there shall come water out of it, that the people may drink. And Moses did so in the sight of the elders of Israel" (Exod. 17:6).

       Bread from the sky and water from a rock. Oh, the total and tender satisfaction of God's salvation. "Who satisfieth thy mouth with good things; so that thy youth is renewed like the eagle's" (Psa. 103:5). "For he satisfieth the longing soul, and filleth the hungry soul with goodness" (Psa. 107:9).

F. The brazen serpent, illustrating that salvation cures us—"And Moses made a serpent of brass, and put it upon a pole, and it came to pass, that if a serpent had bitten any man, when he beheld the serpent of brass, he lived" (Num. 21:9).

       In the New Testament Christ applied this Old Testament event to himself and led

Nicodemus to salvation: "And as Moses lifted up the serpent in the wilderness, even so must the Son of man be lifted up" (John 3:14).

G. Naaman, illustrating that salvation cleanses us—This Syrian pagan was the only man in the entire Old Testament to be cleansed from the dreadful scourge of leprosy. (See 2 Kings 5:1-14.) Note the following: "Purge me with hyssop, and I shall be clean: wash me, and I shall be whiter than snow" (Psa. 51:7).

H. The tabernacle, illustrating that salvation restores lost fellowship—"And there I will meet with thee, and I will commune with thee from above the mercy seat, from between the two cherubims which are upon the ark of the testimony, of all things which I will give thee in commandment unto the children of Israel" (Exod. 25:22).

One of Israel's most tragic moments in the Old Testament was the worship of a devilish Egyptian golden calf god (see Exod. 32). Both idolatry and immorality were involved in that sordid affair. But the newly constructed tabernacle was able to once again assure Israel's fellowship with God. "He restoreth my soul: he leadeth me in the paths of righteousness for his name's sake" (Psa. 23:3).

IX. The Vocabulary of Salvation—There are 15 key words in the vocabulary of salvation. These are:

conversion	redemption	justification
substitution	regeneration	sanctification
reconciliation	imputation	glorification
propitiation	adoption	preservation
remission	supplication	origination

We shall now examine each of these important terms.

A. Conversion—The word *conversion* (Hebrew, *shub*; Greek, *epistrophe*) is found some 14 times in the Bible. (See Pss. 19:7; 51:13; Isa. 1:27; 6:10; Matt. 13:15; 18:3; Mark 4:12; Luke 22:32; John 12:40; Acts 3:19; 15:3; 28:27; James 5:19-20.)

Here are some examples of its usage: "The law of the LORD is perfect, converting the soul: the testimony of the LORD is sure, making wise the simple" (Psa. 19:7). "Restore unto me the joy of thy salvation; and uphold me with thy free spirit. Then will I teach transgressors thy ways; and sinners shall be converted unto thee" (Psa. 51:12-13).

"And said, Verily I say unto you, Except ye be converted, and become as little children, ye shall not enter into the kingdom of heaven" (Matt. 18:3). "Repent ye therefore, and be converted, that your sins may be blotted out, when the times of refreshing shall come from the presence of the Lord" (Acts 3:19). "And being brought on their way by the church, they passed through Phoenicia and Samaria, declaring the conversion of the Gentiles: and they caused great joy unto all the brethren" (Acts 15:3). "Let him know, that he which converteth the sinner from the error of his way shall save a soul from death, and shall hide a multitude of sins" (James 5:20).

In essence, both Hebrew and Greek meanings have reference to a twofold turning on the part of an individual. One has to do with *repentance* (a turning from), and the other with *faith* (a turning to).

1. Repentance (Greek, *metanoia*)
   a. What repentance is not
      (1) It is not reformation, that act of turning over a new leaf.

(2) It is not remorse, that act of regretting the *fruit* of one's crime, but not the *root*.

Here we have two biblical examples:

(a) Esau—"For ye know how that afterward, when he would have inherited the blessing, he was rejected: for he found no place of repentance, though he sought it carefully with tears" (Heb. 12:17). (For the full background of this, read Gen. 27.)

(b) Judas—"Then Judas, which had betrayed him, when he saw that he was condemned, repented himself, and brought again the thirty pieces of silver to the chief priests and elders" (Matt. 27:3). That this was only remorse and not true repentance is shown in the following passage: "And he cast down the pieces of silver in the temple, and departed, and went and hanged himself" (Matt. 27:5).

(3) It is not penitence, that act of attempting to make up for one's sins through good works.

b. What repentance is—It is a voluntary and sincere change in the mind of the sinner, causing him to turn from his sin. It should be noted here I said *sin* and not *sins*. True repentance involves the turning from one specific sin, the previous rejection of Christ. Jesus spelled this out very clearly for us. "Nevertheless I tell you the truth; It is expedient for you that I go away: for if I go not away, the Comforter will not come unto you; but if I depart, I will send him unto you. And when he is come, he will reprove the world of sin, and of righteousness, and of judgment: of sin, because they believe not on me; of righteousness, because I go to my Father, and ye see me no more; of judgment, because the prince of this world is judged" (John 16:7-11).

God is not primarily interested in convincing a sinner to give up smoking, swearing, drinking, and illicit sex, as bad as these may be, for this will never save him. His great sin which will eventually condemn him forever is the rejection of Jesus Christ. Repentance, therefore, deals with a turning from this horrible crime of spurning Calvary.

(1) As expressed in the ministry of John the Baptist: "And saying, Repent ye: for the kingdom of heaven is at hand" (Matt. 3:2). "Bring forth therefore fruits meet for repentance" (Matt. 3:8).

(2) As expressed in the ministry of Jesus: "I am not come to call the righteous, but sinners to repentance" (Matt. 9:13). "I tell you, Nay: but, except ye repent, ye shall all likewise perish" (Luke 13:5). "I say unto you, that likewise joy shall be in heaven over one sinner that repenteth, more than over ninety and nine just persons, which need no repentance" (Luke 15:7). "And that repentance and remission of sins should be preached in his name among all nations, beginning at Jerusalem" (Luke 24:47).

(3) As expressed in the ministry of Peter: "Then Peter said unto them, Repent, and be baptized every one of you in the name of Jesus Christ for the remission of sins, and ye shall receive the gift of the Holy Ghost" (Acts 2:38). "Repent ye therefore, and be converted, that your sins may be blotted out, when the times of refreshing shall come from the presence of the Lord" (Acts 3:19).

(4) As expressed in the ministry of Paul: "But [Paul] shewed first unto them of Damascus, and at Jerusalem, and throughout all the coasts of Judaea,

and then to the Gentiles, that they should repent" (Acts 26:20). "And the times [prior to the cross] of this ignorance God winked at [overlooked]; but now commandeth all men every where to repent" (Acts 17:30).

2. Faith

   a. What it is not

     (1) It is not a "blind leap into the dark."

     (2) It is not supposition.

     (3) It is not speculation.

     (4) It is not opinion or hypothesis.

   b. What it is—It is a voluntary and sincere change in the mind of the sinner, causing him to turn to the Savior.

   c. When it occurs—It occurs the instant a sinner involves both his head and heart concerning the claims of Christ. It is *not* enough to simply possess an intellectual knowledge of the gospel. Biblical faith demands both head acknowledgment and heart acceptance. Note: "And every one that heareth these sayings of mine, and doeth them not, shall be likened unto a foolish man, which built his house upon the sand" (Matt. 7:26). "King Agrippa, believest thou the prophets? I know that thou believest. Then Agrippa said unto Paul, Almost thou persuadest me to be a Christian" (Acts 26:27-28). "Thou believest that there is one God; thou doest well: the devils also believe, and tremble" (James 2:19).

   d. How it is produced—"So then faith cometh by hearing, and hearing by the word of God" (Rom. 10:17). Here Paul is saying that faith comes from hearing the message and the message comes through preaching Christ.

   e. Why it is so necessary—"But without faith it is impossible to please him: for he that cometh to God must believe that he is, and that he is a rewarder of them that diligently seek him" (Heb. 11:6).

     (1) The sinner is saved by faith—"Therefore being justified by faith, we have peace with God through our Lord Jesus Christ" (Rom. 5:1). "For by grace are ye saved through faith; and that not of yourselves: it is the gift of God: not of works, lest any man should boast" (Eph. 2:8-9).

     (2) The saint is sanctified (grows in grace) by faith.

       Thus, by faith:

     (a) We live—"For therein is the righteousness of God revealed from faith to faith: as it is written, The just shall live by faith" (Rom. 1:17).

     (b) We stand—"Not for that we have dominion over your faith, but are helpers of your joy: for by faith ye stand" (2 Cor. 1:24).

     (c) We walk—"For we walk by faith, not by sight" (2 Cor. 5:7).

     (d) We fight—"Fight the good fight of faith, lay hold on eternal life, whereunto thou art also called, and hast professed a good profession before many witnesses" (1 Tim. 6:12).

     (e) We overcome—"For whatsoever is born of God overcometh the world: and this is the victory that overcometh the world, even our faith" (1 John 5:4).

We have now seen both sides of the coin of conversion. Repentance is a turning *from* sin, and faith is a turning *to* Christ. Paul includes both concepts during his farewell message to the Ephesian elders. "Testifying both to the Jews, and also to the Greeks, repentance toward God, and faith toward our Lord Jesus Christ" (Acts 20:21).

B. Substitution—"For Christ also hath once suffered for sins, the just for the unjust, that he might bring us to God" (1 Pet. 3:18). Substitution refers to that act whereby someone or something replaces, or stands in the stead of someone else or something else. The Scriptures present two kinds of substitution.

   1. Temporary substitution—In Old Testament times, prior to Calvary, the sheep died for the shepherd.

     a. As illustrated by a ram on a mountain—"And it came to pass after these things, that God did tempt Abraham, and said unto him, Abraham: and he said, Behold, here I am. And he said, Take now thy son, thine only son Isaac, whom thou lovest, and get thee into the land of Moriah; and offer him there for a burnt offering upon one of the mountains which I will tell thee of. . . . And Abraham stretched forth his hand, and took the knife to slay his son. And the angel of the LORD called unto him out of heaven, and said, Abraham, Abraham: and he said, Here am I. And he said, Lay not thine hand upon the lad, neither do thou any thing unto him: for now I know that thou fearest God, seeing thou hast not withheld thy son, thine only son from me. And Abraham lifted up his eyes, and looked, and behold behind him a ram caught in a thicket by his horns: and Abraham went and took the ram, and offered him up for a burnt offering in the stead of his son" (Gen. 22:1-2, 10-13).

     b. As illustrated by a lamb in Egypt—"Speak ye unto all the congregation of Israel, saying, In the tenth day of this month they shall take to them every man a lamb, according to the house of their fathers, a lamb for an house. . . . And ye shall keep it up until the fourteenth day of the same month: and the whole assembly of the congregation of Israel shall kill it in the evening. And they shall take of the blood, and strike it on the two side posts and on the upper door post of the houses, wherein they shall eat it. . . . For I will pass through the land of Egypt this night, and will smite all the firstborn in the land of Egypt, both man and beast; and against all the gods of Egypt I will execute judgment: I am the LORD. And the blood shall be to you for a token upon the houses where ye are: and when I see the blood, I will pass over you, and the plague shall not be upon you to destroy you, when I smite the land of Egypt" (Exod. 12:3, 6-7, 12-13).

   2. Permanent substitution—"For it is not possible that the blood of bulls and of goats should take away sins" (Heb. 10:4). In New Testament times, after Calvary, the Shepherd died for the sheep. "I am the good shepherd: the good shepherd giveth his life for the sheep" (John 10:11).

     Thus, Christ became on the cross what he was not—namely, sin—that we might become what we were not—namely, righteous. The Son of God became the Son of man that sons of men might become the sons of God. "For he hath made him to be sin for us, who knew no sin; that we might be made the righteousness of God in him" (2 Cor. 5:21). (Also read carefully Isa. 53.)

C. Reconciliation

   1. The meaning of reconciliation

     a. The Old Testament meaning—The Hebrew word *kaphar*, which means "to cover something," is found some 83 times in the Old Testament. Of these, it is translated "atonement" 76 times and "reconciliation" 7 times.

       Robert Lightner writes: "The Old Testament words for reconciliation do not represent a final dealing with sin. Rather, they present sin as being covered temporarily from God, awaiting final reconciliation through Christ (see Lev. 6:30; 8:15; 2 Chron. 29:24; 1 Sam. 29:4; Ezek. 45:15)" (*Evangelical Dictionary*, p. 195).

  b. The New Testament meaning—The Greek word *allasso* means to change from that of enmity to that of friendship. In essence, it indicates a change of relationship *from* that of hostility *to* that of harmony between two parties.
2. The need for reconciliation—"Behold, the LORD's hand is not shortened, that it cannot save; neither his ear heavy, that it cannot hear: But your iniquities have separated between you and your God, and your sins have hid his face from you, that he will not hear" (Isa. 59:1-2). "And you, that were sometime alienated and enemies in your mind by wicked works, yet now hath he reconciled" (Col. 1:21).
3. The example of reconciliation
  a. That of a man and his brother—"Therefore if thou bring thy gift to the altar, and there rememberest that thy brother hath ought against thee; leave there thy gift before the altar, and go thy way; first be reconciled to thy brother, and then come and offer thy gift" (Matt. 5:23-24).
  b. That of husband and wife—"But and if she depart, let her remain unmarried, or be reconciled to her husband: and let not the husband put away his wife" (1 Cor. 7:11).
  c. That of God and the sinner—"And all things are of God, who hath reconciled us to himself by Jesus Christ, and hath given to us the ministry of reconciliation" (2 Cor. 5:18). "For if, when we were enemies, we were reconciled to God by the death of his Son, much more, being reconciled, we shall be saved by his life. And not only so, but we also joy in God through our Lord Jesus Christ, by whom we have now received the atonement" (Rom. 5:10-11).
4. The implications of reconciliation
  a. That a previous animosity once existed
  b. That the offended party (or parties) now views things differently
5. The two phases of reconciliation
  a. God has reconciled himself to the world through Christ—"To wit, that God was in Christ, reconciling the world unto himself, not imputing their trespasses unto them; and hath committed unto us the word of reconciliation" (2 Cor. 5:19).
  b. Man is now to reconcile himself to God through Christ—"Now then we are ambassadors for Christ, as though God did beseech you by us: we pray you in Christ's stead, be ye reconciled to God" (2 Cor. 5:20).
      Paul Enns writes:

> There are two parts to reconciliation. The objective aspect of reconciliation is that in which man is reconciled to God prior to faith and man is rendered savable (2 Cor. 5:18a, 19a). This is provisional reconciliation. The subjective aspect of reconciliation is that in which man is reconciled to God when he believes (2 Cor. 5:18b, 19b). This is experimental reconciliation. (*Moody Handbook of Theology*, p. 324)

6. The chronology of reconciliation
  a. In Eden, God and man faced each other in fellowship.
  b. After the Fall, God and man turned from each other.

       c. At Calvary, God, through Christ, turned his face toward man.

       d. At conversion (through repentance and faith), man turns his face toward God.

D. Propitiation

   1. The meaning of propitiation—The Greek word *hilasmos* means "to render favorable, to satisfy, to appease." On one occasion the Greek word is translated "mercy seat."

      In essence the doctrine of propitiation states that the death of Christ fully satisfies all the righteous demands of God toward the sinner. "And he is the propitiation for our sins: and not for ours only, but also for the sins of the whole world" (1 John 2:2). "Herein is love, not that we loved God, but that he loved us, and sent his Son to be the propitiation for our sins" (1 John 4:10).

   2. The method of propitiation—How could God possibly reconcile his holiness and righteousness to his mercy and grace? This problem was of course gloriously solved by Christ who was "set forth to be a propitiation" (Rom. 3:25). This then became the grand fulfillment of the prediction: "Mercy and truth are met together; righteousness and peace have kissed each other" (Psa. 85:10).

      Thus Paul could write with absolute confidence: "To declare, I say, at this time his righteousness: that he might be just, and the justifier of him which believeth in Jesus" (Rom. 3:26). "Being justified freely by his grace through the redemption that is in Christ Jesus: Whom God hath set forth to be a propitiation through faith in his blood" (Rom. 3:24-25).

   3. The necessity for propitiation—It was necessary because of God's wrath (that stern reaction of the divine nature to evil in man).

       a. The current wrath of God—"He that believeth on the Son hath everlasting life: and he that believeth not the Son shall not see life; but the wrath of God abideth on him" (John 3:36). "For the wrath of God is revealed from heaven against all ungodliness and unrighteousness of men, who hold the truth in unrighteousness" (Rom. 1:18). "Let no man deceive you with vain words: for because of these things cometh the wrath of God upon the children of disobedience" (Eph. 5:6).

       b. The coming wrath of God—"And said to the mountains and rocks, Fall on us, and hide us from the face of him that sitteth on the throne, and from the wrath of the Lamb" (Rev. 6:16). "And the nations were angry, and thy wrath is come, and the time of the dead, that they should be judged, and that thou shouldest give reward unto thy servants the prophets, and to the saints, and them that fear thy name, small and great; and shouldest destroy them which destroy the earth" (Rev. 11:18). "The same shall drink of the wine of the wrath of God, which is poured out without mixture into the cup of his indignation; and he shall be tormented with fire and brimstone in the presence of the holy angels, and in the presence of the Lamb" (Rev. 14:10). "And out of his mouth goeth a sharp sword, that with it he should smite the nations: and he shall rule them with a rod of iron: and he treadeth the winepress of the fierceness and wrath of Almighty God" (Rev. 19:15).

   4. The place of propitiation

       a. The Old Testament temporary place: the mercy seat in the tabernacle (typically)—Note: The mercy seat in the Holy of Holies beneath the glory cloud of God was actually the golden lid belonging to the boxlike structure known as the Ark of the Covenant that contained, among other things, the tablets of the Ten Commandments.

Once each year on the Day of Atonement the high priest would enter the Holy of Holies and sprinkle blood upon the mercy seat. The spiritual significance of this act cannot be overstated; namely, the only thing separating the righteous demands of God (as seen by the glory cloud) from the sinful condition of man (as seen by the Ten Commandments he had already broken) was the blood of a sacrificial animal.

"And there I will meet with thee, and I will commune with thee from above the mercy seat, from between the two cherubims which are upon the ark of the testimony, of all things which I will give thee in commandment unto the children of Israel" (Exod. 25:22). "And over it the cherubims of glory shadowing the mercy seat; of which we cannot now speak particularly. Now when these things were thus ordained, the priests went always into the first tabernacle, accomplishing the service of God. But into the second went the high priest alone once every year, not without blood, which he offered for himself, and for the errors of the people" (Heb. 9:5-7).

b. The New Testament permanent place: the center cross on Golgotha (actually)—"For if, when we were enemies, we were reconciled to God by the death of his Son, much more, being reconciled, we shall be saved by his life" (Rom. 5:10). "And, having made peace through the blood of his cross, by him to reconcile all things unto himself; by him, I say, whether they be things in earth, or things in heaven" (Col. 1:20).

5. The results of propitiation
   a. God is justified in forgiving sin.
   b. God is justified in bestowing righteousness—"Whom God hath set forth to be a propitiation through faith in his blood, to declare his righteousness for the remission of sins that are past, through the forbearance of God; to declare, I say, at this time his righteousness: that he might be just, and the justifier of him which believeth in Jesus" (Rom. 3:25-26). Stated another way, Jesus' blood as it covered God's mercy seat totally satisfied the righteous demands of the Law.

E. Remission—"To him (Jesus) give all the prophets witness, that through his name whosoever believeth in him shall receive remission of sins" (Acts 10:43). "For this is my blood of the new testament, which is shed for many for the remission of sins" (Matt. 26:28). "And that repentance and remission of sins should be preached in his name among all nations, beginning at Jerusalem" (Luke 24:47). "And almost all things are by the law purged with blood; and without shedding of blood is no remission" (Heb. 9:22).

1. The meaning of remission—This concept is practically synonymous with the word *forgiveness*. It refers to a sending back, a putting away.
   a. "Put away"—In the following passages it is translated "put away."
      (1) In regard to Joseph—"Then Joseph her husband, being a just man, and not willing to make her a publick example, was minded to put her away privily" (Matt. 1:19).
      (2) In regard to a wife—"It hath been said, Whosoever shall put away his wife, let him give her a writing of divorcement" (Matt. 5:31).
      (3) In regard to believers—"Wherefore putting away lying, speak every man

truth with his neighbour: for we are members one of another" (Eph. 4:25).

(4) In regard to apostates—"Holding faith, and a good conscience; which some having put away concerning faith have made shipwreck" (1 Tim. 1:19).

(5) In regard to Christ—"For then must he often have suffered since the foundation of the world: but now once in the end of the world hath he appeared to put away sin by the sacrifice of himself" (Heb. 9:26).

b. "Forgive"—In the following passages it is translated "forgive." "Judge not, and ye shall not be judged: condemn not, and ye shall not be condemned: forgive, and ye shall be forgiven" (Luke 6:37). "And be ye kind one to another, tenderhearted, forgiving one another, even as God for Christ's sake hath forgiven you" (Eph. 4:32). "And you, being dead in your sins and the uncircumcision of your flesh, hath he quickened together with him, having forgiven you all trespasses" (Col. 2:13).

2. The Old Testament example of remission—A classic illustration is found in Leviticus 16, where the high priest brought two goats to the tabernacle during the great Day of Atonement. One goat was killed, and its blood was sprinkled upon the mercy seat. Concerning the other goat we read: "And Aaron shall lay both his hands upon the head of the live goat, and confess over him all the iniquities of the children of Israel, and all their transgressions in all their sins, putting them upon the head of the goat, and shall send him away by the hand of a fit man into the wilderness: and the goat shall bear upon him all their iniquities unto a land not inhabited: and he shall let go the goat in the wilderness" (Lev. 16:21-22).

In light of this, carefully note Paul's words in the following verses: "Wherefore Jesus also, that he might sanctify the people with his own blood, suffered without the gate. Let us go forth therefore unto him without the camp, bearing his reproach" (Heb. 13:12-13).

3. The problem of remission—As the Old Testament closed, a great problem remained to be solved. It centered around the two words *remission* and *forbearance*. "Whom God hath set forth to be a propitiation through faith in his blood, to declare his righteousness for the remission of sins that are past, through the forbearance of God" (Rom. 3:25).

a. The word *remission*—The word *remission* (as we have already seen) refers to the act of letting something pass by, in this case, the sins of the Old Testament saints.

b. The word *forbearance*—The word *forbearance* refers to the act of holding something back, in this case, the wrath of God upon those sins. "Who in times past suffered all nations to walk in their own ways" (Acts 14:16). "And the times of this ignorance God winked at; but now commandeth all men every where to repent" (Acts 17:30). (See also Psa. 50:16-22.)

4. The uniqueness of remission—Of the 15 key words in the vocabulary of salvation, remission alone has to do with *subtraction*, whereas all other terms speak of glorious *addition*.

F. Redemption—"Blessed be the Lord God of Israel; for he hath visited and redeemed his people" (Luke 1:68). "Christ hath redeemed us from the curse of the law" (Gal. 3:13). "And they sung a new song, saying, Thou art worthy to take the book, and to open the seals thereof: for thou wast slain, and hast redeemed us to God by thy blood out of every kindred, and tongue, and people, and nation" (Rev. 5:9).

1. The threefold meaning of redemption

    a. To pay a ransom price for something or someone—"Neither by the blood of goats and calves, but by his own blood he entered in once into the holy place, having obtained eternal redemption for us" (Heb. 9:12).

    b. To remove from a slave marketplace—"Christ hath redeemed us from the curse of the law, being made a curse for us: for it is written, Cursed is every one that hangeth on a tree" (Gal. 3:13).

    c. To effect a full release

        (1) The current, immediate release—"Being justified freely by his grace through the redemption that is in Christ Jesus" (Rom. 3:24). But of him are ye in Christ Jesus, who of God is made unto us wisdom, and righteousness, and sanctification, and redemption" (1 Cor. 1:30). "In whom we have redemption through his blood, even the forgiveness of sins" (Col. 1:14).

        (2) The coming, ultimate release—"For we know that the whole creation groaneth and travaileth in pain together until now. And not only they, but ourselves also, which have the firstfruits of the Spirit, even we ourselves groan within ourselves, waiting for the adoption, to wit, the redemption of our body" (Rom. 8:22-23). "And grieve not the holy Spirit of God, whereby ye are sealed unto the day of redemption" (Eph. 4:30).

        Charles Ryrie observes:

> Redemption may be summarized around three basic ideas. (1) People are redeemed *from* something; namely, from the market place or slavery of sin. (2) People are redeemed *by* something; namely, by the payment of a price, the blood of Christ. (3) People are redeemed *to* something; namely, to a state of freedom; and then they are called to renounce that freedom for slavery to the Lord who redeemed them. (*Basic Theology*, p. 292)

2. The Old Testament example of redemption—One of the most important Old Testament offices was that of a *goel*, or kinsman-redeemer. *Baker's Dictionary of Theology* describes this office as follows:

> It is used in the regaining possession of a property which had been sold for debt (Lev. 25:25). It is used in the restoring or preserving of the name of one who had died without offspring: his brother is then to take his wife (Levirate marriage), and raise up seed to him, that his name be not forgotten in Israel (Deut. 25:5). Boaz is the most familiar example of this (Ruth 3–4). (p. 252)

There were three requirements a *goel* had to fulfill:

    a. He must be a near kinsman—"After that he is sold he may be redeemed again; one of his brethren may redeem him: Either his uncle, or his uncle's son, may redeem him, or any that is nigh of kin unto him of his family may redeem him; or if he be able, he may redeem himself" (Lev. 25:48-49).

    "And now it is true that I am thy near kinsman: howbeit there is a kinsman nearer than I. Tarry this night, and it shall be in the morning, that if he will perform unto thee the part of a kinsman, well; let him do the kinsman's part: but if he will not do the part of a kinsman to thee, then will I do the part of a kinsman to thee, as the LORD liveth: lie down until the morning" (Ruth 3:12-13).

   b. He must be able to redeem—"Their Redeemer is strong; the LORD of hosts is his name: he shall throughly plead their cause, that he may give rest to the land, and disquiet the inhabitants of Babylon" (Jer. 50:34).

   c. He must be willing to redeem—Jesus Christ, of course, successfully fulfilled all three of these requirements.

   (1) He became a near kinsman—"Forasmuch then as the children are partakers of flesh and blood, he also himself likewise took part of the same; that through death he might destroy him that had the power of death, that is, the devil; and deliver them who through fear of death were all their lifetime subject to bondage. For verily he took not on him the nature of angels; but he took on him the seed of Abraham" (Heb. 2:14-16). "For we have not an high priest which cannot be touched with the feeling of our infirmities; but was in all points tempted like as we are, yet without sin" (Heb. 4:15).

   (2) He was able to redeem—"I am the good shepherd: the good shepherd giveth his life for the sheep. . . . No man taketh it from me, but I lay it down of myself. I have power to lay it down, and I have power to take it again. This commandment have I received of my Father" (John 10:11, 18).

   (3) He was willing to redeem—"For it is not possible that the blood of bulls and of goats should take away sins. Wherefore when he cometh into the world, he saith, Sacrifice and offering thou wouldest not, but a body hast thou prepared me: In burnt offerings and sacrifices for sin thou hast had no pleasure. Then said I, Lo, I come (in the volume of the book it is written of me,) to do thy will, O God. Above when he said, Sacrifice and offering and burnt offerings and offering for sin thou wouldest not, neither hadst pleasure therein; which are offered by the law; then said he, Lo, I come to do thy will, O God. He taketh away the first, that he may establish the second. By the which will we are sanctified through the offering of the body of Jesus Christ once for all" (Heb. 10:4-10).

3. The costliness of redemption—"Forasmuch as ye know that ye were not redeemed with corruptible things, as silver and gold, from your vain conversation received by tradition from your fathers; but with the precious blood of Christ, as of a lamb without blemish and without spot" (1 Pet. 1:18-19).

   Note: The Bible is in reality the record concerning God's two great works, that of creation (Gen. 1–2) and that of *redemption* (Gen. 3—Rev. 22). It took only a command ("And God said, let there be . . .") to effect the work of creation, but that of a cross to accomplish the work of redemption.

G. Regeneration—"Not by works of righteousness which we have done, but according to his mercy he saved us, by the washing of regeneration, and renewing of the Holy Ghost" (Titus 3:5).

   1. The definition of regeneration—It is that process whereby God, through a second birth, imparts to the believing sinner a new nature. "Jesus answered and said unto him (Nicodemus), Verily, verily, I say unto thee, Except a man be born again, he cannot see the kingdom of God" (John 3:3). "But as many as received him, to them gave he power to become the sons of God, even to them that believe on his name: Which were born, not of blood, nor of the will of the flesh,

nor of the will of man, but of God" (John 1:12-13). "Whosoever believeth that Jesus is the Christ is born of God: and every one that loveth him that begat loveth him also that is begotten of him" (1 John 5:1).

2. The necessity for regeneration—It is necessary because of the corruptness of human nature. "Can the Ethiopian change his skin, or the leopard his spots? then may ye also do good, that are accustomed to do evil" (Jer. 13:23). "As it is written, There is none righteous, no, not one: There is none that understandeth, there is none that seeketh after God. They are all gone out of the way, they are together become unprofitable; there is none that doeth good, no, not one. Their throat is an open sepulchre; with their tongues they have used deceit; the poison of asps is under their lips: Whose mouth is full of cursing and bitterness: Their feet are swift to shed blood: Destruction and misery are in their ways: And the way of peace have they not known: There is no fear of God before their eyes" (Rom. 3:10-18).

"For I know that in me (that is, in my flesh,) dwelleth no good thing: for to will is present with me; but how to perform that which is good I find not" (Rom. 7:18). "Because the carnal mind is enmity against God: for it is not subject to the law of God, neither indeed can be" (Rom. 8:7). "Now the works of the flesh are manifest, which are these; adultery, fornication, uncleanness, lasciviousness, idolatry, witchcraft, hatred, variance, emulations, wrath, strife, seditions, heresies, envyings, murders, drunkenness, revellings, and such like: of the which I tell you before, as I have also told you in time past, that they which do such things shall not inherit the kingdom of God" (Gal. 5:19-21).

   a. By nature all men are dead to God—"And you hath he quickened, who were dead in trespasses and sins" (Eph. 2:1).
   b. By nature all men are children of wrath—"Among whom also we all had our conversation in times past in the lusts of our flesh, fulfilling the desires of the flesh and of the mind; and were by nature the children of wrath, even as others" (Eph. 2:3).
   c. By nature all men are sons of disobedience—"Wherein in time past ye walked according to the course of this world, according to the prince of the power of the air, the spirit that now worketh in the children of disobedience" (Eph. 2:2).
   d. By nature all men are cursed with Adam's sin nature—"Wherefore, as by one man sin entered into the world, and death by sin; and so death passed upon all men, for that all have sinned" (Rom. 5:12). "The first man is of the earth, earthy: the second man is the Lord from heaven" (1 Cor. 15:47).

3. The extent of regeneration
   a. Individual—"Not by works of righteousness which we have done, but according to his mercy he saved us, by the washing of regeneration, and renewing of the Holy Ghost" (Titus 3:5).
   b. Universal—Universal here refers to the redemption of nature itself. This will transpire during the Millennium. "And Jesus said unto them, Verily I say unto you, That ye which have followed me, in the regeneration when the Son of man shall sit in the throne of his glory, ye also shall sit upon twelve thrones, judging the twelve tribes of Israel" (Matt. 19:28).

   "For the earnest expectation of the creature waiteth for the manifestation of the sons of God. For the creature was made subject to vanity, not willingly, but by reason of him who hath subjected the same in hope, because the creature itself also shall be delivered from the bondage of corruption into the glorious liberty of the children of God. For we know that the whole creation groaneth and travaileth in pain together until now. And not only they, but ourselves also, which have the firstfruits of the Spirit, even we ourselves groan within ourselves, waiting for the adoption, to wit, the redemption of our body" (Rom. 8:19-23).

4. The results of regeneration
   a. It provides us a new mind, allowing us to know God (1 Cor. 2:16).
   b. It provides us a new heart, allowing us to love God (Rom. 5:5; 1 John 4:9).
   c. It provides us a new will, allowing us to obey God (Rom. 6:13).

5. The means of regeneration—Three factors are vital for a sinner to experience redemption.
   a. The Word of God—"Jesus answered, Verily, verily, I say unto thee, Except a man be born of water and of the Spirit, he cannot enter into the kingdom of God" (John 3:5). "That he might sanctify and cleanse it with the washing of water by the word" (Eph. 5:26). "Not by works of righteousness which we have done, but according to his mercy he saved us, by the washing of regeneration, and renewing of the Holy Ghost" (Titus 3:5). "Of his own will begat he us with the word of truth, that we should be a kind of firstfruits of his creatures" (James 1:18). "Being born again, not of corruptible seed, but of incorruptible, by the word of God, which liveth and abideth for ever" (1 Pet. 1:23).
   b. The man of God—"For whosoever shall call upon the name of the Lord shall be saved. How then shall they call on him in whom they have not believed? and how shall they believe in him of whom they have not heard? and how shall they hear without a preacher? And how shall they preach, except they be sent? as it is written, How beautiful are the feet of them that preach the gospel of peace, and bring glad tidings of good things!" (Rom. 10:13-15).

    "For though ye have ten thousand instructors in Christ, yet have ye not many fathers: for in Christ Jesus I have begotten you through the gospel" (1 Cor. 4:15). "And all things are of God, who hath reconciled us to himself by Jesus Christ, and hath given to us the ministry of reconciliation; to wit, that God was in Christ, reconciling the world unto himself, not imputing their trespasses unto them; and hath committed unto us the word of reconciliation. Now then we are ambassadors for Christ, as though God did beseech you by us: we pray you in Christ's stead, be ye reconciled to God" (2 Cor. 5:18-20). "My little children, of whom I travail in birth again until Christ be formed in you" (Gal. 4:19).
   c. The Spirit of God—"Jesus answered, Verily, verily, I say unto thee, Except a man be born of water and of the Spirit, he cannot enter into the kingdom of God. That which is born of the flesh is flesh; and that which is born of the Spirit is spirit" (John 3:5-6). "But the natural man receiveth not the things of the Spirit of God: for they are foolishness unto him: neither can he know them, because they are spiritually discerned" (1 Cor. 2:14). (See also Titus 3:5.)

    These three factors should not be lightly passed over. They teach that no sinner has ever been saved since Adam apart from them. Some may deny the necessity of the second factor, however (the man of God), pointing out that people often came to Christ while alone, after reading a gospel tract. But just how was that tract written, printed, and distributed in the first place? Obviously saved human beings were involved. If the above is true, then it is not unreasonable to conclude that as the Holy Spirit looks for a human instrument (mothers) to bring living souls into this world, he likewise seeks out human instruments (soul winners) to usher sinners into the kingdom of God.

6. The biblical illustrations of regeneration—Among the many conversions in the Bible the two which perhaps most vividly demonstrate the life-changing process effected by regeneration are those of Manasseh in the Old Testament and Saul of Tarsus in the New Testament.

a. Manasseh (2 Kings 21:1-18; 2 Chron. 33:1-20)

(1) Manasseh, the unique king

(a) He was the fourteenth king of Judah.

(b) He ruled for 55 years, longer than any other king in the Bible (2 Kings 21:1).

(c) He was 12 years old when he began to reign (2 Kings 21:1).

(2) Manasseh, the ungodly king (2 Kings 21:2-16; 2 Chron. 33:2-10)

(a) He rebuilt the pagan high places his father Hezekiah had destroyed.

(b) He erected altars to Baal and made an Asherah pole.

(c) He bowed down to the starry hosts and worshipped them.

(d) He rebuilt pagan altars in the temple of God.

(e) He sacrificed his own sons in the fire in the Valley of Hinnom, outside Jerusalem.

(f) He practiced sorcery, divination, and witchcraft.

(g) He consulted mediums and spiritists.

(h) He did more evil than the original Canaanites in the land had done.

(i) He filled Jerusalem from end to end with the blood of innocent people who were slaughtered at his command.

(j) Tradition says he ordered Isaiah to be sawn asunder (Heb. 11:37).

(k) He continued to do all these things in spite of repeated warnings from God.

(l) Jeremiah the prophet later referred to Manasseh as a symbol of evil (Jer. 15:4).

(3) Manasseh, the upright king

(a) The record of his conversion

i) The prison—God punished Manasseh for all this by allowing the Assyrians to take him prisoner, put a hook in his nose, bind him with bronze shackles, and take him to Babylon (2 Chron. 33:11).

ii) The prayer—In his distress, Manasseh turned to God and begged for forgiveness (2 Chron. 33:12). God heard his prayer, saved him, and brought him back to Jerusalem (2 Chron. 33:13, 18-19).

(b) The results of his conversion

i) Military accomplishments—Manasseh rebuilt the outer wall of the city of David, making it much higher, and stationed military commanders in all the fortified cities of Judah (2 Chron. 3:14).

ii) Moral accomplishments—He got rid of the foreign gods and altars, removing them from the temple (2 Chron. 33:15). He urged all Judah to serve God (3 Chron. 33:16).

b. Saul of Tarsus
  (1) His war against the Savior
    (a) He "kept the raiment" of those that murdered Stephen, and consented to his death (Acts 7:57-58; 8:1-2; 22:20).
    (b) He made havoc of the church (Acts 8:3)—This word describes the act of a wild hog viciously uprooting a vineyard.
    (c) He entered the homes of Christians and dragged them off to prison (Acts 8:3).
    (d) He hounded Christians to their death in various cities (Acts 22:5).
    (e) He beat believers (Acts 22:19).
    (f) He voted to have them put to death (Acts 26:10).
    (g) He attempted through torture to force them into cursing Christ (Acts 26:11).
    (h) He persecuted the church beyond measure and "wasted it" (Gal. 1:13).
  (2) His witness to the Savior—Following his conversion Saul, once Satan's most ferocious wolf, then became God's most faithful sheepdog.
7. The fruits of regeneration
  a. The twice-born person now loves other Christians—"We know that we have passed from death unto life, because we love the brethren. He that loveth not his brother abideth in death" (1 John 3:14).
  b. The twice-born person now loves Jesus—"Whosoever believeth that Jesus is the Christ is born of God: and every one that loveth him that begat loveth him also that is begotten of him. By this we know that we love the children of God, when we love God, and keep his commandments" (1 John 5:1-2).
  c. The twice-born person now loves the separated life—"Love not the world, neither the things that are in the world. If any man love the world, the love of the Father is not in him. For all that is in the world, the lust of the flesh, and the lust of the eyes, and the pride of life, is not of the Father, but is of the world" (1 John 2:15-16). "For whatsoever is born of God overcometh the world: and this is the victory that overcometh the world, even our faith" (1 John 5:4).
  d. The twice-born person now loves his enemies—"Ye have heard that it hath been said, Thou shalt love thy neighbour, and hate thine enemy. But I say unto you, Love your enemies, bless them that curse you, do good to them that hate you, and pray for them which despitefully use you, and persecute you; that ye may be the children of your Father which is in heaven: for he maketh his sun to rise on the evil and on the good, and sendeth rain on the just and on the unjust" (Matt. 5:43-45).
  e. The twice-born person now loves the Word of God—"And I will delight myself in thy commandments, which I have loved. . . . The law of thy mouth is better unto me than thousands of gold and silver. . . . O how love I thy law! it is my meditation all the day. . . . How sweet are thy words unto my taste! yea, sweeter than honey to my mouth! . . . Therefore I love thy commandments above gold; yea, above fine gold. . . . Thy word is very pure: therefore thy servant loveth it. . . . Great peace have they which love thy law: and nothing shall offend them" (Psa. 119:47, 72, 97, 103, 127, 140, 165).
  f. The twice-born person now loves the souls of men—"I say the truth in Christ, I lie not, my conscience also bearing me witness in the Holy Ghost, that I have great heaviness and continual sorrow in my heart. For I could

wish that myself were accursed from Christ for my brethren, my kinsmen according to the flesh" (Rom. 9:1-3). "Brethren, my heart's desire and prayer to God for Israel is, that they might be saved" (Rom. 10:1). "For the love of Christ constraineth us; because we thus judge, that if one died for all, then were all dead" (2 Cor. 5:14).

    g. The twice-born person now loves prayer—"Speaking to yourselves in psalms and hymns and spiritual songs, singing and making melody in your heart to the Lord; giving thanks always for all things unto God and the Father in the name of our Lord Jesus Christ" (Eph. 5:19-20).

H. Imputation—"Blessed is the man to whom the Lord will not impute sin" (Rom. 4:8).

    1. Definition of imputation—To impute is for one person to add something good or bad to the account of another person.

    2. Kinds of imputation—In the Bible there are three main theological imputations.

        a. The imputation of Adam's sin upon the human race—"Wherefore, as by one man sin entered into the world, and death by sin; and so death passed upon all men, for that all have sinned" (Rom. 5:12). "For as in Adam all die" (1 Cor. 15:22). "For all have sinned, and come short of the glory of God" (Rom. 3:23).

           This first imputation seems at first to be totally unjust. Why should Adam's sin be imputed to me when it happened in a remote part of this world thousands of years before I was even born? If the story ended here it might be unjust, but it doesn't. Read on.

        b. The imputation of the race's sin upon Christ—"But he was wounded for our transgressions, he was bruised for our iniquities: the chastisement of our peace was upon him; and with his stripes we are healed" (Isa. 53:5). "My righteous servant justify many; for he shall bear their iniquities" (Isa. 53:11). "That he by the grace of God should taste death for every man" (Heb. 2:9). "Who his own self bare our sins in his own body on the tree, that we, being dead to sins, should live unto righteousness: by whose stripes ye were healed" (1 Pet. 2:24). (See also 2 Cor. 5:14-21.)

           The first imputation was an unwilling one (for no human would voluntarily accept Adam's guilt), but the second imputation was effected upon a totally willing volunteer. "I am the good shepherd: the good shepherd giveth his life for the sheep. . . . No man taketh it from me, but I lay it down of myself" (John 10:11, 18).

        c. The imputation of God's righteousness upon the believing sinner—"But what things were gain to me, those I counted loss for Christ. Yea doubtless, and I count all things but loss for the excellency of the knowledge of Christ Jesus my Lord: for whom I have suffered the loss of all things, and do count them but dung, that I may win Christ, and be found in him, not having mine own righteousness, which is of the law, but that which is through the faith of Christ, the righteousness which is of God by faith" (Phil. 3:7-9).

           This imputation, like the second, must be voluntary. God forces the righteousness of Christ upon no one.

    3. Biblical examples of imputation

        a. Abraham—"And the scripture was fulfilled which saith, Abraham believed God, and it was imputed unto him for righteousness: and he was called the Friend of God" (James 2:23). "And he believed in the LORD; and he counted

it to him for righteousness" (Gen. 15:6). "For what saith the scripture? Abraham believed God, and it was counted unto him for righteousness" (Rom. 4:3).
   b. David—"Even as David also describeth the blessedness of the man, unto whom God imputeth righteousness without works, saying, Blessed are they whose iniquities are forgiven, and whose sins are covered. Blessed is the man to whom the Lord will not impute sin" (Rom. 4:6-8). "Blessed is he whose transgression is forgiven, whose sin is covered. Blessed is the man unto whom the LORD imputeth not iniquity, and in whose spirit there is no guile" (Psa. 32:1-2).
   c. Onesimus—Dr. J. Dwight Pentecost writes:

> Paul's prison cell in Rome became a pulpit from which the gospel went out to multitudes in the capital city of the Roman Empire. Among those to whom the gospel came in transforming power was a runaway slave, Onesimus, who had stolen from his master and made his way from the city of Colosse in Asia Minor over to Rome. While Paul could have used this new-found son in the faith to minister to his needs as a prisoner, he purposed to send Onesimus back to Philemon, his master.
>
> Paul wrote the letter to Philemon to exhort him to forgive and restore his runaway slave, and to count him as a brother in Christ. Paul recognized that before such a restoration could be made, the debt which Onesimus had incurred must be paid. Onesimus had nothing with which he could discharge that debt, and so in penning his epistle the Apostle says (vv. 17-18), "If thou count me therefore a partner, receive him as myself. If he hath wronged thee, or oweth thee ought, put that on mine account; I Paul have written it with mine own hand, I will repay it." And in those words the Apostle was giving a classic example of the great Christian doctrine of imputation. (*Things Which Become Sound Doctrine*, p. 40)

   d. Stephen—"And they stoned Stephen, calling upon God, and saying, Lord Jesus, receive my spirit. And he kneeled down, and cried with a loud voice, Lord, lay not this sin to their charge. And when he had said this, he fell asleep" (Acts 7:59-60).
   e. Paul—"At my first answer no man stood with me, but all men forsook me: I pray God that it may not be laid to their charge" (2 Tim. 4:16).
I. Adoption—"But when the fulness of the time was come, God sent forth his Son, made of a woman, made under the law, to redeem them that were under the law, that we might receive the adoption of sons" (Gal. 4:4-5).
   1. The theology of adoption (Rom. 8:15-23)
      a. Clarified—The word literally means "the placing of a son." Adoption logically follows regeneration. Regeneration gives one his nature as a child of God, whereas adoption gives him his position as a son of God.
         "And will be a Father unto you, and ye shall be my sons and daughters, saith the Lord Almighty" (2 Cor. 6:18). "But when the fulness of the time was come, God sent forth his Son, made of a woman, made under the law, to redeem them that were under the law, that we might receive the adoption of sons. And because ye are sons, God hath sent forth the Spirit of his Son into your hearts, crying, Abba, Father" (Gal. 4:4-6). "Having predestinated us

unto the adoption of children by Jesus Christ to himself, according to the good pleasure of his will" (Eph. 1:5).

b. Contrasted—How spiritual adoption differs from civil adoption

   (1) We never adopt our own children, but God never adopts any other.

   (2) Civil adoption provides comfort for the childless, but God had a beloved Son prior to adopting us—"And lo a voice from heaven, saying, This is my beloved Son, in whom I am well pleased" (Matt. 3:17). "While he yet spake, behold, a bright cloud overshadowed them: and behold a voice out of the cloud, which said, This is my beloved Son, in whom I am well pleased; hear ye him" (Matt. 17:5).

   (3) There are usually many pleasing characteristics in a civil adopted child, but not in God's children prior to their adoption—See Romans 3:10-18.

   (4) Civil adoption could never give the child the nature of the father, but God's adopted are given the very mind of Christ—"For who hath known the mind of the Lord, that he may instruct him? But we have the mind of Christ" (1 Cor. 2:16).

   (5) In some cases, civil adoption could be declared null and void, but God's adopted are absolutely secure.

c. Compared—How spiritual adoption compares with civil adoption

   (1) The Father must begin the action leading to adoption—"Come now, and let us reason together, saith the LORD: though your sins be as scarlet, they shall be as white as snow; though they be red like crimson, they shall be as wool" (Isa. 1:18). "For God so loved the world, that he gave his only begotten Son, that whosoever believeth in him should not perish, but have everlasting life" (John 3:16).

   (2) Both adoptions give an inheritance to one who previously had none—"And if children, then heirs; heirs of God, and joint-heirs with Christ; if so be that we suffer with him, that we may be also glorified together" (Rom. 8:17).

   (3) Both adoptions provide a new name—"And he brought him to Jesus. And when Jesus beheld him, he said, Thou art Simon the son of Jona: thou shalt be called Cephas, which is by interpretation, A stone" (John 1:42). "He that hath an ear, let him hear what the Spirit saith unto the churches; To him that overcometh will I give to eat of the hidden manna, and will give him a white stone, and in the stone a new name written, which no man knoweth saving he that receiveth it" (Rev. 2:17).

2. The Trinity in adoption

a. There is an intimacy toward the Father—"Whereby we cry, Abba, Father" (Rom. 8:15). This is a very personal name for one's Father. Only Jesus himself had used this until now. "He went away again the second time, and prayed, saying, O my Father, if this cup may not pass away from me, except I drink it, thy will be done" (Matt. 26:42). "And he said, Abba, Father, all things are possible unto thee; take away this cup from me: nevertheless not what I will, but what thou wilt" (Mark 14:36).

b. There is an illumination by the Spirit—He both leads us and assures us. "For as many as are led by the Spirit of God, they are the sons of God" (Rom. 8:14). "The Spirit itself beareth witness with our spirit, that we are the children of God" (Rom. 8:16).

c. There is an inheritance with the Son—"And if children, then heirs; heirs of

God, and joint-heirs with Christ; if so be that we suffer with him, that we may be also glorified together" (Rom. 8:17). (See also 1 Pet. 1:3-9.)

J. Supplication (prayer)—"I exhort therefore, that, first of all, supplications, prayers, intercessions, and giving of thanks, be made for all men" (1 Tim. 2:1). "Praying always with all prayer and supplication in the Spirit" (Eph. 6:18). "Be careful for nothing; but in every thing by prayer and supplication with thanksgiving let your requests be made known unto God" (Phil. 4:6).

It may be said that no sinner is saved without prayer and no believer is sanctified (to grow in grace) apart from prayer. The prayer may be like Solomon's prayer (one of the longest in the Bible, with 31 verses; see 1 Kings 8:23-53) or like Peter's prayer (one of the shortest, with 1 verse containing three words, see Matt. 14:30), but in any case, prayer must be exercised.

1. Definition of prayer—Prayer may be best defined as "having fellowship with God." It is more than simply talking *to* God, but rather talking *with* God. It implies a two-way give-and-take.

2. Elements in prayer—"After this manner therefore pray ye: Our Father which art in heaven, Hallowed be thy name. Thy kingdom come. Thy will be done in earth, as it is in heaven. Give us this day our daily bread. And forgive us our debts, as we forgive our debtors. And lead us not into temptation, but deliver us from evil: For thine is the kingdom, and the power, and the glory, for ever. Amen" (Matt. 6:9-13).

According to this model prayer of Jesus', which was given to us at the request of the disciples, prayer includes 10 elements:

a. A personal relationship with God: "Our Father"—The word *our* signifies the believer's brotherly relationship between himself and all other Christians. While the Bible nowhere presents the universal fatherhood of God, it does declare the universal brotherhood of believers. The word *Father* signifies the relationship between God and the believer.

b. Faith: "which art in heaven"—Paul declares that without this element, our prayers are useless. "But without faith it is impossible to please him: for he that cometh to God must believe that he is, and that he is a rewarder of them that diligently seek him" (Heb. 11:6).

c. Worship: "hallowed be thy name"—David felt this part of prayer to be so important that he appointed a select group of men who did nothing else in the temple but praise and worship God. "Moreover four thousand were porters; and four thousand praised the LORD with the instruments which I made, said David, to praise therewith" (1 Chron. 23:5). "Moreover David and the captains of the host separated to the service of the sons of Asaph, and of Heman, and of Jeduthun, who should prophesy with harps, with psalteries, and with cymbals. . . . So the number of them, with their brethren that were instructed in the songs of the LORD, even all that were cunning, was two hundred fourscore and eight" (1 Chron. 25:1, 7).

In the book of Revelation John sees four special angels who exist solely to worship God and who "rest not day and night, saying, Holy, holy, holy, Lord God Almighty, which was, and is, and is to come" (Rev. 4:8).

See also Christ's statement to the Samaritan woman: "But the hour cometh, and now is, when the true worshippers shall worship the Father in spirit and in truth: for the Father seeketh such to worship him. God is a

Spirit: and they that worship him must worship him in spirit and in truth" (John 4:23-24).

d. Expectation: "Thy kingdom come"—This kingdom is that blessed millennial kingdom spoken of so much in the Old Testament: "And it shall come to pass in the last days, that the mountain of the LORD's house shall be established in the top of the mountains, and shall be exalted above the hills; and all nations shall flow unto it. And many people shall go and say, Come ye, and let us go up to the mountain of the LORD, to the house of the God of Jacob; and he will teach us of his ways, and we will walk in his paths: for out of Zion shall go forth the law, and the word of the LORD from Jerusalem. And he shall judge among the nations, and shall rebuke many people: and they shall beat their swords into plowshares, and their spears into pruninghooks: nation shall not lift up sword against nation, neither shall they learn war any more" (Isa. 2:2-4).

This kingdom was later previewed by John in the New Testament. (See Rev. 20:1-6.)

e. Submission: "Thy will be done in earth, as it is in heaven"—Jesus would later give the finest example of this element in Gethsemane. "And he went a little further, and fell on his face, and prayed, saying, O my Father, if it be possible, let this cup pass from me: nevertheless not as I will, but as thou wilt" (Matt. 26:39).

f. Petition: "Give us this day our daily bread"—This suggests that our praying should be as our eating—daily.

g. Confession: "And forgive us our debts"—The blood of Christ will forgive us of every sin, but not one excuse. Only confessed sin can be forgiven. "If we confess our sins, he is faithful and just to forgive us our sins, and to cleanse us from all unrighteousness" (1 John 1:9).

h. Compassion: "as we forgive our debtors"—"If a man say, I love God, and hateth his brother, he is a liar: for he that loveth not his brother whom he hath seen, how can he love God whom he hath not seen?" (1 John 4:20). (See also Matt. 18:21-35.)

i. Dependence: "And lead us not into temptation, but deliver us from evil"—It should be understood that, while God has never promised to keep us *from* temptation, he has promised to preserve us *in* and *through* temptation. "There hath no temptation taken you but such as is common to man: but God is faithful, who will not suffer you to be tempted above that ye are able; but will with the temptation also make a way to escape, that ye may be able to bear it" (1 Cor. 10:13).

j. Acknowledgement: "For thine is the kingdom, and the power, and the glory forever"—See David's great prayer in 1 Chronicles 29:10-19, where he actually anticipates the final part of Jesus' model prayer.

3. Reasons for prayer—Why should we pray?

a. Because of the repeated command of God—"Moreover as for me, God forbid that I should sin against the LORD in ceasing to pray for you: but I will teach you the good and the right way" (1 Sam. 12:23). "Rejoicing in hope; patient in tribulation; continuing instant in prayer" (Rom. 12:12). "Continue in prayer, and watch in the same with thanksgiving" (Col. 4:2). "Pray without ceasing" (1 Thess. 5:17). "I will therefore that men pray every where, lifting up holy hands, without wrath and doubting" (1 Tim. 2:8).

b. Because of the example of Christ—"Who in the days of his flesh, when he had offered up prayers and supplications with strong crying and tears unto him that was able to save him from death, and was heard in that he feared" (Heb. 5:7). "For even hereunto were ye called: because Christ also suffered for us, leaving us an example, that ye should follow his steps: Who did no sin, neither was guile found in his mouth: Who, when he was reviled, reviled not again; when he suffered, he threatened not; but committed himself to him that judgeth righteously" (1 Pet. 2:21-23).

c. Because of the example of the early church—"These all continued with one accord in prayer and supplication, with the women, and Mary the mother of Jesus, and with his brethren" (Acts 1:14). "And they continued stedfastly in the apostles' doctrine and fellowship, and in breaking of bread, and in prayers" (Acts 2:42). " But we will give ourselves continually to prayer, and to the ministry of the word" (Acts 6:4). "Peter therefore was kept in prison: but prayer was made without ceasing of the church unto God for him" (Acts 12:5).

d. Because prayer is God's chosen method for the following:
   (1) Defeating the devil—"But I have prayed for thee, that thy faith fail not: and when thou art converted, strengthen thy brethren" (Luke 22:32). "But the end of all things is at hand: be ye therefore sober, and watch unto prayer" (1 Pet. 4:7).
   (2) Saving the sinner—"And the publican, standing afar off, would not lift up so much as his eyes unto heaven, but smote upon his breast, saying, God be merciful to me a sinner" (Luke 18:13).
   (3) Restoring the backslider—"Confess your faults one to another, and pray one for another, that ye may be healed. The effectual fervent prayer of a righteous man availeth much. . . . Brethren, if any of you do err from the truth, and one convert him; let him know, that he which converteth the sinner from the error of his way, shall save a soul from death, and shall hide a multitude of sins" (James 5:16, 19-20).
   (4) Strengthening the saint—"But ye, beloved, building up yourselves on your most holy faith, praying in the Holy Ghost" (Jude 20).
   (5) Sending forth laborers—"Pray ye therefore the Lord of the harvest, that he will send forth labourers into his harvest" (Matt. 9:38). "As they ministered to the Lord, and fasted, the Holy Ghost said, Separate me Barnabas and Saul for the work whereunto I have called them. And when they had fasted and prayed, and laid their hands on them, they sent them away" (Acts 13:2-3).
   (6) Curing the sick—"Is any among you afflicted? let him pray. Is any merry? let him sing psalms. Is any sick among you? let him call for the elders of the church; and let them pray over him, anointing him with oil in the name of the Lord: And the prayer of faith shall save the sick, and the Lord shall raise him up; and if he have committed sins, they shall be forgiven him" (James 5:13-15).
   (7) Glorifying God's name—And when he had taken the book, the four beasts and four and twenty elders fell down before the Lamb, having every one of them harps, and golden vials full of odours, which are the prayers of saints" (Rev. 5:8). "And I saw the seven angels which stood before God; and to them were given seven trumpets. And another angel

came and stood at the altar, having a golden censer; and there was given unto him much incense, that he should offer it with the prayers of all saints upon the golden altar which was before the throne. And the smoke of the incense, which came with the prayers of the saints, ascended up before God out of the angel's hand" (Rev. 8:2-4).

(8) Accomplishing the impossible—"And all things, whatsoever ye shall ask in prayer, believing, ye shall receive" (Matt. 21:22). "And he said unto them, This kind can come forth by nothing, but by prayer and fasting" (Mark 9:29). "Elias was a man subject to like passions as we are, and he prayed earnestly that it might not rain: and it rained not on the earth by the space of three years and six months. And he prayed again, and the heaven gave rain, and the earth brought forth her fruit" (James 5:17-18). (See also Acts 12:5-17.)

(9) Giving good things—"He will regard the prayer of the destitute, and not despise their prayer" (Psa. 102:17). "Ask, and it shall be given you; seek, and ye shall find; knock, and it shall be opened unto you: For every one that asketh receiveth; and he that seeketh findeth; and to him that knocketh it shall be opened. Or what man is there of you, whom if his son ask bread, will he give him a stone? Or if he ask a fish, will he give him a serpent? If ye then, being evil, know how to give good gifts unto your children, how much more shall your Father which is in heaven give good things to them that ask him?" (Matt. 7:7-11). (See also Matt. 21:22.)

(10) Imparting wisdom—"If any of you lack wisdom, let him ask of God, that giveth to all men liberally, and upbraideth not; and it shall be given him" (James 1:5).

(11) Bestowing peace—"Let your moderation be known unto all men. The Lord is at hand. Be careful for nothing; but in every thing by prayer and supplication with thanksgiving let your requests be made known unto God. And the peace of God, which passeth all understanding, shall keep your hearts and minds through Christ Jesus" (Phil. 4:5-7).

(12) Keeping one from sin—"Watch and pray, that ye enter not into temptation: the spirit indeed is willing, but the flesh is weak" (Matt. 26:41).

(13) Revealing the will of God—"And I say unto you, Ask, and it shall be given you; seek, and ye shall find; knock, and it shall be opened unto you. For every one that asketh receiveth; and he that seeketh findeth; and to him that knocketh it shall be opened" (Luke 11:9-10).

e. Because of the example of the greatest Christian of all time—Paul

(1) Paul began and ended his Christian life by prayer.

(a) The beginning—"And the Lord said unto him, Arise, and go into the street which is called Straight, and enquire in the house of Judas for one called Saul, of Tarsus: for, behold, he prayeth" (Acts 9:11).

(b) The ending—"At my first answer no man stood with me, but all men forsook me: I pray God that it may not be laid to their charge" (2 Tim. 4:16).

(2) Paul prayed everywhere he went.

(a) In a prison (Acts 16:25)—"And at midnight Paul and Silas prayed, and sang praises unto God: and the prisoners heard them" (Acts 16:25).

(b) On a seashore
  i) At Miletus—"And when he had thus spoken, he kneeled down, and prayed with them all" (Acts 20:36).
  ii) At Tyre—"And when we had accomplished those days, we departed and went our way; and they all brought us on our way, with wives and children, till we were out of the city: and we kneeled down on the shore, and prayed" (Acts 21:5).
(c) In Jerusalem (Acts 22:17)
(d) On an island—"And it came to pass, that the father of Publius lay sick of a fever and of a bloody flux: to whom Paul entered in, and prayed, and laid his hands on him, and healed him" (Acts 28:8).
(3) Paul prayed for almost everyone he met.
  (a) For the churches (Rom. 1:9; 1 Cor. 1:4; 2 Cor. 13:7; Gal. 4:19; Eph. 1:16; 3:14; Phil. 1:4, 9; Col. 1:3, 9; 1 Thess. 1:2; 3:10; 5:23; 2 Thess. 1:3, 11; 2:13)
  (b) For Philemon (Philem. 4)
  (c) For Timothy (2 Tim. 1:3)
  (d) For Onesiphorus (2 Tim. 1:16-18)
  (e) For those who forsook him in Rome (2 Tim. 4:16)
  (f) For Israel—"Brethren, my heart's desire and prayer to God for Israel is, that they might be saved" (Rom. 10:1).
  (g) For all men (1 Tim. 2:1-3, 8; 4:4-5)
(4) Paul constantly asked others to pray for him (1 Thess. 5:25; 2 Thess. 3:1; Philem. 22; Rom. 15:30; Col. 4:3).
4. Direction of prayer—To whom should we pray? To the Father? Son? Spirit? The basic New Testament rule is this: Prayer should be made *to* the Father, *through* the Spirit, *in the name* of Jesus. (See Rom. 8:15-16, 26-27.)
5. Objects of prayer—For whom should we pray?
  a. For ourselves—In the Scriptures Abraham's servant, Peter, and the dying thief prayed for themselves. The first prayer was for guidance, the second for survival from drowning, and the third for salvation.
    (1) Abraham's servant—"And he said, O LORD God of my master Abraham, I pray thee, send me good speed this day, and shew kindness unto my master Abraham" (Gen. 24:12).
    (2) Peter—"But when he saw the wind boisterous, he was afraid; and beginning to sink, he cried, saying, Lord, save me" (Matt. 14:30).
    (3) The dying thief—"And he said unto Jesus, Lord, remember me when thou comest into thy kingdom" (Luke 23:42).
  b. For one another—"Confess your faults one to another, and pray one for another, that ye may be healed. The effectual fervent prayer of a righteous man availeth much" (James 5:16). "For God is my witness, whom I serve with my spirit in the gospel of his Son, that without ceasing I make mention of you always in my prayers" (Rom. 1:9).
  c. For pastors—The apostle Paul requested prayer for himself from both Ephesian and Colossian believers. "And for me, that utterance may be given unto me, that I may open my mouth boldly, to make known the mystery of the gospel, for which I am an ambassador in bonds: that therein I may speak boldly, as I ought to speak" (Eph. 6:19-20). "Withal praying also for us, that God would open unto us a door of utterance, to speak the mystery of Christ, for which I am also in bonds" (Col. 4:3).

d. For sick believers—"Is any sick among you? let him call for the elders of the church; and let them pray over him, anointing him with oil in the name of the Lord: And the prayer of faith shall save the sick, and the Lord shall raise him up; and if he have committed sins, they shall be forgiven him" (James 5:14-15).

e. For rulers—"I exhort therefore, that, first of all, supplications, prayers, intercessions, and giving of thanks, be made for all men; for kings, and for all that are in authority; that we may lead a quiet and peaceable life in all godliness and honesty. For this is good and acceptable in the sight of God our Saviour" (1 Tim. 2:1-3).

How easy it is (and how sinful) to criticize our leaders but never remember to pray for them.

f. For our enemies—"But I say unto you, Love your enemies, bless them that curse you, do good to them that hate you, and pray for them which despitefully use you, and persecute you" (Matt. 5:44). "Bless them that curse you, and pray for them which despitefully use you" (Luke 6:28). "And they stoned Stephen, calling upon God, and saying, Lord Jesus, receive my spirit. And he kneeled down, and cried with a loud voice, Lord, lay not this sin to their charge. And when he had said this, he fell asleep" (Acts 7:59-60).

g. For Israel—"Pray for the peace of Jerusalem: they shall prosper that love thee" (Psa. 122:6). "I have set watchmen upon thy walls, O Jerusalem, which shall never hold their peace day nor night: ye that make mention of the LORD, keep not silence, and give him no rest, till he establish, and till he make Jerusalem a praise in the earth" (Isa. 62:6-7).

h. For all men—See 1 Timothy 2:1.

6. Positions for prayer—No specific position is required. It is the heart that counts. Note the various positions as described in the Bible.

a. Standing (suggested by Jesus)—"And when ye stand praying, forgive, if ye have ought against any: that your Father also which is in heaven may forgive you your trespasses" (Mark 11:25).

b. Sitting (done by David)—"And David the king came and sat before the LORD, and said, Who am I, O LORD God, and what is mine house, that thou hast brought me hitherto?" (1 Chron. 17:16). (See 1 Chron. 17:16-27.)

c. Bowing (Moses)—"And Moses made haste, and bowed his head toward the earth, and worshipped" (Exod. 34:8).

d. Lying (David)—"I am weary with my groaning; all the night make I my bed to swim; I water my couch with my tears" (Psa. 6:6).

e. With lifted hands (David)—"Hear the voice of my supplications, when I cry unto thee, when I lift up my hands toward thy holy oracle" (Psa. 28:2).

f. On one's face (Jesus)—"And he went a little further, and fell on his face, and prayed, saying, O my Father, if it be possible, let this cup pass from me: nevertheless not as I will, but as thou wilt" (Matt. 26:39).

g. On one's knees (Solomon, Daniel, Jesus, Paul)
(1) Solomon—"And it was so, that when Solomon had made an end of praying all this prayer and supplication unto the LORD, he arose from before the altar of the LORD, from kneeling on his knees with his hands spread up to heaven" (1 Kings 8:54).
(2) Daniel—"Now when Daniel knew that the writing was signed, he went into his house; and his windows being open in his chamber toward

Jerusalem, he kneeled upon his knees three times a day, and prayed, and gave thanks before his God, as he did aforetime" (Dan. 6:10).

    (3) Jesus—"And he was withdrawn from them about a stone's cast, and kneeled down, and prayed" (Luke 22:41).

    (4) Paul—"And when he had thus spoken, he kneeled down, and prayed with them all" (Acts 20:36).

  h. With the face between the knees (Elijah)—"So Ahab went up to eat and to drink. And Elijah went up to the top of Carmel; and he cast himself down upon the earth, and put his face between his knees" (1 Kings 18:42).

7. Time of prayer—Anytime

  a. Early in the morning—"And in the morning, rising up a great while before day, he went out, and departed into a solitary place, and there prayed" (Mark 1:35).

  b. At noon—"Evening, and morning, and at noon, will I pray, and cry aloud: and he shall hear my voice" (Psa. 55:17).

  c. Late in the afternoon—"Now Peter and John went up together into the temple at the hour of prayer, being the ninth hour" (Acts 3:1).

  d. In the evening—"Let my prayer be set forth before thee as incense; and the lifting up of my hands as the evening sacrifice" (Psa. 141:2).

  e. At midnight—"And at midnight Paul and Silas prayed, and sang praises unto God: and the prisoners heard them" (Acts 16:25).

8. Hindrances to prayer

  a. Known sin—"If I regard iniquity in my heart, the Lord will not hear me" (Psa. 66:18).

  b. Insincerity—"And when thou prayest, thou shalt not be as the hypocrites are: for they love to pray standing in the synagogues and in the corners of the streets, that they may be seen of men. Verily I say unto you, They have their reward" (Matt. 6:5).

  c. Carnal motives—"Ye ask, and receive not, because ye ask amiss, that ye may consume it upon your lusts" (James 4:3).

  d. Unbelief—"If any of you lack wisdom, let him ask of God, that giveth to all men liberally, and upbraideth not; and it shall be given him. But let him ask in faith, nothing wavering. For he that wavereth is like a wave of the sea driven with the wind and tossed" (James 1:5-6).

  e. Satanic activity—"And, behold, an hand touched me, which set me upon my knees and upon the palms of my hands. And he said unto me, O Daniel, a man greatly beloved, understand the words that I speak unto thee, and stand upright: for unto thee am I now sent. And when he had spoken this word unto me, I stood trembling. Then said he unto me, Fear not, Daniel: for from the first day that thou didst set thine heart to understand, and to chasten thyself before thy God, thy words were heard, and I am come for thy words. But the prince of the kingdom of Persia withstood me one and twenty days: but, lo, Michael, one of the chief princes, came to help me; and I remained there with the kings of Persia" (Dan. 10:10-13).

    On certain occasions the sovereign God for a short period of time may allow satanic interference to block the prayer line of the believer. This is usually for the purpose of testing and purifying his child, as the book of Job and tenth chapter of Daniel so vividly illustrate.

  f. Domestic problems—"Likewise, ye husbands, dwell with them according to knowledge, giving honour unto the wife, as unto the weaker vessel, and as being heirs together of the grace of life; that your prayers be not hindered" (1 Pet. 3:7).

g. Pride—"Two men went up into the temple to pray; the one a Pharisee, and the other a publican. The Pharisee stood and prayed thus with himself, God, I thank thee, that I am not as other men are, extortioners, unjust, adulterers, or even as this publican. I fast twice in the week, I give tithes of all that I possess. And the publican, standing afar off, would not lift up so much as his eyes unto heaven, but smote upon his breast, saying, God be merciful to me a sinner. I tell you, this man went down to his house justified rather than the other: for every one that exalteth himself shall be abased; and he that humbleth himself shall be exalted" (Luke 18:10-14).

h. Robbing God—"Will a man rob God? Yet ye have robbed me. But ye say, Wherein have we robbed thee? In tithes and offerings. Ye are cursed with a curse: for ye have robbed me, even this whole nation. Bring ye all the tithes into the storehouse, that there may be meat in mine house, and prove me now herewith, saith the LORD of hosts, if I will not open you the windows of heaven, and pour you out a blessing, that there shall not be room enough to receive it" (Mal. 3:8-10).

i. Refusing to help the needy—"Whoso stoppeth his ears at the cry of the poor, he also shall cry himself, but shall not be heard" (Prov. 21:13). "Hereby perceive we the love of God, because he laid down his life for us: and we ought to lay down our lives for the brethren. But whoso hath this world's good, and seeth his brother have need, and shutteth up his bowels of compassion from him, how dwelleth the love of God in him?" (1 John 3:16-17).

j. Refusing to submit to biblical teaching—"He that turneth away his ear from hearing the law, even his prayer shall be abomination" (Prov. 28:9). (See also Prov. 1:24-31; Zech. 7:11-14.)

k. Refusing to forgive or to be forgiven—"Therefore if thou bring thy gift to the altar, and there rememberest that thy brother hath aught against thee; leave there thy gift before the altar, and go thy way; first be reconciled to thy brother, and then come and offer thy gift" (Matt. 5:23-24). "And forgive us our debts, as we forgive our debtors. . . . For if ye forgive men their trespasses, your heavenly Father will also forgive you" (Matt. 6:12, 14).

9. Qualifications of prayer—What are the ground rules of prayer? The following points absolutely must be met.

a. Prayer should be humble—"LORD, thou hast heard the desire of the humble: thou wilt prepare their heart, thou wilt cause thine ear to hear" (Psa. 10:17). (See also Luke 18:13-14.)

b. Prayer should be bold—"These things have I written unto you that believe on the name of the Son of God; that ye may know that ye have eternal life, and that ye may believe on the name of the Son of God. And this is the confidence that we have in him, that, if we ask any thing according to his will, he heareth us: And if we know that he hear us, whatsoever we ask, we know that we have the petitions that we desired of him" (1 John 5:13-15).

c. Prayer should be in faith—"But without faith it is impossible to please him: for he that cometh to God must believe that he is, and that he is a rewarder of them that diligently seek him" (Heb. 11:6).

d. Prayer should be sincere—"The LORD is nigh unto all them that call upon him, to all that call upon him in truth" (Psa. 145:18).

e. Prayer should be simple—"But when ye pray, use not vain repetitions, as the heathen do: for they think that they shall be heard for their much speaking" (Matt. 6:7).

f. Prayer should be persistent—"And shall not God avenge his own elect, which cry day and night unto him, though he bear long with them?" (Luke 18:7). "Continue in prayer, and watch in the same with thanksgiving" (Col. 4:2).

g. Prayer should be definite—"One thing have I desired of the LORD, that will I seek after; that I may dwell in the house of the LORD all the days of my life, to behold the beauty of the LORD, and to enquire in his temple" (Psa. 27:4). "Peter therefore was kept in prison: but prayer was made without ceasing of the church unto God for him" (Acts 12:5).

All too often our prayers are so vague and indefinite as to render them totally meaningless. Petitions such as "Lord, save that soul nearest hell," or "Heal all the sick and comfort all the lonely," simply provide no basis for divine action.

h. Prayer should be in accord with Scripture—"And this is the confidence that we have in him, that, if we ask any thing according to his will, he heareth us" (1 John 5:14). Prayer must be grounded in and bounded by the Word of God if we are to find his will for our life.

K. Justification

1. The definition of justification

a. Negative considerations (what it is *not*)

(1) It does not mean to be acquitted, that is, to successfully defend oneself against all charges—"Now we know that what things soever the law saith, it saith to them who are under the law: that every mouth may be stopped, and all the world may become guilty before God" (Rom. 3:19).

(2) It does not mean to be pardoned, that is, to be found guilty but given a second chance.

(3) It does not mean to be paroled, that is, to be guilty and set free with certain restrictions.

b. Positive considerations (what it *is*)—The great theologian A. H. Strong has defined justification in the following way: "By *justification* we mean that judicial act of God which, on account of Christ, to whom the sinner is united by faith, He declares that sinner to be no longer exposed to the penalty of the law, but restored to His favor" (*Systematic Theology*, p. 849).

Justification is thus that legal act whereby man's status before God is changed for the good.

2. The need for justification—In his Epistle to the Romans, the Apostle Paul presents sinful man in a courtroom on trial for his very life. The *charge* is high treason against the King of the universe. "For all have sinned, and come short of the glory of God" (Rom. 3:23).

a. The presiding *Judge* is the Lord Jesus Christ himself—"For the Father judgeth no man, but hath committed all judgment unto the Son" (John 5:22). "Because he hath appointed a day, in the which he will judge the world in righteousness by that man whom he hath ordained; whereof he hath given assurance unto all men, in that he hath raised him from the dead" (Acts 17:31).

b. The *jury* is made up of the Law of God and the deeds of man—"Who will render to every man according to his deeds. . . . For as many as have sinned without law shall also perish without law: and as many as have sinned in the law shall be judged by the law" (Rom. 2:6, 12).

After proper deliberation a just and fair *verdict* of "guilty" is returned. (See Rom. 3:9-20.)

c. A terrifying *sentence* is then imposed—spiritual death, meaning to be forever separated from God to suffer throughout all eternity in the lake of fire— "For the wages of sin is death" (Rom. 6:23). "Then shall he say also unto them on the left hand, Depart from me, ye cursed, into everlasting fire, prepared for the devil and his angels" (Matt. 25:41). "And whosoever was not found written in the book of life was cast into the lake of fire" (Rev. 20:15).

In light of all this, it can be readily seen that a desperate need for justification existed.

3. The miracle of justification—Up to this point the case of God against man has pretty well followed the format of earthly jurisprudence. But suddenly something totally different and unexpected takes place that would surely cause every earthly court reporter to gasp in utter amazement. After the Judge has carefully heard all the evidence and patiently listened to all the pleas, he finds no other choice but to invoke the supreme penalty, lest true justice be denied. But before the terrible sentence can be carried out, this same Judge quietly closes the case book, lays down the heavenly gavel, rises to his feet, takes off his judicial robes, and goes out to die for these convicted defendants. This and this alone is justification.

The corrupt, doomed, and naked sinner may now be cleansed, delivered, and clothed in the very righteousness of Christ himself.

Stated yet another way, an earthly judge might approach a guilty defendant in one of three possible ways.

a. He could *condemn* the man, and thus fulfill the demands of justice.

b. He could *compromise* with the man, and thus frustrate the demands of justice.

c. He could seek to somehow *clear* the man—The divine Judge, of course, chose the third approach; namely, clearing the guilty defendant through justification.

4. The method of justification—"How then can man be justified with God? or how can he be clean that is born of a woman?" (Job 25:4). "Therefore it is of faith, that it might be by grace" (Rom. 4:16).

a. It is by faith—"Therefore being justified by faith, we have peace with God through our Lord Jesus Christ" (Rom. 5:1). This is the only way for the sinner to be saved.

One of the great Old Testament examples of salvation can be found in Numbers 21 (and referred to in John 3). At that time many sinning Israelites had suffered fatal wounds by poisonous snakes. But God offered a cure, requiring only that, by faith, the stricken victim gaze upon a brass serpent atop a pole.

(1) The events as reported by Moses—"And Moses made a serpent of brass, and put it upon a pole, and it came to pass, that if a serpent had bitten any man, when he beheld the serpent of brass, he lived" (Num. 21:9).

(2) The event as recalled by Jesus—"And as Moses lifted up the serpent in the wilderness, even so must the Son of man be lifted up" (John 3:14).

b. It is by grace—"Being justified freely by his grace through the redemption that is in Christ Jesus" (Rom. 3:24). "That being justified by his grace, we should be made heirs according to the hope of eternal life" (Titus 3:7). This is the best way for God to be glorified. (See Eph. 2:1-10.)

Man justifies only the innocent; but God, only the guilty. Man justifies on the basis of self-merit; but God, on the basis of the Savior's merit.

5. The two great examples of justification
a. Abraham—He was justified apart from circumcision. "And he believed in the LORD; and he counted it to him for righteousness" (Gen. 15:6).

We are informed he was *86* at the time of his conversion. "And Abram was fourscore and six years old, when Hagar bare Ishmael to Abram" (Gen. 16:16). We are told he was *99* when circumcision took place. "And Abraham was ninety years old and nine, when he was circumcised in the flesh of his foreskin" (Gen. 17:24). (See especially Rom. 4:1-5, 9-25.)

Note: Some have imagined a contradiction between *Paul* and *James* concerning the justification of Abraham. "Now to him that worketh is the reward not reckoned of grace, but of debt. But to him that worketh not, but believeth on him that justifieth the ungodly, his faith is counted for righteousness" (Rom. 4:4-5). "Ye see then how that by works a man is justified, and not by faith only" (James 2:24).

There exists no such contradiction. Let us note what these two men say about justification. *Paul* says that through *faith* a man is justified before *God*. *James* says that through *works* a man is justified before *men*. *Paul* says *faith* is the *root* of justification. *James* says *works* are the *fruit* of justification.

The teaching of the Reformation was: "Good works make not a good man, but a good man doeth good works."

b. David—He was justified apart from the Levitical offerings. "Blessed is he whose transgression is forgiven, whose sin is covered. Blessed is the man unto whom the LORD imputeth not iniquity, and in whose spirit there is no guile" (Psa. 32:1-2). "For thou desirest not sacrifice; else would I give it: thou delightest not in burnt offering. The sacrifices of God are a broken spirit: a broken and a contrite heart, O God, thou wilt not despise" (Psa. 51:16-17). "Even as David also describeth the blessedness of the man, unto whom God imputeth righteousness without works, saying, Blessed are they whose iniquities are forgiven, and whose sins are covered. Blessed is the man to whom the Lord will not impute sin" (Rom. 4:6-8).

6. The results of justification
a. The remission of sin's penalty—"Be it known unto you therefore, men and brethren, that through this man is preached unto you the forgiveness of sins: And by him all that believe are justified from all things, from which ye could not be justified by the law of Moses" (Acts 13:38-39). (See also Rom. 8:1, 33-34.)

b. The restoration to divine favor—See Romans 5:1-11.

c. The imputation of Christ's righteousness—"For what saith the scripture? Abraham believed God, and it was counted unto him for righteousness. . . . Now it was not written for his sake alone, that it was imputed to him; but for us also, to whom it shall be imputed, if we believe on him that raised up Jesus our Lord from the dead" (Rom. 4:3, 23-24). "For he hath made him to be sin for us, who knew no sin; that we might be made the righteousness of God in him" (2 Cor. 5:21).

L. Sanctification—"And for their sakes I sanctify myself, that they also might be sanctified through the truth" (John 17:19). "Husbands, love your wives, even as Christ also loved the church, and gave himself for it; that he might sanctify and cleanse it with the washing of water by the word" (Eph. 5:25-26). "For this is the will of God, even your sanctification" (1 Thess. 4:3). "And the very God of peace sanctify you wholly" (1 Thess. 5:23).

1. Sanctification defined

a. Negative considerations (what it is *not*)

(1) It is *not* the eradication of the sinful nature—In fact, those who boast of the eradication of their sinful natures actually claim that which Paul, James, and John admit they had not attained.

(a) Paul's testimony—"Not as though I had already attained, either were already perfect: but I follow after, if that I may apprehend that for which also I am apprehended of Christ Jesus. Brethren, I count not myself to have apprehended: but this one thing I do, forgetting those things which are behind, and reaching forth unto those things which are before, I press toward the mark for the prize of the high calling of God in Christ Jesus" (Phil. 3:12-14).

(b) James's testimony—"For in many things we offend all. If any man offend not in word, the same is a perfect man, and able also to bridle the whole body" (James 3:2).

(c) John's testimony—"If we say that we have no sin, we deceive ourselves, and the truth is not in us. If we confess our sins, he is faithful and just to forgive us our sins, and to cleanse us from all unrighteousness" (1 John 1:8-9).

Note: The opposite and equally erroneous position of eradicationism is *antinomianism*, which means literally "against the law." This was the theory that a Christian was under no moral obligation whatsoever to observe the commandments. Thus, the first view was an attempt to *eliminate* sin, while the second simply *enjoyed* it. Both sinless perfection and sinful imperfections are unscriptural doctrines. Although the Christian cannot be sinless, he can, nevertheless, through sanctification, *sin less*.

(2) It is *not* the "second blessing"—In 2 Corinthians Paul writes: "And in this confidence I was minded to come unto you before, that ye might have a second benefit" (2 Cor. 1:15).

Some have taken their theology of the second blessing from this verse. However, Paul describes the Corinthian believers in his first epistle as already being sanctified: "Unto the church of God which is at Corinth, to them that are sanctified in Christ Jesus, called to be saints, with all that in every place call upon the name of Jesus Christ our Lord, both theirs and ours" (1 Cor. 1:2). "And such were some of you: but ye are washed, but ye are sanctified, but ye are justified in the name of the Lord Jesus, and by the Spirit of our God" (1 Cor. 6:11).

(3) It is *not* the baptism by the Holy Spirit—Paul states *all* believers have

been baptized by the Holy Spirit, regardless of their personal spiritual condition. "For by one Spirit are we all baptized into one body, whether we be Jews or Gentiles, whether we be bond or free; and have been all made to drink into one Spirit" (1 Cor. 12:13).

Compare this with the following: "And I, brethren, could not speak unto you as unto spiritual, but as unto carnal, even as unto babes in Christ. I have fed you with milk, and not with meat: for hitherto ye were not able to bear it, neither yet now are ye able. For ye are yet carnal: for whereas there is among you envying, and strife, and divisions, are ye not carnal, and walk as men? For while one saith, I am of Paul; and another, I am of Apollos; are ye not carnal?" (1 Cor. 3:1-4).

b. Positive considerations (what it *is*)—Sanctification occurs in various forms some 300 times in the New Testament and 760 times in the Old Testament, for a total of 1,060 in the Bible. The basic meaning in all these instances is "to set apart." Thus:

(1) Days and seasons were sanctified—"And God blessed the seventh day, and sanctified it: because that in it he had rested from all his work which God created and made" (Gen. 2:3). "Keep the sabbath day to sanctify it, as the LORD thy God hath commanded thee" (Deut. 5:12). "Sanctify ye a fast, call a solemn assembly, gather the elders and all the inhabitants of the land into the house of the LORD your God, and cry unto the LORD" (Joel 1:14). "Blow the trumpet in Zion, sanctify a fast, call a solemn assembly" (Joel 2:15). (See also Neh. 13:19-22.)

(2) Physical objects were sanctified.

   (a) Mount Sinai—"And Moses said unto the LORD, The people cannot come up to mount Sinai: for thou chargedst us, saying, Set bounds about the mount, and sanctify it" (Exod. 19:23).

   (b) The Levitical offerings—"And thou shalt sanctify the breast of the wave offering, and the shoulder of the heave offering, which is waved, and which is heaved up, of the ram of the consecration, even of that which is for Aaron, and of that which is for his sons" (Exod. 29:27).

   (c) The fields—"And if a man sanctify unto the LORD a field which he hath bought, which is not of the fields of his possession" (Lev. 27:22).

   (d) The tabernacle—"And I will sanctify the tabernacle of the congregation, and the altar: I will sanctify also both Aaron and his sons, to minister to me in the priest's office" (Exod. 29:44).

   (e) The city gates—"Then Eliashib the high priest rose up with his brethren the priests, and they builded the sheep gate; they sanctified it, and set up the doors of it; even unto the tower of Meah they sanctified it, unto the tower of Hananeel" (Neh. 3:1).

   (f) Houses—"And when a man shall sanctify his house to be holy unto the LORD, then the priest shall estimate it, whether it be good or bad: as the priest shall estimate it, so shall it stand" (Lev. 27:14).

(3) People were to sanctify themselves—"For I am the LORD your God: ye shall therefore sanctify yourselves, and ye shall be holy; for I am holy: neither shall ye defile yourselves with any manner of creeping thing that creepeth upon the earth" (Lev. 11:44).

(4) One man could sanctify another—"Sanctify unto me all the firstborn,

whatsoever openeth the womb among the children of Israel, both of man and of beast: it is mine" (Exod. 13:2).

(5) Evildoers sanctified themselves—"They that sanctify themselves, and purify themselves in the gardens behind one tree in the midst, eating swine's flesh, and the abomination, and the mouse, shall be consumed together, saith the LORD" (Isa. 66:17).

(6) Israel was punished for not sanctifying God—"Because ye trespassed against me among the children of Israel at the waters of Meribah-Kadesh, in the wilderness of Zin; because ye sanctified me not in the midst of the children of Israel" (Deut. 32:51).

(7) God sanctified Christ—"Say ye of him, whom the Father hath sanctified, and sent into the world, Thou blasphemest; because I said, I am the Son of God?" (John 10:36).

(8) Christ sanctified his disciples—"I pray for them: I pray not for the world, but for them which thou hast given me; for they are thine" (John 17:9).

(9) A believing married partner can sanctify the unbelieving partner—"For the unbelieving husband is sanctified by the wife, and the unbelieving wife is sanctified by the husband: else were your children unclean; but now are they holy" (1 Cor. 7:14).

(10) Carnal Christians are said to be sanctified—"Unto the church of God which is at Corinth, to them that are sanctified in Christ Jesus, called to be saints, with all that in every place call upon the name of Jesus Christ our Lord, both theirs and ours" (1 Cor. 1:2). "For ye are yet carnal: for whereas there is among you envying, and strife, and divisions, are ye not carnal, and walk as men?" (1 Cor. 3:3).

(11) Believers are to sanctify God—"But sanctify the Lord God in your hearts: and be ready always to give an answer to every man that asketh you a reason of the hope that is in you with meekness and fear" (1 Pet. 3:15).

2. Sanctification contrasted—At this point it may help to contrast sanctification with justification.

   a. Justification deals with our *standing,* while sanctification deals with our *state.*

   b. Justification is that which God does *for* us, while sanctification is that which God does *in* us.

   c. Justification is an *act,* while sanctification is a *work.*

   d. Justification is the *means,* while sanctification is the *end.*

   e. Justification makes us *safe,* while sanctification makes us *sound.*

   f. Justification *declares* us good, while sanctification *makes* us good.

   g. Justification removes the *guilt* and *penalty* of sin, while sanctification checks the *growth* and *power* of sin.

   h. Justification furnishes the *track* that leads to heaven, while sanctification furnishes the *train.*

3. Sanctification achieved—In Romans 6 Paul clearly lays out the program leading to that lifelong process of growing in grace and spiritual maturity, which is sanctification. The plan involves three simple commands.

   a. "Know ye"—See Romans 6:1-10.

      (1) That we have been "buried with him [Christ] by baptism into death"—"Therefore we are buried with him by baptism into death: that like as Christ was raised up from the dead by the glory of the Father, even so we also should walk in newness of life" (Rom. 6:4).

Here Paul says Christ not only died *for* me, but *as* me. The word *baptism* simply means "identification." This identification with Christ on Calvary is one of many "dry baptisms" in the Bible. Others would include:

(a) The baptism of sin and suffering upon Christ—"But Jesus answered and said, Ye know not what ye ask. Are ye able to drink of the cup that I shall drink of, and to be baptized with the baptism that I am baptized with? They say unto him, We are able" (Matt. 20:22).

(b) The baptism of the Holy Spirit upon believers at Pentecost—"For John truly baptized with water; but ye shall be baptized with the Holy Ghost not many days hence" (Acts 1:5).

(c) The baptism of believers into the body of Christ—"For by one Spirit are we all baptized into one body, whether we be Jews or Gentiles, whether we be bond or free; and have been all made to drink into one Spirit" (1 Cor. 12:13).

(d) The baptism "for the dead"—"Else what shall they do which are baptized for the dead, if the dead rise not at all? why are they then baptized for the dead?" (1 Cor. 15:29). Note: This is thought to refer to the act of living believers identifying themselves with martyred believers by picking up their fallen banners.

(e) The baptism "unto Moses"—"And were all baptized unto Moses in the cloud and in the sea" (1 Cor. 10:2).

(f) The baptism of judgment during the tribulation (Matt. 3:11-12)

(2) That we have been "planted together . . . in the likeness of his resurrection"—"For if we have been planted together in the likeness of his death, we shall be also in the likeness of his resurrection" (Rom. 6:5).

The believer has now been "transplanted" three times:

(a) To the Garden of Eden, where he sinned with Adam

(b) To the cross, where he died with Christ

(c) To the tomb, where he arose with Christ

(3) That because of these two facts, the believer is:

(a) Delivered from his sin—"God forbid. How shall we, that are dead to sin, live any longer therein? . . . Knowing this, that our old man is crucified with him, that the body of sin might be destroyed, that henceforth we should not serve sin. For he that is dead is freed from sin" (Rom. 6:2, 6-7).

(b) Delivered to his Savior—"Now if we be dead with Christ, we believe that we shall also live with him: Knowing that Christ being raised from the dead dieth no more; death hath no more dominion over him. For in that he died, he died unto sin once: but in that he liveth, he liveth unto God" (Rom. 6:8-10).

Death cancels all obligations. Sin here is personified as a cruel tyrant who taxes his subjects beyond endurance. The only way to beat the rap is to die. This then renders inactive (but does not remove) the body of sin and makes it powerless. (See Eph. 4:22-24; Col. 3:9-10.)

b. "Reckon ye"—See Romans 6:11-12. This simply means that by faith we are to act upon these facts regardless of any personal feelings.

c. "Yield ye"—Romans 6:13-23

(1) We are to stop yielding (present tense) our body members as instruments of unrighteousness.

(2) We are to once for all (aorist tense) yield our body members as instruments of righteousness.

There are three Latin theological terms that may clarify this precious doctrine. These are:

(a) *Non posse non pecare*—not able not to sin. This refers to believers before their salvation.

(b) *Posse non pecare*—able not to sin. This describes them after their salvation. They now have the power to live victorious lives.

(c) *Non posse pecare*—not able to sin. This describes their existence after the Rapture.

M. Glorification—"Moreover whom he did predestinate, them he also called: and whom he called, them he also justified: and whom he justified, them he also glorified" (Rom. 8:30). "By whom also we have access by faith into this grace wherein we stand, and rejoice in hope of the glory of God" (Rom. 5:2). "For I reckon that the sufferings of this present time are not worthy to be compared with the glory which shall be revealed in us" (Rom. 8:18).

"It is sown in dishonour; it is raised in glory: it is sown in weakness; it is raised in power" (1 Cor. 15:43). "When Christ, who is our life, shall appear, then shall ye also appear with him in glory" (Col. 3:4). "The elders which are among you I exhort, who am also an elder, and a witness of the sufferings of Christ, and also a partaker of the glory that shall be revealed" (1 Pet. 5:1).

1. The meaning of glorification—It refers to the ultimate and absolute physical, mental, and spiritual perfections of all believers. (See Rom. 8:22-23; 1 Cor. 15:41-44; 15:51-55; 2 Cor. 4:14-18; Jude 24-25.)

2. The time of glorification—It will begin at the Rapture and continue throughout all eternity. "Behold, I shew you a mystery; We shall not all sleep, but we shall all be changed, in a moment, in the twinkling of an eye, at the last trump: for the trumpet shall sound, and the dead shall be raised incorruptible, and we shall be changed. For this corruptible must put on incorruption, and this mortal must put on immortality" (1 Cor. 15:51-53). (See also 1 Thess. 4:13-18.)

3. The purpose of glorification—Glorification is both the logical and necessary final side of the great salvation triangle. It completes justification and sanctification.

a. In the past—Christ the Prophet saved us from the penalty of sin through justification (Eph. 2:8; Titus 3:5).

b. In the present—Christ the Priest saves us from the power of sin through sanctification (Heb. 7:25).

c. In the future—Christ the King shall save us from the presence of sin through glorification (Rom. 5:9-10).

4. The results of glorification—What kind of body will the believer possess?

a. It will be a body like Christ's body—"Who shall change our vile body, that it may be fashioned like unto his glorious body, according to the working whereby he is able even to subdue all things unto himself" (Phil. 3:21). "Beloved, now are we the sons of God, and it doth not yet appear what we shall be: but we know that, when he shall appear, we shall be like him; for we shall see him as he is" (1 John 3:2).

b. It will be a body of flesh and bone—"Behold my hands and my feet, that it is

I myself: handle me, and see; for a spirit hath not flesh and bones, as ye see me have" (Luke 24:39).

c. It will be a recognizable body—"For now we see through a glass, darkly; but then face to face: now I know in part; but then shall I know even as also I am known" (1 Cor. 13:12).

d. It will be a body in which the Spirit predominates—"It is sown a natural body; it is raised a spiritual body. There is a natural body, and there is a spiritual body" (1 Cor. 15:44). "And as we have borne the image of the earthy, we shall also bear the image of the heavenly" (1 Cor. 15:49).

This situation is, of course, reversed today, as seen in the following verse: "Watch ye and pray, lest ye enter into temptation. The spirit truly is ready, but the flesh is weak" (Mark 14:38).

e. It will be a body unlimited by time, gravity, or space—On at least three occasions during the early days following his resurrection, our Lord defied all natural laws by suddenly appearing in and out of locked rooms to comfort his disciples.

(1) First occasion—He disappears from the home of two disciples in Emmaus. "And their eyes were opened, and they knew him; and he vanished out of their sight" (Luke 24:31).

(2) Second occasion—He appears to the apostles in Jerusalem. "Then the same day at evening, being the first day of the week, when the doors were shut where the disciples were assembled for fear of the Jews, came Jesus and stood in the midst, and saith unto them, Peace be unto you" (John 20:19).

(3) Third occasion—He appears (eight days later) to 11 apostles in Jerusalem. "And after eight days again his disciples were within, and Thomas with them: then came Jesus, the doors being shut, and stood in the midst, and said, Peace be unto you" (John 20:26).

f. It will be an eternal body—"For we know that if our earthly house of this tabernacle were dissolved, we have a building of God, an house not made with hands, eternal in the heavens" (2 Cor. 5:1).

g. It will be a glorious body—"For I reckon that the sufferings of this present time are not worthy to be compared with the glory which shall be revealed in us" (Rom. 8:18). (See 1 Cor. 15:43.)

The Hebrew word for glory is *kabod*, which means literally "to be heavy," lending itself to that one laden down with riches (Gen. 31:1), power (Isa. 8:7), and position (Gen. 45:13). It can also refer to moral beauty (Exod. 33:18-23).

The Greek word for glory is *doxa*, which means literally "to manifest an honorable opinion." Both words often suggest the brightness and brilliance of supernatural light. Putting all these meanings together, it may be suggested that the believer's glorified body will be supernaturally enriched and empowered to serve God in an appointed position by radiating the brightness of grace to angels and the universe.

N. Preservation—"And the very God of peace sanctify you wholly; and I pray God your whole spirit and soul and body be preserved blameless unto the coming of our Lord Jesus Christ. Faithful is he that calleth you, who also will do it" (1 Thess. 5:23-24). "Jude, the servant of Jesus Christ, and brother of James, to them that are sanctified by God the Father, and preserved in Jesus Christ, and called" (Jude 1).

This word, which deals with the burning question, "Can a saved person ever lose his or her salvation?" will be fully considered in section XI, "The Security of Salvation."

O. Origination—"Wherefore David blessed the LORD before all the congregation: and David said, Blessed be thou, LORD God of Israel our father, for ever and ever. Thine, O LORD, is the greatness, and the power, and the glory, and the victory, and the majesty: for all that is in the heaven and in the earth is thine; thine is the kingdom, O LORD, and thou art exalted as head above all. Both riches and honour come of thee, and thou reignest over all; and in thine hand is power and might; and in thine hand it is to make great, and to give strength unto all. Now therefore, our God, we thank thee, and praise thy glorious name. But who am I, and what is my people, that we should be able to offer so willingly after this sort? for all things come of thee, and of thine own have we given thee" (1 Chron. 29:10-14).

We now briefly (and bravely) discuss the final word concept in the vocabulary of salvation. It deals with what is, without doubt, the most profound (and often perverted) subject in the entire Word of God. Throughout church history (especially from the sixteenth century onward) no other single theme has stirred such thunder and turmoil as has this subject. Some detest it, while others delight in it, but no honest Bible student can ignore it. By what means and for what reasons was the plan of salvation originated? Why are not all men saved? Can indeed all men be saved?

1. The terms included within the subject of salvation origination—Eight words here must be considered: *decree, ordain, foreknowledge, election, counsel, predestination, purpose,* and *called.*

   a. Decree—"For by him were all things created, that are in heaven, and that are in earth, visible and invisible, whether they be thrones, or dominions, or principalities, or powers: all things were created by him, and for him" (Col. 1:16). "Thou art worthy, O Lord, to receive glory and honour and power: for thou hast created all things, and for thy pleasure they are and were created" (Rev. 4:11).

   The decree of God is defined by the Westminster *Shorter Catechism* as follows: "The decree of God is His eternal purpose according to the counsel of His will, whereby, for His own glory, He hath foreordained whatsoever comes to pass."

   Louis Berkhof lists seven characteristics involved in this decree.

   (1) It is founded in divine wisdom (Eph. 3:9-11; Psa. 104:24; Prov. 3:19).
   (2) It is eternal (Acts 15:18; Eph. 1:4; 2 Tim. 1:9).

   > The divine decree is eternal in the sense that it lies entirely in eternity. In a certain sense it can be said that all acts of God are eternal, since there is no succession of moments in the Divine Being. But some of them terminate in time, as, for instance, creation and justification. Hence we do not call them eternal but temporal acts of God. The decree, however, while it relates to things outside of God, remains in itself an act within the Divine Being, and is therefore eternal in the strictest sense of the word. (*Systematic Theology,* pp. 103–104)

   (3) It is efficacious (effective) (Psa. 33:11; Prov. 19:21; Isa. 46:9-10; 14:24).

   > This does not mean that God has determined to bring to pass Himself

by a direct application of His power all things which are included in His decree, but only that what He has decreed will certainly come to pass; that nothing can thwart His purpose. (Ibid., p. 104)

(4) It is immutable (Acts 2:22-24).

Man may and often does alter his plans for various reasons. It may be that in making his plans he lacked seriousness of purpose, that he did not fully realize what the plan involved or that he is wanting the power to carry it out. But in God nothing of the kind is conceivable. He is not deficient in knowledge, veracity, or power. Therefore, He need not change His decree because of a mistake of ignorance, nor because of inability to carry it out. And He will not change it, because He is the immutable God, and because He is faithful and true. (Ibid., pp. 104–105)

(5) It is unconditional or absolute (Eph. 2:8; 1 Pet. 1:2)—This means that it is not dependent in any of its particulars on anything that is not part and parcel of the decree itself.
(6) It is universal or all-comprehensive.

The decree includes whatsoever comes to pass in the world, whether it be in the physical or in the moral realm, whether it be good or evil, Eph. 1:11. It includes: (a) the good actions of men, Eph. 2:10; (b) their wicked acts, Prov. 16:4; Acts 2:23; 4:27, 28; (c) contingent events, Gen. 45:8; 50:20; Prov. 16:33; (d) the means as well as the end, Psa. 119:89-91; 2 Thess. 2:13; Eph. 1:4 (e) the duration of man's life, Job 14:5; Psa. 39:4, and the place of his habitation, Acts 17:26. (Ibid., p. 105)

(7) With reference to sin, it is permissive.

It is customary to speak of the decree of God respecting moral evil as permissive. By His decree God rendered the sinful actions of man infallibly certain without deciding to effectuate them by acting immediately upon and in the finite will. This means that God does not positively work in man "both to will and to do" when man goes contrary to His revealed will. . . . It is a decree which renders the future sinful act absolutely certain, but in which God determines (a) not to hinder the sinful self-determination of the finite will; and (b) to regulate and control the result of this sinful self-determination. (Ibid., p. 105)

"So they did eat, and were well filled: for he gave them their own desire" (Psa. 78:29). "And he gave them their request; but sent leanness into their soul" (Psa. 106:15). "Who in times past suffered all nations to walk in their own ways" (Acts 14:16).
   b. Ordain—The Greek word for *ordain* is *tasso*, also translated "appoint." To ordain means "to place or put in order, to arrange."
   (1) In the New Testament we have three nontheological examples of this—"Then the eleven disciples went away into Galilee, into a mountain where Jesus had appointed them" (Matt. 28:16). "For I also am a man set under authority, having under me soldiers, and I say unto one, Go, and he goeth; and to another, Come, and he cometh; and to my servant, Do

this, and he doeth it" (Luke 7:8). "Let every soul be subject unto the
higher powers. For there is no power but of God: the powers that be are
ordained of God" (Rom. 13:1).

(2) In the theological usage of the word, note—"And when the Gentiles
heard this, they were glad, and glorified the word of the Lord: and as
many as were ordained to eternal life believed" (Acts 13:48). "Forasmuch
as ye know that ye were not redeemed with corruptible things, as silver
and gold, from your vain conversation received by tradition from your
fathers; but with the precious blood of Christ, as of a lamb without
blemish and without spot: Who verily was foreordained before the
foundation of the world, but was manifest in these last times for you"
(1 Pet. 1:18-20).

c. Foreknowledge—The Greek word for *foreknowledge* is *proginosko,* meaning
"to know experientially, to know beforehand." This prior knowledge is seen
operating in the following areas:

(1) The realm of creation itself—"Known unto God are all his works from
the beginning of the world" (Acts 15:18).

(2) The nation Israel—"Hear this word that the LORD hath spoken against
you, O children of Israel, against the whole family which I brought up
from the land of Egypt, saying, You only have I known of all the families
of the earth: therefore I will punish you for all your iniquities" (Amos
3:1-2). "I say then, Hath God cast away his people? God forbid . . . God
hath not cast away his people which he foreknew" (Rom. 11:1-2).

(3) The crucifixion and resurrection of Christ—"And truly the Son of man
goeth, as it was determined: but woe unto that man by whom he is
betrayed!" (Luke 22:22). "Him, being delivered by the determinate
counsel and foreknowledge of God, ye have taken, and by wicked hands
have crucified and slain: Whom God hath raised up, having loosed the
pains of death: because it was not possible that he should be holden
of it" (Acts 2:23-24). "Who [Christ] verily was foreordained before the
foundation of the world" (1 Pet. 1:20). "And all that dwell upon the earth
shall worship him, whose names are not written in the book of life of the
Lamb slain from the foundation of the world" (Rev. 13:8).

(4) The believer

(a) His physical condition—See Psalm 139.

(b) His spiritual condition—"For whom he did foreknow, he also did
predestinate" (Rom. 8:29). "Elect according to the foreknowledge of
God the Father" (1 Pet. 1:2).

d. Election—The Greek word for *election* is *eklektos.* To elect is "to pick or
choose from a number." It means to select for an appointed task.

(1) Christ was God's elect—"A living stone, disallowed indeed of men, but
chosen of God, and precious" (1 Pet. 2:4). (See also Isa. 42:1; 49:5; Luke
23:35; 1 Pet. 2:6.)

(2) A certain group of angels have been elected—"I charge thee before God,
and the Lord Jesus Christ, and the elect angels" (1 Tim. 5:21).

(3) Old Testament Israel was an elect nation—"The God of this people of
Israel chose our fathers" (Acts 13:17). (See also Deut. 4:37; 7:6-8; 1 Kings
3:8; Isa. 44:1-2; Matt. 24:22, 24, 31; Rom. 9:25-27.)

(4) Believing Jews today are an elect group—"Even so then at this present

time also there is a remnant according to the election of grace" (Rom.
11:5).
(5) Certain men were elected to perform important tasks in God's ministry.
   (a) Jeremiah—"Before I formed thee in the belly I knew thee; and before
        thou camest forth out of the womb I sanctified thee, and I ordained
        thee a prophet unto the nations" (Jer. 1:5).
   (b) David—"And he sent, and brought him in. Now he was ruddy, and
        withal of a beautiful countenance, and goodly to look to. And the
        LORD said, Arise, anoint him: for this is he" (1 Sam. 16:12). (See also
        2 Sam. 7:8; Psa. 78:70-72.)
   (c) Abraham (Gen. 12:1-3)
   (d) John the Baptist (Luke 1:13-17)
   (e) Paul—"But the Lord said unto him, Go thy way: for he is a chosen
        vessel unto me, to bear my name before the Gentiles, and kings, and
        the children of Israel" (Acts 9:15).
   (f) Isaac—"Neither, because they are the seed of Abraham, are they all
        children: but, in Isaac shall thy seed be called" (Rom. 9:7).
   (g) Jacob—"(For the children being not yet born, neither having done any
        good or evil, that the purpose of God according to election might
        stand, not of works, but of him that calleth)" (Rom. 9:11).
(6) The 12 apostles were elected by God—"And when he had called unto
     him his twelve disciples" (Matt. 10:1). "Ye have not chosen me, but I have
     chosen you, and ordained you" (John 15:16). "Jesus answered them,
     Have not I chosen you twelve, and one of you is a devil?" (John 6:70).
     (See also Acts 1:2, 24; 10:41.)
(7) The plan of salvation was chosen by God—"But God hath chosen the
     foolish things of the world to confound the wise; and God hath chosen
     the weak things of the world to confound the things which are mighty;
     and base things of the world, and things which are despised, hath God
     chosen, yea, and things which are not, to bring to nought things that are"
     (1 Cor. 1:27-28).
(8) The people of salvation were chosen by God—"Who shall lay any thing
     to the charge of God's elect?" (Rom. 8:33). "According as he hath chosen
     us in him before the foundation of the world" (Eph. 1:4). (See also 2 Thess
     2:13; 2 Tim. 2:10; Titus 1:1-2; James 2:5; 1 Pet. 1:1-2; 2:9; Rev. 17:14.)
e. Counsel—The Greek word for *counsel* is *boulema*, referring to "deliberate and
   willful intention." Biblical examples are:
(1) The intention of the Pharisees to kill Christ—"Then from that day forth
     they took counsel together for to put him to death" (John 11:53).
(2) The intention of the Pharisees to kill Peter and John—"When they heard
     that, they were cut to the heart, and took counsel to slay them" (Acts
     5:33).
(3) The intention of the centurion to save Paul—"But the centurion, willing
     to save Paul, kept them from their purpose; and commanded that they
     which could swim should cast themselves first into the sea, and get to
     land" (Acts 27:43).
(4) The intention of God to offer up Christ—"Him, being delivered by the
     determinate counsel and foreknowledge of God, ye have taken, and by

wicked hands have crucified and slain" (Acts 2:23). (See also Acts 4:26-28.)

(5) The intention of God to save the elect (Eph. 1:11; Heb. 6:17)

(6) The intention of God to control all things—"Declaring the end from the beginning, and from ancient times the things that are not yet done, saying, My counsel shall stand, and I will do all my pleasure" (Isa. 46:10). (See Psa. 33:11; Prov. 14:21; Isa. 25:1; 46:10.)

f. Predestination—The Greek words for *predestination* are *proorizo* and *horizo*. To predestinate is to "mark out beforehand, to determine a boundary." The English word *horizon* comes from *horizo*. It is our horizon, of course, that marks out the earth from the sky. The Greek word is also translated as "determination" and "declaration." This word is used in reference to:

(1) The declaration of the deity of Christ—"And declared to be the Son of God with power, according to the spirit of holiness, by the resurrection from the dead" (Rom. 1:4). While Jesus was on earth, God the Father marked off the true identity and nature of his beloved Son, Jesus Christ.

(2) The predetermination of the death of Christ at the hands of wicked men—"Him, being delivered by the determinate counsel and fore-knowledge of God, ye have taken, and by wicked hands have crucified and slain" (Acts 2:23). (See also Luke 22:22; Acts 4:27-28.)

(3) The predetermining of national boundaries—See Acts 17:24-26.

(4) The predetermining of believers to be conformed to Christ—See Romans 8:29-30; Ephesians 1:9-12.

The Westminster Confession of Faith states this act of God as follows: "God from all eternity did by the most wise and holy counsel of His own Will, freely and unchangeable ordain whatsoever to pass: yet so as thereby neither is God the author of sin, nor is violence offered to the Will of the creatures, nor is the liberty of contingency of second causes taken away, but rather established."

g. Purpose—The Greek word for *purpose* is *prothesis*, literally meaning a "setting forth."

(1) The setting forth of the shewbread in the tabernacle (Luke 6:4; Heb. 9:2)

(2) The setting forth of nations for judgment

   (a) Assyria (Isa. 14:26)
   (b) Tyre (Isa. 23:9)
   (c) Babylon (Isa. 46:11)
   (d) Israel (Jer. 4:28; 51:29)

(3) The setting forth of Pharaoh as an object of God's judgment—"For the scripture saith unto Pharaoh, Even for this same purpose have I raised thee up, that I might shew my power in thee, and that my name might be declared throughout all the earth" (Rom. 9:17).

(4) The setting forth of the divine plan to work through Isaac (instead of Ishmael) and Jacob (instead of Esau)—See Romans 9:6-13.

h. Called—The Greek words for *called* are *kaleo* and *klesis*, meaning "to officially summon."

(1) As used in reference to Jesus' parables

   (a) The parable of the Lord of the vineyard—"So when even was come, the lord of the vineyard saith unto his steward, Call the labourers, and

give them their hire, beginning from the last unto the first" (Matt.
20:8).

(b) The parable of the departing master—"For the kingdom of heaven is
as a man travelling into a far country, who called his own servants,
and delivered unto them his goods" (Matt. 25:14).

(2) As used in reference to the call of the elect—"Moreover whom he did
predestinate, them he also called: and whom he called, them he also
justified: and whom he justified, them he also glorified" (Rom. 8:30).
"God is faithful, by whom ye were called unto the fellowship of his Son
Jesus Christ our Lord" (1 Cor. 1:9). (See also Eph. 4:1; 1 Thess. 2:12;
2 Thess. 1:11; 2 Tim. 1:9; Phil. 3:4; Heb. 9:25; 3:1; 2 Pet. 1:10.)

2. The two basic positions concerning the subject of salvation origination—Why
are some people saved and others lost? Does man have *any* say in his salvation?
Does he have *all* say? No serious Bible student denies the *fact* of God's election.
However, good men do disagree concerning the *nature* of this election.

a. Position number one

(1) Defined

The only people that God predestinates to be saved are those whom
He did foreknow, that is, those who, in His infinite knowledge, God
knows will, when given the opportunity, come to trust in Christ to be
saved. It is not that predestination *causes* people to trust Christ and be
saved. No, they are only predestinated to be saved because God
knows that they will put their trust in Christ. Predestination is based
wholly on God's foreknowledge. (John R. Rice, *Predestinated for Hell?
No!* p. 90)

Perhaps one of the most qualified theologians to hold this position is
Henry Thiessen. He writes:

Furthermore, He chose who He foreknew would accept Christ. The
Scriptures definitely base God's election on His foreknowledge:
"Whom He foreknew, He also foreordained, . . . and whom He foreordained, them He also called" (Romans 8:29-30); "to the elect . . .
according to the foreknowledge of God the Father" (1 Peter 1:1, 2).
Although we are nowhere told what it is in the foreknowledge of God
that determines His choice, the repeated teaching of Scripture that
man is responsible for accepting or rejecting salvation necessitates our
postulating that it is man's reaction to the revelation God has made of
Himself that is the basis of His election. May we repeat: Since mankind is hopelessly dead in trespasses and sins and can do nothing to
obtain salvation, God graciously restores to all men sufficient ability
to make a choice in the matter of submission to Him. This is the salva-
tion-bringing grace of God that has appeared to all men. In His foreknowledge He perceives what each one will do with this restored
ability, and elects men to salvation in harmony with His knowledge of
their choice of Him. There is no merit in this transaction. (*Systematic
Theology*, pp. 344–345)

(2) Defended—A number of scriptural principles are offered to support this
first position. Some are as follow:

(a) Because Christ is said to have died for all men—"In him was life; and the life was the light of men. The same came for a witness, to bear witness of the Light, that all men through him might believe" (John 1:4, 7). "And I, if I be lifted up from the earth, will draw all men unto me. This he said, signifying what death he should die. . . . And if any man hear my words, and believe not, I judge him not: for I came not to judge the world, but to save the world" (John 12:32-33, 47). "Therefore as by the offence of one judgment came upon all men to condemnation; even so by the righteousness of one the free gift came upon all men unto justification of life" (Rom. 5:18). (See also Rom. 8:32; 1 Tim. 2:6; 4:10; Heb. 2:9; 2 Pet. 2:1; 3:9; 1 John 2:2.)

(b) Because of the justice of God—Henry Thiessen writes:

> It is admitted that God is under no obligation to provide salvation for anyone, since all are responsible for their present lost condition. It is also admitted that God is not obliged actually to save anyone, even though Christ has provided salvation for men. But it is difficult to see how God can choose some from the mass of guilty and condemned men, provide salvation for them and efficiently secure their salvation, and do nothing about all the others, if, as we read, righteousness is the foundation of His throne. God would not be partial if He permitted all men to go to their deserved doom; but how can He be other than partial if He selects some from this multitude of men and does things for them and in them that He refuses to do for the others, if there is not something about the two classes that makes the difference? We hold that common grace is extended to all, and that everyone has the ability restored to him to "will to do His will." The salvation-bearing grace of God has appeared to all men; but some receive the grace of God in vain. It seems to us that only if God makes the same provisions for all and makes the same offers to all, is He truly just. (Ibid., pp. 346–347)

(c) Because Christ bore all our iniquities—"All we like sheep have gone astray; we have turned every one to his own way; and the LORD hath laid on him the iniquity of us all" (Isa. 53:6).

(d) Because of the command for all men to repent—"And the times of this ignorance God winked at; but now commandeth all men every where to repent" (Acts 17:30).

(e) Because of the universal "whosoever will" invitation—"For God so loved the world, that he gave his only begotten Son, that whosoever believeth in him should not perish, but have everlasting life" (John 3:16). "For whosoever shall call upon the name of the Lord shall be saved" (Rom. 10:13). "And the Spirit and the bride say, Come. And let him that heareth say, Come. And let him that is athirst come. And whosoever will, let him take the water of life freely" (Rev. 22:17).

Note the words of John R. Rice in concluding this first view:

> There is a Bible doctrine of God's foreknowledge, predestination and election. Most great bodies of Christians not strictly Calvinists, or not Calvinists at all, agree that God has His controlling hand on

the affairs of men. They agree that according to the Bible, He selects individuals like Abraham, Isaac, Jacob, David, and King Cyrus, as instruments to do certain things He has planned. He raised up Pharaoh who was already "a vessel of wrath," with many years of hardened heart and wicked rejection, to make him an example of punishment. Christians agree that God may choose a nation, particularly that He did choose Israel, through which He would give the law, the prophets, and eventually through whom the Saviour would come. It is a Bible doctrine that God foreknows who will trust in Christ, and that He has predestined or purposed to see that they are justified and glorified. He will keep the saved, will glorify those He saves. You see, Calvin did not originate those teachings. They are taught in the Bible, believed by multitudes who are not Calvinists.

But the doctrine that God predestined some men to Hell, that some cannot be saved, that they are born to be damned by God's own choice, is a doctrine of Calvinism, a philosophy developed by John Calvin. It is a sectarian tenet strictly followed only by hyper-Calvinists. It is a radical heresy, not taught in the Bible.

The term *Calvinism* is loosely used by people who do not hold Calvin's teaching on predestination. To thousands who may call themselves Calvinists, the word means only that they believe in salvation by grace, without human merit, as Calvin did, and so believe in everlasting life for the believer, since he is kept by the power of God. One who says he is a Calvinist generally means simply that he is not an Arminian, that he is kept by the grace of God, and is not saved or kept by his own works or life.

So those who are generally, but mistakenly, called Calvinists only rarely follow Calvin in his doctrine that some are predestined to be lost, born to be damned, by God's own plan, and cannot be saved.

John Calvin was a great theologian, was right in saying that people are saved by grace alone. But extreme Calvinism, the teaching that some people, by the foreordained plan of God, are predestined to be saved and some are predestined to be lost and that their destinies were settled before they were born, is a wicked heresy contrary to the Bible, that dishonors God and has done incalculable harm. The heresy of extreme Calvinism is particularly appealing to people from four viewpoints.

First, it appeals to the scholarly intellect, the self-sufficient and proud mind. So brilliant, philosophical, scholarly preachers are apt to be misled on this matter more than the humble-hearted Bible-believer.

Second, this doctrine appeals particularly to those who hold "covenant theology," that is, the Presbyterian doctrine that believers and their children should be received in the church alike, that babies sprinkled in infancy are in a covenant relationship with God without any choice of their own, etc.

Third, the hyper-Calvinistic heresy is particularly appealing to the carnal nature, unwilling to have the heartbreak, the burden for soul-winning, unwilling to pay the price of separation and perhaps ostracism which goes with all-out-soulwinning, unwilling to pay the price for the fullness of the Spirit in continual self-crucifixion and waiting on God.

Fourth, Calvinism especially appeals to those who think that hyper-Calvinism is the only answer to Arminianism. They do not believe that a saved person is "on probation" and may lose his salvation at any moment. They know that the Bible clearly teaches salvation by grace and not of works. Hyper-Calvinists would like to make people believe, and do make many believe that, if one does not teach universal salvation, he must be either a Calvinist or an Arminian. The Arminian position does such violence to the grace of God that many would rather be Calvinists. I am convinced that Whitefield and Spurgeon were both influenced by the pressure of Arminian theology in their day, to call themselves Calvinists, although neither was hyper-Calvinistic in actual practice and emphasis.

Note some of the foolish statements of hyper-Calvinists. It has been said that 'There are babes in Hell not a span long," that is, little ones who died in infancy or before birth, predestined to Hell with no choice in the matter! This is wholly unscriptural. (*Predestined for Hell? No!* pp. 6–9)

b. Position number two
   (1) Defined—A. H. Strong explains this view.

   Election is that eternal act of God, by which in His sovereign pleasure, and on account of no foreseen merit in them, he chooses certain out of the number of sinful men to be the recipients of the special grace of His Spirit, and so to be made voluntary partakers of Christ's salvation. (*Systematic Theology*, p. 779)

   Years before Strong, church father Augustine had written in similar fashion: "He chooses us, not because we believe but that we may believe; lest we should say that we first chose him."
   (2) Defended—Charles F. Baker writes the following in defense of the second position.

   In approaching the doctrine of Election, we must keep certain Scriptural facts in mind. The first is that God is absolutely righteous. As Paul introduces the subject of Election in Romans 9 he asks the question which comes to the mind of everyone who has ever seriously considered the doctrine: "What shall we say then? Is there unrighteousness with God?" (vs. 14). And he immediately answers: "Perish the thought." The second fact we need to consider is the estate of man under sin. Man is a responsible being who is fully accountable to God. He is responsible for his apostasy from God and his lost condition. He merits only the judgment of God. The third thing which Scripture presents is that no man of himself seeks after God. In other words, Scripture teaches that, even though God provided a salvation for the whole world, not one would accept it and be saved unless God first of all took the initiative by Himself seeking after man.

—What election is not:

It is not an arbitrary act of God or capriciousness. Election is according to God's eternal purpose and foreknowledge (Romans 8:28, 29; 9:11; Ephesians 1:4-11; 1 Peter 1:2).

It is not an act to choose some to be lost or a decree of reprobation. Election is to salvation, not to condemnation (1 Thessalonians 1:4; 2 Thessalonians 2:13).

It is not merely God's purpose to save them that believe, although it is true that only those who believe will be saved.

It is not man's choosing of himself, although man must himself choose if he is to be saved. Election is God's choice. Christ said to His apostles: "Ye have not chosen me, but I have chosen you" (John 15:16).

It is not merely to a place of service, although God chooses men for special tasks. Election is also unto salvation (2 Thessalonians 2:13).

—What election is:

It is a choice on the part of God which includes some, but not all. This fact is substantiated by three lines of proof. The fact that some are lost is proof that not all were chosen. The word itself, to elect, would be meaningless if all were to be saved. When an election is held, it is evident from the use of the word that only certain ones will be appointed to office. In the third place the Scripture speaks over and over of those who are lost, so that these are definitely not among the elect.

It is a choice which God made before the foundation of the world (Ephesians 1:4). It is sometimes helpful to consider the fact that God is a timeless Being, that He lives in an eternal now. Hence, it is not as though He made a choice a billion years before He really knew what we would do, but rather He knew us then as we are today.

It is a choice based upon something that is in God, and not something that is in man. Paul states that election is according to grace (Romans 11:5), and he also definitely states that it is not of works (Romans 9:11). Election, like salvation, is all of grace and not of works. Therefore, it should be evident that God did not choose to save certain ones because He foresaw any goodness or merit in them.

It is a choice based upon foreknowledge, which in turn is based upon the determinate counsel and purpose of God. It is evident that God has purposed everything that He has done, and the reason God foreknows what will happen is because He has purposed it.

It is a choice which is absolutely sure of fulfillment; no power can overthrow it. Romans 8:28-30 indicates that every one who is foreknown of God will be called, justified, and glorified. Verse 33 states that no one will ever be able to lay anything to the charge of God's elect, and the chapter ends with the assurance that nothing shall ever be able to separate the elect from the love of God which is in Christ

Jesus. Acts 13:48 states, "As many as were ordained to eternal life believed."

It is a choice which is in harmony with human freedom. Election does not coerce or force the elect to believe. No man upon believing the gospel has the consciousness of being forced against his will to believe. It is probably at this point that human knowledge is most lacking in understanding how God can move upon the will of man without violating man's freedom. Even the apostle Paul, after discussing the elective purposes of God with Israel, had to confess: "O the depth of the riches both of the wisdom and knowledge of God! how unsearchable are his judgments, and his ways past finding out! For who hath known the mind of the Lord? or who hath been his counsellor? . . . For of him, and through him, and to him, are all things: to whom be glory forever. Amen (Romans 11:33-36). (*A Dispensational Theology*, pp. 389–390)

3. The objections leveled against these views of salvation's origination
   a. First position
      (1) It leaves salvation wholly in the hands of man
          (a) The soul winner has 100 percent power to decide who will get a chance to go to heaven.
          (b) The sinner (upon hearing the message) has 100 percent power to decide whether he will go to heaven.
      (2) It does violence to the word *election*—If God merely knew who would accept him, he would be thus limited to crystal-ball gazing and not electing or choosing in any sense of the word whatsoever. It would be like "electing" all those who will be born in the USA next year to become Americans.
      (3) It limits God's purpose and his glory to the actions of men.
   b. Second position
      (1) It makes God a respecter of persons.
      (2) It forces salvation upon the elect.
      (3) It denies the freedom of man.
      (4) It views election as an arbitrary act of God.
      (5) It discourages evangelism and missionary activity.
      (6) It generates pride in the mind of the elect.
      (7) It does violence to the word *whosoever.*
      (8) It leads to the doctrine of reprobation, the decree that certain ones should be lost.
4. Some conclusions on salvation's origination—In light of all we have just discussed, what position is the correct one? What are we to believe and teach?

One is almost tempted when asked for his view on all this to respond as a politician once did. Upon being asked his position concerning a burning issue he replied: "Some of my friends are violently opposed to this issue, while other friends of mine are 100 percent in favor of it. But I want to tell you that *I'm for my friends!*"

In a more serious tone, it seems to this author that rather than ask which position is *correct*, one should inquire concerning which position is *complete*. Is either view able to work in all the Scriptures involved and harmonize them? It would appear not. Whatever interpretation one holds, he *must* consider the following principles.

a. The Bible clearly presents in the strongest language *both* the sovereignty of God *and* the responsibility of man—The sovereignty of God and the responsibility of man cannot be totally reconciled in the mind of man. To do so would be like attempting to pour the Atlantic Ocean into a small bucket.

Consider the following illustration. Here is a mighty river flowing from eternity past to eternity future. Its ultimate destination is the glory of God and the good of the elect. On either side of the river is a clay bankside. One side is called the Sovereignty of God Bank, and the other side is the Responsibility of Man Bank. Some of the elect can be seen standing on both banks discussing (and on occasion perhaps denouncing) the theology of the opposite bank dwellers. But in doing this, the great and glorious River of Grace flowing at their feet is overlooked. The perfect will of God would direct both sides to embark upon that river and experience all its bountiful blessings. It takes two bank sides to make a river.

As a final thought here, what happens to a river if one of its supporting banks is removed? This, of course, has happened to earthly rivers through earthquakes or enemy bombs. When this occurs, the once life-giving waters cease flowing and the river becomes an ill-smelling, insect-ridden swamp.

To overemphasize one aspect of election and ignore or deny the other side is to turn salvation's river of redemption into a theological and sectarian swamp.

b. We do not possess all the facts about anything—"And if any man think that he knoweth any thing, he knoweth nothing yet as he ought to know" (1 Cor. 8:2).

God has indeed told us everything he wants *us* to know, but certainly not everything *he* knows. "For we know in part, and we prophesy in part. . . . For now we see through a glass, darkly; but then face to face: now I know in part; but then shall I know even as also I am known" (1 Cor. 13:9, 12).

Following a discussion concerning the sovereignty of God, Paul freely confesses his ignorance and breaks into singing over the marvelous and matchless wisdom of God: "O the depth of the riches both of the wisdom and knowledge of God! how unsearchable are his judgments, and his ways past finding out! For who hath known the mind of the Lord? or who hath been his counsellor? Or who hath first given to him, and it shall be recompensed unto him again? For of him, and through him, and to him, are all things: to whom be glory for ever. Amen" (Rom. 11:33-36).

c. God cannot do *anything* that is either unfair or unreasonable—It is not simply that he *wouldn't* but that he *couldn't*. "That by two immutable things, in which it was impossible for God to lie, we might have a strong consolation, who have fled for refuge to lay hold upon the hope set before us" (Heb. 6:18).

We must therefore interpret anything God *does* by what he *is*. "He is the Rock, his work is perfect: for all his ways are judgment: a God of truth and without iniquity, just and right is he" (Deut. 32:4). (See also Gen. 18:25; Mark 7:35-37.)

The words penned by King Solomon some 30 centuries ago are appropriate as we bring this chapter to a close. "The preacher sought to find out acceptable words: and that which was written was upright, even words of truth. The words of the wise are as goads, and as nails fastened by the masters of assemblies, which are given from one shepherd. And further, by these, my son, be admonished: of making many books there is no end; and much study is a weariness of the flesh. Let us hear the conclusion of the whole matter: Fear God, and keep his commandments: for this is the whole duty of man" (Eccles. 12:10-13).

X. The Completeness of Salvation—A modern proverb runs: "Youth is such a wonderful thing, but it's a shame to waste it all upon teenagers!" Be that as it may, one can rephrase the proverb in the area of salvation to read: "Salvation is such a wonderful thing, but it's a shame to waste it all upon the soul!"

The truth of the matter is that when we speak of winning souls to Christ, we imply salvation is limited to this area. However God's salvation fully embraces man's soul, spirit, and body.

A. Salvation in regard to man's body—"It is sown a natural body; it is raised a spiritual body. There is a natural body, and there is a spiritual body" (1 Cor. 15:44). "Who shall change our vile body, that it may be fashioned like unto his glorious body, according to the working whereby he is able even to subdue all things unto himself" (Phil. 3:21). "And not only they, but ourselves also, which have the firstfruits of the Spirit, even we ourselves groan within ourselves, waiting for the adoption, to wit, the redemption of our body" (Rom. 8:23).

B. Salvation in regard to man's soul—"Which hope we have as an anchor of the soul, both sure and stedfast, and which entereth into that within the veil" (Heb. 6:19). "Wherefore lay apart all filthiness and superfluity of naughtiness, and receive with meekness the engrafted word, which is able to save your souls" (James 1:21). "Receiving the end of your faith, even the salvation of your souls" (1 Pet. 1:9). "Wherefore let them that suffer according to the will of God commit the keeping of their souls to him in well doing, as unto a faithful Creator" (1 Pet. 4:19).

C. Salvation in regard to man's spirit—"The Spirit itself beareth witness with our spirit, that we are the children of God" (Rom. 8:16). "The Lord Jesus Christ be with thy spirit. Grace be with you. Amen" (2 Tim. 4:22). "To the general assembly and church of the firstborn, which are written in heaven, and to God the Judge of all, and to the spirits of just men made perfect" (Heb. 12:23).

XI. The Security of Salvation—Does the Bible present a *whole* (unconditional and permanent) salvation, or does it offer a *holey* (conditional and temporary) salvation?

A. The problems of eternal security—Dr. John F. Walvoord writes:

> While most believers in Christ accept the doctrine that they can have assurance of salvation at any given moment in their experience, the question is often raised, "Can a person once saved become lost again?" Since the fear of losing salvation could seriously affect a believer's peace of mind, and because his future is so vital, this question is a most important aspect of the doctrine of salvation.
>
> The claim that one who is once saved may be lost again is based on certain biblical passages which seem to raise questions concerning the continuance of salvation. In the history of the church, there have been opposing systems of interpretation known as Calvinism, in support of eternal security, and Arminianism, in opposition to eternal security (each named after its foremost apologist, John Calvin or Jacob Arminius). (*Major Bible Themes*, p. 220)

Those holding the Arminian position confidently assure us their view is amply supported by some 100 biblical passages. It will prove helpful to all at this point to examine the more important of these verses.

They can be arranged under the following topical headings:

1. Passages dealing with false teachers—Matthew 7:15-23; 24:11; 2 Corinthians 11:13-15; 1 Timothy 4:1; 2 Peter 2:1-22; 3:16-17; 1 John 2:19; 2 John 7; Jude 4, 10-16; Revelation 22:18-19.

    a. The above-mentioned passages considered—The men described in the above verses are apostates. An apostate is one who has received light but not life. He knows something of the Word of God, but nothing about the God of the Word. He then refuses to give even mental assent to the great truths of the Bible. His description and deeds are as follows:

        (1) He is a grievous and ravening wolf dressed in sheep's clothing—"Beware of false prophets, which come to you in sheep's clothing, but inwardly they are ravening wolves" (Matt. 7:15).

        (2) He hates real sheep—"For I know this, that after my departing shall grievous wolves enter in among you, not sparing the flock" (Acts 20:29).

        (3) He will deceive many through great signs and wonders—"And many false prophets shall rise, and shall deceive many. . . . For there shall arise false Christs, and false prophets, and shall shew great signs and wonders; insomuch that, if it were possible, they shall deceive the very elect" (Matt. 24:11, 24).

        (4) He is a perverse empire-builder—"Also of your own selves shall men arise, speaking perverse things, to draw away disciples after them" (Acts 20:30).

        (5) He is divisive and materialistic—"Now I beseech you, brethren, mark them which cause divisions and offences contrary to the doctrine which ye have learned; and avoid them" (Rom. 16:17).

        (6) He gives impressive speeches, using flowery language—"For they that are such serve not our Lord Jesus Christ, but their own belly; and by good words and fair speeches deceive the hearts of the simple" (Rom. 16:18).

        (7) He deceives by allowing Satan to disguise him as an angel of light, rather than a demon of darkness—"For such are false apostles, deceitful workers, transforming themselves into the apostles of Christ. . . . Therefore it is no great thing if his ministers also be transformed as the ministers of righteousness; whose end shall be according to their works" (2 Cor. 11:13, 15).

        (8) His nature and message are demon-controlled—"Now the Spirit speaketh expressly, that in the latter times some shall depart from the faith, giving heed to seducing spirits, and doctrines of devils; speaking lies in hypocrisy; having their conscience seared with a hot iron; forbidding to marry, and commanding to abstain from meats, which God hath created to be received with thanksgiving of them which believe and know the truth" (1 Tim. 4:1-3).

        (9) He perverts the doctrine of the Son of God—"For many deceivers are entered into the world, who confess not that Jesus Christ is come in the flesh. This is a deceiver and an antichrist" (2 John 7). (See also 2 Pet. 2:1; Jude 4.)

        (10) He perverts the Word of God (2 Pet. 3:16; Rev. 22:18-19).

(11) He perverts the grace of God (Jude 4).

(12) He can be identified by his fruits—"They went out from us, but they were not of us; for if they had been of us, they would no doubt have continued with us: but they went out, that they might be made manifest that they were not all of us" (1 John 2:19). (See also Matt. 7:16-20; James 3:11-12.)

b. Two of the above-mentioned passages considered in more detail

(1) Matthew 7:21-23—"Not every one that saith unto me, Lord, Lord, shall enter into the kingdom of heaven; but he that doeth the will of my Father which is in heaven. Many will say to me in that day, Lord, Lord, have we not prophesied in thy name? and in thy name have cast out devils? and in thy name done many wonderful works? And then will I profess unto them, I never knew you: depart from me, ye that work iniquity."

Some day Jesus will say to all false teachers and preachers, "I never knew you." It does *not* read, "I *once* knew you," or "I *used* to know you," but rather, "I *never* knew you."

(2) 2 Peter 2:20-22—"For if after they have escaped the pollutions of the world through the knowledge of the Lord and Saviour Jesus Christ, they are again entangled therein, and overcome, the latter end is worse with them than the beginning. For it had been better for them not to have known the way of righteousness, than, after they have known it, to turn from the holy commandment delivered unto them. But it is happened unto them according to the true proverb, The dog is turned to his own vomit again; and the sow that was washed to her wallowing in the mire."

While these false teachers had (for a time) escaped the evils of alcohol, sexual diseases, cancer from tobacco, etc. by loosely applying (as do, for example, the Mormons) the *principles* of the gospel, they nevertheless had *never* accepted the *person* of the gospel, the Lord Jesus Christ.

These cannot be Christians who became unsaved, for nowhere in the Bible does God call a believer a hog or a dog (2 Pet. 2:22). The "sow that was washed" here in the Greek language is in the middle voice, and thus should read, "The sow that washed itself." Here is a clear case of moral reformation, *not* Messiah regeneration.

2. Passages dealing with the act of conversion itself—Matthew 10:32-33; John 8:51; 1 Corinthians 15:1-2; 2 Corinthians 13:5; Colossians 1:23; Hebrews 2:1-4; 12:25, 29; James 2:14-26; 1 John 3:6, 8-9; 5:18; 2 John 9.

Note a few of these passages:

a. John 8:51—"Verily, verily, I say unto you, If a man keep my saying, he shall never see death."

Just what "saying" (teaching, commandment) is Jesus referring to here? In a previous conversation (John 6:28) a crowd had asked him: "What shall we do, that we might work the works of God?" Our Lord answered: "This is the work of God, that ye believe on him [Christ] whom he [the Father] hath sent" (John 6:29).

b. 1 Corinthians 15:1-2—"Moreover, brethren, I declare unto you the gospel which I preached unto you, which also ye have received, and wherein ye stand; by which also ye are saved, if ye keep in memory what I preached unto you, unless ye have believed in vain."

The key phrase here is "unless ye have believed in vain." What does this mean? Paul explains it in the following passage: "Now if Christ be preached that he rose from the dead, how say some among you that there is no resurrection of the dead?" (1 Cor. 15:12).

There were apparently in Corinth some professing believers who denied the resurrection of Christ. The apostle, thus, says they were not saved in the first place and their faith was in vain since it is impossible for a denier of Christ's resurrection to experience the new birth.

The little word *if* in 15:2 has also bothered some. But here in the Greek New Testament it is the first-class condition and should be rendered *since*. This is also true concerning the *if* in the following passage: "If ye continue in the faith grounded and settled, and be not moved away from the hope of the gospel, which ye have heard, and which was preached to every creature which is under heaven; whereof I Paul am made a minister" (Col. 1:23).

c. 1 John 3:9—"Whosoever is born of God doth not commit sin; for his seed remaineth in him: and he cannot sin, because he is born of God."

Greek scholar Kenneth Wuest writes:

> The infinitive in the present tense in Greek always speaks of continuous, habitual action, never the mere fact of the action . . . the translation therefore is, "He is not able to habitually sin." The Greek text here holds no warrant for the erroneous teaching of sinless perfection. (*In the Last Days*, p. 150)

The same Greek construction also holds true for the following verses: "Whosoever abideth in him sinneth not: whosoever sinneth hath not seen him, neither known him" (1 John 3:6). "We know that whosoever is born of God sinneth not; but he that is begotten of God keepeth himself, and that wicked one toucheth him not" (1 John 5:18).

d. Matthew 10:32-33—"Whosoever therefore shall confess me before men, him will I confess also before my Father which is in heaven. But whosoever shall deny me before men, him will I also deny before my Father which is in heaven."

At the beginning of this chapter Jesus is instructing his apostles before sending them out to preach for the first time. In the above-quoted verses he reminds them of the seriousness of their task. They are to warn their hearers that to personally reject the Messiah here on earth would someday mean his rejection of them in heaven.

3. Passages dealing with Christian rewards—1 Corinthians 3:11-15; 2 Corinthians 5:9-10; Galatians 6:9; Colossians 3:24-25; 2 Timothy 2:12; James 1:12; 2 John 18; Revelation 2:7, 11, 17, 26; 3:5, 12, 21.

a. 2 Timothy 2:12—"If we suffer, we shall also reign with him: if we deny him, he also will deny us."

The *deny* here can be tied into 1 Corinthians 3:15: "If any man's work shall be burned, he shall suffer loss: but he himself shall be saved; yet so as by fire." Thus the denial here is that of rewards.

b. Colossians 3:24-25—"Knowing that of the Lord ye shall receive the reward of the inheritance: for ye serve the Lord Christ. But he that doeth wrong shall receive for the wrong which he hath done: and there is no respect of persons."

4. Passages dealing with missing God's best—1 Corinthians 9:27; 10:5; Hebrews 3:11-19; 4:1-16; 12:14-15.

   a. 1 Corinthians 9:27—"But I keep under my body, and bring it into subjection: lest that by any means, when I have preached to others, I myself should be a castaway."

   The word *castaway* here is *adokimos,* which means "disapproved." Paul was not in the least concerned about his *salvation* from God (2 Tim. 1:12), but he was very concerned about his *service* for God. He did not want to be set on a spiritual shelf somewhere.

   b. 1 Corinthians 10:5—"But with many of them God was not well pleased: for they were overthrown in the wilderness."

   c. Hebrews 3:11—"So I sware in my wrath, They shall not enter into my rest."

   These verses review the tragic Old Testament account of Israel's unbelief at Kadesh-barnea in Numbers 14, where they refused to enter Palestine. Because of this, God would not allow anyone under 20 (Joshua and Caleb excepted) to enter. Even Moses (because of a later sin) was refused passage. However, all this had nothing whatever to do with spiritual damnation, but rather with physical destruction. It simply (and sadly) meant that most of that generation would never get out of the hot desert into a land flowing with milk and honey.

   In Psalms we are told of God's reaction to Israel's terrible sin in the wilderness. Note: "For their heart was not right with him, neither were they stedfast in his covenant. But he, being full of compassion, forgave their iniquity, and destroyed them not: yea, many a time turned he his anger away, and did not stir up all his wrath" (Psa. 78:37-38). "Many times did he deliver them; but they provoked him with their counsel, and were brought low for their iniquity. Nevertheless he regarded their affliction, when he heard their cry" (Psa. 106:43-44).

   Moses' eventual salvation certainly cannot be questioned even though he was not allowed to enter the land. However, he is mentioned in the New Testament. (See Matt. 17:1-4.)

   The point of all the above is simply this: the author of Hebrews uses this historical example to exhort believers to press on in their Christian lives and enter into God's perfect will. "Let us therefore fear, lest, a promise being left us of entering into his rest, any of you should seem to come short of it. . . . Let us labour therefore to enter into that rest, lest any man fall after the same example of unbelief" (Heb. 4:1, 11).

5. Passages dealing with God's discipline

   a. Romans 14:23—"And he that doubteth is damned if he eat, because he eateth not of faith: for whatsoever is not of faith is sin."

   b. 1 Corinthians 11:29—"For he that eateth and drinketh unworthily, eateth and drinketh damnation to himself, not discerning the Lord's body."

   c. 1 Timothy 5:12—"Having damnation, because they have cast off their first faith."

   The problem word found in each of these three verses is the word *damnation.* In each case the Greek word could be better rendered by the word *judgment.* In the first passage Paul refers to a believer eating certain foods he was not sure God wanted him to eat. In the second passage the apostle speaks of believers partaking of the Lord's table with known sin in their lives. In the third passage he describes young believing widows who had displayed a worldly attitude toward sex and marriage. While *none* of these parties involved faced damnation, they all would, however, be judged by God.

Peter summarizes all this and uses the same Greek word. "For the time is come that judgment must begin at the house of God: and if it first begin at us, what shall the end be of them that obey not the gospel of God?" (1 Pet. 4:17). (See also Heb. 12:50-11.)

6. Passages dealing with fruit bearing, testimony, and Christian maturity
   a. Matthew 5:13—"Ye are the salt of the earth: but if the salt have lost his savour, wherewith shall it be salted? it is thenceforth good for nothing, but to be cast out, and to be trodden under foot of men."
   b. John 8:30-32—"As he spake these words, many believed on him. Then said Jesus to those Jews which believed on him, If ye continue in my word, then are ye my disciples indeed; and ye shall know the truth, and the truth shall make you free."

   Our Lord would later amplify this statement: "I am come that they might have life, and that they might have it more abundantly (John 10:10). While all Christians have *life*, only fruit-bearing Christians enjoy *abundant* life.
   c. John 15:6—"If a man abide not in me, he is cast forth as a branch, and is withered; and men gather them, and cast them into the fire, and they are burned."

   We note that it is *men* here who gather these fruitless branches and burn them, and *not* God. A similar example is given by Christ during the Sermon on the Mount. (See also Acts 13:43; 14:22; James 1:26; 2 Pet. 1:9-11; 1 John 2:24.) These verses thus describe useless testimony before men, not lost salvation before God.

7. Passages dealing with a believer being influenced by false doctrines—2 Corinthians 11:2-4; Galatians 5:4; Colossians 2:4, 8, 18; 1 Thessalonians 3:5; 1 Timothy 1:6, 19-20; 6:20-21; 2 Timothy 2:18, 26.

   One of the reasons why a Christian is to mature in the faith is: "That we henceforth be no more children, tossed to and fro, and carried about with every wind of doctrine, by the sleight of men, and cunning craftiness, whereby they lie in wait to deceive" (Eph. 4:14).

   Here Paul sadly admits it is tragically possible for a true believer to become entangled with false doctrine.
   a. The false doctrine of legalism—"Christ is become of no effect unto you, whosoever of you are justified by the law; ye are fallen from grace" (Gal. 5:4).

   This verse is probably the favorite proof-text of Arminian theology, especially the phrase "ye are fallen from grace." But it must be asked just what had caused them to fall? It was a frantic (and fruitless) effort to fulfill the Mosaic Law. Does this then mean that a Christian who does his very best to perform good works will lose his salvation? It does not. Paul faults the Galatians *not* because of their *evil* against the law, but because of their *effort* to keep the law. Thus, to fall from grace is the act of allowing the legalism of law to prevent one from enjoying the full liberty of love. It is possible that both Peter (Gal. 2:11-14) and James (Acts 21:18-26) "fell from grace" for awhile over this matter. (See also 1 Tim. 1:6-7.)
   b. The false doctrine of worldly wisdom and philosophy (Col. 2:8)

    c. The false doctrine of angel worship (Col. 2:18)

    d. The false doctrine of a past resurrection theory (1 Tim. 1:19-20; 2 Tim. 2:18)

8. Passages dealing with the sin unto death—Acts 5:1-11; Romans 6:16; 8:13; 1 Corinthians 5:5; 11:30; Hebrews 6:4-20; 10:26; James 1:13-15; 5:19-20; 1 John 5:16.

This sin unto death is a sin only a believer can commit. It refers not to his eternal soul, but to his earthly service. It is committed when he allows his life to become so carnal and unproductive that God simply takes him home early via physical death. This sin (or perhaps sins) can vary among Christians.

    a. Ananias and Sapphira committed this sin (Acts 5:1-11).

    b. Some of the Corinthian believers committed it—"For this cause many are weak and sickly among you, and many sleep" (1 Cor. 11:30).

    c. The man in 1 Corinthians 5 was in danger of committing it (1 Cor. 5:1-5).

    d. Hymenaeus and Alexander were in danger of committing it—"Of whom is Hymenaeus and Alexander; whom I have delivered unto Satan, that they may learn not to blaspheme" (1 Tim. 1:20).

    e. Some to whom the book of Hebrews was addressed were in danger of committing it—"For it is impossible for those who were once enlightened, and have tasted of the heavenly gift, and were made partakers of the Holy Ghost, and have tasted the good word of God, and the powers of the world to come, if they shall fall away, to renew them again unto repentance; seeing they crucify to themselves the Son of God afresh, and put him to an open shame" (Heb. 6:4-6). "For if we sin wilfully after that we have received the knowledge of the truth, there remaineth no more sacrifice for sins. . . . For we know him that hath said, Vengeance belongeth unto me, I will recompense, saith the Lord. And again, The Lord shall judge his people. It is a fearful thing to fall into the hands of the living God" (Heb. 10:26, 30-31).

9. Passages dealing with the unpardonable sin—"Wherefore I say unto you, All manner of sin and blasphemy shall be forgiven unto men: but the blasphemy against the Holy Ghost shall not be forgiven unto men. And whosoever speaketh a word against the Son of man, it shall be forgiven him: but whosoever speaketh against the Holy Ghost, it shall not be forgiven him, neither in this world, neither in the world to come" (Matt. 12:31-32).

These verses have bothered many Christians and unsaved alike. Two basic questions must be asked here.

    a. To whom did Jesus speak these words? They were directed toward the wicked Pharisees. "But when the Pharisees heard it, they said, This fellow doth not cast out devils, but by Beelzebub the prince of the devils. And Jesus knew their thoughts, and said unto them, Every kingdom divided against itself is brought to desolation; and every city or house divided against itself shall not stand" (Matt. 12:24-24).

    b. What grievous sin had they committed? For many months they had the priceless privilege of hearing the Savior's sermons and viewing his mighty miracles. But instead of believing, they degraded the Son of God, accusing him of performing miracles through satanic energy. By doing this they committed the unpardonable sin. What else could God himself possibly do to convince them? It was not, of course, that they *couldn't* believe, but that they *wouldn't* believe.

In light of the above, the unpardonable sin cannot be committed today, as Jesus is not walking about in his earthly body performing miracles.

10. Passages dealing with the nation Israel and the tribulation—Matthew 22:1-13; 24:13, 45-51; 25:1-30; Luke 13:23-30.

   a. Unsaved Israeli individuals—Each of these passages deals with those unsaved Israeli individuals who survive the tribulation but find themselves spiritually unprepared to meet their returning Messiah. Jesus uses the parabolic method to relate this sad truth in each of the five passages.

   (1) The parable of the wedding guest without a wedding garment (Matt. 22:1-13)
   (2) The parable of the unfaithful servant (Matt. 24:45-51)
   (3) The parable of the 10 virgins (Matt. 25:1-13)
   (4) The parable of the eight talents (Matt. 25:14-30)
   (5) The parable of the shut door (Luke 13:23-30)

   b. Physical survival during the tribulation—One passage deals with sheer physical survival during the tribulation. Note: "But he that shall endure unto the end, the same shall be saved" (Matt. 24:13).

   What "end" is he referring to here? Verses 21 and 29 make it clear he is talking about the coming great tribulation. "For then shall be great tribulation, such as was not since the beginning of the world to this time, no, nor ever shall be" (Matt. 24:21).

11. Passage dealing with Gentile nations—Romans 11:13-24 (especially to be noted are verses 21-22). "For if God spared not the natural branches, take heed lest he also spare not thee. Behold therefore the goodness and severity of God: on them which fell, severity; but toward thee, goodness, if thou continue in his goodness: otherwise thou also shalt be cut off" (Rom. 11:21-22).

   In dealing with this entire passage, let us consider four questions.

   a. To whom is Paul talking? Paul is talking to Gentile people (v. 13).
   b. What is he talking about? He tells about the opportunity of Gentiles to share in the spiritual blessings of Abraham. (See especially Rom. 4:23-25.)
   c. Who are the broken-off branches mentioned in 11:17? They represent the nation Israel, which had just rejected its own Messiah. (See also Matt. 21:42-43.)
   d. Who are the grafted branches here? They represent Gentile people.

   The conclusion is that this passage has nothing whatsoever to do with individuals losing their salvation, but rather with that of the Gentiles receiving (during the Church Age) those blessings forfeited by Israel.

12. Passages dealing with the testimony of local churches—Revelation 2–3. Note especially the following verses:

   "Nevertheless I have somewhat against thee, because thou hast left thy first love. Remember therefore from whence thou art fallen, and repent, and do the first works; or else I will come unto thee quickly, and will remove thy candlestick out of his place, except thou repent" (Rev. 2:4-5). "I know thy works, that thou art neither cold nor hot: I would thou wert cold or hot. So then because thou art lukewarm, and neither cold nor hot, I will spue thee out of my mouth" (Rev. 3:15-16).

   The last verse in chapter 1 makes it perfectly clear that Jesus speaks these words to local churches, and the issue in question concerns itself with that of the personal testimony of each local church, not to the individual members within the church.

13. Passages dealing with head assent instead of heart acceptance—Matthew 13:1-8, 18-23; Luke 11:24-28; John 6:66.

   a. The seed and the four soils (Matt. 13:1-8, 18-23)—Some have mistakenly concluded that all four individuals here (as represented by different kinds of soil) were originally saved, but only one retained this salvation. However, a little logic will show the error of this position. Does the Bible teach that every person who hears the gospel will be saved? It does not. Furthermore, Scripture teaches that a person cannot be saved without eventually showing *some* kind of fruit, however small. Thus, the only born-again individual here was the fourth, as proven by his fruit.

   b. The man and the unclean spirits—"When the unclean spirit is gone out of a man, he walketh through dry places, seeking rest; and finding none, he saith, I will return unto my house whence I came out. And when he cometh, he findeth it swept and garnished. Then goeth he, and taketh to him seven other spirits more wicked than himself; and they enter in, and dwell there: and the last state of that man is worse than the first" (Luke 11:24-26).

   Here is clearly a case of moral reformation without regeneration. A demon (let alone eight) cannot dwell in the heart of a saved man.

   c. The defecting disciples—"From that time many of his disciples went back, and walked no more with him" (John 6:66). The word *disciple* simply means "one who learns." Many of those who followed Christ were simply band-wagon, fair-weather friends. When the sun grew hot and the road bumpy, they just drifted away. For a while they may have *professed* salvation, but they never *possessed* it. (See also John 2:23-25; 12:42-43.)

14. Passages dealing with the destruction of Jerusalem by Nebuchadnezzar—Ezekiel 3:17-21; 33:8.

   One of the most important rules in rightly understanding any passage in the Bible is to put it into its proper context. Ezekiel wrote these words around 597 B.C. from Babylon (where he had been taken captive by Nebuchadnezzar) prior to the final destruction of Jerusalem, which occurred in 586 B.C. While Ezekiel was in exile, God had commissioned him to be a "watchman unto the house of Israel."

   "Son of man, I have made thee a watchman unto the house of Israel: therefore hear the word at my mouth, and give them warning from me" (Ezek. 3:17). "So thou, O son of man, I have set thee a watchman unto the house of Israel; therefore thou shalt hear the word at my mouth, and warn them from me" (Ezek. 33:7).

   He was to warn those still living in Jerusalem that, unless they repented immediately, a similar fate awaited them. In other words, those arrogant Jerusalem citizens felt that, inasmuch as they had already escaped Nebuchad-nezzar's first (605 B.C.) and second (597 B.C.) siege, they had nothing to fear and need not repent.

15. Passages dealing with the Book of Life—Here two separate books apparently are in mind.

   a. The book of physical life—"And it came to pass on the morrow, that Moses said unto the people, Ye have sinned a great sin: and now I will go up unto the LORD; peradventure I shall make an atonement for your sin. And Moses returned unto the LORD, and said, Oh, this people have sinned a great sin, and have made them gods of gold. Yet now, if thou wilt forgive their sin—; and if not, blot me, I pray thee, out of thy book which thou hast written" (Exod. 32:30-32). Moses here may have been offering himself as a physical substitute for the nation Israel which nation had just grieved and angered God through the sin of golden calf worship.

"Let them be blotted out of the book of the living, and not be written with the righteous" (Psa. 69:28). Here David obviously refers to the physical death of his enemies.

b. The book of eternal life—"Notwithstanding in this rejoice not, that the spirits are subject unto you; but rather rejoice, because your names are written in heaven" (Luke 10:20). (See also Dan. 12:1; Rom. 9:3; Phil. 4:3; Rev. 3:5; 13:8, 17:8; 20:12, 15; 21:27; 22:19.)

16. Passages dealing with certain individuals

a. Esau—"Lest there be any fornicator, or profane person, as Esau, who for one morsel of meat sold his birthright. For ye know how that afterward, when he would have inherited the blessing, he was rejected: for he found no place of repentance, though he sought it carefully with tears" (Heb. 12:16-17).

The account here has reference to events recorded in Genesis 25:27-34; 27:1-46. They concern themselves with the birthright and blessing of the eldest son and have nothing to do with the doctrine of salvation. There is not the slightest evidence that Esau was ever a saved man.

b. Balaam (Num. 22–24.)— Balaam was a typical hireling prophet, seeking only to make a market of his gift. He was, to King Balak (his employer), the best prophet money could buy. Three New Testament passages make it clear that he was never a saved man (2 Pet. 2:15; Jude 11; Rev. 2:14).

c. Saul—Was the first king of Israel a saved man? Some have advocated that he was, on the basis of the following verses: 1 Samuel 10:6-12; 11:6, 13-15; 12:13; 14:35; 15:30-31. However, the bulk of Bible students have held that he was not. A great number of passages would seem to bear this out: 1 Samuel 13:13-14; 14:37, 44; 15:22-23, 35; 16:14; 18:10-12; 20:30-33; 22:17; 28:6, 16.

d. Judas—Was the world's most notorious traitor ever saved? The Scriptures answer with a resounding *no.*

"Then entered Satan into Judas surnamed Iscariot, being of the number of the twelve" (Luke 22:3). And truly the Son of man goeth, as it was determined: but woe unto that man by whom he is betrayed!" (Luke 22:22). "Jesus answered them, Have not I chosen you twelve, and one of you is a devil? He spake of Judas Iscariot the son of Simon: for he it was that should betray him, being one of the twelve" (John 6:70-71). (See also John 12:4-6; 13:27.)

Dr. Robert Gromacki has written:

> The *repentance* of Judas has caused some perplexity. Matthew wrote, "Then Judas, which had betrayed him, when he saw that he was condemned, repented himself and brought again the thirty pieces of silver to the chief priest and elders, Saying, I have sinned in that I have betrayed the innocent blood. And they said, What is that to us? see thou to that. And he cast down the pieces of silver in the temple, and departed, and went and hanged himself" (Matt. 27:3-5).

What kind of repentance was this? This particular Greek word indicates an emotional regret (*metamelomai*), not a repentance of moral and spiritual guilt (*metanoeo*). Judas was sorry over what had happened to Jesus because he did not realize that it would go that far. After being with Jesus three years he knew that Jesus was not worthy of death.

He tried to reverse the trial action by returning the money, but it was too late. In remorse, he hanged himself. If this had been genuine repentance, he would have sought out Jesus or the eleven apostles. When the disciples prayed about the appointment of the twelfth apostle, they said, "Thou, Lord, which knowest the hearts of all men, shew whether of these two thou hast chosen, that he may take part of this ministry and apostleship, from which Judas by transgression fell, that he might go to his own place" (Acts 1:24-25).

Judas did not fall from salvation; he fell from the apostleship. There is a vast difference. Judas is a perfect example of those unsaved Christian workers mentioned by Jesus in the conclusion of the Sermon on the Mount: "Not every one that saith unto me, Lord, Lord, shall enter into the kingdom of heaven; but he that doeth the will of my Father which is in heaven. Many will say to me in that day, Lord, Lord, have we not prophesied in thy name? and in thy name have cast out devils? and in thy name done many wonderful works? And then will I profess unto them, I never knew you: depart from me, ye that work iniquity" (Matt. 7:21-23).

Judas had done all of these things (Matt. 10; Luke 10). He had performed a ministry for Christ, but he did not know Christ as his Savior from sin. He was a totally unsaved man, from the beginning to the end. (*Salvation Is Forever*, pp. 166–167)

e. Simon—In John 2:23-25 it is recorded that a number of bandwagon jumpers believed in Jesus "when they saw the miracles which he did." But, we are told that "Jesus did not commit himself to them, because he knew all men." These fickle men were interested in his *miracles*, but were deaf concerning his *message*. (See Acts 8:5-25.)

The passage in Acts 8 records a similar thing. Even though Simon "believed" (probably based on the miracles performed by Philip—see 8:6) and was actually baptized (8:13), there is no indication he was ever saved.

"And the people with one accord gave heed unto those things which Philip spake, hearing and seeing the miracles and signs which he did" (Acts 8:6). "Then Simon himself believed also: and when he was baptized, he continued with Philip, and wondered, beholding the miracles and signs which were done" (Acts 8:13). "But Peter said unto him, Thy money perish with thee, because thou hast thought that the gift of God may be purchased with money. Thou hast neither part nor lot in this matter: for thy heart is not right in the sight of God. Repent therefore of this thy wickedness, and pray God, if perhaps the thought of thine heart may be forgiven thee. For I perceive that thou art in the gall of bitterness, and in the bond of iniquity" (Acts 8:20-23).

f. The Prodigal Son—What was the purpose of Jesus in relating this parable? It was to emphasize the joy in heaven over men repenting here on earth. This is clearly indicated in Luke 15, especially in the following verses: "I say unto you, that likewise joy shall be in heaven over one sinner that repenteth, more than over ninety and nine just persons, which need no repentance. . . . Likewise, I say unto you, there is joy in the presence of the angels of God over one sinner that repenteth. . . . It was meet that we should make merry, and be glad: for this thy brother was dead, and is alive again; and was lost, and is found" (Luke 15:7, 10, 32).

Is the repentance in this story that of a lost man being saved or of a saved man being restored to fellowship? The latter is true. This son did not lose his salvation and then regain it, for in the depths of sin and despair he could still say, "I will arise and go to my father." No unsaved man can ever refer to God in such a manner.

g. Demas—"For Demas hath forsaken me, having loved this present world, and is departed unto Thessalonica" (2 Tim. 4:10). Whatever else one may conclude here, this is a sad commentary on one of Paul's companions. We had previously read of him fellowshipping with both the apostle and Luke (Col. 4:12-14).

The truth of the matter is that, as John Mark had once done (Acts 13:13), Demas failed Paul in an hour of great need. The John Mark story had a happy ending, however (2 Tim. 4:11). Perhaps the Demas story had a better ending also if we were told all the facts.

Before leaving this topic of the problems of eternal security, let us attempt to answer two oft-repeated charges against the doctrine.

1. "Why, if I believed that way, I could go out tonight, get drunk, lie, cheat, steal, commit adultery, and live like the devil, and still be saved."

I would like to relate a personal experience here. Some years ago an Arminian friend of mine would often repeat the above words to me. One day I said: "Glen, you're always bringing this up. Let me ask you a personal question. Are you telling me that the *only* reason holding you back from going out tonight and doing all these things is the knowledge that *if* you did, you'd be lost?"

He quickly assured me: "Oh no! That's not the main reason why. I don't do them because I love my family and the Lord!"

I then told him: "I feel the same way! I simply have no desire to do those things. My belief in eternal security has nothing whatsoever to do with the matter."

I believe it can be further demonstrated that the person believing in eternal security has, in reality, a *bigger* club hanging over his head than the one who does not believe in it. Consider the following:

Here are two salesmen from the same company located in a small town. One we will call Pentecostal Pete and the other Baptist Bill. Both men are saved and faithful workers in their respective churches. Both are sent by their company to a sales meeting in New York City. After the final meeting on a Friday each man is tempted to go out on the town and live it up before leaving the next day, as he used to do before his conversion. Let us suppose that, to their shame, both men given in to the temptation. What happens next? After a few drinks, Pentecostal Pete would conclude he had probably lost his salvation. He could then reason that since this was the case, he might as well enjoy himself and get saved again after the weekend! But what about poor Baptist Bill? Regardless of what he does, he realizes God is still his Father, that he cannot escape his ever-watching eye, that he is grieving the Holy Spirit of God within him, and that, due to all this, he is probably in for the spiritual spanking of his life.

2. "But what about the person who got saved and later on became a drunkard?"

To answer this, let me make a statement that may, at first glance, smack of pride, but it does not. Here is the statement: The *only* person that I can know beyond *any* shadow of doubt who is going to heaven is myself! Does this sound arrogant? Think about it for a moment. Actually, the only person *you* can be absolutely sure of in the same light is *yourself.* You see, we simply have no total insight into the mind of another person as we do our own heart.

We are, of course (as much as possible), confident that *all* our professing Christian friends are heavenbound with us, but again, the *only* person I can *know* will be there is *myself.* But what about the Christian who later becomes a drunkard? To begin with, we do not know whether he was saved in the first place. We *do* know, however, that *if* his conversion was real, God will step in somewhere along the line and chasten him to repentance.

As a personal note, to my shame, I did not start drinking until *after* my conversion. The reason for this is that I began running with a crowd of unsaved boys. I'm sure an Arminian would have pointed to me back then as an example of someone who "had it," but through booze had "lost it." Of course, they had no way of knowing the terrible struggle and conviction that were raging inside me during that period. The Spirit of God literally had my carnal soul in a divine vise, applying the pressure that only he can. Part of my carnality in those days was an attempt to escape the call of God to preach. I knew he was calling me, but, like Jonah, I turned and ran. Finally, unable to bear it any longer, I submitted my will to him. What peace and joy then filled my heart as I enrolled in the Moody Bible Institute to prepare for the gospel ministry.

The point of all the above is simply this: we cannot make a final judgment concerning the salvation of any professing Christian, for only God knows those who truly belong to him. "Nevertheless the foundation of God standeth sure, having this seal, The Lord knoweth them that are his. And, Let every one that nameth the name of Christ depart from iniquity" (2 Tim. 2:19).

As a final illustration, imagine yourself in the vicinity of the Garden of Gethsemane on a warm April night some 2,000 years ago. As you watch, a man walks up to Jesus and begins kissing him. You would probably conclude, "How this man must love the Master!" Shortly after this you are shocked to hear another man bitterly cursing Christ. Now your conclusion would be, "How this man must hate the Master!" But both times you would be wrong. Judas, the man who kissed Christ, really hated him, and Peter, the one who cursed Him, really loved Him.

In closing this point it should be noted that the honest Arminian must attempt to answer two key questions.

First, the Bible clearly teaches that salvation is wholly of grace and totally apart from any good works by man. "For by grace are ye saved through faith; and that not of yourselves: it is the gift of God: not of works, lest any man should boast" (Eph. 2:8-9). "Not by works of righteousness which we have done, but according to his mercy he saved us, by the washing of regeneration, and renewing of the Holy Ghost" (Titus 3:5).

Now *if* good works play no part whatsoever in *obtaining* salvation, how can they help in *keeping* it? *If* one must maintain good works to keep it, then salvation is simply not of grace at all. One cannot have it both ways.

Secondly, *if* one could be saved and then lost, how could he *ever* know at any given time whether he had retained or forfeited that salvation? For example, how many cigarettes could he smoke before becoming unsaved? Would he be able to feel his salvation leaving him when he reached the fatal number?

B. The proofs of eternal security—We have discussed at some length the problems concerning eternal security. Now what are the proofs of this precious biblical doctrine? Does the Bible indeed teach once saved always saved? It most certainly does. In fact, the work of the entire Trinity guarantees it.

  1. The work of the Father

   a. Because of his plan and program—"And we know that all things work together for good to them that love God, to them who are the called according to his purpose" (Rom. 8:28). (See also Eph. 1:3-11; 2:7.) Note the features of this plan:

    (1) To predestinate all those he foreknew to be conformed to the image of Christ—"For whom he did foreknow, he also did predestinate to be conformed to the image of his Son, that he might be the firstborn among many brethren" (Rom. 8:29).

    (2) To accept all those in Christ—"To the praise of the glory of his grace, wherein he hath made us accepted in the beloved" (Eph. 1:6). "For ye are dead, and your life is hid with Christ in God" (Col. 3:3). This means that the believer has as much right to be in heaven as Christ does, for he is in Christ.

    (3) To call, justify, and glorify all those accepted in Christ—"Moreover whom he did predestinate, them he also called: and whom he called, them he also justified: and whom he justified, them he also glorified" (Rom. 8:30).

      Note especially the last phrase of this verse, "them he also glorified." Glorification, of course, will not take place until the Rapture. (See 1 Cor. 15:51-54.) But in Romans 8:30 Paul puts the word in the past tense. In other words, in God's sight the believer is *already* glorified in heaven with Christ. This is the strongest verse in the Bible on eternal security.

    (4) To gather them all in Christ in the fullness of time—"That in the dispensation of the fulness of times he might gather together in one all things in Christ, both which are in heaven, and which are on earth; even in him" (Eph. 1:10).

    (5) To display those he has gathered in Christ as trophies of his grace throughout eternity—"That in the ages to come he might shew the exceeding riches of his grace in his kindness toward us through Christ Jesus" (Eph. 2:7).

   b. Because of his power—"My Father, which gave them me, is greater than all; and no man is able to pluck them out of my Father's hand" (John 10:29). (See also Rom. 4:21; 14:4; 1 Cor. 1:8-9; Eph. 3:20; Phil. 1:6; 2 Tim. 1:12; 4:18; Heb. 7:25; 1 Pet. 1:5; Jude 24.)

   c. Because of his love—"But God commendeth his love toward us, in that, while we were yet sinners, Christ died for us" (Rom. 5:8). (See also Rom. 8:31-33.)

    d. Because of his faithfulness in chastening his own—"For whom the Lord loveth he chasteneth, and scourgeth every son whom he receiveth" (Heb. 12:6).

2. The work of the Son

    a. Because of his promises—"Verily, verily, I say unto you, He that heareth my word, and believeth on him that sent me, hath everlasting life, and shall not come into condemnation; but is passed from death unto life" (John 5:24). (See also John 6:37; 10:27-28.)

    b. Because of his prayer—"And now I am no more in the world, but these are in the world, and I come to thee. Holy Father, keep through thine own name those whom thou hast given me, that they may be one, as we are. . . . Sanctify them through thy truth: thy word is truth. . . . Father, I will that they also, whom thou hast given me, be with me where I am; that they may behold my glory, which thou hast given me: for thou lovedst me before the foundation of the world" (John 17:11, 17, 24).

    c. Because of his death—"But he was wounded for our transgressions, he was bruised for our iniquities: the chastisement of our peace was upon him; and with his stripes we are healed" (Isa. 53:5). "For this is my blood of the new testament, which is shed for many for the remission of sins" (Matt. 26:28). "When Jesus therefore had received the vinegar, he said, It is finished: and he bowed his head, and gave up the ghost" (John 19:30).

        Here the law of double jeopardy is seen. This law states that a man cannot be tried or punished twice for the same crime. Through his death Christ was punished for my sin. By accepting him as Savior I agreed to allow him to pay my sin debt. But if I must eventually pay for my own sin in hell because I fell from grace prior to death, then the righteous Judge of the universe becomes guilty of breaking the law of double jeopardy.

    d. Because of his resurrection—"For if we have been planted together in the likeness of his death, we shall be also in the likeness of his resurrection: Knowing this, that our old man is crucified with him, that the body of sin might be destroyed, that henceforth we should not serve sin. For he that is dead is freed from sin. Now if we be dead with Christ, we believe that we shall also live with him: Knowing that Christ being raised from the dead dieth no more; death hath no more dominion over him" (Rom. 6:5-9).

    e. Because of his present ministry

       (1) His work as our *advocate* in heaven assures our eternal security—"Who is he that condemneth? It is Christ that died, yea rather, that is risen again, who is even at the right hand of God, who also maketh intercession for us" (Rom. 8:34). "For Christ is not entered into the holy places made with hands, which are the figures of the true; but into heaven itself, now to appear in the presence of God for us" (Heb. 9:24). "My little children, these things write I unto you, that ye sin not. And if any man sin, we have an advocate with the Father, Jesus Christ the righteous" (1 John 2:1).

       (2) His work as our *intercessor* in heaven assures our eternal security—"And they truly were many priests, because they were not suffered to continue by reason of death: But this man, because he continueth ever, hath an unchangeable priesthood. Wherefore he is able also to save them to the uttermost that come unto God by him, seeing he ever liveth to make intercession for them" (Heb. 7:23-25). (See also John 17:1-26; Rom. 8:34.)

Dr. John Walvoord writes:

> The present ministry of Christ in glory has to do with the eternal security of those on earth who are saved. Christ both intercedes and serves as our advocate. As intercessor, He has in view the weakness, ignorance, and immaturity of the believer—things concerning which there is no guilt. In this ministry Christ not only prays for His own who are in the world and at every point of their need (Luke 22:31-32; John 17:9, 15, 20; Rom. 8:34), but on the grounds of His own sufficiency in his unchanging priesthood, He guarantees that they will be kept saved forever (John 14:19; Rom. 5:10; Heb. 7:25). (*Major Bible Themes*, p. 226)

The summary statement of all the above is as follows: "For if, when we were enemies, we were reconciled to God by the death of his Son, much more, being reconciled, we shall be saved by his life" (Rom. 5:10). The glorious truth Paul is literally shouting about here is this: Jesus Christ died to get me saved, but he now lives to keep me saved. This is why he is said to be the author of *eternal* salvation: "And being made perfect, he became the author of eternal salvation unto all them that obey him" (Heb. 5:9).

3. The work of the Holy Spirit
   a. He regenerates the believer (John 3:3-7; Titus 3:5; James 1:18; 1 Pet. 1:23)—This means the Christian now has a new nature that desires the things of God.
   b. He baptizes the believer into the body of Christ (Rom. 6:3-4; 1 Cor. 12:13; Gal. 3:27; Eph. 4:4-5)—The believer thus becomes bone of his bone and flesh of his flesh.
   c. He indwells the believer (1 Cor. 3:16; 6:19; John 14:16; 1 John 3:24).
   d. He seals the believer (2 Cor. 1:22; 5:5; Eph. 1:13-14)—It has been noted that Romans 8:30 is probably the strongest verse in the Bible concerning eternal security. The second strongest would doubtless be found in Ephesians: "And grieve not (literally, stop grieving) the holy Spirit of God, whereby ye are sealed unto the day of redemption" (Eph. 4:30).
      What is this day of redemption? According to Romans 8:23, it is a reference to the Rapture. In other words, the child of God is sealed by the Spirit of God until the day of the Rapture itself.
   e. He strengthens the believer (Eph. 3:16).
   f. He prays for the believer (Rom. 8:26).
4. Conclusion—Let us now hear the conclusion of the matter. Can a saved person ever be lost? Absolutely not. If he could, then he would be forced to admit to the following *unthinkable* things:
   a. That it is possible for one who has been purged from sin by the blood of Christ to become *unpurged*—This claim is refuted by the following passage: "Who being the brightness of his glory, and the express image of his person, and upholding all things by the word of his power, when he had by himself purged our sins, sat down on the right hand of the Majesty on high" (Heb. 1:3).
   b. That it is possible for one who has been forever perfected to become *unperfected*—Refuted by: "For by one offering he hath perfected for ever them that are sanctified" (Heb. 10:14).

c. That God does remember that which he promised to forget—Refuted by: "And their sins and iniquities will I remember no more" (Heb. 10:17).

d. That God does that which he dares anyone else to do: namely, to lay something to the charge of his elect—Refuted by: "Who shall lay any thing to the charge of God's elect? It is God that justifieth. Who is he that condemneth? It is Christ that died, yea rather, that is risen again, who is even at the right hand of God, who also maketh intercession for us" (Rom. 8:33-34).

e. That it is possible for one born of God to become *unborn*—Refuted by: "Jesus answered, Verily, verily, I say unto thee, Except a man be born of water and of the Spirit, he cannot enter into the kingdom of God" (John 3:5).

f. That it is possible for one who has been sealed to become *unsealed*—Refuted by: "And grieve not the holy Spirit of God, whereby ye are sealed unto the day of redemption" (Eph. 4:30).

g. That it is possible for one who has been baptized to become *unbaptized*—Refuted by: "For by one Spirit are we all baptized into one body, whether we be Jews or Gentiles, whether we be bond or free; and have been all made to drink into one Spirit" (1 Cor. 12:13).

h. That it is possible for one who has been joined to the body of Christ to suffer amputation—Refuted by: "For no man ever yet hated his own flesh; but nourisheth and cherisheth it, even as the Lord the church: For we are members of his body, of his flesh, and of his bones" (Eph. 5:29-20). "Now ye are the body of Christ, and members in particular" (1 Cor. 12:27). (See also 1 Cor. 12:13.)

i. That it is possible for God's very elect to be defeated by Satan—Refuted by: "Jude, the servant of Jesus Christ, and brother of James, to them that are sanctified by God the Father, and preserved in Jesus Christ, and called" (Jude 1). (See also Rom. 8:33.)

j. That God did not really mean "shall never perish"—Refuted by: "For God so loved the world, that he gave his only begotten Son, that whosoever believeth in him should not perish, but have everlasting life" (John 3:16). "My sheep hear my voice, and I know them, and they follow me: And I give unto them eternal life; and they shall never perish, neither shall any man pluck them out of my hand. My Father, which gave them me, is greater than all; and no man is able to pluck them out of my Father's hand" (John 10:27-29).

k. That God did not really mean "shall never hunger or thirst"—Refuted by: "But whosoever drinketh of the water that I shall give him shall never thirst; but the water that I shall give him shall be in him a well of water springing up into everlasting life" (John 4:14).

l. That God did not really mean "shall never be judged"—Refuted by: "Who shall also confirm you unto the end, that ye may be blameless in the day of our Lord Jesus Christ. God is faithful, by whom ye were called unto the fellowship of his Son Jesus Christ our Lord" (1 Cor. 1:8-9).

m. That God did not really mean "shall never taste of death"—Refuted by: "Then said the Jews unto him, Now we know that thou hast a devil. Abraham is dead, and the prophets; and thou sayest, If a man keep my saying, he shall never taste of death" (John 8:52).

n. That God did not really mean "shall never be forsaken"—Refuted by:

"Being confident of this very thing, that he which hath begun a good work in you will perform it until the day of Jesus Christ" (Phil. 1:6). "Let your conversation be without covetousness; and be content with such things as ye have: for he hath said, I will never leave thee, nor forsake thee" (Heb. 13:5).

    o. That God did not really mean "shall never be moved"—Refuted by: "Cast thy burden upon the LORD, and he shall sustain thee: he shall never suffer the righteous to be moved" (Psa. 55:22).

Thus, if a Christian can be lost, then, according to Paul in Romans 8:35-39, he himself must be able to do that which the Father, the Son, the Holy Spirit, angels, demons, life, death, persecutions, distresses, things present, or things to come *cannot* do. "Who shall separate us from the love of Christ? shall tribulation, or distress, or persecution, or famine, or nakedness, or peril, or sword? As it is written, For thy sake we are killed all the day long; we are accounted as sheep for the slaughter. Nay, in all these things we are more than conquerors through him that loved us. For I am persuaded, that neither death, nor life, nor angels, nor principalities, nor powers, nor things present, nor things to come, nor height, nor depth, nor any other creature, shall be able to separate us from the love of God, which is in Christ Jesus our Lord" (Rom. 8:35-39).

XII. The Assurances of Salvation—"These things have I written unto you that believe on the name of the Son of God; that ye may know that ye have eternal life, and that ye may believe on the name of the Son of God" (1 John 5:13). "Examine yourselves, whether ye be in the faith; prove your own selves. Know ye not your own selves, how that Jesus Christ is in you, except ye be reprobates?" (2 Cor. 13:5).

In his excellent book on salvation, Dr. Robert Gromacki lists 12 things by which one may test his salvation experience. They are:

A. First, have you enjoyed spiritual fellowship with God, with Christ, and with fellow believers? (1 John 1:3-4)

B. Second, do you have a sensitivity to sin? (1 John 1:5-10)

C. Third, are you basically obedient to the commandments of Scripture? (1 John 2:3-5)

D. Fourth, what is your attitude toward the world and its values? (1 John 2:15)

E. Fifth, do you love Jesus Christ and look forward to his coming? (2 Tim. 4:8; 1 John 3:2-3)

F. Sixth, do you practice sin less now that you have professed faith in Christ? (1 John 3:5-6)

G. Seventh, do you love other believers? (1 John 3:14)

H. Eighth, have you experienced answered prayer? (1 John 3:22; 5:14-15)

I. Ninth, do you have the inner witness of the Holy Spirit? (Rom. 8:15; 1 John 4:13)

J. Tenth, do you have the ability to discern between spiritual truth and error? (John 10:3-5, 27; 1 John 4:1-6)

K. Eleventh, do you believe the basic doctrines of the faith? (1 John 5:1)

L. Twelfth, have you experienced persecution for your Christian position? (John 15:18-20; Phil. 1:28) (*Salvation Is Forever*, pp. 177–182)

THE DOCTRINE OF THE CHURCH

INTRODUCTION
In the book of Ephesians the Apostle Paul warned his readers against "the wiles of the devil," and the "fiery darts of the wicked." "Put on the whole armour of God, that ye may be able to stand against the wiles of the devil" (Eph. 6:11). "Above all, taking the shield of faith, wherewith ye shall be able to quench all the fiery darts of the wicked" (Eph. 6:16).

Satan has always, of course, bitterly opposed both the work and workers of God. His battle with Jesus began in the Garden of Eden (Gen. 3:15) and continued without pause throughout the Old Testament. With the advent of the incarnation, life, crucifixion, resurrection and ascension of Christ, the intensity of the struggle increased a thousandfold. During the first few centuries of church history, the devil attacked the doctrine of the deity of Christ. Then (after a terrible defeat in A.D. 325) he moved against the doctrine of justification by faith. But he had not counted on the actions of one Martin Luther. Again, turning in another direction, he lashed out against the inspiration of the Scriptures. This reached its high point during the final years of the nineteenth century and early years of the twentieth century, about the time God was raising up great schools of the Scripture, such as the Moody Bible Institute in Chicago, and other Bible centers to counteract this satanic attack.

Finally, in a desperate effort to corrupt and confuse the work of God (before the coming of the Son of God), Satan has boldly and brazenly declared all-out war upon the very bride of Christ, the church itself. Perhaps the most disturbing factor about this attack, unlike all others, is that the devil has been successful in deceiving a number of both professing and possessing Christians into joining his ranks.

The author once wrote an article entitled "If I Were the Devil." The following is taken from this article:

> If I were the devil I would viciously attack those four divine institutions so graciously given by God to man, namely, the institutions of marriage, human government, the nation Israel, and the church.
>
> Concerning the church, I would continue to attack it from the outside (just to keep in practice), but would concentrate the bulk of my evil efforts from within. "The church is dead" would become my creed and cry. If I were the devil I would do my utmost to convince professing Christians that the local church is finished! Not weak, not ineffective, but dead and decaying! I would encourage them to dig a hole, carve an epitaph, and bury it as quietly and quickly as possible. "Christianity" could then proceed to new glories where private cell groups would replace Sunday assemblies, and sermons would be set aside for buzz sessions! (*Baptist Bulletin*, Dec. 1971)

Today one need only scan the horizon of Christendom to discover just how successful Satan has been along these lines. There is a desperate need for the study of and subsequent return to the scriptural teachings of the church. This must be, "Lest Satan should get an advantage of us: for we are not ignorant of his devices" (2 Cor. 2:11).

I. The Meaning of the Word *Church*

The Greek word in the New Testament for our English word *church* is *ekklesia.* It is derived from the verb *ekkaleo.* The compound *ek* means "out," and *kaleo* means "to call or summon." Thus, the literal meaning is "to call out."

Charles Ryrie, however, cautions, "If the word is going to be translated on the basis of etymology, then it should be translated "called together," not "called out" (*Basic Theology,* p. 394).

A. Its connection with the Hebrew world of the Old Testament—The New Testament Greek word *ekklesia* has a loose connection with the Hebrew word *qahal,* which is found some 100 times in the Old Testament. It is translated by the English words *congregation, assembly, company. Qahal* may refer to those assemblies gathered for purposes of:

1. Evil counsel—"I have hated the congregation of evildoers; and will not sit with the wicked" (Psa. 26:5).
2. Civil affairs—"That they sent and called him. And Jeroboam and all the congregation of Israel came, and spake unto Rehoboam, saying . . . , If thou wilt be a servant unto this people this day, and wilt serve them, and answer them, and speak good words to them, then they will be thy servants for ever" (1 Kings 12:3, 7). In this passage, Israel's elders had gathered together at Shechem to discuss a very important civil affair, the coronation of Rehoboam, Solomon's son, as their next king.
3. War—"And the chief of all the people, even of all the tribes of Israel, presented themselves in the assembly of the people of God, four hundred thousand footmen that drew sword" (Judg. 20:2). This relates to the sad meeting of Israel's 11 tribes who had gathered to go to war against the twelfth tribe, Benjamin.
4. Religious worship of God—"And Jehoshaphat stood in the congregation of Judah and Jerusalem, in the house of the Lord, before the new court" (2 Chron. 20:5).

B. Its connection with the secular Greek world—In secular Greek, *ekklesia* referred only to an assembly or meeting and never to the people which composed that assembly. Even a wild and ignorant lynch mob could be referred to as an *ekklesia* (Acts 19:32).

C. Its connection to the theological world of the New Testament—The New Testament reveals a development of the word *ekklesia* from the simple nontechnical meaning of "assembly" to the full-blown technical and theological designation for "the people of God." Of its 114 occurrences in the New Testament, with but five exceptions (Acts 7:38; 19:32, 39, 41; Heb. 2:12), the *ekklesia* church is presented in this light.

Note these exceptions:

1. "This is he, that was in the church in the wilderness with the angel which spake to him in the mount Sinai, and with our fathers: who received the lively oracles to give unto us" (Acts 7:38).

This passage deals with Stephen's address before the Sanhedrin during which he described the nation Israel at Mount Sinai as "the church in the wilderness."

2. "Some therefore cried one thing, and some another: for the assembly was confused; and the more part knew not wherefore they were come together" (Acts 19:32). "But if ye inquire any thing concerning other matters, it shall be determined in a lawful assembly" (Acts 19:39). "And when he had thus spoken, he dismissed the assembly" (Acts 19:41).

These three verses occur in reference to the wild Greek mob at Ephesus.

3. "Saying, I will declare thy name unto my brethren, in the midst of the church will I sing praise unto thee" (Heb. 2:12).

This passage apparently describes Christ's song of praise to the Father concerning all the elect, both Old Testament and New Testament saints.

II. The Origin of the Church—When and where did the church actually begin? Here we are confronted with several different views.

A. It began with Adam in Genesis 3—In a discussion of this question, Dr. Earl Radmacher quotes R. B. Kuiper, who says:

> And if we assume, as undoubtedly we may, that Adam and Eve believed the promise of God that the seed of the serpent would indeed bruise the heel of the woman, but that the woman's seed would bruise the serpent's head . . . then it may be asserted that they constituted the first Christian church. (*The Nature of the Church*, pp. 193–194)

B. It began with Abraham in Genesis 12—This is the position of most covenant theologians. The logic behind this view is the belief that as Israel once functioned as God's church in the Old Testament, so the church now functions as God's Israel in the New Testament.

C. It began with John the Baptist in Matthew 3—Here the argument is that John was Scripture's first baptizer, and inasmuch as Christ later commanded his church to practice this worldwide (Matthew 28:19), the conclusion is that the church began with John: "Go ye therefore, and teach all nations, baptizing them in the name of the Father, and of the Son, and of the Holy Ghost" (Matt. 28:19).

D. It began with Christ—Here four different time periods are advocated by those who believe it began with the Savior.

1. At the call of the 12 apostles in Matthew 10—Thomas P. Simmons holds this view. He writes:

> In locating the founding of the church we must find a time when something that answers to the description of the church came into existence. This rule points us to the time when, after a night of prayer, Christ selected the twelve disciples. With this selection, these twelve men, for the first time, became a body. They had a head—Christ. They had a treasurer—Judas. They were supposed to be baptized believers. They banded together to carry out Christ's will. What more than this did they become . . . ? (*A Systematic Study of Bible Doctrine*, p. 354)

2. With Peter's confession in Matthew 16—Advocates of this position place the church at this point for the simple reason that it is first mentioned by Christ here: "And I say also unto thee, That thou art Peter, and upon this rock I will build my church; and the gates of hell shall not prevail against it" (Matt. 16:18).

3. With the Last Supper—(See Matt. 26; Mark 14; Luke 22; John 13.) Those who

defend this view believe that it was at this time that Christ instituted the ordinance of the Lord's Supper, indicating the church now existed.

4. On the first Easter night after Jesus' resurrection (John 20)—"Then said Jesus to them again, Peace be unto you: as my Father hath sent me, even so send I you. And when he had said this, he breathed on them, and saith unto them, Receive ye the Holy Ghost" (John 20:21-22). Here it is argued that the final element necessary for the composition of the promised church is now given, namely, the person and power of the Holy Spirit.

E. It began at Pentecost in Acts 2.

F. It began with Paul—Here, as in the case of Christ, several time periods are offered.

1. At the time of his conversion in Acts 9—Proponents of this position remind us that the church could hardly have begun until the conversion of its most famous theologian and epistle writer, the Apostle Paul.

2. At the time of his first missionary trip in Acts 13—Some are convinced that the assembly at Jerusalem, even though referred to as a church, was in reality not one, but rather a group of mainly Jewish believers operating under a modified Old Testament economy. However, in Acts 13 Paul begins his lifelong ministry of establishing 100 percent Christian local churches.

3. At the time of his Roman imprisonment in Acts 28—During this (his first) Roman imprisonment, Paul wrote Philippians, Philemon, Colossians, and Ephesians. Disciples of this last view feel these four New Testament church epistles alone (later to include Paul's two letters to Timothy and Titus) compose God's message to local churches, thus their Acts 28 church origin position.

G. Here, then, are the theories. Which are we to believe? Godly and able men may be cited to support each view, but the bulk of Bible students hold the position that the church began at Pentecost. This view has been amply defended by Dr. Lewis Sperry Chafer, Dr. Charles Ryrie, and Dr. Robert Lightner. These men write:

1. Chafer:

> Apparently for want of due consideration of all that enters into the case, some theologians have sustained the idea that those things which characterize the Old Testament revelation are carried forward without change into the New Testament. The necessity of observing dispensational distinctions arises in connection with the abrupt abandonment of existing features and the introduction of new features which mark the transition from one dispensation to the next. This line of demarcation is especially clear between the present age and that which preceded it, and between the present age and that which is to follow. Certain events which serve to reproduce these changes are properly styled age-transforming. Things cannot be the same in this age as they were in the past age, after the death of Christ has taken place, His resurrection, His ascension, and the advent of the Spirit on Pentecost. In like manner, things cannot be the same in the coming age as they are in this age, after there is brought about the second advent of Christ to reign on the earth, the binding of Satan, the removal of the Church, and the restoration of Israel. Those who see no force in this declaration have hardly considered the measureless meaning of these age-transforming occurrences. In the light of these determining issues, it may be seen (a) that there could be no Church in the world— constituted as she is and distinctive in all her features—until Christ's

death; for her relation to that death is not a mere anticipation, but is based wholly on His finished work and she must be purified by His precious blood. (b) There could be no Church until Christ arose from the dead to provide her with resurrection life. (c) There could be no Church until He had ascended up on high to become her Head; for she is a New Creation with a new federal headship in the resurrected Christ. He is, likewise, to her as the head is to the body. Nor could the Church survive for a moment were it not for His intercession and advocacy in heaven. (d) There could be no Church on earth until the advent of the Holy Spirit; for the most basic and fundamental reality respecting the Church is that she is a temple for the habitation of God through the Spirit. She is regenerated, baptized, and sealed by the Spirit. (*Systematic Theology*, vol. IV, p. 45)

2. Ryrie:

That the day of Pentecost marked the beginning of the church seems evident for the following reasons:

a. The Lord spoke of the church as being future in Matthew 16:18. This apparently means that the church did not exist in Old Testament times.

b. The resurrection and ascension of Christ are essential to the functioning of the church. It is built on the resurrection (Eph. 1:19-20), and the giving of gifts is required for its operation, which giving of gifts in turn is dependent on Christ's being ascended (Eph. 4:7-12). If by some stretch of imaginative theology the body of Christ could be said to have been in existence before the ascension of Christ, then it will have to be concluded that it was an ungifted and inoperative body. The church's being built on the resurrection and ascension of Christ makes it distinctive to this age.

c. But the principal evidence that the church began on the day of Pentecost concerns the baptizing work of the Holy Spirit. The Lord declared that this particular and distinctive ministry of the Spirit was still future just before his ascension (Acts 1:5). On the day of Pentecost it first occurred (the record does not say so in Acts 2 but it does in Acts 11:15, 16). Now, what is it that Spirit baptism does? The answer to this is found in 1 Corinthians 12:13; it places the believer in the body of Christ. Since this is the only way to enter the body (i.e., by the baptizing work of the Spirit), and since this work of the Spirit first occurred on the day of Pentecost, then the conclusion seems obvious that the church, the body of Christ, began on the day of Pentecost. (*A Survey of Bible Doctrine*, pp. 157–158)

3. Lightner:

The beginning of the church is definitely related to the day of Pentecost (Acts 2). First, the Spirit's baptism is future from the ascension of Christ (Acts 1:5). Second, the day of Pentecost is the time when the promise in Acts 1:5 was fulfilled. Third, we know this because of Peter's reference to prophecy and his discussion of what happened in the house of Cornelius (Acts 11:15-16). Fourth, Paul declared that as a result of the baptism of the Spirit the body was formed (1 Cor. 12:12-13). Fifth, we are told that the body formed by the Spirit's baptism is the church (Eph. 1:22-23; Col. 1:18). (*Evangelical Theology*, p. 241)

III. The Nature of the Church—Before attempting to determine what it *is*, let us consider some things the church *is not*.
  A. The church considered from a negative viewpoint
    1. It is not a new name for Israel—Covenant theologians teach that the church has become God's elect people, as Israel once was. But this is not the case, as seen by the following arguments:
      a. The promises are different.
        (1) The promises and provisions concerning Israel were basically earthly in scope—"And said, If thou wilt diligently hearken to the voice of the LORD thy God, and wilt do that which is right in his sight, and wilt give ear to his commandments, and keep all his statutes, I will put none of these diseases upon thee, which I have brought upon the Egyptians: for I am the LORD that healeth thee" (Exod. 15:26). (See also Deut. 28.)
        (2) The promises concerning the church are basically heavenly in scope—"Blessed be the God and Father of our Lord Jesus Christ, who hath blessed us with all spiritual blessings in heavenly places in Christ" (Eph. 1:3). "If ye then be risen with Christ, seek those things which are above, where Christ sitteth on the right hand of God. Set your affection on things above, not on things on the earth. For ye are dead, and your life is hid with Christ in God" (Col. 3:1-3).
      b. The seed is different
        (1) Abraham's physical seed refers to Israel—"Neither, because they are the seed of Abraham, are they all children: but, In Isaac shall thy seed be called" (Rom. 9:7).
        (2) Abraham's spiritual seed refers to the church—"Know ye therefore that they which are of faith, the same are the children of Abraham" (Gal. 3:7).
      c. The births are different
        (1) Israel celebrated its birthday at the base of Mount Sinai. (See Exod. 19–20.)
        (2) The church celebrated its birthday at Pentecost. (See Acts 2.) The author of Hebrews brings out the great contrast between these two entities. (See Heb. 12:18-24.)
        (3) Israelites became what they were by physical birth.
        (4) Believers become what they are by spiritual birth.
      d. The nationality is different.
        (1) Israel belonged to this earth and to the world system.
        (2) The church is composed of all nations and has no citizenship down here, but its members are strangers and pilgrims. "Dearly beloved, I beseech you as strangers and pilgrims, abstain from fleshly lusts, which war against the soul" (1 Pet. 2:11).
      e. The relationship with the Father is different.
        (1) God is never presented as the Father of individual Israelites in the Old Testament.
        (2) God is presented as the Father of all New Testament believers—"For ye have not received the spirit of bondage again to fear; but ye have received the Spirit of adoption, whereby we cry, Abba, Father" (Rom. 8:15). "Behold, what manner of love the Father hath bestowed upon us, that we should be called the sons of God: therefore the world knoweth us not, because it knew him not" (1 John 3:1).

(3) Israel is now under God's judgment—"But to Israel he saith, All day long I have stretched forth my hands unto a disobedient and gainsaying people" (Rom. 10:21). "(According as it is written, God hath given them the spirit of slumber, eyes that they should not see, and ears that they should not hear;) unto this day" (Rom. 11:8).

(4) The church is free from all present judgment—"And you, being dead in your sins and the uncircumcision of your flesh, hath he quickened together with him, having forgiven you all trespasses; blotting out the handwriting of ordinances that was against us, which was contrary to us, and took it out of the way, nailing it to his cross; and having spoiled principalities and powers, he made a shew of them openly, triumphing over them in it" (Col. 2:13-15).

(5) Israel was God's servant—"But thou, Israel, art my servant, Jacob whom I have chosen, the seed of Abraham my friend" (Isa. 41:8).

(6) The church—each believer—is God's son—"But as many as received him, to them gave he power to become the sons of God, even to them that believe on his name" (John 1:12). (See also 1 John 3:1.)

f. The relationship with the Son is different.

(1) Israel is pictured as an unfaithful wife—"They say, If a man put away his wife, and she go from him, and become another man's, shall he return unto her again? shall not that land be greatly polluted? but thou hast played the harlot with many lovers; yet return again to me, saith the LORD. . . . Turn, O backsliding children, saith the LORD; for I am married unto you: and I will take you one of a city, and two of a family, and I will bring you to Zion" (Jer. 3:1, 14). "Surely as a wife treacherously departeth from her husband, so have ye dealt treacherously with me, O house of Israel, saith the LORD" (Jer. 3:20). (See also Isa. 54:1-17; Ezek. 16:1-59; Hos. 2:1-23.)

(2) The church is pictured as a chaste virgin bride yet to be married in heaven—"For I am jealous over you with godly jealousy: for I have espoused you to one husband, that I may present you as a chaste virgin to Christ" (2 Cor. 11:2). "Let us be glad and rejoice, and give honour to him: for the marriage of the Lamb is come, and his wife hath made herself ready. And to her was granted that she should be arrayed in fine linen, clean and white: for the fine linen is the righteousness of saints. And he saith unto me, Write, Blessed are they which are called unto the marriage supper of the Lamb. And he saith unto me, These are the true sayings of God" (Rev. 19:7-9).

(3) Christ was a stumbling stone to Israel—"But we preach Christ crucified, unto the Jews a stumbling block, and unto the Greeks foolishness" (1 Cor. 1:23). "And a stone of stumbling, and a rock of offence, even to them which stumble at the word, being disobedient: whereunto also they were appointed" (1 Pet. 2:8).

(4) Christ is the foundation and chief Cornerstone of the church—"And are built upon the foundation of the apostles and prophets, Jesus Christ himself being the chief corner stone; in whom all the building fitly framed together groweth unto an holy temple in the Lord: In whom ye also are builded together for an habitation of God through the Spirit" (Eph. 2:20-22). "To whom coming, as unto a living stone, disallowed

indeed of men, but chosen of God, and precious, ye also, as lively stones, are built up a spiritual house, an holy priesthood, to offer up spiritual sacrifices, acceptable to God by Jesus Christ" (1 Pet. 2:4-5).

(5) Christ is Israel's Messiah and King—"Nathanael answered and saith unto him, Rabbi, thou art the Son of God; thou art the King of Israel" (John 1:49).

(6) Christ is the church's Savior, Bridegroom, and Head—"For the husband is the head of the wife, even as Christ is the head of the church: and he is the saviour of the body" (Eph. 5:23).

g. The relationship with the Holy Spirit is different.

(1) The Holy Spirit rarely came upon individual Old Testament Israelites.

(2) The Holy Spirit actually lives inside each New Testament believer—"What? know ye not that your body is the temple of the Holy Ghost which is in you, which ye have of God, and ye are not your own?" (1 Cor. 6:19).

h. The temple is different.

(1) Israel had a temple—"And let them make me a sanctuary; that I may dwell among them" (Exod. 25:8).

(2) The church is a temple—"In whom all the building fitly framed together groweth unto an holy temple in the Lord" (Eph. 2:21).

The above contrasts should make it crystal clear that the church is not Israel. Paul carefully distinguished these two separate entities when he wrote: "Give none offence, neither to the Jews, nor to the Gentiles, nor to the church of God" (1 Cor. 10:32).

2. It is not the kingdom—The church is to be built up during this present time (Eph. 4:12), while the kingdom will be set up at a future time (Acts 15:16; Rev. 11:15). "For the perfecting of the saints, for the work of the ministry, for the edifying of the body of Christ" (Eph. 4:12). "After this I will return, and will build again the tabernacle of David, which is fallen down; and I will build again the ruins thereof, and I will set it up" (Acts 15:16). "And the seventh angel sounded; and there were great voices in heaven, saying, The kingdoms of this world are become the kingdoms of our Lord, and of his Christ; and he shall reign for ever and ever" (Rev. 11:15).

Charles Ryrie aptly summarizes this aspect: "Much confusion exists because of the failure to carefully define, distinguish, and compare the church and the kingdom. Based on Augustine's *City of God*, the equation of the church and the kingdom resulted in the absolute authority of the church on earth. Postmillennialism builds the earthly kingdom on the growth and success of the church. The mistaken concept of theonomy sees the church's mission as establishing the Old Testament Law of God in the kingdoms of the world today. Reformed theology, less frontal than theonomy, builds on the concept of the lordship of Christ over all the structures of the world, and sees the church as a principal agent in accomplishing this. What is the relation between the church and the kingdom?"

a. The meaning of the kingdom—"The dictionary defines kingdom as a politically organized community. It therefore involves ruler(s), ruled, and realm. To define a particular kingdom, one needs to ask several questions: Who is the ruler? Who are the ruled? When and where is the kingdom? The various kingdoms of Scripture can and need to be distinguished by asking such questions."

b. The various concepts of kingdom

(1) The universal kingdom—"The Scriptures reveal God as Ruler of the whole world (1 Chron. 29:11; Psa. 145:13). As such He exercises jurisdiction over the nations of the world, appointing rulers of His choosing and judging the world (Psa. 96:13; Dan. 2:37). In Jewish thought this concept of the kingdom began with Adam, was disfigured when sin entered, yet continued on until Abraham who recalled people to the kingdom with only partial success (witness the rebellion of Sodom and Gomorrah). However, when Israel accepted the Mosaic Law, this kingdom was reestablished, though rebellion erupted almost immediately (with the golden calf) and repeatedly throughout Israel's history. Only the godly remnant revived the kingdom. Only Messiah would bring the full realization of this kingdom.

"Christian theology acknowledges this concept of a universal kingdom (though usually including angels in it which Judaism did not). God is Ruler of the nations (Rev. 15:3), and ultimately they will answer to Him when He judges them (Psa. 110:6).

"In summary, in the universal kingdom of God, God is the Ruler; He rules over all; and He does it in all time and eternity."

(2) The Davidic/Messianic kingdom—"Both Judaism and premillennial Christian theology give a major place to this concept of kingdom. It is Davidic in that the promises concerning the kingdom were made in the great covenant with David (2 Sam. 7:12-16). It is messianic since Messiah will be the Ruler. It will be realized at the second advent of Christ when He will establish His kingdom and fulfill those promises made to David.

"In summary, in the Davidic messianic kingdom Christ is the Ruler; He will rule over the earth and its inhabitants during the 1,000 years that follow His second coming."

(3) The mystery form of the kingdom—"In Matthew 13 Christ revealed mysteries concerning the concept of the kingdom (v. 11). In accord with the meaning of 'mystery,' this means He told the disciples some things about the kingdom which were previously unknown. This idea of the kingdom, then, began when the Lord was teaching and will end at His second advent (vv. 39-40). In other words, it is the concept of kingdom used to encompass the period between the two advents of Christ. The Ruler is God. The ruled are people on the earth who have related themselves in a positive, neutral, or negative way to 'Christendom' (including true believers, professing people, rejecters, and even opponents). The time is the period between His comings."

(4) The spiritual kingdom—"Spiritual may not be the best label (I take it from James Buswell, *Systematic Theology* [Grand Rapids: Zondervan, n.d.], 2:346), but nothing seems better to characterize this concept of kingdom. It refers to the kingdom into which all believers have been placed (Col. 1:13), and it is entered by the new birth. The Ruler is Christ; in this concept of the kingdom He rules over believers only; and the relationship exists now."

c. The relationship of the church to these kingdoms

    (1) To the universal kingdom—"In the sense that the church is in the world it is part of God's universal kingdom. He designed it, brought it into being, and rules over it, as He does all aspects of His universe."

    (2) To the Davidic/messianic kingdom—"The church is not a part of this kingdom at all. When this kingdom is established the church will have been resurrected and will reign with Christ over the millennial kingdom."

    (3) To the mystery form of the kingdom—"Since the church is part of Christendom, she is part of this concept of kingdom."

    (4) To the spiritual kingdom—"The true church, the body of Christ, is equivalent to this concept of kingdom.

        "If one were to try to summarize the relationship of the church to the kingdom, he would have to say that it is related but not equivalent to certain concepts of the kingdom; it is unrelated to another concept; and it is equivalent to another. The concept of kingdom must be defined before one can determine the relationship of the church to it" (*Basic Theology,* pp. 397–398).

3. It is not a building structure composed of wood, bricks, nails and mortar.

4. It is not a state or national organization—Earl Radmacher writes:

> It is common today, especially in European countries, to witness a close connection between the state and the church so that one particular church is governed and supported by the state. It is interesting to note that all of the leading reformers, who so heroically freed the church from the Roman Catholic Church and the Pope, fastened a state church upon the people wherever they went and the churches which stood for absolute religious liberty were persecuted by these state churches. (*The Nature of the Church,* p. 149)

5. It is not a denominational organization—Again, Radmacher writes: "People often speak of the various denominations or churches, as, for instance, the Episcopal Church, the Lutheran Church, the Presbyterian Church; but this use of *ekklesia* is never found in the Scriptures" (Ibid., p. 150).

6. It is not what the Roman Catholic theologians say it is.

> It has been seen that the Roman Catholic doctrine of the church falls into two divisions, namely, the mystical body of Christ and the church on earth. These do not refer to two different churches, for the constituency of each one is the same; but they refer to two aspects of the church. Because of the identification of the mystical body with the visible church, their conclusion is that there is no salvation outside of the visible church. Although there are numerous books on the Protestant-Catholic dialogue and their ecumenical interests, it has been noted that any "return" of Protestants to Rome must involve the recognition of the Pope as the viceregent of Christ. (Ibid., p. 368)

7. It is not what the liberal theologians say it is.

> Liberalism, being strongly influenced by the social gospel, saw little need for the local churches, which simply impeded the progress of the transformation of society by feverishly clinging to their ecclesiastical dogmas and traditions. The church was regarded as being extraneous to the Christian faith, and a strictly human, mundane organization. (Ibid., p. 369)

8. It is not what the neo-liberal theologians say it is.

Neo-liberalism, reacting against the worldly, human organization of the liberals, brought in a new sense of the importance of the church. They have come to believe that there is a church over and beyond the split denominations. It is a living society, begun in the work of Jesus and continuing that work through the ages. Thus, it is not simply a social organization; it is a divine institution, founded by God. This institution is often referred to by neo-liberals as the *koinonia*, the spiritual fellowship of all those who have committed themselves to the reign of God. One must not be deceived by the seeming orthodoxy, for in reality it is a subtle form of existentialism in which the church is simply a subjective state of being as regards the I-Thou encounter. Neo-liberalism denies that the organized church was in the plan of Christ. (Ibid., p. 369)

9. It is not what the neo-orthodox theologians say it is.

Neo-orthodoxy has some striking similarities to neo-liberalism as regards the doctrine of the church, especially concerning the fluid nature of it. The church is an "event," that is, "The church is not constituted once for all, but that it is continually being recreated by renewed divine activity." There are striking differences, however. Not only does Barth give much greater place to the Holy Spirit as Creator of the church, but, whereas neo-liberalism tends to think of the organized church as a necessary evil, Barth feels that it is *the church*. Finally, he believes that the one, holy, universal church exists in each of the local congregations. (Ibid., p. 369)

10. It is not what the neo-evangelical theologians say it is.

Neo-evangelicalism finds one of its most serious differences with fundamentalism in its doctrine of the church. Neo-evangelicalism tends to sacrifice the purity of the church for the peace and unity of the church. It is their opinion that heretics and unbelievers within the church do not affect the nature of the church. Thus, they are willing to sacrifice purity for unity and opportunity. The job of separating the wheat from the tares, they say, will be Christ's at the second advent. Little attention is given to the New Testament passages demanding definite discipline and purgation in the church. Because the neo-evangelicalist believes that rapprochement can be effected with liberalism and neo-orthodoxy, he is willing to subordinate doctrinal particularity. (Ibid., p. 369)

B. The church considered from a positive viewpoint—We have briefly examined some 10 things that the church is *not*. Now the question: What *is* the church?
  1. The concepts involved—Here three distinct positions may be seen:
    a. First position—This view holds that the *ekklesia* of the New Testament refers only to those geographical groups of baptized believers who regularly assemble, led by pastors and deacons, for the purpose of worship, instruction, fellowship, and evangelism. This position, of course, would categorically deny the existence of a universal and invisible church.

      Thomas Paul Simmons holds this view. He writes:

Now the imaginary universal, invisible church never functions collectively. It holds no services, observes no ordinances, sends out and

supports no missionaries. It is simply a colossal nonentity, without function, purpose, or reason for existence. It is the local church that functions
for Christ. And it is the local church alone that can rightly be called the
body of Christ. (*A Systematic Study of Bible Doctrine*, p. 353)

The extreme of this view is the bride-of-Christ position that says only a
select group will compose the Savior's bride. Robert Lightner observes, "The
view of the above is not too dissimilar from Roman Catholicism, which also
denies the universal church. It teaches that no one can be a part of Christ's
mystical body who is not a member of the visible Roman Catholic church"
(*Evangelical Theology*, p. 237).

b. Second position—This view holds that the *ekklesia* of the New Testament
refers primarily (if not only) to that invisible body of Christ, composed
of all believers, saved from the day of Pentecost to the Rapture. The extreme
of this view is to downplay, if not actually deny the worth of local church
assemblies, substituting instead swimming pool baptismal parties, coffee-
house evangelism, and ecumenical religious dialogues and buzz sessions.

c. Third position—This view holds that the *ekklesia* of the New Testament
embraces both the total body of Christ (including living and departed
believers) and individual local assemblies, with the main emphasis being
placed on the latter meaning. This position is held by most Bible students.

2. The conclusion involved—Assuming the third position is the correct one,
consider the following:

a. The references:

(1) Passages describing the universal church—Matthew 16:18; 1 Corinthians
12:13; 15:9; Galatians 1:13; 3:28; Ephesians 1:22-23; 4:4; 5:25-32; Colossians
1:18; Hebrews 12:23; Revelation 19:6-9. Note especially the following:

(a) "And I say also unto thee, That thou art Peter, and upon this rock I
will build my church; and the gates of hell shall not prevail against it"
(Matt. 16:18).

(b) "For by one Spirit are we all baptized into one body, whether we be
Jews or Gentiles, whether we be bond or free; and have been all made
to drink into one Spirit" (1 Cor. 12:13).

(c) "For I am the least of the apostles, that am not meet to be called an
apostle, because I persecuted the church of God" (1 Cor. 15:9).

(d) "There is neither Jew nor Greek, there is neither bond nor free, there is
neither male nor female: for ye are all one in Christ Jesus" (Gal. 3:28).

(e) "Husbands, love your wives, even as Christ also loved the church,
and gave himself for it" (Eph. 5:25).

(f) "To the general assembly and church of the firstborn, which are
written in heaven, and to God the Judge of all, and to the spirits of just
men made perfect" (Heb. 12:23).

(g) "Let us be glad and rejoice, and give honour to him: for the marriage
of the Lamb is come, and his wife hath made herself ready" (Rev.
19:7).

(2) Passages describing the local church—There are some 27 specific local
churches referred to in the New Testament. Here are but a few of the
biblical passages referring to the local church: Acts 11:26; 13:1; Romans

16:1; 1 Corinthians 1:2; Galatians 1:2; 1 Thessalonians 1:1; 2 Thessalonians 1:1; Philemon 2; Revelation 1:4.

(a) "And when he had found him, he brought him unto Antioch. And it came to pass, that a whole year they assembled themselves with the church, and taught much people. And the disciples were called Christians first in Antioch" (Acts 11:26).

(b) "Unto the church of God which is at Corinth, to them that are sanctified in Christ Jesus, called to be saints, with all that in every place call upon the name of Jesus Christ our Lord, both theirs and ours" (1 Cor. 1:2).

(c) "We give thanks to God always for you all, making mention of you in our prayers" (1 Thess. 1:1).

(d) "John to the seven churches which are in Asia: Grace be unto you, and peace, from him which is, and which was, and which is to come; and from the seven Spirits which are before his throne" (Rev. 1:4).

b. The requirements—In a certain sense of the word it may be stated there is a twofold requirement imposed by the Scriptures for belonging to both the universal and local church. These have to do with the subjects of the new birth and baptism. Consider:

(1) Universal church requirements

(a) That a person be born again—"Jesus answered and said unto him, Verily, verily, I say unto thee, Except a man be born again, he cannot see the kingdom of God" (John 3:3).

(b) That a person be baptized—"For by one Spirit are we all baptized into one body, whether we be Jews or Gentiles, whether we be bond or free; and have been all made to drink into one Spirit" (1 Cor. 12:13). The baptism here, of course, is spirit baptism into the body of Christ. (See also Rom. 6:3-5; Eph. 4:5; Col. 2:12.)

(2) Local church requirements:

(a) That a person be born again—"And all that believed were together, and had all things common; praising God, and having favour with all the people. And the Lord added to the church daily such as should be saved" (Acts 2:44, 47).

(b) That a person be baptized—"Then they that gladly received his word were baptized: and the same day there were added unto them about three thousand souls" (Acts 2:41). "But when they believed Philip preaching the things concerning the kingdom of God, and the name of Jesus Christ, they were baptized, both men and women" (Acts 8:12).

The baptism in mind here is water baptism, a public testimony to one's faith in Christ. Charles Ryrie asks:

> What constitutes a local church? Does a church exist wherever and whenever two or three believers are gathered in the name of Christ? If so, then every Christian home would also be a Christian church. How much organization is necessary to have a local church? Some say the less the better while others opt for a developed organization.
>
> The New Testament does not contain a formal definition of a local church. However, it does describe the normal features of a

local assembly. On the basis of these features we can formulate a definition of a local church. It is an assembly of professing believers in Christ who have been baptized and who are organized to carry out God's will. Notice the important facets of that definition. (1) Those who do not make a profession of faith are excluded. The profession may not be genuine, but it must be made. (2) Without debating the mode of baptism, it is clear that the New Testament knows nothing of unbaptized church members. (3) A church always has some kind of organization, and in the New Testament organization was instituted as soon as possible (Acts 14:23). (4) A church exists for a purpose—to do God's will. This includes a number of things: observing the ordinances, evangelizing, building up believers, worship, giving, ministering to all age groups, etc. A specialized ministry to a particular age group cannot be a church even though it may have features and activities similar to a church. But because it does not open its doors to all professing believers it is not a church. (*Basic Theology,* p. 405)

IV. The Purpose of the Church
  A. Its purpose considered from a negative viewpoint
    1. The purpose of the church is not to save the world—The leaven of Matthew 13:33 is certainly not a picture of the gospel permeating and purifying society, thus turning it into the golden age of the Millennium. To the contrary, world events will sour and become much worse before they get better.
       "This know also, that in the last days perilous times shall come. For men shall be lovers of their own selves, covetous, boasters, proud, blasphemers, disobedient to parents, unthankful, unholy, Without natural affection, trucebreakers, false accusers, incontinent, fierce, despisers of those that are good, Traitors, heady, highminded, lovers of pleasures more than lovers of God; Having a form of godliness, but denying the power thereof: from such turn away. For of this sort are they which creep into houses, and lead captive silly women laden with sins, led away with divers lusts, Ever learning, and never able to come to the knowledge of the truth" (2 Tim. 3:1-7). (See also 2 Pet. 3:1-5.)
    2. The purpose of the church is not to serve the world—Nowhere in the New Testament is the church told to lobby for stronger pollution laws, or march for civil rights, or stage "pray-ins" for unpopular wars. This is not, of course, to say that individual believers cannot be involved in social action.
    3. The purpose of the church is not to fight the world—All too often Bible believers fall victim to this error. Although there are those special occasions when local churches simply must stand up and thunder out against immorality and sin, the church's job is not to expend all its energies and resources fighting dictatorships and alcoholism.
    4. The purpose of the church is not to imitate the world—It has been sadly observed that today the church is so worldly and (on occasion) the world so churchy that angels themselves could not separate the two. For the first three centuries of its history, the church was bitterly opposed by Satan from without. Then, with the advent of Constantine and "Christendom," the devil abruptly changed his tactics, put on his Easter Sunday clothes, walked the church aisle,

and applied for church membership. The church is in the world, but not to be of the world.

   5. The purpose of the church is not to isolate itself from the world—This is the opposite error from that of imitation. About the time of Constantine there arose a new religious movement known as "monasticism." The philosophy of monasticism was that one could escape the perversions of the world by removing himself from the peoples of this world. From this interesting but totally unrealistic belief came the monks and monasteries of the Middle Ages. But the job of the church is not to spend its life in silent contemplation high in the mountains somewhere.

B. Its purpose considered from a positive viewpoint—One of the great Bible teachers of this century was C. I. Scofield, author of the Scofield Reference Edition of the Bible. But many cannot agree with him concerning the purpose of the church. Scofield writes:

> Much is said concerning the "mission of the church." The "church which is his body" has for its mission to build itself up until the body is complete (Eph. 4:11-16; Col. 2:19), but the visible church, as such, is charged with no mission. The commission to evangelize the world is personal, and not corporate. So far as the Scripture story goes, the work of evangelization was done by individuals called directly of the Holy Spirit to that work. Churches and individuals helped the work of these men, but there is no trace of any corporate responsibility attaching to "the church" as such. (*Bible Correspondence Course*, III, p. 431)

It is almost inconceivable to read these words from the pen of such a scriptural giant. Surely Paul would not have agreed with him. The driving force behind his evil actions prior to conversion was to destroy every single local church. "As for Saul, he made havoc of the church, entering into every house, and haling men and women committed them to prison" (Acts 8:3). The burning purpose after his salvation was to start local churches. "And when they had ordained them elders in every church, and had prayed with fasting, they commended them to the Lord, on whom they believed"Acts 14:23).

The sole reason for his second missionary trip was to establish those churches. "And some days after Paul said unto Barnabas, Let us go again and visit our brethren in every city where we have preached the word of the Lord, and see how they do. And he went through Syria and Cilicia, confirming the churches" (Acts 15:36, 41). (See also Acts 16:5.)

One of his heaviest burdens was for the welfare of those local churches. "Beside those things that are without, that which cometh upon me daily, the care of all the churches" (2 Cor. 11:28). Of his 13 known New Testament epistles, 9 are directly written to local churches, and 3 to pastors of local churches. In these epistles he gives detailed instruction concerning the worship services (see 1 Cor. 11:1-16), communion (see 1 Cor. 11:17-343), gifts (see 1 Cor. 12), and officer responsibilities (see 1 Tim. 3; Titus 1) for local churches.

In view of the above, it is difficult indeed to conclude that Paul looked upon the church as an institution without program, plan, or purpose. The facts are that Christ has literally loaded down his church with many and manifold responsibilities and tasks.

   1. Responsibilities concerning the Savior

a. It is to love God—"Nevertheless I have somewhat against thee, because thou hast left thy first love" (Rev. 2:4).

During the heyday of Hollywood in the forties and fifties, there developed in our country the concept of the fan club. These gatherings consisted of admirers of a Hollywood movie star. The basic purpose of the fan club was thus to propagate the name and fame of that one so honored. In a very real sense local churches may be viewed in this light. They are fan clubs to elevate and exalt, promote and praise the name of Jesus that "name which is above every name" (Phil. 2:9).

b. It is to glorify God—"Having predestinated us unto the adoption of children by Jesus Christ to himself, according to the good pleasure of his will, to the praise of the glory of his grace, wherein he hath made us accepted in the beloved. In whom also we have obtained an inheritance, being pre-destinated according to the purpose of him who worketh all things after the counsel of his own will: That we should be to the praise of his glory, who first trusted in Christ. . . . [The Holy Spirit] is the earnest of our inheritance until the redemption of the purchased possession, unto the praise of his glory" (Eph. 1:5-6, 11-12, 14). (See also Eph. 3:21.) "That the name of our Lord Jesus Christ may be glorified in you, and ye in him, according to the grace of our God and the Lord Jesus Christ" (2 Thess. 1:12).

How do we glorify God?

(1) Through our praise and prayer—"Whoso offereth praise glorifieth me: and to him that ordereth his conversation aright will I show the salvation of God" (Psa. 50:23). "And whatsoever ye shall ask in my name, that will I do, that the Father may be glorified in the Son" (John 14:13). "By him therefore let us offer the sacrifice of praise to God continually, that is, the fruit of our lips giving thanks to his name" (Heb. 13:15).

(2) Through our fruit bearing—"Herein is my Father glorified, that ye bear much fruit; so shall ye be my disciples" (John 15:8).

(3) Through our giving—"But I have all, and abound: I am full, having received of Epaphroditus the things which were sent from you, an odour of a sweet smell, a sacrifice acceptable, well-pleasing to God" (Phil. 4:18). "But to do good and to communicate forget not: for with such sacrifices God is well pleased" (Heb. 13:16).

(4) Through our preaching and ministry—"If any man speak, let him speak as the oracles of God; if any man minister, let him do it as of the ability which God giveth: that God in all things may be glorified through Jesus Christ, to whom be praise and dominion for ever and ever. Amen" (1 Pet. 4:11)

(5) Through our loving—"Now the God of patience and consolation grant you to be likeminded one toward another according to Christ Jesus: That ye may with one mind and one mouth glorify God, even the Father of our Lord Jesus Christ" (Rom. 15:5-6).

(6) Through our acknowledging of God's Son—"Wherefore God also hath highly exalted him, and given him a name which is above every name: That at the name of Jesus every knee should bow, of things in heaven, and things in earth, and things under the earth; and that every tongue should confess that Jesus Christ is Lord, to the glory of God the Father" (Phil. 2:9-11).

(7) Through our believing of God's Word—"He staggered not at the promise of God through unbelief; but was strong in faith, giving glory to God" (Rom. 4:20).

(8) Through our suffering—"Verily, verily, I say unto thee, When thou wast young, thou girdedst thyself, and walkedst whither thou wouldest: but when thou shalt be old, thou shalt stretch forth thy hands, and another shall gird thee, and carry thee whither thou wouldest not. This spake he, signifying by what death he should glorify God. And when he had spoken this, he saith unto him, Follow me" (John 21:18-19). "If ye be reproached for the name of Christ, happy are ye; for the spirit of glory and of God resteth upon you: on their part he is evil spoken of, but on your part he is glorified. Yet if any man suffer as a Christian, let him not be ashamed; but let him glorify God on this behalf" (1 Pet. 4:14, 16).

(9) Through our witnessing—"Finally, brethren, pray for us, that the word of the Lord may have free course, and be glorified, even as it is with you" (2 Thess. 3:1).

c. It is to display God's grace—"That in the ages to come he might show the exceeding riches of his grace in his kindness toward us through Christ Jesus" (Eph. 2:7). "That the Gentiles should be fellow heirs, and of the same body, and partakers of his promise in Christ by the gospel: To the intent that now unto the principalities and powers in heavenly places might be known by the church the manifold wisdom of God" (Eph. 3:6, 10). "But ye are a chosen generation, a royal priesthood, an holy nation, a peculiar people; that ye should show forth the praises of him who hath called you out of darkness into his marvellous light" (1 Pet. 2:9).

2. Responsibilities concerning the Scriptures

a. It is to read it—"Till I come, give attendance to reading, to exhortation, to doctrine" (1 Tim. 4:13).

b. It is to heed it—"Take heed unto thyself, and unto the doctrine; continue in them: for in doing this thou shalt both save thyself, and them that hear thee" (1 Tim. 4:16).

c. It is to deed it—"Thou therefore, my son, be strong in the grace that is in Christ Jesus. And the things that thou hast heard of me among many witnesses, the same commit thou to faithful men, who shall be able to teach others also" (2 Tim. 2:1-2). "Preach the word; be instant in season, out of season; reprove, rebuke, exhort with all longsuffering and doctrine" (2 Tim. 4:2).

3. Responsibilities concerning the saints

a. It is to baptize believers (Matt. 28:19).

b. It is to instruct believers—Paul Enns writes:

> Teaching is an important factor in edification, and it made up a vital part of the New Testament church. Members of the early church steadfastly devoted themselves to the teaching of the apostles (Acts 2:42). They taught the doctrine of the resurrection of Christ (Acts 4:2); they taught continually, as they had opportunity (Acts 5:21, 25), to the extent that the entire city of Jerusalem was saturated with the teaching about Christ and His atonement (Acts 5:28). The heart of their message was that Jesus was

indeed the Messiah (Acts 5:42; 17:3). Teaching the new believers resulted in their maturity (Acts 11:26; 15:35).

The goal of Paul's teaching was to present a believer mature in Christ (Col. 1:28); hence, teaching was to be an ongoing practice to succeeding generations (2 Tim. 2:2). Failure to do so or failure to respond to teaching resulted in spiritual babyhood (Heb. 5:12). A simple concordance study will reveal the importance of teaching as a New Testament emphasis.

Teaching is the antidote to false doctrine (1 Tim. 1:3); it produces love among believers (1 Tim. 1:5); it provides spiritual nourishment (1 Tim. 4:6); godliness (1 Tim. 4:6-16); submission (1 Tim. 5:17; 6:2); and a proper focus on life (1 Tim. 6:17). Paul instructed Timothy to teach others in order to reproduce himself (2 Tim. 2:2; cf. 1 Tim. 4:14, 16; 6:20). (*Moody Handbook of Theology*, pp. 353, 365)

c. It is to edify believers—"How is it then, brethren? when ye come together, every one of you hath a psalm, hath a doctrine, hath a tongue, hath a revelation, hath an interpretation. Let all things be done unto edifying" (1 Cor. 14:26). "Wherefore comfort yourselves together, and edify one another, even as also ye do" (1 Thess. 5:11). "And he gave some, apostles; and some, prophets; and some, evangelists; and some, pastors and teachers; For the perfecting of the saints, for the work of the ministry, for the edifying of the body of Christ" (Eph. 4:11-12).

d. It is to discipline believers—"For the time is come that judgment must begin at the house of God: and if it first begin at us, what shall the end be of them that obey not the gospel of God?" (1 Pet. 4:17).

Note: The reason for and recipients of church discipline will be discussed at a later point of our study.

e. It is to provide fellowship for believers—"And they continued stedfastly in the apostles' doctrine and fellowship, and in breaking of bread, and in prayers" (Acts 2:42). "God is faithful, by whom ye were called unto the fellowship of his Son Jesus Christ our Lord" (1 Cor. 1:9). "Praying us with much entreaty that we would receive the gift, and take upon us the fellowship of the ministering to the saints" (2 Cor. 8:4). "The grace of the Lord Jesus Christ, and the love of God, and the communion of the Holy Ghost, be with you all. Amen" (2 Cor. 13:14).

"And when James, Cephas, and John, who seemed to be pillars, perceived the grace that was given unto me, they gave to me and Barnabas the right hands of fellowship; that we should go unto the heathen, and they unto the circumcision" (Gal. 2:9). "That which we have seen and heard declare we unto you, that ye also may have fellowship with us: and truly our fellowship is with the Father, and with his Son Jesus Christ. If we say that we have fellowship with him, and walk in darkness, we lie, and do not the truth: But if we walk in the light, as he is in the light, we have fellowship one with another, and the blood of Jesus Christ his Son cleanseth us from all sin" (1 John 1:3, 6-7).

John MacArthur, Jr., writes:

The New Testament word for fellowship is *koinonia*. It means communion or fellowship—intimate communication. God designed men for fellowship. In Genesis 2:18, God says, "It is not good that the man should be alone." Man was not made to be isolated; being alone is not the will of God. People were made for fellowship. And the church, the body of Christ, is the epitome of fellowship. The church was never intended to be only a building—a place where lonely people walk in, listen, and walk out still alone—but a place of fellowship.

Bruce Larson says, "The neighborhood bar is possibly the best counterfeit there is to the fellowship Christ wants to give His Church. It's an imitation dispensing liquor instead of grace, escape rather than reality. But it is a permissive, accepting, and inclusive fellowship. It is unshockable, it is democratic. You can tell people secrets and they usually don't tell others, or want to. The bar flourishes, not because most people are alcoholics, but because God has put into the human heart the desire to know and be known, to love, and be loved, and so many seek a counterfeit at the price of a few beers."

This need for fellowship is the genius of the church. (*The Church, The Body of Christ,* p. 169)

MacArthur goes on to discuss the basis, nature, dangers, and responsibilities involved within this blessed fellowship.

(1) The basis of Christian fellowship: the person of Christ—"That which we have seen and heard declare we unto you, that ye also may have fellowship with us: and truly our fellowship is with the Father, and with his Son Jesus Christ" (1 John 1:3).

(2) The nature of Christian fellowship: sharing—"And all that believed were together, and had all things common; And sold their possessions and goods, and parted them to all men, as every man had need. And they, continuing daily with one accord in the temple, and breaking bread from house to house, did eat their meat with gladness and singleness of heart, Praising God, and having favour with all the people. And the Lord added to the church daily such as should be saved" (Acts 2:44-47).

"And the multitude of them that believed were of one heart and of one soul: neither said any of them that ought of the things which he possessed was his own; but they had all things common. Neither was there any among them that lacked: for as many as were possessors of lands or houses sold them, and brought the prices of the things that were sold, And laid them down at the apostles' feet: and distribution was made unto every man according as he had need" (Acts 4:32, 34-35).

(3) The dangers of losing Christian fellowship: sin—"The cup of blessing which we bless, is it not the communion of the blood of Christ? The bread which we break, is it not the communion of the body of Christ? Ye cannot drink the cup of the Lord, and the cup of devils: ye cannot be partakers of the Lord's table, and of the table of devils" (1 Cor. 10:16, 21).

(4) The responsibilities of Christian fellowship:

   (a) Confess our faults—"And the prayer of faith shall save the sick, and the Lord shall raise him up; and if he have committed sins, they shall be forgiven him" (James 5:16).

   (b) Rebuke sin in each other—"And have no fellowship with the unfruitful works of darkness, but rather reprove them" (Eph. 5:11).

"Them that sin rebuke before all, that others also may fear" (1 Tim. 5:20).

(c) Forgive one another—"Sufficient to such a man is this punishment, which was inflicted of many. . . . Wherefore I beseech you that ye would confirm your love toward him" (2 Cor. 2:6, 8). "And be ye kind one to another, tenderhearted, forgiving one another, even as God for Christ's sake hath forgiven you" (Eph. 4:32). "Forbearing one another, and forgiving one another, if any man have a quarrel against any: even as Christ forgave you, so also do ye" (Col. 3:13).

(d) Bear one another's burdens—"Bear ye one another's burdens, and so fulfil the law of Christ" (Gal. 6:2).

(e) Gently restore one another—"Brethren, if a man be overtaken in a fault, ye which are spiritual, restore such an one in the spirit of meekness; considering thyself, lest thou also be tempted" (Galatians 6:1).

(f) Prefer the weaker brother—"Let us not therefore judge one another any more: but judge this rather, that no man put a stumblingblock or an occasion to fall in his brother's way" (Rom. 14:13). "We then that are strong ought to bear the infirmities of the weak, and not to please ourselves" (Rom. 15:1).

(g) Comfort and exhort each other—"But I would not have you to be ignorant, brethren, concerning them which are asleep, that ye sorrow not, even as others which have no hope" (1 Thess. 4:18). "Wherefore comfort one another with these words" (1 Thess. 5:11).

(h) Pray one for another—"Confess your faults one to another, and pray one for another, that ye may be healed. The effectual fervent prayer of a righteous man availeth much" (James 5:16).

(i) Edify one another—"Let us therefore follow after the things which make for peace, and things wherewith one may edify another" (Rom. 14:19). "And let us consider one another to provoke unto love and to good works" (Heb. 10:24; see also 1 Thess. 5:11).

(j) Admonish one another—"And I myself also am persuaded of you, my brethren, that ye also are full of goodness, filled with all knowledge, able also to admonish one another" (Rom. 15:14).

f. It is to care for its own in time of need.

(1) Those needy believers without the local church—This would include hurting Christians who are members of another local church. "And in these days came prophets from Jerusalem unto Antioch. And there stood up one of them named Agabus, and signified by the Spirit that there should be great dearth throughout all the world: which came to pass in the days of Claudius Caesar. Then the disciples, every man according to his ability, determined to send relief unto the brethren which dwelt in Judaea. Which also they did, and sent it to the elders by the hands of Barnabas and Saul" (Acts 11:27-30).

(2) Those needy believers within the local church

(a) The poverty-stricken—"If a brother or sister be naked, and destitute of daily food, And one of you say unto them, Depart in peace, be ye warmed and filled; notwithstanding ye give them not those things which are needful to the body; what doth it profit?" (James 2:15-16).

"But whoso hath this world's good, and seeth his brother have need, and shutteth up his bowels of compassion from him, how dwelleth the love of God in him?" (1 John 3:17).

(b) The fatherless (James 1:27)

(c) Widows—Charles Ryrie comments:

> At the time of Christ there existed a fund in the temple which was used to support widows and orphans. When many Jewish widows were converted to Christianity the church undertook their continued support. However, Paul makes it crystal clear in the central passage on the subject that a widow's family has the first and primary obligation to care for the widow. This is true of both younger, unenrolled widows (1 Tim. 5:4, 8) and of any older, enrolled widows (v. 16).
>
> If there are no relatives to support a widow, then the church must assume that obligation, regardless of the age of the widow. A "widow indeed" is not necessarily an enrolled widow but one who is destitute in that she has no family to support her (v. 5). Therefore, her church family must underwrite her support. Younger widows are encouraged to remarry (v. 14); widows who qualify can be put on the church roll after age sixty (vv. 9-10).
>
> What should a church do about this responsibility in a day of social security, insurance, annuities, and other financial provisions often made for a widow? The principles seem clear: to whatever extent her own family cannot support her (whether through living relatives or through the provision of relatives who have died), the church should assume the obligation whether it means partial or full support. Needs often exist today for widows of Christian workers who are left in need through no fault of their own. (*Basic Theology*, p. 435.

(d) Missionaries—"And now, brothers, we want you to know about the grace that God has given the Macedonian churches. Out of the most severe trial, their overflowing joy and their extreme poverty welled up in rich generosity. For I testify that they gave as much as they were able, and even beyond their ability. Entirely on their own" (2 Cor. 8:1-3, NIV).

4. Responsibilities concerning sinners—"I am debtor both to the Greeks, and to the Barbarians; both to the wise, and to the unwise. So, as much as in me is, I am ready to preach the gospel to you that are at Rome also" (Rom. 1:14-15).

In a sentence, it is to evangelize the world. "Go ye therefore, and teach all nations, baptizing them in the name of the Father, and of the Son, and of the Holy Ghost: Teaching them to observe all things whatsoever I have commanded you: and, lo, I am with you alway, even unto the end of the world. Amen" (Matt. 28:19-20). "And he said unto them, Go ye into all the world, and preach the gospel to every creature" (Mark 16:15). "And that repentance and remission of sins should be preached in his name among all nations, beginning at Jerusalem" (Luke 24:47). "Then said Jesus to them again, Peace be unto you: as my Father hath sent me, even so send I you" (John 20:21). "But ye shall receive power, after that the Holy Ghost is come upon you: and ye shall be witnesses unto me both in Jerusalem, and in all Judaea, and in Samaria, and unto the uttermost part of the earth" (Acts 1:8).

Gordon G. Johnson writes:

> One day Dr. Wilfred Grenfell, medical missionary to Labrador, was guest at dinner in London, together with a number of socially prominent British men and women. During the course of the dinner the lady seated next to him turned and said, "Is it true, Dr. Grenfell, that you are a missionary?" Dr. Grenfell looked at her for a moment before replying. Then he said, "Is it true, madam, that you are not?" (*My Church*, p. 88)

5. Responsibilities concerning society
   a. It is to act as a restraining and enlightening force in this present world—
      "Ye are the salt of the earth: but if the salt have lost his savour, wherewith shall it be salted? it is thenceforth good for nothing, but to be cast out, and to be trodden under foot of men. Ye are the light of the world. A city that is set on an hill cannot be hid. Neither do men light a candle, and put it under a bushel, but on a candlestick; and it giveth light unto all that are in the house. Let your light so shine before men, that they may see your good works, and glorify your Father which is in heaven" (Matt. 5:13-16).
   b. It is to promote all that is good—"As we have therefore opportunity, let us do good unto all men, especially unto them who are of the household of faith" (Gal. 6:10).

Henry Thiessen writes:

> While the believer is to separate from all worldly alliances (2 Cor. 6:14-18), he is yet to support all causes that seek to promote the social, economic, political, and educational welfare of the community. Paul says: "So then, as we have opportunity, let us work that which is good toward all men, and especially toward them that are of the household of the faith" (Gal. 6:10).
>
> Here we note that we have a primary duty toward fellow believers, but that we also have a duty toward the rest of the world. In this day of social service it is necessary to be clear as to the place of this ministry toward the world. Jesus' practice is the best example to follow. He always subordinated physical and other material help to the spiritual. He went about doing good and healing all that were oppressed of the devil, though his principal mission was never lost sight of (Acts 10:38-43). We should devote ourselves to social service on the same principle on which a man picks up sharp nails that he finds in the street on the way to his work. It is one thing for him to devote his entire time to ridding the streets of nails, and another to remove such nails as he can without interfering with his main task. That is, the work of reformation must be definitely subordinated to the work of evangelization. So also in the case of philanthropy. The Christian should make all his benevolences bear testimony to Christ. Jesus may have fed the five thousand as a humanitarian act; but He certainly did it primarily as a testimony to His own power and deity. Clearly, He went to dinners and suppers in order to testify to the truth. It appears that he healed the man born blind in order to win his

soul (John 9:35-38). In other words, the Christian must make all his good works testify to Christ. (*Lectures in Systematic Theology*, p. 436)

In summary, it may be said that the job of a local church is to make as many people as much like Jesus in the shortest time possible. God the Father is so much in love with his beloved Son that he desires to populate the entire universe throughout eternity with those individuals which resemble Jesus Christ. "Beloved, now are we the sons of God, and it doth not yet appear what we shall be: but we know that, when he shall appear, we shall be like him; for we shall see him as he is" (1 John 3:2). But he desires to start the work in repenting sinners down here right now.

An unknown poet has written the following:

I want my church to be a place, where I can meet God face to face.
I want each worship hour so sweet, that I can feel each time we meet,
   the Lord Himself will take His seat.
I want my church to be far more than table, window, pew and door,
   or carpet laid upon the floor.
But oh, I know it cannot be more than that which is found in me,
So teach me Lord, to live for thee!

6. Responsibilities concerning the seed of Abraham (Israel)—In essence, it is to provoke Israel to jealousy. Robert L. Saucy writes:

The extension of the blessings of salvation to those outside Israel during the age of the church when Israel is judicially blinded is designed by God to effect the final salvation of Israel and the fulfillment of her covenant promises. This in turn will bring the full Messianic blessing upon all nations (Rom. 11:11-15). The apostle explains this intent of God when he says of Israel, "They did not stumble so as to fall, did they? May it never be! But by their transgression salvation has come to the Gentiles, to make them jealous" (v. 11, NASB: cf. 10:10). The apostle magnified his ministry as an apostle to the Gentiles according to his testimony that "somehow I might move to jealousy my fellow countrymen and save some of them" (11:14, NASB).

Through the grafting in of the Gentiles into the root of the Abrahamic blessing which initially belonged to Israel, God purposes by the church to bring a jealousy upon Israel which will cause her to desire to return to the place of blessing through repentance and the acknowledgment of Christ as her true Messiah. (*The Church in God's Program*, p. 89)

V. The Founding of the Church—One of the most important events in the life of Christ prior to his crucifixion took place at Caesarea Philippi in northern Galilee perhaps at the base of mighty Mount Hermon.
 A. The information involved
  1. The probing of Christ—"When Jesus came into the coasts of Caesarea Philippi, he asked his disciples, saying, Whom do men say that I the Son of man am?" (Matt. 16:13)
   a. The rumors—"And they said, Some say that thou art John the Baptist: some, Elias; and others, Jeremias, or one of the prophets. He saith unto them, But whom say ye that I am?" (Matt. 16:14-15).

      b. The recognition—"And Simon Peter answered and said, Thou art the Christ, the Son of the living God" (Matt. 16:16).

      c. The revelation—"And Jesus answered and said unto him, Blessed art thou, Simon Barjona: for flesh and blood hath not revealed it unto thee, but my Father which is in heaven" (Matt. 16:17).

   2. The promise of Christ

      a. What he would provide for his disciples—"And I say also unto thee, That thou art Peter, and upon this rock I will build my church; and the gates of hell shall not prevail against it" (Matt. 16:19).

      b. What he would present to his disciples—"And I will give unto thee the keys of the kingdom of heaven: and whatsoever thou shalt bind on earth shall be bound in heaven: and whatsoever thou shalt loose on earth shall be loosed in heaven" (Matt. 16:19).

   3. The passion of Christ—"From that time forth began Jesus to show unto his disciples, how that he must go unto Jerusalem, and suffer many things of the elders and chief priests and scribes, and be killed, and be raised again the third day" (Matt. 16:21).

   4. The provoking of Christ—"Then Peter took him, and began to rebuke him, saying, Be it far from thee, Lord: this shall not be unto thee. But he turned, and said unto Peter, Get thee behind me, Satan: thou art an offence unto me: for thou savourest not the things that be of God, but those that be of men" (Matt. 16:22-23).

B. The interpretation involved

   1. Was Jesus building his church upon Peter and planning to make him its first pope? It may be clearly stated that he was not.

      a. Because Christ later gave the same responsibilities to the other apostles that he here gives to Peter. (Compare Matt. 16:19 with John 20:22-23.)

      b. Because the New Testament clearly presents Christ and Christ only as the Foundation of his church. (See Acts 4:11-12; 1 Cor. 3:11; 1 Pet. 2:4-8.)

      c. Because the New Testament clearly presents Christ and Christ only as the Head of his church. (See Eph. 1:20-23; 5:23; Col. 1:18; 2:18-19.)

      d. Because of the Greek language—There is a play upon words here. Jesus said, "Thou art Peter [*petros,* a little stone], and upon this rock [*petra,* a massive cliff or rock] I will build my church."

      e. Because of Peter's personal testimony. (See 1 Pet. 5:1-4.)

      f. Because James, not Peter, later officiated at the Jerusalem church. (See Acts 15:13, 19.)

   2. What then, was Christ doing? The answer is given in Ephesians. "Now therefore ye are no more strangers and foreigners, but fellow citizens with the saints, and of the household of God; And are built upon the foundation of the apostles and prophets, Jesus Christ himself being the chief corner stone; In whom all the building fitly framed together groweth unto an holy temple in the Lord: In whom ye also are builded together for an habitation of God through the Spirit" (Eph. 2:19-22).

   3. What did he mean by "The gates of hell shall not prevail against it?" J. Vernon McGee writes: "The gates of hell refer to the 'gates of death.' The word used here is the hades and sheol of the Old Testament which refers to the unseen world and means death. The gates of death shall not prevail against Christ's church" (*Matthew,* vol. II, p. 23).

4. What were the "keys of the kingdom of heaven" that Jesus gave Peter? A key, of course, unlocks doors and makes available something that was previously closed. Jesus here predicts that Peter would be given the privilege of opening the door of salvation to various peoples. This he later did.
   a. He opened the door of Christian opportunity to Israel at Pentecost (Acts 2:38-42).
   b. He did the same thing for the Samaritans (Acts 8:14-17).
   c. He performed this ministry to the Gentiles at Cornelius's house at Caesarea (Acts 10).
5. What did Christ mean by the binding and loosing of Matthew 16:19? This authority was given to all the apostles and even other believers. (See Matt. 18:18; John 20:22-23.) W. A. Criswell writes:

> In Greek the future perfect tense is used to express the double notion of an action terminated in the past but whose effects are still existing in the present. "Having been bound and still bound," and "having been loosed and still loosed." The meaning is: if the disciples act in their proper capacity as stewards, they will be acting in accordance with the principles and elective purposes ordained beforehand in heaven. (*Expository Notes on Matthew*, p. 101)

In other words, all the actions of the Spirit-filled believer, whether positive or negative in nature, will carry with it the awesome authority of heaven itself.

C. The illustration involved—Matthew 16 can be favorably compared with Genesis 11 and John 6.
   1. The Matthew 16/Genesis 11 comparison
      a. Both chapters describe the beginning of a church—Genesis 11:1-9 records the origin of Satan's church. Archaeological evidence has proven the tower of Babel was in reality a religious temple, probably given over to the worship of the stars.
      b. Both chapters describe God's dealings with those churches.
         (1) Satan's church was punished by God (Gen. 11:8).
         (2) Christ's church will be preserved by God (Matt. 16:18).
         (3) Satan's church will be destroyed by the Antichrist during the great tribulation (Rev. 17:16)
         (4) Christ's church will be delivered by the true Christ from the great tribulation (1 Thess. 4:16-17)
   2. The Matthew 16/John 6 comparison
      a. Both chapters record the testimony of Peter
         (1) The John 6 testimony—"From that time many of his disciples went back, and walked no more with him. Then said Jesus unto the twelve, Will ye also go away? Then Simon Peter answered him, Lord, to whom shall we go? thou hast the words of eternal life. And we believe and are sure that thou art that Christ, the Son of the living God" (John 6:66-69)
         (2) The Matthew 16 testimony—"And Simon Peter answered and said, Thou art the Christ, the Son of the living God" (Matt. 16:16).
      b. Both chapters record the treachery of the devil.
         (1) The treachery in John 6—"Jesus answered them, Have not I chosen you twelve, and one of you is a devil? He spake of Judas Iscariot the son of

Simon: for he it was that should betray him, being one of the twelve" (John 6:70-71).

(2) The treachery seen in Matthew 16—"But he turned, and said unto Peter, Get thee behind me, Satan: thou art an offence unto me: for thou savourest not the things that be of God, but those that be of men" (Matt. 16:23).

VI. The History, Growth, and Character of the Various New Testament Churches—In 1 Corinthians 10:11 Paul writes: "Now all these things happened unto them for ensamples: and they are written for our admonition, upon whom the ends of the world are come."

Here, he refers to those Old Testament events. But we may with scriptural justification apply these same words to the events recorded for us in the New Testament. Present-day church leaders will profit greatly by examining the joys, sorrows, sins, and strong points of these early churches. The following is a brief summary of 27 such New Testament churches.

A. The church in Jerusalem (Acts 1–7, 11–12, 15; Epistle of James)

1. Its origin—It began on the day of Pentecost, 10 days after the ascension, in the Upper Room at the advent of the Holy Spirit. "For John truly baptized with water; but ye shall be baptized with the Holy Ghost not many days hence" (Acts 1:8). And when the day of Pentecost was fully come, they were all with one accord in one place. And suddenly there came a sound from heaven as of a rushing mighty wind, and it filled all the house where they were sitting" (Acts 2:1-2).

2. Its duration—How long did it exist? It functioned for some 40 years. Jesus ascended in A.D. 30 and the city of Jerusalem was destroyed in A.D. 70. Just prior to its destruction, the Christians in Jerusalem escaped to an area east of the Jordan River.

3. Its size—To say the very least, the Jerusalem church experienced both a phenomenal, and probably, unprecedented numerical growth. Consider:

   a. It began with 120 (Acts 1:15)

   b. It soon jumped to 3,120—"Then they that gladly received his word were baptized: and the same day there were added unto them about three thousand souls" (Acts 2:41).

   c. From there it leaped to 8,120—"Howbeit many of them which heard the word believed; and the number of the men was about five thousand" (Acts 4:4). Note: The 5,000 figure here refers only to men. Doubtless many women and children were also added to the church, making the actual count much higher.

   d. It continued to mushroom in its growth—"And believers were the more added to the Lord, multitudes both of men and women. And the word of God increased; and the number of the disciples multiplied in Jerusalem greatly; and a great company of the priests were obedient to the faith" (Acts 5:14; 6:7).

4. Its leaders—Perhaps no other Christian assembly in history has had the various kinds of leaders and leadership as did the Jerusalem Church. This included:

   a. Pastor—There is evidence that James, the half brother of Christ and author of the New Testament book of James, served as pastor. Consider:

   (1) For some reason he was afforded a personal, post-resurrection appearance by Christ himself. (See 1 Cor. 15:7.)

(2) For some reason his book was the first New Testament epistle to be written.

(3) Peter refers to him personally after being released from prison—"But Peter continued knocking: and when they had opened the door, and saw him, they were astonished. But he, beckoning unto them with the hand to hold their peace, declared unto them how the Lord had brought him out of the prison. And he said, Go show these things unto James, and to the brethren. And he departed, and went into another place" (Acts 12:16-17).

(4) Paul refers to him personally when describing his first trip to Jerusalem following the Damascus Road conversion—"But other of the apostles saw I none, save James the Lord's brother. . . . And when James, Cephas, and John, who seemed to be pillars, perceived the grace that was given unto me, they gave to me and Barnabas the right hands of fellowship; that we should go unto the heathen, and they unto the circumcision" (Gal. 1:19; 2:9).

(5) It was James who presided over the Jerusalem Council and who announced its decision concerning whether saved Gentiles should be circumcised—"And after they had held their peace, James answered, saying, Men and brethren, hearken unto me. . . . Wherefore my sentence is, that we trouble not them, which from among the Gentiles are turned to God" (Acts 15:13, 19).

(6) It was James who welcomed Paul back to Jerusalem following the apostle's third missionary journey—"And the day following Paul went in with us unto James; and all the elders were present" (Acts 21:18).

b. Apostles—In addition to the original 12 apostles (with Matthias replacing Judas Iscariot; Acts 1:23-25), there were several other men appointed to the high office of apostleship. These included:

(1) Joseph called Barsabas (Acts 1:23)

(2) Judas (Acts 15:22)

(3) Silas (1 Thess. 1:1; Acts 15:22)

(4) Barnabas (Acts 15:22)

(5) James (Gal. 1:19)

(6) Paul (Rom. 1:1)

With the single exception of Paul all the apostles originally ministered in the Jerusalem church.

c. Prophets

(1) Agabus—"And in these days came prophets from Jerusalem unto Antioch. And there stood up one of them named Agabus, and signified by the Spirit that there should be great dearth throughout all the world: which came to pass in the days of Claudius Caesar" (Acts 11:27-28).

(2) Judas and Silas—"And Judas and Silas, being prophets also themselves, exhorted the brethren with many words, and confirmed them" (Acts 15:32).

d. Priests—"And the word of God increased; and the number of the disciples multiplied in Jerusalem greatly; and a great company of the priests were obedient to the faith" (Acts 6:7).

e. Elders (Acts 11:30; 15:2, 4, 6, 22-23; 16:4; 21:18)—These elders may have served as associate pastors along with James, the half brother of Christ.

f. Teachers (Acts 5:21, 25, 42)—Apparently the apostles themselves served in this capacity.

g. Deacons (Acts 6:1-6)—"Wherefore, brethren, look ye out among you seven men of honest report, full of the Holy Ghost and wisdom, whom we may appoint over this business. And the saying pleased the whole multitude: and they chose Stephen, a man full of faith and of the Holy Ghost, and Philip, and Prochorus, and Nicanor, and Timon, and Parmenas, and Nicolas a proselyte of Antioch" (Acts 6:3, 5).

h. Missionaries
  (1) Philip, who was sent to Samaria and Gaza strip (Acts 8:5, 26)
  (2) Peter and John, who were sent to Samaria (Acts 8:14)
  (3) Barnabas, who was sent to Antioch (Acts 11:19-22)

i. Evangelists
  (1) Stephen seemed to serve in this capacity (Acts 6:8–7:60).
  (2) John Mark (nephew of Barnabas and author of the Gospel of Mark) may have become an evangelist.
  (3) Philip became an evangelist (Acts 8:5, 26, 39-40).

5. Its accomplishments
  a. It observed the ordinances.
    (1) That of baptism—"Then they that gladly received his word were baptized: and the same day there were added unto them about three thousand souls" (Acts 2:41).
    (2) That of the Lord's Supper—"And they continued stedfastly in the apostles' doctrine and fellowship, and in breaking of bread, and in prayers" (Acts 2:42).
  b. It enjoyed unity—"And when the day of Pentecost was fully come, they were all with one accord in one place. And they, continuing daily with one accord in the temple, and breaking bread from house to house, did eat their meat with gladness and singleness of heart" (Acts 2:1, 46).
  c. It practiced a form of commonism—Note, there is a vast difference between this and communism.
    (1) Communism says, "What is thine is mine, if I can take it from you!"
    (2) Commonism says, "What is mine is thine if you need it!" "And all that believed were together, and had all things common; And sold their possessions and goods, and parted them to all men, as every man had need" (Acts 2:44-45). (See also Acts 4:32-37.)
  d. It was a praying church—"But we will give ourselves continually to prayer, and to the ministry of the word" (Acts 6:4). (See also Acts 2:42; 3:1; 4:24-31; 12:12.)
  e. It was a Spirit-led church—"And when they had prayed, the place was shaken where they were assembled together; and they were all filled with the Holy Ghost, and they spake the word of God with boldness" (Acts 4:31).
    (1) As reflected by a champion in the church—"But he, being full of the Holy Ghost, looked up stedfastly into heaven, and saw the glory of God, and Jesus standing on the right hand of God, And they stoned Stephen, calling upon God, and saying, Lord Jesus, receive my spirit" (Acts 7:55, 59).
    (2) As reflected by a conclusion by the church—"For it seemed good to the

Holy Ghost, and to us, to lay upon you no greater burden than these necessary things" (Acts 15:28).

f. It continually evangelized (Acts 2:41; 4:4; 5:14; 6:7)—"And believers were the more added to the Lord, multitudes both of men and women" (Acts 5:14). "And the word of God increased; and the number of the disciples multiplied in Jerusalem greatly; and a great company of the priests were obedient to the faith" (Acts 6:7).

g. It preached a threefold message—"And daily in the temple, and in every house, they ceased not to teach and preach Jesus Christ" (Acts 5:42).
   (1) His crucifixion (Acts 2:23, 36; 3:15; 5:30)
   (2) His resurrection (Acts 2:24, 31-32; 3:15; 4:2, 33; 5:30)
   (3) His ascension (Acts 2:33; 3:13; 5:34)

h. It was a miracle-working church—"And fear came upon every soul: and many wonders and signs were done by the apostles" (Acts 2:43). (See also Acts 3:8; 5:12, 15-16; 6:8; 8:6; 9:34, 40.)

i. It was ministered to by angels.
   (1) An angel released the imprisoned apostles (Acts 5:17-20).
   (2) An angel sent Philip to the Gaza desert (Acts 8:26).
   (3) An angel delivered Peter from death row (Acts 12:7).
   (4) An angel slew a bitter enemy of the church, Herod Agrippa I (Acts 12:23).

j. It rebuked sin (Acts 2:23; 5:3; 7:51-53; 8:20-21).
   (1) As demonstrated by Simon Peter—"But Peter said, Ananias, why hath Satan filled thine heart to lie to the Holy Ghost, and to keep back part of the price of the land?" (Acts 5:3).
   (2) As demonstrated by Stephen—"Ye stiffnecked and uncircumcised in heart and ears, ye do always resist the Holy Ghost: as your fathers did, so do ye. Which of the prophets have not your fathers persecuted? and they have slain them which showed before of the coming of the Just One; of whom ye have been now the betrayers and murderers" (Acts 7:51-52).

k. It displayed great boldness—"And they called them, and commanded them not to speak at all nor teach in the name of Jesus. But Peter and John answered and said unto them, Whether it be right in the sight of God to hearken unto you more than unto God, judge ye. For we cannot but speak the things which we have seen and heard. Then Peter and the other apostles answered and said, We ought to obey God rather than men" (Acts 4:18-20; 5:29).

l. It experienced severe persecution.
   (1) It was ridiculed—"Others mocking said, These men are full of new wine" (Acts 2:13).
   (2) It was threatened (Acts 4:21).
   (3) It was imprisoned (Acts 4:1-3; 5:18; 12:5).
   (4) It was slandered (Acts 6:12-13).
   (5) It was beaten (Acts 5:40-41)—"And to him they agreed: and when they had called the apostles, and beaten them, they commanded that they should not speak in the name of Jesus, and let them go. And they departed from the presence of the council, rejoicing that they were counted worthy to suffer shame for his name" (Acts 5:40-41).
   (6) It was scattered (Acts 8:2-3).
   (7) It was stoned to death (Acts 7:57-60).

(8) It was beheaded (Acts 12:1-2).

m. It hosted the first church conference (Acts 15).

n. It anointed its sick with oil and prayed for them (James 5:14-16).

6. Its problems

a. It backslid into legalism on occasion, especially in matters of circumcision.

(1) Peter was criticized for ministering to and fellowshipping with uncircumcised Gentile believers (Acts 11:1-3).

(2) Some in the church felt believing Gentiles should be forced to circumcise themselves—"And certain men which came down from Judaea taught the brethren, and said, Except ye be circumcised after the manner of Moses, ye cannot be saved" (Acts 15:1).

(3) Peter himself was later rebuked by Paul for refusing to fellowship with uncircumcised Gentile believers (Gal. 2:11-13)—"But when Peter was come to Antioch, I withstood him to the face, because he was to be blamed" (Gal. 2:11).

(4) Apparently both James, the half brother of Christ, and Barnabas were also guilty of this (Gal. 2:12-13).

b. It was on occasion guilty of discrimination.

(1) Favoring the Hebrew widows over the Greek widows—"And in those days, when the number of the disciples was multiplied, there arose a murmuring of the Grecians against the Hebrews, because their widows were neglected in the daily ministration" (Acts 6:1).

(2) Favoring the rich over the poor (James 2:1-9)—"My brethren, have not the faith of our Lord Jesus Christ, the Lord of glory, with respect of persons. For if there come unto your assembly a man with a gold ring, in goodly apparel, and there come in also a poor man in vile raiment; And ye have respect to him that weareth the gay clothing, and say unto him, Sit thou here in a good place; and say to the poor, Stand thou there, or sit here under my footstool: Are ye not then partial in yourselves, and are become judges of evil thoughts?" (James 2:1-4)

c. It may have had members who were long on faith but short on works—"But be ye doers of the word, and not hearers only, deceiving your own selves" (James 1:22). "What doth it profit, my brethren, though a man say he hath faith, and have not works? can faith save him? If a brother or sister be naked, and destitute of daily food, And one of you say unto them, Depart in peace, be ye warmed and filled; notwithstanding ye give them not those things which are needful to the body; what doth it profit? Even so faith, if it hath not works, is dead, being alone. For as the body without the spirit is dead, so faith without works is dead also" (James 2:14-17, 26).

d. It may have had members who continually gossiped and perhaps even slandered others—"If any man among you seem to be religious, and bridleth not his tongue, but deceiveth his own heart, this man's religion is vain. For in many things we offend all. If any man offend not in word, the same is a perfect man, and able also to bridle the whole body. Speak not evil one of another, brethren. He that speaketh evil of his brother, and judgeth his brother, speaketh evil of the law, and judgeth the law: but if thou judge the law, thou art not a doer of the law, but a judge" (James 1:26; 3:2; 4:11).

Note: These passages in James have been quoted on the assumption that the author was indeed the pastor of the Jerusalem church and that he was probably addressing various situations within that assembly.

B. The church in Samaria (Acts 8:1-25)

1. Its origin—The church was founded by those believers from Jerusalem who had been scattered following the martyrdom of Stephen (Acts 8:1-2, 4).

2. Its leaders

a. Philip—"Then Philip went down to the city of Samaria, and preached Christ unto them. And the people with one accord gave heed unto those things which Philip spake, hearing and seeing the miracles which he did. For unclean spirits, crying with loud voice, came out of many that were possessed with them: and many taken with palsies, and that were lame, were healed. And there was great joy in that city. But when they believed Philip preaching the things concerning the kingdom of God, and the name of Jesus Christ, they were baptized, both men and women" (Acts 8:5-8, 12).

b. Peter and John—"Now when the apostles which were at Jerusalem heard that Samaria had received the word of God, they sent unto them Peter and John" (Acts 8:14).

3. Its importance

a. It signified a partial fulfillment of Christ's final prophecy before his ascension—"But ye shall receive power, after that the Holy Ghost is come upon you: and ye shall be witnesses unto me both in Jerusalem, and in all Judaea, and in Samaria, and unto the uttermost part of the earth" (Acts 1:8).

b. It marked the first recorded instance involving direct Satanic opposition leveled against a local church.

(1) The person involved—"But there was a certain man, called Simon, which beforetime in the same city used sorcery, and bewitched the people of Samaria, giving out that himself was some great one" (Acts 8:9).

(2) The perversion involved—"And when Simon saw that through laying on of the apostles' hands the Holy Ghost was given, he offered them money, Saying, Give me also this power, that on whomsoever I lay hands, he may receive the Holy Ghost" (Acts 8:18-19).

(3) The punishment involved—"But Peter said unto him, Thy money perish with thee, because thou hast thought that the gift of God may be purchased with money. Thou hast neither part nor lot in this matter: for thy heart is not right in the sight of God. Repent therefore of this thy wickedness, and pray God, if perhaps the thought of thine heart may be forgiven thee. For I perceive that thou art in the gall of bitterness, and in the bond of iniquity" (Acts 8:20-23).

c. It continued to grow and mature in the Lord (Acts 9:31).

C. The church in Lydda (Acts 9:32-35)—"To the saints which dwelt at Lydda" (9:32b).

1. Peter healed a man in Lydda named Aeneas who had been paralyzed and bedridden for eight years.

2. This miracle led to the conversion of many in Lydda and also nearby Sharon.

D. The church in Joppa (Acts 9:36-43)

1. A godly believer named Dorcas died in Joppa.

a. She was always doing kind things for others, especially for the poor (9:36).

b. She had made many coats and garments for the widows (9:39).

2. Upon being summoned, Peter arrived and raised her from the dead (9:40).

3. This led to the salvation of many in Joppa (9:42).

E. The church in Caesarea (Acts 10:1-48)
1. Through a vision, Simon Peter was instructed to visit Caesarea and lead
   Cornelius, a Roman military man and a seeking sinner, to Christ (Acts 10:1-23).
2. Peter arrived in Caesarea and related the gospel to Cornelius—"How God
   anointed Jesus of Nazareth with the Holy Ghost and with power: who went
   about doing good, and healing all that were oppressed of the devil; for God was
   with him. And we are witnesses of all things which he did both in the land of
   the Jews, and in Jerusalem; whom they slew and hanged on a tree: Him God
   raised up the third day, and showed him openly. . . . And he commanded us to
   preach unto the people, and to testify that it is he which was ordained of God
   to be the Judge of quick and dead. To him give all the prophets witness, that
   through his name whosoever believeth in him shall receive remission of sins"
   (Acts 10:38-40, 42-43).
3. Cornelius and his household accepted the message and spoke in tongues
   (10:44-46).
4. Peter baptized them and remained for awhile to instruct them in the faith
   (10:47-48).
5. Philip the evangelist and his family would apparently assume a leadership role
   in the Caesarean church at a later date—Luke describes the visit he and Paul
   made to Philip's home during the apostle's final missionary journey. "And the
   next day we that were of Paul's company departed, and came unto Caesarea:
   and we entered into the house of Philip the evangelist, which was one of the
   seven; and abode with him. And the same man had four daughters, virgins,
   which did prophesy" (Acts 21:8-9).
F. The church in Antioch of Syria (Acts 11:19-30; 13:1-3)
1. Its origin. The church was founded during the persecution that followed the
   martyrdom of Stephen (Acts 8:1; 11:19-20).
2. Its early growth—"And the hand of the Lord was with them: and a great
   number believed, and turned unto the Lord" (Acts 11:21).
3. Its leaders
   a. Barnabas—"Then tidings of these things came unto the ears of the church
      which was in Jerusalem: and they sent forth Barnabas, that he should go as
      far as Antioch. Who, when he came, and had seen the grace of God, was
      glad, and exhorted them all, that with purpose of heart they would cleave
      unto the Lord. For he was a good man, and full of the Holy Ghost and of
      faith: and much people was added unto the Lord" (Acts 11:22-24).
   b. Saul—"Then departed Barnabas to Tarsus, for to seek Saul: And when he
      had found him, he brought him unto Antioch. And it came to pass, that a
      whole year they assembled themselves with the church, and taught much
      people. And the disciples were called Christians first in Antioch" (Acts
      11:25-26).
   c. Symeon, Lucius, and Manaen (Acts 13:1)
   d. John Mark (Acts 12:25; 13:2,5)
   e. Silas (Acts 15:30, 34)
4. Its importance
   a. This is where believers were first called Christians (Acts 11:26).
   b. It was the first church where both believing Jews and converts from Gentile
      paganism came together to form a Christian congregation (Acts 11:19-20).
   c. It was the first church to minister to the needs of another church. Believers in

Antioch sent a love gift to those in Jerusalem suffering because of a famine (Acts 11:27-30).

d. It was a praying, fasting, teaching, worshipping, and Spirit-led church—"As they ministered to the Lord, and fasted, the Holy Ghost said, Separate me Barnabas and Saul for the work whereunto I have called them. And when they had fasted and prayed, and laid their hands on them, they sent them away" (Acts 13:2-3).

e. It was the church from where Paul's three missionary journeys began and where two of them would end.
(1) His first trip (Acts 13:4; 14:26)
(2) His second trip (Acts 15:36; 18:22)
(3) His third trip (Acts 18:23)

f. It was where Paul would set Peter straight on matters of legalism—"But when Peter was come to Antioch, I withstood him to the face, because he was to be blamed" (Gal. 2:11).

G. The church in Antioch of Pisidia (Acts 13:14-50)
1. The origin—It was founded by Paul during his first missionary journey (Acts 13:14).
2. The occasion
a. Paul and Barnabas visited the Jewish synagogue and were invited to address the congregation—"And after the reading of the law and the prophets the rulers of the synagogue sent unto them, saying, Ye men and brethren, if ye have any word of exhortation for the people, say on" (Acts 13:15).

b. At this time Paul delivered his first recorded sermon (Acts 13:16-41)—"Then Paul stood up, and beckoning with his hand said, Men of Israel, and ye that fear God, give audience" (13:16). Paul stressed two key points in this message:
(1) The preparation for the Messiah
(a) the Exodus stage (Acts 13:17-18)
(b) the conquest stage (Acts 13:19)
(c) the judges stage (Acts 13:20)
(d) the United Kingdom stage (Acts 13:21-22)
(2) The manifestation of the Messiah
(a) The forerunner involved (Acts 13:24-25)—"When John had first preached before his coming the baptism of repentance to all the people of Israel" (Acts 13:24).
(b) The fruits involved—Paul concluded by talking about the death, resurrection, and saving ministry of Jesus Christ (Acts 13:26-41). "And though they found no cause of death in him, yet desired they Pilate that he should be slain. . . . But God raised him from the dead. Be it known unto you therefore, men and brethren, that through this man is preached unto you the forgiveness of sins" (Acts 13:28, 30, 38).

3. The opposition (Acts 13:45, 50)—"But the Jews stirred up the devout and honourable women, and the chief men of the city, and raised persecution against Paul and Barnabas, and expelled them out of their coasts" (Acts 13:50).

4. The open hearts (Acts 13:44, 48-49)—"And the next sabbath day came almost the whole city together to hear the word of God. . . . And when the Gentiles heard this, they were glad, and glorified the word of the Lord: and as many as

were ordained to eternal life believed. And the word of the Lord was published throughout all the region."

5. The outcome (Acts 13:45-47)—"But when the Jews saw the multitudes, they were filled with envy, and spake against those things which were spoken by Paul, contradicting and blaspheming. Then Paul and Barnabas waxed bold, and said, It was necessary that the word of God should first have been spoken to you: but seeing ye put it from you, and judge yourselves unworthy of everlasting life, lo, we turn to the Gentiles."

H. The church in Iconium (Acts 14:1-6)

1. The witnesses concerning the gospel—"And it came to pass in Iconium, that they went both together into the synagogue of the Jews, and so spake, that a great multitude both of the Jews and also of the Greeks believed" (Acts 14:1).

2. The wickedness against the gospel—"But the unbelieving Jews stirred up the Gentiles, and made their minds evil affected against the brethren" (Acts 14:2).

3. The wonders accompanying the gospel—"Long time therefore abode they speaking boldly in the Lord, which gave testimony unto the word of his grace, and granted signs and wonders to be done by their hand" (Acts 14:3).

I. The church in Lystra (Acts 14:8-20)

1. The miracle—"And there sat a certain man at Lystra, impotent in his feet, being a cripple from his mother's womb, who never had walked: The same heard Paul speak: who stedfastly beholding him, and perceiving that he had faith to be healed, Said with a loud voice, Stand upright on thy feet. And he leaped and walked" (Acts 14:8-10).

2. The misunderstanding—"And when the people saw what Paul had done, they lifted up their voices, saying in the speech of Lycaonia, The gods are come down to us in the likeness of men. And they called Barnabas, Jupiter; and Paul, Mercurius, because he was the chief speaker. Then the priest of Jupiter, which was before their city, brought oxen and garlands unto the gates, and would have done sacrifice with the people" (Acts 14:11-13).

3. The message—"Which when the apostles, Barnabas and Paul, heard of, they rent their clothes, and ran in among the people, crying out, and saying, Sirs, why do ye these things? We also are men of like passions with you, and preach unto you that ye should turn from these vanities unto the living God, which made heaven, and earth, and the sea, and all things that are therein: Who in times past suffered all nations to walk in their own ways. Nevertheless he left not himself without witness, in that he did good, and gave us rain from heaven, and fruitful seasons, filling our hearts with food and gladness" (Acts 14:14-17).

4. The malice—"And there came thither certain Jews from Antioch and Iconium, who persuaded the people, and, having stoned Paul, drew him out of the city, supposing he had been dead" (Acts 14:19).

5. The man of God—"But thou, O man of God, flee these things; and follow after righteousness, godliness, faith, love, patience, meekness" (1 Tim. 6:11). Paul later wrote these words concerning Timothy, whom he would select as a team member during the second missionary journey. Timothy's Christian grandmother (Lois) and his mother (Eunice) lived in Lystra. All three were doubtless faithful members in the church there (Acts 16:1-3; 2 Tim. 1:5).

J. The church in Derbe (Acts 14:6-7, 21)—"And when they had preached the gospel to that city, and had taught many, they returned again to Lystra, and to Iconium, and Antioch" (Acts 14:21).

Note: A commonly held theory is that Paul originally wrote his first epistle, the book of Galatians, to the three churches in Iconium, Lystra, and Derbe. If this be true, then the following characteristics found in Galatians apply to the members in these churches:

1. They had been turned from the grace of God to the legalism of works by the Judaizers (Gal. 1:6-8; 2:1-3).
    a. They desired to be back under the law (4:9, 21; 5:4).
    b. They observed days and months, seasons and years (4:10).
    c. They practiced circumcision (5:3).
2. "The Galatians were noted for their impetuosity, fickleness, and love for new and curious things" (*New Scofield Bible*, p. 1264).
3. They were guilty of slandering each other (5:15, 26).
4. In spite of all this, they loved Paul and he dearly loved them (4:13-15, 19).

K. The church in Philippi (Acts 16:12-40; 2 Cor. 8:1-6; 11:9; Philippians)
    1. The circumstances involved
        a. Paul went to Philippi as the result of his Macedonian vision (Acts 16:9-10).
        b. He quickly led three people to Christ.
            (1) A businesswoman named Lydia (16:14-15)—Note: It is possible he established the original church in her home. "And when she was baptized, and her household, she besought us, saying, If ye have judged me to be faithful to the Lord, come into my house, and abide there. And she constrained us" (Acts 16:15).
            (2) A demon-possessed girl (Acts 16:16-18)
            (3) A jailor (Acts 16:19-34)
        c. While in a Roman prison, he wrote a letter (book of Philippians) to this church.
        d. It may have been his favorite church (Phil. 1:7-8).
    2. The characteristics involved—What kind of a church was the assembly in Philippi?
        a. It was an evangelistic church (Phil. 1:5).
        b. It had suffered for Christ (Phil. 1:29).
        c. It repeatedly gave sacrificially to Paul's support (Phil. 4:15-16; 2 Cor. 8:1-5; 11:9).
        d. It sent one of its most trusted members, Epaphroditus, to minister to the imprisoned Paul in Rome (Phil. 2:25).
        e. It may have leaned toward legalism (Phil. 3:2).
        f. It apparently had some selfish and complaining members (Phil. 2:3-4, 14).
        g. Two of its leading women were at odds with each other (Phil. 4:2-3).

L. The church in Thessalonica (Acts 17:1-9; 1 & 2 Thess.)
    1. The circumstances involved
        a. It was founded during Paul's second missionary trip following three Sabbath days preaching in the Jewish synagogue (Acts 17:1-4).
        b. The church may have first met in the house of Jason (Acts 17:5-7).
        c. Many Greek men and important women in the city were among the early converts (Acts 17:4).
        d. Paul was later hindered by Satan when he attempted to revisit this church (1 Thess. 2:18).
        e. It was later ministered to by Timothy (1 Thess. 3:1-3).

2. The characteristics involved.
   a. It was an example to the believers in Greece (1 Thess. 1:7).
   b. It had a ringing testimony (1 Thess. 1:8-9).
   c. It had a great interest in prophecy (1 Thess. 1:10)—It was, however, confused about certain aspects of prophecy.
      (1) Concerning the nature of the Rapture (1 Thess. 4:13)
      (2) Concerning the nature of the great tribulation (2 Thess. 2:1-3)
   d. It had received Paul's message gladly (1 Thess. 2:13).
   e. It had not, however, supported the apostle, as did the Philippian church (1 Thess. 2:9).
   f. It had suffered persecution from its own countrymen (1 Thess. 2:14; 2 Thess. 1:4-5).
   g. The members were not the diligent Bible students, as were the Berean believers (Acts 17:10-11).
   h. The church may have been tolerating immorality (1 Thess. 4:1-9).
   i. It had some lazy members (2 Thess. 3:6-10).
   j. It had some gossipers (2 Thess. 3:11).
   k. It had some disobedient members (2 Thess. 3:14).
M. The church in Berea (Acts 17:10-14)
   1. It was founded by Paul during his second missionary journey.
   2. Some of its early converts consisted of several prominent Greek men and women (Acts 17:12).
   3. Its members were diligent Bible students—"These were more noble than those in Thessalonica, in that they received the word with all readiness of mind, and searched the scriptures daily, whether those things were so" (Acts 17:11).
N. The church in Athens (Acts 17:16-34)
   1. The circumstances involved
      a. It was founded by Paul during his second missionary journey.
      b. Paul was invited to preach the gospel to the Epicureans and Stoics (Greek philosophers) on Mars Hill in Athens—"Then Paul stood in the midst of Mars' hill, and said, Ye men of Athens, I perceive that in all things ye are too superstitious. For as I passed by, and beheld your devotions, I found an altar with this inscription, TO THE UNKNOWN GOD. Whom therefore ye ignorantly worship, him declare I unto you. . . . Because he hath appointed a day, in the which he will judge the world in righteousness by that man whom he hath ordained; whereof he hath given assurance unto all men, in that he hath raised him from the dead" (Acts 17:22-23, 31).
   2. The contempt—"And when they heard of the resurrection of the dead, some mocked: and others said, We will hear thee again of this matter" (Acts 17:32).
   3. The conversions—"Howbeit certain men clave unto him, and believed: among the which was Dionysius the Areopagite, and a woman named Damaris, and others with them" (Acts 17:34).
O. The church in Corinth (Acts 18:1-18; 1 & 2 Cor.)
   1. The circumstances involved
      a. It was founded during Paul's second missionary journey.
      b. Its original members included Aquila and Priscilla (Acts 18:2); a Gentile named Titus Justus (Acts 18:7); Crispus, the leader of the synagogue (Acts 18:8); and Sosthenes, the leader who succeeded Crispus (Acts 18:17; 1 Cor. 1:1).
      c. Paul stayed here 18 months (Acts 18:11).

d. He would later write several letters to this church, two of which are included in the New Testament canon.
  (1) The canonical letters: First and Second Corinthians
  (2) The noncanonical letters—"I wrote unto you in an epistle not to company with fornicators" (1 Cor. 5:9). (See also 2 Cor. 10:9-10.)
e. Paul later sent both Timothy (1 Cor. 4:17) and Titus (2 Cor. 7:6-7) to help the church.
f. Apollos apparently pastored the church for awhile (1 Cor. 3:6).
2. The characteristics involved
  a. It was filled with immaturity, carnality, and strife—"For it hath been declared unto me of you, my brethren, by them which are of the house of Chloe, that there are contentions among you. . . . And I, brethren, could not speak unto you as unto spiritual, but as unto carnal, even as unto babes in Christ. I have fed you with milk, and not with meat: for hitherto ye were not able to bear it, neither yet now are ye able. For ye are yet carnal: for whereas there is among you envying, and strife, and divisions, are ye not carnal, and walk as men?" (1 Cor. 1:11; 3:1-3).
  b. The church had degenerated into little cliques with membership dependent upon who had baptized them (1:10-17)—"Now this I say, that every one of you saith, I am of Paul; and I of Apollos; and I of Cephas; and I of Christ. Is Christ divided? was Paul crucified for you? or were ye baptized in the name of Paul?" (1 Cor. 1:12-13).
  c. Many were puffed up with pride, considering themselves to be intellectual giants (1 Cor. 3:18; 4:7, 19; 2 Cor. 11:19-20)—"Let no man deceive himself. If any man among you seemeth to be wise in this world, let him become a fool, that he may be wise" (1 Cor. 3:18).
  d. They felt in need of nothing (1 Cor. 4:8).
  e. They tolerated gross immorality within the church (1 Cor. 5:1-2; 6:15-18; 2 Cor. 12:21)—"It is reported commonly that there is fornication among you, and such fornication as is not so much as named among the Gentiles, that one should have his father's wife. And ye are puffed up, and have not rather mourned, that he that hath done this deed might be taken away from among you" (1 Cor. 5:1-2).
      Note: Some of this no doubt was a carry over from their past lives (1 Cor. 6:10-11).
  f. They were taking each other to pagan courts (1 Cor. 6:1-6).
  g. They were ignorant and confused about various issues.
    (1) That of marriage (1 Cor. 7)
    (2) That of eating meat sacrificed to an idol (1 Cor. 8)
    (3) That of Christian liberty (1 Cor. 8-10)
    (4) That of spiritual gifts (1 Cor. 12)
  h. They were making a mockery of the Lord's Table (1 Cor. 11:17-34).
  i. They were abusing the gift of tongues (1 Cor. 14).
  j. Some were denying the doctrine of the resurrection (1 Cor. 15)—"Now if Christ be preached that he rose from the dead, how say some among you that there is no resurrection of the dead? But if there be no resurrection of the dead, then is Christ not risen" (1 Cor. 15:12-13).
  k. They were gullible (1 Cor. 11:3-4).
  l. They were fickle and unstable

(1) They refused to remove from their fellowship an unrepentant member (1 Cor. 5:1-2).

(2) They refused to restore to their fellowship the same repentant member (2 Cor. 2:5-8; 7:11-12).

m. They were being influenced by false teachers (2 Cor. 3:1; 5:12; 10:12; 11:13-15)—"For such are false apostles, deceitful workers, transforming themselves into the apostles of Christ" (2 Cor. 11:13).

n. They tended to be critical of Paul, especially in matters involving money (2 Cor. 1:17; 7:2; 8:21; 10:1, 10; 11:7-9; 12:13-18).

P. The church in Ephesus (Acts 18:19–20:1, 17-38; Eph.; Rev. 2:1-7)

1. The circumstances involved

a. Paul had visited this city at the end of his second missionary journey (Acts 18:19-21), but probably established the church at the beginning of his third trip (Acts 19:1). Between these two visits, Apollos came to Ephesus and doubtless helped pave the way for the church (Acts 18:24-28).

b. Paul was there for three years (Acts 20:31).

c. During that time he went door-to-door telling people about Christ (Acts 20:20).

d. Twelve former disciples of John the Baptist may have been some of the original members of the church (Acts 19:1-7).

e. The first meeting place was at the lecture hall of Tyrannus (Acts 19:9-10).

f. God used Paul's miracles in bringing many people in Ephesus to Christ—Thus the church experienced rapid growth. "And God wrought special miracles by the hands of Paul: So that from his body were brought unto the sick handkerchiefs or aprons, and the diseases departed from them, and the evil spirits went out of them. . . . And many that believed came, and confessed, and showed their deeds. Many of them also which used curious arts brought their books together, and burned them before all men: and they counted the price of them, and found it fifty thousand pieces of silver. So mightily grew the word of God and prevailed" (Acts 19:11-12, 18-20).

g. The work was at first violently opposed by Demetrius, an influential pagan silversmith (Acts 19:24).

h. This was the only Christian church ever to receive letters from two New Testament writers—Paul directed the book of Ephesians to them (Ephesians 1:1), and John the apostle would later direct a portion of Revelation to them (Rev. 2:1-7).

i. Paul wrote the Ephesian epistle while he was a prisoner in Rome (Eph. 3:1).

j. He had previously written them another noncanonical letter (Eph. 3:2).

k. Paul utters two of Scripture's most beautiful prayers for this church (Eph. 1:15-23; 3:14-21).

l. Paul later sent Tychicus to help the Ephesian church (Eph. 6:21-22).

m. Timothy would later pastor the church at Ephesus (1 Tim. 1:3).

2. The characteristics involved

a. It had many patient and hardworking members (Rev. 2:2).

b. The church possessed high standards and was intolerant of sin (Rev. 2:2).

c. It had exposed the false teachers and apostles in its own fellowship (Rev. 2:2).

d. Paul had previously warned of this—"For I know this, that after my departing shall grievous wolves enter in among you, not sparing the flock.

Also of your own selves shall men arise, speaking perverse things, to draw away disciples after them" (Acts 20:29-30).

    Note: Paul's sad prediction had apparently later been fulfilled by two such "grievous wolves." "And their word will eat as doth a canker: of whom is Hymenaeus and Philetus; Who concerning the truth have erred, saying that the resurrection is past already; and overthrow the faith of some" (2 Tim. 2:17-18). (See also 1 Tim. 1:3-8.)

  e. It hated the deeds of the licentious Nicolaitans. Ken Taylor observes, "*Nicolaitans*, when translated from Greek to Hebrew, becomes *Balaamites*; followers of the men who induced the Israelites to fall by lust (see Rev. 2:14 and Num. 31:15-16)." (*The Living New Testament*, p. 615, footnote.)

  f. It had suffered for Christ without quitting (Rev. 2:3).

  g. It had, however, left its first love (Rev. 2:4).

    (1) It was therefore, to *remember* this first love.

    (2) It was to *rekindle* this first love.

    (3) It was to *return* to this first love.

  h. This had resulted in its grieving of the Holy Spirit by various sins (Eph. 4:25-31; 5:3-4).

Q. The church at Troas (Acts 16:8, 9; 20:6-12)

  1. Paul had received his Macedonian vision at Troas during his second missionary journey (Acts 16:8-9).

  2. He revisited Troas at the end of his third missionary trip (Acts 20:6-12).

  3. He was here for only a week (Acts 20:6).

  4. The highlight of this visit centered in a midnight message and a midnight miracle.

    a. The message—"And upon the first day of the week, when the disciples came together to break bread, Paul preached unto them, ready to depart on the morrow; and continued his speech until midnight. And there were many lights in the upper chamber, where they were gathered together. And there sat in a window a certain young man named Eutychus, being fallen into a deep sleep: and as Paul was long preaching, he sunk down with sleep, and fell down from the third loft, and was taken up dead" (Acts 20:7-9).

    b. The miracle—"And Paul went down, and fell on him, and embracing him said, Trouble not yourselves; for his life is in him. When he therefore was come up again, and had broken bread, and eaten, and talked a long while, even till break of day, so he departed. And they brought the young man alive, and were not a little comforted" (Acts 20:10-12).

R. The church in Rome (Acts 28:24; Rom.; Phil. 1:12-17; 4:21-22)

  1. The circumstances involved

    a. Paul was not the founder of this church.

    b. It probably was not begun by Peter either (compare Rom. 1:11 with 15:20).

    c. Both Paul and Peter were, however, later martyred in Rome (2 Tim. 4:6; 2 Pet. 1:14).

    d. The church was probably begun by those converts returning from Pentecost (Acts 2:10).

    e. The membership consisted of both Jews and Gentiles, but mostly Gentiles (Rom. 1:13; 11:13; 15:16).

    f. They probably met in several houses (Rom. 16:5, 10-11, 14).

    g. Paul was especially anxious to visit this church.

(1) He had expressed this to the church when he wrote them from Corinth— "For I long to see you, that I may impart unto you some spiritual gift, to the end ye may be established" (Rom. 1:11).

(2) He repeated this desire when in Ephesus (Acts 19:21).

(3) He was later assured by God himself that this indeed would be the case—"And the night following the Lord stood by him, and said, Be of good cheer, Paul: for as thou hast testified of me in Jerusalem, so must thou bear witness also at Rome" (Acts 23:11).

h. He knew many believers there. In fact, he sent greetings to 26 of his friends (Rom. 16).

i. Phoebe, a godly believer from Corinth, probably carried the epistle of Romans to the church (Rom. 16:1).

j. Onesiphorus and his family, who were members of the Roman church, ministered greatly to the imprisoned Paul (2 Tim. 1:16-18).

2. The characteristics involved

a. Paul's imprisonment had apparently served to identify the sincere and insincere church members—"As a result, it has become clear throughout the whole palace guard and to everyone else that I am in chains for Christ. Because of my chains, most of the brothers in the Lord have been encouraged to speak the word of God more courageously and fearlessly. It is true that some preach Christ out of envy and rivalry, but others out of good will. The latter do so in love, knowing that I am put here for the defense of the gospel. The former preach Christ out of selfish ambition, not sincerely, supposing that they can stir up trouble for me while I am in chains" (Phil. 1:13-17, NIV).

b. The church in general however, gave forth a ringing gospel testimony— "First, I thank my God through Jesus Christ for you all, that your faith is spoken of throughout the whole world" (Rom. 1:8).

c. In fact, converts could be found in Caesar's very household (Phil. 1:13; 4:22).

d. Some, however, had not consecrated their bodies to Christ (Rom. 12:1-2).

e. Others were confused concerning Christian liberty (Rom. 14:1-8, 14-15, 20-23).

f. The church also had its share of critics and faultfinders (Rom. 14:10-13).

g. A few were outright troublemakers—"I urge you, brothers, to watch out for those who cause divisions and put obstacles in your way that are contrary to the teaching you have learned. Keep away from them. For such people are not serving our Lord Christ, but their own appetites. By smooth talk and flattery they deceive the minds of naive people" (Rom. 16:17-18, NIV).

S. The church in Crete (book of Titus)

1. Titus was instructed by Paul to appoint the various pastors over local assemblies as needed (Titus 1:5).

2. The Cretan church was plagued by the legalistic Judaizers (Titus 1:10-11, 14).

3. The Cretans themselves tended to be dishonest, lazy, and carnal (Titus 1:12).

T. The church in Colosse (books of Colossians and Philemon)

1. The church was founded by Epaphras during Paul's third missionary journey (Col. 1:7).

2. It apparently had a close relationship with the church at Laodicea (Col. 2:1; 4:16).

3. Philemon may have been the pastor, as the church met in his home (Philem. 1-2).

4. No doubt the converted runaway slave Onesimus who returned to his master Philemon became a faithful member (Col. 4:9; Philem.).

5. Paul sent Tychicus to help in the church (Col. 4:7-8).

6. The church was plagued by the legalistic Judaizers (Col. 2:20-23).

U. The church in Babylon (1 and 2 Pet.)—"The church that is at Babylon, elected together with you, saluteth you; and so doth Marcus my son" (1 Pet. 5:13).

1. Some feel Peter uses Babylon here as a code name for Rome.

2. Whatever the location, Peter served as an elder (1 Pet. 5:1).

V. The church in Smyrna (Rev. 2:8-13)

1. The church had suffered much for Christ.

2. Some of this suffering involved poverty.

3. They had been slandered by those from the synagogue of Satan.

4. The devil had actually imprisoned some of them.

W. The church in Pergamos (Rev. 2:12-17)

1. The good things

a. It was located in a city that had become the center of satanic worship.

b. In spite of this, the church had remained loyal to Christ.

c. Antipas, a godly member, had been martyred by the followers of Satan.

2. The grievous things—Christ rebuked this church, however, in one major area: Some of the members were guilty of sexual immorality and had attended idol feasts. The church thus received a stern warning: "Repent; or else I will come unto thee quickly, and will fight against them with the sword of my mouth" (Rev. 2:16).

X. The church in Thyatira (Rev. 2:18-29)

1. The good things

a. They were kind to the poor.

b. They were growing in love, faith, and patience.

2. The grievous things—"Notwithstanding I have a few things against thee, because thou sufferest that woman Jezebel, which calleth herself a prophetess, to teach and to seduce my servants to commit fornication, and to eat things sacrificed unto idols" (Rev. 2:20).

Y. The church in Sardis (Rev. 3:1-6)

1. The good things—"Thou hast a few names even in Sardis which have not defiled their garments; and they shall walk with me in white: for they are worthy" (Rev. 3:4).

2. The grievous things

a. They had a reputation as a live and active church, but they were dead.

b. They were at the very point of death.

Z. The church in Philadelphia (Rev. 3:7-13)

1. Even though weak, they had obeyed and had not denied Christ.

2. Because of this, God would cause their enemies to acknowledge the relationship the church enjoyed with Christ.

AA. The church in Laodicea (Rev. 3:14-22)

1. This was the worst single church described in the New Testament.

2. How the church viewed itself

a. "I am rich, with everything I want."

b. "I don't need a thing."

3. How God viewed the church
   a. "You are wretched and miserable."
   b. "You are poor, and blind, and naked." "As many as I love, I rebuke and chasten: be zealous therefore, and repent. Behold, I stand at the door, and knock: if any man hear my voice, and open the door, I will come in to him, and will sup with him, and he with me" (Rev. 3:19-20).

VII. The Symbols for the Church—There are seven main symbols depicting the relationship between Christ and his church in the New Testament. These are:

A. The Head and the body (Rom. 12:4-5; 1 Cor. 12:12-31; Eph. 1:22-23; 4:12, 16; 5:23, 30; Col. 1:18)—"Christ is the head of the church: and he is the saviour of the body" (Eph. 5:23) "For we are members of his body, of his flesh, and of his bones. And he is the head of the body, the church: who is the beginning, the firstborn from the dead; that in all things he might have the preeminence" (Eph. 5:30; Col.1:18).

Blessings resulting from this relationship: unity and direction.

   1. The unity of the body—"For as the body is one, and hath many members, and all the members of that one body, being many, are one body: so also is Christ" (1 Cor. 12:12). In 12:12-27, Paul links the body of Christ and its many spiritually gifted members to that of the body of man with its many physical members.
      a. Each member in both bodies performs a vital task, appointed by God himself (12:18, 25).
      b. No member is to be independent of the other members.
         (1) The foot and the ear are not to show envy toward the hand and the eye (1 Cor. 12:15-17).
         (2) The eye and the head are not to show pride toward the hand and the feet (1 Cor. 12:21).
      c. Every member is to rejoice and suffer with the other members—"And whether one member suffer, all the members suffer with it; or one member be honoured, all the members rejoice with it" (1 Cor. 12:26).
   2. The direction of the body—As the human head both controls and guides its body, so Christ desires to direct his body.

B. The Bridegroom and the bride (2 Cor. 11:2; Eph. 3:19-21; 5:25-32; Rev. 19:7-9; 21:9)— "For the husband is the head of the wife, even as Christ is the head of the church" (Eph. 5:23). "Husbands, love your wives, even as Christ also loved the church, and gave himself for it; That he might sanctify and cleanse it with the washing of water by the word, That he might present it to himself a glorious church, not having spot, or wrinkle, or any such thing; but that it should be holy and without blemish" (Eph. 5:25-27). "For I am jealous over you with godly jealousy: for I have espoused you to one husband, that I may present you as a chaste virgin to Christ" (2 Cor. 11:2). "And to her was granted that she should be arrayed in fine linen, clean and white: for the fine linen is the righteousness of saints" (Rev. 19:8).

Blessings resulting from this relationship: love and devotion. Paul Enns writes:

This illustration is apt because it reveals the magnitude of Christ's love for the church (Eph. 5:2, 25). A second emphasis of the illustration is the exalted position of the bride. As in the Oriental wedding custom, at the engagement (betrothal) the bride receives the promise of future blessing with her husband. Similarly, the church today is an espoused bride, awaiting her husband's return from glory. The second stage of the Oriental marriage was the wedding itself, when the husband came to take the bride to be with him. In an analogous figure, the church awaits the return of Christ, when she will be espoused to her husband (John 14:1-3; 1 Thess. 4:16-17). In Oriental weddings, the wedding feast followed; similarly the church, as Christ's bride, awaits the husband's return (Rev. 19:7-9) and the glory of the millennial kingdom to follow. (*Moody Handbook of Theology*, pp. 149–150)

C. The Vine and the branches (John 15:1-16)—"I am the vine, ye are the branches" (John 15:5).

Blessings resulting from this relationship: sustenance and fruit.

1. The source involved—"I am the true vine, and my Father is the husbandman" (John 15:1).
2. The steps involved
   a. Abide in Christ—"Abide in me, and I in you. As the branch cannot bear fruit of itself, except it abide in the vine; no more can ye, except ye abide in me. I am the vine, ye are the branches: He that abideth in me, and I in him, the same bringeth forth much fruit: for without me ye can do nothing" (John 15:4-5).
   b. Study the Word—"Now ye are clean through the word which I have spoken unto you" (John 15:3).
   c. Submit to pruning—"Every branch in me that beareth not fruit he taketh away: and every branch that beareth fruit, he purgeth it, that it may bring forth more fruit. . . . If a man abide not in me, he is cast forth as a branch, and is withered; and men gather them, and cast them into the fire, and they are burned" (John 15:2, 6).
3. The success involved—"If ye abide in me, and my words abide in you, ye shall ask what ye will, and it shall be done unto you. Herein is my Father glorified, that ye bear much fruit; so shall ye be my disciples" (John 15:7-8).
4. The stability involved—"Ye have not chosen me, but I have chosen you, and ordained you, that ye should go and bring forth fruit, and that your fruit should remain: that whatsoever ye shall ask of the Father in my name, he may give it you" (John 15:16).
5. The summary involved
   a. The believer, as a branch is to bear (not produce) fruit—A branch is useless for anything else. Its wood cannot be used for furniture, firewood, or building purposes.
   b. The believer, as a branch, is to do what Old Testament Israel refused to do, namely, bear fruit—"Thou hast brought a vine out of Egypt: thou hast cast out the heathen, and planted it" (Psa. 80:8). "Israel is an empty vine, he bringeth forth fruit unto himself: according to the multitude of his fruit he hath increased the altars; according to the goodness of his land they have made goodly images" (Hosea 10:1). "And when he saw a fig tree in the way, he came to it, and found nothing thereon, but leaves only, and said unto it, Let no fruit grow on thee henceforward for ever. And presently the fig tree withered away" (Matt. 21:19).

D. The Shepherd and the sheep (John 10:1-16)—"A Psalm of David. The LORD is my shepherd; I shall not want" (Psa. 23:1).

Blessing resulting from this relationship: provision and protection. "Verily, verily, I say unto you, He that entereth not by the door into the sheepfold, but climbeth up some other way, the same is a thief and a robber" (John 10:1). "Now the

God of peace, that brought again from the dead our Lord Jesus, that great shepherd of the sheep, through the blood of the everlasting covenant" (Heb. 13:20). "And when the chief Shepherd shall appear, ye shall receive a crown of glory that fadeth not away" (1 Pet. 5:4).

Thus, to his church, Christ is the Good Shepherd (because of what he has accomplished in the past, namely justification—see Psa. 22), the Great Shepherd (because of what he accomplishes in the present, namely, Sanctification—see Psa. 23), and the Chief Shepherd (because of what he shall accomplish in the future, namely, glorification—see Psa. 24).

> A beautiful, tender image depicting the relationship of believers to the Lord is found in John 10:16 where the church is called a flock (cf. Acts 20:28; 1 Pet. 5:3). Israel had a relationship to the Lord as sheep to a shepherd (Psa. 23) and was called a flock (Psa. 80:1; Jer. 13:17), but in the Old Testament that figure was restricted to Israel. The uniqueness about the church being a flock and Christ the Shepherd is that this flock is composed of both Jews and Gentiles. Jesus declared, "I have other sheep [Gentiles], which are not of this fold [Jews]; I must bring them also, and they shall hear my voice; and they shall become one flock [the church composed of Jews and Gentiles] with one Shepherd" (John 10:16).
>
> The image emphasizes that members of the church as the sheep of Christ belong to Him. Jesus emphasizes that the flock is "My sheep" (John 10:26-27) and that they are secure in His hand. Moreover, the sheep respond to the Shepherd's voice—there is intimacy for the Shepherd knows His sheep individually, and they recognize His voice and respond to Him. (Paul Enns, *Moody Handbook of Theology,* p. 351)

E. The High Priest and a kingdom of priests (Heb. 5:1-10; 1 Pet. 2:5, 9; Rev. 1:6; 5:10; 20:6b)—"Now of the things which we have spoken this is the sum: We have such an high priest, who is set on the right hand of the throne of the Majesty in the heavens" (Heb. 8:1). "But ye are a chosen generation, a royal priesthood, an holy nation, a peculiar people; that ye should show forth the praises of him who hath called you out of darkness into his marvelous light" (1 Pet. 2:9). "And hath made us kings and priests unto God and his Father to him be glory and dominion for ever and ever. Amen" (Rev. 1:6).

Blessings resulting from this relationship: intercession and service.

1. Intercession: Christ's ministry for us in heaven (Rom. 8:34; Heb. 4:14-16; 7:25-27; 9:24; 10:12-13)—"Who is he that condemneth? It is Christ that died, yea rather, that is risen again, who is even at the right hand of God, who also maketh intercession for us" (Rom. 8:34). "Wherefore he is able also to save them to the uttermost that come unto God by him, seeing he ever liveth to make intercession for them" (Heb. 7:25).

2. Service: Our ministry for Christ on earth—En route to the promised land God had on two occasions expressed his intention of accepting the firstborn son in all 12 tribes as a priest. Note these occasions:

   a. Upon leaving Egypt—"And the LORD spake unto Moses, saying, Sanctify unto me all the firstborn, whatsoever openeth the womb among the children of Israel, both of man and of beast: it is mine" (Exod. 13:1-2).

   b. At Mount Sinai—"And ye shall be unto me a kingdom of priests, and an holy nation. These are the words which thou shalt speak unto the children of Israel" (Exod. 19:6).

However, during the tragic golden calf incident, only the tribe of Levi remained true to God (Exod. 32:26-29). "Then Moses stood in the gate of the camp, and said, Who is on the LORD's side? let him come unto me. And all the sons of Levi gathered themselves together unto him" (Exod. 32:26). This resulted in God's selection of this tribe alone to serve as his priests (Num. 8:14-18).

The Old Testament priest was to offer up an animal sacrifice. The New Testament priest is to offer up sacrifices also, but of a different kind. He is to offer up:

1) The sacrifice of his body as a living offering—"I beseech you therefore, brethren, by the mercies of God, that ye present your bodies a living sacrifice, holy, acceptable unto God, which is your reasonable service" (Rom. 12:1).

2) The sacrifice of praise—"Ye also, as lively stones, are built up a spiritual house, an holy priesthood, to offer up spiritual sacrifices, acceptable to God by Jesus Christ. . . . But ye are a chosen generation, a royal priesthood, an holy nation, a peculiar people; that ye should show forth the praises of him who hath called you out of darkness into his marvelous light" (1 Pet. 2:5, 9). "By him therefore let us offer the sacrifice of praise to God continually, that is, the fruit of our lips giving thanks to his name" (Heb. 13:15).

3) The sacrifice of doing good—"But to do good and to communicate forget not: for with such sacrifices God is well pleased" (Heb. 13:16).

4) The sacrifice of substance—"And do not forget to do good and to share with others, for with such sacrifices God is pleased" (Heb. 13:16, NIV).

F. The Cornerstone and the living stones (Isa. 28:16; Dan. 2:34; Matt. 21:42; Acts 4:11; Eph. 2:20-22; 1 Pet. 2:4-7)—"And what is the exceeding greatness of his power to us-ward who believe, according to the working of his mighty power, Which he wrought in Christ, when he raised him from the dead, and set him at his own right hand in the heavenly places, Far above all principality, and power, and might, and dominion, and every name that is named, not only in this world, but also in that which is to come: And hath put all things under his feet, and gave him to be the head over all things to the church" (Eph. 2:19-22).

Blessings resulting from this relationship: security and stability.

1. Passages relating to the Cornerstone (Isa. 28:16; Dan. 2:34; Matt. 21:42; Acts 4:11; Eph. 2:20; 1 Pet. 2:4, 6-7)

2. Passages related to the living stones (Eph. 2:21-22; 1 Pet. 2:5)—"In whom all the building fitly framed together groweth unto an holy temple in the Lord" (Eph. 2:21).

Note: There are two Greek words translated by the one English word "temple."

a. *Naos*, referring to the holy place and the Holy of Holies

b. *Hieron*, having in mind the entire temple structure, outer courts, porches, porticoes, etc.

The temple mentioned in Ephesians 2:21 is *naos*. While upon earth Christ never entered the *naos* area, which was restricted to the Levitical priests alone. He drove the moneychangers from the *hieron* temple, not the *naos* temple. But now his church has actually *become* that which he could not *enter* during his earthly ministry.

Dr. Earl Radmacher writes the following concerning the role of Christ as cornerstone: "In Christ, Jew and Gentile have been united in one as the cornerstone by which the two partitions of the building are united. In Christ the building has coherence and stability in its structure. In Christ, the rest of the building finds its inner harmony, oneness, correspondence, and design" (*The Nature of the Church*, p. 262).

G. The last Adam and the new creation (Rom. 5:11-21; 1 Cor. 15:20-50)—"For as by one man's disobedience many were made sinners, so by the obedience of one shall many be made righteous" (Rom. 5:19). "For as in Adam all die, even so in Christ shall all be made alive. So also is the resurrection of the dead. It is sown in corruption; it is raised in incorruption: And as we have borne the image of the earthy, we shall also bear the image of the heavenly" (1 Cor. 15:22, 42, 49).

Blessings resulting from this relationship: righteousness and resurrection.

VIII. The Old Testament Foreshadowing of the Church—The institution of the church, of course, was not revealed in the Old Testament. Paul makes this clear in Ephesians 3:1-12. However, there are two special brides mentioned in the Old Testament whose lives beautifully lend themselves as remarkable foreshadowing of the coming New Testament church. These two women are Eve and Rebekah.

A. The bride Eve

1. Eve proceeded from Adam's side as the church came from Christ's side.

   a. The (literal) creation of Eve—"And the LORD God caused a deep sleep to fall upon Adam, and he slept: and he took one of his ribs, and closed up the flesh instead thereof; and the rib, which the LORD God had taken from man, made he a woman, and brought her unto the man" (Gen. 2:21-22).

   b. The (symbolic) creation of the church—"But one of the soldiers with a spear pierced his side, and forthwith came there out blood and water" (John 19:34).

2. Eve became espoused to the first head of creation, while the church will be joined to the final Head of creation.

3. Both brides were to reign with their husband over all creation.

   a. Eve's joint-rule—"And God blessed them, and God said unto them, Be fruitful, and multiply, and replenish the earth, and subdue it: and have dominion over the fish of the sea, and over the fowl of the air, and over every living thing that moveth upon the earth" (Gen. 1:28).

   b. The church's joint-rule—"And if children, then heirs; heirs of God, and joint-heirs with Christ; if so be that we suffer with him, that we may be also glorified together" (Rom. 8:17). "And they lived and reigned with Christ a thousand years" (Rev. 20:4).

4. Both brides become bone and flesh of their spouse—"And Adam said, This is now bone of my bones, and flesh of my flesh: she shall be called Woman, because she was taken out of Man. Therefore shall a man leave his father and his mother, and shall cleave unto his wife: and they shall be one flesh" (Gen. 2:23-24). "For we are members of his body, of his flesh, and of his bones. For this cause shall a man leave his father and mother, and shall be joined unto his wife, and they two shall be one flesh" (Eph. 5:30-31).

5. Eve was deceived by Satan, but the church will be delivered from Satan.

   a. The deception—"And the serpent said unto the woman, Ye shall not surely die" (Gen. 3:4).

   b. The deliverance—"And the God of peace shall bruise Satan under your feet
       shortly. The grace of our Lord Jesus Christ be with you. Amen" (Rom. 16:20).
B. The bride Rebekah—Genesis 24 is the greatest single typical chapter in the entire
   Old Testament. The four key individuals involved in this chapter are Abraham,
   Isaac, the servant, and Rebekah.
   1. Abraham sends his trusted servant to a distant land to fetch a bride for Isaac,
      his son—He becomes a type of the Father who has done the same for his Son.
      "But thou shalt go unto my country, and to my kindred, and take a wife unto
      my son Isaac" (Gen. 24:4). "The kingdom of heaven is like unto a certain king,
      which made a marriage for his son, and sent forth his servants to call them that
      were bidden to the wedding: and they would not come" (Matt. 22:2-3).
   2. Isaac, having been previously offered up on Mount Moriah, is content to await
      the arrival of his bride—He becomes a type of the Son who now awaits the
      arrival of his bride in heaven. "And Isaac went out to meditate in the field at
      the eventide: and he lifted up his eyes, and saw, and, behold, the camels were
      coming" (Gen. 24:63). "But this man, after he had offered one sacrifice for sins
      for ever, sat down on the right hand of God; from henceforth expecting till his
      enemies be made his footstool. For by one offering he hath perfected for ever
      them that are sanctified" (Heb. 10:12-14).
   3. The servant arrives in that distant land for the sole purpose of taking a bride—
      He becomes a foreshadow of the Holy Spirit.
      a. Christ was sent by the Father—"And I will pray the Father, and he shall give
          you another Comforter, that he may abide with you for ever" (John 14:16).
      b. Christ came at Pentecost to take a bride—"For by one Spirit are we all
          baptized into one body, whether we be Jews or Gentiles, whether we be
          bond or free; and have been all made to drink into one Spirit" (1 Cor. 12:13).
      c. God elevates Christ as the servant did Isaac—"And Sarah my master's wife
          bare a son to my master when she was old: and unto him hath he given all
          that he hath" (Gen. 24:36). "Howbeit when he, the Spirit of truth, is come, he
          will guide you into all truth: for he shall not speak of himself; but whatso-
          ever he shall hear, that shall he speak: and he will show you things to come.
          He shall glorify me: for he shall receive of mine, and shall show it unto you"
          (John 16:13-14).
   4. Rebekah, upon hearing about Isaac, agrees to go with the servant—She became
      a foreshadow of the church.
      a. Like the church and Christ, she loved her bridegroom even before seeing
          him—"Whom having not seen, ye love; in whom, though now ye see him
          not, yet believing, ye rejoice with joy unspeakable and full of glory" (1 Pet.
          1:8).
      b. Like the church and Christ, she received an earnest from the riches of
          Isaac—"And the servant brought forth jewels of silver, and jewels of gold,
          and raiment, and gave them to Rebekah: he gave also to her brother and to
          her mother precious things" (Gen. 24:53). "Who hath also sealed us, and
          given the earnest of the Spirit in our hearts" (2 Cor. 1:22). "Which is the
          earnest of our inheritance until the redemption of the purchased possession,
          unto the praise of his glory" (Eph. 1:14).
      c. Like the church and Christ, she began her long pilgrimage to meet her
          bridegroom—"And they sent away Rebekah their sister, and her nurse, and
          Abraham's servant, and his men" (Gen. 24:59). "Dearly beloved, I beseech

you as strangers and pilgrims, abstain from fleshly lusts, which war against the soul" (1 Pet. 2:11).

d. Like the church and Christ, she is prayed for by her bridegroom—"And Isaac went out to meditate in the field at the eventide: and he lifted up his eyes, and saw, and, behold, the camels were coming" (Gen. 24:63). "Who is he that condemneth? It is Christ that died, yea rather, that is risen again, who is even at the right hand of God, who also maketh intercession for us" (Rom. 8:34).

e. Like the church and Christ, she is received into the home of her father-in-law—"And Isaac brought her into his mother Sarah's tent, and took Rebekah, and she became his wife; and he loved her: and Isaac was comforted after his mother's death" (Gen. 24:67). "In my Father's house are many mansions: if it were not so, I would have told you. I go to prepare a place for you" (John 14:2).

IX. The Organization of the Church—Henry Thiessen writes:

There have been individuals and groups of believers who have taught that the Scriptures give no warrant for our present-day organized churches. It is held that believers should get together, observe the Lord's Supper, study God's Word, and cooperate in Christian service without anything resembling a formal organization. But that this is an extreme view of the matter is clear. There are indications that very early in Jerusalem the Church must have had at least a loose kind of organization, and there is conclusive evidence that soon thereafter local churches were definitely organized.

That there must have been a simple organization even in the Church in Jerusalem is evident from a number of things. The believers adhered to a definite doctrinal standard (Acts 2:42; cf. Eph. 20); they met for spiritual fellowship (*ibia*) they united in prayer (Acts 2:4-2; Matt. 18:19-20); they practiced baptism (Acts 2:41) and observed the Lord's Supper (Acts 2:42, 46); they kept account of the membership (Acts 2:14, 41; 4:4); they met for public worship (Acts 2:4-6); and they provided material help for the needy of their number (Acts 2:44-45). The Apostles were the ministers in this Church, but they soon added the seven men of Acts 6:1-7 to take care of the ministration to the poor. On the day of Pentecost they were assembled in "the upper room" (Acts 1:13, 21; 2:1) . . . though for some services apparently they still visited the temple (Acts 2:46; 3:1). All these factors indicate the beginnings of organization in the Jerusalem Church.

A. They had church officers. There are, besides the example of this first Church, many other indications that the Scriptures teach the propriety and necessity of organizing local groups of believers into churches. Paul, when retracing his steps from Derbe on his first journey, "appointed for them elders in every church" (Acts 14:23). The original indicates that this was done by a show of hands and not by apostolic authority. He definitely asks Titus to "appoint elders" (Titus 1:5). We have already seen that the Jerusalem Church appointed stewards to look after the needs of the poor (Acts 6:1-7). There must have been a way of ascertaining the sentiment of the people, and a regulation that stated who was entitled to vote on the question (Acts 6:2-6). In the Church at Ephesus there were "elders" (Acts 20:1 7), in the Church at Antioch, "prophets and teachers" (Acts 13:1), and in the Church at Philippi, "bishops and deacons" (Phil. 1:1).

B. They had stated times of meeting. We are informed that the disciples met on the "first day of the week," immediately following Christ's resurrection (John 20:19, 26). In his first letter to the Corinthians Paul instructs the readers to lay by them in store as the Lord has prospered them on the first day of the week (1 Cor. 16:2). That is, on that day the collection was to be taken. On Paul's last journey to Jerusalem he stops at Troas and meets with the disciples there on the first day of the week (Acts 20:7). And in the Revelation John tells us that he was in the Spirit on the "Lord's day" (1:10). We have already referred to Canright's work, in which he proves that Sunday observance originated with the apostles. There must have been an action taken with regard to the day to be observed and business transactions presuppose an organization.

C. They regulated church decorum (1 Cor. 14:34) and exercised church discipline. Jesus had given instructions that in the case of a believer who refused to bow to private admonition, the dispute was to be referred to the church for discipline (Matt. 18:17). Paul requests the Corinthians most definitely to exercise church discipline (1 Cor. 5:13). He gives similar instructions to the Church at Rome (Rom. 16:17). In 3 John 10 we are told that Diotrophes acted high-handedly in church discipline. Here again organization is presupposed; for it is necessary to draw the line in such matters.

D. They raised money for the Lord's work. Writing to the Corinthian church from Ephesus, Paul says that he has already given orders to the churches of Galatia, and then gives them instructions to contribute to the collection for the saints (1 Cor. 16:1-2). They are to give systematically (on the first day of the week), proportionately (as each may prosper), and purposefully (for the saints). In his Second Epistle to the Corinthians he urges them to give liberally (2 Cor. 8:7-9; 9:6) and cheerfully (2 Cor. 9:7). He commends the Macedonian churches for their great liberality in this connection (2 Cor. 8:1-5) and urges the Corinthian church to follow their example (2 Cor. 8:6-9:5). In his Epistle to the Romans he tells of the offering which he is taking to Jerusalem (Rom. 15:25-28). Before Felix, Paul refers to this offering which he had brought to his nation (Acts 24:17). It is clear that he thinks of this contribution as coming from the "churches of Galatia" and the "churches of Macedonia." The same thing is implied when Paul says that the Corinthians began a year ago (2 Cor. 8:10; 9:2). They did this as individuals composing the church; and yet he addresses them as a group. Organized effort seems to be implied in his exhortation to carry out their earlier intention (2 Cor. 8:11; 9:3-5).

E. They sent letters of commendation to the other churches. This was done when Apollos left Ephesus and went to Corinth (Acts 18:24—28). It is also implied in Paul's sarcastic question, whether he will have to bring letters of commendation when he returns to Corinth (2 Cor. 3:1). Romans 16:1-2 is probably a sample of such a letter with regard to Phoebe. Insofar as this practice grew, it must have become necessary to ascertain the mind of the church as to who was worthy of such a letter. Organization is to be presupposed in such a procedure. The Council at Jerusalem rendered a decision with reference to the conditions on which Gentiles might be admitted into fellowship (Acts 15:22-29). This, too, presupposes an organization of some sort or another. (*Lectures in Systematic Theology*, pp. 415-417)

X. The Government of the Church—Within the confines of organized Christianity today, four separate church systems of government exist. These are:

A. The papal form—Here the pope of Rome functions as the supreme religious authority. When he speaks from the chair of St. Peter in matters of faith and morals, his words, like the Scriptures themselves, are infallible. The pope thus governs the faithful through the College of Cardinals, archbishops, bishops, and priests assigned to pastor local churches. The basis for this form is said to be given by Christ himself.

"And I say also unto thee, That thou art Peter, and upon this rock I will build my church; and the gates of hell shall not prevail against it. And I will give unto thee the keys of the kingdom of heaven: and whatsoever thou shalt bind on earth shall be bound in heaven: and whatsoever thou shalt loose on earth shall be loosed in heaven" (Matt. 16:18-19).

John Davis observes however: "The Roman Catholic Church points to these verses as the foundation of the papacy. Note, however, that nothing whatsoever is mentioned here concerning a *succession* of 'bishops' following Peter. And in John 20:22-23, the 'power of the keys' is given not just to Peter, but to all the disciples" (*Handbook of Basic Bible Texts*, p. 114).

B. The Episcopal form—This approach is espoused by the Orthodox church, the Episcopal, Lutheran, and Methodist churches. It is a government by bishops, aided by priests and deacons. The essential concept is that the right to consecrate other bishops and ordain both priests and deacons belongs only to the bishops themselves. This provides a succession of bishops and their rulership over the two subordinate ministries.

Scriptures used to support this form are Acts 6:6; 14:21-23; Philippians 1:1; 1 Timothy 3:1; 2 Timothy 1:6; Galatians 1:19; 2:9. It would seem from these cited biblical references that this form has ample Scriptural support. However, note the evaluation by Paul Enns:

> In evaluating this form of church government, the *episcopal* form is based partly on the authority of the apostles, which really does not have a counterpart in the New Testament church beyond the apostolic era. Christ had given a unique authority to the Twelve (Luke 9:1) that cannot be claimed by any person or group, nor is there a biblical basis for any form of apostolic succession. The authority Jesus gave to Peter (Matt. 16:18-19) was given to all the apostles (Matt. 18:18; John 20:23) but to no successive group. The episcopal form of church government can be seen in the second century but not in the first. (*Moody Handbook of Theology*, p. 358)

C. The federal, representative form—This is also known as the Presbyterian system, taken from the Greek word *presbuteros.* This word, found 62 times (in its noun form) is always translated by the English word "elder." Its system of government is best illustrated by the Presbyterian and Reformed churches of today. The federal system operates somewhat similar to that of the U.S. government. Each local church duly elects ruling elders to represent them. This group forms the church session. A distinction is usually made in this session between those ruling elders who govern but do not teach, preach, or administer the ordinances, and those elders (the chief being the pastor) who do.

The next high-ranking body in this system is the presbytery, which includes all ordained ministers or teaching elders and one ruling elder from each local congregation in a given district. Although pastors are elected by their own congregations, they must be approved by the presbytery. Above the presbytery is the synod (from a Greek word meaning "company"), and over the synod is the general assembly, the Supreme Court of its kind. Charles Ryrie writes the following:

Arguments in support of the federal type include the fact that elders were appointed by the apostles (Acts 14:23; Titus 1:5), there were obviously rulers over the churches besides the apostles (Heb. 13:7, 17), in matters of discipline the leaders gave instructions as to what to do (1 Cor. 5; 1 Tim. 5:20), and ordination passages imply the federal system. (*A Survey of Bible Doctrine*, p. 146)

W. L. Lingle suggests that the Jerusalem Council in Acts 15 illustrates this form of government. He writes:

If the church at Antioch had been entirely independent it could have settled this question for itself, and with such men as Paul and Barnabas present it was abundantly clear, to do so. As a matter of fact the Church at Antioch referred this question to a church council at Jerusalem. . . . Note well that it was composed of apostles and elders. It must have looked a good deal like a Presbyterian Synod or General Assembly. Note also that this council composed of apostles and elders, after full deliberations, settled the question author- itatively, and that the Church at Antioch and other churches accepted its decisions. (*Presbyterians: Their Ministry and Beliefs*, p. 16)

D. The congregational, democratic form—This type of government is clearly seen in Baptist, Congregational, Evangelical Free, Disciples of Christ, and Independent Bible churches. Followers of this form believe no outside man or group of men should exercise authority over a local assembly. Therefore, the government should be in the hands of the members themselves. The pastor is considered to be the sin- gle elder in the church. He is called and elected by the church congregation. Dea- cons are then chosen to assist him in shepherding the flock.

Again, to quote from Charles Ryrie:

Arguments in favor of this form of government include the many passages that speak of the responsibilities of the entire church (1 Cor. 1:10; Phil. 1:26), the passages which seem to commit the ordinances of the church to the entire group, not just leaders (Matt. 28:19-20; 1 Cor. 11:2, 20), the apparent involve- ment of the whole church in choosing leaders (Acts 6:3, 5; 15:2, 30; 2 Cor. 8:19), and the fact that the whole church was involved in exercising discipline (Matt. 18:17; 1 Cor. 5; 2 Thess. 3:14ff.).

Under the congregational system, the pastor is usually considered to be the single elder in the church. This is supported by the fact that the seven churches of Revelation 2 and 3 apparently had a single leader (called the "angel" but referring to a human leader), and by the fact that in 1 Timothy 3 the first part of the passage speaks of *the* bishop (elder) while the latter part (vv. 8-13) mentions the deacons. This would seem to indicate that there was only one elder in each church although there were several deacons. (*A Survey of Bible Doctrine*, p. 147)

Scriptures used to support this position are Matthew 18:17; Acts 6:3, 5; 15:12, 22-25; 2 Corinthians 2:6-7; 8:19; Colossians 1:18; 2 Thessalonians 3:14-15; 1 Peter 2:9; Jude 2.

Paul Enns offers the following conclusion:

The *presbyterian* form of church government has strong support for its view of the elders; there are many New Testament examples. The New Testament, however, reveals no organization beyond the local church.

The *congregational* form of church government finds biblical support for all the people being involved in the decision-making of the church. It can safely be said that elements of both the presbyterian and congregational forms of church government find support in Scripture. (*Moody Handbook of Theology,* p. 358)

XI. The Officers of the Church

Whatever be a person's or organization's preferences concerning the classes of leadership, no one can deny that leadership was considered necessary in New Testament churches. Recall a few facts. (1) Early in the life of the churches, relief funds were sent from Antioch to the elders in the churches in Judea (Acts 11:29). (2) Paul appointed elders almost immediately in the churches founded on the first missionary journey (14:23). (3) The council at Jerusalem was called, conducted, and concluded by leaders (chap. 15). (4) Elders and deacons appear as part of the normal picture of the life of various churches (20:17; Phil. 1:1). (5) Paul seemed to consider leaders a necessity for the proper functioning of churches (Titus 1:5). (6) Leadership is one of the spiritual gifts (Rom. 12:8) that functions in local churches (Heb. 13:7, 17). (Charles Ryrie, *A Survey of Bible Doctrine,* p. 412)

A. The designation of church officers (who they are)
   1. Bishops—"This is a true saying, If a man desire the office of a bishop, he desireth a good work" (1 Tim. 3:1). "For this cause left I thee in Crete, that thou shouldest set in order the things that are wanting, and ordain elders in every city, as I had appointed thee" (Titus 1:5).

   The Greek word for *bishop* is *episkopos,* and it refers to an overseer. Here Paul had in mind the office of the pastor. Another name found in the New Testament that may refer to this same position is "elder" (*presbuteros* in the Greek). These two terms, *bishop* and *elder,* are often used interchangeably (Acts 20:17-28; Titus 1:5-7). The former term (*bishop*) speaks of his office responsibility, while the latter term (*elder*) refers to his spiritual maturity. (See 1 Tim. 3:1-7; Titus 1:5-9.)

   Robert Lightner asks:

   Must there always be a plurality of elders, bishops, or pastors—whatever they are called—in every local church if it is to be true to the New Testament pattern? I do not believe so. Though the term "elder" does appear consistently in the plural, there are strong reasons why plurality is not always demanded, even though many evangelicals insist this is the case.

   First, there were house churches rather than large public meeting places in New Testament times. Therefore the use of the plural need not mean that each and every church had a plurality of elders. It may be understood to refer to one elder for each of the house churches in the city. Second, there is an interesting switch from the singular bishop to the plural deacons (1 Tim. 3:1-2, 8). This change lends some support to the validity of having only one elder or bishop in some instances. Third, the "angel," or messenger, in Revelation 2–3 most likely referred to the single elder of each of those churches. It would seem strange to give divine messages regarding human conduct to angelic beings. There are other instances where the same word obviously refers to humans (e.g., Mark 1:2; Luke 7:24; 9:52; 2:25). (*Evangelical Theology,* (pp. 241–242)

2. Deacons—"Likewise must the deacons be grave, not double-tongued, not given to much wine, not greedy of filthy lucre" (1 Tim. 3:8). The exact nature and duties of this office are nowhere set forth in any systematic way in the New Testament. It seems almost certain that the office was created to solve the organizational problem of the early church, due in part to its rapid growth (Acts 6:1-8). The Greek word for "deacon" is *diakonos*. (See also Rom. 12:7, here translated "ministry," and Phil. 1:1.)

B. The description of church officers (how they qualify)

1. Bishop

a. He must be a male—It has been correctly observed that, without exception, the principle church offices in the New Testament were held by men. Especially is this true regarding the offices of pastors and deacons. One of the chief qualifications for each of these offices is that the individual involved be "the husband of one wife" (1 Tim. 3:2, 12) To say the least, a woman could scarcely meet this requirement.

b. He must be blameless—Note, it does not say sinless. In essence, he must be without reproach, that is, of such character that no accusation can be levelled against him.

c. He must be the husband of one wife—Few New Testament statements have been the object of so much speculation as verse 2: "The husband of one wife." There are two main interpretations to the verse.

(1) The prohibition of polygamy view—According to this theory, Paul is simply saying no church member who had several wives in his home could qualify as a bishop. However, this view has serious problems.

(a) Paul had already forbidden this years ago (Rom. 7:1-3; 1 Cor. 7:2).

(b) The Roman government had outlawed polygamy at this time.

(c) There is no evidence that the early church ever had this problem.

(d) This term literally says a "one-woman man" and is found again in 1 Timothy 5:9 (though here reversed) where it speaks of a widow as a "one-man woman."

(2) The prohibition of divorce view—According to this theory a divorced and remarried man is prohibited from occupying the office of the pastorate, regardless of the circumstances that may have surrounded the divorce.

The vast majority of conservative Bible students hold to this view. Those opposing this second theory often accuse its advocates of simply underestimating the saving grace of God that totally wipes out the sinner's past. Spiritually speaking, this is absolutely correct. However, it does not change in the least many earthly circumstances. For example, a man saved in prison remains a prisoner.

Furthermore, it must be kept in mind that Paul here in this chapter is not discussing the salvation of a sinner, but the qualification of an officer. Finally, of all the qualifications mentioned here, this is the only one that cannot be corrected in the closet of prayer. For example, if a bishop has problems with greed (a qualification mentioned in 1 Tim. 3:3), he may confess this and rid himself of it. But he simply cannot pray away the existence of more than one living former wife.

d. He must be vigilant (temperate).

e. He must be sober (serious-minded).

      f. He must be of good behavior (orderly)—This would be reflected in his sermons, clothes, and life manner.

      g. He must be given to hospitality (a lover of strangers).

      h. He must be "apt to teach" (having the ability and love for teaching)—"And he gave some, apostles; and some, prophets; and some, evangelists; and some, pastors and teachers" (Eph. 4:11).

      i. He must not be given to wine.

      j. He must not be a striker (not pugnacious).

      k. He must not be greedy of money.

      l. He must not be a brawler (not contentious).

      m. He must not covet (not desire something belonging to someone else).

      n. He must rule his own house well—"One that ruleth well his own house, having his children in subjection with all gravity; (For if a man know not how to rule his own house, how shall he take care of the church of God?)" (1 Tim. 3:4-5).

      o. He must not be a novice (a new convert)—"Not a novice, lest being lifted up with pride he fall into the condemnation of the devil" (1 Tim. 3:6).

      p. He must maintain a good report from without (a good public testimony in his immediate community).

  2. Deacon (See 1 Tim. 3:8-13.)

      a. He must be grave (held in high respect).

      b. He must not be double-tongued (two-faced, a talebearer).

      c. He must not be given over to wine.

      d. He must not be greedy.

      e. He must hold forth the mystery of the faith (know, explain, and defend the great theological truths of the Bible).

      f. He must maintain a pure conscience.

      g. He must be tested and proven (his testimony within the church must be good).

      h. He must be blameless (his testimony without the church must be good).

C. The duties of church officers (what they do)

  1. Pastors—"But if I tarry long, that thou mayest know how thou oughtest to behave thyself in the house of God, which is the church of the living God, the pillar and ground of the truth" (1 Tim. 3:15).

      a. He is to administer the ordinances (Matt. 28:19-20).

      b. He is to be a man of prayer (1 Tim. 2:1).

      c. He is to warn his flock (1 Tim. 4:1-6)—"Now the Spirit speaketh expressly, that in the latter times some shall depart from the faith, giving heed to seducing spirits, and doctrines of devils. . . . If thou put the brethren in remembrance of these things, thou shalt be a good minister of Jesus Christ, nourished up in the words of faith and of good doctrine, whereunto thou hast attained" (1 Tim. 4:1, 6).

      d. He is to study the Word—"Study to show thyself approved unto God, a workman that needeth not to be ashamed, rightly dividing the word of truth" (2 Tim. 2:15).

      e. He is to preach the Word—"Preach the word; be instant in season, out of season; reprove, rebuke, exhort with all longsuffering and doctrine" (2 Tim. 4:2). (See also 1 Tim. 4:11-16; Acts 6:2-4.)

      f. He is to exhort and rebuke (1 Thess. 5:12; Titus 2:15).

g. He is to watch over souls.
  (1) His own—"Take heed therefore unto yourselves, and to all the flock, over the which the Holy Ghost hath made you overseers, to feed the church of God, which he hath purchased with his own blood" (Acts 20:28). "Take heed unto thyself, and unto the doctrine; continue in them: for in doing this thou shalt both save thyself, and them that hear thee" (1 Tim. 4:16).
  (2) Those of others—"Obey them that have the rule over you, and submit yourselves: for they watch for your souls, as they that must give account, that they may do it with joy, and not with grief: for that is unprofitable for you" (Heb. 13:17). (See also Acts 20:28-31.)
h. He is to feed and lead his flock—"Take heed therefore unto yourselves, and to all the flock, over the which the Holy Ghost hath made you overseers, to feed the church of God, which he hath purchased with his own blood" (Acts 20:28). "Feed the flock of God which is among you, taking the oversight thereof, not by constraint, but willingly; not for filthy lucre, but of a ready mind" (1 Pet. 5:2).
i. He is to be an example to all—"Let no man despise thy youth; but be thou an example of the believers, in word, in conversation, in charity, in spirit, in faith, in purity" (1 Tim. 4:12).

Pastor John MacArthur, Jr., writes concerning Paul's fourfold perspective of pastoral priorities in Acts 20:19-22 (*Leadership, God's Priority for the Church,* p.15):
  (1) A right perspective toward *God.* "Serving the Lord with all humility of mind, and with many tears, and trials, which befell me by the lying in wait of the Jews."
  (2) A right perspective toward the *church.* "And how I kept back nothing that was profitable unto you, but have shown you, and have taught you publicly."
  (3) A right perspective toward the *lost.* "And from house to house, testifying both to the Jews and also to the Greeks, repentance toward God, and faith toward our Lord Jesus Christ."
  (4) A right perspective toward *himself.* "And now, behold, I go bound in the spirit unto Jerusalem, not knowing the things that shall befall me there."

2. Deacons—In Philippians 1:1 Paul writes to "all the saints in Jesus Christ which are at Philippi, with the bishops and deacons."

Three well-known authors write concerning these officers and their duties. The first is Dr. John Walvoord.

> The mention of bishops and deacons indicates the advanced state of organization of the Church at Philippi now composed of mature and gifted believers from whom recognized leaders had come. As A. R. Fausset notes, "This is the earliest epistle where bishops and deacons are mentioned and the only one where they are separately addressed." Of course, as early as Acts 6, men were appointed in the church to serve in a way similar to deacons. Although not called deacons, the prominence of this appointment of men to special service in Acts seems to recognize its significance. Elders were appointed in every church as early as Acts 14:23, and are mentioned in Acts 11:30; 20:27-28; 1 Thess. 5:12-13. (*Philippians, Triumph in Christ,* p. 24)

Greek scholar Kenneth Wuest writes:

> The word bishop is the translation of a Greek word used in secular pursuits of an overseer in any capacity, for instance, the official in charge of the repairing of a temple or an officer in an army. The word itself means "to look upon." Paul uses it as another name for an elder, the latter being the title of the office so far as statutes in the church is concerned, the former being the title that indicated the responsibility and activity of the office, that of overseeing the spiritual welfare of the local church. He brings the two names together as designating one individual in Acts 20:17, 28.
>
> The word deacon is the English spelling of a Greek word that was used as a general term to designate a servant. It covered both slaves and hired servants. It represented a servant, not in his relation to his master, but in his activity. The same word is translated "minister" in 1 Corinthians 3:5; 2 Corinthians 3:6; Ephesians 3:7. Here it refers to a distinct class of officers in the apostolic church. The origin of the office is given us in Acts 6. (*Word Studies in Philippians,* p. 28)

As a final note here, consider the comments of J. Dwight Pentecost:

> The word "deacon" comes from a compound Greek word that means "to stir up the dust." It presents the picture of one who is moving so rapidly through the dusty lanes of the villages of Palestine to discharge his duty that his feet kick up dust as he goes. There was so much for the deacons to do they could not loiter nor tarry. They went about their ministry with such diligence that they were stirring up the dust; thus those who were set apart to this ministry were called "those who stir up the dust" or deacons. (*The Joy Of Living,* p. 114)

XII. The Ordinances of the Church—The meaning of an ordinance: An ordinance is an outward and visible symbolic rite commanded in the Bible to be practiced by the church that sets forth a central truth of the Christian faith. It is a memorial or reminder of some precious historical event of great significance.

The distinction between an ordinance and a sacrament: "A sacrament is something presented to the senses, which has the power by divine institution, not only signifying, but also of efficiently conveying grace" (as defined by the Roman Catholic Council of Trent in 1551). An ordinance therefore differs from a sacrament in that it is performed not to obtain grace, but because the one observing it has already obtained that grace.

The number of the ordinances: The Roman Catholic church teaches there are seven sacraments. These are: ordination, confirmation, matrimony, extreme unction, penance, baptism, the Eucharist (Communion). Of these seven the New Testament lists but two, and (as we have already seen) regards them as memorial ordinances and not sacraments. These two are the Lord's Supper and baptism.

A. The Lord's Supper—"Now before the feast of the passover, when Jesus knew that his hour was come that he should depart out of this world unto the Father, having loved his own which were in the world, he loved them unto the end" (John 13:1).

1. The original Lord's Supper—"And the disciples did as Jesus had appointed them; and they made ready the passover. Now when the even was come, he sat down with the twelve. . . . And as they were eating, Jesus took bread, and blessed it, and brake it, and gave it to the disciples, and said, Take, eat; this is

my body. And he took the cup, and gave thanks, and gave it to them, saying, Drink ye all of it; For this is my blood of the new testament, which is shed for many for the remission of sins" (Matt. 26:19-20, 26-28). (See also Mark 14:22-26; Luke 22:17-20; 1 Cor. 11:23-25.)

Note: The actual details of the Lord's Supper are not mentioned in John's Gospel. However, some believe Jesus referred to it during his Bread of Life sermon as recorded by John (see John 6:31-58; especially note 6:51, 53-56).

2. The names for the Lord's Supper

a. The *Eucharist* (Greek word for the "giving of thanks")—This name is taken from 1 Corinthians 11:24. "And when he had given thanks, he brake it, and said, Take, eat: this is my body, which is broken for you: this do in remembrance of me."

b. The *eulogia* (Greek word for "blessing")—This name is taken from 1 Corinthians 10:16, "the cup of blessing." "The cup of blessing which we bless, is it not the communion of the blood of Christ?"

c. The *prosphora* (Greek word for "offering")—This name came into being because gifts or offerings for the poor were made at the celebration of the Supper.

d. Communion—This name derives from 1 Corinthians 10:16, "the communion of the blood of Christ."

e. The breaking of bread—This expression is found in Acts 2 and is thought by some to refer to the Lord's Supper. "And they continued stedfastly in the apostles' doctrine and fellowship, and in breaking of bread, and in prayers" (Acts 2:42).

3. The views concerning the Lord's Supper

a. Transubstantiation—This Roman Catholic doctrine teaches that the bread and wine actually become the body and blood of Christ when consecrated by the priest during Mass, even though they still look and taste the same. Thus the one partaking literally eats Christ's flesh and drinks his blood. Needless to say, this is without scriptural support. In fact, it is totally refuted by the book of Hebrews.

Paul Enns observes:

> There are several serious problems with this view. (1) It views the work of Christ as unfinished, the sacrifice of Christ continuing in the Mass. Yet Christ declared His work completed (John 19:30) as did also the writer of Hebrews (Heb. 10:10-14). (2) Christ's human body would have to be omnipresent if this teaching were true; however, Christ's human body is localized in heaven (Acts 7:56). (3) In instituting the Supper, Christ used a common figure of speech—the metaphor ("This is my body . . . my blood")—in referring to the bread and cup. He was physically present yet distinct from the elements when He referred to them as His body and blood. Similarly, in the John 6 passage, Jesus used a powerful metaphor ("eat my flesh . . . drink my blood") to vividly picture a saving faith-relationship to Himself. To insist that these expressions are literal language is to do violence to fundamental hermeneutical principles. (4) It was forbidden for Jews to drink blood (Lev. 17:10-16), yet this is what Jesus would be asking them to do if transubstantiation was what He intended. (*Moody Handbook of Theology*, pp. 360–361)

    b. Consubstantiation—This Lutheran doctrine teaches that, while the bread and wine remain the same, the presence of the body of Christ is nevertheless "in, with, and under" both elements. While this error is not as severe as the above, it too is unscriptural.

    c. Spiritualization—This is also known as the Reformed view. According to the Reformed position, Christ is not literally present in the elements (bread and wine), but there is nevertheless a spiritual presence of the Savior. Again, one searches the Scriptures in vain to find this position.

    d. Memorialization—This doctrine teaches that the bread and wine are mere symbols to remind and aid the believer in observing both the first and second comings of our Lord. This practice is both scriptural and sensible.
        Paul Enns writes:

> The memorial view has much to commend it in the Scriptures. An examination of the passages reveals the significance of the Lord's Supper. It is a memorial to His death (1 Cor. 11:24, 25): the recurring statement, "in remembrance of me," makes this clear, the bread symbolizing His perfect body offered in sin-bearing sacrifice (1 Pet. 2:24), and the wine His blood shed for forgiveness of sins (Eph. 1:7). It is a proclamation of the death of Christ while waiting for His coming (1 Cor. 11:26): it involves a looking back to the historical event of the cross and an anticipating of His return in the future (Matt. 26:29). It is a communion of believers with each other (1 Cor. 10:17): they eat and drink the same symbolic elements, focusing on their common faith in Christ." (Ibid., p. 362)

4. The Old Testament type of the Lord's Supper—A beautiful type is seen in the Passover Lamb, the sprinkled blood of which saved the Israelite home from the death plague in Egypt prior to the Exodus.

    "For I will pass through the land of Egypt this night, and will smite all the firstborn in the land of Egypt, both man and beast; and against all the gods of Egypt I will execute judgment: I am the LORD. And the blood shall be to you for a token upon the houses where ye are: and when I see the blood, I will pass over you, and the plague shall not be upon you to destroy you, when I smite the land of Egypt" (Exod. 12:12-13).

    "Then Moses called for all the elders of Israel, and said unto them, Draw out and take you a lamb according to your families, and kill the passover. And ye shall take a bunch of hyssop, and dip it in the blood that is in the basin, and strike the lintel and the two side posts with the blood that is in the basin; and none of you shall go out at the door of his house until the morning" (Exod. 12:21-22). "And it shall come to pass, when your children shall say unto you, What mean ye by this service? That ye shall say, It is the sacrifice of the LORD's passover, who passed over the houses of the children of Israel in Egypt, when he smote the Egyptians, and delivered our houses. And the people bowed the head and worshipped" (Exod. 12:26-27).

    In the New Testament Paul connects the Passover Lamb with that of the Lord's Table. Note: "Purge out therefore the old leaven, that ye may be a new lump, as ye are unleavened. For even Christ our passover is sacrificed for us: Therefore let us keep the feast, not with old leaven, neither with the leaven of malice and wickedness; but with the unleavened bread of sincerity and truth" (1 Cor. 5:7-8).

5. The rules governing the Lord's Supper
   a. The person involved—The Lord Jesus Christ: It is not the church's supper, or the elders' supper, but the Lord's Supper. Thus, the table of the Lord is to magnify the Lord of the table.
   b. The procedure involved—"For I have received of the Lord that which also I delivered unto you, That the Lord Jesus the same night in which he was betrayed took bread: And when he had given thanks, he brake it, and said, Take, eat: this is my body, which is broken for you: this do in remembrance of me. After the same manner also he took the cup, when he had supped, saying, This cup is the new testament in my blood: this do ye, as oft as ye drink it, in remembrance of me" (1 Cor. 11:23-25).
   c. The purpose involved—A threefold purpose is seen:
     (1) It serves as a backward look to the Cross—"For as often as ye eat this bread, and drink this cup, ye do show the Lord's death" (1 Cor. 11:26).
     (2) It serves as an inward look to the conscience—"But let a man examine himself, and so let him eat of that bread, and drink of that cup" (1 Cor. 11:28).
     (3) It serves as a forward look to the crown—"Till he come" (1 Cor. 11:26).
   d. The partakers involved
     (1) Generally speaking—all believers, but only believers
     (2) Specifically speaking—two groups are forbidden to partake:
       (a) The unsaved sinners—they may qualify by obeying John 3:16
       (b) the unclean saints—they may qualify by obeying 1 John 1:9
   e. The penalty involved—"For he that eateth and drinketh unworthily, eateth and drinketh damnation to himself, not discerning the Lord's body. For this cause many are weak and sickly among you, and many sleep" (1 Cor. 11:29-30).
     Here several words deserve our consideration.
     (1) Unworthily—The word here is an adverb and not an adjective. Paul does not say, "If anyone who is not worthy partakes," but rather, "If anyone partakes in an unworthy manner."
     (2) Damnation—In the Greek this is the word *krina* and should here be translated "judgment." (See Rom. 11:33; 1 Pet. 4:17; and Rev. 20:4, where the same word appears.) This judgment may be manifested in a twofold manner:
       (a) Through physical sickness (11:30)
       (b) Through physical death—"And many sleep." The Greek word for sleep here is *koimao* and refers to physical death. (See John 11:11-12; Acts 7:60; 1 Cor. 15:18, 20, 51.)
   f. The profit involved
     (1) It can be used for the judging of ourselves—"For if we would judge ourselves, we should not be judged. But when we are judged, we are chastened of the Lord, that we should not be condemned with the world" (1 Cor. 11:31-32).
     (2) It can be used for the giving of ourselves—"So, dear brothers, when you gather for the Lord's Supper—the communion service—wait for each other" (1 Cor. 11:33, TLB).
B. Baptism—"Go ye therefore, and teach all nations, baptizing them in the name of the Father, and of the Son, and of the Holy Ghost" (Matt. 28:19).

1. The theological meaning of baptism—Most Bible students would agree that the act of baptism is, in essence, the act of identifying with someone or something.
2. The examples of baptism—Following is a list of eight kinds of baptism in the New Testament. Each may be correctly defined by the concept of identification.
   a. The baptism of sin upon Christ at Calvary—"But I have a baptism to be baptized with; and how am I straitened till it be accomplished!" (Luke 12:50).
   b. The baptism of the Holy Spirit upon believers at Pentecost—"I indeed baptize you with water unto repentance: but he that cometh after me is mightier than I, whose shoes I am not worthy to bear: he shall baptize you with the Holy Ghost, and with fire" (Matt. 3:11). "For John truly baptized with water; but ye shall be baptized with the Holy Ghost not many days hence." (Acts 1:5). "And when the day of Pentecost was fully come, they were all with one accord in one place. And suddenly there came a sound from heaven as of a rushing mighty wind, and it filled all the house where they were sitting. And there appeared unto them cloven tongues like as of fire, and it sat upon each of them. And they were all filled with the Holy Ghost, and began to speak with other tongues, as the Spirit gave them utterance" (Acts 2:1-4).
   c. The baptism of all Christians by the Holy Spirit into the body of Christ—"For by one Spirit are we all baptized into one body, whether we be Jews or Gentiles, whether we be bond or free; and have been all made to drink into one Spirit" (1 Cor. 12:13).
   d. The baptism of Israel unto Moses—"And were all baptized unto Moses in the cloud and in the sea" (1 Cor. 10:2).
   e. The baptism of John the Baptist (national baptism of repentance)—"John did baptize in the wilderness, and preach the baptism of repentance for the remission of sins" (Mark 1:4). "When John had first preached before his coming the baptism of repentance to all the people of Israel" (Acts 13:24).
   f. The baptism of Jesus
      (1) With water by John—"And Jesus answering said unto him, Suffer it to be so now: for thus it becometh us to fulfil all righteousness. Then he suffered him" (Matt. 3:15).
      (2) With the Holy Spirit by the Father—"And Jesus, when he was baptized, went up straightway out of the water: and, lo, the heavens were opened unto him, and he saw the Spirit of God descending like a dove, and lighting upon him" (Matt. 3:16).
   g. The baptism for the dead—"Else what shall they do which are baptized for the dead, if the dead rise not at all? why are they then baptized for the dead?" (1 Cor. 15:29).
      Note: Whatever this verse teaches, it does not in the slightest even remotely support the "proxy baptism" position held by the Mormon church. This false view says, in effect, a living person today (Mormon believer) can be baptized in place of a dead friend or relative (who was not a convert to Mormonism) and thus impute the faith to the deceased one. In reality, Paul was refuting the senseless claims of some who denied the resurrection of the dead. Here (1 Cor. 15:29) he says (in suggested paraphrase fashion): "If there is no resurrection, then what is the logic of the living (current Christians) in picking up the fallen banners once held high by the dead (departed Christians)?"

h. The water baptism of new converts in the book of Acts

(1) At Pentecost—Here 3,000 were baptized by Peter and the apostles. "Then they that gladly received his word were baptized: and the same day there were added unto them about three thousand souls" (Acts 2:41).

(2) At Samaria—Here many were baptized by Philip the Evangelist. "But when they believed Philip preaching the things concerning the kingdom of God, and the name of Jesus Christ, they were baptized, both men and women" (Acts 8:12).

(3) At Gaza—Here the Ethiopian eunuch was baptized by Philip. "And he commanded the chariot to stand still: and they went down both into the water, both Philip and the eunuch; and he baptized him" (Acts 8:38).

(4) At Damascus—Here Paul was baptized by Ananias. "And immediately there fell from his eyes as it had been scales: and he received sight forthwith, and arose, and was baptized" (Acts 9:18).

(5) At Caesarea—Here Peter baptized Cornelius and his friends. "And he commanded them to be baptized in the name of the Lord. Then prayed they him to tarry certain days" (Acts 10:48).

(6) At Philippi—Here Paul baptized Lydia and the Philippian jailor. "And when she was baptized, and her household, she besought us, saying, If ye have judged me to be faithful to the Lord, come into my house, and abide there. And she constrained us" (Acts 16:15).

(7) At Corinth—Here Paul baptized Crispus, Gaius, Stephanas, and others. "And Crispus, the chief ruler of the synagogue, believed on the Lord with all his house; and many of the Corinthians hearing believed, and were baptized" (Acts 18:8). "I thank God that I baptized none of you, but Crispus and Gaius. . . . And I baptized also the household of Stephanas: besides, I know not whether I baptized any other" (1 Cor. 1:14, 16).

(8) At Ephesus—Here Paul baptized some followers of John the Baptist. "And he said unto them, Unto what then were ye baptized? And they said, Unto John's baptism. Then said Paul, John verily baptized with the baptism of repentance, saying unto the people, that they should believe on him which should come after him, that is, on Christ Jesus. When they heard this, they were baptized in the name of the Lord Jesus" (Acts 19:3-5).

3. The importance of baptism—Charles Ryrie observes:

The importance of baptism is underscored by the following considerations.

a. Christ was baptized (Matt. 3:16). Though the meaning of His baptism was entirely different from the significance of Christian baptism, nevertheless there exists a sense in which we follow the Lord when we are baptized. To be sure, we can never fully imitate a sinless Person; yet we are to follow His steps, and baptism was one of them (1 Pet. 2:21).

b. The Lord approved of His disciples baptizing (John 4:1-2).

c. Christ commanded that people be baptized in this age (Matt. 28:19). Clearly this command was not only for the apostles who heard it but for His followers throughout the entire age, since He promised His presence to the end of the age.

d. The early church gave an important place to baptism (Acts 2:38, 41;

8:12-13, 36, 38; 9:18; 10:47-48; 16:15, 33; 18:8; 19:5). The early church never conceived of a believer remaining unbaptized.

e. The New Testament uses the ordinance to picture or symbolize important theological truths (Rom. 6:1-10; Gal. 3:27; 1 Pet. 3:21).

f. The writer to the Hebrews terms baptism a foundational truth (6:1-2). It is no more optional or less significant than the doctrines of repentance, resurrection, and judgment. (*Basic Theology,* pp. 421–422)

4. The various views concerning baptism

a. That baptism is necessary for salvation (also known as baptismal regeneration)

(1) This is totally erroneous—Dozens of key passages make it crystal clear that salvation is by grace through faith plus nothing. Note but a few:

"What shall we say then that Abraham our father, as pertaining to the flesh, hath found? For if Abraham were justified by works, he hath whereof to glory; but not before God. For what saith the scripture? Abraham believed God, and it was counted unto him for righteousness. Now to him that worketh is the reward not reckoned of grace, but of debt. But to him that worketh not, but believeth on him that justifieth the ungodly, his faith is counted for righteousness. Even as David also describeth the blessedness of the man, unto whom God imputeth righteousness without works" (Rom. 4:1-6).

"For by grace are ye saved through faith; and that not of yourselves: it is the gift of God: Not of works, lest any man should boast" (Eph. 2:8-9). "Not by works of righteousness which we have done, but according to his mercy he saved us, by the washing of regeneration, and renewing of the Holy Ghost" (Titus 3:5).

(2) The strongest refutation of baptismal regeneration is found in 1 Corinthians 1—"For Christ sent me not to baptize, but to preach the gospel: not with wisdom of words, lest the cross of Christ should be made of none effect" (1 Cor. 1:17).

(3) In 1 Corinthians 15 Paul explains what the gospel is, and baptism is definitely not a part of it—"Moreover, brethren, I declare unto you the gospel which I preached unto you, which also ye have received, and wherein ye stand; By which also ye are saved, if ye keep in memory what I preached unto you, unless ye have believed in vain. For I delivered unto you first of all that which I also received, how that Christ died for our sins according to the scriptures; And that he was buried, and that he rose again the third day according to the scriptures" (1 Cor. 15:1-4).

(4) An oft-repeated "proof-text" for baptismal regeneration is Acts 2: "Then Peter said unto them, Repent, and be baptized every one of you in the name of Jesus Christ for the remission of sins, and ye shall receive the gift of the Holy Ghost" (Acts 2:38).

The Greek preposition *eis* (here translated "for") can also be rendered "upon." In other words, Peter was saying in effect: "Repent and submit to baptism upon (showing evidence of) your new relationship with the Messiah."

(5) Another favorite verse used by those advocating this false position is Acts 22:16—"And now why tarriest thou? arise, and be baptized, and wash away thy sins, calling on the name of the Lord" (Acts 22:16).

Stanley Toussaint writes:

> Two questions revolve about this verse. *First,* when was Paul saved—
> on the Damascus Road or at Judas' house? Several factors suggest he
> was saved on the Damascus Road: (1) The gospel was presented to
> him directly by Christ (Gal. 1:11-12), not later by Ananias. (2) Already
> (Acts 22:10) Paul said he had submitted in faith to Christ. (3) Paul was
> filled with the Spirit *before* his baptism with water (9:17-18). (4) The
> Greek aorist participle *epikalesamenos,* translated "calling on His
> name" refers either to action, which is simultaneous with, or before
> that of the main verb. Here Paul's calling on Christ's name (for salva-
> tion) preceded his water baptism. The participle may be translated,
> "having called on His name."
>   *Second,* what then do the words "wash your sins away" mean? Do
> they teach that salvation comes by water baptism? Because Paul was
> already cleansed spiritually (see comments in preceding par.), these
> words must refer to the symbolism of baptism. Baptism is a picture of
> God's inner work of washing away sin (cf. 1 Cor. 6:11; 1 Pet. 3:21). (In
> John Walvoord and Roy Zuck, *The Bible Knowledge Commentary,* New
> Testament ed., p. 418)

b. That baptism replaces circumcision—Paul Enns states:

> This is the view of Reformed and Presbyterian churches. The sacraments
> of baptism and the Lord's Supper are "signs and seals of an inward and
> invisible thing by means whereof God works in us by the power of the
> Holy Spirit . . . like circumcision in the Old Testament, baptism makes
> us sure of God's promises." . . . The act of baptism is both the means of
> initiation into the covenant and a sign of salvation. (*Moody Handbook of
> Theology,* p. 363)

This cannot be, however, for several reasons.
   (1) Circumcision was performed upon male babies only, but in the New
       Testament we have the baptism of women mentioned—"But when they
       believed Philip preaching the things concerning the kingdom of God,
       and the name of Jesus Christ, they were baptized, both men and women"
       (Acts 8:12). (See also Acts 16:15.)
   (2) Circumcision had nothing to do with the faith of the baby—Only his
       nationality was in mind.
   (3) Baptism has nothing to do with the nationality of the believer—Only his
       faith is in mind.
   (4) Circumcision continued to be practiced among Jewish believers even
       after the institution of baptism—"Him would Paul have to go forth with
       him; and took and circumcised him because of the Jews which were in
       those quarters: for they knew all that his father was a Greek" (Acts 16:3).
   c. That baptism serves as a sign of one's salvation—This is the position of
      Baptists and others. Stated another way, baptism becomes a public, outward
      testimony giving evidence to a personal, inward faith. This view is totally
      supported by all nine events recorded in the book of Acts where people
      were baptized. Without exception, immediately following their conversion
      they were baptized as a public testimony of their newfound faith. Note:

(1) The converts at Pentecost (Acts 2:41)

(2) The converts at Samaria (Acts 8:12)

(3) The Ethiopian eunuch (Acts 8:36-37)

(4) Saul of Tarsus (Acts 9:15-18)

(5) Cornelius and his household (Acts 10:47-48)

(6) Lydia (Acts 16:15)

(7) The Philippian jailor and his household (Acts 16:33)

(8) Crispus (Acts 18:8)

(9) The 12 disciples of John the Baptist (Acts 19:1-7)—Note: Two key truths are clearly seen coming from these various baptismal experiences:

(1) That *all* believers be baptized—F. F. Bruce writes, "The idea of an unbaptized Christian is simply not entertained in the New Testament" (*The Book of Acts*, p. 77). Baptism is therefore not a personal choice, but a divine command.

(2) That *only* believers be baptized—The two words *belief* and *baptism* are inseparably linked together in the New Testament. Belief is always assumed to be the *root* of which baptism becomes the *fruit*. In the light of Scriptures the practice of baptizing infants must be completely ruled out.

5. The mode of baptism—There are three main views concerning the mode of baptism.

   a. Sprinkling—A defense:

     (1) Because of the logistical problems involved concerning pouring or immersion in various baptismal accounts, such as:

      (a) The huge number baptized at Pentecost (Acts 2:41)

      (b) The scarcity of water when the eunuch was baptized in the desert (Acts 8:38)

     (2) Because various Old Testament cleansings involved sprinkling (Exod. 24:6-7; Lev. 14:7; Num. 8:5-7; 19:4, 8), and these are later classified as "baptism" in Heb. 9:10.

     (3) Because Cyprian, a third century church father, approved of it.

   b. Pouring—A defense:

     (1) Pouring is permitted in the Didache (a second century manual devoted to moral instruction and church order).

     (2) The early pictorial illustrations in the catacombs show the baptismal candidate standing in the water with the minister pouring water on his head.

   c. Immersion—A defense:

     (1) Lexical studies of the Greek word *baptizo* indicate it means "to dip, immerse."

     (2) Secular employment of the word used it in regards to the sinking of a ship, to drown, to immerse something.

     (3) The Greek words for sprinkle, *rontizo*, and pour, *ekcheo, ballo*, are not used in the baptismal passages.

     (4) Proselytes to Judaism were self-immersed.

     (5) Immersion was the mode practiced by the early church until the third century, when pouring was permitted in case of illness.

     (6) The first record of the use of sprinkling was about A.D. 250, when Novatian lay sick in bed and thought he was to die. He had water poured all over him on the bed as an act of baptism.

(7) John Calvin and Martin Luther (two of the most famous non-immersionists) both freely acknowledged that the Greek word *baptizo* refers to dipping, or submerging something into water, oil, blood, etc.

6. The symbolism of baptism—What exactly does baptism symbolize? One's interpretation of this will determine his view on the *mode* of baptism also. Here there are two views concerning the symbolism of baptism.

    a. The view of the affusionist—He is one who sprinkles or pours the baptismal water. The affusionist believes the object lying behind baptism is to represent the coming of the Holy Spirit upon the believer. He reasons that inasmuch as Calvary is represented by one ordinance (the Lord's Supper) then there would be no need of a second ordinance representing the same event.

    b. The view of the immersionist—He is one who requires the complete submerging of the believer in water. The immersionist relates baptism to Christ's death, burial, and resurrection on the ground of the fact that the believer is said to have been baptized into his death, burial, and resurrection, according to Romans 6:1-10 and Colossians 2:11-13.

        While it is true that there is a similarity here to that of the Lord's Supper, there are also important differences. Note:

        (1) The Lord's Supper speaks primarily of Christ's death.

        (2) Baptism speaks primarily of the believer's death.

        (3) The return of Christ is seen in the Lord's Supper.

        (4) The resurrection of Christ is seen in baptism.

        (5) Justification (the cross) and glorification (the crown) are in view in the Lord's Supper.

        (6) Sanctification is seen in baptism—"Therefore we are buried with him by baptism into death: that like as Christ was raised up from the dead by the glory of the Father, even so we also should walk in newness of life" (Rom. 6:4).

XIII. The Worship of the Church—"Give unto the LORD the glory due unto his name; worship the LORD in the beauty of holiness" (Psa. 29:2). "But the hour cometh, and now is, when the true worshippers shall worship the Father in spirit and in truth: for the Father seeketh such to worship him. God is a Spirit: and they that worship him must worship him in spirit and in truth" (John 4:23-24).

  A. The definition of worship—There are three Greek verbs translated by the one English word *worship*. These words are:

    1. *Proskuneo*—"To bow or prostrate oneself in submissive lowliness and deep reverence," "to kiss one's hand."

    2. *Sebomai*—"To look upon with awe."

    3. *Latreuo*—"To render priestly service for."

        Andrew W. Blackwood has defined it thus: "Worship is man's response to God's revelation of Himself." To worship God is therefore to ascribe to him the supreme homage of which he alone is worthy.

        Charles Ryrie writes: "The worship of the church, then, consists of individual, corporate, public, and private service for the Lord which is generated by a reverence for and submission to Him who is totally worthy" (*Basic Theology*, p. 428).

B. The importance of worship—"And God said, Let us make man in our image, after our likeness. . . . So God created man in his own image" (Gen. 1:26-27).

How was man made in the image of God? In essence, God fashioned a creature that, in some areas, would share similar experiences with the animal, such as breathing, sleeping, eating, etc. But this creature would be able to do something no dog, dandelion, or dinosaur could do, namely, to bow its head and thank God for the food it was about to eat.

The difference between Adam and all other creatures in the Garden was not in his size or strength, but in his ability (and command) to worship the Creator. God did not make the first man to build the largest Sunday school in Eden or to "win that soul nearest hell," but rather to fellowship with and follow after his Maker.

C. The reasons for worship

1. We are to worship God because of who he is—"Give unto the LORD the glory due unto his name; worship the LORD in the beauty of holiness" (Psa. 29:2). "And all the angels stood round about the throne, and about the elders and the four beasts, and fell before the throne on their faces, and worshipped God, Saying, Amen: Blessing, and glory, and wisdom, and thanksgiving, and honour, and power, and might, be unto our God for ever and ever. Amen. . . . And a voice came out of the throne, saying, Praise our God, all ye his servants, and ye that fear him, both small and great" (Rev. 7:11-12; 19:5).

    He and he alone is the only eternal, infinite, omnipresent, omniscient, omnipotent, sovereign, righteous, faithful, holy, gracious, and loving God.

2. We are to worship God because of what he has done—It can be said that everything God has already done, is doing, or will do, can be correctly placed under one of two categories, namely, his twin works of creation and redemption. These two works are highlighted by God through a sevenfold scriptural reminder:

    a. The two heavens and earths

      (1) The heaven and earth of creation—"In the beginning God created the heaven and the earth" (Gen. 1:1).

      (2) The heaven and earth of redemption—"And I saw a new heaven and a new earth: for the first heaven and the first earth were passed away; and there was no more sea" (Rev. 21:1).

    b. The two gardens

      (1) Creation's garden—"And the LORD God planted a garden eastward in Eden; and there he put the man whom he had formed. And out of the ground made the LORD God to grow every tree that is pleasant to the sight, and good for food; the tree of life also in the midst of the garden, and the tree of knowledge of good and evil" (Gen. 2:8-9).

      (2) Redemption's garden—"Then cometh Jesus with them unto a place called Gethsemane, and saith unto the disciples, Sit ye here, while I go and pray yonder" (Matt. 26:36). "When Jesus had spoken these words, he went forth with his disciples over the brook Cedron, where was a garden, into the which he entered, and his disciples" (John 18:1)

    c. The two marriages

      (1) Creation's marriage—Eve to Adam (Gen. 2:23-24)

      (2) Redemption's marriage—The church to Christ (Rev. 19:7-9)

    d. The nine feasts in Leviticus 23

      (1) Feasts reminding us of creation

(a) The weekly Sabbath rest

(b) The 7-year rest

(c) The 50-year rest

(2) Feasts reminding us of redemption

(a) The Passover (speaking of Calvary)

(b) The first fruits (speaking of the Resurrection)

(c) The seven-week feast (speaking of Pentecost)

(d) The Feast of Trumpets (speaking of Christ's return)

(e) The Day of Atonement (speaking of the great tribulation)

(f) The Feast of Tabernacles (speaking of the Millennium)

e. The two special days

(1) Saturday, reminding us of creation—"Remember the sabbath day, to keep it holy. . . . For in six days the LORD made heaven and earth, the sea, and all that in them is, and rested the seventh day: wherefore the LORD blessed the sabbath day, and hallowed it" (Exod. 20:8, 11).

(2) Sunday, reminding us of redemption—"Now when Jesus was risen early the first day of the week, he appeared first to Mary Magdalene, out of whom he had cast seven devils" (Mark 16:9).

f. The two special chapters

(1) Genesis 1—The creation account, describing how man was made in the image of God.

(2) Luke 2—The redemption account, describing how God was made in the image of man.

g. The two songs in Revelation

(1) The song of creation—"Thou art worthy, O Lord, to receive glory and honour and power: for thou hast created all things, and for thy pleasure they are and were created" (Rev. 4:11).

(2) The song of redemption—"And they sung a new song, saying, Thou art worthy to take the book, and to open the seals thereof: for thou wast slain, and hast redeemed us to God by thy blood out of every kindred, and tongue, and people, and nation" (Rev. 5:9).

D. The aspects of worship—How do we worship God?

1. Through our handling of the Word of God

a. We are to read it.

b. We are to heed it.

c. We are to deed it (to our children).

d. We are to seed it (in the fields of society)—"Hold fast the form of sound words, which thou hast heard of me, in faith and love which is in Christ Jesus. . . . Study to show thyself approved unto God, a workman that needeth not to be ashamed, rightly dividing the word of truth" (2 Tim. 1:13; 2:15). "So then faith cometh by hearing, and hearing by the word of God" (Rom. 10:17). "I charge you by the Lord that this epistle be read unto all the holy brethren" (1 Thess. 5:27). "Therefore, brethren, stand fast, and hold the traditions which ye have been taught, whether by word, or our epistle" (2 Thess. 2:15).

2. Through our prayers (Acts 4:24; 6:4; 10:9; 12:5; 13:3; 1 Tim. 2:1-8)—"But we will give ourselves continually to prayer, and to the ministry of the word" (Acts 6:4). "I exhort therefore, that, first of all, supplications, prayers, intercessions, and

giving of thanks, be made for all men; I will therefore that men pray every where, lifting up holy hands, without wrath and doubting" (1 Tim. 2:1, 8).

3. Through our obedience in observing the ordinances of baptism and the Lord's Supper (Matt. 28:19; 1 Cor. 11:23-25)

4. Through our singing—"Speaking to yourselves in psalms and hymns and spiritual songs, singing and making melody in your heart to the Lord" (Eph. 5:19). "Let the word of Christ dwell in you richly in all wisdom; teaching and admonishing one another in psalms and hymns and spiritual songs, singing with grace in your hearts to the Lord" (Col. 3:16). "Is any among you afflicted? let him pray. Is any merry? let him sing psalms" (James 5:13).

Several New Testament passages may contain parts of hymns that the early church used. Example: "And without controversy great is the mystery of godliness: God was manifest in the flesh, justified in the Spirit, seen of angels, preached unto the Gentiles, believed on in the world, received up into glory" (1 Tim. 3:16).

5. Through the offering up of sacrifices—According to 1 Peter 2:5-9 and Revelation 1:6, every New Testament believer is a priest unto God. The main function of the Old Testament priest was to sacrifice. So it is with the New Testament priests. Their priestly service toward God is fourfold.

   a. The sacrifice of our bodies—"I beseech you therefore, brethren, by the mercies of God, that ye present your bodies a living sacrifice, holy, acceptable unto God, which is your reasonable service" (Rom. 12:1).

   b. The sacrifice of our praise—"By him therefore let us offer the sacrifice of praise to God continually, that is, the fruit of our lips giving thanks to his name" (Heb. 13:15).

   c. The sacrifice of our good works—"But to do good and to communicate forget not: for with such sacrifices God is well pleased" (Heb. 13:16).

   d. The sacrifice of our substance—"But I have all, and abound: I am full, having received of Epaphroditus the things which were sent from you, an odour of a sweet smell, a sacrifice acceptable, well pleasing to God" (Phil. 4:18).

XIV. The Stewardship of the Church—"But I have all, and abound: I am full, having received of Epaphroditus the things which were sent from you, an odour of a sweet smell, a sacrifice acceptable, well pleasing to God" (Phil. 4:18). ". . . As good stewards of the manifold grace of God" (1 Pet. 4:10).

In the New Testament world a steward was the manager of a household or estate. He was appointed by the owner and entrusted to keep the estate running smoothly. Both Paul and Peter write with this background in view, reminding us we are God's stewards. The estate responsibilities entrusted to us are threefold.

A. How we use our time—David Jeremiah writes: "There is a gift which comes to us from a royal source each day of our lives, bright and sparkling, absolutely untouched, unspoiled. What is this gift? The priceless gift of time. Each day we receive a fresh, new supply—24 hours, 1,440 minutes, 86,400 seconds. Twenty-four hours we have never lived before—twenty-four hours we shall never live again" (*Biblical Stewardship,* p. 9).

The following Scripture passages point out the importance God places upon the stewardship of time: "For we are strangers before thee, and sojourners, as were all our fathers: our days on the earth are as a shadow, and there is none abiding"

(1 Chron. 29:15). "My days are swifter than a weaver's shuttle, and are spent without hope" (Job 7:6).

"LORD, make me to know mine end, and the measure of my days, what it is; that I may know how frail I am. Behold, thou hast made my days as an handbreadth; and mine age is as nothing before thee: verily every man at his best state is altogether vanity. Selah" (Psa. 39:4-5). "Remember how short my time is: wherefore hast thou made all men in vain?" (Psa. 89:47). "So teach us to number our days, that we may apply our hearts unto wisdom" (Psa. 90:12).

"And that, knowing the time, that now it is high time to awake out of sleep: for now is our salvation nearer than when we believed. The night is far spent, the day is at hand: let us therefore cast off the works of darkness, and let us put on the armour of light" (Rom. 13:11-12). "Redeeming the time, because the days are evil" (Eph. 5:16). "Walk in wisdom toward them that are without, redeeming the time" (Col. 4:5). "Whereas ye know not what shall be on the morrow. For what is your life? It is even a vapour, that appeareth for a little time, and then vanisheth away. For that ye ought to say, If the Lord will, we shall live, and do this, or that" (James 4:14-15).

Yesterday is a canceled check. Tomorrow is a promissory note. Today is the only cash you have.

B. How we use our talents—"For the kingdom of heaven is as a man travelling into a far country, who called his own servants, and delivered unto them his goods. And unto one he gave five talents, to another two, and to another one; to every man according to his several ability; and straightway took his journey" (Matt. 25:14-15).

"Now concerning spiritual gifts, brethren, I would not have you ignorant" (1 Cor. 12:1). "But unto every one of us is given grace according to the measure of the gift of Christ" (Eph. 4:7). (See also Rom. 12:6-8; 1 Cor. 12:4-31; Eph. 4:8-13.)

C. How we use our money

In the New Testament there are thirty-eight parables. Twelve of these are about money. One out of every six verses in Matthew, Mark, and Luke has to do with money. Because 100% of what we have comes from God, we are responsible to use it all wisely and in accordance with God's will. Like every other area of stewardship, God is interested in the whole picture, not just a percentage. What we do with all our treasure is important to Him. (*Biblical Stewardship*, p. 23)

Perhaps the most accurate barometer to measure the spiritual condition of a man is to observe his relationship concerning money. Jesus dealt with money matters because money matters. We shall consider this vital area among the following lines of thought.

1. How do I feel about money?

a. I must recognize that money comes from God—"But thou shalt remember the LORD thy God: for it is he that giveth thee power to get wealth, that he may establish his covenant which he sware unto thy fathers, as it is this day" (Deut. 8:18). "Thine, O LORD, is the greatness, and the power, and the glory, and the victory, and the majesty: for all that is in the heaven and in the earth is thine; thine is the kingdom, O LORD, and thou art exalted as head above all. Both riches and honour come of thee, and thou reignest over all; and in thine hand is power and might; and in thine hand it is to make great, and to give strength unto all" (1 Chron. 29:11-12). "Every good gift and every perfect gift is from above, and cometh down from the Father of lights, with whom is no variableness, neither shadow of turning" (James 1:17).

b. I must recognize that money in itself cannot satisfy—"Ho, every one that thirsteth, come ye to the waters, and he that hath no money; come ye, buy, and eat; yea, come, buy wine and milk without money and without price. Wherefore do ye spend money for that which is not bread? and your labour for that which satisfieth not? hearken diligently unto me, and eat ye that which is good, and let your soul delight itself in fatness" (Isa. 55:1-2).

It has been said that there are two kinds of unhappy people on this earth. The first group is unhappy because they didn't get those things they wanted, while the second group is sad because they did.

c. I must refuse to substitute silver for the Savior—"No servant can serve two masters: for either he will hate the one, and love the other; or else he will hold to the one, and despise the other. Ye cannot serve God and mammon" (Luke 16:13). "For the love of money is the root of all evil: which while some coveted after, they have erred from the faith, and pierced themselves through with many sorrows. . . . Charge them that are rich in this world, that they be not highminded, nor trust in uncertain riches, but in the living God, who giveth us richly all things to enjoy" (1 Tim. 6:10, 17).

d. I must believe that God will graciously supply all my needs that I cannot honestly provide for myself—"Therefore take no thought, saying, What shall we eat? or, What shall we drink? or, Wherewithal shall we be clothed? (For after all these things do the Gentiles seek:) for your heavenly Father knoweth that ye have need of all these things" (Matt. 6:31-32). "But my God shall supply all your need according to his riches in glory by Christ Jesus" (Phil. 4:19).

2. How do I secure my money? Money may be secured through three methods.

a. By earning it—"In the sweat of thy face shalt thou eat bread, till thou return unto the ground; for out of it wast thou taken: for dust thou art, and unto dust shalt thou return" (Gen. 3:19). "In all labour there is profit: but the talk of the lips tendeth only to penury" (Prov. 14:23). "He that tilleth his land shall have plenty of bread: but he that followeth after vain persons shall have poverty enough" (Prov. 28:19). "Let him that stole steal no more: but rather let him labour, working with his hands the thing which is good, that he may have to give to him that needeth" (Eph. 4:28). "For even when we were with you, this we commanded you, that if any would not work, neither should he eat" (2 Thess. 3:10).

b. By investing it—"Thou oughtest therefore to have put my money to the exchangers, and then at my coming I should have received mine own with usury" (Matt. 25:27).

c. By inheriting it—"A good man leaveth an inheritance to his children's children: and the wealth of the sinner is laid up for the just" (Prov. 13:22).

3. How do I share my money?

a. The prerequisite of giving—The giver is first of all to have given himself. God desires the dedication of our wills before that of our wallets. "I beseech you therefore, brethren, by the mercies of God, that ye present your bodies a living sacrifice, holy, acceptable unto God, which is your reasonable service" (Rom. 12:1). "And this they did, not as we hoped, but first gave their own selves to the Lord, and unto us by the will of God" (2 Cor. 8:5).

b. The percentage of giving—In the Old Testament there were two kinds of giving—required (Lev. 27:32, 10 percent) and free will (Exod. 25:1, 2; 36:5-7; 1 Chron. 29:9; Prov. 3:9, as much as desired).

But what of the New Testament? Endless arguments have been advanced concerning whether New Testament believers are still bound to the law of Old Testament tithing. Whatever else may be said, it seems unthinkable that one under grace could possibly give anything less than one under the law had to give.

c. The place of giving—Does the Bible teach storehouse tithing? Again, good men have differed over this issue. A general rule is that one should pay his room and board bill. This means I am expected to support that local church from which my soul draws its weekly strength. Other ministries should not be neglected, but giving, like charity, still begins at home.

d. The pattern of giving
   (1) The example of the Macedonians (2 Cor. 8:1-3)
       (a) They surrendered their bodies to the Lord.
       (b) They surrendered their wills to the apostle.
       (c) They sacrificially shared their wealth with the saints.
   (2) The example of the Son—"For ye know the grace of our Lord Jesus Christ, that, though he was rich, yet for your sakes he became poor, that ye through his poverty might be rich" (2 Cor. 8:9).
   (3) The example of the Father—"Thanks be unto God for his unspeakable gift" (2 Cor. 9:15).

e. The paradox of giving—A paradox is an apparent (but not real) contradiction. Here is the paradox. If I have $100 and give God $15, I should wind up with $85. But somehow that $85 will, in the long run, pay more bills and buy more necessities than the original $100 could possibly have done. The classic example of this is seen by the two small fishes and five barley loaves given to Christ by a little lad. (See John 6:9-13.) "One man gives freely, yet gains even more; another withholds unduly, but comes to poverty. A generous man will prosper; he who refreshes others will himself be refreshed" (Prov. 11:24-25, NIV).

f. The principles of giving
   (1) It is initiated by God himself (2 Cor. 8:1; 9:8).
   (2) It is to be done thoughtfully (2 Cor. 9:7).
   (3) It is to voluntary (2 Cor. 8:3-4, 8, 12; 9:7).
   (4) It is to be liberal (2 Cor. 8:2; 9:6).
   (5) It is to be preceded by a giving of self to the Lord (2 Cor. 8:5).
   (6) It is to come from our joy in Christ (2 Cor. 8:2; 9:7).
   (7) It is to be based on what we have (2 Cor. 8:12).
   (8) It is associated with the spiritual gifts (2 Cor. 8:7).
   (9) It is therefore to be regarded as a ministry (2 Cor. 9:1).

g. The purpose of giving
   (1) It serves as an example for others (2 Cor. 9:2).
   (2) It shows our love for God (2 Cor. 8:8, 24).
   (3) It guarantees our own spiritual growth (2 Cor. 9:9-10).
   (4) It assures us our own needs will be provided (2 Cor. 9:11).
   (5) It results in God giving us more that we might in turn give back more (2 Cor. 9:8).
   (6) It provides for the needs of deserving saints (2 Cor. 9:12).

(7) It results in God receiving glory from those needy saints who have been ministered to (2 Cor. 9:12-13).

(8) It enriches the giver, as he is prayed for by the saints he has helped (2 Cor. 9:14).

h. The privilege of giving—Whether we realize it or not, God does not need our money. "If I were hungry, I would not tell thee: for the world is mine, and the fulness thereof. Will I eat the flesh of bulls, or drink the blood of goats? Offer unto God thanksgiving; and pay thy vows unto the most High: And call upon me in the day of trouble: I will deliver thee, and thou shalt glorify me" (Psa. 50:12-15).

But he has graciously allowed us to give back to him—and actually get credit for it—that which is already his.

4. How do I spend money?

a. I am to pay my debts—"Then she came and told the man of God. And he said, Go, sell the oil, and pay thy debt, and live thou and thy children of the rest" (2 Kings 4:7). "And when they were come to Capernaum, they that received tribute money came to Peter, and said, Doth not your master pay tribute?" (Matt. 17:24). "Owe no man any thing, but to love one another: for he that loveth another hath fulfilled the law" (Rom. 13:8).

b. I am to provide for my family—David Jeremiah aptly summarizes this area as follows:

(1) We should prepare for the winter in the summer (Prov. 30:25).

(2) We should place our money where it will grow (Matt. 25:27).

(3) We should plan in light of our Lord's imminent return (James 4:13-16) (From *Biblical Stewardship*, p. 29).

XV. The Discipline of the Church

A. The definition of discipline—To discipline is to penalize an individual for breaking the laws of a unit of society to which he belongs with the view of restoring him back to those laws.

B. The kinds of discipline—There are three kinds of New Testament discipline.

1. Self-discipline—"For if we would judge ourselves, we should not be judged" (1 Cor. 11:31).

2. Sovereign discipline—"But when we are judged, we are chastened of the Lord, that we should not be condemned with the world" (1 Cor. 11:32). "For the time is come that judgment must begin at the house of God: and if it first begin at us, what shall the end be of them that obey not the gospel of God?" (1 Pet. 4:17). "For we know him that hath said, Vengeance belongeth unto me, I will recompense, saith the Lord. And again, The Lord shall judge his people" (Heb. 10:30). (See also Acts 5:1-10.)

3. Sanctuary discipline—"And if he shall neglect to hear them, tell it unto the church: but if he neglect to hear the church, let him be unto thee as a heathen man and a publican" (Matt. 18:17).

C. The basis of discipline—The basis of discipline of a local church is the holiness of God. "Thy testimonies are very sure: holiness becometh thine house, O LORD, for ever" (Psa. 93:5). "Because it is written, Be ye holy; for I am holy" (1 Pet. 1:16).

D. The authority to discipline—The ultimate authority resides in Christ, who authorizes his church to exercise it when needed. "And I will give unto thee the keys of the kingdom of heaven: and whatsoever thou shalt bind on earth shall be bound in heaven: and whatsoever thou shalt loose on earth shall be loosed in heaven" (Matt.

16:19). "In the name of our Lord Jesus Christ, when ye are gathered together, and my spirit, with the power of our Lord Jesus Christ" (1 Cor. 5:4).

E. The recipients of discipline—Who deserves church discipline?

1. Troublemakers and those who sow discord—"These six things doth the LORD hate: yea, seven are an abomination unto him: A false witness that speaketh lies, and he that soweth discord among brethren" (Prov. 6:16, 19). "Now I beseech you, brethren, mark them which cause divisions and offences contrary to the doctrine which ye have learned; and avoid them (Rom. 16:17).

2. The unruly, disorderly, and undisciplined—"Now we exhort you, brethren, warn them that are unruly, comfort the feebleminded, support the weak, be patient toward all men" (1 Thess. 5:14). "Now we command you, brethren, in the name of our Lord Jesus Christ, that ye withdraw yourselves from every brother that walketh disorderly, and not after the tradition which he received of us. For we hear that there are some which walk among you disorderly, working not at all, but are busybodies" (2 Thess. 3:6, 11).

3. Those who disobey the great doctrines of faith—"And if any man obey not our word by this epistle, note that man, and have no company with him, that he may be ashamed" (2 Thess. 3:14).

4. Those who deny the great doctrines of the faith—"If any man teach otherwise, and consent not to wholesome words, even the words of our Lord Jesus Christ, and to the doctrine which is according to godliness; . . . Perverse disputings of men of corrupt minds, and destitute of the truth, supposing that gain is godliness: from such withdraw thyself" (1 Tim. 6:3, 5). "But shun profane and vain babblings: for they will increase unto more ungodliness. Who concerning the truth have erred, saying that the resurrection is past already; and overthrow the faith of some" (2 Tim. 2:16-18).

"A man that is an heretic after the first and second admonition reject" (Titus 3:10). "If there come any unto you, and bring not this doctrine, receive him not into your house, neither bid him God speed: For he that biddeth him God speed is partaker of his evil deeds" (2 John 10-11).

5. The immoral—"It is reported commonly that there is fornication among you, and such fornication as is not so much as named among the Gentiles, that one should have his father's wife. And ye are puffed up, and have not rather mourned, that he that hath done this deed might be taken away from among you" (1 Cor. 5:1-2).

F. The procedures in discipline—Church discipline is to be handled prayerfully, carefully, and justly.

1. First step—Note and mark those who are in need of discipline. "Now I beseech you, brethren, mark them which cause divisions and offences contrary to the doctrine which ye have learned; and avoid them" (Rom. 16:17). (See 2 Thess. 3:14.)

2. Second step—Arrange a private meeting with the offender. "Moreover if thy brother shall trespass against thee, go and tell him his fault between thee and him alone: if he shall hear thee, thou hast gained thy brother" (Matt. 18:15).

3. Third step—If this fails, set up a second meeting, this time with several others present. "But if he will not hear thee, then take with thee one or two more, that in the mouth of two or three witnesses every word may be established" (Matt. 18:16).

During these preliminary private and semiprivate meetings the individual should be repeatedly admonished (Titus 3:10), rebuked (2 Tim. 4:2), and warned (1 Thess. 5:14).

4. Fourth step—As a final resort, the unrepentant one is to be brought before the entire church. "Them that sin rebuke before all, that others also may fear" (1 Tim. 5:20). (See also Matt. 18:17.)

5. Fifth step—Upon refusal to submit to church discipline the guilty party is to be spiritually excommunicated. This constitutes two fearful things, a *denial* and a *deliverance.*

   a. He is to be denied Christian fellowship.

     (1) "Avoid them" (see Rom. 16:17).

     (2) "Withdraw yourselves from" (see 2 Thess. 3:6).

     (3) "From such withdraw thyself" (see 1 Tim. 6:3, 5).

     (4) "Reject" (see Titus 3:10).

     (5) "Have no company with him" (see 2 Thess. 3:14).

   b. He is to be delivered over to Satan—"To deliver such an one unto Satan for the destruction of the flesh, that the spirit may be saved in the day of the Lord Jesus" (1 Cor. 5:5). "Of whom is Hymenaeus and Alexander; whom I have delivered unto Satan, that they may learn not to blaspheme" (1 Tim. 1:20).

     What does it mean to do this? The Greek word for destruction in 1 Corinthians 5:5 is *olethros,* a reference to the act of spoiling or marring something. Apparently Paul was here saying, "If this fellow [the church member living in adultery] is having so much fun in his sin, then remove him entirely from your fellowship and let Satan kick him around a little! Let him taste what it's like to face a hostile world without the prayers and ministry of a local church."

     Thus, when a local Bible-believing church removes a person like this, it literally fulfills the divine command of Job 2:6: "And the Lord said unto Satan, Behold, he is in thine hand; but save his life" (Job 2:6).

G. The heart attitude in discipline

1. We are told to avoid both vengeance and arrogance—"Brethren, if a man be overtaken in a fault, ye which are spiritual, restore such an one in the spirit of meekness; considering thyself, lest thou also be tempted" (Gal. 6:1).

2. We are to view the individual as an erring brother and not a bitter enemy— "Yet count him not as an enemy, but admonish him as a brother" (2 Thess. 3:15).

3. We are to approach him with sorrow and not sarcasm—"For out of much affliction and anguish of heart I wrote unto you with many tears; not that ye should be grieved, but that ye might know the love which I have more abundantly unto you" (2 Cor. 2:4). (See also 1 Cor. 5:2.)

4. We are to be ready to forgive him when repentance occurs (2 Cor. 2:7; 7:10-11)—This last attitude is of supreme importance for two reasons.

   a. "Lest perhaps such a one should be swallowed up with overmuch sorrow" (2 Cor. 2:7).

   b. "Lest Satan should get an advantage of us: for we are not ignorant of his devices" (2 Cor. 2:11).

H. The purpose of discipline

1. It is to maintain the standards of the church before a watching world—"Ye are the salt of the earth: but if the salt have lost his savour, wherewith shall it be salted? it is thenceforth good for nothing, but to be cast out, and to be trodden

under foot of men. Ye are the light of the world. A city that is set on an hill cannot be hid. Neither do men light a candle, and put it under a bushel, but on a candlestick; and it giveth light unto all that are in the house. Let your light so shine before men, that they may see your good works, and glorify your Father which is in heaven" (Matt. 5:13-16).

God does not want the church to have the same bad testimony as Israel once had. "For the name of God is blasphemed among the Gentiles through you, as it is written" (Rom. 2:24).

One reason why the church has so little influence in the world today is because the world has so much influence in the church.

2. It is to keep sin from spreading throughout the church—"Your glorying is not good. Know ye not that a little leaven leaveneth the whole lump? Purge out therefore the old leaven, that ye may be a new lump, as ye are unleavened. For even Christ our passover is sacrificed for us" (1 Cor. 5:6-7).

3. It is to help the guilty person find his way back to God—"Sufficient to such a man is this punishment, which was inflicted of many. So that contrariwise ye ought rather to forgive him, and comfort him, lest perhaps such a one should be swallowed up with overmuch sorrow. Wherefore I beseech you that ye would confirm your love toward him" (2 Cor. 2:6-8).

4. It is to escape God's twofold judgment upon habitually sinning saints.
   a. Sickness—"For this cause many are weak and sickly among you" (1 Cor. 11:30a).
   b. Physical death—"And many sleep. For if we would judge ourselves, we should not be judged" (1 Cor. 11:30b-31).

I. The scope of discipline (1 Cor. 5:9-13)—The church is called upon to discipline (if needed) all believers, but only believers. It has no authority to judge individual worldly unbelievers for their smoking, swearing, sexual activities, etc. Its only duty to an unsaved person is to lead him or her to Jesus Christ. "But them that are without God judgeth. Therefore put away from among yourselves that wicked person" (1 Cor. 5:13).

J. The reaction to discipline—How will the guilty person react when disciplined either by God himself or by a local church?

1. He can despise it, that is, treat it too lightly (as did Esau concerning his birthright)—"And ye have forgotten the exhortation which speaketh unto you as unto children, My son, despise not thou the chastening of the Lord, nor faint when thou art rebuked of him" (Heb. 12:5).

2. He can faint under it, that is, treat it too seriously. (See Heb. 12:5.)

3. He can be exercised by it—"For they verily for a few days chastened us after their own pleasure; but he for our profit, that we might be partakers of his holiness. Now no chastening for the present seemeth to be joyous, but grievous: nevertheless afterward it yieldeth the peaceable fruit of righteousness unto them which are exercised thereby" (Heb. 12:10-11).

The real question is not so much what I have done wrong (though this, of course, is important), but what is my attitude about it.

XVI. The Destiny of the Church—Everyone likes a story that has a happy ending. They story of the church has such a happy ending. The Bridegroom gets the bride, and together they live happily ever after

The glorious destiny of the church is as follows:

A. To be caught up by the Bridegroom at the Rapture—"Behold, I show you a mystery; We shall not all sleep, but we shall all be changed, In a moment, in the twinkling of an eye, at the last trump: for the trumpet shall sound, and the dead shall be raised incorruptible, and we shall be changed. For this corruptible must put on incorruption, and this mortal must put on immortality" (1 Cor. 15:51-53).

"For this we say unto you by the word of the Lord, that we which are alive and remain unto the coming of the Lord shall not prevent them which are asleep. For the Lord himself shall descend from heaven with a shout, with the voice of the archangel, and with the trump of God: and the dead in Christ shall rise first: Then we which are alive and remain shall be caught up together with them in the clouds, to meet the Lord in the air: and so shall we ever be with the Lord" (1 Thess. 4:15-17).

B. To be examined and rewarded at the judgment seat of Christ—"But why dost thou judge thy brother? or why dost thou set at nought thy brother? for we shall all stand before the judgment seat of Christ. For it is written, As I live, saith the Lord, every knee shall bow to me, and every tongue shall confess to God. So then every one of us shall give account of himself to God" (Rom. 14:10-12).

"Every man's work shall be made manifest: for the day shall declare it, because it shall be revealed by fire; and the fire shall try every man's work of what sort it is" (1 Cor. 3:13). "For we must all appear before the judgment seat of Christ; that every one may receive the things done in his body, according to that he hath done, whether it be good or bad" (2 Cor. 5:10).

C. To be united with Christ at the marriage service of the Lamb—"For I am jealous over you with godly jealousy: for I have espoused you to one husband, that I may present you as a chaste virgin to Christ" (2 Cor. 11:2). "Let us be glad and rejoice, and give honour to him: for the marriage of the Lamb is come, and his wife hath made herself ready. And to her was granted that she should be arrayed in fine linen, clean and white: for the fine linen is the righteousness of saints" (Rev. 19:7-8).

D. To be seated with Christ at the marriage supper of the Lamb—"And he saith unto me, Write, Blessed are they which are called unto the marriage supper of the Lamb. And he saith unto me, These are the true sayings of God" (Rev. 19:9).

E. To reign with Christ during the Millennium—"And hath made us kings and priests unto God and his Father; to him be glory and dominion for ever and ever. Amen" (Rev. 1:6). "To him that overcometh will I grant to sit with me in my throne, even as I also overcame, and am set down with my Father in his throne" (Rev. 3:21). "Blessed and holy is he that hath part in the first resurrection: on such the second death hath no power, but they shall be priests of God and of Christ, and shall reign with him a thousand years" (Rev. 20:6).

F. To share the new Jerusalem with Christ throughout all eternity—"And I saw a new heaven and a new earth: for the first heaven and the first earth were passed away; and there was no more sea. And I John saw the holy city, new Jerusalem, coming down from God out of heaven, prepared as a bride adorned for her husband" (Rev. 21:1-2). (See also Rev. 21:9-27.)

G. To illustrate the glory of Christ throughout all eternity—"To the praise of the glory of his grace, wherein he hath made us accepted in the beloved" (Eph. 1:6). "That we should be to the praise of his glory, who first trusted in Christ" (Eph. 1:12). "To the intent that now unto the principalities and powers in heavenly places might be known by the church the manifold wisdom of God" (Eph. 3:10). (See also Eph. 2:1-7.)

THE DOCTRINE OF PROPHECY

INTRODUCTION
This study will feature both a topical and a chronological summary of biblical prophecy.

Section one: A topical overview of prophecy featuring the subjects involved, viewing the what of the matter.
  I. A General Consideration
    A. Prophecies concerning individuals (40 in number)
    B. Prophecies concerning births (7 in number)
    C. Prophecies concerning Christ (63 in number)
    D. Prophecies concerning Satan (5 in number)
    E. Prophecies concerning the Antichrist (21 in number)
    F. Prophecies concerning the false prophet (11 in number)
    G. Prophecies concerning false teachers (14 in number)
    H. Prophecies concerning cities (6 in number)
    I. Prophecies concerning Gentile nations (10 in number)
    J. Prophecies concerning the nation Israel (38 in number)
    K. Prophecies concerning the 70 weeks (3 in number)
    L. Prophecies concerning judgments (18 in number)
    M. Prophecies concerning the last days (24 in number)
    N. Prophecies concerning the great tribulation (46 in number)
    O. Prophecies concerning the Millennium (38 in number)
    P. Prophecies concerning hell (9 in number)
    Q. Prophecies concerning heaven (56 in number)
    R. Prophecies concerning the glorified body (7 in number)
  II. A Specific Consideration
    A. Prophecies concerning individuals
      1. Adam
        Prediction—That he would die if he disobeyed God (Gen. 2:17)
        Fulfillment
        a. Adam died spiritually (Gen. 3:7).
        b. Adam died physically (Gen. 5:5).
      2. Noah
        a. Prediction—That God would destroy the earth but save him and his family (Gen. 6:13, 18)
          Fulfillment—Genesis 7:23
        b. Prediction—That God would never again destroy the world by a flood (Gen. 8:21; 9:11)
          Fulfillment—Testimony of history

    c. Prediction—That God would preserve the four seasons and the day and night arrangements (Gen. 8:22)
       Fulfillment—Testimony of history

    d. Prediction—Noah predicted the future of the peoples his three sons would found (Gen. 9:25-27).
       Fulfillment—Testimony of history

3. Abraham

    a. Prediction—That God would father a great nation through him (Gen. 12:2; 15:5)
       Fulfillment—Testimony of history

    b. Prediction—That God would reward or punish nations according to their treatment of Israel (Gen. 12:3)
       Fulfillment—Testimony of history

    c. Prediction—That God would give Abraham and his seed a land (Gen. 12:7; 15:18-21; 17:8)
       Fulfillment—Testimony of history

    d. Prediction—That Abraham would have a son in his old age (Gen. 15:4; 18:10, 14)
       Fulfillment—Genesis 21:1-3

    e. Prediction—That the nation Abraham founded would serve in a foreign land for 400 years (Gen. 15:13)
       Fulfillment—Exodus 12:40

    f. Prediction—That God would lead them out with great riches (Gen. 15:14)
       Fulfillment—Exodus 12:35-36

    g. Prediction—That God would destroy Sodom (Gen. 18:20-21)
       Fulfillment—Genesis 19:24

4. Ishmael

   Prediction—That he would found a violent and powerful people (Gen. 16:12; 17:20)
   Fulfillment—Testimony of history

5. Jacob

    a. Prediction—That he and his seed would be served by Esau and his seed (Gen. 25:23)
       Fulfillment—Testimony of history

    b. Prediction—That God would bring him back to the land of Canaan (Gen. 28:15)
       Fulfillment—Genesis 35:1-7

    c. Prediction—Jacob predicted the life-style of his 12 sons and the tribes they would found (Gen. 49).
       Fulfillment—Testimony of history

6. Esau

   Prediction—That he would found a people who lived by the sword (Gen. 27:40)
   Fulfillment—Testimony of history

7. Joseph

    a. Prediction—That his 11 brothers would someday bow down to him (Gen. 37:5-7)
       Fulfillment—Genesis 42:6; 44:14

    b. Prediction—That the Middle East would experience seven years of bumper crops, followed by seven years of famine (Gen. 41:29-31)

Fulfillment—Genesis 41:53-54

8. Moses

  a. Prediction—That he would deliver Israel from the Egyptian captivity (Exod. 3:10)
    Fulfillment—Exodus 12:40-41

  b. Prediction—That the deliverance would be effected by divine miracles (Exod. 3:20)
    Fulfillment—Exodus 7–12

  c. Prediction—That Israel would leave Egypt with great wealth (Exod. 3:21-22)
    Fulfillment—Exodus 12:35-36

  d. Prediction—That God would divide the Red Sea waters, bringing escape for Israel and death for the Egyptians (Exod. 14:16-17)
    Fulfillment—Exodus 14:21-30

  e. Prediction—That God would feed Israel with manna (Exod. 16:4)
    Fulfillment—Exodus 16:14-15

  f. Prediction—That a rock, when struck, would provide water for the thirsty Israelites (Exod. 17:6a)
    Fulfillment—Exodus 17:6b

  g. Prediction—That the Sabbath would be observed by Israel throughout the ages (Exod. 31:16-17)
    Fulfillment—Testimony of history

  h. Prediction—That Israel would worship God at Mount Sinai (Exod. 3:12)
    Fulfillment—Exodus 19:1-8

  i. Prediction—That Moses would see God's glory (Exod. 32:21-23)
    Fulfillment—Exodus 34:5-7

  j. Prediction—That a brass serpent would bring healing to those bitten by deadly serpents (Num. 21:8)
    Fulfillment—Numbers 21:9

  k. Prediction—That Moses would bring Israel up to the promised land (Exod. 3:17)
    Fulfillment—Numbers 36:13; Deuteronomy 1:1

  l. Prediction—That Moses, because of a previous sin, would not enter the promised land (Num. 20:12; Deut. 3:23-26)
    Fulfillment—Deuteronomy 34:5

  m. Prediction—That Moses, however, would be allowed to see it (Deut. 3:27)
    Fulfillment—Deuteronomy 34:1

9. Joshua

  a. Prediction—That he would enter Canaan after a period of 40 years (Num. 14:24, 33-34, 38)
    Fulfillment—Joshua 3:17

  b. Prediction—That Joshua would be given victory over his enemies in Canaan (Josh. 1:1-9)
    Fulfillment—Joshua 11:23

  c. Prediction—That the Jordan River would be parted (Josh. 3:13)
    Fulfillment—Joshua 3:16

  d. Prediction—That the walls of Jericho would fall after the sounding of trumpets (Josh. 6:5)
    Fulfillment—Joshua 6:20

10. Barak

Prediction—That he would defeat Sisera through the help of a woman (Judg. 4:6-9)

Fulfillment—Judges 4:21

11. Gideon

Prediction—That he would defeat a mighty Midianite army with but 300 soldiers (Judg. 6:14; 7:7)

Fulfillment—Judges 7:19-22

12. Samson

Prediction—That he would deliver Israel from the Philistines (Judg. 13:5)

Fulfillment—Judges 15:15

13. Eli

a. Prediction—That his wicked sons, Hophni and Phinehas, would die on the same day (1 Sam. 2:3-4)

Fulfillment—1 Samuel 4:11

b. Prediction—That the priesthood would be removed from his line (1 Sam. 2:27-36; 3:11-14)

Fulfillment—Testimony of Old Testament history

14. Samuel

a. Prediction—That Saul would visit him within 24 hours looking for some lost animals (1 Sam. 9:15-16)

Fulfillment—1 Samuel 9:17-20

b. Prediction—That Saul's kingdom would not continue (1 Sam. 13:4)

Fulfillment—1 Samuel 24:20

c. Prediction—That the next king would be a son of Jesse, a Bethlehem farmer (1 Sam. 16:1)

Fulfillment—1 Samuel 16:12-13

d. Prediction—That Saul and his sons would die in a battle with the Philistines (1 Sam. 28:19)

Fulfillment—1 Samuel 31:6

15. David

a. Prediction—That both sword and sorrow would be a part of his household because of his sins of adultery and murder (2 Sam. 12:11)

Fulfillment—2 Samuel 13:28-29; 15:13-14

b. Prediction—That Bathsheba's first infant son would die (2 Sam. 12:14)

Fulfillment—2 Samuel 12:18

c. Prediction—That David's kingdom would eventually be established forever (2 Sam. 7:16)

Fulfillment—To occur during the Millennium (Jer. 30:9; Ezek. 34:23; Hos. 3:5)

d. Prediction—That Solomon, not David, would build the temple (1 Chron. 17:1-12; 22:8-10; 28:2-6)

Fulfillment—1 Kings 7:51

16. Solomon

a. Prediction—That he would be given much wisdom, riches, and honor (1 Kings 3:12)

Fulfillment—1 Kings 4:29-31; 10:1-9, 23, 27

b. Prediction—That God would rend the kingdom from his son because of Solomon's sin (1 Kings 11:11-13)

Fulfillment—1 Kings 12:16

17. Jeroboam
    a. Prediction—Ahijah predicted he would become ruler over 10 of Israel's 12 tribes (1 Kings 11:29-31).
    Fulfillment—1 Kings 12:20
    b. Prediction—Ahijah later predicted Jeroboam's dynasty would be cut off (1 Kings 14:10-11).
    Fulfillment—1 Kings 15:29-30
18. Elijah
    a. Prediction—That it would not rain for three and one-half years (1 Kings 17:1)
    Fulfillment—1 Kings 17:7; James 5:17
    b. Prediction—That there would be an abundance of rain (1 Kings 18:41)
    Fulfillment—1 Kings 18:45; James 5:18
    c. Prediction—That a starving widow and her son would be supernaturally fed by God (1 Kings 17:14)
    Fulfillment—1 Kings 17:16
    d. Prediction—That wicked King Ahab would have his blood shed and die in the same place where he had godly Naboth killed (1 Kings 21:19)
    Fulfillment—1 Kings 22:37-38
    e. Prediction. That Ahab's wife, Jezebel, would be eaten by dogs (1 Kings 21:23)
    Fulfillment—2 Kings 9:30-37
    f. Prediction—That Ahaziah, king of the northern 10 Israelite tribes, would die for his idol worship (2 Kings 1:4)
    Fulfillment—2 Kings 1:17
    g. Prediction—That Elijah would leave this earth without dying by way of a whirlwind (2 Kings 2:1)
    Fulfillment—2 Kings 2:11
19. Elisha
    a. Prediction—That a widow's oil would be supernaturally increased (2 Kings 4:1-4)
    Fulfillment—2 Kings 4:6-7
    b. Prediction—That a barren Shunnamite woman would have a son (2 Kings 4:16)
    Fulfillment—2 Kings 4:17
    c. Prediction—That Naaman's leprosy would be healed by washing in the Jordan River (2 Kings 5:10)
    Fulfillment—2 Kings 5:14
    d. Prediction—That Gehazi, Elisha's servant, would be punished with leprosy because of his greed (2 Kings 5:27a)
    Fulfillment—2 Kings 5:27b
    e. Prediction—That the starving citizens of besieged Samaria would enjoy an abundance of food within 24 hours (2 Kings 7:1)
    Fulfillment—2 Kings 7:16, 18
    f. Prediction—That the skeptic who ridiculed the abundant food prediction would live to see it fulfilled but would not eat the food (2 Kings 7:2)
    Fulfillment—2 Kings 7:17
    g. Prediction—That there would be a seven-year famine in northern Israel (2 Kings 8:1)
    Fulfillment—2 Kings 8:3

h. Prediction—That northern Israel's King Jehoash would defeat the Syrians on three occasions (2 Kings 13:14-19)
Fulfillment—2 Kings 13:25

20. Hezekiah

a. Prediction—That a divine plague would supernaturally deliver both King Hezekiah and the people of Jerusalem from Assyrian troops who had surrounded the city (2 Kings 19:6-7a; Isa. 37:33-35)
Fulfillment—2 Kings 19:35-36; 2 Chronicles 32:21a; Isaiah 37:36

b. Prediction—That the Assyrian king Sennacherib would be killed upon returning to Nineveh (Isa. 37:7)
Fulfillment—2 Chronicles 32:21b; Isaiah 37:37-38

c. Prediction. That God would heal and add an additional 15 years to the life of Hezekiah (2 Kings 20:1-6; 2 Chron. 32:24; Isa. 38:1-5)
Fulfillment. (2 Kings 20:8-11; Isa. 38:9)

21. Jehoshaphat

Prediction—That God would save the hopelessly outnumbered people of Judah from a threatened Moabite and Ammonite invasion (2 Chron. 20:14-17)
Fulfillment—2 Chronicles 20:20-25

22. Josiah

Prediction—That this godly Judean king would burn the decayed bones of ungodly Israelite king Jeroboam's pagan priests upon the false altar the wicked ruler had once constructed (1 Kings 13:1-3)
Fulfillment—2 Kings 23:4-6

23. Jehoahaz

Prediction—That this wicked Judean king, captured by the Assyrians, would die in Egypt (Jer. 22:10-12)
Fulfillment—2 Kings 23:31-34

24. Jehoiachin

Prediction—That both this godless Judean ruler and his mother would be carried away into Babylon, never to return (Jer. 22:25-27)
Fulfillment—2 Kings 24:15

25. Hananiah

Prediction—That this false Judean prophet would be struck dead by the Lord in less than a year (Jer. 28:15-16)
Fulfillment—Jeremiah 28:17

26. Zedekiah

Prediction—That Judah's final and wicked king:
a. Would be forced to look into the eyes of Nebuchadnezzar (Jer. 32:4-5)
b. Would not see the land of Babylon even though he would be carried there (Ezek. 12:13)
Fulfillment—Jeremiah 39:7

27. Nebuchadnezzar

a. Prediction—That he would be victorious over the Egyptians at the world-famous battle of Carchemish (Jer. 46)
Fulfillment—Testimony of history

b. Prediction—That Nebuchadnezzar would then invade and destroy Egypt (Jer. 43:9-13; 46:26; Ezek. 29:19-20)
Fulfillment—Testimony of history

    c. Prediction—That Nebuchadnezzar would lose his mind and live like an animal for seven years because of his pride (Dan. 4:24-25)
       Fulfillment—Daniel 4:28-33
    d. Prediction—That after seven years, Nebuchadnezzar would have his kingdom restored (Dan. 4:26)
       Fulfillment—Daniel 4:34-37

28. Belshazzar
   Prediction—That God would judge this wicked Babylonian ruler by immediately allowing the Persians to take his kingdom (Dan. 5:25-28)
   Fulfillment—Daniel 5:30-31

29. Cyrus
    a. Prediction—That this Persian warrior would be allowed to build a world empire (Isa. 45:1-4)
       Fulfillment—Testimony of history and 2 Chronicles 36:23
    b. Prediction—That he would permit the Jews to return to Jerusalem and rebuild both their temple and city, which were previously destroyed by Nebuchadnezzar (Isa. 44:28; 45:13)
       Fulfillment—2 Chronicles 36:23; Ezra 1:2-4

30. Alexander the Great
    a. Prediction—That he would utterly defeat the Persians and establish a world empire (Dan. 2:32-39; 7:6; 8:5-8, 21; 11:3)
       Fulfillment—Testimony of history
    b. Prediction—That he would suddenly die and his kingdom would be divided into four parts (Dan. 8:8, 22; 11:4)
       Fulfillment—Testimony of history

31. Antiochus Epiphanes
    a. Prediction—That this Syrian Jew-hater would persecute the Jews and profane their temple (Dan. 8:9-13)
       Fulfillment—Testimony of history
    b. Prediction—That the temple would be cleansed after a period of 2,300 days (Dan. 8:14)
       Fulfillment—Testimony of history

32. Malachi and Isaiah
   Prediction—Both these Old Testament prophets foretold of the New Testament ministry of John the Baptist (Isa. 40:3-5; Mal. 3:1)
   Fulfillment—Matthew 3:1-3; 11:10; Mark 1:2-3; Luke 3:4-6; 7:27

33. Zacharias
    a. Prediction—That his barren wife would give birth to a son (Luke 1:13a)
       Fulfillment—Luke 1:57
    b. Prediction—That his son would be named John (Luke 1:13b)
       Fulfillment—Luke 1:60-63
    c. Prediction—That the son would become a Nazarite (Luke 1:15)
       Fulfillment—Luke 1:80
    d. Prediction—That his ministry would turn many to the Lord (Luke 1:16-17)
       Fulfillment—Matthew 3:5-6; Mark 1:4; Luke 3:7-14
    e. Prediction—That John would serve as the Messiah's forerunner (Luke 1:76-79)
       Fulfillment—John 1:29

   f. Prediction—That Zacharias would be unable to speak until John was born
      (Luke 1:20)
      Fulfillment—Luke 1:22, 63
34. Simeon
    Prediction—That he would live to see the Messiah (Luke 2:25-26)
    Fulfillment—Luke 2:27-35
35. A man born blind
    Prediction—That he would see after washing himself in the pool of Siloam
    (John 9:7a)
    Fulfillment—John 9:7b
36. Martha and the disciples
    Prediction—That Lazarus would be raised from the dead (John 11:11, 23)
    Fulfillment—John 11:43-44
37. Peter
    a. Prediction—That he would deny Jesus (Matt. 26:34; Mark 14:30; Luke 22:34;
       John 13:38)
       Fulfillment—Matthew 26:69-75; Mark 14:66-72; Luke 22:54-62; John 18:24-27
    b. Prediction—That Peter would suffer martyrdom for Jesus (John 21:18-19;
       2 Pet. 1:12-14)
       Fulfillment—Testimony of history
38. Judas
    a. Prediction—That he would be possessed and controlled by Satan (John 6:70)
       Fulfillment—Luke 22:3; John 13:27
    b. Prediction—That he would betray Christ (Matt. 26:21-25; Mark 14:18-21;
       Luke 22:21-23; John 13:18, 21-26)
       Fulfillment—Matthew 26:14-16, 47-48; Mark 14:42-45; Luke 22:47-48; John
       18:2-3
39. Agabus
    Prediction—That there would be a great famine in the Holy Land (Acts 11:28a)
    Fulfillment—Acts 11:28b-29
40. Paul
    a. Prediction—That he would suffer much for Jesus (Acts 9:16)
       Fulfillment—2 Corinthians 11:23-28; 12:7-10; Galatians 6:17; Philippians
       1:29-30
    b. Prediction—That he would serve as a minister to the Gentiles (Acts 9:15)
       Fulfillment—Acts 13:46; 18:6; 22:21; 26:17; 28:28; Romans 11:13; Ephesians
       3:1; 1 Timothy 2:7; 2 Timothy 1:11)
    c. Prediction—That he would preach before kings (Acts 9:15)
       Fulfillment—Acts 24–26
    d. Prediction—That he would be arrested by the Jews when he arrived in
       Jerusalem (Acts 21:4, 11)
       Fulfillment—Acts 21:27-36
    e. Prediction—That he would eventually go to Rome (Acts 23:11)
       Fulfillment—Acts 28:16
    f. Prediction—That all the 276 people (including Paul) would safely leave a
       sinking ship, caused by a terrible storm at sea (Acts 27:22, 26, 37)
       Fulfillment—Acts 27:44
B. Prophecies concerning births
   1. Isaac's birth

Prediction—Genesis 15:4; 17:19, 21; 18:10, 14
Fulfillment—Genesis 21:1-3
2. Jacob and Esau's birth
Prediction—Genesis 25:19-23
Fulfillment—Genesis 25:24-26
3. Samson's birth
Prediction—Judges 13:5
Fulfillment—Judges 13:24
4. Samuel's birth
Prediction—1 Samuel 1:17-18
Fulfillment—1 Samuel 1:20
5. Birth of the Shunammite woman's son
Prediction—2 Kings 4:16
Fulfillment—2 Kings 4:17
6. John the Baptist's birth
Prediction—Luke 1:13-17
Fulfillment—Luke 1:57-64
7. Jesus' birth
Prediction—Luke 1:26-33
Fulfillment—Luke 2:4-7
C. Prophecies concerning Christ
Study number one: The Old Testament prophecies he fulfilled
1. Prediction—That he would be born of a woman (Gen. 3:15)
Fulfillment—Luke 2:7; Galatians 4:4
2. Prediction—That he would be from the line of Abraham (Gen. 12:3, 7; 17:7)
Fulfillment—Romans 9:5; Galatians 3:16
3. Prediction—That he would be from the tribe of Judah (Gen. 49:10)
Fulfillment—Hebrews 7:14; Revelation 5:5
4. Prediction—That he would be from the house of David (2 Sam. 7:12-13)
Fulfillment—Luke 1:31-33; Romans 1:3
5. Prediction—That he would be born of a virgin (Isa. 7:14)
Fulfillment—Matthew 1:22-23
6. Prediction—That he would be given the throne of David (2 Sam. 7:11-12; Psa. 132:11; Isa. 9:6-7; 16:5; Jer. 23:5; Luke 1:31-32)
Fulfillment—Revelation 5:1-7; 22:16
7. Prediction—That this throne would be an eternal throne (Dan. 2:44; 7:14, 27; Mic. 4:7; Luke 1:33)
Fulfillment—Revelation 11:15; 20:4
8. Prediction—That he would be called Emmanuel (Isa. 7:14)
Fulfillment—Matthew 1:23
9. Prediction—That he would have a forerunner (Isa. 40:3-5; Mal. 3:1)
Fulfillment—Matthew 3:1-3; Luke 1:76-78; 3:3-6)
10. Prediction—That he would be born in Bethlehem (Mic. 5:2)
Fulfillment—Matthew 2:5-6; Luke 2:4-6
11. Prediction—That he would be worshipped by wise men and presented with gifts (Psa. 72:10; Isa. 60:3, 6, 9)
Fulfillment—Matthew 2:11
12. Prediction—That he would be in Egypt for a season (Num. 24:8; Hos. 11:1)
Fulfillment—Matthew 2:15

13. Prediction—That his birthplace would suffer a massacre of infants (Jer. 31:15)
    Fulfillment—Matthew 2:17-18
14. Prediction—That he would be called a Nazarene (Isa. 11:1)
    Fulfillment—(Matthew 2:23
15. Prediction—That he would be zealous for the Father (Psa. 69:9; 119:139)
    Fulfillment—John 6:37-40
16. Prediction—That he would be filled with God's Spirit (Psa. 45:7; Isa. 11:2; 61:1-2)
    Fulfillment—Luke 4:18-19
17. Prediction—That he would heal many (Isa. 53:4)
    Fulfillment—Matthew 8:16-17
18. Prediction—That he would deal gently with the Gentiles (Isa. 9:1-2; 42:1-3)
    Fulfillment—Matthew 4:13-16; 12:17-21
19. Prediction—That he would speak in parables (Isa. 6:9-10)
    Fulfillment—Matthew 13:10-15
20. Prediction—That he would be rejected by his own (Psa. 69:8; Isa. 53:3)
    Fulfillment—John 1:11; 7:5
21. Prediction—That he would make a triumphal entry into Jerusalem (Zech. 9:9)
    Fulfillment—Matthew 21:4-5
22. Prediction—That he would be praised by little children (Psa. 8:2)
    Fulfillment—Matthew 21:16
23. Prediction—That he would be the rejected cornerstone (Psa. 118:22-23)
    Fulfillment—Matthew 21:42
24. Prediction—That his miracles would not be believed (Isa. 53:1)
    Fulfillment—John 12:37-38
25. Prediction—That his friend would betray him for 30 pieces of silver (Psa. 41:9;
    55:12-14; Zech. 11:12-13)
    Fulfillment—Matthew 26:14-16, 21-25
26. Prediction—That he would be a man of sorrows (Isa. 53:3)
    Fulfillment—Matthew 26:37-38
27. Prediction—That he would be forsaken by his disciples (Zech. 13:7)
    Fulfillment—Matthew 26:31, 56
28. Prediction—That he would be scourged and spat upon (Isa. 50:6)
    Fulfillment—Matthew 6:67; 27:26
29. Prediction—That his price money would be used to buy a potter's field (Jer.
    18:1-4; 19:1-4; Zech. 11:12-13)
    Fulfillment—Matthew 27:9-10
30. Prediction—That he would be crucified between two thieves (Isa. 53:12)
    Fulfillment—Matthew 27:38; Mark 15:27-28; Luke 22:37
31. Prediction—That he would be given vinegar to drink (Psa. 69:21)
    Fulfillment—Matthew 27:34, 48; John 19:28-30
32. Prediction—That he would suffer the piercing of his hands and feet (Psa. 22:16;
    Zech. 12:10)
    Fulfillment—Mark 15:25; John 19:34, 37; 20:25-27
33. Prediction—That his garments would be parted and gambled for (Psa. 22:18)
    Fulfillment—Luke 23:34; John 19:23-24
34. Prediction—That he would be surrounded and ridiculed by his enemies (Psa.
    22:7-8)
    Fulfillment—Matthew 27:39-44; Mark 15:29-32
35. Prediction—That he would thirst (Psa. 22:15)

Fulfillment—John 19:28
36. Prediction—That he would commend his spirit to the Father (Psa. 31:5)
Fulfillment—Luke 23:46
37. Prediction—That his bones would not be broken (Exod. 12:46; Num. 9:12; Psa. 34:20)
Fulfillment—John 19:33-36
38. Prediction—That he would be stared at in death (Zech. 12:10)
Fulfillment—Matthew 27:36; John 19:37
39. Prediction—That he would be buried with the rich (Isa. 53:9)
Fulfillment—Matthew 27:57-60
40. Prediction—That he would be raised from the dead (Psa. 16:10)
Fulfillment—Matthew 28:2-7
41. Prediction—That he would ascend (Psa. 24:7-10)
Fulfillment—Mark 16:19; Luke 24:51
42. Prediction—That he would then become a greater high priest than Aaron (Psa. 110:4)
Fulfillment—Hebrews 5:4-6, 10; 7:11-28
43. Prediction—That he would be seated at God's right hand (Psa. 110:1)
Fulfillment—Matthew 22:44; Hebrews 10:12-13
44. Prediction—That he would become a smiting scepter (Num. 24:17: Dan. 2:44-45)
Fulfillment—Revelation 19:15
45. Prediction—That he would rule the heathen (Psa. 2:8)
Fulfillment—Revelation 2:27

Study number two: The New Testament prophecies he foretold
  1. Concerning the church
     a. Its symbol (Matt. 13:45)
     b. Its foundation—Christ himself (Matt. 16:13-19)
        Fulfillment—Acts 2
     c. Its ministry (Matt. 28:19-20; Acts 1:8)
        Fulfillment—Book of Acts and the testimony of history
     d. Its field of service (Matt. 28:19-20; Acts 1:8)
        Fulfillment—Book of Acts and the testimony of history
     e. Its authority (Matt. 16:19; 18:18; John 20:23)
     f. Its persecution (Matt. 10:16-23, 34; John 15:18-21; 16:1-3, 33)
        Fulfillment—Book of Acts and the testimony of history
     g. Its discipline (Matt. 18:15-17)
     h. Its removal (John 14:2-3)
        Fulfillment—1 Thessalonians 4:13-17
  2. Concerning himself
     a. His transfiguration (Matt. 16:28)
        Fulfillment—Matthew 17:1-12
     b. His betrayal by Judas
        (1) Predicted in Galilee
            (a) First occasion (John 6:70-71)
            (b) Second occasion (Matt. 17:22)
        (2) Predicted in the Upper Room (Matt. 26:21, 25)
            Fulfillment—Matthew 26:14-16, 45-50
     c. His denial by Peter

        (1) Predicted in the Upper Room (John 13:37-38)

        (2) Predicted en route to the Mount of Olives and Gethsemane (Matt. 26:30, 34)

        Fulfillment—Matthew 26:69-75

    d. His abandonment by the twelve (Matt. 26:31)

      Fulfillment—Matthew 26:56

    e. His sufferings

        (1) Predicted in Caesarea Philippi (Matt. 16:21a)

        (2) Predicted on the Mount of Transfiguration (Matt. 17:12b)

        Fulfillment—Matthew 26:67; 27:26-30)

    f. His death

        (1) The fact of his death (John 10:11, 15; Matt. 17:23)

        (2) The place of his death (Matt. 20:18)

           Fulfillment—Luke 23:33

        (3) The method of his death (John 3:14; 12:32; Matt. 20:18-19)

           Fulfillment—Matthew 27:35

    g. His resurrection

        (1) The fact of his resurrection (John 10:17-18)

        (2) The time element in his resurrection (Matt. 12:40; John 2:19)

           Fulfillment—Matthew 27:64; 1 Corinthians 15:3-4

    h. His appearance in Galilee (Matt. 26:32)

    Fulfillment—John 21

    i. His ascension (John 7:33; 16:28)

    Fulfillment—Acts 1:9-11

    j. His return

        (1) In the air (John 14:3)

           Fulfillment—1 Thessalonians 4:16-17

        (2) On the earth (Matt. 16:27; 24:30; 26:63, 64)

           Fulfillment—Revelation 19:11-21

3. Concerning the resurrection of Lazarus (John 11:11)

    Fulfillment—John 11:43-44

4. Concerning the destruction of Jerusalem and the temple

    a. The destruction of Jerusalem (Luke 19:43-44)

      Fulfillment—Testimony of history

    b. The destruction of the temple (Mark 13:1-2)

      Fulfillment—Testimony of history

5. Concerning the death of Peter (John 21:18-19)

    Fulfillment—2 Peter 1:14 and the testimony of history

6. Concerning Pentecost and the ministry of the Holy Spirit

    Fulfillment—Acts 2; 8; 10; 19

    a. The fact of his ministry (John 7:37-39; Luke 24:49)

    b. The duration of his ministry (John 14:16)

    c. The location of his ministry (John 14:17)

    d. The nature of his ministry

        (1) Regarding the Savior (John 15:26; 16:14)

        (2) Regarding the saved (John 14:26; 16:13)

        (3) Regarding the sinner (John 16:8)

7. Concerning the last days (Luke 17:26-30; Matt. 24:32-34)

8. Concerning the nation Israel

      a. Its blindness (Matt. 23:37-39)
        Fulfillment—Romans 11:7
      b. Its rejection (Matt. 21:43)
        Fulfillment—Testimony of history
      c. Its regathering (Matt. 24:31)
        Fulfillment—Revelation 7:2-8; 21:10-12
    9. Concerning the great tribulation (Matt. 24:21, 29; Luke 21:22-26)
      Fulfillment: Revelation 6–19
  10. Concerning the coming of Elijah (Matt. 17:11)
      Fulfillment—Revelation 11:3-6
  11. Concerning the coming Antichrist (John 5:43; Matt. 24:15)
      Fulfillment—Revelation 13
  12. Concerning the battle of Armageddon (Luke 17:34-37; Matt. 24:28)
      Fulfillment—Revelation 19
  13. Concerning the resurrection of the dead (John 5:28-29)
      Fulfillment—1 Thessalonians 4:16; 1 Corinthians 15:51-55; Revelation 20:4-6
  14. Concerning the future rewards (Matt. 10:41-42; 19:29)
      Fulfillment—Revelation 22:14
  15. Concerning the Millennium (Matt. 8:11; 13:43; 19:28; 25:34)
      Fulfillment—Revelation 20:1-6
  16. Concerning the Great White Throne Judgment (Matt. 25:31-33)
      Fulfillment—Revelation 20:11-15
  17. Concerning hell (Matt. 13:49-50; 18:8-9; 5:28-29)
      Fulfillment—Revelation 20:15
  18. Concerning heaven (John 14:2-3)
      Fulfillment—Revelation 21–22
D. Prophecies concerning Satan—"And the God of peace shall bruise Satan under your feet shortly. The grace of our Lord Jesus Christ be with you. Amen" (Rom. 16:20).
  1. He will be removed from the heavenlies and restricted to planet earth (Rev. 12:7, 9).
  2. He will launch an all-out, genocide-type attack against Israel during the great tribulation (Rev. 12:13-17).
  3. He will be cast into the bottomless pit at the beginning of the Millennium (Rev. 20:1-3).
  4. He will be released at the end of the Millennium (Rev. 20:7-9).
  5. He will be thrown into the lake of fire forever (Rev. 20:10).
E. Prophecies concerning the Antichrist
  1. He will be an intellectual genius (Dan. 8:23).
  2. He will be an oratorical genius (Dan. 11:36).
  3. He will be a political genius (Rev. 17:11-12).
  4. He will be a commercial genius (Dan. 11:43; Rev. 13:16-17).
  5. He will be a military genius (Rev. 6:2; 13:2).
  6. He will be a religious genius (2 Thess. 2:4; Rev. 13:8).
  7. He will begin by controlling the Western power block (Rev. 17:12).
  8. He will make a seven-year covenant with Israel, but will break it after three and a half years (Dan. 9:27).
  9. He will attempt to destroy all of Israel (Rev. 12).

10. He will destroy the false religious system so that he may rule unhindered (Rev. 17:16-17).
11. He will set himself up as God (Dan. 11:36-37; 2 Thess. 2:4, 11; Rev. 13:5).
12. He will do everything according to his own selfish will (Dan. 11:36).
13. He will not regard the God of his fathers (Dan. 11:37).
14. He will not have the desire of women (Dan. 11:37).
15. His god will be the god of power (Dan. 11:38).
16. He will be a master of deceit (2 Thess. 2:10).
17. He will profane the temple (Matt. 24:15).
18. He will be energized by Satan himself (Rev. 13:2).
19. He will briefly rule over all nations (Psa. 2; Dan. 11:36; Rev. 13:16).
20. He will be utterly crushed by the Lord Jesus Christ at the battle of Armageddon (Rev. 19).
21. He will be the first creature thrown into the lake of fire (Rev. 19:20).

F. Prophecies concerning the false prophet
1. He may be a citizen of Israel, if the word "earth" is a reference to the Holy Land (Rev. 13:11a).
2. He will be gentle in appearance, but will possess a devilish character (Rev. 13:11b).
3. He will brutally exercise all the authority and power given him by the Antichrist (Rev. 13:12a).
4. He will force all the world to worship the Antichrist (Rev. 13:12b).
5. He will perform great miracles, such as causing fire to come down from heaven (Rev. 13:13).
6. He will deceive the entire earth (Rev. 13:14a).
7. He will build a great statue of the Antichrist and cause it to speak (Rev. 13:14-15).
8. He will kill those who refuse to worship this statue (Rev. 13:15b).
9. He will require the rest to receive the mark of the statue, which is 666 (Rev. 13:18).
10. Without this mark, no one will be able to buy or sell (Rev. 13:16-17).
11. He will be cast into the lake of fire at the end of the great tribulation (Rev. 19:20).

G. Prophecies concerning false teachers
1. They will come disguised as harmless sheep but are in reality vicious wolves (Matt. 7:15; Acts 20:29).
2. They will pretend to honor Christ, cast out demons, and do many other wonderful miracles (Matt. 7:22).
3. They will, however, be denied by Christ himself at the final judgment (Matt. 7:23).
4. They will have a form of godliness, but will deny its power (2 Tim. 3:5).
5. They will distort the truth (Acts 20:30).
6. They will tell lies with straight faces so often that their conscience won't bother them (1 Tim. 4:2).
7. They will promise peace, but will reject the Prince of peace (1 Thess. 5:2-3).
8. They will fall from the faith (1 Tim. 4:1a).
9. They will deny the deity of Jesus (1 John 2:22-23; 4:1-3).
10. Some will actually claim to be the Messiah and will lead many astray (Matt. 24:5, 11, 24; 1 John 2:18).
11. They will be demon-possessed (1 John 4:3).

12. They will introduce destructive heresies (2 Pet. 2:1).
13. They will always be learning, but will never be able to come to the knowledge of the truth (2 Tim. 3:7).
14. They will mock the Second Coming and final judgment (2 Pet. 3:3-4).

H. Prophecies concerning cities
    1. Sodom—"But the men of Sodom were wicked and sinners before the LORD exceedingly" (Gen. 13:13).
       a. The foretelling of Sodom's destruction by God (Gen. 18:20-21; 19:13, 15)
       b. The fulfilling of Sodom's destruction by God (Gen. 19:24-25).
    2. Tyre—Ezekiel's prophecy in chapter 26 concerning the city of Tyre is surely one of the greatest in the entire Bible. Tyre was actually two cities, one on the coastline, some sixty miles northwest from Jerusalem, and the other on an island, a half mile out in the Mediterranean Sea. In this prophecy, Ezekiel predicts:
       a. The Babylonian king, Nebuchadnezzar, was to capture the city.
       b. Other nations would later participate in Tyre's destruction.
       c. The city was to be scraped and made flat, like the top of a rock.
       d. It was to become a place for the spreading of nets.
       e. Its stones and timber were to be laid in the sea (Zech. 9:3-4).
       f. The city was never to be rebuilt.
    Has all this taken place? Consider the following historical facts:
       a. Ezekiel wrote all this around 590 B.C. Some four years later, in 586 B.C., Nebuchadnezzar surrounded the city of Tyre. The siege lasted 13 years, and in 573 B.C. the coastal city was destroyed. But he could not capture the island city. During the next 241 years the island city of Tyre dwelt in safety and would have doubtless ridiculed Ezekiel's prophecy concerning total destruction.
       b. But in 332 B.C. Alexander the Great arrived upon the scene, and the island city was doomed. Alexander built a bridge leading from the coastline to the island by throwing the debris of the old city into the water. In doing this he literally scraped the coastline clean. (Some years ago an American archaeologist named Edward Robinson discovered 40 or 50 marble columns beneath the water along the shores of ancient Tyre.) After a seven-month siege, Alexander took the island city and destroyed it. From this point on, the surrounding coastal area has been used by local fishermen to spread and dry their nets.
       c. Tyre has never been rebuilt, in spite of the well-known nearby freshwater springs of Roselain, which yield some 10,000 gallons of water daily.
    3. Jericho
       a. Concerning its destruction
         (1) The foretelling—"And ye shall compass the city, all ye men of war, and go round about the city once. Thus shalt thou do six days. And seven priests shall bear before the ark seven trumpets of rams' horns: and the seventh day ye shall compass the city seven times, and the priests shall blow with the trumpets. And it shall come to pass, that when they make a long blast with the ram's horn, and when ye hear the sound of the trumpet, all the people shall shout with a great shout; and the wall of the city shall fall down flat, and the people shall ascend up every man straight before him" (Josh. 6:3-5).

(2) The fulfilling—"So the people shouted when the priests blew with the trumpets: and it came to pass, when the people heard the sound of the trumpet, and the people shouted with a great shout, that the wall fell down flat, so that the people went up into the city, every man straight before him, and they took the city" (Josh. 6:20).

b. Concerning its rebuilding—In the sixth chapter of Joshua we see described the fall of Jericho's walls and the subsequent destruction of the city. Immediately after this, Joshua made an amazing threefold prophecy about this fallen city. He stated:

(1) That Jericho would be rebuilt again by one man

(2) That the builder's oldest son would die when the work on the city had begun

(3) That the builder's youngest son would die when the work was completed (see Josh. 6:26)—Joshua uttered these words around 1400 B.C. Did this happen? Some five centuries after this, in 930 B.C., we are told:

- That a man named Hiel from Bethel rebuilt Jericho
- That as he laid the foundations, his oldest son, Abiram, died
- That when he completed the gates, his youngest son, Segub, died (see 1 Kings 16:34)

4. Nineveh (Nah. 1–3)—During the time of Jonah, God had spared the wicked city of Nineveh by using that Hebrew prophet (after an unpleasant submarine trip) to preach repentance. But the city had soon returned to its evil ways. So around 650 B.C. another prophet, Nahum, predicted the complete overthrow of Nineveh.

At the time of this prophecy, Nineveh appeared to be impregnable; her walls were 100 feet high and broad enough for chariots to drive upon. The city had a circumference of 60 miles and was adorned by more than 1,200 strong towers.

In spite of all this, the city fell, less than 40 years after Nahum's prophecy. An alliance of Medes and Babylonians broke through her walls in August 612 B.C., after a two-month siege. The victory was due in part to the releasing of the city's water supply by traitors within. The destruction was so total that Alexander the Great marched his troops over the desolate ground that had once given support to her mighty buildings, and he never knew there had once been a city there.

5. Babylon

a. The historical city

(1) The foretelling—That it would be given over to the Medes and Persians (Isa. 21:1-10; Dan. 2:39a; 5:26-28; 7:5; 8:20)

(2) The fulfilling (Dan. 5:30-31)

b. The prophetical city—Will the ancient city of Babylon be rebuilt? At least six biblical chapters strongly indicate this will indeed occur. These chapters are Isaiah 13–14; Jeremiah 50–51; Revelation 17–18. The reason for holding this view centers in various prophecies concerning the city of Babylon that have yet to be fulfilled. Consider:

(1) Ancient Babylon was never suddenly destroyed as predicted in Isaiah 13:19. Nebuchadnezzar's Babylon simply changed hands one night from the Babylonians to the Persians in a bloodless takeover (see Dan. 5).

(2) The description of Babylon given by both Isaiah and Jeremiah is very

similar to the one given by John in Revelation 18, where the apostle describes the fate of future Babylon. Note the comparisons:

(a) This Babylon would become the narcotic of the nations (Jer. 51:7; Rev. 18:3, 9).

(b) It would be abandoned by the righteous just prior to its destruction (Jer. 51:6, 45; Rev. 18:4).

(c) Babylon would be destroyed by God himself (Jer. 51:6, 55; Rev. 18:5).

(d) This destruction would be sudden (Jer. 51:8; Rev. 18:10, 19).

(e) This destruction would be by fire (Isa. 13:19; Jer. 51:58; Rev. 18:8-9, 18).

(f) It would never be inhabited following this destruction and its materials would never be used (Jer. 51:26; Rev. 18:23).

Note: None of the above held true concerning Nebuchadnezzar's Babylon. To the contrary (in regards to point f), archaeological discoveries have shown that bricks and stones from ancient Babylon have been reused for building purposes.

(3) Babylon will be destroyed during the day of the Lord, an Old Testament term referring to the great tribulation (Isa. 13:9-13).

(4) Isaiah 14 predicts the Millennium will follow Babylon's destruction (Isa. 14:4-7).

6. Jerusalem

a. It would become God's chosen place (Deut. 12:5-6, 11; 26:2; Josh. 9:27; 10:1; 1 Kings 8:29; 11:36; 15:4; 2 Kings 21:4, 7; 2 Chron. 7:12; Psa. 78:68).
Fulfillment—Testimony of history

b. It would be spared from invasion by Israel (10 northern tribes) and Syria (Isa. 7:1-7).
Fulfillment—Testimony of Old Testament history

c. It would be spared from invasion by the Assyrians (Isa. 37:33-35)
Fulfillment—Isaiah 37:36-37

d. It would be destroyed by the Babylonians (Isa. 3:8; Jer. 11:9; 26:18; Mic. 3:12).
Fulfillment—2 Kings 25:1-10

e. The temple of Solomon would suffer destruction (1 Kings 9:7-9; Psa. 79:1; Jer. 7:11-14; 26:18; Ezek. 7:21-22; 24:21; Mic. 3:12).
Fulfillment—2 Chronicles 36:19

f. The temple vessels would be carried to Babylon and later returned to Jerusalem (Jer. 28:3).
Fulfillment—2 Kings 25:14-15; 2 Chronicles 36:18; Ezra 1:7-11

g. It would be rebuilt by the Jews after spending 70 years in Babylonian captivity (Isa. 44:28; Jer. 25:11-12; 29:10).
Fulfillment—Ezra 1:1-4

h. It would have its streets and walls rebuilt during a period of trouble (Dan. 9:25).
Fulfillment—Ezra 4–5; Nehemiah 2:6

i. The walls would be rebuilt 483 years prior to the crucifixion of Jesus (Dan. 9:26).
Fulfillment—Testimony of history

j. It would be destroyed by the Romans (Luke 19:41-44).

k. The temple of Herod would also be burned at this time (Matt. 24:1-2).
Fulfillment—Testimony of history. Accomplished by Titus in A.D. 70.

    l. It would be trodden down by Gentiles until the Second Coming (Luke
      21:24).
      Fulfillment—Testimony of history
    m. It will be occupied by the Antichrist during the tribulation (Zech. 12:2; 14:2).
    n. It will become the worship center of the world during the Millennium (Isa.
      2:2-3; Mic. 4:1).

I. Prophecies concerning Gentile nations
  1. Edom—Esau, Jacob's brother, was the founder of the nation Edom (see Gen.
    36). Years after his death, Edom refused to help Israel, the nation founded
    by Jacob (see Num. 20) and actually delighted in persecuting them. Because
    of this, God pronounced doom upon them. According to various biblical
    prophecies:
    a. Their commerce was to cease.
    b. Their race was to become extinct.
    c. Their land was to be desolate. (See Jer. 49:17-18; Ezek.35:3-7; Obad. 1-21; Mal.
      1:4.)
    All this has taken place in spite of her unbelievably strong fortified capital,
    Petra. In A.D. 36 Petra was captured by Mohammed, and shortly after this Petra
    and Edom drop from the pages of history.
  2. Egypt
    a. It was to experience seven years of plenty and seven years of famine (Gen.
      (41:1-7, 17-24; 45:6, 11).
      Fulfillment—Genesis 41:47-48, 53-57; 47:13, 20
    b. It was to host Israel for 400 years and afflict them (Gen. 15:13).
      Fulfillment—Exodus 12:40; Acts 7:6
    c. Egypt would be judged for this by the 10 plagues (Gen. 15:14; Exod. 3:20;
      6:1; 7:5).
      Fulfillment—Exodus 7:14; 12:29
    d. It would pursue Israel but fail and perish (Exod. 14:3-4).
      Fulfillment—Exodus 14:5-9, 23-28, 30-31
    e. It would defeat Israel at Megiddo (Jer. 2:16-17, 19, 36-37).
      Fulfillment—2 Kings 23:29-35
    f. It would stumble and fall before Babylon at Charchemish (Jer. 46:5-6, 10-12).
      Fulfillment—Testimony of history
    g. Egypt would be invaded by Nebuchadnezzar (Jer. 43:7-13; 46:13-26).
      Fulfillment—Testimony of history
    h. It would decline from its exalted position and become a base nation (Ezek.
      29:1-2, 15).
      Fulfillment—Testimony of history
    i. It will suffer (perhaps to be double-crossed) at the hand of the Antichrist
      during the tribulation (Dan. 11:40-43; Joel 3:19).
    j. It will be restored and blessed by God along with Assyria and Israel during
      the Millennium (Isa. 19:21-25).
  3. Assyria
    a. It would conquer the 10 northern Israelite tribes (Mic. 1).
      Fulfillment—2 Kings 17
    b. It would suffer the death of many of its troops outside the city of Jerusalem
      (2 Kings 19:6-7a; Isa. 37:33-35).
      Fulfillment—2 Kings 19:35-36; 2 Chronicles 32:21a; Isaiah 37:36

c. It would be overthrown by the Babylonians (Isa. 10:12; 14:24-27; Nah. 1–3).
Fulfillment—Testimony of history

4. Babylon
   a. Fulfilled prophecies
      (1) It would expand under Nebuchadnezzar (Hab. 1:5-10).
      Fulfillment—Testimony of history
      (2) It would defeat the Egyptians at Carchemish (Jer. 46).
      Fulfillment—Testimony of history
      (3) It would defeat the Assyrians (Nah.).
      Fulfillment—Testimony of history
      (4) It would be defeated by the Medes and Persians (Isa. 13:17; Jer. 51:11; Dan. 5:28).
      Fulfillment—Daniel 5:30-31
   b. Unfulfilled prophecies—Will the land of ancient Babylon (modern Iraq) become an important nation in the kingdom of the Antichrist during the great tribulation? Does one of Zechariah's visions speak of this?
      Zechariah, the Old Testament prophet, saw a flying sin-filled bushel basket with a woman inside. An angel told him she represented the ultimate in wickedness. Upon being asked by the prophet concerning its destination, the angel replied, "To build it an house in the land of Shinar: and it shall be established, and set there upon her own base" (Zech. 5:11).
      Note two significant phrases in this vision:
      (1) A wicked woman (Zech. 5:7-8)—Compare this with Rev. 17:4-5: "And the woman was arrayed in purple and scarlet colour, and decked with gold and precious stones and pearls, having a golden cup in her hand full of abominations and filthiness of her fornication: And upon her forehead was a name written, MYSTERY, BABYLON THE GREAT, THE MOTHER OF HARLOTS AND ABOMINATIONS OF THE EARTH."
      (2) The land of Shinar (Zech. 5:11)—Compare this with Gen. 11:1-2: "And the whole earth was of one language, and of one speech. And it came to pass, as they journeyed from the east, that they found a plain in the land of Shinar; and they dwelt there."
      Who will rebuild Babylon and for what reason? The Antichrist may rebuild it, for this city that once served as Satan's headquarters could again become his capital.

5. Persia
   a. Fulfilled prophecies
      (1) It would consist of an alliance between two peoples (the Medes and Persians) (Dan. 8:1-4, 20).
      Fulfillment—Testimony of history
      (2) It would defeat the Babylonians (Dan. 2:39; 7:5).
      Fulfillment—Daniel 5
      (3) It would be defeated by the Greeks (Dan. 8:5-8, 21-22).
      Fulfillment—Testimony of history
   b. Unfulfilled prophecies
      (1) It will join forces with Russia in an attack against Israel during the great tribulation (Ezek. 38:5-12).
      (2) It will be utterly routed by God himself, resulting in the death of many troops (Ezek. 38:21–39:4, 12).

6. Greece
   a. It would be invaded by Persia (Dan. 11:2).
      Fulfillment—Testimony of history
   b. Alexander the Great would conquer Greece and establish a world empire
      (Dan. 2:32-39; 7:6; 8:5-8, 21; 11:3).
      Fulfillment—Testimony of history
   c. It would defeat the Persians (Dan. 8:5-8).
      Fulfillment—Testimony of history
   d. It was to be divided into four parts after Alexander's death (Dan. 8:8, 22;
      11:4).
      Fulfillment—Testimony of history
7. Rome
   a. It would defeat the Greeks (Dan. 2:40; 7:7; 11:18-19).
      Fulfillment—Testimony of history
   b. It would destroy Jerusalem (Matt. 23:37-39).
      Fulfillment—Testimony of history
   c. It will be revived during the tribulation (Dan. 2:41; 7:7-8; Rev. 13:1; 17:12).
   d. It will be destroyed by Jesus at the Second Coming (Dan. 2:34-35, 44; 7:9, 14,
      27).
8. Germany and the Eastern European nations—Nearly six centuries before the
   Bethlehem event, God revealed to Daniel that in the final days prior to Christ's
   return the Antichrist would succeed in reviving and controlling the old Roman
   Empire (see Dan. 2; 7). John the Apostle would later receive the same basic
   information (see Rev. 13; 17).
      The ancient empire of Rome is now (for the most part) occupied by
   European nations and the USA. In essence, these prophesies stated the
   Antichrist would rule over the Western world. According to Daniel 11 and
   Ezekiel 39, however, he would not control Russia. However, at the close of
   the 1980s these predictions seemed highly unlikely to be fulfilled, for
   practically all of Eastern Europe and half of Germany suffered under the
   bondage of Russian communism. But then the impossible and incredible
   occurred. Consider:
   a. Germany was reunified on October 3, 1990.
   b. Romanian president Nicolae Ceausescu was executed by his own country-
      men on Christmas Day 1989, and a democratic government was instituted.
   c. On December 29, 1989, Vaclav Havel, a dissident playwright who had been
      imprisoned by the Communists, was elected president of Czechoslovakia.
   d. Lech Walesa, hero of the Solidarity movement, became president of Poland
      in November 1990.
   e. In October 1989 Hungary proclaimed itself to be a free republic.
   f. Yugoslavia began exploring paths toward democracy in the fall of 1990.
   g. The Bulgarian parliament approved free multiparty elections in April 1989.
   h. Albania, the smallest and most isolated of the Eastern European countries,
      made at least cosmetic gestures toward democratic reforms in May 1990.
9. America—Edgar C. James writes:

   Does the Bible say anything about the future of the United States? Some, in
   reading the Scripture, believe various passages may allude to the United
   States. But such conclusions are very remote. For instance, some hold the

"young lions" (Ezekiel 38:13, KJV), and "islands" (Psalm 72:10) refer to England's colonies; namely, America. But a careful check shows those are villages or islands of Tarshish, the area of southern Spain (cf. Jonah 1:3).

Others find America as the "great eagle" (Rev. 12:14) or the "land shadowing with wings" (Isaiah 18:1, KJV). But the Revelation passage is showing the speed with which the woman fled into the wilderness, not a nation. The Isaiah passage refers to a nation with "whirling wings" (Isaiah 18:1), most likely a reference to the insects of Ethiopia. (*Armageddon,* pp. 102–103)

However, simply because the United States is not mentioned in prophecy does not mean it has no role in the latter days. To the contrary, it would appear tragically possible the United States will function as the most important member of the Antichrist's 10-nation Western confederation. In fact, it may well be that the Antichrist will be an American citizen. Consider:
- a. The Antichrist will no doubt hold citizenship from one of the 10 nations he eventually controls.
- b. Following the rapture of the church, no other nation on earth will suffer the loss of so many key (saved) leaders in the areas of government, business, education, medicine, sports, etc., as America.
- c. In light of this above, it is not unreasonable to envision a United States citizen (Antichrist) quickly moving in to fill the tremendous power vacuum which will of necessity exist.
10. Russia
    - a. It will invade Israel during the Tribulation (Ezek. 28:8-11, 16).
    - b. It will be joined by various allies (Ezek. 38:4-7).
    - c. It will come down for a "spoil" (Ezek. 38:12).
    - d. It will suffer a disastrous defeat at the hand of God, losing some 83 percent of its troops (Ezek. 39:2).
J. Prophecies concerning Israel
    1. The people of Shem would be especially blessed of God (Gen. 9:26).
       Fulfillment—Matthew 1:1; John 4:22
    2. A great nation would come from Abraham (Gen 12:2).
       Fulfillment—Numbers 23:10
    3. This nation would exist forever (Jer. 31:35-37).
       Fulfillment—Testimony of history
    4. Israel's kings would come from the tribe of Judah (Gen. 49:10).
       Fulfillment—1 Samuel 16:1-2; 1 Chronicles 28:4; Luke 1:26-27
    5. Canaan will be given to Israel forever (Gen. 13:15).
       Partial fulfillment—Joshua 21:43-45
       Future fulfillment—Isaiah 60:21; Ezekiel 37:25
    6. Israel would sojourn in another land (Egypt) for 400 years, there to serve and be afflicted (Gen. 15:13).
       Fulfillment—Exodus 12:40
    7. This oppressive nation (Egypt) would be judged by God (Gen. 15:14).
       Fulfillment—Exodus 7:14–12:29
    8. Israel would leave Egypt with great substance (Gen. 15:14).
       Fulfillment—Exodus 12:35-36
    9. Israel would return to Canaan from Egypt in the fourth generation (Gen. 15:16).
       Fulfillment—Joshua 3:16-17

10. Israel would conquer Canaan gradually (Exod. 23:29-30).
    Fulfillment—Judges 1:19-36
11. Those (over 20) who sinned at Kadesh-barnea would not see the promised land, but would wander 40 years in the wilderness (Num. 14:32-34).
    Fulfillment—Numbers 26:63-65
12. Israel would set a king over them (Deut. 17:14-20).
    Fulfillment—1 Samuel 10:24
13. Israel would suffer a tragic civil war after the death of Solomon (1 Kings 11:11, 31).
    Fulfillment—1 Kings 12:16-17, 19-20
14. The Northern Kingdom would be carried away into Assyrian Captivity (1 Kings 14:15-16; Hos. 1:5; 10:1, 6).
    Fulfillment—2 Kings 17:6-7, 22-23
15. This would happen 65 years after the Isaiah and Ahaz meeting (Isa. 7:8).
    Fulfillment—2 Kings 17:24
16. The Southern Kingdom would be carried away into Babylonian Captivity (Jer. 13:19; 20:4-5; 21:10; Mic. 4:10).
    Fulfillment—2 Kings 24–25
17. The temple would be destroyed (1 Kings 9:7; 2 Chron. 7:20-21; Jer. 7:14).
    Fulfillment—2 Kings 25:9
18. The length of the Babylonian captivity would be 70 years (Jer. 25:11; 29:10).
    Fulfillment—Dan. 9:2
19. Israel would then return to the land (Jer. 29:10).
    Fulfillment—Ezra 1
20. The temple vessels once carried into Babylon would be brought back to the land (2 Kings 25:14-15; Jer. 28:3; Dan. 5:1-4).
    Fulfillment—Ezra 1:7-11
21. Israel eventually would be scattered among the nations of the world (Lev. 26:33; Deut. 4:27-28; 28:25-68; Hos. 9:17).
    Fulfillment—Testimony of history
22. Israel would "abide many days" without a king, an heir apparent, the Levitical offerings, the temple, or the Levitical priesthood (Hos. 3:4).
    Fulfillment—Testimony of history
23. Israel also would be free from idolatry during this terrible time (Hos. 3:4).
    Fulfillment—Testimony of history
24. Israel would become a byword among the nations (Deut. 28:37).
    Fulfillment—Testimony of history
25. Israel would loan to many nations, but borrow from none (Deut. 28:12).
    Fulfillment—Testimony of history
26. Israel would be hounded and persecuted (Deut. 28:65-67).
    Fulfillment—Testimony of history
27. Israel nevertheless would retain her identity (Lev. 26:44; Jer. 46:28).
    Fulfillment—Testimony of history
28. Israel would remain alone and aloof among the nations (Num. 23:9).
    Fulfillment—Testimony of history
29. Israel would reject her Messiah (Isa. 53:1-9).
    Fulfillment—(Luke 23:13-25)
30. Israel would return to Palestine in the latter days prior to the second coming of Jesus (Deut. 30:3; Ezek. 36:24; 37:1-14).

Fulfillment—Testimony of history since 1948

31. Israel will be deceived into signing a seven-year peace treaty with the Western leader (Antichrist) during the great tribulation (Isa. 28:18; Dan. 9:27).
32. Israel will rebuild its temple (Matt. 24:15; 2 Thess. 2:3-4; Rev. 11:1).
33. Israel will experience a hellish onslaught by Satan himself (Rev. 12:13, 17).
34. Israel will suffer terribly from this future attempted holocaust (Zech. 13:8; 14:2).
35. Israel nevertheless, as a nation, will survive the hellish great tribulation (Zech. 13:9a; Rev. 12:14-16).
36. Israel will recognize Christ as its Messiah (Zech. 12:10; 13:9b).
37. Israel will be regenerated, regathered, and restored to the land following the great tribulation (Jer. 33:8; Ezek. 11:17).
38. Israel will become God's witnesses during the Millennium (Isa. 44:8; 61:6).

K. Prophecies concerning the 70 weeks—"Seventy weeks are determined upon thy people and upon thy holy city, to finish the transgression, and to make an end of sins, and to make reconciliation for iniquity, and to bring in everlasting righteousness, and to seal up the vision and prophecy, and to anoint the most Holy. Know therefore and understand, that from the going forth of the commandment to restore and to build Jerusalem unto the Messiah the Prince shall be seven weeks, and threescore and two weeks: the street shall be built again, and the wall, even in troublous times. And after threescore and two weeks shall Messiah be cut off, but not for himself: and the people of the prince that shall come shall destroy the city and the sanctuary; and the end thereof shall be with a flood, and unto the end of the war desolations are determined. And he shall confirm the covenant with many for one week: and in the midst of the week he shall cause the sacrifice and the oblation to cease, and for the overspreading of abominations he shall make it desolate, even until the consummation, and that determined shall be poured upon the desolate" (Dan. 9:24-27).

  1. To whom does this prophecy refer? It refers to Israel: "Thy people" (9:24).
  2. What is meant by the term "70 weeks"? The Hebrew word refers to 70 sevens of years, or a total of 490 years.
  3. When was the 70-week period to begin? It was to begin with the command to rebuild Jerusalem's walls (9:25).
  4. What are the distinct time periods mentioned within the 70-week prophecy and what was to happen during each period?
      a. First period—7 weeks (49 years), from 445 B.C. to 396 B.C. The key events during this time were the building of the streets and walls of Jerusalem "even in troublous times" (9:25).
      b. Second period—62 weeks (434 years), from 396 B.C. to A.D. 30. At the end of this second period the Messiah was to be crucified.
          The brilliant British scholar and Bible student Sir Robert Anderson has reduced the first two periods into their exact number of days. This he has done by multiplying 483 (the combined years of the first two periods) by 360 (the days in a biblical year). The total number of days in the first 69 weeks (or 483 years) is 173,880. Anderson then points out that if one begins counting on March 14, 445 B.C., and goes forward in history, these days would run out on April 6, A.D. 32. It was on this very day that Jesus made his triumphal entry into the city of Jerusalem. Surely our Lord must have had Daniel's prophecy in mind when he said: "Saying, If thou hadst known, even thou, at least in this thy day, the things which belong unto thy peace!

but now they are hid from thine eyes" (Luke 19:42). Of course, it was on this same day that the Pharisees plotted to murder Christ (Luke 19:47).

Thus, Daniel, writing some five and a half centuries earlier, correctly predicted the very day of Christ's presentation and rejection.

   c. Third period—One week (7 years) from the Rapture until the Millennium.

5. Do the 70 weeks run continuously?. This is to say, is there a gap somewhere between these 490 years or do they run without pause until they are completed?

Dispensational theology teaches that these weeks do not run continuously, but that there has been a gap or parenthesis of nearly 2,000 years between the sixty-ninth and seventieth week. This is known as the age of the church. The chronology may be likened to a 70-minute basketball game. For 69 minutes the game has been played at a furious and continuous pace. Then the referee for some reason calls time out with the clock in the red and showing one final minute of play. No one knows for sure when the action will start again, but at some point the referee will step in and blow his whistle. At that time the teams will gather to play out the last minute of the game. God has stepped in and stopped the clock of prophecy at Calvary. This divine "time out" has already lasted some 20 centuries, but soon the Redeemer will blow his trumpet, and the final "week" of action will be played upon this earth.

L. Prophecies concerning judgments
  1. Past judgments
    a. The Garden of Eden judgment (Gen. 2:15-17)
      Fulfillment—Genesis 3:7-19; 5:5
    b. The flood judgment (Gen. 6:7, 13, 17)
      Fulfillment—Genesis 7:10-12, 17-24
    c. The Babylonian judgment of God upon sinful Israel (Jer. 13:19; 20:4-5; 21:10)
      Fulfillment—2 Kings 24–25
    d. The Calvary judgment (Isa. 53:1-10; Psa. 22:1-18)
      Fulfillment—Matthew 27; Mark 15; Luke 23; John 19; 1 Peter 3:18
    e. The Roman judgment of God upon sinful Israel (Matt. 24:2; Luke 19:41-44)
      Fulfillment—Testimony of history
  2. Future judgments
    a. The judgment seat of Christ (Rom. 14:10; 1 Cor. 3:9-15; 2 Cor. 5:10; Rev. 22:12)
    b. The tribulational judgment upon man's religious systems (Rev. 17)
    c. The tribulational judgment upon man's economic and political systems (Rev. 18)
    d. The tribulational judgment upon man's military systems (Rev. 19:11-21)
    e. The tribulational judgment upon man himself (Rev. 6; 8–9; 16)
    f. The lamp and talent judgment on Israel (Matt. 24:45-51; 25:1-30; Ezek. 20:33-38)
    g. The sheep and goat judgment on the Gentiles (Matt. 25:31-46)
    h. The judgment upon the Antichrist and false prophet (Rev. 19:20)
    i. The judgment upon Satan in the bottomless pit for 1,000 years (Rev. 20:1-3)
    j. The judgment upon Satan in the lake of fire forever (Rev. 20:10)
    k. The fallen angel judgment (1 Cor. 6:3; 2 Pet. 2:4; Jude 6)
    l. The Great White Throne Judgment (Rev. 20:11-15)
    m. The worldwide fire judgment (2 Pet. 3:7-12)
M. Prophecies concerning the last days

1. Increase of wars and rumors of war (Joel 3:9-10; Matt. 24:6-7)
2. Extreme materialism (2 Tim. 3:1-2; Rev. 3:14-19)
3. Lawlessness (Psa. 78:8; Prov. 30:11-14; 2 Tim. 3:2-3)
4. Population explosion (Gen. 6:1; Luke 17:26)
5. Increasing speed and knowledge (Dan. 12:4)
6. Departure from the Christian faith (2 Thess. 2:3; 1 Tim. 4:1, 3-4; 2 Tim. 3:5; 4:3-4; 2 Pet. 3:3-4)
7. Intense demonic activity (Gen. 6:1-4; 1 Tim. 4:1-3)
8. Unification of the world's religious, political, and economic systems (Rev. 13:4-8, 16-17; 17:1-18; 18:1-24)
9. The absence of gifted leadership among the nations, thus making it easy for the Antichrist to take over
10. Universal drug usage ("Sorceries" here can also refer to drugs.) (Rev. 9:21)
11. Abnormal sexual activity (Rom. 1:17-32; 2 Pet. 2:10, 14; 3:3; Jude 18)
12. Mass slaughter of innocents by unconcerned mothers (abortion) (Rom. 1:31; 2 Tim. 3:3)
13. Widespread violence (Gen. 6:11, 13; 2 Tim. 3:1; Rev. 9:21)
14. Rejection of God's Word (2 Tim. 4:3-4; 2 Pet. 3:3-4, 16)
15. Rejection of God himself (Psa. 2:1-3)
16. Blasphemy (2 Tim. 3:2; 2 Pet. 3:3; Jude 18)
17. Self-seeking and pleasure-seeking (2 Tim. 3:2, 4)
18. Men minus a conscience (1 Tim. 4:2)
19. Religious hucksters (2 Pet. 2:3)
20. Outright devil worshippers (Rev. 9:20; 13:11-14)
21. Rise of false prophets and antichrists (Matt. 24:5, 11; 2 Pet. 2:1-2)
22. False claims of peace (1 Thess. 5:1-3)
23. Rapid advances in technology (Gen. 4:22; Luke 17:26)
24. Great political and religious upheavals in the Holy Land (Matt. 24:32-34)

N. Prophecies concerning the nature of the tribulation
1. Unbelievably bloody wars (Matt. 24:6-7; Rev. 6:2-4; 14:20)
2. Drunkenness (Matt. 24:38; Luke 17:27)
3. Illicit sex (Matt. 24:38; Luke 17:27; Rev. 9:21)
4. Gross materialism (Luke 17:28; Rev. 18:12-14)
5. Rise of false messiahs and prophets (Matt. 24:5, 11-24)
6. Horrible persecution of believers (Matt. 24:10; Rev. 16:6; 17:6)
7. Men to hide in the caves (Isa. 2:19-21; Rev. 6:15-17)
8. The pangs and sorrows of death to seize men, similar to the pains of women in labor (Isa. 13:8; Jer. 30:6)
9. Terrible worldwide famines (Rev. 6:5-6, 8)
10. Humans to be slaughtered by predatory wild beasts (Rev. 6:8)
11. Disastrous earthquakes (Rev. 6:12; 11:13; 16:18)
12. Fearful heavenly signs and disturbances (Luke 21:25; Rev. 6:12-14; 8:12)
13. Universal tidal waves and ocean disasters (Luke 21:25; Rev. 8:8-9; 16:3)
14. The stars, moon, and sun to be darkened (Isa. 13:10; Joel 2:30-31; 3:15)
15. The moon to be turned into blood (Joel 2:31; Rev. 6:12)
16. The heavens to be rolled together like a scroll (Isa. 34:4; Joel 2:10; Rev. 6:14)
17. Massive hailstones composed of fire and blood to fall upon the earth (Rev. 8:7; 16:21)
18. Huge meteorites to fall upon the earth (Rev. 8:8-11)

19. Stars of the heavens to fall upon the earth (Rev. 6:13)
20. Both salt waters and fresh waters to become totally polluted (Rev. 8:8-11; 11:6; 16:3-4)
21. Universal disaster of land ecology (Rev. 8:7)
22. Events to steadily go from bad to worse (Amos 5:19)
23. A time of thick darkness and utter depression (Joel 2:2)
24. No period in history to even compare to it (Jer. 30:7; Dan. 12:1; Matt. 24:21-22)
25. A time of famine of the very Word of God itself (Amos 8:11-12)
26. A time of absolutely no escape from God's fierce judgment (Amos 9:2-3)
27. Worldwide drug usage (Rev. 9:21)
28. Universal idolatry and devil worship (Rev. 9:20; 13:11-17)
29. Murderous demonic invasions (Rev. 9:3-20)
30. Subterranean eruptions (Rev. 9:1-2)
31. Scorching solar heat (Rev. 16:8-9)
32. Terrifying periods of total darkness (Rev.16:10)
33. Unchecked citywide fires (Rev. 18:8-9, 18)
34. A plague of cancerous sores (Rev. 16:2)
35. The total destruction of the earth's religious, political, and economic systems (Rev. 17–18)
36. A universal dictatorial rule by the Antichrist (Rev. 13)
37. An all-out, no-holds-barred attempt to destroy Israel (Rev. 12:1-17)
38. Survivors of this period to be more rare than gold (Isa. 13:12)
39. Men's blood to be poured out like dust and their flesh like dung (Zeph. 1:17)
40. The slain to remain unburied and the mountains to be covered with blood (Isa. 34:3; 66:24)
41. The earth to be moved out of its orbit (Isa. 13:13)
42. The earth to be turned upside down (Isa. 24:1, 19)
43. The earth to reel to and fro like a drunkard (Isa. 24:20)
44. The most frightful physical plague in all history (Zech. 14:12)
45. A 200-mile river of human blood to flow (Rev. 14:20)
46. Scavenger birds to eat the rotted flesh of entire armies of men (Matt. 24:28; Rev. 19:17-19)

O. Prophecies concerning the Millennium
1. The final temple to be rebuilt (Isa. 2:2; Ezek. 40–48; Joel 3:18; Hag. 2:7-9; Zech. 6:12-13)
2. Israel to be regathered (Isa. 43:5-6; Jer. 24:6; 29:14; 31:8-10; Ezek. 11:17; 36:24-25, 28; Amos 9:14-15; Zech. 8:6-8; Matt. 24:31)
3. Israel to recognize her Messiah (Isa. 8:17; 25:9; 26:8; Zech. 12:10-12; Rev. 1:7)
4. Israel to be cleansed (Jer. 33:8; Zech. 13:1)
5. Israel to be regenerated (Jer. 31:31-34; 32:39; Ezek. 11:19-20; 36:26)
6. Israel to once again be related to God by marriage (Isa. 54:1-17; 62:2-5; Hos. 2:14-23)
7. Israel to be exalted above the Gentiles (Isa. 14:1-2; 49:22-23; 60:14-17; 61:6-7)
8. Israel to become God's witnesses (Isa. 44:8; 61:6; 66:21; Ezek. 3:17; Mic. 5:7; Zeph. 3:20; Zech. 8:3)
9. Jesus to rule from Jerusalem with a rod of iron (Psa. 2:6-8, 11; Isa. 2:3; 11:4)
10. David to aid in this rule as vice-regent (Isa. 55:3-4; Jer. 30:9; Ezek. 34:23; 37:24; Hos. 3:5)
11. All sickness to be removed (Isa. 33:24; Jer. 30:17; Ezek. 34:16)

12. The original curse upon creation to be removed (Isa. 11:6-9; 35:9; 65:25; Joel 3:18; Amos 9:13-15; see Gen. 3:17-19)
13. The wolf, lamb, calf, and lion to lie down together in peace (Isa. 11:6-7; 65:25)
14. A little child to safely play with once-poisonous serpents and spiders (Isa. 11:8)
15. Physical death to be swallowed up in victory (Isa. 25:8)
16. All tears to be dried (Isa. 25:8; 30:19)
17. The deaf to hear, the blind to see, and the lame to walk (Isa. 29:18; 35:5-6; 61:1-2; Jer. 31:8)
18. Man's knowledge about God to be vastly increased (Isa. 41:19-20; 54:13; Hab. 2:14)
19. No social, political, or religious oppression (Isa. 14:3-6; 49:8-9; Zech. 9:11-12)
20. Full ministry of the Holy Spirit (Isa. 32:15; 45:3; 59:21; Ezek. 36:27; 37:14; Joel 2:28-29)
21. Jesus himself to be the Good, Great, and Chief Shepherd (Isa. 40:11; 49:10; 58:11; Ezek. 34:11-16)
22. A time of universal singing (Isa. 35:6; 52:9; 54:1; 55:12; Jer. 33:11)
23. A time of universal praying (Isa. 56:7; 65:24; Zech. 8:22)
24. A unified language (Zeph. 3:9)
25. The wilderness and deserts to bloom (Isa. 35:1-2)
26. God's glory to be seen by all nations (Isa. 60:1-3; Ezek. 39:21; Mic. 4:1-5; Hab. 2:14)
27. Longevity of man to be restored (Isa. 65:20)
28. Universal peace (Isa. 2:4; 32:18)
29. Universal holiness (Zech. 13:20-21)
30. Solar and lunar light to increase (Isa. 4:5; 30:26; 60:19-20; Zech. 2:5)
31. Palestine to become greatly enlarged and changed (Isa. 26:15; Obad. 17-21)
32. A river to flow east-west from the Mount of Olives into both the Mediterranean and Dead seas (Ezek. 47:8-9, 12; Joel 3:18; Zech. 14:4, 8, 10)
33. Jerusalem to become known as Jehovah Tsidkenu (the Lord our righteousness), and Jehovah Shammah (the Lord is there) (Jer. 33:16; Ezek. 48:35)
34. Jerusalem to become the worship center of the world (Isa. 2:2-3; Mic. 4:1)
35. Jerusalem's streets to be filled with happy boys and girls playing (Zech. 8:5)
36. The city to occupy an elevated site (Zech. 14:10)
37. The earthly city to be six miles in circumference (Ezek. 48:35)
38. The heavenly, suspended city (new Jerusalem) to be 1,400 by 1,400 by 1,400 miles (Rev. 21:10, 16)

P. Prophecies concerning hell
1. Hell will be a place of unquenchable fire (Matt. 3:12; 13:41-42; Mark 9:43).
2. It will be a place of memory and remorse (Luke 16:19-31).
3. It will be a place of thirst (Luke 16:24).
4. It will be a place of misery and pain (Rev. 14:10-11).
5. It will be a place of frustration and anger (Matt. 13:42; 24:51).
6. It will be a place of separation (Rev. 2:11; 20:6, 15).
7. It will be a place of undiluted divine wrath (Hab. 3:2; Rev. 14:10).
8. It was originally prepared for Satan and his hosts (Matt. 25:41).
9. It will be a place created for all eternity (Dan. 12:2; Matt. 25:46; Jude 7).

Q. Prophecies concerning heaven
1. Heaven is being prepared by Christ himself (John 14:3).
2. It is only for those who have been born again (John 3:3).

3. It is described as a glorious city, likened to pure gold and clear glass (Rev. 21:11, 18).
4. The name of this city is the new Jerusalem (Rev. 21:2).
5. It is in the shape of a cube, with the length, width, and height being equal (Rev. 21:16).
6. Its size is 12,000 furlongs, roughly 1,400 miles long, wide, and high (Rev. 21:16).
7. The city rests upon 12 layers of foundational stones, with each layer being inlaid with a different precious gem (Rev. 21:19-20).
8. Each foundation has one of the names of the 12 apostles on it (Rev. 21:14).
9. The wall around the city is made of pure jasper (Rev. 21:18).
10. The height of the wall is approximately 216 feet (Rev. 21:17).
11. The wall has 12 gates, 3 on each of the 4 sides (Rev. 21:12).
12. Each gate is made of solid pearl (Rev. 21:21).
13. Each gate has on it the name of one of the 12 tribes of Israel (Rev. 21:12).
14. An angel stands guard at each gate (Rev. 21:12).
15. The gates will never be shut (Rev. 21:25).
16. The palaces may possibly be made of ivory (Psa. 45:8).
17. The River of Life is there, to insure everlasting life (Rev. 22:1).
18. The Tree of Life is there, to ensure abundant life (Rev. 2:7; 22:19).
19. The Tree of Life will bear its fruit each month (Rev. 22:2).
20. The throne of God will occupy the central palace (Rev. 4:2; 22:1).
21. This throne is likened to wheels of burning fire with an emerald rainbow canopy (Dan. 7:9; Rev. 4:3).
22. It is surrounded by 24 small thrones (Rev. 4:4).
23. Near it stands the brazen laver, described as "a sea of glass, like crystal" (Rev. 4:6).
24. Beside the throne are four special angels who worship God continually (Rev. 4:8).
25. The golden altar is there, with bowls of incense (Rev. 5:8; 8:3; 9:13).
26. The menorah, or seven-branched lamp stand, is there (Rev. 1:12; 4:5).
27. The holy ark of God may be there (Rev. 11:19).
28. The main street of the city is composed of transparent gold (Rev. 21:21).
29. The city will shine with and be enlightened by God's glory (John 17:24; Rom. 8:18; Rev. 21:11, 23; 22:5).
30. It is a place of holiness (Rev. 21:27).
31. It is a place of beauty (Psa. 50:2).
32. It is a place of unity (Eph. 1:10).
33. It is a place of perfection (1 Cor. 13:10).
34. It is a place of joy (Psa. 16:11).
35. It is a place for all eternity (John 3:15; Psa. 23:6).
36. There may be a tabernacle (Rev. 15:5; 21:3).
37. There will be no temple (Rev. 21:22).
38. There will be no sea (Rev. 21:1).
39. There will be no tears (Rev. 7:17; 21:4).
40. There will be no sickness (Rev. 22:2).
41. There will be no pain (Rev. 21:4).
42. There will be no death (Isa. 25:8; 1 Cor. 15:26; Rev. 21:4).
43. There will be no more thirst or hunger (Rev. 7:16).
44. There will be no more sin (Rev. 21:27).

45. There will be no more judgment upon sin (Rev. 22:3).
46. There will be no need for the sun or moon (Rev. 21:23).
47. There will be no night (Rev. 21:25; 22:5).
48. The city will be the Bridegroom's gift to the bride, Christ's church (Rev. 21:2, 10).
49. It will be shared by saved Israel (Heb. 11:10, 16).
50. It will be shared by the holy angels (Dan. 7:10; Heb. 12:22; Rev. 5:11).
51. The Father will be there (Dan. 7:9; Rev. 4:2-3).
52. The Son will be there (Rev. 5:6; 7:17).
53. The Holy Spirit will be there (Rev. 14:13; 22:17).
54. Heaven will be a place of singing (Isa. 44:23; Heb. 2:12; Rev. 14:3; 15:3).
55. Heaven will be a place of serving (Rev. 7:15; 22:3).
56. Heaven will be a place of learning (1 Cor. 13:9-10).
R. Prophecies concerning the glorified body
    1. It will be a recognizable body (1 Cor. 13:12).
    2. It will be a body like Christ's body (1 John 3:2).
    3. It will be a body that will permit eating (Luke 24:41-43; John 21:12-13).
    4. It will be a body in which the spirit predominates (1 Cor. 15:44, 49).
    5. It will be a body unlimited by time, gravity, or space (Luke 24:31; John 20:19, 26).
    6. It will be an eternal body (2 Cor. 5:1).
    7. It will be a glorious body (Rom. 8:18; 1 Cor. 15:43).

Section two: A chronological overview of prophecy featuring the sequence involved, viewing the *when* of the matter.
  I. A General Consideration
    A. The Rapture of the church
    B. The bema judgment seat of Christ
    C. The marriage service of the Lamb
    D. The singing of two special songs
    E. The great tribulation
    F. The battle of Armageddon
    G. The second coming of Christ
    H. The glorious Millennium
    I. Satan's final revolt
    J. The Great White Throne Judgment
    K. The destruction of this present earth and heaven
    L. The creation of the new earth and heaven
  II. A Specific Consideration
    A. The Rapture of the church
      1. The meaning of the word *rapture*—Actually, the word *rapture* is from *rapere*, found in the expression "caught up" in the Latin translation of 1 Thessalonians 4:17. However, if one so desires, the rapture could be scripturally referred to as the *harpazo*, which is the Greek word translated "caught up" in 1 Thessalonians 4:17. The identical phrase is found in Acts 8:39, where Philip was caught away by the Holy Spirit, and in 2 Corinthians 12:2, 4, when Paul was caught up into the third heaven. Or, if you'd rather, the rapture could be known as the *allasso*, from the Greek translated "changed" in 1 Corinthians 15:51-52. *Allasso* is used in describing the final renewal and transformation of the heavens and the earth. (See Heb. 1:12.) So then, use whatever name suits your fancy. Of course, the important thing is not what you name it, but rather, can you *claim it?* That is,

will you participate in it? Thus, the next scheduled event predicted in the Word of God will take place when the Savior himself appears in the air to catch up his own.

2. The first mention of the Rapture—The first mention of the Rapture in the Bible is found in John 14:1-3. "Let not your heart be troubled: ye believe in God, believe also in me. In my Father's house are many mansions: if it were not so, I would have told you. I go to prepare a place for you. And if I go and prepare a place for you, I will come again, and receive you unto myself; that where I am, there ye may be also" (John 14:1-3).

While the Old Testament prophets spoke in glowing terms of the Messiah's eventual return to earth and the establishment of his perfect kingdom upon the earth (Isa. 2:2-5; 9:6-7; 11:1-16; 32:1; 35:1-10; etc.), they knew absolutely nothing of that event whereby God himself would (for a brief period of time) remove his people from the earth.

3. The participants of the Rapture—For whom will Jesus come? It is the view of this theological summary that Christ will come again for his church, which is composed of all saved people from Pentecost up to the Rapture itself.

4. Two descriptions of the Rapture—The two most important passages describing the Rapture are found in 1 Thessalonians 4 and 1 Corinthians 15. Let us briefly examine these two passages.

   a. 1 Thessalonians 4:13-18—In this great passage Paul answers a question that had bothered the Thessalonians. When he was among them (Acts 17), they had doubtless learned many precious truths about the glorious return of Christ to earth someday and the establishing of his kingdom. In fact, to some this all seemed to be just around the corner. But since the apostle's departure, a number of believers had died. They obviously then would not be on earth at the time of Christ's return. Did this mean they would miss everything? This then is the background to the great Rapture passage before us here in chapter 4. These six verses thus present for us:

   (1) A realization: "But I would not have you to be ignorant, brethren, concerning them which are asleep, that ye sorrow not, even as others which have no hope" (4:13). This is but one of four key areas that Paul would not have us to be ignorant. The other three are:

     (a) The events in the Old Testament (1 Cor. 10:1)

     (b) The restoration of Israel (Rom. 11:25)

     (c) The manifestation of spiritual gifts (1 Cor. 12:1)

   (2) A repose: "For if we believe that Jesus died and rose again, even so them also which sleep in Jesus will God bring with him" (4:14). The death of a believer is looked upon as a peaceful sleep. (See Matt. 27:52; John 11:11; Acts 7:60; 13:36; 1 Cor. 15:6; 18, 20, 51; 2 Pet. 3:4.) However, it should be quickly stated that this verse in no way teaches soul sleep. That unscriptural doctrine is refuted by Matthew 17:3 and Revelation 6:9-11.

   (3) A revelation: "For this we say unto you by the word of the Lord, that we which are alive and remain unto the coming of the Lord shall not prevent [precede] them which are asleep" (4:15). Note Paul's usage of the pronoun "we." The apostle apparently hoped at this time to be here when Christ came. He would later know otherwise. (See 2 Tim. 4:6.)

   (4) A return: "For the Lord himself shall descend from heaven with a shout, with the voice of the archangel, and with the trump of God" (4:16). It is

often supposed that Michael will be this archangel, on the basis of Daniel 12:1-2. However, it is not unreasonable to suggest that Gabriel will be the angel involved at this time because of the vital part he played in the events surrounding the first coming of Christ. (See Luke 1:19, 26; Matt. 1:20; 2:13.) Note the little phrase "with a shout." This is the final of three instances in which Christ shouted. On each occasion a resurrection took place. The other two are:

(a) The shout at Bethany (John 11:43-44)

(b) The shout at Calvary (Matt. 27:50-53)

(5) A resurrection: "And the dead in Christ shall rise first" (4:16).

(6) A removal: "Then we which are alive and remain shall be caught up together with them in the clouds" (4:17).

(7) A reunion: "To meet the Lord in the air: and so shall we ever be with the Lord" (4:17).

(8) A reassurance: "Wherefore comfort one another with these words" (4:18).

b. 1 Corinthians 15:51-53—In many respects, this passage complements the other major passage in 1 Thessalonians 4. In 1 Thessalonians 4:13-18, the question was whether those who had died in Christ would have the same benefits and experience as those who were translated. In 1 Corinthians 15, the question is whether those who are translated will have the same experience and benefits as those who have died and who are resurrected.

Observe some phrases from 1 Corinthians 15:51-53:

(1) "I shew you a mystery" (15:51)—What is this mystery or secret concerning the Rapture? Let us suppose you began reading the Bible in Genesis 1, and read through 1 Corinthians 14. If you stopped your reading there, you would already have learned about many important facts, such as Creation, man's sin, the flood, Bethlehem, Calvary, the Resurrection, and the existence of heaven and hell. But you would be forced to conclude that a Christian could get to heaven only after physically dying. You would of course note the two exceptions of Enoch (Gen. 5:24) and Elijah (2 Kings 2:11), but apart from these it would be clear that believers have to travel the path of the grave to reach the goal of glory. But now the secret is out, and here it is: Millions of Christians will someday reach heaven without dying. "Behold, I show you a mystery; we shall not all sleep, but we shall all be changed" (1 Cor. 15:51). This, then, is the mystery of the Rapture.

(2) "In a moment, in the twinkling of an eye . . . and we shall be changed" (15:52)—"Moment" here is the Greek word *atomos,* from which we get the word *atom,* and it denotes that which cannot be cut or divided, the smallest conceivable quantity. "Twinkling" is *rhipe,* referring to the fastest movement possible.

(3) "For the trumpet shall sound" (15:52)—In at least three biblical passages concerning the Rapture a trumpet is mentioned (1 Cor. 15:52; 1 Thess. 4:16; Rev. 4:1). How are we to understand this? In the Old Testament the trumpet was used for two things—to summon to battle and to summon to worship. Which of the two meanings, however, is involved at the Rapture? It is suggested that both meanings are in mind, one directed toward angels and the other toward believers.

(a) To angels the trumpet blast will mean "Prepare for battle!" According to various New Testament passages (John 14:30; Eph. 6:12; 1 John 5:19), this present world lies in the hands of the evil one, the devil, and the very atmosphere is filled with his wicked power and presence. Satan will obviously resist believers being caught up through his domain and becoming freed from his wicked worldly system. Therefore, the trumpet commands the angels, "Prepare for battle! Clear the way for the catching up of those resurrected bodies and those living believers!"

(b) To all believers the trumpet blast will mean "Prepare to worship!" In Numbers 10:1-3 we read, "And the Lord spake unto Moses, saying, Make thee two trumpets of silver . . . that thou mayest use them for the calling of the assembly . . . and when they shall blow with them, all the assembly shall assemble themselves to thee at the door of the tabernacle."

Regarding the Rapture trumpet, Numbers 10:4 seems to be especially significant: "If they blow but with one trumpet, then the princes, which are heads of the thousands of Israel, shall gather themselves unto thee." At the Rapture only one trumpet is sounded, suggesting that in God's sight all believers occupy a place of utmost importance. We are all "head princes" in the mind of God.

(4) "For this corruptible must put on incorruption, and this mortal must put on immortality" (15:53)— This describes the supernatural act whereby the bodies of departed believers ("corruptible") will be resurrected, and whereby the bodies of living believers ("mortal") will be transformed.

5. Some false views of the Rapture
   a. The Rapture and Second Coming are one and the same event—Although these two are inseparably linked together, they are not the same. In essence, the Rapture introduces the great tribulation, while the Second Coming will conclude it. Other distinguishing features are:
   (1) The Rapture
      (a) Christ comes in the air (1 Thess. 4:16-17).
      (b) He comes for his saints (1 Thess. 4:16-17).
      (c) The rapture is a mystery, i.e., a truth unknown in Old Testament times (1 Cor. 15:51).
      (d) Christ's coming for his saints is never said to be preceded by signs in the heavens.
      (e) The rapture is identified with the day of Christ (1 Cor. 1:8; 2 Cor. 1:14; Phil. 1:6, 10).
      (f) The rapture is presented as a time of blessing (1 Thess. 4:18).
      (g) The rapture takes place in a moment, "in the twinkling of an eye" (1 Cor. 15:52). This strongly implies that it will not be witnessed by the world.
      (h) The rapture seems to involve the church primarily (John 14:1-4; 1 Cor. 15:51-58; 1 Thess. 4:13-18).
      (i) Christ comes as the bright and morning star (Rev. 22:16).
   (2) The Second Coming
      (a) He comes to the earth (Zech. 14:4).
      (b) He comes with his saints (1 Thess. 3:13; Jude 14).

(c) The revelation is not a mystery; it is the subject of many Old Testament prophecies (Psa. 72; Isa. 11; Zech. 14).

(d) Christ's coming with his saints will be heralded by celestial portents (Matt. 24:29-30).

(e) The revelation is identified with the day of the Lord (2 Thess. 2:1-12, ASV).

(f) The main emphasis of the revelation is on judgment (2 Thess. 2:8-12).

(g) The revelation will be visible worldwide (Matt. 24:27; Rev. 1:7).

(h) The revelation involves Israel primarily, then also the Gentile nations (Matt. 24:1; 25:46).

(i) Christ comes as the sun of righteousness with healing in his wings (Mal. 4:2).

b. The Rapture will include only "spiritual" Christians, leaving carnal believers behind to endure a seven-year "Protestant purgatory" of some sort. Maybe this is what God should do, as it would serve most of us right—but it is not what he is going to do. The Rapture is, in a sense, the proof of redemption, and both are based on grace and not human works. Thus, the partial rapture theory is to be rejected for the following three reasons:

(1) First, it confuses grace with rewards.

(2) Second, it divides the bride of Christ—How can the marriage of the Lamb take place if part of the bride is left on earth?

(3) Third, it ignores the clear scriptural teaching to the contrary (See 1 Thess. 1:9-10; 2:19; 4:14-16; 5:4-11; Rev. 22:12.)—Perhaps the most conclusive evidence against the partial rapture theory is 1 Corinthians 15:51. This church was one of the most carnal in the history of Christianity, yet Paul declares in this verse that if the Rapture occurred in their day, *all* of the saved in that church would be raptured.

c. The Rapture will not occur until the middle of the tribulation, thus forcing the entire church to go through the first three and a half years of God's wrath. This theory is called mid-tribulationism. However, this seems to be refuted by 1 Thessalonians 5:9. "For God hath not appointed us to wrath, but to obtain salvation by our Lord Jesus Christ."

The New Testament pictures the church as the body and bride of Christ. If the mid-tribulation or post-tribulation view were correct, then a part of his body would suffer amputation, and a section of the bride would be left behind. In addition to this, one would be forced to conclude that all bodies of carnal departed Christians would likewise be left in the grave. This simply is not the clear teaching of the Word of God.

The Bible teaches clearly that the Rapture is pretribulational in nature and includes all believers. (See 1 Thess. 1:10 and Rom. 5:9.) Perhaps the strongest proof of this statement is the fact that up to chapter 6 of Revelation the church is mentioned many times, but from chapter 6 to chapter 19 (the period of the tribulation) there is no mention whatsoever of the church on earth. In fact, the only godly group Satan can find to persecute is the nation Israel. (See Rev. 12.) In Revelation 4:1 John declares, "After this I looked, and, behold, a door was opened in heaven: and the first voice which I heard was as it were of a trumpet talking with me; which said, Come up hither." We are told that Christians are God's ambassadors on earth (2 Cor. 5:20) and that he will someday declare war on this earth. The first thing a king or president does after he declares war on another country is to call his ambassadors home. Thus, we conclude that the church will escape the tribulation.

6. The Old Testament foreshadowing of the Rapture
   a. Seen in Enoch, who was taken from the world before the flood judgment (Gen. 5:24)
   b. Seen in Lot, who was taken from Sodom before the fire judgment (Gen. 19:22-24)

7. The challenges of the Rapture—Because of this glorious coming event, the child of God is instructed to do many things.
   a. He is to attend the services of the Lord's house regularly—"Not forsaking the assembling of ourselves together, as the manner of some is; but exhorting one another; and so much the more, as ye see the day approaching" (Heb. 10:25).
   b. He is to observe the Lord's Supper with the Rapture in mind—"For as often as ye eat this bread, and drink this cup, ye do show the Lord's death till he come" (1 Cor. 11:26).
   c. He is to love believers and all men—"And the Lord make you to increase and abound in love one toward another, and toward all men, even as we do toward you: To the end he may stablish your hearts unblamable in holiness before God, even our Father, at the coming of our Lord Jesus Christ with all his saints" (1 Thess. 3:12-13).
   d. He is to be patient—"Be ye also patient; stablish your hearts: for the coming of the Lord draweth nigh" (James 5:8).
   e. He is to live a separated life—"Beloved, now are we the sons of God, and it doth not yet appear what we shall be: but we know that, when he shall appear, we shall be like him; for we shall see him as he is. And every man that hath this hope in him purifieth himself, even as he is pure" (1 John 3:2-3).

   "Teaching us that, denying ungodliness and worldly lusts, we should live soberly, righteously, and godly, in this present world; Looking for that blessed hope, and the glorious appearing of the great God and our Saviour Jesus Christ" (Titus 2:12-13). "And now, little children, abide in him; that, when he shall appear, we may have confidence, and not be ashamed before him at his coming" (1 John 2:28).
   f. He is to refrain from judging others—"Therefore judge nothing before the time, until the Lord come, who both will bring to light the hidden things of darkness, and will make manifest the counsels of the hearts: and then shall every man have praise of God" (1 Cor. 4:5).
   g. He is to preach the Word—"I charge thee therefore before God, and the Lord Jesus Christ, who shall judge the quick and the dead at his appearing and his kingdom; Preach the word; be instant in season, out of season; reprove, rebuke, exhort with all longsuffering and doctrine" (2 Tim. 4:1-2). "Feed the flock of God which is among you, taking the oversight thereof, not by constraint, but willingly; not for filthy lucre, but of a ready mind. . . . And when the chief Shepherd shall appear, ye shall receive a crown of glory that fadeth not away" (1 Pet. 5:2, 4).
   h. He is to comfort the bereaved—"For the Lord himself shall descend from

heaven with a shout, with the voice of the archangel, and with the trump of God: and the dead in Christ shall rise first" (1 Thess. 4:16).

    i. He is to win souls—"Keep yourselves in the love of God, looking for the mercy of our Lord Jesus Christ unto eternal life. And of some have compassion, making a difference: And others save with fear, pulling them out of the fire; hating even the garment spotted by the flesh" (Jude 21-23).

    j. He is to be concerned with heaven—"If ye then be risen with Christ, seek those things which are above, where Christ sitteth on the right hand of God. Set your affection on things above, not on things on the earth. For ye are dead, and your life is hid with Christ in God. When Christ, who is our life, shall appear, then shall ye also appear with him in glory" (Col. 3:1-4).

8. The event that may trigger the Rapture—Does anything have to happen before the Rapture can take place and this glorious change be effected? The surprising answer seems to be yes. One final event must transpire, and that event is the adding of the last repenting sinner into the body of Christ by the Holy Spirit. Thus, when the body is complete, the Head will appear, or, to use another scriptural analogy, the Bridegroom will come for his beloved bride. The entire book of Ephesians seems to suggest this. See especially 1:10, 22-23; 2:21; 4:4, 13, 16; 5:22-33.

    A very practical truth may be seen here. According to Acts 2, the first convert was added to the body of Christ at Pentecost. What an occasion that must have been, with 3,000 answering Peter's "altar call." And God had provided 120 "personal workers" to deal with them (Acts 1:15; 2:1). We know that God himself keeps all the records. Perhaps someday at the judgment seat of Christ one of these 120 will hear the Master say: "Well done, thou good and faithful servant. You led the first individual into that spiritual body!" If this be true, and if Christ's coming is at hand, it is entirely possible that a soul winner reading these very words might one day hear similar words from Jesus: "Well done, thou good and faithful servant. You led the last individual into that spiritual body!" At any rate, someday a soul winner will point some seeking sinner to the Savior, and it will all be over.

    In closing our study on the Rapture, consider the words of German theologian Erich Sauer:

> The present age is Easter time. It begins with the resurrection of the Redeemer (Matt. 28), and ends with the resurrection of redeemed (1 Thess. 4; 1 Cor. 15). Between lies the spiritual "resurrection" of those called into life (Rom. 6:4-11; Col. 3:1). So we live between two Easters, as those who have been raised between two resurrections, as burning and shining lights. . . . And in the power of the First Easter we go to meet the Last Easter. The resurrection of the Head guarantees the resurrection of the members. The tree of life of the resurrection bears fully ripe fruit. (*The Triumph of the Crucified*, p. 101)

B. The bema judgment seat of Christ

    1. The fact of the bema judgment—Many New Testament verses speak of this. "But why dost thou judge thy brother? or why dost thou set at nought thy brother? for we shall all stand before the judgment seat of Christ. For it is written, As I live, saith the Lord, every knee shall bow to me, and every tongue shall confess to God. So then every one of us shall give account of himself to

God" (Rom. 14:10-12). "Every man's work shall be made manifest: for the day shall declare it" (1 Cor. 3:13). "For we must all appear before the judgment seat of Christ" (2 Cor. 5:10). (To these passages could be added Gal. 6:7; Col. 3:24-25; Heb. 10:30.)

2. The meaning of the bema judgment

The Greek word *bema* (translated "judgment seat" in the KJV) was a familiar term to the people of Paul's day. Dr. Lehman Strauss writes:

> In the large Olympic arenas, there was an elevated seat on which the judge of the contest sat. After the contests were over, the successful competitors would assemble before the *bema* to receive their rewards or crowns. The *bema* was not a judicial bench where someone was condemned; it was a reward seat. Likewise, the Judgment Seat of Christ is not a judicial bench. The Christian life is a race, and the divine umpire is watching every contestant. After the church has run her course, He will gather every member before the *bema* for the purpose of examining each one and giving the proper reward to each. (*God's Plan for the Future*, p. 111)

The Apostle Paul seemed to have such an Olympic arena in mind when he penned Hebrews 12:1: "Wherefore seeing we also are compassed about with so great a cloud of witnesses, let us lay aside every weight, and the sin which doth so easily beset us, and let us run with patience the race that is set before us."

This amazing human being was many things. He was a missionary, a soul winner, a pastor, a great theologian, a tentmaker, etc. But in his spare time he also seemed to be a sports lover. Often in his writings Paul used sports as an analogy to get his point across. For example:

a. Wrestling—"For we wrestle not against flesh and blood, but against principalities, against powers, against the rulers of the darkness of this world, against spiritual wickedness in high places" (Eph. 6:12).

b. Boxing—"I have fought a good fight" (2 Tim. 4:7). "So fight I, not as one that beateth the air" (1 Cor. 9:26).

c. Racing—"Know ye not that they which run in a race run all, but one receiveth the prize? So run that ye may obtain. . . . I therefore so run" (1 Cor. 9:24, 26). Here in Hebrews 12 Paul chooses the third analogy—that of a foot race. This chapter may be titled God's Superbowl. J. Vernon McGee writes: "The Christian life is likened to a Greek race. Along the way the Christian as a soldier is to stand, as a believer he is to walk, and as an athlete he is to run. One day he will fly—space travel to the New Jerusalem" (*Studies in Hebrews*, p. 240).

At the time Paul wrote, King Herod had built a thronelike seat in the theater at Caesarea (his headquarters), where he sat to view the games and make speeches to the people.

3. The purpose of the bema judgment.

a. Negative considerations.

(1) The purpose of the bema judgment is not to determine whether a particular individual enters heaven or not, for every man's eternal destiny is already determined before he leaves this life.

(2) The purpose of the bema judgment is not to punish believers for sins committed either before or after their salvation. The Scriptures are very clear that no child of God will have to answer for his sins after this life.

"He hath not dealt with us after our sins; nor rewarded us according to our iniquities. For as the heaven is high above the earth, so great is his mercy toward them that fear him. As far as the east is from the west, so far hath he removed our transgressions from us" (Psa. 103:10-12).

"Behold, for peace I had great bitterness: but thou hast in love to my soul delivered it from the pit of corruption: for thou hast cast all my sins behind thy back" (Isa. 38:17). "I have blotted out . . . thy transgressions and . . . thy sins" (Isa. 44:22). "Thou wilt cast all their sins into the depths of the sea" (Mic. 7:19).

"For I will be merciful . . . and their sins and their iniquities will I remember no more" (Heb. 8:12). "The blood of Jesus Christ his Son cleanseth us from all sin" (1 John 1:7).

  b. Positive considerations—What then is the purpose of the *bema* judgment? In 1 Corinthians 4:2 Paul says that all Christians should conduct themselves as faithful stewards of God: "Moreover it is required in stewards, that a man be found faithful." The Apostle Peter later writes in a similar way: "Minister . . . as good stewards of the manifold grace of God" (1 Pet. 4:10).

  In the New Testament world, a steward was the manager of a large household or estate. He was appointed by the owner and was entrusted to keep the estate running smoothly. He had the power to hire and fire and to spend and save, being answerable to the owner alone. His only concern was that periodic meeting with his master, at which time he was required to give account for the condition of the estate up to that point. With this background in mind, it may be said that someday at the bema judgment all stewards will stand before their Lord and Master and be required to give an accounting of the way they have used their privileges and abilities from the moment of their conversion.

  In conclusion, it can be seen that:
  (1) In the past, God dealt with us as sinners (Rom. 5:6-8; 1 Cor. 6:9-11; Eph. 2:1-3).
  (2) In the present, God deals with us as sons (Rom. 8:14; Heb. 12:5-11; 1 John 3:1-2).
  (3) In the future, God will deal with us (at the bema) as stewards.
4. The materials to be tested at the bema judgment—In 1 Corinthians 3:11 the Apostle Paul explains the glorious fact that at the moment of salvation a repenting sinner is firmly placed on the foundation of the death, burial, and resurrection of Christ himself. His continuing instruction after his salvation is to rise up and build upon this foundation.

  Paul says, "But let every man take heed how he buildeth thereupon. . . . Now if any man build upon this foundation gold, silver, precious stones, wood, hay, stubble; every man's work shall be made manifest: for the day shall declare it, because it shall be revealed by fire; and the fire shall try every man's work of what sort it is" (1 Cor. 3:10, 12-13).

  a. Negative considerations—It should be noted immediately that this passage does not teach the false doctrine known as purgatory, for it is the believer's works and not the believer himself that will be subjected to the fires.

  b. Positive considerations—From these verses it is apparent that God classifies the works of believers into one of the following six areas: gold, silver, precious stones, wood, hay, stubble. There has been much speculation about the kinds of work down here that will constitute gold or silver up there. But it seems more appropriate to note that the six objects can be readily placed into two categories: Those indestructible and worthy objects that will survive and thrive in the fires: gold, silver, and precious stones. Those destructible and worthless objects that will be totally consumed in the fires: wood, hay, and stubble. Thus, what the fire cannot purify, it destroys, and what the fire cannot destroy, it purifies.

Though it is difficult to know just what goes to make up a "golden work" or a "stubble work," we are nevertheless informed of certain general areas in which God is particularly interested.

(1) How we treat other believers—"For God is not unrighteous to forget your work and labour of love, which ye have showed toward his name, in that ye have ministered to the saints, and do minister" (Heb. 6:10; see also Matt. 10:41-42). It is tragic but all too factual that often the shabbiest treatment suffered by a believer comes from the hand of another believer.

(2) How we exercise our authority over others—"Obey them that have the rule over you, and submit yourselves: for they watch for your souls, as they that must give account, that they may do it with joy, and not with grief: for that is unprofitable for you" (Heb. 13:7; see also James 3:1). Almost every Christian at one time or another has had a measure of authority over another believer. This leadership role may have been that of a parent, pastor, teacher, employer, etc. It has been remarked that while some grow with authority, others simply swell.

(3) How we employ our God-given abilities—"Now there are varieties of gifts, but the same Spirit. . . . But one and the same Spirit works all these things, distributing to each one individually just as He wills" (1 Cor. 12:4, 11, NASB). "Wherefore I put thee in remembrance that thou stir up the gift of God, which is in thee" (2 Tim. 1:6). "As each one has received a special gift, employ it in serving one another, as good stewards of the manifold grace of God" (1 Pet. 4:10, NASB).

To these verses can be added the overall teaching of Jesus' parables of the 10 pounds (Luke 19:11-26) and the eight talents (Matt. 25:14-29). A spiritual gift is a supernatural ability to glorify God, given by the Holy Spirit to the believer at the moment of salvation. Each Christian has at least one gift (1 Cor. 7:7; 12:7, 11; Eph. 4:7; 1 Pet. 4:10). There are 18 of these gifts (Rom. 12; 1 Cor. 12; Eph. 4). Thus, it is vital for every child of God to discover and employ his own gift, in light of the bema.

(4) How we use our money—"Upon the first day of the week let every one of you lay by him in store, as God hath prospered him, that there be no gatherings when I come" (1 Cor. 16:2; see also 2 Cor. 9:6-7; 1 Tim. 6:17-19).

Perhaps the most accurate barometer to measure the spiritual condition of a Christian is to observe his or her relationship concerning money. Jesus himself often dealt with money matters, because money matters. In the New Testament there are some 38 parables. Twelve of them are about money. How much of our money belongs to God? According to 1 Corinthians 6:19-20 it all belongs to him, because we are his, purchased with an awesome price (1 Pet. 1:18-19). What does all this mean? It means that if I gross $250 per week, I am not only responsible for the tithe ($25) but I will, at the *bema,* be held accountable concerning the remaining $225.

(5) How we spend our time—"So teach us to number our days, that we may apply our hearts unto wisdom" (Psa. 90:12). "Redeeming the time, because the days are evil" (Eph. 5:16). "Walk in wisdom . . . redeeming the time" (Col. 4:5). "And if ye call on the Father, who without respect of persons judgeth according to every man's work, pass the time of your sojourning here in fear" (1 Pet. 1:17).

(6) How much we suffer for Jesus—"Blessed are ye, when men shall revile you, and persecute you, and shall say all manner of evil against you falsely, for my sake. Rejoice, and be exceeding glad: for great is your reward in heaven: for so persecuted they the prophets which were before you" (Matt. 5:11-12; see also Mark 10:29-30; Rom. 8:18; 2 Cor. 4:17; 1 Pet. 4:12-13).

(7) How we run that particular race which God has chosen for us—"Know ye not that they which run in a race run all, but one receiveth the prize? So run, that ye may obtain" (1 Cor. 9:24). "Let us lay aside every weight, and the sin which doth so easily beset us, and let us run with patience the race that is set before us" (Heb. 12:1).

Especially to be observed are the words found in Hebrews 12:1. Note the implications of this statement: Every believer has been entered in this race by God himself. It is not just for pastors and missionaries. Note: The usual word for race (*dromos*) is not used here, but rather the Greek word *agon,* from which we get our English word agony. This is a serious race. The pace of each runner is set by God. The object of the race is to please God and win rewards. Its goal is not heaven. Every runner is expected to win.

(8) How effectively we control the old nature—"And every man that striveth for the mastery is temperate in all things. Now they do it to obtain a corruptible crown; but we an incorruptible. I therefore so run, not as uncertainly; so fight I, not as one that beateth the air: But I keep under my body, and bring it into subjection: lest that by any means, when I have preached to others, I myself should be a castaway" (1 Cor. 9:25-27).

The Greek word for "castaway" here (*adoimos*) means disapproved. Without the *a* prefix it speaks of approval. A key passage where *doimos* is used can be seen in 2 Timothy 2:15: "Study to shew thyself approved unto God." (See also 1 Cor. 16:3; Phil.1:10; 1 Thess. 2:4, where the identical word is used.) The point of the above is that Paul desired above all things to keep his old nature in check, lest he be disapproved of, reward-wise, at the bema.

(9) How many souls we witness to and win to Christ—"The fruit of the righteous is a tree of life; and he that winneth souls is wise" (Prov. 11:30). "And they that be wise shall shine as the brightness of the firmament; and they that turn many to righteousness as the stars for ever and ever" (Dan. 12:3).

(10) How we react to temptation—"My brethren, count it all joy when ye fall into divers temptations; Knowing this, that the trying of your faith worketh patience" (James 1:2-3). "Fear none of those things which thou shalt suffer: behold, the devil shall cast some of you into prison, that ye

may be tried; and ye shall have tribulation ten days: be thou faithful unto death, and I will give thee a crown of life" (Rev. 2:10).

(11) How much the doctrine of the Rapture means to us—"Henceforth there is laid up for me a crown of righteousness, which the Lord, the righteous judge, shall give me at that day: and not to me only, but unto all them also that love his appearing" (2 Tim. 4:8).

(12) How faithful we are to the Word of God and the flock of God—"Feed the flock of God which is among you, taking the oversight thereof, not by constraint, but willingly; not for filthy lucre, but of a ready mind; Neither as being lords over God's heritage, but being ensamples to the flock. And when the chief Shepherd shall appear, ye shall receive a crown of glory that fadeth not away" (1 Pet. 5:2-4; see also Acts 20:26-28; 2 Tim. 4:1-2).

5. The results of the bema judgment seat of Christ—Some will receive rewards. "If any man's work abide which he hath built thereupon, he shall receive a reward" (1 Cor. 3:14).

The Bible mentions at least five rewards. These are:

(1) The incorruptible crown—given to those who master the old nature

(2) The crown of rejoicing—given to soul winners (Prov. 11:30; Dan. 12:3; 1 Thess. 2:19-20)

(3) The crown of life—given to those who successfully endure temptation (James 1:2-3; Rev. 2:10)

(4) The crown of righteousness—given to those who especially love the doctrine of the Rapture (2 Tim. 4:8)

(5) The crown of glory—given to faithful preachers and teachers (Acts 20:26-28; 2 Tim. 4:1-2; 1 Pet. 5:2-4). It has been suggested that these "crowns" will actually be talents and abilities with which to glorify Christ. Thus, the greater the reward, the greater the ability.

6. The Old Testament foreshadowing of the bema judgment seat of Christ— Although the church is nowhere mentioned in the Old Testament, there is nevertheless a passage that can very easily be applied to the bema judgment. This can be found in the words of Boaz (a foreshadowing of Christ) to Ruth (a foreshadowing of the church) when he says, "It hath fully been shewed me, all that thou hast done. . . . The Lord recompense thy work, and a full reward be given thee of the Lord God of Israel, under whose wings thou art come to trust" (Ruth 2:11-12).

C. The marriage service of the Lamb—A number of weddings are described in the Bible. The first was performed by a very special guest minister. Whatever religious ceremony he may have chosen, it did not include those familiar words: "If any man can show just cause why these two should not be lawfully joined together, let him now speak, or else forever hold his peace." This phrase was unnecessary, for the minister was God himself, and the couple was Adam and Eve (Gen. 2:18-25).

Then there was a very unusual wedding in which the bridegroom found out the next morning, by light of day, that he had married the wrong girl (Gen. 29:21-25). One of the most beautiful wedding stories began in a barley field outside the little town of Bethlehem (Ruth 2). Perhaps the most tragic wedding was that between Ahab, King of Israel, and Jezebel, a godless Baal worshipper. This marriage would result in much sorrow and suffering for God's people (1 Kings 16:29-31). Finally, the

Savior of men chose a wedding in the city of Cana to perform his first miracle (John 2:1-11).

However, the most fantastic and wonderful wedding of all time is yet to take place.

1. The fact of this marriage
   a. This marriage is described through the parables of Jesus—"The kingdom of heaven is like unto a certain king, which made a marriage for his son" (Matt. 22:2). "Then shall the kingdom of heaven be likened unto ten virgins, which took their lamps, and went forth to meet the bridegroom" (Matt. 25:1). "Let your loins be girded about, and your lights burning; and ye yourselves like unto men that wait for their lord, when he will return from the wedding; that when he cometh and knocketh, they may open unto him immediately" (Luke 12:35-36).
   b. This marriage is described through the vision of John—"Let us be glad and rejoice, and give honour to him: for the marriage of the Lamb is come, and his wife hath made herself ready" (Rev. 19:7).

2. The Host of the marriage—The New Testament very clearly presents the Father as the divine Host who gives this marriage. He is pictured as preparing it, then sending his servants out to invite the selected guests (Luke 14:16-23).

3. The Bridegroom of the marriage—The Father's beloved Son (Matt. 3:17; 17:5), the Lord Jesus, is the Bridegroom.
   a. As stated by John the Baptist (John 3:27-30)
   b. As stated by Jesus (Luke 5:32-35)

4. The bride of the marriage—"For I am jealous over you with godly jealousy: for I have espoused you to one husband, that I may present you as a chaste virgin to Christ" (2 Cor. 11:2). "For the husband is the head of the wife, even as Christ is the head of the church: and he is the saviour of the body. Husbands, love your wives, even as Christ also loved the church, and gave himself for it" (Eph. 5:23, 25).

5. The guests of the marriage—"And he saith unto me, Write, blessed are they which are called unto the marriage supper of the Lamb" (Rev. 19:9).
   Who are these invited guests of the Lamb's marriage to the church?
   a. In general—A group that would include all believing Gentiles who were converted prior to Pentecost or after the Rapture. This is so, for all those individuals saved between the day of Pentecost and the Rapture make up the bride of Christ at this wedding.
   b. In particular—A group that would include all saved Israelites everywhere. The 10 virgins mentioned in Matthew 25 are Israelites; the 5 wise represent saved Israelites, and the 5 foolish represent unsaved ones. They cannot represent the church, for the church is the bride, inside with the Bridegroom. The virgins are guests who have been invited to the wedding. Note that a bride is never invited to her own wedding. If she refuses to come, there is no wedding.

6. The service schedule of the marriage—The marriage of Christ to the church will follow the oriental pattern of marriage as described for us in the New Testament. It consisted of three separate stages:
   a. The betrothal stage—New Testament marriage contracts were often initiated when the couple was very young (sometimes even prior to birth) by the groom's father. He would sign a legal enactment before the proper judge,

pledging his son to a chosen girl. The father would then offer the proper dowry payment. Thus, even though the bride had never seen the groom, she was nevertheless betrothed or espoused to him. A New Testament example of this first step is the marriage of Mary and Joseph. "Now the birth of Jesus Christ was on this wise: When as his mother Mary was espoused to Joseph, before they came together, she was found with child of the Holy Ghost" (Matt. 1:18).

Both Mary and Joseph had come from Bethlehem and had perhaps been betrothed, or promised to each other, since childhood. But now Mary was found to be with child before the marriage could be consummated, and of course Joseph could arrive at only one conclusion—she had been untrue to him. Then the angel of the Lord explained to Joseph the glories of the Virgin Birth. Thus the betrothal stage consisted of two steps: The selection of the bride and the payment of the dowry. With this in mind we can state that the marriage of the Lamb is still in its betrothal stage

(1) The bride had been selected—"Blessed be the God and Father of our Lord Jesus Christ, who hath blessed us with all spiritual blessings in heavenly places in Christ: According as he hath chosen us in him before the foundation of the world, that we should be holy and without blame before him in love" (Eph. 1:3-4).

(2) The dowry had been paid—"What? know ye not that your body is the temple of the Holy Ghost which is in you, which ye have of God, and ye are not your own? For ye are bought with a price: therefore glorify God in your body, and in your spirit, which are God's" (1 Cor. 6:19-20). "Forasmuch as ye know that ye were not redeemed with corruptible things, as silver and gold, from your vain conversation received by tradition from your fathers; but with the precious blood of Christ, as of a lamb without blemish and without spot" (1 Pet. 1:18-19).

b. The presentation stage—At the proper time the father would send to the house of the bride servants carrying the proper legal contract. The bride would then be led to the home of the groom's father. When all was ready, the father of the bride would place her hand in the hand of the groom's father. He would then place her hand in that of his son. Applying this background to the marriage of the Lamb, the church still awaits this second phase, the presentation stage, which we know as the Rapture.

Note now the events involved in the second stage:

(1) The heavenly Father will send for the bride—"After this I looked, and, behold, a door was opened in heaven: and the first voice which I heard was as it were of a trumpet talking with me; which said, Come up hither" (Rev. 4:1).

(2) The proper legal papers of marriage will be shown—"Nevertheless the foundation of God standeth sure, having this seal, The Lord knoweth them that are his. And, Let every one that nameth the name of Christ depart from iniquity" (2 Tim. 2:19).

(3) The bride will be taken to the Father's home—"In my Father's house are many mansions: if it were not so, I would have told you. I go to prepare a place for you. And if I go and prepare a place for you, I will come again, and receive you unto myself; that where I am, there ye may be also" (John 14:2-3).

c. The celebration stage—After the private marriage service was completed, the public marriage supper would begin. Many guests would be invited to this celebration. It was during such a supper that our Lord performed his first miracle, that of changing water into wine (see John 2:1-11). Jesus later made reference to this third step when he spoke the following words: "Then said he unto him, A certain man made a great supper, and bade many: And sent his servant at supper time to say to them that were bidden, Come; for all things are now ready" (Luke 14:16-17).

7. The time of the marriage—When does the wedding transpire? In view of what has already been said, it would seem that the wedding service (the presentation stage) will be privately conducted in heaven, perhaps shortly after the bema judgment seat of Christ. The wedding supper (the celebration stage) will be publicly conducted on earth shortly after the second coming of Christ.

It is no accident that the Bible describes the Millennium as occurring right after the celebration supper has begun. (The supper is described in Rev. 19, while the Millennium is described in Rev. 20.) In New Testament times the length and cost of this supper was determined by the wealth of the father. Therefore, when his beloved Son is married, the Father of all grace (whose wealth is unlimited) will rise to the occasion by giving his Son and the bride a hallelujah celebration that will last for a thousand years.

8. The certainty of the marriage—Earthly marriages may be prevented because of various unexpected problems.

a. In an earthly wedding there can be a last-minute refusal on the part of either the bride or groom, but not with the heavenly marriage.

(1) The Bridegroom has already expressed his great love for his bride (Eph. 5:25), and he never changes. "Which also said, Ye men of Galilee, why stand ye gazing up into heaven? this same Jesus, which is taken up from you into heaven, shall so come in like manner as ye have seen him go into heaven." (Acts 1:11). "Jesus Christ, the same yesterday, and today, and forever" (Heb. 13:8).

(2) The bride has already been glorified and is sinless, and therefore cannot be tempted into changing her mind or losing her love for the Bridegroom. "A glorious church, not having spot, or wrinkle . . . but . . . holy and without blemish" (Eph. 5:27). "For by one offering he hath perfected forever them that are sanctified" (Heb. 10:14).

b. In an earthly wedding a serious legal problem might arise, such as lack of age, or even that of a previous marriage, but not in the heavenly wedding (see Rom. 8:33-39).

c. In an earthly wedding the tragedy of death might intervene, but not in the heavenly wedding.

(1) The bride will never die—"And whosoever liveth and believeth in me shall never die. Believest thou this?" (John 11:26).

(2) The Bridegroom will never die—"I am he that liveth, and was dead; and, behold, I am alive for evermore, Amen; and have the keys of hell and of death" (Rev. 1:18).

D. The singing of two special songs—The events described here in Revelation 4–5 are all too often overlooked in the study of prophecy. This is unfortunate, for the account records two songs which in themselves summarize God's two great works, that of Creation and redemption.

1. The Creation hymn of worship (Rev. 4)
   a. The place (4:1)—John the apostle has been caught up into heaven where he writes about the marvelous things he sees and hears.
   b. The persons
      (1) He sees the Father—"And immediately I was in the spirit; and, behold, a throne was set in heaven, and one sat on the throne. And he that sat was to look upon like a jasper and a sardine stone: and there was a rainbow round about the throne, in sight like unto an emerald" (Rev. 4:2-3).

      Here the jasper, a white stone, and the sardine, a fiery red stone, may refer to God's two basic characteristics: his glory and his grace. These were also the first and last stones among the 12 that the Old Testament high priest bore upon his breastplate. These stones represented the 12 tribes of Israel, arranged according to the births of the 12 sons of Jacob (Exod. 28). Reuben was the first tribe, which name meant "Behold a son," and Benjamin was the last, meaning "Son of my right hand." This then may be God's way of reminding all creatures throughout eternity of:
      (a) The incarnation of Christ (his humanity) via the jasper stone, Reuben, "Behold a son."
      (b) The exaltation of Christ (his deity) via the sardine stone, Benjamin, "Son of my right hand."
      (2) He sees 24 with golden crowns (Rev.4:4). These 24 may consist of a special representative body of both Old Testament and New Testament saints. The Greek text tells us they are all wearing *stephanos* crowns, or martyrs' crowns, rather than diadems, or monarchs' crowns. Thus they must be humans rather than angels.

      He sees and hears lightnings and thunderings, which means that the awful storm of the great tribulation is about to unleash its fury (Rev. 4:5). He sees a crystal sea of glass (Rev. 4:6). This is a reference to the brazen laver (a basin filled with water) found both in the tabernacle and temple for the cleansing of the priests. Donald Barnhouse writes:

      > Here the priests came for their cleansing. Each time before they entered the holy place they stopped for the cleansing ceremony. But thank God the laver will be turned to crystal. The day will come when none of the saints will ever need confession. One of the greatest joys in the anticipation of Heaven is that the laver is of crystal. I shall never have to go to the Heavenly Father again to tell Him I have sinned. I shall never have to meet that gaze of Christ that caused Peter to go out and weep bitterly. The laver is of crystal only because I and all the saints of all the ages will have been made like unto the Lord Jesus Christ. (*Revelation: An Expository Commentary*, p. 94)

      (3) He sees and hears the testimony of four special angelic creatures (Rev. 4:6-8). The first of the creatures had the characteristics of a lion, the second of a calf, the third of a man, and the fourth of an eagle. It is possible that these beings are the same as described by Ezekiel, the Old Testament prophet (see Ezek. 1). In chapter 10 he identified what he previously saw as the cherubims (10:20-22). Some believe these four creatures may have inherited Lucifer's responsibilities after his terrible rebellion against God (see Isa. 14:12-15; Ezek. 28:11-19). At any rate, there

is a definite similarity between the appearance of the four living creatures and the manner by which the four Gospel writers present the earthly ministry of Christ. For example: Matthew presents Christ as the Lion of the tribe of Judah. Mark pictures him as the lowly ox. Luke describes the Savior as the perfect man. John paints him to be the lofty eagle. Thus by their very features, these four heavenly beings may serve to remind redeemed sinners throughout all eternity of the Savior's blessed earthly ministry.

    c. The praises—"The four and twenty elders fall down before him that sat on the throne, and worship him that liveth for ever and ever, and cast their crowns before the throne, saying, Thou art worthy, O Lord, to receive glory and honour and power: for thou hast created all things, and for thy pleasure they are and were created" (Rev. 4:10-11).

    This then, is the backdrop for the singing of the first song, praising God for his work of Creation.

2. The redemption hymn of worship (Rev. 5)

    a. The proclamation—"And I saw in the right hand of him that sat on the throne a book written within and on the backside, sealed with seven seals. And I saw a strong angel proclaiming with a loud voice, Who is worthy to open the book, and to loose the seals thereof?" (Rev. 5:1-2).

    What is this book (really a rolled-up scroll), sealed so securely with seven seals? Whatever it contained, the scroll was extremely important, for history informs us that under Roman law all legal documents pertaining to life and death were to be sealed seven times. A number of theologians believe that this is actually the legal title deed to the earth. Thus the angel's proclamation was, in effect, "Who is worthy to reclaim the earth's title deed? Who is able to pour out the seven-sealed judgment, to purify this planet, and to usher in the long-awaited golden-age Millennium?" Who indeed was worthy?

    b. The investigation—"And no man in heaven, nor in earth, neither under the earth, was able to open the book, neither to look thereon" (Rev. 5:3).

      (1) The search in heaven—Was there any among the redeemed worthy to claim the earth's title deed? There was not.

        (a) Adam originally possessed this title deed (Gen. 1:28-29), but was cheated out of it by the devil (Gen 3:1-19).

        (b) Noah, the hero of the flood, subsequently became the drunkard of the vineyard, thus disqualifying himself (Gen. 6–9).

        (c) Abraham, the father of Israel, backslid and went to Egypt temporarily (Gen. 12).

        (d) David, the man after God's own heart (1 Sam. 16:7), later broke God's heart through lust and murder (2 Sam. 11).

        (e) John the Baptist, the forerunner of Christ, in a moment of weakness doubted that same Messiah (Matt. 11:3).

        (f) Peter, the "rock," denied his Lord in the hour of need (Matt. 26:70).

        (g) Paul, perhaps the greatest Christian who ever lived, compromised his testimony (Acts 21).

      (2) The search on earth—Who could accomplish in the sinful environment of earth what no man could achieve even in the sinless environment of heaven? Preachers and priests might minister to the earth, and kings rule over sections of it, but claim it they could not.

(3) The search under the earth (in hades)—If no saint or angel could purify this earth, then certainly no sinner or demon would, even if this were possible.

c. The lamentation—"And I wept much, because no man was found worthy to open and to read the book, neither to look thereon" (Rev. 5:4). Why did John weep? Perhaps because (among other things) he realized that the ultimate resurrection and glorification of his own body was directly connected with the removal of the curse placed upon this earth. (See Rom. 8:17-23.)

d. The manifestation—"And one of the elders saith unto me, Weep not: behold, the Lion of the tribe of Judah, the Root of David, hath prevailed to open the book, and to loose the seven seals thereof. And I beheld, and, lo, in the midst of the throne and of the four beasts, and in the midst of the elders, stood a Lamb as it had been slain, having seven horns and seven eyes, which are the seven Spirits of God sent forth into all the earth. And he came and took the book out of the right hand of him that sat upon the throne" (Rev. 5:5-7).

Who is this heavenly hero who so boldly removes the scroll from the Father's right hand? We need not speculate for one second about his identity, for he is the Lord Jesus Christ himself. The proof is overwhelming.

Thus John sees Christ as a lamb, since he once came to redeem his people. This was his past work. John also sees him as a lion, for he shall come again to reign over his people. This will be his future work. The source of his claim to the earth's scepter is therefore related to his slain-lamb characteristics, while the strength of his claim is due to his mighty lion characteristics.

We are now given the words to the next song. "And they sung a new song, saying, Thou art worthy to take the book, and to open the seals thereof: for thou wast slain, and hast redeemed us to God by thy blood out of every kindred, and tongue, and people, and nation; and hast made us unto our God kings and priests: and we shall reign on the earth" (Rev. 5:9-10).

e. The adoration—"And I beheld, and I heard the voice of many angels round about the throne and the beasts and the elders: and the number of them was ten thousand times ten thousand, and thousands of thousands; saying with a loud voice, Worthy is the Lamb that was slain to receive power, and riches, and wisdom, and strength, and honour, and glory, and blessing. And every creature which is in heaven, and on the earth, and under the earth, and such as are in the sea, and all that are in them, heard I saying, Blessing, and honour, and glory, and power, be unto him that sitteth upon the throne, and unto the Lamb for ever and ever" (Rev. 5:11-13).

E. The great tribulation—"For then shall be great tribulation, such as was not since the beginning of the world to this time, no, nor ever shall be. Immediately after the tribulation of those days shall the sun be darkened, and the moon shall not give her light, and the stars shall fall from heaven, and the powers of the heavens shall be shaken" (Matt. 24:21, 29).

1. The names for this period—No less than 12 titles for this blood-chilling period can be found in the Bible. These are:

a. The Day of the Lord—This title is used more frequently than any other. See, for example, Isaiah 2:12; 13:6, 9; Ezekiel 13:5; 30:3; Joel 1:15; 2:1, 11, 31; 3:14; Amos 5:18, 20; Obadiah 15; Zephaniah 1:7, 14; Zechariah 14:1; Malachi 4:5;

Acts 2:20; 1 Thessalonians 5:2; 2 Thessalonians 2:2; 2 Peter 3:10. A distinction should be made between the Day of the Lord and the day of Christ. The day of Christ is a reference to the Millennium. See 1 Corinthians 1:8; 5:5; 2 Corinthians 1:14; Philippians 1:6, 10; 2:16.

b. The indignation (Isa. 26:20; 34:2)

c. The day of God's vengeance (Isa. 34:8; 63:1-6)

d. The time of Jacob's trouble (Jer. 30:7)

e. The overspreading of abominations (Dan. 9:27)

f. The time of trouble such as never was (Dan. 12:1)

g. The seventieth week (Dan. 9:24-27)

h. The time of the end (Dan. 12:9)

i. The great day of his wrath (Rev. 6:17)

j. The hour of his judgment (Rev. 14:7)

k. The end of this world (Matt. 13:40, 49)

l. The tribulation (Matt. 24:21, 29)—The word *tribulation* is derived from the Latin *tribulem,* which was an agricultural tool used for separating the husks from the corn. As found in the Bible, the theological implications would include such concepts as a pressing together, an affliction, a burdening with anguish and trouble, a binding with oppression. Keeping this in mind, it would seem that of all the 12 names for the coming calamity, the last one would most accurately describe this period. Therefore, from this point on, the term *tribulation* will be employed.

2. The nature of this period—The following passages aptly describe this future and fearful time. "Howl ye; for the day of the LORD is at hand; it shall come as a destruction from the Almighty. Therefore shall all hands be faint, and every man's heart shall melt: For the stars of heaven and the constellations thereof shall not give their light: the sun shall be darkened in his going forth, and the moon shall not cause her light to shine. And I will punish the world for their evil, and the wicked for their iniquity; and I will cause the arrogancy of the proud to cease, and will lay low the haughtiness of the terrible" (Isa. 13:6-7, 10-11).

"And they shall go into the holes of the rocks, and into the caves of the earth, for fear of the LORD . . . when he ariseth to shake terribly the earth" (Isa. 2:19). "Behold, the LORD maketh the earth empty . . . turneth it upside down, and scattereth abroad the inhabitants thereof. . . . The earth is utterly broken down, the earth is clean dissolved, the earth is moved exceedingly. The earth shall reel to and fro like a drunkard" (Isa. 24:1, 19-20).

"For the indignation of the LORD is upon all nations, and his fury upon all their armies. . . . Their slain also shall be cast out, and their stink shall come up out of their carcases, and the mountains shall be melted with their blood. And all the host of heaven shall be dissolved, and the heavens shall be rolled together as a scroll" (Isa. 34:2-4). (See also Isa. 63:3-4, 6; Jer. 25:32-33; Joel 2:1-2; Zeph. 1:14-15; Matt. 24:7, 11-12, 21-22; Luke 21:25-26; 1 Thess. 5:2-3; Rev. 6:12-17.)

3. The length of this period—A careful study of Daniel 9:24-27 reveals the time element here to be seven years. For a detailed summary of this, see Prophecies concerning the 70 weeks (letter *K*) listed under section one of this study.

4. The purpose for this period—Why this terrible time? There are at least seven reasons given by the Scriptures.

a. To harvest the crop that has been sown throughout the ages by God, Satan, and man—Our Lord himself took an entire sermon to expound upon this. Note his words: "He answered and said unto them, He that soweth the good seed is the Son of man; the field is the world; the good seed are the children of the kingdom; but the tares are the children of the wicked one; the enemy that sowed them is the devil; the harvest is the end of the world; and the reapers are the angels. As therefore the tares are gathered and burned in the fire; so shall it be in the end of this world. The Son of man shall send forth his angels, and they shall gather out of his kingdom all things that offend, and them which do iniquity; And shall cast them into a furnace of fire: there shall be wailing and gnashing of teeth. Then shall the righteous shine forth as the sun in the kingdom of their Father. Who hath ears to hear, let him hear" (Matt. 13:37-43).

b. To prove the falseness of the devil's claim—Since his fall (Isa. 14:12-14), Satan has been attempting to convince a skeptical universe that he rather than Christ is the logical and rightful ruler of Creation. Therefore, during the tribulation the sovereign God will give him a free and unhindered hand to make good his boast. Needless to say, Satan will fail miserably.

c. To prepare a great martyred multitude for heaven—"After this I beheld, and, lo, a great multitude, which no man could number, of all nations, and kindreds, and people, and tongues, stood before the throne, and before the Lamb, clothed with white robes, and palms in their hands" (Rev. 7:9).

d. To prepare a great living multitude for the Millennium—"And before him shall be gathered all nations: and he shall separate them one from another, as a shepherd divideth his sheep from the goats: And he shall set the sheep on his right hand, but the goats on the left. Then shall the King say unto them on his right hand, Come, ye blessed of my Father, inherit the kingdom prepared for you from the foundation of the world" (Matt. 25:32-34).

e. To punish the Gentiles—"For the wrath of God is revealed from heaven against all ungodliness and unrighteousness of men" (Rom. 1:18). "And for this cause God shall send them strong delusion, that they should believe a lie: That they all might be damned who believed not the truth, but had pleasure in unrighteousness" (2 Thess. 2:11-12). "And out of his mouth goeth a sharp sword, that with it he should smite the nations" (Rev. 19:15).

f. To purge Israel—"And I will cause you to pass under the rod. . . . And I will purge out from among you the rebels" (Ezek. 20:37-38). "And it shall come to pass, that in all the land, saith the LORD, two parts therein shall be cut off and die; but the third shall be left therein. And I will bring the third part through the fire, and will refine them as silver is refined, and will try them as gold is tried: they shall call on my name, and I will hear them: I will say, It is my people: and they shall say, The LORD is my God" (Zech. 13:8-9). "And he shall sit as a refiner and purifier of silver: and he shall purify the sons of Levi, and purge them as gold and silver, that they may offer unto the LORD an offering in righteousness" (Mal. 3:3).

g. To prepare the earth itself for the Millennium—The Bible indicates that prior to the great flood our earth was surrounded by a watery canopy (Gen. 1:6-7; 7:11) resulting in a universal semitropical paradise of a climate. The discovery of vast oil and coal deposits in the area of both the north and south poles bears strong witness to this. In addition there were probably no deserts, ice caps, rugged mountains, or deep canyons, all of which so radically affect our weather today. But then came the flood, changing all this. (The psalmist may have written about this in Psalm 104:5-9.) However, during the Millennium, pre-flood conditions will once again prevail. (See Isa. 4:5; 30:26; 40:3-5; 60:19-20.) Mankind will once again experience longevity. (Compare Gen. 5 with Isa. 65:20.)

But by what process will all these tremendous changes come about? It is interesting that the King James Version translators used the word *regeneration* on but two occasions. One is in reference to the conversion of repenting sinners (Titus 3:5), and the other describes the salvation of nature itself. Note: "And Jesus said unto them, Verily I say unto you, That ye which have followed me, in the regeneration when the Son of man shall sit in the throne of his glory, ye also shall sit upon twelve thrones, judging the twelve tribes of Israel" (Matt. 19:28).

In other words, mother nature herself will be gloriously regenerated and give up her evil habits (droughts, tornadoes, floods, cyclones, earthquakes, volcanic action, etc.) at the beginning of the Millennium. Here are the conditions that will lead up to her marvelous conversion:

(1) Between the sixth and seventh judgment seals the winds of heaven will be held back—"And after these things I saw four angels standing on the four corners of the earth, holding the four winds of the earth, that the wind should not blow on the earth, nor on the sea, nor on any tree" (Rev. 7:1).

(2) During the fourth vial judgment, great solar heat will proceed from the sun—"And the fourth angel poured out his vial upon the sun; and power was given unto him to scorch men with fire. And men were scorched with great heat, and blasphemed the name of God, which hath power over these plagues: and they repented not to give him glory" (Rev. 16:8-9).

(3) As a result of the seventh vial judgment, the mightiest earthquake yet will take place—"And there were voices, and thunders, and lightnings; and there was a great earthquake, such as was not since men were upon the earth, so mighty an earthquake, and so great. . . . And every island fled away, and the mountains were not found" (Rev. 16:18, 20).

(4) During the tribulation the sun will boil away great quantities of water into the upper atmosphere.

(5) However, the absence of wind will prohibit the formation of clouds, thus making it impossible for rain to fall. As a result, the original pre-flood canopy will be reestablished.

(6) The world's greatest earthquake will level the mountains and fill up the deep canyons, thus the gentle geographical terrain existing before the flood.

What a wonderful and gracious God we have, who will use the very wrath of the tribulation as an instrument to prepare for the glories of the Millennium. In performing this, God will answer a prayer once uttered by the prophet Habakkuk some six centuries B.C. "O Lord . . . revive thy work in the midst of the years . . . in wrath remember mercy" (Hab. 3:2).

5. Personalities appearing during this period—As in a play, a number of actors will render their parts and say their lines during the earth's most sobering drama, the tribulation.

a. The Holy Spirit—Contrary to some, the Holy Spirit will not be removed when the church is raptured. He will instead, it would seem, perform a ministry similar to his work in the Old Testament. It is concluded that he will remain on earth due to the fact that many will be saved during the tribulation (Rev. 7:9-17). The Word of God makes it crystal clear that no mortal can ever be saved apart from the convicting ministry of the Holy Spirit. (See John 3:5-8; 16:8-11; 1 Cor. 2:13.) At any rate, his presence will be felt in the tribulation, as indicated by the prophet Joel. (See Joel 2:28, 30-32; Rev. 11:11; 17:3.)

b. The devil—"Therefore rejoice, ye heavens, and ye that dwell in them. Woe to the inhabiters of the earth and of the sea! for the devil is come down unto you, having great wrath, because he knoweth that he hath but a short time" (Rev. 12:12).

c. Two special Old Testament witnesses—"And I will give power unto my two witnesses, and they shall prophesy a thousand two hundred and threescore days, clothed in sackcloth" (Rev. 11:3).

d. The Antichrist—"Let no man deceive you by any means: for that day shall not come, except there come a falling away first, and that man of sin be revealed, the son of perdition; Who opposeth and exalteth himself above all that is called God, or that is worshipped; so that he as God sitteth in the temple of God, showing himself that he is God. Even him, whose coming is after the working of Satan with all power and signs and lying wonders" (2 Thess. 2:3-4, 9).

e. The false prophet—"And I beheld another beast coming up out of the earth; and he had two horns like a lamb, and he spake as a dragon" (Rev. 13:11).

f. A multitude of angels—Angels have been employed throughout the Bible to perform God's work, but at no other time will they be as busy as during the tribulation. The book of Revelation describes the following for us:
   (1) An angel with the seal of the living God (Rev. 7:2)
   (2) Seven angels with seven trumpets (Rev. 8–9; 11)
   (3) An angel with a golden censer (Rev. 8:3)
   (4) An angel with a little book and a measuring reed (Rev. 10:1-2; 11:1)
   (5) An angel with the everlasting gospel (Rev. 14:6)
   (6) An angel with a harvest sickle (Rev. 14:19)
   (7) Seven angels with seven vials of wrath (Rev. 16)
   (8) An angel with a message of doom (Rev. 18:1, 21)
   (9) An angel with a strange invitation (Rev. 19:17)
   (10) An angel with a key and a great chain (Rev. 20:1)
   In the Old Testament, the prophet Daniel (Dan. 12:1) informs us that one of these angels will be Michael the Archangel himself.

g. 144,000 Israelite preachers—"And I heard the number of them which were sealed: and there were sealed an hundred and forty and four thousand of all the tribes of the children of Israel" (Rev. 7:4).

h. An army of locustlike demons from the bottomless pit—"And he opened the bottomless pit; and there arose a smoke out of the pit, as the smoke of a great furnace; and the sun and the air were darkened by reason of the smoke of the pit. And there came out of the smoke locusts upon the earth: and unto them was given power, as the scorpions of the earth have power" (Rev. 9:2-3).

    i. An army of horse and rider demons from the Euphrates River—"And the number of the army of the horsemen were two hundred thousand thousand: and I heard the number of them" (Rev. 9:16).

    j. Three evil spirits—"And I saw three evil spirits disguised as frogs leap from the mouth of the Dragon, the Creature, and his False Prophet. These miracle-working demons conferred with all the rulers of the world to gather them for battle against the Lord on that great coming Judgment Day of God Almighty" (Rev. 16:13-14, TLB).

    k. A cruel, power-mad ruler from the north—"And the word of the LORD came unto me, saying, Son of man, set thy face against Gog, the land of Magog, the chief prince of Meshech and Tubal, and prophesy against him, And say, Thus saith the Lord GOD; Behold, I am against thee, O Gog, the chief prince of Meshech and Tubal" (Ezek. 38:1-3).

    l. Four symbolic women

        (1) A persecuted woman (Israel)—"And there appeared a great wonder in heaven; a woman clothed with the sun, and the moon under her feet, and upon her head a crown of twelve stars" (Rev. 12:1).

        (2) A vile and bloody harlot (the false church)—"So he carried me away in the spirit into the wilderness: and I saw a woman sit upon a scarlet coloured beast, full of names of blasphemy, having seven heads and ten horns. And the woman was arrayed in purple and scarlet colour, and decked with gold and precious stones and pearls, having a golden cup in her hand full of abominations and filthiness of her fornication: And upon her forehead was a name written, MYSTERY, BABYLON THE GREAT, THE MOTHER OF HARLOTS AND ABOMINATIONS OF THE EARTH" (Rev. 17:3-5).

        (3) An arrogant queen (the world's political and economic systems)—"And he cried mightily with a strong voice, saying, Babylon the great is fallen, is fallen, and is become the habitation of devils, and the hold of every foul spirit, and a cage of every unclean and hateful bird. . . . How much she hath glorified herself, and lived deliciously, so much torment and sorrow give her: for she saith in her heart, I sit a queen, and am no widow, and shall see no sorrow" (Rev. 18:2, 7).

        (4) A pure, chaste bride (the true church)—"Let us be glad and rejoice, and give honour to him: for the marriage of the Lamb is come, and his wife hath made herself ready. And to her was granted that she should be arrayed in fine linen, clean and white: for the fine linen is the righteousness of saints" (Rev. 19:7-8).

    m. A mighty warrior from heaven—"And I saw heaven opened, and behold a white horse; and he that sat upon him was called Faithful and True, and in righteousness he doth judge and make war. . . . And he hath on his vesture and on his thigh a name written, KING OF KINGS, AND LORD OF LORDS" (Rev. 19:11, 16).

6. A chronology of this period

    a. First part (three and one-half years)

        (1) The appearance of the Antichrist

            (a) His nature—"And he shall speak great words against the most High, and shall wear out the saints of the most High" (Dan. 7:25) "And the king shall do according to his will; and he shall exalt himself, and magnify himself above every god, and shall speak marvellous things against the God of gods" (Dan. 11:36). "And that man of sin be revealed, the son of perdition; who opposeth and exalteth himself above all that is called God, or that is worshipped; so that he as God sitteth in the temple of God, showing himself that he is God. . . . Even him, whose coming is after the working of Satan with all power and signs and lying wonders" (2 Thess. 2:3-4, 9).

"Who is a liar but he that denieth that Jesus is the Christ? He is antichrist, that denieth the Father and the Son" (1 John 2:22). "And I saw, and behold a white horse: and he that sat on him had a bow; and a crown was given unto him: and he went forth conquering, and to conquer" (Rev. 6:2). "And I stood upon the sand of the sea, and saw a beast rise up out of the sea. . . . And the beast which I saw was like unto a leopard, and his feet were as the feet of a bear, and his mouth as the mouth of a lion: and the dragon gave him his power, and his seat, and great authority. And he opened his mouth in blasphemy against God" (Rev. 13:1-2, 6).

(b) His names and titles
   i) The little horn (Dan. 7:8)
   ii) The willful king (Dan. 11:36)
   iii) The man of sin (2 Thess. 2:3)
   iv) The son of perdition (2 Thess. 2:3)
   v) The wicked one (2 Thess. 2:8)
   vi) The beast (Rev. 11:7—this title is found 36 times in the book of Revelation).
   vii) The Antichrist (1 John 2:18, 22; 4:3)

(c) Attempts to identify him
   i) He will be a Gentile, based on Daniel 8:8, 9; 9:26 ; Revelation 13:1.
   ii) He will be a Jew, based on Ezekiel 21:25; Daniel 11:37; John 5:43.
   iii) He will come from the tribe of Dan, based on Genesis 49:17; Jeremiah 8:16-17.
   iv) He will be Judas Iscariot, based on Luke 22:3; John 13:27; 6:70-71; 17:12; 2 Thessalonians 2:3.
   v) The Antichrist is Nero.
   vi) The Antichrist is Titus.
   vii) The Antichrist is Domitian.
   viii) The Antichrist is Constantine the Great.
   ix) The Antichrist is Muhammad
   x) The Antichrist is various Roman Catholic popes.
   xi) The Antichrist is Napoleon.
   xii) The Antichrist is Benito Mussolini.
   xiii) The Antichrist is Hitler.
   xiv) The Antichrist is Henry Kissinger.
   xv) The Antichrist is whomever you don't like.

(d) Old Testament forerunners of him—Just as there are many Old Testament characters who depict the person and work of the Lord Jesus (such as Melchizedek in Gen. 14 and Isaac in Gen. 22), there are a number of Old Testament men who describe for us the coming ministry of the Antichrist.

i) Cain, by his murder of the chosen seed (Gen. 4:5-14; Jude 11; 1 John 3:12)

ii) Nimrod, by his creation of Babylon and the tower of Babel (Gen. 10; 11).

iii) Pharaoh, by his oppression of God's people (Exod. 1:8-22).

iv) Korah, by his rebellion (Num. 16:1-3; Jude 11).

v) Balaam, by his attempt to curse Israel (Num. 23–24; 2 Pet. 2:15; Jude 11; Rev. 2:14)

vi) Saul, by his intrusion into the office of the priesthood (1 Sam. 13:9-13)

vii) Goliath, by his proud boasting (1 Sam. 17)

viii) Absalom, by his attempt to steal the throne of David (2 Sam. 15:1-6)

ix) Jeroboam, by his substitute religion (1 Kings 12:25-31)

x) Sennacherib, by his efforts to destroy Jerusalem (2 Kings 18:17)

xi) Nebuchadnezzar, by his golden statue (Dan. 3:1-7)

xii) Haman, by his plot to exterminate the Jews (Esther 3)

xiii) Antiochus Epiphanes, by his defilement of the temple (Dan. 11:21-35)

(e) His personal characteristics

i) He will be an intellectual genius (Dan. 8:23).

ii) He will be an oratorical genius (Dan. 11:36).

iii) He will be a political genius (Rev.17:11-12).

iv) He will be a commercial genius (Dan. 11:43; Rev. 13:16-17).

v) He will be a military genius (Rev. 6:2; 13:2).

vi) He will be a religious genius (2 Thess. 2:4; Rev. 13:8).

Thus, to use various American presidents as an analogy, here is a world leader possessing: (a) the leadership of a Washington and Lincoln, (b) the eloquence of a Franklin Roosevelt, (c) the charm of a Teddy Roosevelt, (d) the charisma of a Kennedy, (e) the political savvy of a Lyndon Johnson, and (f) the intellect of a Jefferson.

vii) He shall do everything according to his own selfish will (Dan. 11:36). (See also Rev. 13:7; 17:13.)

viii) He shall magnify himself and malign God (11:36). (See also 2 Thess. 2:4; Rev. 13:6.)

ix) He will not regard "the gods of his fathers" (11:37)—The word for God is plural. The Antichrist will carry out a vendetta against all organized religion. In fact, it is he who will destroy that great harlot, bloody Babylon, which is the super world church. (See Rev. 17:5, 16.) He will not have the desire for (or of) women (11:37). Here three theories are offered to explain this phrase: (a) the normal desire for love, marriage, and sex (see 1 Tim. 4:3); (b) those things characteristic of women, such as mercy, gentleness, and kindness; (c) that desire of Hebrew women to be the mother of the Messiah (1 Tim. 2:15).

x) His god will be the god of fortresses (11:38)—The Antichrist will spend all his resources on military programs.

(f) His rise to power

i) Through the power of Satan (2 Thess. 2:3, 9-12; Rev. 13:2)

ii) Through the permission of the Holy Spirit—His present-day manifestation is being hindered by the Holy Spirit until the Rapture of the church. God is in control of all situations down here and will continue to be. (See Job 1–2, 2 Thess. 2:6-7.)

iii) Through the formation of a 10-nation organization—He will proceed from a 10-dictatorship confederation that will come into existence during the tribulation. These dictators are referred to as "ten horns" in Daniel 7:7; Revelation 12:3; 13:1; 17:11-12.) In his rise to power he will defeat three of these dictators (Dan. 7:8, 24). This 10-horned confederation is the revived Roman Empire. This is derived from the fact that the most important prophetic details concerning the old Roman Empire in Daniel 2:40-44 are still unfulfilled.

The revived Roman Empire is the last of seven Gentile world powers to plague the nation Israel. These powers are referred to as seven heads in Revelation 12:3; 13:1; 17:7. They are:
- Egypt, which enslaved Israel for 400 years (Exod. 1–12)
- Assyria, which captured the Northern Kingdom of Israel (2 Kings 17)
- Babylon, which captured the Southern Kingdom of Israel (2 Kings 24)
- Persia, which produced wicked Haman (Esther 3)
- Greece, which produced, indirectly, Antiochus Epiphanes (Dan. 11)
- Rome, which destroyed Jerusalem in A.D. 70 (see Luke 21) and which will hound Israel in the revived empire as never before in all history (Rev. 2)

iv) Through the cooperation of the false religious system (Rev. 17)

v) Through his personal charisma and ability

vi) Through a false (or real?) resurrection (Rev. 13:3)

vii) Through a false peace program, probably in the Middle East (Dan. 8:25)

viii) Through a master plan of deception and trickery (Matt. 24:24; 2 Thess. 2:9; Rev. 13:14)—Out of the 91 occurrences in the New Testament of the words meaning "to deceive," or "to go astray," 22 of them belong definitely to passages dealing with the Antichrist and the tribulation. (See Matt. 24:4-5, 11, 24; 2 Thess. 2:3, 9-11; 2 Tim. 3:13; Rev. 12:9; 18:23; 19:20; 20:3, 8, 10.) Three reasons explain this fearful deception: (a) universal ignorance of God's Word (see Matt. 22:29); (b) fierce demonic activity (see 1 Tim. 4:1); (c) the empty soul (see Luke 11:24-26).

(g) His activities

i) He begins by controlling the Western power block (Rev. 17:12)—The Antichrist will defeat 3 of these 10 kingdoms (horns) in his rise to power (Dan. 7:8).

ii) He makes a seven-year covenant with Israel but breaks it after three and a half years (Dan. 9:27).

iii) He gains absolute control over the Middle East after the Russian invasion (Ezek. 38, 39).

iv) He attempts to destroy all of Israel (Rev. 12).

v) He destroys the false religious systems so that he may rule unhindered (Rev. 17:16-17).

vi) He thereupon sets himself up as God (Dan. 11:36-37; 2 Thess. 2:4, 11; Rev. 13:5).

vii) He briefly rules over all nations (Psa. 2; Dan. 11:36; Rev. 13:16)—He will have a universal rule during the final three and a half years of the tribulation (Dan. 7:25). (See also Rev. 13:5; Matt. 24:21.)

viii) He will shed blood upon this earth in unprecedented manner (Dan. 7:7, 19).

ix) He will wear out the saints of God (Israel) (7:25). (See also Rev. 12:13.)

x) He will attempt to change seasons and laws (7:25).

xi) He will blaspheme God (7:25). (See also Rev. 13:5-6.)

xii) He is utterly crushed by the Lord Jesus Christ at the battle of Armageddon (Rev. 19).

xiii) He is the first creature to be thrown into the lake of fire (Rev. 19:20).

(h) His ability to imitate—The Antichrist could surely be a tremendously successful mimic on any late-night TV talk show. Note the following areas in which he will attempt to imitate the person and work of Christ.

i) The Antichrist comes in the very image of Satan, as Christ came in the image of God (2 Thess. 2:9; Rev. 13:4; cf. Col. 1:15 and Heb. 1:3).

ii) The Antichrist is the second person in the hellish trinity, as Christ is in the heavenly Trinity (Rev. 16:13; cf. Matt. 28:19).

iii) The Antichrist comes up from the abyss, while Christ comes down from heaven (Rev. 11:7; 17:8; cf. John 6:38).

iv) The Antichrist is a savage beast, while Christ is a sacrificial lamb (Rev. 13:2; cf. 5:6-9).

v) The Antichrist receives his power from Satan, as Christ received his power from his Father (Rev. 13:2; cf. Matt. 28:18).

vi) The Antichrist will experience a resurrection (perhaps a fake one), just as Christ experienced a true one (Rev. 13:3, 12; cf. Rom. 1:4).

vii) The Antichrist will receive the worship of all unbelievers, as Christ did of all believers (John 5:43; Rev. 13:3-4, 8; cf. Matt. 2:11; Luke 24:52; John 20:28; Phil. 2:10-11).

viii) The Antichrist will deliver mighty speeches, as did Christ (Dan. 7:8; Rev. 13:5; cf. John 7:46). Satan will doubtless give to the Antichrist his vast knowledge of philosophy, science, and human wisdom accumulated through the centuries (Ezek. 28:12).

ix) The greater part of the Antichrist's ministry will last some three and a half years, about the time span of Christ's ministry (Rev. 13:5; 12:6, 14; cf. John 2:13; 6:4; 11:55).

x) The Antichrist will attempt (unsuccessfully) to combine the three Old Testament offices of prophet, priest, and king, as someday Christ will successfully do.

xi) The Antichrist's symbolic number is six, while the symbolic number of Christ is seven (Rev. 13:18; cf. 5:6, 12).

xii) The Antichrist will someday kill his harlot wife, while Christ will someday glorify his holy bride (Rev. 17:16-17; cf. 21:1-2)

(2) The appearance of the false prophet—"And I beheld another beast coming up out of the earth; and he had two horns like a lamb, and he spake as a dragon" (Rev. 13:11).

(a) His identity—Who is this second beast of Revelation 13 who is also called on three later occasions "the false prophet"? (See Rev. 16:13; 19:20; 20:10.) Some believe he will be a Jew (while the Antichrist will be a Gentile), and that he will head up the apostate church. It is entirely possible that the Antichrist will come from the United Nations, while the false prophet may well proceed from the World Council of Churches.

(b) His activities—It has already been pointed out that the Antichrist will attempt to mimic Christ. It would appear that the false prophet will try to copy the work of the Holy Spirit. Thus the following analogy has been suggested between the Spirit of God and the second beast:

   i) The Holy Spirit is the Third Person of the heavenly Trinity (Matt. 28: 19), while the false prophet is the third person of the hellish trinity (Rev. 16:13).

   ii) The Holy Spirit leads men into all truth (John 16:13), while the false prophet seduces men into all error (Rev. 13:11, 14).

   iii) The Holy Spirit glorifies Christ (John 16:13-14), while the false prophet glorifies the Antichrist (Rev. 13:12).

   iv) The Holy Spirit made fire to come down from heaven at Pentecost (Acts 2:3), while the false prophet will do likewise on earth in view of men (Rev. 13:13).

   v) The Holy Spirit gives life (Rom. 8:2), while the false prophet kills (Rev. 13:15).

   vi) The Holy Spirit marks with a seal all those who belong to God (Eph. 1:13), while the false prophet marks those who worship Satan (Rev. 13:16-17).

(c) His mark—"Here is wisdom. Let him that hath understanding count the number of the beast: for it is the number of a man; and his number is Six hundred threescore and six" (Rev. 13:18). Whatever is involved in this hellish mark, it is apparently important, for it is referred to again no less than six times. (See Rev. 14:9, 11; 15:2; 16:2; 19:20; 20:4.)

(3) The formal organization of the super-harlot church

(a) The harlot viewed historically

   i) Satan's church began officially at the tower of Babel in Genesis 11:1-9, nearly 24 centuries B.C. Here, in the fertile plain of Shinar, probably very close to the original Garden of Eden, the first spade of dirt was turned for the purpose of devil-worship.

   ii) The first full-time minister of Satan was Nimrod, Noah's wicked and apostate grandson (Gen. 10:8-10). Secular history and tradition tell us that Nimrod married a woman who was as evil and demonic as himself. Her name was Semerimus. Knowing God's promise of a future Savior (Gen. 3:15), Semerimus brazenly claimed that Tammuz, her first son, fulfilled this prophecy, which made both her and her son the objects of divine worship. She herself became the first high priestess. Thus began the mother-child cult that later spread all over the world.

What was the teaching of Semerimus's satanic church? That Semerimus herself was the way to God. She actually adopted the title "Queen of Heaven." Adherents believed that she alone could administer salvation to the sinner through various sacraments, such as the sprinkling of holy water. They believed that her son Tammuz was tragically slain by a wild bear during a hunting trip, but was, however, resurrected from the dead 40 days later. Thus, each year afterward the temple virgins of this cult would enter a 40-day fast as a memorial to Tammuz's death and resurrection.

Both Jeremiah and Ezekiel warned against this hellish thing. "The children gather wood, and the fathers kindle the fire, and the women knead their dough, to make cakes to the queen of heaven . . . to burn incense to the queen of heaven, and to pour out drink offerings unto her" (Jer. 7:18; 44:25). "Then he brought me to the door of the gate of the LORD's house which was toward the north; and, behold, there sat women weeping for Tammuz" (Ezek. 8:14).

(b) The harlot viewed currently—Is mystery Babylon at work today? She is indeed, stronger and more sinful than ever. At least three New Testament writers describe her latter-day activities and characteristics.
  i) Paul (see 2 Tim. 3:1-5; 4:3-4)
  ii) Peter (see 2 Pet. 2:1)
  iii) John (see Rev. 3:15-17)

(c) The harlot viewed prophetically—"So he carried me away in the spirit into the wilderness: and I saw a woman sit upon a scarlet coloured beast, full of names of blasphemy, having seven heads and ten horns. And the woman was arrayed in purple and scarlet colour, and decked with gold and precious stones and pearls, having a golden cup in her hand full of abominations and filthiness of her fornication: And upon her forehead was a name written, MYSTERY, BABYLON THE GREAT, THE MOTHER OF HARLOTS AND ABOMINATIONS OF THE EARTH" (Rev. 17:3-5).

Mystery Babylon is composed of apostate masses from Protestantism, Catholicism, Judaism, and every other major world religion.

(4) The revival of the old Roman Empire (Dan. 2:41; 7:7-8; Rev. 13:1; 17:12)—In Daniel 2, the prophet interprets a frightening dream experienced by King Nebuchadnezzar in Babylon.

(a) The information in the king's dream—He saw a huge and powerful statue of a man. It was made up of various materials. Its head was gold. Its breast and arms were silver. Its belly and thighs were brass. Its legs were iron, and its feet part iron and clay. This statue was then utterly pulverized into small powder by a special rock, supernaturally cut from a mountainside. The rock then grew until it filled the entire earth.

(b) The interpretation of the king's dream—Just what did Nebuchadnezzar's dream mean? From Daniel 2 and secular history, we learn:
  i) Four major powers (or kingdoms) would rule over Palestine.

ii) These powers are viewed by mankind as gold, silver, brass, iron, and clay.

iii) The four powers stand for: Babylon, from 625 B.C. to 539 B.C.; Medo-Persia, from 539 B.C. to 331 B.C.; Greece, from 331 B.C. to 323 B.C.; and Rome. For Rome, three periods are to be noted here: (a) the first period, the original empire from 300 B.C. to A.D. 476; (b) the second period, the intervening influence from A.D.476 to the present; and (c) the third period, the revived empire from the Rapture to Armageddon. This is definitely implied, for the prophecies concerning the fourth power were not fulfilled in the history of ancient Rome. The smiting rock (Christ himself) did not shatter those earthly kingdoms. On the contrary, he was put to death by the sentence of an official representing the fourth power.

iv) Thus, it is concluded, this last empire—the Roman Empire—will be revived at the end of the age, and during its revival will be utterly crushed by Christ himself.

v) This revived Roman Empire will consist of 10 nations—The Antichrist will personally unite these Western nations. One has only to consult his newspaper in order to follow the rapid present-day fulfillment of this revived Roman Empire prophecy.

(5) The Antichrist's seven-year covenant with Israel—"And your covenant with death shall be disannulled, and your agreement with hell shall not stand; when the overflowing scourge shall pass through, then ye shall be trodden down by it" (Isa. 28:18). "And he shall confirm the covenant with many for one week" (Dan. 9:27).

(a) The background for this covenant—The Word of God indicates that Israel's already intolerable situation will worsen. Then (shortly after the Rapture), to Israel's astonishment and relief, a powerful Western leader (the Antichrist) will pretend to befriend Israel. In fact, he will propose a special seven-year security treaty, guaranteeing to maintain the status quo in the Middle East. Israel will swallow this poisoned bait—hook, line, and sinker.

(b) The betrayal of the covenant—"This king will make a seven-year treaty with the people, but after half that time, he will break his pledge and stop the Jews from all their sacrifices and their offerings; then, as a climax to all his terrible deeds, the Enemy shall utterly defile the sanctuary of God. . ." (Dan. 9:27, TLB).

(6) The mass return of the Jews to the land of Israel—One of the most remarkable chapters in all the Bible concerns itself with the latter-day return of the Jews to their ancient homeland.

Ezekiel the prophet wrote the following: "The power of the Lord was upon me and I was carried away by the Spirit of the Lord to a valley full of old, dry bones that were scattered everywhere across the ground. He led me around among them, and then he said to me: 'Son of dust, can these bones become people again?' I replied, 'Lord, you alone know the answer to that.' Then he told me to speak to the bones and say: 'O dry bones, listen to the words of God, for the Lord God says, "See! I am going to make you live and breathe again! I will replace the flesh and muscles on you and cover you with skin. I will put breath into you, and you shall live and know I am the Lord." So I spoke these words from God, just as he told me to; and suddenly there was a rattling noise from all across the valley, and the bones of each body came together and attached to each other as they used to be. Then, as I watched, the muscles and flesh formed over the bones, and skin covered them, but the bodies had no breath. Then he told me to call to the wind and say: 'The Lord God says: Come from the four winds, O Spirit, and breathe upon these slain bodies, that they may live again.' So I spoke to the winds as he commanded me, and the bodies began breathing; they lived and stood up—a very great army. Then he told me what the vision meant: 'These bones,' he said, 'represent all the people of Israel. They say: "We have become a heap of dried-out bones—all hope is gone." But tell them, "The Lord God says: My people, I will open your graves of exile and cause you to rise again and return to the land of Israel. And, then at last, O my people, you will know I am the Lord. I will put my Spirit into you, and you shall live and return home again to your own land. Then you will know that I, the Lord, have done just what I promised you"'" (Ezek. 37:1-14, TLB).

Even today we see the beginning of this future Israelite ingathering. Note the following figures. In 1882 there were approximately 25,000 Jews in Palestine. In 1900 there were 50,000. In 1922 there were 84,000. In 1931 there were approximately 175,000. In 1948 there were 650,000. In 1952 there were 1,421,000. Today there are approximately 4,000,000 Jews in ancient Palestine. Thus the number of Jews has increased over 150 times in the last 100 years. They have been gathered from over one hundred countries. Three additional passages bear out his latter-day Jewish return.

"For thus saith the Lord GOD; Behold, I, even I, will both search my sheep, and seek them out. As a shepherd seeketh out his flock in the day that he is among his sheep that are scattered; so will I seek out my sheep, and will deliver them out of all places where they have been scattered in the cloudy and dark day. And I will bring them out from the people, and gather them from the countries, and will bring them to their own land" (Ezek. 34:11-13).

"For I will take you from among the heathen, and gather you out of all countries, and will bring you into your own land" (Ezek. 36:24). "Fear not: for I am with thee: I will bring thy seed from the east, and gather thee from the west; I will say to the north, Give up; and to the south, Keep not back: bring my sons from far, and my daughters from the ends of the earth" (Isa. 43:5-6).

(7) The ministry of two special witnesses (Rev. 11:3-6)—"And I will give power unto my two witnesses, and they shall prophesy a thousand two hundred and threescore days, clothed in sackcloth" (Rev. 11:3).

(a) Their identity—Some hold that they are Elijah and Enoch. Hebrews 9:27 states that all men are appointed to die, and since the two men did not experience physical death, they will be sent back to witness and to eventually die a martyr's death. Some believe, however, that they are Elijah and Moses.

i) Elijah—(a) Because of Malachi 4:5-6, which predicts that God will send Elijah during that great and dreadful day of the Lord;

(b) because Elijah appeared with Moses on the Mount of Transfiguration to talk with Jesus (Matt. 17:3); and (c) because Elijah's Old Testament ministry of preventing rain for some three years will be repeated by one of the witnesses during the tribulation. (Compare 1 Kings 17:1 with Rev. 11:6.)

    ii) Moses—(a) Because of Jude 9, where we are informed that after the death of Moses Satan attempted to acquire his dead body, so that God would not be able to use him against the Antichrist during the tribulation; (b) because Moses' Old Testament ministry of turning water into blood will be repeated by one of the witnesses during the tribulation (compare Exod. 7:19 with Rev. 11:6); and (c) because Moses appeared with Elijah on the Mount of Transfiguration (Matt. 17:3).

(b) Their ministry

    i) To prophesy in sackcloth before men as God's anointed lamp stands

    ii) To destroy their enemies in the same manner that their enemies would attempt to destroy them

    iii) To prevent rain for three and a half years

    iv) To turn waters into blood

    v) To smite the earth with every kind of plague

(8) The conversion and call of the 144,000 (Rev. 7:1-8)—"And I saw another angel ascending from the east, having the seal of the living God: and he cried with a loud voice to the four angels, to whom it was given to hurt the earth and the sea, saying, Hurt not the earth, neither the sea, nor the trees, till we have sealed the servants of our God in their foreheads. And I heard the number of them which were sealed: and there were sealed an hundred and forty and four thousand of all the tribes of the children of Israel" (Rev. 7:2-4).

No ink will be wasted here refuting the unscriptural claim of that sect known as the Jehovah's Witnesses, who brazenly claim that their group today makes up this 144,000. The Bible clearly teaches that the 144,000 will consist of 12,000 saved and commissioned preachers from each of the 12 tribes of Israel.

This passage does not mean that God will save only Jews during the tribulation, for in Revelation 7:9-17 the Bible declares that a great multitude from every nation will be saved. What this chapter does teach, however, is that God will send out 144,000 "Hebrew Billy Sundays" to evangelize the world. This will be a massive number indeed, especially when we consider that there are less than 15,000 missionaries of all persuasions in the world today. Our Lord doubtless had the ministry of the 144,000 in mind when he said, "And this gospel of the kingdom shall be preached in all the world for witness unto all nations; and then shall the end come" (Matt. 24:14).

(9) The rebuilding of the Jewish temple—The worship history of Israel can be aptly summarized by the study of three special buildings:

(a) The tabernacle of Moses

    i) Built in 1444 B.C. by Moses (Exod. 40)

    ii) Destroyed in 1100 B.C. by the Philistines (1 Sam. 4)

(b) The first temple
   i) Built in 959 B.C. by Solomon (1 Kings 6)
   ii) Destroyed in 586 B.C. by the Babylonians (2 Kings 25)
(c) The second temple
   i) Built in 516 B.C. (original building) by Zerubbabel (Ezra 6); greatly
     enlarged by Herod in 4 B.C.
   ii) Destroyed in A.D. 70 by the Romans (Matt. 24:1-2); thus, for 2,000
     years the Jews have had no temple.
(d) The third temple—There is ample scriptural evidence to show that the
   Antichrist will allow (and perhaps even encourage) the building of a
   third temple, sometimes known as the tribulational temple. The
   Levitical sacrifices will then be reinstituted, only to be stopped after
   three and one-half years when the man of sin breaks his covenant
   with Israel.
     "And he [Antichrist] shall confirm the covenant with many for
   one week [seven years]: and in the midst of the week he shall cause
   the sacrifice and the oblation to cease, and for [because of] the overspreading of abominations he shall make it [the temple] desolate"
   (Dan. 9:27). "When ye therefore shall see the abomination of desolation, spoken of by Daniel the prophet, stand in the holy place"
   (Matt. 24:15). "That man of sin . . . the son of perdition; who opposeth
   and exalteth himself above all that is called God, or that is worshipped; so that he as God sitteth in the temple of God, showing himself
   that he is God" (2 Thess. 2:3-4). "And there was given me a reed like
   unto a rod: and the angel stood, saying, Rise, and measure the temple
   of God, and the altar, and them that worship therein" (Rev. 11:1). (See
   also Rev. 13.)
     Several questions may be raised at this point.
   i) Where will the third temple be built? There seems little doubt it
     will be constructed on the same spot where the first and second
     temples once stood—Mount Moriah. In ancient times Moriah cov-
     ered 25 acres. Today it occupies 35 acres. It is 2,425 feet above sea
     level.
   ii) What will happen to the Dome of the Rock, which must be
     removed to allow the construction of the third temple? Of course,
     no one knows. Perhaps an earthquake will destroy it, or it may be
     bombed or burned. It could be the Antichrist himself will relocate it
     on another nearby site.
   iii) Is there any present day interest in the rebuilding of the Jewish
     Temple? Two recent and remarkable news articles illustrate the
     growing desire among a number of Israelis concerning the rebuild-
     ing of the third temple.

       Jerusalem-Rabbi Yisrael Ariel sees himself as a dreamer, but
      most Israelis would not be so generous.
       Along with a handful of other rigorously observant Jews,
      Rabbi Ariel is dedicating himself to the rebuilding of the temple
      of Herod on the man-made plateau the Jews call the Temple
      Mount.

The rabbi's organization, called the Temple Institute, has made and displayed a variety of ornaments and furnishings similar to those that once adorned the temple and its priests: a silver menorah, trumpets, goblets, ritual slaughtering knives, priestly garments and so on.

The idea is to be sure all the accessories are ready for use when the new temple is completed. Like many Jews, members of the Temple Institute dream of that day. But they don't have any clear ideas about how it will be brought about.

"We're promised by the prophets of Israel that the Temple will be rebuilt," Ariel said.

During six years of research, the institute has reconstructed 38 of the ritual implements that will be required when Temple sacrifices are restored: it will complete the other 65 items as funds permit. A museum of the completed pieces has drawn 10,000 visitors during the current holy days. In addition to such items as trumpets, lyres and lots, the institute is preparing vestments for the priests-in-waiting. According to Scripture, the clothing must be painstakingly made with flax spun by hand into six-stranded threads.

One difficulty is the requirement (as in Numbers 19:1-10) that priests purify their bodies with the cremated ashes of an unblemished red heifer before they enter the Temple. Following a go-ahead from the Chief Rabbinate, institute operatives spent two weeks in August scouting Europe for heifer embryos that will shortly be implanted into cows at an Israeli cattle ranch.

Two Talmudic schools located near the Western (Wailing) Wall are teaching nearly 200 students the elaborate details of Temple service. Other groups are researching the family lines of Jewish priests who alone may conduct sacrifices. Next year an organizing convention will be held for those who believe themselves to be of priestly descent. Former Chief Rabbi, Shlomo Goren, who heads another Temple Mount organization, believes his research has fixed the location of the ancient Holy of Holies so that Jews can enter the Mount without sacrilege. He insists, "I cannot leave this world without assuring that the Jews will once again pray on the Mount."

A 1983 newspaper poll showed that a surprising 18.3% of Israelis thought it was time to rebuild; a mere 3% wanted to wait for the Messiah. (Richard N. Ostling, "Time for a New Temple?" *Time*, 16 October 1989, 64–65)

(10) The pouring out of the first six seal judgments (Matt. 24:4-8; Rev. 6:1-17)

   (a) The first seal (Rev. 6:2)—"And I saw, and behold a white horse: and he that sat on him had a bow; and a crown was given unto him: and he went forth conquering, and to conquer." The uneasy peace the rider on the white horse brings to earth is temporary and counterfeit. The Antichrist promises peace, but only God can actually produce it. As

Isaiah wrote, "But the wicked are like the troubled sea, when it cannot rest, whose waters cast up mire and dirt. There is no peace, saith my God, to the wicked" (Isa. 57:20-21).

(b) The second seal (Rev. 6:3-4)—"And when he had opened the second seal, I heard the second beast say, Come and see. And there went out another horse that was red: and power was given to him that sat thereon to take peace from the earth, and that they should kill one another: and there was given unto him a great sword."

(c) The third seal (Rev. 6:5-6)—And when he had opened the third seal, I heard the third beast say, Come and see. And I beheld, and lo a black horse; and he that sat on him had a pair of balances in his hand. And I heard a voice in the midst of the four beasts say, A measure of wheat for a penny, and three measures of barley for a penny; and see thou hurt not the oil and the wine."

> The third judgment brings famine to the world. The black horse forebodes death, and the pair of balances bespeaks a careful rationing of food. Normally, a "penny" (a Roman denarius, a day's wages in Palestine in Jesus' day, Matt. 20:2) would buy eight measures of wheat or twenty-four of barley. Under these famine conditions the same wage will buy only one measure of wheat or three of barley. In other words, there will be one-eighth of the normal supply of food. The phrase "see thou hurt not the oil and the wine" is an ironic twist in this terrible situation. Apparently luxury food items will not be in short supply, but of course most people will not be able to afford them. This situation will only serve to taunt the populace in their impoverished state. (Charles Ryrie, *Revelation*, pp. 45–46)

(d) The fourth seal (Rev. 6:7-8)—"And when he had opened the fourth seal, I heard the voice of the fourth beast say, Come and see. And I looked, and behold a pale horse: and his name that sat on him was Death, and Hell followed with him. And power was given unto them over the fourth part of the earth, to kill with sword, and with hunger, and with death, and with the beasts of the earth."

   i) The identity of these riders—John calls them "death" and "hell," apparently referring to physical and spiritual death. Thus the devil will destroy the bodies and damn the souls of multitudes of unbelievers during this, their seal plague.

   ii) The damage done by these riders—One-fourth of all humanity perishes during this plague. It is estimated that during the Second World War 1 out of 40 persons lost his life, but this seal judgment alone will claim 1 out of 4 persons—over one billion human beings.

(e) The fifth seal (Rev. 6:9-11)—"And when he had opened the fifth seal, I saw under the altar the souls of them that were slain for the word of God, and for the testimony which they held: And they cried with a loud voice, saying, How long, O Lord, holy and true, dost thou not judge and avenge our blood on them that dwell on the earth? And white robes were given unto every one of them; and it was said unto them, that they should rest yet for a little season, until their fellow-servants also and their brethren, that should be killed as they were, should be fulfilled."

Here is religious persecution as never before. These three verses are loaded with theological implications.

i) They refute the false doctrine of soul-sleep.
ii) They correct the error of one general resurrection—It is evident that the martyred souls did not receive their glorified bodies at the Rapture, as did the church-age saints. Therefore it can be concluded that these are Old Testament saints who will experience the glorious bodily resurrection after the tribulation. (See Rev. 20:4-6.)
iii) They suggest the possibilities of an intermediate body. (See also 2 Cor. 5:1-3.)

(f) The sixth seal (Rev. 6:12-17)—"And I beheld when he had opened the sixth seal, and, lo, there was a great earthquake; and the sun became black as sackcloth of hair, and the moon became as blood; and the stars of heaven fell unto the earth, even as a fig tree casteth her untimely figs, when she is shaken of a mighty wind. And the heaven departed as a scroll when it is rolled together; and every mountain and island were moved out of their places. And the kings of the earth, and the great men, and the rich men, and the chief captains, and the mighty men, and every bondman, and every free man, hid themselves in the dens and in the rocks of the mountains; and said to the mountains and rocks, Fall on us, and hide us from the face of him that sitteth on the throne, and from the wrath of the Lamb: For the great day of his wrath is come; and who shall be able to stand?"

As it can be seen, this fearful judgment ushers in:

i) The greatest earthquake in history—However, at the end of the tribulation there will be one even worse than the one occurring in the sixth seal. (See Rev. 16:18.)
ii) The greatest cosmic disturbances in history
iii) The greatest prayer meeting in history—But they prayed for the wrong thing. The only object to protect the sinner from the wrath of the Lamb is the righteousness of the Lamb.

b. Middle part (brief undetermined period)
(1) The Gog and Magog invasion into Palestine (Ezek. 38–39)—"Son of man, set thy face toward Gog, of the land of Magog, the prince of Rosh Meshech, and Tubal, and prophesy against him, and say, Thus saith the Lord Jehovah; Behold, I am against thee, O Gog, prince of Rosh, Meshech, and Tubal" (Ezek. 38:2-3; ASV).

In these two remarkable chapters, Ezekiel describes for us an invasion into Palestine by a wicked nation north of Israel in the latter days.

(a) The identity of the invaders—Where is the land of Magog? It seems almost certain that these verses in Ezekiel refer to none other than Russia. Note the following threefold proof of this.
i) Geographical proof—Ezekiel tells us in three distinct passages (38:6, 15; 39:2) that this invading nation will come from the "uttermost part of the north" (as the original Hebrew renders it). A quick

glance at any world map will show that only Russia can fulfill this description.

ii) Historical proof—The ancient Jewish historian Josephus (first century A.D.) assures us that the descendants of Magog (who was Japheth's son and Noah's grandson) migrated to an area north of Palestine. But even prior to Josephus, the famous Greek historian Herodotus (fifth century B.C.) writes that Meshech's descendants settled north of Palestine.

iii) Linguistic proof—Dr. John Walvoord writes concerning this:

> In Ezekiel 38, Gog is described as "the prince of Rosh" (ASV). The Authorized Version expresses it as the "chief prince." The translation "the prince of Rosh" is a more literal rendering of the Hebrew. "Rosh" may be the root of the modern term "Russia." In the study of how ancient words come into modern language, it is quite common for the consonants to remain the same and the vowels to be changed. In the word "Rosh," if the vowel "o" is changed to "u" it becomes the root of the modern word "Russia" with the suffix added. In other words, the word itself seems to be an early form of the word from which the modern word "Russia" comes. Gesenius, the famous lexicographer, gives the assurance that this is a proper identification, that is, that Rosh is an early form of the word "Meshech" and "Tubal" also corresponds to some prominent words in Russia. The term "Meshech" is similar to the modern name "Moscow" and "Tubal" is obviously similar to the name of one of the prominent Asiatic provinces of Russia, the province of Tobolsk. When this evidence is put together, it points to the conclusion that these terms are early references to portions of Russia; therefore the geographic argument is reinforced by the linguistic argument and supports the idea that this invading force comes from Russia. (*The Nations in Prophecy*, pp. 107–108)

(b) The allies in the invasion—Ezekiel lists five nations who will join Russia during her invasion. These are Persia, Ethiopia, Libya, Gomer, and Togarmah. These may (although there is some uncertainty) refer to the following present-day nations:

  i) Persia—modern Iran

  ii) Ethiopia—Black African nations (South Africa)

  iii) Libya—Arabic African nations (North Africa)

  iv) Gomer—Eastern Europe

  v) Togarmah—Southern Russia and the Cossacks, or perhaps Turkey.

(c) The reasons for the invasion.

  i) To cash in on the riches of Palestine (Ezek. 38:11, 12).

  ii) To control the Middle East—Ancient conquerors have always known that he who would control Europe, Asia, and Africa must first control the Middle East bridge that leads to the three continents.

  iii) To challenge the authority of the Antichrist (Dan. 11:40-44).

(d) The chronology of the invasion—Here it is utterly impossible to be dogmatic. The following is therefore only a suggested possibility, based on Ezekiel 38 and Daniel 11:40-44.

 i) Following a preconceived plan, Egypt attacks Palestine from the south (Dan. 11:40a).

 ii) Russia invades Israel from the north by both an amphibious and a land attack (Dan. 11:40b).

 iii) Russia continues southward and doublecrosses her ally by occupying Egypt also (Dan. 11:42-43).

 iv) While in Egypt, Russia hears some disturbing news coming from the east and north and hurriedly returns to Palestine. We are not told what the content of this news is. Several theories have been offered: (a) that it contains the electrifying news that the Antichrist has been assassinated, but has risen from the dead (see Rev. 13:3); (b) that it concerns itself with the impending counterattack of the Western leader (the Antichrist); (c) that it warns of a confrontation with China and India ("Kings of the East"), who may be mobilizing their troops.

It should be noted at this point, however, that some Bible students identify the "he" of Daniel 11:42 as being the Antichrist, and not the Russian ruler. If this is true, then the above chronology would have to be rearranged accordingly.

 v) Upon her return, Russia is soundly defeated upon the mountains of Israel. This smashing defeat is effected by the following events, caused by God himself: (a) a mighty earthquake (Ezek. 38:19-20); (b) mutiny among the Russian troops (Ezek. 38:21); (c) a plague among the troops (Ezek. 38:22); (d) floods, great hailstones, fire and brimstone (Ezek. 38:22; 39:6).

(e) The results of the invasion.

 i) Five-sixths (83 percent) of the Russian soldiers are destroyed (Ezek. 39:2).

 ii) The first grisly feast of God begins (Ezek. 39:4, 17-20)—A similar feast would seem to take place later, after the battle of Armageddon (Rev. 19:17-18; Matt. 24:28).

 iii) Seven months will be spent in burying the dead (Ezek. 39:11-15).

 iv) Seven years will be spent in burning the weapons of war (Ezek. 39:9-10).

(2) The two witnesses

(a) Their martyrdom (Rev. 11:7-13)—The Antichrist is finally allowed to kill them. The word *beast* is first mentioned here in 11:7. There are 35 other references to him in Revelation. It should also be noted that he could not kill the witness until "they shall have finished their testimonies." Satan cannot touch one hair on the head of the most humble saint until God gives him specific permission. (See Job 1:12; 2:6.)

These two, like Paul, finished their testimonies (2 Tim. 4:7). Contrast this with Belshazzar's sad death (Dan. 5:26). To show his contempt for them, the Antichrist refuses to permit their dead bodies to be buried, but leaves them to rot in the street of Jerusalem. All the earth celebrates their deaths through a hellish Christmas; men actually send gifts to each other. This is the only reference to the word "rejoice" in the entire tribulation.

The dead bodies of these two prophets are viewed in a three-and-a-half-day period. Their bodies will be on display in Jerusalem (11:8). It is called Sodom because of its immorality, and Egypt because of its worldliness. It is interesting to note that this prophecy (Rev. 11:9) could not have been fulfilled until the middle 1960s. The following article explains why: "The first link in a worldwide, live television system was taken on May 2, 1965, when the Early Bird Satellite, hovering 22,300 miles in space between Brazil and Africa, united millions of American and European viewers in an international television exchange" (*Reader's Digest Almanac*).

(b) Their resurrection—"And after three days and an half the Spirit of life from God entered into them, and they stood upon their feet; and great fear fell upon them which saw them. And they heard a great voice from heaven saying unto them, Come up hither. And they ascended up to heaven in a cloud; and their enemies beheld them. And the same hour was there a great earthquake, and the tenth part of the city fell, and in the earthquake were slain of men seven thousand: and the remnant were affrighted, and gave glory to the God of heaven" (Rev. 11:11-13).

(3) The victory song of the 144,000—"And I looked, and, lo, a Lamb stood on the mount Sion, and with him an hundred forty and four thousand, having his Father's name written in their foreheads. And I heard a voice from heaven, as the voice of many waters, and as the voice of a great thunder: and I heard the voice of harpers harping with their harps: And they sung as it were a new song before the throne, and before the four beasts, and the elders: and no man could learn that song but the hundred and forty and four thousand, which were redeemed from the earth. These are they which were not defiled with women; for they are virgins. These are they which follow the Lamb whithersoever he goeth. These were redeemed from among men, being the firstfruits unto God and to the Lamb. And in their mouth was found no guile: for they are without fault before the throne of God" (Rev. 14:1-5).

What a far-reaching and fruitful ministry these Hebrew evangelists will have performed. The amazing results of their labor are recorded in Revelation 7:9, 13-14. "After this I beheld, and, lo, a great multitude, which no man could number, of all nations, and kindreds, and people, and tongues, stood before the throne, and before the Lamb, clothed with white robes, and palms in their hands; and one of the elders answered, saying unto me, What are these which are arrayed in white robes? and whence came they? And I said unto him, Sir, thou knowest. And he said to me, These are they which came out of great tribulation, and have washed their robes, and made them white in the blood of the Lamb."

Jesus himself during his Mount Olive sermon predicted the tremendous scope of their ministry: "And this gospel of the kingdom shall be preached in all the world for a witness unto all nations" (Matt. 24:14). In other words the future evangelists will accomplish in a few short years that which the Christian church has not been able to do in the past 20 centuries, namely, fulfill the great commission. "Go ye therefore, and teach all nations, baptizing them in the name of the Father, and of the Son, and of the Holy Ghost: Teaching them to observe all things whatsoever I have commanded you: and, lo, I am with you alway, even unto the end of the world. Amen" (Matt. 28:19-20).

(4) The casting out of heaven's monster (Rev. 12:3-15).

   (a) The identity of this monster—There is no doubt whatever concerning the identity of this "creature from the clouds." He is pinned down by no less than five titles.

   i) The great red dragon (12:3)—He is great because of his vast power (see Matt. 4:8-9), red because he was the first murderer (see John 8:44), and a dragon because of his viciousness (see 2 Cor. 6:15).

   ii) The old serpent (12:9)—He is old, which takes us back to the Garden of Eden (Gen. 3), and a serpent, which reminds us of the first body he used (Gen. 3).

   iii) The devil (12:9), one who slanders (see 12:10; also Job 1-2; Zech. 3:1-7; Luke 22:31)

   iv) Satan (12:9), the adversary (see 1 Pet. 5:8)

   v) The deceiver of the world (12:9)—Note: He deceives not only men but angels as well. In 12:4 we are told that his tail "drew [literally, 'pulled down,' or 'dragged'; see Acts 14:19 where the same word is used] the third part of the stars of heaven." This is apparently a reference to the number of angels Satan persuaded to join him in his original revolt against God (Isa. 14:12-15; Ezek. 28:11-19).

   (b) . The location of this monster—Satan has been, is now, or shall be in one of the following locations:

   i) In heaven, as God's anointed angel (past location, Ezek. 28:14)

   ii) In heaven, as God's chief enemy (present location, Job 1–2)

   iii) On earth, as the Antichrist's spiritual guide (future location during the final part of the tribulation, Rev. 12:12)

   iv) In the bottomless pit (future, during the Millennium, Rev. 20:1-3)

   v) On earth again (future, after the Millennium, Rev. 20:8-9)

   vi) In the lake of fire (future and forever, Rev. 20:10)

   (c) The activities of this monster

   i) He deceives all living unbelievers (Rev. 12:9).

   ii) He accuses all living believers (Rev. 12:10).

   iii) He persecutes the nation Israel (Rev. 12:13).

(5) The destruction of the false church—"And the ten horns which thou sawest upon the beast, these shall hate the whore, and shall make her desolate and naked, and shall eat her flesh, and burn her with fire. For God hath put in their hearts to fulfil his will, and to agree, and give their kingdom unto the beast, until the words of God shall be fulfilled" (Rev. 17:16-17).

One of the most ironical turn of events in all history will be the destruction of the false church. For this evil organization will meet its doom not at the hands of Gabriel, or the Father, or the Son, or the Spirit, but the Antichrist.

What will the future hold for this vile and vicious vixen? According to Revelation 17, the false church lends all her evil strength to elevate the Antichrist during the first part of the tribulation. For awhile she flourishes, luxuriating in surpassing wealth and opulence. But suddenly things change drastically. The scarlet animal and his 10 horns (which represent 10 kings who will reign with him) all hate the woman, and will attack her and leave her naked and ravaged by fire (17:16).

The probable reason for all this is that after she has put the Antichrist into power, the harlot then attempts to control him. History gives us many examples of the Roman Catholic church (and indeed other religious systems) attempting to control kings and rulers.

c. Final part (three and one-half years)

(1) The full manifestation of the Antichrist—"Let no man deceive you by any means: for that day shall not come, except there come a falling away first, and that man of sin be revealed, the son of perdition; who opposeth and exalteth himself above all that is called God, or that is worshipped; so that he as God sitteth in the temple of God, showing himself that he is God. . . . Even him, whose coming is after the working of Satan with all power and signs and lying wonders" (2 Thess. 2:3-4, 9). At this point the man of sin drops all pretense, reveals his true colors, and declares himself to be God.

Here the Antichrist will attempt to do that which his master, Satan, once tried to do: "For thou hast said in thine heart, I will ascend into heaven, I will exalt my throne above the stars of God: I will sit also upon the mount of the congregation, in the sides of the north: I will ascend above the heights of the clouds; I will be like the most High" (Isa. 14:13-14).

(2) The worldwide persecution of Israel—"And there appeared a great wonder in heaven; a woman clothed with the sun, and the moon under her feet, and upon her head a crown of twelve stars" (Rev. 12:1).

These words are unquestionably symbolic, but to whom do they refer?

(a) Identification of this woman

i) She is not Mary—Mary never spent three and a half years in the wilderness, as does this woman (Rev. 12:6, 14). Neither was Mary personally hated, chased, and persecuted, as we see here (Rev. 12:13, 17). While Mary did give birth to that One who will someday "rule all nations with a rod of iron" (Rev. 12:5), the language in this chapter has a wider reference than to Mary.

ii) She is not the church—The church did not bring the man-child into existence, as does this woman (Rev. 12:5), but rather the opposite. (See Matt. 16:18.)

iii) She is Israel—A Jewish Christian who reads Revelation 12:1 will undoubtedly think back to the Old Testament passage in which Joseph describes a strange dream to his father and 11 brothers: "Behold, I have dreamed a dream . . . the sun and the moon and the eleven stars made obeisance to me" (Gen. 37:9). This was of course fulfilled when Joseph's 11 brothers bowed down to him in Egypt (Gen. 43:28).

(b) Persecution of this woman

i) Persecution in the past—Throughout history Satan has made every attempt to exterminate Israel. This he has done by resorting to:
- Enslaving (Exod. 2)
- Drowning (Exod. 14)
- Starving (Exod. 16)
- Tempting (Exod. 32; Num. 14)
- Capturing (2 Kings 17, 24)
- Swallowing (Jon. 2)
- Burning (Dan. 3)
- Devouring (Dan. 6)
- Hanging (Esther 3)
- Gassing (the gas ovens of Adolf Hitler)

ii) Persecution in the future—The most vicious attack is yet to come. John Phillips writes:

> What a time of terror lies ahead for Israel! The world has seen dress rehearsals for this coming onslaught already—the knock on the door at the dead of night; the dreaded secret police; the swift ride through the darkened streets to the sidings where the boxcars wait; the dreadful ordeal of days and nights without food, drink or sanitation, with men and women and children herded like cattle in the dark, and with little babies flung on top of the struggling heap of humanity like so many sacks of flour; the lonely sidings; the barbed wire; the concentration camps; the callous treatment and cruel tortures; and then the gas ovens and the firing squads. It has been rehearsed already in preparation for the full-stage production of terror. (*Exploring Revelation,* p. 174)

"And at that time shall Michael stand up, the great prince which standeth for the children of thy people: and there shall be a time of trouble, such as never was since there was a nation even to that same time" (Dan. 12:1). "For, lo, I will raise up a shepherd in the land, which shall not visit those that be cut off, neither shall seek the young one, nor heal that that is broken, nor feed that that standeth still: but he shall eat the flesh of the fat, and tear their claws in pieces" (Zech. 11:16). "For then shall be great tribulation, such as was not since the beginning of the world to this time, no, nor ever shall be" (Matt. 24:21). "And when the dragon saw that he was cast unto the earth, he persecuted the woman which brought forth the man child" (Rev. 12:13).

This marks the last and most severe anti-Semitic movement in history. It will apparently begin at the recognition by Israel that the Roman world dictator is really the Antichrist and at their refusal to worship him as God or receive his mark (Matt. 21:15-24).

(c) Preservation of this woman—At this point the Jews of the world will travel down one of three roads:
   i) Many Israelites will be killed by the Antichrist (Zech. 13:8).
   ii) Some Israelites will follow the Antichrist (Matt. 24:10-12; Rev. 2:9; 3:9)

iii) A remnant of Israel will be saved—"And to the woman were given two wings of a great eagle, that she might fly into the wilderness, into her place, where she is nourished for a time, and times, and half a time, from the face of the serpent" (Rev. 12:14). "And I will bring the third part through the fire, and will refine them as silver is refined, and will try them as gold is tried: they shall call on my name, and I will hear them: I will say, It is my people: and they shall say, The LORD is my God" (Zech. 13:9).

Thus, it would seem that at least one-third of Israel will remain true to God and be allowed by him to escape into a special hiding place for the duration of the tribulation. We shall now consider the location of this hiding place. While it is not actually specified in Scripture, many Bible students believe that this place will be Petra. This is based on the following three passages.

"And ye shall flee to the valley of the mountains; for the valley of the mountains shall reach unto Azal: yea, ye shall flee . . . and the LORD my God shall come, and all the saints with thee" (Zech. 14:5). The "Azal" mentioned here is thought to be connected with Petra.

"Who is this that cometh from Edom, with dyed garments from Bozrah?" (Isa. 63:1). The first few verses of Isaiah 63 deal with the second coming of Christ. He comes to Edom (of which Petra is capital) and Bozrah (a city in Edom) for some reason, and many believe that reason is to receive the Hebrew remnant who are hiding there.

"He shall enter also into the glorious land, and many countries shall be overthrown: but these shall escape out of his hand, even Edom" (Dan. 11:41).

(3) The pouring out of the last seal judgment (Rev. 8-9; 11:15-19)—"And when he had opened the seventh seal, there was silence in heaven about the space of half an hour" (Rev. 8:1). This marks the only occasion in recorded history that heaven is silent. There is not the slightest sound or movement.

(a) The purpose of the silence—During the sixth seal, mankind seemed to weaken for the first time during the tribulation. A merciful and patient God now awaits further repentance, but to no avail. God takes no pleasure in the death of the wicked (Ezek. 33:11).

(b) The duration of the silence—It was for 30 minutes. The number 30 in the Bible is often associated with mourning. Israel mourned for 30 days over the death of both Aaron (Num. 20:29) and Moses (Deut. 34:8).

We now examine the contents of the seventh seal, which consists of seven trumpet judgments.

(a) The first trumpet (Rev. 8:7)—"The first angel sounded, and there followed hail and fire mingled with blood, and they were cast upon the earth: and the third part of trees was burnt up, and all green grass was burnt up" (Rev. 8:7). It has been observed that plant life was the first to be created, and it is the first to be destroyed (Gen. 1:11-12).

(b) The second trumpet (Rev. 8:8-9)—"And the second angel sounded, and as it were a great mountain burning with fire was cast into the sea: and the third part of the sea became blood; And the third part of the creatures which were in the sea, and had life, died; and the third part of the ships were destroyed."

Dr. Herman A. Hoyt writes:

> Here we read of a great mountain burning with fire. This may refer to a meteoric mass from the sky falling headlong into the sea, perhaps the Mediterranean Sea. The result is to turn a third part of the sea a blood-red color and bring about the death of a third part of the life in the sea. Death may be caused by the chemical reaction in the water, such as radioactivity following atomic explosion. The third part of ships may be destroyed by the violence of the waters produced by the falling of the mass. (*Revelation*, p. 49)

(c) The third trumpet (8:10-11)—"And the third angel sounded, and there fell a great star from heaven, burning as it were a lamp, and it fell upon the third part of the rivers, and upon the fountains of waters; And the name of the star is called Wormwood: and the third part of the waters became wormwood; and many men died of the waters, because they were made bitter."

This star could refer to a meteor containing stifling and bitter gases, which might fall on the Alps or some other freshwater source. During the second trumpet, a third of the salt water was contaminated. Now a third of earth's fresh water suffers a similar fate. Many species of wormwood grow in Palestine. All species have a strong, bitter taste.

(d) The fourth trumpet (8:12)—"And the fourth angel sounded, and the third part of the sun was smitten, and the third part of the moon, and the third part of the stars; so as the third part of them was darkened, and the day shone not for a third part of it, and the night likewise."

Our Lord may have had this trumpet judgment in mind when he spoke the following words: "And except those days should be shortened, there should no flesh be saved: but for the elect's sake those days shall be shortened" (Matt. 24:22). "And there shall be signs in the sun, and in the moon, and in the stars; and upon the earth distress of nations, with perplexity; the sea and the waves roaring" (Luke 21:25).

The Old Testament prophecy of Amos is also significant here: "And it shall come to pass in that day, saith the Lord God, that I will cause the sun to go down at noon, and I will darken the earth in the clear day" (Amos 8:9).

(e) The fifth trumpet (Rev. 9:1-12) The first demonic invasion

"And the fifth angel sounded, and I saw a star fall from heaven unto the earth: and to him was given the key of the bottomless pit" (Rev. 9:1).

i) Their location—The bottomless pit (9:2)

ii) Their target and torment—"And there came out of the smoke locusts upon the earth: and unto them was given power, as the scorpions of the earth have power. And it was commanded them that they should not hurt the grass of the earth, neither any green thing, neither any tree; but only those men which have not the seal of God in their foreheads. . . . And in those days shall men seek death, and shall not find it; and shall desire to die, and death shall flee from them" (Rev. 9:3-4, 6).

iii) Their duration—Five months (9:5)

iv) Their description—"And the shapes of the locusts were like unto horses prepared unto battle; and on their heads were as it were crowns like gold, and their faces were as the faces of men. And they had hair as the hair of women, and their teeth were as the teeth of lions. And they had breastplates, as it were breastplates of iron; and the sound of their wings was as the sound of chariots of many horses running to battle. And they had tails like unto scorpions, and there were stings in their tails: and their power was to hurt men five months" (Rev. 9:7-10).

v) Their leader—"And they had a king over them, which is the angel of the bottomless pit, whose name in the Hebrew tongue is Abaddon, but in the Greek tongue hath his name Apollyon" (Rev. 9:11).

(f) The sixth trumpet (Rev. 9:13-19)—The second demonic invasion: "And the sixth angel sounded, and I heard a voice from the four horns of the golden altar which is before God" (Rev. 9:13).

i) Their leaders—"Saying to the sixth angel which had the trumpet, Loose the four angels which are bound in the great river Euphrates" (Rev. 9:14).

ii) Their mission—"And the four angels were loosed, which were prepared for an hour, and a day, and a month, and a year, for to slay the third part of men" (Rev. 9:15).

iii) Their number—"And the number of the army of the horsemen were two hundred thousand thousand: and I heard the number of them" (Rev. 9:16).

iv) Their description—"And thus I saw the horses in the vision, and them that sat on them, having breastplates of fire, and of jacinth, and brimstone: and the heads of the horses were as the heads of lions; and out of their mouths issued fire and smoke and brimstone" (Rev. 9:17).

v) Their torment—"By these three was the third part of men killed, by the fire, and by the smoke, and by the brimstone, which issued out of their mouths. For their power is in their mouth, and in their tails: for their tails were like unto serpents, and had heads, and with them they do hurt" (Rev. 9:18-19).

(g) The seventh trumpet (11:15-19)—"And the seventh angel sounded; and there were great voices in heaven, saying, The kingdoms of this world are become the kingdoms of our Lord, and of his Christ; and he shall reign for ever and ever" (Rev. 11:15). This seventh angel proclaims the glorious news that very soon now the Lord Jesus Christ will take over the nations of this world as their rightful ruler. The announcement produces a twofold reaction:

i) The citizens of heaven rejoice.

ii) The nations of the earth become angry.

The seventh angel prepares us not only for the consummation of the ages, but also for the explanation of all things. "But in the days of the voice of the seventh angel, when he shall begin to sound, the mystery of God should be finished" (Rev. 10:7).

(4) The sights and sounds of the temple in heaven (Rev. 15:1-8)—Note: At the sounding of the seventh trumpet, "The temple of God was opened in heaven, and there was seen in this temple the ark of his testament" (11:19). It would appear an actual tabernacle exists in heaven from this and other verses. (See Isa. 6:1-8; Exod. 25:9, 20; Heb. 8:2, 5; 9:24; Rev. 14:15, 17; 15:5-6, 8; 16:1, 17.)

(a) John hears the songs of the triumphal (15:2-4)
    i) What they sing—They sing the song of Moses and the song of the Lamb (15:3). Note the contrast between the songs.
- The song of Moses was sung beside the Red Sea (Exod. 15); the song of the Lamb will be sung beside the crystal sea.
- The song of Moses was sung over Egypt; the song of the Lamb will be sung over Babylon.
- The song of Moses described how God brought his people out; the song of the Lamb will describe how God brings his people in.
- The song of Moses was Scripture's first song; the song of the Lamb will be Scripture's last song.

    ii) Why they sing—"For thou only art holy . . . for thy judgments are made manifest" (15:4).

(b) John sees the smoke of the temple (15:5-8)—"And one of the four beasts gave unto the seven angels seven golden vials full of the wrath of God, who liveth for ever and ever. And the temple was filled with smoke from the glory of God, and from his power; and no man was able to enter into the temple, till the seven plagues of the seven angels were fulfilled" (Rev. 15:7-8). (See also Isa. 6:1-8; Exod. 25:9, 40; Heb. 8:2, 5; 9:24; Rev. 14:15, 17; 16:1, 17.)

John Phillips writes:

Since Calvary, the way into the holiest in heaven has been opened to all, because the blood of Christ has blazed a highway to the heart of God. But now, for a brief spell, that royal road is barred. God's wrath , once poured out upon His Son on man's behalf, is to be out-poured again. The world which crucified the Lamb and which now has crowned its rebellions with the worship of the beast, is to be judged to the full. So bright glory burns within the temple, filling it with smoke and standing guard at the door. The way into the holiest is barred again for a while. (*Exploring Revelation*, p. 198)

(5) The pouring out of the seven bowl or vial judgments (Rev. 16)
(a) The first vial judgment—"And the first went, and poured out his vial upon the earth; and there fell a noisome and grievous sore upon the men which had the mark of the beast, and upon them which worshipped his image" (Rev. 16:2).

J. Vernon McGee writes, "God is engaged in germ warfare upon the followers of Antichrist. . . . These putrefying sores are worse than leprosy or cancer. This compares to the sixth plague in Egypt, and is the same type of sore or boil (Exod. 9:8-12)" (*Reveling Through Revelation*, p. 36).

(b) The second vial judgment—"And the second angel poured out his vial upon the sea; and it became as the blood of a dead man; and every living soul died in the sea" (Rev. 16:3).

Dr. Charles Ryrie writes the following concerning this plague:

> The second bowl is poured on the sea, with the result that the waters became blood and every living thing in the sea dies. The "as" is misplaced in the Authorized Version, the correct reading being "became blood as of a dead man." The vivid image is of a dead person wallowing in his own blood. The seas will wallow in blood. Under the second trumpet, one-third of the sea creatures died (8:9); now the destruction is complete. The stench and disease that this will cause along the shores of the seas of the earth are unimaginable. (*Revelation*, p. 97)

(c) The third vial judgment—"And the third angel poured out his vial upon the rivers and fountains of waters; and they became blood. And I heard the angel of the waters say, Thou art righteous, O Lord, which art, and wast, and shalt be, because thou hast judged thus. For they have shed the blood of saints and prophets, and thou hast given them blood to drink; for they are worthy. And I heard another out of the altar say, Even so, Lord God Almighty, true and righteous are thy judgments" (Rev. 16:4-7).

Two significant things may be noted in these verses:

i) This third vial judgment is, among other things, an answer to the cry of the martyrs under the altar at the beginning of the tribulation. Their prayer at that time was, "How long, O Lord, holy and true, dost thou not judge and avenge our blood on them that dwell on the earth?" (Rev. 6:10).

ii) These verses indicate that God has assigned a special angel as superintendent on earth's waterworks. When we compare this with Revelation 7:1, where we are told that four other angels control the world's winds, we realize that even during the hellishness of the tribulation this world is still controlled by God.

(d) The fourth vial judgment—"And the fourth angel poured out his vial upon the sun; and power was given unto him to scorch men with fire. And men were scorched with great heat, and blasphemed the name of God, which hath power over these plagues: and they repented not to give him glory" (Rev. 16:8-9). (See also Deut. 32:24; Isa. 24:6; 42:25; Mal. 4:1; Luke 21:25.)

Perhaps the two most illuminating passages in Scripture about man's total depravity can be found in Revelation 9:20-21 and 16:9. Both sections deal with the world's attitude toward God during the tribulation. "And the rest of the men which were not killed by these plagues yet repented not of the works of their hands, that they should not worship devils, and idols of gold, and silver, and brass, and stone, and of wood: which neither can see, nor hear, nor walk: Neither repented they of their murders, nor of their sorceries, nor of their fornication, nor of their thefts" (Rev. 9:20-21). "And they repented not to give him glory (Rev. 16:9).

What do the verses prove? They prove that in spite of horrible wars, of terrible famine, of darkened skies, of raging fires, of bloody seas, of stinging locusts, of demonic persecutions, of mighty earthquakes, of falling stars, and of cancerous sores, sinful mankind still will not repent.

(e) The fifth vial judgment—"And the fifth angel poured out his vial upon the seat of the beast; and his kingdom was full of darkness; and they gnawed their tongues for pain, and blasphemed the God of heaven because of their pains and their sores, and repented not of their deeds" (Rev. 16:10-11). (See also Isa. 60:2; Joel 2:1-2, 31; Amos 5:18; Nah. 1:6, 8; Zeph. 1:15.)

This plague, poured out upon "the seat of the beast" (literally, his "throne"), will apparently concentrate itself upon the 10 nations of the revived Roman Empire. Again we read those tragic words "and repented not of their deeds."

(f) The sixth vial judgment—"And the sixth angel poured out his vial upon the great river Euphrates; and the water thereof was dried up, that the way of the kings of the east might be prepared. And I saw three unclean spirits like frogs come out of the mouth of the dragon, and out of the mouth of the beast, and out of the mouth of the false prophet. For they are the spirits of devils, working miracles, which go forth unto the kings of the earth and of the whole world, to gather them to the battle of that great day of God Almighty" (Rev. 16:12-14).

Here the God of heaven employs psychological warfare upon his enemies, conditioning them to gather themselves together in the near future at Armageddon. The Euphrates River is 1,800 miles long and in some places 3,600 feet wide. It is 30 feet deep. This river has been the dividing line between Western and Eastern civilization since the dawn of history. It served as the eastern border of the old Roman Empire. Thus, the Euphrates becomes both the cradle and grave of man's civilization. Here the first godless city (Enoch, built by Cain; see Gen. 4:16-17) went up, and here the last rebellious city will be constructed (Babylon, built by the Antichrist; see Rev. 18).

(g) The seventh vial judgment—"And the seventh angel poured out his vial into the air; and there came a great voice out of the temple of heaven, from the throne, saying, It is done. And there were voices, and thunders, and lightnings; and there was a great earthquake, such as was not since men were upon the earth, so mighty an earthquake, and so great. And the great city was divided into three parts, and the cities of the nations fell: and great Babylon came in remembrance before God, to give unto her the cup of the wine of the fierceness of his wrath. And every island fled away, and the mountains were not found. And there fell upon men a great hail out of heaven, every stone about the weight of a talent: and men blasphemed God because of the plague of the hail; for the plague thereof was exceeding great" (Rev. 16:17-21).

The intensity of an earthquake is measured on an instrument called a Richter scale. The greatest magnitude ever recorded so far has been 8.9. The greatest loss of life due to an earthquake occurred on January 23, 1556, in Shensi Province, China, and killed some 830,000 people. However, that earthquake will be but a mild tremor compared to the tribulation earthquake, which, we are told, will level all the great cities of the world. The world's greatest shower of hailstones comes crashing down on mankind. These gigantic icy chunks will weigh up to 125 pounds apiece.

(6) The sudden destruction of economic and political Babylon (Rev. 18)—"And there followed another angel, saying, Babylon is fallen, is fallen, that great city, because she made all nations drink of the wine of the wrath of her fornication" (Rev. 14:8). "And great Babylon came in remembrance before God, to give unto her the cup of the wine of the fierceness of his wrath" (Rev. 16:19). "And he cried mightily with a strong voice, saying, Babylon the great is fallen, is fallen, and is become the habitation of devils, and the hold of every foul spirit, and a cage of every unclean and hateful bird" (Rev. 18:2).

Dr. J. Vernon McGee says:

In chapters 17 and 18 two Babylons are brought before us. The Babylon of chapter 17 is ecclesiastical. The Babylon of chapter 18 is economic. The first is religious—the apostate church. The second is political and commercial. The apostate church is hated by the kings of the earth (Rev. 17:16); the commercial center is loved by the kings of the earth (Rev. 8:9). The apostate church is destroyed by the kings of the earth; political Babylon is destroyed by the judgment of God (verses 5, 8).

Obviously, mystery Babylon is destroyed first—in the midst of the Great Tribulation; while commercial Babylon is destroyed at the Second Coming of Christ. These two Babylons are not one and the same city. (*Reveling Through Revelation*, p. 58)

(a) The description of the city
   i) It had become the habitation of demons and false doctrines (Rev. 18:2; Matt. 13:32).
   ii) Both rulers and merchants had worshiped at her shrine of silver (Rev. 18:3).
   iii) Her sins had reached into the heavens (Rev. 18:5).
   iv) She had lived in sinful pleasure and luxury (Rev. 18:7).
   v) Her prosperity had blinded her to the judgment of God (Rev. 18:7)— There is in this chapter a list (Rev. 18:11-17) of no less than 75 of the world's most expensive luxury items. Again the words of J. Vernon McGee are revealing:

Everything listed here is a luxury item. Babylon will make these luxury items necessities. You will not find a cotton dress or a pair of overalls anywhere in this list. First there is the jewelry department—". . . the merchandise of gold, and silver and precious stones, and of pearls." Then we move from the

jewelry department to the ladies' ready-to-wear— ". . . and
fine linen, and purple, and silk, and scarlet." Then to the luxury
gift department— ". . . and all thyine wood, and every vessel
of ivory, and every vessel made of most precious wood, and
of brass, and marble." We move on to the spice and cosmetic
department— ". . . and cinnamon, and spice, and odors, and
ointment, and frankincense." To the liquor department and the
pastry center— "and wine, and oil, and fine flour, and wheat."
On to the meat department for T-bone steaks and lamb chops—
". . . and cattle, and sheep." (Ibid., p. 62)

    vi) She had deceived all nations with her sorceries (Rev. 18:23).
   vii) She was covered with the blood of many of God's saints (Rev.
      18:24).

(b) The destruction of the city
    i) The source of Babylon's destruction—God himself
   ii) The means of Babylon's destruction—It would almost seem that
     atomic power of some sort is used to accomplish this. This is
     strongly suggested by the swiftness of the judgment, the raging
     fires, and the distance kept by those who watch her burn—possibly
     due to fear of radioactive fallout. (See Rev. 18:9-10, 15, 17, 19.)
  iii) The reaction to her destruction
     • By those on earth—"And they cast dust on their heads, and cried,
      weeping and wailing, saying, Alas, alas, that great city, wherein
      were made rich all that had ships in the sea by reason of her
      costliness! for in one hour is she made desolate" (Rev. 18:19).
      There are three classes of people who weep over Babylon. They
      are the monarchs (18:9), the merchants (18:11), and the mariners
      (18:17).
     • By those in heaven—"Rejoice over her, thou heaven, and ye holy
      apostles and prophets; for God hath avenged you on her" (Rev.
      18:20).
       There are three events in the tribulation which cause all of
     heaven to rejoice: when Satan is cast out (Rev. 12:12); when
     Babylon is destroyed (Rev. 18:20); and when the Lamb is married
     to the church (Rev. 19:7).
   iv) The reasons for her destruction—The city will become the head-
     quarters of all demonic activity during the tribulation (Rev. 18:2).
     • Her devilish pride (Rev. 18:7)
     • Her gross materialism—This wicked city will import and export
      28 principal items of merchandise, beginning with gold and
      ending with the bodies of men (Rev. 18:12-13).
     • Her drug activities (Rev. 18:23)
     • Her blood shedding (Rev. 18:24)
   v) The Old Testament foreshadows her destruction—On the night of
    October 13, 539 B.C., the Babylon of the Old Testament was cap-
    tured by the Medes and Persians. Just prior to this, Daniel the
    prophet had read the fearful words of God to a frightened Belshaz-
    zar: "God hath numbered thy kingdom, and finished it. . . . Thou

art weighed in the balances, and art found wanting. . . . Thy kingdom is divided" (Dan. 5:26-28). Someday God himself will once again write these fearsome words across the skies of Babylon.

F. The battle of Armageddon—"And he gathered them together into a place called in the Hebrew tongue Armageddon" (Rev. 16:16).

   1. The nature of this battle—The Holy Spirit of God has chosen five capable authors to describe for us in clear and chilling language that culmination of all battles—Armageddon. These five authors include David, Isaiah, Joel, Zechariah, and John.

      a. According to David (Psa. 2:1-5, 9)

      b. According to Isaiah (Isa. 34:1-6; 63:3-4, 6)

      c. According to Joel (Joel 3:2, 9-16)

      d. According to Zechariah (Zech. 14:2-3, 12)

      e. According to John (Rev. 14:14-20; 19:11-21)

Observe but a sampling concerning the nature of this fierce battle: "For the indignation of the LORD is upon all nations, and his fury upon all their armies: he hath utterly destroyed them, he hath delivered them to the slaughter. Their slain also shall be cast out, and their stink shall come up out of their carcases, and the mountains shall be melted with their blood. And all the host of heaven shall be dissolved, and the heavens shall be rolled together as a scroll: and all their host shall fall down, as the leaf falleth off from the vine, and as a falling fig from the fig tree" (Isa. 34:2-4). "And the angel thrust in his sickle into the earth, and gathered the vine of the earth, and cast it into the great winepress of the wrath of God. And the winepress was trodden without the city, and blood came out of the winepress, even unto the horse bridles, by the space of a thousand and six hundred furlongs" (Rev. 14:19-20).

   2. The narration of this battle—This coming war of Armageddon will be by far the biggest, boldest, bloodiest, most brazen, and most blasphemous of all time. We shall now consider the negative and positive elements of this war.

      a. Negative.

         (1) Armageddon is not the same as the Russian invasion of Ezekiel 38—Note the difference: Russia invades from the north, but at Armageddon the nations come from all directions. Russia invades to capture Israel's wealth, but this invasion is to destroy the Lamb and his people. Gog leads the Russian invasion, but the Antichrist leads this one.

         (2) Armageddon is not the final war in the Bible—The final war occurs after the Millennium (Rev. 20:7-9); Armageddon takes place at the end of the tribulation.

      b. Positive

         (1) The location of the battle—Dr. Herman A. Hoyt aptly describes the location:

> The staggering dimensions of this conflict can scarcely be conceived by man. The battlefield will stretch from Megiddo on the north (Zech. 12:11; Rev. 1:16) to Edom on the South (Isa. 34:5-6; 63:1), a distance of sixteen hundred furlongs—approximately two hundred miles. It will reach from the Mediterranean Sea on the west to the hills of Moab on the east, a distance of almost one hundred miles. It will include the

Valley of Jehoshaphat (Joel 3:2, 12) and the Plains of Esdraelon. At the center of the entire area will be the city of Jerusalem (Zech. 14: 1-2).

Into this area the multiplied millions of men, doubtless approaching 400 million, will be crowded for the final holocaust of humanity. The kings with their armies will come from north and the south, from the east and from the west. . . . In the most dramatic sense this will be the "Valley of decision" for humanity (Joel 3:14) and the great winepress into which will be poured the fierceness of the wrath of Almighty God (Rev. 19:15). (*The End Times*, p. 163)

Thus there would seem to be at least four important names involved in Armageddon:

(a) The Valley of Jehoshaphat—A valley just east of Jerusalem, between the Holy City and the Mount of Olives (Joel 3:2, 12). This valley, known in the New Testament as the Kidron Valley, plays an important role in the Bible.

   i) David crossed over this valley, weeping as he fled from his rebellious son Absalom (2 Sam. 15:23).

   ii) King Asa burned the idols of his own mother here (1 Kings 15:13).

   iii) Hezekiah destroyed some idols here also (2 Chron. 30:14).

   iv) Josiah destroyed the idols previously placed in the Temple by Ahaz and Manasseh (2 Kings 23:4, 6, 12).

   v) Jesus crossed over this valley en route to the Garden of Gethsemane (John 18:1).

The Valley of Jehoshaphat has been a favorite burial ground for Jews for thousands of years. They believed the final resurrection trumpet would sound from here. Some even taught that the bodies of the righteous, regardless of where they were originally buried on earth, would roll back underground to the Valley of Jehoshaphat on that glad day.

As we have already seen, the ground area involved at Armageddon is unbelievably massive—running some 200 miles north and south, and 100 miles east and west, for a total of 20,000 square miles. But the climax will happen in the Valley of Jehoshaphat.

(b) The Valley of Esdraelon—A valley 20 miles long and 14 miles wide, north and west of Jerusalem between the Holy City and the Mediterranean Sea.

(c) Megiddo—A flat plain in the Valley of Esdraelon (Zech. 12:11)

(d) Bozrah—A city in Edom, east of the Jordan River and near Petra, the capital city of Edom. These two cities will play an important role during the second coming of our Lord (Isa. 34:6; 63:1).

(2) The reasons for the battle—What will draw all the nations of the world into the area of Armageddon? They will gather themselves there for various reasons. It would seem that the following are three of the more important reasons.

(a) Because of the sovereignty of God—In at least five distinct passages we are told that God himself will gather the nations here. "He hath delivered them to the slaughter" (Isa. 34:2). "I will also gather all nations, and will bring them down into the valley of Jehoshaphat" (Joel 3:2). "For I will gather all nations against Jerusalem to battle"

(Zech. 14:2). "For my determination is to gather the nations, that I may assemble the kingdoms, to pour upon them mine indignation, even all my fierce anger" (Zeph. 3:8). "And he gathered them together into a place called in the Hebrew tongue Armageddon" (Rev. 16:16).

(b) Because of the deception of Satan (Rev. 16:13-14)—In this passage we are told that three special unclean spirits will trick the nations into gathering at Armageddon.

(c) Because of the hatred of the nations for Christ—A number of passages tell us of this devilish hatred (Psa. 2:1-3; Rev. 11:18). The nations, led by the Antichrist, will doubtless realize the imminent return of Christ (Rev. 11:15; 12:12). They will also be aware of his touching down on the Mount of Olives (Zech. 14:4; Acts 1:9-12). Thus it is not unreasonable to assume they will gather in that area to try to destroy Christ at the moment of his return to earth.

(3) The chronology of the battle

(a) The drying up of the Euphrates River (Rev. 16:12)—Dr. Donald Barnhouse quotes Seiss in describing this:

> From time immemorial the Euphrates with its tributaries has been a great and formidable boundary between the peoples east of it and west of it. It runs a distance of 1,800 miles, and is scarcely fordable anywhere or any time. It is from three to twelve hundred yards wide, and from ten to thirty feet in depth; and most of the time it is still deeper and wider. It was the boundary of the dominion of Solomon, and is repeatedly spoken of as the northeast limit of the lands promised to Israel. . . . History frequently refers to the great hindrance the Euphrates has been to military movements; and it has always been a line of separation between the peoples living east of it and those living west of it. (*Revelation*, p. 301)

> Thus when this watery barrier is removed, tens of millions of soldiers from China, India, and other Asian nations will march straight for Armageddon and destruction.

(b) The destruction of Jerusalem—Perhaps the saddest event during the tribulation will be the siege and destruction of the Holy City. This will be the forty-seventh and last takeover of the beloved city of David. The following passages bear this out.

"Behold, I will make Jerusalem a cup of trembling unto all the people round about, when they shall be in the siege both against Judah and against Jerusalem" (Zech. 12:2). "For I will gather all nations against Jerusalem to battle; and the city shall be taken, and the houses rifled, and the women ravished; and half of the city shall go forth into captivity, and the residue of the people shall not be cut off from the city" (Zech. 14:2). "And when ye shall see Jerusalem compassed with armies, then know that the desolation thereof is nigh" (Luke 21:20).

When these two events transpire, both the angels in paradise and the demons in perdition will surely hold their breath.

(4) The results of the battle—Two authors aptly describe this battle for us.

Palestine is to be given a blood bath of unprecedented proportions which will flow from Armageddon at the north down through the valley of Jehoshaphat, will cover the land of Edom, and will wash over all Judea and the city of Jerusalem. John looks at this scene of carnage and he describes it as blood flowing to the depths of the horses' bridles. It is beyond human imagination to see a lake that size that has been drained from the veins of those who have followed the purpose of Satan to try to exterminate God's chosen people in order to prevent Jesus Christ from coming to reign. (J. Dwight Pentecost, *Prophecy for Today*, p. 118)

The Battle of Armageddon will result in wholesale carnage among the legions of the beast. The brilliance of Christ's appearing will produce a trembling and demoralization in the soldiers (Zech. 12:2; 14:13). The result of this demoralization and trembling will be the desertion from the Antichrist and the rendering of him inoperative (2 Thess. 2:8). This tremendous light from heaven will produce astonishment and blindness in animals and madness in men (Zech. 12:4).

A plague will sweep through the armies from this light and men will not fight where they stand (Zech. 14:12). The blood of animals and men will form a lake two hundred miles long and bridle deep (Rev. 14:19, 20). The stench of this rotting mass of flesh and blood will fill the entire region (Isa. 34:3). The mangled forms of men and beasts will provide a feast for the carrion birds (Rev. 19:17, 18, 21). The beast and the false prophet will then be cast alive into the lake of fire forever (Rev. 19:20). (Herman A. Hoyt, *The End Times*, p. 165)

G. The second coming of Christ—"And Enoch . . . the seventh from Adam, prophesied . . . saying, Behold, the Lord cometh with ten thousands of his saints" (Jude 14). This message on Christ's second coming was preached long before his first coming by Enoch who ministered even prior to the great flood in Noah's day. His was the very first prophecy concerning the second coming.

The greatest day in history occurred during an April Sunday morning some 2,000 years ago, when the crucified Savior rose from the dead. But God is preparing an even greater, grander, and more glorious day than the resurrection of his beloved Son—and that event is his return to earth again.

1. The chronology of the second coming of Christ
   a. It begins with fearful manifestations in the skies—"Immediately after the tribulation of those days shall the sun be darkened, and the moon shall not give her light, and the stars shall fall from heaven, and the powers of the heavens shall be shaken" (Matt. 24:29) "And there shall be signs in the sun, and in the moon, and in the stars; and upon the earth distress of nations, with perplexity; the sea and the waves roaring; men's hearts failing them for fear . . . for the powers of heaven shall be shaken" (Luke 21:25-26)
   b. In the midst of this, the heavens open and Jesus comes forth—"And then shall appear the sign of the Son of man in heaven: and then shall all the tribes of the earth mourn, and they shall see the Son of man coming in the clouds of heaven with power and great glory" (Matt. 24:30) "Lord Jesus shall be revealed from heaven with his mighty angels" (2 Thess. 1:7). "Behold, he cometh with clouds; and every eye shall see him" (Rev. 1:7).

"And I saw heaven opened, and behold a white horse; and he that sat upon him was called Faithful and True" (Rev. 19:11).

c. The returning Savior touches down upon the Mount of Olives, causing a great earthquake (Zech. 14:4, 8). The Mount of Olives is one of the most important mountains in both biblical history and prophecy.

(1) It towers over Mount Moriah by 318 feet.

(2) It rises to a height of 2,743 feet above sea level.

(3) Its name is derived from the olives grown there.

(4) Sometimes it was called the Mount of Lights (designating the beginning of a new month, year, etc.).

(5) David paused here, wept, and worshipped God after being driven from Jerusalem by Absalom, his son (2 Sam. 15:30, 32).

(6) Tradition says that Christ first spoke the Lord's Prayer on this mountain.

(7) The Church of the Lord's Prayer, built in 1868, has the prayer engraved in 32 languages on 32 marble slabs, each three feet wide and six feet long.

(8) The Bible says Jesus often visited here—"And he came out, and went, as he was wont, to the mount of Olives; and his disciples also followed him" (Luke 22:39).

(9) From here he sent for a colt to ride during the Triumphal Entry of Palm Sunday (Matt. 21:1).

(10) Here he delivered the Mount Olivet Discourse (Matt. 24–25).

(11) He visited here after leaving the Upper Room and may have uttered his high priestly prayer (John 17) from this spot (Matt. 26:30).

(12) He slept here on occasion during the passion week (Luke 21:37).

(13) He ascended from here (Acts 1).

d. After touching down on the Mount of Olives, Christ proceeds to Petra and Bozrah, two chief cities in Edom. While it is impossible to be dogmatic here, it would seem that he goes to Edom to gather the hiding Israelite remnant. Accompanied by the holy angels, the church, and the remnant, Christ marches toward Armageddon (Isa. 34:6; 63:1).

2. The purpose of the second coming of Christ

a. To defeat the Antichrist and the world's nations assembled at Armageddon

b. To regather, regenerate, and restore faithful Israel—Perhaps the most frequent promise in all the Old Testament concerns God's eventual restoration of Israel. The prophets repeat this so often that it becomes a refrain, a chorus of confidence.

Note the following: "Fear not: for I am with thee: I will bring thy seed from the east, and gather thee from the west; I will say to the north, Give up; and to the south, Keep not back; bring my sons from far, and my daughters from the ends of the earth" (Isa. 43:5-6). "And he shall send his angels with a great sound of a trumpet, and they shall gather together his elect from the four winds, from one end of heaven to the other" (Matt. 24:31).

Thus will our Lord gather Israel when he comes again and, as we have already observed, he will begin by appearing to the remnant hiding in Petra. Here we note:

(1) Their temporary sorrow—"And I will pour upon the house of David, and upon the inhabitants of Jerusalem, the spirit of grace and of supplications: and they shall look upon me whom they have pierced, and they shall mourn for him, as one mourneth for his only son, and shall be in

bitterness for him, as one that is in bitterness for his firstborn. In that day shall there be a great mourning in Jerusalem . . . in the valley of Megiddon. And the land shall mourn, every family apart; the family of the house of David apart, and their wives apart" (Zech. 12:10-12). "Behold, he cometh with clouds; and every eye shall see him, and they also which pierced him: and all kindreds of the earth shall wail because of him. Even so, Amen" (Rev. 1:7).

(2) Their ultimate joy—"He will swallow up death in victory; and the Lord GOD will wipe away tears from off all faces; and the rebuke of his people shall he take away from off all the earth: for the LORD hath spoken it. And it shall be said in that day, Lo, this is our God; we have waited for him, and he will save us: this is the LORD . . . we will be glad and rejoice in his salvation" (Isa. 25:8-9). "Moreover the light of the moon shall be as the light of the sun, and the light of the sun shall be sevenfold, as the light of seven days, in the day that the LORD bindeth up the breach of his people, and healeth the stroke of their wound" (Isa. 30:26).

"He shall feed his flock like a shepherd: he shall gather the lambs with his arm, and carry them in his bosom, and shall gently lead those that are with young" (Isa. 40:11). "I, even I, am he that blotteth out thy transgressions for mine own sake, and will not remember thy sins" (Isa. 43:25). "Can a woman forget her sucking child, that she should not have compassion on the son of her womb? yea, they may forget, yet will I not forget thee" (Isa. 49:15).

c. To judge and punish faithless Israel—In the book of Romans the great Apostle Paul makes two significant statements concerning his beloved nation Israel. He writes: "For they are not all Israel, which are of Israel" (Rom. 9:6). "And so all Israel shall be saved: as it is written, There shall come out of Sion the Deliverer, and shall turn away ungodliness from Jacob" (Rom. 11:26).

By the first statement Paul of course meant that all faithful Israel would be saved. As we have previously seen, this blessed event will occur during the tribulation. By the second statement Paul writes concerning faithless Israel. In other words, all that glitters is not gold. From the very moment God began working through Abraham (the first Hebrew), Satan also began working through members of that same race. Thus, as the Bible has been advanced by faithful Israel throughout history, it has likewise been opposed by faithless Israel.

Therefore, when the master of all Israel returns, he will be especially gracious to true Israel but specially harsh with false Israel. Note the tragic record of false Israel.

(1) Her sins against the Father
   (a) Rebelling (Num. 14:22-23)
   (b) Rejecting (1 Sam. 8:7)
   (c) Robbing (Mal. 3:2-5)

(2) Her sins against the Son
   (a) She refused him (John 1:11).
   (b) She crucified him (Acts 2:22-23; 3:14-15; 4:10; 5:30; 1 Thess. 2:14-16).

(3) Her sins against the Holy Spirit—stubborn resistance. (See Acts 7:51.)

d. To separate the Gentile sheep from the goats—"And before him shall be gathered all nations: and he shall separate them one from another, as a shepherd divideth his sheep from the goats: And he shall set the sheep on his right hand, but the goats on the left" (Matt. 25:32-33).

    (1) His words to the sheep—"Then shall the King say unto them on his right hand, Come, ye blessed of my Father, inherit the kingdom prepared for you from the foundation of the world" (Matt. 25:34).

    (2) His words to the goats—"Then shall he say also unto them on the left hand, Depart from me, ye cursed, into everlasting fire, prepared for the devil and his angels" (Matt. 25:41).

  e. To bind Satan—"And the God of peace shall bruise Satan under your feet shortly" (Rom. 16:20). "And I saw an angel come down from heaven, having the key of the bottomless pit and a great chain in his hand. And he laid hold on the dragon, that old serpent, which is the Devil, and Satan, and bound him a thousand years, and cast him into the bottomless pit, and shut him up, and set a seal upon him, that he should deceive the nations no more, till the thousand years should be fulfilled" (Rev. 20:1-3).

  f. To resurrect Old Testament and tribulational saints—It is the view of this study guide that at the Rapture of the church God will raise only those believers who have been saved from Pentecost till the Rapture. According to this view, all other believers will be resurrected just prior to the Millennium at this time.

    (1) The fact of this resurrection—At least nine passages bring out this resurrection. "For I know that my redeemer liveth, and that he shall stand at the latter day upon the earth: And though after my skin worms destroy this body, yet in my flesh shall I see God" (Job 19:25-26). (See Psa. 49:15; Isa. 25:8; 26:19; Dan. 12:2; Hos. 13:14; John 5:28-29; Heb. 11:35; Rev. 20:4-5.)

    (2) The order of this resurrection—This is the third of four major biblical resurrections. These are:

      (a) The resurrection of Christ (1 Cor. 15:23)

      (b) The resurrection of believers at the Rapture (1 Thess. 4:16; 1 Cor. 15:51-53)

      (c) The resurrection of Old Testament and tribulational saints

      (d) The resurrection of the unsaved (Rev. 20:5, 11-14)— Thus one of the reasons for the Second Coming will be to resurrect those non-church-related saints. For many long centuries Father Abraham has been patiently awaiting that city "which hath foundations, whose builder and maker is God" (Heb. 11:10). God will not let him down.

  g. To judge fallen angels—"Know ye not that we shall judge angels?" (1 Cor. 6:3). All fallen angels are of course, included in this judgment. But they fall into two main categories: chained and unchained.

    (1) Unchained fallen angels (See Luke 8:30-31; Mark 1:23-24; Eph. 6:12.)

    (2) Chained angels (See 1 Pet. 3:18-20; Jude 6.)

3. The time element involved in the second coming of Christ—According to Daniel 12:11-12, there will be a period of 75 days between the second coming of Christ and the millennial reign. Dr. S. Franklin Logsdon has written:

    We in the United States have a national analogy. The President is elected in the early part of November, but he is not inaugurated until January 20th.

There is an interim of 70-plus days. During this time, he concerns himself with the appointment of Cabinet members, foreign envoys and others who will comprise his government. In the period of 75 days between the termination of the Great Tribulation and the Coronation, the King of glory likewise will attend to certain matters. (*Profiles of Prophecy*, p. 81)

H. The glorious Millennium—"And they lived and reigned with Christ a thousand years" (Rev. 20:4). Dr. J. Dwight Pentecost writes:

A larger body of prophetic Scripture is devoted to the subject of the millennium, developing its character and conditions, than any other one subject. This millennial age, in which the purposes of God are fully realized on the earth, demands considerable attention. An attempt will be made to deduce from the Scriptures themselves the essential facts and features of this theocratic kingdom. While much has been written on the subject of the millennium, that which is clearly revealed in the Word can be our only true guide as to the nature and character of that period. (*Things to Come*, p. 476)

1. The fact of the Millennium.—The word itself is a Latin term that signifies "one thousand years." "And they lived and reigned with Christ a thousand years" (Rev. 20:4).

In the first seven verses of Revelation 20, John mentions the 1000-year period no less than six times. In spite of this some have argued that, since this number is found in only one New Testament passage, one cannot insist that the 1000-year period will really come to pass.

Dr. Rene Pache writes the following helpful words:

Let us notice again this fact: the teaching of the Old Testament concerning the millennium is so complete that the Jews in the Talmud succeeded in developing it entirely themselves, without possessing the gift furnished later by the New Testament. For example, they had indeed affirmed before the Apocalypse that the messianic kingdom would last one thousand years. One should not, therefore, claim (as some have done) that without the famous passage of Revelation 20:1-10 the doctrine of the millennium would not exist. (*The Return of Jesus Christ*, p. 380)

2. Three views concerning the Millennium
   a. Postmillennialism—This theory says that through the preaching of the gospel the world will eventually embrace Christianity and become a universal "society of saints." At this point Christ will be invited to assume command and reign over man's peaceful planet. Thus, postmillennialists believe in a literal thousand-year reign. Their position is false, however, for the Bible clearly teaches that the world situation will become worse and worse prior to Christ's second coming—not better and better. (See 1 Tim. 4:1; 2 Tim. 3:1-5.) This position was popularized by a Unitarian minister named Daniel Whitby (1638–1726).
   b. Amillennialism—This view teaches that there will be no 1000-year reign at all and that the New Testament church inherits all the spiritual promises and prophecies of Old Testament Israel. In this view Isaiah's beautiful prophecy of the bear and the cow lying together and the lion eating straw like the ox (Isa. 11:7) simply doesn't mean what it says at all. However, if

the eleventh chapter of Isaiah cannot be taken literally, what proof do we have that the magnificent fifty-third chapter should not likewise be allegorized away?

c. Premillennialism—This view teaches that Christ will return just prior to the Millennium and will personally rule during this glorious thousand-year reign. This position alone is scriptural and is the oldest of these three views. From the apostolic period on, the premillennial position was held by the early church fathers.

3. The wedding at the beginning of the Millennium—"Let us be glad and rejoice, and give honour to him: for the marriage of the Lamb is come, and his wife hath made herself ready. And to her was granted that she should be arrayed in fine linen, clean and white: for the fine linen is the righteousness of saints. And he saith unto me, write, Blessed are they which are called unto the marriage supper of the Lamb. And he saith unto me, These are the true sayings of God" (Rev. 19:7-9).

Note: As previously stated (see "The marriage service of the Lamb" in this chapter), the wedding service is private and takes place in heaven shortly after the Rapture, while the wedding supper is public and occurs on earth at the beginning of the Millennium.

4. The purpose of the Millennium

a. To reward the saints of God—"Verily there is a reward for the righteous" (Psa. 58:11). "To him that soweth righteousness shall be a sure reward" (Prov. 11:18). "Behold, the Lord GOD will come with strong hand, and his arm shall rule for him: behold, his reward is with him" (Isa. 40:10).

"Rejoice, and be exceeding glad: for great is your reward in heaven" (Matt. 5:12). "For the Son of man shall come in the glory of his Father with his angels; and then he shall reward every man according to his works" (Matt. 16:27). "Then shall the King say . . . , Come, ye blessed of my Father, inherit the kingdom prepared for you from the foundation of the world" (Matt. 25:34). "Knowing that of the Lord ye shall receive the reward of the inheritance" (Col. 3:24). "And, behold, I come quickly; and my reward is with me" (Rev. 22:12).

b. To answer the oft-prayed model prayer—In Luke 11:1-4 and Matthew 6:9-13 our Lord, at the request of his disciples, suggested a pattern prayer to aid all believers in their praying. One of the guidelines was this: "Thy kingdom come." Here the Savior was inviting his followers to pray for the Millennium. Someday he will return to fulfill the untold millions of times these three little words have wafted their way to heaven by Christians: "Thy kingdom come."

c. To redeem creation—In Genesis 3 God cursed nature because of Adam's sin. From that point on, man's paradise became a wilderness. The roses suddenly contained thorns, and the docile tiger became a hungry meat-eater. But during the Millennium all this will change. Paul describes the transformation for us in his Epistle to the Romans: "For all creation is waiting patiently and hopefully for that future day when God will resurrect his children. For on that day thorns and thistles, sin, death, and decay—the things that overcame the world against its will at God's command—will all disappear, and the world around us will share in the glorious freedom from sin which God's children enjoy. For we know that even the things of nature, like animals and plants, suffer in sickness and death as they await this great event" (Rom. 8:19-22, TLB).

d. To fulfill three important Old Testament covenants.

   (1) The Abrahamic Covenant—God promised Abraham two basic things

      (a) That his seed (Israel) would become a mighty nation (Gen. 12:1-3; 13:16; 15:5; 17:7; 22:17-18)

      (b) That his seed (Israel) would someday own Palestine forever (Gen. 12:7; 13:11-15, 17; 15:7, 18-21; 17:8)

   (2) The Davidic Covenant (2 Sam. 7:12-16; 23:5)—Here the promise was threefold

      (a) That from David would come an everlasting throne

      (b) That from David would come an everlasting kingdom

      (c) That from David would come an everlasting King

In a very real sense many of the conditions within these first two covenants have already come to pass. For example, concerning the Abrahamic Covenant, God did form a mighty nation from Abraham and today approximately 25 percent of that nation lives in the promised land. Then, in the fullness of time, God sent a babe from the seed of David to rule over the seed of Abraham in the land. (See Luke 1:30-33.) But a problem soon arose, for when the ruler from David presented himself, he was rejected by Abraham's seed (Luke 23:18, 21; John 19:15). Thus, a third covenant was needed that would bring to completion the blessings of the first two. This God will wondrously accomplish through the New Covenant.

   (3) The New Covenant (Jer. 31:31-34; Isa. 42:6; Heb. 8:7-12)—This promise was also threefold:

      (a) That he would forgive their iniquity and forget their sin

      (b) That he would give them new hearts

      (c) That he would use Israel to reach and teach the Gentiles

e. To prove a point—This is the point regardless of his environment or heredity: mankind apart from God's grace will inevitably fail. For example:

   (1) The age of innocence ended with willful disobedience (Gen. 3).

   (2) The age of conscience ended with universal corruption (Gen. 6).

   (3) The age of human government ended with devil-worshipping at the tower of Babel (Gen. 11).

   (4) The age of promise ended with God's people out of the promised land and enslaved in Egypt (Exod. 1).

   (5) The age of the law ended with the creatures killing their Creator (Matt. 27).

   (6) The age of the church will end with worldwide apostasy (1 Tim. 4).

   (7) The age of the tribulation will end with the battle of Armageddon (Rev. 19).

   (8) The age of the Millennium will end with an attempt to destroy God himself (Rev. 20). (Note: Just where and how Satan will gather this unsaved human army at the end of the Millennium will be discussed later in this chapter.)

   Dr. J. Dwight Pentecost writes:

> The millennial age is designed by God to be the final test of fallen humanity under the most ideal circumstances, surrounded by every

enablement to obey the rule of the king, from whom the outward sources of temptation have been removed, so that man may be found and proved to be a failure in even this last testing of fallen humanity. (*Things to Come*, p. 538)

f. To fulfill the main burden of biblical prophecy—All Bible prophecy concerning the Lord Jesus Christ is summarized in one tiny verse by the Apostle Peter: "the sufferings of Christ, and the glory that should follow" (1 Pet. 1:11).

Here Peter connects Christ's first coming (the sufferings) with his second coming (the glory). This in a nutshell is a panorama of the purpose, plan, and program of almighty Jehovah God. Note this beautiful outline as we trace it through the Word of God.

(1) The sufferings—a Baby, wrapped in swaddling clothes (Luke 2:12); the glory—a King, clothed in majestic apparel (Psa. 93:1)

(2) The sufferings—he was the wearied traveler (John 4:6); the glory—he will be the untiring God (Isa. 40:28-29).

(3) The sufferings—he had nowhere to lay his head (Luke 9:58); the glory—he will become heir to all things (Heb. 1:2).

(4) The sufferings—he was rejected by tiny Israel (John 1:11); The glory—he will be accepted by all the nations (Isa. 9:6).

(5) The sufferings—wicked men took up stones to throw at him (John 8:59); the glory—wicked men will cry for stones to fall upon them to hide them from him (Rev. 6:16).

(6) The sufferings—a lowly Savior, acquainted with grief (Isa. 53:3); the glory—the mighty God, anointed with the oil of gladness (Heb. 1:9)

(7) The sufferings—he was clothed with a scarlet robe in mockery (Luke 23:11); the glory—he will be clothed with a vesture dipped in the blood of his enemies (Rev. 19:13).

(8) The sufferings—he was smitten with a reed (Matt. 27:30); the glory—he will rule the nations with a rod of iron (Rev. 19:15).

(9) The sufferings—wicked soldiers bowed their knee and mocked (Mark 15:19); the glory—every knee shall bow and acknowledge him (Phil. 2:10).

(10) The sufferings—he wore a crown of thorns (John 19:5); the glory—he will wear a crown of gold (Rev. 14:14).

(11) The sufferings—his hands were pierced with nails (John 20:25); the glory—his hands will carry a sharp sickle (Rev. 14:14).

(12) The sufferings—his feet were pierced with nails (Psa. 22:16); the glory—his feet will stand on the Mount of Olives (Zech. 14:4).

(13) The sufferings—he had no form or comeliness (Isa. 53:2); the glory—he will be the fairest of 10,000 (Psa. 27:4).

(14) The sufferings—he delivered up his spirit (John 19:30); the glory—he is alive forevermore (Rev. 1:18).

(15) The sufferings—he was laid in the tomb (Matt. 27:59-60); the glory—he will sit on his throne (Heb. 8:1).

Here, then, is the "suffering-glory story" of the Savior. Furthermore, when a sinner repents and becomes a part of the body of Christ, he too shares in this destiny. "For I reckon that the sufferings of this present time are not worthy to be compared with the glory which shall be revealed in us" (Rom. 8:18). "And our hope of you is stedfast, knowing, that as ye are partakers of the sufferings, so shall ye be also of the consolation" (2 Cor. 1:7). "If we suffer, we shall also reign with him" (2 Tim. 2:12). "Beloved, think it not strange concerning the fiery trial which is to try you, as though some strange thing happened unto you: But rejoice, inasmuch as ye are partakers of Christ's sufferings; that, when his glory shall be revealed, ye may be glad also with exceeding joy" (1 Pet. 4:12-13). "The elders which are among you I exhort, who am also an elder, and a witness of the sufferings of Christ, and also a partaker of the glory that shall be revealed" (1 Pet. 5:1).

5. The titles of the Millennium
   a. The world to come (Heb. 2:5)
   b. The kingdom of heaven (Matt. 5:10)
   c. The kingdom of God (Mark 1:14)
   d. The last day (John 6:40)
   e. The regeneration (Matt. 19:28)—"And Jesus said unto them, Verily I say unto you, That ye which have followed me, in the regeneration when the Son of man shall sit in the throne of his glory, ye also shall sit upon twelve thrones, judging the twelve tribes of Israel" (Matt. 19:28).

   The word *regeneration* is found only twice in the English Bible, here and in Titus 3:5, where Paul is speaking of the believer's new birth. The word literally means "re-creation." Thus the Millennium will be to the earth what salvation is to the sinner.
   f. The times of refreshing (Acts 3:19)
   g. The restitution of all things (Acts 3:21)
   h. The day of Christ—This is by far the most common biblical name for the Millennium. (See 1 Corinthians 1:8; 5:5; 2 Corinthians 1:14; Philippians 1:6; 2:16.)

   Thus, during the Millennium our blessed Lord will have the opportunity to exercise his rightful and eternal fourfold sonship.
   (1) His racial sonship—Son of Abraham (Gen. 17:8; Matt. 1:1; Gal. 3:16)
   (2) His royal sonship—Son of David (Isa. 9:7; Matt. 1:1; Luke 1:32-33)
   (3) His human sonship—Son of Man (John 5:27; Acts 1:11).
   (4) His divine sonship—Son of God (Isa. 66:15-18, 23; 41:10, 17-18; Psa. 46:1, 5; 86:9; Zech. 14:16-19)

6. Old Testament examples of the Millennium
   a. The Sabbath—This word literally means "rest." In Old Testament times God wisely set aside a Sabbath or rest time after a period of activity.
   A rest was to be observed:
   (1) After six workdays (Exod. 20:8-11; Lev. 23:3)
   (2) After six workweeks (Lev. 23:15-16)
   (3) After six work months (Lev. 23:24-25, 27, 34)
   (4) After six work years (Lev. 25:2-5)
   b. The jubilee year (Lev. 25:10-12)
   c. The tabernacle—because God's glory dwelt in the Holy of Holies (Exod. 25:8; 29:42-46; 40:34)
   d. The Feast of Tabernacles (Lev. 23:34-42)
   e. The promised land (Deut. 6:3; Heb. 4:8-10)
   f. The reign of Solomon

(1) Because of the vastness of his kingdom (1 Kings 4:21)
(2) Because of its security (1 Kings 4:25)
(3) Because of his great wisdom (1 Kings 4:29, 34)
(4) Because of the fame of his kingdom (1 Kings 10:7)
(5) Because of the riches of his kingdom (1 Kings 10:27)

7. The nature of the Millennium—What will the 1000-year reign of Christ be like? Dr. J. Dwight Pentecost has compiled the following extended and impressive facts (*Things to Come*, pp. 487–490):

a. Peace—The cessation of war through the unification of the kingdoms of the world under the reign of Christ, together with the resultant economic prosperity (since nations need not devote vast proportions of their expenditure on munitions), is a major theme of the prophets. National and individual peace is the fruit of Messiah's reign (Isa. 2:4; 9:4-7; 11:6-9; 32:17-18; 33:5-6; 54:13; 55:12; 60:18; 65:25; 66:12; Ezek. 28:26; 34:25, 28; Hos. 2:18; Mic. 4:2-3; Zech. 9:10).

b. Joy—The fullness of joy will be a distinctive mark of the age (Isa. 9:3-4; 12:3-6; 14:7-8; 25:8-9; 30:29; 42:1, 10-12; 52:9; 60:15; 61:7, 10; 65:18-19; 66:10-14; Jer. 30:18-19; 31:13-14; Zeph. 3:14-17; Zech. 8:18-19; 10:6-7).

c. Holiness—The theocratic kingdom will be a holy kingdom, in which holiness is manifested through the King and the King's subjects. The land will be holy, the city holy, the temple holy, and the subjects holy unto the Lord (Isa. 1:26-27; 4:3-4; 29:18-23; 31:6-7; 35:8-9; 52:1; 60:21; 61:10; Jer. 31:23; Ezek. 36:24-31; 37:23-24; 43:7-12; 45:1; Joel 3:21; Zeph.3:11, 13; Zech. 8:3; 13:1-2; 14:20-21).

d. Glory—The kingdom will be a glorious kingdom, in which the glory of God will find full manifestation (Isa. 4:2; 24:34; 35:2; 40:5; 60:1-9).

e. Comfort—The King will personally minister to every need, so that there will be the fullness of comfort in that day (Isa. 12:1-2; 29:22-23; 30:26; 40:1-2; 49:13; 51:3; 61:3-7; 66:13-14; Jer. 31:23-25; Zeph. 3:18-20; Zech. 9:11-12; Rev. 21:4).

f. Justice—There will be the administration of perfect justice to every individual (Isa. 9:7; 11:5; 32:16; 42:1-4; 65:21-23; Jer. 23:5; 31:23; 31:29-30).

g. Full knowledge—The ministry of the King will bring the subjects of his kingdom into full knowledge. Doubtless there will be an unparalleled teaching ministry of the Holy Spirit (Isa. 11:1-2, 9; 41:19-20; 54:13; Hab. 2:14).

h. Instruction—This knowledge will come about through the instruction that issues from the King (Isa. 2:2-3; 12:3-6; 25:9; 29:17-24; 30:20-21; 32:3-4; 49:10; 52:8; Jer. 3:14-15; 23:1-4; Mic. 4:2).

i. Removal of the curse—The original curse placed upon creation (Gen. 3:17-19) will be removed, so that there will be abundant productivity to the earth. Animal creation will be changed so as to lose its venom and ferocity (Isa. 11:6-9; 35:9; 65:25).

j. Sickness removed—The ministry of the King as a healer will be seen throughout the age, so that sickness and even death, except as a penal measure in dealing with overt sin, will be removed (Isa. 33:24; Jer. 30:17; Ezek. 34:16).

k. Healing of the deformed—Accompanying this ministry will be the healing of all deformity at the inception of the Millennium (Isa. 29:17-19; 35:3-6; 61:1-2; Jer. 31:8; Mic. 4:6-7; Zeph. 3:19).

l. Protection—There will be a supernatural work of preservation of life in the millennial age through the King (Isa. 41:8-14; 62:8-9; Jer. 32:27; 23:6; Ezek. 34:21; Joel 3:16-17; Amos 9:15; Zech. 8:14-15; 9:8; 14:10-11).

m. Freedom from oppression—There will be no social, political, or religious oppression in that day (Isa. 14:3-6; 42:6-7; 49:8-9; Zech. 9:11-12).

n. No immaturity—The suggestion seems to be that there will not be the tragedies of feeble-mindedness nor of dwarfed bodies in that day (Isa. 65:20). Longevity will be restored.

o. Reproduction by the living people—The living saints who go into the Millennium in their natural bodies will beget children throughout the age. The earth's population will soar. Those born in this age will not be born without a sin nature, so salvation will be required (Jer. 30:20; 31:29; Ezek. 47:22; Zech. 10:8).

p. Labor—The period will not be characterized by idleness, but there will be a perfect economic system, in which the needs of men are abundantly provided for by labor in that system, under the guidance of the King. There will be a fully developed industrialized society, providing for the needs of the King's subjects (Isa. 62:8-9; 65:21-23; Jer. 31:5; Ezek. 48:18-19). Agriculture as well as manufacturing will provide employment.

q. Economic prosperity—The perfect labor situation will produce economic abundance, so that there will be no want (Isa. 35:1-2, 7; 30:23-25; 62:8-9; 65:21-23; Jer. 31:5, 12; Ezek. 34:26; 36:29-30; Joel 2:21-27; Amos 9:13-14; Micah 4:1, 4; Zech. 8:11-12; 9:16-17).

Willard Cantelon writes:

> Some who studied the riches of earth estimated the combined value of the gold and silver, the grain and oil and timber, the fish and fruit and minerals, etc., at one decillion dollars! This figure of course, was beyond my comprehension, but slowly I repeated, "Million, billion, trillion, quadrillion, quintillion, sextillion, septillion, octillion, novillion, decillion!"? Taking pen and paper, I divided the four billion of earth's population into this figure, and saw that everyone would be a billionaire, if he shared such wealth! The Psalmist said: "The earth is full of thy riches!" (Psa. 104:24). (*Money Master of the World*, p. 137)

r. Increase of light—There will be an increase of solar and lunar light in the age. This increased light probably is a major cause in the increased productivity of the earth (Isa. 4:5; 30:26; 60:19-20; Zech. 2:5).

s. Unified language—The language barriers will be removed so that there can be free social interchange (Zeph. 3:9).

t. Unified worship—All the world will unite in the worship of God and God's Messiah (Isa. 45:23; 52:1, 7-10; 66:17-23; Zeph. 3:9; Zech. 13:2; 14:16; 8:23; 9:7; Mal. 1:11; Rev. 5:9-14).

u. The manifest presence of God—God's presence will be fully recognized and fellowship with God will be experienced to an unprecedented degree (Ezek. 37:27-28; Zech. 2:2, 10-13; Rev. 21:3).

v. The fullness of the Spirit—Divine presence and enablement will be the experience of all who are in subjection to the authority of the King (Isa. 32:13-15; 41:1; 44:3; 59:19, 21; 61:1; Ezek. 11:10-20; 36:26-27; 37:14; 39:29; Joel 2:28-29).

w. The perpetuity of the millennial state—That which characterizes the millennial age is not viewed as temporary, but eternal (Isa. 51:6-8; 55:3, 13; 56:5; 60:19-20; 61:8; Jer. 32:40; Ezek. 16:60; 37:26-28; 43:7-9; Dan. 9:24; Hos. 2:19-23; Joel 3:20; Amos 9:15).

8. The citizens of the Millennium
   a. Considered negatively—No unsaved persons will enter the Millennium (Isa. 35; Jer. 31:33-34; Ezek. 20:37-38; Zech. 13:9; Matt. 18:3; 25:30, 46; John 3:3). However, millions of babies will evidently be reared in the Millennium. They will be born of saved but mortal Israelite and Gentile parents who survived the tribulation and entered the Millennium in that state of mortality (thus the possible reason for the tree of life in Rev. 22:2). As they mature, some of these babies will refuse to submit their hearts to the new birth, though outward acts will be subjected to existing authority. Thus Christ will rule with a rod of iron (Rev. 2:27; 12:5; 19:15; Zech. 14:17-19).
   Dr. Rene Pache writes concerning this:

   > As beautiful as the Millennium is, it will not be heaven. . . . Sin will still be possible during the thousand years (Isa. 11:4; 65:20). Certain families and certain nations will refuse to go up to Jerusalem to worship the Lord (Zech. 14:17-19). Such deeds will be all the more inexcusable because the tempter will be absent and because the revelations of the Lord will be greater. . . . Those who have been thus smitten will serve as examples to all those who would be tempted to imitate them (Isa. 66:24). (*The Return of Christ*, pp. 428–429)

   b. Considered positively
      (1) Saved Israel
         (a) Israel will once again be related to God by marriage (Isa. 54:1-17; 62:2-5; Hos. 2:14-23).
         (b) Israel will be exalted above the Gentiles (Isa. 14:1-2; 49:22-23; 60:14-17; 61:6-7).
         (c) Israel will become God's witnesses during the Millennium (Isa. 44:8; 61:6; 66:21; Jer. 16:19-21; Micah 5:7; Zeph. 3:20; Zech. 4:1-7; 8:3).
      (2) Saved Old Testament and tribulation Gentiles (Rev. 5:9-10; Isa. 2:4; 11:12)
      (3) The church (1 Cor. 6:2; 2 Tim. 2:12; Rev. 1:6; 2:26-27; 3:21)
      (4) The elect angels (Heb. 12:22)

9. The King of the Millennium—The Lord Jesus Christ will of course be King supreme, but there are passages that suggest he will graciously choose to rule through a vice-regent, and that vice-regent will be David. Note the following Scripture: "But they shall serve the LORD their God, and David their king, whom I will raise up unto them" (Jer. 30:9). Jeremiah wrote those words some 400 years after the death of David, so he could not have been referring to his earthly reign here.

   "And I will set up one shepherd over them, and he shall feed them, even my servant David; he shall feed them, and he shall be their shepherd" (Ezek. 34:23). (See also Ezek. 37:24.) "Afterward shall the children of Israel return, and seek the LORD their God, and David their king; and shall fear the LORD and his goodness in the latter days" (Hos. 3:5).

   If we take these passages literally, David will once again sit upon the throne of Israel. He will thus be aided in his rule by:

　　　　a. The church (1 Cor. 6:3)
　　　　b. The apostles (Matt. 19:28)
　　　　c. Nobles (Jer. 30:21)
　　　　d. Princes (Isa. 32:1; Ezek. 45:8-9)
　　　　e. Judges (Zech. 3:7; Isa. 1:26)
　　10. The geography of the Millennium
　　　　a. Palestine
　　　　　　(1) To be greatly enlarged and changed (Isa. 26:15; Obad. 17-21)—For the
　　　　　　　　first time Israel will possess all the land promised to Abraham in Genesis
　　　　　　　　15:18-21.
　　　　　　(2) A great fertile plain to replace the mountainous terrain
　　　　　　(3) A river to flow east-west from the Mount of Olives into both the
　　　　　　　　Mediterranean and the Dead seas—The following passages from *The
　　　　　　　　Living Bible* bear this out:
　　　　　　　　　　"The Mount of Olives will split apart, making a very wide valley
　　　　　　　　running from east to west, for half the mountain will move toward
　　　　　　　　the north and half toward the south. . . . Life-giving waters will flow
　　　　　　　　out from Jerusalem, half toward the Dead Sea and half toward the
　　　　　　　　Mediterranean, flowing continuously both in winter and in summer. . . .
　　　　　　　　All the land from Geba (the northern border of Judah) to Rimmon (the
　　　　　　　　southern border) will become one vast plain" (Zech. 14:4, 8, 10). "Sweet
　　　　　　　　wine will drip from the mountains, and the hills shall flow with milk.
　　　　　　　　Water will fill the dry stream beds of Judah, and a fountain will burst
　　　　　　　　forth from the Temple of the Lord to water Acacia valley" (Joel 3:18).
　　　　　　　　　　"He told me: 'This river flows east through the desert and the Jordan
　　　　　　　　Valley to the Dead Sea, where it will heal the salty waters and make them
　　　　　　　　fresh and pure. Everything touching the water of this river shall live. Fish
　　　　　　　　will abound in the Dead Sea, for its waters will be healed. . . . All kinds of
　　　　　　　　fruit trees will grow along the river banks. The leaves will never turn
　　　　　　　　brown and fall, and there will always be fruit. There will be a new crop
　　　　　　　　every month—without fail! For they are watered by the river flowing
　　　　　　　　from the Temple. The fruit will be for food and the leaves for medicine'"
　　　　　　　　(Ezek. 47:8-9, 12).
　　　　b. Jerusalem
　　　　　　(1) The city will become the worship center of the world—"But in the last
　　　　　　　　days Mount Zion will be the most renowned of all the mountains of the
　　　　　　　　world, praised by all nations; people from all over the world will make
　　　　　　　　pilgrimages there" (Mic. 4:1, TLB). "In the last days Jerusalem and the
　　　　　　　　Temple of the Lord will become the world's greatest attraction, and
　　　　　　　　people from many lands will flow there to worship the Lord, 'Come,'
　　　　　　　　everyone will say, 'Let us go up the mountain of the Lord, to the Temple
　　　　　　　　of the God of Israel; there he will teach us his laws, and we will obey
　　　　　　　　them'" (Isa. 2:2-3, TLB).
　　　　　　(2) The city will occupy an elevated site (Zech. 14:10).
　　　　　　(3) The city will be six miles in circumference (Ezek. 48:35). (In the time of
　　　　　　　　Christ the city was about four miles.)
　　　　　　(4) The city will be named "Jehovah-Shammah," meaning "the Lord is
　　　　　　　　there" (Ezek. 48:35), and "Jehovah Tsidkenu," meaning, "the Lord our
　　　　　　　　righteousness" (Jer. 23:6; 33:16).

These two will be the final names for God's beloved city. It has been called by many titles in the Bible.

(a) The city of David (2 Sam. 6:12)
(b) The city of the great King (Matt. 5:35)
(c) The Holy City (Isa. 48:2; 51:1; Matt. 4:5)
(d) Salem (Gen. 14:18)
(e) The city of God (Psa. 46:4; 48:1; 87:3)
(f) The city of the Lord of Hosts (Psa. 48:8)
(g) The city of righteousness (Isa. 1:26)
(h) The city of truth (Zech. 8:3)
(i) The city of the Lord (Isa. 60:14)
(j) The perfection of beauty (Lam. 2:15)
(k) The joy of the whole earth (Lam. 2:15)

11. The temple in the Millennium
   a. Its biblical order—The millennial temple is the last of seven great scriptural temples. These are:
   (1) The tabernacle of Moses—Exodus 40 (1500–1000 B.C.)
   (2) The temple of Solomon—1 Kings 8 (1000–586 B.C.)
   (3) The temple of Zerubbabel (rebuilt later by Herod)—Ezra 6; John 2 (516 B.C.–A.D. 70)
   (4) The temple of the body of Jesus—John 2:21 (4 B.C.–A.D. 30)
   (5) The spiritual temple, the church—Acts 2; 1 Thessalonians 4 (from Pentecost till the Rapture)
       (a) The whole church (Eph. 2:21)
       (b) The local church (1 Cor. 3:16-17)
       (c) The individual Christian (1 Cor. 6:19)
   (6) The tribulational temple—Revelation 11 (from the Rapture till Armageddon)
   (7) The millennial temple—Isaiah 2:3; 60:13; Ezek. 40–48; Dan. 9:24; Joel 3:18; Haggai 2:7, 9
   b. Its holy oblation—Palestine will be redistributed among the 12 tribes of Israel during the Millennium. The land itself will be divided into three areas. Seven tribes will occupy the northern area and five the southern ground. Between these two areas there is a section called "the holy oblation," that is, that portion of ground that is set apart for the Lord. Dr. J. Dwight Pentecost quotes Merrill F. Unger on this:

   > The holy oblation would be a spacious square, thirty-four miles each way, containing about 1,160 square miles. This area would be the center of all the interests of the divine government and worship as set up in the Millennial earth. . . . The temple itself would be located in the middle of this square (the holy oblation) and not in the City of Jerusalem, upon a very high mountain, which will be miraculously made ready for that purpose when the temple is to be erected (see Isa. 2:4; Mic. 4:1-4; Ezek. 37:26). (*Things to Come,* p. 510)

   c. Its priesthood—On four specific occasions we are told that the sons of Zadok will be assigned the priestly duties (Ezek. 40:46; 43:19; 44:15; 48:11). Zadok was a high priest in David's time (the eleventh in descent from Aaron). His loyalty to the king was unwavering. Because of this, he was promised that his seed would have this glorious opportunity (1 Sam. 2:35; 1 Kings 2:27, 35).

d. Its prince—In his description of the temple, Ezekiel refers to a mysterious "prince" some 17 times. Whoever he is, he occupies a very important role in the temple itself, apparently holding an intermediary place between the people and the priesthood. We are sure that it is not Christ, since he prepares a sin offering for himself (Ezek. 45:22), and is married and has sons (Ezek. 46:16). Some suggest that the prince is from the seed of King David, and that he will be to David what the false prophet was to the Antichrist.

e. Its negative aspects—Several articles and objects present in the temple of Moses, Solomon, and Herod will be absent from the millennial temple.

(1) There will be no veil—This was torn in two from top to bottom (Matt. 27:51) and will not reappear in this temple. Thus there will be no barrier to keep man from the glory of God.

(2) There will be no table of shewbread—This will not be needed, for the living Bread himself will be present.

(3) There will be no lampstands—These will not be needed either, since the Light of the World himself will personally shine forth.

(4) There will be no Ark of the Covenant—This will also be unnecessary, since the Shekinah Glory himself will hover over all the world, as the glory cloud once did over the Ark.

(5) The east gate will be closed—Observe the words of Ezekiel: "This gate shall be shut, and no man shall enter in by it; because the Lord, the God of Israel, hath entered in by it, therefore it shall be shut" (Ezek. 44:2). This gate, it has been suggested, will remain closed for the following reasons:

(a) This will be the gate by which the Lord Jesus Christ enters the temple—As a mark of honor to an eastern king, no person could enter the gate by which the king entered.

(b) It was from the eastern gate that the glory of God departed for the last time in the Old Testament (Ezek. 10:18-19)—By sealing the gate, God reminds all those within that his glory will never again depart from his people.

f. Its sacrifices—As we have already seen, several pieces of furniture in the Old Testament temple will be missing in the millennial edifice. However, the brazen altar of sacrifice will again be present. There are at least four Old Testament prophecies that speak of animal sacrifices in the millennial temple: Isaiah 56:6-7; 60:7; Jeremiah 33:10; Zechariah 14:16-21. But why the need of these animal blood sacrifices during the golden age of the Millennium? In a nutshell, they will serve as a reminder, an object lesson, an example, and an illustration.

(1) A reminder to all of the necessity of the new birth

(2) An object lesson of the costliness of salvation

(3) An example of the awfulness of sin

(4) An illustration of the holiness of God

I. Satan's final revolt—"And when the thousand years are expired, Satan shall be loosed out of his prison, and shall go out to deceive the nations which are in the four quarters of the earth, Gog and Magog, to gather them together to battle: the number of whom is as the sand of the sea. And they went up on the breadth of the earth, and compassed the camp of the saints about, and the beloved city" (Rev. 20:7-9).

Dr. J. Vernon McGee writes the following words concerning these verses:

> When the late Dr. Chafer (founder of Dallas Theological Seminary) was once asked why God loosed Satan after he once had him bound, he replied, "If you will tell me why God let him loose in the first place, I will tell you why God lets him loose the second time." Apparently Satan is released at the end of the Millennium to reveal that the ideal conditions of the kingdom, under the personal reign of Christ, do not change the human heart. This reveals the enormity of the enmity of man against God. Scripture is accurate when it describes the heart as "desperately wicked" and incurably so. Man is totally depraved. The loosing of Satan at the end of the 1,000 years proves it. (*Reveling Through Revelation*, pp. 74–75)

We have already discussed the purposes accomplished by the sacrifices during the Millennium. Apparently millions of maturing children will view these sacrifices and hear the tender salvation plea of the priests, but will stubbornly harden their sinful hearts. The fact that earth's mighty King at Jerusalem once bled as a lowly lamb at Calvary will mean absolutely nothing to them. Outwardly they will conform, but inwardly they will despise.

Finally, at the end of the Millennium, the world will be offered for the first time in ten centuries "a choice, and not an echo." Millions will make a foolish and fatal choice. Dr. J. Dwight Pentecost quotes F. C. Jennings, who writes:

> Has human nature changed, at least apart from sovereign grace? Is the carnal mind at last in friendship with God? Have a thousand years of absolute power and absolute benevolence, both in unchecked activity, done away with all war forever and forever? These questions must be marked by a practical test. Let Satan be loosed once more from his prison. Let him range once more earth's smiling fields that he knew of old. He saw them last soaked with blood and flooded with tears, the evidence and accompaniments of his own reign; he sees them now "laughing with abundance." . . . But as he pursues his way further from Jerusalem, the center of this blessedness, these tokens become fainter, until, in the far-off "corner of the earth," they cease altogether, for he finds myriads who have instinctively shrunk from close contact with that holy center, and are not unprepared once more to be deceived. (*Things to Come*, p. 549)

However, this insane and immoral insurrection is doomed to utter and complete failure. As a war correspondent, the Apostle John duly records this final battle: "And fire came down from God out of heaven, and devoured them. And the devil that deceived them was cast into the lake of fire and brimstone, where the beast and the false prophet are, and shall be tormented day and night for ever and ever" (Rev. 20:9-10).

Obviously, this battle referred to as Gog and Magog is not the same as the one in Ezekiel 38–39. Dr. J. Vernon McGee writes concerning this:

> Because the rebellion is labeled "Gog and Magog," many Bible students identify it with Gog and Magog of Ezekiel 38 and 39. This, of course, is not possible, for the conflicts described are not parallel as to time, place, or participants—only the name is the same. The invasion from the north by Gog

and Magog of Ezekiel 38 and 39 breaks the false peace of the Antichrist and causes him to show his hand in the midst of the Great Tribulation. That rebellion of the godless forces from the north will have made such an impression on mankind that after 1,000 years the last rebellion of man bears the same label. We have passed through a similar situation in this century. World War I was so devastating that when war again broke out in Europe, it was labeled again "World War," but differentiated by the number 2. Now World War III is being predicted! likewise the war in Ezekiel 38 and 39 is Gog and Magog I, while this reference in verse 8 is Gog and Magog II. (*Thru the Revelation*, p. 77)

J. The Great White Throne Judgment
   1. The fact of this throne (Heb. 9:27)—"And I saw a great white throne, and him that sat on it, from whose face the earth and the heaven fled away; and there was found no place for them. And I saw the dead, small and great, stand before God; and the books were opened: and another book was opened, which is the book of life: and the dead were judged out of those things which were written in the books, according to their works. And the sea gave up the dead which were in it; and death and hell delivered up the dead which were in them: and they were judged every man according to their works. And death and hell were cast into the lake of fire. This is the second death. And whosoever was not found written in the book of life was cast into the lake of fire" (Rev. 20:11-15).
      "I beheld till the thrones were cast down, and the Ancient of days did sit, whose garment was white as snow, and the hair of his head like the pure wool: his throne was like the fiery flame, and his wheels as burning fire. A fiery stream issued and came forth from before him: thousand thousands ministered unto him, and ten thousand times ten thousand stood before him: the judgment was set, and the books were opened" (Dan. 7:9-10).
   2. The Judge of this throne, Christ himself—"For the Father judgeth no man, but hath committed all judgment unto the Son. . . . And hath given him authority to execute judgment also, because he is the Son of man" (John 5:22, 27). "Him God raised up the third day, and showed him openly. . . . And he commanded us to preach unto the people, and to testify that it is he which was ordained of God to be the Judge of quick and dead" (Acts 10:40, 42). "I charge thee therefore before God, and the Lord Jesus Christ, who shall judge the quick and the dead at his appearing and his kingdom" (2 Tim. 4:1).
   3. The books referred to at this judgment
      a. In regards to man
         (1) The book of conscience—"Because that which may be known of God is manifest in them; for God hath showed it unto them. . . . (Which show the work of the law written in their hearts, their conscience also bearing witness, and their thoughts the mean while accusing or else excusing one another)" (Rom. 1:19; 2:15).
         (2) The book of words—"But I say unto you, That every idle word that men shall speak, they shall give account thereof in the day of judgment. For by thy words thou shalt be justified, and by thy words thou shalt be condemned" (Matt. 12:36-37).
         (3) The book of deeds—"Who will render to every man according to his deeds" (Rom. 2:6).

(a) Private deeds—"In the day when God shall judge the secrets of men by Jesus Christ according to my gospel" (Rom. 2:16). "For God shall bring every work into judgment, with every secret thing, whether it be good, or whether it be evil" (Eccles. 12:14).

(b) Public deeds—"For the Son of man shall come in the glory of his Father with his angels; and then he shall reward every man according to his works" (Matt. 16:27). "Therefore it is no great thing if his ministers also be transformed as the ministers of righteousness; whose end shall be according to their works" (2 Cor. 11:15).

b. In regards to God

(1) The works of God—"For the invisible things of him from the creation of the world are clearly seen, being understood by the things that are made, even his eternal power and Godhead; so that they are without excuse" (Rom. 1:20).

(2) The Word of God—"He that rejecteth me, and receiveth not my words, hath one that judgeth him: the word that I have spoken, the same shall judge him in the last day" (John 12:48).

(3) The witness of God, the Lamb's Book of Life (Rev. 13:8; 17:8; 20:15; 21:27)

4. The judged at this throne—As has previously been discussed (see "The judgment seat of Christ"), only unsaved people will stand before this great white throne. "The wicked shall be turned into hell, and all the nations that forget God" (Psa. 9:17).

5. The judgment at this throne—The eternal lake of fire (Rev. 20:14-15; Matt. 25:41, 46)

K. The destruction of this present earth and heaven

1. The fact of this destruction—"Heaven and earth shall pass away, but my words shall not pass away" (Matt. 24:35). "And, Thou, Lord, in the beginning hast laid the foundation of the earth; and the heavens are the works of thine hands: They shall perish; but thou remainest; and they all shall wax old as doth a garment; and as a vesture shalt thou fold them up, and they shall be changed: but thou art the same, and thy years shall not fail" (Heb. 1:10-12).

"But the day of the Lord will come as a thief in the night; in the which the heavens shall pass away with a great noise, and the elements shall melt with fervent heat, the earth also and the works that are therein shall be burned up. . . . Looking for and hasting unto the coming of the day of God, wherein the heavens being on fire shall be dissolved, and the elements shall melt with fervent heat" (2 Pet. 3:10, 12).

2. The reason for this destruction—At this stage in the Bible the final rebellion has been put down, the false prophet, the Antichrist, and the devil himself are all in the lake of fire forever, and the wicked dead have been judged. In light of this, why the necessity for this awesome destruction?

To help illustrate, consider the following: let us suppose that some crackpot breaks into the money vaults of Fort Knox, Kentucky, and begins pouring filthy crankcase oil on the stacked bars of gold and silver. Upon leaving, however, he is caught, tried, and confined to prison. The authorities thereupon close their books on the Fort Knox case. But the gunk on the gold remains. In this illustration, the vandal would represent the devil, the crankcase oil would stand for sin, and the gold and silver for God's perfect creation. God will someday arrest the devil, of course, and forever confine him to prison. But what about the oily sin stains that remain on his gold and silver creation? To solve the problem, God does what the Fort Knox authorities might consider doing—he purges the stains in a fiery wash. And it works. For the hotter the flame, the more rapidly the oil evaporates and the brighter the gold becomes.

God will someday do to creation what he did to His beloved Israel in the Old Testament: "Behold, I have refined thee . . . I have chosen thee in the furnace of affliction" (Isa. 48:10).

L. The creation of the new earth and heaven—"For, behold, I create new heavens and a new earth: and the former shall not be remembered, nor come into mind" (Isa. 65:17). "For as the new heavens and the new earth, which I will make, shall remain before me, saith the LORD, so shall your seed and your name remain" (Isa. 66:22). "Nevertheless we, according to his promise, look for new heavens and a new earth, wherein dwelleth righteousness" (2 Pet. 3:13). "And I saw a new heaven and a new earth: for the first heaven and the first earth were passed away; and there was no more sea" (Rev. 21:1).

BIBLIOGRAPHY

Adler, Mortimer J. *Great Ideas from the Great Books.* New York: Washington Square Press, 1972.

Anderson, J. Kerby. *Confronting.* Dallas: Dallas Theological Seminary, 1987.

Baker, Charles F. *A Dispensational Theology.* Grand Rapids, Mich.: Grace Bible College Publications, 1971.

Bales, James. *Atheism's Faith and Fruits.* Boston: W. A. Wilde Co., 1951.

Bancroft, Emery. *Christian Theology.* Grand Rapids, Mich.: Zondervan, 1961.

————. *Elemental Theory.* Grand Rapids, Mich.: Academic Books, 1977.

Barackman, Floyd. *Practical Christian Theology.* Tarrytown, N.Y.: Fleming H. Revell, 1984.

Barnhouse, Donald. *Revelation, An Expository Commentary.* Grand Rapids, Mich.: Zondervan, 1971.

Belcher, Richard. *The Inerrancy Debate.* Chicago: Moody Press, 1980.

Berkhof, Louis. *Systematic Theology.* Grand Rapids, Mich.: Eerdmans, 1953.

Braun, John. *Whatever Happened to Hell?* Nashville, Tenn.: Thomas Nelson, 1979.

Bromiley, Geoffery W., ed. *International Standard Bible Encyclopedia.* Vol. 4. Grand Rapids, Mich.: Eerdmans, 1988.

Bruce, F. F. *The Book of Acts.* Grand Rapids, Mich.: Eerdmans, 1977.

Bryson, Harold T. *Yes, Virginia, There Is a Hell.* Nashville, Tenn.: Broadman, 1975.

Buswell, J. Oliver. *A Systematic Theology of the Christian Religion.* Grand Rapids, Mich.: Zondervan, 1968.

Cantelon, Willard. *Money Master of the World.* Plainfield, N.J.: Logos International, 1976.

Chafer, Lewis S. *He That Is Spiritual.* Findlay, Ohio: Dunham Publishing, 1983.

————. *Systematic Theology.* Vol. II. Dallas: Dallas Seminary Press, 1948.

————. *Systematic Theology.* Vol. IV. Dallas: Dallas Seminary Press, 1953.

Cornwall, Judson. *Heaven.* Van Nuys, Calif.: Bible Voice Publishers, 1978.

Criswell, W. A. *The Bible for Today's World.* Grand Rapids, Mich.: Zondervan, 1965.

————. *Expository Notes on Matthew.* Grand Rapids, Mich.: Zondervan, 1961.

Culver, Robert. *The Living God.* Wheaton, Ill.: Victor Books, 1978.

Davis, John. *Handbook of Basic Bible Texts.* Grand Rapids, Mich.: Zondervan, 1984.

Day, G. M. *The Wonder of the Word.* Chicago: Moody Press, 1957.

Dickason, Fred. *Angels, Elect and Evil.* Chicago: Moody Press, 1975.

Elwell, Walter, ed. *Evangelical Dictionary of Theology.* Grand Rapids, Mich.: Baker Book House, 1984.

Enns, Paul. *Moody Handbook of Theology.* Chicago: Moody Press, 1989.

Fuller, David Otis. *Which Bible?* Grand Rapids, Mich.: Grand Rapids International Publications, 1970.

Geisler, Norman L., and J. Yutaka Amano. *The Infiltration of the New Age.* Wheaton, IL: Tyndale House, 1989.

Geisler, Norman, and William E. Nix. *A General Introduction to the Bible*. Chicago: Moody Press, 1968.

Gish, Duane T. *Evolution? The Fossils Say No*. San Diego, Calif.: Creation-Life Publishers, 1974.

Goodrick, Edward. *Is My Bible the Inspired Word of God?* Portland, Oreg.: Multnomah, 1988.

Graham, Billy. *Angels: God's Special Agents*. Waco, Tex.: Word, 1986.

Gray, James M. *Spiritism and the Fallen Angels in Light of the Old and New Testaments*. Tarrytown, N.Y.: Fleming H. Revell, 1920.

Gromacki, Robert. *Salvation Is Forever*. Chicago: Moody Press, 1973.

Grounds, Vernon. *The Reason for Our Hope*. Chicago: Moody Press, 1945.

Harrison, Everett F., ed. *Baker's Dictionary of Theology*. Grand Rapids, Mich.: Baker Book House, 1966.

Hodge, Charles. *Systematic Theology*. Vol. I. Grand Rapids, Mich.: Eerdmans, 1940.

Hoyt, Herman A. *The End Times*. Winona Lake, Ind.: Brethren Missionary Herald Books, 1978.

—————. *Revelation*. Winona Lake, Ind.: Brethren Missionary Herald Books, 1966.

Inge, William. *The Church in the World*. London: Longmans, Green and Co., 1927.

Ironside, H. A. *Revelation*. New York: Loizeaux Brothers.

James, Edgar C. *Armageddon*. Chicago: Moody Press, 1981.

Jennings, F. C. *Satan, His Person, Work, Place, and Destiny*. Neptune, N.J.: Loizeaux Brothers, 1975.

Jeremiah, David. *Biblical Stewardship*. Fort Wayne, Ind.: DJ Publications, 1977.

Johnson, Gordon G. *My Church*. Chicago: Harvest Publishers, 1963.

Johnson, Otto, ed. *1991 Information Please Almanac*. Boston: Houghton Mifflin Company, 1991.

Joppie, A. S. *All about Angels*. Grand Rapids, Mich.: Baker Book House, 1973.

Lightner, Robert. *Biblical Theology*. Grand Rapids, Mich.: Baker Book House, 1986.

—————. *Evangelical Dictionary*. Grand Rapids, Mich.: Baker Book House, 1987.

—————. *Evangelical Theology: A Survey and Review*. Grand Rapids, Mich.: Baker Book House, 1987.

—————. *The God of the Bible*. Grand Rapids, Mich.: Baker Book House, 1978.

Lingle, Walter L., and John W. Kuykendall, *Presbyterians: Their Ministry and Beliefs*. Louisville, Ky.: Westminster/John Knox, 1978.

The Living New Testament. Wheaton, Ill.:Tyndale House, 1967.

Logsdon, S. Franklin. *Profiles of Prophecy*. Grand Rapids, Mich.: Zondervan, 1971.

Lutzer, Erwin. *Coming to Grips with Heaven*. Chicago: Moody Press, 1990.

—————. *Coming to Grips with Hell*. Chicago: Moody Press, 1990.

MacArthur, John, Jr. *The Church, The Body of Christ*. Grand Rapids, Mich.: Zondervan, 1973.

—————. *God, Satan, and Angels*. Chicago: Moody Press, 1989.

—————. *Leadership, God's Priority for the Church*. Sun Valley, Calif.: Grace Community Church, 1975.

McDowell, Josh. *Handbook of Today's Religions*. San Bernardino, Calif.: Here's Life Publishers, 1983.

McGee, J. Vernon. *Matthew*. Vol. 2. Nashville, Tenn.: Thomas Nelson, 1982.

—————. *Reveling through Revelation*. Nashville, Tenn.: Thomas Nelson, 1982.

—————. *Studies in Hebrews*. Pasadena, Calif.: Thru the Bible Publications, 1983

—————. *Thru the Revelation*. Pasadena, Calif.: Thru the Bible Publications, 1983.

McMillen, S. I. *None of These Diseases*. Tarrytown, N.Y.: Fleming H. Revell, 1963.

Miller, H. S. *General Biblical Introduction*. Houghton, N.Y.: The Word Bearer Press, 1952.

Morris, Henry. *The Biblical Basis for Modern Science*. Grand Rapids, Mich.: Baker Book House, 1985.

New Scofield Reference Bible. New York: Oxford University Press, 1967.

Orr, James, ed. *International Standard Bible Encyclopedia*. Vol. 5. Grand Rapids, Mich.: Eerdmans, 1930.

Oursler, William C. *Protestant Power and the Coming Revolution*. Garden City, N.Y.: Doubleday, 1971.

Pache, Rene. *The Return of Jesus Christ*. Chicago: Moody Press, 1955.

Paulk, Earl. *Satan Unmasked*. Decatur, Ga.: K-Dimension Publishers, 1984.

Pentecost, J. Dwight. *The Joy Of Living*. Grand Rapids, Mich.: Zondervan, 1953.

————. *Prophecy for Today*. Chicago: Moody Press, 1969.

————. *Things to Come*. Findlay, Ohio: Dunham Publishing, 1958.

————. *Things Which Become Sound Doctrine*. Westwood, N.J.: Fleming H. Revell, 1965.

————. *Your Adversary, the Devil*. Grand Rapids, Mich.: Zondervan, 1990.

Petersen, William J. *Those Curious New Cults*. New Canaan, Conn.: Keats Publishing, 1973.

Phillips, John. *Exploring Revelation*. Chicago: Moody Press, 1974.

Pinnock, Clark. *Set Forth Your Case*. Nutley, N.J.: The Craig Press, 1968.

Price, Walter. *The Coming Antichrist*. Chicago: Moody Press, 1974.

Radmacher, Earl. *The Nature of the Church*. Portland, Oreg.: Western Baptist Press, 1972.

Ramsay, William. *The Bearing of Recent Discovery on the Trustworthiness of the New Testament*. London: Hodder and Stoughton, 1915.

Reader's Digest editors. *Reader's Digest Almanac*. New York: Reader's Digest Assn., 1966.

————. *Strange Stories, Amazing Facts*. New York: Reader's Digest Assn., 1981.

Rice, John R. *Predestinated for Hell? No!* Murfreesboro, Tenn.: Sword of the Lord Foundation, 1971.

Robinson, John A. T. *But That I Can't Believe*. New York: The New American Library, 1967.

Rosten, Leo, ed. *A Guide to the Religions of America*. New York: Simon and Schuster, 1955.

Ryrie, Charles. *Basic Theology*. Victor Books: Wheaton, IL, 1987.

————. *Revelation*. Chicago: Moody Press, 1968.

————. *A Survey of Bible Doctrine*. Chicago: Moody Press, 1972.

Saucy, Robert L. *The Church in God's Program*. Chicago: Moody Press, 1972.

Sauer, Erich. *The Triumph of the Crucified*. Grand Rapids, Mich.: Eerdmans, 1955.

Schnabel, A. O. *Has God Spoken?* San Diego: Creation-Life Publishers, 1974.

Shedd, William. *Dogmatic Theology*. Vol. II. Nashville: Thomas Nelson, 1980.

Simmons, Thomas Paul. *A Systematic Study of Bible Doctrine*. Daytona Beach, Fla.: Associated Publishers, 1972.

Smith, Wilbur. *The Biblical Doctrine of Heaven*. Chicago: Moody Press, 1968.

Strauss, Lehman. *God's Plan for the Future*. Grand Rapids, Mich.: Zondervan, 1969.

Strong, A. H. *Systematic Theology*. Valley Forge, Pa.: Judson Press, 1907.

Swaggart, Jimmy. *Questions and Answers*. Baton Rouge, La.: Swaggart Ministries, 1985.

Tan, Paul Lee. *The New Jerusalem*. Rockville, Md.: Assurance Publishers, 1978.

Taylor, Richard S., ed. *Beacon Dictionary of Theology*. Kansas City, Mo.: Beacon Hill Press, 1983.

Thiessen, Henry. *Lectures in Systematic Theology*. Grand Rapids, Mich.: Eerdmans, 1979.

Toon, Peter. *Heaven and Hell*. Nashville, Tenn.: Thomas Nelson, 1986.

Tozer, A. W. *The Knowledge of the Holy*. Lincoln, Nebr.: Back to the Bible Broadcast, 1971.

————. *The Pursuit of God*. Harrisburg, Penn.: Christian Publications, 1958.

Unger, Merrill F., ed. *Unger's Bible Dictionary.* Chicago: Moody Press, 1957.

————. *Unger's Bible Handbook.* Chicago: Moody Press, 1956.

Wagner, C. Peter. *Your Spiritual Gifts Can Help Your Church Grow.* Ventura, Calif.: Regal Books, 1979.

Walvoord, John. *The Holy Spirit: A Comprehensive Study of the Person and Work of the Holy Spirit.* Grand Rapids, Mich.: Zondervan, 1991.

————. *Jesus Christ, Our Lord.* Chicago: Moody Press, 1969.

————. *Major Bible Themes.* Grand Rapids, Mich.: Zondervan, 1974.

————. *The Nations in Prophecy.* Grand Rapids, Mich.: Zondervan, 1967.

————. *Philippians, Triumph in Christ.* Chicago: Moody Press, 1971.

Walvoord, John, and Roy Zuck, *The Bible Knowledge Commentary.* New Testament ed. Wheaton, Ill.: Victor Books, 1983.

Warfield, Benjamin. *Biblical and Theological Studies.* Phillipsburg, N.J.: Presby and Reformed, 1952.

Whitcomb, John C., Jr. *Creation according to God's Word.* Grand Rapids, Mich.: Baker Book House, 1966.

Wiersbe, Warren. *Be Rich (Ephesians).* Wheaton, Ill.: Victor, 1989.

Wouk, Herman. *This Is My God.* New York: Pocket Books, 1970.

Wuest, Kenneth. *In the Last Days.* Grand Rapids, Mich.: Eerdmans, 1954.

————. *Word Studies in Philippians.* Grand Rapids, Mich.: Eerdmans, 1953.

Yohn, Rick. *Discover Your Spiritual Gift and Use It.* Wheaton, Ill.: Tyndale House, 1974.

Young, Robert. *Young's Analytical Concordance to the Bible.* Grand Rapids, Mich.: Eerdmans, 1955.